KEATING ON BUILDING CONTRACTS

AUSTRALIA
The Law Book Company
Sydney

CANADA
The Carswell Company
Toronto, Ontario

INDIA
N. M. Tripathi Private Ltd.
Bombay
and
Eastern Law House Private Ltd.
Calcutta

M.P.P. House
Bangalore

Universal Book Traders
Delhi

ISRAEL
Steimatzky's Agency Ltd.
Tel Aviv

PAKISTAN
Pakistan Law House
Karachi

KEATING ON BUILDING CONTRACTS

FIFTH EDITION

BY

HON. SIR ANTHONY MAY, M.A.
One of Her Majesty's Justices of Inner Temple

With Commentaries on JCT Forms of Contract

BY

ADRIAN WILLIAMSON, M.A.,
of Middle Temple, Barrister

and a Commentary on the I.C.E. Conditions of Contract

BY

JOHN UFF, Q.C.,
B.Sc.(Eng.), Ph.D., C.Eng., F.I.C.E., F.C.I.Arb.,
of Gray's Inn
Director, Centre of Construction Law and Management,
King's College, London

Original Author and Consultant Editor

DONALD KEATING, Q.C., B.A., F.C.I.Arb.,
of Lincoln's Inn

LONDON
SWEET & MAXWELL
1991

Published in 1991 by
Sweet & Maxwell Limited of
South Quay Plaza, 183 Marsh Wall,
London, E14 9FT
Phototypeset by
MFK Typesetting Limited of
Hitchin, Herts.
Printed in Great Britain by
Bath Press, Bath, Avon

First Edition	1955
Second Impression	1956
Second Edition	1963
Third Edition	1969
Fourth Edition	1978
Fifth Edition	1991

A catalogue record for this book is available from the British Library

ISBN 0421 3273 08

EDITOR'S ACKNOWLEDGMENT

All the primary research for the first 17 chapters of this edition and much other work besides was carried out by the Members of 10 Essex Street whose names are given below. The Editor wishes to express his warmest thanks for their sustained work and support and to acknowledge that without them this edition could not have been produced.

IAN PENNICOTT, B.A., LL.M.(Cantab.),
of Middle Temple, Barrister

PAUL DARLING, B.A.(Oxon.), B.C.L.,
of Middle Temple, Barrister

FINOLA O'FARRELL, B.A.(Dunelm.),
of Inner Temple, Barrister

ALEXANDER NISSEN, LL.B.,
of Middle Temple, Barrister

NERYS A. JEFFORD, M.A.(Oxon.), LL.M.(Virginia),
of Gray's Inn, Barrister

MICHAEL BOWSHER, B.A.(Oxon.),
of Middle Temple, Barrister

PUBLISHER'S ACKNOWLEDGMENT

The copyright documents appearing at the following pages are reproduced with permission of R.I.B.A. Publications and BEC Publications.

1980 JCT Local Authorities with Quantities Main Contract	466
NSC/4	699
NSC/2	793
TNS/2	805
Architect's Appointment	950

Copyright in the I.C.E. Conditions of Contract (6th edition) appearing at page 810 is held by and reproduced with permission of:
Institution of Civil Engineers
Federation of Civil Engineering Contractors
Association of Consulting Engineers

PREFACE

It has been the greatest privilege to have been able to produce a new edition of Donald Keating's book during his active professional career. I have learnt as no one else could the sheer quality of his fourth edition. Although my word processor has enabled me to do some rearranging on a scale which a manual edition would never have contemplated, there is very little of the fourth edition which does not reappear somewhere in this book, and unaltered except where later authority demanded a change. Donald's calm acceptance on the first floor of 10 Essex Street that I on the second floor was probably murdering his book may have been induced in part by the thought that, for the first time for over 35 years, he was going to be able to submit credibly in Court that the content of the book which bears his name is wrong. Long may he be able to do so.

The most outstanding development in the law relating to building contracts since the publication of the fourth edition of this book happened in July 1990, when a Committee of the House of Lords, consisting of seven Law Lords, decided *Murphy* v. *Brentwood District Council*. In departing from *Anns* v. *Merton London Borough Council* and overruling *Dutton* v. *Bognor Regis Urban District Council*, they not only swept away 13 years and more of the English law of negligence, but demonstrated that many decisions of the past decade, not all at first instance, were wrongly decided. (It is tempting to question whether an appellate system which produces this kind of upheaval in such a comparatively short time is best suited to the needs of the customer.) The law of negligence has in general gone back to where it was in 1970. Chapter 7 of this edition, written in the immediate aftermath of *Murphy*, attempts to state without undue nostalgia what the law now is and to grapple with those problems which *Murphy* does not clearly resolve. It is suggested, for instance, that the law of professional negligence needs reconsideration. Should a professional person's normal obligation to his client continue to exist in tort as well as in contract?

Besides many instances where cases decided since the publication of the fourth edition have required a revision or recasting of the text or addition to it, I have spent some time with concurrent causes in Chapter 8, bonds in Chapter 10 and ICC arbitration in Chapter 16, where I have also wrestled with *Crouch*. There is a new Chapter 14 about the impact of The European Economic Community on building contracts, and a new Chapter 15 discusses a number of statutes including the Limitation Act 1980, the Building Act 1984 and the Insolvency Act 1986. Adrian Williamson has rewritten the commentaries on the 1980 JCT Forms of Main Contract and Sub-Contract and John Uff has written a new commentary on the sixth edition of the I.C.E. Conditions recently published.

As my acknowledgment following the title page says, I have been helped and supported beyond measure by the team at 10 Essex Street. The editorial staff of Sweet & Maxwell have given me every possible help and I am particularly grateful for being provided at the outset with a scanned text on disk of the fourth edition of the book. Alison Wilmot did much of the initial typing of the commentaries in Chapters 18–21 for Adrian Williamson and John Uff and we are most grateful. And I am grateful not least to 10 Essex Street as a whole for sustained practical and personal encouragement.

This edition aims to state the law on January 1, 1991. Cases reported after October 12, 1990, have been included at proof stage and therefore under some space constraint.

Anthony May
10 Essex Street
London
WC2A 3AA

CONTENTS

Contents

Contents

Contents

Contents

Contents

Contents

ABBREVIATIONS

In addition to standard abbreviation references to Law Reports which may be found in such other works as Current Law Year Book, the following are used in this Edition:

C.A.	=	Court of Appeal
D.C.	=	Divisional Court
H.L.	=	House of Lords
P.C.	=	Privy Council
B.L.R.	=	Building Law Reports
Const. L.J.	=	Construction Law Journal
Con. L.R.	=	Construction Law Reports
C.I.L.L.	=	Construction Industry Law Letter
Halsbury	=	Halsbury's Laws of England
H.B.C.	=	Hudson's Building Contracts
R.S.C.	=	Rules of the Supreme Court

CROSS-REFERENCES

In an appropriate context, references to a chapter or page are to that chapter or page of this book.

TABLE OF CASES

Table of Cases

Table of Cases

xlix

Table of Cases

Table of Cases

Table of Cases

Table of Cases

TABLE OF EUROPEAN CASES

TABLE OF STATUTES

TABLE OF STATUTORY INSTRUMENTS

TABLE OF RULES

County Court Rules

TABLE OF EUROPEAN LEGISLATION

THE NATURE OF A BUILDING CONTRACT

1. Introduction

"A building contract is an entire contract for the sale of goods and work and labour for a lump sum price payable by instalments as the goods are delivered and the work is done."[1]

Relation to the general law of contract. The phrase "building contract" in this book is used to include any contract where one person[2] agrees for valuable consideration to carry out building or engineering works for another. It thus covers every contract from, for example, a simple oral agreement to repair a garage roof to elaborate public works contracts. The law of building contracts is a part of the general law of contract[3] and is not governed by any codifying statute. All the elements of a simple contract must be present[4] and the general rules of performance and discharge of contract apply to a building contract. Where the general principles of the law of contract apply to problems of common occurrence in building contracts they have been dealt with in detail in this book. But where they apply to problems which rarely arise in building contracts, *e.g.* mistake avoiding a contract, a mere outline has been given and for further information reference must be made to one of the standard works on the law of contract.[5]

2. The Persons Concerned in a Building Contract

The employer and the contractor. The employer for whose benefit the

---

[1] Lord Diplock in *Modern Engineering* v. *Gilbert-Ash* [1974] A.C. 689 at 717 (H.L.). For entire contracts, see p. 70. This is not a completely comprehensive definition.

[2] This includes a corporation—see Chap. 2.

[3] English law is referred to throughout the book unless the contrary is indicated. A reader who has not previously studied any law may find it useful to read Professor Glanville Williams, *Learning the Law* (11th ed., 1982).

[4] See Chap. 2.

[5] *e.g. Chitty on Contracts* (26th ed., 1989).

work is carried out and the contractor who must carry out the work are the principal parties to a building contract. The employer has frequently been termed "the building owner," and the contractor the "builder"[6] or the "building contractor." For the sake of clarity and because the Standard Form of Building Contract[7] uses the terms, the parties are generally referred to in this book as "employer" and "contractor," unless a reference to a decided case involves the use of other terms.

In addition to the parties to the contract, there are usually in a large contract several other persons involved. These may include the architect or engineer, the quantity surveyor and other consultants. Although they are not parties, they may materially affect the legal relationship between the contractor and the employer. A short note on their position is given in this chapter although a full account, where appropriate, will be found in other chapters. There is no requirement of the law that there shall be such persons employed in a building contract and many smaller contracts are entered into and completed without their employment.

The architect. The term is ordinarily used in this book to describe the person who is engaged by the employer to carry out the duties of an architect referred to in Chapter 13.[8] In the broadest sense his duties are to prepare plans and specifications and supervise the execution of the works on behalf of the employer so that they may be completed in accordance with the contract. He is therefore the agent of the employer and owes him a contractual duty of professional care, notwithstanding that the employer and contractor ordinarily contract on the understanding that many matters may arise under the contract where the architect has to make a decision in a fair and unbiased manner.[9] A surveyor or some other person may carry out the duties and occupy the position of an architect in a building contract.

The engineer. In an engineering contract the person who carries out the duties and occupies a position similar to that of an architect in a building contract is normally termed the engineer.[10]

---

[6] This term received judicial consideration under a now repealed statute formerly relating to bankruptcy law—see H.B.C. (7th ed., 1946), p. 105. It has also been defined for the purpose of the London Building Acts 1930–1939 in s.4 of the London Building Acts (Amendment) Act 1939. See also ss.121–123 of the Building Act 1984.

[7] Joint Contracts Tribunal Standard Form of Building Contract (1980 ed.). See further Chap. 18. This is the successor of the document referred to in previous editions of this book as the "R.I.B.A. Form." Further references will normally be to the "Standard Form of Building Contract."

[8] See Chap. 13. Thus references to "architect" do not refer to a person who, though he may have qualified as an architect, does not practise as such but acts as, say, an expert adviser or salaried assistant to a large contractor.

[9] *Sutcliffe* v. *Thackrah* [1974] A.C. 727 (H.L.). See further p. 114. The architect may also owe his client a parallel professional duty in tort, but it is suggested under "Professional negligence" at p. 172 that this needs judicial reconsideration.

[10] See generally Chap. 13, Section 3. Note that surveyors, engineers and others may not term themselves architects unless registered under the Architects Registration Act 1931–1969.

The quantity surveyor.   The quantity surveyor is employed by or on behalf of the employer to estimate the quantities of the proposed works and set them out in the form of bills of quantities for the purposes of tender. He may also be employed to measure and value variations and to do such other works of measurement and valuation as the architect may require.[11] In some cases the architect takes out his own quantities and does his own measuring of the works.

Consultants.   In large building contracts, consultants other than the architect and quantity surveyor are often engaged by the employer for special purposes. There may for instance be a structural engineer, a mechanical and electrical engineer, an acoustics consultant or others. Their roles are often imprecisely defined in the contract, but generally their functions are more limited than those of the architect and confined to the design and supervision of those parts of the works within their special expertise.

Project manager.   In some large building contracts, the employer may engage a project manager in addition to the architect and some or all of the consultants mentioned above. A project manager's role is organisational, but his exact relationship with the architect, consultants, contractor and sub-contractors varies from one contract to another. Contractors also sometimes employ a person whom they call the project manager.

Sub-contractors.[12]   The contractor frequently subcontracts, or, as it is sometimes termed, sublets, much of the work to sub-contractors. If the architect or the employer has nominated the sub-contractor he is termed a nominated sub-contractor.

Sureties.   Persons known as sureties may give various guarantees. They may guarantee the performance of the works by the contractor or due payment by the employer, or less commonly the good faith of the architect or other persons having control of money.[13]

3. Contract Documents

Contract documents contain the terms of the contract and are to be distinguished from other documents such as invitations to tender[14] or mere representations[15] not intended to form part of the contract. It is a question partly of fact and partly of construction[16] to determine which documents are contractual, but those here briefly referred to are common.[17]

---

[11] See generally Chap. 13.
[12] See generally Chap. 12.
[13] See generally Chap. 10, Section 5.
[14] See Chap. 2, Section 2.
[15] See Chap. 6, Section 1.
[16] See Chap. 3.
[17] See Chap. 18 for a discussion of the contract documents in the various versions of the Standard Form of Building Contract.

3

Agreement or articles of agreement.   This usually sets out the date, the parties, the intended works and the consideration. It may also name the architect and quantity surveyor and provide in certain circumstances for their replacement.

Conditions.   Elaborate conditions are often made part of the contract and attempt to provide for the various problems which can arise during and after the execution of the works.

Architects' plans and drawings.   In some smaller contracts these may show the works in full detail, but in larger contract often do not aim to do so. Further detailed drawings and instructions are therefore necessary and their timely production can be a source of much dispute.

Bills of quantities.   Bills of quantities quantify the works in detail and are ordinarily prepared in accordance with an agreed standard method of measurement. Their purpose "is to put into words every obligation or service which will be required in carrying out the building project."[18] They may not form part of the contract although submitted to the contractor for tender.[19] Generally it requires express words in the articles of agreement to make the bills of quantities a contract document.[20]

Specification.   This term is much less exact in meaning than "bills of quantities." It usually means a document which describes the work to be done and the goods to be supplied. There is no standard or customary method for the preparation of a specification and its meaning must be considered in each contract. Thus in the Standard Form of Building Contract where quantities do not form part of the contract, it has the meaning, just stated, whereas it does not have such meaning in the version where quantities form part.[21] In the I.C.E. Conditions it has the meaning stated above but does not give quantities of work, this function being performed by a separate Bill of Quantities.

Other documents.   A variety of other documents such as letters, estimates, memoranda, and in some cases the tender or invitation to tender, may contain terms of the contract. Where parties have apparently finally stated their agreement in a document, it may be difficult to show that other documents (or oral statements) not expressly incorporated or referred to contain terms of the contract.[22]

---

[18] Simon Report, para. 55. See n. 23 below for the Simon Report.
[19] See pp. 83 and 132.
[20] See p. 84.
[21] See Chap. 18. In the 1980 Standard Form of Building Contract, with quantities, there is no reference to a specification, although clause 5 does refer to "descriptive schedules or other like documents necessary for use in carrying out the Works"—see p. 498.
[22] See Chap. 3.

4

4. A Typical Building Operation—Traditional Procedure

The scope of the law of building contracts and some of the problems which may arise are illustrated in the following summary.[23]

The employer obtains a sufficient interest in the land upon which he proposes to build to enable him to give the contractor possession of the site. If the contract is of any substance he usually employs an architect who, if authorised to do so, engages a quantity surveyor on behalf of the employer. The architect translates the employer's wishes into detailed plans and the quantity surveyor measures the amount of work and materials necessary to complete the plans and sets this out in detail in bills of quantities. Any appropriate planning consents are obtained and all statutory requirements taken into account.[24] The contract must then be placed. This is done either by open or limited competition[25] or by individual negotiation.[26] Forms of tender are sent out with bills of quantities, specification, plans and conditions of contract, or such other information as the architect may think desirable. If good practice is followed the documents intended to form part of the contract will be clearly stated. The contractor estimates the cost of the works on the basis of the amount of work and materials shown on the plans and described in the bills of quantities and the specification or other documents supplementing or replacing the bills of quantities. He then submits his estimate, *i.e.* tender, and it is the normal practice that such tender is an offer capable of acceptance. Where there is more than one tender the employer with the advice and assistance of his architect selects one of the tenders, usually, though not necessarily, the lowest. When the employer notifies the contractor of his unqualified acceptance, a binding contract comes into existence. The contract is frequently expressed in a formal document such as the Standard Form of Building Contract or, for engineering works, the I.C.E. Conditions.

The works are carried out by the contractor under the supervision of the architect. It is usual for interim payments of the contract sum to be made from time to time as the architect certifies that work of a certain value has been carried out. Such payments are subject to the retention of a percentage of the value of the work carried out, the money retained ("retention money") being held by way of security until completion of the works. After the completion of the works it is usual for the contractor to be under an express obligation to

---

[23] For further reading see the Government publications: *The Placing and Management of Building Contracts* (H.M.S.O., 1944) (the Simon Report); *The Placing and Management of Contracts for Building and Civil Engineering Work* (H.M.S.O., 1964) (the Branwell Report). Procedure can, of course, vary at the will of the parties.

[24] Town and country planning law, the detail of Building Regulations and special statutory controls are outside the scope of this book.

[25] For a suggested procedure for limited competitive tendering, see *A Code of Procedure for Single Stage Selective Tendering* (April 1989) obtainable from the National Joint Consultative Committee for Building.

[26] See "Prohibition of contracting restrictions" at p. 357 for relevant EEC legislation.

make good defects which appear during a certain period often termed the "defects liability" or "maintenance" period.[27]

Numerous difficulties may arise. For example, the completion of the works may be delayed by the ordering of variations, by late or inadequate instructions, by shortage of materials or delay on the part of sub-contractors. The contractor may find that he is required to execute more work or spend more money to complete than he originally estimated. A third party injured by a falling object or annoyed by dust and noise may make a claim against the contractor or the employer. One or both of the parties may become bankrupt or go into liquidation. A breach of contract by one of the parties may give rise to a claim by the other for damages or even to bring the contract to an end, either by virtue of an express clause or under the general law of contract. After completion, disputes may arise about defects alleged to exist or to have appeared during the defects liability or maintenance period. Any of these events may affect the obligations of a surety.[28]

When the works have been completed the architect usually has the power to decide the amount of money payable to the contractor and to state his decision in the form of a certificate. In arriving at the final sum he may have to take into account many matters some of which are mentioned above. The result may be that the final certificate is for a very different sum from that stated as the original contract sum.[29] If the parties cannot agree on the amount to be paid under the contract or on some other matter which has arisen during the course of the building operations, there may have to be legal proceedings, but the parties may have expressly limited their right to litigate in two ways. Firstly, the contract may provide that the architect's decision on certain matters shall be binding and conclusive. Secondly it may provide for the arbitration of any disputes arising between them.[30]

The Joint Contracts Tribunal publishes a number of versions of its Standard Form of Building Contract, of which the 1980 Local Authorities version With Quantities is reproduced with a commentary in Chapter 18. This Form generally follows the traditional procedure.

5. Design and Build Contracts

The traditional procedure outlined above has developed since the early days of railway contracts in the nineteenth century, and is probably still applied today in a majority of large building or engineering contracts. It is based upon the principle that, in general, the employer, through his agents, provides the design which the contractor carries out. This principle is often not consistently

---

[27] See Chap. 10, Section 4.
[28] Discussion of the various matters appearing in this paragraph appears in subsequent chapters.
[29] Under the Standard Form of Building Contract, the contract sum can be varied by the operation of numerous clauses.
[30] See n. 28 above.

6

applied,[31] and in any event there have always been some contracts where the contractor has, to greater or lesser degree, accepted responsibility for design.

In recent times it has become increasingly common for contractors to offer, in addition to building the works, to perform some or all of the duties of architect, engineer or even surveyor, as performed in traditional contracts. The commercial argument for such an approach is either that it is necessary because the contractor alone possesses the specialist knowledge and skill to design and carry out specialist works or, in other cases, that there will be savings of costs or time or both compared with the traditional procedure. Such contracts are sometimes termed "package deal" contracts.[32]

Documents proffered for consideration by contractors require scrutiny to see whether they afford reasonable protection for the employer. In particular it should be considered how far, if at all, by express terms they affect the term of suitability for purpose which is ordinarily implied. This implied term is valuable. If the design turns out to be unsuitable it is no defence to the contractor that he had exercised reasonable skill and care in its preparation. It thus affords greater protection to the employer than he obtains under the traditional procedure where, ordinarily, it is a defence for the architect or engineer to show that he used reasonable skill and care in preparing the design.[33]

The Standard Form of Building Contract and the I.C.E. Conditions (see Chapters 18 and 21) are each wholly unsuitable for use as design and build contracts. The Joint Contracts Tribunal publish a Standard Form of Building Contract With Contractor's Design. This provides for the contractor to complete the design of the Works as well as their construction, and the contractor has an equivalent liability to the employer for the design as would an architect acting independently under a separate contract with the employer. Subject to the application of the Defective Premises Act 1972 for dwellings,[34] the contractor's design liability for consequential loss may be limited to a specific agreed sum.

Construction of contract. The ordinary rules of construction apply.[35] In so far as the contractor is performing duties of architects, engineers and surveyors, cases dealing with such duties when performed by persons as independent professional men[36] and women may be of some assistance although care must be taken to have regard to the different subject-matter. Again when considering the performance of duties similar to those carried out

---

[31] See p. 53 for fitness for purpose; p. 291 for design by specialist sub-contractors; p. 476 for the contractor's position under the Standard Form of Building Contract.

[32] For an example judicially considered, see *Viking Grain Storage* v. *T. H. White Installations* (1985) 33 B.L.R. 103.

[33] See Chap. 13 generally and in particular "The degree of skill required" at p. 312.

[34] See p. 362 for the Defective Premises Act 1972.

[35] See Chap. 3.

[36] See Chap. 13.

by a contractor in a traditional contract some of the decided cases may help but caution is required. Apparently identical terms of contract may, because of the different subject-matter, have a different meaning. An obvious example is that relating to a "defects" clause.[37] In the traditional type of contract it ordinarily excludes defects of design, while in design and build contracts it ordinarily includes them.

Suitability for purpose.   In a design and build contract there is ordinarily an implied term that the finished work will be reasonably suitable for the purpose for which the contractor knows it is required.[38] But one must always exercise caution when placing a contract into a particular category. Thus it appears that where a contractor is invited to tender to design and build, and submits a design which is adopted by the employer's architect acting in the traditional sense and thereafter a formal contract is entered into whereby the contractor's obligations are limited to performing specific works described in the contract, the contractor is not liable in damages for breach of contract if the works do not fulfil the result which, to his knowledge, was sought to be achieved by the employer.[39] But he may be liable if he has expressly guaranteed the result.[40] And he might in special circumstances be liable in tort.[41]

"Turnkey".   This term is sometimes used in design and build contracts. It may be that it is intended to indicate that upon completion the key can be turned and everything will be ready. It has been said that it is not a term of art,[42] *i.e.* it has no precise legal meaning.[43]

Professional men.   Contractors sometimes engage independent professional men to carry out design and other services to fulfil part of the contractor's obligations to the employer. Arising out of such engagement they owe the contractor a duty to carry out their work properly. The requisite standard will be at least one of reasonable skill and care.[44] Where they know that the contractor is under an absolute duty to provide finished work reasonably suitable for a purpose of which they have knowledge they are, it seems, ordinarily under such a duty themselves to the contractor in carrying out design or other services.[45] Further, although not engaged by the employer, they might in certain circumstances owe him a duty of care in tort.[46]

---

[37] See Chap. 10, Section 4.

[38] *Greaves & Co. Ltd.* v. *Baynham Meikle* [1975] 1 W.L.R. 1095 at 1098 (C.A.). See further "Fitness for purpose of completed works" and "Package deals" at p. 55.

[39] *Cable (1956) Ltd.* v. *Hutcherson Ltd.* (1969) 43 A.L.J.R. 321 (Australian High Court).

[40] *Steel Co. of Canada Ltd.* v. *Willand Management Ltd.* [1966] S.C.R. 746 (Canadian Supreme Court).

[41] See generally Chap. 7 and in particular "Contractor's pre-contract information" at p. 178.

[42] *Cable (1956) Ltd.* v. *Hutcherson Ltd.* (1969) 43 A.L.J.R. 321 at 324 (Australian High Court).

[43] See "Term of art" at p. 40.

[44] See p. 312.

[45] *Greaves & Co. Ltd.* v. *Baynham Meikle* [1975] 1 W.L.R. 1095 (C.A.).

[46] See generally "Negligent misstatement" at p. 174 and in particular "Consultants" at p. 180. For the position of salaried architects and comparable employees of the contractor see p. 304.

The employer may himself engage independent professional men to protect his interests. They owe him a duty of care arising out of the engagement.[47] An architect or engineer in such a position usually is, or is supposed to be, an inspector only, whether of the design, the works or both. If such architect or engineer is given authority as agent of the employer, the terms of such agency and his actions should be such as not to interfere with the duties of design, administration and supervision undertaken by the contractor towards the employer. If there is such interference, liabilities may be confused and the employer may find himself deprived of, or hindered in the enforcement of, his remedy against the contractor by the operation of doctrines of law such as variation, waiver or estoppel.[48]

Employers sometimes engage a surveyor to check the contractor's valuations, to price variations and to perform some other duties comparable with those carried out by a quantity surveyor in the the traditional procedure. This can usually be accommodated without great difficulty in a design and build contract and some contractors encourage it, presumably on the basis that it will help to avoid disputes over payment.

6. Management Contracts

For large building projects, management contracts are now fairly common.[49] They are more akin to the traditional procedure than to design and build contracts. They have varying procedures, but the main feature is that there is a management contractor who generally does little or no direct construction work himself, but organises and co-ordinates those who do. The management contractor is usually paid the prime cost of the works[50] plus a fee which may be increased by a bonus related to the amount by which the actual cost of the works is less than a target cost. The construction works are carried out by works contractors who may be sub-contractors of the management contract or, less frequently, in direct contract with the employer. Architects, quantity surveyors and other consultants are usually engaged by the employer as with the traditional procedure. The increasing use of management contracts reflects among other things an appreciation that the complexity of modern building requires the planning and organisational skills of specialists. On the other hand, with the employer engaging a larger number of parties, responsibility is diffused and theoretical legal liability more difficult to enforce in

---

[47] See n. 44 above.

[48] See pp. 262 *et seq.*

[49] The JCT publishes a Standard Form of Management Contract with related standard Works Contract Conditions.

[50] Most management contracts define "prime cost" in an elaborate schedule. The expression usually in essence in this context denotes the basic cost to the management contractor of carrying out the works. His profit and overheads, and sometimes his site and supervision costs, are taken to be covered by the fee. Compare "P.C. or prime cost sums" at p. 86.

practice. By comparison, a design and build contract is likely to be more straightforward for employers.

7. Smaller Contracts

The 1980 Standard Form of Building Contract reproduced with a commentary in Chapter 18 is a sophisticated contract suitable for large projects. One of its features is that there are most elaborate provisions for nominating sub-contractors. For smaller contracts, there are several other standard possibilities. The 1963 Standard Form of Building Contract, which the 1980 Form superseded, was also for large projects but was less sophisticated and is still sometimes used. It should be appreciated by anyone considering using this now outdated Form that it contains difficulties and deficiencies which the 1980 Form has sought to deal with.

The JCT publishes a Standard Intermediate Form of Building Contract[51] and a Standard Agreement for Minor Building Works. The Intermediate Form has provision for Named Sub-contractors, being sub-contractors who are named in the contract documents and whom the contractor is obliged to employ as sub-contractors upon a standard form of Named Sub-contract. The Minor Works Form is a comparatively simple contract where sub-contracting is forbidden without the written consent of the architect which is not to be unreasonably withheld.

---

[51] See generally Darryl Royce, "Tugging at the Contract: Some Preliminary Reflections on the JCT Intermediate Form of Building Contract" (1984) 1 Const.L.J. 97.

FORMATION OF CONTRACT

1. Elements of Contract

The essence of a building contract, like any other contract, is agreement. In deciding whether there has been an agreement and what its terms are the court looks for an offer to do or forbear from doing something by one party and an acceptance[1] of that offer by the other party, turning the offer into a promise.[2] The law further requires that a party suing on a promise must show that he has given consideration for the promise, unless the promise was given by deed. There is consideration where "an act or forbearance of the one party or the promise thereof is the price for which the promise of the other is bought."[3] In

---

[1] See Section 2 below.

[2] See *Chitty* (26th ed.), Vol. 1, Chap. 2.

[3] *Pollock on Contracts* (12th ed.), p. 130, adopted by Lord Dunedin in *Dunlop* v. *Selfridge* [1915] A.C. 847 at 855 (H.L.). See also *Currie* v. *Misa* (1875) L.R. 10 Ex. 153 at 162. For a case where forbearance was held to be valuable consideration see *Comyn Ching* v. *Oriental Tube* (1979) 17 B.L.R. 47 at 79 (C.A.); *cp. I.B.A.* v. *E.M.I. and B.I.C.C.* (1980) 14 B.L.R. 1 (H.L.), where forbearance did not result in a collateral warranty.

the ordinary building contract the consideration given by the employer is the price paid or the promise to pay,[4] and by the contractor is the carrying out of the works or promise to carry them out. The parties must have the capacity to make a contract,[5] and any formalities required by law must be complied with.[6] Both the consideration and the objects of the contract must not be illegal.[7] If there is fraud or misrepresentation the contract may be voidable,[8] while if there is a mutual mistake about some fundamental matter of fact this may have the effect of making the contract void.[9]

2. Offer and Acceptance

(a) *Invitation to tender*

The employer, normally acting through his architect, sends out an invitation to tender for the proposed works. This document usually includes the proposed conditions of contract, plans, and a specification and often unpriced bills of quantities, *i.e.* a bill with the quantities of work set out but the price column blank. An invitation to tender is not normally an offer binding the employer to accept the lowest or any tender. It is comparable to an advertisement that one has a stock of books to sell or houses to let and such advertisements have been described as "offers to negotiate—offers to receive offers—offers to chaffer."[10] It follows that the clause frequently inserted in tenders to the effect that the employer does not undertake to accept the lowest or any tender is probably unnecessary in law.[11] But an express offer to accept

---

[4] For the consideration given where the employer was not to pay, see *Charnock* v. *Liverpool Corporation* [1968] 1 W.L.R. 1498 at 1505 (C.A.). For performance of an existing contractual duty as consideration, see *New Zealand Shipping Co. Ltd.* v. *A. M. Satterthwaite & Co. Ltd.* [1975] A.C. 154 (P.C.); *North Ocean Shipping Co. Ltd.* v. *Hyundai Construction Co. Ltd.* [1979] Q.B. 705; *Pao On* v. *Lau Yiu Long* [1980] A.C. 614 (P.C.); *Comyn Ching* v. *Oriental Tube* (1979) 17 B.L.R. 47 (C.A.); *Williams* v. *Roffey Brothers* [1990] 2 W.L.R. 1153 (C.A.).
[5] See Section 4 of this chapter.
[6] See Section 3 of this chapter.
[7] See Chap. 6, Section 8.
[8] See Chap. 6, Sections 1 and 2.
[9] See *Bell* v. *Lever Bros.* [1932] A.C. 161 (H.L.) reviewed by Steyn J. in *Associated Japanese Bank* v. *Credit du Nord* [1989] 1 W.L.R. 255 at 264; *Chitty* (26th ed.), Vol. 1, Chap. 5. Mistake in this sense does not appear to have been argued in a reported building contract case, neither does it seem important in practice. For these reasons it is not discussed further in this book. For rectification where there has been a mistake in expressing the contract, see Chap. 11, Section 4. For the equitable powers of the court in cases of mistake, see *Solle* v. *Butcher* [1950] 1 K.B. 671 (C.A.); *Grist* v. *Bailey* [1967] 1 Ch. 532; *Curtin* v. *G.L.C.* (1970) 114 S.J. 932 (C.A.). See also *Magee* v. *Pennine Insurance Co. Ltd.* [1969] 2 Q.B. 507 (C.A.); *Laurence* v. *Lexcourt Holdings* [1978] 1 W.L.R. 1128 (H.L.). For mistake as to the nature of a document, see *Saunders* v. *Anglia Building Society* [1971] A.C. 1004 (H.L.).
[10] Bowen L.J. in *Carlill* v. *Carbolic Smoke Ball Co.* [1893] 1 Q.B. 256 at 268 (C.A.); *Grainger & Son* v. *Gough* [1896] A.C. 325 at 334 (H.L.). See also the building contract case of *Moore* v. *Shawcross* [1954] C.L.Y. 342; [1954] J.P.L. 431.
[11] *cf. Pauling* v. *Pontifex* (1852) 2 Saund. & M. 59.

the lowest tender can be binding and have the effect of turning the invitation to tender into an offer,[12] or it may possibly be a unilateral or "if contract," being an offer which the offeror may be free to revoke until the offeror starts to perform its condition.[13] To be in law an offer, an invitation to tender must be construed as a contractual offer capable of being converted by acceptance into a legally enforceable contract.[14] Where tenders are solicited from selected parties all of them known to the invitor and the invitation prescribes a clear, orderly and familiar procedure, a tenderer submitting a conforming tender before the prescribed deadline may be contractually entitled at least to have his tender opened and considered in conjunction with all other conforming tenders. An invitor who failed to open or consider such a tender was held to be in breach of contract.[15]

Statements of fact in the invitation to tender about such matters as the quantities or the site or existing structures may, if a contract is entered into, have no legal effect at all, or they may take effect as representations, or they may form collateral warranties or they may give rise to a claim for negligent misstatement or they may subsequently become incorporated into the contract.[16] It is a question partly of fact, partly of construction to determine the nature of such statements.

(b) *Tender*

The contractor's offer to carry out the works is usually termed a tender.[17] It may well happen that as a result of negotiation[18] it is the employer who eventually makes the offer. In any event a statement, to amount to an offer, must be definite and unambiguous.[19] The person making the offer is for the purposes of this part of the law termed the offeror; the person to whom it is made, the offeree.

Costs of tendering. The cost to the contractor of preparing his tender, including any amended tender necessitated by bona fide alterations in the bills

---

[12] *cf. South Hetton Coal Co.* v. *Haswell Coal Co.* [1898] 1 Ch. 465 (C.A.) approved in *Harvela Ltd.* v. *Royal Trust Co.* [1986] A.C. 207 (H.L.); *Warlow* v. *Harrison* (1859) 1 E. & E. 309.

[13] See Lord Diplock in *Harvela Ltd.* v. *Royal Trust Co.* [1986] A.C. 207 at 224 (H.L.); *Daulia Ltd.* v. *Four Millbank* [1978] 1 Ch. 231 at 238 (C.A.).

[14] See *Gibson* v. *Manchester City Council* [1979] 1 W.L.R. 294 (H.L.), where a statement that "the corporation may be prepared to sell the house to you at the purchase price of £2,725 . . ." was not an offer.

[15] *Blackpool and Fylde Aero Club* v. *Blackpool Borough Council* [1990] 1 W.L.R. 1195 (C.A.).

[16] For a full discussion, see Chap. 6 and for negligent misstatement Chap. 7, Section 3(a).

[17] The term is here used in a completely different sense from that of the tender of goods or money which may amount to a defence under a contract—see *Chitty* (26th ed.), Vol. 1, para. 1555.

[18] See "Lengthy negotiations for a contract" at p. 19; "Unconditional acceptance" at p. 19; "Negotiations after contract" at p. 24.

[19] *Falck* v. *Williams* [1900] A.C. 176 (P.C.); *Harvey* v. *Facey* [1893] A.C. 552 (P.C.); *Bigg* v. *Boyd Gibbins Ltd.* [1971] 1 W.L.R. 913 (C.A.). An acceptance also must be unambiguous, see *Peter Lind & Co. Ltd.* v. *Mersey Docks and Harbour Board* [1972] 2 Lloyd's Rep. 234.

of quantities and plans, may be considerable, but in ordinary circumstances there is no implication that the tenderer will be paid for this work.[20] "[H]e undertakes this work as a gamble, and its cost ... he hopes will be met out of the profits of such contracts as are made as a result of tenders which prove to be successful."[21] But the contractor may be able to recover a reasonable sum for work done at the employer's request which falls outside the normal work which a contractor performs gratuitously.[22] In *William Lacey (Hounslow) Ltd.* v. *Davis*,[23] the contractor submitted a tender for the rebuilding of war-damaged premises. The tender was not accepted, but in the belief that the contract would be placed with him the contractor subsequently prepared various further estimates, schedules and the like which the employer made use of in negotiation with the War Damage Commission, but he never placed any contract with the contractor. It was held that the contractor was entitled to a reasonable sum for the work carried out subsequent to the tender. There was held to be an implied promise to pay. The modern legal analysis may be that the obligation to pay sounds "in quasi-contract or, as we now say, restitution."[24]

If the employer invites a tender without any intention of entering into a contract and the contractor, believing the invitation to tender to be genuine, incurs expense in tendering, the contractor may have a claim for damages in fraud against the employer.[25]

Design costs.　As part of the process of tendering, specialist contractors sometimes carry out works of design. It is thought that, in the absence of agreement,[26] the costs of such works are part of the costs of tendering so that by analogy with the *Lacey* case if there is no contract they are irrecoverable unless the employer makes some use of the design or causes the contractor to carry out work beyond what is normal in the circumstances.

Restrictive tendering arrangements.　There is United Kingdom and European Community legislation aimed at promoting competition, preventing restrictive tendering agreements and prohibiting national or local restrictions on contracting. This is discussed in Sections 3 and 4 of Chapter 14.

(c) *Letter of intent*

Documents so described are frequently sent. It is a question upon the facts of

---

[20] *William Lacey (Hounslow) Ltd.* v. *Davis* [1957] 1 W.L.R. 932. The principle is based on custom; *ibid.* at 934, 935. For expenses of entering an architectural competition, *cp. Jepson & Partners* v. *Severn Trent Water Authority* (1982) 20 B.L.R. 53 (C.A.).
[21] *William Lacey (Hounslow) Ltd.* v. *Davis* [1957] 1 W.L.R. 932 at 934.
[22] *Ibid.*
[23] [1957] 1 W.L.R. 932.
[24] *British Steel* v. *Cleveland Bridge* [1984] 1 All E.R. 504, 511 and 24 B.L.R. 94 at 122; *Chitty* (26th ed.), Vol. 1 para. 2040; see also *Marston Construction Co.* v. *Kigass* (1989) 46 B.L.R. 109; *cp. Turriff Construction* v. *Regalia* (1971) 9 B.L.R. 20.
[25] *cf. Richardson* v. *Silvester* (1873) L.R. 9 Q.B. 34. For fraud, see p. 122.
[26] For an example of such an agreement arising out of a letter of intent, see *Turriff Construction* v. *Regalia* (1971) 9 B.L.R. 20.

each case whether the sending of a letter of intent can give rise to any, and if any, what, liability.[27]

A letter of intent ordinarily expresses an intention to enter into a contract in the future but creates no liability in regard to that future contract. Construed in its factual context, it may have no binding effect. It may exceptionally take effect as an executory ancillary contract entitling the recipient to interim costs if the intended future contract is not made and, perhaps, imposing liabilities, *e.g.* for the quality or suitability of work done. It may effect an "if" contract under which the writer asks the recipient to carry out a certain performance and promises that, if he does so, he will receive remuneration in return. It may result in no contract, but the law may nevertheless impose an obligation on the party who makes a request to pay a reasonable sum for such work as has been done pursuant to the request if the intended future contract is not made. If the intended future contract is made, the rights of the parties are normally governed by that contract, the letter of intent ceasing to have effect.[28]

In *Turriff Construction* v. *Regalia*,[29] a design and build contractor[30] offered to the employer to undertake certain urgent works of design necessary to obtain estimates and planning permission provided he obtained an assumption of liability to pay for such work. He indicated that he would regard receipt of a letter of intent as an acceptance of his offer. The employer sent a letter of intent and it was held that he was liable to pay for the work carried out. In *British Steel* v. *Cleveland Bridge*,[31] suppliers of steel castings were held entitled to a reasonable sum in quasi-contract or restitution. In *Wilson Smithett* v. *Bangladesh Sugar*,[32] a letter of intent was construed as an acceptance of an offer binding both parties.

(d) *Estimates*

There may be an offer although the contractor makes it on a document called an estimate. Thus in *Croshaw* v. *Pritchard*[33] the employer's architect sent a letter to the defendants asking them if they "would be willing to give us a tender in competition for the work," and wrote later enclosing information required for tender. In a letter headed "Estimate" the defendants wrote to the architect saying "our estimate ... amounts to the sum of £1,230." This was accepted. The defendants then purported to withdraw their estimate and, when sued for the difference between £1,230 and the cost incurred in having the work

---

[27] See generally S. N. Ball, "Work carried out in pursuance of Letters of Intent—Contract of Restitution?" (1983) 99 L.Q.R. 572.

[28] This paragraph is based on *British Steel* v. *Cleveland Bridge* [1984] 1 All E.R. 504 and *Turriff Construction* v. *Regalia* (1971) 9 B.L.R. 20. See also *Kleinwort Benson* v. *Malaysia Mining* [1989] 1 W.L.R. 379 (C.A.) at 391 for the concept of a "comfort letter." See also S. N. Ball, *op. cit.*

[29] (1971) 9 B.L.R. 20.

[30] For a discussion of such contracts see p. 6.

[31] [1984] 1 All E.R. 504.

[32] [1986] 1 Lloyd's Rep. 378.

[33] (1899) 16 T.L.R. 45; *sub nom. Crowshaw* v. *Pritchard*, H.B.C. (4th ed.), Vol. 2, p. 274.

executed by another contractor, claimed that they had made no offer capable of acceptance. This defence was rejected and the damages claimed awarded to the plaintiff. It was further held that there was no custom that a letter such as that written by the defendants could not amount to an offer, and it was said that if such a custom existed it would be bad and not enforceable.[34]

In a Canadian case, an employer was liable for the inaccuracy of an "estimate" of the cost of part of the works, it being intended as a reliable basis for a tenderer's calculations.[35]

(e) *Standing offers*

Tenders are sometimes invited for the periodic carrying out of work.[36] If the contractor tenders and there is an acceptance, the result depends upon the construction of the documents, but can have one of three well-known consequences.[37] Firstly, there may be a contract for the carrying out of a definite amount of work during a certain period. Secondly, there may be a contract in which the employer agrees to order such work as he needs during the period. In such a case the employer is in breach of contract if during the period he places orders for the work elsewhere, and the contractor is in breach if he refuses to carry out the work during the period.[38] Thirdly, there may be a standing offer on the part of the contractor to carry out certain work during the period if and when the employer chooses to give an order.[39] The contractor may revoke his offer for future orders unless there is consideration to keep it open or the documents are under seal,[40] but if before revocation an order in the terms of the agreement is given, a contract comes into existence for that order and the contractor must carry it out.[41] If no order at all is given during the period,[42] or if less work is ordered than the probable amount indicated in the invitation to tender, whether because the work is given to another contractor or otherwise,[43] the contractor has no action for breach of contract.[44] Contracts of indefinite or very long duration may be construed as determinable upon reasonable notice, particularly if they are affected by inflation.[45]

---

[34] H.B.C. Report p. 276.

[35] *Cana Construction* v. *The Queen* (1973) 37 D.L.R. (3d) 418.

[36] Most of the cases deal with the supply of goods but the principle applies to contracts of work and labour, *R.* v. *Demers* [1900] A.C. 103 (P.C.).

[37] *Percival Ltd.* v. *L.C.C. Asylums Committee* (1918) 87 L.J.K.B. 677 at 678.

[38] *Ibid.* at 679. *cf. Att.-Gen.* v. *Stewards & Co. Ltd.* (1901) 18 T.L.R. 131 (H.L.); *Kelly Pipelines* v. *British Gas* (1989) 48 B.L.R. 126.

[39] *Percival Ltd.* v. *L.C.C. Asylums Committee* (1918) 87 L.J.K.B. 677 at 67.

[40] *Offord* v. *Davies* (1862) 12 C.B.(N.S.) 748; *G.N. Railway* v. *Witham* (1873) L.R. 9 C.P. 16 at 19.

[41] *G.N. Railway* v. *Witham* (1873) L.R. 9 C.P. 16.

[42] See *R.* v. *Demers* [1900] A.C. 103 (P.C.).

[43] See *Att.-Gen.* v. *Stewards & Co. Ltd.* (1901) 18 T.L.R. 131 (H.L.).

[44] *Ibid.*; *Gilmour* v. *McLeod*, 12 N.Z.L.R. S.C. 334; *Pitcaithly & Co.* v. *Mclean & Son* (1911) 31 N.Z.L.R. 648.

[45] *Re Spenborough Urban District Council's Agreement*; *Spenborough Corporation* v. *Cooke Sons & Co. Ltd.* [1968] Ch. 139; *Staffordshire Health Authority* v. *South Staffordshire Waterworks* [1978] 1 W.L.R. 1387; *cp. Kirklees M.B.C.* v. *Yorkshire Woollen* (1978) 77 L.G.R. 448; and see Article, 96 L.Q.R. 177. See p. 332 for Architect's Engagements.

16

(f) *Rejection and revocation of offer*

Rejection. A rejection, which takes effect when it is communicated to the offeror, kills the offer so that it cannot thereafter be accepted.[46] It is a matter of construction whether a particular statement does or does not constitute a rejection.

Counter-offer. A counter-offer operates as a rejection killing the offer which it addresses, and a purported acceptance may in law be a counter-offer if it materially alters the terms proposed.[47]

Revocation. An offer may be revoked at any time before acceptance unless consideration has been given to keep it open[48]; or the offeror is, in special circumstances, estopped from acting inconsistently with the existence of the offer.[49] Revocation of the offer is not effective until it has been communicated to the offeree.[50] In the ordinary case an offeree who has acted on the offer cannot recover damages in tort if the offer is revoked before acceptance.[51]

Lapse of offer. An offer can expressly state the time within which it is open for acceptance. If that time expires without acceptance the offer lapses. Where negotiations were taking place between contractor and employer in the course of which the contractor's offer lapsed but the contractor proceeded to carry out the work without ever concluding an express contract with the employer the contractor recovered a reasonable sum.[52] If no time is stated the offer remains in force for a reasonable time and upon the expiry of that time it lapses.[53] What is reasonable depends on whether on the facts the offeree should, in fairness to both parties, be regarded as having refused the offer. The parties' conduct after the making of the offer is relevant.[54]

Death. "It is admitted law that, if a man who makes an offer dies, the offer cannot be accepted after he is dead."[55]

---

[46] *Tinn* v. *Hoffman and Co.* (1873) 29 L.T.R. 271 at 278; *Trollope & Colls* v. *Atomic Power Constructions Ltd.* [1963] 1 W.L.R. 333 at 337. See also *Chitty* (26th ed.), paras. 95–97; *cp.* "Acceptance by post, telex or fax" at p. 25.

[47] *Trollope & Colls* v. *Atomic Power Constructions Ltd.* [1963] 1 W.L.R. 333 applied in *Butler Machine Tool* v. *Ex-Cell-O Corporation* [1979] 1 W.L.R. 401 (C.A.), and see *Chitty* (26th ed.), Vol. 1, paras. 56, 78 and 95. See also "Battle of forms" at p. 19.

[48] *Byrne* v. *Van Tienhoven* (1880) 5 C.P.D. 344.

[49] *Watson* v. *Canada Permanent Trust Co.* (1972) 27 D.L.R. (3d) 735, British Columbia Supreme Court applying the principle sometimes known as that stated in *Central London Property Trust Ltd.* v. *High Trees House Ltd.* [1947] K.B. 130. See p. 263.

[50] *Byrne* v. *Van Tienhoven* (1880) 5 C.P.D. 344; *cf. Dickinson* v. *Dodds* (1876) 2 Ch.D. 463 (C.A.).

[51] *Holman Construction Ltd.* v. *Delco Timber Co. Ltd.* [1972] N.Z.L.R. 1081 (New Zealand Supreme Court), discussed at p. 178.

[52] *Peter Lind & Co. Ltd.* v. *Mersey Docks & Harbour Board* [1972] 2 Lloyd's Rep. 234.

[53] *Ramsgate Victoria Hotel Co. v. Montefiore* (1866) L.R. 1 Ex. 109.

[54] See *Manchester Diocesan Council for Education* v. *Commercial & General Investments Ltd.* [1970] 1 W.L.R. 241 at 248.

[55] Mellish L.J. in *Dickinson* v. *Dodds* (1876) 2 Ch.D. 463 at 475 (C.A.); *cf.* "Death" at p. 133.

(g) *Notice of terms*

A party to a contract cannot be bound by a term of which he has no notice. In particular, if the other party seeks to rely on some clause limiting his common law obligations he must prove strictly that the clause on which he seeks to rely is part of the contract.[56] He can do this by a signed contract which includes the clause, for a person who has signed a contract is ordinarily, in the absence of fraud or misrepresentation[57] or undue influence,[58] bound by its terms whether he has read it or not.[59] Failing such a document it is a question in each case whether reasonably sufficient steps have been taken to give notice of the terms.[60]

To succeed in enforcing a particularly onerous or unusual printed clause, a party has to show that it was brought fairly and reasonably to the attention of the other party.[61] Where work was done in pursuance of a typewritten offer which had on the face of it, in very small print, an exemption clause relating to delay caused by strikes, it was held that the employer was bound by the clause although he had never read it.[62] If in such a case the clause had been on the back of the document with no reference to its existence on the face of the document the contractor might not have been able to rely on it.[63]

An offer "subject to our General Conditions of Contract obtainable on request" was held to refer to the conditions current at the time of the offer.[64]

Course of dealing. "If two parties have made a series of similar contracts each containing certain conditions, and then they make another without expressly referring to those conditions it may be that those conditions ought to

---

[56] *Olley* v. *Marlborough Court* [1949] 1 K.B. 532 at 549 (C.A.); *Mendelssohn* v. *Normand Ltd.* [1970] 1 Q.B. 177 (C.A.); *Thornton* v. *Shoe Lane Parking Ltd.* [1971] 2 Q.B. 163 (C.A.); *Hollier* v. *Rambler Motors (A.M.C.) Ltd.* [1972] 2 Q.B. 71 (C.A.); *cf.* Unfair Contract Terms Act 1977, s.11(2) and Sched. 2, para. (c).

[57] See, *e.g. Curtis* v. *Chemical Cleaning Co.* [1951] 1 K.B. 805 (C.A.); *Mendelssohn* v. *Normand Ltd.* [1970] 1 Q.B. 177 (C.A.). See also *Dietz* v. *Lennig Chemicals Ltd.* [1969] 1 A.C. 170 (H.L.); *J. Evans & Son* v. *Andrea Merzario* [1976] 1 W.L.R. 1078 (C.A.).

[58] *National Westminster Bank* v. *Morgan* [1985] A.C. 686.

[59] *Parker* v. *S.E. Railway* (1877) 2 C.P.D. 416 at 421; *L'Estrange* v. *Graucob* [1934] 2 K.B. 394 at 403 (C.A.). For mistake as to nature of document, see *Saunders* v. *Anglia Building Society* [1971] A.C. 1004 (H.L.); *United Dominions Trust* v. *Western* [1976] Q.B. 513 (C.A.).

[60] *Parker* v. *S.E. Railway* (1877) 2 C.P.D. 416; *Thornton* v. *Shoe Lane Parking Ltd.* [1971] 2 Q.B. 163 (C.A.). For a person not bound by notice in foreign language, see *Geier* v. *Kujawa Western & Warne Bros. (Transport) Ltd.* [1970] 1 Lloyd's Rep. 364.

[61] *Interfoto Picture Library* v. *Stiletto Visual Programmes* [1989] Q.B. 433 (C.A.); *cf.* Unfair Contract Terms Act 1977, s.11(2) and Sched. 2, para. (c).

[62] *Frederick Sage & Co. Ltd.* v. *Spiers & Ponds Ltd.* (1915) 31 T.L.R. 104; *cf. L'Estrange* v. *Graucob* [1934] 2 K.B. 394 (C.A.). See also *British Road Services* v. *Crutchley (Arthur V.) Ltd.* [1968] 1 All E.R. 811 (C.A.).

[63] *Parker* v. *S.E. Railway* (1877) 2 C.P.D. 416; *Olley* v. *Marlborough Court* [1949] 1 K.B. 532 (C.A.) and other authorities referred to in n. 56 above; see also *Chapelton* v. *Barry Urban District Council* [1940] 1 K.B. 532 (C.A.).

[64] *Smith* v. *South Wales Switchgear* [1978] 1 W.L.R. 165 (H.L.).

be implied."[65] This principle occasionally applies in building contracts.[66] More often, the complexity of both subject-matter and of the terms usually contained in express written contracts precludes it.

(h) *Unconditional acceptance*

There is an acceptance of the offer bringing a binding contract into existence when the offeree makes an unconditional acceptance.[67] If he suggests any new terms there cannot be an acceptance and this may amount to a fresh offer[68] although a mere request for information about the terms of an offer does not amount to a counter-offer.[69]

"Battle of forms." This expression refers to an offer followed by a series of counter-offers where each party successively seeks to stipulate different terms, often their own standard printed terms. "In some cases the battle is won by the man who fires the last shot,"[70] the other party being taken to have agreed his terms by conduct in proceeding to perform the agreement without objection. Sometimes agreement is reached by an amalgamation of both parties' proposed terms and conditions construed together.[71] Such battles quite often occur with building contracts.[72]

Lengthy negotiations for a contract. It is sometimes difficult to determine whether a concluded contract has come into existence when there have been lengthy negotiations between the parties but no formal contract has ever been signed. It is suggested that a useful approach is to ask whether the following can be answered in the affirmative[73]:

---

[65] Lord Reid in *McCutcheon* v. *David MacBrayne Ltd.* [1964] 1 W.L.R. 125 at 127 (H.L.); see also *Hardwick Game Farm* v. *Suffolk, etc., Association* [1969] 2 A.C. 31 at 90, 104, 105, 130 (H.L.); *Mendelssohn* v. *Normand Ltd.* [1970] 1 Q.B. 177 (C.A.); *Hollier* v. *Rambler Motors (A.M.C.) Ltd.* [1972] 2 Q.B. 71 (C.A.); *Roberts* v. *Elwells Engineers Ltd.* [1972] 2 Q.B. 586 (C.A.); *British Crane Hire Corporation Ltd.* v. *Ipswich Plant Hire Ltd.* [1975] Q.B. 303 (C.A.); *Amalgamated Investment and Property Co. Ltd.* v. *Texas Thomas International Bank Ltd.* [1982] Q.B. 84 (C.A.), commented on in *Keen* v. *Holland* [1984] 1 W.L.R. 251 (C.A.); *The "Leila"* [1985] 2 Lloyd's Rep. 172 at 178.
[66] *e.g. Rees-Hough Ltd.* v. *Redland* (1985) 2 Cons.L.R. 109; *Hanson* v. *Rapid Civil Engineering* (1987) 38 B.L.R. 106.
[67] See *Nicolene* v. *Simmonds* [1953] 1 Q.B. 543 (C.A.). Problems as to the existence of a contract and as to its meaning when it is decided that there is a contract are closely related and it may be useful to refer to the next chapter on construction of contracts.
[68] *Hyde* v. *Wrench* (1840) 3 Beav. 334; *cf. Leslie & Co.* v. *Commissioners of Works* (1914) 78 J.P. 462; *Peter Lind & Co. Ltd.* v. *Mersey Docks & Harbour Board* [1972] 2 Lloyd's Rep. 235; and see "Counter-offer" at p. 17.
[69] *Stevenson* v. *McLean* (1880) 5 Q.B.D. 346.
[70] *Butler Machine Tool* v. *Ex-Cell-O Corporation* [1979] 1 W.L.R. 401 at 404 (C.A.).
[71] *Ibid.*
[72] *e.g. Rees Hough* v. *Redland* 2 Cons.L.R. 109; *Sauter Automation* v. *Goodman* (1986) 34 B.L.R. 81; *Chichester Joinery* v. *John Mowlem* (1987) 42 B.L.R. 100.
[73] See *Pagnan* v. *Feed Products* [1987] 2 Lloyd's Rep. 601 at 610 and 619 (C.A.) and propositions applied by Megaw J. in *Trollope & Colls Ltd.* v. *Atomic Power Constructions Ltd.* [1963] 1 W.L.R. 333 at 336. See also *British Guiana Credit Corp.* v. *Da Silva* [1965] 1 W.L.R. 248 (P.C.); *Bushwall Properties Ltd.* v. *Vortex Properties Ltd.* [1976] 1 W.L.R. 591 at 603 (C.A.).

(1) in the relevant period of negotiation did the parties intend to contract?[74]

(2) at the time when they are alleged to have contracted, had they agreed with sufficient certainty upon the terms which they then regarded as being required in order that a contract should come into existence?

(3) did those terms include all the terms which, even though the parties did not realise it, were in fact essential[75] to be agreed if the contract was to be legally enforceable and commercially workable?

(4) was there a sufficient indication of acceptance by the offeree of the offer as then made complying with any stipulation in the offer itself as to the manner of acceptance?[76]

Some of these matters are discussed further below.

All negotiations should be considered.[77] This is important, especially where there have been meetings at which oral statements were made showing that essential terms, not referred to in certain correspondence, were still awaiting agreement at the time of such correspondence.[78]

Essential terms.   Subject to the question at (3) above, "the parties are to be regarded as masters of their contractual fate" in determining what terms are essential.[79] "It is for the parties to decide whether they wish to be bound and, if so, by what terms, whether important or unimportant."[80]

It is thought that agreement as to parties, price, time and description of works is normally the minimum necessary to make the contract commercially workable. Lack of agreement as to parties can arise when companies have common directors and there is confusion as to which company is intended to be a contracting party.[81] It can also arise when there is an issue as to whether a contract is with an agent or his principal.[82] Price is discussed at page 23 and time at page 218. Silence by the parties as to either price or time may not alone prevent a contract coming into existence, for if the other essential terms are agreed a reasonable charge or time for completion will be implied by the

---

[74] For the requirement that the parties intended to create a legal relationship, see *Edwards* v. *Skyways Ltd.* [1964] 1 W.L.R. 349 and authorities referred to therein (offer to make *ex gratia* payment does not carry necessary or even probable implication that the agreement is to be without legal effect). See also *Horrocks* v. *Forray* [1976] 1 W.L.R. 230 (C.A.); *ZIC* v. *NK* [1987] 2 Lloyd's Rep. 596 (which reaches no conclusion on the point there at issue but lists some of the main authorities); *Kleinwort Benson* v. *Malaysia Mining* [1989] 1 W.L.R. 379 (C.A.).

[75] "If some particulars essential to the agreement still remain to be settled afterwards there is no contract"; Lord Blackburn in *Rossiter* v. *Miller* (1878) 3 App.Cas. 1124 at 1151 (H.L.).

[76] *Holwell Securities Ltd.* v. *Hughes* [1974] 1 W.L.R. 155 (C.A.); *Wettern Electric* v. *Welsh Agency* [1983] Q.B. 796 at 802; *Chitty* (26th ed.), paras. 77–80.

[77] *Pagnan* v. *Granaria* [1986] 2 Lloyd's Rep. 547; *Pagnan* v. *Feed Products* [1987] 2 Lloyd's Rep. 601 (C.A.).

[78] *Hussey* v. *Horne-Payne* (1879) 4 App.Cas. 311 at 316 (H.L.); *Panorama Developments (Guildford) Ltd.* v. *Fidelis Furnishing Fabrics Ltd.* [1971] 2 Q.B. 711 (C.A.).

[79] *Pagnan* v. *Feed Products* [1987] 2 Lloyd's Rep. 601 at 611 (C.A.).

[80] *Ibid.* at 619.

[81] *cp. Damon* v. *Hapag-Lloyd* [1985] 1 W.L.R. 435.

[82] See *Panorama Developments (Guildford) Ltd.* v. *Fidelis Furnishing Fabrics Ltd.* [1971] 2 Q.B. 711 (C.A.). See also p. 307.

Supply of Goods and Services Act 1982.[83] The description of the works may be in wide terms[84] and it may be subject to the retrospective operation of a variation clause. Thus in *Trollope & Colls Ltd.* v. *Atomic Power Constructions Ltd.*[85] an offer was made in February 1959 to carry out certain works for £x. In June 1959, while the parties were still negotiating the terms of the contract, work commenced and was still continuing in April 1960 when the parties agreed upon all the essential terms including a clause providing for the variation of the contract work. By April 1960, as a result of variations, the work to be carried out and the price to be paid if there was a contract differed from the work and price referred to in the February 1959 offer, but it was held that a contract came into existence upon the terms finally agreed in April 1960.[86]

"Subject to contract". If a purported acceptance is expressed to be "subject to contract," or some other words[87] are used which show that further negotiations or events are contemplated, there is no concluded contract.[88] The words "subject to contract" have acquired a definite ascertained legal meaning,[89] but very exceptionally they may be used in relation to an agreement which is nevertheless binding.[90] There may be a concluded contract where the parties have agreed upon all the terms and merely agree that these shall later be embodied in a formal document.[91]

---

[83] See p. 45.

[84] See p. 81; see also *Malcolm* v. *Chancellor, Masters and Scholars of the University of Oxford, The Times*, December 19, 1990 (C.A.).

[85] [1963] 1 W.L.R. 333.

[86] It followed that the contractors were bound to complete and accept payment in accordance with the contract and were not entitled to stop work and claim payment on a *quantum meruit*.

[87] *e.g.* "subject to strike and lock-out clauses": *Love & Stewart Ltd.* v. *S. Instone* (1917) 33 T.L.R. 475; "subject to surveyor's report": *Marks* v. *Board* (1930) 46 T.L.R. 424; "subject to satisfactory survey": *Astra Trust Ltd.* v. *Adams & Williams* [1969] 1 Lloyd's Rep. 81; "subject to satisfactory running trials": *John Howard & Co.* v. *J. P. Knight Ltd.* [1969] 1 Lloyd's Rep. 364; "subject to satisfactory completion of two trial voyages": *Albion Sugar* v. *William Tankers* [1977] 2 Lloyd's Rep. 457, resulting in an agreement for the two trials but no time charter-party; "subject to satisfactory mortgage": *Lee Parker* v. *Izzet (No. 2)* [1972] 1 W.L.R. 775; "subject to details": *Star Steamship* v. *Beogradska* [1988] 2 Lloyd's Rep. 583. *cf. Mackay* v. *Dick* (1881) 6 App.Cas. 251 (H.L.). For a contract subject to ratification by the principal of the person purporting to make it, see *Warehousing, etc., Ltd.* v. *Jafferali & Sons Ltd.* [1964] A.C. 1 (P.C.).

[88] *Rossiter* v. *Miller* (1878) 3 App.Cas. 1124 (H.L.); *Bozson* v. *Altrincham Urban District Council* (1903) 67 J.P. 397 (C.A.); *Chillingworth* v. *Esche* [1924] 1 Ch. 97 (C.A.); *cf. Branca* v. *Cobarro* [1947] K.B. 854 (C.A.); *Smallman* v. *Smallman* [1972] Fam. 25, 32 (C.A.); *Brown* v. *Gould* [1972] Ch. 53; *Tiverton Estates Ltd.* v. *Wearwell Ltd.* [1975] Ch. 146 (C.A.); *Munton* v. *G.L.C.* [1976] 1 W.L.R. 649 (C.A.). For a discussion of the principles relating to a contract subject to a suspensive condition, see *Cranleigh Precision Engineering Ltd.* v. *Bryant* [1965] 1 W.L.R. 1293.

[89] *Chillingworth* v. *Esche* [1924] Ch. 97 (C.A.). The words, once introduced, can only cease to apply if the parties expressly or by necessary implication so agree, see *Cohen* v. *Nessdale* [1987] 2 All E.R. 97 (C.A.).

[90] As in *Alpenstow* v. *Regalian* [1985] 1 W.L.R. 721.

[91] *Rossiter* v. *Miller* (1878) 3 App.Cas. 1124 (H.L.); *Lewis* v. *Brass* (1877) 3 Q.B.D. 667 (C.A.); *Love & Stewart Ltd.* v. *S. Instone* (1917) 33 T.L.R. 475. See also the very special case of *Richards (Michael) Properties Ltd.* v. *St. Saviours Parish, Southwark* [1975] 3 All E.R. 416 where the words "subject to contract" were added by mistake to a concluded contract and therefore were rejected as surplusage. In *Munton* v. *G.L.C.* [1976] 1 W.L.R. 649 at 656 (C.A.), the Court of Appeal emphasised that this was a very special case which in no way altered the "sanctity of the words subject to contract."

Certainty of terms.   "In order to constitute a valid contract the parties must so express themselves that their meaning can be determined with a reasonable degree of certainty."[92] Thus agreements for the sale of goods "on hire-purchase terms over two years,"[93] and "subject to war clause,"[94] have been held to be too vague.[95] But "a distinction must be drawn between a clause which is meaningless and a clause which is yet to be agreed. A clause which is meaningless can often be ignored while still leaving the contract good; whereas a clause which has yet to be agreed may mean that there is no contract at all because the parties have not agreed on all the essential terms."[96]

Reference to reasonable requirements or standards is not too vague; the court (or arbitrator when there is an arbitration clause) can, in default of agreement, determine what is reasonable.[97]

Meaningless words.   An apparent agreement containing meaningless words may be treated in one of three ways: the meaningless words may be ignored and the rest of the clause in which they appear enforced; or the clause in which they appear may be struck out but the rest of the agreement enforced; or the whole agreement may exceptionally be vitiated. Which of these may occur depends on the importance which the parties are considered to have attached to the clause and, presumably, on the remaining integrity of the agreement shorn of the meaningless words.[98] If a clause taken literally is almost incomprehensible, the court may be prepared to "translate" it if the parties' intention is clear, even though this might involve using words not to be found in the contract.[99]

Where an otherwise clear acceptance was expressed to be subject to "the usual conditions of acceptance" and there were no usual conditions of acceptance so that the words were meaningless, the court ignored the words quoted and held that the writer of the words was bound by the clear terms of the rest of

---

[92] Lord Maugham in *Scammell* v. *Ouston* [1941] A.C. 251 at 255 (H.L.); *Bushwall Properties Ltd.* v. *Vortex Properties Ltd.* [1976] 1 W.L.R. 591 (C.A.); *cf.* Lord Wright, *Hillas & Co. Ltd.* v. *Arcos Ltd.* (1932) 147 L.T. 503 at 504 (H.L.) and see "Valid meaning" at p. 41.

[93] *Scammell* v. *Ouston* [1941] A.C. 251 (H.L.).

[94] *Bishop & Baxter* v. *Anglo-Eastern Co. Ltd.* [1944] 1 K.B. 12 (C.A.).

[95] See also *British Electrical, etc., Ltd.* v. *Patley Pressings Ltd. and others* [1953] 1 W.L.R. 280—"Subject to force majeure conditions" too vague; but see Denning L.J. in *Nicolene* v. *Simmonds*, [1953] 1 Q.B. 543 at 552 (C.A.), and *cf. Hong Guan & Co. Ltd.* v. *R. Jumabhoy & Sons Ltd.* [1960] A.C. 684 at 700. (P.C.), a sale "subject to force majeure and shipment" valid; *Three Rivers Trading Co.* v. *Gwinear and District Farmers* (1967) 111 S.J. 831 (C.A.)—sale of "400 tons (approx.)" of barley not void for uncertainty; and see *Edwards* v. *Skyways Ltd.* [1964] 1 W.L.R. 349.

[96] Denning L.J. in *Nicolene* v. *Simmonds*, [1953] 1 Q.B. 543 at 551 (C.A.); *Lovelock Ltd.* v. *Exportles* [1968] 1 Lloyd's Rep. 163 (C.A.). See also "subject to contract" above; *cf. Shamrock SS. Co. Ltd.* v. *Storey* (1899) 81 L.T. 413 (C.A.); *Hobbs Padgett and Co. (Reinsurance)* v. *C. Kirkland Ltd.* [1969] 2 Lloyd's Rep. 547 (C.A.).

[97] See *Sweet & Maxwell Ltd.* v. *Universal News Services Ltd.* [1964] 2 Q.B. 699 (C.A.).

[98] *Nicolene* v. *Simmonds*, [1953] 1 Q.B. 543 (C.A.); *Gola Sports* v. *General Sportcraft Co.* [1982] Com.L.R. 51 (C.A.); for another example of the first possibility, see *Adamastos Shipping* v. *Anglo-Saxon Petroleum* [1959] A.C. 133 (H.L.).

[99] *Esmil* v. *Fairclough* (1981) 19 B.L.R. 129.

the document and there was a contract in existence.[1] A contract made upon "usual terms" as to one of its incidents can be valid, and the term will be enforced if the contents of the term and its general use by the class of persons who make such contracts is proved.[2]

Price.   In the vast majority, at least, of substantial transactions the price will be an essential term, but it is a question of construction whether it indeed is.[3] It is thought that an agreement to do specified work which is silent as to price can be binding if the price is not in the circumstances essential. If there is a binding agreement, the law implies a promise on the part of the employer to pay a reasonable charge.[4] If there is an agreement to do work "at a price to be agreed" by the parties and the agreement is executory (*i.e.* nothing done by either party in performance of the agreement), there is no binding contract.[5] If the agreement is executed wholly or in part, the employer must pay a reasonable price for work done, and it seems, the terms of the contract are binding.[6]

An agreement where there is a formula or other machinery for determining the price is valid. If the machinery breaks down for any reason, the court may substitute its own machinery to determine a fair and reasonable price if, on the true construction of the agreement, the machinery was a subsidiary and non-essential part of the contract.[7] Arguments that contractual machinery is inadequate "exert minimal attraction."[8]

An agreement to do work at a price to be agreed or, in default of agreement, to be determined by arbitration is valid,[9] it being a question of construction whether a document containing an arbitration clause has this effect.[10] Where there is such an agreement there is an obligation on the parties to try to agree the price and refusal to discuss is a repudiation.[11] Where work was carried out

---

[1] *Nicolene* v. *Simmonds* [1953] 1 Q.B. 543 (C.A.).

[2] *Shamrock SS. Co. Ltd.* v. *Storey* (1899) 81 L.T. 413 (C.A.).

[3] *B.S.C.* v. *Cleveland Bridge Co.* [1984] 1 All E.R. 504 and the cases there cited.

[4] See Supply of Goods and Service Act 1982, s.15 and p. 78.

[5] *May & Butcher Ltd.* v. *The King* [1934] 2 K.B. 17 (H.L.); *British Bank for Foreign Trade Ltd.* v. *Novinex Ltd.* [1949] 1 K.B. 623; *King's Motors (Oxford) Ltd.* v. *Lax* [1970] 1 W.L.R. 426; *Smith* v. *Morgan* [1971] 1 W.L.R. 803; *Brown* v. *Gould* [1972] Ch. 53; *Courtney & Fairbairn Ltd.* v. *Tolaini Brothers (Hotels) Ltd.* [1975] 1 W.L.R. 297 (C.A.).

[6] *Foley* v. *Classique Coaches* [1934] 2 K.B. 1 (C.A.); *National Coal Board* v. *Galley* [1958] 1 W.L.R. 16 (C.A.); see also *Hillas* v. *Arcos* (1932) 147 L.T. 503 (H.L.).

[7] *Sudbrooke Trading* v. *Eggleton* [1983] 1 A.C. 444 (H.L.); *Didymi Corporation* v. *Atlantic Lines* [1988] 2 Lloyd's Rep. 108 (C.A.); *cp. Northern Regional Health Authority* v. *Derek Crouch* [1984] Q.B. 644 (C.A.) discussed at p. 389.

[8] *Queensland Electricity* v. *New Hope Collieries* [1989] 1 Lloyd's Rep. 205 at 210 (P.C.).

[9] *May & Butcher Ltd.* v. *The King* [1934] 2 K.B. 17 (H.L.); *Hillas* v. *Arcos* (1932) 147 L.T. 503 (H.L.); *Foley* v. *Classique Coaches* [1934] 2 K.B. 1 (C.A.); *F. & G. Sykes (Wessex) Ltd.* v. *Fine Fare Ltd.* [1966] 2 Lloyd's Rep. 205, *affd.* [1967] 1 Lloyd's Rep. 53 (C.A.), although reversed in part on different grounds. See also *Brown* v. *Gould* [1972] Ch. 53; *Courtney & Fairbairn Ltd.* v. *Tolaini Brothers (Hotels) Ltd.* [1975] 1 W.L.R. 297 (C.A.); *Thomas Bates Ltd.* v. *Wyndhams Ltd.* [1981] 1 W.L.R. 505 at 519.

[10] *Ibid.; Vosper Thorneycroft Ltd.* v. *Ministry of Defence* [1976] 1 Lloyd's Rep. 58; *Voest Alpine* v. *Chevron* [1987] 2 Lloyd's Rep. 547.

[11] *F. & G. Sykes (Wessex) Ltd.* v. *Fine Fare Ltd.* [1966] 2 Lloyd's Rep. 205, 213, *Foley* v. *Classique Coaches* [1934] 2 K.B. 1 at 12 (C.A.). For meaning and effect of repudiation, see p. 146. See also *Smallman* v. *Smallman* [1972] Fam. 25 at 32 (C.A.).

pursuant to an offer stating "The above quotations will remain fixed price until June 3, 1975; any work carried out after this date to be negotiated," it was held that there was a concluded contract which continued after June 3, 1975, and that it was subject to an implied term that rates for subsequent work would be reasonable.[12]

The parties may agree upon the price after work has commenced but so as to show that they intended the agreement to operate retrospectively to cover the work already carried out.[13]

Contract to negotiate. The law does not recognise such a contract because it would be too uncertain to have any binding force.[14] But a clause dependant on future agreement between the parties may be unenforceable without vitiating the whole contract.[15]

Price payable by another. There can be a contract with the employer to do work for the employer, subject to implied duties owed to the employer to exercise reasonable skill and complete within a reasonable time, but upon terms that payment is not to be by the employer but by another person,[16] and such a contract can exist at the same time as a separate contract with that other person.[17]

Negotiations after contract. "Where negotiations are in progress between parties intending to enter into a contract the whole of those negotiations must be looked at to determine when if at all, the contract comes into being. . . . Once the contract comes into being, however, subsequent negotiations by either party seeking, for example, to obtain better terms will not affect the existence of the previously concluded contract."[18]

(i) *Acceptance by conduct*

The offeror cannot bind the offeree by a stipulation that silence will amount to acceptance,[19] but acceptance can be by conduct showing an intention to accept

---

[12] *Constable Hart & Co. Ltd.* v. *Peter Lind & Co. Ltd.* (1978) 9 B.L.R. 4 (C.A.).

[13] See *Trollope & Colls Ltd.* v. *Atomic Power Ltd.* [1963] 1 W.L.R. 333.

[14] *Courtney & Fairbairn Ltd.* v. *Tolaini Brothers (Hotels) Ltd.* [1975] 1 W.L.R. 297 (C.A.); unanimous decision of the court disapproving the dictum of Lord Wright in *Hillas & Co. Ltd.* v. *Arcos Ltd.* (1932) 147 L.T. 503 at 515 (H.L.). But in principle why should there not be such a contract where the parties contemplate negotiations by skilled and experienced persons? As to damages, consider *Chaplin* v. *Hicks* [1911] 2 K.B. 786 (C.A.).

[15] *Mallozzi* v. *Carapelli* [1976] 1 Lloyd's Rep. 407.

[16] *Charnock* v. *Liverpool Corporation* [1968] 1 W.L.R. 1498 (C.A.), a car repair case. For the consideration given, see *ibid.* 1505. See also *Brown and Davis* v. *Galbraith* [1972] 1 W.L.R. 997 (C.A.). For the implied duty of skill, see p. 52, and the implied duty as to time, p. 218.

[17] *Charnock* v. *Liverpool Corporation* [1968] 1 W.L.R. 1498 (C.A.).

[18] *British Guiana Credit Corp.* v. *Da Silva* [1965] 1 W.L.R. 248, 255 (P.C.). See further at p. 35, "Subsequent conduct."

[19] *Felthouse* v. *Bindley* (1862) 11 C.B.(N.S.) 869.

the terms of the offer.[20] It is a question in each case whether conduct, known to the offeror, shows such an intention.[21] Thus if an offer is made to a contractor for the performance of certain work upon stated terms, and without making any express acceptance, or counter-offer, the contractor carries out the work, he is bound by the terms of the offer.[22] The same principles apply to an employer who, without any express acceptance, or counter-offer, permits a contractor to carry out work the subject-matter of an offer subject to certain terms. He is bound by those terms.[23]

(j) *Acceptance by post, telex or fax*

The general rule is that acceptance must be communicated to the offeror, and does not become effective until it reaches him[24] but if the acceptance is by post special rules may apply. Where the circumstances are such that the parties must have contemplated that the post might be used as a means of communication the acceptance is complete as soon as it is posted[25]although the ordinary rule still applies that revocation of the offer is not effective until it reaches the offeree. Therefore if in such circumstances an acceptance is posted before the offeree knows of the revocation of the offer a contract comes into existence.[26]

The special rules as to acceptance by post do not apply where there is a contract by telex. Where telex communication is instantaneous and between principals the contract is concluded where and when acceptance is communicated to the offeror. Where communication is not instantaneous no universal rule applies. Reference must be made to the intentions of the parties, sound business practice and in some cases to a judgment where the risks should lie.[27]

There is no authority yet about the formation of a contract using fax machines, although the Court of Appeal has held that some documents in court proceedings can be validly served by fax.[28] It is submitted that there is no essential difference between acceptance by fax and acceptance by telex.

The artificial concept of acceptance by posting yields to the express terms of the offer. Thus where an option to purchase a freehold was exercisable by

---

[20] *Charnock* v. *Liverpool Corporation* [1968] 1 W.L.R. 1498 at 1507 (C.A.).

[21] See as examples *Shields Furniture Ltd.*v. *Golt* [1973] 2 All E.R. 655; *Fairline Shipping Corporation* v. *Adamson* [1975] Q.B. 180; *Wettern Electric* v. *Welsh Agency* [1983] Q.B. 796 at 802.

[22] *Brogden* v. *Metropolitan Railway* (1877) 2 App.Cas. 666 (H.L.); *Dartford Union* v. *Trickett* (1888) 59 L.T. 754; *Greenwood* v. *Hawkings* (1907) 23 T.L.R. 72; *Robophone Facilities Ltd.* v. *Blank* [1966] 1 W.L.R. 1428; *Peter Lind & Co. Ltd.* v. *Mersey Docks & Harbour Board* [1972] 2 Lloyd's Rep. 235; *New Zealand Shipping Co. Ltd.* v. *Satterthwaite & Co. Ltd.* [1975] A.C. 154 (P.C.).

[23] *Ibid.* For the position where no price is fixed see p. 23.

[24] *Entores Ltd.* v. *Miles Far East Corporation* [1955] 2 Q.B. 327 (C.A.).

[25] *Henthorn* v. *Fraser* [1892] 2 Ch. 27 at 33; *Holwell Securities Ltd.* v. *Hughes* [1974] 1 W.L.R. 155 (C.A.).

[26] *Byrne* v. *Van Tienhoven* (1880) 5 C.P.D. 344; see also *Household Insurance Co.* v. *Grant* (1879) 4 Ex.D. 216.

[27] *Brinkibon Ltd.* v. *Stahag Stahl* [1983] 2 A.C. 34 (H.L.) applying *Entores* v. *Miles Far East Corporation* [1955] 2 Q.B. 327 (C.A.).

[28] *Hastie and Jenkerson* v. *McMahon* [1990] 1 W.L.R. 1575 (C.A.).

"notice in writing to . . ." the defendant, it was held that actual communication of the acceptance was necessary notwithstanding that the parties contemplated that the post might be used.[29] Accordingly there was no valid exercise of the option where the notice was lost in the post.[30]

3. Formalities of Contract

The general rule of law is that no formalities are required for the formation of a contract. It may be written, oral or partly oral and partly in writing.[31] To this rule there are, for the purposes of the law relating to building contracts, two exceptions: first, contracts for the sale of land can now only be in writing and secondly contracts of guarantee must be written or evidenced in writing.

(a) *Contracts requiring writing*

Contracts for the sale of land.   A contract for the sale or other disposition of an interest in land can only be made in writing and only by incorporating all the terms which the parties have expressly agreed in one document or, where contracts are exchanged, in each.[32] Terms may be incorporated by reference to some other document.[33] The document incorporating the terms must be signed by or on behalf of each party to the contract.[34] Since a contract to which these rules apply can only be made in writing, contracts which do not comply are, it seems, void and the former law relating to part performance no longer applies.[35] If the parties fail to record all the terms of an agreement in writing, either party may apply to the Court for rectification or there may be possible remedies in estoppel or by means of a collateral contract.[36]

A normal building contract is not a contract for the sale or other disposition of an interest in land because the contractor is merely given a licence to enter the land.[37] A contract to grant a building lease, *i.e.* a lease, part of the consideration for the grant of which consists of a promise by the lessee to build on the demised land must be evidenced in writing.[38]

---

[29] *Holwell Securities Ltd.* v. *Hughes* [1974] 1 W.L.R. 155 at 157 (C.A.). Lawton L.J. in his judgment at 161 set out other qualifications to the concept. See also *Yates Building* v. *Pulleyn, The Times,* February 26, 1975 (C.A.).

[30] *Holwell Securities Ltd.* v. *Hughes* [1974] 1 W.L.R. 155 (C.A.).

[31] See "Contract only partly in writing" at p. 39.

[32] Law of Property (Miscellaneous Provisions) Act 1989, s.2(1). This section came into force on September 29, 1989. For the law before that date under s.40 of the Law of Property Act 1925, see the 4th edition of this book, p. 22.

[33] s.2(2) of the 1989 Act.

[34] s.2(3) of the 1989 Act.

[35] See Law Commission No. 164 (1987).

[36] *Ibid.* For rectification, see p. 266; for estoppel, see p. 262, for collateral contracts, see p. 130.

[37] *Camden* v. *Batterbury* (1860) 7 C.B.(N.S.) 864; *cf. Lavery* v. *Pursell* (1888) 39 Ch.D. 508. See also *Hounslow, London Borough Council* v. *Twickenham Gardens Development Ltd.* [1971] 1 Ch. 233 discussed at p. 270; *cf. Surrey Heath Borough Council* v. *Lovell Construction* (1988) 42 B.L.R. 25 at 51.

[38] See Law of Property (Miscellaneous Provisions) Act 1989, s.2(6) and Law of Property Act 1925, s.205(1).

Contracts of suretyship and guarantee.[39]   A contract of guarantee is a promise to answer for the debt, default or miscarriage of another and must be contained in, or evidenced by, a note or memorandum in writing signed by the surety or his agent,[40] although the writing need not show the consideration for which the promise was given.[41] A contract of guarantee intended to be made by more than one co-surety is not binding unless all anticipated parties become bound.[42]

It may sometimes be difficult to distinguish between a guarantee which is required to be evidenced in writing and an indemnity which is not. A leading case is *Lakeman* v. *Mountstephen*[43] where the contractor, M, was carrying out drainage work for a local board. Certain private persons disregarded notices to make connections with the drain. The chairman of the board, L, said to M:

"What objection have you to making the connections?"

M replied:

"None, if you or the board will order the work, or become responsible for the payment."

L replied:

"Go on and do the work, and I will see you paid."

It was held that L had given an indemnity and was liable personally despite the absence of writing. He had assumed a primary liability to pay M and had not entered into a mere contract of guarantee, for this requires that there be a principal debtor who is primarily liable, and a surety who becomes liable only on his default.[44]

(b) *Deeds*

Deeds,[45] sometimes called specialty contracts, were formerly always documents which effected contracts under seal. This no longer need apply to deeds executed by individuals for which a seal is no longer required.[46] A deed is

---

[39] For guarantees generally, see p. 248.

[40] Statute of Frauds 1677, s.4.

[41] Mercantile Law Amendment Act 1856, s.3. There were formerly certain other contracts required to be evidenced in writing, and a large body of law, some of which is now obsolete, developed. As the subject is now of such limited application to building contracts, it is not further dealt with here.

[42] *James Graham and Co.* v. *Southgate-Sands* [1986] Q.B. 80 (C.A.).

[43] (1874) L.R. 7 H.L. 17 (H.L.). See also *Guild & Co.* v. *Conrad* [1894] 2 Q.B. 885 at 895 (C.A.).

[44] For a full discussion of the distinction between guarantee and indemnity, see *Chitty* (26th ed.), Vol. 2, para. 5016. See also *Goulston Discount Co. Ltd.* v. *Clark* [1967] 2 Q.B. 493 (C.A.). For a case of novation, *i.e.* substitution of one debtor for another, see *Commercial Bank of Tasmania* v. *Jones* [1893] A.C. 313 (P.C.).

[45] See "Construction of Deeds" at p. 58.

[46] Law of Property (Miscellaneous Provisions) Act 1989, s.1(1)(b). This section came into force on July 31, 1990. It does not apply to instruments delivered as deeds before that date—see s.1(11).

validly executed by an individual if it is signed by him in the presence of a witness who attests the signature and if it is delivered as a deed.[47] An instrument is not a deed unless it makes clear on its face that it is intended to be a deed by the person making it and is validly executed as a deed. Sealing is still required by parties other than individuals. Modern practice does not require a wax or wafer seal.[48]

The main characteristics of deeds are that they do not require consideration and that they have a 12-year limitation period.[49]

4. Capacity of Parties

There are certain categories of persons whose capacity to make contracts is less than that of the ordinary person, or in respect of whose contracts special rules apply.

(a) *Minors (or Infants)*[50]

A minor is a person under 18 years of age.[51] The general position is that contracts made by a minor are not binding on him save that he must pay a reasonable price for necessaries which he has received.[52] So far as goods are concerned necessaries are defined as "goods suitable to the condition in life of the minor ... and to his actual requirements at the time of the sale and delivery."[53] Necessaries can include services, such as lodging and even attendance if the minor's position in society warrants it, and an infant was held liable on a contract for the burial of his wife and children.[54] There seems therefore to be no reason in principle why a contract for building work could not be a contract for necessaries,[55] but a contractor is ill-advised to enter into a contract with a minor. Apart from the perils of the law relating to necessaries, a minor cannot hold any legal estate in land,[56] and might not therefore be able to grant possession of the site for completion of the works. The contractor's better

---

[47] s.1(3).

[48] *First National Securities* v. *Jones* [1978] Ch. 109 (C.A.). For a strange case where a local authority was estopped by convention from denying that an agreement was under seal, see *Whittal Builders* v. *Chester-le-Street District Council* (1987) 40 B.L.R. 82.

[49] For the 12-year limitation period, see p. 366.

[50] See Family Law Reform Act 1969, s.12.

[51] Family Law Reform Act 1969, s.1.

[52] Sale of Goods Act 1979, s.3 (goods sold and delivered)—it is not clear whether the same rule applies to necessaries which are not goods, *i.e.* that he pays a reasonable price, not necessarily the contract sum; probably it does—*Nash* v. *Inman* [1908] 2 K.B. 1 at 8 (C.A.); *cp.* s.2 of the Minors' Contracts Act 1987 for guarantees of minors' obligations and s.3 of the Act for the Court's power to order restitution.

[53] Sale of Goods Act 1979, s.3(3).

[54] *Chapple* v. *Cooper* (1844) 13 M. & W. 252.

[55] There is no such case reported.

[56] Law of Property Act 1925, s.1(6).

course where he has been negotiating with a minor is to make the contract with the trustees of the land in which the minor has a beneficial interest.

(b) *Aliens*

An alien is liable upon, and can enforce, contracts within the jurisdiction of the English courts unless he is an alien enemy. For the purpose of the enforceability of contracts an alien enemy is a person, whatever his nationality, resident in or carrying on business in the enemy's country, or in a country within the effective control of the enemy.[57]

(c) *Bankrupts*

An undischarged bankrupt may enter into any contract provided that he does not commit the criminal offences of:

(1) either alone or jointly with any other person obtaining credit to the extent of the prescribed amount[58] or more from any person without informing that person that he is an undischarged bankrupt; or
(2) engaging in any business under a name other than that in which he was adjudicated bankrupt without disclosing to all persons with whom he enters into any business transaction the name in which he was adjudicated bankrupt.[59]

(d) *Persons of unsound mind*

Contracts with persons of unsound mind whose affliction is not apparent and whose consequent incapacity is not known to the other contracting party are to be judged by the same standards as those made by a person of sound mind. Such contracts will not be rescinded for incapacity and unfairness if the other party is guilty of no unconscionable conduct.[60]

(e) *Corporations*

A corporation is a legal person, that is to say it is regarded by the law as a legal entity quite distinct from the person or persons who may for the time being be the member or members of the corporation. A corporation sole is composed of one office holder such as a bishop or the Public Trustee,[61] and a corporation

---

[57] *Porter* v. *Freudenberg* [1915] 1 K.B. 857 (C.A.); see further *Chitty* (26th ed.), Vol. 1, para. 750.
[58] Currently £250 (S.I. 1986 No. 1996) Art. 3, Sched., Pt. II.
[59] Insolvency Act 1986, s.360. See *Fisher* v. *Raven* [1964] A.C. 210 (H.L.); *R.* v. *Hartley* [1972] 2 Q.B. 1 (C.A. Crim.Div.).
[60] *Hart* v. *O'Connor* [1985] A.C. 1000 (P.C.).
[61] The provision, noted above under "Deeds," that a seal is no longer required for an individual's deed does not apply to a corporation sole—see s.1(10) of the Law of Property (Miscellaneous Provisions) Act 1989.

aggregate of more than one person such as the members of a company.[62] Local authorities are corporations.

The *ultra vires* doctrine.   Corporations may be broadly classified as those incorporated by charter, either express or implied, and those incorporated as the result of an Act of Parliament. A chartered corporation has at common law the power "to bind itself to such contracts as an ordinary person can bind himself to."[63] But a statutory corporation being a statutory creature can only enter into such contracts as are necessary to attain the objects of its creation. Any purported contract for purposes beyond these objects is *ultra vires* (*i.e.* beyond its powers) and therefore void. For a person dealing with a company registered under the Companies Act 1985, which includes the ordinary commercial company, the position is much simplified.[64] Any transaction decided on by the directors shall, in favour of a person dealing with the company in good faith,[65] be deemed to be one which it is in the capacity of the company to enter into, and the power of the directors to bind the company is deemed to be free of any limitation under the memorandum or articles of association; and a party to a transaction so decided on is not bound to inquire as to the capacity of the company to enter into it or as to any such limitation on the powers of the directors, and is presumed to have acted in good faith unless the contrary is proved.

The formalities required of contracts made by corporations are for practical purposes the same as those for individuals,[66] except that a corporation's deed has to be sealed.[67]

Corporation acts through its agents.   A corporation acts through its agents and, even though a contract purported to be entered into is within the powers of the corporation, to be binding it must be within the express or ostensible authority of the agent. Directors of a company registered under the Companies Act 1985 have authority to bind the company and the position of a person dealing with them is dealt with above. At one time the secretary of such a company had very little authority on its behalf. It has now been held that he has ostensible authority to make contracts on its behalf in connection with the administrative side of its affairs such as employing staff and ordering cars and

---

[62] See *Chitty* (26th ed.), Vol. 1, para. 632.

[63] *Wenlock (Baroness) Ltd.* v. *River Dee Co.* (1887) 36 Ch.D. 674 at 685 (C.A.).

[64] Companies Act 1985, s.35 first enacted by European Communities Act 1972, s.9(1). Before January 1, 1973, a person was at risk of it being held that a contract was not within the powers of the company as set out within its memorandum of association, or of the directors as limited by the articles—see *Royal British Bank* v. *Turquand* (1856) 6 E.B. 327; *Ashbury Railway* v. *Riche* (1875) L.R. 7 (H.L.) 653 (H.L.); *Bell Houses Ltd.* v. *City Wall Properties Ltd.* [1966] 2 Q.B. 656 (C.A.). See also s.36(4) of the 1985 Act which makes the promoter of a company personally liable where the company has not been formed.

[65] For the test of lack of good faith, see *International Sales* v. *Marcus* [1982] 3 All E.R. 551 at 559.

[66] See s.36 of the Companies Act 1985 and s.1 of the Corporate Bodies' Contracts Act 1960.

[67] See Section 3 of this chapter under "Deeds" and generally.

so forth.[68] It is thought that such authority extends to works of repair and maintenance of a company's premises, but it must be a matter of doubt how far it extends to building contracts generally.

Where a person represents that he has authority which he does not possess, and thereby induces another to enter into a contract which is void for want of authority, that other person, if he has suffered loss, can sue the first for breach of warranty of authority.[69]

(f) *Contracts by local authorities*

A local authority must make standing orders with regard to the making of contracts by them or on their behalf for the execution of works,[70] but a person entering into a contract with a local authority is not bound to inquire whether the standing orders have been complied with and non-compliance does not invalidate any contract entered into by or on its behalf.[71]

Local authority contracts do not have to be under seal.[72] In practice local authorities frequently do enter into substantial contracts under seal. This gives them the benefit of a 12-year limitation period[73] and avoids questions whether a person had authority to contract on their behalf. Senior officers are likely to be held to have such authority.[74]

The making by local authorities of public supply or works contracts is regulated by Part II of the Local Government Act 1988, the local authority being required to exercise certain functions without reference to non-commercial matters.[75] The use by local authorities of Direct Labour Organisations is regulated by Part III of the Local Government, Planning and Land Act 1980.[76]

Members of local authorities and river authorities. Where they have a pecuniary interest in any contract or proposed contract they must disclose the fact, and must not take part in the consideration or discussion of, or vote on any question with respect to, the contract.[77] A person failing to comply with these requirements commits a criminal offence.[78]

---

[68] *Panorama Development (Guildford) Ltd.* v. *Fidelis Furnishing Fabrics Ltd.* [1971] 2 Q.B. 711 (C.A.).

[69] See cases cited at p. 308. For the authority of the architect, see p. 305. For the authority of senior officers of local authorities, see below.

[70] Local Government Act 1972, s.135(2). The London Government Act 1963 applies to London.

[71] Local Government Act 1972, s.135(4). See *North West Leicestershire District Council* v. *East Midlands Housing Association* [1981] 1 W.L.R. 1396 for a consideration of its statutory predecessor.

[72] The Corporate Bodies' Contracts Act 1960.

[73] See p. 366.

[74] See, *e.g. Carlton Contractors* v. *Bexley Corporation* (1962) L.G.R. 331—borough surveyor; *Roberts & Co. Ltd.* v. *Leicestershire County Council* [1961] Ch. 555—officers of county architect's department; *cp. North West Leicestershire District Council* v. *East Midlands Housing Association* [1981] 1 W.L.R. 1396 where a clerk of the council did not have authority. See also p. 305.

[75] s.17(1) of the Act. For a case applying the provisions, see *R.* v. *London Borough of Islington* (1989) 45 B.L.R. 45.

[76] As amended by s.32 of the Local Government Act 1988.

[77] See Local Government Act 1972, ss.94–98, 105, 272; Water Resources Act 1963, s.6(6).

[78] *Ibid.* s.94(2). See *Brown* v. *D.P.P.* [1956] 2 Q.B. 369; *Rands* v. *Oldroyd* [1959] 1 Q.B. 204.

(g) *Government contracts*

Contracts with government departments can be enforced by or against the Crown.[79]

(h) *Partnerships*

Partnership is "the relationship which subsists between persons carrying on business in common with a view to profit."[80] A partnership is not a corporation and in general a partner acting for the purposes of the partnership can enter into a contract on behalf of the other partners so as to make them liable.[81]

(i) *Unincorporated associations*

An unincorporated association is a general term given to a group of persons neither a corporation nor a partnership who act together for certain purposes.[82] A typical example is a club. As it has no corporate existence contracts cannot be made on its behalf and a member is not liable unless he made the contract or authorised or ratified it.[83] Members of the committee who enter into the contract are liable, and in general a person dealing with a club is normally entitled to look to the members of the committee of management.[84]

---

[79] For the right to sue the Crown and the procedure, see the Crown Proceedings Act 1947.

[80] Partnership Act 1890, s.1; *Keith Spicer Ltd.* v. *Mansell* [1970] 1 W.L.R. 333 (C.A.).

[81] s.5 of the 1890 Act. See generally *Lindley on Partnership* (15th ed.) and, *e.g. Mann* v. *D'Arcy* [1968] 1 W.L.R. 893.

[82] See further *Chitty* (26th ed.), Vol. 1, paras. 675 *et seq.* For Trade Unions, see *Chitty*, paras. 686 *et seq.*

[83] *Bradley Egg Farm Ltd.* v. *Clifford* [1943] 2 All E.R. 378 (C.A.); *Wise* v. *Perpetual Trustee Co.* [1903] A.C. 139 (P.C.).

[84] *Steele* v. *Gourley* (1887) 3 T.L.R. 118, 119; *Bradley Egg Farm Ltd.* v. *Clifford* [1943] 2 All E.R. 378 (C.A.); *cf. Draper* v. *Manvers (Earl)* (1892) 9 T.L.R. 73.

CHAPTER 3

CONSTRUCTION OF CONTRACTS

A. CONSTRUCTION OF CONTRACTS

Many of the problems likely to arise under a building contract are concerned with the meaning to be given to words in a written contract. The process by which the courts arrive at this meaning is termed construing a contract, and the meaning, as determined by the court, the construction of the contract.[1]

"The object sought to be achieved in construing any commercial contract is to ascertain ... what each [party] would have led the other reasonably to assume were the acts that he was promising to do or to refrain from doing by the words in which the promises on his part were expressed."[2]

1. Expressed Intention

In construing a contract the court applies the rule of law that, "while it seeks to

---

[1] For a full exposition, see *Norton on Deeds*, and for a shorter account, see *Odgers on the Construction of Deeds and Statutes*. See also *Chitty* (26th ed.), paras. 808 *et seq*. Problems of construction and of formation of contract are often closely related and reference should also be made to Chap. 2, especially the sections dealing with offer and acceptance.

[2] Lord Diplock in *Pioneer Shipping* v. *B.T.P. Tioxide* [1982] A.C. 724 at 736 (H.L.).

give effect to the intention of the parties, [it] must give effect to that intention as expressed, that is, it must ascertain the meaning of the words actually used."[3] For the purposes of construction "intention" does not mean motive, purpose, desire or a state of mind but intention as expressed, and the common law adopts an objective standard of construction excluding general evidence of actual intention of the parties. Thus while, as will be shown below, it permits evidence of the circumstances in which the contractual document was made, of the special meaning of words, of customs and certain other matters to assist the court in arriving at the expressed intention of the parties, nevertheless the fundamental rule is that the words must speak for themselves.[4] The parties cannot come into court to give evidence of what they intended to say.[5] If the rule were otherwise, "all certainty would be taken from the words in which the parties have recorded their agreement."[6]

(a) *Extrinsic evidence—not normally admissible*

It follows from the principle just stated that, for a written contract, no evidence outside the document itself, *i.e.* extrinsic evidence, may normally be adduced to contradict, vary, add to or subtract from the written terms.[7]

Blanks. Where a complete blank is left in a material part of the contract evidence is not admissible to fill it.[8] Thus where the date for completion was omitted, and to insert it would result in the imposition of an onerous obligation under a liquidated damages clause, the court refused to admit evidence that each party had been told of the date.[9]

Preliminary negotiations. Although restricted evidence of the factual background is admissible,[10] when the parties have entered into a final concluded contract in writing the preliminary negotiations such as letters cannot

---

[3] *Inland Revenue Commissioners* v. *Raphael* [1935] A.C. 96 at 142 (H.L.); *Schuler A.G.* v. *Wickman Machine Tool Sales Ltd.* [1974] A.C. 235 (H.L.).

[4] *Ibid.*

[5] But note that in certain circumstances equity will rectify a contract mistakenly expressed. See p. 266.

[6] *Inland Revenue Commissioners* v. *Raphael* [1935] A.C. 96 at 142 (H.L.); see also *London County Council* v. *Henry Boot & Sons Ltd.* [1959] 1 W.L.R. 1069 at 1077 (H.L.).

[7] *Bank of Australia* v. *Palmer* [1897] A.C. 540 at 545 (P.C.); *National Westminster Bank* v. *Halesowen Presswork* [1972] A.C. 785 at 818 (H.L.); *O'Connor* v. *Hume* [1954] 1 W.L.R. 824 at 830 (C.A.); *Rabin* v. *Gerson Berger* [1986] 1 W.L.R. 526 (C.A.).

[8] *In the goods of De Rosaz* (1877) 2 P.D. 66 at 69. For an exceptional case where, under s.11 of the Employment Protection (Consolidation) Act 1978, gaps in a contract of employment were filled, see *Mears* v. *Safecar Security* [1983] 1 Q.B. 54 at 80.

[9] *Kemp* v. *Rose* (1858) 1 Giff. 258. For a case where the expression "£ nil" in a liquidated damages clause was construed *not* to be equivalent to a blank, see *Temloc* v. *Errill Properties* (1987) 22 B.L.R. 30 (C.A.).

[10] See "Factual background" at p. 36.

be referred to for the purpose of explaining the parties' intention.[11] In one case[12] a covering letter sent with the tender stated that the tender was "subject to" a certain term. After negotiations a formal contract was signed which defined the contract documents without including the letter, although in the contract documents, as defined, there was a reference to part of the letter for a different purpose. It was held that that term was not part of the contract.

Subsequent conduct. "[I]t is not legitimate to use as an aid in the construction of the contract anything which the parties said or did after it was made,"[13] and this rule applies even where there is an ambiguity in the contract.[14] The rule applies particularly where a contract is arrived at in the course of correspondence. All the letters must be looked at in order to determine whether, and at what stage, the parties intended to make themselves contractually liable, but when that stage has been established subsequent correspondence cannot be taken into account in construing the contract.[15]

Deletions from printed documents. It is unclear whether in construing a contract it is permissible to look at deletions from printed documents and, if it is permissible, for what purpose. There are two schools of thought. One school, supported by weighty, if elderly, authority[16] but followed recently,[17] says that you may not take account of such deletions at all. The other school holds that "when the parties use a printed form and delete parts of it one can, in my opinion, pay regard to what has been deleted as part of the surrounding circumstances in the light of which one must construe what they have chosen

---

[11] *Inglis* v. *Buttery* (1878) 3 App.Cas. 552 (H.L.); *Leggott* v. *Barrett* (1880) 15 Ch.D. 306 at 311 (C.A.); *Kinlen* v. *Ennis Urban District Council* [1916] 2 I.R. 299 (H.L.); *Davis Contractors Ltd.* v. *Fareham Urban District Council* [1956] A.C. 696 (H.L.); *L.C.C.* v. *Boot* [1959] 1 W.L.R. 1069 (H.L.); *Prenn* v. *Simmonds* [1971] 1 W.L.R. 1381 (H.L.). For building contract cases, see, *e.g. Wates Ltd.* v. *G.L.C.* (1983) 25 B.L.R. 1 at 22; *Viking Grain* v. *T. H. White* (1985) 33 B.L.R. 103 at 116—evidence of negotiations not admissible on questions of implication of terms, but see n. 32 below. Contrast "Agreed factual assumption" and "Parties' own dictionary" at p. 38.

[12] *Davis Contractors Ltd.* v. *Fareham Urban District Council* [1956] A.C. 696 (H.L.).

[13] Lord Reid in *Whitworth Street Estates (Manchester) Ltd.* v. *James Miller & Partners Ltd.* [1970] A.C. 583 at 603 (H.L.). See also *Wates Ltd.* v. *G.L.C.* (1983) 25 B.L.R. 1 at 29.

[14] *Schuler A.G.* v. *Wickman Machine Tool Sales Ltd.* [1974] A.C. 235 at 252, 265 (H.L.). In the *Schuler* case doubt was expressed as to the authority of *Watcham* v. *East African Protectorate* [1919] A.C. 533 (P.C.) which dealt with an ambiguous title to land.

[15] *Bushwall Properties Ltd.* v. *Vortex Properties Ltd.* [1976] 1 W.L.R. 591 at 603 (C.A.). For an exceptional case where, under s.11 of the Employment Protection (Consolidation) Act 1978, evidence of subsequent conduct was held to be admissible, see *Mears* v. *Safecar Security* [1983] 1 Q.B. 54 at 80.

[16] *Inglis* v. *Buttery* (1878) 3 App.Cas. 552 (H.L.); *Ambatielos* v. *Jurgens* [1923] A.C. 175 at 185 (H.L.); *M. A. Sassoon & Sons* v. *International Banking Corporation* [1927] A.C. 711 at 712 (P.C.); see also *City & Westminster Properties (1934) Ltd.* v. *Mudd* [1959] Ch. 129; *Prenn* v. *Simmonds* [1971] 1 W.L.R. 1381 (H.L.).

[17] *Compania Naviera Termar* v. *Tradax Export* [1965] 1 Lloyd's Rep. 198 at 204; *Ben Shipping* v. *An-Board Bainne* [1986] 2 Lloyd's Rep. 285 at 291; *Wates Construction* v. *Franthom Property* H.H. Judge Newey Q.C. (unreported) July 31, 1990, who nevertheless misinterpreted, it is submitted, Lord Reid in *Timber Shipping Co.* v. *London & Overseas Freighters* [1972] A.C. 1 at 15 (H.L.).

to leave in."[18] Applying this principle, the House of Lords referred to the deletion in an existing contract of a clause giving the employer an express right of set-off as part of the surrounding circumstances showing that the parties directed their minds to the question of set-off and decided that it should not be allowed. This second school has support to the effect that the court is entitled to look at deleted words to see if any assistance can be derived from them in solving an ambiguity in words retained,[19] and that a word or phrase in the deleted part of a clause may throw light on the meaning of the same word or phrase in what remains of the clause.[20] But by deleting a provision parties are not to be deemed to have agreed the converse. They may have had all sorts of reasons for making the deletion.[21]

In this confusion, it is submitted that the second school is to be preferred. Where parties have made a contract in a document which contains deletions, to look at the deletions does not offend the principle discussed above which prevents reference to preliminary negotiations. The deletion is physically contained in the concluded contract. It is submitted that the court should first construe the retained words. If they are unambiguous, reference to the deletion is unnecessary. If they are ambiguous, reference to deletions from printed documents should be permitted to see whether objectively they throw light on the meaning of the retained words.

(b) *Extrinsic evidence—when admissible*

To the general rule that extrinsic evidence is not admissible to interpret a written contract there are many qualifications and exceptions relevant to building contracts of which the most important are now discussed.

Factual background. Contracts are not made in a vacuum. There is always a setting in which they have to be placed.[22] Restricted evidence is admissible "of the factual background known to the parties at or before the date of the contract, including evidence of the 'genesis' and objectively the 'aim' of the transaction."[23] "What the court must do must be to place itself in thought in the same factual matrix as that in which the parties were."[24]

---

[18] Lord Cross, stating the majority view in *Mottram Consultants Ltd.* v. *Bernard Sunley & Sons* [1975] 2 Lloyd's Rep. 197 at 209 (H.L.), Lords Hodson and Wilberforce agreeing; Lords Morris and Salmon dissenting, but on another point and not dealing with this issue. See further p. 440. For earlier cases consistent with the *Mottram* case, see *Chitty* (26th ed.), Vol. 1, para. 825, n. 46. For discussion relating to the Standard Form, see p. 575.

[19] Diplock J. in *Louis Dreyfus* v. *Parnaso Cia. Naviera* [1959] 1 Q.B. 498 at 513.

[20] Lloyd J. *Mineralimportexport* v. *Eastern Mediterranean Maritime* [1980] 2 Lloyd's Rep. 572 at 575. See also Lord Reid in *Timber Shipping Co.* v. *London & Overseas Freighters* [1972] A.C. 1 at 15 (H.L.); Slade L.J. in *Jefco Mechanical Services Ltd.* v. *Lambeth* (1983) 24 B.L.R. 1 at 8 (C.A.).

[21] *Mineralimportexport* v. *Eastern Mediterranean Maritime* [1980] 2 Lloyd's Rep. 572 at 575.

[22] *Reardon Smith Line* v. *Hansen-Tangen* [1976] 1 W.L.R. 989 at 995 (H.L.); *cf. A. Bell & Son* v. *CBF Residential Care and Housing* (1989) 46 B.L.R. 102 at 107.

[23] *Prenn* v. *Simmonds* [1971] 1 W.L.R. 1381 at 1385 (H.L.).

[24] *Reardon Smith Line* v. *Hansen-Tangen* [1976] 1 W.L.R. 989 at 997 (H.L.).

Surrounding circumstances.   The court does not ascertain the intention of the parties by an interpretation based purely on internal linguistic considerations.[25] It must "inquire beyond the language and see what the circumstances were with reference to which the words were used, and the object, appearing from those circumstances, which the person using them had in view."[26] Thus evidence can be given to identify persons and things referred to in the document and to explain the circumstances existing at the time of its making.[27] "In construing all instruments you must know what the facts were when the agreement was entered into."[28] "Such facts give very little help in the construction if the words of the deed[29] are clear, but they will help very much if the words are ambiguous."[30] They may assist in deciding what terms, if any, are to be implied.[31] But this principle does not permit evidence to be made available of negotiations before contract or of the parties' subjective intentions.[32]

Foreign and technical words.   The meaning of foreign and technical words can be proved.[33] If there is no dispute about the meaning of technical words the court can inform itself about them by any means that is reliable and ready to hand, such as an explanation by counsel or by reference to dictionaries or in cases of difficulty by calling in aid an assessor.[34]

Custom and usage.   Evidence is admissible to show that words were used according to a special custom or usage attaching to the trade or locality applicable to the contract.[35] The custom must be strictly proved and must be notorious so that everybody in the trade or locality concerned enters into a contract with that custom as an implied term.[36] It must not be inconsistent

---

[25] *Prenn* v. *Simmonds* [1971] 1 W.L.R. 1381 at 1384 (H.L.); see also n. 11 above.
[26] *Ibid.*
[27] *Shore* v. *Wilson* (1842) 9 Cl. & F. 355 (H.L.).
[28] Jessel M.R. in *Cannon* v. *Villars* (1878) 8 Ch.D. 415 at 419; *Hart* v. *Hart* (1881) 18 Ch.D. 670 at 693. See also *Bank of New Zealand* v. *Simpson* [1900] A.C. 182 at 187 (P.C.), *A/s Tankexpress* v. *Compagnie Financiere Belges des Petroles S.A.* [1949] A.C. 76 (H.L.).
[29] The principle applies to all written instruments—*Shore* v. *Wilson* (1842) 9 Cl. & F. 355 (H.L.).
[30] Lord Esher M.R. in *Roe* v. *Siddons* (1888) 22 Q.B.D. 224 at 233 (C.A.). For a case, upon rather special facts, discussing the duty of an arbitrator to decide whether there is an ambiguity which requires the admission of extrinsic evidence, see *F. G. Whitley & Sons* v. *Clwyd County Council* (1982) 22 B.L.R. 48 (C.A.).
[31] See *British Movietonews Ltd.* v. *London and District Cinemas Ltd.* [1952] A.C. 166 at 183 (H.L.).
[32] See n. 25 above and *Viking Grain* v. *T. H. White* (1985) 33 B.L.R. 103 at 116—evidence of negotiations (as distinct from circumstances) not admissible on questions of implication of terms. It is suggested that *Viking Grain* is correct on this point, although *British Movietonews Ltd.* v. *London and District Cinemas Ltd.* [1952] A.C. 166 (H.L.) was not considered in the judgment.
[33] *Shore* v. *Wilson* (1842) 9 Cl. & F. 355 (H.L.); *R.* v. *Patents Appeal Tribunal, ex p. Baldwin & Francis Ltd.* [1959] 1 Q.B. 105 (C.A.); affd. *sub nom. Baldwin & Francis Ltd.* v. *Patents Appeal Tribunal* [1959] A.C. 663 (H.L.).
[34] *Baldwin & Francis Ltd.* v. *Patents Appeal Tribunal* [1959] A.C. 663 at 679, 691 (H.L.).
[35] See *Symonds* v. *Lloyd* (1859) 6 C.B.(N.S.) 691 ("Reduced brickwork" means brickwork nine inches thick); *cf. Crowshaw* v. *Pritchard* (1899) H.B.C. (4th ed., 1914), Vol. 2, p. 274; also 16 T.L.R. 45. See p. 15.
[36] *Nelson* v. *Dahl* (1879) 12 Ch.D. 568 at 575 (C.A.); *Brown* v. *Inland Revenue Commissioners* [1965] A.C. 244, 258, 262, 266 (H.L.); *General Reinsurance* v. *Fennia* [1983] Q.B. 856 at 872 (C.A.).

with the express or necessarily implied terms of the contract,[37] must be reasonable and not against the law.[38]

Parties' own dictionary.   Where words in a contract are capable of more than one meaning but the parties have negotiated on the agreed basis that the words have one meaning only, it is permissible to look at the negotiations to find out "their own dictionary meaning."[39]

Agreed factual assumption.   When parties have acted in a transaction upon an agreed assumption that a particular state of facts between them is to be accepted as true, each is to be regarded as estopped as against the other from questioning as regards that transaction the truth of the facts so assumed.[40] Evidence to establish the agreed assumption is admissible which, it is suggested, might conceivably include evidence of facts occurring after the making of the contract in so far as they go to establish the existence at the time the contract was made of the agreed assumption.

Attacking the contract.   Evidence is admissible to show an unfulfilled condition precedent, *e.g.* to show that an obligation was not to arise until an event, such as a third person's approval, had taken place and the event has not occurred either at all or within the time limited by the agreement[41] or that a contract is void or voidable because of misrepresentation, fraud, mistake, illegality, duress, minority or made by a mentally disordered person[42] or that the contract has been varied, rescinded, or is subject to an estoppel.[43] Evidence of rescission can be given even though the original contract was by deed and the rescission was oral,[44] or if the original contract was required to be evidenced in writing and has been orally rescinded.[45]

To claim rectification.   See page 266.

To show collateral warranties.   Where it is alleged that the written contract does not contain the whole of the agreement entered into and that there is a collateral warranty (sometimes termed collateral contract)[46] evidence of

---

[37] *Ibid.*; *London Export Corporation Ltd.* v. *Jubilee Coffee Roasting Co. Ltd.* [1958] 1 W.L.R. 661 at 675, 677 (C.A.).

[38] *Ibid.*; *Crowshaw* v. *Pritchard* (1899) H.B.C. (4th ed., 1914), Vol. 2, p. 274; also 16 T.L.R. 45; *Three Rivers Trading Co.* v. *Gwinear and District Farmers* (1967) 111 S.J. 831 (C.A.), sale of "400 tons (approx.)" of barley; custom that seller could deliver 10 per cent. less than figure stated held to be unreasonable.

[39] *The Karen Oltmann* [1976] 1 Lloyd's Rep. 708 at 712.

[40] See "Estoppel by convention" at p. 263.

[41] *Pym* v. *Campbell* (1856) 6 E. & B. 370 at 374.

[42] *Norton on Deeds* (2nd ed.), p. 151; *Chitty* (26th ed.), Vol. 1, para. 862.

[43] *Schuler* v. *Wickman* [1974] A.C. 235 at 261 (H.L.). For variation and estoppel, see pp. 262 and 265.

[44] *Berry* v. *Berry* [1929] 2 K.B. 316.

[45] *Morris* v. *Baron* [1918] A.C. 1 (H.L.).

[46] For meaning, see p. 130.

such a warranty is admissible.[47] But so far as there is a collateral contract the sole effect of which is to vary or add to the terms of the principal contract, it is viewed with suspicion by the law and must be strictly proved, for any laxity on this point would enable parties to escape from the full performance of their obligations and lessen the authority of written contracts.[48] There must be a clear intention to contract.[49] Although the reluctance of the courts to find collateral warranties or collateral contracts has been said to be out of date,[50] the reluctance seems to continue.[51]

To show consideration. "There is no doubt ... that extrinsic evidence is admissible to prove the real consideration where (a) no consideration, or a nominal consideration, is expressed in the instrument, or (b) the expressed consideration is in general terms or ambiguously stated, or (c) a substantial consideration is stated, but an additional consideration exists. The additional consideration must not, however, be inconsistent with the terms of the written instrument."[52]

Contract only partly in writing. Different considerations apply when the contract is in truth, not exclusively in writing, but partly in writing and partly oral and/or by conduct.[53] In such a case the court admits evidence of the oral part of the contract and/or the conduct and construes the contract according to all its terms gathered from the documents, words and conduct comprising the contract.[54]

2. Rules of Construction[55]

A rule of law takes effect although the parties may have expressed a contrary intention, but a rule of construction merely "points out what a court shall do in the absence of express or implied intention to the contrary."[56] It is therefore only applied to assist the court where there is some ambiguity or inconsistency, for if the words are plain the court gives effect to them.[57] No rule of construction

---

[47] *De Lassalle* v. *Guildford* [1901] 2 K.B. 215 (C.A.).

[48] *Heilbut Symons & Co.* v. *Buckleton* [1913] A.C. 30 at 47 (H.L.); *Routledge* v. *McKay and Others* [1954] 1 W.L.R. 615 (C.A.); *Dick Bentley Ltd.* v. *Harold Smith (Motors) Ltd.* [1965] 1 W.L.R. 623 (C.A.); *Quickmaid Rental Services Ltd.* v. *Reece* (1970) 114 S.J. 372 (C.A.).

[49] *Heilbut Symons & Co.* v. *Buckleton* [1913] A.C. 30 (H.L.); *Howard Marine* v. *A. Ogden & Sons* [1978] Q.B. 574 (C.A.); *I.B.A.* v. *E.M.I. and B.I.C.C.* (1980) 14 B.L.R. 1 at 22 (H.L.).

[50] *Evans & Sons* v. *Andrea Merzario* [1976] 1 W.L.R. 1078 at 1081 (C.A.).

[51] See, *e.g. I.B.A.* v. *E.M.I. and B.I.C.C.* (1980) 14 B.L.R. 1 (H.L.).

[52] *Pao On* v. *Lau Yiu Long* [1980] A.C. 614 at 631 (P.C.).

[53] *Evans & Sons* v. *Andrea Merzario* [1976] 1 W.L.R. 1078 at 1081 (C.A.). The majority of the Court of Appeal did not seem to agree wholly with the approach of Lord Denning and dealt with the case as a contract partly in writing, partly oral and partly by conduct.

[54] *Ibid.*

[55] Sometimes termed "canons of construction."

[56] *Re Coward* (1887) 57 L.T. 285 at 291 (C.A.).

[57] *Leader* v. *Duffey* (1888) 13 App.Cas. 294 at 301 (H.L.); *James Archdale & Co.* v. *Comservices* [1954] 1 W.L.R. 459 at 463 (C.A.).

is individually of such importance that it is regarded as paramount.[58] There are no special rules of construction applicable to building contracts.[59]

Ordinary meaning. With an ordinary English word and where it is not contended that there is anything in the context which would result in it having a special meaning, the court adopts the ordinary meaning and decides as a matter of fact whether the facts of the case are within the ordinary meaning or not.[60]

> "The grammatical and ordinary sense of the words is to be adhered to unless that would lead to some absurdity, or some repugnance or inconsistency with the rest of the instrument, in which case the grammatical and ordinary sense of the words may be modified so as to avoid that absurdity or inconsistency, but no further."[61]

The "absurdity" in the last sentence is, apparently, limited to that which would arise if reading the document as a whole it is clear that the parties intended a special meaning to be given to a word and that to give it its ordinary meaning would therefore create an absurdity.[62]

In a contract relating to any art or trade or business, the court gives words any special technical, trade, or customary meaning which the parties must have intended the words to bear.[63]

Term of art. This is used to describe words or phrases which have acquired a precise legal meaning ordinarily applied by the courts, but "where a word or phrase which is a 'term of art' is used by an author who is not a lawyer, particularly in a document which he does not anticipate may have to be construed by a lawyer, he may have meant by it something different from its meaning when used by a lawyer as a term of art."[64]

Reasonable meaning. "When the terms of a contract are ambiguous and one construction would lead to an unreasonable result, the court will be

---

[58] Parker L.J. in *Sabah Flour* v. *Comfez* [1988] 2 Lloyd's Rep. 18 at 20 (C.A.).

[59] *cf. National Coal Board* v. *William Neill & Son* [1985] Q.B. 300.

[60] *Commonwealth Smelting* v. *G.R.E.* [1986] 1 Lloyd's Rep. 121 at 126 (C.A.) considering *Brutus* v. *Cozens* [1973] A.C. 854 (H.L.).

[61] Lord Wensleydale in *Grey* v. *Pearson* (1857) 6 H.L.Cas. 61 at 106 (H.L.); *cf.* Lord Blackburn in *Caledonian Railway* v. *North British Railway* (1881) 6 App.Cas. 114 at 131 (H.L.).

[62] *Rhodes* v. *Rhodes* (1882) 7 App.Cas. 192 at 205 (H.L.); *cf. Staffordshire Area Health Authority* v. *Staffordshire Waterworks* [1978] 1 W.L.R. 1387. See also *Sir Lindsay Parkinson & Co. Ltd.* v. *Commissioners of Works* [1949] 2 K.B. 632 at 662 (C.A.), but *cf. British Movietonews Ltd.* v. *London and District Cinemas Ltd.* [1952] A.C. 166 at 183 (H.L.).

[63] *Produce Brokers Co. Ltd.* v. *Olympia Oil & Cake Co. Ltd.* [1916] 1 A.C. 314 at 324 (H.L.); *cf. Reardon Smith Line* v. *Hansen-Tangen* [1976] 1 W.L.R. 989 at 996 (H.L.) and see also "Custom and usage" at p. 37 and "Parties' own dictionary," at p. 38.

[64] Diplock L.J. in *Sydall* v. *Castings Ltd.* [1967] 1 Q.B. 302 at 314 (C.A.). In *L.C.C.* v. *Boot (Henry) & Sons Ltd.* [1959] 1 W.L.R. 1069 at 1075 (H.L.) it was said that, in construing a contract, no help could be got from the then Working Rule Agreement, which was "not an artistically drawn document."

unwilling to adopt that construction."[65] "If detailed semantic and syntactical analysis of words in a commercial contract is going to lead to a conclusion that flouts business common sense, it must be made to yield to the business common sense."[66] The court is unlikely to be driven by semantic niceties to adopt an improbable and unbusinesslike interpretation, if a sensible and businesslike one is reasonably available.[67] There are other cases which suggest that if there is no ambiguity the court will enforce the terms however absurd or unreasonable they may be,[68] and there are examples of contractors being held to the harsh terms of plainly worded contracts.[69] But it is thought that, with the complexity of modern building contracts both factually and in their drafting, these cases may now have limited application.

Internal consistency.   A legal draftsman is presumed to aim at uniformity. The same words will be presumed to have the same meaning throughout the document and different words to refer to a different thing or concept.[70]

Valid meaning.   "Where a clause is ambiguous a construction which will make it valid is to be preferred to one which will make it void."[71] This principle is sometimes expressed by the maxim *verba ita sunt intelligenda ut res magis valeat quam pereat*, which has particular reference to documents prepared by businessmen who "often record the most important agreements in crude and summary fashion."[72]

Clerical errors corrected.   Where there is a manifest error in a document, the court will put a sensible meaning on it by correcting or reading the error as corrected.[73]

Contract read as a whole.   "The contract must be construed as a whole, effect being given, so far as practicable, to each of its provisions."[74] Construing

---

[65] Lord Esher M.R. in *Dodd* v. *Churton* [1897] 1 Q.B. 562 at 566 (C.A.); *Schuler A.G.* v. *Wickman Machine Tool Sales Ltd.* [1974] A.C. 235 at 251, 256, 265, 272 (H.L.).

[66] *Antaios Compania* v. *Salen A.B.* [1985] A.C. 191 at 201 (H.L.); *cf. Home and Overseas Insurance* v. *Mentor Insurance* [1990] 1 W.L.R. 153 for the effect of an "honourable engagement" provision in a reinsurance contract.

[67] *Mitsui* v. *Att.-Gen. of Hong Kong* (1986) 33 B.L.R. 1 at 14 (P.C.).

[68] *Jones* v. *St. John's College, Oxford* (1870) L.R. 6 Q.B. 115, distinguished in *Dodd* v. *Churton* [1897] 1 Q.B. 562 (C.A.); *Adamastos Shipping* v. *Anglo Saxon Petroleum* [1959] A.C. 133 at 177 (H.L.).

[69] *e.g. Jackson* v. *Eastbourne Local Board* (1886) H.B.C. (4th ed., 1914), Vol. 2, p. 88 (H.L.).

[70] *John Jarvis* v. *Rockdale Housing Association* (1986) 36 B.L.R. 48 at 61 (C.A.) applying *Prestcold (Central) Ltd.* v. *Minister of Labour* [1969] 1 W.L.R. 89 at 97.

[71] Kay L.J. in *Mills* v. *Dunham* [1891] 1 Ch. 576 at 590 (C.A.).

[72] Lord Wright in *Hillas* v. *Arcos* (1932) 147 L.T. 503 at 514 (H.L.); *Adamastos Shipping* v. *Anglo-Saxon Petroleum* [1959] A.C. 133 at 161 (H.L.); *Nea Agrex S.A.* v. *Baltic Shipping Co. Ltd.* [1976] 2 W.L.R. 925 at 934 (C.A.); for a building contract case, see *Gold* v. *Patman & Fotheringham Ltd.* [1958] 1 W.L.R. 697 at 702 (C.A.); *cp. Esmil* v. *Fairclough* (1981) 19 B.L.R. 129. See also "Certainty of terms" at p. 22.

[73] *Burchell* v. *Clark* (1876) 2 C.P.D. 88 at 97. For an example, see *Townsend (Builders) Ltd.* v. *Cinema News, etc., Ltd.* [1959] 1 W.L.R. 119 at 122 (C.A.)—the case is more fully reported at (1958) 20 B.L.R. 118 (C.A.).

[74] Lord Atkinson in *Brodie* v. *Cardiff Corp.* [1919] A.C. 337 at 355 (H.L.); *National Coal Board* v. *William Neill & Son* [1985] Q.B. 300 at 319. See also "Ordinary meaning" at p. 40.

a contract may involve two stages; first, the court may have to determine which documents are contractual[75] secondly, having decided which documents form part of the contract, it must give effect to all the terms and endeavour to reconcile inconsistencies by the rules of construction. In doing this it will be assisted if the parties have expressly[76] or impliedly[77] indicated that certain clauses or documents are to prevail in the event of an inconsistency.

Written words prevail. Where there is a contract contained in a printed form with clauses inserted or filled in which are inconsistent with printed words, "the written words are entitled to have a greater effect attributed to them than the printed words, inasmuch as the written words were the immediate language and terms selected by the parties themselves for the expression of their meaning."[78] If printed words by an express clause state that the printed form is to prevail over written words a difficult question of construction arises,[79] but it seems that if the clause is sufficiently clear the printed form will prevail.[80] Provisions in a written document generally prevail over those in a document which the written document incorporates.[81]

Ejusdem generis **rule.** This rule is that where there are words of a particular class followed by general words, the general words are treated as referring to matters of the same class. Thus a ship was exempted from liability for non-delivery of a cargo if the port was unsafe "in consequence of war, disturbance or any other cause." It was held that danger from ice was not within the meaning of "any other cause" which must be limited to causes similar to war or disturbance.[82] In a clause permitting an extension of time to be granted to the contractor, if the works were "delayed by reason of any alteration or addition . . . or in case of combination of workmen, or strikes, or by default of the sub-contractors . . . or other causes beyond the contractor's control," the

---

[75] *e.g.* whether quantities are part of the contract—see Chap. 4. See also, as to offer and acceptance, Chap. 2.

[76] *e.g. Brodie* v. *Cardiff Corp.* [1919] A.C. 337 at 344 (H.L.); and see clause 2.2.1 of the Standard Form of Building Contract. Engineering contracts frequently have a clause specifying the order of priority of a number of incorporated documents.

[77] As where there are written and printed parts of the contract—see below.

[78] Lord Ellenborough in *Robertson* v. *French* (1803) 4 East 130; *Glynn* v. *Margetson* [1893] A.C. 351 (H.L.); *Adamastos Shipping* v. *Anglo-Saxon Petroleum* [1959] A.C. 133 (H.L.); *Renton (G. H.) & Co. Ltd.* v. *Palmyra Trading Corp.* [1957] A.C. 149 (H.L.); *The Brabant* [1967] 1 Q.B. 588; *A. Davies & Co. (Shopfitters)* v. *William Old* (1969) 113 S.J. 262 (C.A.). See also *Neuchatel Asphalte Co. Ltd.* v. *Barnett* [1957] 1 W.L.R. 356 (C.A.).

[79] *English Industrial Estates* v. *Wimpey* [1973] 1 Lloyd's Rep. 118 (C.A.); *Henry Boot* v. *Central Lancashire New Town District Council* (1980) 15 B.L.R. 1 at 19; see further p. 488.

[80] *Gold* v. *Patman & Fotheringham Ltd.* [1958] 1 W.L.R. 697 at 701 (C.A.); *N.W. Metropolitan Regional Hospital Board* v. *T. A. Bickerton & Son Ltd.* [1970] 1 W.L.R. 607 at 617 (H.L.); *English Industrial Estates* v. *Wimpey* [1973] 1 Lloyd's Rep. 118 (C.A.).

[81] *Adamastos Shipping* v. *Anglo-Saxon Petroleum* [1959] A.C. 133 (H.L.); *Sabah Flour* v. *Comfez* [1988] 2 Lloyd's Rep. 18 at 20 (C.A.).

[82] *S. S. Knutsford Ltd.* v. *Tillmans & Co.* [1908] A.C. 406.

"other causes" were limited to those *ejusdem generis* with the causes particularised, and did not therefore include the employer's own default in failing to give possession of the site.[83] Where the words "*et cetera*" were inserted between words describing a particular class and general words it was held that their meaning was too vague to prevent the operation of the rule.[84]

For the rule to operate, it is necessary to construe a class from the particular words.[85] This will not normally be possible unless there are at least two particular things which precede the general words.[86]

"The tendency of the more modern authorities is to attenuate the application of the rule of *ejusdem generis*,"[87] and it does not apply if the parties show that they intended its exclusion.[88] It has been suggested that the rule, ordinarily applied to deeds, wills and statutes, is of less force with a contract and still less force with a commercial contract.[89] "Where you find the word 'whatsoever' following ... upon certain substantives, it is often intended to repel ... the implication of the so-called doctrine of *ejusdem generis*."[90] Thus where there was a clause somewhat similar to those cited above save that the general words "of what kind soever" were used the rule did not apply, and these words were given their ordinary unrestricted meaning.[91]

Contra proferentem rule. This expression means "against the profferer," *i.e.* against the person who drafted or tendered the document. If there is an ambiguity in a document which all the other methods of construction have failed to resolve so that there are two alternative meanings to certain words, the court may construe the words against the party who put forward the document and give effect to the meaning more favourable to the other party.[92] Where there was a clause enabling the architect to extend the time for completion and the employer sought to rely on the clause to enable him to claim liquidated damages,[93] it was held for various reasons that the employer could not rely on it. It was said that in case those reasons were wrong, then in

---

[83] *Wells* v. *Army & Navy Co-op. Society* (1902) H.B.C. (4th ed., 1914), Vol. 2, p. 353 at 357 (C.A.). See further p. 231.

[84] *Herman* v. *Morris* (1919) 35 T.L.R. 574 (C.A.).

[85] *Henry Boot* v. *Central Lancashire New Town District Council* (1980) 15 B.L.R. 1 at 15.

[86] *Re Ellwood* [1927] 1 Ch. 455 at 461.

[87] *Allen* v. *Emmerson* [1944] K.B. 362 at 367 (D.C.). Note that this decision dealt with the construction of a statute.

[88] *Jersey (Earl of)* v. *Guardians of Neath* (1889) 22 Q.B.D. 555 (C.A.).

[89] *Henry Boot* v. *Central Lancashire New Town District Council* (1980) 15 B.L.R. 1, where H.H. Judge Fay Q.C. declined to apply the rule to clause 23(h) of the 1963 JCT Standard Form of Building Contract.

[90] Fry L.J. in *Jersey (Earl of)* v. *Guardians of Neath* (1889) 22 Q.B.D. 555 at 566 (C.A.); *cf. Gillespie Brothers* v. *Roy Bowles* [1973] Q.B. 400 (C.A.) and contrast *Sonat* v. *Amerada Hess* [1988] 1 Lloyd's Rep. 145 (C.A.).

[91] *Larsen* v. *Sylvester* [1908] A.C. 295 (H.L.).

[92] *John Lee & Son* v. *Railway Executive* [1949] 2 All E.R. 581 at 583 (C.A.); *Billyack* v. *Leyland Construction Co. Ltd.* [1968] 1 W.L.R. 471 at 477. See also *Adams* v. *Richardson & Starling Ltd.* [1969] 1 W.L.R. 1645 (C.A.), discussed at p. 247.

[93] See Chap. 9.

any event the employer could not rely on the clause for it was ambiguous and would therefore be given the construction favourable to the contractor.[94] Of a form of contract devised by the employer, it was said "The liquidated damages and extension of time clauses in printed forms of contract must be construed strictly *contra proferentem*."[95]

In principle, the *contra proferentem* rule should not be applied to standard forms of contract drafted, not by the parties, but by representative bodies such as the Joint Contracts Tribunal or the Institution of Civil Engineers.[96]

The expression is sometimes more loosely used to refer to a strict construction of certain kinds of clause, *e.g.* exemption clauses[97] or liquidated damages clauses,[98] against the person seeking to rely on them. For such cases, a strict construction applies from the nature of the clause, not because one party drafted or tendered the document.[99]

Recitals. A recital is an introductory part of a document, usually beginning with the word "Whereas ... ," which indicates what the parties want to effect by their contract. Recitals often intentionally or in effect contain definitions or descriptions of the subject-matter of the succeeding contract.

> "If there is any doubt about the construction of that document the recital may be looked at in order to determine what is the true construction; but if there is no doubt about the construction the rights of the parties are governed entirely by the operative part of the writing or deed."[1]

Irreconcilable clauses. The court always endeavours to resolve an apparent inconsistency,[2] but if two clauses cannot be reconciled it will give effect to that which states the intention of the parties. Finally, if it is unable otherwise to ascertain which clause should prevail, it will give effect to the earlier clause and reject the later.[3]

---

[94] *Miller* v. *L.C.C.* (1934) 50 T.L.R. 479 at 482, discussed further at p. 232.

[95] Salmon L.J. in *Peak Construction (Liverpool) Ltd.* v. *McKinney Foundations Ltd.* (1970) 1 B.L.R. 111 at 121; also at (1971) 69 L.G.R. 1 at 11 (C.A.); *cf. Bramall & Ogden* v. *Sheffield City Council* (1983) 29 B.L.R. 73.

[96] *Tersons Ltd.* v. *Stevenage Development Corporation* [1963] 2 Lloyd's Rep. 333 at 368 (C.A.); *cf. R. W. Green Ltd.* v. *Cade Bros. Farms* [1978] 1 Lloyd's Rep. 602 at 607; and consider the approach to demurrage clauses—*Suisse Atlantique* v. *N.V. Rotterdamsche, etc.* [1967] A.C. 361 (H.L.). See Chaps. 18–21 for consideration of standard forms of contract of the kind referred to in the text.

[97] See p. 63.

[98] See *Miller* v. *L.C.C.* (1934) 50 T.L.R. 479; *Peak Construction (Liverpool) Ltd.* v. *McKinney Foundations Ltd.* (1970) 1 B.L.R. 111; see also p. 222.

[99] *cf. I.B.A.* v. *E.M.I. and B.I.C.C.* (1978) 11 B.L.R. 29 at 55 (C.A.), where a true *contra proferentem* argument would have yielded in the face of a strict construction of an exception clause. The case went to the House of Lords (reported at (1980) 14 B.L.R. 1) where the point was not disapproved.

[1] Brett L.J in *Leggott* v. *Barrett* (1880) 15 Ch.D. 306 at 311 (C.A.). For misstatement of facts in recitals in deeds, see p. 59.

[2] *Bush* v. *Watkins* (1851) 14 Beav. 425 at 432.

[3] *Forbes* v. *Git* [1922] 1 A.C. 256 at 259 (P.C.). See also "Meaningless words" at p. 22.

3. Alterations

Alterations made before a contract is signed are binding.[4] It is presumed that alterations apparent on a document were made before execution.[5] Alterations or erasures made after execution by one party without the consent of the other are of no effect.[6] If both parties alter a document after execution by agreement this is a variation of the contract.

4. Implied Terms

There is a distinction between construction, which is determining the meaning of words which are in the contract, and implication which is (in effect) supplying words which are not in the contract.

It has been said that there are three different senses in which the expression "implied term" is used.[7] The first is a term which does not depend on the actual intention of the parties but on a rule of law such as the implied terms in a contract for the sale of goods.[8] This is discussed under "Statutory implication" below. The second is where the law in some circumstances holds that a contract is dissolved if there is a vital change of conditions.[9] The third is where a term is sought to be implied based on an intention imputed to the parties from their actual circumstances. This sense is discussed under "Necessary implication" below.

(a) *Statutory implication*[10]

Supply of Goods and Services Act 1982. Part II of this Act applies to contracts, made on or after July 4, 1983,[11] "for the supply of a service,"[12] and a

---

[4] For the effect of deletions in a printed form, see p. 35.

[5] *Doe d. Tatum* v. *Catomore* (1851) 16 Q.B. 745.

[6] See *Pattinson* v. *Luckley* (1875) L.R. 10 Ex. 330.

[7] Lord Wright in *Luxor (Eastbourne) Ltd.* v. *Cooper* [1941] A.C. 108 at 137 (H.L.); *cf. Sterling Engineering Co. Ltd.* v. *Patchett* [1955] A.C. 534 at 547 (H.L.). See also *Tsakiroglou & Co. Ltd.* v. *Noblee Thorl G.m.b.H.* [1962] A.C. 93 at 122 (H.L.); *Young & Marten* v. *McManus Childs* [1969] 1 A.C. 454 at 465 (H.L.); *Gloucestershire County Council* v. *Richardson* [1969] 1 A.C. 480 at 503 (H.L.). For another use of the term see "Custom and Usage" at p. 37. For an interesting discussion of terminology, see *Halsbury* (4th ed.), Vol. 9, paras. 351 *et seq.* For a classification by Lord Denning, see *Shell U.K. Ltd.* v. *Lostock Garage Ltd.* [1976] 1 W.L.R. 1187 at 1195 (C.A.).

[8] See Sale of Goods Act 1979, ss.12–15; Supply of Goods (Implied Terms) Act 1973, ss.1–3; Supply of Goods and Services Act 1982, ss.13–15 discussed below. A building contract is a contract for the supply of services but is not a contract for the sale of goods, but see "Implication of 'usual' terms" at p. 48.

[9] This approach to the judicial basis of frustration is, it seems, now in disfavour, see "Frustration generally" at p. 134 but it is convenient to retain this classification of meaning given to the expression "implied term" as there are numerous reported cases, including decisions of the House of Lords, where the words are used in this second sense.

[10] See also n. 8 above.

[11] S.I. 1982 No. 1770 and s.20(5) of the Act.

[12] s.12.

building contract is such a contract. In general the effect of the Act is to put into statutory form minimum terms which the law ordinarily implies in a contract for services.

In a contract for the supply of a service where the supplier is acting in the course of a business, there is an implied term that he will carry out the service with reasonable care and skill (section 13). Subject to time being fixed in a manner agreed by the contract or determined by the course of dealing between the parties, there is an implied term that the supplier will carry out the service within a reasonable time (section 14). Subject to equivalent qualifications, there is an implied term to pay the supplier a reasonable charge (section 15). The implied terms may be negatived or varied by express agreement or by the course of dealing between the parties or by a binding usage, but an express term does not negative a term implied by the Act unless it is inconsistent with it (section 16). The Act does not prejudice any rule of law which imposes a duty stricter than that imposed by sections 13 and 14 (section 16).

(b) *Necessary implication*

There are varieties of implication which the courts make in seeking to establish the imputed or presumed intention of the parties,[13] and categories of implication have been referred to as shades of a "continuous spectrum."[14] Within the spectrum, two broad areas or categories may be discerned.[15] The first appears where the parties have drawn up a detailed contract but it is necessary to insert a term to make it work. This is sometimes termed "*The Moorcock*[16] approach." The second is where in all contracts of a certain type, such as building contracts, the law implies certain usual terms unless the parties have shown an intention to exclude or modify them.[17] In each category the implication must be necessary and the term must be reasonable, but terms which are not necessary will not be implied merely because the court regards them as reasonable.[18] It seems that in the first category it is for the party putting forward the term to establish its existence, and in the second for the party denying the term to establish its absence.

(i) *Implication to make contract work*

The court does not make or improve contracts.

---

[13] *Liverpool City Council* v. *Irwin* [1977] A.C. 239 at 253 (H.L.).

[14] *Ibid.* Lord Wilberforce at 254. For a useful discussion relating to a building contract, see *London Borough of Merton* v. *Leach* (1985) 32 B.L.R. 51 at 73 *et seq.*

[15] *Liverpool City Council* v. *Irwin* [1977] A.C. 239 at 255, 257 (H.L.); *National Bank of Greece* v. *Pinios Co. No. 1* [1990] A.C. 637 at 644 (C.A.) unaffected by the decision in the House of Lords, *ibid.* at 637 (H.L.); *cp.* also *Greaves & Co. Ltd.* v. *Baynham Meikle* [1975] 1 W.L.R. 1095 at 1099, 1103 (C.A.); *George Hawkins* v. *Chrysler* (1986) 38 B.L.R. 36 at 47 (C.A.).

[16] (1889) 14 P.D. 64 (C.A.).

[17] See n. 15 above.

[18] *Liverpool City Council* v. *Irwin* [1977] A.C. 239 at 262 (H.L.); *George Hawkins* v. *Chrysler* (1986) 35 B.L.R. 36 at 49 (C.A.).

Its "function is to interpret and apply the contract which the parties have made for themselves. If the express terms are perfectly clear and free from ambiguity, there is no choice to be made between different possible meanings; the clear terms must be applied even if the court thinks some other terms would have been more suitable. An unexpressed term can be implied if and only if the court finds that the parties must have intended that term to form part of their contract; it is not enough for the court to find that such a term would have been adopted by the parties as reasonable even if it had been suggested to them; it must have been a term that went without saying, a term *necessary* to give business efficacy to the contract, a term which, though tacit, formed part of the contract which the parties made for themselves."[19]

The test of implication, therefore, is necessity—"such obligation should be read into the contract as the nature of the contract itself implicitly requires, no more, no less." The term sought to be implied must be one without which the whole transaction would become "inefficacious, futile and absurd."[20] The implication may be necessary because "language is imperfect and there may be, as it were, obvious interstices in what is expressed which have to be filled up."[21] What the court does, if so persuaded, is in effect "to rectify a particular—often a very detailed—contract by inserting in it a term which the parties have not expressed."[22]

A term sought to be implied under this heading has to be what the parties must have intended and therefore is not implied if it provides only one of several possible solutions to the matter in question.[23]

In *Trollope & Colls Ltd.* v. *North West Metropolitan Regional Hospital Board*,[24] the contract provided for the work to be carried out in phases.[25] Phase III was to commence six months after the issue of the certificate of practical completion of phase I and was to be completed on April 30, 1972. There was delay in completing phase I, so that the period for completion of phase III which would

---

[19] Lord Pearson in *Trollope & Colls Ltd.* v. *North West Metropolitan Regional Hospital Board* [1973] 1 W.L.R. 601 at 609 (H.L.); see also *The Moorcock* (1889) 14 P.D. 64 (C.A.); *Reigate* v. *Union Manufacturing Co. Ltd.* [1918] 1 K.B. 592 at 605 (C.A.). See *Shirlaw* v. *Southern Foundries (1926) Ltd.* [1939] 2 K.B. 206 at 227 (C.A.) for the test of what answer the parties would give to the "officious bystander"; *G.L.C.* v. *Cleveland Bridge* (1984) 34 B.L.R. 50 at 78 (C.A.)—no implied term of due diligence beyond contractor's express obligation to comply with key dates.

[20] *Tai Hing* v. *Liu Chong Hing Bank* [1986] A.C. 80 at 104 (P.C.), citing *Liverpool City Council* v. *Irwin* [1977] A.C. 239 at 254 and 262 (H.L.).

[21] *Luxor (Eastbourne) Ltd.* v. *Cooper* [1941] A.C. 108 at 137 (H.L.).

[22] Lord Cross in *Liverpool City Council* v. *Irwin* [1977] A.C. 239 at 258 (H.L.); *cf. Duke of Westminster* v. *Gould* [1985] 1 Q.B. 688 at 697 *et seq.* (C.A.); *Wettern Electric* v. *Welsh Development Agency* [1983] Q.B. 796.

[23] *Trollope & Colls Ltd.* v. *North West Metropolitan Regional Hospital Board* [1973] 1 W.L.R. 601 at 610, 614 (H.L.); see also *Brown & Davis Ltd.* v. *Galbraith* [1972] 1 W.L.R. 997 (C.A.); *El Awadi* v. *Bank of Credit S.A.* [1990] Q.B. 606 at 623.

[24] [1973] 1 W.L.R. 601 (H.L.).

[25] Such contracts seem to give rise to problems of construction; for the position where the Standard Form of Building Contract is used, see p. 534. In the *Trollope & Colls* case there was one contract but three sets of conditions based on the 1963 Standard Form of Building Contract.

have been 30 months if there had been no such delay became 16 months. There was express provision for extension of time for the completion of phase I but not for the extension of the completion date for phase III if phase I was delayed. The House of Lords refused to imply a term extending the time for completion of phase III by a period equal to the extension of time for completion of phase I properly allowable in respect of phase I. The express terms were clear so there was no room for implication and the parties must be taken to have accepted the risks involved; in any event there were four or five different ways in which the question of extension of time in the event of delay in completion of phase I might have been dealt with.

(ii) *Implication of "usual" terms—employer*

Where there is a comprehensive written contract such as the Standard Form of Building Contract there may be very little room for the implication of any terms, for if the parties have dealt expressly with a matter in the contract, no term dealing with the same matter can be implied.[26] But where there is no express contract, or its terms do not deal with the matters about to be mentioned, certain terms are usually implied. Such terms are often referred to as "warranties."

Co-operation. "Generally speaking, where B is employed by A to do a piece of work which requires A's co-operation ... it is implied that the necessary co-operation will be forthcoming."[27] The employer impliedly agrees to do all that is necessary on his part to bring about completion of the contract.[28] For example, he must give possession of the site within a reasonable time.[29] He may be obliged to obtain planning permission or Building Regulation consent

---

[26] See, *e.g. Lynch* v. *Thorne* [1956] 1 W.L.R. 303 (C.A.); *Jones* v. *St. John's College, Oxford* (1870) L.R. 6 Q.B. 115 at 126; *cf. Euro-Diam Ltd.* v. *Bathurst* [1990] Q.B. 1 at 40 (C.A.). The principle is sometimes expressed *expressio unius est exclusio alterius*. But if certain warranties are expressly excluded, the principle cannot be relied on to imply warranties as to matters where warranties are not expressly excluded, *Thorn* v. *London Corp.* (1876) 1 App.Cas. 120 at 131 (H.L.). See generally *Halsbury* (4th ed.), Vol. 12, para. 1476.

[27] Lord Simon in *Luxor (Eastbourne) Ltd.* v. *Cooper* [1941] A.C. 108 at 118 (H.L.). See L. F. Burrows (1968) 31 M.L.R. 390.

[28] *Mackay* v. *Dick* (1881) 6 App.Cas. 251 at 263 (H.L.); *London Borough of Merton* v. *Leach* (1985) 32 B.L.R. 51 at 81, adopting the sentence in the text. *Cf. Hamlyn* v. *Wood* [1891] 2 Q.B. 488 (C.A.); *Holland Hannen & Cubitts* v. *W.H.T.S.O.* (1983) 18 B.L.R. 80 at 117; *Lorne Stewart* v. *William Sindall* (1986) 35 B.L.R. 109 at 127 *et seq.*—co-operation by main contractor in relation to a sub-contractor's name borrowing arbitration.

[29] *Freeman* v. *Hensler* (1900) H.B.C. (4th ed.), Vol. 2, p. 292 (C.A.); *The Queen* v. *Walter Cabott Ltd.* (1975) 21 B.L.R. 46 (Canadian Federal Court of Appeals), where it was held on the facts that more than the actual site upon which the structure stands was required to erect the structure; *Canterbury Pipe Lines* v. *Christchurch Drainage* (1979) 16 B.L.R. 76 at 90 (New Zealand Court of Appeal); *Hounslow London Borough Council* v. *Twickenham Garden Developments* [1971] Ch. 233 at 247—implied negative obligation on the employer not to revoke the contractor's licence to occupy the site otherwise than in accordance with the contract; *cp. L.R.E. Engineering* v. *Otto Simon Carves* (1981) 24 B.L.R. 127; *Surrey Heath B.C.* v. *Lovell Construction* (1988) 42 B.L.R. 25 at 51.

in sufficient time to enable the contractor to proceed without delay.[30] If an architect is to supervise the work the employer must appoint an architect.[31]

Where a certifier is failing to apply the terms of a contract properly to the detriment of the contractor and where the contract does not contain a relevant arbitration clause,[32] it is ordinarily an implied term on the part of the employer that he will require the certifier to perform his duties properly.[33]

The negative aspect of the same principle is that the employer should not interfere with the proper performance by the certifier of the duties imposed upon him by the contract.[34] If to the employer's knowledge the architect persists in applying the contract wrongly in regard to those matters where the architect must act fairly between the parties, he must dismiss him and appoint another.[35]

If, however, the contract contains a wide arbitration clause, there may not be any need or scope for the positive implications referred to in the previous paragraph. In *Lubenham* v. *South Pembrokeshire District Council*,[36] such terms were held not to be implied where the arbitration clause in a 1963 Standard Form of Building Contract expressly permitted arbitration upon interim certificates during the currency of the contract and before practical completion.[37] There was one simple remedy[38] available to the contractor needing no implied term, namely to go to arbitration and have the certificates corrected. It is submitted that the mere presence of a wide arbitration clause may not alone be decisive. In addition, the court may consider the precise state of the employer's knowledge. In the *Lubenham* case, it was said on the facts that the employers were doubtless content to be guided by the architects as experts and that such acquiescence did not expose them to liability to pay sums higher than had been certified. If it were established that an employer knew perfectly well that his architect was failing to certify in accordance with the contract, it is thought that he would not be allowed to shelter behind the arbitration clause.

---

[30] This will depend on the facts and the express terms of the contract, but see *Ellis-Don* v. *Parking Authority of Toronto* (1978) 28 B.L.R. 98 at 110; *cf. Townsend* v. *Cinema News & Property Management* (1958) 20 B.L.R. 118 at 142. For statutory obligations under the Standard Form of Building Contract, see p. 503.

[31] *Hunt* v. *Bishop* (1853) 8 Ex. 675.

[32] See *Lubenham* v. *South Pembrokeshire District Council* (1986) 33 B.L.R. 39 (C.A.) discussed below.

[33] *Panamena* v. *Leyland* in the Court of Appeal, (1943) 76 Lloyd's Rep. 113, explained in the judgment of Macfarlan J. in the Supreme Court of New South Wales in *Perini Corporation* v. *Commonwealth of Australia* (1969) 12 B.L.R. 82. See also *Canterbury Pipe Lines Ltd.* v. *Christchurch Drainage Board* (1979) 16 B.L.R. 76 (New Zealand Court of Appeal)—contractor had no implied right to suspend work where Engineer wrongly refused to certify.

[34] *Perini Corporation* v. *Commonwealth of Australia* (1969) 12 B.L.R. 82; Devlin J. in *Minster Trust Ltd.* v. *Traps Tractors Ltd.* [1954] 1 W.L.R. 963 at 975; *Panamena* v. *Leyland* [1947] A.C. 428 (H.L.); *Sutcliffe* v. *Thackrah* [1974] 2 A.C. 727.

[35] *Panamena* v. *Leyland* [1947] A.C. 428 at 436 (H.L.), discussed at p. 104.

[36] (1986) 33 B.L.R. 39 at 58 (C.A.). See also *Croudace* v. *London Borough of Lambeth* (1986) 33 B.L.R. 20 at 34 (C.A.).

[37] For the substantially similar arbitration clause in the current Standard Form of Building Contract, see p. 673.

[38] In practice, the remedy may not be at all simple.

The implied term of co-operation extends to those things which the architect must do to enable the contractor to carry out the work and the employer is liable for any breach of this duty by the architect.[39] If instructions, nominations, information, plans or details are required, they must be supplied at reasonable times.[40] This may include a duty to give instructions to a nominated sub-contractor and may extend to instructions relating to the sub-contractor's bad design.[41] What is reasonable depends upon the express terms of the contract in question and all the circumstances.[42] But the particular terms should always be carefully considered. In *Neodox* v. *Swinton and Pendlebury Borough Council*,[43] it was said that what was reasonable did not depend solely upon the convenience and financial interests of the contractor. It depended also on the point of view of the engineer and his staff and the employer. The contract there provided for the works, including the order of the works, to be carried out on the direction of the engineer. It is thought that it may not be appropriate to consider reasonableness from the point of view of the architect or engineer or employer where the order of the works is a matter solely for the contractor. The prime consideration is, it is suggested, that instructions should be given at such times and in such manner as not to hinder or prevent the contractor from performing his duties under the contract.[44] Since the principal relevant contractor's duty is to complete within the stipulated time, the obligation of the architect or engineer to furnish drawings and instructions "could validly be performed within a reasonable time of the conclusion of the contract."[45]

Where a contract is running late so that, unless the contractor increases the rate of progress, it will not be completed to time, it is sometimes said that it is reasonable to supply instructions at such a rate as will enable the contractor to continue with the works at the existing rate of progress. Expressed thus the proposition is, it is submitted, too wide. The actual rate of progress is, ordinarily, a factor to be considered. But there may well be other factors, such as the contractor's expressed intention to increase the rate of progress and his

---

[39] *London Borough of Merton* v. *Leach* (1985) 32 B.L.R. 51 at 81; *Neodox* v. *Swinton and Pendlebury Borough Council* (1958) 5 B.L.R. 38 at 41.

[40] *Roberts* v. *Bury Commissioners* (1870) L.R. 5 C.P. 310 at 325; *McAlpine* v. *Lanarkshire, etc., Railway* (1889) 17 R. 113; *Wells* v. *Army & Navy Co-op. Society* (1902) H.B.C. (4th ed.), Vol. 2, p. 346 at 352 (C.A.); *Neodox* v. *Swinton and Pendlebury Borough Council* (1958) 5 B.L.R. 38. See also *McAlpine & Son* v. *Transvaal Provincial Administration* [1974] 3 S.A.L.R. 506, particularly the minority judgments of Corbett A.J.A. and Jansen J.A. *cp. Fischbach & Moore of Canada* v. *Noranda Mines* (1978) 84 D.L.R. (3d) 465. For claims for damages by the contractor arising out of breach of these duties, see pp. 208 *et seq.* and 444.

[41] *Holland, Hannen and Cubitts Ltd.* v. *W.H.T.S.O.* (1981) 18 B.L.R 80.

[42] Guidance can be obtained from *Wells* v. *Army & Navy Co-op. Society* and the *Neodox* and *McAlpine* cases and referred to in n. 40 above.

[43] (1958) 5 B.L.R. 38.

[44] This passage (in the terms of the First Supplement to the 4th edition, p. 6) quoted with apparent approval in *Glenlion Construction* v. *The Guinness Trust* (1987) 39 B.L.R. 89 at 103.

[45] Corbett A.J.A. in *McAlpine & Son* v. *Transvaal Provincial Administration* [1974] 3 S.A.L.R. 506 at 535; *cf. Glenlion Construction* v. *The Guinness Trust* (1987) 39 B.L.R. 89.

ability to achieve that intention. Further, it is sometimes said[46] that the prime consideration is the contractor's own stated requirements of the time when he is to be supplied with instructions. Again, it is thought that this is too wide. The contractor's stated requirements are a factor but not decisive. The contractor cannot unilaterally determine what is a reasonable time, and a contractor does not prove a claim based on late instructions merely by establishing non-compliance with requests for instructions or a schedule of dates for instructions which he has sent to the architect. Agreement by the architect with such a schedule, or even acquiescence, may, it is submitted, be relevant evidence on the question what is reasonable. In most cases, the critical question will be to determine on all the facts when the contractor really needs the instructions.

Sometimes contractors, at the commencement of or early in the course of a contract, prepare and submit to the architect a programme of works showing completion at a date materially before the contract date. The architect may approve such programme or accept it without comment. It is then argued that the contractor has a claim for damages for failure by the architect to issue instructions at times necessary to comply with the programme. Every case must depend upon the particular express terms and circumstances. In *Glenlion Construction* v. *The Guinness Trust*,[47] it was held, under a 1963 JCT Standard Form of Contract, firstly that the contractor was entitled to programme to complete before the contractual completion date and to complete on the earlier date, but secondly that there was no implied term that the employer should so perform the agreement as to enable the contractor to complete by the earlier date. The contractor was not *obliged* to complete by the earlier date and the unilateral imposition of an earlier completion date would result in the whole balance of the contract being lost.[48]

Not to prevent completion.   "In general . . . a term is necessarily implied in any contract, the other terms of which do not repel the implication, that neither party shall prevent the other from performing it."[49] A term of this nature cannot be implied if it is illegal[50] or contrary to an express term of the contract.[51] The particular implied term relied on should be expressly pleaded, and "except possibly in the rare cases where the wrongful act alleged is independent of the contract" it is circumlocution to add a general allegation of

---

[46] Relying upon the *dictum* of Wright J. in the *Wells* v. *Army & Navy Co-op. Society* (1902) H.B.C. (4th ed.), Vol. 2, p. 346 at 352 (C.A.).

[47] (1987) 39 B.L.R. 89.

[48] *Ibid.* at 105, quoting with apparent approval a passage from the Supplement to the 4th edition of this book, p. 6, substantially reproduced in this and the preceding paragraph.

[49] Lord Asquith in *Cory Ltd.* v. *City of London Corp.* [1951] 2 K.B. 476 at 484 (C.A.); see *Lawson* v. *Wallasey Local Board* (1883) 48 L.T. 507 (C.A.); *Bywaters* v. *Curnick* (1906) H.B.C. (4th ed.), Vol. 2, p. 393 (C.A.); *London Borough of Merton* v. *Leach* (1985) 32 B.L.R. 51 at 79.

[50] *Cory Ltd.* v. *City of London Corp.* [1951] 2 K.B. 476 (C.A.).

[51] *Farr* v. *The Admiralty* [1953] 1 W.L.R. 965; *Martin Grant* v. *Sir Lindsay Parkinson* (1984) 29 B.L.R. 31—a case between contractor and sub-contractor.

prevention.[52] The employer does not impliedly warrant the fitness of the site,[53] nor, it seems, that there will be no wrongful interference by third parties.[54] The employer is not, in the absence of fraud or collusion, responsible for delay caused by a sub-contractor, even though under the terms of the contract the sub-contractor was nominated by the employer or his architect without consultation with the contractor.[55] The employer is liable for delay caused by his servants and agents.[56] This liability usually extends to delay on the part of the architect or the engineer under a typical building or engineering contract.[57] There is, it is submitted, an implied term that the employer will not so act as to disqualify the architect.[58]

Unjustified interference by the employer in the supply of goods necessary for the contract is a breach of the implied term, notwithstanding that the supplier has no contract direct with the contractor.[59]

(iii) *Implication of "usual" terms—contractor*

Workmanship. The contractor must do the work with all proper skill and care.[60] It is suggested that this is a continuing duty during construction and not only upon completion.[61] In deciding what degree of skill is required the

---

[52] Devlin J. in *Mona, etc., Ltd.* v. *Rhodesia Rys. Ltd.* [1949] 2 All E.R. 1014 at 1016; *Luxor* v. *Cooper* [1941] A.C. 108 at 149 (H.L.); *cf.* Lord Atkin in *Southern Foundries* v. *Shirlaw* [1940] A.C. 701 at 717 (H.L.); *Thompson* v. *ASDA-MFI Plc.* [1988] Ch. 241 considering *Cheal* v. *A.P.E.X.* [1983] 1 A.C. 180 at 189.

[53] *Appleby* v. *Myers* (1867) L.R. 2 C.P. 651, and see pp. 82 and 137.

[54] *Porter* v. *Tottenham Urban District Council* [1915] 1 K.B. 776 (C.A.); *L.R.E. Engineering* v. *Otto Simon Carves* (1981) 24 B.L.R. 127.

[55] *Leslie & Co. Ltd.* v. *The Managers of the Metropolitan Asylums District* (1901) 68 J.P. 86 (C.A.); *Kirk & Kirk* v. *Croydon Corporation* [1956] J.P.L. 585. *Cp. Thomas Bates & Son Ltd.* v. *Thurrock Borough Council, The Times,* October 23, 1975 (C.A.) where, contrary to the ordinary rule, the employer was held liable for a nominated sub-contractor's default upon the special wording of the contract. Under the 1980 Standard Form of Building Contract, there are extensive express provisions relating to nominated sub-contractors—see p. 626.

[56] *Russell* v. *Sa da Bandeira* (1862) 13 C.B.(N.S.) 149.

[57] See *Sutcliffe* v. *Thackrah* [1974] 2 A.C. 727 (H.L.). The case of *Re de Morgan Snell & Co.* (1891) H.B.C. (4th ed.), Vol. 2, p. 185 (C.A.), so far as it is to contrary effect, should no longer be considered as of general application.

[58] See *Sutcliffe* v. *Thackrah* [1974] 2 A.C. 727 (H.L.). For the meaning of disqualification of a certifier see p. 114. For whether acts by an employer in breach of the implied term can be treated as repudiation see p. 156.

[59] *Acrow (Automation) Ltd.* v. *Rex Chainbelt Inc.* [1971] 1 W.L.R. 1676 at 1680 (C.A.).

[60] *Young & Marten* v. *McManus Childs* [1969] 1 A.C. 454 at 465 (H.L.); *Charnock* v. *Liverpool Corporation* [1968] 1 W.L.R. 1498 (C.A.); *Duncan* v. *Blundell* (1820) 3 Stark. 6; *Pearce* v. *Tucker* (1862) 3 F. & F. 136. The duty is sometimes expressed as one to do the work in a good and workmanlike manner. For compliance with Building Regulations, see p. 143 and Chap. 15, Section 4.

[61] See *Surrey Heath B.C.* v. *Lovell Construction* (1988) 42 B.L.R. 25 at 34 considering Lord Diplock (dissenting) in *P. & M. Kaye* v. *Hosier & Dickinson* [1972] 1 W.L.R. 146 at 165 (H.L.) and unaffected by the decision in the Court of Appeal at (1990) 48 B.L.R. 108 (C.A.); *Lintest Builders Ltd.* v. *Roberts* (1978) 10 B.L.R. 120 and (1980) 13 B.L.R. 38 (C.A.); *William Tomkinson* v. *Parochial Church Council of St. Michael* (1990) 6 Const.L.J. 319. At least, the employer acquires a right to require the contractor to remedy the bad work at the time it is done—see *Lintest* at 13 B.L.R. 43.

court will, it is submitted, consider all the circumstances of the contract including the degree of skill expressly or impliedly professed by the contractor.[62] Breach of the duty includes the use of materials containing patent defects, even though the source of such materials has been chosen by the employer.[63]

Materials. The law as to implied warranties[64] was considered fully by the House of Lords in the cases of *Young & Marten* v. *McManus Childs*[65] and *Gloucestershire County Council* v. *Richardson*.[66]

Warranties of fitness for purpose and good quality. If the contractor is to supply materials he warrants that the materials he will use are:

(1) reasonably fit for the purpose for which they will be used; and

(2) of good quality,

unless the express terms of the contract and any admissible surrounding circumstances show that the parties intended to exclude either or both warranties.[67]

The two warranties correspond substantially with the warranties implied by section 14 of the Sale of Goods Act 1979[68] upon a contract for the sale of goods,[69] so that where there is no limitation upon the contractor's right of recourse against his supplier he will in the case of defective materials[70] or goods have his remedy over against his supplier who in turn will have his remedy over and so on down the chain of contracts until the manufacturer or other author of the defect is reached.[71]

The effect of the second warranty is, in the ordinary case, to make the contractor liable for latent defects even though the employer may have chosen the materials or nominated the supplier and there has been no lack of care and

---

[62] *Duncan* v. *Blundell* (1820) 3 Stark. 6 at 7; *Harmer* v. *Cornelius* (1858) 5 C.B.(N.S.) 236; *Young & Marten* v. *McManus Childs* [1969] 1 A.C. 454 at 468, 472 (H.L.).

[63] *Young & Marten* v. *McManus Childs* [1969] 1 A.C. 454 at 469, 470 (H.L.).

[64] Used here in the sense of "implied terms."

[65] [1969] 1 A.C. 454 (H.L.).

[66] [1969] 1 A.C. 480 (H.L.).

[67] *Young & Marten* v. *McManus Childs* [1969] 1 A.C. 454 (H.L.); *Gloucestershire County Council* v. *Richardson* [1969] A.C. 480 (H.L.); *Myers* v. *Brent Cross Service Co.* [1934] 1 K.B. 46 (D.C.), explained in *Young & Marten's* case at pp. 467, 471, 474, 478; *Samuels* v. *Davies* [1943] 1 K.B. 526 (C.A.); *Stewart* v. *Reavell's Garage* [1952] 2 Q.B. 545; *Ingham* v. *Emes* [1955] 2 Q.B. 366 (C.A.); *cf. I.B.A.* v. *E.M.I. and B.I.C.C.* (1980) 14 B.L.R. 1 at 48.

[68] For cases which consider this section, see, *e.g. Aswan Engineering Co.* v. *Lupdine* [1987] 1 W.L.R. 1 (C.A.); *Rogers* v. *Parish Ltd.* [1987] 2 W.L.R. 353 (C.A.) and note that s.14(6) has a statutory definition of "merchantable quality" in terms introduced by s.7(2) of the Supply of Goods (Implied Terms) Act 1973.

[69] *Young & Marten* v. *McManus Childs* [1969] 1 A.C. 454 (H.L.) noting that Lord Upjohn's view, at 475, was that the obligation upon the contractor in respect of materials was higher than that upon the seller of goods.

[70] Materials are "goods" for the purposes of the Sale of Goods Act 1979.

[71] *Young & Marten* v. *McManus Childs* [1969] 1 A.C. 454 at 466 (H.L.); *Gloucestershire County Council* v. *Richardson* [1969] A.C. 480 (H.L.).

skill on the part of the contractor.[72] Thus in *Young & Marten* v. *McManus Childs*,[73] the agent of the employer,[74] a highly skilled and experienced person, relied on his own skill and judgment in the choice of "Somerset 13" tiles to be fixed by the contractor. After fixing and exposure to weather, defects appeared which required the replacement of the tiles. It was held that although the warranty of fitness for purpose was excluded the warranty of quality was not, and the contractor was liable. Lord Pearce stated by way of illustration of the general principle: "It is frequent for builders to fit baths, sanitary equipment, central heating and the like, encouraging their clients to choose from the wholesaler's display rooms which they prefer. It would, I think, surprise the average householder if it were suggested that simply by exercising a choice he had lost all right of recourse in respect of the quality of the fittings against the builder who normally has a better knowledge of these matters."[75]

Exclusion of warranties.   Reference is sometimes made to the practical convenience of having a chain of contractual liability from employer to main contractor to sub-contractor or supplier.[76] But the chain can be broken.[77] Exclusion of usual warranties depends upon the contract and surrounding circumstances.[78] So far as it is a question of surrounding circumstances, it is a question of fact and degree,[79] but some principles can be stated.

The warranty of fitness for purpose is excluded if in the selection of the materials in question the employer placed no reliance on the contractor's skill and judgment.[80] The facts of *Young & Marten* v. *McManus Childs*[81] illustrate the point. The warranty is excluded where the employer fails to disclose some relevant abnormal circumstance relating to the use of the material and thus does not make known to the contractor the particular purpose for which the materials are required.[82] The warranty is excluded if it is inconsistent with

---

[72] It makes him ". . . an insurer in respect of the defects which he could not prevent and of which he did not know": Lord Wilberforce in *Young & Marten* v. *McManus Childs* [1969] 1 A.C. 454 at 479 (H.L.).

[73] [1969] 1 A.C. 454 (H.L.).

[74] In fact the main contractor contracting with his subcontractor, but the principle is the same as in the case of employer and contractor, and for convenience the usual terminology is used.

[75] [1969] 1 A.C. 454 at 470 (H.L.).

[76] *e.g.* Lord Fraser in *I.B.A.* v. *E.M.I. and B.I.C.C.* (1980) 14 B.L.R. 1 at 44 (H.L.) with reference to *Young & Marten* v. *McManus Childs* [1969] 1 A.C. 454 (H.L.); *University of Warwick* v. *Sir Robert McAlpine* (1988) 42 B.L.R. 1 at 11.

[77] As, *e.g.* in the Irish case of *Norta* v. *John Sisk Ltd.* (1977) 14 B.L.R. 49 referred to with apparent approval by Lord Fraser in *I.B.A.* v. *E.M.I. and B.I.C.C.* (1980) 14 B.L.R. 1 (H.L.); *University of Warwick* v. *Sir Robert McAlpine* (1988) 42 B.L.R. 1.

[78] See n. 67 above.

[79] *Young & Marten* v. *McManus Childs* [1969] 1 A.C. 454 at 471 (H.L.).

[80] See cases cited in n. 67 above; *Cammell Laird & Co. Ltd.* v. *Manganese Bronze and Brass Co. Ltd.* [1934] A.C. 402 (H.L.), a case on the Sale of Goods Act 1893, but the principle is the same; *Young & Marten* v. *McManus Childs* [1969] 1 A.C. 454 at 472, 479 (H.L.); *Comyn Ching* v. *Oriental Tube* (1979) 17 B.L.R. 47 at 81; *Norta* v. *John Sisk* (1977) 14 B.L.R. 49 cited in *I.B.A.* v. *E.M.I. and B.I.C.C* (1980) 14 B.L.R. 1 at 25 and 45; *University of Warwick* v. *Sir Robert McAlpine* (1988) 42 B.L.R. 1.

[81] [1969] 1 A.C. 454 (H.L.).

[82] *Ingham* v. *Emes* [1955] 2 Q.B. 366 (C.A.).

express terms[83] or if the contractor contracts on the basis of a disclaimer of responsibility.[84]

Circumstances will not often exclude the warranty of quality as they did not in *Young & Marten* v. *McManus Childs*.[85] The court will, however, infer an intention to exclude the warranty of quality if the employer chooses materials which he and the contractor know can only be obtained from a supplier upon terms which remove or substantially limit the contractor's right of recourse against his supplier for defects of quality in such materials.[86] In *Gloucestershire County Council* v. *Richardson*,[87] the contractor was directed to enter into a contract for the supply of concrete columns at a price and upon terms which had been fixed by the employer. One of the terms limited liability for defective goods to free replacement and excluded liability for consequential loss. It was held[88] that this showed an intention that the contractor should not be liable for latent defects due to bad manufacture. Other circumstances which influenced the House were that the design, materials, specification, quality and price of the columns were fixed without reference to the contractor,[89] and that under the form of contract used[90] there was no right to object to the nomination or to insist on an indemnity.[91]

As to repairing contracts it has been said:

"... less cogent circumstances may be sufficient to exclude an implied warranty of quality where the use of spare parts is only incidental to what is in essence a repairing operation where the customer's main reliance is on the skill of the tradesman, than in a case where the main element is the supply of an article, the installation being merely incidental."[92]

Fitness for purpose of completed works. Where the employer makes known to the contractor the particular purpose for which the work is to be done and the work is of a kind which the contractor holds himself out as performing, and the circumstances show that the employer relied on the contractor's skill and judgment in the matter, there is an implied warranty that the work as

---

[83] *Young & Marten* v. *McManus Childs* [1969] 1 A.C. 454 at 471 (H.L.); *Gloucestershire County Council* v. *Richardson* [1969] A.C. 480 at 495 (H.L.); see also *Lynch* v. *Thorne* [1956] 1 W.L.R. 303 (C.A.).

[84] *Young & Marten* v. *McManus Childs* [1969] 1 A.C. 454 at 471 (H.L.); *cp. Wormell* v. *RHM Agriculture* [1987] 3 All E.R. 75.

[85] See above and see also *Rumbelow* v. *A.M.K.* (1980) 19 B.L.R. 25 at 42.

[86] *Young & Marten* v. *McManus Childs* [1969] 1 A.C. 454 at 466, 471 (H.L.); *Gloucestershire County Council* v. *Richardson* [1969] A.C. 480 at 497, 503, 504, 507 (H.L.).

[87] [1969] A.C. 480 (H.L.).

[88] By a majority, Lord Pearson dissenting.

[89] See the speeches of Lord Pearce and Lord Wilberforce.

[90] R.I.B.A. Form, 1939 edition, printed in the 1st and 2nd editions of this book.

[91] As there was in the case of nominated sub-contractors under clause 21 of the contract—see Lord Pearce at 495, and Lord Wilberforce at 507. Lord Upjohn at 502, 503 expressed a different view.

[92] Lord Reid in *Young & Marten* v. *McManus Childs* [1969] 1 A.C. 454 at 468 (H.L), commenting on dictum of du Parcq J. in *Myers* v. *Brent Cross* [1934] 1 K.B. 46 at 55 (D.C.). See also Lord Wilberforce in *Young & Marten's* case at 476.

completed will be reasonably fit for the particular purpose.[93] The contractor's duty includes, it is submitted, the performance of any works of design necessary to complete the work to the requisite standard.[94] The warranty may apply only to a part or parts of the works.[95] The warranty is excluded in the same circumstances as those set out above relating to materials alone.[96] It follows that, in a building contract where the contractor is bound to complete according to detailed plans and specification or bills of quantities for which he was not responsible, the room for the operation of such an implied warranty is small.[97] But where a contractor had expressly warranted the fitness of the works, it was held that such warranty overrode the duty to comply with the detailed specification[98] and contractors generally have an obligation to warn of design defects which they believe exist.[99] Where a contractor undertook to build a house in accordance with plans supplied by the employer's architect, but there was no supervision by the architect and the employer relied upon the experience, judgment and skill of the contractor to supervise the construction, it was held that the contractor was liable to the employer for failing to warn him of obvious defects in the plans which resulted in defects.[1]

Package deals.   Where a contractor agrees in the course of his business both to design and construct works, a term of fitness for purpose of the completed works will readily be implied unless excluded by the express terms of the contract or other particular circumstances.[2] Where the package is to design and construct dwellings for a local authority, there may be an implied term that the dwellings will on completion be fit for habitation.[3] In *I.B.A.* v. *E.M.I. and B.I.C.C.*,[4] a main contractor was held liable for negligent design on the part

---

[93] *Greaves & Co. Ltd.* v. *Baynham Meikle* [1975] 1 W.L.R. 1095 at 1098 (C.A.); *cp. National Coal Board* v. *Neill* [1985] Q.B. 300 at 317; see also cases cited in n. 80 above; *Smith & Snipes Hall Farm Ltd.* v. *River Douglas Catchment Board* [1949] 2 K.B. 500 (C.A.) and *Cable (1956) Ltd.* v. *Hutcherson Ltd.* (1969) 43 A.L.J.R. 321, discussed at p. 8. See also "Licences" at p. 57.

[94] See n. 93 above.

[95] *Cammell Laird & Co. Ltd.* v. *Manganese Bronze & Brass Co. Ltd.* [1934] A.C. 402 (H.L.).

[96] See n. 93 above.

[97] See *Lynch* v. *Thorne* [1956] 1 W.L.R. 303 at 311 (C.A.). Note comment on the application of this principle to this case at p. 58.

[98] *Steel Co. of Canada Ltd.* v. *Willand Management Ltd.* [1966] S.C.R. 746 (Supreme Court of Canada).

[99] *Equitable Debenture* v. *William Moss* (1984) 1 Constr.L.J. 131 at 134; *Victoria University of Manchester* v. *Hugh Wilson* (1984) 1 Constr.L.J. 162; *cp. University of Glasgow* v. *William Whitfield* (1988) 42 B.L.R. 66. See generally Hilary Nicholls, "Contractors' Duty to Warn" (1989) 5 Const.L.J. 175.

[1] *Brunswick Construction* v. *Nowlan* (1974) 49 D.L.R. (3d) and 21 B.L.R. 27 (Supreme Court of Canada). It is thought that this case would now be readily followed in England, and that *Lynch* v. *Thorne* [1956] 1 W.L.R. 303 (C.A.) would be distinguished. Upon the particular facts, the dissenting judgment of Dickson J. is attractive.

[2] See, *e.g. Viking Grain* v. *T. H. White* (1985) 33 B.L.R. 103; *cp. Bacal Construction* v. *Northampton District Council* (1975) 8 B.L.R. 88 where there was an implied term or warranty by the employer that the ground conditions would accord with the hypotheses upon which the contractor had been instructed to design the foundations. Contrast the position of the professional consultant who does not construct as in *George Hawkins* v. *Chrysler* (1986) 38 B.L.R. 36 (C.A.).

[3] *Test Valley Borough Council* v. *G.L.C.* (1979) 13 B.L.R. 63 (C.A.); *Basildon District Council* v. *J. E. Lesser* [1985] 1 All E.R. 20. See also "Sale of buildings" at p. 57.

[4] (1980) 14 B.L.R. 1 (H.L.).

of a nominated sub-contractor upon the express terms of the main contract, but the view was expressed that he might well have been liable upon an implied term as to fitness for purpose.[5]

Licences.   Where there was a licence to occupy a new factory unit for 12 months while the licensee's factory, held under a lease from the licensor, was extended, it was held to be an implied term of the licence that the licensed premises would be sound and suitable for the licensee's manufacturing purposes.[6] Under a lease, there would have been no such implication.[7]

Specialist contractors.   The implication of fitness more readily arises where a contractor is employed because of a specialist skill he professes.[8]

Sale of buildings.   Where there is a contract for the sale of a house to be erected, or in the course of erection, there is, subject to the express terms of the contract, ". . . a threefold implication: that the builder will do his work in a good and workmanlike manner; that he will supply good and proper materials; and that it will be reasonably fit for human habitation."[9] The implication extends to the whole house including the parts, if any, built before the contract of sale was made,[10] but it does not arise if the contractor merely sells a house which he has already completed.[11]

The contractor may become liable for breach of statutory duty in respect of dwellings provided to the order of a person, to that person and others who acquire an interest in the dwelling.[12] He has a statutory duty to visitors under the Occupiers' Liability Act 1957,[13] and to persons other than visitors, *e.g.* trespassers, under the Occupiers' Liability Act 1984. He may also be liable in tort to persons who suffer physical injury to their person or property as a result of his negligence.[14]

---

[5] *Ibid.* at 26, 44, and 47. The Irish case of *Norta* v. *John Sisk* (1977) 14 B.L.R. 49, where a contractor was held not liable for his sub-contractor's design, turned on different facts—see *I.B.A.* case at 25 and 45. See also *George Hawkins* v. *Chrysler* [1986] 38 B.L.R. 36 at 55. See generally Michael Regan, "Fitness, Quality and Skill and Care" (1987) 3 Const.L.J. 241.
[6] *Wettern Electric* v. *Welsh Development Agency* [1983] Q.B. 796.
[7] *Ibid.* at 808.
[8] See cases cited in n. 80 above. See also *Adams* v. *Richardson and Starling Ltd.* [1969] 1 W.L.R. 1645 (C.A.)—specialists in eradication of dry rot. See also p. 6 for design and build contracts; p. 291 for nominated sub-contractors; p. 312 for the analogous position of the professional man.
[9] *Hancock* v. *B. W. Brazier (Anerley) Ltd.* [1966] 1 W.L.R. 1317 at 1332 (C.A.). See also *Miller* v. *Cannon Hill Estates* [1931] 2 K.B. 113; *Perry* v. *Sharon Development Co.* [1937] 4 All E.R. 390 (C.A.); *Jennings* v. *Taverner* [1955] 1 W.L.R. 932; *Lynch* v. *Thorne* [1956] 1 W.L.R. 303 (C.A.); *Greaves & Co.* v. *Baynham Meikle* [1975] 1 W.L.R. 1095 at 1098; *I.B.A.* v. *E.M.I. and B.I.C.C.* (1978) 11 B.L.R. 29 at 51 (C.A.); *Test Valley Borough Council* v. *Greater London Council* (1979) 13 B.L.R. 63 (C.A.)—one local authority so liable to another.
[10] *Hancock* v. *B. W. Brazier (Anerley) Ltd.* [1966] 1 W.L.R. 1317 (C.A.).
[11] See cases cited in n. 9 above; *Hoskins* v. *Woodham* [1938] 1 All E.R. 692; *Minster Trust Ltd.* v. *Traps Tractors Ltd.* [1954] 1 W.L.R. 963 at 975.
[12] Defective Premises Act 1972; see p. 362.
[13] As amended by the Defective Premises Act 1972.
[14] See Chap. 7, Section 2 and in particular "Personal injury" at p. 163. For the letting of houses at a low rent, see the Housing Act 1957, s.6.

Effect of express terms. "[I]f a builder has done his work badly, and defects afterwards appear, he is not to be excused from liability except by clear words."[15] So where a house was sold and defects appeared it was held that a clause providing for the making good of defects discovered within six months did not deprive the purchaser of damages for defects discovered after six months.[16] But in *Lynch* v. *Thorne*[17] a builder agreed to sell a house to be completed according to a detailed specification which provided for nine-inch solid brick walls with no rendering. One of the walls when completed permitted the entry of driving rain which made a room uninhabitable. It was held that there was no implied warranty of fitness with regard to the wall because it had been constructed exactly in accordance with the specification and to have built it with cavities or with rendering so as to make it waterproof would not have been a compliance with the contract. Accordingly the purchaser failed in his claim against the builder in respect of the wall.[18] It is possible that the case is distinguishable where no sale of land is involved and the employer does not rely on his own skill and judgment in the choice of the specified item.[19] It is thought that today it would be necessary to consider both the Defective Premises Act 1972[20] and whether the purchaser had a claim for breach of the Building Regulations.[21]

Effect of price. The standard of work to be carried out depends upon the terms of the contract express or implied. The question whether the price is high or low in relation to the work is, it is submitted, irrelevant in considering what standard of work is required,[22] unless the parties have expressly or impliedly agreed that the amount of the price is to affect the standard of the work.

5. Construction of Deeds

Deeds[23] are construed in the same way as other documents save that where one

---

[15] *Hancock* v. *B. W. Brazier (Anerley) Ltd.* [1966] 1 W.L.R. 1317 at 1334 (C.A.); see also *Billyack* v. *Leyland Construction Co. Ltd.* [1968] 1 W.L.R. 471.

[16] *Ibid.*

[17] [1956] 1 W.L.R. 303 (C.A.); *cp. Test Valley Borough Council* v. *G.L.C.* (1979) 13 B.L.R. 63 at 80 (C.A.), where it is said that the building owner in *Lynch* v. *Thorne* "insisted on providing a specification which formed part of the contract." It is not clear that *insistence* can be derived from *Lynch* v. *Thorne.*

[18] Note that for a claim relating to a window it was conceded that the purchaser could succeed for breach of implied warranty because the specification did not so precisely identify the nature of the work, at 309. See also Lord Parker C.J. at 311.

[19] Contracts for the sale of land and for work and labour differ in that in the former but not the latter the rule of *caveat emptor* still applies fundamentally (*Young & Marten Ltd.* v. *McManus Childs Ltd.* [1969] 1 A.C. 454 (H.L.), Lord Upjohn at 472).

[20] See p. 362.

[21] See p. 374.

[22] *cf. Cotton* v. *Wallis* [1955] 1 W.L.R. 1168 (C.A.), but note that this case, discussed at p. 486, was a dispute between architect and employer and is not, it is submitted, an authority on disputes between employer and contractor.

[23] For the formal requirements of deeds, see p. 27.

party wishes to deny the truth of a statement in the deed he may be estopped (*i.e.* prevented) from doing so by the application of a further rule known as estoppel by deed. This is a rule of evidence found in the principle that a solemn and unambiguous statement or engagement in a deed must be taken as binding between parties and privies and therefore as not admitting any contradictory proof.[24] Statements of fact in recitals are subject to the rule.[25] Statements in the deed may bind all or only one or some of the parties according to the construction of the deed.[26] The estoppel does not operate where the deed was fraudulent or, in general, where it was illegal,[27] nor where there was a common mistake of fact giving rise to a right to rectification,[28] nor where the party seeking to set up the estoppel caused the misstatement of fact to appear in the deed.[29]

6. The Value of Previous Decisions

Common form contracts.   The court is very reluctant to depart from a previous long-standing decision upon the meaning of a common form of contract in constant use because the parties are taken thereafter to have contracted upon the basis of that meaning.[30] But one version of a Standard Form of Building Contract should not, it is submitted, be construed with reference to a later version,[31] although the court sometimes comments on such later versions.[32]

Similar contracts.   Different shades of caution have been expressed.

> "To some extent decisions on one contract may help by way of analogy or illustration in the decision of another contract. But however similar the contracts may appear the decision as to each must depend on the consideration of the language of the particular contract read in the light of the material circumstances of the parties in view of which the contract is made."[33]

By contrast, "comparison of one contact with another can seldom be a useful aid to construction and may be . . . positively misleading."[34] There are however

---

[24] Lord Maugham in *Greer* v. *Kettle* [1938] A.C. 156 at 171 (H.L.).

[25] *Ibid.*

[26] *Ibid.*; see also generally *Halsbury* (4th ed.), Vol. 12, paras. 1353 *et seq.*

[27] *Ibid.*

[28] *Wilson* v. *Wilson* [1969] 1 W.L.R. 1470 and for rectification, see p. 266.

[29] *Greer* v. *Kettle* [1938] A.C. 156 (H.L.).

[30] *Dunlop & Sons* v. *Balfour Williamson & Co.* [1892] 1 Q.B. 507 at 518 (C.A.); *The Annefield* [1971] P. 169, 183, 185 (C.A.). For the importance of certainty in the construction of contracts in standard terms, see *Pioneer Shipping* v. *B.T.P. Tioxide* (*The Nema*) [1982] A.C. 724 at 743 (H.L.); *cp. Ashville Investments* v. *Elmer Contractors* [1989] Q.B. 488 at 495 (C.A.).

[31] *H. W. Nevill* v. *William Press & Son* (1981) 20 B.L.R. 78 at 91.

[32] See, *e.g. F. G. Minter* v. *W.H.T.S.O.* (1980) 13 B.L.R. 1 at 20 (C.A.).

[33] Lord Wright in *Luxor* v. *Cooper* [1941] A.C. 108 at 130 (H.L.).

[34] Lord Bridge in *Mitsui* v. *Att.-Gen. of Hong Kong* (1986) 33 B.L.R. 1 at 18 (P.C.).

many instances in which one building contract has been used to assist in the construction of another.[35]

B. RISK, INDEMNITY AND EXCLUSION CLAUSES

These three types of clauses are dealt with together because their subject-matter overlaps and common problems of construction arise. In particular, a consideration of loss caused by negligence is potentially relevant to all three types of clause.

Loss caused by negligence. There are statutory limitations on the extent to which a person can exclude or limit his liability for loss or damage resulting from negligence.[36] Even where these limitations do not apply, it is inherently improbable that one party to a contract should intend to absolve the other party from the consequences of the latter's negligence,[37] and even more inherently improbable that one party should agree to discharge by indemnity the liability of the other party for acts for which the other is responsible.[38] To achieve either of these improbabilities, very clear words must be used. Equally, a person is not exempted from liability for the negligence of his servants unless adequate words are used.[39]

If a clause contains language which expressly[40] exempts the person in whose favour it is made from the consequences of his own negligence, effect is given to that provision. If there is no express reference to negligence, the court considers whether the words used are wide enough, in their ordinary meaning, to cover the person's negligence. If a doubt arises here, it is resolved against the person relying on the clause. If the words used are wide enough, the court considers whether the exempted head of damage may be based on some other possible ground than negligence. If there is such another ground which is not too fanciful or remote, the clause is construed as not exempting from negli-

---

[35] *e.g. Re Ford & Bemrose* (1902) H.B.C. (4th ed.), Vol. 2, p. 324 (C.A.); also (1902) 18 T.L.R. 443. In H.B.C. (7th ed.), Chap. IV, there is a collection of words and phrases judicially interpreted.

[36] See s.2 of the Unfair Contract Terms Act discussed at p. 66. See generally Professor N. E. Palmer, "Limiting Liability for Negligence" (1982) 45 M.L.R. 322.

[37] *Gillespie Bros. & Co.* v. *Roy Bowles Transport* [1973] Q.B. 400 at 419 (C.A.).

[38] *Smith* v. *South Wales Switchgear* [1978] 1 W.L.R. 165 at 168 (H.L.).

[39] *Rutter* v. *Palmer* [1922] 2 K.B. 87 at 92 (C.A.); *cf. Canada Steamship Lines* v. *The King* [1952] A.C. 192 (P.C.); *Lamport & Holt Lines* v. *Coubro & Scrutton* [1982] 2 Lloyd's Rep. 42 (C.A.).

[40] Use of the word "negligence" or a synonym is necessary. An indemnity against "all claims or demands whatsoever" or "any liability, loss, claim or proceedings whatsoever" was not an express reference to negligence—*Smith* v. *South Wales Switchgear* [1978] 1 W.L.R. 165 at 169, 173 (H.L.). Accordingly, *Farr* v. *The Admiralty* [1953] 1 W.L.R. 965, cited in the 4th edition of this book, might not be followed today.

gence. But if there is no such other ground, the clause is construed as applying to losses caused by negligence.[41]

This approach of construction is applied, in the light of other provisions of the contract, both to exclusion clauses and to indemnity clauses,[42] and has been applied, for instance, to the indemnity in clause 14(b) of the 1939 R.I.B.A. Standard Form of Building Contract.[43] It has also been applied to payment clauses where the benefit for which the payment is stipulated may cease because of the payee's negligence.[44]

By contrast limitation clauses, although they are read *contra proferentem*[45] and must be clearly expressed, are not judged by the specially exacting standards which are applied to exclusion and indemnity clauses. This is because there is no high degree of improbability that one party would agree to limit the other's liability, especially where the potential liability may be very great in proportion to the sums which could reasonably be charged for the services to be provided by that party.[46] In this context it appears that a limitation clause is one which limits liability without purporting to exclude it altogether. It follows that negligence on the part of a person in breach of contract does not prevent him from relying upon a limitation clause.[47] Further, it would appear that the clause can be relied upon by him to limit a clause in tort.[48]

By further contrast, where a party expressly assumes the sole risk of classes of events causing damage (*e.g.* fire) against which he is obliged to insure, the contract is likely to be construed as imposing on that party the whole risk of such damage including that caused by the negligence of the other party. Such was the conclusion of the House of Lords in *Scottish Special Housing Association* v. *Wimpey*[49] considering clauses 18(2) and 20[C] of a 1963 Standard Form of

---

[41] *Canada Steamship Lines* v. *The King* [1952] A.C. 192 at 208 (P.C.) considering *Alderslade* v. *Hendon Laundry* [1945] K.B. 189 (C.A.); *Smith* v. *South Wales Switchgear* [1978] 1 W.L.R. 165 (H.L.); *Smith* v. *U.B.M. Chrysler (Scotland)* (1978) S.C.(H.L.) 1; *Lamport & Holt Lines* v. *Coubro & Scrutton* [1982] 2 Lloyd's Rep. 42 (C.A.); *Dorset County Council* v. *Southern Felt Roofing* (1989) 48 B.L.R. 96 (C.A.); *cf. Rutter* v. *Palmer* [1922] 2 K.B. 87 at 92 (C.A.); *Comyn Ching* v. *Oriental Tube* [1979] 17 B.L.R. 47 at 88 (C.A.); and see the summary of the law in *Industrie Chimiche* v. *Nea Ninemia Shipping* [1983] 1 Lloyd's Rep. 310 at 312.

[42] *Smith* v. *South Wales Switchgear* [1978] 1 W.L.R. 165 (H.L.); *cf. Hollier* v. *Rambler Motors (AMC) Ltd.* [1972] 2 Q.B. 71 (C.A.).

[43] *A.M.F. International* v. *Magnet Bowling* [1968] 1 W.L.R. 1028 following *Walters* v. *Whessoe* (1960) 6 B.L.R. 23 (C.A.); *City of Manchester* v. *Fram Gerrard* (1974) 6 B.L.R. 70 at 89.

[44] See *Sonat Offshore* v. *Amerada Hess Development* (1987) 39 B.L.R. 1 (C.A.).

[45] See p. 43.

[46] *Ailsa Craig Fishing* v. *Malvern Fishing* [1983] 1 W.L.R. 964 at 970 (H.L.); *George Mitchell* v. *Finney Lock Seeds* [1983] 2 A.C. 803 at 814 (H.L.).

[47] *George Mitchell* v. *Finney Lock Seeds* [1983] 2 A.C. 803 at 814 (H.L.).

[48] *William Hill* v. *Bernard Sunley* (1982) 22 B.L.R. 1 at 29 (C.A.).

[49] [1986] 1 W.L.R. 995 (H.L.) approving *James Archdale & Co.* v. *Comservices* [1954] 1 W.L.R. 459 (C.A.); *cf. Coleman Street Properties* v. *Denco Miller* (1982) 31 B.L.R. 32; *Mark Rowlands* v. *Bernie Inns* [1986] Q.B. 211 (C.A.); *Norwich City Council* v. *Harvey* [1989] 1 W.L.R. 828 (C.A.). See generally J. Kodwo Bentil, "Liability for Fire Damage under the Standard Form of Building Contract" (1987) 3 Const.L.J. 83.

Building Contract.[50] Clauses relevant to the negligent operation of plant have been similarly construed.[51]

1. Risk Clauses

In the absence of express provisions dealing with the risk of damage to the works, the contractor's liability depends upon what he has undertaken to perform, but it seems that where he has to complete the works he must, as an incident of the duty to complete, make good any damage to the works occurring before completion,[52] unless the damage is so great and the circumstances such that the contract is frustrated[53] or the damage was caused by the employer's default.[54] In practice written contracts frequently contain a clause stating upon whom rests the risk of damage to the works.[55] It may be coupled with a clause providing for insurance against the risk.[56] It seems that if the contractor is required to effect insurance his duty is to insure himself and does not extend to insuring the employer unless express words are used.[57]

2. Indemnity Clauses

An indemnity clause is a clause where one party (*e.g.* an insurer) agrees to make good a loss suffered by another. One of the parties may indemnify the other against certain losses, *i.e.* he may promise to make good any loss suffered by the other party in respect of damage or claims arising out of various matters such as injury to persons or property.[58] An indemnity can be expressed to apply to liabilities occurring before, as well as after, the date on which the

---

[50] See now clauses 20.2 and 22C of the 1980 Form discussed at p. 544.

[51] See *Arthur White (Contractors)* v. *Tarmac Civil Engineering* [1967] 1 W.L.R. 1508 (H.L.); *Thompson* v. *T. Lohan (Plant Hire)* [1987] 1 W.L.R. 649 (C.A.); *cp. McConkey* v. *Amec, The Times*, February 28, 1990 (C.A.).

[52] *Gold* v. *Patman & Fotheringham Ltd.* [1958] 1 W.L.R. 697 at 703 (C.A.); *Charon (Finchley)* v. *Singer Sewing Machine Co.* (1968) 112 S.J. 536.

[53] For frustration, see p. 134.

[54] See cases cited at p. 60 under "Loss caused by negligence."

[55] *e.g. Kellett* v. *York Corp.* (1894) 10 T.L.R. 662; *Scottish Special Housing Association* v. *Wimpey Construction* [1986] 1 W.L.R. 995 (H.L.); and see clause 20 of the Standard Form of Building Contract at p. 542.

[56] *e.g. James Archdale & Co. Ltd.* v. *Comservices Ltd.* [1954] 1 W.L.R. 459 (C.A.); clauses 21 and 22 of the Standard Form of Building Contract at pp. 548 and 550; *cf. Swiss Bank Corporation* v. *Brink's-Mat* [1986] 2 Lloyd's Rep. 79 at 95.

[57] *Gold* v. *Patman & Fotheringham Ltd.* [1958] 1 W.L.R. 697 (C.A.).

[58] See, *e.g.* clause 20 of the Standard Form of Building Contract discussed at p. 543. See also *Kirby* v. *Chessum & Sons Ltd.* (1914) 79 J.P. 81 (C.A.), where despite a clause in the employer's favour the contractor was entitled to an indemnity from the employer where the adjoining owner recovered damages from the contractor for trespass committed by him while he was obeying the architect's orders. For cases on the indemnity clause in the I.C.E. Conditions (1955 ed.), see *C. J. Pearce & Co.* v. *Hereford Corp.* (1968) 66 L.G.R. 647; *Richardson* v. *Buckinghamshire County Council* (1970) 68 L.G.R. 662.

indemnity itself is given.[59] It is no defence to an employer sued by a third person that he is indemnified by the contractor,[60] although he can join the contractor as third party to the proceedings between himself and the third person.[61]

Where the contractor gives the employer an indemnity against claims by third parties and there is an exception to the indemnity the courts tend to construe the exception so that it does not operate to deprive the indemnity of effect.[62]

The discussion of "Loss caused by negligence" above applies to indemnity clauses and the Unfair Contract Terms Act 1977 limits the extent to which a person can rely on an unreasonable indemnity clause in a consumer contract.[63]

Subrogation.   An indemnifier who makes good a loss suffered by another party is entitled to be subrogated to the rights of the person indemnified against third parties. But these rights can only be pursued in the name of the person indemnified even if the indemnifier has an independent direct claim of his own.[64]

Limitation period for liability under indemnity clauses.   Where there is an obligation to indemnify against loss, the cause of action does not arise until the loss has been established,[65] so that the limitation period runs from the date when the liability or loss indemnified against is established or incurred.[66] This may be after the expiry of the ordinary limitation period. Such clauses are therefore potentially very onerous.

Insurance policy—exceptions.   Where a loss is caused by two causes, one within the general words describing the risk insured and one within the exception to those words, the insurer is not liable.[67] Where, however, there were two effective causes of loss, one within the insurance and the other not, it was held that the insured could recover under the policy.[68]

3. Exclusion Clauses

This term is intended to refer to clauses variously termed exclusion, exception,

---

[59] See *Basildon District Council* v. *J. E. Lesser* (*Properties*) (1984) 8 Con.L.R. 89 at 101.

[60] *Dalton* v. *Argus* (1881) 6 App.Cas. 740 at 829 (H.L.).

[61] See R.S.C., Ord. 16.

[62] See *Hosking* v. *De Havilland Ltd.* [1949] 1 All E.R. 540; *Murfin* v. *United Steel Companies Ltd.* [1957] 1 W.L.R. 104 (C.A.), and see further p. 543.

[63] See p. 66.

[64] *Esso Petroleum* v. *Hall Russell* [1989] A.C. 643 (H.L.) applying *Simpson* v. *Thomson* (1877) 3 App.Cas. 279 (H.L.) and *Castellain* v. *Preston* (1883) 11 Q.B.D. 380 (C.A.).

[65] *Collinge* v. *Hayward* (1839) 9 Ad. & El. 633 and other cases cited in *Halsbury* (3rd ed.), Vol. 24, para. 393; *County & District Properties* v. *C. Jenner & Son Ltd.* [1976] 2 Lloyd's Rep. 728.

[66] *R. & H. Green & Silley Wier* v. *British Railways Board* (1980) 17 B.L.R. 94; *Telfair Shipping Corporation* v. *Inersea Carriers* [1985] 1 W.L.R. 553.

[67] *Wayne Tank & Pump Co. Ltd.* v. *Employers Liability Ltd.* [1974] 1 Q.B. 57 (C.A.).

[68] *J. J. Lloyd Instruments* v. *Northern Star Insurance* [1987] 1 Lloyd's Rep. 32 (C.A.). See also "Causation and Concurrent Causes" at pp. 191 *et seq.*

exemption or limitation clauses.[69] It is a convenient description of clauses relied on by a party who would otherwise be under a certain liability on contract[70] to exclude or limit that liability. Such clauses must be distinguished from those which define the parties' rights and duties, such as agreed damages clauses[71] or defects clauses which confer additional rights,[72] and which are construed like any other clauses in the contract whereas exclusion clauses are construed against the party seeking to rely on them.[73]

The leading case on the construction of exclusion clauses is *Photo Production* v. *Securicor Transport*.[74] Securicor for a very modest charge agreed to provide a night patrol service for four visits per night. Their contract incorporated printed standard conditions which exempted them from any loss "except in so far as such loss is solely attributable to the negligence of the company's employees acting within the course of their employment. ..." On a Sunday night the duty employee of Securicor deliberately started a fire which got out of control and a large part of the premises were burned down causing loss of £615,000. Although the starting of the fire was deliberate, it was not established that he intended to destroy the factory. The House of Lords held that upon the construction of the clause and having regard to the surrounding circumstances, which included the very modest charge for its services provided by Securicor, the clause exempted Securicor from liability.

"Any persons capable of making a contract are free to enter into any contract they may choose: and providing the contract is not illegal or avoidable it is binding upon them. ... In the end, everything depends upon the true construction of the clause in dispute. ..."[75]

"Parties are free to agree to whatever exclusion or modification of all types of obligations as they please within the limits that the agreement must retain the legal characteristics of a contract; and must not offend against the equitable rule against penalties ... Since the presumption is that the parties by entering into the contract intended to accept the implied obligations exclusion clauses are to be construed strictly and the degree of strictness appropriate to be applied to their construction may properly depend upon the extent to which they involve departure from the implied obligations."[76]

---

[69] For a classification see *Kenyon, Son & Craven* v. *Baxter Hoare & Co.* [1971] 1 W.L.R. 519.
[70] In tort the issue is whether the defendant by his words has shown that he does not intend to undertake any liability towards the plaintiff—see *Hedley Byrne* v. *Heller & Partners* [1964] A.C. 465 (H.L.); see also "Disclaimer" at p. 182.
[71] *Suisse Atlantique, etc.* v. *N.V. Rotterdamsche Kolen Centrale* [1967] A.C. 361 (H.L.); *Arthur White (Contractors) Ltd.* v. *Tarmac Civil Engineering Ltd.* [1967] 1 W.L.R. 1508 at 1520 (H.L.).
[72] See p. 247.
[73] *Adams* v. *Richardson & Starling Ltd.* [1969] 1 W.L.R. 1645 at 1653 (C.A.).
[74] [1980] A.C. 827 (H.L.); *cf. George Mitchell* v. *Finney Lock Seeds* [1983] 2 A.C. 803 at 812 (H.L.)
[75] Lord Salmon in *Photo Production* v. *Securicor Transport* [1980] A.C. 827 at 853 (H.L.).
[76] Lord Diplock in *Photo Production* v. *Securicor Transport* [1980] A.C. 827 at 850 (H.L.).

"In commercial contracts between business-men capable of looking after their own interests and of deciding how risks inherent in the performance of various kinds of contract can be most economically borne (generally by insurance), it is, in my view, wrong to place a strained construction upon words in an exclusion clause which are clear and fairly susceptible of one meaning only even after due allowance has been made for the presumption in favour of the implied primary and secondary obligations."[77]

In considering exclusion clauses, reference must be made to the Unfair Contract Terms Act 1977,[78] but this Act:

"applies to consumer contracts and those based on standard terms and enables exception clauses to be applied with regard to what is just and reasonable. It is significant that Parliament refrained from legislating over the whole field of contract. After this Act, in commercial matters generally, when the parties are not of unequal bargaining power, and when risks are normally borne by insurers, not only is the case for judicial intervention undemonstrated, but there is everything to be said, and this seems to be parliament's intention, for leaving the parties free to apportion the risks as they think fit and for respecting their decisions."[79]

Third parties.   Third parties to a contract cannot rely upon an exclusion clause in the contract,[80] unless it was made as agent for the third party and certain other conditions are fulfilled.[81] Thus sub-contractors did not have the benefit of contractual protection resulting from main contract taking-over certificates, since they were not parties to the main contract which the main contractor had not entered into as agent for the sub-contractors.[82] On the other hand, notices of disclaimer are capable in principle, subject to the Unfair Contract Terms Act 1977, of negativing a duty of care in tort,[83] and a contractual exclusion clause in a contract between A and B is sometimes relevant to the existence of a duty of care between B and C.[84]

---

[77] Lord Diplock in *Photo Production* v. *Securicor Transport* [1980] A.C. 827 at 851 (H.L.); *cf. Spriggs* v. *Sotherby Parke Bernet* [1986] 1 Lloyd's Rep. 487 at 495 (C.A.).

[78] See p. 66.

[79] Lord Wilberforce in *Photo Production* v. *Securicor Transport* [1980] A.C. 827 at 843 (H.L.); for the meaning of the exclusion of "any consequential loss or damage" in a contract for the supply of masonry blocks, see *Croudace Construction* v. *Cawoods Concrete Products* [1978] 2 Lloyd's Rep. 55 (C.A.).

[80] *Scruttons Limited* v. *Midland Silicones Ltd.* [1962] A.C. 446 (H.L.).

[81] *New Zealand Shipping Co. Ltd.* v. *Satterthwaite Ltd.* [1975] A.C. 154 (P.C.—majority 3:2); *Port Jackson Stevedoring* v. *Salmond and Spraggon* [1981] 1 W.L.R. 138 (P.C.).

[82] *Southern Water Authority* v. *Carey* [1985] 2 All E.R. 1077. Note that the consideration of potential tortious liability in this case has to be reconsidered in the light of *Murphy* v. *Brentwood District Council* [1990] 3 W.L.R. 414 (H.L.). See generally Chap. 7.

[83] See *Hedley Byrne* v. *Heller & Partners* [1964] A.C. 465 (H.L.).

[84] See, *e.g. Pacific Associates* v. *Baxter* [1990] Q.B. 993 (C.A.); *cf. Smith* v. *Eric S. Bush* [1990] A.C. 831 at 858 (H.L.) where the disclaimer was held not to satisfy the test of reasonableness under the Unfair Contract Terms Act 1977; *Southern Water Authority* v. *Carey* [1985] 2 All E.R. 1077 subject to the *caveat* in n. 82 above; *Norwich City Council* v. *Harvey* [1989] 1 W.L.R. 828 (C.A.).

4. Unfair Contract Terms Act 1977[85]

This Act imposes limits on the extent to which civil liability for breach of contract, or for negligence or other breach of duty, can be avoided by means of contract terms or otherwise.[86] Apart from its effect upon notices or contract terms purporting to exclude or limit liability for negligence,[87] the Act's application to substantial building contracts may be limited to cases where large contractors contract on their own domestic standard forms.[88] But the Act may more frequently apply to private house building or house purchase. So far as is likely to be relevant to building contracts, it applies only to "business liability" as defined in section 1(3) of the Act. It does not apply to contracts where goods are sold or supplied and which are made between parties whose places of business are in the territories of different States.[89] The material provisions of the Act do not apply where English law is the proper law of the contract only by choice of the parties. But conversely the Act can apply where a choice of law clause applies the law of some country outside the United Kingdom wholly or mainly for the purpose of evading the operation of the Act.[90]

Negligence liability. For the purposes of the Act, "negligence" means the breach of a contractual obligation to take reasonable care or to exercise reasonable skill or breach of an equivalent common law duty.[91] A person cannot by reference to any contract term or to a notice given generally or to particular persons exclude or restrict his liability for death or personal injury resulting from negligence.[92] In the case of other loss or damage, a person cannot so exclude or restrict his liability for negligence except in so far as the term or notice satisfies the requirement of reasonableness.[93] The requirement of reasonableness in relation to a contract term is stated in section 11(1) of the Act as:

"... *that the term shall have been a fair and reasonable one to be included having regard to the circumstances which were, or ought reasonably to have been, known to or in the contemplation of the parties when the contract was made.*"[94]

---

[85] See generally Adams and Brownsword, "The Unfair Contract Terms Act: A Decade of Discretion" (1988) 104 L.Q.R. 94.

[86] Evasion of the provisions of the Act by means of a secondary contract is ineffective—see s.10 of the Act. See also s.13 of the Act. For the relation between the doctrine of freedom of contract and of statutory intervention for the protection of persons entering into contracts, see *Johnson* v. *Moreton* [1980] A.C. 37 at 65 *et seq.* (H.L.).

[87] See "Negligence liability" below.

[88] See "Liability arising in contract" at p. 68.

[89] s.26 of the Act.

[90] s.27 of the Act.

[91] s.1(1) of the Act.

[92] s.2(1) of the Act.

[93] s.2(2) of the Act; *cf.* s.3 of the Misrepresentation Act 1967 as amended discussed at p. 129.

[94] For the purposes of s.2 of the Act, the court or arbitrator is not, it seems, specifically required to have regard to the matters specified in Sched. 2 of the 1977 Act. There would be such a requirement if ss.6 or 7 of the Act also applied to relevant transaction—see s.11(2) and *cf. Rees Hough* v. *Redland Reinforced Plastics* (1984) 27 B.L.R. 136 at 151. See also s.11(4).

In relation to a non-contractual notice, the requirement of reasonableness is:

"*. . . that it should be fair and reasonable to allow reliance on it, having regard to all the circumstances obtaining when the liability arose or (but for the notice) would have arisen.*"[95]

It is for those claiming that a contract term or notice satisfies the requirement of reasonableness to show that it does.[96] Where reliance upon a relevant contract term has to satisfy the requirement of reasonableness, it may be found to do so and have effect notwithstanding that the contract has been terminated by breach or by the acceptance of a repudiation.[97] In considering whether the requirement of reasonableness is satisfied, appellate courts treat original decisions with the utmost respect and refrain from interfering with them unless satisfied that they proceeded upon some erroneous principle or were plainly and obviously wrong.[98]

The House of Lords has held that a disclaimer by a building society on its own behalf and on behalf of a surveyor carrying out a valuation of a modest dwelling house for mortgage purposes which purports to exclude liability for negligence is a notice within the Act which, to be effective, has to satisfy the requirement of reasonableness. It was further held that on the facts of that case the requirement of reasonableness was not satisfied.[99] The decision applies generally to valuations in broadly similar circumstances. But it is not necessarily unreasonable for professional men in all circumstances to seek to exclude or limit their liability for negligence and the decision might not apply to valuations of industrial property, large blocks of flats or very expensive houses.[1]

Section 2(1) of the Act is concerned with protecting victims of negligence and not the arrangements between wrongdoers and other persons for the sharing or bearing of the burden of compensating victims.[2] A clause in a plant hire agreement, making the plant owner's driver the servant or agent of the hirer, was held not to satisfy the requirement of reasonableness in section 2(2) of the Act when the owner tried to rely on the clause to avoid liability to the hirer for the driver's negligence.[3] But a similar clause was not affected by the Act where a third party was killed as a result of the plant driver's negligence,

---

[95] See also s.11(4).

[96] s.11(5) of the Act.

[97] s.9 of the Act. For repudiation, see p. 146 and in particular "Acceptance of repudiation" at p. 151.

[98] See *George Mitchell* v. *Finney Lock Seeds* [1983] 2 A.C. 803 at 816 (H.L.)—a decision on the rather different wording of the now obsolete s.55(3) of the Sale of Goods Act 1979. The decisive factor in that case in the decision that reliance on the term in question was not fair and reasonable was evidence that the seller, who was seeking to rely on the term, had a practice of waiving it in genuine cases thus demonstrating a recognition that it was unreasonable.

[99] *Smith* v. *Eric S. Bush* [1990] A.C. 831 (H.L.).

[1] See Lord Griffiths in *Smith* v. *Eric S. Bush* [1990] A.C. 831 at 858, 859 (H.L.) and see his list of considerations at 858.

[2] *Thompson* v. *T. Lohan (Plant Hire)* [1987] 1 W.L.R. 649 (C.A.).

[3] *Philips Products* v. *Hyland* [1987] 1 W.L.R. 659 (C.A.).

since there was no exclusion or restriction of liability to the plaintiff widow sought to be achieved by reliance on the clause.[4]

Liability arising in contract.   Where one contracting party deals as a consumer[5] or on the other's written standard terms of business,[6] that other party cannot by reference to any contract term exclude or restrict any liability of his for breach of contract except in so far as the contract term satisfies the requirement of reasonableness.[7] A house purchaser and an individual contracting for the construction of a dwelling house will both, it seems, normally deal as consumers. A company entering into a transaction which is merely incidental to the carrying on of a business deals as a consumer unless a degree of regularity is established so as to make the transaction an integral part of the business.[8] It may be, therefore, that a business company which makes a single building contract with a contractor to build a headquarters office building and for that purpose engages an architect deals in each instance as a consumer. It is thought that a contract made on a standard form of contract drafted, not by the contractor, but by a representative body such as the Joint Contracts Tribunal or the Institution of Civil Engineers would not be a contract on the contractor's written standard terms of business, even if it was a form of contract which the contractor frequently entered into.[9]

Unreasonable indemnity clauses.   A person dealing as a consumer cannot by reference to any contract term be made to indemnify another person (whether a party to the contract or not) in respect of liability that may be incurred by the other for negligence or breach of contract, except in so far as the contract terms satisfies the requirement of reasonableness.[10]

---

[4] *Thompson* v. *T. Lohan (Plant Hire)* [1987] 1 W.L.R. 649 at 656 (C.A.).

[5] See s.12 of the Act. See also s.5 of the Act for "guarantees" of consumer goods, and s.6 of the Act for other provisions where possession or ownership of goods passes.

[6] For a building contract case where reliance on standard conditions of sale did not satisfy the requirement of reasonableness, see *Rees Hough* v. *Redland Reinforced Plastics* (1984) 27 B.L.R. 136; *cf. Stag Line* v. *Tyne Shiprepair Group* [1984] 2 Lloyd's Rep. 211 at 222.

[7] s.3 of the Act. For the requirement of reasonableness, see "Negligence liability" at p. 66.

[8] *R. & B. Customs Brokers* v. *United Dominions Trust* [1988] 1 W.L.R. 321 (C.A.).

[9] See *Tersons Ltd.* v. *Stevenage Development Corporation* [1963] 2 Lloyd's Rep. 333 at 368 (C.A.); *cf. R. W. Green Ltd.* v. *Cade Bros. Farms* [1978] 1 Lloyd's Rep. 602 at 607.

[10] s.4 of the Act. For the requirement of reasonableness, see "Negligence liability" at p. 66.

CHAPTER 4

THE RIGHT TO PAYMENT AND VARIED WORK

A. THE RIGHT TO PAYMENT

The contractor's right to payment depends upon the wording of the contract. Within the limits of legality parties can make what arrangements they please, but there are three broad heads under which the right can arise, *viz.*:

(1) a lump sum contract;
(2) an express contract other than for a lump sum; and
(3) a claim for a reasonable sum frequently called a *quantum meruit*.

1. Lump Sum Contracts

A lump sum contract is a contract to complete a whole[1] work for a lump sum, *e.g.* to build a house for £60,000. If the house is completed in every detail required by the contract[2] the contractor is entitled to £60,000,[3] and if extra work was carried out he may be able to recover further payment.[4] If he does

---

[1] Sometimes termed an "entire" or a "specific" work.
[2] See Part B of this chapter for discussion of work which may be impliedly included in the contract.
[3] Subject to any unfulfilled condition precedent such as an architect's certificate—see Chap. 5.
[4] See Part B of this chapter. The contract may provide many other ways in which an amount different from the original contract sum may eventually become payable—see, *e.g.* Commentary on the Articles of Agreement of the Standard Form of Building Contract, Chap. 18.

not complete the house, detailed clauses may provide what amount, if any, he is to receive.[5] But parties entering into a contract do not always contemplate its breach, and in the absence of such clauses, and even to some extent when they are present, a difficult problem may arise. This has two aspects. The first is what payment, if any, the contractor can recover. The second is what claim, if any, the employer has for damages. This chapter is concerned with the first aspect, Chapter 8 with the second.

If a contractor agrees to do a whole work according to a specification which consists of 40 items for a lump sum of £5,000 and fails to carry out 20 of the items, it is obvious that he is not entitled to recover the whole of the £5,000 and that the employer may have an action against him for damages. But is the contractor entitled to recover any of the £5,000? Can the employer say to him, "You agreed to complete the whole and to be paid when the whole was completed.[6] The work is incomplete, therefore you are entitled to nothing?" And can the employer rely on the same argument where only two out of the 40 items are omitted? These problems, which have greatly exercised the courts,[7] require discussion of entire contracts and substantial performance.

(a) *Entire contracts*

An entire contract is one where entire performance by one party is a condition precedent to the liability of the other party[8] and where therefore the contractor's right to payment depends on entire performance on his part. "An entire contract is an indivisible contract, one where the entire fulfilment of the promise by either party is a condition precedent to the right to call for the fulfilment of any part of the promise by the other."[9] Whether a contract is an entire one is a matter of construction.[10]

Clear words are needed to bring an entire contract into existence.[11] The type of contract which may be entire is that where the contractor undertakes some simple clear obligation such as to put some broken article or part of a house in working order and completely fails to do so. In such a case he may be entitled to nothing although he has expended much work and labour, for the main

---

[5] See, *e.g.* Standard Form of Building Contract, clause 27.4.4.
[6] See *Appleby* v. *Myers* (1867) L.R. 2. C.P. 651 at 661.
[7] See cases cited at n. 8 below and in Notes to *Cutter* v. *Powell* (1795) 2 Sm.L.C. 1. For a useful judicial summary, see *Holland Hannen & Cubitts* v. *W.H.T.S.O.* (1981) 18 B.L.R. 80 at 122. The text which follows does not, however, precisely follow that summary.
[8] *Cutter* v. *Powell* (1795) 6 T.R. 320; *Munro* v. *Butt* (1858) 8 E.B. 739; *Appleby* v. *Myers* (1867) L.R. 2 C.P. 651; *Hoenig* v. *Isaacs* [1952] 2 All E.R. 176 (C.A.). See also *Heywood* v. *Wellers* [1976] Q.B. 446 (C.A.)—solicitor's contract.
[9] H.B.C. (7th ed.), p. 165, citing *Cutter* v. *Powell* (1795) 2 Sm.L.C. 1; note Somervell L.J.'s interpretation of *Cutter* v. *Powell* in *Hoenig* v. *Isaacs* [1952] 2 All E.R. 176 at 178 (C.A.).
[10] *Hoenig* v. *Isaacs* [1952] 2 All E.R. 176 at 178, 180.
[11] *Appleby* v. *Myers* (1867) L.R. 2 C.P. 651 at 661; *Hoenig* v. *Isaacs* [1952] 2 All E.R. 176 at 180 (C.A.); Smith's L.C. Notes to *Cutter* v. *Powell* (13th ed.), Vol. 2, p. 26.

purpose of the contract is that the article or part of the house shall work and there is no scope in the contract for terms collateral to the main purpose.[12]

It is perhaps academically debateable whether or not a lump sum contract is by definition an entire contract.[13] It is submitted that, subject to provisions for instalments:

(1) most lump sum contracts are entire contracts in the sense that "the builder can recover nothing on the contract if he stops work before the work is completed in the ordinary sense—in other words abandons the contract"[14]; but

(2) most lump sum contracts are not entire contracts in the sense that they are construed as excluding the principle of substantial performance.[15]

Instalments. A contract which gives the contractor an enforceable right to instalments cannot to that extent be an entire contract because the contractor has the right to call for fulfilment of part of the employer's promise before he has entirely completed his own promise.[16] But entire contract considerations may still apply to incompletely earned instalments.

The right to instalments may arise expressly or by implication. The nature of the right under an express provision is a matter of construction of the words. The inference of an implied right is governed by the usual rules,[17] but it has been said that:

"a man who contracts to do a long costly piece of work does not contract, unless he expressly says so that he will do all the work, standing out of pocket until he is paid at the end. He is entitled to say '. . . there is an understanding all along that you are to give me from time to time, at the reasonable times, payments for work done.' "[18]

It was held that a shipwright who had undertaken to put a ship into thorough repair—apparently no price was agreed—was entitled to demand payment for part of the work he had carried out.[19] It seems to be implied in the absence of clear words that a person carrying out repairing work to another's property is entitled to payment from time to time before completion.[20]

---

[12] *Duncan* v. *Blundell* (1820) 3 Stark, 6; *Sinclair* v. *Bowles* (1829) 9 B. & C. 92; *Portman* v. *Middleton* (1858) 4 C.B.(N.S.) 322; see *Hoenig* v. *Isaacs* [1952] 2 All E.R. 176 at 178 (C.A.). See also *Vigers* v. *Cook* [1919] 2 K.B. 475 (C.A.)—an undertaker's contract.

[13] Contrast the analysis of the law in Law Commission Report 121 (1983) with Denning L.J. in *Hoenig* v. *Isaacs* [1952] 2 All E.R. 176 (C.A.) and with *Holland Hannen & Cubitts* v. *W.H.T.S.O.* (1981) 18 B.L.R. 80 at 122.

[14] Somervell L.J. in *Hoenig* v. *Isaacs* [1952] 2 All E.R. 176 at 178 (C.A.).

[15] See p. 72.

[16] *Terry* v. *Duntze* (1779) 2 Hy.Bl. 389.

[17] See Chap. 3.

[18] Phillimore J. in *The Tergeste* [1903] P. 26 at 34; *cf. Rees* v. *Lines* (1837) 8 C. & P. 126.

[19] *Roberts* v. *Havelock* (1832) 3 B. & Ad. 404.

[20] *Menetone* v. *Athawes* (1764) 3 Burr. 1592; *Roberts* v. *Havelock* (1832) 3 B. & Ad. 404; *Appleby* v. *Myers* (1867) L.R. 2 C.P. 651 at 660.

Retention money.   The contract may provide:

"for progress payments to be made as the work proceeds, but for retention money to be held until completion. Then entire performance is usually a condition precedent to payment of the retention money but not, of course, to the progress payments. The contractor is entitled to payment *pro rata* as the work proceeds, less a deduction for retention money. But he is not entitled to the retention money until the work is entirely finished, without defects or omissions."[21]

This, however, again depends on the words of the contract, as for example whether the expression "practical completion," giving the contractor a right to release of part of the retention money, means "apparent perfect completion" or "completion in the ordinary sense" or something else.[22]

Recovery of money paid.   If the employer pays money under a contract which the contractor fails to complete, the employer can recover that money in an action for money had and received if there has been a total failure of consideration.[23] If the employer has received any of the benefit bargained for from performance by the contractor, there has not been a total failure of consideration[24] and any payment is not recoverable even though it was made in advance of performance.[25] In such circumstances the employer can claim damages for breach of contract.[26] In his claim he has to give credit for the value of work performed by the contractor.[27] The combined effect of the rules relating to recovery of money paid and damages for breach of contract can operate somewhat capriciously to favour employer or contractor according to whether the contract price was high or low, and the value of the partial performance by the contractor in relation to the amount of money, if any, paid to the contractor by way of instalments or advance upon the contract price.[28]

(b) *Substantial performance*

In the ordinary lump sum contract[29] the employer cannot refuse to pay the

---

[21] Denning L.J. in *Hoenig* v. *Isaacs* [1952] 2 All E.R. 176 at 181 (C.A.), where it was also held that the £400 not paid by the employer could not be treated as retention money because it formed so large a proportion of the contract sum. If the parties so desired they could expressly make such a large sum retention money. See also *National Coal Board* v. *Neill* [1985] Q.B. 300 at 309, 321.

[22] For a discussion relating to the retention provisions of the Standard Form of Building Contract, see p. 614.

[23] *Fibrosa Spolka Akcyjna* v. *Fairbairn Lawson Ltd.* [1943] A.C. 32 (H.L.).

[24] *Ibid.*; *The Julia* [1949] A.C. 293 (H.L.).; *Rover International* v. *Cannon Film* [1989] 1 W.L.R. 912 (C.A.).

[25] *Fibrosa Spolka Akcyjna* v. *Fairbairn Lawson Ltd.* [1943] A.C. 32 (H.L.); *Whincup* v. *Hughes* (1871) L.R. 6 C.P. 78.

[26] See Chap. 8.

[27] *Fibrosa Spolka Akcyjna* v. *Fairbairn Lawson Ltd.* [1943] A.C. 32 (H.L.) and see especially *Mertens* v. *Home Freeholds Co.* [1921] 2 K.B. 526 (C.A.) the facts of which are set out at p. 202.

[28] See the Law Commission Report No. 121 (1983), whose recommendations are apparently not going to be adopted; Goff and Jones, *The Law of Restitution* and consider the effect of applying various different figures to the facts of *Mertens* v. *Home Freeholds Co.* [1921] 2 K.B. 526 (C.A.).

[29] Denning L.J. said of the contract in *Hoenig* v. *Isaacs* (for the facts see below) "I think this contract should be regarded as an ordinary lump sum contract."

contractor merely because there are a few defects and omissions. If there is substantial completion he must pay the contract price[30] subject to a deduction by way of set-off or counterclaim for the defects.[31]

In *Hoenig* v. *Isaacs*,[32] the plaintiff was employed to decorate a one-room flat and provide it with certain furniture for a sum of £750, the terms of payment being "net cash, as the work proceeds, and balance on completion." The plaintiff claimed that he had carried out the work under the contract and asked for payment of the unpaid balance of £350 of the contract price. The defendant entered into occupation of the flat and used the furniture but refused to pay, complaining of faulty design and bad workmanship. The Official Referee found that the door of a wardrobe required replacing, and that a bookshelf, which was too short, would have to be remade, which would require alterations being made to a bookcase. He held that there had been substantial compliance with the contract and awarded £294, being the £350 claimed less £56, the cost of remedying the defects. This finding was upheld by the Court of Appeal which rejected the defendant's contention that there had been non-performance of an entire contract, and that therefore the plaintiff was not entitled to any further payment under the contract, but could only claim on a *quantum meruit*.[33]

The principle applied by the court in *Hoenig* v. *Isaacs* is usually traced back to Lord Mansfield C.J. who said:

> "Where mutual covenants go to the whole of the consideration on both sides, they are mutual conditions, the one precedent to the other. But where they go only to a part, where a breach may be paid for in damages, there the defendant has a remedy on his covenant and shall not plead it as a condition precedent."[34]

The principle is illustrated by the law relating to sale of goods which makes a distinction between conditions, breach of which gives a right to reject the goods, and warranties, breach of which gives no right to reject the goods but leaves the buyer to his claim for damages.[35] In applying the principle to

---

[30] Subject to any unfulfilled condition precedent imposed by the contract, *e.g.* an architect's certificate.

[31] *Hoenig* v. *Isaacs* [1952] 2 All E.R. 176 (C.A.); *cf. Williams* v. *Roffey Brothers* [1990] 2 W.L.R. 1153 (C.A.); *Hutchinson* v. *Harris* (1978) 10 B.L.R. 19 appears to be authority for the proposition that this principle can apply to an architect's right to payment under the stages of the R.I.B.A. Conditions of Engagement. For set-off and counterclaim, see p. 438.

[32] [1952] 2 All E.R. 176 (C.A.).

[33] It was not necessary for the defendant to argue that the plaintiff was entitled to nothing because apparently the defendant was satisfied that if the work were measured and valued on a *quantum meruit* basis the amount found due to the plaintiff would not exceed the £400 already paid. (See pp. 181, 183 of the report.) Presumably it was conceded by the defendant that he had accepted the work and impliedly promised to pay a reasonable sum.

[34] *Boone* v. *Eyre* (1779) 1 Hy.Bl. 273, cited by Somervell L.J., *Hoenig* v. *Isaacs* [1952] 2 All E.R. 176 at 178 (C.A.).

[35] *Hoenig* v. *Isaacs* [1952] 2 All E.R. 176 at 178 (C.A.). For a sale of goods case *cf. Regent* v. *Francesco of Jermyn St.* [1981] 3 All E.R. 327.

building contracts, although the question is one of construction, "when a contract provides for a specific sum to be paid on completion of specified work, the courts lean against a construction which would deprive the contractor of any payment at all simply because there are some defects or omissions."[36] It is suggested that words at least as strong as "complete in every particular" relating to the payment provisions would be needed to exclude the principle.

What is substantial completion.   One test to be applied is whether the work was "finished" or "done" in the ordinary sense even though part of it is defective.[37] And "it is relevant to take into account both the nature of the defects and the proportion between the cost of rectifying them and the contract price."[38] Thus it is not sufficient to consider the cost of rectification alone. In one case where the contract price was £520 and the cost of remedying the defects was £200 the Court of Appeal upheld a finding that there had been substantial completion.[39] But in *Bolton* v. *Mahadeva*[40] where the cost of remedying defects was £174 against a contract price of £560 the Court of Appeal allowed an appeal against a finding that there had been substantial completion. The contract was to provide central heating and the defects were such that the system did not heat the house adequately and fumes were given out so as to make living rooms uncomfortable. The work was ineffective for its primary purpose.[41]

(c) *Non-completion*

This may occur by express or implied agreement, because the employer prevents completion, because the contractor in breach of contract fails to complete or because the contract is frustrated. If the contractor fails to complete in breach of contract, his breach will normally amount to repudiation. Prevention by the employer may amount to repudiation.[42]

When entire completion[43] is a condition precedent to payment, the contractor cannot recover anything either under the contract or on a *quantum meruit* if he has failed to complete in every detail.[44] For an ordinary lump sum contract,

---

[36] Denning L.J. in *Hoenig* v. *Isaacs* [1952] 2 All E.R. 176 at 181 (C.A.). For the analogy with the grant of specific performance in contracts for the sale of land when a vendor fails to make title to some insignificant part, see the judgment of Romer L.J. in *Hoenig* v. *Isaacs*.

[37] See *Hoenig* v. *Isaacs* [1952] 2 All E.R. 176 at 179 (C.A.), referring to *Dakin* v. *Lee* [1916] 1 K.B. 566 (C.A.) and *Appleby* v. *Myers* (1867) L.R. 2 C.P. 651 at 661. See also *Forman & Co. Proprietary* v. *The Ship "Liddesdale"* [1900] A.C. 190 at 200 (P.C.).

[38] *Bolton* v. *Mahadeva* [1972] 1 W.L.R. 1009 at 1013 (C.A.).

[39] *Kiely & Sons* v. *Medcraft* (1965) 109 S.J. 829 (C.A.). See also *Ibmac Ltd.* v. *Marshall (Homes) Ltd.* 208 E.G. 851, November 23, 1968 (C.A.)—one-third value not substantial completion.

[40] [1972] 1 W.L.R. 1009 (C.A.).

[41] See also *Technistudy Ltd.* v. *Kelland* [1976] 1 W.L.R. 1042 at 1045 (C.A.).

[42] For repudiation, see p. 146 and especially "Work partly carried out" at p. 207.

[43] See p. 70.

[44] *Cutter* v. *Powell* (1795) 2 Sm.L.C. 1; *Sinclair* v. *Bowles* (1829) 9 B. & C. 92; see also *Ellis* v. *Hamlen* (1810) 3 Taunt. 52, but see Ridley J. in *Dakin* v. *Lee* [1916] 1 K.B. 566 at 572 (C.A.); *Stegmann* v. *O'Connor* (1899) 81 L.T. 627 (C.A.); *Vigers* v. *Cook* [1919] 2 K.B. 475 (C.A.).

the contractor cannot recover anything either under the contract or on a *quantum meruit* unless he shows substantial completion.[45] These propositions are subject to exceptions discussed below.

It has been said that the rule that a contractor who has not substantially completed cannot recover payment does not work hardly upon him if only he is prepared to remedy the defects before seeking to resort to litigation to recover the lump sum.[46] It seems to follow that ordinarily there is an implied duty upon an employer to give a willing contractor an opportunity to remedy defects, breach of which duty amounts to prevention. Such duty does not, it is submitted, arise if the defects are so grave as to show that the contractor is unable to perform the contract.[47]

Express agreement or implied promise to pay. If there is an express agreement, its terms will govern the contractor's right to payment. In obvious cases where agreement is clearly reached, there will be little problem. In less obvious cases, the court may nevertheless spell out an agreement by conduct,[48] and an implied promise to pay a reasonable sum for the work done can arise from acceptance or waiver.

Acceptance. If the contractor can prove a fresh contract to pay for the work done he can recover on that contract.[49] Such a contract may be inferred from the acceptance by the employer of the work done with the full knowledge of the failure to complete,[50] but it is difficult to prove acceptance from mere occupation and use of the building works.[51] Thus in *Sumpter* v. *Hedges*,[52] S contracted to build a house for H for £565. S did work to the value of £333, received part payment and then abandoned the contract. H completed the house, incorporating the work carried out by S. S sued for the difference between the money he had received and the value of his work, but did not recover.[53] It was said that:

---

[45] See p. 72.

[46] *Bolton* v. *Mahadeva* [1972] 1 W.L.R. 1009 at 1025 (C.A.).

[47] See "Repudiation—generally" at p. 146.

[48] See *Holland Hannen & Cubitts* v. *W.H.T.S.O.* (1981) 18 B.L.R. 80 at 125. See also "Acceptance" below.

[49] *Hoenig* v. *Isaacs* [1952] 2 All E.R. 176 at 181 (C.A.); *Holland Hannen & Cubitts* v. *W.H.T.S.O.* (1981) 18 B.L.R. 80.

[50] *Munro* v. *Butt* (1858) 8 E. & B. 738; *Appleby* v. *Myers* (1867) L.R. 2 C.P. 651. Acceptance does not prevent the employer counterclaiming for damages for defects—see p. 265.

[51] "In the case of goods sold and delivered, it is easy to show a contract from the retention of goods; but this is not so where work is done on real property," Bramwell B. in *Pattinson* v. *Luckley* (1875) 10 Ex. 330 at 334.

[52] [1898] 1 Q.B. 673 (C.A.).

[53] In earlier editions of this book it was suggested that it was just possible that this case might be decided differently today having regard to developments in the doctrine of restitution and unjust enrichment. But the approach of the Court of Appeal in *Bolton* v. *Mahadeva* [1972] 1 W.L.R. 1009 suggests that this is unlikely. See also *Holland Hannen & Cubitts* v. *W.H.T.S.O.* (1981) 18 B.L.R. 80 at 123. It seems that any change in the law to deal with a principle which can sometimes cause injustice must come from Parliament—see The Law Commission's Working Paper No. 65. For statutory recognition of the doctrine of unjust enrichment in relation to goods, see the Torts (Interference with Goods) Act 1977, s.7(4).

"there are cases in which though the plaintiff has abandoned the performance of a contract, it is possible for him to raise the inference of a new contract to pay but in order that that may be done the circumstances must be such as to give an option to the defendant to take or not to take the benefit of the work done. . . . The mere fact that a defendant is in possession of what he cannot help keeping or even has done work upon it affords no ground for such an inference. He is not bound to keep unfinished a building which in an incomplete state would be a nuisance on his land."[54]

Waiver. "It is always open to a party to waive a condition which is inserted for his benefit."[55] On the facts in *Hoenig* v. *Isaacs*,[56] the court held that, even if entire performance was a condition precedent, the employer by entering into occupation and using the furniture had waived the condition and could no longer rely on it. This is not inconsistent with *Sumpter* v. *Hedges*[57] because the contract included a number of chattels which the employer could have avoided using, but did in fact use and therefore put himself "in the same position as a buyer of goods who by accepting them elects to treat a breach of condition as a breach of warranty."[58]

Unpaid instalments. The cancellation or rescission of a contract (other than for sale of land or goods) in consequence of repudiation does not affect accrued rights to the payment of instalments of the contract price, unless the contract so provides.[59] Accordingly unless there is some provision to the contrary not amounting to a penalty,[60] or unless there has been a total failure of consideration,[61] the employer cannot, subject to set-off, refuse to pay unpaid instalments which have become payable to the contractor under the terms of the contract.[62]

Impossibility or frustration. If the failure to complete is due to impossibility or performance or frustration and the employer has obtained a valuable benefit from the work done, the contractor can recover from the employer such sum as the court considers just.[63]

---

[54] Collins L.J. in *Sumpter* v. *Hedges* [1898] 1 Q.B. 673 at 676 (C.A.); see also *Whitaker* v. *Dunn* (1887) 3 T.L.R. 602 (D.C.), a very strong case, where substantial performance might perhaps have been argued, and *Wheeler* v. *Stratton* (1911) 105 L.T. 786.

[55] Denning L.J. in *Hoenig* v. *Isaacs* [1952] 2 All E.R. 176 at 181 (C.A.).

[56] [1952] 2 All E.R. 176 (C.A.).

[57] [1898] 1 Q.B. 673 (C.A.).

[58] Somervell L.J. in *Hoenig* v. *Isaacs* [1952] 2 All E.R. 176 at 180 (C.A.). In *Sumpter* v. *Hedges* [1898] 1 Q.B. 673 (C.A.) the employer was held liable to account for the value of unfixed materials which he had used in the works. For goods, see the Torts (Interference with Goods) Act 1977.

[59] *Hyundai Heavy Industries Co. Ltd.* v. *Papadopoulos* [1980] 1 W.L.R. 1129 (H.L.); *Bank of Boston* v. *European Grain* [1989] 2 W.L.R. 440 at 445 (H.L.).

[60] See Chap. 9, Part B.

[61] See "Recovery of money paid" at p. 72.

[62] See further Chap. 10, Section 1, "Forfeiture Clauses."

[63] Law Reform (Frustrated Contracts) Act 1943—see p. 140. For a case where payment on termination was contractually provided for, see *National Coal Board* v. *Leonard & Partners* (1985) 31 B.L.R. 117.

2. Contracts Other than for a Lump Sum

Generally. The manner of payment can be arranged in a variety of ways and it is impossible to attempt any exhaustive classification. A contract to do a whole work in consideration of the payment of different sums for different parts of the work is prima facie subject to the same rules about completion as an ordinary lump sum contract.[64] A contract to do a whole work with a provision for payment of each completed part of the whole may be a divisible contract in the sense that if the whole is not completed through the default of the contractor, he may be entitled to payment under the contract for those parts he has completed subject to the employer's right to counterclaim for non-completion of the whole.[65]

Measurement and value contracts. A contract where the amount of work when completed is to be measured and valued according to a schedule,[66] or formula, or at cost plus a fixed fee[67] or percentage of the cost, or at a reasonable price, is usually described as a measurement and value contract and is contrasted with a lump sum contract.[68] If the agreement is to do a whole work to be measured and valued and paid for on completion, entire completion may be a condition precedent to payment.[69] But it is submitted that normally the rule of substantial completion will apply, so that if the work is substantially performed, the contractor will be entitled to have it measured and valued and to be paid at the contract rate for the work done, subject to the employer's counterclaim for damages for defects and omissions.[70] It seems that in a repairing or jobbing contract the contractor is prima facie entitled to be paid for the work he has carried out,[71] though he may if he chooses contract not to be paid until completion.[72]

Cost plus percentage contracts. Such contracts sometimes contain an elaborate description of the method of calculating the cost. Where they do not and there is a simple agreement to pay a percentage upon the cost of labour and materials, "cost" means, it is submitted, the actual cost honestly and

---

[64] *Appleby* v. *Myers* (1867) L.R. 2 C.P. 651.
[65] *Newfoundland Government* v. *Newfoundland Ry.* (1888) 13 App.Cas. 199 (P.C.).
[66] For an example of a Schedule of Rates contract, see *Arcos* v. *Electricity Commission* (1973) 12 B.L.R. 65 (New South Wales C.A.), where it was said (at 75) that "the reason for having a schedule of rates contract is that the extent of the work cannot at the outset be predicated so that a contract price may be firmly stated. The nature of the work is certain, but its extent is not." For an example of a hybrid contract, see *Commissioner for Roads* v. *Reed & Stuart* (1974) 12 B.L.R. 55 (High Court of Australia).
[67] See "Management Contracts" at p. 9.
[68] See *Re Ford & Bemrose* (1902) H.B.C. (4th ed.), Vol. 2, p. 324 at 333 (C.A.) (18 T.L.R. 443). See also p. 85.
[69] *Whitaker* v. *Dunn* (1887) 3 T.L.R. 602 (D.C.).
[70] *cf. Newfoundland Government* v. *Newfoundland Ry.* (1888) 13 App.Cas. 199 (P.C.).
[71] *Appleby* v. *Myers* (1867) L.R. 2 C.P. 651.
[72] *Ibid.* at 661.

properly expended in carrying out the works. The contractor is not, it is submitted, disentitled from such cost merely because it exceeds what was anticipated. But is is thought that there would normally be an implied term that the contractor would carry out the works with reasonable economy so that expenditure in excess of what was reasonable would be irrecoverable. It would be a question of fact and degree in each case.[73] A formally drafted cost plus contract will usually have a clause intended to protect an employer against waste or extravagance on the part of the contractor.[74]

3. Quantum Meruit

The expression *quantum meruit* means "the amount he deserves" or "what the job is worth" and in most instances denotes a claim for a reasonable sum. It is used to refer to various circumstances where the court awards a money payment whose amount at least is not determined by a contract. In some instances, the basis for the payment also is less than contractual.

> "A *quantum meruit* claim (like the old actions for money had and received and for money paid) straddles the boundaries of what we now call contract and restitution; so the mere framing of a claim as a *quantum meruit* claim, or a claim for a reasonable sum, does not assist in classifying the claim as contractual or quasi-contractual."[75]

A claim on a *quantum meruit* cannot arise if there is an existing contract between the parties to pay an agreed sum.[76] But there may be a *quantum meruit* claim where there is:

(1) *an express agreement to pay a reasonable sum.*
(2) *no price fixed.* If the contractor does work under a contract express or implied and no price is fixed by the contract, he is entitled to be paid a reasonable sum for his labour and the materials supplied.[77] If such a contract, or an express agreement to be paid a reasonable sum, is for a whole work, completion may be made a condition precedent to payment, but it seems that in the absence of clear words the contractor is entitled from time to time to demand payment on account of the value of the work he has done.[78]

---

[73] In the 4th edition of this book, reference was made to remarks by H.H. Sir Brett Cloutman V.C. in an unreported case to the effect that the contractor is not disentitled from recovering actual cost merely because through some lack of efficiency on his part it exceeds a reasonable sum, but is disentitled from the cost of labour or materials expended in so wasteful a manner that it cannot truly be said to be part of the cost of the contract works. The formulation in the text is now preferred.

[74] See also "Management Contracts" at p. 9.

[75] Robert Goff J. in *British Steel Corporation* v. *Cleveland Bridge and Engineering* [1984] 1 All E.R. 504 at 509; *cf. Holland Hannen & Cubitts* v. *W.H.T.S.O.* (1981) 18 B.L.R. 80 at 123. See also Goff & Jones, *The Law of Restitution* (3rd ed.) and an article by Professor Jones (1977) 93 L.Q.R. 273.

[76] *Gilbert & Partners* v. *Knight* [1968] 2 All E.R. 248 (C.A.), the facts of which appear at p. 334.

[77] *Moffatt* v. *Laurie* (1855) 15 C.B. 583; *Turriff Construction Ltd.* v. *Regalia Knitting Mills Ltd.* (1971) 9 B.L.R. 20 discussed at p. 15; *cf. Holland Hannen & Cubitts* v. *W.H.T.S.O.* (1981) 18 B.L.R. 80 at 125—the decision on the 12th Issue. See also s.15 of the Supply of Goods and Services Act 1982.

[78] *Roberts* v. *Havelock* (1832) 3 B. & Ad. 404; *Appleby* v. *Myers* (1867) L.R. 2 C.P. 651.

(3) *a quasi-contract*. This may occur where, for instance, there are failed negotiations. If work is carried out while negotiations as to the terms of the contract are proceeding but agreement is never reached upon essential terms, the contractor is entitled to be paid a reasonable sum for the work carried out.[79]

"Both parties confidently expected a contract to eventuate. In these circumstances, to expedite performance under that anticipated contract, one requested the other to commence the contract work, and the other complied with that request.... if, contrary to their expectation, no contract was entered into, then the performance of the work is not referable to any contract of which the terms can be ascertained, and the law simply imposes an obligation on the party who made the request to pay a reasonable sum for such work as has been done pursuant to that request, such an obligation sounding in quasi-contract or, as we now say, in restitution."[80]

(4) *work outside a contract*.[81] Where there is a contract for specified work but the contractor does work outside the contract at the employer's request the contractor is entitled to be paid a reasonable sum for the work outside the contract on the basis of an implied contract.[82] In *Parkinson* v. *Commissioners of Works*[83] the contractor agreed under a varied contract to carry out certain work to be ordered by the Commissioners on a cost plus profit basis subject to a limitation as to the total amount of profit. The Commissioners ordered work to a total value of £6,600,000 but it was held that on its true construction the varied contract only gave the Commissioners authority to order work to the value of £5,000,000. It was held that the work that had been executed by the contractors included more than was covered, on its true construction, by the variation deed, and that the cost of the uncovenanted addition had therefore to be paid for by a *quantum meruit*.[84] The contractor thus recovered more than the total fixed profit.[85]

[79] *Trollope & Colls Ltd.* v. *Atomic Power Constructions Ltd.* [1963] 1 W.L.R. 333; *Peter Lind & Co. Ltd.* v. *Mersey Docks and Harbour Board* [1972] 2 Lloyd's Rep. 234.

[80] Robert Goff J. in *British Steel Corporation* v. *Cleveland Bridge and Engineering* [1984] 1 All E.R. 504 at 511; *cf. William Lacey (Hounslow) Ltd.* v. *Davis* [1957] 1 W.L.R. 932; *Brewer Street Investments* v. *Barclays Woollens* [1954] 1 Q.B. 428 (C.A.).

[81] See also "Work outside the contract" at p. 93.

[82] *Thorn* v. *London Corporation* (1876) 1 App.Cas. 120 at 127 (H.L.); *Parkinson & Co.* v. *Commissioners of Works* [1949] 2 K.B. 632 (C.A.); *Greenmast Shipping* v. *Jean Lion* [1986] 2 Lloyd's Rep. 277; see also *Cana Construction Co.* v. *The Queen* (1973) 37 D.L.R. (3d) 418 (Canadian Supreme Court); 21 B.L.R. 12.

[83] [1949] 2 K.B. 632 (C.A.).

[84] See Viscount Simon in *British Movietonews* v. *London and District Cinemas* [1951] A.C. 166 at 184 (H.L.); *cf. Thorn* v. *London Corporation* (1876) 1 App.Cas. 120 at 128 (H.L.). *Parkinson's* case should be treated with caution since it relies heavily on the now discredited case of *Bush* v. *Whitehaven Trustees* (1888) 52 J.P. 392 (C.A.) and H.B.C. (4th ed.), Vol. 2, p. 122 which is not "worth recording as an exposition of any principle of law"—Lord Radcliffe in *Davis Contractors* v. *Fareham Urban District Council* [1956] A.C. 696 at 732 (H.L.).

[85] See also "Rate of Payment" at p. 94.

(5) *work under a void contract.* If a contractor carries out work or renders services under a contract subsequently found to be void, he is entitled to a *quantum meruit* for the work or services.[86]

Assessment of a reasonable sum. The courts have laid down no rules limiting the way in which a reasonable sum is to be assessed. Where a *quantum meruit* is recoverable for work done outside a contract, it is wrong to regard the work as though it had been performed to any extent under the contract. The contractor should be paid at a fair commercial rate for the work done.[87] Where a *quantum meruit* is recoverable for work done pursuant to a void contract, it is wrong in principle to apply the provisions of the void contract to the assessment of the *quantum meruit.*[88] But it is unclear whether, in determining what is a reasonable sum, it is permissible or relevant to consider the plaintiff's conduct in performing the work and whether by reason of such conduct the defendant has suffered any unnecessary additional costs.[89] Useful evidence in any particular case may include abortive negotiations as to price,[90] a calculation based on the net cost of labour and materials used plus a sum for overheads and profit, measurements of work done and materials supplied, and the opinion of quantity surveyors, experienced builders or other experts as to a reasonable sum. Although expert evidence is often desirable there is no rule of law that it must be given and in its absence the court normally does the best it can on the materials before it to assess a reasonable sum.[91]

B. Varied Work

Introduction. A contractor frequently carries out, or is asked to carry out, work for which he considers he is entitled to payment in excess of the original contract sum. To recover such payment he must be prepared to prove:

(1) that it is extra work not included in the work for which the contract sum is payable;
(2) that there is a promise express or implied to pay for the work;
(3) that any agent who ordered the work was authorised to do so; and
(4) that any condition precedent to payment imposed by the contract has been fulfilled.

If he cannot prove these requirements, or those of them which are in dispute and are relevant, he may be able to recover payment if he can rely upon an

---

[86] *Craven-Ellis* v. *Canons Ltd.* [1936] 2 K.B. 403 (C.A.); *Rover International* v. *Cannon Film* [1989] 1 W.L.R. 912 (C.A.).
[87] *Greenmast Shipping* v. *Jean Lion* [1986] 2 Lloyd's Rep. 277 at 279.
[88] *Rover International* v. *Cannon Film* [1989] 1 W.L.R. 912 at 927 (C.A.).
[89] See *Crown House Engineering* v. *Amec Projects* (1989) 48 B.L.R. 32 (C.A.).
[90] *Way* v. *Latilla* [1937] 3 All E.R. 759, 764, 766 (H.L.); *M.R. Hornibrook (Pty.) Ltd.* v. *Eric Newham* (1971) 45 A.L.J.R. 523.
[91] See generally "Expert witnesses" at p. 426 and "Contingency" at p. 198.

architect's final and conclusive certificate or an arbitrator's award in his favour. These matters are dealt with in detail below.

1. What is Extra Work?

Meaning. There is no generally accepted definition of extra work, but in a lump sum contract it may be defined as work not expressly or impliedly included in the work for which the lump sum is payable.[92] If work is included in the original contract sum the contractor must carry it out and cannot recover extra payment for it, although he may not have thought at the time of entering into the contract that it would be necessary for the completion of the contract.[93] The question is one of construction in each case, but lump sum contracts may be broadly classified into those in which the contractor's obligation is defined in wide terms, such as "to build a house," and those in which it is defined in exact terms, such as "to execute so many cubic metres of digging."

(a) *Lump sum contract for whole work—widely defined*

Indispensably necessary works. Where the contractor must complete a whole work,[94] such as a house, or a railway from A to B, for a lump sum, the courts readily infer a promise on his part to provide everything indispensably necessary to complete the whole work.[95] Such necessary works are not extras for they are impliedly included in the lump sum.[96] Examples of the applications of this principle are as follows:

(i) Work not expressly specified. In *Williams* v. *Fitzmaurice*[97] there was a contract to build a house "to be completed and dry and fit for Major Fitzmaurice's occupation by August 1, 1858." In the specification the contractor undertook to provide "the whole of the materials mentioned or otherwise in the foregoing particulars necessary for the completion of the work," and "to perform all the works of every kind mentioned and contained in the foregoing specification for the sum of £1,100." Flooring was omitted from the specification, and the contractor, on this ground, refused to put it in unless it was paid for as an extra. The employer thereupon turned the contractor off the site, seized flooring boards brought upon the site by the contractor and used them to complete. It was held that the contractor could recover neither the amount outstanding under the contract nor the cost of the floorboards, for,

---

[92] *cf. Kemp* v. *Rose* (1858) 1 Giff. 258 at 268.
[93] *Sharpe* v. *San Paul Railway* (1873) L.R. 8 Ch.App. 597.
[94] Sometimes referred to as a "specific" or an "entire" work.
[95] *Williams* v. *Fitzmaurice* (1858) 3 H. & N. 844; *Coker* v. *Young* (1860) 2 F. & F. 98; *Sharpe* v. *San Paul Railway* (1873) L.R. 8 Ch.App. 597.
[96] *Ibid.*
[97] (1858) 3 H. & N. 844.

81

although they were omitted from the specification, "it was clearly to be inferred from the language of the specification that the plaintiff was to do the flooring."[98]

(ii) Work not taken out on the quantities supplied to the contractor for tender,[99] or wrongly stated on the drawings. In *Sharpe* v. *San Paulo Railway*[1] the contractor had undertaken to make a railway line "from terminus to terminus complete."[2] In carrying out the work it was found that the engineer's original plan was quite inadequate and had to be replaced by another. As a result the contractor, upon the engineer's orders, carried out nearly two million cubic yards of excavation in excess of the quantities of work set out in a schedule to the contract, and thus nearly doubled the excavation originally contemplated. It was held that these works were not "in any sense of the words extra works."[3]

(iii) Unexpected labour caused by difficulties of the terrain,[4] or by the proposed method of carrying out the works.[5]

(iv) Work caused by the lawful and not unreasonable exercise by the employer of statutory powers existing at the time of entering into the contract.[6]

(v) Work carried out in a manner directed by the engineer, where the contract set out no specific method of carrying out particular operations necessary to complete the works but provided that the works should be carried out under the engineer's directions and in the best manner to his satisfaction.[7]

No implied warranties by employer. A contractor who has been put to unexpected expense because of inaccurate quantities or drawings or imprac-

---

[98] *Ibid.* at 851.

[99] *Scrivener* v. *Pask* (1866) L.R. 1 C.P. 715; *Re Ford and Bemrose* (1902) H.B.C. (4th ed.), Vol. 2, p. 324 (C.A.).

[1] (1873) L.R. 8 Ch. App. 597.

[2] *Ibid.* at 608, and note clause 25 of the contract set out at p. 599.

[3] *Ibid.* See also *Thorn* v. *London Corporation* (1876) 1 App.Cas. 120 (H.L.), explained in *Re Ford and Bemrose* (1902) H.B.C. (4th ed.), Vol. 2, p. 324 at 332 (C.A.).

[4] *Bottoms* v. *York Corporation* (1892) H.B.C. (4th ed.), Vol. 2, p. 208 (C.A.); *McDonald* v. *Workington Corporation* (1892) H.B.C. (4th ed.), Vol. 2, p. 228 (C.A.); *Re Nuttall & Lynton & Barnstaple Railway* (1899) H.B.C. (4th ed.), Vol. 2, p. 279 and (1899) 82 L.T. 17 (C.A.). See *Jackson* v. *Eastbourne Local Board* (1885) H.B.C. (4th ed.), Vol. 2, p. 81 at 90 (H.L.), for statement of principle.

[5] *Thorn* v. *London Corporation* (1876) 1 App.Cas. 120 (H.L.); *Tharsis Sulphur & Copper Co.* v. *M'Elroy & Sons and others* (1878) 3 App.Cas. 1040 (H.L.); *Canterbury Pipe Lines* v. *Canterbury Drainage* (1979) 16 B.L.R. 76 at 121. *cf. Bacal Construction* v. *Northampton District Council* (1975) 8 B.L.R. 88 (C.A.) discussed at p. 732; *Simplex* v. *Borough of St. Pancras* (1958) 14 B.L.R. 80—architect's instruction held to be a variation even though without it the contractor would have been in breach of contract.

[6] *Rigby* v. *Bristol Corporation* (1860) 29 L.J. Ex. 359.

[7] *Neodox* v. *Swinton and Pendlebury Borough Council* (1958) 5 B.L.R. 34; *cf. Leedsford* v. *City of Bradford* (1956) 24 B.L.R. 45 (C.A.)—artificial stone to be obtained from X Ltd. "or other approved firm" did not give contractor option to submit any firm for approval, the approval not to be unreasonably withheld. Insistence on X Ltd. did not entitle contractor to additional payment.

ticable plans cannot usually recover the expense by bringing an action for breach of an implied warranty that the plans, drawings or bills of quantities are accurate or practicable. No such warranties are implied merely from the fact that these documents are submitted to the contractor for tender,[8] nor even from their attachment to the contract as a schedule[9] but the express words of the invitation to tender may show an intention to warrant the accuracy of statements which it contains.[10] Where tender documents contain a notice that the tenderer must satisfy himself of the correctness of statements in the documents, "the notice may, at the least, have validity as an element in determining whether there was a misrepresentation upon which [the tenderer] relied."[11]

Two Australian cases have considered whether an employer owed a duty of care to a tendering contractor in relation to information supplied. In one case,[12] the possible existence of a duty of care was not ruled out at an interlocutory stage before all the relevant facts had been established, it being held that certain contractual provisions did not by themselves necessarily amount to a disclaimer sufficient to negative the duty. In the other,[13] the employer was held not to have assumed responsibility for the completeness or accuracy of tender information about special site conditions. Both cases addressed the question with reference to *Hedley Byrne* v. *Heller & Partners.*[14]

(b) *Lump sum contract for whole work—exactly defined*

Bills of quantities contract.   The term bills of quantities contract is used here to describe a contract where the bills of quantities form part of the contract and describe the work to be carried out for which a lump sum is payable.[15] The quantities "are introduced into the contract as part of the description of the contract work" and "the plans do not go to quantity."[16] The contractor may be, and usually is, bound by the terms of the contract to carry out work in excess of that stated in the bills of quantities if it is necessary to complete the contract, but in a bills of quantities contract such excess work is

---

[8] *Thorn* v. *London Corporation* (1876) 1 App.Cas. 120 (H.L.); *Re Ford and Bemrose* (1902) H.B.C. (4th ed.), Vol. 2, p. 324 (C.A.). See further pp. 118 *et seq.* for a full discussion of inaccurate statements and when they give rise to a remedy.

[9] *Ibid.*

[10] See *Bacal Construction* v. *Northampton District Council* (1975) 8 B.L.R. 88 (C.A.).

[11] *Cremdean Properties* v. *Nash* (1977) 241 E.G. 837 at 841 upheld at (1977) 244 E.G. 547 (C.A.). For misrepresentation, see Chap. 6, Sections 3, 4 and 5.

[12] *Morrison-Knudsen International* v. *Commonwealth of Australia* (1972) 13 B.L.R. 114 (Australian High Court).

[13] *Dillingham Construction* v. *Downs* (1972) 13 B.L.R. 97 (New South Wales Supreme Court).

[14] [1964] A.C. 465 (H.L.). For a full discussion, see Chap. 7 and in particular "Employer's pre-contract information" at p. 176.

[15] Bills of quantities may be an important contract document without describing the work for which a lump sum is payable; see p. 85. In such a case the contract is not a bills of quantities contract in the sense used here.

[16] *Patman and Fotheringham* v. *Pilditch* (1904) H.B.C. (4th ed.), Vol. 2, p. 368 at 373.

extra work.[17] This type of contract has been said to be "obviously unsafe" for an employer because it can hardly ever be known beforehand what exact quantities of work may be necessary to complete[18]; conversely it may save the contractor much trouble and loss.[19]

It is sometimes a difficult question of construction to determine whether the quantities form part of the contract. The mere fact that quantities are submitted to the contractor for the purposes of tender does not make them form part.[20] They have been held not to form part where there was an express power reserved under the contract to the architect to rectify any mistakes in the quantities upon which the contractor's tender was based,[21] where they were a schedule to a contract to do work according to a specification,[22] and where there was a contract to erect certain buildings in accordance with plans and specification and the specification consisted of a bill of quantities with rather fuller description than usual.[23] But quantities were held to form part of the contract where the contract was to do work "according to the plans and the quantities there given by the architect."[24] In *Patman & Fotheringham* v. *Pilditch*,[25] the contract was to erect and complete, fit for occupation, a block of flats for a lump sum "according to the plans, invitation to tender, specification and bills of quantities signed by the contractors." Channell J. decided, though not "by any means without doubt,"[26] that the quantities signed by the contractors formed part of the contract. They were therefore entitled to recover for all work done by them in completing the contract which had been omitted from or understated in the bills of quantities. The judge expressly reserved[27] the case of "things that everybody must understand are to be done, but which happen to be omitted from the quantities," and thought that it would be covered by *Williams* v. *Fitzmaurice*.[28]

Other exactly defined contracts. A bills of quantities contract is the most exact way of defining the amount of work for which the unadjusted lump sum is payable. Where bills of quantities do not so define the amount of work, that information obviously has to be derived from elsewhere. It may come from the drawings read with any specification or other description of the work. Such

---

[17] *Kemp* v. *Rose* (1858) 1 Giff. 258; *Patman and Fotheringham* v. *Pilditch* (1904) H.B.C. (4th ed.), Vol. 2, p. 368.

[18] *Kemp* v. *Rose* (1858) 1 Giff. 258 at 268.

[19] See the advice of Stephen J. to contractors in *Priestley* v. *Stone* (1888) H.B.C. (4th ed.), Vol. 2, p. 134 at 140.

[20] *Re Ford and Bemrose* (1902) H.B.C. (4th ed.), Vol. 2, p. 324 (C.A.).

[21] *Young* v. *Blake* (1887) H.B.C. (4th ed.), Vol. 2, p. 110.

[22] *Sharpe* v. *San Paulo Railway* (1873) L.R. 8 Ch.App. 597.

[23] *In Re Ford and Bemrose* (1902) H.B.C. (4th ed.), Vol. 2, p. 324 (C.A.).

[24] *Kemp* v. *Rose* (1858) 1 Giff. 258,

[25] (1904) H.B.C. (4th ed.), Vol. 2, p. 368.

[26] *Ibid.* p. 372. It was necessary to distinguish the very strong case of *Re Ford and Bemrose* (1902) H.B.C. (4th ed.), Vol. 2, p. 324 (C.A.) and the dictum of Lord Esher at 330.

[27] *Ibid.* p. 373.

[28] (1858) 3 H. & N. 844 and see p. 81.

other forms of contract may define the work with considerable precision, especially if the contract incorporates detailed and fully dimensioned drawings. It was said of the contract in *Williams* v. *Fitzmaurice*[29] that, "the contract was that the house should be complete and fit for occupation by August 1, 1858, and not that the works therein before mentioned should be completed by that day."[30] It follows that the contractor could conversely, by clear words, limit his obligation to works expressly described in, *e.g.* a specification. Work not so described would be extra work.[31]

Contractor's implied obligations. Even in an exactly defined contract there is usually room for the implication of some obligations by the contractor so that their performance is not extra work. But the greater the detail used in the bills of quantities or other contract documents to describe the obligation for which the lump sum is payable the less scope there is for such implication.[32]

(c) *Measurement and value contracts*

In a measurement and value contract[33] it is usually immaterial whether any particular item of work that a contractor has to do is in the contract or not, because the contractor is entitled to be paid for it at the contract rate if it is applicable, or at a reasonable price if it is not.[34] But where such a contract provides for the payment of a specified sum of money for a specified item of work, it is a question of construction to determine what work is impliedly included in that item of work and is not therefore extra work. It is submitted that the principles of construction applicable to lump sum contracts apply to each item.[35] And it may be important to determine whether work is of the type contemplated by the contract and therefore governed by the conditions of the contract including price, or is work outside the contract[36] and not therefore subject to the contract conditions or price.

Comparison with bills of quantities contract. A bills of quantities contract is not a measurement and value contract in the sense in which the term is used in this book. Where the contract was for a "lump sum," the bills of quantities forming part of the contract, and "all variations to be ... added to, or deducted from the lump sum," it was held that the final account must be taken by adjusting the lump sum for variations, and not by remeasuring the

---

[29] *Ibid.*

[30] *Ibid.* at 851.

[31] See notes to Standard Form of Building Contract, dealing with the position where quantities do not form part at p. 480.

[32] See cases cited above in this chapter, and for implication of terms generally, see Chap. 3. For design and build contracts, see Chap. 1.

[33] For meaning, see p. 77.

[34] *Re Walton-on-the-Naze Urban District Council* v. *Moran* (1905) H.B.C. (4th ed.), Vol. 2, p. 376 at 380.

[35] *cf. Appleby* v. *Myers* (1867) L.R. 2 C.P. 651.

[36] For meaning, see p. 93.

works as carried out and applying the bill rates to the quantities so found.[37] But bills of quantities can form part of a measurement and value contract where they do not define the work for which a lump sum is payable but constitute a schedule defining units of measurement and rates for pricing those units.[38]

Pricing errors.   The difference between a contract to do the work described in the bills of quantities for a lump sum and a measurement and value contract is important when considering pricing errors.[39] Assume two contracts, one for a lump sum, the other one measurement and value. Bills of quantities are in each case a contract document. Say the contractor in pricing the bills of quantities has correctly stated his price per unit of measurement but has incorrectly extended the price and this error has been incorporated into the lump sum in the one contract and into his estimated total of prices in the other. Neither party noticed the error before the contract was made and there is no ground for rectification.[40] If the contract is for a lump sum there is, it is submitted, no implied right to have the contract price adjusted to take account of the error.[41] If the contract is one of measure and value where the contractor is to be paid £x per unit of measurement, the error will disappear on valuation of the measured work at completion.

(d) *Other common features*

Omissions.   The contract usually gives the employer or the architect power to order part of the work to be omitted with a consequent adjustment of the contract price. There is little English authority dealing with the exercise of such a power. On the construction of the contract it may not extend to the ordering of variations,[42] and it may not give the employer the right to omit part of the work from the contract with the object of giving it or similar work in substitution to another contractor.[43]

P.C. or prime cost sums.   The contractor sometimes undertakes to do work or provide materials at the "P.C." or at the "prime cost sum" of £x. These terms are usually defined in the contract. In the Standard Form of Building Contract, prime cost work or materials can only be carried out or supplied by

---

[37] *London Steam Stone Sawmills Co.* v. *Lorden* (1900) H.B.C. (4th ed.), Vol. 2, p. 301 (D.C.).

[38] See below and see I.C.E. Conditions, clause 56 at p. 895; *cp. Mitsui* v. *A.G. of Hong Kong* (1986) 33 B.L.R. 1 (P.C.).

[39] See p. 95 for effect of pricing errors on pricing variations.

[40] See p. 266.

[41] The unreported case of *M. V. Gleeson Ltd.* v. *Sleaford Urban District Council* (1953) noted in H.B.C. (10th ed.), p. 521, may be of assistance.

[42] *R.* v. *Peto* (1826) 1 Y. & J. Ex. 37.

[43] See the American case of *Gallagher* v. *Hirsch* (1899) N.Y. 45 App.Div. 467; *Simplex Floor Finishing* v. *Duranceau* (1941) D.L.R. 260 (Canadian Supreme Court); the Australian cases of *Carr* v. *J. A. Berriman Pty. Ltd.* (1953) 27 A.L.J.R. 273; *Commissioner of Main Roads* v. *Reed & Stuart* (1974) 12 B.L.R. 55 (Australian High Court).

nominated sub-contractors or suppliers[44] and the cost resulting from the nomination is substituted in the final account for the prime cost sum in the contract.[45] If there is no contractual definition and where there is no question of nomination, the ordinary meaning[46] of prime cost is, it is submitted, estimate[47] of net cost, and the intention is therefore that the contractor should only charge the employer the actual cost to himself. If this cost is less or more than that stated in the contract the contract sum is adjusted accordingly, subject always to the principles relating to extra work set out in this chapter.

Provisional sums. The contract sum may include a provisional sum or provisional amount to cover some expenditure the amount of which is not known at the time of entering into the contract. Thus it may be for extras, or for some item which cannot be exactly estimated, or for a subcontract which has to be placed after the main contract is entered into.[48] The term is usually defined, but the general rule is that the original contract sum is adjusted according to whether the actual expenditure ordered is greater or less than the provisional sum. It is usual to provide for an adjustment of the contractor's profit in accordance with the alteration of the contract sum.

Effect of Building Regulations. Compliance with Building Regulations as the works are carried out may require unanticipated work to be done.[49] Subject to relevant express terms[50] there is, it is submitted, normally an implied term by the contractor not to complete the work in a manner which contravenes relevant Building Regulations or other statutory requirements as to methods of construction. Can the contractor recover extra payment for unanticipated work required to comply with the Building Regulations? The answer depends, it is submitted, upon the application of the principles set out earlier in this chapter and in particular on:

(1) whether the work for which the contract sum is payable is defined in terms wide enough to include work unspecified but necessary to comply with Building Regulations[51]; and

---

[44] *Bickerton* v. *N.W. Metropolitan Regional Hospital Board* [1970] 1 W.L.R. 607 at 610, 623 (H.L.). Lord Reid said at 610 that the ordinary meaning of "prime cost sums" was "sums entered or provided in bills of quantities for work to be executed by nominated sub-contractors."

[45] See p. 626.

[46] See p. 40.

[47] See *Bickerton* v. *N.W. Metroplitan Regional Hospital Board* [1970] 1 W.L.R. 607 at 610 (H.L.); *cf. Tuta Products* v. *Hutcherson Bros.* (1972) 46 A.L.J.R. 549 (Australian High Court), where there was said to be an inference that prime cost sums, which were only estimates over which the builder had no control, were inherently subject to adjustment when the true cost emerged.

[48] See further p. 286. For the meaning of the term in the Standard Form of Building Contract, see p. 520.

[49] See generally "Building Act 1984 and the Building Regulations" at p. 372.

[50] *e.g.* clause 6 of the Standard Form of Building Contract at p. 501; and see *Townsend (Builders)* v. *Cinema News* [1959] 1 W.L.R. 119 (C.A.) more fully reported at 20 B.L.R. 118 (C.A.); *Acrecrest* v. *Hattrell* [1983] Q.B. 260 at 267 (C.A.); *Equitable Debenture Assets Corporation* v. *Williams Moss* (1984) 2 Con. L.R. 1. For implied terms, see pp. 45 *et seq.*

[51] See p. 81.

(2) where the contract work was not defined in such wide terms, whether the contractor sought the employer's instructions before carrying out the unanticipated work necessary to comply with the Building Regulations or can he otherwise show a promise to pay.[52]

2. Agent's Authority

An architect or other agent of the employer in the position of the architect has no implied power to vary the terms of the contract,[53] or to vary the contract works such as by ordering extras,[54] or to order as extras works impliedly included in the work for which the contract sum is payable.[55] If therefore the contractor has carried out extra work under the authority of the architect he must show:

(1) that the architect had an authority to order extra work; and
(2) that the particular work for which he is claiming was properly ordered within the scope of that authority.[56] If there is a written contract the question is one of construction, otherwise it is a question of fact.[57]

A contract to do a whole work usually gives the architect an express power to order extras. Such a power will not, in the absence of express words, be construed as extending beyond the scope of the original whole work.[58] It is possible that, if there is a provisional sum for extras, its amount might place some limit on the extent of the architect's authority.[59]

An architect who gives instructions to the contractor which are not empowered by any provision in the contract does not "saddle the employer with liability. The architect is not the employer's agent in that respect. He has no authority to vary the contract. Confronted with such acts, the parties may either acquiesce, in which case the contract may be *pro tanto* varied and the acts cannot be complained of, or a party may protest and ignore them. But he cannot saddle the employer with responsibility for them."[60] If work outside the contract is ordered to the knowledge of the employer the contractor will

---

[52] See p. 91.
[53] *Sharpe* v. *San Paulo Railway* (1873) L.R. 8 Ch.App. 597; *Stockport M.B.C.* v. *O'Reilly* [1978] 1 Lloyd's Rep. 595 at 601.
[54] *R.* v. *Peto* (1826) 1 Y. & J. Ex. 37; *Cooper* v. *Langdon* (1842) 10 M. & W. 785; *Ranger* v. *G.W. Railway* (1854) 5 H.L.C. 72 (H.L.); *Carlton Contractors* v. *Bexley Corporation* (1962) 60 L.G.R. 331.
[55] *Sharpe* v. *San Paulo Railway* (1873) L.R. 8 Ch.App. 597.
[56] See n. 54 above.
[57] *Wallis* v. *Robinson* (1862) 3 F. & F. 307, N.P.; *R.* v. *Peto* (1826) 1 Y. & J. Ex. 37 noting the remarks of Moulton L.J. in the unreported case of *Stevens* v. *Mewes & Davis* (1910) June 8 (C.A.), cited H.B.C. (10th ed.), p. 532.
[58] *R.* v. *Peto* (1826) 1 Y. & J. Ex. 37; *Russell* v. *Sa da Bandeira* (1862) 13 C.B.(N.S.) 149; *cf. Sir Lindsay Parkinson & Co. Ltd.* v. *Commissioners of Works* [1949] 2 K.B. 632 (C.A.), discussed at p. 79.
[59] For provisional sums, see p. 87.
[60] *Stockport M.B.C.* v. *O'Reilly* [1978] 1 Lloyd's Rep. 595 at 601.

normally be able to recover a reasonable price for such work on a fresh contract.[61]

An architect who orders extras without or in excess of his authority may be liable to the contractor for breach of warranty of authority. An architect who orders work without disclosing that he is acting as agent for an employer may be held personally liable. The fact that such a person is acting in a professional capacity does not necessarily exclude his personal liability.[62]

3. Payment for Extra Work

The mere fact that a contractor has carried out extra work does not of itself entitle him to demand extra payment. He must show an express or implied contract to pay.[63] This he may do either by proving that the work was properly ordered under a provision in the original contract entitling him to payment,[64] or that there is a fresh contract to pay for the work.[65]

Production of agreement. Where the agreement is in writing and the contractor is claiming payment for extra work he must produce the written agreement to prove that the work claimed for is an extra,[66] unless the extra work is work outside the contract and was therefore carried out under a separate contract express or implied.[67]

Work done without request. If the contractor has undertaken to do specified work with certain materials for an agreed price, and without request uses better materials or does more work, this does not entitle him to demand extra payment[68]; and if the materials or work are not in accordance with the contract he may not be able to recover the contract price because he has not completed the contract.[69] Mere permission by the employer to do work different from that contracted for must be distinguished from a request. Thus contractors had undertaken as part of a lump sum contract to make certain girders. They found that it was impracticable or very expensive to make them in the specified way and applied for, and were granted, permission to make them thicker. Lord

---

[61] *Russell* v. *Sa da Bandeira* (1862) 13 C.B.(N.S.) 149; *Astilleros Canarios* v. *Cape Hatteras Shipping* [1982] 1 Lloyd's Rep. 518.

[62] *Sika Contracts* v. *Gill and Closeglen Properties* (1978) 9 B.L.R. 11.

[63] *Tharsis Sulphur and Copper Co.* v. *M'Elroy & Sons and others* (1878) 3 App.Cas. 1040 at 1053 (H.L.).

[64] See "Written orders" at p. 91.

[65] See "Implied promise to pay" at p. 91, and "Work outside the contract" at p. 93.

[66] *Vincent* v. *Cole* (1828) 1 M. & M. 257.

[67] *Vincent* v. *Cole* (1828) 1 M. & M. 257; *Reid* v. *Batte* (1829) Moo. & M. 413; *Parton* v. *Cole* (1841) 11 L.J.Q.B. 70.

[68] *Wilmot* v. *Smith* (1828) 3 C. & P. 453; *Bottoms* v. *York Corporation* (1892) H.B.C. (4th ed.), Vol. 2, p. 208 (C.A.).

[69] *Forman* v. *The Liddesdale* [1900] A.C. 190 (P.C.); *Ashwell and Nesbit Ltd.* v. *Allen & Co.* (1912) H.B.C. (4th ed.), Vol. 2, p. 462 (C.A.); *Holland Hannen & Cubitts* v. *W.H.T.S.O.* (1981) 18 B.L.R. 80 at 121—the decision on the eleventh issue.

Blackburn said: "I think there is nothing in that to imply that there was to be a payment for that additional thickness."[70]

Emergency.   It is possible that a contractor who in an emergency, when it is impossible to obtain instructions from the employer, expends money in preserving the employer's property can recover payment.[71]

No knowledge of increased expense.   If the contractor has undertaken to carry out certain work at an agreed price and the employer consents to the execution of different work, the employer is not liable for any increased cost unless he knows, or must be taken to know, that the different work will cost more.[72]

Absence of consideration.[73]   The contractor may refuse to carry out certain work unless the employer promises to pay for it as extra work. If it appears that the work is not in fact extra work because it is included in the work for which the original contract sum is payable, the employer's promise may not be binding for lack of consideration.[74] Where a contract is silent on some particular, it may be possible to argue that better definition in that particular is a matter of mutual benefit and that acceptance of the definition by each party is supported by consideration moving from the other.[75]

An agreement to pay an additional sum for no extra work may not always fail for lack of consideration. Where a sub-contract carpenter was in financial difficulties and the agreed price for his work was too low, it was held that there was consideration for the main contractor's promise to pay an additional amount for the same work in that the main contractor thereby secured benefits or obviated disbenefits from the continuing relationship with the sub-contractor.[76] The benefits were:

---

[70] *Tharsis Sulphur and Copper Co.* v. *M'Elroy & Sons and others* (1878) 3 App.Cas. 1040 at 1053 (H.L.). The majority of the House of Lords seem to have decided the case on the grounds that: (a) the work was not an extra; (b) there was no order in writing as required by the contract. See also *Kirk & Kirk Ltd.* v. *Croydon Corporation* [1956] J.P.L. 585; *cf. Simplex Concrete Piles Ltd.* v. *St. Pancras Borough Council* (1958) 14 B.L.R. 80.

[71] *Falcke* v. *Scottish Imperial Insurance Co.* (1886) 34 Ch.D 234 at 248–249 (C.A.) appears to be an authority to the contrary, but the court might imply a request; consider the authorities collected and the comment in Goff and Jones, *The Law of Restitution* (3rd ed.), Chap. 15. And see the statements of principle in *China Pacific* v. *Food Corporation of India* [1982] A.C. 939 at 961 and 965 (H.L.)—a case about salvage of goods; *Owen* v. *Tate* [1976] Q.B. 402 (C.A.). See also (1977) 93 L.Q.R. 273. See also clause 6.1.4 of the 1980 Standard Form of Building Contract.

[72] *Lovelock* v. *King* (1831) 1 Moo. & Rob. 60; *Johnson* v. *Weston* (1859) 1 F. & F. 693; *Thames Iron Works, etc., Co.* v. *Royal Mail, etc., Co.* (1861) 13 C.B.(N.S.) 358 at 378.

[73] *Sharpe* v. *San Paulo Railway* (1873) L.R. 8 Ch. App. 597 at 608, James L.J. "it is perfectly *nudum pactum.*" See also Chap. 2, nts. 3 and 4 at pp. 11–12. For the right to set up by way of an equitable defence, despite the absence of consideration, a promise acted upon by the promisee so as to affect his legal position and for the limitations to that right, see "Promissory estoppel" at p. 263. For a promise to perform a duty owed to another, see *New Zealand Shipping Co. Ltd.* v. *A. M. Satterthwaite & Co. Ltd.* [1975] A.C. 154 (P.C.); *Pao On* v. *Lau Yiu Long* [1980] A.C. 614 at 632 (P.C.).

[74] But *cp. Simplex Concrete Piles* v. *St. Pancras Borough Council* (1958) 14 B.L.R. 80.

[75] See *Ficom* v. *Sociedad Cadex* [1980] 2 Lloyd's Rep. 118 at 132.

[76] *Williams* v. *Roffey Brothers* [1990] 2 W.L.R. 1153 (C.A.); *cf.* "Economic duress" at p. 145.

(1) seeking to ensure that the sub-contractor did not stop work in breach of contract;
(2) avoiding the penalty for delay; and
(3) avoiding the trouble and expense of engaging others to complete the work.

Work exceeding contract limit.   Contracts sometimes have clauses limiting the value of variations which can be ordered. Problems can arise in determining whether the value has been exceeded.[77] If the value is exceeded, it is suggested that the principles discussed in this chapter would determine whether the contractor was entitled to payment. An architect would have no implied authority to order work in excess of the limit. The contractor might be able to establish a new contract or implied promise by the employer to pay.

Written orders.   Contracts frequently provide that extras must be ordered in a certain manner. The purpose of these provisions is usually to prevent unauthorised or extravagant claims for extras. A frequent requirement is that there must be a written order signed by the architect and that no extras will be paid for unless so ordered. In such a contract a proper written order is a condition precedent to payment for extras.[78]

The form of the order will depend upon the wording of the contract, but in general the writing relied on must be a clear definite order and not a mere passing reference to some extra work. Thus progress certificates referring to work claimed to be an extra,[79] and unsigned sketches and drawings prepared in the architect's office[80] have been held not to be written orders. The contract may require that such orders must be given before the extra work is carried out,[81] but it may be that if an otherwise valid written order is given retrospectively the courts will treat this as a waiver of the requirement.

Recovery without written orders.   The general rule is that in the absence of written orders, or other formalities which are conditions precedent to payment, the contractor cannot recover either under the contract, or on a fresh contract to pay a reasonable sum, even though the employer has had the benefit of the extra work.[82] To this rule there are certain exceptions discussed in the following paragraphs.

Implied promise to pay.   "When there is a condition in the contract that extras shall not be paid for unless ordered in writing by the architect ... and

---

[77] See, *e.g. Arcos Industries* v. *Electricity Commission of N.S.W.* (1973) 12 B.L.R. 65 (New South Wales Supreme Court); *cf.* the form of contract in *McAlpine & Son.* v. *Transvaal Provincial Administration* (1974) 3 S.A.L.R. 506.

[78] *Russell* v. *Sa da Bandeira* (1862) 13 C.B.(N.S.) 149; *Taverner & Co. Ltd.* v. *Glamorgan County Council* (1941) 57 T.L.R. 243; *cf. Astilleros Canarios* v. *Cape Hatteras Shipping* [1982] 1 Lloyd's Rep. 518.

[79] *Tharsis Sulphur and Copper Co.* v. *M'Elroy & Sons and others* (1878) 3 App.Cas. 1040 (H.L.).

[80] *Myers* v. *Sarl* (1860) 3 E. & E. 306.

[81] *Lamprell* v. *Billericay Union* (1849) 18 L.J. Ex. 282.

[82] *Kirk* v. *Bromley Union* (1848) 12 Jur. 85; *Ranger* v. *G.W. Railway* (1854) 5 H.L.C. 72 (H.L.); *Taverner & Co. Ltd.* v. *Glamorgan County Council* (1941) 57 T.L.R. 243.

the employer orders work which he knows, or is told, will cause extra cost, a jury[83] or an arbitrator may find that there was an implied promise by the employer that the work should be paid for as an extra and especially so in cases where any other inference from the facts would be to attribute dishonesty to the employer."[84] Such a promise may be implied where there has been a waiver of the condition. "In order to constitute a waiver there must be conduct which leads the other party reasonably to believe that the strict legal rights will not be insisted on."[85] Thus in principle a written waiver by the employer would be effective,[86] and even an oral waiver would be sufficient if it were a clear undertaking not to rely on the condition.[87] In *Molloy* v. *Liebe* the contractor maintained that certain work was extra work. The employer said that it was not and insisted on the work being done. Upon arbitration the arbitrator held that the work was extra work, and inferred a promise on the part of the employer to pay for it if it should be found to be extra work, although it was not ordered in writing as an extra in the manner required by the contract. The arbitrator's award was upheld, and it was said that it was difficult to see how he could have drawn any other inference without attributing dishonesty to the employer.[88]

In *Holland Hannen & Cubitts* v. *W.H.T.S.O.*,[89] windows installed by a nominated sub-contractor in a partly constructed hospital were defective and remedial works were carried out. Most of the remedial works were held to include design changes, but the architect had refused to issue a variation instruction to effect the changes. It was held that the resulting windows were not in accordance with the main contract or the sub-contract so that neither the main contractor nor the sub-contractor could recover payment under those contracts. But it was further held that, notwithstanding the architect's refusal to issue a variation instruction, the employer and the architect had by their words and conduct agreed to the arrangement whereby the sub-contractor provided the altered windows. The result was a new contract between the sub-contractor and the employer, to which the main contractor was not a party, that in consideration of the sub-contractor providing windows for the hospital the employer would pay them a *quantum meruit*.[90]

---

[83] Note that juries do not decide such matters today. The judge decides questions of fact, or remits them to a referee—see Chap. 17.

[84] Extract from H.B.C. (6th ed.), p. 313, referred to with approval by Humphreys J., *Taverner & Co. Ltd.* v. *Glamorgan County Council* (1941) 57 T.L.R. 243 at 245. See also *Tool Metal Manufacturing Co. Ltd.* v. *Tungsten Electric Co. Ltd.* [1955] 1 W.L.R. 761 (H.L.) and other authorities referred to at n. 73 above and consider restitution referred to in n. 48 above.

[85] Denning L.J. in *Rickards* v. *Oppenheim* [1950] 1 K.B. 616 at 626 (C.A.)—see "Waiver" at p. 264.

[86] See *Taverner & Co. Ltd.* v. *Glamorgan County Council* (1941) 57 T.L.R. 243 at 245.

[87] See *Molloy* v. *Liebe* (1910) 102 L.T. 616; *cf. Franklin* v. *Darke* (1862) 6 L.T. 291. In certain circumstances the contractor may be able to say that the employer is estopped from setting up the absence of a written order as a defence. For estoppel there must be a clear unequivocal representation by the employer, see *Woodhouse Ltd.* v. *Nigerian Produce Ltd.* [1972] A.C. 741 (H.L.). See also p. 262.

[88] *Molloy* v. *Liebe* (1910) 102 L.T. 616 at 617.

[89] (1981) 18 B.L.R. 80.

[90] *Ibid.* at 125.

Acceptance of work orally ordered by the architect does not show an implied promise to pay,[91] neither has the architect any implied authority to waive a term of the contract requiring extras to be ordered in writing.[92] But the court may find that, where the employer has desired the execution of extra works, and has stood by and seen the expenditure on them, and taken the benefit of that expenditure, it would be a fraud on the part of the employer to refuse to pay on the ground that the work was not properly ordered. In such a case the employer will be ordered to account for the value of the extra work.[93] The mere fact that work was done on oral orders by an agent and payment is then refused is by itself no indication of fraud.[94]

A contractor cannot, it seems, rely on the absence of a written order to avoid the subsequent necessity of giving notice of an intention to claim where the contractual validity of the oral instruction is not challenged by the employer.[95]

Work outside the contract.   Extra work may be of the kind contemplated by clauses of the contract which provide for the ordering of extras or it may be so peculiar and so different that it is outside the contract.[96] It may be work outside the contract if it is carried out after completion of the original contract work.[97] Extra work outside the contract is not governed by the terms of the contract, and need not therefore be ordered in writing. The employer is liable to pay a reasonable price for such work carried out at his request,[98] but may exceptionally not be so liable if the original contract is not expressly or by implication replaced by a new contract[99] and if there is no other basis for liability as, *e.g.* an implied promise to pay. "In order to make a person liable on a *quantum meruit* there has to be a necessary implication that the person liable is agreeing to pay."[1] It is unlikely to be sufficient for a contractor to claim after the works are completed that extra work is outside the terms of the contract.[2]

Arbitration clause.   If there is an arbitration clause in the contract it may be so worded as to give the arbitrator, on a proper reference being made, "power to dispense with the conditions precedent and to order that, notwithstanding the non-performance of those conditions precedent a liability may be

---

[91] *Taverner* v. *Glamorgan County Council* (1941) 57 T.L.R. 243; *Kirk* v. *Bromley Union* (1848) 12 Jur. 85.

[92] *Sharpe* v. *San Paulo Railway* (1873) L.R. 8 Ch.App. 597.

[93] *Hill* v. *South Staffs Railway* (1865) 12 L.T.(N.S.) 63 at 65 also at (1874) L.R. 18 Eq. 154; *cf. Kirk* v. *Bromley Union* (1848) 12 Jur. 85.

[94] *Taverner & Co. Ltd.* v. *Glamorgan County Council* (1941) 57 T.L.R. 243 at 246.

[95] *Hersent* v. *Burmah Oil* [1978] 2 Lloyd's Rep. 565.

[96] *Thorn* v. *London Corporation* (1876) 1 App.Cas. 120 (H.L.); *Goodyear* v. *Weymouth Corporation* (1865) 35 L.J.C.P. 12; *Blue Circle Industries* v. *Holland Dredging* (1987) 37 B.L.R. 40 (C.A.); *cf. Sir Lindsay Parkinson & Co. Ltd.* v. *Commissioners of Works* [1949] 2 K.B. 632 (C.A.), discussed at p. 79.

[97] *Russell* v. *Sa da Bandeira* (1862) 13 C.B.(N.S.) 149.

[98] *Reid* v. *Batte* (1829) Moo. & M. 413; *Russell* v. *Sa da Bandeira* (1862) 13 C.B.(N.S.) 149; *Astilleros Canarios* v. *Cape Hatteras Shipping* [1982] 1 Lloyd's Rep. 518.

[99] *Gilbert & Partners* v. *Knight* [1968] 2 All E.R. 248 (C.A.); *cf. Thorn* v. *London Corporation* (1876) 1 App.Cas. 120 at 134 (H.L.).

[1] *Ibid.* Davis L.J. at 251.

[2] See *McAlpine & Son* v. *Transvaal Provincial Administration* (1974) 3 S.A.L.R. 506.

established on which money may be ordered to be paid."[3] In *Brodie* v. *Cardiff Corporation*[4] the architect refused to issue a written order for extras on the ground that work required to be carried out was included in the contract price. On a reference the arbitrator awarded sums of money to be paid in respect of the extras despite the absence of an order in writing and his decision was upheld.

Architect's final certificate.   The parties may by the contract give the architect power to decide various matters finally between them, and to state his decision in the form of a certificate.[5] Having given the architect this power they are not allowed by the courts, in the absence of fraud or other special circumstances, to attack his decision upon such matters. His certificate is binding and conclusive upon them.[6] Thus where architects have certified by final certificates that certain money is due to the contractor, employers have not been allowed to go behind the certificate and say that a smaller sum was due because the certificate included payment for extras not ordered in writing[7] or not otherwise ordered properly,[8] or for work which was not extra work,[9] or for work which had not been done at all.[10] It is a matter of construction in each case to determine whether the architect's decision is intended to be binding and conclusive on matters relating to extras.[11] It seems that "conclusive evidence" clauses are construed neither more nor less strictly than other clauses since, unlike clauses which seek to exclude liability, they can work to the benefit of either party.[12]

4. Rate of Payment

Work within the contract.   Extra work of the kind contemplated by the

---

[3] Greer L.J. in *Prestige & Co. Ltd.* v. *Brettell* [1938] 4 All E.R. 346 at 354 (C.A.), referring to *Brodie* v. *Cardiff Corporation* [1919] A.C. 337 (H.L.) and *Neale* v. *Richardson* [1938] 1 All E.R. 753 (C.A.); *cf. Northern Regional Health Authority* v. *Derek Crouch* [1984] Q.B. 644 (C.A.) and see "Crouch" at p. 389. For arbitration generally, see Chap. 16.

[4] [1919] A.C. 337 (H.L.).

[5] For mistakes of law by architects and grounds for attacking their certificates, see Chap. 5.

[6] See generally Chap. 5.

[7] *Goodyear* v. *Weymouth Corporation* (1865) 35 L.J.C.P. 12; *Laidlaw* v. *The Hastings Pier Co.* (1874) H.B.C. (4th ed.), Vol. 2, p. 13.

[8] *Lapthorne* v. *St. Aubyn* (1885) 1 Cab. & El. 486.

[9] *Laidlaw* v. *The Hastings Pier Co.* (1874) H.B.C. (4th ed.), Vol. 2, p. 13; *Richards* v. *May* (1883) 10 Q.B.D. 400 (D.C.).

[10] *Laidlaw* v. *The Hasting Pier Co.* (1874) H.B.C. (4th ed.), Vol. 2, p. 13. For a sale of goods case where a mistake subsequently admitted by an official certifier did not invalidate the certificate, see *Toepfer, Alfred C.* v. *Continental Grain Co.* [1974] 1 Lloyd's Rep. 11 (C.A.), but note that this was a certificate *in rem, i.e.* upon which numerous persons in a chain of transactions would rely. The *Toepfer* case was approved in *Gill & Duffus* v. *Berger (No. 2)* [1984] A.C. 382 at 394 (H.L.) and applied in *Gill & Duffus* v. *Berger* [1982] 1 Lloyd's Rep. 101.

[11] See *Pashby* v. *Birmingham Corporation* (1856) 18 C.B. 2; *Re Meadows & Kenworthy* (1896) H.B.C. (4th ed.), Vol. 2, p. 265 (C.A., aff. H.L.). See further Chap. 5.

[12] *Gill & Duffus* v. *Berger* [1982] 1 Lloyd's Rep. 101 at 104.

contract will be paid for in the manner provided by the terms of the contract.[13] Payment will usually be at or with reference to the contract rates. If there are no relevant rates, it will be a reasonable sum. Where the contract provided that "Additional work shall be paid for at rates pro rata to the estimate" and there were no rates in the estimate which was for a lump sum, it was held that these words had no application to the pricing of extra work for which a reasonable sum was therefore payable.[14]

Effect of pricing errors.   When the contractor has made an error in his pricing of the tender for a lump sum contract and there are no grounds for rectification,[15] and the contract provides for payment of variations at rates shown in the tender, a difficult question can arise when pricing variations and the error is apparent. Should any, and if any, what, adjustment be made in the rates shown in the tender to arrive at the new rate for pricing variations?[16] Many surveyors in practice claim to make an adjustment.[17] It is thought that there is no generally accepted custom and that the question must always be one of construction. The matter can conveniently be dealt with by an express term.[18]

Work outside the contract.[19]   For work outside the contract the contractor is entitled to a reasonable sum.[20] The normal rule is that however great the amount of work outside the contract, the work within the contract is paid for at the contract rates and only work outside the contract is paid for at a reasonable rate[21]; but "if a man contracts to work by a certain plan, and that plan is so entirely abandoned that it is impossible to trace the contract, and to what part of it the work shall be applied, in such a case the workman shall be permitted to charge for the whole work done by measure and value, as if no contract at all had ever been made."[22]

5. Appropriation of Payments

An employer may from time to time pay money generally on account without appropriating it to any particular items or part of the work. If the contractor

---

[13] *Thorn* v. *London Corporation* (1876) 1 App.Cas. 120 at 134, 127 (H.L.); *Canterbury Pipe Lines* v. *Christchurch Drainage* (1979) 16 B.L.R. 76 at 122 (New Zealand Court of Appeal).
[14] *Reliance Shopfitters Ltd.* v. *Hyams* (1960) (unreported) H.H. Percy Lamb Q.C., Official Referee.
[15] See p. 266.
[16] The lump sum is not altered, see p. 86.
[17] *e.g.* assume a lump sum of £1,000 is £45 less than it would have been for an error in extending a unit price; it is sometimes said that a reduction of 45/1045 should be made in pricing variations.
[18] See, *e.g. A Code of Procedure for Single Stage Selective Tendering* (April 1989) obtainable from the National Joint Consultative Committee for Building.
[19] See also p. 93.
[20] See p. 79.
[21] *Sir Lindsay Parkinson & Co. Ltd.* v. *Commissioners of Works* [1949] 2 K.B. 632 (C.A.).
[22] Lord Kenyon in *Pepper* v. *Burland* (1792) 1 Peake N.P. 139.

has carried out extra work for which he has no claim for payment from the employer because of the failure of a condition precedent or for some other reason, the contractor cannot appropriate the money to payment of such extra work.[23] The general rule is that in the absence of a specific appropriation by the debtor the creditor may appropriate payments on account to whatever debts he pleases, but "before such a question can arise, it must be plain that there must be two debts. The doctrine never has been held to authorise a creditor receiving money on account to apply it towards the satisfaction of what does not, nor ever did, constitute any legal or equitable demand against the party making the payments."[24]

---

[23] *Lamprell* v. *Billericay Union* (1849) 18 L.J. Ex. 282.
[24] *Ibid.* A similar rule was applied to work illegal under the Defence Regulations. See p. 145.

Chapter 5

EMPLOYER'S APPROVAL AND ARCHITECT'S CERTIFICATES

A. EMPLOYER'S APPROVAL

Construction against employer. A contract may provide that work must be completed to the approval of the employer. "There is, after all, nothing to prevent a party from requiring that work shall be done to his own satisfaction."[1] Such a provision if construed in the employer's favour would be very onerous. If goods do not meet with the approval of a buyer and he rejects them the seller can sell the goods for what they are worth. But in the case of a building contract, when the work is fixed to the land it becomes the property of the owner of the land.[2] If the employer is entitled to say, "I do not approve of the work; you have not carried out your contract, therefore you cannot recover on the contract," the contractor is in an unfortunate position. He cannot sell the work to a third party because it is not his property. He cannot recover on the contract because he has not fulfilled it. He will have great difficulty even in showing an implied promise to pay a reasonable sum, because mere use and occupation of building work is not evidence of such a promise.[3] For these reasons, and perhaps also because of the maxim "no man shall be a judge in his own cause,"[4] clauses of this nature are given a reasonable construction and are construed against the employer as discussed in the following two paragraphs.[5]

Not usually a condition precedent to payment. The court leans against a construction making the approval of the employer a condition precedent to

---

[1] *Minster Trust* v. *Traps Tractors* [1954] 1 W.L.R. 963 at 973.
[2] See p. 241.
[3] See p. 75.
[4] See *Dimes* v. *Grand Junction Canal* (*Proprietors*) (1852) 3 H.L.Cas. 794 (H.L.).
[5] *Dallman* v. *King* (1837) 7 L.J.C.P. 6; *Stadhard* v. *Lee* (1863) 32 L.J.Q.B. 75.

payment, and prefers a construction making the promise to complete according to the employer's approval, and the promise to pay independent of one another.[6] In such a case if the work does not meet with the employer's approval he cannot refuse to pay under the contract, but can only seek a reduction in the contract price by way of set-off, or counterclaim for damages."[7]

Reasonable, honest and not capricious. Normally the employer's approval must not be unreasonably, or dishonestly, or capriciously withheld.[8] What is reasonable is a question of fact.[9] The right to withhold approval may by the terms of the contract be limited to certain parts or qualities of the work.[10] If approval is subject to the completion of certain tests which the employer through his own default fails to carry out, he cannot withhold his approval because the work has not satisfied other tests not agreed upon in the contract.[11]

Express words. Exceptionally, however, the court may be constrained by express words.

> "Where from the whole tenor of the agreement it appears that however unreasonable and oppressive a stipulation or condition may be, the one party intended to insist upon and the other to submit to it, a court of justice cannot do otherwise than give full effect to the terms which have been agreed upon between the parties . . . without stopping to consider how far they may be reasonable or not."[12]

Thus a sub-contract provided that if the sub-contract works did not proceed as rapidly and satisfactorily as required by the main contractors or their agent, the main contractors could put on extra men themselves and deduct the additional cost from the money due under the sub-contract. The court was satisfied that the intention was that this power could be exercised if the main contractors "were dissatisfied, whether with or without sufficient reason," with the progress of the work. It was added that, in the circumstances, the clause was not unreasonable as the main contractors were probably under stringent terms themselves to complete to time.[13]

Where a contractor had undertaken to complete a carriage to B's "convenience and taste," it was held (despite a jury's verdict in favour of the

---

[6] *Dallman* v. *King* (1837) 7 L.J.C.P. 6 at 9, 11. Another way of stating the effect of this proposition is to say that the court treats the promise to complete to the employer's approval as a mere term and not as a condition.

[7] *Ibid*. See "Substantial performance" at p. 72.

[8] *Dallman* v. *King* (1837) 7 L.J.C.P. 6; *Parsons* v. *Sexton* (1847) 4 C.B. 899; *Andrews* v. *Belfield* (1857) 2 C.B.(N.S.) 779. See also *Cammell Laird & Co.* v. *The Manganese Bronze and Brass Co.* [1934] A.C. 402 (H.L.)—sale of goods to be completed to "entire satisfaction" of a third party; *Minster Trust* v. *Traps Tractors* [1954] 1 W.L.R. 963 at 973.

[9] *Ripley* v. *Lordan* (1860) 2 L.T. 154.

[10] *Ibid*.

[11] *Mackay* v. *Dick* (1881) 6 App.Cas. 251 (H.L.).

[12] Cockburn C.J. in *Stadhard* v. *Lee* (1863) 32 L.J.Q.B. 75 at 78; *Diggle* v. *Ogston Motor Co.* (1915) 112 L.T. 1029. See also *Minster Trust Ltd.* v. *Traps Tractors* [1954] 1 W.L.R. 963 at 973.

[13] *Ibid*.

contractor) that B was entitled to reject it if it did not accord with his convenience and taste, assuming that his rejection was bona fide and not capricious.[14] But the rejection of goods which can be resold differs in substance from that of work to land which cannot.

Approval by alter ego.   If work is to be done to the satisfaction of an agent it may, on the construction of the contract, "be plain that he is to function only as the *alter ego* of his master,"[15] and not to act in the independent manner of an architect as the term "architect" is used in this chapter. Approval by such an agent is, it is submitted, subject to the same principles as apply to the employer's approval.

Approval by employer and architect.   Where work was to be carried out to the approval of both the employer and the architect and they had expressed their approval, and the architect had given a final certificate of satisfaction which the contract made binding upon the parties, it was held that the employer, in the absence of fraud or collusion, could not claim for damages for defects.[16]

B. ARCHITECT'S CERTIFICATES

1. Types of Certificate

In building contracts, the certifier is usually an architect or surveyor. In engineering contracts, he is usually an engineer. In other construction contracts, there may be provision for other professionals or individuals to certify. The text which follows refers to "architect" and "architect's certificate" generally to apply to all such persons and their certificates.

Formal requirements.[17]   The formal requirements of an architect's certificate depend on the terms of the contract, but building contracts seldom stipulate precise formalities. In any event, minor immaterial errors will not invalidate a certificate if no one is misled.[18] It must, however, clearly and unambiguously appear that the document relied upon is the physical expression of a certifying process and regard should be had to its "form," "substance" and "intent."[19] The document should be "the expression in a definite form of

---

[14] *Andrews* v. *Belfield* (1857) 2 C.B.(N.S.) 779. See also *Docker* v. *Hyams* [1969] 1 W.L.R. 1060 at 1065 (C.A.) where the effect of cases dealing with agreements to provide ships or goods to the purchaser's approval is reviewed.

[15] *Minster Trust Ltd.* v. *Traps Tractors* [1954] 1 W.L.R. 963 at 973.

[16] *Bateman (Lord)* v. *Thompson* (1875) H.B.C. (4th ed.), Vol. 2, p. 36 (C.A.).

[17] See also "Form of certificate" at p. 111.

[18] *Emson Contractors* v. *Protea Estates* (1987) 39 B.L.R. 126.

[19] *Token Construction* v. *Charlton Estates* (1973) 1 B.L.R. 48 at 52 (C.A.) citing *Minster Trust* v. *Traps Tractors Ltd.* [1954] 1 W.L.R. 963.

the exercise of the judgment, opinion or skill of the engineer, architect or surveyor in relation to some matter provided for by the terms of the contract."[20] It is crucially important that any certificate should be clear and unambiguous so that the parties know where they are and should not be left in doubt or dispute as to their consequent mutual rights and liabilities.[21] The use of the word "certify" is not, in most contracts, mandatory but the architect would be well advised to use the word[22] and to follow as closely as he can the language of the clause from which his power to certify derives.

A certificate is not normally effective unless it is issued or delivered. Mere signature is not enough.[23] What constitutes issuance or delivery will depend on the terms of the contract and many contracts deal expressly with the service of notices and certificates.[24] Where a local authority contract required certificates to be issued to the local authority employer with a duplicate to be sent to the contractor, it was held that, to be issued, the certificate had to be sent to the employer's Treasury Department so that payment could be effected.[25] It is thought that, if the contract is silent, delivery of the certificate to both the employer and the contractor is likely to be an implied requirement.

The nature and effect of an architect's certificate depends upon the construction of the particular contract, but in general such certificates may be divided into:

(1) progress or interim certificates;
(2) final certificates; and
(3) other certificates.

These are discussed in the following paragraphs.

Progress or interim certificates. These certificates are issued from time to time during the course of the work certifying that, in the opinion of the architect, work has been carried out, and, in some cases, materials supplied, to the value of £x. They are approximate estimates, made in some instances for the purpose of determining whether the employer is safe in making a payment in advance of the contract sum,[26] in others whether he is under a duty to pay an

---

[20] *Ibid.* adopting H.B.C. (10th ed.), p. 479. Contrast *Costain International Ltd.* v. *Att.-Gen.* (1983) 23 B.L.R. 48 (Hong Kong Court of Appeal) where it was held that an "order in writing signed by the engineer" effecting a "variation in time for completion of the contract" was not a "certificate" for the purposes of an arbitration clause similar to clause 66(2) of the I.C.E. Conditions limiting arbitration before completion, *inter alia*, to disputes concerning the withholding of any certificate.

[21] *Token Construction* v. *Charlton Estates* (1973) 1 B.L.R. 48 at 58 (C.A.); *cf. Pyrok Industries* v. *Chee Tat Engineering* (1988) 41 B.L.R. 124 (Hong Kong High Court).

[22] *Token Construction* v. *Charlton Estates* (1973) 1 B.L.R. 48 at 57 (C.A.).

[23] *London Borough of Camden* v. *Thomas McInerney* (1986) 2 Const. L.J. 293; *cf. Token Construction* v. *Charlton Estates* (1973) 1 B.L.R. 48 (C.A.) where the point was not decided.

[24] *cf. Anglian Water Authority* v. *R.D.L. Contracting* (1988) 43 B.L.R. 98 holding that notice of an engineer's decision under clause 66 of the I.C.E. Conditions was on the facts properly served on the employer.

[25] *London Borough of Camden* v. *Thomas McInerney* (1986) 2 Const. L.J. 293.

[26] See *Tharsis Sulphur and Copper Co.* v. *M'Elroy* (1878) 3 App.Cas. 1040 (H.L.); *cf. Canterbury Pipe Lines* v. *Christchurch Drainage* (1979) 16 B.L.R. 76 at 95 (New Zealand Court of Appeal).

instalment and if so, how much he is to pay.[27] Such certificates are not normally binding upon the parties as to quality or amount and are subject to adjustment on completion.[28] It has, however, been held under the 1963 Standard Form of Building Contract that the employer is not obliged to pay more than the amount stated as due on the face of an interim certificate. Whatever the cause of an undervaluation, the contractor's remedy is to request the architect to make an appropriate adjustment in a subsequent certificate or to take the dispute to arbitration.[29] An employer who has a bona fide arguable contention that an interim certificate overvalues the contractor's right to payment has an equivalent remedy and can resist proceedings for summary judgment on that ground.[30]

Subject to the effect of words showing that it is merely intended to make advances on money not legally due until completion,[31] a progress certificate properly given creates a debt due.[32] Subject to rights of set-off, the contractor can seek summary judgment for the amount certified upon the issue of a certificate for payment of an instalment.[33] If an employer's claim to set-off raises issues which have to be referred to arbitration, payment of the amount due in an interim certificate is not, without express words, a condition precedent to the employer's right to go to arbitration.[34]

Final certificates.   A final certificate may certify the amount finally payable to the contractor under the contract, or the satisfaction of the architect that work conforms with the contract, or both.[35] Upon these matters the architect's decision embodied in his certificate is often binding and conclusive on the parties. This is discussed below. If an architect or engineer issues an unqualified certificate authorising final payment, that is in practice likely to be irrebuttable evidence of his satisfaction, whether or not the contract contains terms providing for certification and whether or not, if it does, they provide for such a certificate to have a final or conclusive effect.[36]

Other certificates.   The contract may empower the architect to certify various matters, such as the happening of an event which entitles the employer to exercise a right of forfeiture,[37] or to record an extension of time given by the

---

[27] See Standard Form of Building Contract, clause 30.2 at p. 605.

[28] *Lamprell* v. *Billericay Union* (1849) 18 L.J.Ex. 282.

[29] *Lubenham* v. *South Pembrokeshire District Council* (1986) 33 B.L.R. 39 at 55 (C.A.).

[30] *C. M. Pillings* v. *Kent Investments* (1985) 30 B.L.R. 80 (C.A.).

[31] See p. 71 and *cf. Canterbury Pipe Lines* v. *Christchurch Drainage* (1979) 16 B.L.R. 76 at 95 (New Zealand Court of Appeal).

[32] *Pickering* v. *Ilfracombe Railway* (1868) L.R. 3 C.P. 235.

[33] *Workman, Clark & Co.* v. *Lloyd Brazileno* [1908] 1 K.B. 968 (C.A.). For summary judgment, see p. 441 and for set-off and counterclaim, see p. 438.

[34] *C. M. Pillings* v. *Kent Investments* (1985) 30 B.L.R. 80 (C.A.).

[35] See, *e.g.* clause 30.7 of the Standard Form of Building Contract discussed at p. 617.

[36] *National Coal Board* v. *Neill* [1985] Q.B. 300 at 308. The judgment expresses it as being factually "conclusive" evidence of satisfaction.

[37] For forfeiture, see p. 236.

architect to the contractor.[38] The architect's decision may be binding and conclusive upon these matters.[39]

Retention money.   It is usual to provide for the retention of a percentage of the value, sometimes subject to a limit as to amount, to provide a fund for the payment of amending defects.[40] In one case the contractor was "entitled ... under certificates ... to payment by the employer from time to time by instalments, when in the opinion of the architect actual work to the value of £1,000 [had] been executed in accordance with the contract, at the rate of 90 per cent. of the value of the work so executed...." It was held that an arbitration award was wrong on the face of it in finding that the contractor was only entitled to 90 per cent. of each completed £1,000; he was entitled to payment of 90 per cent. of the value of work actually executed at the time of granting a certificate.[41]

2. Certificates as Condition Precedent

The contract may show by express words, or upon reading it as a whole, that the architect's[42] certificate is a condition precedent to payment whether interim or final. It is a condition precedent if upon the true construction of the contract, the employer only agrees to pay what is certified by the architect,[43] or only to pay upon a certificate of satisfactory completion by the architect.[44] In such a case if the contractor fails to obtain the certificate required for payment he has no present claim at law or in equity,[45] unless he can show one of the special circumstances discussed in the next section of this chapter. He may, however, have an immediate right of arbitration to seek to secure a certificate or alter the contents of an existing one.[46]

The Court of Appeal of New Zealand has held that a contractor has no implied right of temporary suspension of the works for non-payment upon the

---

[38] See *Sattin* v. *Poole* (1901) H.B.C. (4th ed.), Vol. 2, p. 306 (D.C.). Contrast *Costain International Ltd.* v. *Att.-Gen.* (1983) 23 B.L.R. 48 (Hong Kong Court of Appeal) referred to in n. 20 above. For liquidated damages and extension of time, see pp. 222 *et seq.*

[39] See p. 106.

[40] See, *e.g.* clause 30.4 of the Standard Form of Building Contract discussed at p. 614.

[41] *F. R. Absalom Ltd.* v. *Great Western (London) Garden Village Society* [1933] A.C. 592 at 611 (H.L.).

[42] "Architect" is used to mean the architect as defined by the contract. See "Given by wrong person" at p. 112.

[43] *Sharpe* v. *San Paulo Railway* (1873) L.R. 8 Ch.App. 597 at 612; *Lubenham* v. *South Pembrokeshire District Council* (1986) 33 B.L.R. 39 at 55 (C.A.) considering the 1963 Standard Form of Building Contract; *cf. South Australian Railways Commissioner* v. *Egan* (1973) 47 A.L.J.R. 140.

[44] *Morgan* v. *Birnie* (1833) 9 Bing. 672; *Grafton* v. *Eastern Counties Railway* (1853) 8 Ex. 699; *Scott* v. *Liverpool Corporation* (1858) 28 L.J.Ch. 230; *Westwood* v. *The Secretary of State for India* (1863) 7 L.T. 736; *Wallace* v. *Brandon & Byshottles Urban District Council* (1903) H.B.C. (4th ed.), Vol. 2, p. 362 (C.A.).

[45] *Scott* v. *Liverpool Corporation* (1858) 28 L.J.Ch. 230 at 239; *Glenn* v. *Leith* (1853) 1 Comm. Law Rep. 569; *Stevenson* v. *Watson* (1879) 4 C.P.D. 148; *Morgan* v. *Lariviere* (1875) L.R. 7 H.L. 423 (H.L.).

[46] *Lubenham* v. *South Pembrokeshire District Council* (1986) 33 B.L.R. 39 (C.A.).

wrongful withholding of a progress certificate whose issue was a condition precedent to payment.[47]

The contractor may be able to show that on the wording of the contract a certificate is not a condition precedent to payment.[48] If the contract only requires a certificate showing the architect's satisfaction, the contractor can sue on the contract when he has obtained such a certificate notwithstanding that it does not certify that a sum of money is payable.[49]

Contracts may provide that the issue of various certificates other than payment certificates is a condition precedent to the exercise of certain rights, *e.g.* to deduct liquidated damages,[50] to the right of a main contractor to claim damages for delay from a sub-contractor[51] or to initiate a process leading to contractual determination of the contractor's employment.[52]

Third parties.   Assignees of the contractor are in no better position than the contractor,[53] but third parties whose rights arise on completion may be able to enforce such rights although no certificate of completion has been given. Thus where H lent money to T, a contractor, on the employer's guarantee to repay upon completion of the contract works in accordance with the building contract, it was held that H could recover from the employer when the works were completed in fact, although no certificate of completion had been given as required by the building contract. The contract of guarantee between H and the employer did not require certificated completion.[54] Similarly a claim against a surety under a bond, whose condition was to satisfy damages suffered by the employer from the contractor's default, succeeded without an architect's certificate of the amount of loss suffered by the employer and caused by the determination of the contractor's employment upon receivership.[55] The certificate under the building contract was held to be irrelevant to a claim under the bond.

3. Recovery of Payment without Certificate

Certificate not a condition precedent.   If a certificate is not a condition precedent to recovery, the contractor will obviously be able to recover without one.[56]

---

[47] *Canterbury Pipe Lines* v. *Christchurch Drainage* (1979) 16 B.L.R. 76; *cf. Lubenham* v. *South Pembrokeshire District Council* (1986) 33 B.L.R. 39 at 70 (C.A.).
[48] See the Scottish case of *Howden* v. *Powell Duffryn Steam Coal Co.*, 1912 S.C. 920; *Re Hohenzollern, etc., and City of London Contract Corporation* (1886) 54 L.T. 596, H.B.C. (4th ed.), Vol. 2, p. 100 (C.A.); *cf. London Gas Light Co.* v. *Chelsea Vestry* (1860) 2 L.T. 217.
[49] *Pashby* v. *Birmingham Corporation* (1856) 18 C.B. 2 at 32.
[50] See p. 233.
[51] *Brightside Kilpatrick* v. *Mitchell Construction* [1975] 2 Lloyd's Rep. 493 at 497.
[52] See p. 236 for determination and p. 588 for clause 27 of the Standard Form of Building Contract, where the requirement is a "notice" not a certificate.
[53] *Lewis* v. *Hoare* (1881) 44 L.T. 66 (H.L.). For assignments, see p. 273.
[54] *Ibid.*
[55] *Nene Housing Society* v. *National Westminster Bank* (1980) 16 B.L.R. 22.
[56] See "Certificates as Condition Precedent" at p. 102.

Waiver of condition precedent.   The requirement of a certificate as a condition precedent to payment is for the benefit of the employer. He may therefore waive his right to insist upon a certificate. It is submitted that the same principles apply as in the case of waiver of a condition requiring written orders.[57]

Disqualification of the certifier.   If as a result of fraud, collusion, or otherwise the architect is disqualified as certifier and fails to grant a certificate the condition precedent goes and the contractor can sue.[58]

Prevention by the employer.   The mere failure of the architect to certify where there has been no fraud or collusion or wrongful interference by the employer does not of itself enable the contractor to recover.[59] But if the employer or his agent prevents the architect giving a certificate, the employer cannot rely on its absence, for "no person can take advantage of the non-fulfilment of a condition the performance of which has been hindered by himself."[60] In *Croudace* v. *London Borough of Lambeth*,[61] the architect under the contract retired and no one was appointed to take his place. It was common ground that the contractor's claim for loss and expense under the agreement could not be maintained by action in the absence of a certificate from the architect. The court held nevertheless that the employer's acts and omissions, including but not limited to their failure to appoint a successor architect, amounted to a failure by them to take such steps as were necessary to enable the contractor's claim for loss and expense to be ascertained and amounted to a breach of contract.[62]

If the architect wrongly neglects, or deliberately, as a result of a mistaken view of his powers, refuses to issue a certificate, and the employer concurs in his action and the contractor has done everything necessary for the issue of the certificate, the employer cannot take advantage of the absence of the certificate,[63] at least if there is no relevant arbitration clause. Thus a contract provided that payment should be made upon the issue by the employer's surveyor (acting in the position of an architect) of a certificate that the work had been satisfactorily carried out. The surveyor contended that his function

---

[57] See p. 91.
[58] *Panamena Europea Navigacion* v. *Frederick Leyland* [1947] A.C. 428 (H.L.); *Hickman* v. *Roberts* [1913] A.C. 229 (H.L.); *Brunsden* v. *Beresford* (1883) 1 Cab. & El. 125. For full discussion of disqualification, see p. 114.
[59] *Neale* v. *Richardson* [1938] 1 All E.R. 753 (C.A.); *Botterill* v. *Ware Guardians* (1886) 2 T.L.R. 621; *Cooper* v. *Uttoxeter Burial Board* (1864) 11 L.T. 565; *cf. Kellett* v. *New Mills Urban District Council* (1900) H.B.C. (4th ed.), Vol. 2, p. 298; *Scott* v. *Liverpool Corporation* (1858) 28 L.J.Ch. 230 at 236.
[60] Blackburn J. in *Roberts* v. *Bury Commissioners* (1870) L.R. 5 C.P. 310 at 326; *Panamena Europea Navigacion* v. *Frederick Leyland* [1947] A.C. 428 (H.L.).
[61] (1986) 33 B.L.R. 20 (C.A.).
[62] The court referred to *Smith* v. *Howden Union* H.B.C. (4th ed.), Vol. 2, p. 156.
[63] *Panamena Europea Navigacion* v. *Frederick Leyland* [1947] A.C. 428 (H.L.); *Hotham* v. *East India Co.* (1787) 1 T.R. 638; *Oshawa (City of)* v. *Brennan Paving Co. Ltd.* [1955] S.C.R. 76 (Canadian Supreme Court); *cp. Perini* v. *Commonwealth of Australia* (1969) 12 B.L.R. 82.

of certification extended to economy of time, labour and materials, and demanded, with the concurrence of the employer, certain information for this purpose. It was not given and the surveyor therefore refused to certify. The court held that on the construction of the contract his function of certifying was confined to whether the work had been satisfactorily carried out and that an "illegitimate condition precedent to any consideration of the granting of a certificate," had been insisted on by the surveyor and the employer. Consequently the employer could not rely on the absence of the certificate. If the employer had, contrary to the surveyor, taken the correct view of the surveyor's functions it would have been his duty to appoint another surveyor. Failure to appoint another surveyor would have absolved the contractor from the necessity of obtaining a certificate.[64] There was, however, no arbitration clause in the contract in question. Where there is a wide arbitration clause, the contractor's remedy may be to take immediate arbitration proceedings to secure the appropriate certificate.[65]

Where the interference of the employer's agents delayed works so that they were not completed to time, the employer was not allowed to resist payment on the ground that the absence of the architect's certificate extending time made the contractor liable to penalties.[66]

Death or incapacity of the certifier. The position upon the death or incapacity of the architect depends upon the construction of the contract. The matter may be dealt with expressly,[67] or it may be an implied term that the employer has a right to appoint a new architect.[68] The right may also be a duty and failure to appoint a new architect a breach of contract by the employer entitling the contractor to damages.[69] If there is no term express or implied providing for the appointment of a new architect, it is submitted that the employer cannot rely upon the absence of a certificate caused by the death or incapacity of the architect.[70]

Award superseding a certificate. An arbitration clause may be so worded that on a proper reference the arbitrator can decide whether the architect was

---

[64] *Panamena Europea Navigacion* v. *Frederick Leyland* [1947] A.C. 428 at 435, 436 (H.L.); see also *Kellett* v. *New Mills Urban District Council* (1900) H.B.C. (4th ed.), Vol. 2, p. 298 at 300.

[65] *Lubenham* v. *South Pembrokeshire District Council* (1986) 33 B.L.R. 39 (C.A.) and see p. 49. Contrast *Canterbury Pipe Lines* v. *Christchurch Drainage* (1979) 16 B.L.R. 76 at 120 (New Zealand Court of Appeal) where the employer "not only refused to meet the progress payment but denied the [contractor] the opportunity to obtain redress for it through arbitration." For an article critical of the *Lubenham* decision, see I. N. Duncan Wallace Q.C., "Interim Certificates—Another Heresy? The *Lubenham* Case" (1987) 3 Const.L.J. 172.

[66] *Russell* v. *Sa da Bandeira* (1862) 13 C.B.(N.S.) 149; see also *Roberts* v. *Bury Commissioners* (1870) L.R. 5 C.P. 310. For penalties, used here in the sense of liquidated damages, see p. 222.

[67] See: Articles of Agreement, Standard Form of Building Contract; cases cited under "Given by wrong person" at p. 112.

[68] *cf. Panamena Europea Navigacion* v. *Frederick Leyland* [1947] A.C. 428 at 436 (H.L.).

[69] *Croudace* v. *London Borough of Lambeth* (1986) 33 B.L.R. 20 (C.A.).

[70] *cf. Kellett* v. *New Mills Urban District Council* (1900) H.B.C. (4th ed.), Vol. 2, p. 298 at 300.

right in withholding a certificate, and if he finds in the contractor's favour award a sum of money to be paid notwithstanding the absence of a certificate, a condition precedent.[71]

The refusal of the arbitrator to deal with the matter may enable the contractor to sue in the courts. Thus where an architect was also the arbitrator he refused both to grant a certificate and to arbitrate. The arbitration clause was wide enough to override the clause making certificates a condition precedent. It was held that, neither party having taken any steps to stay the proceedings or appoint a new arbitrator, the court had jurisdiction to deal with the contractor's claim.[72]

4. Binding and Conclusive Certificates

Certificate may be binding and conclusive. An architect in granting ordinary certificates in building contracts is not an arbitrator.[73] But his decision as stated in his certificate may be as binding and conclusive between the parties as if it were an award.[74] Because he is not an arbitrator he cannot be compelled to state his reasons for the purposes of an appeal under Section 1 of the Arbitration Act 1979,[75] and he may not be obliged to observe the rules of natural justice by giving both parties a hearing or other opportunity to state their case.[76] It has been said that the object of making the architect's decision in a final certificate binding and conclusive is to have the benefit of his skill and knowledge as an independent man to decide what is finally due between the parties without recourse to the enormous expense and trouble often involved

---

[71] *Brodie* v. *Cardiff Corporation* [1919] A.C. 337 (H.L.); *Neale* v. *Richardson* [1938] 1 All E.R. 753 (C.A.); *Prestige & Co.* v. *Brettell* [1938] 4 All E.R. 346 (C.A.); *cf. Northern Regional Health Authority* v. *Derek Crouch* [1984] Q.B. 644 (C.A.) and see "Crouch" at p. 389. For arbitration generally, see Chap. 16.

[72] *Neale* v. *Richardson* [1938] 1 All E.R. 753 (C.A.); *cf. Northern Regional Health Authority* v. *Derek Crouch* [1984] Q.B. 644 (C.A.) and see "Crouch" at p. 389. For arbitration generally, see Chap. 16.

[73] *Sutcliffe* v. *Thackrah* [1974] A.C. 727 (H.L.); *cf. Pacific Associates* v. *Baxter* [1990] Q.B. 993 (C.A.) where it was decided that an engineer did not owe the contractor a duty of care in relation to certification. See also p. 340.

[74] *Goodyear* v. *Weymouth Corporation* (1865) 35 L.J.C.P. 12 at 17. It is difficult to be consistent in the use of terms, for words such as "conclusive," "final and conclusive," "binding and conclusive," "final," have been used to describe an architect's certificate or decision against which there is no appeal to the courts, or to arbitration. Such certificates or decisions are frequently called "final," but this is not completely satisfactory, as a final certificate in the sense defined at p. 101 may be conclusive on some matters only, or not conclusive at all—*Robins* v. *Goddard* [1905] 1 K.B. 294 (C.A.), discussed in *East Ham Borough Council* v. *Bernard Sunley & Sons Ltd.* [1966] A.C. 406 at 434, 441, 447 (H.L.).

[75] See p. 412.

[76] See *Hounslow London Borough Council* v. *Twickenham Garden Developments* [1971] Ch. 233 at 259—a decision with reference to a notice under clause 25(1) of the 1963 Standard Form of Building Contract. Most certificates in practice depend on the architect receiving information from the contractor. It is thought that architects would normally be ill advised to issue certificates adverse to the contractor in avoidable ignorance of his case. See further "Parties not heard" at p. 112.

in judicial proceedings.[77] But it may be that the court[78] would entertain an application for a declaration and other relief if the architect has departed from his instructions in a material respect so that either party would be able to say that the certificate was not binding because he had not done what he was appointed to do.[79]

Effect of such certificates.   When parties have agreed that the architect shall decide matters finally between them they are not allowed in the absence of fraud or special circumstances[80] to go behind his decision upon such matters merely because they are dissatisfied with it. Thus, if the question of extras is within the architect's jurisdiction to decide finally, the contractor cannot recover more than the amount allowed by the certificate.[81] Conversely, the employer cannot go behind the certificate and say that a lesser sum is due.[82] If a certificate is given which the contract shows was intended to be a final expression of the architect's satisfaction, the employer is not allowed subsequently to allege that there are any defects.[83]

When is a certificate binding and conclusive?   It is a question of construction in each case to determine whether it was intended that a particular certificate should be conclusive upon the matter with which it purports to deal. Beyond this, it is not possible to formulate a comprehensive test to determine whether a certificate is binding and conclusive.[84] Express words are frequently used such as, for example that "the certificate of the engineer ... shall be binding and conclusive on both parties."[85] It seems that prima facie a final certificate which is a condition precedent to payment is conclusive.[86] Progress certificates are usually not conclusive.[87] An arbitration clause may prevent a certificate from being conclusive.[88]

---

[77] *Sharpe* v. *San Paulo Railway* (1873) L.R. 8 Ch.App. 597, 609, 611; *Tullis* v. *Jacson* [1892] 3 Ch. 441 at 444.

[78] Or arbitrator, if there is a comprehensive arbitration clause—see p. 117.

[79] *Jones* v. *Sherwood Computer Services, The Times,* December 14, 1989 (C.A.), otherwise unreported. See further "Mistake by architect" at p. 113; and consider *Re Davstone Estates Ltd.'s Leases* [1969] 2 Ch. 378 applying *Lee* v. *Showmen's Guild of Great Britain* [1952] 2 Q.B. 329 at 342, 354 (C.A.); *Kaye (P. & M.) Ltd.* v. *Hosier & Dickinson* [1972] 1 W.L.R. 146 at 157 (H.L.)—"The court retains ultimate control in seeing that the architect acts properly and honestly and in accordance with the contract"—Lord Wilberforce.

[80] See pp. 110 *et seq.*

[81] *Sharpe* v. *San Paulo Railway* (1873) L.R. 8 Ch.App. 597; *Brunsden* v. *Staines Local Board* (1884) 1 Cab. & El. 272.

[82] See p. 94.

[83] *Harvey* v. *Lawrence* (1867) 15 L.T. 571; *Bateman (Lord)* v. *Thompson* (1875) H.B.C. (4th ed.), Vol. 2, p. 36 (C.A.); *Dunaberg Railway* v. *Hopkins* (1877) 36 L.T. 733; *Kaye (P. & M.) Ltd.* v. *Hosier & Dickinson* [1972] 1 W.L.R. 146 (H.L.), discussed further on p. 108; *cf. Billyack* v. *Leyland Construction Co. Ltd.* [1968] 1 W.L.R. 471.

[84] *cf. Halsbury* (4th ed.), Vol. 4, p. 616, para. 1209.

[85] *Kennedy* v. *Barrow-in-Furness Corporation* (1909) H.B.C. (4th ed.), Vol. 2, p. 411 at 413 (C.A.). See p. 618 for a discussion of the effect of clause 30.9 of the Standard Form of Building Contract.

[86] *Sharpe* v. *San Paulo Railway* (1873) L.R. 8 Ch.App. 597.

[87] See p. 100.

[88] See p. 117.

In *National Coal Board* v. *Neill*,[89] it was held on a review of the authorities that there was no rule of law or principle of construction applicable to building contracts that, where the contract contains a term that a structure is to be erected in a prescribed manner and to the satisfaction of the employer's architect or engineer, the contractor fulfils that obligation if the architect or engineer is in fact satisfied even though the structure has not been erected in the prescribed manner. The general principles of construction apply and the meaning of any clause must be ascertained from within the particular contract by construing the contract as a whole and giving effect so far as possible to every part of it. In the *National Coal Board* case, the engineer had issued an unqualified certificate of satisfaction, but the obligation to satisfy the engineer was held to be cumulative upon other obligations. The balance of English authority was said to favour a cumulative approach, but there was in fact held to be no particular applicable rule of law.[90]

The paramount consideration is that the question whether, and if so to what extent, a certificate is binding and conclusive "must depend upon the construction of [the] particular contractual documents and though a consideration of the opinions of courts on other words in other contracts in other cases is of assistance the adjudication . . . involves thereafter a return to a study of the contract under review."[91] Modern cases to which reference might with caution[92] be made include:

(i) *East Ham Corporation* v. *Bernard Sunley*,[93] where the arbitration clause in the 1950 Revision of the R.I.B.A. Standard Form of Building Contract was held to be subject to the final certificate clause so that the architect's final certificate was conclusive and could not be reopened by the arbitrator save in the exceptional circumstances therein stated.

(ii) *P. & M. Kaye* v. *Hosier & Dickinson*,[94] where a majority of the House of Lords held that a final certificate issued under a 1963 JCT Standard Form of Building Contract was conclusive in proceedings begun both before and after the date of its issue. The majority refused on procedural grounds to entertain a construction raised for the first time in the House of Lords. Lord Diplock, dissenting, considered that construction and held that the final certificate was conclusive that everything which had to be done had by the date of the certificate been done and all defects made good but that there was no exclusion of claims for alleged earlier defects and their consequences.[95]

---

[89] [1985] Q.B. 300.

[90] *cp.* however, the older cases cited in the *National Coal Board* judgment and also *Stratford Borough Council* v. *Ashman* (1960) N.Z.L.R. 503 at 517 and *Major* v. *Greenfield* (1965) N.Z.L.R. 1035 at 1061.

[91] *Ata Ul Haq* v. *City Council of Nairobi* (1962) 28 B.L.R. 76 at 95 (P.C.); *cp. Mitsui* v. *Att.-Gen. of Hong Kong* (1986) 33 B.L.R. 1 at 18 (P.C.).

[92] It should be particularly noted that the final certificate clause in the Standard Form of Building Contract has been amended on a number of occasions over the years, most recently in 1987.

[93] [1966] A.C. 406 (H.L.).

[94] [1972] 1 W.L.R. 146 (H.L.).

[95] This case is discussed further at p. 248.

(iii) *Ata Ul Haq* v. *City Council of Nairobi*,[96] where it was held that a certificate issued at the beginning of the maintenance period terminated the contractor's obligations subject only to the maintenance period provisions.

(iv) *Fairweather* v. *Asden Securities*,[97] where an Official Referee held under a pre-1976 version of the 1963 JCT Standard Form of Building Contract and following the majority decision in *P. & M. Kaye* v. *Hosier & Dickinson*[98] that the final certificate was conclusive as to time. Once the architect had issued a final certificate, he was *functus officio* and was precluded from subsequently issuing any valid certificate under clause 22.[99]

(v) *H. W. Nevill (Sunblest)* v. *Wm. Press*,[1] where a different Official Referee followed Lord Diplock's dissenting judgment in *P. & M. Kaye* v. *Hosier & Dickinson* in holding that a final certificate under a pre-1976 version of the 1963 JCT Standard Form of Building Contract was not conclusive as to consequential losses suffered by the employer between practical completion and the date of the final certificate.

(vi) *William Hill* v. *Bernard Sunley*,[2] where the Court of Appeal held that a final certificate which was conclusive to bar a contractual claim also barred an equivalent claim in tort.[3]

(vii) *Crestar* v. *Carr*,[4] where the Court of Appeal decided that the final certificate under a pre-1980 JCT Minor Works Contract had no conclusive effect.

"And" clauses. A contractor must frequently complete work according to a specification or to a certain standard *and* to the satisfaction of the architect. It is a question of construction in each case whether this imposes a double obligation on the contractor.[5] In some cases it has been held that it does not, in the sense that when the architect had given a certificate of satisfaction the employer was not permitted to give evidence showing that the work was not according to the specification or the required standard.[6] Where work was to be completed in accordance with plans and a specification, the work to be carried

---

[96] (1962) 28 B.L.R. 76 (P.C.); see also *Loke Hong Kee* v. *United Overseas Land* (1982) 23 B.L.R. 35 (P.C.), a one-off decision reached as a matter of pure construction without reference to any previous authority.

[97] (1979) 12 B.L.R. 40.

[98] [1972] 1 W.L.R. 146 (H.L.).

[99] *cf. E.C.C. Quarries* v. *Merriman* (1988) 45 B.L.R. 90.

[1] (1981) 20 B.L.R. 78.

[2] (1982) 22 B.L.R. 1 (C.A.). See also *Wharf Properties* v. *Eric Cumine Associates* (1984) 29 B.L.R. 106 (Hong Kong High Court)—deciding that a subcontractor's final certificate was conclusive and following *William Hill* v. *Bernard Sunley* on the tort point.

[3] For tortious claims generally, see Chap. 7 and in particular pp. 170 *et seq.*

[4] (1987) 37 B.L.R. 113 (C.A.).

[5] *National Coal Board* v. *Neill* [1985] Q.B. 300.

[6] *Harvey* v. *Lawrence* (1867) 15 L.T. 571; *Bateman (Lord)* v. *Thompson* (1875) H.B.C. (4th ed.), Vol. 2, p. 36 (C.A.); *Dunaberg Railway* v. *Hopkins* (1877) 36 L.T. 733.

out to the satisfaction of the surveyor and local sanitary inspector, and they expressed their satisfaction upon completion, and defects then appeared, it was held that their approval was merely an added protection to the employer. It was not conclusive, so that the employer was entitled to recover damages.[7]

Expiration of time.   The contract may provide that a certificate is not to become conclusive until the expiration of a certain period from its issue,[8] or that it shall not be conclusive if either party takes prescribed steps, *e.g.* starts arbitration proceedings, within a prescribed time.[9]

5. Attacking a Certificate

In addition to questions of construction whose answer may be that the certificate is not conclusive, there may be other grounds on which a particular certificate, when given, can be successfully attacked and set aside. This involves a consideration not only of the parties' intention to be derived from the contract, but of their conduct and that of the architect.

(a) *Not within the architect's jurisdiction*

The architect's decision is not conclusive upon matters which are not within his jurisdiction to decide.[10] His decision may be conclusive on some matters but not on others.[11]

Employer's breach of contract.   It seems that clear language is required before an architect's powers of certification extend to cover breaches of contract by the employer,[12] so that in the absence of such words if an architect gives a certificate for payment and the contractor has been put to loss and expense by the employer's breach of contract, such as delay or interference, the certificate is not conclusive upon the contractor's claim for damages unless it is

---

[7] *Newton Abbot Development Co. Ltd.* v. *Stockman Bros.* (1931) 47 T.L.R. 616, followed in *Billyack* v. *Leyland Construction Co. Ltd.* [1968] 1 W.L.R. 471; see also *Bird* v. *Smith* (1848) 12 Q.B. 786; *Petrofina S.A. of Brussels* v. *Compagnia Italiana, etc.* (1937) 53 T.L.R. 650 at 653 (C.A.)—dealing with the construction of a charterparty; *Minster Trust Ltd.* v. *Traps Tractors* [1954] 1 W.L.R. 963.

[8] See, *e.g. Bateman (Lord)* v. *Thompson* (1875) H.B.C. (4th ed.), Vol. 2, p. 36 (C.A.).

[9] See p. 610 for the relevant provision of the Standard Form of Building Contract.

[10] See *Northampton Gaslight Co.* v. *Parnell* (1855) 24 L.J.C.P. 60; *Russell* v. *Sa da Bandeira* (1862) 13 C.B.(N.S.) 149; *Roberts* v. *Bury Commissioners* (1870) L.R. 5 C.P. 310; *Ashwell and Nesbit* v. *Allen* (1912) H.B.C. (4th ed.), Vol. 2, p. 462 (C.A.); *Panamena, etc.* v. *Frederick Leyland & Co. Ltd.* [1947] A.C. 428 (H.L.).

[11] See *Re Meadows and Kenworthy* (1896) H.B.C. (4th ed.), Vol. 2, p. 265 (C.A. affd. H.L.); *East Ham Borough Council* v. *Bernard Sunley & Sons Ltd.* [1966] A.C. 406 (H.L.), explaining the final certificate under the 1939 edition R.I.B.A. form (pre-1957 revision). See also *Kaye (P. & M.) Ltd.* v. *Hosier & Dickinson* [1972] 1 W.L.R. 146 (H.L.) referred to in the text above.

[12] *Russell* v. *Sa da Bandeira* (1862) 13 C.B.(N.S.) 149; *Roberts* v. *Bury Commissioners* (1870) L.R. 5 C.P. 310; *Lawson* v. *Wallasey Local Board* (1883) 48 L.T. 507 (C.A.).

an award upon a proper reference of the dispute.[13] However, the contractor may waive his rights to object to the certificate by expressly seeking the architect's decision on the matter.[14]

New contract.   The architect's power of certifying under a contract cannot extend to matters which have arisen under a new and independent contract.[15]

Outside time limit.   If there is a time limit for the giving of a certificate, a purported certificate given after the expiry of the time limit is void and of no effect unless the parties agree to extend the time.[16]

(b) *Not properly made*

A certificate is invalid, and therefore not conclusive, if it is not properly made in accordance with the contract.[17] This will also be so if any necessary pre-condition as to its issue has not been fulfilled.[18]

Form of certificate.   The certificate must be in the form, if any, required by the contract.[19] Thus a mere checking of the contractor's account for extras was held not to be a certificate of satisfactory completion.[20] Where, under clause 66 of the I.C.E. Conditions (1955 edition), a "decision" was required as a condition precedent to arbitration, an informal rejection of the contractor's claims was held not to amount to such decision.[21] If the architect is merely required to certify his satisfaction with no express requirement for a written certificate, an oral statement of satisfaction is sufficient.[22] In all cases it must be clear that there was an intention to issue the certificate in question and that it was in substance what the contract required.[23] The ordinary rules of

---

[13] *Lawson* v. *Wallasey Local Board* (1883) 48 L.T. 507 (C.A.), upholding the Divisional Court (1883) 11 Q.B.D. 229, but on different grounds; *cf. Sattin* v. *Poole* (1901) H.B.C. (4th ed.), Vol. 2, p. 306 (D.C.). For extension of time, see Chap. 9, p. 233. Note that a valid extension of times does not necessarily extinguish the contractor's claim for damages—*Roberts* v. *Bury Commissioners* (1870) L.R. 5 C.P. 310 at 327.

[14] *Sattin* v. *Poole* (1901) H.B.C. (4th ed.), Vol. 2, p. 306 (D.C.).

[15] *Trade Indemnity Co.* v. *Workington Harbour and Dock Board* [1937] A.C. 1 (H.L.).

[16] *E.C.C. Quarries* v. *Merriman* (1988) 45 B.L.R. 90. The engineer's decision under clause 66 of the I.C.E. Conditions, given with the contractor's agreement after the stipulated time had expired, was held to be final and binding when there was no reference to arbitration within the subsequent three months' time limit. It is understood, however, that in fact the employer did not consent to the time extension for the engineer's decision.

[17] *Lamprell* v. *Billericay Union* (1849) 18 L.J. Ex. 282; *Coleman* v. *Gittins* (1884) 1 T.L.R. 8, where an employer successfully resisting payment on a technicality was not awarded his costs; *Kaye (P. & M.) Ltd.* v. *Hosier & Dickinson* [1972] 1 W.L.R. 146 at 157 (H.L.).

[18] *Crestar* v. *Carr* (1987) 37 B.L.R. 113 (C.A.).

[19] See also "Formal requirements" at p. 99.

[20] *Morgan* v. *Birnie* (1833) 9 Bing. 672; *Elmes* v. *Burgh Market Co.* (1891) H.B.C. (4th ed.), Vol. 2, p. 170 at 171.

[21] *Monmouthshire County Council* v. *Costelloe and Kemple* (1965) 63 L.G.R. 429 (C.A.) also 5 B.L.R. 83.

[22] *Roberts* v. *Watkins* (1863) 14 C.B.(N.S.) 592; *Elmes* v. *Burgh Market Co.* (1891) H.B.C. (4th ed.), Vol. 2, p. 170.

[23] See *Token Construction Company Ltd.* v. *Charlton Estates Ltd.* (1973) 1 B.L.R. 48 (C.A.) (not overruled on this point by *Modern Engineering (Bristol) Ltd.* v. *Gilbert Ash (Northern) Ltd.* [1974] A.C. 689 (H.L.)) applying a passage from *Minster Trust Ltd.* v. *Traps Tractors Ltd.* [1954] 1 W.L.R. 963 at 982, Devlin J.

construction apply[24] so that the test of intention, it is submitted, is objective. It is thought that evidence of surrounding circumstances such as relevant letters or conversations would frequently be admissible in deciding whether a document (or, in the unusual case, an oral statement) was the certificate. Thus in *London Borough of Merton* v. *Lowe*,[25] a certificate was held upon the facts of the case to be the final certificate, although not so expressed upon its face, by reference in particular to an accompanying letter which said "We are enclosing the final certificate."

Delegation of duties.   In giving his certificate, the architect is entitled to make use of the assistance of others, such as, for example, a quantity surveyor, for detailed matters of measurement and valuation, but the certificate must be his. He cannot delegate his whole function of certifying.[26] An engineer may receive help from his resident or project engineer. "In the commercial world many decisions are made by people such as [the engineer], who append their signatures to the letters drafted by others. It would require compelling evidence to establish in such circumstances that the decision was not that of the signatory."[27]

Given by wrong person.   A certificate must be given by the person or persons authorised by the contract.[28] Thus, if a particular person is named as the certifier, in the absence of a term indicating the contrary, that person and no other can give the certificate.[29] Where the contract identifies the certifier by description, as, for example, "anyone whom from time to time the (employer) might choose to select as chief engineer,"[30] or "AB or other the engineer" of the employer,[31] then the person who is the properly appointed engineer (or architect as the case may be) at the time when the certificate is required to be given has power to certify.[32]

Parties not heard.   The architect is not normally bound to give anything in the nature of a formal hearing.[33] Where the contract provided that the certi-

---

[24] See Chap. 3.

[25] (1981) 18 B.L.R. 130 (C.A.).

[26] *Clemence* v. *Clarke* (1880) H.B.C. (4th ed.), Vol. 2, p. 54 at 59 (C.A.); *cf. Burden Ltd.* v. *Swansea Corporation* [1957] 1 W.L.R. 1167 at 1173 (H.L.); *cf.* also *Croudace* v. *London Borough of Lambeth* (1986) 33 B.L.R. 20 (C.A.) where the finding of the employer's breach of contract in not appointing a new architect implicitly assumes that his duties cannot be delegated.

[27] *Anglian Water Authority* v. *R.D.L. Contracting* (1988) 43 B.L.R. 98 at 112.

[28] *Lamprell* v. *Billericay Union* (1849) 18 L.J. Ex. 282.

[29] *Ess* v. *Truscott* (1837) 2 M. & W. 385; *Att.-Gen.* v. *Briggs* (1855) 1 Jur.(N.S.) 1084.

[30] *Ranger* v. *G.W. Railway* (1854) 5 H.L.C. 72 at 91 (H.L.).

[31] *Kellett* v. *Mayor of Stockport* (1906) 70 J.P. 154. See also *Cunliffe* v. *Hampton Wick Local Board* (1893) H.B.C. (4th ed.), Vol. 2, p. 250 (C.A.); also 9 T.L.R. 378.

[32] *Ranger* v. *G.W. Railway* (1854) 5 H.L.C. 72 (H.L.); *cp. Croudace* v. *London Borough of Lambeth* (1986) 33 B.L.R. 20 at 33 (C.A.)—the architect under the contract was the employer's "Chief Architect," but the Court of Appeal's decision seems to be that a successor had to be nominated under the contract, not merely to the office.

[33] See Megarry J. in *Hounslow London Borough Council* v. *Twickenham Garden Developments* [1971] 1 Ch. 233 at 259, applying *Panamena, etc.* v. *Leyland* [1947] A.C. 428; *A. C. Hatrick (N.Z.) Ltd.* v. *Nelson Carlton Construction Co. Ltd.* [1964] N.Z.L.R. 72.

fier's decision on a wide range of matters was to "be final and without appeal" it was said that he could if he wished hear arguments from the parties, and state his own view to obtain their opinions, provided that he gave equal opportunity to each party and did not allow his judgment to be influenced by directions given to him in his capacity solely as agent for the employer.[34] On the special wording of another contract it was said that he must hear the parties before giving his certificate in relation to any dispute.[35]

Mistake by architect. A certificate of the architect intended to be binding and conclusive "cannot be impeached for mere negligence, or mere mistake or mere idleness on the part of the architect."[36] The position was formerly said to be different where there is a valuation.[37] But in *Campbell* v. *Edwards*,[38] Lord Denning M.R. said that the law has been transformed because the parties now have, since the decisions of the House of Lords in *Sutcliffe* v. *Thackrah*[39] and *Arenson* v. *Arenson*,[40] a claim for negligence against architects and valuers.[41] The distinction sometimes made between a speaking and a non-speaking valuation is not a relevant distinction, the real question being whether it is possible to say from all the evidence which is properly before the court what the valuer or certifier has done and why he has done it. The first step is to see what the parties have agreed as a matter of contract to remit to the expert. If he has departed from his instructions in a material respect, either party would be able to say that the certificate was not binding because he had not done what he was appointed to do.[42] Otherwise, "it is simply the law of contract. If two persons agree that the price of property should be fixed by a valuer on whom they agree, and he gives that valuation honestly and in good faith, they are bound

---

[34] Channell J. in *Page* v. *Llandaff, etc., District Council* (1901) H.B.C. (4th ed.), Vol. 2, p. 316 at 320. For employer's influence, see p. 116.

[35] *Eaglesham* v. *McMaster* [1920] 2 K.B. 169 at 174—a contract in which the architect was both certifier and arbitrator. Such a contract is unlikely today because of the effect of the Arbitration Act 1950, s.24(1), see p. 395. See also *Armstrong* v. *South London Tramways Co.* (1891) 7 T.L.R. 123 (C.A.).

[36] Lindley L.J. in *Clemence* v. *Clarke* (1880) H.B.C. (4th ed.), Vol. 2, p. 54 at 65 (C.A.); *Goodyear* v. *Weymouth Corporation* (1865) 35 L.J.C.P. 12; *Sharpe* v. *San Paulo Railway* (1873) L.R. 8 Ch.App. 597. See also *Campbell* v. *Edwards* [1976] 1 W.L.R. 403 (C.A.)—valuation not impeachable for mistake; *Toepfer* v. *Continental Grain Co.* [1974] 1 Lloyd's Rep. 11 (C.A.)—grain purchase— "Official ... certificates of inspection to be final as to quality." Binding, despite admitted mistake—but it was a certificate *in rem* (see p. 94).

[37] *Collier* v. *Mason* (1858) 25 Beav. 200; approved in *Dean* v. *Prince* [1954] Ch. 409 (C.A.), distinguished in *Toepfer* v. *Continental Grain Co.* [1974] 1 Lloyd's Rep. 11 (C.A.) and said by Lord Denning M.R. in *Campbell* v. *Edwards* [1976] 1 W.L.R. 403 at 407 (C.A.) to require reconsideration. See now *Jones* v. *Sherwood Computer Services, The Times,* December 14, 1989 (C.A.) (otherwise unreported).

[38] *Campbell* v. *Edwards* [1976] 1 W.L.R. 403 at 407 (C.A.).

[39] [1974] A.C. 727 (H.L.).

[40] [1977] A.C. 405 (H.L.).

[41] Whereas an employer may have a claim against his architect, the better view appears to be that a contractor normally does not—see *Pacific Associates* v. *Baxter* [1990] Q.B. 993 (C.A.) and see generally pp. 340 *et seq.*

[42] *Jones* v. *Sherwood Computer Services, The Times,* December 14, 1989 (C.A.) (otherwise unreported).

by it. Even if he has made a mistake they are still bound by it. The reason is because they have agreed to be bound by it."[43]

It has never been held that the law relating to valuations also applies to a conclusive architect's certificate. The point is unlikely to arise factually since it is improbable both that an architect's certificate would be open to the limited challenge indicated in the previous paragraph and that the parties had failed to take steps to prevent it becoming conclusive, *e.g.* by starting arbitration proceedings within the prescribed time. It is suggested, however, that there is no relevant distinction in principle between conclusive share valuations and conclusive architects' certificates.

(c) *Disqualification of the certifier*

Professional independence. An architect is not an arbitrator but he has "two different types of function to perform. In many matters he is bound to act on his client's instructions, whether he agrees with them or not; but in many other matters requiring professional skill he must form and act on his own opinion."[44] This was said with reference to the architect's position under the Standard Form of Building Contract but it may be taken as applicable to most forms of building contract where the architect performs the traditional duties as agent for the employer of supervision and of certification.

The employer and the contractor make their contract on the understanding that in all matters where the architect has to apply his professional skill he will act in a fair and unbiased[45] manner in applying the terms of the contract.[46] Such matters include not only certificates for payment and for satisfaction with the works but many instances where the architect has to form a professional opinion upon matters which will affect the amount paid to (or to be deducted from) the contractor.

If the architect fails to act fairly where the contract requires him to do so he is said to be disqualified as a certifier and his certificates are of no effect,[47] and

---

[43] Lord Denning M.R. in *Campbell* v. *Edwards* [1976] 1 W.L.R. 403 at 407 (C.A.); *Jones* v. *Sherwood Computer Services, The Times*, December 14, 1989 (C.A.) (otherwise unreported), not following *Burgess* v. *Puchase & Sons* [1983] Ch. 216; *cf. Baber* v. *Kenwood Manufacturing* [1978] 1 Lloyd's Rep. 175 (C.A.).

[44] Lord Reid in *Sutcliffe* v. *Thackrah* [1974] A.C. 727 at 737 (H.L.). There are many old cases (excerpts from which are set out in earlier editions of this book) referring to the dual function or dual capacity as it was sometimes called of the architect. Their basis is not, it is submitted, essentially different from the exposition by the House of Lords in *Sutcliffe* v. *Thackrah* but they frequently use words which speak in terms of the architect as an adjudicator or quasi-arbitrator and these terms should no longer be used. It is suggested that it is still, however, correct and useful when referring to those functions where the architect must act fairly to say that he must act "independently."

[45] See further on this the heading "Known interests do not disqualify" at p. 116.

[46] *Sutcliffe* v. *Thackrah* [1974] A.C. 727 at 737 (H.L.). Lord Morris at 751 and Lord Salmon at 759 also use the term "impartially" as part of the description of the duty of the architect. But in the context they do not use it as suggesting that the architect should or could have the impartiality of an arbitrator. As to this see Lord Dilhorne at 756–757.

[47] *Hickman* v. *Roberts* [1913] A.C. 229 (H.L.).

he remains disqualified unless the contractor with full knowledge of the facts waives the breach.[48] An employer may, however, be able to rely on an erroneous certificate issued by an honest but incompetent architect.[49]

Fraud, collusion, dishonesty.   Fraud or collusion with one of the parties, or dishonesty, disqualifies the certifier.[50] It has been held that a clause providing that the architect's certificate should not be set aside or attempted to be set aside on the ground of fraud or collusion was not void as against public policy, and consequently an allegation of fraud on the part of the architect in giving a certificate was not entertained by the court.[51] The decision has been strongly criticised by Scrutton L.J.,[52] and is, it is submitted, open to review by the Court of Appeal.[53]

Failure to certify independently.   Without any fraud or turpitude on the part of the architect he may so mistake his position, or lack the firmness to repel unworthy communications by one of the parties, that he loses the independence required of him and therefore becomes disqualified.[54] Thus in *Hickman* v. *Roberts*[55] the architect failed to issue certificates at the proper time, and wrote to the contractor saying, "had you better not call and see my clients, because in the face of their instructions to me I cannot issue a certificate whatever my own private opinion in the matter." It was held that he had become so much under the influence of the employer that he had lost his independence, and had not recovered it when he gave a final certificate. It was therefore set aside.

Unknown interests.   A certifier is disqualified if he conceals any unusual interest which might influence his mind as certifier, such as a promise to the employer (as opposed to a mere estimate) that the final cost should not exceed a certain figure.[56]

---

[48] *Ibid.* at 233, 235, 238. See also *Thornton Hall & Partners* v. *Wembley Electrical Appliances Ltd.* [1947] 2 All E.R. 630 at 634 (C.A.).

[49] *Lubenham* v. *South Pembrokeshire District Council* (1986) 33 B.L.R. 39.

[50] *South Eastern Railway* v. *Warton* (1861) 2 F. & F. 457; *Sharpe* v. *San Paulo Railway* (1873) L.R. 8 Ch.App. 597.

[51] *Tullis* v. *Jacson* [1892] 3 Ch. 441.

[52] *Czarnikow* v. *Roth, Schmidt & Co.* [1922] 2 K.B. 478 at 488 (C.A.); *cf. Scott* v. *Liverpool Corporation* (1856) 25 L.J.Ch. 230 at 232.

[53] See Denning L.J. in *Lazarus Estates Ltd.* v. *Beasley* [1956] 1 Q.B. 702 at 712 (C.A.)—"Fraud unravels everything. . . . It vitiates judgments, contracts and all transactions whatsoever." See also *Re Davstone Estates Ltd.'s Leases* [1969] 2 Ch. 378.

[54] *Hickman* v. *Roberts* [1913] A.C. 229 (H.L.); *Panamena* v. *Frederick Leyland & Co.* [1947] A.C. 428 at 437 (H.L.). For a discussion of the position of certifiers who are not, or are not in the position of, architects, see the case, not on a building contract, of *Minster Trust Ltd.* v. *Traps Tractors Ltd.* [1954] 1 W.L.R. 963.

[55] [1913] A.C. 229 (H.L.).

[56] *Kimberley* v. *Dick* (1871) L.R. 13 Eq. 1; *Kemp* v. *Rose* (1858) 1 Giff. 258. The giving of an estimate is part of an architect's duties under the R.I.B.A. Architect's Appointment (at p. 950) and this must be known to contractors.

Known interests do not disqualify.   The known interests of the architect at the time of entering into the contract do not disqualify him.[57] The interests of the architect which the contractor knows of, or, it is submitted, must be taken to know of, at the time of entering into the contract include:

(1)   that the architect will have given an estimate of the cost to the employer;
(2)   that he is paid by and is liable to dismissal by or in damages for negligence to the employer; and
(3)   that he "has in diverse ways to look after the interest"[58] of the employer, including supervising the works to see that they comply with the contract.

There is "neither unfairness nor partisanship in ensuring that the work is properly carried out."[59] A contractor cannot therefore claim that the architect "must be in the position of an independent arbitrator, who has no other duty which involves acting in the interests of one of the parties."[60]

The architect may consult with the employer, and report to him on the quality of the work, and upon the contractor's expenditure and give him an estimate of the proper sum to be paid to the contractor. Such actions, in the absence of fraud or collusion, do not disqualify him, provided he does not submit to the employer's control and influence[61] so as to be incapable of forming an independent view when he comes to give his certificate.[62] On a legal matter such as the construction of the contract the architect is entitled to consult with the employer's solicitor and counsel,[63] provided, it is submitted, he treats what they say not as a direction but as advice only which he is in no way bound to follow. Architects often in practice may think it more appropriate to take independent advice.

An architect is not disqualified merely because he is a shareholder in,[64] or even the president of,[65] the employer company, or is the employee of the

---

[57] *Bristol Corporation* v. *Aird* [1913] A.C. 241 at 258 (H.L.); *cf.* the position of an arbitrator under the Arbitration Act 1950, s.24(1). See p. 395.

[58] *Sutcliffe* v. *Thackrah* [1974] A.C. 727 at 741 (H.L.).

[59] *Ibid.* See also *Scott* v. *Carluke Local Authority* (1879) 6 R. 616 at 617; *Cross* v. *Leeds Corporation* (1902) H.B.C. (4th ed.), Vol. 2, p. 339 (C.A.); but noting that the terminology now should be that used in *Sutcliffe* v. *Thackrah.* See also p. 312 for a full discussion of the architect's duties to the employer of which duties the contractor must, it is submitted, at least in outline, be treated as having knowledge.

[60] *Panamena* v. *Frederick Leyland & Co.* [1947] A.C. 428 at 437 (H.L.).

[61] See, *e.g.* the facts of *Hickman* v. *Roberts* [1913] A.C. 229 (H.L.).

[62] *Panamena* v. *Frederick Leyland & Co.* [1947] A.C. 428 (H.L.) distinguishing *Hickman* v. *Roberts* [1913] A.C. 229 (H.L.) and approving the Scottish cases of *Scott* v. *Carluke L.A.* (1879) 6 R. 616 and *Halliday* v. *Hamilton's Trustees* (1903) 5 F. 800. For what amounts to interference or obstruction in the issue of certificates where the Standard Form of Building Contract is used, see excerpt from *Burden* v. *Swansea Corporation* [1957] 1 W.L.R. 1167 at 1180 (H.L.) at p. 599. Such conduct would, it is submitted, if acquiesced in by the architect, disqualify him.

[63] See *Panamena* v. *Frederick Leyland & Co.* [1947] A.C. 428 at 437, 444 (H.L.).

[64] *Ranger* v. *G.W. Railway* (1854) 5 H.L.C. 72 (H.L.); *Hill* v. *South Staffs Railway* (1865) 12 L.T. 63, 65.

[65] *Panamena* v. *Frederick Leyland & Co.* [1947] A.C. 428 (H.L.).

employer,[66] provided that the contractor knows, or it seems, must be taken to know, of the architect's interest.[67] With local authority contracts, the architect is very often an employee of the employer.

(d) *Effect of an arbitration clause*

The effect of an arbitration clause in a contract upon the conclusiveness of a certificate must depend upon the words of each contract. The following are possibilities:

  (i) *No effect.* The certificate may remain conclusive in a court of law and not be within the scope of the arbitration agreement.[68]

 (ii) *Certificate not conclusive at all.* Where a contract provides that either the architect's certificate or the arbitrator's award is a condition precedent to payment the courts of law do not have jurisdiction to open up the architect's certificate merely because there was a right of appeal against it to an arbitrator.[69] But the wording of the arbitration clause may show that the certificate was not intended to be binding at all.[70]

(iii) *Certificate conclusive except upon arbitration.* The certificate may be conclusive in a court of law, but subject to review by arbitration under an arbitration clause in the contract.[71] Where an arbitration clause empowers the arbitrator to open up, review and revise certificates, it may be that the court does not have equivalent powers[72] other than by agreement between the parties under section 43A of the Supreme Court Act 1981[73] when this comes into force.

 (iv) *Certificate or award conclusive.* It seems that if a contract provides that either a certificate of the architect or an award of the arbitrator is to be conclusive, the certificate is conclusive if given before a dispute had arisen but not if given thereafter.[74]

---

[66] *Cross* v. *Leeds Corporation* (1902) H.B.C. (4th ed.), Vol. 2, p. 339 (C.A.).

[67] *Ranger* v. *G.W. Railway* (1854) 5 H.L.C. 72 (H.L.).

[68] *Re Meadows and Kenworthy* (1896) H.B.C. (4th ed.), Vol. 2, p. 265 (C.A., affd. H.L.); *Brunsden* v. *Staines Local Board* (1884) 1 Cab. & El. 272; *East Ham Borough Council* v. *Bernard Sunley & Sons Ltd.* [1966] A.C. 406 (H.L.).

[69] *Sharpe* v. *San Paulo Railway* (1873) L.R. 8 Ch.App. 597 at 613; *Eaglesham* v. *McMaster* [1920] 2 K.B. 169.

[70] *Robins* v. *Goddard* [1905] 1 K.B. 294 (C.A.) a decision correct on its facts but not apparently authority for any general principle—*East Ham Borough Council* v. *Bernard Sunley & Sons Ltd.* [1966] A.C. 406 at 434, 441, 447 (H.L.). See also *Ranger* v. *G.W. Railway* (1854) 5 H.L.C. 72 (H.L.); *National Coal Board* v. *Neill* [1985] Q.B. 300 at 309.

[71] *Sharpe* v. *San Paulo Railway* (1873) L.R. 8 Ch.App. 597; *Clemence* v. *Clarke* (1880) H.B.C. (4th ed.), Vol. 2, p. 54 at 65; *Eaglesham* v. *McMaster* [1920] 2 K.B. 169.

[72] See *Northern Regional Health Authority* v. *Derek Crouch* [1984] Q.B. 644 (C.A.) and see "Crouch" at p. 389.

[73] As inserted by s.100 of the Courts and Legal Services Act 1990.

[74] *Lloyd Bros.* v. *Milward* (1895) H.B.C. (4th ed.), Vol. 2, p. 262 (C.A.); *Milestone* v. *Yates* [1938] 2 All E.R. 439.

CHAPTER 6

EXCUSES FOR NON-PERFORMANCE

1. Inaccurate Statements Generally

Many disputes arise as to the effect of inaccurate statements. In the invitation to tender and other negotiations leading up to the conclusion of a contract, statements of fact may be made by the employer or his agent about such matters as the quantities of work involved, the nature of the site or the methods by which the work can be carried out. Such statements, if they are intended to be acted upon by the contractor, are termed representations.[1]

Contractual term.   If a statement has been expressly made a term of a contract, *e.g.* where a report about soil conditions is incorporated into the contract and expressly warranted to be true, the plaintiff's remedy, if its inaccuracy causes him loss, is to claim damages for breach of the contract.[2] If such a statement does not form part of the contract, and did not act as an inducement to the contractor to enter into the contract, it is of no legal effect.[3]

---

[1] *Priestley* v. *Stone* (1888) 4 T.L.R. 730; H.B.C. (4th ed.), Vol. 2, p. 134 (C.A.). For a case where a statement of belief as to a fact involved a representation of having reasonable grounds for that belief, see *Brown* v. *Raphael* [1958] Ch. 636 (C.A.). The general principles set out in this section and Section 4 of this chapter apply equally to the employer seeking a remedy although the difference in circumstances reduces the opportunities for their application.

[2] See Chap. 8.

[3] See *Edginton* v. *Fitzmaurice* (1885) 29 Ch.D. 459 (C.A.).

Misrepresentation. An untrue representation is a misrepresentation. A misrepresentation which induces[4] the making of a contract and causes[5] loss may result in legal liability:

(1) if it is made fraudulently[6]; or

(2) if it is an actionable negligent misstatement[7]; or

(3) under the Misrepresentation Act 1967[8]; or

(4) if it is or becomes a collateral warranty.[9]

Additionally innocent misrepresentation may in certain circumstances entitle the other party to an order rescinding the contract or to elect to rescind it.[10]

Mere "puff." A "puff" is a statement which by its nature, and in the context in which it is made, is not intended to have legal effect[11]—a statement which any ordinary reasonable man would take "with a large pinch of salt."[12] An announcement by a builder that he is the best builder in town is likely to be a mere "puff."

Honest opinion. A mere statement of honest opinion not impliedly involving a statement of fact is not actionable.[13] But "the word 'representation' is an extremely wide term; I cannot see why one should not be making a representation when giving information or when stating one's opinion or belief."[14] Circumstances which can impliedly give rise to a statement of opinion involving a statement of fact include those where facts are not equally known to both sides, where a statement of opinion by one who knows the facts best very often involves a statement by him of material fact.[15] A misstatement of material fact is one of the elements in a claim for, or based on, misrepresentation.[16] The category of a mere statement of honest opinion is to be distinguished from that of the negligent misstatement made by a person in circumstances in which he owes a duty of care to the plaintiff.[17]

---

[4] Whether there has been a misrepresentation inducing a contract depends on all the facts including, in an appropriate case, the contents and effect of a non-contractual notice requiring the party to satisfy himself of the correctness of statements made—*Cremdean* v. *Nash* (1977) 241 E.G. 837 upheld at (1977) 244 E.G. 547; *cf. JEB Fasteners* v. *Marks Bloom & Co.* [1983] 1 All E.R. 583 (C.A.).

[5] See *Strover* v. *Harrington* [1988] Ch. 390 at 411.

[6] See "Fraudulent misrepresentation" at p. 122.

[7] See generally Chap. 7, Section 3 and in particular "Negligent misstatement" at p. 174.

[8] See Section 4 of this chapter.

[9] See Section 5 of this chapter.

[10] See "Innocent misrepresentation" below.

[11] *Carlill* v. *Carbolic Smokeball Company* [1893] 1 Q.B. 256 at 261, 266 (C.A.).

[12] See *De Beers Limited* v. *International Company Limited* [1975] 1 W.L.R. 972 at 978.

[13] *Bisset* v. *Wilkinson* [1927] A.C. 177 (P.C.).

[14] Bridge L.J. in *Cremdean Properties* v. *Nash* (1977) 244 E.G. 547 at 551 (C.A.) with reference to use of "representation" in the Misrepresentation Act 1967.

[15] *Bisset* v. *Wilkinson* [1927] A.C. 177 at 182 (P.C.). *Esso Petroleum Company Limited* v. *Mardon* [1976] Q.B. 801 at 826, 830 (C.A.) discussed at p. 132.

[16] See above.

[17] Discussed at pp. 174 *et seq.*

2. Misrepresentation—before 1964

Two landmarks in the development of the law of misrepresentation are the case in 1964 of *Hedley Byrne* v. *Heller & Partners*[18] which developed the tort of negligent misstatement and the Misrepresentation Act 1967 which introduced a statutory cause of action for misrepresentation for statements made after April 21, 1967. Before 1964 it was thought that no claim could arise out of a negligent misstatement which was not a breach of contract or a breach of a fiduciary duty.[19] The Misrepresentation Act is not a code of law but a statutory amendment to existing law and an understanding of the old law is still necessary since many cases still of importance cannot otherwise be understood. The developments are in the main additions to the previous law whose principles and remedies largely remain.

Innocent misrepresentation. Before 1964, the general principle was that a person induced to enter into a contract by an innocent misrepresentation of a material fact was entitled, upon discovering the falsity of the representation, to rescission of the contract, but was not entitled to recover damages unless the misrepresentation was also a breach of contract.[20] The remedy of rescission remains.[21] The injured party either takes proceedings for an order rescinding the contract, or elects to rescind and refuses to carry out the contract and, if sued for breach, sets up the misrepresentation by way of defence.[22] The rescission is ineffective until it is communicated to the other party unless that other party prevented communication fraudulently.[23] Subject to matters discussed in the next paragraph, any misrepresentation which in fact induces a person to enter into a contract entitles him to rescind it and the question whether or not the misrepresentation would have induced a reasonable person to enter into the contract relates only to matters of proof.[24]

Rescission is an equitable remedy and is subject to certain bars. There must be *restitutio in integrum*, *i.e.* the parties must be restored to their original positions. If this cannot be done rescission will not be granted. Contractors after completing the contract works, a branch railway, claimed rescission of the contract and a reasonable sum on a *quantum meruit* on the ground of the innocent misrepresentation of the railway company's engineer as to the nature of the strata through which the railway passed. The remedy was refused because the contractors had completed the railway after full knowledge of the

---

[18] [1964] A.C. 465 (H.L.).

[19] See the exposition of the law in *Hedley Byrne* v. *Heller & Partners* [1964] A.C. 465 (H.L.).

[20] *Redgrave* v. *Hurd* (1881) 20 Ch.D. 1 (C.A.); see also *Dietz* v. *Lennig Chemicals Ltd.* [1969] 1 A.C. 170 (H.L.).

[21] See, *e.g. Laurence* v. *Lexcourt Holdings* [1978] 1 W.L.R. 1128.

[22] *Dietz* v. *Lennig Chemicals Ltd.* [1969] 1 A.C. 170 (H.L.).

[23] *Car and Universal Finance Co. Ltd.* v. *Caldwell* [1965] 1 Q.B. 525 (C.A.).

[24] *Museprime Properties* v. *Adhill Properties*, *The Times*, March 13, 1990, approving a passage from Goff and Jones, *The Law of Restitution* (3rd ed.), p. 168.

facts, and *restitutio* had become impossible.[25] It seems likely that, where any building works have been carried out pursuant to the contract materially affecting the employer's land,[26] rescission will be refused even where the work was carried out without knowledge of the untruth of the representation. Affirmation of the contract by taking some substantial[27] step towards its performance after discovery of the untruth bars rescission.[28] Delay in seeking rescission, or the acquisition of an interest in the subject-matter of the contract by a purchaser innocent of the untruth of the representation bars rescission.[29] It was formerly the law that "if the contract has been executed by the completion of a conveyance or lease or the formal assignment of a chattel, then rescission cannot be obtained on the ground of innocent misrepresentation by the vendor or lessor."[30] This principle, known as the rule in *Seddon* v. *North Eastern Salt Co.*,[31] was removed by section 1(b) of the Misrepresentation Act 1967.[32]

If the misrepresentation complained of had become a term of the contract, rescission for innocent misrepresentation was not granted at common law,[33] but this impediment to rescission was removed by section 1(a) of the Misrepresentation Act 1967.[34]

The right of rescission for a misrepresentation not forming part of the contract must be carefully distinguished from the right of a party to treat a contract as at an end (also sometimes called rescission) if the other party repudiates the contract. Where the injured party accepts such repudiation he is not only released from further performance but is entitled to damages for breach of contract.[35] Damages are never awarded for an innocent misrepresentation which does not form part of the contract.[36]

---

[25] *Glasgow and South Western Railway* v. *Boyd & Forrest* [1915] A.C. 526 (H.L.), reported fully *sub nom. Boyd & Forrest* v. *Glasgow and South Western Railway*, 1915 S.C. (H.L.) 20; *cf. Moss* v. *Swansea Corp.* (1910) 74 J.P. 351; *Thorn* v. *London Corp.* (1876) 1 App.Cas. 120 at 127 (H.L.); *Abram Steamship Co. Ltd.* v. *Westville Shipping Co. Ltd.* [1923] A.C. 773 (H.L.)—a shipbuilding case.

[26] No case deals with partial completion of building works as a bar to rescission on the ground of the impossibility of *restitutio.*

[27] See *Abram Steamship Co. Ltd.* v. *Westville Shipping Co. Ltd.* [1923] A.C. 773 (H.L.); *cf. Senanayake* v. *Cheng* [1966] A.C. 63 (P.C.)—a partnership case.

[28] *Boyd & Forrest* v. *Glasgow and South Western Railway*, 1915 S.C. (H.L.) 20; *Leaf* v. *International Galleries* [1950] 2 K.B. 86 (C.A.); *Long* v. *Lloyd* [1958] 1 W.L.R. 753 (C.A.).

[29] *Clough* v. *London & N.W. Railway* (1871) L.R. 7 Exch. 26. See also *Allen* v. *Robles* [1969] 1 W.L.R. 1193 (C.A.)—a repudiation case.

[30] McCardie J. in *Armstrong* v. *Jackson* [1917] 2 K.B. 822 at 825.

[31] (1905) 1 Ch. 326. The existence of the rule was judicially doubted, see, *e.g. Leaf* v. *International Galleries* [1950] 2 K.B. 86 (C.A.).

[32] See p. 125.

[33] *Pennsylvania Shipping Co.* v. *Cie. Nat. de Navigacion* [1936] 2 All E.R. 1167 at 1171; *Leaf* v. *International Galleries* [1950] 2 K.B. 86 at 93, 95 (C.A.); *Cremdean Properties* v. *Nash* (1977) 244 E.G. 547 (C.A.).

[34] See p. 125.

[35] For repudiation, see p. 146.

[36] *Redgrave* v. *Hurd* (1881) 20 Ch.D. 1 (C.A.); *Heilbut, Symons & Co.* v. *Buckleton* [1913] A.C. 30 at 51 (H.L.); *Hedley Byrne & Co. Ltd.* v. *Heller* [1964] A.C. 465 at 539 (H.L.).

Protection against misrepresentation.   An agreement could be so worded as to afford "... complete protection against innocent misrepresentation."[37]

Fraudulent misrepresentation.   In the leading case of *Derry* v. *Peek*,[38] Lord Herschell said:

> "fraud is proved when it is shown that a false representation has been made (1) knowingly, (2) without belief in its truth, or (3) recklessly, careless whether it is true or false. Although I have treated the second and third as distinct cases, I think the third is but an instance of the second, for one who makes a statement under such circumstances can have no real belief in the truth of what he states. To prevent a false statement being fraudulent there must always be an honest belief in its truth ... If fraud be proved, the motive of the person guilty of it is immaterial; it matters not that there was no intention to cheat or injure the person to whom the statement is made."[39]

Fraud in this sense always involves dishonesty even if the motive is not personal gain.[40] A statement made carelessly or negligently, as where, for example, a quantity surveyor carelessly misstates the quantities,[41] cannot in itself be fraudulent,[42] neither is it fraud merely because a person honestly but erroneously believes his statement to be true although according to its objective meaning it is not true[43] but recklessness may be of such a degree as to be dishonesty and the fact that an alleged belief in the truth of a statement is destitute of all reasonable foundation may suffice in itself to convince the court that it was not really entertained and that the representation was fraudulent.[44]

In *Pearson* v. *Dublin Corporation*[45] the contractor undertook to carry out a high-level outfall sewer and outfall works for a lump sum. It was an elaborate scheme, an essential feature of which was the use of a wall shown on the maps and drawings supplied by the employer's engineers as extending for a depth of nine feet below the ordnance datum line. In fact it rarely extended as much as three feet. It was therefore useless for the purpose proposed and the contractor was put to extra expense. The defendant's engineers responsible for the

---

[37] Lord Shaw in *Boyd & Forrest* v. *Glasgow and South Western Railway*, 1915 S.C. (H.L.) 20 at 36 referring to a typical clause warning the contractor that no allowance would be made if the soil should turn out to be different from what it was stated to be.

[38] (1889) 14 App.Cas. 337 (H.L.).

[39] *Ibid.* at 374.

[40] *Ibid.*; *Armstrong* v. *Strain* [1952] 1 K.B. 232 (C.A.); *Dutton* v. *Louth Corp.* (1955) 116 E.G. 128 (C.A.). For the standard of proof, see *Hornal* v. *Neuberger Products* [1957] 1 Q.B. 247 (C.A.). Contrast *Applegate* v. *Moss* [1971] 1 Q.B. 406 (C.A.) and *King* v. *Victor Parsons* [1973] 1 W.L.R. 29 (C.A.) for the lesser meaning of "fraud" in s.26 of the Limitation Act 1939 (now replaced by s.32 of the Limitation Act 1980) see pp. 369 *et seq.*

[41] *Priestley* v. *Stone* (1888) 4 T.L.R. 730; H.B.C. (4th ed.), Vol. 2, p. 134 (C.A.).

[42] *Derry* v. *Peek* (1889) 14 App.Cas. 337 (H.L.).

[43] *Akerhielm* v. *De Mare* [1959] A.C. 789 (P.C.). See also *Gross* v. *Lewis Hillman Ltd.* [1970] Ch. 445 (C.A.).

[44] Lord Herschell in *Derry* v. *Peek* (1889) 14 App.Cas. 337 at 375 (H.L.); *Akerhielm* v. *De Mare* [1959] A.C. 789 (P.C.).

[45] [1907] A.C. 351 (H.L.).

drawings and description had carried out no accurate survey and had doubts whether the wall existed or was of the description stated, and "rashly and without inquiry represented nine feet of wall where no wall existed."[46] This was held to be evidence of fraud. The case is also of interest in that the contract provided that "the contractor is to satisfy himself as to the dimensions . . . of all existing works," and that the corporation did not hold itself responsible for the accuracy of statements about existing works. It was held that while such clauses might have furnished a complete answer to any claim for breach of warranty[47] they afforded no defence to an action for fraud, for they might well be part of the fraud being inserted in the hope that no tests would be made.[48] Lord Loreburn said:

> "no one can escape liability for his own fraudulent statements by inserting in a contract a clause that the other party shall not rely upon them. I will not say that a man himself innocent may not under any circumstances, however peculiar, guard himself by apt and express clauses from liability for the fraud of his own agents. It suffices to say that in my opinion the clauses before us do not admit of such a construction."[49]

The plaintiff must always prove that the fraudulent misrepresentation was an inducement,[50] but the defendant cannot succeed in his defence by showing that there were other more weighty causes which contributed to the plaintiff's decision, "for in this field the court does not allow an examination into the relative importance of contributory causes."[51] It seems, however, that if a material statement in a notice is made recklessly, without an honest belief in its truth, the notice is a nullity and it is irrelevant whether the recipient of the notice was in fact deceived.[52]

Fraudulent misrepresentation must be specifically pleaded in the claim and an amendment so to plead outside the limitation period may not be allowed.[53] Section 2(1) of the Misrepresentation Act 1967 may enable a plaintiff to sue without having to allege fraud, but if it becomes necessary to allege fraud for

---

[46] *Pearson* v. *Dublin Corp.* (1906) H.B.C. (3rd ed.), Vol. 2, p. 453. Note: a fuller account of the facts can be found in H.B.C. (3rd ed.), Vol. 2 than in the reports of the House of Lords decision.

[47] [1907] A.C. 351 at 366 (H.L.).

[48] *Ibid.* Lord Ashbourne at 360.

[49] [1907] A.C. 351 at 353 (H.L.); *cf. Tullis* v. *Jacson* [1892] 3 Ch. 441, discussed at p. 115. See also *John Carter (Fine Worsteds) Ltd.* v. *Hanson Haulage (Leeds) Ltd.* [1965] 2 Q.B. 495 (C.A.). For a detailed discussion of the liability of the employer where there is an agent such as the architect, see p. 309.

[50] See, *e.g. Convent Hospital* v. *Eberlin & Partners* (1988) 14 Con.L.R. 1.

[51] *Barton* v. *Armstrong* [1976] A.C. 104 at 118 (P.C.). The "field" referred to includes duress. This means "the compulsion under which a person acts through fear of personal suffering"—*Halsbury* (4th ed.), Vol. 9, para. 297. Duress is not further referred to in this book as it is not thought likely to be of much importance in building contracts, but "Economic duress" is discussed at p. 145.

[52] See *Earl of Stradbroke* v. *Mitchell, The Times*, October 4, 1990 (C.A.)—a case concerning a notice to quit served under the Agricultural Holdings Act 1986.

[53] See *Garden Neptune Shipping* v. *Occidental* [1990] 1 Lloyd's Rep. 330 (C.A.); see also "Amendments" at p. 371.

some other reason, it must be properly pleaded.[54] No action may be brought for a fraudulent representation as to character or credit unless the representation is in writing signed by the defendant.[55]

Pricing errors.   Where before the contract is signed an error is discovered by the employer in the pricing of the contractor's tender operating in favour of the employer, mere failure clearly to draw the contractor's attention to the error before the contract is signed is not in itself evidence of fraud,[56] although the employer is under a moral duty to the contractor to draw his attention to the errors.[57]

Remedies for fraud.   Where the contractor has been induced to enter into the contract by a fraudulent misrepresentation he can on discovering the fraud avoid the contract[58] and treat it as at an end, or he can affirm the contract and complete. In either event he can recover damages in an action for the tort of deceit.[59] The correct measure of damages in the tort of deceit is an award which will put the plaintiff into the position he would have been in if the fraudulent representation had not been made to him.[60]

3. Negligent Misstatement

A negligent misstatement or misrepresentation may give rise to an action in tort for damages for financial loss since the law will imply a duty of care when a party seeking information from a party possessed of special skill trusts him to exercise due care, and that party knew or ought to have known that reliance was being placed on his skill and judgment. The leading case which developed this liability is *Hedley Byrne* v. *Heller & Partners.*[61] There is a full discussion in Chapter 7, Section 3 at pages 174 *et seq.*

4. Misrepresentation Act 1967

The Misrepresentation Act 1967 is short but, in some aspects, difficult to

---

[54] *Ibid.* and see p. 125 for the Misrepresentation Act.

[55] s.6 of the Statute of Frauds Amendment Act 1828; *Banbury* v. *Bank of Montreal* [1918] A.C. 626; *UBAF Ltd.* v. *European American Banking Corporation* [1984] Q.B. 713 (C.A.).

[56] *Dutton* v. *Louth Corp.* (1955) 116 E.G. 128 (C.A.). *cf. Bottoms* v. *York Corp.* (1892) H.B.C. (4th ed.), Vol. 2, p. 208 (C.A.).

[57] *Dutton* v. *Louth Corp.* (1955) 116 E.G. 128 (C.A.). See also p. 268. The contractor might have had a remedy in rectification had he sought it.

[58] Unless, it seems, *restitutio* is impossible or the rights of innocent purchasers have arisen—see cases cited at p. 120.

[59] See *Archer* v. *Brown* [1985] Q.B. 401 and generally *Chitty* (26th ed.), Vol. 1. For a summary of the elements of an action for deceit, see *Bradford Building Soc.* v. *Borders* [1941] 2 All E.R. 205 at 211 (H.L.).

[60] *Doyle* v. *Olby (Ironmongers) Ltd.* [1969] 2 Q.B. 158 (C.A.); *Smith Kline & French* v. *Long* [1989] 1 W.L.R. 1 (C.A.); *Saunders* v. *Edwards* [1987] 1 W.L.R. 1116 at 1121 (C.A.). In certain circumstances the measure of damages in tort differ from contract; see *McGregor on Damages* (15th ed.), paras. 1718 *et seq.*; *Archer* v. *Brown* [1985] Q.B. 401.

[61] [1964] A.C. 464 (H.L.).

understand,[62] and it made the law more complex. It enlarged the right of rescission for innocent misrepresentation (section 1). It introduced two statutory rights to damages for misrepresentation. One is a statutory cause of action for damages for misrepresentations made during contractual negotiations unless the representor proves that he had reasonable ground to believe that the facts represented were true (section 2(1)). The other is linked to the right to rescind (section 2(2)). The Act also makes contractual provisions purporting to exclude liability for misrepresentation ineffective unless the party relying on it establishes that the provision is fair and reasonable (section 3).

The main parts of the Act are printed below with a discussion. The headings are the side headings of the Act.

Section 1. Removal of certain bars to rescission for innocent misrepresentation

"Where a person has entered into a contract after a misrepresentation has been made to him, and—

    (a) the misrepresentation has become a term of the contract; or

    (b) the contract has been performed;

or both, then, if otherwise he would be entitled to rescind the contract without alleging fraud, he shall be so entitled, subject to the provisions of this Act, notwithstanding the matters mentioned in paragraphs (a) and (b) of this section."

Subsection (b) removes "the rule in *Seddon* v. *North Eastern Salt Co. Ltd.*" For this and the effect upon the right to rescission of a misrepresentation becoming a term of the contract, see page 120. Other bars to rescission, *e.g.* affirmation, impossibility of *restitutio*, delay, rights of the innocent purchaser, remain.[63]

Section 2. Damages for misrepresentation

"(1) Where a person has entered into a contract after a misrepresentation has been made to him by another party thereto and as a result thereof he has suffered loss, then, if the person making the misrepresentation would be liable to damages in respect thereof had the misrepresentation been made fraudulently, that person shall be so liable notwithstanding that the misrepresentation was not made fraudulently, unless he proves that he had reasonable ground to believe and did believe up to the time the contract was made that the facts represented were true.

(2) Where a person has entered into a contract after a misrepresentation has been made to him otherwise than fraudulently, and he would be entitled, by reason of the misrepresentation, to rescind the contract, then, if it is claimed, in any proceedings arising out

---

[62] Many articles have been written about the Act—see Current Law Statute Citator 1947–71, p. 432; in particular see Fairest [1967] C.L.J. 239; Atiyah and Treitel (1967) 30 M.L.R. 396—a highly critical analysis. See also *Chitty* (26th ed.), Vol. 1, paras. 438 *et seq.* and 455; Cheshire & Fifoot, *Contract* (11th ed.), pp. 282 *et seq.*

[63] See further commentary on Section 2(2) below.

of the contract, that the contract ought to be or has been rescinded, the court or arbitrator may declare the contract subsisting and award damages in lieu of rescission, if of opinion that it would be equitable to do so, having regard to the nature of the misrepresentation and the loss that would be caused by it if the contract were upheld, as well as to the loss that rescission would cause to the other party.

(3) Damages may be awarded against a person under subsection (2) of this section whether or not he is liable to damages under subsection (1) thereof, but where he is so liable any award under the said subsection (2) shall be taken into account in assessing his liability under the said subsection (1)."

Section 2(1).   Section 2(1) has the effect of enabling a plaintiff to sue for misrepresentation without having to allege fraud.[64] The ungainly reference to fraudulent misrepresentation derives from the common law anomaly that a plaintiff could recover damages for fraudulent, but not for innocent mis-representation.[65] It is submitted that the statutory cause of action requires the same elements as are required for fraudulent misrepresentation but without the fraud. There must be a misrepresentation of fact[66] which intentionally induces the other party to enter into a contract[67] and which causes loss. "To succeed in an action for misrepresentation, a plaintiff must show that the loss he has suffered is caused by, and is the result of, the misrepresentation."[68]

It is no defence to the misrepresentation to say that the person misled could have checked and found out the facts for himself,[69] but if he knows the misrepresentation to be false and knows the true position he cannot complain.[70]

The statutory cause of action is wider than that arising in a plea of fraudu-lent misrepresentation, since it includes cases where the defendant did believe up to the time the contract was made that the facts represented were true but did not have reasonable ground for that belief.[71] Dishonesty is not an essential element as it is in fraud.[72] But there can be cases where there is an exact coincidence of fact between the statutory cause of action and a cause of action in fraudulent misrepresentation, where the issue is whether the alleged repre-sentors had reasonable ground for believing, and did believe, that the facts alleged to have been represented were true.[73]

---

[64] *Garden Neptune Shipping* v. *Occidental* [1990] 1 Lloyd's Rep. 330 (C.A.).
[65] See Section 2 of this chapter.
[66] *Andre & Cie S.A.* v. *Ets. Michel Blanc* [1979] 2 Lloyd's Rep. 427 (C.A.)—a misrepresentation of foreign law is misrepresentation of fact. For the width of the word "representation," see "Honest opinion" at p. 119.
[67] See *Howard Marine* v. *Ogden & Sons* [1978] Q.B. 574 at 596 (C.A.); *cf. JEB Fasteners* v. *Marks Bloom & Co.* [1983] 1 All E.R. 583 (C.A.); *Convent Hospital* v. *Eberlin & Partners* (1988) 14 Con.L.R. 1.
[68] *Strover* v. *Harrington* [1988] Ch. 390 at 411.
[69] *Laurence* v. *Lexcourt Holdings* [1978] 1 W.L.R. 1128 at 1137.
[70] *Strover* v. *Harrington* [1988] Ch. 390 at 407.
[71] See, *e.g. Walker* v. *Boyle* [1982] 1 W.L.R. 495 at 508.
[72] See p. 122.
[73] *Garden Neptune Shipping* v. *Occidental* [1989] 1 Lloyd's Rep. 305, but see [1990] 1 Lloyd's Rep. 330 (C.A.).

The test of whether the defendant had reasonable ground to believe that the facts represented were true is objective.[74] It does not depend on the existence of a duty to check the accuracy of the facts, although it may perhaps loosely be equivalent to the question whether the defendant was negligent. Facts such as are necessary to establish a claim in negligence must ordinarily exist but it is not for the plaintiff to prove negligence, but for the defendant to prove the statutory defence. "In the course of negotiations leading to a contract the statute imposes an absolute obligation not to state facts which the representor cannot prove he had reasonable grounds to believe."[75]

The right to damages under section 2(1) is not linked to the right of rescission, so that damages under the subsection may be claimed despite the existence of bars to rescission such as affirmation of the contract.

Servants or agents. Problems arise as to the knowledge, or lack of it, of servants or agents. The employer is, it is submitted, liable where his servants lacked reasonable grounds for their belief. He is probably also liable for his agents, such as independent architects or engineers, who are employed to act for the project in question, so that a claim under the section would lie on the facts of *Pearson* v. *Dublin Corporation*.[76] But it is thought unlikely that the employer is liable for the lack of reasonable grounds of belief of the independent expert whose opinion he sought on some special matter, such as, *e.g.* water levels or strata, provided the employer had reasonable grounds for believing and did believe the expert's report to be true. It is not clear how far the knowledge or lack of knowledge of the employer and his servants or agents, or of various servants and agents, can be added together so as to prevent proof of reasonable grounds of belief.[77]

The Act is concerned with representations between contracting parties and liability rests with principals. Accordingly an agent, acting within his express or ostensible authority, cannot be held personally liable under the Act when he makes a statement which is untrue in circumstances where he did not have reasonable grounds to believe that it was true.[78]

In normal conveyancing transactions, the purchaser's solicitors have actual or at least ostensible authority to receive information and information given to them correcting a misrepresentation will be imputed to the purchaser.[79] This could, depending on the facts, also apply to other circumstances.

---

[74] *Howard Marine* v. *Ogden & Sons* [1978] Q.B. 574 at 598 (C.A.).

[75] Bridge L.J. in *Howard Marine* v. *Ogden & Sons* [1978] Q.B. 574 at 596 (C.A.); *cf. Resolute Maritime* v. *Nippon Kaiji* [1983] 1 W.L.R. 857 at 861; *Cremdean Properties* v. *Nash* (1977) 244 E.G. 547 (C.A.). For the loose equivalence with negligence, see Lord Denning M.R. in *Howard Marine* (dissenting in the result) at 593. For the separate cause of action of negligent misstatement, see p. 124.

[76] See p. 122.

[77] *cf. Armstrong* v. *Strain* [1952] 1 K.B. 232 (C.A.) discussed at p. 310 and in Atiyah and Treitel, *op. cit.* at 374. For a case of a principal not liable for an agent acting outside the limits of his authority which limits had been made clear to the plaintiff, see *Overbrooke Estates Ltd.* v. *Glencombe Properties Ltd.* [1974] 1 W.L.R. 1335.

[78] *Resolute Maritime* v. *Nippon Kaiji* [1983] 1 W.L.R. 857.

[79] *Strover* v. *Harrington* [1988] Ch. 390 at 409.

Section 2(2).   This gives a right to apply for a discretionary remedy of damages where the misrepresentation is wholly innocent, *i.e.* neither fraudulent nor made with that element of fault which prevents a defence being established under section 2(1). But it is thought to be of limited value to a contractor because, it is submitted, he must prove that he would be entitled to rescission if damages were not awarded,[80] and in consequence his claim for damages fails if one of the bars to rescission exists, such as affirmation, delay or impossibility of *restitutio*. If the contractor discovers the misrepresentation before work starts he can, as before the Act, in the ordinary case, rescind, and the section now gives him a right to apply for damages. But if, as seems likely, the right to rescission must exist at the date of hearing,[81] and meanwhile the employer has had the works carried out by another contractor, the court cannot, or alternatively, would not, it is thought, declare the contract subsisting so as to be able to award damages.

Repudiation.   The terms "rescind," "rescinded" and "rescission" are not, it is submitted, intended to have the meaning of an acceptance of repudiation[82] so as to bring the contract to an end.

Damages.   Section 2(3) seems to contemplate that the measure of damages under subsection (1) is greater than under subsection (2). No other guidance is given, but it seems that the court assimilates the award of damages under subsection (1) to that for the tort of deceit.[83] This means that the plaintiff is not merely to be put in the same position as if a contract had been performed but can recover actual loss directly flowing from the misrepresentation.[84] The result is that in some cases he recovers more damages than if his claim is for breach of contract,[85] which, for this purpose, includes breach of collateral warranty.

Misrepresentation incorporated into the contract.   A statement of fact by the employer as to the nature of the soil, or the site or the like is often made

---

[80] See discussion, Atiyah and Treitel, *op. cit.* at 377.

[81] *Ibid.*

[82] This is sometimes also called "rescission," see p. 147.

[83] *Gosling* v. *Anderson* [1972] E.G.D. 709 at 713 (C.A.); *Jarvis* v. *Swan's Tours Ltd.* [1973] 1 Q.B. 233 at 237 (C.A.); *Davis & Co. Ltd.* v. *Afa-Minerva Ltd.* [1974] 2 Lloyd's Rep. 27; *Watts* v. *Spence* [1976] Ch. 165; see also *Andre & Cie S.A.* v. *Ets. Michel Blanc* [1979] 2 Lloyd's Rep. 427 (C.A.) upholding Ackner J. who had held that the appropriate measure of damages under s.2(1) was the measure appropriate to claims in tort; *Walker* v. *Boyle* [1982] 1 W.L.R. 495 at 508—loss of interest on a deposit as damages. See also *Sharneyford* v. *Edge* [1987] Ch. 305 at 323 where it is said that the criticism of *Watts* v. *Spence* in McGregor (14th ed.), paras. 1486–1489 (now 15th ed., para 1746) is entirely convincing.

[84] *Jarvis* v. *Swan's Tours Ltd.* [1973] 1 Q.B. 233 (C.A.); *Davis & Co. Ltd.* v. *Afa-Minerva Ltd.* [1974] 2 Lloyd's Rep. 27; *Watts* v. *Spence* [1976] Ch. 165—criticised at 91 L.Q.R. 308 for awarding damages for loss of bargain, but this is the measure of damages for fraud in contracts for the sale of land, see the review of the authorities in *Watts* v. *Spence* [1976] Ch. 165 at 174.

[85] See *Doyle* v. *Olby (Ironmongers) Ltd.* [1969] 2 Q.B. 158 (C.A.).

in the tender documents and is at that stage a representation. When the contract is signed such statements are often expressly incorporated into the contract. It is thought that the remedies under the Act apply notwithstanding such incorporation, so that the contractor may seek damages for breach of contract or under this section or both in the alternative. Matters to be considered include:

(1) In certain circumstances he may recover more damages under the Act than for breach of contract—see above.

(2) If there is no clause in the contract excluding or restricting the employer's liability or the contractor's remedy and he has lost the right to rescission, he may prefer the claim for breach of contract so as not to have to meet the statutory defence of reasonable ground of belief under section 2(1).

(3) If there is such a clause he may prefer his remedy under the Act so as to be able to apply to have the clause set aside or reduced in its effect under section 3 of the Act.

Section 3. Avoidance of provision excluding liability for misrepresentation[86]

"If a contract contains a term which would exclude or restrict—

    (a) any liability to which a party to a contract may be subject by reason of any misrepresentation made by him before the contract was made; or

    (b) any remedy available to another party to the contract by reason of such a misrepresentation;

that term shall be of no effect except in so far as it satisfies the requirement of reasonableness as stated in section 11(1) of the Unfair Contract Terms Act 1977; and it is for those claiming that the term satisfies the requirement to show that it does."

The requirement of reasonableness as stated in section 11(1) of the Unfair Contract Terms Act 1977 is:

". . . that the term shall have been a fair and reasonable one to be included having regard to the circumstances which were, or ought reasonably to have been, known to or in the contemplation of the parties when the contract was made."[87]

The "agreement." A notice which is not a term of a contract is not within the section.[88] The contract must, it is submitted, be enforceable[89] and can be

---

[86] This section was substituted for the section originally enacted by s.8(1) of the Unfair Contract Terms Act 1977. For an application of the originally enacted wording, which included the words "fair and reasonable," see *Howard Marine* v. *Ogden & Sons* [1978] Q.B. 574 (C.A.).

[87] For the purposes of s.3 of the Misrepresentation Act alone, the court or arbitrator is not, it seems, specifically required to have regard to the matters specified in Sched. 2 of the 1977 Act. There would be such a requirement if ss.6 or 7 of that Act also applied to relevant transaction—see s.11(2).

[88] *Collins* v. *Howell-Jones* (1981) 259 E.G. 331 (C.A.).

[89] *cf.* Atiyah and Treitel, *op. cit.* at 379, who canvass the idea of a "subject to contract" agreement (see p. 21), but this is, it is submitted, in law a nullity. *cf.* definition of "agreement" in the Restrictive Trade Practices Act 1976—see p. 353.

made before the contract in question and even before the commencement of the Act. It can also, it is submitted, be contained within the "contract" referred to in the section and includes, it is submitted, a provision relating to misrepresentations which have become incorporated into the contract. It is doubtful whether a contractual term could be devised which would be allowed to defeat the purpose of section 3, *e.g.* by deeming statements of fact not to be representations within the Act. Such a term is likely to be treated as one excluding or restricting liability and within section 3.[90]

"Fair and reasonable."   The presumption is against allowing reliance on the provision, the burden of proof being explicitly placed on the party relying on it. Subject to this, no principle applies save as stated in the section. Effect is only given to the provision to the extent (if any) that may be "fair and reasonable" having regard to the circumstances contemplated by the parties or which they ought reasonably to have contemplated.[91] This may introduce a substantial element of uncertainty as to the ultimate apportionment of risks in some contracts and make the estimator's task very difficult. A common form clause in a standard printed contract may not achieve the "accolade of fairness and reasonableness."[92]

Agent's authority.   The section only applies to a provision which would exclude or restrict liability for a misrepresentation made by a party or his duly authorised agent. It has no application to a notice limiting the authority of an agent.[93]

5. Collateral Warranty

In Chapter 20, certain written subsidiary standard forms of contract are discussed. They and similar contracts are sometimes referred to as "collateral contracts," "collateral warranties" or "warranties." The word "collateral" imports that the contract is subsidiary to a main or principal contract. The word "warranty" in this context means "enforceable contractual promise" and in substance means the same as "contract." These contracts have in law all the manifestations and requirements of ordinary contracts and in principle they have no special features. The legal consideration for the subsidiary promise is often the making of the principal contract or a promise to nominate the other party as a sub-contractor or supplier.

---

[90] Bridge L.J. in *Cremdean Properties* v. *Nash* (1977) 244 E.G. 547 at 551 (C.A.). See Scarman L.J. *ibid.* for Humpty Dumpty's wrong approach.

[91] For a case which considered and applied the originally enacted version of this section, see *Howard Marine* v. *Ogden & Sons* [1978] Q.B. 574 (C.A.).

[92] *Walker* v. *Boyle* [1982] 1 W.L.R. 495 at 508.

[93] *Overbrooke Estates Ltd.* v. *Glencombe Properties Ltd.* [1974] 1 W.L.R. 1335; *Collins* v. *Howell-Jones* (1980) 259 E.G. 331 (C.A.), discussed at (1981) 97 L.Q.R. 522.

The term "collateral warranty" in this section is used to refer to essentially the same legal relationship but arising in a less structured way. If a contractor can show that, although a statement is not a term of the building contract, nevertheless it was, in effect, a promise by the employer that, in consideration of the contractor entering into the contract, the employer would warrant or guarantee the accuracy of the statement, then if the statement is incorrect the contractor can recover damages from the employer for breach of warranty.[94] There is, in effect, a collateral contract. "Such collateral contracts, the sole effect of which is to vary or add to the terms of the principal contract, are viewed with suspicion by the law. They must be proved strictly."[95] It is not every representation, whether made innocently, negligently or fraudulently, which is intended to be acted on and which is acted on that creates a contractual relationship. There has to be an intention to make a contract.[96] If the court is satisfied that on the totality of the evidence the parties intended or must be taken to have intended the statement to form part of the basis of the contractual relations between them then it will award damages for its inaccuracy.[97] The court will more readily find such an intention if the party by whom it was made had, or professed to have special knowledge and skill in relation to the subject-matter of the statement and made it with the intention of inducing the other party, who had less knowledge, to enter into the contract.[98]

In *I.B.A.* v. *E.M.I. and B.I.C.C.*,[99] there was a contract for the construction of three television masts to be designed, supplied and erected by nominated sub-contractors. There was an occasion when one of the masts began to oscillate violently and the plaintiff employer wrote directly to the sub-contractor suggesting that design data should be investigated and confirmed. The sub-contractor replied saying that they were "well satisfied that the structures will not oscillate dangerously." On receiving this assurance, the plaintiffs took no further action. When one of the masts subsequently collapsed, the plaintiffs contended that the assurance was a contractual warranty. The judge and the Court of Appeal held in their favour on this issue. The House of Lords reversed this decision holding that there was no evidence that, at the time when the assurance was given, either party intended to make a contract.

---

[94] *Heilbut, Symons & Co.* v. *Buckleton* [1913] A.C. 30 (H.L.); *Routledge* v. *McKay and others* [1954] 1 W.L.R. 615 (C.A.); *Esso Petroleum Co. Ltd.* v. *Mardon* [1976] Q.B. 801 (C.A.). For employer relying on collateral warranty of fitness, see *Miller* v. *Cannon Hill Estates Ltd.* [1931] 2 K.B. 113 (D.C.); *Birch* v. *Paramount Estates Ltd.* (1956) 16 E.G. 396 (C.A.)—"as good as show house." For employer recovering damages for breach of collateral warranty from manufacturer who supplied contractor, see *Shanklin Pier Ltd.* v. *Detel Products Ltd.* [1951] 2 K.B. 854, discussed at p. 284.

[95] *Heilbut, Symons & Co.* v. *Buckleton* [1913] A.C. 30 at 47 (H.L.); *Oscar Chess Ltd.* v. *Williams* [1957] 1 W.L.R. 370 (C.A.). See also p. 39 and discussion based on *Evans (J.) & Sons (Portsmouth) Ltd.* v. *Andrea Merzario Ltd.* [1976] 1 W.L.R. 1078 (C.A.).

[96] See *I.B.A.* v. *E.M.I. and B.I.C.C.* (1980) 14 B.L.R. 1 at 23 and 41 (H.L.) discussed below; *cf. Howard Marine* v. *Ogden & Sons* [1978] Q.B. 574 at 591.

[97] *Esso Petroleum Co. Ltd.* v. *Mardon* [1976] Q.B. 801 at 826 (C.A.).

[98] *Esso Petroleum Co. Ltd.* v. *Mardon* [1976] Q.B. 801 (C.A.); *Dick Bentley, etc., Ltd.* v. *Harold Smith (Motors) Ltd.* [1965] 1 W.L.R. 623 (C.A.).

[99] (1980) 14 B.L.R. 1 (H.L.).

Not all warranties of the kind described above are collateral in the sense of being subsidiary to the making of a main or principal contract.[1] If an alleged warranty is collateral in this sense, the intention to make a contract may be less difficult to establish and the making of the principal contract can be consideration for the collateral promise. If it is not so collateral, the warranty can only have contractual force if a separate independent contract is made and that requires an intention to make a contract on both sides.[2]

There is no rule that a statement of future fact or a forecast cannot be a warranty.[3] Thus where the agent of an intending lessor stated to the prospective lessee of a petrol station that there was an anticipated throughput of 200,000 gallons per year this, upon the facts, was found to be a warranty that the statement was arrived at after careful consideration and the lessor was liable in damages for loss resulting from his lack of such care.[4]

Where the employer, an architect, was in breach of his promise either to obtain licences or stop the work if he could not, the contractor recovered damages for breach of warranty.[5]

In *Bacal (Midland) Limited* v. *Northampton Development Corporation*,[6] the contract was for the contractor to design and build.[7] He was instructed by the employer to design the foundations upon certain hypotheses as to the nature of the ground conditions. It was held that there was an implied warranty on the part of the employer that such conditions would accord with the hypotheses.

It has been frequently held that the mere inclusion of plans, bills of quantities and specification in the invitation to tender does not show that the employer is warranting their accuracy.[8] The same rule has been applied even where such statements have been incorporated in schedules to the contract.[9] The principle upon which these decisions are based is that a contractor who has undertaken to complete a whole work such as a house, a railway line or a bridge, should satisfy himself that any statements about the amount of work involved, or the condition of the site, or the methods of carrying out the work are accurate and practicable; he is not therefore entitled to assume that such

---

[1] *I.B.A.* v. *E.M.I. and B.I.C.C.* (1980) 14 B.L.R. 1 at 41 (H.L.); *cp. Dick Bentley, etc., Ltd.* v. *Harold Smith (Motors) Ltd.* [1965] 1 W.L.R. 623 (C.A.);

[2] See Lord Fraser in *I.B.A.* v. *E.M.I. and B.I.C.C.* (1980) 14 B.L.R. 1 at 41 (H.L.).

[3] *Esso Petroleum Co. Ltd.* v. *Mardon* [1976] Q.B. 801 (C.A.).

[4] *Ibid.*

[5] *Strongman (1945) Ltd.* v. *Sincock* [1955] 2 Q.B. 525 (C.A.). For the architect's authority as agent, see p. 305.

[6] (1976) 8 B.L.R. 88 (C.A.).

[7] For such contracts generally, see Chap. 1.

[8] *Scrivener* v. *Pask* (1866) L.R. 1 C.P. 715; *Thorn* v. *London Corp.* (1876) 1 App.Cas. 120 (H.L.); *Jackson* v. *Eastbourne Local Board* (1886) H.B.C. (4th ed.), Vol. 2, p. 81 (H.L.); *Young* v. *Blake* (1887) H.B.C. (4th ed.), Vol. 2, p. 110; *Bottoms* v. *York Corp.* (1892) H.B.C. (4th ed.), Vol. 2, p. 208 (C.A.); *McDonald* v. *Workington Corp.* (1892) 9 T.L.R. 230; H.B.C. (4th ed.), Vol. 2, p. 228 (C.A.); *Re Nuttall and Lynton and Barnstaple Railway* (1899) H.B.C. (4th ed.), Vol. 2, p. 279 (C.A.) also (1899) 82 L.T. 17; *Re Ford and Bemrose* (1902) H.B.C. (4th ed.), Vol. 2, p. 324 (C.A.).

[9] *Sharpe* v. *San Paulo Railway* (1873) L.R. 8 Ch.App. 597; *Re Ford and Bemrose* (1902) H.B.C. (4th ed.), Vol. 2, p. 324 (C.A.).

statements are warranties.[10] He can accept them as honest representations made by skilled persons, but beyond that they do not go.[11]

The preceding paragraph, largely based on nineteenth century cases, was quoted with apparent approval in a 1972 Australian case.[12] It is thought that the paragraph still states the law but that it has to be read subject to considerations arising from the Misrepresentation Act and the law about collateral warranties and negligent misstatement.[13]

Facts which support a claim for breach of collateral warranty may also prompt a claim under the Misrepresentation Act.[14] Material differences are that:

(1) if a contractual warranty is established, there is liability independent of fault, whereas reasonable ground to believe the truth of the representation is a defence under the Act;
(2) under the Act it is not necessary to establish that the representation was contractual, only that it induced the making of the principal contract;
(3) the measure of damages is tortious under the Act but contractual for breach of collateral warranty.

6. Death[15]

The general rule. Upon the death of either the contractor or the employer the benefit and burden of existing contracts other than personal contracts pass to their respective legal personal representatives.[16] The personal representatives must honour those obligations of the deceased that could have been enforced against him even if the contract is not beneficial to the estate,[17] although in the case of an enforceable onerous contract they ought not "to neglect any opportunity that may present itself of coming to terms with the other contracting party that may benefit the estate."[18]

Personal contracts. The liability of a person to perform personal obligations ceases with his death, the contract having been rendered impossible.[19]

---

[10] *McDonald* v. *Workington Corp.* (1892) 9 T.L.R. 230; H.B.C. (4th ed.), Vol. 2, p. 228 at 231 (C.A.); *Re Ford and Bemrose* (1902) H.B.C. (4th ed.), Vol. 2, p. 324 (C.A.).

[11] *Re Ford and Bemrose* (1902) H.B.C. (4th ed.), Vol. 2, p. 324 at 330 (C.A.).

[12] *Dillingham Construction* v. *Downs* [1972] 2 N.S.W.L.R. 49 at 56 (New South Wales High Court) also 13 B.L.R. 97 at 107—a claim for negligent misstatement failed on the facts because there was held to be no assumption by the employer of the responsibility to provide full and accurate information about site conditions. The quotation was from the 3rd edition of this book, but the same text is retained in this edition.

[13] See Chap. 7, Section 3 at p. 174.

[14] Or possibly for negligent misstatement, but see under "Contractual influences" at p. 170.

[15] *cf.* "Death" at p. 17.

[16] *Marshall* v. *Broadhurst* (1831) 1 Cr. & J. 403; *Cooper* v. *Jarman* (1866) L.R. 3 Eq. 98; *Ahmed Anguillia, etc.* v. *Estate & Trust Agencies (1927) Ltd.* [1938] A.C. 624 (P.C.).

[17] *Ahmed Anguillia, etc.* v. *Estate & Trust Agencies (1927) Ltd.* [1938] A.C. 624 at 634, 639 (P.C.).

[18] *Ibid.* at 635.

[19] *Stubbs* v. *Holywell Railway* (1867) L.R. 2 Ex. 311.

Thus in a contract of master and servant the death of either party brings the contract to an end.[20] In a contract of personal confidence such as that with an architect the death of the architect brings the contract to an end,[21] although the death of the employer does not normally have this effect.[22]

The employment of the contractor may be personal in that his obligations cannot be performed by his personal representatives. In such a case the position will be similar to that·on the death of the architect.

7. Frustration and Impossibility

Impossibility at time of contract. Actual physical impossibility of performing the contract, whatever means are employed[23] which exists at the time of entering into the contract is, subject to express terms or warranties, an excuse for non-performance.[24] But the contractor is liable in damages if he has warranted the possibility of the work[25] or if he has positively and absolutely contracted to do the work.[26]

Frustration generally. Very rarely[27] after the contract has been lawfully entered into and is in course of operation there may arise some intervening event or change of circumstances of so catastrophic[28] or fundamental a nature as to determine the contract prematurely[29] by the operation of the doctrine of frustration.[30] At least five theories have been advanced at different times of the

---

[20] *Farrow* v. *Wilson* (1869) L.R. 4 C.P. 744.

[21] *Stubbs* v. *Holywell Railway* (1867) L.R. 2 Ex. 311; see also "Duration of architect's duties" at p. 332.

[22] *Davison* v. *Reeves* (1892) 8 T.L.R. 391 (the employment of a civil engineer by a contractor).

[23] Note that, in the cases of *Thorn* v. *London Corp.* (1876) 1 App.Cas. 120 (H.L.), *Bottoms* v. *York Corp.* (1892) H.B.C. (4th ed.), Vol. 2, p. 208 (C.A.); *McDonald* v. *Workington Corp.* (1892) 9 T.L.R. 230; H.B.C. (4th ed.), Vol. 2, p. 228 (C.A.) and *Jackson* v. *Eastbourne Local Board* (1885) H.B.C. (4th ed.), Vol. 2, p. 81 (H.L.), it was in each case possible to complete the work at great expense. Physical impossibility is an express excuse under the I.C.E. Conditions, clause 13—see p. 836.

[24] *Taylor* v. *Caldwell* (1863) 3 B. & S. 826; *Clifford* v. *Watts* (1870) L.R. 5 C.P. 577; *cf. Tharsis, etc.* v. *M'Elroy and Sons* (1878) 3 App.Cas. 1040 at 1052–1053 (H.L.). See also *Bell* v. *Lever Bros.* [1932] A.C. 161 (H.L.) for mistake avoiding the contract.

[25] *Clifford* v. *Watts* (1870) L.R. 5 C.P. 577 at 588.

[26] *Jones* v. *St. John's College, Oxford* (1870) L.R. 6 Q.B. 115; *cf. Baily* v. *De Crespigny* (1869) L.R. 4 Q.B. 180 at 185; *Dodd* v. *Churton* [1897] 1 Q.B. 562 (C.A.), and see further p. 232.

[27] "Frustration is a doctrine only too often invoked by a party to a contract who finds performance difficult or unprofitable, but it is very rarely relied on with success. It is in fact a kind of last ditch," Harman L.J. in *Tsakiroglou & Co. Ltd.* v. *Noblee Thorl G.m.b.H.* [1960] 2 Q.B. 318 at 370 (C.A.); affd. [1962] A.C. 93 (H.L.); *cf. Lauritzen* v. *Wijsmuller* [1990] 1 Lloyd's Rep. 1 at 8 (C.A.).

[28] See Asquith L.J. In *Sir Lindsay Parkinson & Co. Ltd.* v. *Commissioners of Works* [1949] 2 K.B. 632 at 665 (C.A.).

[29] "It kills the contract itself," Lord Simon in *Constantine Ltd.* v. *Imperial Smelting Ltd.* [1942] A.C. 154 at 163 (H.L.).

[30] *Cricklewood Property & Investment Trust Ltd.* v. *Leighton's Investment Trust Ltd.* [1945] A.C. 221 at 228 (H.L.); *British Movietonews Ltd.* v. *London & District Cinemas Ltd.* [1952] A.C. 166 (H.L.); *Davis Contractors Ltd.* v. *Fareham Urban District Council* [1956] A.C. 696 (H.L.). It will be observed that the Law Reform (Frustrated Contracts) Act 1943 treats impossibility of performance as an aspect of frustration.

jurisprudential foundation for the doctrine of frustration.[31] But the formulation in *Davis Contractors* v. *Fareham*[32] is now usually regarded as "the classic statement of the doctrine."[33] It was there said that frustration "occurs wherever the law recognises that without default of either party a contractual obligation has become incapable of being performed because the circumstances in which performance is called for would render it a thing radically different from that which was undertaken by the contract. *Non haec in foedera veni*. It was not this that I promised to do."[34]

In deciding whether a contract has been frustrated, "the data for decision are, on the one hand, the terms and construction of the contract, read in the light of the then existing circumstances, and on the other hand the events which have occurred."[35]

> "In the nature of things there is often no room for any elaborate inquiry. The court must act upon a general impression of what its rule requires. It is for this reason that special importance is necessarily attached to the occurrence of any unexpected event that, as it were, changes the face of things. But, even so, it is not hardship or inconvenience or material loss itself which calls the principle of frustration into play. There must be as well such a change in the significance of the obligation that the thing undertaken would if performed, be a different thing from that contracted for."[36]

In *Davis Contractors* v. *Fareham*,[37] the contractors entered into a contract to build 78 houses for a fixed price within a contract period of eight months. Attached to their tender had been a letter stating that their tender was subject to adequate supplies of labour being available as and when required, but it was held that this letter was not a contract document.[38] There were unanticipated shortages of labour and materials and, although work never actually stopped, the shortages caused such delay that the contract took 22 months to complete and as a result cost the contractors about £17,000 more than the contract price. These facts were held not to frustrate the contract and the contractors had to bear the loss themselves, even though in one sense it might be said that the

---

[31] See Lord Roskill in *National Carriers* v. *Panalpina* [1981] A.C. 675 at 717 (H.L.); and see *ibid.* at 687, 693 and 702.
[32] [1956] A.C. 696 (H.L.).
[33] *Wates* v. *Greater London Council* (1983) 25 B.L.R. 1 at 27 (C.A.); see in particular *National Carriers* v. *Panalpina* [1981] A.C. 675 at 688, 717 (H.L.); *Wong Lai Ying* v. *Chinachem* (1979) 13 B.L.R. 81 (P.C.); *Pioneer Shipping* v. *B.T.P. Tioxide* (*The Nema*) [1982] A.C. 724 at 744 and 751 (H.L.) where Lord Roskill said that it should be unnecessary in future cases to search back beyond *Davis Contractors Ltd.* v. *Fareham Urban District Council* [1956] A.C. 696 (H.L.).
[34] Lord Radcliffe in *Davis Contractors Ltd.* v. *Fareham Urban District Council* [1956] A.C. 696 at 729 (H.L.), echoing the language of Lord Cairns in *Thorn* v. *London Corp.* (1876) 1 App.Cas. 120, 127 (H.L.); see also *The Eugenia* [1964] 2 Q.B. 226 at 239 (C.A.); *Amalgamated Investment Ltd.* v. *John Walker Ltd.* [1977] 1 W.L.R. 164 (C.A.).
[35] Lord Wright in *Denny, Mott & Dickinson Ltd.* v. *James B. Fraser & Co. Ltd.* [1944] A.C. 265, 274–275 (H.L.).
[36] *Davis Contractors Ltd.* v. *Fareham Urban District Council* [1956] A.C. 696 at 729 (H.L.).
[37] [1956] A.C. 696 (H.L.).
[38] See "Preliminary negotiations" at p. 34.

"basis" or "footing" of the contract, *i.e.* adequate supplies of labour and materials, had gone, for "it by no means follows that disappointed expectations lead to frustrated contracts,"[39] and the risk of loss to the contractors caused through the delay which occurred was on the contractors.[40]

Whether a contract is frustrated is in the ultimate analysis a question of law.[41] But often it will be a question of degree whether the effect of, for instance, delay suffered and likely to be suffered will be such as to bring about frustration.[42] In such cases the question may be one of mixed law and fact.[43] In some cases it is possible to determine at once whether or not the doctrine can be legitimately invoked. In others, where there is delay caused in the performance of contractual obligations, it is often necessary to wait upon events to see whether actual and prospective delay result in frustration.[44] The fact that after the happening of an event the parties treated the contract as still subsisting is not conclusive that the event did not frustrate the contract.[45] The court appears reluctant to interfere with an arbitrator's decision that a contract has been frustrated if it is reached by applying right legal test.[46]

When frustration occurs both parties are automatically[47] discharged from any further obligation unless the party alleging that there is a breach can prove that the circumstances leading to the frustration were brought about by the default of the other party, in which case that other party will be liable in damages.[48] Thus where a contractor deliberately delayed work hoping that by so doing completion would be prevented by a government prohibition against construction of houses, and it was in fact so prevented, he was held to be liable in damages.[49]

Express terms. If the terms of the contract show that the parties contemplated and provided for a particular event, that event cannot frustrate the

---

[39] Lord Simonds in *Davis Contractors Ltd.* v. *Fareham Urban District Council* [1956] A.C. 696 at 715 (H.L.).

[40] *Bush* v. *Whitehaven Trustees* (1888) H.B.C. (4th ed.), Vol. 2, p. 130 (C.A.), strongly relied on by the contractors, was held not to be an authority for any proposition of law.

[41] *Pioneer Shipping* v. *B.T.P. Tioxide* (*The Nema*) [1982] A.C. 724 at 752 (H.L.).

[42] *Ibid.*

[43] *National Carriers* v. *Panalpina* [1981] A.C. 675 at 688 (H.L.).

[44] *Pioneer Shipping* v. *B.T.P. Tioxide* (*The Nema*) [1982] A.C. 724 at 752 (H.L.).

[45] *Kissavos Shipping* v. *Empresa Cubana* (*The Agathon*) [1982] 2 Lloyd's Rep. 211 (C.A.).

[46] *Pioneer Shipping Ltd.* v. *B.T.P. Tioxide Ltd.* (*The Nema*) [1982] A.C. 724 (H.L.); *Kodros Shipping* v. *Empresa Cubana* (*No. 2*) [1983] 1 A.C. 736 (H.L.); *Wates* v. *Greater London Council* (1983) 25 B.L.R. 1 at 33 (C.A.).

[47] See, *e.g. National Carriers* v. *Panalpina* [1981] A.C. 675 at 712 (H.L.); *Lauritzen* v. *Wijsmuller* [1990] 1 Lloyd's Rep. 1 at 8 (C.A.).

[48] *Constantine Ltd.* v. *Imperial Smelting Ltd.* [1942] A.C. 154 (H.L.). A custodial sentence imposed on an employee is capable of frustrating a contract of employment and the employee could not say that the frustration was self-induced in order to gain an advantage—*Shepherd & Co.* v. *Jerrom* [1987] Q.B. 301 (C.A.).

[49] *Mertens* v. *Home Freeholds Co.* [1921] 2 K.B. 526 (C.A.). See further p. 202 for the measure of damages. See also *Lauritzen* v. *Wijsmuller* [1989] 1 Lloyd's Rep. 148 for an extensive analysis by Hobhouse J. of varieties of "self-induced" frustration; and see further *Lauritzen* v. *Wijsmuller* [1990] 1 Lloyd's Rep. 1 (C.A.) upholding Hobhouse J.

contract.[50] But in considering a clause relied on as expressly providing for the event alleged to frustrate the contract the court determines whether that event is in fact so abnormal or of such a nature as to fall outside what the parties could possibly have contemplated in the clause.[51] An example is given below[52] of a case where the court held that an interruption in the work was of such a kind as to frustrate the contract despite an express provision for interruption.

Arbitration agreements. An arbitration agreement cannot be frustrated by such delay by either or both parties in preparing for the arbitration and bringing it to a hearing that a satisfactory trial is no longer possible. Both parties have a mutual obligation to progress the arbitration and a failure so to do is a default which excludes the operation of the doctrine of frustration. Further, there is no sufficient frustrating event.[53]

Leases. The doctrine of frustration can apply to a lease so as to bring it to an end if a frustrating event occurs, but it is "hardly ever" likely to apply in practice.[54]

Difficulty or expense no excuse. Unexpected difficulty or expense is in general no excuse for non-performance.[55] The contractor in such a case cannot rely on his ignorance of such matters as defects in the soil[56] nor on any implied warranty by the employer that the bills of quantities, plans and specification are accurate[57] or that the work is capable of performance in the manner set out in the invitation to tender.[58] He should make his own investigations[59] or limit his liability to exactly stated quantities of work.[60]

---

[50] *Cricklewood Property & Investment Trust Ltd.* v. *Leighton's Investment Trust Ltd.* [1945] A.C. 221 at 228 (H.L.); *cf. Wates* v. *Greater London Council* (1983) 25 B.L.R. 1 (C.A.).

[51] *Sir Lindsay Parkinson Ltd.* v. *Commissioners of Works* [1949] 2 K.B. 632 at 665 (C.A.); see also *Bank Line Ltd.* v. *Capel* [1919] A.C. 435 (H.L.); *Wong Lai Ying* v. *Chinachem* (1979) 13 B.L.R. 81 (P.C.); *Kodros Shipping* v. *Empresa Cubana (The Evia) (No. 2)* [1983] 1 A.C. 736 (H.L.); *cf. B.P. Exploration Co.* v. *Hunt (No. 2)* [1983] 2 A.C. 352 (H.L.) for the application of s.2(3) of the Law Reform (Frustrated Contracts) Act 1943 and see p. 140.

[52] See discussion in the text of *Metropolitan Water Board* v. *Dick Kerr & Co. Ltd.* [1918] A.C. 119 (H.L.).

[53] *Paal Wilson* v. *Partenreederei* [1983] 1 A.C. 854 (H.L.) applying *Bremer Vulkan* v. *South India Shipping* [1981] A.C. 909 (H.L.). For delay in arbitrations, see pp. 405 *et seq.* and s.13A of the Arbitration Act 1950 as inserted by s.102 of the Courts and Legal Services Act 1990 (not yet in force).

[54] *National Carriers* v. *Panalpina* [1981] A.C. 675 (H.L.).

[55] *Bottoms* v. *York Corp.* (1892) H.B.C. (4th ed.), Vol. 2, p. 208 (C.A.); *McDonald* v. *Workington Corp.* (1893) 9 T.L.R. 230; H.B.C. (4th ed.), Vol. 2, p. 228 (C.A.); *Brauer Ltd.* v. *Clark Ltd.* [1952] 2 All E.R. 497 (C.A.); *Davis Contractors Ltd.* v. *Fareham Urban District Council* [1955] 1 Q.B. 302 (C.A.); *The "Captain George K"* [1970] 2 Lloyd's Rep. 21.

[56] *Bottoms* v. *York Corp.* (1892) H.B.C. (4th ed.), Vol. 2, p. 208 (C.A.); *McDonald* v. *Workington Corp.* (1893) 9 T.L.R. 230; H.B.C. (4th ed.), Vol. 2, p. 228 (C.A.).

[57] See Section 5 of this chapter.

[58] *Thorn* v. *London Corp.* (1876) 1 App.Cas. 120 (H.L.).

[59] *McDonald* v. *Workington Corp.* (1893) 9 T.L.R. 230; H.B.C. (4th ed.), Vol. 2, p. 228 (C.A.).

[60] *e.g. Bryant* v. *Birmingham Hospital Saturday Fund* [1938] 1 All E.R. 503 (defects in soil); and see generally "Bills of quantities contract" at p. 83.

Prohibition by law.   If after entering into the contract the completion of the works becomes permanently prohibited by law this normally frustrates the contract.[61] If the prohibition is not permanent the test would seem to be "whether the interruption (caused by the prohibition) was so long as to destroy the identity of the work and service when resumed, with the work and service when interrupted."[62] Thus in *Metropolitan Water Board* v. *Dick Kerr & Co. Ltd.*,[63] the contractors in July 1914, before the outbreak of war, entered into a contract to construct reservoirs at an agreed price within a period of six years. In February 1916 the government prohibited the continuance of the work and seized and sold the contractor's plant and materials, and the work was still prohibited when the case came before the House of Lords in 1918. It was held that the contract was at an end, and this notwithstanding that the engineer had power to extend the time for completion "prospectively or retrospectively" in the event of any "difficulties, impediments, obstructions, oppositions . . . whatsoever and howsoever occasioned."[64]

War.   "Except in cases of supervening illegality, arising from the fact that the contract involves a party in trading with someone who has become an enemy, a declaration of war does not prevent the performance of a contract; it is the acts done on furtherance of the war which may or may not prevent performance, depending on the individual circumstances of the case. If there is any presumption at all, it relates to the duration of the state of war, not to the effects which the war may have on the performance of the contract."[65] Building contracts often have clauses providing contractual consequences of the outbreak of hostilities.[66]

Delay.   Increased cost to the contractor caused by unforeseen delay due to shortage of labour and materials or other causes not the fault of the employer is a risk which, in the absence of express terms to the contrary, is undertaken by the contractor,[67] and it seems unlikely[68] that delay which does not result in a stoppage of work[69] can be sufficient to frustrate the contract.

---

[61] *Baily* v. *de Crespigny* (1869) L.R. 4 Q.B. 180. *cf. Walton Harvey Ltd.* v. *Walker and Homfrays Ltd.* [1931] 1 Ch. 274 (C.A.); *Amalgamated Investment Ltd.* v. *John Walker Ltd.* [1977] 1 W.L.R. 164 (C.A.).

[62] Lord Wright in *Cricklewood Property & Investment Trust Ltd.* v. *Leighton's Investment Trust Ltd.* [1945] A.C. 221 at 236 (H.L.); *Woodfield Co. Ltd.* v. *Thompson & Sons Ltd.* (1919) 367 T.L.R. 43 (C.A.).

[63] [1918] A.C. 119 (H.L.).

[64] See also *Fibrosa, etc.* v. *Fairbairn, etc., Ltd.* [1943] A.C. 32 (H.L.); *New Zealand Shipping Co.* v. *Ateliers, etc., de France* [1919] A.C. 1 (H.L.). It has been held on rather special facts by a majority of 4:1 of the Australian High Court (Brennan J. dissenting) that an injunction restraining noisy building operations between certain hours frustrated a contract to build an underground railway—*Codelfa Construction* v. *State Railway Authority of New South Wales* (1982) 149 C.L.R. 337.

[65] *Finelvelt A.G.* v. *Vinava Shipping Co. Ltd.* [1983] 1 W.L.R. 1469 at 1481.

[66] See pp. 623 and 917.

[67] See *Davis Contractors Ltd.* v. *Fareham Urban District Council* [1956] A.C. 696 (H.L.). For shipping cases, see *The "Captain George K"* [1970] 2 Lloyd's Rep. 21; *The Anglia* [1973] 1 W.L.R. 210.

[68] In view of *Davis Contractors Ltd.* v. *Fareham Urban District Council* [1956] A.C. 696 (H.L.).

[69] *cf. Metropolitan Water Board* v. *Dick Kerr & Co. Ltd.* [1918] A.C. 119 (H.L.) where work stopped; *Pioneer Shipping* v. *B.T.P. Tioxide (The Nema)* [1982] A.C. 724 (H.L.)—arbitrator's decision that a charterparty was frustrated by delay caused by a strike upheld.

Change in prices.   The contract is not affected by an unanticipated and wholly abnormal rise or fall in prices or a sudden depreciation in the currency unless these events, upon the principles set out above, are of such gravity as to frustrate the contract.[70] It is thought that little short of a catastrophe[71] to the currency would suffice.

Destruction by fire, flood, landslip, etc.   Where a contractor undertakes to complete a whole work for a specified price and the contract works are destroyed by fire, flood or the like, he is not, subject to the express terms of the contract, released from his obligation to complete, and normally the contract is not frustrated.[72] If he undertakes to do work on another's building and that building is destroyed the contract may or may not be frustrated according to the application of the principles set out above.[73] If the soil upon which he has undertaken to build is destroyed by flood and the like, then, it is submitted, normally the contract is frustrated.[74] Where in Hong Kong an unforeseeable landslip brought a 13-storey block of flats and hundreds of tons of earth onto the site obliterating the building works, killing 67 people and resulting in lengthy and uncertain delay, it was held that this was "a major interruption fundamentally changing the character and the duration of the contract performance" and thus a frustrating event.[75]

Weather and acts of God.   Bad weather and storms do not generally excuse a contractor for he must be taken to have contemplated their possibility.[76] But if there is an exceptional and extraordinary rainfall[77] or snowfall,[78] or flooding[79] or earthquake,[80] or other weather "such as could not reasonably be anticipated," it may be an act of God.[81] This in itself does not excuse a breach

---

[70] *British Movietonews Ltd.* v. *London & District Cinemas Ltd.* [1952] A.C. 166, 185 (H.L.); *cp. Staffordshire Area Health Authority* v. *South Staffordshire Water Works* [1978] 1 W.L.R 1387 at 1398 (C.A.).

[71] See Asquith L.J. in *Sir Lindsay Parkinson & Co. Ltd.* v. *Commissioners of Works* [1949] 2 K.B. 632 at 665 (C.A.). There was little enthusiasm to argue that rates of inflation current in 1975 (about 25 per cent.) had this effect on building contracts. Such an argument did not succeed in *Wates* v. *Greater London Council* (1983) 25 B.L.R. 1 (C.A.).

[72] *Appleby* v. *Myers* (1867) L.R. 2 C.P. 651; *Gold* v. *Patman & Fotherington Ltd.* [1958] 1 W.L.R. 697 at 704 (C.A.).

[73] See *Appleby* v. *Myers* where on the facts of the contract it was held to be frustrated (although the modern term "frustration" was not used). Many contracts today expressly provide for fire to the employer's building—see *e.g.* clause 22 of the Standard Form of Building Contract at p. 550.

[74] See *Taylor* v. *Caldwell* (1863) 3 B. & S. 826.

[75] *Wong Lai Ying* v. *Chinachem* (1979) 13 B.L.R. 81 (P.C.).

[76] *Maryon* v. *Carter* (1830) 4 C. & P. 295; *Jackson* v. *Eastbourne Local Board* (1885) H.B.C. (4th ed.), Vol. 2, p. 81 (H.L.); *Electric Power Equipment* v. *R.C.A. Victor Co.* (1964) 46 D.L.R. (2d) 722 (British Columbia C.A.).

[77] *Dixon* v. *Metropolitan Board of Works* (1881) 7 Q.B.D. 418.

[78] *Briddon* v. *G.N. Railway* (1858) 28 L.J.Ex. 51.

[79] *Nichols* v. *Marsland* (1876) 2 Ex.D. 1 (C.A.).

[80] *Ibid.*

[81] Fry L.J. in *Nitrophosphate and Odams' Chemical Manure Co.* v. *London & St. Katherine Docks Co.* (1878) 9 Ch.D. 503 at 516 (C.A.). See "force majeure" at p. 576.

of contract,[82] but the parties may, on the construction of the contract, have intended that an act of God should bring the contract to an end.[83] There is as yet no reported case arising out of the hurricane in October 1987.

Strikes.   Strikes do not ordinarily frustrate contracts,[84] although the principles set out above must be applied to the circumstances of any particular case to see whether, exceptionally, there is such certainty of a long duration of the strike or other effect as to frustrate the contract.[85] It is usual to provide expressly for delay caused by strikes.

Compliance with building regulations.[86]   This may require heavy expenditure as, for example, when the site is opened up and it is found that elaborate foundations are necessary for a simple building. It is thought that in some cases the expenditure required in comparison with that contemplated may be so heavy that the contract is frustrated.[87]

Effect of discharge by impossibility or frustration.   Frustration of the contract discharges the parties from further obligations,[88] and at common law the contractor under the ordinary lump sum contract for a whole work could not recover the cost of work he had carried out.[89] Money paid under a contract thereafter frustrated was recoverable, but only if the consideration for the payment had wholly failed.[90]

Law Reform (Frustrated Contracts) Act 1943.[91]   The Act provides that where a contract governed by English law has become impossible of performance or has been otherwise frustrated and the employer has obtained a valuable benefit from the contract works, the contractor can recover from the employer such sum not exceeding the value of the benefit as the court having

---

[82] *Baily* v. *de Crespigny* (1869) L.R. 4 Q.B. 180 at 185.

[83] *Ibid.*

[84] *Metropolitan Water Board* v. *Dick, Kerr & Co.* [1917] 2 K.B. 1, 35; *Reardon Smith Line* v. *Min. of Agriculture* [1962] 1 Q.B. 42 at 81 (C.A.). For meaning of "strike" in a charterparty, see *Tramp Shipping Corp.* v. *Greenwich Marine Inc.* [1975] 1 W.L.R. 1042 at 1046–1047 (C.A.). For delay caused by a strike where the obligation is to complete within a reasonable time, see p. 219.

[85] *cf. Matsoukis* v. *Priestman & Co.* [1915] 1 K.B. 681; *Pioneer Shipping* v. *B.T.P. Tioxide* (*The Nema*) [1982] A.C. 724 (H.L.).

[86] See generally p. 372.

[87] There is no authority directly in point. The argument would be difficult; see "Difficulty or expense no excuse," at p. 137 and consider *Walton Harvey Ltd.* v. *Walker and Homfrays Ltd.* [1931] 1 Ch. 274 (C.A.); *Amalgamated Investment Ltd.* v. *John Walker Ltd.* [1977] 1 W.L.R. 164 (C.A.).

[88] See p. 136. The ordinary arbitration clause remains effective—see p. 388.

[89] *Appleby* v. *Myers* (1867) L.R. 2 C.P. 651. For the position of the employer, see *Fibrosa Spolka* v. *Fairbairn Lawson* [1943] A.C. 32 (H.L.).

[90] *Fibrosa Spolka* v. *Fairbairn Lawson* [1943] A.C. 32 (H.L.); see also *B.P. Exploration Co.* v. *Hunt* (*No. 2*) [1979] 1 W.L.R. 783 at 798.

[91] There is a full exposition of the operation of the Act, particularly s.3(1), by Robert Goff J. in *B.P. Exploration Co.* v. *Hunt* (*No. 2*) [1979] 1 W.L.R. 783. The Court of Appeal, at [1981] 1 W.L.R. 232, upheld his decision although they said that they got no help from the use by the judge of the term "unjust enrichment" which is not in the Act. The House of Lords, at [1983] 2 A.C. 352, dismissed the further appeal on grounds which do not materially affect the original exposition.

regard to all the circumstances of the case considers just.[92] Conversely money paid by the employer is recoverable, or if payable, ceases to be payable provided that if the contractor has incurred expenses in performance of the contract the court may, if it considers it just to do so, having regard to all the circumstances of the case, allow the contractor to retain or, as the case may be, recover the whole or any part of the money paid or payable before frustration up to the amount of the expenses incurred.[93] The Act takes effect subject to the provisions of the contract.[94] It does not require a detailed accountancy exercise.[95] Interest can be awarded under section 3(1) of the Law Reform (Miscellaneous Provisions) Act 1934.[96]

A contractor, under an entire contract,[97] who relies solely on the Act may be in no better position than at common law. He must show that the employer has received a valuable benefit, and the amount he can recover cannot exceed the value of such benefit.[98] So where the contract works are totally destroyed before use or occupation by the employer he may recover nothing.[99] It is probably more in the interest of both parties to deal expressly with matters most likely to frustrate the contract, and in particular to provide for insurance[1] against the more common risks.[2]

8. Illegality

No assistance from the court. If at the time of entering into a contract its performance or its object or the consideration for performance is illegal or contrary to sound morals, the contract is void.[3] If its completion becomes illegal after performance has commenced, the contract is frustrated and both parties are discharged from further performance.[4] No enforceable rights can, in general, accrue under an illegal or immoral contract for "no court will lend its aid to a man who founds his cause of action upon an immoral or illegal act."[5] If the contract is illegal in the sense that its performance is absolutely

---

[92] s.1(1), (3).

[93] s.1(2).

[94] s.2(3). See *B.P. Exploration Co.* v. *Hunt (No. 2)* [1981] 1 W.L.R. 232 (C.A.); *cf.* clauses 6, 22, 25, 26, 28, 32, 33 and 34 of the Standard Form of Building Contract.

[95] *B.P. Exploration Co.* v. *Hunt (No. 2)* [1981] 1 W.L.R. 232 at 242 (C.A.).

[96] *B.P. Exploration Co.* v. *Hunt (No. 2)* [1983] 2 A.C. 352 (H.L.).

[97] For meaning, see p. 70 and cases there cited, in particular *Appleby* v. *Myers* (1867) L.R. 2 C.P. 651.

[98] s.1(3). For difficulties in the interpretation and application of the Act, see *Chitty* (26th ed.), Vol. 1, paras. 1686 *et seq.*

[99] See *B.P. Exploration Co.* v. *Hunt (No. 2)* [1979] 1 W.L.R. 783 at 801.

[1] Note the effect of s.1(5).

[2] For reinstatement by insurers after destruction by fire, see the Fires Prevention (Metropolis) Act 1774, ss.83, 84. See also *Gold* v. *Patman & Fotheringham Ltd.* [1958] 1 W.L.R. 697 (C.A.), discussed at p. 550.

[3] See generally *Chitty* (26th ed.), Vol. 1, Chap. 16.

[4] See *Metropolitan Water Board* v. *Dick, Kerr & Co.* [1918] A.C. 119 (H.L.). See also p. 138.

[5] Lord Mansfield C.J. in *Holman* v. *Johnson* (1775) 1 Cowp. 341 at 343; *Brightman* v. *Tate* [1919] 1 K.B. 463; *Brown Jenkinson & Co. Ltd.* v. *Percy Dalton (London) Ltd.* [1957] 2 Q.B. 621, 635, 639 (C.A.); *Palaniappa Chettiar* v. *Arunasalam Chettiar* [1962] A.C. 294 (P.C.).

prohibited, or only permitted under a licence which is not obtained, the general rule is that the contractor cannot recover payment for illegal work even if he did not know of the illegality,[6] while the employer cannot recover instalments which he has paid under the contract.[7] If the contract is one where only the object of the building's use is immoral or illegal, it would seem that a contractor who was ignorant of such object would be able to recover for the work done and materials supplied, provided that he ceased work as soon as he became aware of the immoral or illegal purpose.[8] The position might arise in a contract to do work on premises to be used for prostitution.[9]

Severance. In cases where an ancillary part of a contract is illegal, it may be possible to sever the illegal part and enforce the lawful remainder.[10]

Contracts tainted with illegality. This is where the contract is not itself illegal, but it has a connection with some other illegal transaction which renders it obnoxious.[11] The courts tend to adopt a pragmatic approach. Where the plaintiff's action in truth arises directly out of illegality, he is likely to fail. Where the plaintiff has a genuine claim, to which allegedly unlawful conduct is incidental, he is likely to succeed.[12]

Return of goods. The owner of goods the possession of which has passed to another under an illegal contract is entitled to the return of the goods or their value provided that the owner does not have to rely on the illegal contract or plead its illegality to support his claim and provided that the claim is not so closely connected with the proceeds of crime as to offend the conscience of the court.[13] The court will look at the contract when it is just and proper to do so, as when it is necessary for the assessment of damages in an action by the owner for conversion of the goods.[14]

---

[6] *Re Mahmoud and Ispahani* [1921] 2 K.B. 716 (C.A.); *Bostel Bros. Ltd.* v. *Hurlock* [1949] 1 K.B. 74 (C.A.); cf. *Yin* v. *Sam* [1962] A.C. 304 (P.C.); *Phoenix Insurance* v. *Halvanon Insurance* [1988] Q.B. 216 (C.A.).

[7] *Smith & Son Ltd.* v. *Walker* [1952] 2 Q.B. 319 at 328 (C.A.); *Kearley* v. *Thomson* (1889) 24 Q.B.D. 742 at 745–746 (C.A.).

[8] See *Clay* v. *Yates* (1856) 1 H. & N. 73; *Pearce* v. *Brooks* (1866) L.R. 1 Ex. 213; *Kiriri Cotton Co. Ltd.* v. *Dewani* [1960] A.C. 192 (P.C.).

[9] cf. *Pearce* v. *Brooks* (1866) L.R. 1 Ex. 213. The case of *Upfill* v. *Wright* [1911] 1 K.B. 506 (D.C.) cited in earlier editions of this book is entertaining, but see now *Heglibiston Establishment* v. *Heyman* (1977) P. & C.R. 351 at 362 (C.A.).

[10] See *Carney* v. *Herbert* [1985] A.C. 301 (P.C.).

[11] Staughton J. in *Euro-Diam Ltd.* v. *Bathurst* [1990] Q.B. 1 at 15 (C.A.) upheld at [1990] Q.B. 1 (C.A.); cf. *Howard* v. *Shirlstar Container Transport* [1990] 1 W.L.R. 1292 (C.A.).

[12] Bingham L.J. in *Saunders* v. *Edwards* [1987] 1 W.L.R. 1116 at 1134 (C.A.). The subject is extensively further dealt with in *Thackwell* v. *Barclays Bank* [1986] 1 All E.R. 676; *Euro-Diam Ltd.* v. *Bathurst* [1990] Q.B. 1 (C.A.)—see especially Kerr L.J. at 34 *et seq.*

[13] *Bowmakers Ltd.* v. *Barnet Instruments Ltd.* [1945] 1 K.B. 65 (C.A.); *Singh* v. *Ali* [1960] A.C. 167 (P.C.), distinguished in *Palaniappa Chettiar* v. *Arunasalam Chettiar* [1962] A.C. 294 (P.C.); *Euro-Diam Ltd.* v. *Bathurst* [1990] Q.B. 1 at 35–36 (C.A.).

[14] *Belvoir Finance Co. Ltd.* v. *Stapleton* [1971] 1 Q.B. 210 at 218 (C.A.).

Contravention of statute.   The general principle is that "what is done in contravention of the provisions of an Act of Parliament cannot be made the subject-matter of action,"[15] but the application of this principle involves careful consideration of the statutory provisions in question and the particular breach complained of.[16] Where a contract is legal but an illegality is committed in the course of performing it, the question is whether Parliament intended that the offender should be precluded from enforcing the contract or whether breaches of the statute should attract only the civil or criminal penalties enacted.[17]

Insurance policies.   In a non-marine insurance policy,[18] there is no implied warranty, in the insurance sense of a term whose breach discharges the insurer from liability even if the breach is unconnected with the loss, that the adventure insured is a lawful one and that so far as the insured can control the matter it must be carried out in a lawful manner.[19]

Building Regulations.   Where contravention of Building Regulations or similar provisions[20] are alleged a distinction is drawn between contracts illegal as formed and contracts illegal only as performed.[21] The contractor cannot recover payment for carrying out work which on the face of the contract must contravene the statutory provision.[22] In *Stevens* v. *Gourley*[23] the contractor undertook to erect and in fact completed a shop made of wood and resting on wooden foundations with the deliberate intention of evading statutory provisions which required that buildings should be made of incombustible material. It was held that he could not recover payment because of the contravention of the statute.[24] But where a contract is on the face of it capable of performance in accordance with the relevant statutory provisions and the contravention arises only in the mode of carrying it out, then the contractor may or may not, according to the particular circumstances, be able to recover payment for work which contravened the statute. Thus in *Townsend (Builder) Ltd.* v. *Cinema News, etc., Ltd.*,[25] the work as specified did not, but as completed did, involve a contravention of a by-law. It was held that there was no "fundamental

[15] Lord Ellenborough C.J. in *Langton* v. *Hughes* 1 M. & S. 593 at 596; *cf. Howell* v. *Falmouth Boat Construction Co. Ltd.* [1951] A.C. 837 (H.L.); see also *Barton* v. *Piggott* (1874) L.R. 10 Q.B. 86.
[16] See, *e.g. Phoenix Insurance* v. *Halvanon Insurance* [1988] Q.B. 216 at 273 (C.A.).
[17] *Shaw* v. *Groom* [1970] 2 Q.B. 504 (C.A.); *Bauche* v. *Woodhouse Drake* [1977] 2 Lloyd's Rep. 516.
[18] For marine policies, see s.41 of the Marine Insurance Act 1906.
[19] *Euro-Diam Ltd.* v. *Bathurst* [1990] Q.B. 1 at 40 (C.A.).
[20] See generally p. 372.
[21] For a full discussion of this principle, see Cheshire and Fifoot, *Contract* (11th ed.), pp. 337 *et seq.* See also *Archbolds (Freightage) Ltd.* v. *S. Spanglett Ltd.* [1961] 1 Q.B. 374 (C.A.); *Ashmore, Benson Ltd.* v. *Dawson Ltd.* [1973] 1 W.L.R. 828 (C.A.).
[22] Cases cited in n. 12 above; *Stevens* v. *Gourley* (1859) 7 C.B.(N.S.) 99; *Townsend (Builders) Ltd.* v. *Cinema News, etc., Ltd.* [1959] 1 W.L.R. 119 (C.A.), also 20 B.L.R. 118.
[23] (1859) 7 C.B.(N.S.) 99.
[24] The building was, on the magistrate's order, removed.
[25] [1959] 1 W.L.R. 119 (C.A.), also 20 B.L.R. 118.

illegality pervading the whole work and the whole contract"[26] and that the contractor was entitled to recover payment[27] having regard to the following: the by-law in question; the contractor's ignorance until the work was far advanced that there would be a contravention; a temporary waiver of the contravention by the local authority and to the ease with which compliance could be secured by the insertion of a partition. It seems that had it not been for the special circumstances just set out the contractor would not have recovered payment.[28]

In the *Townsend* case, the employer recovered as damages the cost of making the works comply with the by-laws on a counterclaim for breach of an express term to comply with by-laws.[29] It is submitted that an employer who knows of, or becomes aware of, the contractor's intention to contravene by-laws cannot recover as damages any loss resulting from the breach.[30] Whether or not he would be debarred from recovering damages for other breaches would seem to depend upon whether the contravention brought about a "fundamental illegality"—see above.

Town and Country Planning Acts. It seems that the same general principles apply to contravention of town and country planning legislation as apply to contravention of Building Regulations.[31]

Obtaining necessary consents. Where consents, *e.g.* of the local authority, must be obtained to make a contract lawful it depends on the particular contract whether the contractor or the employer must obtain them and whether, if they are not obtained, the parties are discharged from further obligations under the contract.[32] It seems that in the absence of express words the party who has to obtain the consent or licence does not give an absolute warranty that he will obtain it, but a warranty to use all due diligence.[33] In a

---

[26] [1959] 1 W.L.R. 119 at 125.
[27] For the architect's liability, see pp. 180 and 319.
[28] See in particular the judgment of Lord Cohen at [1959] 1 W.L.R. 119 at 126. See also *One Hundred Simcoe Street* v. *Frank Burger Contractors* (1968) 66 D.L.R. (2d) 602, (Ontario C.A.); *Fielding & Platt Ltd.* v. *Najjar* [1969] 1 W.L.R. 357 (C.A.).
[29] R.I.B.A. form (1939 edition), clause 3, printed at p. 274 of the 2nd edition of this book. For the current clause, see clause 6 of the Standard Form of Building Contract at p. 501.
[30] *Ashmore Benson Ltd.* v. *Dawson Ltd.* [1973] 1 W.L.R. 828 (C.A.).
[31] *cf. Best* v. *Glenville* [1960] 1 W.L.R. 1198 (C.A.)—a landlord and tenant case; see also *Shaw* v. *Groom* [1970] 1 Q.B. 504 (C.A.).
[32] See *Ellis-Don* v. *Parking Authority of Toronto* (1978) 28 B.L.R. 98 (Ontario Supreme Court) for a case where the employer was in breach of contract for not obtaining necessary permits in time and the contractor was entitled to assume that a proper application had been made.
[33] See *Smith* v. *Mayor of Harwich* (1857) 26 L.J.C.P. 257; *Baily* v. *de Crespigny* (1869) L.R. 4 Q.B. 180; *Brauer & Co. Ltd.* v. *Clark, etc., Ltd.* [1952] 2 All E.R. 497 (C.A.); *cp. Pagnan* v. *Tradax Ocean* [1987] 2 Lloyd's Rep. 342 (C.A.)—absolute obligation to obtain export certificate coupled with a cancellation clause if export prohibited or restricted. See also clause 6 of the Standard Form at p. 501; *Re Northumberland Avenue Hotel Co.* (1887) 56 L.T. 833 (C.A.)—approval of plans by third party not obtained; *A. V. Pound & Co. Ltd.* v. *M. W. Hardy & Co. Inc.* [1956] A.C. 588 (H.L.); *Compagnie Algerienne, etc.* v. *Katana Societa, etc.* [1960] 2 Q.B. 115 (C.A.); *Smallman* v. *Smallman* [1972] Fam. 25 at 31 (C.A.); *Agroexport* v. *Cie. Europeene* [1974] 1 Lloyd's Rep. 499.

commercial case where a seller had an obligation to obtain an export licence, this was held not to amount to a warranty to maintain the licence in the face of supervening government intervention.[34]

Building Licences. Earlier editions of this book had discussion of the Defence Regulations 1939 and the Building Control Act 1966[35] under which certain building work was unlawful without a licence. Reference is retained here as a means only of finding the material if necessary.[36]

The Trade Description Act 1968. The Act imposes criminal sanctions for its contravention. Its purpose as regards goods is to prevent sellers of them of from attaching false descriptions to the goods, and when providing services "to make it an offence if the person providing the services recklessly makes a false statement as to what he has done."[37] In *Beckett* v. *Cohen*[38] a builder who promised to build a garage in about 10 days "as the existing" neighbouring garage did not commit an offence when he did not complete it in 10 days and it was not exactly like the other garage. "Parliament never intended . . . to make a criminal offence out of what is really a breach of warranty."[39]

9. Economic Duress

An agreement made under duress in the form of illegitimate economic pressure which amounts to a coercion of will and which vitiates consent may be voidable.[40] "It must be shown that the payment made or the contract entered into was not a voluntary act."[41] It must also be shown that the pressure exerted was illegitimate.[42] It is not clear precisely what is meant by "illegitimate,"[43] but a sufficiently coercive threat to break a contract may amount to economic duress. This may occur typically where a party to an existing contract compels by coercion uncovenanted additional payment by threatening not to perform

---

[34] *Czarnikow Ltd.* v. *Rolimpex* [1979] A.C. 351 (H.L.).

[35] Suspended in 1968 and eventually repealed by the Housing and Building Control Act 1984.

[36] See the 2nd edition of the book for the Defence Regulations and the 4th edition for the Building Control Act.

[37] *Beckett* v. *Cohen* [1972] 1 W.L.R. 1593 at 1596 (D.C.); see also *British Airways Board* v. *Taylor* [1976] 1 W.L.R. 13 (H.L.).

[38] [1972] 1 W.L.R. 1593 (D.C.).

[39] *Beckett* v. *Cohen* [1972] 1 W.L.R. 1593 at 1596 (D.C.).

[40] *Occidental Worldwide Investment* v. *Skibs A/S Avanti* [1976] 1 Lloyd's Rep. 293; *North Ocean Shipping* v. *Hyundai Construction* [1979] Q.B. 705; *Pao On* v. *Lau Yiu Long* [1980] A.C. 614 at 635 (P.C.); *Universe Tankships* v. *International Transport Workers Federation* [1983] 1 A.C. 366 at 384, 400 (H.L.). The prevailing conceptual analysis of the law of economic duress has been strongly questioned by P. S. Atiyah, "Economic Duress and the 'Overborne Will' " (1982) 98 L.Q.R. 197.

[41] Lord Scarman in *Pao On* v. *Lau Yiu Long* [1980] A.C. 614 at 636 (P.C.).

[42] *Universe Tankships* v. *International Transport Workers Federation* [1983] 1 A.C. 366 at 384, 400 (H.L.).

[43] *cf. B. & S. Contracts and Design* v. *Victor Green Publications* [1984] I.C.R. 419 at 423 (C.A.).

the contract if his demand is not met.[44] It could in principle occur in a building contract if, for example, a sub-contractor has undertaken work at a fixed price and, before he has completed the work, he declines to continue with it unless the contractor agrees to pay an increased price. Such an agreement could be voidable for economic duress if the sub-contractor was held guilty of securing the contractor's promise by taking unfair advantage of the difficulties he would cause if he did not complete the work.[45]

But commercial pressure without coercion is insufficient. If there is no sufficient coercion, a threat to repudiate a pre-existing contractual obligation or an unfair use of a dominant bargaining position is insufficient to invalidate the consideration for the agreement.[46]

> "In determining whether there was coercion of will such that there was no true consent, it is material to inquire whether the person alleged to have been coerced did or did not protest; whether, at the time he was allegedly coerced into making the contract, he did or did not have an alternative course open to him such as an adequate legal remedy; whether he was independently advised; and whether after entering the contract he took steps to avoid it."[47]

10. Default of Other Party

(a) *Repudiation generally*

The word "repudiation" is ambiguous and has several meanings,[48] but it is the most convenient term to describe circumstances where "one party so acts or so expresses himself as to show that he does not mean to accept the obligations of a contract any further."[49] Such a repudiation if accepted by the innocent party releases the innocent party from further performance.[50]

Every breach of contract entitles the other party to damages to compensate for the loss sustained in consequence of the breach. But, with the exceptions discussed below and subject to express contractual rights of determination,[51]

---

[44] *North Ocean Shipping* v. *Hyundai Construction* [1979] Q.B. 705 at 719; *B. & S. Contracts and Design* v. *Victor Green Publications* [1984] I.C.R. 419 (C.A.); *Atlas Express* v. *Kafco (Importers and Distributors)* [1989] Q.B. 833; *Vantage Navigation* v. *Suhail and Saud Bahwan Building Materials* [1989] 1 Lloyd's Rep. 138 at 145.

[45] See *Williams* v. *Roffey Bros.* [1990] 2 W.L.R. 1153 at 1163 (C.A.). (This case may be appealed to the House of Lords, but Glidewell L.J.'s reference to economic duress was not central to the main decision.)

[46] *Pao On* v. *Lau Yiu Long* [1980] A.C. 614 at 634, 635 (P.C.). A plea of economic duress is closely allied to, but different from, a plea of absence of consideration—see pp. 11 and 39.

[47] Lord Scarman in *Pao On* v. *Lau Yiu Long* [1980] A.C. 614 at 635 (P.C.); *cf. Alec Lobb (Garages)* v. *Total Oil* [1983] 1 W.L.R. 87 at 93—not affected by the decision in the Court of Appeal [1985] 1 W.L.R. 173 (C.A.).

[48] See *Heyman* v. *Darwins* [1942] A.C. 356 at 378, 398 (H.L.).

[49] *Ibid.* Lord Simon at 361.

[50] *Heyman* v. *Darwins* [1942] A.C. 356 (H.L.).

[51] See p. 236 for such determination clauses.

breach of contract by one party does not discharge the other party from performance of his unperformed obligations.[52]

There are two circumstances in which breach of contract by one party entitles the other to elect to put an end to all remaining primary obligations of both parties.[53] These are:

(1) where the contracting parties have agreed, whether by express words or implication of law that *any* breach of the contractual term in question shall entitle the other party to elect to put an end to all remaining primary obligations of both parties, *i.e.* where there is a *breach of condition*;

(2) where the event resulting from the breach of contract has the effect of depriving the other party of substantially the whole benefit which it was the intention of the parties that he should obtain from the contract, *i.e.* where there is a *fundamental breach*.[54]

Operation of the election to put an end to all remaining primary obligations of both parties is variously referred to as the "determination" or "rescission" of the contract or as "treating the contract as repudiated" or "accepting the repudiation" of the contract breaker. The first two of these expressions are, however, misleading if it is thought that for all purposes the contract is at an end and can be disregarded.[55]

Where there is a breach of condition or fundamental breach, the cause of action in *damages* does not depend on the innocent party electing to rescind the contract. Depending on the circumstances, the election may occur later.[56] The innocent party may alternatively elect not to rescind the contract, but the breach will nevertheless in principle sustain a claim for damages.

Breach of condition. A condition in this context is a contractual term breach of which entitles the other party to operate the election referred to above irrespective of the nature or seriousness of the breach.[57] Whether a contractual term is a condition is a question of construction. A term may be a condition:

(1) by statutory implication[58]; or

(2) because the parties have explicitly made it so; or

(3) because the court so construes it.

---

[52] See, *e.g. Photo Production* v. *Securicor* [1980] A.C. 827 at 849 (H.L.); *Decro-Wall International S.A.* v. *Practitioners in Marketing* [1971] 1 W.L.R. 361 (C.A.).

[53] For the meaning of "primary obligations" here, see Lord Diplock in *Photo Production* v. *Securicor* [1980] A.C. 827 at 848 (H.L.).

[54] Lord Diplock in *Photo Production* v. *Securicor* [1980] A.C. 827 at 849 (H.L.).

[55] *Ibid.* and see Lord Wilberforce *ibid.* at 845.

[56] *Tilcon* v. *Land and Real Estate* [1987] 1 W.L.R. 46 (C.A.).

[57] See, *e.g. Suisse Atlantique* v. *N.V. Rotterdamsche Kolen Centrale* [1967] 1 A.C. 361 at 422 (H.L.).

[58] See, *e.g.* ss.12–15 of the Sale of Goods Act 1979 and contrast, *e.g.* ss.13–15 of the Supply of Goods and Services Act 1982 where there are "implied terms."

Condition by explicit agreement. It is open to the parties to agree that, as regards any particular obligation, any breach shall entitle the party not in default to treat the contract as repudiated,[59] *i.e.* to make the term a condition, even if it would not be so in the absence of such a provision.[60] The parties may use language which explicitly says that a contractual term is to be so regarded. The actual use of the word "condition" is not required. "Any term or terms of the contract, which, fairly read, have the effect indicated are sufficient."[61] A common instance is where it is stipulated that "time is of the essence."[62]

Condition by construction. Although the parties may not have explicitly agreed that a contractual term is a condition, the court may find that it is. If the parties have not expressly ascribed a degree of importance to the consequences of breach, the court asks what consequences ought to be attached to it having regard to the contract as a whole.[63] This must inevitably involve a value judgment about the commercial significance of the term in question.[64] The court does not here consider the breach actually committed since parties to commercial transactions should be entitled to know their rights at once and should not, when possible, be required to wait upon events before those rights can be determined.[65] The court will not be over ready, unless required by statute or previous authority, to construe a term in a contract as a condition,[66] and will be unlikely to do so where the effect of some breaches of the term is trivial.[67]

If a term is described as a "condition," this is a strong indication that the parties intended any breach, however small, to be repudiatory, but the description is not conclusive and yields to the discovery of the parties' intention as disclosed by the contract read as a whole.[68] Conversely the use of the word "warranty" to describe a term is not conclusive that that term is not a condition. In insurance law, breach of warranty is treated as breach of condition[69] and it may well be that in a building contract the parties intend an express "warranty" of performance or as to the result or use of the works to have the effect of a condition.

---

[59] *Bunge Corporation* v. *Tradax* [1981] 1 W.L.R. 711 at 715 (H.L.); *Scandinavian Trading* v. *Flota Ecuatoriana* [1983] 2 A.C. 694 at 702 (H.L.).

[60] See *Lombard* v. *Butterworth* [1987] Q.B. 527 at 535 (C.A.).

[61] Lord Wilberforce in *Bunge Corporation* v. *Tradax* [1981] 1 W.L.R. 711 at 716 (H.L.).

[62] See p. 219 *cf. Scandinavian Trading* v. *Flota Ecuatoriana* [1983] 2 A.C. 694 at 703 (H.L.).

[63] *Bunge Corporation* v. *Tradax* [1981] 1 W.L.R. 711 at 715 (H.L.).

[64] See *State Trading Corporation of India* v. *Golodetz* [1989] 2 Lloyds's Rep. 277 (C.A.).

[65] Lord Roskill in *Bunge Corporation* v. *Tradax* [1981] 1 W.L.R. 711 at 725 (H.L.); see also Lord Wilberforce *ibid.* at 715.

[66] *Cehave N.V.* v. *Bremer m.b.H.* [1976] 1 Q.B. 44 at 70 (C.A.), Roskill L.J.

[67] *Cehave N.V.* v. *Bremer m.b.H* [1976] 1 Q.B. 44 (C.A.); *Hong Kong Fir Shipping* v. *Kawasaki Kison Kaisha* [1962] 2 Q.B. 26 (C.A.); *Schuler (L.) A.G.* v. *Wickman Machine Tool Sales* [1974] A.C. 235 (H.L.).

[68] *Schuler (L.) A.G.* v. *Wickman Machine Tool Sales* [1974] A.C. 235 (H.L.).

[69] *Ibid.* at. 256.

Fundamental breach. Contractual terms are classified as either:

(1) conditions in the sense discussed above; or

(2) warranties, being terms whose breach sounds in damages but does not terminate or entitle the other party to terminate the contract; or

(3) "intermediate" or "innominate" terms.[70]

Intermediate terms are terms capable of operating as conditions or warranties according to the gravity of the breach[71] and it is thought that, in building contracts, most terms which are not conditions are intermediate.[72] There is thus fundamental breach when the gravity of the breach of an intermediate term has the effect of depriving the other party of substantially the whole benefit which it was the intention of the parties that he should obtain from the contract. To amount to repudiation a breach must go to the root of the contract.[73]

Other tests have been to ask whether the breach is total[74] or fundamental[75] or whether the effect of the breach is such that it would be unfair to leave the injured party to a remedy in damages.[76] In commercial contracts, in particular those relating to shipping, a prime test seems to be whether the commercial purpose of the enterprise is frustrated.[77] It is submitted that, in relation to building contracts, to ask whether the breach goes to the root of the contract is often more helpful. The deliberate character of a breach makes it easier for, but does not compel, the court to find that it was fundamental.[78]

"Repudiation is a drastic conclusion which should only be held to arise in clear cases of a refusal, in a matter going to the root of the contract, to perform contractual obligations.[79] It may consist of a renunciation, an absolute refusal to perform the contract,[80] or it may arise as the result of a breach, or breaches of contract such that 'the acts and conduct of the party evince an intention no

---

[70] *Hong Kong Fir Shipping* v. *Kawasaki Kison Kaisha* [1962] 2 Q.B. 26 (C.A.); see also Lord Scarman in *Bunge Corporation* v. *Tradax* [1981] 1 W.L.R. 711 at 717 (H.L.); Lord Simon in *United Scientific Holdings* v. *Burnley Council* [1978] A.C. 904 at 945 (H.L.); Robert Goff J. in *Compagnie General Maritime* v. *Diakan Spirit* [1982] 2 Lloyd's Rep. 574 at 583 *et seq.* See also F. M. B. Reynolds, "Discharge of Contract by Breach" (1981) 97 L.Q.R. 541 who argues convincingly that *three* categories are unnecessary and that classification into (1) conditions and (2) other promises, to which the "gravity of the breach" test (see below in the text) can be applied, is preferable.

[71] See Diplock L.J. in *Hong Kong Fir Shipping* v. *Kawasaki Kison Kaisha* [1962] 2 Q.B. 26 at 70 (C.A.); *Bunge Corporation* v. *Tradax* [1981] 1 W.L.R. 711 at 717 (H.L.).

[72] See Lord Scarman in *Bunge Corporation* v. *Tradax* [1981] 1 W.L.R. 711 at 717H (H.L.).

[73] *Federal Commerce* v. *Molena Alpha* [1979] A.C. 757 at 779 (H.L.). See also the cases there cited; *Cehave N.V.* v. *Bremer m.b.H.* [1976] 1 Q.B. 44 at 60 (C.A.).

[74] *Heyman* v. *Darwins* [1942] A.C. 356 at 397 (H.L.).

[75] *Suisse Atlantique* v. *N.V. Rotterdamsche Kolen Centrale* [1967] 1 A.C. 361 at 397, 410 (H.L.).

[76] *Decro-Wall International S.A.* v. *Practitioners in Marketing* [1971] 1 W.L.R. 361 at 380 (C.A.).

[77] *Hong Kong Fir Shipping* v. *Kawasaki Kison Kaisha* [1962] 2 Q.B. 26 (C.A.).

[78] *Suisse Atlantique* v. *N.V. Rotterdamsche Kolen Centrale* [1967] 1 A.C. 361 at 394, 398, 415, 429, 435 (H.L.).

[79] Lord Wilberforce in *Woodar* v. *Wimpey* [1980] 1 W.L.R. 277 at 283 (H.L.). See also *Ross T. Smyth & Co. Ltd.* v. *T. D. Bailey, Son & Co.* [1940] 3 All E.R. 60 at 71 (H.L.).

[80] *Suisse Atlantique* v. *N.V. Rotterdamsche Kolen Centrale* [1967] 1 A.C. 361 at 412, 421 (H.L.); *Mersey Steel & Iron Co. Ltd.* v. *Naylor* (1884) 9 App.Cas. 434 at 439, 443 (H.L.).

longer to be bound by the contract.' "[81] Repudiation before performance is due is termed an anticipatory breach.[82]

Erroneous expression of view. There can be repudiation where a party intends to fulfil a contract, but "is determined to do so only in a manner substantially inconsistent with his obligations and not in any other way."[83] But it is not a repudiation merely to put forward in good faith an interpretation of the contract which is wrong,[84] the more especially if it is put forward in such a way as to show that it is open to correction.[85] A party who bona fide relies upon an express stipulation in a contract in order to rescind or terminate the contract is not, by that fact alone, treated as having repudiated his contractual obligations if he turns out to be mistaken as to his rights.[86] It is necessary to pay proper regard to the impact of the party's conduct on the other party.[87] It is thought that, if either party to a building contract operates contractual determination machinery upon a mistaken, albeit bona fide, view of the facts or his legal rights, that will normally be repudiation. The impact of such conduct on the other party suggests no other conclusion.[88]

Subsequent excuses for alleged repudiation. A party who is alleged to have repudiated a contract can subsequently rely on any defence notwithstanding that at the time of the alleged repudiation he gave other or no reasons by way of excuse,[89] unless he is estopped by his conduct and the other party's reliance thereon from relying upon a reason different from that which he gave at the time of the alleged repudiation.[90]

---

[81] *General Billposting Co. Ltd.* v. *Atkinson* [1909] A.C. 118 at 122 (H.L.).

[82] *The Mihalis Angelos* [1971] 1 Q.B. 164 (C.A.); *Federal Commerce* v. *Molena Alpha* [1979] A.C. 757 at 778 (H.L.); *Afovos Shipping* v. *Pagnan* [1983] 1 W.L.R. 195 at 203 (H.L.). For a discussion and sub-classification of anticipatory breach into (a) breach by evinced intention and (b) breach by impossibility, see *Chilean Nitrate Sales* v. *Marine Transportation* [1982] 1 Lloyd's Rep. 570 at 572 *et seq.* (C.A.).

[83] *Ross T. Smyth & Co. Ltd.* v. *T. D. Bailey, Son & Co.* [1940] 3 All E.R. 60 at 72 (H.L.).

[84] *Ibid.*; *Mersey Steel & Iron Co. Ltd.* v. *Naylor* (1884) 9 App.Cas. 434 (H.L.); *James Shaffer Ltd.* v. *Findlay, Durham & Brodie* [1953] 1 W.L.R. 106 (C.A.); *Peter Dumenil* v. *James Ruddin* [1953] 1 W.L.R. 815 (C.A.); *Sweet & Maxwell Ltd.* v. *Universal News Services Ltd.* [1964] 2 Q.B. 699 (C.A.); *Toepfer* v. *Cremer* [1975] 2 Lloyds's Rep. 118 at 125 (C.A.).

[85] *Ibid.* especially *Ross T. Smith & Co. Ltd.* v. *T. D. Bailey, Son & Co.* [1940] 3 All E.R. 60 at 72 (H.L.); *Sweet & Maxwell Ltd.* v. *Universal News Services Ltd.* [1964] 2 Q.B. 699 at 737 (C.A.).

[86] Lord Wilberforce in *Woodar* v. *Wimpey* [1980] 1 W.L.R. 277 at 283 (H.L.) expressing the conclusion of the majority—Lords Salmon and Russell (dissenting) held that contractual rescission on grounds unjustified in law is always repudiation.

[87] *Ibid.* Lord Scarman at 299.

[88] *cf. Canterbury Pipe Lines* v. *Christchurch Drainage* (1979) 16 B.L.R. 76.

[89] *British and Beningtons* v. *North Western Cachar Tea* [1923] A.C. 48 at 71 (H.L.); *Scammell* v. *Ouston* [1941] A.C. 251 at 268 (H.L.); *The Mihalis Angelos* [1971] 1 Q.B. 164 at 195 (C.A.); *Scandinavian Trading* v. *Zodiac Petroleum* [1981] 1 Lloyds's Rep. 81.

[90] *Panchaud Freres S.A.* v. *Etablissements General Grain Co.* [1970] 1 Lloyds's Rep. 53 (C.A.). The text of the 4th edition of this book is here retained, but see the discussion of *Panchaud Freres* by Hirst J. in *Procter & Gamble* v. *Peter Cremer* [1988] 3 All E.R. 843 concluding at 852 that "no distinctive principle of law can be distilled from the *Panchaud* case." For determination under the Standard Form of Building Contract, see clauses 27, 28 discussed at pp. 590 *et seq.*

Arbitration agreements. In certain limited circumstances, one party to an arbitration agreement may treat the other party as guilty of repudiatory breach of that agreement.[91]

Acceptance of repudiation.[92] "Repudiation by one party standing alone does not terminate the contract. It takes two to end it, by repudiation on the one side, and acceptance of the repudiation on the other."[93] The innocent party must make it plain that "in view of the wrongful act of the party who has repudiated he claims to treat the contract as at an end."[94] By doing this he is usually said to rescind[95] the contract. He is released from further performance of primary obligations[96] and can sue at once for damages even though the time for performance has not yet arisen.[97] Acceptance of repudiation by the employer does not affect the contractor's accrued rights to the payment of instalments of the contract price unless the contract otherwise provides.[98]

> "[T]he contract is not rescinded as from the beginning. Both parties are discharged from the further performance of the contract, but rights are not divested or discharged which have already been unconditionally acquired. ... The contract is discharged so far as it is executory only."[99]

But advance payments may be recoverable if the contractor has provided no consideration in the nature of part performance.[1]

A full arbitration clause will normally continue to apply to disputes arising upon an acceptance of repudiation.[2] A clause barring liability unless suit was brought within one year after an event was held to be "indistinguishable from an arbitration clause, or a forum clause, which, on clear authority, survive a

---

[91] See *Bremer Vulkan* v. *South India Shipping Corporation* [1981] A.C. 909 at 980 (H.L.); *Turriff* v. *Richards & Wallington* (1981) 18 B.L.R. 19; see also pp. 388 and 405 and s.13A of the Arbitration Act 1950 as inserted by s.102 of the Courts of Legal Services Act 1990 (not yet in force).

[92] Note that *Harbutt's "Plasticine"* v. *Wayne Tank and Pump* [1970] 1 Q.B. 447 (C.A.), discussed in this context in the 4th edition of this book was overruled in *Photo Production* v. *Securicor* [1980] A.C. 827 (H.L.).

[93] Lord Simon in *Heyman* v. *Darwins* [1942] A.C. 356 at 361 (H.L.); *White & Carter (Councils) Ltd.* v. *McGregor* [1962] A.C. 413 at 432 (H.L.); *Lakshmijt* v. *Sherani* [1974] A.C. 605 at 616 (P.C.); *Aquis Estates Ltd.* v. *Minton* [1975] 1 W.L.R. 1452 (C.A.). Where there is no acceptance the injured party cannot obtain a bare declaration that there was conduct constituting a repudiation—*Howard* v. *Pickford Tool Co. Ltd.* [1951] 1 K.B. 417 (C.A.).

[94] Lord Simon in *Heyman* v. *Darwins* [1942] A.C. 356 at 361 (H.L.).

[95] See p. 120 for misrepresentation and p. 128 for the view that references in the Misrepresentation Act 1967 to rescission are not to acceptance of repudiation.

[96] See n. 53 above.

[97] Lord Simon in *Heyman* v. *Darwins* [1942] A.C. 356 at 361 (H.L.); *Hochster* v. *de la Tour* (1853) 2 E. & B. 678. This type of repudiation is termed "anticipatory breach."

[98] *Hyundai Industries* v. *Papadopoulos* [1980] 1 W.L.R. 1129 (H.L.).

[99] Dixon J. in *McDonald* v. *Dennys Lascelles Ltd.* (1933) 48 C.L.R. 457 at 476, quoted with approval by Lord Wilberforce in *Johnson* v. *Agnew* [1980] A.C. 367 at 396 (H.L.); *cf. Damon Compania Naviera* v. *Hapag-Lloyd* [1985] 1 W.L.R. 435 (C.A.); *Bank of Boston* v. *European Grain* [1989] A.C. 1056 at 1098 (H.L.). See also s.9 of the Unfair Contract Terms Act 1977 discussed at p. 67.

[1] *Rover International* v. *Cannon Film* [1989] 1 W.L.R. 912 at 932 (C.A.).

[2] *Heyman* v. *Darwins* [1942] A.C. 356 (H.L.).

repudiatory breach."[3] The terms of the contract may be referred to for the purpose of assessing damages.[4]

If the innocent party does not elect to accept the repudiation but affirms[5] the contract, the defaulting party may continue to rely on the terms of the contract, including any agreed damages or cancellation clause,[6] unless on its true construction any term excluding or limiting his liability was not intended to cover the kind of breach which has been committed.[7] Where the time for performance has not yet arisen, the defaulting party "has the opportunity of withdrawing from his false position, and even if he does not, may escape ultimate liability because of some supervening event"[8] which frustrates the contract.[9] Where the contract remains in existence the innocent party's obligations continue, and he cannot thereafter terminate the contract for a breach he has waived,[10] although if the breach is not remedied or excused before performance is due, he can then enforce his claim under or for breach of the contract.[11]

The innocent party is not, it seems, in the ordinary case, bound to accept a repudiation before performance is completed in order to reduce the amount ultimately payable to him by the defaulting party,[12] but it is doubtful whether this principle can have any application to repudiation by the employer in the ordinary building contract where the employer's assent is required to go on his land for its performance.[13] In an extreme case[14] where an innocent party has no legitimate interest, financial or otherwise, in performing the contract rather than claiming damages, the court may decline in the exercise of its general

[3] *Port Jackson* v. *Salmond & Spraggon* [1981] 1 W.L.R. 138 at 145 (P.C.).
[4] *Bloeman (F.J.) Pty. Ltd.* v. *Gold Coast City* [1973] A.C. 115 (P.C.); *Lep Air Services Ltd.* v. *Rolloswin Ltd.* [1973] A.C. 331 (H.L.). For arbitration, see Chap. 16.
[5] Affirmation must be unequivocal and with knowledge of the facts giving rise to the right to rescind and of the right to rescind itself—*Peyman* v. *Lanjani* [1985] Ch. 457 (C.A.).
[6] See *Fercometal* v. *Mediterranean Shipping* [1989] A.C. 788 at 805 (H.L.), Lord Ackner concluding that the innocent party has two choices only, to affirm the contract or treat it as finally and conclusively discharged.
[7] *Suisse Atlantique* v. *N.V. Rotterdamsche Kolen Centrale* [1967] 1 A.C. 361 (H.L.).
[8] *Heyman* v. *Darwins* [1942] A.C. 356 at 361 (H.L.).
[9] *Ibid.*; *Avery* v. *Bowden* (1855) 6 E. & B. 953, where after refusal but before the time for performance the contract became illegal because of the outbreak of war.
[10] *Frost* v. *Knight* (1872) L.R. 7 Ex. 111 at 112; *Hughes* v. *Metropolitan Railway* (1877) 2 App.Cas. 439 (H.L.); *Suisse Atlantique* v. *N.V. Rotterdamsche Kolen Centrale* [1967] 1 A.C. 361 (H.L.); *Allen* v. *Robles* [1969] 1 W.L.R. 1193 (C.A.).
[11] *Frost* v. *Knight* (1872) L.R. 7 Ex. 111; *Heyman* v. *Darwins* [1942] A.C. 356 (H.L.); *White & Carter (Councils) Ltd.* v. *McGregor* [1962] A.C. 413 (H.L.).
[12] *White & Carter (Councils) Ltd.* v. *McGregor* [1962] A.C. 413 (H.L.)—a Scottish appeal where the majority (3:2) of the House of Lords held that an advertising contractor who did not accept a repudiation was entitled to perform his contract and recover the full contract price. See also p. 190.
[13] See *Finelli* v. *Dee* (1968) 67 D.L.R. (2d) 393 (Ontario C.A.); *Hounslow (London Borough)* v. *Twickenham Garden Developments* [1971] Ch. 233 at 252–254, but note comments at p. 270; *Mayfield Holdings* v. *Moana Reef* [1973] 1 N.Z.L.R. 309 (New Zealand Supreme Court). See also *Barker, George (Transport) Ltd.* v. *Eynon* [1974] 1 W.L.R. 462 (C.A.); *Attica Sea Carriers* v. *Ferrostaal-Poseidon GmbH* [1976] 1 Lloyd's Rep. 250 (C.A.).
[14] See *Gator Shipping Corporation* v. *Trans-Asiatic Oil* [1978] 2 Lloyd's Rep. 357 at 374 (C.A.).

equitable jurisdiction to allow the innocent party to enforce his full contractual rights.[15]

Repudiation and contractual determination clauses. A party who purports to operate a contractual determination clause when he is not entitled to do so either factually or legally is likely to repudiate the contract.[16] This is because a party who acts upon a contractual determination clause usually refuses or ceases to perform his own obligations. If this is not in accordance with the contract, he will usually himself be in fundamental breach.

Contractual determination clauses do not exclude common law remedies available upon repudiation unless the agreement expressly provides that the contractual rights are to be the exclusive remedy for the breaches in question.[17] It is theoretically possible that such an exclusion might also arise by implication, but it is thought that in practice this is unlikely.

It is an open question whether an employer, faced with default by the contractor which might both amount to repudiation and entitle the employer to operate a contractual determination clause, can hedge his position so as to avail himself of both opportunities. Logically this may not be possible, since to operate the contract is to affirm it, which is inconsistent with accepting a repudiation.[18] It may, however, depend on the order in which the alternatives are effected. An acceptance of repudiation followed in the alternative by a contractual determination expressed to be without prejudice to the acceptance of repudiation might achieve the contractual determination if there was held to have been no repudiation to accept.[19] A single notice which is not framed in the alternative may or may not serve to effect either possibility. A notice explicitly operating a contractual determination clause will normally not serve in the alternative as an acceptance of repudiation.[20] A notice expressed neutrally may serve as an acceptance of repudiation if a contractual determination relying on it is held to be ineffective.[21]

(b) *Repudiation by contractor*[22]

Refusal or abandonment. An absolute refusal to carry out the work or an

---

[15] See *Clea Shipping Corporation* v. *Bulk Oil International (No. 2)* [1983] 2 Lloyd's Rep. 645, where the authorities are reviewed.

[16] See, *e.g. Architectural Installation Services* v. *James Gibbons* (1989) 16 Con.L.R. 68 at 73.

[17] *Modern Engineering (Bristol)* v. *Gilbert-Ash* [1974] A.C. 689 (H.L.); *Architectural Installation Services* v. *James Gibbons Windows* (1989) 46 B.L.R. 91 at 100; *Sutcliffe* v. *Chippendale & Edmondson* (1971) 18 B.L.R. 149 at 160 *et seq.*; see also *Chitty* (26th ed.), para. 1614.

[18] *cf. Fercometal* v. *Mediterranean Shipping* [1989] A.C. 788 at 805 (H.L.).

[19] See *Scarf* v. *Jardine* (1882) 7 A.C. 345 at 360 (H.L.); *United Australia* v. *Barclays Bank* [1941] A.C. 1 at 30 (H.L.).

[20] *E. R. Dyer* v. *Simon Build/Lind Partnership* (1983) 23 B.L.R. 23 at 33; *cf. Mvita Construction* v. *Tanzania Harbours Authority* (1988) 46 B.L.R. 19 at 33 (Tanzanian Court of Appeal).

[21] *Architectural Installation Services* v. *James Gibbons Windows* (1989) 46 B.L.R. 91 at 100. See also "Forfeiture clauses" at p. 236 and in particular "Ascertainment of the event" at p. 238.

[22] The specific matters discussed must be read with "Repudiation—generally" above.

abandonment of the work before it is substantially completed, without any lawful excuse, is a repudiation.[23]

Defects. A breach consisting of mere negligent omissions or bad workmanship where the work is substantially completed does not go to the root of the contract in the ordinary lump sum contract,[24] and is not therefore a repudiation.

Can omissions or bad work as they occur during the course of the work be treated as repudiation? It is submitted that in the ordinary case they cannot if they are not such as to prevent substantial completion, but that there is a repudiation where, having regard to the construction of the contract and all the facts and circumstances, the gravity of the breaches is such as to show that the contractor does not intend to or cannot substantially perform his obligations under the contract.[25] In *Sutcliffe* v. *Chippendale and Edmondson*,[26] it was held that the contractor's:

> "manifest inability to comply with the completion date requirements, the nature and number of complaints from subcontractors and [the architect's] own admission that in May and June the quality of work was deteriorating and the number of defects was multiplying, many of which he had tried unsuccessfully to have put right, all point to the truth of the plaintiff's expressed view that the contractors had neither the ability, competence or the will by this time to complete the work in the manner required by the contract."

Hence the plaintiff was justified in ordering the contractors off the site.[27]

Delay. Delay on the part of the contractor where time is not of the essence of the contract does not amount to a repudiation unless it is such as to show that he will not, or cannot, carry out the contract.[28] In *Hill* v. *London Borough of Camden*,[29] it was held on the facts that a contractor, who had reduced his workforce to such an extent that it might have been said that they were not

---

[23] *Mersey Steel & Iron Co. Ltd.* v. *Naylor* (1884) 9 App.Cas. 434 (H.L.); *Marshall* v. *Mackintosh* (1898) 78 L.T. 750; *Hoenig* v. *Isaacs* [1952] 2 All E.R. 176 (C.A.).

[24] *Hoenig* v. *Isaacs* [1952] 2 All E.R. 176 (C.A.); see generally Chap. 4.

[25] *Suisse Atlantique* v. *N.V. Rotterdamsche Kolen Centrale* [1967] 1 A.C. 361 at 422 (H.L.); see also *Wayne Tank Co. Ltd.* v. *Employers Liability Ltd.* [1974] Q.B. 57 at 73 (C.A.) subject to the qualification that the effect of an acceptance of repudiation on exception clauses there stated (at 74A) was overruled in *Photo Production* v. *Securicor* [1980] A.C. 827 (H.L.).

[26] (1971) 18 B.L.R. 157 at 161. This was the first instance decision leading to *Sutcliffe* v. *Thackrah* [1974] A.C. 727 (H.L.). The quoted part of the first instance decision was not appealed against.

[27] *cf. Wathes (Western)* v. *Austins (Menswear)* (1975) 9 B.L.R. 113—but cases concerning repudiation in the context of exclusion clauses decided before *Photo Production* v. *Securicor* [1980] A.C. 827 (H.L.) should be treated with some caution. For a case where a contractor's defects did not amount to repudiation, see *Sheffield* v. *Conrad* (1987) C.I.L.L. 381 (C.A.).

[28] *Felton* v. *Wharrie* (1906) H.B.C. (4th ed.), Vol. 2, p. 398 (C.A.); *Chandler Bros.* v. *Boswell* [1936] 3 All E.R. 179 at 185 (C.A.); *Suisse Atlantique* v. *N.V. Rotterdamsche Kolen Centrale* [1967] 1 A.C. 361 (H.L.).

[29] (1980) 18 B.L.R. 31 (C.A.).

proceeding "regularly and diligently" within the meaning of clause 25 of the JCT Form, had not by such conduct repudiated the contract.

In most cases[30] it is desirable to give notice that continuance of the delay will be treated as repudiation before purporting to accept the repudiation by dismissing the contractor. In *Felton* v. *Wharrie*[31] the contractor had not finished the work by the completion date, and when asked by the employer's agent whether it would take one, two, three or four months, replied that he could not say. He proceeded with the work and two weeks later the employer without any express right under the contract, and without any warning forcibly ejected the contractor from the site. It was held that the employer had no right to determine the contract.

> "If he were going to act upon the plaintiff's conduct as being evidence of his not going on, he ought to have told him of it, and to have said, 'I treat that as a refusal,' and the man would know of it; but the fact of allowing him to go on cannot be any evidence of justification of re-entry."[32]

Where time is of the essence either by the terms of the contract, or as a result of a notice making it of the essence,[33] and the contractor fails to complete to time the employer is entitled to treat the contract as at an end and to dismiss the contractor from the site.[34]

Other breaches of contract. It is a question in each case whether other breaches of contract go to the root of the contract. For example, it has been held that sub-letting part of the contract works contrary to an express provision was not a repudiation.[35]

Repudiation and forfeiture.[36] A distinction must be made between the acceptance of repudiation bringing a contract to an end, and the determination of the contract under an express power.[37] If the event giving rise to the exercise of an express right to determine was a repudiation by the contractor, the employer is, subject to the express terms of the contract, entitled to all the damages that flow from non-completion, including the enhanced cost of completing by another contractor.[38] But such damages may not be payable if the event relied on was not a repudiation. This in *Feather* v. *Keighley Corporation*,[39] the contractor undertook not to sub-let work without consent, the

---

[30] *cf. Etablissements Chainbaux* v. *Harbormaster Ltd.* [1955] 1 Lloyd's Rep. 303.

[31] (1906) H.B.C. (4th ed.), Vol. 2, p. 398 (C.A.).

[32] *Ibid.* Lord Alverstone L.C.J. at 400. For express rights, see Chap. 10, "Forfeiture Clauses."

[33] See pp. 219 *et seq.*

[34] *Rickards* v. *Oppenheim* [1950] 1 K.B. 616 at 628 (C.A.).

[35] *Feather* v. *Keighley Corp.* (1953) 52 L.G.R. 30.

[36] See also "Repudiation and contractual determination clauses" at p. 153.

[37] *cf. E. R. Dyer* v. *Simon Build/Lind* (1983) 23 B.L.R. 23 and see Chap. 10, "Forfeiture Clauses."

[38] See *Marshall* v. *Mackintosh* (1898) 78 L.T. 750. For the measure of damages see p. 201.

[39] (1953) 52 L.G.R. 30.

contract providing that for breach of this term the employer could either absolutely determine the contract, or could claim £100 by way of liquidated damages. The contractor sub-let without consent, and the employer thereupon determined the contract and claimed as damages the increased cost of completing by another contractor. It was held that there had only been a breach of a collateral term, not a repudiation, and that the employer having chosen his remedy of determining the contract was not entitled to claim damages.

(c) *Repudiation by employer*[40]

Refusal.   An absolute refusal by the employer to carry out his part of the contract, whether made before the works commenced or while they are being carried out is a repudiation of the contract.[41]

Rendering completion impossible.   It is, in general, a repudiation if the employer wrongfully by his own acts, and without lawful excuse,[42] renders completion impossible.[43]

Possession of site.   The employer repudiates the contract if he fails to give possession of the site at all, or without lawful excuse ejects the contractor from the site before completion.[44]

Order not to complete.   A clear unjustified order not to complete the works is a repudiation.[45]

Failure to pay instalments.   This cannot be a repudiation if there is no contractual duty to pay them.[46] Where there is such a duty it is a question in each case whether failure to pay is a repudiation. Failure to pay one instalment out of many due under the terms of the contract is not ordinarily sufficient to amount to a repudiation.[47] It was held to be a repudiation where a company

---

[40] The specific matters discussed must be read with "Repudiation—generally" above.
[41] *Hochster* v. *de la Tour* (1853) 2 E. & B. 678; *Mersey Steel & Iron Co. Ltd.* v. *Naylor* (1884) 9 App.Cas. 434 (H.L.).
[42] See *Cory Ltd.* v. *City of London Corp.* [1951] 2 K.B. 476 (C.A.).
[43] *Stirling* v. *Maitland* (1864) 5 B. & S. 840, 852; *Roberts* v. *Bury Commissioners* (1870) L.R. 4 C.P. 755; *Southern Foundries* v. *Shirlaw* [1940] A.C. 701 at 717, 741 (H.L.). For the employer's duty to co-operate and not to prevent completion, see p. 48.
[44] *Ibid.; Felton* v. *Wharrie* (1906) H.B.C. (4th ed.), Vol. 2, p. 398 (C.A.); *cf. Earth & General Contractors Ltd.* v. *Manchester Corp.* (1958) 108 L.J. 665—interference with possession not repudiation.
[45] *Cort* v. *Ambergate Railway* (1851) 17 Q.B. 127.
[46] *Rees* v. *Lines* (1837) 8 C. & P. 126; see p. 70.
[47] *Mersey Steel & Iron Co. Ltd.* v. *Naylor* (1884) 9 App.Cas. 434 (H.L.); *Decro-Wall International S.A.* v. *Practitioners in Marketing* [1971] 1 W.L.R. 361 (C.A.); *Lakshmijit* v. *Faiz Sherani* [1974] A.C. 605 at 616 (P.C.); *Afovos Shipping* v. *Pagnan* [1983] 1 W.L.R. 195 at 202 (H.L.); *cf. Fenton Insurance* v. *Gothaer Versicherungsbank, The Times,* July 4, 1990.

had only paid £10,000 out of £24,000 then due.[48] A failure to pay is less likely to be a repudiation if it occurs towards the end of a contract.[49]

Under-certification. Can an employer who pays certificates issued by the architect be guilty of repudiation if those certificates are substantially too low?[50] There are difficulties in saying that he can because prima facie he is doing what the contract requires of him. But it has now been settled that the architect is the employer's agent when giving his certificate.[51] It has been held that an employer cannot stand by and take advantage of his architect applying a wrong principle in certifying.[52] It has been more recently held that, where there was a wide arbitration clause and where the employer had not interfered with or obstructed the issue of certificates, the employer was not obliged to pay more than the amount stated on the certificate. The contractor's simple remedy was to go to arbitration and have the certificates corrected.[53] There is thus a narrow dividing line between cases where an employer who has paid certified amounts may be in breach of contract and cases where he may not. In principle, if there are circumstances in which he may be in breach, he could also in extreme cases be in repudiatory breach. But it seems that this would at least require both clear knowledge by the employer that the architect was persistently undercertifying and a contract without a relevant arbitration clause.[54]

No general right to suspend work. Although particular contracts may give the contractor express rights if certificates are not paid, there is no general right to suspend work if payment is wrongly withheld.[55] This is consistent with the principle that, except where there is a breach of condition or fundamental breach of contract, breach of contract by one party does not discharge the other party from performance of his unperformed obligations.[56]

Other breaches. It depends upon the construction of the contract and the circumstances whether the acts and conduct of the employer show that he no

---

[48] *Lep Air Services Ltd.* v. *Rolloswin Ltd.* [1973] A.C. 331 at 344, 346, 353 (H.L.).

[49] *Cornwall* v. *Henson* [1900] 2 Ch. 298 (C.A.).

[50] For certificates generally, see Chap. 5.

[51] *Sutcliffe* v. *Thackrah* [1974] A.C. 727 (H.L.).

[52] *Panamena, etc.* v. *Frederick Leyland & Co. Ltd.* [1947] A.C. 428 (H.L.), discussed at p. 104. See also the *Panamena* case in the Court of Appeal at [1943] 76 Lloyd's Rep. 113 at 124 where it was said that the interference there was a repudiation; and *cf.* the judgment of Macfarlan J. in the New South Wales Supreme Court in *Perini Corporation* v. *Commonwealth of Australia* (1969) 12 B.L.R. 82.

[53] *Lubenham* v. *South Pembrokeshire District Council* (1986) 33 B.L.R. 39 (C.A.). See discussion at p. 49.

[54] For the principles which the architect must apply when certifying under the Standard Form of Building Contract, see clause 30.

[55] *Lubenham* v. *South Pembrokeshire District Council* (1986) 33 B.L.R. 39 at 70 (C.A.); *cf. Canterbury Pipe Lines* v. *Christchurch Drainage* (1979) 16 B.L.R. 76 (New Zealand Court of Appeal); *Supamarl* v. *Federated Homes* (1981) 9 Con. L.R. 25.

[56] See p. 146.

longer intends to be bound by the contract. Thus, assuming there is a breach, it may or may not be a repudiation if the employer fails to appoint an architect,[57] or to supply plans[58] or materials,[59] or to make a fresh nomination of a sub-contractor.[60]

Where a contractor was carrying out work for an employer under two separate contracts, he was held not to be entitled to stop work on one contract because the employer had not paid on the other contract.[61]

If the employer interferes with the architect in the performance of those functions where he has to act fairly between the employer and the contractor[62] it is, it is submitted, a question in each case depending both upon the nature of the employer's acts and their effect whether such interference amounts to a repudiation.

(d) *Party cannot rely on own wrong*

Where one party has failed to perform a condition of the contract, the other party cannot rely on its non-performance if it was caused by his own wrongful acts.[63] This principle has been considered elsewhere in respect of the contractor's failure to complete the contract work,[64] to obtain written orders for extras,[65] to obtain the architect's certificate,[66] and to complete to time.[67] To attract the principle that a party to a contract is not permitted to take advantage of his own breach of duty, the duty must be one that is owed to the other party under the contract. A duty, whether contractual or non-contractual, owed to a stranger to the contract does not suffice.[68] The principle is probably a rule of construction and not an absolute rule of law.[69] It applies to a party seeking to obtain a benefit under a continuing contract on account of his

[57] *Coombe* v. *Greene* (1843) 11 M. & W. 480; *Hunt* v. *Bishop* (1853) 8 Ex. 675; *Ctr. Jones* v. *Cannock* (1852) 3 H.L.C. 700.
[58] *Wells* v. *Army & Navy Co-op. Society* (1902) 86 L.T. 764; H.B.C. (4th ed.), Vol. 2, p. 356 (C.A.); *Trollope & Colls* v. *Singer* (1913) H.B.C. (4th ed.), Vol. 1, p. 849; *cf. Stevens* v. *Taylor* (1860) 2 F. & F. 419.
[59] *Macintosh* v. *Midland Counties Railway* (1845) 14 L.J. Ex. 338; *cf. Gaze Ltd.* v. *Port Talbot Corp.* (1929) 93 J.P. 89.
[60] See *Bickerton (T. A.) & Son Ltd.* v. *N.W. Regional Hospital Board* [1970] 1 W.L.R. 607 (H.L.); *cf. Percy Bilton* v. *Greater London Council* [1982] 1 W.L.R. 794 (H.L.). The circumstances in which such a breach might be repudiatory are not discussed. See also p. 293.
[61] *Small & Sons Ltd.* v. *Middlesex Real Estates Ltd.* [1921] W.N. 245.
[62] See *Sutcliffe* v. *Thackrah* [1974] A.C. 727 at 737 (H.L.) and submission at p. 52 that there is an implied term that the employer will not so act as to disqualify the architect. For disqualification, see p. 114.
[63] *Roberts* v. *Bury Commissioners* (1870) L.R. 4 C.P. 755; *cp. Lubenham* v. *South Pembrokeshire District Council* (1986) 33 B.L.R. 39 at 57 (C.A.). See article by J. F. Burrows (1965) 31 M.L.R. 390. For clauses purporting to exempt a party from the consequences of his own negligence, see p. 60.
[64] See p. 74.
[65] See p. 92.
[66] See p. 104.
[67] See p. 231.
[68] *Cheal* v. *A.P.E.X.* [1983] 2 A.C. 180 at 189; *cf. Thompson* v. *ASDA-MFI Plc.* [1988] Ch. 241 at 266.
[69] See *Alghussein Establishment* v. *Eton College* [1988] 1 W.L.R. 587 at 595 (H.L.).

own breach as much as to a party who relies on his own breach to avoid a contract and thereby escape his obligations.[70]

A similar principle is applied to the construction of contracts which provide that, upon the happening of certain events, the contract shall become void. When such an event occurs either party may declare the contract void provided he has not himself in breach of a duty owed to the other party been the means of bringing about the event[71]; for example, an insolvent contractor cannot rely on his own insolvency to escape from the contract.[72]

---

[70] *Ibid.* at 594.

[71] *New Zealand Shipping Co.* v. *Ateliers, etc., de France* [1919] A.C. 1 (H.L.); *Cheal* v. *A.P.E.X.* [1983] 2 A.C. 180 at 189.

[72] *New Zealand Shipping Co.* v. *Ateliers, etc., de France* [1919] A.C. 1 at 13 (H.L.).

CHAPTER 7

NEGLIGENCE AND ECONOMIC LOSS

1. Introduction

Between the publication of the 4th and 5th editions of this book, there was an astonishing revolution and counter-revolution in the English law of negligence. In July 1990, a Judicial Committee of seven Law Lords deciding *Murphy* v. *Brentwood District Council*[1] unanimously departed from the 1977 House of Lords decision of *Anns* v. *Merton London Borough Council*[2] and overruled the 1971 Court of Appeal decision of *Dutton* v. *Bognor Regis Urban District Council*.[3] In addition "all decisions subsequent to *Anns* which purported to follow it" were overruled.[4] It is accordingly necessary to read all English authorities concerning negligence decided between 1971 and 1990 with extreme caution. There are very many of them and many of these contain decisions or dicta which are wrong. Many of them concerned building contracts. Even some House of Lords decisions not specifically departed from in *Murphy* are nevertheless suspect.[5] Some cases cited in this chapter on points for which it is thought that they remain authority are nevertheless *Anns* cases and should be treated cautiously. However, the counter-revolution began historically in about 1985,[6] and for the most part Court of Appeal decisions between then and 1990 adopted a restrictive approach to *Anns* which anticipated its eventual demise.

Summary.[7]   To establish a claim in negligence, a plaintiff must show that the defendant owes him a duty of care and that there has been a breach of that

---

[1] [1990] 3 W.L.R. 414 (H.L.); see also *Department of Environment* v. *Thomas Bates* [1990] 3 W.L.R. 457 (H.L.); *D. & F. Estates* v. *Church Commissioners* [1989] A.C. 177 (H.L.).

[2] [1978] A.C. 728 (H.L.).

[3] [1972] 1 Q.B. 373 (C.A.).

[4] See *Murphy* v. *Brentwood District Council* [1990] 3 W.L.R. 414 at 419, 433, 442, 451 (H.L.).

[5] *e.g. Junior Books* v. *Veitchi Co.* [1983] 1 A.C. 520 (H.L.); *Pirelli* v. *Oscar Faber & Partners* [1983] 2 A.C. 1 (H.L.). These are discussed below.

[6] See, for its progress, *e.g. Governors of the Peabody Donation Fund* v. *Sir Lindsay Parkinson* [1985] A.C. 210 (H.L.); *Leigh and Sillivan* v. *Aliakmon Shipping* [1986] A.C. 785 (H.L.); *Curran* v. *Northern Ireland Co-ownership Housing Association* [1987] A.C. 718 (H.L.); *Yuen Kun Yeu* v. *Att.-Gen. of Hong Kong* [1988] A.C. 175 (P.C.); *Hill* v. *Chief Constable of West Yorkshire* [1989] A.C. 53 (H.L.); *D. & F. Estates* v. *Church Commissioners* [1989] A.C. 177 (H.L.).

[7] The bare summary in this paragraph is developed in the rest of the chapter.

duty causing actionable damage.[8] Definition of the circumstances in which a defendant owes a duty of care is closely related to definition of what is actionable damage. The critical question is whether the scope of the duty of care in the circumstances of the case is such as to embrace damage of the kind which the plaintiff claims to have suffered.[9] Generally, the damage necessary to sustain a claim in negligence must be actual physical injury to person or property other than property which is the product of the negligence itself. Normally a plaintiff claiming in negligence cannot recover economic loss. Economic loss is only recoverable where there is a special relationship amounting to reliance by the plaintiff on the defendant or where the economic loss is truly consequential upon actual physical injury to person or property. There are a few rogue cases which do not accord with this summary. Since damage is an essential ingredient of the cause of action in negligence, the limitation period will not start to run until the damage has occurred.[10]

Negligence contrasted with breach of contract. It may be helpful to summarise dogmatically[11] that liabilities under a contract are governed by its terms. Necessary terms may in appropriate circumstances be implied and implied terms to the effect that a contracting party will exercise due skill and care in performing what he agrees to do are not uncommon. Breaches of express or implied contractual terms give rise to a liability to pay damages. Those damages may extend to the consequences naturally arising or actually contemplated by the parties and are intended to put the injured party as nearly as money can in the same position as if the contract had been performed. Such consequences can and frequently do include pure economic loss. By contrast, the damage which will sustain a claim in negligence does not normally extend to economic loss and a negligence claim cannot normally be equated with a claim for breach of contractual warranty.[12] The essential difference is that between a dangerous defect which causes external physical damage and a defect of quality. A builder who builds defectively will ordinarily be liable for breach of contract to the employer with whom he contracts. But he will not normally be liable *in negligence*[13] to the employer, nor to a third party with whom he did not contract, on account of a mere defect even if the third party now owns the building. Such a liability would only normally arise if, for example, the building collapsed and caused physical injury to the third party

---

[8] See, *e.g. Grant* v. *Australian Knitting Mills* [1936] A.C. 85 at 103 (P.C.); *Overseas Tankship* v. *Morts Dock and Engineering* [1961] A.C. 388 at 425 (P.C.).

[9] *Murphy* v. *Brentwood District Council* [1990] 3 W.L.R. 414 at 445 (H.L.); *Caparo Industries* v. *Dickman* [1990] A.C. 605 at 627 (H.L.).

[10] *Pirelli* v. *Oscar Faber & Partners* [1983] 2 A.C. 1 (H.L.); *Ketteman* v. *Hansel Properties* [1987] A.C. 189 (H.L.). For limitation generally, see p. 366.

[11] See this book *passim* for full consideration of the matters covered by this summary.

[12] See Lord Brandon in *Junior Books* v. *Veitchi* [1983] 1 A.C. 520 at 551 (H.L.); *D. & F. Estates* v. *Church Commissioners* [1989] A.C. 177 at 203 (H.L.).

[13] He might however be liable in other ways, *e.g.* upon an assignment or a collateral warranty—see pp. 273 and 130 respectively.

personally or to his property other than the building itself. Equivalent considerations will normally apply as between an employer and a sub-contractor with whom the employer has no contractual relationship.[14]

2. Liability for Physical Damage

The modern law derives from and is limited by the leading case of *Donoghue* v. *Stevenson*,[15] a decision of the House of Lords by a majority of three to two. The case was about the supposed snail in the ginger beer bottle which was supposed to have caused the Scottish pursuer physical injury. It was held that the manufacturer of an article of food, medicine or the like, sold by him to a distributor in circumstances which prevent the distributor or the ultimate purchaser or consumer from discovering by inspection any defect, is under a legal duty to the ultimate purchaser or consumer to take reasonable care that the article is free from defect likely to cause injury to health. Lord Atkin's famous passage[16] says this:

> "*At present I content myself with pointing out that in English law there must be, and is, some general conception of relations giving rise to a duty of care, of which the particular cases found in the books are but instances. . . . The rule that you are to love your neighbour becomes in law, you must not injure your neighbour; and the lawyer's question, Who is my neighbour? receives a restrictive reply. You must take reasonable care to avoid acts or omissions which you can reasonably foresee would be likely to injure your neighbour. Who, then, in law is my neighbour? The answer seems to be—persons who are so closely and directly affected by my act that I ought reasonably to have them in contemplation as being so affected when I am directing my mind to the acts or omissions which are called in question.*"

He then referred with approval to cases[17] which indicated that the duty was to avoid physical injury to person or property.[18] There may also be limited circumstances where one person may owe a plaintiff a duty to prevent another person from damaging the plaintiff's person or property where there is a manifest risk of such damage if the duty is neglected.[19]

A chattel which causes physical injury to person or property is to be contrasted with a chattel which is merely defective in quality even to the extent

---

[14] This notwithstanding *Junior Books* v. *Veitchi* [1983] 1 A.C. 520 (H.L.)—see "Specialist sub-contractors" at p. 178.

[15] [1932] A.C. 562 (H.L.).

[16] [1932] A.C. 562 at 580 (H.L.); see Lord Reid in *Dorset Yacht Co.* v. *Home Office* [1970] A.C. 1004 at 1027 (H.L.)—the passage "should I think be regarded as a statement of principle. It is not to be treated as if it were a statutory definition. It will require qualification in new circumstances. But I think that the time has come when we can and should say that it ought to apply unless there is some justification or valid explanation for its exclusion." See also Lord Diplock at 1060.

[17] *Heaven* v. *Pender* (1883) 11 Q.B.D. 503 (C.A.); *Le Lievre* v. *Gould* [1893] 1 Q.B. 491 (C.A.).

[18] See Lord Brandon in *Junior Books* v. *Veitchi* [1983] 1 A.C. 520 at 549 (H.L.); *D. & F. Estates* v. *Church Commissioners* [1989] A.C. 177 at 202 (H.L.).

[19] *Dorset Yacht Co.* v. *Home Office* [1970] A.C. 1004 (H.L.); but see *Hill* v. *Chief Constable of West Yorkshire* [1989] A.C. 53 (H.L.).

of being valueless. For mere quality defects, "the manufacturer's liability at common law arises only under and by reference to the terms of any contract to which he is a party in relation to the chattel; the common law does not impose on him any liability in tort to persons to whom he owes no duty in contract but who, having acquired the chattel, suffer economic loss because the chattel is defective in quality."[20] This applies also to dangerous defects once they are discovered because the danger is then known. "The chattel is either capable of repair at economic cost or it is worthless and must be scrapped. In either case the loss sustained by the owner or hirer of the chattel is purely economic."[21]

Donoghue v. *Stevenson*[22] itself was confined to "articles of common household use, where every one, including the manufacturer, knows that the articles will be used by other persons than the actual ultimate purchaser."[23] But the principle applies so as to place the builder of premises under a duty to take reasonable care to avoid injury through latent defects in the premises to the person or property of those whom he should have in contemplation as likely to suffer injury if care is not taken.[24] For a plaintiff to have a right to claim in negligence for loss caused to him by reason of loss of or damage to property, he has to have either the legal ownership in or a possessory title to the property when the damage occurs. Contractual rights relating to the property are insufficient.[25]

In the absence of a contractual duty or a special relationship of proximity, a builder owes no duty of care in tort in respect of the quality of his work,[26] and the principle does not extend to bring home liability towards an occupier who knows the full extent of the defect yet continues to occupy the building. He has discovered the defect in time to avert any possibility of injury and his loss is purely economic and irrecoverable in negligence. "It is the latency of the defect which constitutes the mischief."[27]

Personal injury.   A contractor will be liable if a plaintiff suffers personal injury because of the contractor's negligence. In one case, contractors were held liable in negligence to a plaintiff who was injured by a falling concrete

---

[20] Lord Bridge in *Murphy* v. *Brentwood District Council* [1990] 3 W.L.R. 414 at 435 (H.L.); see also Lord Oliver at 447; *cf. D. & F. Estates* v. *Church Commissioners* [1989] A.C. 177 at 206 (H.L.); *Candlewood Navigation* v. *Mitsui O.S.K. Lines* [1986] A.C. 1 (H.L.).

[21] *Ibid.*

[22] [1932] A.C. 562 (H.L.).

[23] Lord Atkin [1932] A.C. 562 at 583 (H.L.).

[24] See Lord Keith in *Murphy* v. *Brentwood District Council* [1990] 3 W.L.R. 414 at 424 (H.L.). See also Lord Bridge at 436; *D. & F. Estates* v. *Church Commissioners* [1989] A.C. 177 (H.L.).

[25] See *Candlewood Navigation* v. *Mitsui O.S.K. Lines* [1986] A.C. 1 (H.L.); *Leigh and Sillivan* v. *Aliakmon Shipping* [1986] A.C. 785 (H.L.).

[26] *D. & F. Estates* v. *Church Commissioners* [1989] A.C. 177 (H.L.); *Murphy* v. *Brentwood District Council* [1990] 3 W.L.R. 414 at 440 (H.L.).

[27] Lord Keith in *Murphy* v. *Brentwood District Council* [1990] 3 W.L.R. 414 at 424 (H.L.); see also *ibid.* at 431; Lord Bridge at 436; *D. & F. Estates* v. *Church Commissioners* [1989] A.C. 177 at 206 (H.L.); *Department of Environment* v. *Thomas Bates* [1990] 3 W.L.R. 457 at 463 (H.L.); *cf. Grant* v. *Australian Knitting Mills* [1936] A.C. 85 at 103 *et seq.* (P.C.).

canopy,[28] and in another, to a plaintiff who fell and was injured when the heel of her ordinary high-heeled shoe went through a negligently repaired hole in a wooden floor board.[29] Where contractors carrying out reconstruction works obstructed the normal approach to a house so that it was impassable, they were held liable when a visitor was injured while using a dangerous alternative route suggested by the contractors' workmen.[30]

"Other property."   To sustain a claim in negligence, physical damage to property must normally be damage to property other than the property which is the product of the negligence.[31] Where a whole building is erected and equipped by the same contractor, the building is ordinarily to be regarded as one unit.[32] If in such a building defective foundations damage the superstructure, that will not be physical damage to other property sufficient to found a claim against the contractor in negligence.[33]

> "The reality is that the structural elements in any building form a single indivisible unit of which the different parts are essentially interdependent. To the extent that there is any defect in one part of the structure it must to a greater or lesser degree necessarily affect all other parts of the structure. Therefore any defect in the structure is a defect in the quality of the whole."

If it weakens the structure, it is not a dangerous defect liable to cause damage to "other property."[34]

But if "some distinct item incorporated in the structure ... positively malfunctions so as to inflict positive damage on the structure in which it is incorporated," there may be liability in tort. If defective electrical wiring installed by a sub-contractor causes a fire which damages the building or if a central heating boiler explodes, the electrical sub-contractor or the boiler manufacturer may be held liable for damages.[35]

---

[28] *Sharpe* v. *E. T. Sweeting & Son Ltd.* [1963] 1 W.L.R. 665.

[29] *Gallagher* v. *McDowell Ltd.* [1961] N.I.L.R. 26 (Northern Ireland C.A.).

[30] *A. C. Billings Ltd.* v. *Riden* [1958] A.C. 240 (H.L.); *cf. George Hawkins* v. *Chrysler (U.K.)* (1986) 38 B.L.R. 36 (C.A.).

[31] *D. & F. Estates* v. *Church Commissioners* [1989] A.C. 177 (H.L.); *cf.* Lord Brandon in *Junior Books* v. *Veitchi* [1983] 1 A.C. 520 at 549, 551 (H.L.).

[32] Lord Keith in *Murphy* v. *Brentwood District Council* [1990] 3 W.L.R. 414 at 431 (H.L.).

[33] Moreover, once the first cracks are detected, the loss is purely economic and irrecoverable in tort—see Lord Bridge in *Murphy* v. *Brentwood District Council* [1990] 3 W.L.R. 414 at 439 (H.L.) and see "Economic loss" at p. 165.

[34] Lord Bridge in *Murphy* v. *Brentwood District Council* [1990] 3 W.L.R. 414 at 438 (H.L.). See also Lord Oliver at 444.

[35] *Murphy* v. *Brentwood District Council* [1990] 3 W.L.R. 414 at 431, 438 (H.L.). It seems that these possibilities may depend more on the severity and speed of the damage than a clear application of the "other property" principle. Lord Keith's formulation at 431 contrasts a single contractor with an electrical *sub*-contractor. This by itself begs the question whether, where a sub-contractor builds defective foundations which cause the superstructure, built by others, to crack slightly but not to collapse, the employer who has no contract with the sub-contractor has a claim in negligence. It is thought that he should not, if only because it would be capricious to hold the sub-contractor liable in this instance when in otherwise identical circumstances the contractor who does not sub-contract the construction of the foundations himself is not liable. But the distinction in principle between the electrical sub-contractor who causes a fire and the foundations sub-contractor who causes cracks in the superstructure is not altogether clear, and

It seems that, if a building collapses when it is unoccupied and causes no damage other than to itself, there is no claim in negligence against the builder nor against the local authority who carelessly passed its plans or inspected its construction.[36] It is an open question whether there would be a claim in negligence against the careless architect, engineer or other professional person.[37]

Negligent instructions. An architect or engineer who issues instructions which he knows or ought to know are likely to cause injury to person or property may be liable in negligence if injury results.[38] It seems that he may also be liable if he fails to issue appropriate instructions to prevent such injury in circumstances when he ought to have done so.

In *Clayton* v. *Woodman & Son*, an architect was held liable at first instance[39] for negligence in issuing instructions which resulted in personal injury to the plaintiff bricklayer. The facts found were that the architect instructed the plaintiff on site to cut a chase in a gable without giving any instructions as to shoring or strutting and against the expressed wishes of the plaintiff, who thought that the gable was unsafe. The chase was cut and later in the day, as the plaintiff removed a small piece of stone from the side of the gable, the whole gable toppled inwards and fell, injuring the plaintiff. This decision was reversed on appeal, but on the facts.[40] In *Clay* v. *A. J. Crump & Sons*,[41] an architect who negligently permitted a demolition contractor to leave a dangerous wall standing was held liable when the wall collapsed and injured a labourer working for building contractors who subsequently came onto the site.

Economic loss. Economic loss is monetary loss and pure economic loss is monetary loss unrelated to physical injury to person or "other" property.[42]

Lord Jauncey at 456 appears to contemplate possible tortious liability where a steel frame erected by a specialist contractor failed to give adequate support to floors or walls built by others. Lord Bridge's formulation at 438 has the building as a single indivisible unit apparently irrespective of whether parts were sub-contracted and his negligent electrician is not in terms a sub-contractor. The clear general message from *Murphy* as a whole is that the "complex structure theory" mooted in *D. & F. Estates* v. *Church Commissioners* [1989] A.C. 177 (H.L.) is, with the electrical fire and boiler explosion exceptions, rejected, but the position of sub-contractors is not yet fully resolved. See also *M/S Aswan Engineering Establishment Co.* v. *Lupdine Ltd.* [1987] 1 W.L.R. 1 at 21 (C.A.).

[36] See *Murphy* v. *Brentwood District Council* [1990] 3 W.L.R. 414 at 430, 440, 456 (H.L.).
[37] See "Professional negligence" below.
[38] *Clay* v. *A. J. Crump & Sons* [1964] 1 Q.B. 533 (C.A.); see also *Caparo Industries* v. *Dickman* [1990] A.C. 605 at 636 (H.L.).
[39] [1962] 2 Q.B. 533 (C.A.).
[40] [1962] 1 W.L.R. 585 (C.A.); see *Clay* v. *A. J. Crump & Sons* [1964] 1 Q.B. 533 at 570 (C.A.).
[41] [1964] 1 Q.B. 533 (C.A.).
[42] The damage in *Anns* v. *Merton London Borough Council* [1978] A.C. 728 (H.L.) was pure economic loss—see Lord Keith in *Murphy* v. *Brentwood District Council* [1990] 3 W.L.R. 414 at 428 (H.L.), adopting Deane J. in *Council of the Shire of Sutherland* v. *Heyman* 157 C.L.R. 424 at 503 (High Court of Australia).

"The infliction of physical injury to the person or property of another universally requires to be justified. The causing of economic loss does not. If it is to be categorised as wrongful it is necessary to find some factor beyond the mere occurrence of the loss and the fact that its occurrence could be foreseen."[43] Pure economic loss may be recoverable against a party who owes the loser a relevant contractual duty. "But it is not recoverable in tort in the absence of a special relationship of proximity imposing on the tortfeasor a duty of care to safeguard the plaintiff from economic loss."[44] The right to recover pure economic loss in tort, not flowing from physical injury, does not extend beyond the situation where the loss is sustained through reliance on negligent misstatements as in *Hedley Byrne* v. *Heller & Partners*.[45]

The loss sustained by a building owner from an ordinary building defect is the cost of rectifying the defect. This is pure economic loss and is ordinarily irrecoverable in tort.[46] The loss sustained by a building owner from a dangerous building defect is also irrecoverable pure economic loss once the defect is detected.[47]

> "The only qualification I would make to this is that, if a building stands so close to the boundary of the building owner's land that after discovery of the dangerous defect it remains a potential source of injury to persons or property on neighbouring land or on the highway, the building owner ought, in principle, to be entitled to recover in tort from the negligent builder the cost of obviating the danger, whether by repair or demolition, so far as the cost is necessarily incurred in order to protect himself from liability to third parties."[48]

Consequential economic loss.   Although pure economic loss is irrecoverable in negligence unless there is a special relationship, economic loss which is consequential upon actionable physical damage to person or property is sometimes recoverable. Consequential economic loss is habitually awarded in personal injury cases, *e.g.* for future loss of earnings. It has also been awarded in commercial cases,[49] but there is no clear principle to determine when such loss is recoverable and when it is not.[50]

---

[43] Lord Oliver in *Murphy* v. *Brentwood District Council* [1990] 3 W.L.R. 414 at 446 (H.L.).

[44] Lord Bridge in *Murphy* v. *Brentwood District Council* [1990] 3 W.L.R. 414 at 435 (H.L.).

[45] [1964] A.C. 465 (H.L.)—see *Murphy* v. *Brentwood District Council* [1990] 3 W.L.R. 414 at 427, 452 (H.L.). *D. & F. Estates* v. *Church Commissioners* [1989] A.C. 177 (H.L.); *cf. Dorset Yacht Co.* v. *Home Office* [1970] A.C. 1004 at 1027 (H.L.); *Governors of the Peabody Donation Fund* v. *Sir Lindsay Parkinson* [1985] A.C. 210 at 241 (H.L.) For other authorities, see *Cattle* v. *Stockton Waterworks Co.* (1875) L.R. 10 Q.B. 453; *Simpson* v. *Thomson* (1877) 3 App.Cas. 279; *Weller & Co.* v. *Foot and Mouth Disease Research Council* [1966] 1 Q.B. 569; *Leigh and Sillivan* v. *Aliakmon Shipping* [1986] A.C. 785 (H.L.). For *Hedley Byrne* and negligent misstatements, see below.

[46] *Department of Environment* v. *Thomas Bates* [1990] 3 W.L.R. 457 at 464 (H.L.).

[47] *D. & F. Estates* v. *Church Commissioners* [1989] A.C. 177 (H.L.); *Murphy* v. *Brentwood District Council* [1990] 3 W.L.R. 414 at 424, 436, 443 (H.L.).

[48] Lord Bridge in *Murphy v. Brentwood District Council* [1990] 3 W.L.R. 414 at 435 (H.L.); but see Lord Oliver at 448 who was "not at the moment convinced."

[49] See in addition to the cases cited below *Liesbosch* v. *Edison* [1933] A.C. 449 (H.L.), usually referred to on the subject of a plaintiff's impecuniosity.

[50] See *Murphy* v. *Brentwood District Council* [1990] 3 W.L.R. 414 at 446 (H.L.).

In *S.C.M. (United Kingdom)* v. *W. J. Whittall & Son*,[51] the defendant contractors damaged an electricity cable serving the plaintiffs' typewriter factory. The plaintiffs had molten materials in machines and the loss of electricity caused damage to the materials and machines and consequent loss of production. It was held that the defendants, knowing that the cable served factory owners, owed the plaintiffs a duty of care and were liable for the material damage and consequent loss of production. A description of the economic loss which the plaintiffs were entitled to recover was that it was "truly consequential" on the material damage.[52] In the similar case of *Spartan Steel & Alloys* v. *Martin & Co. (Contractors)*,[53] defendant contractors damaged an electricity cable serving the plaintiffs' factory. The plaintiffs had molten materials in machines and had to empty the furnace to prevent damage. The metal depreciated in value—(this loss was admitted); they lost the profit on that melt—(not greatly disputed); and they lost four further melts while the electricity was off. It was held by a majority that the loss of profit on the immediate melt was recoverable but that on the other four was not because that was economic loss independent of physical damage. A description of the economic loss which plaintiffs may recover was when it is the "immediate consequence" of a breach of duty to safeguard the plaintiff from that kind of loss.[54]

It is also possible that where economic loss suffered by a distributor in a chain between the manufacturer and the ultimate consumer consists of a liability to pay damages to the ultimate consumer for physical injuries sustained by him, or consists of a liability to indemnify a distributor lower in the chain of distribution for its liability to the ultimate consumer for damages for physical injuries, such economic loss is recoverable under the *Donoghue* v. *Stevenson* principle from the manufacturer.[55] If this principle is correct and extends to circumstances where the ultimate consumer suffers damage to his property, a contractor might, for instance, recover in tort from the negligent manufacturer of a boiler, if the boiler exploded and damaged the employer's property so that the contractor was liable to the employer for breach of contract.

Liability for negligence of sub-contractors. "It is trite law that the employer of an independent contractor is, in general, not liable for the negligence or other torts committed by the contractor in the course of the execution of the work. To this general rule, there are certain well-established exceptions or apparent exceptions."[56] Thus a main contractor is not generally liable,

---

[51] [1971] 1 Q.B. 337 (C.A.).

[52] See Lord Denning M.R. at 342. See also *ibid.* at 346 for Lord Denning's answer to the question "where is the line to be drawn?"

[53] [1973] Q.B. 27 (C.A.); see also *Muirhead* v. *Industrial Tank Specialists Ltd.* [1986] Q.B. 507 (C.A.).

[54] *Ibid.* Lord Denning M.R. at 39 and Lawton L.J. at 47.

[55] See *Lambert* v. *Lewis* [1982] A.C. 225 at 278 (H.L.).

[56] Lord Bridge in *D. & F. Estates* v. *Church Commissioners* [1989] A.C. 177 at 208 (H.L.). Exceptionally a special relationship between a defendant and a third party may render the defendant liable for the acts of the third party—see *Dorset Yacht Co.* v. *Home Office* [1970] A.C. 1004 (H.L.); *P. Perl (Exporters)* v. *Camden London Borough Council* [1984] Q.B. 342 (C.A.).

other than in contract, for the negligence of his sub-contractors. But "if in the course of supervision the main contractor in fact comes to know that the sub-contractor's work is being done in a defective and foreseeably dangerous way and if he condones that negligence on the part of the sub-contractor, he will no doubt make himself potentially liable for the consequences as a joint tortfeasor."[57]

Local authorities.   The liability of a local authority for any negligence in performing their statutory functions of securing compliance with the Building Regulations is no greater than that of the negligent builder whose fault was the primary cause of the damage.[58] Thus the local authority is not liable if the building is defective in quality nor for economic loss in the terms discussed above.[59] Local authorities owe no duty to activate their statutory powers to warn a building owner that he is heading for financial disaster.[60] It is an open question whether a local authority might be liable in negligence for carelessly passing defective plans or for careless inspection of building works if this causes physical damage to person or property other than the product of the negligence.[61] If there is such a liability, it may not nevertheless extend to benefit an original building owner who is himself obliged to comply with the Building Regulations.[62]

3. Other Categories of Negligence

Apart from claims for physical injury to person or property, there is no "single general principle to provide a practical test which can be applied to every situation to determine whether a duty of care is owed and, if so, what is its scope."[63] Rather, there are "distinct and recognisable situations as guides to

---

[57] *Ibid.* at 209.

[58] *Murphy* v. *Brentwood District Council* [1990] 3 W.L.R. 414 at 439, 441, 443 (H.L.); *Department of Environment* v. *Thomas Bates* [1990] 3 W.L.R. 457 at 463 (H.L.). See also "liability of local authority" at p. 375.

[59] *Murphy* v. *Brentwood District Council* [1990] 3 W.L.R. 414 (H.L.). For non-liability of public regulatory authorities generally, see *Curran* v. *Northern Ireland Co-ownership Housing Association* [1987] A.C. 718 (H.L.); *Yuen Kun Yeu* v. *Att.-Gen. of Hong Kong* [1988] A.C. 175 (P.C.); *Hill* v. *Chief Constable of West Yorkshire* [1989] A.C. 53 (H.L.); *Davis* v. *Radcliffe* [1990] 1 W.L.R. 821 (P.C.).

[60] *Governors of the Peabody Donation Fund* v. *Sir Lindsay Parkinson* [1985] A.C. 210 (H.L.).

[61] The builder is liable in negligence for physical injury to person or property caused by his carelessness—see, *e.g.* Lord Keith in *Murphy* v. *Brentwood District Council* [1990] 3 W.L.R. 414 at 424 (H.L.)—the liability of the local authority is not greater than that of the builder but it may not be co-extensive. In *Murphy*, the local authority appear to have conceded a limited duty of care, but Lord Mackay L.C. (at 419), Lord Keith (at 425) and Lord Jauncey (at 451) all reserved the question.

[62] See *Investors in Industry* v. *South Bedfordshire District Council* [1986] Q.B. 1034 (C.A.); *Richardson* v. *West Lindsey District Council* [1990] 1 W.L.R. 522 (C.A.)—both cases decided before *Anns* v. *Merton London Borough Council* [1978] A.C. 728 (H.L.) was departed from.

[63] Lord Bridge in *Caparo Industries* v. *Dickman* [1990] A.C. 605 at 617 (H.L.) citing *Governors of the Peabody Donation Fund* v. *Sir Lindsay Parkinson* [1985] A.C. 210 at 239 *et seq.* (H.L.); *Yuen Kun Yeu* v. *Att.-Gen. of Hong Kong* [1988] A.C. 175 at 190 *et seq.* (P.C.); *Rowling* v. *Takaro Properties* [1988] A.C. 473 at 501 (P.C.); *Hill* v. *Chief Constable of West Yorkshire* [1989] A.C. 53 at 60 (H.L.). See also Lord Roskill in *Caparo Industries* at 628, and Lord Oliver *passim*.

the existence, the scope and the limits of the varied duties of care which the law imposes."[64] "At the margin, the boundaries of a man's responsibilities for acts of negligence have to be fixed as a matter of policy."[65] It is thought however that, with limited exceptions and apart from cases of physical injury to person or property, the situations where the law has recognised a duty of care to guard against economic loss are limited to those derived from *Hedley Byrne* v. *Heller & Partners*.[66] These are discussed under "Negligent misstatement" at page 174.

During the counter-revolution referred to in the opening paragraph of this chapter and before the House of Lords departed from *Anns* v. *Merton London Borough Council*[67] in *Murphy* v. *Brentwood District Council*,[68] a number of cases considered the circumstances in which a defendant could be under a duty of care to safeguard a plaintiff from economic loss.[69] Many of these cases concluded that the plaintiff's claim in negligence failed in circumstances where, after *Murphy*, such a claim would probably not be advanced at all. The principles which emerged necessarily assumed that *Anns* was correctly decided and to that extent should be viewed with caution. Nevertheless and with the qualification expressed in the previous paragraph, it is thought that these principles may remain helpful.

In addition to the requirement that the loss should be foreseeable, the requirements which emerged for the existence of a duty of care were:

(1) a special relationship of proximity;
(2) reliance by the plaintiff on the defendant; and
(3) that the existence of the duty should be just and reasonable.[70]

"The true question in each case is whether the particular defendant owed to the particular plaintiff a duty of care having the scope which is contended for, and whether he was in breach of that duty with consequent loss to the plaintiff. A relationship of proximity in Lord Atkin's sense must exist before any duty of care can arise, but the scope of the duty must depend on all the circumstances of the case."[71]

"In determining whether or not a duty of care of particular scope was incumbent upon a defendant it is material to take into consideration whether it is just and reasonable that it should be so."[72]

---

[64] Lord Bridge in *Caparo Industries* v. *Dickman* [1990] A.C. 605 at 618.

[65] Lord Wilberforce in *McLoughlin* v. *O'Brian* [1983] 1 A.C. 410 at 420 (H.L.).

[66] [1964] A.C. 464 (H.L.).

[67] [1978] A.C. 728 (H.L.).

[68] [1990] 3 W.L.R. 414 (H.L.).

[69] See, *e.g. Simaan General Contracting* v. *Pilkington Glass* [1988] Q.B. 758 (C.A.).

[70] See, *e.g. Smith* v. *Bush* and *Harris* v. *Wyre Forest D.C.* [1990] A.C. 831 at 865 (H.L.); *Simaan General Contracting Co.* v. *Pilkington Glass* (*No. 2*) [1988] Q.B. 758 at 781 (C.A.); *Caparo Industries* v. *Dickman* [1989] Q.B. 653 at 678 (C.A.).

[71] Lord Keith in *Governors of the Peabody Donation Fund* v. *Sir Lindsay Parkinson* [1985] 1 A.C. 210 at 240 (H.L.).

[72] *Ibid.* at 241; see also Lord Oliver in *Caparo Industries* v. *Dickman* [1990] A.C. 605 at 633 (H.L.).

Assuming responsibility.   "Proximity" is an elusive concept[73] and what is just and reasonable can be cynically measured as the length of the particular judge's boot.[74] Another approach considers whether the defendant can be properly said to have assumed responsibility to guard against the plaintiff's loss. "The question in any given case is whether the nature of the relationship is such that one party can fairly be said to have assumed responsibility to the other as regards the reliability of the advice or information."[75] Although this approach is not universally favoured,[76] it is frequently adopted in practice. In one case, the Court of Appeal was:

> "prepared to accept . . . that in some cases (if rare) of pure economic loss the court may be willing to find the existence of a duty of care owed by a defendant to a plaintiff even in the absence of evidence of any actual voluntary assumption by the defendant of such duty and/or of any reliance on such assumption. We shall accordingly proceed on the basis that, on appropriate facts, the court may be willing to hold that, having regard to the special circumstances and the relationship between the parties, a defendant should be treated *in law* (even though not in fact) as having assumed responsibility to the plaintiff which is capable of giving rise to a claim for damages for pure economic loss."[77]

On this analysis, there must usually, but not always, be some factual manifestation by the defendant of assuming responsibility. Where there is not such a manifestation but the law treats the defendant as having assumed responsibility, the linguistic result is to discard the word "voluntary." The defendant is taken to have assumed responsibility.[78] Although this shorthand formulation is nothing like definitive, it is thought to be useful in that it directs some attention to what may be taken to be the legitimate expectations of the defendant. It also fits in with considerations discussed below under the heading "Contractual influences."

Contractual influences.   Although it has been said that there is a duty of care "wherever there is a relationship equivalent to contract,"[79] there has been

---

[73] See, *e.g.* Bingham L.J. in *Caparo Industries* v. *Dickman* [1989] Q.B. 653 at 678 (C.A.).

[74] *cf. James McNaughton Paper Group* v. *Hicks Anderson & Co., The Times*, October 2, 1990 (C.A.), where the concept of fairness was said to be elusive and perhaps no more than one of the criteria by which proximity is to be judged.

[75] Richmond P. in *Scott Group Ltd.* v. *McFarlane* [1978] 1 N.Z.L.R. 553 (New Zealand Court of Appeal) cited with agreement by Lord Bridge in *Caparo Industries* v. *Dickman* [1990] A.C. 605 at 624 (H.L.); see also *Hedley Byrne* v. *Heller & Partners* [1964] A.C. 464 (H.L.).

[76] See *Smith* v. *Bush* and *Harris* v. *Wyre Forest District Council* [1990] A.C. 831 at 862 (H.L.); Lord Roskill in *Caparo Industries* v. *Dickman* [1990] A.C. 605 at 628 (H.L.); see also *Caparo Industries* v. *Dickman* in the Court of Appeal [1989] Q.B. 653 at 684, 698; *Reid* v. *Rush and Tompkins* [1989] 2 Lloyd's Rep. 167 (C.A.).

[77] *Banque Keyser Ullman S.A.* v. *Skandia (U.K.) Insurance* [1990] Q.B. 665 at 797 (C.A.).

[78] See Lord Jauncey in *Smith* v. *Bush* and *Harris* v. *Wyre Forest District Council* [1990] A.C. 831 at 871 (H.L.).

[79] Lord Devlin in *Hedley Byrne* v. *Heller & Partners* [1964] A.C. 464 at 530 (H.L.).

uncertainty about the effect upon tortious relationships of contractual exclusion clauses[80] and in a wider context there has been growing concern about how, or indeed whether, claims in negligence can exist in an essentially contractual context. These questions are related to the problems with claims for professional negligence discussed below.

The trend is towards denying a remedy in tort at all where the responsibility in question was assumed contractually. In a case concerning banks, the Privy Council have said:

> "*Their Lordships do not believe that there is anything to the advantage of the law's development in searching for a liability in tort where the parties are in a contractual relationship. This is particularly so in a commercial relationship. Though it is possible as a matter of legal semantics to conduct an analysis of the rights and duties inherent in some contractual relationships . . . either as a matter of contract law when the question will be what, if any, terms are to be implied or as a matter of tort law when the task will be to identify a duty arising from the proximity and character of the relationship between the parties, their Lordships believe it to be correct in principle and necessary for the avoidance of confusion in law to adhere to the contractual analysis: on principle because it is a relationship in which the parties have, subject to a few exceptions, the right to determine their obligations to each other, and for the avoidance of confusion because different consequences do follow according to whether liability arises from contract or tort, e.g. in the limitation of action. . . . Their Lordships do not, however, accept that the parties mutual obligations in tort can be any greater than those to be found expressly or by necessary implication in their contract.*"[81]

It seems, therefore, that you cannot sidestep a contractual limitation defence by bringing your claim in negligence and, where there is a contract, if there are parallel obligations in tort at all, they cannot be greater than those deriving from the contract.

In *William Hill Organisation* v. *Bernard Sunley & Sons*,[82] there was a claim for allegedly defective stone cladding and mosaic which failed in contract on final certificate and limitation defences. The Court of Appeal further held that the contract itself circumscribed the boundaries of the defendants' duty in tort and defined its content. Accordingly it was not open to the plaintiffs to disregard those clauses of the contract which provided for the conclusive effect of the Final Certificate but to claim a remedy for breaches which were only ascertainable by reference to the contract itself. The plaintiffs were not entitled to claim a remedy in tort which was wider than the obligations assumed by the defendants under their contract.

Where assignees of a long lease of an office development claimed in negligence against engineers, nominated mechanical subcontractors and ductwork

---

[80] See, *e.g.* Lord Roskill in *Junior Books* v. *Veitchi Co.* [1983] 1 A.C. 520 at 546 (H.L.); *cf.* Lord Brandon in *Leigh and Sillivan* v. *Aliakmon Shipping Co.* [1986] A.C. 785 at 817 (H.L.).
[81] *Tai Hing Cotton Mill* v. *Liu Chong Haing Bank* [1986] A.C. 80 at 107 (P.C.).
[82] [1982] 22 B.L.R. 1 (C.A.).

sub-contractors for deficiencies in air conditioning ductwork, it was held that the damage was exclusively comprehended within the defendants' contracts to construct and the contractual obligations of the plaintiffs and of their assignees to repair under the lease.[83] Where sub-contractors entered into a JCT collateral warranty covering design and selection of materials, this direct limited contract was held to be inconsistent with any assumption of responsibility beyond that which had been expressly undertaken. The rights and obligations of the parties should be solely dependent on the contract.[84] A claim by contractors in negligence against engineers under a FIDIC Engineering Contract for breach of an alleged duty to act impartially in certifying failed by reference to terms in the contract between the contractors and the employer.[85] And a claim by an employer in tort against sub-contractors failed where the sub-contractors were in effect held entitled to the benefit of a Taking-Over Certificate issued under the main contract between the employer and the main contractor.[86]

It seems therefore that, not only will a relevant direct contract negative a duty of care in tort owed by one party to the contract to the other (other than for physical injury deriving from *Donoghue* v. *Stevenson*[87]), but also that such a duty of care is unlikely to be found between parties who are both in a contractual chain but who are not in direct contract.[88] It is difficult to see how a person can assume responsibility towards someone with whom he is not in contract to any greater extent than he has assumed responsibility towards the person with whom he is most closely related commercially, *i.e.* the person with whom he is in contract.

Professional negligence. Breach of a professional person's obligations to his client is habitually referred to as professional negligence. The duties of architects, engineers and surveyors to their employer are discussed in Chapter 13 and the standard of professional skill and care which the law requires is discussed mainly under the heading "The degree of skill required" at page 312. There is usually a contract between the employer and the professional and in the contractual context professional negligence is a breach of contract. It is here considered whether the duty can at the same time be tortious. If it were, not only would the employer have the benefit of a potentially more favourable limitation period, but the employer could recover in a negligence action, brought outside the contractual limitation period against his architect or engineer, economic loss which he could not recover in a negligence action against the contractor or a sub-contractor.

---

[83] *Ernst & Whinney* v. *Willard* (1987) 40 B.L.R. 67.

[84] *Greater Nottingham Co-operative Society* v. *Cementation Piling* [1989] Q.B. 71 (C.A.); *cf. Reid* v. *Rush and Tompkins* [1989] 2 Lloyd's Rep. 167 (C.A.).

[85] *Pacific Associates* v. *Baxter* [1990] Q.B. 993 (C.A.); *cf. Norwich City Council* v. *Harvey* [1989] 1 W.L.R. 828 (C.A.).

[86] *Southern Water* v. *Lewis & Duvivier* (1984) 27 B.L.R. 111.

[87] [1932] A.C. 562 (H.L.)—see above.

[88] *Pacific Associates* v. *Baxter* [1990] Q.B. 993 (C.A.); *Norwich City Council* v. *Harvey* [1989] 1 W.L.R. 828 (C.A.); *cf. Ernst & Whinney* v. *Willard* (1987) 40 B.L.R. 67.

There are cases before 1976 which hold that a professional person's liability to his client is normally a liability in contract alone.[89] The view was that:

"where the breach of duty alleged arises out of a liability independently of the personal obligation undertaken by contract, it is tort, and it may be tort even though there may happen to be a contract between the parties, if the duty in fact arises independently of that contract. Breach of contract occurs where that which is complained of is a breach of duty arising out of the obligations undertaken by the contract."[90]

Thus an architect's obligation was held to be founded in contract alone.[91]

However, in *Esso Petroleum* v. *Mardon*,[92] Lord Denning M.R. suggested that cases referred to in the previous paragraph were in conflict with other cases of high authority[93] and that "in the case of a professional man, the duty to use reasonable care arises not only in contract, but is also imposed by the law apart from contract, and is therefore actionable in tort."[94] Since then, the balance of direct authority and dicta supports the view that the professional man owes a duty to exercise that standard of skill and care appropriate to his professional status and will be liable both in contract and in tort for all losses which his client may suffer by reason of any breach of that duty.[95]

It is submitted that this question needs reconsideration in the light of recent House of Lords and Privy Council decisions for two distinct reasons.[96] Firstly, unless professional people's contracts are to be singled out for special adverse

---

[89] See *Jarvis* v. *Moy, Davies, Smith, Vanderville* [1936] 1 K.B. 399 (C.A.); *Groom* v. *Crocker* [1939] 1 K.B. 194 (C.A.); *Clark* v. *Kirby-Smith* [1964] Ch. 506; *Bagot* v. *Stevens Scanlan* [1966] 1 Q.B. 197; *cf. Sealand of the Pacific* v. *McHaffie* (1975) 51 D.L.R. (3d) 702 (British Columbia Court of Appeal).

[90] Greer L.J. in *Jarvis* v. *Moy, Davies, Smith, Vanderville* [1936] 1 K.B. 399 at 405 (C.A.); *cf. Greater Nottingham Co-operative Society* v. *Cementation Piling* [1989] Q.B. 71 (C.A.).

[91] *Bagot* v. *Stevens Scanlan* [1966] 1 Q.B. 197—Diplock L.J. sitting as an additional Queen's Bench Judge.

[92] [1976] Q.B. 801 (C.A.).

[93] He cited *Boorman* v. *Brown* (1842) 3 Q.B. 511 at 525 and *Nocton* v. *Lord Ashburton* [1914] A.C. 932 at 956 (H.L.); and, for the relationship of master and servant, *Lister* v. *Romford Ice and Cold Storage* [1957] A.C. 555 at 587 (H.L.)—which does not appear to support the thesis—and *Matthews* v. *Kuwait Bechtel Corporation* [1959] 2 Q.B. 57 (C.A.).

[94] *Ibid.* at 819. Lord Denning went on to say (at 820) that the damages should be the same whether the professional person is sued in contract or in tort. In disapproving *Bagot* v. *Stevens Scanlan* [1966] 1 Q.B. 197, he must be taken to be accepting that the plaintiff can have the benefit of the more favourable limitation period in tort—for that was the point of *Bagot*—but he does not address the problem of exclusion clauses.

[95] See, *e.g. Caparo Industries* v. *Dickman* [1990] A.C. 605 at 619 (H.L.); *Arenson* v. *Arenson* [1977] A.C. 405 at 434; *Batty* v. *Metropolitan Property Realisations* [1978] Q.B. 554 (C.A.); *Midland Bank Trust Co.* v. *Hett, Stubbs & Kemp* [1979] Ch. 384 where there is an extensive review; *Ross* v. *Caunters* [1980] Ch. 297 at 322; *Pirelli* v. *Oscar Faber & Partners* [1983] 2 A.C. 1 (H.L.); *Richard Roberts* v. *Douglas Smith Stimson* (1988) 46 B.L.R. 50 at 57.

[96] Consideration would also need to be given to the relationship of master and servant, said by Lord Denning M.R. in *Esso Petroleum* v. *Mardon* [1976] Q.B. 801 at 819 to impose mutual duties of care both in contract and tort; but *cf.* Lord Radcliffe (dissenting) in *Lister* v. *Romford Ice and Cold Storage* [1957] A.C. 555 at 587 (H.L.)—who did not think that authorities cited by Denning L.J. in the Court of Appeal in *Lister* proved that the action against a servant must be founded on tort.

treatment, the prevailing law now appears to be inconsistent with the Privy Council view quoted above[97] and other recent decisions referred to above to the effect that a relevant direct contract will negative a duty of care in tort owed by one party to the contract to the other. There does not seem to be any reason in the modern commercial world why the architect, for instance, should be treated differently from the sub-contractor. The giving of gratuitous advice by a professional person may be a sufficient assumption of responsibility to found a claim for negligent misstatement as discussed below. But if the relationship is contractual, the logic of recent cases ought to preclude a parallel tortious claim. Secondly, take the facts in *Pirelli* v. *Oscar Faber & Partners*[98] as an example. There was a claim against consulting engineers for negligence resulting in damage to a factory chimney which cracked and it was held that the cause of action accrued when the damage came into existence, not when it was discovered or should with reasonable diligence have been discovered. Not surprisingly in the then state of the law, the defendants did not argue (at least in the House of Lords) that the plaintiffs' only claim was in contract. But since the counter-revolution referred to in the opening paragraph of this chapter, there would be no claim in negligence against the contractor who built such a chimney nor the local authority who passed its plans or inspected its construction, since the cracking, once known, would be damage to the thing itself and irrecoverable economic loss. Is the engineer alone to be liable in negligence in these circumstances for pure economic loss?[99] Is he alone to be subject to a potentially longer limitation period? And is he not to have the benefit of a contractual limitation of liability provision in his contract if there is one?

Even if the law capriciously remains that a professional person owes his client a duty of care in tort as well as in contract, it is thought that architects, engineers and surveyors are not ordinarily to be taken to have assumed responsibility to third parties who are not their clients to any greater extent than contractors or local authorities. Thus a careless professional would be liable if his carelessness caused physical injury to a third party's person or property other than property which is itself the product of the negligence,[1] but would not be liable for a third party's economic loss to the extent discussed under "Economic loss" above.

(a) *Negligent misstatement*

Apart from cases where there is physical injury as discussed above and possible claims for professional negligence by a client against his professional adviser,[2] claims in negligence are now, it seems, limited to cases where there is

---

[97] *Tai Hing Cotton Mill* v. *Liu Chong Haing Bank* [1986] A.C. 80 at 107 (P.C.).

[98] [1983] 2 A.C. 1 (H.L.).

[99] *cf.* on this question Ralph Gibson L.J. in *London Congregational Union* v. *Harriss* [1988] 1 All E.R. 15 at 25C (C.A.), but note that the damage to property to which he there refers would now probably be regarded as pure economic loss—see "Economic loss" at p. 165.

[1] See also "Negligent instructions" at p. 165.

[2] See "Professional negligence" at p. 172.

a special relationship of proximity imposing on the tortfeasor a duty of care to safeguard the plaintiff from economic loss.[3] Such cases may be gathered under the umbrella of negligent misstatement and derive from *Hedley Byrne* v. *Heller & Partners*.[4] A negligent misstatement or misrepresentation may give rise to an action for damages for financial loss since the law will imply a duty of care when a party seeking information from a party possessed of special skill trusts him to exercise due care, and that party knew or ought to have known that reliance was being placed on his skill and judgment. Liability for economic loss due to negligent misstatement is confined to cases where the statement or advice is given to a known recipient for a specific purpose of which the maker of the statement is aware and upon which the recipient has relied and acted upon to his detriment.[5] The law adopts a restrictive approach to any extension of the scope of the duty of care beyond the person directly intended by the maker of the statement to act upon it. Matters to be considered are the purpose for which the statement was made and the purpose for which it was communicated to the plaintiff; the relationships between the maker and receiver of the statement and any relevant third party; the size of the class to which the plaintiff belongs; the state of knowledge of the defendant; and whether and to what extent the plaintiff was entitled to rely on the statement.[6] The misstatement must play a real and substantial part in inducing the plaintiff to act, though it need not by itself be decisive.[7] No duty arises if the person making the statement shows that he is not assuming or accepting a duty to be careful.[8] Thus a banker in a situation where a duty would otherwise have arisen, was not liable to an inquirer where he gave a favourable reference, but said it was given "without responsibility."[9]

There is no general rule that claims in negligence may succeed on proof of foreseeable economic loss caused by the defendant.[10] For liability in negligence, there must be something more than mere misstatement.[11] There is the additional requirement that expressly or by implication from the circumstances the speaker or writer has undertaken some responsibility.[12] If a person assumes a responsibility to tender deliberate advice, there can be a liability if

---

[3] See *Murphy* v. *Brentwood District Council* [1990] 3 W.L.R. 414 at 435 (H.L.); *cf. Simaan General Contracting* v. *Pilkington Glass* [1988] Q.B. 758 (C.A).

[4] [1964] A.C. 464 (H.L.).

[5] *Hedley Byrne* v. *Heller & Partners* [1964] A.C. 464 (H.L.); *Cann* v. *Willson* 39 Ch.D. 39; the dissenting judgment of Denning L.J. in *Candler* v. *Crane Christmas & Co.* [1951] 2 K.B. 164 at 174 (C.A.); *Caparo Industries* v. *Dickman* [1990] A.C. 605 (H.L.); *James McNaughton Paper Group* v. *Hicks Anderson & Co., The Times,* October 2, 1990 (C.A.).

[6] *James McNaughton Paper Group* v. *Hicks Anderson & Co., The Times,* October 2, 1990 (C.A.).

[7] *J.E.B. Fasteners* v. *Marks Bloom and Co.* [1983] 1 All E.R. 583 (C.A.).

[8] *Hedley Byrne* v. *Heller & Partners* [1964] A.C. 464 at 492, 504, 511, 533, 540 (H.L.); *McInerny* v. *Lloyds Bank Ltd.* [1974] 1 Lloyd's Rep. 246 (C.A.).

[9] *Hedley Byrne* v. *Heller & Partners* [1964] A.C. 464 (H.L.); but see "Disclaimer" below.

[10] *Simaan General Contracting* v. *Pilkington Glass* [1988] Q.B. 758 at 782 (C.A.).

[11] There may in appropriate circumstances be liability under the Misrepresentation Act 1967 or for fraudulent misrepresentation—see pp. 122 and 124.

[12] *Hedley Byrne* v. *Heller & Partners* [1964] A.C. 465 at 483 (H.L.).

175

the advice is given negligently.[13] There may be liability deriving from relationships which are " 'equivalent to contract,' that is, where there is an assumption of responsibility in circumstances in which, but for the absence of consideration, there would be a contract."[14]

If reliance on a careless statement results in direct physical injury, the maker of the statement may be liable in negligence.[15]

It has been said that the persons who may be potentially liable for negligent misstatement are:

"those persons such as accountants, surveyors, valuers and analysts, whose profession and occupation it is to examine books, accounts and other things, and to make reports on which other people—other than their clients—rely in the ordinary course of business."[16]

This list is obviously not exhaustive and *Hedley Byrne* itself at least adds bankers. The majority of the Privy Council were of the view that the duty of care was limited to persons who carry on or hold themselves out as carrying on the business or profession of giving advice.[17] This view is not binding upon the English courts and has been rejected by the Court of Appeal.[18]

"To import such a duty [of care] the representation must normally, I think, concern a business or professional transaction whose nature makes clear the gravity of the enquiry and the importance and influence attached to the answer. . . . A most important circumstance is the form of the enquiry and of the answer."[19]

Possible circumstances discussed.   Circumstances where a liability for negligent misstatement has been held or might be held to arise are discussed below. The discussion should be treated cautiously, since all the cases cited were decided before *Anns* v. *Merton London Borough Council*[20] was departed from.[21]

Employer's pre-contract information. It is common in building contracts, and more particularly engineering contracts, for information to be given in tender documents about the soil and other relevant conditions. Such information is

---

[13] *Hedley Byrne* v. *Heller & Partners* [1964] A.C. 465 at 494, 497, 529 (H.L.).
[14] Lord Devlin in *Hedley Byrne* v. *Heller & Partners* [1964] A.C. 465 at 429 (H.L.).
[15] *Caparo Industries* v. *Dickman* [1990] A.C. 605 at 636 (H.L.). See also "Negligent instructions" above.
[16] Denning L.J. in *Candler* v. *Crane Christmas & Co.* [1951] 2 K.B. 164 at 174 (C.A.)—part of a longer passage cited as "a masterly analysis" by Lord Bridge in *Caparo Industries* v. *Dickman* [1990] A.C. 605 at 623 (H.L.).
[17] *Mutual Life Ltd.* v. *Evatt* [1971] A.C. 793 (P.C.).
[18] *Esso Petroleum* v. *Mardon* [1976] Q.B. 801 (C.A.); see also *Caparo Industries* v. *Dickman* [1990] A.C. 605 at 637 (H.L.).
[19] Lord Pearce in *Hedley Byrne* v. *Heller & Partners* [1964] A.C. 464 at 539 (H.L.); *cf. Howard Marine and Dredging* v. *A. Ogden & Sons* [1978] 1 Q.B. 574 at 591, 600 (C.A.).
[20] [1978] A.C. 728 (H.L.).
[21] See the opening paragraph of this chapter.

usually accompanied by a clause purporting to prevent a duty of care arising or otherwise to avoid liability in so far as the information is incorrect. Apart from the effect of such a disclaimer,[22] it seems that an employer who has, or professes himself as having, special knowledge of such matters as soil conditions and represents to the contractor that his statements are accurate or have been made after reasonable care and inquiry and does not use words showing a refusal to assume liability can be liable to the contractor in damages if he was negligent.[23] Upon such facts the contractor may also have a claim for damages for breach of collateral warranty or for misrepresentation under the Misrepresentation Act 1967.[24]

The New South Wales case of *Dillingham Ltd.* v. *Downs*[25] provides an interesting discussion of the principles to be applied. The plaintiffs, engineering contractors, undertook to carry out certain works in a harbour, involving, *inter alia*, the breaking up and removal of rock on the sea floor. The employer was the Government and had for many years had the management and control of dredging and rock removal from the harbour. For a period of two years prior to calling for tender it had extensive surveys, soundings and borings carried out to provide basic material for incorporation in the specification and attached drawings. Much of this material was incorporated into the tender documents. The question was whether the government department was under an obligation to exercise reasonable care in the assembling and presentation to the plaintiff of material relative to the existence of worked-out mines beneath the surface and other faults in the soil which, in the event, disrupted the contract and caused great expense to the contractor.

It was said that the matters to be considered to decide whether a duty arose and its nature and extent were "the material provisions of the contract documents, the position, conduct, knowledge and intention of each of the parties and the communications passing between them."[26]

There were terms of the specification requiring that the tenderer "should fully inform himself on these aspects" (the site conditions) and that though relevant information was given "in good faith and is believed to be accurate" the tenderer "must satisfy himself regarding the adequacy and accuracy of his information on site conditions."[27] It was apparent from the documents that the information as to site conditions supplied was not intended to be complete and

---

[22] Discussed under "Disclaimer" at p. 182.

[23] See *Esso Petroleum* v. *Mardon* [1976] Q.B. 801 (C.A.).

[24] See p. 130 for collateral warranties and p. 124 for the Misrepresentation Act 1967.

[25] [1972] 130 N.S.W.L.R. 49 and 13 B.L.R. 97 (New South Wales Supreme Court); see also *Morrison-Knudsen International* v. *Commonwealth of Australia* (1972) 46 A.L.J.R. 265 and 13 B.L.R. 114 (Australian High Court); *Post Office* v. *Mears Construction Ltd.* [1979] 2 All E.R. 813.

[26] *Ibid.* Hardie J. at 56 and at 106 in the B.L.R. report. This statement of principle appears to be consistent with the approach of the Court of Appeal in *Esso Petroleum* v. *Mardon* [1976] Q.B. 801 (C.A.).

[27] Compare the clause relied on by the employer in *Pearson* v. *Dublin Corporation* [1907] A.C. 351 (H.L.), the facts of which are set out at p. 122, but note that in the *Dillingham* case fraud was not alleged, and on the facts appearing in the report could not have been alleged.

exhaustive. The tenderers made a site visit but never sought advice from a geologist or an engineer and were obviously anxious to obtain the contract. Upon the particular facts it was held that there had been no assumption of liability by the employer so as to make it liable in negligence and in any event there had been no reliance by the contractor.

Contractor's pre-contract information. In a New Zealand case,[28] a builder was held liable to an employer in negligence in relation to precontractual estimates of the likely cost of the construction of residential units on the basis of which the employer committed himself to the scheme. In so far as this case relies on *Anns* v. *Merton London Borough Council*,[29] it should now be treated with caution, but it is thought that such a claim might still succeed on appropriate facts.[30] If a contractor provided a pre-contract design which was adopted by the employer's architect, and the subsequent building contract did not make the contractor contractually liable for the design, he might nevertheless be held liable in tort if the employer had sufficiently relied on his design.

In another New Zealand case,[31] a contractor asked a sub-contractor to tender for the delivery of timber. A tender was made on September 15, 1970. In reliance on the tender price the contractor made up his contract figure and entered into a main contract on September 23, 1970. The sub-contractor then discovered an error in his tender and withdrew it before acceptance. It was held that the contractor could have no remedy in negligence against the sub-contractor on the *Hedley Byrne*[32] principle.

Contractor's duty to warn. Since the contractor almost invariably has a contract with the employer, any duty to warn for instance that the design is or may be defective must derive, if at all, from an express or implied term of the contract.[33] The contractor does not ordinarily owe a duty of care to the architect to guard the architect from a potential liability to his client for a defective design, since the architect's loss is purely economic.[34]

Specialist sub-contractors. In *Junior Books* v. *Veitchi Co.*,[35] specialist flooring sub-contractors laid a floor at the pursuers factory which the pursuers alleged was negligently defective. They claimed the cost of relaying the floor and various items of economic and financial loss consequential on replacement. They did not allege that there was any danger of injury to people or property. It was held that, where the relationship was sufficiently close, a duty in tort extended to avoid causing pure economic loss consequential on defects in the work. It is thought that the facts do not sustain a *Donoghue* v. *Stevenson*[36]

---

[28] *J. & J. C. Abrams* v. *Ancliffe* [1978] 2 N.Z.L.R. 420.

[29] [1978] A.C. 728 (H.L.).

[30] In addition to *Anns*, the court also cited and followed *Hedley Byrne* v. *Heller & Partners* [1964] A.C. 464 (H.L.) and *Esso Petroleum* v. *Mardon* [1976] Q.B. 801 (C.A.).

[31] *Holman Construction Ltd.* v. *Delta Timber Co. Ltd.* [1972] N.Z.L.R. 108 (New Zealand Supreme Court).

[32] *Hedley Byrne* v. *Heller & Partners* [1964] A.C. 465 (H.L.).

[33] See "Fitness for purpose of completed works" at p. 55.

[34] *University of Glasgow* v. *William Whitfield* (1988) 42 B.L.R. 66.

[35] *Junior Books* v. *Veitchi Co.* [1983] 1 A.C. 520 (H.L.).

[36] [1932] A.C. 562 (H.L.).

negligence claim as now understood.[37] There was no physical damage, let alone to "other property."[38] Lord Roskill's leading opinion overtly applies the *Anns* two stage test[39] and, were it not a decision of the House of Lords itself, *Junior Books* would stand overruled by *Murphy* v. *Brentwood District Council.*[40]

It is however still judicially suggested that *Junior Books* might be understood on the basis that there was a special relationship of proximity between the building owner and the sub-contractor which was sufficiently akin to contract to introduce the element of reliance so that the scope of the sub-contractor's duty of care was wide enough to embrace economic loss.[41] But it is not clear that the case was decided on such a basis nor is it clear what features of its commonplace facts support a sufficient special relationship. The duties were all averred to flow from the defenders' position as reasonably competent flooring contractors, and not from any relationship which they had as such with the pursuers.[42] The case has been classified as "unique"[43] and it is thought that it should at most be regarded as a case of no general application.[44]

Usually, where an employer obtains advice from a specialist, there is a direct contract or collateral warranty and this is likely to negative a duty of care in tort.[45] It is, however, possible that special factual circumstances may arise where an employer relies on specific advice from a specialist with whom he is not in contract so that the specialist assumes a duty to guard the employer against economic loss.[46]

---

[37] See Section 2 of this chapter.

[38] See *Junior Books* v. *Veitchi Co.* [1983] 1 A.C. 520 at 545B (H.L.) and see Lord Brandon's dissenting opinion at 547 which is now acknowledged to state the law—*D. & F. Estates* v. *Church Commissioners* [1989] A.C. 177 at 202 (H.L.).

[39] See *Junior Books* v. *Veitchi Co.* [1983] 1 A.C. 520 at 548 (H.L.).

[40] [1990] 3 W.L.R. 414 (H.L.). See the opening paragraph of this chapter.

[41] See *Murphy* v. *Brentwood District Council* [1990] 3 W.L.R. 414 at 427, 441 (H.L.); *Yuen Kun Yeu* v. *Att.-Gen. of Hong Kong* [1988] A.C. 175 at 196 (P.C.).

[42] See the extract from the opinion of the Lord Ordinary at [1983] 1 A.C. 523 and see Lord Keith at 535 who said that *Hedley Byrne* v. *Heller & Partners* [1964] A.C. 464 (H.L.) was not in point except in so far as it established that reasonable anticipation of physical injury is not a *sine qua non* for the existence of a duty of care.

[43] See *D. & F. Estates* v. *Church Commissioners* [1989] A.C. 177 at 202, 215 (H.L.).

[44] It is thought that the House of Lords must have departed from *Junior Books* in *Murphy* v. *Brentwood District Council* [1990] 3 W.L.R. 414 (H.L.) had they been specifically invited to do so. For other strictures, see *Muirhead* v. *Industrial Tank Specialists* [1986] Q.B. 507 at 523 *et seq.* (C.A.); *Simaan General Contracting Company* v. *Pilkington Glass* [1988] Q.B. 758 at 773, 784 (C.A.); *Greater Nottingham Co-operative Society* v. *Cementation Piling and Foundation* [1989] Q.B. 71 (C.A.).

[45] See *Greater Nottingham Co-operative Society* v. *Cementation Piling and Foundation* [1989] Q.B. 71 (C.A.); and see generally "Contractual influences" above and p. 130 for collateral warranties.

[46] See *Simaan General Contracting Co.* v. *Pilkington Glass (No. 2)* [1988] Q.B. 758 at 781 (C.A.). For the reasons explained in the text, it is thought that *Junior Books* v. *Veitchi Co.* [1983] 1 A.C. 520 (H.L.) does not exemplify such special factual circumstances. Such a claim against a specialist sub-contractor failed in the Court of Appeal in *Warwick University* v. *Sir Robert McAlpine* unreported May 4, 1990 (C.A.), it being held on the facts that the employer had not relied on the specialist; see also *Hindustan Steam Shipping Co. Ltd.* v. *Siemans Bros. & Co. Ltd.* [1955] 1 Lloyd's Rep. 167; *The Diamantis Pateras* [1966] 1 Lloyd's Rep. 179—shipbuilding cases at first instance where a duty of care was held to exist as between employer and sub-contractor, although in each case the claim failed on the facts.

In *I.B.A.* v. *E.M.I. and B.I.C.C.*,[47] the contractor undertook to design and supply for the employer a television mast designed by the sub-contractor. The mast failed, and, it being accepted by the sub-contractor that they owed a duty of care to the employer, it was held that they were in breach of that duty in respect of the design. Further, after the works had started, defects appeared in a similar mast being erected elsewhere and the employer was concerned whether tests should be carried out. The sub-contractor gave the employer certain assurances as to the mast as a consequence of which no tests were carried out. The assurances were given negligently and the sub-contractor was also liable to the employer in respect of the negligent assurances.

Consultants. It is thought that an architect, engineer, surveyor or other consultant may in appropriate circumstances be liable in negligence to the employer for careless statements made before entering into a contract of engagement with the employer in so far as such matters are not encompassed by the subsequent engagement. Each might, in exceptional circumstances, be held to have assumed responsibility for gratuitous advice unrelated to a subsequent engagement.[48] It is thought that an architect or other consultant engaged by a design and build contractor[49] might be liable in negligence to the employer, if there was sufficient particular evidence that the consultant had assumed such responsibility and that the employer had relied on the particular consultant. This might happen if, for instance, there had been a pre-contract meeting at which the contractor in the presence of the consultant proffered the consultant's expertise to encourage the employer to enter into the contract. Consultants may also, in some circumstances, become liable to the contractor for loss caused by reliance on a negligent misstatement,[50] particularly in respect of an answer to some specific inquiry on a matter and in circumstances where the contractor reasonably relies upon the architect's judgment or skill or his ability to make careful inquiry. But the consultant would probably not be liable if he expresses his statement to be given "without responsibility" or otherwise in such a way as to show that he does not accept a duty of care towards the contractor.[51]

An architect may in some circumstances be liable in tort to a contractor or others. In *Townsends Ltd.* v. *Cinema News, etc., Ltd.*,[52] there was a statutory duty upon the contractor to serve notice upon the sanitary authority before executing certain work, but there was proved to be a clear practice that the contractor "relies upon the architect to do all the work and give the notices and see that regulations are complied with."[53] The contractor relied in this case upon the

[47] (1980) 14 B.L.R. 1 (H.L.).

[48] See *Hedley Byrne* v. *Heller & Partners* [1964] A.C. 464 (H.L.); *Yuen Kun Yeu* v. *Att.-Gen. of Hong Kong* [1988] A.C. 175 at 192 (P.C.); *cf. Chaudhry* v. *Prabhakar* [1989] 1 W.L.R. 29 (C.A.).

[49] For design and build contracts see p. 6.

[50] *Hedley Byrne* v. *Heller & Partners* [1964] A.C. 465, 503, 530, 539 (H.L.). *Priestley* v. *Stone* (1888) 4 T.L.R. 730; H.B.C. (4th ed.), Vol. 2, p. 134 (C.A.) so far as it is to the contrary must be considered as overruled.

[51] *Ibid.*; and see "Disclaimer" at p. 182. See also "Negligent certificate" at p. 340.

[52] [1959] 1 W.L.R. 119 (C.A.) more fully reported at (1958) 20 B.L.R. 118 (C.A.).

[53] Lord Evershed M.R. at (1958) 20 B.L.R. 118 at 142 (C.A.).

architect serving the proper notice and seeing that the by-laws were complied with. The architect failed to carry out these tasks properly. There was a breach of the by-laws causing loss to the employer which he was entitled to recover from the contractor. In turn the contractor recovered this loss from the architect who, having undertaken a duty towards the contractor, was liable to him for its negligent performance although it was undertaken gratuitously.

Building Society valuations. Where a surveyor agrees to carry out a mortgage valuation of a modest house for a prospective mortgagee knowing that the prospective mortgagor has paid a valuation fee and will probably rely on the valuation in deciding whether or not to purchase the house, the surveyor owes a duty of care to the mortgagor to exercise reasonable skill and care in carrying out the valuation.[54] It is thought that such a duty of care may not necessarily arise where there is a survey of commercial premises and no contractual relationship with the prospective purchasers.[55] A disclaimer purporting to exclude the surveyor's liability for negligence is subject to the requirement of reasonableness in the Unfair Contract Terms Act 1977.[56] In the ordinary case the surveyor is unlikely to establish that such a disclaimer was a fair and reasonable one.[57] If there is specific ground for suspicion, the surveyor's duty requires him to take reasonable steps to follow the trail of suspicion behind furniture or under carpets.[58] By obtaining and disclosing a valuation, a mortgagee does not assume responsibility to the purchaser for the valuation,[59] although he does owe a duty to take reasonable care to select a reasonably competent valuer.[60]

Financial advice. In *Hedley Byrne* v. *Heller & Partners*,[61] the appellant advertising agents placed orders which they were liable to pay for themselves. They asked their bankers to inquire into the financial stability of their client company. The bankers made inquiries of the Respondents, who gave favourable references "without responsibility." In reliance on the references, the Appellants placed the orders which resulted in loss. It was held that a negligent misrepresentation may give rise to an action for damages for financial loss since the law will imply a duty of care when a party seeking information from a party possessed of special skill trusts him to exercise due care, and that party

---

[54] *Smith* v. *Bush* and *Harris* v. *Wyre Forest District Council* [1990] A.C. 831 (H.L.) approving *Yianni* v. *Edwin Evans & Sons* [1982] Q.B. 438; *cf. Beaumont* v. *Humberts, The Times,* July 17, 1990 (C.A.); *cp. Curran* v. *Northern Ireland Co-ownership Housing Association* [1987] A.C. 718 (H.L.) For the principles on which damages are awarded, see "Negligent survey" at p. 330.

[55] See *Smith* v. *Bush* and *Harris* v. *Wyre Forest District Council* [1990] A.C. 831 at 859 (H.L.).

[56] See ss.2(2) and 11 of the Act and see generally p. 66.

[57] See *Smith* v. *Bush* and *Harris* v. *Wyre Forest District Council* [1990] A.C. 831 (H.L.); *cf. Davies* v. *Parry* (1988) H.L.R. 452; *Beaton* v. *Nationwide Anglia Building Society, The Times,* October 8, 1990.

[58] See *Smith* v. *Bush* and *Harris* v. *Wyre Forest District Council* [1990] A.C. 831 at 851 (H.L.) citing *Roberts* v. *J. Hampson & Co.* [1990] 1 W.L.R. 94; *cp. Bere* v. *Slades* [1989] 2 E.G.L.R. 160.

[59] *Smith* v. *Bush* and *Harris* v. *Wyre Forest District Council* [1990] A.C. 831 at 841 (H.L.); but *cp. Beresforde* v. *Chesterfield Borough Council* [1989] 2 E.G.L.R. 149 (C.A.).

[60] *Ibid.* at 865.

[61] [1964] A.C. 465 (H.L.); *cf. Mutual Life Ltd.* v. *Evatt* [1971] A.C. 793 at 801 (P.C.); *Cherry* v. *Allied Insurance Brokers* [1978] 1 Lloyd's Rep. 274 at 280.

knew or ought to have known that reliance was being placed on his skill and judgment. The disclaimer, however, negatived the duty. In other circumstances, there has been held to be no negligence[62] or no duty of care.[63]

Other examples. A large oil company, who had special knowledge and skill in estimating the throughput of filling stations and who induced a prospective tenant of a filling station to enter into a written tenancy agreement by carelessly representing its potential throughput, were held to be liable to the tenant in damages for their misrepresentation.[64] There has been held to be liability where inquiry is made of a public servant who "knows, or ought to know, that, others, being his neighbours in this regard, would act on the faith of the statement being accurate."[65] It is possible that a duty may be owed to others, such as the contractor, engaged in a building project where a person, such as the architect or the engineer, makes statements before or during that project which he knows, or ought to know, may be acted upon by those others as being accurate.[66]

Disclaimer. In some instances, a disclaimer has been held to negative a duty of care.[67] In others, the Unfair Contract Terms Act 1977 has prevented the defendant from relying on a disclaimer.[68]

It is common in building contracts, and more particularly engineering contracts, for there to be a clause in the tender documents referring to certain information about the soil and other relevant conditions purporting to prevent a duty of care arising or otherwise to avoid liability in so far as the information is incorrect. Each case depends on its own facts and circumstances and particularly the terms of the disclaimer. If there is a clear disclaimer at tender stage, it is thought that a contractor, who is unable to recover under the resulting contract nor under a collateral warranty nor under the Misrepresentation Act 1967, is unlikely to succeed in tort except perhaps exceptionally where the Unfair Contract Terms Act 1977 prevents the employer from relying on the disclaimer.[69] But in an Australian case,[70] where there was a

---

[62] See, *e.g. McInerny* v. *Lloyds Bank Ltd.* [1974] 1 Lloyd's Rep. 246 (C.A.).
[63] See, *e.g. Caparo Industries* v. *Dickman* [1990] A.C. 605 (H.L.); *Al Saudi Bank* v. *Clarke Pixley* [1990] Ch. 313; *James McNaughton Paper Group* v. *Hicks Anderson & Co., The Times,* October 2, 1990 (C.A.).
[64] *Esso Petroleum* v. *Mardon* [1976] Q.B. 801 (C.A.); *cf. Anderson (W. B.) & Sons Ltd.* v. *Rhodes Ltd.* [1967] 2 All E.R. 850.
[65] *Ministry of Housing* v. *Sharp* [1970] 2 Q.B. 223 at 268 (C.A.)—this case is not, however, a clear reliance case—see *Murphy* v. *Brentwood District Council* [1990] 3 W.L.R. 414 at 446 (H.L.).
[66] See cases cited above; *Arenson* v. *Arenson* [1977] A.C. 405 at 438 (H.L.).
[67] See, *e.g. Hedley Byrne* v. *Heller & Partners* [1964] A.C. 464 (H.L.); *Post Office* v. *Mears Construction Ltd.* [1979] 2 All E.R. 813.
[68] *Smith* v. *Bush* and *Harris* v. *Wyre Forest District Council* [1990] A.C. 831 (H.L.); see p. 66 for the Unfair Contract Terms Act 1977; *cf. Beaton* v. *Nationwide Anglia Building Society, The Times,* October 8, 1990.
[69] See "Employer's pre-contract information" at p. 176; the Misrepresentation Act 1967, p. 124; collateral warranties, p. 130 and the Unfair Contract Terms Act 1977, p. 66.
[70] *Morrison-Knudsen International* v. *Commonwealth of Australia* (1972) 46 A.L.J.R. 265 and 13 B.L.R. 114 (Australian High Court).

"contractor must satisfy himself" clause in the contract, it was held as a matter of law, and without any decision upon the facts, that the terms of the contract did not prevent the contractor setting up a duty upon the employer in negligence for failure to take reasonable care to ensure that information was accurate and not false or misleading.

(b) *Possible further categories*

It is not necessarily to be supposed that the reliance cases are the only possible category of cases in which a duty to take reasonable care to avoid or prevent pecuniary loss can arise.[71] The law is prepared to develop new categories of negligence incrementally,[72] and there are a few cases, apparently still to be regarded as correctly decided, which do not readily fit into the two main categories discussed above.[73] These rogue cases include:

Morrison Steamship Co. Ltd. v. *Greystoke Castle (Cargo Owners)*[74] where there was a ship collision and cargo owners became liable for general average contribution. The cargo was not damaged. It was held by a narrow majority that the cargo owners had a direct claim against the owners of the colliding ship on the ground that their obligation was to share in the expenditure *ab initio* and not merely to contribute by way of idemnity towards the owners' expenditure. The case may turn on specialities of maritime law.[75]

Ross v. *Caunters*,[76] where a gift to a beneficiary under a will was void because the beneficiary's husband had witnessed the will due to negligence of the testator's solicitors. It was held that the solicitors owed a duty of care to the beneficiary sufficient to sustain a claim for financial loss and there were no considerations to negative or reduce or limit the scope of the duty. Megarry V.-C. examined the authorities and various possible tests for liability, but appears in the end to have decided the case according to its "feel."[77]

It is thought that no identifiable category of negligence emerges from either of these cases beyond a general point that solicitors may occasionally owe a duty

---

[71] *Murphy* v. *Brentwood District Council* [1990] 3 W.L.R. 414 at 446 (H.L.).

[72] *Yuen Kun Yeu* v. *Att.-Gen. of Hong Kong* [1988] A.C. 175 at 191 (P.C.) citing Brennan J. in *Council of the Shire of Sutherland* v. *Heyman* (1985) 59 A.L.J.R. 564 at 588.

[73] See *Murphy* v. *Brentwood District Council* [1990] 3 W.L.R. 414 at 446 (H.L.) and note that *Minister of Housing* v. *Sharp* [1970] 2 Q.B. 223 (C.A.) there referred to has been cited in this chapter under "Negligent misstatement" at p. 182.

[74] [1947] A.C. 265 (H.L.).

[75] See *Murphy* v. *Brentwood District Council* [1990] 3 W.L.R. 414 at 429, 445 (H.L.); *cf. Hedley Byrne* v. *Heller & Partners* [1964] A.C. 465 at 518 (H.L.); *Simaan General Contracting Company* v. *Pilkington Glass* [1988] Q.B. 758 at 771 (C.A.); *cp. Simpson* v. *Thomson* (1877) 3 App.Cas. 279 (H.L.).

[76] [1980] Ch. 297; *cf. Al-Kandari* v. *J. R. Brown & Co.* [1987] Q.B. 514. In so far as *Ross* v. *Caunters* applies *Anns* v. *Merton London Borough Council* [1978] A.C. 728 (H.L.), it could be said to have been overruled by *Murphy* v. *Brentwood District Council* [1990] 3 W.L.R. 414 (H.L.), but it seems from *Murphy* that the House of Lords did not so regard it—see Lord Oliver at 446. See, however, *Clarke* v. *Bruce Lance & Co.* [1988] 1 W.L.R. 881 (C.A.). *Ross* v. *Caunters* might not now survive a direct attack.

[77] See [1980] Ch. 297 at 321.

of care to guard against financial loss to third parties who are not their clients and who do not themselves rely upon their advice. The relevance to building contracts is that it seems unlikely that a negligence claim will succeed which does not come within one of the two main categories.

DEFAULT OF THE PARTIES—DAMAGES

Introduction. A breach of contract which has not been excused gives the injured party the right to bring an action for damages. If he merely proves the breach, but no loss, he is awarded nominal damages, *e.g.* £1 or less.[1] If he proves actual loss, he is awarded substantial damages as compensation.[2] This chapter is concerned with the amount of damages recoverable where there is actual loss. A short account of the general principles upon which the courts award damages for breach of contract will be given, with a discussion of causation followed by a discussion of the application of those principles to breaches by the contractor and the employer.

1. Principles upon which Damages are Awarded

Damages are awarded to put the plaintiff as nearly as possible "in the same position as he would have been in if he had not sustained the wrong for which he is now getting compensation or reparation."[3] Accordingly, the approach to assessing damages for breach of contract, where the wrong is a failure to perform an enforceable promise, differs from that in tort, where the wrong is damage caused by a breach of duty.[4] "Where a party sustains a loss by reason of a breach of contract, he is, so far as money can do it, to be placed in the same

---

[1] See *McGregor on Damages* (15th ed.), Chap. 10. For aggravated and exemplary damages, neither of which normally apply in building contracts, see *Rookes* v. *Barnard* [1964] A.C. 1129 (H.L.); *Broome* v. *Cassell* [1972] A.C. 1027 (H.L.); *Drane* v. *Evangelou* [1978] 1 W.L.R. 455 (C.A.).

[2] *Ibid.*

[3] Lord Blackburn in *Livingstone* v. *Rawyards Coal Company* (1880) 5 App.Cas. 25 at 39 (H.L.).

[4] See, however, Scarman L.J. in *Parsons* v. *Uttley Ingham* [1978] Q.B. 791 at 807 (C.A.).

situation with regard to damages, as if the contract had been performed."[5] In tort the measure is the loss caused by the wrong and a greater sum is sometimes recoverable.[6] This chapter is concerned mainly with damages for breach of contract.

Damages for breach of contract. "The governing purpose of damages is to put the party whose rights have been violated in the same position,[7] so far as money can do, as if his rights had been observed."[8] But if this purpose were relentlessly pursued it would lead to the party in default having to pay "for all loss *de facto* resulting from a particular breach however improbable, however unpredictable."[9] The courts therefore set a limit to the loss for which damages are recoverable, and loss beyond such limit is said to be too remote.

The famous rule as stated in the case of *Hadley* v. *Baxendale*[10] is:

> "Where two parties have made a contract which one of them has broken the damages which the other party ought to receive in respect of such breach of contract should be such as may fairly and reasonably be considered either [1] arising naturally, *i.e.* according to the usual course of things from such breach of contract itself, or [2] such as may reasonably be supposed to have been in the contemplation of both parties at the time they made the contract, as the probable result of the breach of it."[11]

The rule has two limbs which have been indicated by the insertion into the quoted text of the figures [1] and [2].[12]

---

[5] *Robinson* v. *Harman* (1848) 1 Ex. 850 at 855, said by Lord Pearce to be "the underlying rule of the common law," *Koufos* v. *Czarnikow Ltd.* [1969] 1 A.C. 350 at 414 (H.L.); *British Westinghouse* v. *Underground Electric Railways* [1912] A.C. 673 at 689 (H.L.); see also *The Albazero* [1977] A.C. 774 at 841 (H.L.); *Johnson* v. *Agnew* [1980] A.C. 367 at 400 (H.L.); *Bevan Investments* v. *Blackhall & Struthers* (1977) 11 B.L.R. 78 at 95 (New Zealand Court of Appeal). Where the defendant has a choice of more than one method of performance, damages are generally assessed by reference to the method which is least unfavourable to him—see *Paula Lee* v. *Robert Zehil* [1983] 2 All E.R. 390.

[6] In tort, "the defendant will be liable for any type of damage which is reasonably foreseeable as liable to happen even in the most unusual case, unless the risk is so small that a reasonable man would in the whole circumstances feel justified in neglecting it."—Lord Reid in *Koufos* v. *Czarnikow* [1969] 1 A.C. 350 at 387 (H.L.). See also *Overseas Tankship (U.K.) Ltd.* v. *Morts Dock & Engineering Co. Ltd.* [1961] A.C. 388 (P.C.); and see discussion in *Salmond on Torts* (19th ed., 1987), Chap. 22. Liability may be wider in tort (*Koufos* case at 385) and comparison between damages in tort and contract is not helpful (*ibid.* at 413). For a claim for deceit, see *Doyle* v. *Olby (Ironmongers) Ltd.* [1969] Q.B. 158 (C.A.). See also *Broome* v. *Cassell* [1972] A.C. 1027 at 1076, 1080, 1130 (H.L.)—exemplary damages not recoverable for deceit; *cf. Archer* v. *Brown* [1985] Q.B. 401 and see p. 124.

[7] But not in a better position—see *C. & P. Haulage* v. *Middleton* [1983] 1 W.L.R. 1461 at 1467 (C.A.).

[8] Asquith L.J. in *Victoria Laundry Ltd.* v. *Newman Ltd.* [1949] 2 K.B. 528 at 539 (C.A.).

[9] *Ibid.*

[10] (1854) 9 Ex. 341.

[11] *Ibid.* Alderson B. at 354.

[12] See *Victoria Laundry Ltd.* v. *Newman Ltd.* [1949] 2 K.B. 528 at 537 (C.A.); *Koufos* v. *Czarnikow* [1969] 1 A.C. 350 at 421 (H.L.); *Wroth* v. *Tyler* [1974] 1 Ch. 30; *Parsons* v. *Uttley Ingham* [1978] Q.B. 791 (C.A.).

The first limb of Hadley v. Baxendale. Two leading cases in which the rule has been discussed are *Victoria Laundry* v. *Newman Industries*[13] and *Koufos* v. *Czarnikow*,[14] the latter considering the former at length with a number of other cases.[15] In the *Victoria Laundry* case, Asquith L.J. in a "classic judgment"[16] stated six propositions which emerged, he said, from the authorities as a whole.[17] Taking account of the opinions of the House of Lords in *Koufos* v. *Czarnikow*, the first limb of the rule may be elaborated into these propositions[18] based on those of Asquith L.J.:

(1) the aggrieved party is only entitled to recover such part of the loss actually resulting as may fairly and reasonably be considered as arising naturally, that is according to the usual course of things, from the breach of contract.

(2) The question is to be judged as at the time of the contract.

(3) In order to make the contract breaker liable it is not necessary that he should actually have asked himself what loss was liable to result from a breach of the kind which subsequently occurred. It suffices that, if he had considered the question, he would as a reasonable man have concluded that the loss of the type in question, not necessarily the specific loss, was "liable to result."

(4) The words "liable to result" should be read in the sense conveyed by the expressions "a serious possibility" and "a real danger" and "not unlikely to occur."[19]

For the first limb, therefore, knowledge of certain basic facts according to the usual course of things is imputed, but no special knowledge.

The second limb of Hadley v. Baxendale. This depends on additional special knowledge by the defendant. The passage from *Hadley* v. *Baxendale* quoted above is followed by:

---

[13] [1949] 2 K.B. 528 (C.A.).

[14] [1969] 1 A.C. 350 (H.L.).

[15] The House of Lords expressed differing views as to the *Victoria Laundry* case, but two years earlier they applied it without criticism in a building contract case—*East Ham Borough Council* v. *Bernard Sunley & Sons Ltd.* [1966] A.C. 406 at 440, 445, 450 (H.L.); see also *Overseas Tankship (U.K.) Ltd.* v. *Morts Dock & Engineering Co. Ltd.* [1961] A.C. 388 at 420 (P.C.). Neither case is referred to in the speeches in the *Koufos* case.

[16] *Aruna Mills Ltd.* v. *Gobindram* [1968] 1 Q.B. 655 at 668; see also *Allan Peters (Jewellers) Ltd.* v. *Brocks Alarms Ltd.* [1968] 1 Lloyd's Rep. 387 at 392.

[17] [1949] 2 K.B. 528 at 539 *et seq.*

[18] With the exception of the last five words (which derive from the opinion of Lord Reid in *Koufos* v. *Czarnikow* [1969] 1 A.C. 350 at 388 (H.L.)) and some words at the end of proposition (3) (which derive from *Parsons* v. *Uttley Ingham* [1978] Q.B. 791 at 813 (C.A.)), these propositions are taken from the judgment of Richmond P. in *Bevan Investments* v. *Blackhall & Struthers* (1977) 11 B.L.R. 78 at 106 (New Zealand Court of Appeal). The case is not binding authority in England, but is thought to contain an accurate and clear synthesis of the two leading English cases on which the passage depends. For a shorter formulation, see Scarman L.J. in *Parsons* v. *Uttley Ingham* at 806.

[19] The phrase "on the cards," used in the *Victoria Laundry* case, was applied by Lord Upjohn and Lord Pearson in *East Ham Borough Council* v. *Bernard Sunley & Sons Ltd.* [1966] A.C. 406 at 445, 451 (H.L.) but is so heavily criticised in the *Koufos* case that it is probably better now not to rely on it. See also *G.K.N. Centrax Gears Ltd.* v. *Marbro Ltd.* [1976] 2 Lloyd's Rep. 555 at 579 (C.A.).

"If the special circumstances were communicated by the plaintiffs to the defendants, and thus known to both parties, the damages resulting from the breach of such a contract, which they would reasonably contemplate, would be the amount of injury which would ordinarily follow from a breach of contract under these special circumstances so known and communicated."[20]

As with the first limb, the question is to be judged at the time of the contract so that damages claimed under the second limb will not be awarded unless the plaintiff has particular evidence to show that the defendant then knew the special circumstances relied on.

The first limb of the rule contains the necessity for knowledge of certain basic facts upon the basis of which there is a "horizon of contemplation." "Additional or 'special' knowledge, however, may extend the horizon to include losses that are outside the natural course of events. And of course the extension of the horizon need not always *increase* the damages; it might introduce a knowledge of particular circumstances, *e.g.* a sub-contract, which show that the plaintiff would in fact suffer *less* damage than a more limited view of the circumstances might lead one to expect."[21]

Propositions (2), (3) and (4) apply to both limbs of the rule. The necessary degree of likelihood of the loss occurring was considered at length in *Koufos* v. *Czarnikow* by reference to phrases such as those given at (4) above. But "the result in any particular case need not depend upon giving pride of place to any one of such phases."[22] It seems that the degree of likelihood can be less than evens,[23] even slight,[24] but that to equate it with what is reasonably foreseeable could be misleading. "To bring in reasonable foreseeability appears to me to be confusing measure of damages in contract with measure of damages in tort. A great many extremely unlikely results are reasonably foreseeable."[25]

In the *Victoria Laundry* case[26] a laundry company, intending to enlarge its business, ordered a boiler from the defendants, delivery to be on a certain date. Owing to the defendant's default delivery was several months late and as a result the laundry lost certain specially lucrative contracts. It was held that, though the defendants were not liable for the loss of profits on these particular contracts of which they had no knowledge, nevertheless they knew, or must be taken to have known from the circumstances and their position as engineers and businessmen, that there was bound to be business loss of some sort, and were liable for such loss on the basis of their knowledge actual or imputed.

---

[20] *Hadley* v. *Baxendale* (1854) 9 Ex. 341 at 354. For a clear modern application, see *Panalpina* v. *Densil Underwear* [1981] 1 Lloyd's Rep. 187 at 191; *cf. Koch Marine* v. *D'Amica Societa Di Navigazione* [1980] 1 Lloyd's Rep. 75 at 87.

[21] Lord Pearce in *Koufos* v. *Czarnikow* [1969] 1 A.C. 350 at 416 (H.L.).

[22] *Ibid.* Lord Morris at 397.

[23] See especially *ibid.* Lord Reid.

[24] *Parsons* v. *Uttley Ingham* [1978] Q.B. 791 at 813 (C.A.).

[25] Lord Reid in *Koufos* v. *Czarnikow* at 389; contrast Scarman L.J. in *Parsons* v. *Uttley Ingham* [1978] Q.B. 791 at 807 (C.A.); *cp. Lamb* v. *Camden Council* [1981] Q.B. 625 (C.A.).

[26] [1949] 2 K.B. 528 (C.A.).

In *Parsons* v. *Uttley Ingham,*[27] the defendants supplied a hopper for pig nuts to feed pigs and when they installed it failed to ensure that the ventilator was open with the result that the pig nuts became mouldy. The pigs died. The defendants who could have contemplated illness caused by their breach but not the particular rare illness which caused the deaths were held liable. It is thought that the principles applied in this case may well be relevant in building contract cases in relation to defects in the works.

"Consequential" loss.   Building and other contracts sometimes have clauses excluding liability for "consequential" loss.[28] The construction of each such clause will depend on its own words and context, but generally consequential loss is likely to approximate to loss within the second limb of *Hadley* v. *Baxendale.* It is loss which is in some way less direct or more remote than that loss or damage which remains recoverable despite the exclusion clause. "Consequential" does not cover loss which directly and naturally results in the ordinary course of events. Where sellers were in breach of contract in supplying masonry blocks, there was a clause in their contract seeking to exclude their liability for consequential loss or damage caused by or resulting from late supply. This clause was held not to exclude claims against the buyers by their sub-contractors for delay in the sub-contractors' work caused by the absence of the materials which the sellers ought to have delivered.[29]

Date of assessment.   With a decrease in the value of money this is often a matter of the greatest moment, although an award of interest may, in theory at least, mitigate the effect of choosing an early date.[30]

The general rule, both in contract and in tort, is that damages should be assessed as at the date when the cause of action arises.[31] But there are many exceptions and it has been said that "this so-called general rule . . . has been so far eroded in recent times . . . that little of practical reality remains of it."[32] Where the measure of damages is the cost of repair or reinstatement, the date of assessment is the date when it was first reasonable in all the relevant circumstances[33] for the plaintiff to undertake the repair or reinstatement works.[34] This is part of the principle that a defendant must mitigate his loss

---

[27] [1978] Q.B. 791 (C.A.).

[28] For exclusion clauses generally, see p. 63.

[29] *Croudace Construction* v. *Cawoods Concrete Products* [1978] 2 Lloyd's Rep. 55 (C.A.); *cf. Millars Machinery* v. *Way* (1934) 40 Comm. Cas. 204; *Saint Line* v. *Richardsons Westgarth* [1940] 2 K.B. 99; *F. G. Minter* v. *W.H.T.S.O.* (1980) 13 B.L.R. 1 at 15 (C.A.).

[30] For awards of interest, see pp. 451 *et seq.* See also generally articles at (1979) 95 L.Q.R. 270; (1980) 96 L.Q.R. 341; (1981) 97 L.Q.R. 445; (1982) 98 L.Q.R. 406.

[31] *Miliangos* v. *George Frank (Textiles) Ltd.* [1976] A.C. 443 at 468 (H.L.); *Dodd Properties* v. *Canterbury City Council* [1980] 1 W.L.R. 433 at 450 and 454 (C.A.).

[32] Ormrod L.J. in *Cory & Son* v. *Wingate Investments* (1980) 17 B.L.R. 104 at 121 (C.A.).

[33] These include the conduct of the defendant—see *Cory & Son* v. *Wingate Investments* (1980) 17 B.L.R. 104 (C.A.).

[34] *Dodd Properties* v. *Canterbury City Council* [1980] 1 W.L.R. 433 at 451 (C.A.); *cf. West Midland Baptist* v. *Birmingham Corporation* [1970] A.C. 874 at 903 (H.L.).

"but, in the ultimate analysis, the question is one of the reasonableness of the plaintiffs actions or inaction."[35] A reasonable date should normally at least include a reasonable time for the employer to survey the defects, obtain any necessary reports and arrange for the repairs.

If the plaintiff has not carried out the works at the date of the hearing, there is a *prima facie* presumption that the costs then prevailing are those which should be adopted. An earlier date will, of course, normally be taken where the plaintiff has already carried out the works and an earlier date will also be taken where the plaintiff, acting reasonably, should have carried out the works at some earlier date than he did or, as the case may be, than the date of the hearing.[36] It may be reasonable for a plaintiff, who starts proceedings which are contested and conducts then with reasonable expedition, to delay carrying out the works until the result of the contested proceedings is known.[37]

In the *Dodd Properties* v. *Canterbury City Council*,[38] the defendants had, in the course of building operations, damaged the plaintiffs' commercial garage premises. The cost of repair had more than doubled between the date of the damage and the date of trial. The plaintiff was held entitled to the higher figure. For various reasons of which "financial stringency" was one, it made commercial good sense to defer the repairs. "A plaintiff who is under a duty to mitigate is not obliged, in order to reduce the damages, to do that which he cannot afford to do: particularly where, as here, the plaintiffs "financial stringency," so far as it was relevant at all, arose, as a matter of common sense, if not as a matter of law, solely as a consequence of the defendants' wrong-doing."[39] It was a relevant factor that the defendants had never admitted liability. Although in the *Dodd Properties* case the claim was in tort, the same principles apply to the date for assessing damages for breach of contract.[40]

Where the measure of damages is the diminution in value of the property, the date of assessment is normally the date when the cause of action arises.[41] Where the damages awarded are for pecuniary loss, these are assessed at the date when the loss is incurred or, for future loss, at the date of trial.[42]

Mitigation of loss. The award of damages as compensation is qualified by a principle, "which imposes on a plaintiff the duty of taking all reasonable

---

[35] *Radford* v. *Froberville* [1977] 1 W.L.R. 1262 at 1287; *cf. Johnson* v. *Agnew* [1980] A.C. 367 at 400 *et seq.* (H.L.).

[36] *Dodd Properties* v. *Canterbury City Council* [1980] 1 W.L.R. 433 at 458 (C.A.); *Cory & Son* v. *Wingate Investments* (1980) 17 B.L.R. 104 (C.A.); *cf. Tito* v. *Waddell (No. 2)* [1977] Ch. 106 at 332.

[37] *Radford* v. *Froberville* [1977] 1 W.L.R. 1262 at 1287; *Dodd Properties* v. *Canterbury City Council* [1980] 1 W.L.R. 433 (C.A.); *cf. Bevan Investments* v. *Blackhall & Struthers* (1977) 11 B.L.R. 78 (New Zealand Court of Appeal).

[38] [1980] 1 W.L.R. 433 (C.A.).

[39] *Ibid.* at 453.

[40] See, *e.g. Cory & Son* v. *Wingate Investments* (1980) 17 B.L.R. 104 (C.A.).

[41] *Dodd Properties* v. *Canterbury City Council* [1980] 1 W.L.R. 433 at 457 (C.A.); *Perry* v. *Sidney Phillips* [1982] 1 W.L.R. 1297 (C.A.).

[42] *Dodd Properties* v. *Canterbury City Council* [1980] 1 W.L.R. 433 (C.A.); *Swingcastle* v. *Gibson* [1990] 1 W.L.R. 1223 at 1236 (C.A.).

steps to mitigate the loss consequent on the breach, and debars him from claiming any part of the damage which is due to his neglect to take such steps."[43] But this "does not impose on the plaintiff an obligation to take any step which a reasonable and prudent man would not ordinarily take in the course of his business."[44] Any gain resulting from the plaintiff's reasonable steps in mitigation must be balanced against the loss caused by the breach. Any loss resulting from such reasonable steps is recoverable.[45] The onus of proof is on the defendant to prove any failure to mitigate.[46] Generally it is legitimate to ask what damage the plaintiff has really suffered as a result of the defendant's breach.[47]

2. Causation and Concurrent Causes

A number of initial distinctions are necessary, *i.e.* firstly, whether the claim is in contract or in tort where different considerations apply; secondly, if it is in contract, whether it is brought under the contract or as damages for breach of it[48]; and thirdly, if there are competing causes one of which is the responsibility of the defendant, whether the other cause is the responsibility of the plaintiff on the one hand, or of another actual or potential defendant or third party or of no one on the other.

Causation generally. "Causation is a mental concept, generally based on inference or induction from uniformity of sequence as between two events that there is a causal connection between them."[49] For a plaintiff to succeed in a claim for damages, he has to establish on the balance of probabilities an effective causal connection between the defendant's breach of contract or negligence and the plaintiff's loss.[50] An intervening act by a third party,[51] or by

---

[43] Lord Haldane in *British Westinghouse* v. *Underground Railways Co.* [1912] A.C. 673 at 689 (H.L.); *The World Beauty* [1970] P. 144 (C.A.); *cp. Sotiros Shipping* v. *Sameiet Solholt* [1983] 1 Lloyd's Rep. 605 at 608 (C.A.).

[44] *British Westinghouse* v. *Underground Railways Co.* [1912] A.C. 673 at 689 (H.L.) referring to James L.J. in *Dunkirk Colliery Co.* v. *Lever* (1878) 9 Ch.D. 20 at 25 (C.A.). For a recent case, see *London and South England Building Society* v. *Stone* [1983] 1 W.L.R. 1242 (C.A.) especially at 1262 *et seq.* For the position where there has been non-acceptance of repudiation, see *White and Carter (Councils) Ltd.* v. *McGregor* [1962] A.C. 413 (H.L.), referred to at p. 152, but it is doubtful whether this case applies to the usual building contract.

[45] *British Westinghouse* v. *Underground Railways Co.* [1912] A.C. 673 at 691 (H.L.); *The World Beauty* [1970] P. 144 (C.A.); *Pagnan (R.) Fratelli* v. *Corbisa Industrial* [1970] 1 W.L.R. 1306 (C.A.); *Koch Marine* v. *D'Amica Societa Di Navigazione* [1980] 1 Lloyd's Rep. 75 at 88.

[46] *British Westinghouse* v. *Underground Railways Co.* [1912] A.C. 673 (H.L.); *Garnac Grain Co. Inc.* v. *Faure & Fairclough Ltd.* [1968] A.C. 1130 at 1140 (H.L.).

[47] *Sealace Shipping* v. *Oceanvoice Shipping, The Times*, September 25, 1990 (C.A.). For an illustration of failure to mitigate, see *Hutchinson* v. *Harris* (1978) 10 B.L.R. 19 at 43 (C.A.).

[48] See "Claims under or for breach of the contract" at p. 209.

[49] Lord Wright in *Monarch Steamship Co.* v. *Karlshamns Oljefabriker* [1949] A.C. 196 at 228 (H.L.).

[50] See *Monarch Steamship Co.* v. *Karlshamns Oljefabriker* [1949] A.C. 196 at 226 (H.L.); *Bonnington Castings* v. *Wardlaw* [1956] A.C. 613 (H.L.); *Hotson* v. *East Berkshire Area Health Authority* [1987] A.C. 750 (H.L.); *Wilsher* v. *Essex Area Health Authority* [1988] A.C. 1074 (H.L.).

[51] See *Lamb* v. *Camden London Borough Council* [1981] Q.B. 625 (C.A.); *P. Perl (Exporters)* v. *Camden London Borough Council* [1984] Q.B. 342 (C.A.); *Ward* v. *Cannock Chase District Council* [1986] Ch. 546.

the plaintiff[52] may break the chain of causation. But an act by the plaintiff will not normally break the chain of causation if it was reasonable.[53]

Contributory negligence. The Law Reform (Contributory Negligence) Act 1945 provides for a claimant's damages to be reduced to such extent as the court or arbitrator[54] thinks just and reasonable where the claimant suffers damage as the result partly of his own fault and partly of the fault of another person.[55] The Act applies to claims in tort.[56] It also applies to claims in contract where the defendant's contractual liability is the same as his liability in the tort of negligence independently of the existence of any contract[57] unless the parties have by their contract varied that position.[58] The Act may also apply where the defendant's liability arises from a contractual obligation which is expressed in terms of taking care but does not correspond to a common law duty to take care which would exist independently of contract.[59] Where the plaintiff admits some negligence or expects it to be found against him, he will seek an apportionment lest such negligence prevents him recovering all.[60] The Act does not apply where the defendant's liability arises from some contractual provision which does not depend on negligence on the part of the defendant.[61]

Statutory contribution. The Civil Liability (Contribution) Act 1978 enables contribution to be recovered from any other person liable in respect of the same damage, whatever the legal basis of his liability, whether it is tort, breach of contract, breach of trust or otherwise. This Act (to which reference for its exact terms must be made) enables a just and equitable apportionment, including a complete indemnity, to be made. It does not affect express or implied contractual or other rights to indemnity or contribution which would be enforceable apart from the Act.

(a) *Concurrent causes—tort*

In tort, the law is reasonably clear. If there are competing causes neither of

---

[52] *Quinn* v. *Burch Bros.* (*Builders*) [1966] 2 Q.B. 370 (C.A.); *cf. Lambert* v. *Lewis* [1982] A.C. 225 at 277 (H.L.).
[53] See *Emeh* v. *Kensington & Chelsea Health Authority* [1985] Q.B. 1012 (C.A.).
[54] See the definition of "court" in s.4 of the Act.
[55] See s.1 of the Act.
[56] See the definition of "fault" in s.4 of the Act.
[57] *Vesta* v. *Butcher* [1989] A.C. 852 (C.A.) upholding Hobhouse J. at [1986] 2 All E.R. 488 (the case went to the House of Lords on other issues—[1989] A.C. 852); *Sayers* v. *Harlow Urban District Council* [1958] 1 W.L.R. 623 (C.A.).
[58] *Vesta* v. *Butcher* [1986] 2 All E.R. 488 at 510.
[59] These are category (2) cases as described by Hobhouse J. in *Vesta* v. *Butcher* [1986] 2 All E.R. 488 at 508; see the *Vesta* case in the Court of Appeal at [1989] A.C. 852 (C.A.) and see also *De Meza* v. *Apple* [1974] 1 Lloyd's Rep. 508; *Rowe* v. *Turner Hopkins & Partners* [1980] 2 N.Z.L.R. 550 (New Zealand High Court); *Basildon District Council* v. *Lesser* [1985] Q.B. 839.
[60] See *Sole* v. *W. J. Hallt Ltd.* [1973] Q.B. 574 at 582; *De Meza* v. *Apple* [1974] 1 Lloyd's Rep. 508.
[61] These are category (1) cases as described by Hobhouse J. in *Vesta* v. *Butcher* [1986] 2 All E.R. 488 at 508; see *ibid.* at 509; *Basildon District Council* v. *Lesser* [1985] Q.B. 839; *Tennant Radiant Heat* v. *Warrington Development Corporation* (1988) 1 E.G.L.R. 41 (C.A.).

which is the responsibility of the plaintiff, he can recover in full if he establishes that the cause for which the defendant is liable caused or materially contributed to his loss.[62] (This is referred to below as *the tortious solution.*) "The question must be determined by applying common sense to the facts of each particular case."[63] The principle was applied in a building case where an aerial television mast collapsed from two separate causes operating at the same time. The less important of the causes was negligent design by sub-contractors, but they were held liable on the basis that their negligence materially contributed to the collapse.[64] There can be contribution between two or more defendants or between a defendant and one or more third parties.[65] If the plaintiff's loss was partly his own fault his damages may be reduced on account of his contributory negligence.[66]

(b) Concurrent causes—contract

In contract, the law is not so clear. There is a confusing number of possible factual permutations which can be illustrated by hypothetical building contract claims, *viz*:

Case A.
> *where an employer claims damages against two defendants, e.g.* for defects caused both by the architect's defective design and the contractor's defective work.

Case B.
> *where a contractor claims payment under the contract, e.g.* for delay resulting from variation instructions and there is a competing cause of delay. The competing cause of delay could be (i) no one's fault, *e.g.* bad weather, or (ii) the contractor's own delay in breach of contract.

Case C.
> *where the contractor claims damages for breach of contract, e.g.* for delay resulting from late instructions and there is a competing cause of delay. The competing cause of delay could be (i) no one's fault, or (ii) the contractor's own delay in breach of contract.

For each of these possibilities and on the assumption that all competing causes at least materially contributed to the loss (see the tortious solution referred to above):

> (1) the competing causes could be of approximately equal efficacy; or

---

[62] *Bonnington Castings* v. *Wardlaw* [1956] A.C. 613 (H.L.); *Hotson* v. *East Berkshire Area Health Authority* [1987] A.C. 750 (H.L.).
[63] Lord Reid in *Stapley* v. *Gypsum Mines* [1953] A.C. 663 at 681 (H.L.).
[64] *I.B.A.* v. *E.M.I. and B.I.C.C.* (1980) 14 B.L.R. 1 at 37 (H.L.); see also *Imperial College* v. *Norman and Dawbarn* (1986) 2 Const. L.J. 280—a claim in tort against architects, as to which see now "Professional negligence" at p. 172.
[65] See "Statutory contribution" above.
[66] See "Contributory negligence" above.

(2) one cause could be of significantly greater efficacy than the other.

Any solution for Cases B and C must take account of the fact that Cases B(ii) and C(ii) have an obverse. Not only does the plaintiff in each of these cases have a claim against the defendant, but the defendant potentially has a counterclaim against the plaintiff in which the concurrent cause problem would also arise. This is referred to as *the obverse problem.*

Claims under the contract.   If a contractor brings a delay claim, for instance, under the contract—Case B above—his entitlement depends on the meaning of the clause or clauses on which he relies. That meaning may exceptionally be determinative without any sophisticated analysis of causation, even if there is more than one competing cause of delay. The meaning may, however, explicitly or indirectly raise a question of causation. Thus, if the contract entitles the contractor to additional payment if the works are delayed by variations, it may be necessary in essence to determine whether the variations *caused* the delay because that is a question which the contract on its true construction raises. In insurance, if there are two approximately equal causes, one within the policy and the other within an exception, the loss cannot be recovered under the policy. The effect of the cover is not to impose on the insurer liability for something which is within the exception.[67] It is thought that this is no more than an example of a causation problem being resolved as a matter of the construction of the contract.

The law unclear—summary conclusion.   It is suggested in summary that the present law is that:

    (1) the plaintiff succeeds in full on Case A against either defendant or both provided he establishes that the relevant cause or causes at least materially contributed to the loss;

    (2) the plaintiff succeeds in Cases B and C, if he establishes that the cause on which he relies was the effective, dominant cause of delay;

    (3) the defendant succeeds on his counterclaim in Cases B(ii) and C(ii), if he establishes that the cause on which he relies was the effective, dominant cause of delay.

The law unclear—discussion.   There is authority of varying weight for a number of (as initially presented) disjointed propositions each of which is for convenience given a label, *viz*:

    (1) *the Devlin approach.* If a breach of contract is one of two causes of a loss,

---

[67] *Wayne Tank Co.* v. *Employers Liability* [1974] Q.B. 57 at 69 (C.A.); *cf. J. J. Lloyd Instruments* v. *Northern Star Insurance* [1987] 1 Lloyd's Rep. 32 (C.A.).

both causes co-operating and both of approximately equal efficacy, the breach is sufficient to carry judgment for the loss[68];

(2) *the dominant cause approach.* If there are two causes, one the contractual responsibility of the defendant and the other the contractual responsibility of the plaintiff, the plaintiff succeeds if he establishes that the cause for which the defendant is responsible is the effective, dominant cause.[69] Which cause is dominant is a question of fact,[70] which is not solved by the mere point of order in time,[71] but is to be decided by applying common sense standards[72];

(3) *the burden of proof approach.* If part of the damage is shown to be due to a breach of contract by the plaintiff, the claimant must show how much of the damage is caused otherwise than by his breach of contract, failing which he can recover nominal damages only.[73]

There is also

(4) *the tortious solution* referred to above, *i.e.* the plaintiff recovers if the cause on which he relies caused or materially contributed to the loss.

The tortious solution as applied in tort is coupled with statutory provisions for reducing the plaintiff's claim if his negligence partly caused the loss. There is as yet no generally applicable provision for reducing a plaintiff's claim in contract.[74] But there can be contribution between two actual or potential defendants, *i.e.* in Case A.[75]

It is submitted that there is a material distinction between Case A on the one hand and Cases B and C on the other. The dominant cause approach does not in terms apply to Case A. It is thought that the right answer for Case A is the Devlin approach coupled with the tortious approach. Thus the employer in Case A can recover in full from either defendant whatever the efficacy of the cause for which that defendant is responsible provided that it materially

---

[68] *Heskell* v. *Continental Express Ltd.* [1950] 1 All E.R. 1033 at 1048 (Devlin J.); *Banque Keyser Ullman* v. *Skandia (U.K.) Insurance* [1990] Q.B. 665 at 717 (Steyn J.); *cf. Ibid.* at 814 (C.A.) unaffected by the decision in the House of Lords [1990] 3 W.L.R. 364 (H.L.); *Fairfield-Mabey* v. *Shell U.K. Ltd.* (1989) C.I.L.L. 514; *cf. J. J. Lloyd Instruments* v. *Northern Star Insurance* [1987] 1 Lloyd's Rep. 32 (C.A.); *cp.* however *Wayne Tank Co.* v. *Employers Liability* [1974] Q.B. 57 at 73 (C.A.) which may nevertheless not affect the general proposition stated in the text.

[69] See *Leyland Shipping* v. *Norwich Union* [1918] A.C. 350 at 370 (H.L.); *Yorkshire Dale Steamship* v. *Minister of War Transport* [1942] A.C. 691 (H.L.); *Monarch Steamship Co.* v. *Karlshamns Oljefabriker* [1949] A.C. 196 at 227 (H.L.); *Boiler Inspection and Insurance Company* v. *Sherwin-Williams* [1951] A.C. 319 (P.C.); *Wayne Tank Co.* v. *Employers Liability* [1974] Q.B. 57 (C.A.).

[70] *Leyland Shipping* v. *Norwich Union* [1918] A.C. 350 at 358, 359, 363, 369 (H.L.).

[71] *Ibid.* at 363 (H.L.).

[72] *Yorkshire Dale Steampship* v. *Minister of War Transport* [1942] A.C. 691 (H.L.).

[73] *Government of Ceylon* v. *Chandris* [1965] 3 All E.R. 48 at 57, Mocatta J. in a damage to cargo case, "applying no authority because there is none, but the result follows, in my view, from the principles involved."

[74] See "Contributory negligence" above. It is thought that Cases B and C in the text are unlikely to come within categories (2) or (3) as described by Hobhouse J. in *Vesta* v. *Butcher* [1986] 2 All E.R. 488 at 508.

[75] See "Statutory contribution" at p. 192.

contributed to the loss and provided that the plaintiff does not recover twice over.[76] The defendants can recover contribution from each other.[77]

It is thought that both the tortious solution and the Devlin approach should be rejected for Cases B and C, if only because of the obverse problem. If you apply either of these tests to the plaintiff's claim, you get an insoluble clash when you apply the same test, as logically you must, also to the defendant's counterclaim. Further, the Devlin approach is not apt for Cases B(i) or C(i) if the competing cause is of greater efficacy than the plaintiff's cause, although it is a possible solution for those cases if the competing causes are of approximately equal efficacy. If the plaintiff's cause is dominant, the Devlin approach necessarily produces the same result as the dominant cause approach.[78]

It is submitted that the burden of proof approach should be rejected for Cases B and C, if only because of the obverse problem. Applying the burden of proof approach would mean that, whatever the relative efficacy of the competing causes, the plaintiff would never succeed on his claim and the defendant would never succeed on his counterclaim. There is some building contract authority suggesting the rejection of the burden of proof approach,[79] which is thought also to be inconsistent with the dominant cause approach. The burden of proof approach is not in terms apt for Cases B(i) and C(i). It is further submitted that the burden of proof should require the plaintiff to establish that the loss resulted from the cause on which he relies and that he will do so if he establishes that it was the dominant cause. He should not be required additionally to disprove lesser alternative causes altogether.

The dominant cause approach is supported as indicated above by authority of great weight in insurance cases. It is thought that the principles, so far as they apply, apply to contracts generally.[80] It is accordingly submitted that the dominant cause approach is or should be the correct approach, as the law now stands,[81] for Case C and for Case B also, unless exceptionally the contract on

---

[76] There is good authority that this is the accepted answer for Case A. See *Imperial Bank of Canada* v. *Begley* [1936] 2 All E.R. 367 at 375 (P.C.); *Hutchinson* v. *Harris* (1978) 10 B.L.R. 19 at 22; *Townsend* v. *Stone Toms & Partners* (1984) 27 B.L.R. 26 (C.A.); *cf. Grant* v. *Sun Shipping Co.* [1948] A.C. 549 at 563 (H.L.); *London Borough of Merton* v. *Lowe* (1981) 18 B.L.R. 130 at 145 (C.A.) *London and South of England Building Society* v. *Stone* [1983] 1 W.L.R. 1242 (C.A.).

[77] See "Statutory contribution" at p. 192.

[78] See *Fairfield-Mabey* v. *Shell U.K. Ltd.* (1989) C.I.L.L. 514 where H.H. Judge Bowsher Q.C. adopted the Devlin approach without considering other possibilities but found on the facts that the competing cause was dominant.

[79] See *Wells* v. *Army & Navy Co-operative Society* (1902) 86 L.T. 764; H.B.C. (4th ed.), Vol. 2, p. 346 at 355 (C.A.) where Vaughan Williams L.J. said: "In law, I wholly deny the proposition Mr. Bray put forward, which was this really in effect: 'Never mind how much delay there may be caused by the conduct of the building owner, the builder will not be relieved from penalties if he too has been guilty of delay in the execution of the works.' I do not accept that proposition in law."

[80] In *H. Fairweather & Co.* v. *London Borough of Wandsworth* (1987) 39 B.L.R. 106, an arbitrator had adopted the dominant cause approach to a contrator's delay claim under a 1963 Standard Form of Building Contract. The court considered *obiter* that this approach was not correct, referring to *Henry Boot Construction* v. *Central Lancashire* (1980) 15 B.L.R. 1 and *London Borough of Merton* v. *Leach* (1985) 32 B.L.R. 31 (which do not directly address the problem), but otherwise without detailed reasons.

[81] But see "Apportionment" below.

its true construction provides an explicit answer without sophisticated analysis. This solution resolves the obverse problem. Although the Devlin approach is possible for Cases B(i) and C(i) where the competing causes are of approximately equal efficacy, the dominant cause approach can accommodate those cases on the basis that the competing cause, *ex hypothesi* of approximately equal efficacy, is a cause which is at the contractor's risk in relation to his own costs. It is thought that consistency and common sense suggest adopting the dominant cause approach throughout for Cases B and C.

Apportionment.   The Law Commission's Working Paper No. 114 (1990) "Contributory Negligence as a Defence in Contract" proceeds on the basis that, broadly speaking, the law does not currently permit apportionment where the defendant is liable only in contract. In a landlord and tenant case, the Court of Appeal made an apportionment of two concurrent causes as between a plaintiff's claim and a defendant's counterclaim where one was a claim in tort and the other a claim in contract.[82] The apportionment was made "as a matter of causation" and explicitly not by any application of the Law Reform (Contributory Negligence) Act 1945. It is thought that such a decision is unlikely in building contracts for Cases B or C above under the present law.[83] But the complexity of the analysis in this section and the uncertainty of its result warrant statutory intervention. The Law Commission's provisional conclusion was that where the loss or damage suffered by the plaintiff results partly from his own conduct and partly from the defendant's breach of contract, it is correct in principle for the damages to be apportioned.[84]

3. Various General Considerations

Impecuniosity.   Damage resulting from the impecuniosity of the innocent party known to the defaulting party at the time of making the contract may not be too remote.[85] In a New Zealand case,[86] the plaintiff had for financial reasons delayed carrying out rectification works necessitated by the defendant's breach of contract beyond the date when he might otherwise have carried them out so that the cost was increased by inflation. It was held that the fact that the plaintiff might find itself in a position of such difficulty, from a

---

[82] *Tennant Radiant Heat* v. *Warrington Development Corporation* (1988) 1 E.G.L.R. 41 (C.A.).

[83] In the Law Commission's Working Paper No. 114, this case is referred to in para. 3.20 as "an unusual application of causation principles"—see also para. 4.26.

[84] See also David I. Bristow Q.C., "Contributory Fault in Construction Contracts" (Toronto, Canada) (1986) 2 Const. L.J. 252.

[85] *Trans Trust S.P.R.L.* v. *Danubian Trading Co. Ltd.* [1952] 2 Q.B. 297 (C.A.); *Wadsworth* v. *Lydall* [1981] 1 W.L.R. 598 at 602 and 605 (C.A.); contrast *Compania Financiera* v. *Hamoor Tanker Corporation* [1981] 1 W.L.R. 274 (C.A.). For the limited application of *The Liesbosch* [1933] A.C. 449 (H.L.), see *Dodd Properties* v. *Canterbury City Council* [1980] 1 W.L.R. 433 at 458 (C.A.); *Perry* v. *Sidney Phillips* [1982] 1 W.L.R. 1297 at 1307 (C.A.); *Archer* v. *Brown* [1985] Q.B. 401 at 417.

[86] *Bevan Industries* v. *Blackhall & Struthers* (1977) 11 B.L.R. 78 (New Zealand Court of Appeal).

commercial and common sense point of view, that it was unable to complete the work although otherwise equipped to do so was within the first limb of the rule in *Hadley* v. *Baxendale*. He accordingly recovered costs calculated at the date of trial. This decision accords in the result, though not entirely in the reasoning, with English decisions discussed under the heading "Date of assessment" above.[87] Where expenditure results from or is increased by the plaintiff's financial inability to pursue a less expensive alternative, the critical question will often be whether in incurring the expenditure the plaintiff acted reasonably.[88]

Contingency. A loss dependent upon a contingency is not necessarily too remote, however difficult the assessment of damages may be,[89] but in order to recover more than nominal damages, there must be proof of some loss.[90] There is a distinction here between causation, which must be established on the balance of probabilities,[91] and quantification, where the court may be persuaded to assess damages on unsatisfactory evidence where it is satisfied nevertheless that the plaintiff has suffered substantial loss.[92] Where evidence is unsatisfactory, there is a presumption that an existing state of things will continue.[93] The court will not, however, indulge in pure speculation where a plaintiff fails to prove that any sum is due.[94]

Loss of profits and loss of good will. Such losses may be recoverable on the principles stated above. It will be necessary to prove facts sufficient to come within one limb or the other of the rule in *Hadley* v. *Baxendale*[95] and in particular that the defendant had sufficient general or specific knowledge that the product of the contract was to be put to profit earning commercial use affecting customers or clients.[96] If the breach is calculated to cause a loss of goodwill a reasonable sum can be awarded without positive proof,[97] but it is

---

[87] See also *Perry* v. *Sidney Phillips* [1982] 1 W.L.R. 1297 at 1307 (C.A.).

[88] See, *e.g. Bacon* v. *Cooper (Metals) Ltd.* [1982] 1 All E.R. 397.

[89] *Chaplin* v. *Hicks* [1911] 2 K.B. 786 (C.A.); *Hall* v. *Meyrick* [1957] 2 W.L.R. 458; this case was subsequently reversed but on different grounds [1957] 2 Q.B. 455 (C.A.).

[90] *Sykes* v. *Midland Bank Executor Co.* [1971] 1 Q.B. 113 (C.A.); *cf. Bevan Investments* v. *Blackhall & Struthers* (1977) 11 B.L.R. 78 at 125 (New Zealand Court of Appeal).

[91] *Hotson* v. *East Berkshire Health Authority* [1987] A.C. 750 (H.L.).

[92] See *Ashcroft* v. *Curtin* [1971] 1 W.L.R. 1731 (C.A.); *Penvidic Contracting Co.* v. *International Nickel of Canada* (1975) 53 D.L.R. (3d) 748 at 757; *Tai Hing Mill* v. *Kamsing Factory* [1979] A.C. 91 at 106 (P.C.); *cf. Sun Valley Poultry* v. *Micro-Biologicals Ltd., The Times,* May 14, 1990 (C.A.). See also "Hudson formula" at p. 211.

[93] *Evans Marshall & Co. Ltd.* v. *Bertola Ltd.* [1976] 2 Lloyd's Rep. 17 at 26 (H.L.).

[94] See *Tate & Lyle* v. *Greater London Council* [1982] 1 W.L.R. 149 at 152, Forbes J., the point being unaffected by subsequent appeals—[1982] 1 W.L.R. 971 (C.A.) and [1983] 2 A.C. 509 (H.L.).

[95] See p. 186 *et seq.*

[96] See, *e.g. Satef-Huttens* v. *Paloma Tercera* [1981] 1 Lloyd's Rep. 175 where on the facts some loss of profits was recoverable but a claim for loss of goodwill was too speculative; *cf. Panalpina* v. *Densil Underwear* [1981] 1 Lloyd's Rep. 187. For problems of proof, see *Bevan Investments* v. *Blackhall & Struthers* (1977) 11 B.L.R. 78 at 110 *et seq.* (New Zealand Court of Appeal).

[97] *Anglo-Continental Holidays* v. *Typaldos (London)* [1967] 2 Lloyd's Rep. 61 (C.A.).

suggested that if it is sought to recover substantial sums under this head particulars should be given and evidence of actual loss adduced.[98] Damages for loss of repeat orders may be recoverable.[99]

Wasted expenditure.   Such losses are recoverable if they are reasonably in the contemplation of the parties as likely to be wasted when the contract is entered into and the innocent party elects to claim wasted expenditure instead of loss of profits.[1] A plaintiff claiming damages for breach of contract has an unfettered choice whether to claim loss of profits or wasted expenditure. But he can only recover wasted expenditure if the expenditure would have been recovered as profit if the contract had been performed. The burden of showing on the balance of probabilities that it would not have been so recovered is on the defendant.[2] Expenditure wasted during the currency of a loss making contract is not recoverable if it resulted from a bad initial bargain and not from the defendant's breach of contract.[3]

Managerial expenses.   The expenditure of managerial time in remedying an actionable wrong done to a trading concern can be claimed as special damages, but the extent to which the trading routine was disturbed must be proved by reference, for example, to records of the time spent by managerial staff on particular projects.[4]

Credit for increased cost.   Since the plaintiff is in principle entitled to be put in the same situation as if the contract had been performed, he may have to give credit for increased costs which he would have incurred on that hypothesis. If, for instance, an engineer's structural design is deficient in breach of contract, it may be that a competent design would have cost more to construct than the deficient design. In those and similar circumstances, if damages are assessed as the cost of repair or reinstatement, the plaintiff has to give credit for that difference in cost,[5] unless perhaps exceptionally the defendant warranted at the outset that a proper design could be achieved at the original cost.

Third party losses.   Generally a plaintiff cannot recover damages for a loss caused by a defendant to a third party[6] so that, for instance, a holding company cannot normally recover a loss caused to its subsidiary where the

---

[98] *Perestrello Ltd.* v. *United Paint Co. Ltd.* [1969] 1 W.L.R. 570 (C.A.).
[99] *G.K.N. Centrax Gears Ltd.* v. *Marbro Ltd.* [1976] 2 Lloyd's Rep. 555 (C.A.).
[1] *Anglia Television Ltd.* v. *Reed* [1972] 1 Q.B. 60 (C.A.), discussed 35 M.L.R. 423.
[2] *C.C.C. Films* v. *Impact Quadrant Films* [1985] Q.B. 16.
[3] *C. & P. Haulage* v. *Middleton* [1983] 1 W.L.R. 1461 (C.A.).
[4] *Tate & Lyle* v. *Greater London Council* [1982] 1 W.L.R. 149 at 152, Forbes J., the point being unaffected by subsequent appeals—[1982] 1 W.L.R. 971 (C.A.) and [1983] 2 A.C. 509 (H.L.). See also "Contingency" above and "Cost of reports" below.
[5] See *Bevan Investments* v. *Blackhall & Struthers* (1977) 11 B.L.R. 78 (New Zealand Court of Appeal).
[6] See *Prudential Assurance* v. *Newman Industries* [1982] Ch. 204 at 210 (C.A.).

subsidiary is a separate company.[7] There are a number of exceptions[8] including perhaps that a person may recover his company's losses as damages where that company is personal to him so that its losses are his losses.[9]

Cost of reports.   Subject to principles discussed in this chapter, it seems that the cost of experts' reports and the like are recoverable as damages if their main purpose was to help the plaintiff deal with the defendant's breach of contract on the ground, but (if at all) as costs in the proceedings if their main purpose was related to the conduct of the proceedings.[10] There may possibly be circumstances where the plaintiff has a choice between making the claim as damages or as costs.[11] A corporate litigant may also sometimes recover as costs the actual direct costs of expert assistance provided by its own staff.[12]

Sums paid in settlement of third party claims.   Where a defendant's breach of contract renders the plaintiff liable to a third party,[13] the plaintiff can normally recover the amount of that liability as damages for the breach.[14] If the plaintiff reasonably compromises the third party liability, the amount paid under the compromise is admissible *prima facie* evidence of the loss caused by the defendant's breach, although further evidence may be adduced to determine the actual loss.[15] It will usually also be necessary to establish the plaintiff's liability to the third party and the defendant's liability to the plaintiff, since evidence of the compromise is relevant only to the measure of damages.[16] It is relevant to prove that the compromise was made upon legal advice, but in such circumstances evidence of the legal advisers is not normally relevant or admissible.[17]

---

[7] *Richard Roberts* v. *Douglas Smith Stimson* (1988) 46 B.L.R. 50 at 69.

[8] See *The Albazero* [1977] A.C. 774 at 846 (H.L.); *Woodar* v. *Wimpey* [1980] 1 W.L.R. 277 at 283, 297 (H.L.) explaining *Jackson* v. *Horizon Holidays* [1975] 1 W.L.R. 1468 (C.A.); *Pan Atlantic* v. *Pine Top* [1988] 2 Lloyd's Rep. 505.

[9] *Lee* v. *Sheard* [1956] 1 Q.B. 192; *Esso Petroleum Co. Ltd.* v. *Mardon* [1976] Q.B. 801 (C.A.). But see *Richard Roberts* v. *Douglas Smith Stimson* (1988) 46 B.L.R. 50 at 71.

[10] *Hutchinson* v. *Harris* (1978) 19 B.L.R. 19 at 39 (C.A.); *cp. Peak Construction (Liverpool)* *McKinney Foundations Ltd.* (1970) 1 B.L.R. 111 at 121 and 69 L.G.R. 1 at 10 (C.A.), damages, and *Bolton* v. *Mahadeva* [1972] 1 W.L.R. 1009 at 1014 (C.A.), costs and see also *Manakee* v. *Brattle* [1970] 1 W.L.R. 1607; *Ross* v. *Caunters* [1980] Ch. 297 at 323—legal expenses of investigating a claim before the issue of the writ only recoverable as costs. For work done by a claims' consultant, see *James Longley* v. *South West Regional Health Authority* (1983) 25 B.L.R. 56.

[11] *Manakee* v. *Brattle* [1970] 1 W.L.R. 1607.

[12] *Re Nossen's Patent* [1969] 1 W.L.R. 639.

[13] As, for instance, where a sub-contractor's breach puts the main contractor in breach of the main contract and liable to the employer. See also "Other losses" at p. 206.

[14] The claim will fail where the defendant's breach did not cause the liability to the third party—see *Fairfield-Mabey* v. *Shell U.K. Ltd.* (1989) C.I.L.L. 514.

[15] *Biggin & Co. Ltd.* v. *Permanite Ltd.* [1951] 2 K.B. 314 (C.A.). See also *MISR Travel* v. *Conference and Reunion Organisers* (1984) 134 New L.J. 150 (C.A.)—"you have to show that the settlement that you came to was a reasonable one altogether"; *Holland Hannen & Cubitts* v. *W.H.T.S.O.* (1985) 35 B.L.R. 1 at 15 (C.A.).

[16] *Fletcher & Stewart* v. *Jay & Partners* (1976) 17 B.L.R. 38 (C.A.); *Comyn Ching* v. *Oriental Tube* (1979) 17 B.L.R. 47 at 89 (C.A.); *cf.* s.1(4) of the Civil Liability (Contribution) Act 1978.

[17] *Biggin & Co. Ltd.* v. *Permanite Ltd.* [1951] 2 K.B. 314 at 321 (C.A.); *cf. Comyn Ching* v. *Oriental Tube* (1979) 17 B.L.R. 47 at 89 (C.A.).

A special difficulty sometimes arises with management contracts, which often provided in substance that the management contractor's liability to the employer for defects or delay shall be limited to any amount which he actually recovers from the sub-contractor responsible. Can the sub-contractor successfully avoid liability by arguing that the management contractor has suffered no loss? It is thought that each case depends on the construction of the particular management contract and the sub-contract that no general principle can be stated. However, the sub-contractor's argument is likely to be thought unmeritorious.[18] A management contract, for instance, which in substance stipulates that the management contractor *shall* be liable but that the liability shall only be enforced to the extent that he recovers from the sub-contractor is likely to be held effective to defeat the sub-contractor's argument.[19]

Tax.   The incidence of actual or hypothetical tax may have to be taken into account in assessing damages. In general deductions for tax are only made where the loss for which the damages are awarded would have been taxable in the hands of the plaintiff *and* the damages themselves are not taxable in his hands.[20] Damages do not currently attract Value Added Tax.[21]

Foreign currency.   A court or arbitrator can give judgment or make an award expressed in a foreign currency where the claim is for a debt due in a foreign currency, where the proper law of the contract is that of a foreign country and when the money of account is of that country or possibly some country other than the United Kingdom.[22] Conversion into sterling for enforcement purposes is at the date when the court authorises enforcement.[23]

4. Contractor's Breach of Contract

Cost of completion.   Where the contractor fails to complete,[24] the measure of damages in the first instance is the difference between the contract price and

---

[18] *cf. Haviland* v. *Long* [1952] 2 Q.B. 80 (C.A.); see also *Hambro Life Assurance* v. *White Young & Partners* (1987) 38 B.L.R. 16 (C.A.).

[19] *cf.* clauses 1.7 and 3.21 of the JCT Standard Form of Management Contract and clause 1.6 of the JCT Works Contract Conditions.

[20] See *British Transport Commission* v. *Gourley* [1956] A.C. 185 (H.L.). For a full discussion, see *McGregor on Damages* (15th ed.), Chap. 13, and *Chitty* (26th ed.), Vol. 1, paras. 1841 *et seq.* For Capital Gains Tax, see *Zim Properties* v. *Procter* [1985] S.T.C. 90.

[21] This includes liquidated damages which under current Customs & Excise practice are not regarded as the consideration for any supply. VAT is regarded as payable on a court award which is the consideration for a specific taxable supply, *e.g.* professional fees of a person registered for VAT.

[22] *Miliangos* v. *George Frank (Textiles)* [1976] A.C. 443 at 467, 501 (H.L.). For the detailed application of this principle, see *McGregor on Damages* (15th ed.), paras. 644 *et seq.*

[23] *Ibid.*

[24] For repudiation by the contractor, see p. 153; for the position where the employer determines the contract or ejects the contractor from the site under an express clause, see p. 236; and for liquidated damages for non-completion, see p. 222.

the amount it would actually cost the employer to complete the contract work substantially as it was originally intended, and in a reasonable manner, and at the earliest reasonable opportunity.[25] Thus in *Mertens* v. *Home Freeholds Co.*,[26] the contractor agreed to build a house in 1916 for £1,900. It was an unprofitable contract and he therefore deliberately delayed the work so that as a result the work was stopped by government decree. The earliest moment at which the employer could build was 1919 when it would have cost him £4,153 to complete.[27] It was held that the employer could recover the difference between £4,153 and £1,900, plus £825 paid to the contractor, less £495 being the value of the work done by the contractor before he ceased work, making a total of £2,583. In one case the plaintiff recovered the cost of rebuilding the premises where the defendant had supplied mortar so inferior that the local authority condemned the building.[28]

Offer to complete.   Where a contractor who has repudiated[29] his contract offers to complete under a new contract it is a question of fact in each case whether an employer who does not accept such offer is acting reasonably in mitigation of his loss.[30] If it is unreasonable to refuse such an offer, damages are calculated as if the offer had been accepted.[31] Each case will depend on its facts, but it is thought that conduct which amounts to repudiation by a contractor is likely to render reasonable an employer's refusal to re-engage him.

Defective work.   Where there has been substantial completion the measure of damages is the amount which the work is worth less by reason of the defects and omissions, and is normally calculated by the cost of making them good,[32] *i.e.* the cost of reinstatement.[33] The plaintiff in such a case has to show that he intends to carry out the reinstatement works and that it is reasonable to do so.[34] He must prove that he has suffered loss, but if the court is satisfied that the plaintiff's property has been or will be repaired in consequence of the defendant's breach of contract, the court is not further concerned with whether the plaintiff has had to pay for the repairs out of his own pocket or whether funds

---

[25] *Mertens* v. *Home Freehold Co.* [1921] 2 K.B. 526 (C.A.); *Radford* v. *De Froberville* [1977] 1 W.L.R. 1262.
[26] [1921] 2 K.B. 526 (C.A.).
[27] *I.e.* all the contract works, not merely the unfinished works.
[28] *Smith* v. *Johnson* (1899) 15 T.L.R. 179.
[29] For meaning, see p. 146.
[30] *Strutt* v. *Whitnell* [1975] 1 W.L.R. 870 (C.A.), and see "Mitigation of loss" at p. 190.
[31] See *Sotiros Shipping* v. *Sameiet Solholt* [1983] 1 Lloyd's Rep. 605 (C.A.).
[32] Denning L.J. in *Hoenig* v. *Isaacs* [1952] 2 All E.R. 176 at 181 (C.A.); for facts, see p. 73.
[33] *East Ham Borough Council* v. *Bernard Sunley & Sons Ltd.* [1966] A.C. 406; *cf. Bevan Investments* v. *Blackhall & Struthers* (1977) 11 B.L.R. 78 (New Zealand Court of Appeal); *Dodd Properties* v. *Canterbury City Council* [1980] 1 W.L.R. 433 at 456 (C.A.); *Radford* v. *De Froberville* [1977] 1 W.L.R. 1262.
[34] *Imodco* v. *Wimpey and Taylor Woodrow* (1987) 40 B.L.R. 1 at 19, 25 (C.A.); *Radford* v. *De Froberville* [1977] 1 W.L.R. 1262 at 1283; *cf. Dean* v. *Ainley* [1987] 1 W.L.R. 1729 (C.A.); *Ward* v. *Cannock Chase District Council* [1986] Ch. 546; *Minscombe Properties* v. *Sir Alfred McAlpine* (1986) 2 Const. L.J. 303 (C.A.); see also "Betterment" below.

have come from some other source.[35] Damages will not normally be reduced because the loss might also be recoverable from public funds[36] or from insurance.[37]

Sometimes, perhaps more often in tort than for breach of contract, the proper measure of damages is not the cost of reinstatement but the difference in value between the work as it is and as it ought to have been.[38] This will be so in particular where the plaintiff has no prospect or intention of rebuilding,[39] or where it would otherwise be unreasonable as between the plaintiff and the defendant to award the cost of reinstatement.[40] A claim for diminution in value will not normally exceed the relevant costs of reinstatement.[41] In one case, however, an employer was awarded as damages the difference between the value of houses as they ought to have been completed by the contractor and their value as they were in fact completed, although the only loss the employer had suffered was the cost of voluntarily putting right defects at the request of subsequent purchasers.[42] If all the necessary remedial works have been successfully carried out, residual diminution in value is not additionally recoverable.[43]

Betterment.   Where works of repair or reinstatement result in the plaintiff having a better or newer building than he would have had but for the wrong for which damages are claimed, a deduction from the damages awarded will usually not be made for betterment if the plaintiff has no reasonable choice,[44] unless perhaps this would be absurd.[45] If a plaintiff chooses to rebuild to a higher standard than is strictly necessary, he can recover the cost of the works less a credit for betterment, unless the new works are so different as to break the chain of causation.[46] If the remedial works are executed as part of a larger programme of work, it may be appropriate to award damages based on the cheapest estimate of the cost of the remedial works by themselves.[47]

---

[35] *Jones* v. *Stroud District Council* [1986] 1 W.L.R. 1141 at 1150 (C.A.).

[36] *Design 5* v. *Keniston Housing Association* (1986) 34 B.L.R. 97.

[37] *Browning* v. *The War Office* [1963] 1 Q.B. 750; *Parry* v. *Cleaver* [1970] A.C. 1 (H.L.); see also *McGregor on Damages* (15th ed.), para. 1482.

[38] *Dodd Properties* v. *Canterbury City Council* [1980] 1 W.L.R. 433 at 465 (C.A.); *Cory & Son* v. *Wingate Investments* (1980) 17 B.L.R. 104 at 121 (C.A.); *Ward* v. *Cannock Chase District Council* [1986] Ch. 546; *cp. County Personnel* v. *Alan R. Pulver* [1987] 1 W.L.R. 916 at 925 (C.A.) for the normal rule where property is acquired following negligent advice by surveyors. See however *Pamela Syrett* v. *Carr and Neave* (1990) 6 Const.L.J. 305.

[39] See, *e.g. C. R. Taylor* v. *Hepworths* [1977] 1 W.L.R. 659; *Ward* v. *Cannock Chase District Council* [1986] Ch. 546; *Hussey* v. *Eels* [1990] 2 W.L.R. 234 (C.A.).

[40] *C. R. Taylor* v. *Hepworths* [1977] 1 W.L.R. 659 at 667.

[41] See *Murphy* v. *Brentwood District Council* [1990] 2 W.L.R. 944 (C.A.)—unaffected by the House of Lords decision at [1990] 3 W.L.R. 414 (H.L.).

[42] *Newton Abbot Development Co. Ltd.* v. *Stockman Bros.* (1931) 47 T.L.R. 616.

[43] *Murphy* v. *Brentwood District Council* [1990] 2 W.L.R. 944 at 972, 978 (C.A.)—unaffected by the House of Lords decision at [1990] 3 W.L.R. 414 (H.L.).

[44] *Harbutt's "Plasticine" Ltd.* v. *Wayne Tank and Pump Co. Ltd.* [1970] 1 Q.B. 447 (C.A.)—overruled in *Photo Production* v. *Securicor* [1980] A.C. 827 (H.L.) but on a different point.

[45] See *Bacon* v. *Cooper (Metals) Ltd.* [1982] 1 All E.R. 397 at 400.

[46] See *Richard Roberts* v. *Douglas Smith Stimson* (1988) 46 B.L.R. 50 at 69. See also *Hospitals for Sick Children* v. *McLaughlin & Harvey* (1990) 19 Con. L.R. 25 at 97 and (1990) 6 Const. L.J. 245 at 248.

[47] See *Jones* v. *Stroud District Council* [1986] 1 W.L.R. 1141 at 1150 (C.A.).

Where the defendant asserts that reinstatement works carried out by the plaintiff were unnecessarily expensive, the question is whether the plaintiff acted reasonably and, in tort at least, may be expressed as whether what he did was reasonably foreseeable.[48] A plaintiff who acts upon apparently competent expert advice will normally be taken to have acted reasonably unless some quite clearly unreasonable course was adopted,[49] and unless perhaps the expert's proposals were outside the range of those which an ordinarily competent equivalent expert would have proposed so as to have been negligent.[50]

Destruction of premises. Where a breach results in the destruction of the premises or part of them and the innocent party has no option but to rebuild, the measure of damages is the cost of replacement.[51] He is not entitled to recover the cost of improvements made voluntarily,[52] but he is not subject to a deduction merely because he gets new for old, nor for improvements which are no more than the result of complying with statutory requirements current at this time of rebuilding. Where rebuilding commercial premises after a fire was more expensive, taking loss of business into account, than acquiring different premises, the court rejected the defendant's contention that damages should be assessed as the diminution in value of the damaged premises and awarded the plaintiff the cost of acquiring the different premises.[53]

Delay. Damages for a contractor's failure in breach of contract to complete on time are often the subject of a provision for liquidated damages.[54] Otherwise his liability is for general damages awarded on the principles discussed at the outset of this chapter and depending on his actual or imputed knowledge at the time when the contract was made. Thus it seems that where the works are for industry or commerce the contractor will almost inevitably be liable for some loss, for example, "in a contract to build a mill the builder knows that a delay on his part will result in the loss of business."[55] If he is building houses or blocks of flats for letting, then on analogy with shipping cases he is probably liable for loss of rent.[56] It may be that in cases where works, such as those for

---

[48] See *Hospitals for Sick Children* v. *McLaughlin & Harvey* (1990) 19 Con. L.R. 25 and (1990) 6 Const. L.J. 245.

[49] *Lodge Holes Colliery* v. *Wednesbury Corporation* [1908] A.C. 323 at 325 (H.L.); see also *Clippens Oil* v. *Edinburgh and District Water* [1907] A.C. 291 at 304 (H.L.); *cp. Murphy* v. *Brentwood District Council* [1990] 2 W.L.R. 944 (C.A.)—the point about delegating performance not affected by the decision in the House of Lords at [1990] 3 W.L.R. 414 (H.L.).

[50] See *Hospitals for Sick Children* v. *McLaughlin & Harvey* (1990) 19 Con. L.R. 25 and (1990) 6 Const. L.J. 245; *cf. Frost* v. *Moody Homes* (1989) C.I.L.L. 504.

[51] *Harbutt's "Plasticine" Ltd.* v. *Wayne Tank and Pump Co. Ltd.* [1970] 1 Q.B. 447 (C.A.).

[52] *Ibid.* at 476.

[53] *Dominion Mosaics* v. *Trafalgar Trucking* (1989) E.G. 101.

[54] For liquidated damages, see Chap. 9, Part B.

[55] Parke B. in *Hadley* v. *Baxendale* (1854) 23 L.J.Ex. 179 at 181; and see *Victoria Laundry Ltd.* v. *Newman Ltd.* [1949] 2 K.B. 528 (C.A.). For loss of a machine, see *Sunley & Co. Ltd.* v. *Cunard White Star Ltd.* [1940] 1 K.B. 740 (C.A.).

[56] See *Fletcher* v. *Tayleur* (1855) 25 L.J.C.P. 65; *Wilson* v. *General Iron Screw Colliery Co. Ltd.* (1877) 47 L.J.Q.B. 239; *Steam Herring Fleet Ltd.* v. *Richards & Co. Ltd.* (1901) 17 T.L.R. 731. *cf. Marshall* v. *Mackintosh* (1898) 78 L.T. 750, but note that this was a building agreement.

public buildings, would not produce rents or profits, the contractor would be liable for loss of interest on capital lying idle.[57] If to the contractor's knowledge the contract works consist of an expansion of a factory or other profit-earning structure, he is liable for loss of business resulting from his breach.[58] The extent of his liability varies according to his knowledge, and only includes loss of profit from specially lucrative contracts if he knew of them at the time of entering into the contract.[59] Loss of profit should be expressly pleaded and is inconsistent with a claim for capital expenditure incurred to make that profit.[60]

Going slow. Interim slowness not resulting in a failure to complete on time may not be a breach of contract at all.[61] If it is, damages solely flowing from a failure of the contractor to perform the works at the contract rate will, if any, ordinarily be small.[62]

Inconvenience, discomfort and distress. Modest[63] damages may be recoverable under these heads where the contract is for works to the plaintiff's own house and home, but not where it is a commercial enterprise[64] unless perhaps the contract was itself one to provide peace of mind or freedom from distress.[65] They are awarded, if at all, for physical consequences of the breach actually suffered and not for the tension or frustration of a person involved in a legal dispute in which the defendant refuses to meet his liabilities.[66] Discretionary interest is not normally awarded on damages under these heads.[67] In *Hutchinson* v. *Harris*,[68] the plaintiff had a house which she intended to convert into maisonettes and a flat for letting, and employed the defendant as architect for these purposes. The defendant was negligent in the performance of her duties of supervision and certification. It was held that damages for distress caused by the negligence were not recoverable because this was a commercial enterprise. They would have been recoverable for distress caused to an owner kept out of his house and home through having to do extensive repairs to it.

---

[57] See *The Hebridean Coast* [1961] A.C. 545 (H.L.); *Birmingham Corporation* v. *Sowsbery* (1969) 113 S.J. 877.

[58] By analogy with *Victoria Laundry Ltd.* v. *Newman Ltd.* [1949] 2 K.B. 528 (C.A.).

[59] *Ibid.*

[60] *Perestrello Ltd.* v. *United Paint Co. Ltd.* [1969] 1 W.L.R. 570 (C.A.).; see also *Cullinane* v. *British "Rema" Manufacturing Co.* [1954] 1 Q.B. 292 (C.A.); *Anglia Television* v. *Reed* [1972] 1 Q.B. 60 (C.A.).

[61] See *Greater London Council* v. *Cleveland Bridge and Engineering* (1984) 34 B.L.R. 50 (C.A.).

[62] *Hill* v. *London Borough of Camden* (1980) 18 B.L.R. 31 at 40 (C.A.).

[63] See *Perry* v. *Sidney Phillips* [1982] 1 W.L.R. 1297 at 1303 (C.A.). For a review of recent awards, see Kim Franklin, "Damages for Heartache" (1988) 4 Const. L.J. 264.

[64] *Hutchinson* v. *Harris* (1978) 10 B.L.R. 19 at 37; *cf. Bolton* v. *Mahadeva* [1972] 1 W.L.R. 1009 (C.A.); *King* v. *Victor Parsons & Co.* [1973] 1 W.L.R. 29 (C.A.); see also *Archer* v. *Brown* [1985] Q.B. 401 at 424. For claims in tort for nervous shock, see *McLoughlin* v. *O'Brian* [1983] 1 A.C. 410 (H.L.).

[65] See *Hayes* v. *James & Charles Dodd, The Times,* July 14, 1988 (C.A.); *Bliss* v. *S.E. Thames R.H.A.* [1987] I.C.R. 700 at 718 (C.A.).

[66] *Perry* v. *Sidney Phillips* [1982] 1 W.L.R. 1297 at 1307 (C.A.); *cf. Ward* v. *Cannock Chase District Council* [1986] Ch. 546.

[67] *Saunders* v. *Edwards* [1987] 1 W.L.R. 1116 (C.A.). See "Discretionary interest" at p. 451.

[68] (1978) 10 B.L.R. 19.

Other losses.   If as a result of defective work by the contractor not in accordance with the contract, a third party is injured, or suffers loss and sues the employer, the latter may be able to recover from the contractor the amount of the damages or the sum paid by way of settlement of the claim.[69] Insofar as employer and contractor may each be liable to a third party in tort for the same damage, there may be contribution under the Civil Liability (Contribution) Act 1978.[70] If the employer himself suffers personal injury or loss as a result of the contractor's defective workmanship or materials he may, subject to the terms of the contract, be able to recover damages.[71]

Lack of inspection by architect.   The contractor is not, subject to the express terms of the contract, entitled to a reduction in damages because the architect, clerk of works or other agent of the employer failed to discover defects as the work was carried out.[72]

5. Employer's Breach of Contract

No work carried out.   If there is a repudiation of the contract by the employer before any work is carried out the damages recoverable are, it seems, *prima facie* the amount of profit which the parties knew, or must be taken to have assumed, the contractor would have made if he had been permitted to complete in the ordinary way.[73] Further damages resulting from unusual circumstances are recoverable according to the employer's knowledge of those circumstances.[74]

Election to claim wasted expenditure.   The contractor may, it seems, elect to claim wasted expenditure instead of loss of profit, and can include pre-contract expenditure made in preparation for performance provided it was such as would have been reasonably in the contemplation of the employer at the time of entering into the contract.[75]

---

[69] *Fisher* v. *Val de Travers* (1876) 45 L.J.Q.B. 479; *Kiddle* v. *Lovett* (1885) 16 Q.B.D. 605; *Mowbray* v. *Merryweather* [1895] 2 Q.B. 640 (C.A.); *Sims* v. *Foster Wheeler Ltd.* [1966] 1 W.L.R. 769 (C.A.); *cp. Lambert* v. *Lewis* [1982] A.C. 225 (H.L.). See also "Sums paid in settlement of third party claims" at p. 200. Note that there is usually a clause in the contract providing for an indemnity by the contractor against such claims—see clause 20 of the Standard Form of Building Contract and see p. 542; for sub-contracts, p. 715.

[70] See "Statutory contribution" at p. 192.

[71] *Kimber* v. *William Willett Ltd.* [1947] K.B. 570 (C.A.). See also p. 260. For the contractor's liability in tort, see Chap. 7.

[72] *East Ham Corp.* v. *Bernard Sunley & Sons Ltd.* [1966] A.C. 406 (H.L.); *A.M.F. International Ltd.* v. *Magnet Bowling Ltd.* [1968] 1 W.L.R. 1028 at 1053; *cf. Oldschool* v. *Gleeson* (1976) 4 B.L.R. 103 at 122.

[73] See *Ranger* v. *G.W. Railway* (1854) 5 H.L.C. 72 (H.L.); *Victoria Laundry Ltd.* v. *Newman Ltd.* [1949] 2 K.B. 528 (C.A.); *Koufos* v. *Czarnikow Ltd.* [1969] 1 A.C. 350 at 424 (H.L.).

[74] See p. 187.

[75] See *Anglia Television Ltd.* v. *Reed* [1972] 1 Q.B. 60 (C.A.)—actor who repudiated contract for leading role in film which was abandoned liable for expenses incurred before contract signed.

Work partly carried out.   Where the contract work has been partly carried out and the contract is brought to an end by the employer's repudiation, the contractor is entitled to be paid the value of the work done at contract prices,[76] and to claim in addition damages, the measure of which is normally the loss of profit on the unfinished balance.

> "If while [the contractor] was duly proceeding to fulfil his contract, he was wrongfully impeded by the Respondents, and by them prevented from doing what he had undertaken to do, they would be answerable to him in damages for all the consequences of their wrongful act. Such damages would of course be in part calculated on the value of the plant and other articles of which he had been wrongfully deprived; but the effect would not be to alter the relative position of the parties as to the contract itself, to entitle the Appellant to say there had been no contract, or that he was to be paid for what he had done without reference to the contract. ... The right of the Appellant would be, to recover such amount of damages as would put him in, as nearly as possible, the same position as if no such wrong had been committed—that is, not as if there had been no contract without interruption."

He was not entitled "to an account of work already done, to be taken on terms different from those for which he had contracted."[77]

> "When a party to a simple contract, upon breach by the other contracting party of a condition of the contract, elects to treat the contract as no longer binding upon him, the contract is not rescinded as from the beginning. Both parties are discharged from further performance of the contract, but rights are not divested or discharged which have already been unconditionally acquired. Rights and obligations which arise from the partial execution of the contract and causes of action which have accrued from its breach alike continue unaffected ... when a contract ... is dissolved at the election of one party because the other has not observed an essential condition or has committed a breach going to its root, the contract is determined so far as it is executory only and the party in default is liable for damages for its breach."[78]

Thus if, when a contractor accepts an employer's repudiation, instalments have become due under the contract, they remain payable.[79] The contractor may additionally be entitled to payment at contractual rates for work done but

---

[76] *Felton* v. *Wharrie* (1906) H.B.C. (4th ed.), Vol. 2, p. 398 (C.A.); see further p. 155.

[77] Lord Cranworth L.C. in *Ranger* v. *G.W. Railway* (1854) 5 H.L.C. 72 at 96 (H.L.); see also Lord Brougham at 118.

[78] Dixon J. in *McDonald* v. *Dennys Lascelles* (1933) 48 C.L.R. 457 at 476 approved and adopted by Lord Wilberforce in *Johnson* v. *Agnew* [1980] A.C. 367 at 396 (H.L.) and by Lord Brandon in *Bank of Boston* v. *European Grain* [1989] A.C. 1056 at 1098 (H.L.); *cf. Heyman* v. *Darwins* [1942] A.C. 356 at 399 (H.L.); *Photo Production* v. *Securicor* [1980] A.C. 827 (H.L.), especially at 849 *et seq.* and in particular at 849F-H; *Rover International* v. *Canon Film* [1989] 1 W.L.R. 912 (C.A.).

[79] *Bank of Boston* v. *European Grain* [1989] A.C. 1056 (H.L.).

not covered by the instalments. If the contract does not provide for instalments, the contractor is entitled to payment at contractual rates for all the work done. It is thought that this applies in principle also where there is an entire contract with a single undivided lump sum, although the court will have to make an assessment of the proportion of the lump sum which represents the contractual value of the work done. In each instance, the contractor is additionally entitled to damages.

It is thought that the contractor does not have an option, as an alternative to the claim outlined above, of ignoring the contract and claiming a reasonable price for work and labour done on a *quantum meruit*. There is authority to the effect that he does have such an option,[80] and this has not uncommonly in the past been taken to be the law.[81] It is now thought however that the alternative claim cannot stand in the face of the logic of the House of Lords authority referred to above.[82] If it were the law, it could result in substantial injustice if a contractor who was losing money heavily on a contract became entitled to payment for past work on a more favourable basis than the contract provided and when his losses were not caused by the employer's breach.

Work completed.   Where the employer's breach does not prevent completion the damages recoverable, if any, will vary according to the circumstances. There may be identifiable additional work the direct cost of which can normally be claimed. Delay caused by the employer may give rise to a claim for damages[83] at least where the contract does not provide for an extension of time on account of the delay.[84] Delay may, for example, turn a summer contract into a winter contract thus causing increased cost of working,[85] or it may keep plant

---

[80] *Planché* v. *Colburn* (1831) 8 Bing. 14; *De Bernardy* v. *Harding* (1853) 8 Exch. 822 at 824; *Prickett* v. *Badger* (1856) 1 C.B. (N.S.) 296; *Appleby* v. *Myers* (1867) L.R. 2 C.P. 651 at 659; *Lodder* v. *Slowey* [1904] A.C. 442 at 453 (P.C.); *Chandler Bros. Ltd.* v. *Boswell* [1936] 3 All E.R. 179 at 186 (C.A.); *Luxor (Eastbourne)* v. *Cooper* [1940] A.C. 108 at 141 (H.L.).

[81] *e.g.* in the 4th edition of this book at p. 152, but with the qualification in n. 77.

[82] Of the cases cited above which support the alternative, *Planché* v. *Colburn* (1831) 8 Bing. 14 is a shortly reported case which does not unambiguously do so—it concerned the repudiation of an entire single lump sum contract and can be reconciled with the view expressed in the text; *De Bernardy* v. *Harding* (1853) 8 Exch. 822 at 824 is *obiter*; *Prickett* v. *Badger* (1856) 1 C.B. (N.S.) 296 is a commission agent case; *Appleby* v. *Myers* (1867) L.R. 2 C.P. 651 at 659 is *obiter*; *Lodder* v. *Slowey* [1904] A.C. 442 at 453 (P.C.) is a decision of the Privy council which takes the matter very shortly; *Chandler Bros. Ltd.* v. *Boswell* [1936] 3 All E.R. 179 at 186 (C.A.) is a clear statement by the Court of Appeal without reference to specific authority of what is said to be "well settled" law; *Luxor (Eastbourne)* v. *Cooper* [1940] A.C. 108 at 141 (H.L.) is *obiter*. The 19th century cases generally seem to assume that, when a contract is "rescinded" upon repudiation, it ceases to be in force at all so that no action would lie for breach of it—see, *e.g.* the argument in *De Bernardy* v. *Harding* (1853) 8 Exch. 822 at 823. This is not the modern law. See also Goff and Jones, *The Law of Restitution* (3rd ed.), pp. 466 *et seq.* and see also their 2nd edition, p. 380 for a passage omitted from the 3rd edition.

[83] *Lawson* v. *Wallasey Local Board* (1883) 48 L.T. 507 (C.A.); *cf. Ellis-Don* v. *Parking Authority of Toronto* (1978) 28 B.L.R. 98 at 121 (Supreme Court of Ontario).

[84] Most such contracts also provide for a consequential *contractual* right to additional payment—see, *e.g.* clause 26 of the Standard Form of Building Contract at p. 580. See also "Claims under or for breach of the contract" below.

[85] *Freeman* v. *Hensler* (1900) H.B.C. (4th ed.), Vol. 2, p. 292 (C.A.).

or machinery or even, in some cases, men, idle. There may be disruption which reduces productivity or causes other losses. All these heads of loss require consideration of the principles discussed at the outset of this chapter.

Claims under or for breach of the contract.   The distinction should always be sharply observed. Most sophisticated building contracts give the contractor *contractual* rights to additional payment in circumstances some of which may also, or might otherwise, be breaches of contract by the employer.[86] Such rights are usually additional to, and not in substitution for, the contractor's common law remedy of damages for breach of contract.[87] A claim under the contract will depend on the relevant terms. It may have the advantage of the right to payment as the work proceeds under the architect's certificate but be subject to the fulfilment of certain conditions precedent, *e.g.* as to notices. Where the claim is for breach of contract the court is the more likely to resolve matters of doubt in the contractor's favour and, even where the evidence of loss is very unsatisfactory, if satisfied that there was substantial loss, will make some award.[88]

Claims for delay or disruption.   Apart from direct additional building costs and other specifically identifiable expenses resulting from the breach, contractor's claims for delay and disruption are commonly brought under one or more of these heads:

(1) increased preliminaries;
(2) overheads;
(3) loss of profit;
(4) loss of productivity or uneconomic working;
(5) increased costs resulting from inflation;
(6) interest for non-payment of money.

Such claims are often for commercial or other reasons greatly exaggerated both as to the extent of delay caused by the employer's breach and in quantification. The basis for calculation is often excessively theoretical ignoring the principles that damages are to compensate for *actual* loss and must be proved. "It is not the function of the Courts where there is a breach of contract knowingly ... to put the plaintiff in a better financial position than if the contract had been properly performed."[89]

Increased preliminaries.   The expression "preliminaries" is a loose term, but it generally refers to the first part of a traditional bill of quantities where

---

[86] See, *e.g.* clause 26 of the Standard Form of Building Contract and clause 52 of the I.C.E. Conditions at pp. 580 and 887 respectively.
[87] See *Modern Engineering* v. *Gilbert-Ash* [1974] A.C. 689 (H.L.). See also clause 26.6 of the Standard Form of Building Contract at p. 582.
[88] See "Contingency" at p. 198.
[89] Ackner L.J. in *C. & P. Haulage* v. *Middleton* [1983] 1 W.L.R. 1461 at 1467 (C.A.).

are commonly collected items of necessary cost which do not usually become part of the finished works. These costs often depend on time. Examples are water and electricity for the works, scaffolding, plant, small tools and site supervision. Delay will increase many of these costs and if so the extra cost is recoverable.

Claims for increased preliminaries are frequently made and for convenience allowed upon a calculation which uses amounts in the contract bills proportioned to the length of the delay compared with the original contract period. For a claim under the contract, such a calculation may be justified by the terms of the contract. It is suggested that for a damages claim it would be wrong in principle, although sometimes not perhaps seriously so in practice. For damages, the calculation should be of the actual additional costs. Items of cost in the preliminary bill are at best estimates before the contract is made and are often in practice somewhat arbitrary. A proportionate amount of relevant bill items might or might not be the same as the contractor's actual additional cost in the event. His actual additional costs ought to be known, recorded and capable of being proved.

For idle plant and machinery there are various ways in which loss may arise. One is hiring charges. This is appropriate where the contractor was hiring the machinery.[90] If he owned the machinery it seems that he can only recover hiring charges if he proves that he has lost the opportunity of hiring it out, and even then it must not be assumed that the machinery could necessarily have been hired for the whole of the equivalent of the period when it was idle. If he does not prove loss of opportunity of hiring, his loss is assessed by such factors as loss of interest on the capital lying idle, depreciation and maintenance.[91]

Overheads.   This is another loose term referring to the costs of running the contractor's general business as distinct from the site costs of the particular contract.[92] If particular head office costs are proved to have been increased by a contract's delay, they are recoverable. Examples would be the cost of extra staff recruited because the particular contract was in difficulties or the cost of extra telephone calls and postage in the period of delay. But substantial claims of this kind are rarely made because most contractors are able to cope with delay on a particular contract with their existing resources whose cost is reasonably constant. Accordingly claims for loss of overheads are usually made on a different basis.

A contractor's overheads are commonly taken to be recovered out of the income from his business as a whole and ordinarily where completion of one

---

[90] *Shore & Horwitz Construction Co. Ltd.* v. *Franki of Canada Ltd.* [1964] S.C.R. 589 (Canadian Supreme Court).

[91] *Ibid.* and see shipping cases applied in *The Hebridean Coast* [1961] A.C. 545 (H.L.).

[92] For some assistance see *Shore & Horwitz Construction Co. Ltd.* v. *Franki of Canada Ltd.* [1964] S.C.R. 589 (Canadian Supreme Court).

contract is delayed the contractor claims to have suffered a loss arising from the diminution of his income from the job and hence the turnover of his business. But he continues to incur expenditure on overheads which he cannot materially reduce or, in respect of the site, can only reduce, if at all, to a limited extent. But for the delay, the workforce would have had the opportunity of being employed on another contract which would have had the effect of contributing to the overheads during the overrun period.[93] There is some authority that a claim on this basis is sustainable.[94] But it is suggested that, in order to succeed, a contractor has in principle to prove that there was other work available which, but for the delay, he would have secured but which in fact because of the delay he did not secure.[95] He might do this by producing invitations to tender which he declined with evidence that the reason for declining was that the delay in question left him insufficient capacity to undertake other work. He might alternatively show from his accounts a drop in turnover and establish that this resulted from the particular delay rather than from extraneous causes. If loss of turnover resulting from delay is not established, the effect of the delay is only that receipt of the money is delayed. It is not lost.

Loss of profit.   Contractor's commonly claim a loss of profit arising out of the diminution in turnover, but it seems that to establish this claim he must show, as with overheads, that at the time of the delay he could have used the lost turnover profitably.[96] A claim for loss of profit does not, it is submitted, fail merely because the contract in question was unprofitable. The question is what the contractor would have done with the money if he had received it at the proper time. Even if, at that time, the contractor's business was making a loss a sum analogous to loss of profit is, it is submitted, recoverable if the loss of turnover increased the loss of the business.

"Hudson formula."   This is a formula[97] for calculating claims for loss of overheads and profit taken together, although with suitable data a similar formula could be devised for either individually. It calculates the loss as the contractor's overhead and profit percentage based on a fair annual average multiplied by the contract sum and the period of delay and divided by the

---

[93] See *Finnegan* v. *Sheffield City Council* (1988) 43 B.L.R. 124 at 134.

[94] *Finnegan* v. *Sheffield City Council* (1988) 43 B.L.R. 124 at 134 (H.H. Sir William Stabb Q.C.); *Whittal Builders* v. *Chester-Le-Street District Council* (unreported) (Mr. Recorder Percival Q.C.)— the report at 11 Con. L.R. 40 is a different part of the case and 40 B.L.R. 82 is a different case altogether; *Shore & Horwitz Construction Co. Ltd.* v. *Franki of Canada Ltd.* [1964] S.C.R. 589 (Supreme Court of Canada); *Ellis-Don* v. *Parking Authority of Toronto* (1978) 28 B.L.R. 98 (Supreme Court of Ontario). See also "Hudson formula" below.

[95] Such facts were found in *Whittal Builders* v. *Chester-Le-Street District Council* (unreported—see n. 94 above) at p. 11 of the transcript and in *Ellis-Don* v. *Parking Authority of Toronto* (1978) 28 B.L.R. 98 at 124 (Ontario Supreme Court) but in neither case is the evidential basis for the findings rehearsed in the judgments.

[96] *Ibid.* and see *Sunley (B.) & Co. Ltd.* v. *Cunard White Star Ltd.* [1940] 1 K.B. 740 (C.A.).

[97] To be found in H.B.C. (10th ed.), p. 599.

contract period.[98] It is suggested that claims for overheads and profit have to be established in principle as described above before use of the formula is considered. There may then be more acceptable ways of proving the loss than by means of a formula. If a formula is to be adopted, it would presumably be on the basis that the court was satisfied that the contractor had suffered a real loss and was doing its best on the evidence available to quantify it.[99] It may be that a formula would not be adopted where better proof of actual loss could have been provided but the contractor failed to provide it.[1]

Loss of productivity or uneconomic working.   This is a head of claim sometimes made where there has been delay in completion or disturbance of the contractor's regular and economic progress even though, on occasions, the ultimate delay in completion is small or does not occur. As regards machinery and plant it is ordinarily comparatively easy to compare the contemplated periods of use with the actual periods and then to apply the measure of damages as discussed above. Labour is more difficult. Some contractors add an arbitrary percentage to the contemplated labour costs. It is difficult to see how this can be sustained.[2] There can be no custom or general rule because the loss will vary in each case. A better starting point is to compare actual labour costs with those contemplated.[3] Thus a particular activity or part of the works is taken and, where the contract price can be ascertained, as by reference to the priced bills, the labour element is extracted. This is a matter for experienced surveyors and is done by taking the unit price and applying constants which are generally accepted in the trade. From the contractor's records the actual labour content for the activity or part is extracted. From the difference must be deducted any expenditure upon labour which was not caused by the breach, *e.g.* delay or disturbance caused by bad weather, strikes, nominated sub-contractors or the contractor's own inefficiency. If the original contract price was arrived at in a properly organised competition or as the result of negotiation with a skilled surveyor acting on behalf of the employer, the adjusted figure for the difference is some evidence of loss of productivity.

Increased costs resulting from inflation.   Claims are sometimes made for increased costs of labour or materials on the basis that these costs were incurred at a later and more expensive time because of the employer's delay.

---

[98] See *Finnegan* v. *Sheffield City Council* (1988) 43 B.L.R. 124 at 136; see also "Overheads" and cases at n. 94 above. For a mathematical illogicality in the formula, see commentary on *Ellis-Don* v. *Parking Authority of Toronto* at 28 B.L.R. 102 and see the same commentary at 103 *et seq.* for United States' judicial criticism of a similar formula.

[99] See "Contingency" at p. 198.

[1] *cf. Tate & Lyle* v. *Greater London Council* [1982] 1 W.L.R. 149 at 152, Forbes J., the point being unaffected by subsequent appeals—[1982] 1 W.L.R. 971 (C.A.) and [1983] 2 A.C. 509 (H.L.).

[2] *cf. Tate & Lyle* v. *Greater London Council* [1982] 1 W.L.R. 149 where a broadly similar claim based on a percentage failed.

[3] Such an approach was adopted in *Whittal Builders* v. *Chester-Le-Street District Council* (unreported—see n. 94 above).

In principle such costs are recoverable and can be proved by reference to actual increases or possibly by using published inflation indices. Many contracts, however, contain fluctuation or cost variation clauses under which the contractor is entitled to additional payment for inflationary increases. He cannot recover twice but might conceivably argue that his actual increased costs were greater than those recovered under the clause so that he was entitled to recover the difference as damages.

Interest for non-payment of money.   If the employer fails to pay money due under the contract the contractor may consider the recovery of interest under one of four heads. The first is under an express term of the contract providing for the payment of interest in specific circumstances at a quantified rate.[4] The second is under an express term of the contract which does not provide for interest as such, but which is construed as giving the contractor a contractual right to a what is in effect an interest payment.[5] The third is where he recovers judgment and applies for interest under section 35A of the Supreme Court Act 1981.[6] The fourth is as damages.

"Direct loss and/or expense."   In principle the court is prepared to construe contracts with appropriate words as giving a contractual right to what are often called "finance charges." In *F. G. Minter* v. *W.H.T.S.O.,*[7] the Court of Appeal construed a contractual right to "direct loss and/or expense" under a 1963 Standard Form of Building Contract as including a right to be paid finance charges on other primary loss and expense. The court was not deterred from this construction by its former reluctance, discussed below, to award interest as damages.

> "I do not think that today we should allow medieval abhorrence to usury to make us shrink from implying a promise to pay interest in a contract if by refusing to imply it we thereby deprive a party of what the contract appears on its natural interpretation to give him. There should be no presumption in favour of an anomaly and an anachronism."[8]

Other provisions of the particular contract confined the right to finance charges to the period between the loss and expense being incurred and the making of a written application for its reimbursement resulting in a need for tedious successive applications. In *Rees & Kirby* v. *Swansea City Council,*[9] the court excluded from a calculation of direct loss and expense under materially the same contractual provisions a period during which delay in paying the primary loss and expense was attributable to an independent cause.

---

[4] *e.g.* clause 60(7), I.C.E. Conditions (1991 edition). There is nothing comparable in the Standard Form of Building Contract.
[5] See "Direct loss and/or expense" below.
[6] See p. 451.
[7] (1980) 13 B.L.R. 1 (C.A.).
[8] Stephenson L.J. in *F. G. Minter Ltd.* v. *W.H.T.S.O.* (1980) 13 B.L.R. 1 at 17 (C.A.).
[9] (1985) 30 B.L.R. 1 (C.A.).

Interest as damages. Formerly, the law was that "interest is not due on money secured by a written instrument, unless it appears on the face of the instrument that interest was intended to be paid, or unless it be implied from the usage of trade."[10] In *London Chatham and Dover Railway* v. *South Eastern Railway*,[11] the House of Lords held that interest could not be given by way of damages for detention of a debt, the law upon the subject, unsatisfactory though it was, then being too long settled to be departed from. The House of Lords would probably have departed from that law in 1984,[12] but for the intervention of statute[13] and an intervening decision,[14] then approved by the House of Lords, which limited the common law denial of interest as damages to claims for general damages as discussed below.

The law now is that the court can award interest as *special* damages in a claim for late payment in breach of contract of a *debt*.[15] It cannot do so in a claim for damages.[16] "There is no such thing as a cause of action in damages for late payment of damages. The only remedy which the law affords for delay in paying damages is the discretionary award of interest pursuant to statute."[17] But interest has been awarded as damages under section 2(1) of the Misrepresentation Act 1967 in a claim for the return of a deposit.[18] Interest cannot be awarded as damages for late payment of a debt where the debt was paid before proceedings were brought.[19]

The distinction between a claim for general damages, where interest cannot be awarded as damages, and a claim for special damages, where interest can be so awarded, is the same as the distinction between the first and second limbs of the rule in *Hadley* v. *Baxendale*.[20]

> "The surviving principle of legal policy is that it is a legal presumption that in the ordinary course of things a person does not suffer any loss by reason of the late payment of money. This is an artificial presumption, but is justified by the fact that the usual loss is an interest loss and that compensation for this has been provided for and limited by statute."[21]

---

[10] Lord Tenterden C.J. in *Page* v. *Newman* (1829) B. & C. 378 at 380 (Court of Kings Bench).

[11] [1893] A.C. 429 (H.L.).

[12] See *President of India* v. *La Pintada Compania* [1985] A.C. 104 (H.L.).

[13] The Law Reform (Miscellaneous Provisions) Act 1934 and the Administration of Justice Act 1982 amending the Supreme Court Act 1981.

[14] *Wadsworth* v. *Lydall* [1981] 1 W.L.R. 598 (C.A.).

[15] *President of India* v. *La Pintada Compania* [1985] A.C. 104 (H.L.); *President of India* v. *Lips Maritime* [1988] A.C. 395 (H.L.).

[16] A claim for liquidated damages is a claim for damages, not debt—see *President of India* v. *Lips Maritime* [1988] A.C. 395 at 424 (H.L.)—unless perhaps there is a contractual provision stipulating that it shall be recoverable as a debt.

[17] Lord Brandon in *President of India* v. *Lips Maritime* [1988] A.C. 395 at 425 (H.L.).

[18] *Walker* v. *Boyle* [1982] 1 W.L.R. 495 at 508.

[19] *President of India* v. *La Pintada Compania* [1985] A.C. 104 (H.L.). See s.35A(2) of the Supreme Court Act 1981 for statutory interest where payment is made after proceedings are instituted but before judgment.

[20] (1854) 9 Ex. 341—see p. 187. See *President of India* v. *La Pintada Compania* [1985] A.C. 104 at 127 (H.L.).

[21] Hobhouse J. in *International Minerals* v. *Karl O. Helm* [1986] 1 Lloyd's Rep. 81 at 104 approved by Neill L.J. in *President of India* v. *Lips Maritime* [1988] A.C. 395 at 410 (C.A.).

On the face of it, this might seem to mean that, where a plaintiff incurs bank interest charges on an overdraft, "the more the defaulting party can show that this was not because of some unusual or 'special' circumstances of the particular contract but because of the well-known way in which the relevant trade or business is normally carried on, the less likely will it be that the plaintiff can cover his loss."[22] This possible anomaly could readily occur in building contracts since "the loss of the interest which [the contractor] has to pay on the capital he is forced to borrow and on the capital which he is not free to invest would be recoverable for the employer's breach of contract within the first rule in *Hadley* v. *Baxendale* (1854) 9 Ex. 341 without resorting to the second."[23] The anomaly would be if the contractor who had said to the employer before making the contract "by the way, my bank charges me 2 per cent. over base rate on my overdraft" was able to claim interest as special damages for late payment, but the contractor who allowed this commonplace fact to be taken for granted could not.[24] It would be further anomalous if a contractor's claim for *compound* interest turned on whether he had added words such as "with quarterly rests" to the remark suggested in the previous sentence.[25]

A claim for interest as special damages must be pleaded and proved[26] either as interest paid to a bank or as interest which would otherwise have been earned from investment.[27]

Simple or compound interest? Where interest is payable under an express term of the contract, simple or compound interest will be awarded according to the express words as construed. Normally a bank is impliedly entitled to charge compound interest on an overdraft and this is not dependent on whether or not the account can be categorised as a mercantile account current for mutual transactions.[28] The court has awarded compound interest in a claim for "direct loss and/or expense" under a contract as discussed above.[29] Discretionary interest pursuant to statute is simple interest only.[30] It

---

[22] Nicholls L.J. in *President of India* v. *Lips Maritime* [1988] A.C. 395 at 413 (C.A.). This case was about currency exchange losses which the House of Lords held did not come within the principle in *President of India* v. *La Pintada Compania* [1985] A.C. 104 (H.L.).

[23] Stephenson L.J. in *F. G. Minter* v. *W.H.T.S.O.* (1980) 13 B.L.R. 1 at 15 (C.A.).

[24] It may be possible to avoid the anomaly by reasoning such as that of Neill L.J. in *President of India* v. *Lips Maritime* [1988] A.C. 395 at 412 (C.A.), reversed on appeal but not on this point; the reasoning was applied in *Holbeach Plant Hire* v. *Anglian Water Authority* (1988) 14 Con L.R. 101; *cf. D.O.E. for Northern Ireland* v. *Farrans* (1981) 19 B.L.R. 1 at 22 (Northern Ireland High Court) applying *Wadsworth* v. *Lydall* [1981] 1 W.L.R. 598 (C.A.). The centenary of the decision in *London Chatham and Dover Railway* v. *South Eastern Railway* [1893] A.C. 429 (H.L.) might be a suitable occasion to abandon what remains of the common law rule. See generally A. W. Foyle, "Recent Developments in the Recovery of Interest and Financing Charges" (1988) 4 Const. L.J. 3.

[25] See "Simple or compound interest?" below.

[26] See *Hutchinson* v. *Harris* (1978) 10 B.L.R. 19 at 42 (C.A.).

[27] See *Brandeis Goldschmidt* v. *Western Transport* [1981] Q.B. 864 at 873 (C.A.); *cf.* the passage from *F. G. Minter* v. *W.H.T.S.O.* (1980) 13 B.L.R. 1 at 15 (C.A.) quoted in the text.

[28] *National Bank of Greece* v. *Pinios Shipping* [1990] A.C. 637 (H.L.).

[29] *Rees & Kirby* v. *Swansea City Council* (1985) 30 B.L.R. 1 (C.A.).

[30] See s.35A of the Supreme Court Act 1981; *cf. Coastal States Trading* v. *Mebro* [1986] 1 Lloyd's Rep. 465.

may be that awards of interest as damages as discussed above can only be for simple interest,[31] although it is suggested that the question ought to turn on the extent of the defendant's knowledge at the time the contract was made.

Bonus. Where an employer's delay prevented the contractor earning a bonus for completion to time, the whole of the bonus was awarded as damages to the contractor,[32] but it seems that for contracts providing for such a bonus the measure of damages is not automatically its full amount.[33]

Unusual circumstances. In all cases the employer's liability for damages resulting from such circumstances depends upon his knowledge at the time of entering into the contract.[34]

Composite claims. Contractors often have claims dependent on a number of separate causes each of which has contributed to delay and extra cost. In principle the loss attributable to each cause should be separately identified and proved but separation may be difficult. In *Crosby Ltd.* v. *Portland Urban District Council*,[35] Donaldson J. considered a lump sum award made by an arbitrator for claims arising under various terms of the contract. He said that since the extra cost incurred depended upon an extremely complex interaction between the consequences of various matters, it might well be difficult or even impossible to make an accurate apportionment between the several causes, and that there was no need to make an artificial apportionment which had no basis in reality. In such circumstances a single lump sum award was proper provided the arbitrator had ensured that there was no duplication and that there was no profit element in the particular award, having regard to the provisions of some of the clauses which denied the contractor extra profit. It is submitted that the same reasoning applies to claims for damages resulting from various causes, although the problem of exclusion of profit does not then arise.[36] The danger of advancing a composite claim is that it might fail completely if any significant part of the delay is not established and the court finds no basis for awarding less than the whole. It might also conceivably fail if the court were to find that proper separate identification of causes and losses could have been made.

Local authorities. When settling a claim for damages, or for money due, by a contractor, local authorities have sometimes taken the point that they cannot

---

[31] See *President of India* v. *La Pintada Compania* [1985] A.C. 104 at 120 (H.L.).

[32] *Bywaters* v. *Curnick* (1906) H.B.C. (4th ed.), Vol. 2, p. 393 (C.A.).

[33] *Ibid.* at 397.

[34] See p. 187.

[35] (1967) 5 B.L.R. 121; *Crosby* was followed in *London Borough of Merton* v. *Leach* (1985) 32 B.L.R. 51 at 98 *et seq.* For a stricter approach at pleading stage, see *Wharf Properties* v. *Eric Cumine* (1988) 45 B.L.R. 72 (Hong Kong Court of Appeal).

[36] See also "Contingency" at p. 198 for the court acting on unsatisfactory evidence.

include a sum for interest because such payment is contrary to law rendering them liable to the possibility of surcharge. It is submitted that, provided the local authority acts bona fide in the interests of the ratepayers and with reasonable business acumen the inclusion of such a sum is not contrary to law[37] and, further, if its exclusion results in litigation they would ordinarily be acting against the interest of the ratepayers. This is because, quite apart from the possibility of a claim for interest as damages, interest is ordinarily awarded under section 35A of the Supreme Court Act 1981. A contractor would normally be justified in refusing a sum offered which did not include simple interest and instituting proceedings in order to obtain such interest[38] and would normally recover costs.

---

[37] *Re Hurle-Hobbs* [1944] 1 All E.R. 249 (D.C.); [1944] 2 All E.R. 261 (C.A.); *cf. Pickwell* v. *Camden London Borough Council* [1983] Q.B. 962 (C.A.)—see Ormrod L.J. at 1004, "The question for the Court is whether the evidence establishes that no reasonable local authority could have made a settlement on such terms."
[38] See pp. 451 *et seq.*

CHAPTER 9

THE TIME FOR COMPLETION AND LIQUIDATED
DAMAGES

A. TIME FOR COMPLETION

Generally.   Formal contracts usually make elaborate provisions for the date of completion and its extension, progress and failure to proceed diligently. If no time is specified for completion of the contract a reasonable time for completion will normally be implied.[1] What is a reasonable time is a question of fact[2] to be considered in relation to circumstances which existed at the time when the contractual services were performed but excluding circumstances which were under the control of the party performing those services.[3] A person obliged to complete within a reasonable time "fulfils his obligation, notwithstanding protracted delay, so long as such delay is attributable to causes beyond his control, and he has acted neither negligently nor unreasonably."[4]

---

[1] Supply of Goods and Services Act 1982, s.14; *Charnock* v. *Liverpool Corp.* [1968] 1 W.L.R. 1498 (C.A.); *Startup* v. *Macdonald* (1843) 6 M. & G. 593. There is no room for implying such a term where damages for non-completion are expressly tied to contractual machinery—see *Temloc* v. *Errill Properties* (1987) 39 B.L.R. 30 at 38 (C.A.).

[2] *Startup* v. *Macdonald* (1843) 6 M. & G. 593; *Hick* v. *Raymond & Reid* [1893] A.C. 22 at 32, 33 (H.L.); *McDougall* v. *Aeromarine Ltd.* [1958] 1 W.L.R. 1126—a shipbuilding case. The test is objective—*Charnock* v. *Liverpool Corp.* [1968] 1 W.L.R. 1498 (C.A.).

[3] *B.S.C.* v. *Cleveland Bridge and Engineering* [1984] 1 All E.R. 504 at 512 reported more fully at 24 B.L.R. 94. "What is reasonable depends upon all the circumstances of the case, including the conditions operating during the period when the work is being done. It would follow that as to whether a reasonable time has been taken up in the doing of the works cannot be decided in advance; it can only be decided after the work has been done."—*Sanders and Forster* v. *A. Mark & Co.* February 6, 1980 (C.A.) (unreported) at p. 14 of transcript.

[4] *Hick* v. *Raymond & Reid* [1893] A.C. 22 at 32 (H.L.).

Thus a strike occurring after the contract was entered into was taken into account.[5] But car repairers, who were under-staffed and were aware of the holiday period approaching and that for commercial reasons they had to give priority to certain other work, were not able to rely on delay caused by these factors in assessing a reasonable time.[6]

Requirements to complete which have been considered by the courts include, "as soon as possible."[7] "within a reasonable time,"[8] "as speedily as possible,"[9] "directly,"[10] "forthwith,"[11] "such delivery date cannot be guaranteed."[12]

It has been suggested that, where there is no express provision as to progress, business efficacy requires the implication of a term that the contractor will proceed with reasonable diligence and maintain reasonable progress.[13] It is thought that while such a term may have to be implied in some cases each contract and its surrounding circumstances must be considered, and that there is no such rule of general application. It may well be that in some cases the contractor's only duty is to complete by the due date.[14] In *G.L.C.* v. *Cleveland Bridge and Engineering*,[15] the contract provided for completion of parts of the works by key dates and for forfeiture for failure to execute the works with due diligence and expedition. It was held that, notwithstanding the forfeiture clause, there was no implication of a requirement to execute the works with due diligence and expedition but only a duty to proceed with such diligence and expedition as were reasonably required in order to meet the key dates and the completion date in the contract.

Time of the essence.   If the contractor fails to comply with the terms of the contract as to time, he is in breach of contract and liable in damages and the employer may have express remedies under the contract.[16] Whether or not the breach enables the employer to treat the contract as at an end requires a consideration of the principles of repudiation of contracts and of time being of

---

[5] *Ibid.*

[6] *Charnock* v. *Liverpool Corp.* [1968] 1 W.L.R. 1498 (C.A.).

[7] *Attwood* v. *Emery* (1856) 26 L.J.C.P. 73.

[8] *Hydraulic Engineering Co.* v. *McHaffie* (1878) 4 Q.B.D. 670 (C.A.).

[9] *Penarth Dock Engineering Co.* v. *Pounds* [1963] 1 Lloyd's Rep. 359.

[10] *Duncan* v. *Topham* (1849) 8 C.B. 225.

[11] *Roberts* v. *Brett* (1865) 34 L.J.C.P. 241.

[12] *McDougall* v. *Aeromarine Ltd.* [1958] 1 W.L.R. 1126.

[13] H.B.C. (10th ed.), p. 314.

[14] This passage in the 4th edition of this book quoted with apparent approval in the result of the case in *G.L.C.* v. *Cleveland Bridge and Engineering* (1984) 34 B.L.R. 57 at 66 (Staughton J.)—upheld in C.A. at (1986) 34 B.L.R. 72.

[15] (1984) 34 B.L.R. 57.

[16] Where a contractor is under an obligation to complete on or before a particular date he has the whole of that day to perform his duty—*Afovos Shipping Co.* v. *Pagnan* [1983] 1 W.L.R. 195 at 201 (H.L.); but a clause providing for completion on a specified day cannot, without clear words, be construed as meaning that completion can take place within a reasonable period after the date fixed—*Raineri* v. *Miles* [1981] A.C. 1050 (H.L.); *cf. Amherst* v. *James Walker* [1983] Ch. 305 at 315 (C.A.).

the essence of the contract. Although the terminology is retained, the rules relating to time being of the essence are no more than a particular application of the law of repudiation,[17] but having regard to the historical development of the law relating to time being of the essence it is convenient to treat it separately.

Time being of the essence means that one or more stipulations as to time are conditions breach of which discharges the other party from the obligation to continue to perform any of his own promises.[18] Delay in performance is treated as going to the root of the contract without regard to the magnitude of the breach.[19] The injured party may elect to terminate the contract and recover damages in respect of the other party's outstanding obligations.[20] But if the right to accept the repudiation has been waived, the injured party may not terminate the contract without serving a notice making time of the essence.[21]

There is no general concept of time being of the essence of a contract as a whole. The question is whether time is of the essence of a particular term. It normally arises in the context of failure to complete a contract on the date specified, but it can arise also in relation to other terms of the contract, *e.g.* the giving of notices.[22] It is quite possible in the same contract to have some time stipulations which are conditions and others which are not.

> "Time will not be considered to be of the essence unless: (1) the parties expressly stipulate that conditions as to time must be strictly complied with; or (2) the nature of the subject-matter of the contract or the surrounding circumstances show that time should be considered to be of the essence."[23]

It is possible by express provision in the contract to make time of the essence even if it would not be so otherwise.[24] Such a provision is not one which purports to fix the damages for breach of the obligation and is not subject to the law governing penalty clauses.[25]

In general time is of the essence in mercantile contracts,[26] although it cannot be so if a date is neither specified nor capable of exact determination by the

---

[17] *United Scientific Holdings Ltd.* v. *Burnley Council* [1978] A.C. 904 at 944 *et seq.* (H.L.). See p. 146 for repudiation generally.

[18] *United Scientific Holdings* v. *Burnley Council* [1978] A.C. 904 at 927, 945 (H.L.).

[19] *Lombard plc.* v. *Butterworth* [1987] Q.B. 527 at 535 (C.A.).

[20] *Ibid.*; *Charles Rickards Limited* v. *Oppenheim* [1950] 1 K.B. 616 (C.A.).; *Peak Construction* v. *McKinney Foundations* (1971) 1 B.L.R. 111 at 120 (C.A.).

[21] *Rickards* v. *Oppenheim* [1950] 1 K.B. 616 (C.A.); *State Trading Corporation* v. *Compagnie Francaise* [1983] 2 Lloyd's Rep. 679; *cf. Nichemen* v. *Gatoil* [1987] 2 Lloyd's Rep. 46 (C.A.).

[22] *British Holding plc.* v. *Quadrex* [1989] 3 W.L.R. 723 at 736 (C.A.).

[23] *Halsbury* (4th ed.), Vol. 9, para. 481, approved in *United Scientific Holdings* v. *Burnley Council* [1978] A.C. 904 at 937, 944, 958 (H.L.); *Bunge Corporation* v. *Tradax S.A.* [1981] 1 W.L.R. 711 at 716, 729 (H.L.).

[24] *Lombard plc.* v. *Butterworth* [1987] Q.B. 527 at 535 (C.A.) and see the cases cited at 536; *cf. United Scientific Holdings* v. *Burnley Council* [1978] A.C. 904 at 923 (H.L.); *Weller* v. *Akehurst* [1981] 3 All E.R. 411 at 415.

[25] *Lombard plc.* v. *Butterworth* [1987] Q.B. 527 at 536, 537 (C.A.). For penalty clauses, see p. 224.

[26] *Bunge Corporation* v. *Tradax S.A.* [1981] 1 W.L.R. 711 (H.L.); *cp. State Trading Corporation of India* v. *Golodetz* [1989] 2 Lloyd's Rep. 277 (C.A.)—time not of the essence of a subsidiary obligation to open a performance guarantee.

parties.[27] Building contracts are not mercantile contracts and the normal rule is that time is not of the essence in building contracts,[28] unless it is expressly so provided.[29] It seems that ordinarily it is not of the essence where the contract includes provisions for extension of time and the payment of liquidated damages for delay.[30] But in one case where there were such provisions, but also the words "time shall be considered as of the essence of the contract on the part of the contractor," it was said "no doubt this gave the Corporation the right to determine the contract at the end of the 24-month period as extended by the architect."[31]

Notice making time of the essence.　Where a reasonable time for performance has elapsed and either time was not originally of the essence or has ceased to be of the essence by waiver[32] or agreement, the employer can serve a notice requiring completion by a certain date.[33] He is really telling the contractor that unless he completes by such date he will treat his failure as a repudiation of the contract.[34] If the notice was not given prematurely, and the date for completion was not unreasonably soon in all the circumstances, judged at the time when the notice was given,[35] and the contractor fails to complete by such date, the employer can treat the contract as at an end and dismiss the contractor from the site.[36] The contractor's financial circumstances are irrelevant, it seems, to the reasonableness of the notice.[37] The employer cannot, however, effectively serve a notice making time of the essence if he is not himself ready, willing and able to complete, *i.e.* apparently, if his own breach of contract is affecting the contractor's ability to complete.[38] A notice making time of the essence does not expunge or cancel a time breach already committed.[39]

---

[27] *British Holdings plc.* v. *Quadrex* [1989] 3 W.L.R. 723 at 737 (C.A.).

[28] *Lucas* v. *Godwin* (1837) 3 Bing. N.C. 737 at 744.

[29] See, *e.g.* Lord Diplock in *United Scientific Holdings* v. *Burnley Council* [1978] A.C. 904 at 923 (H.L.) referring to a lease but the principle applies also to building contracts.

[30] *Lamprell* v. *Billericay Union* (1849) 3 Ex. 283 at 308; *Felton* v. *Wharrie* (1906) H.B.C. (4th ed.), Vol. 2, p. 398 at 400 (C.A.).

[31] Salmon L.J. in *Peak Construction* v. *McKinney Foundations* (1971) 1 B.L.R. 111 at 120 (C.A.). The other members of the court did not deal with the point.

[32] Time does not cease to be of the essence by waiver where one party by indulgence grants the other fixed extensions of time—*Nichemen* v. *Gatoil* [1987] 2 Lloyd's Rep. 46 (C.A.).

[33] *United Scientific Holdings* v. *Burnley Council* [1978] A.C. 904 at 946 (H.L.); *Rickards* v. *Oppenheim* [1950] 1 K.B. 616 (C.A.); *Felton* v. *Wharrie* (1906) H.B.C. (4th ed.), Vol. 2, p. 398 (C.A.), the facts of which appear at p. 155; *cf. Behzadi* v. *Shaftesbury Hotels, The Times,* October 1, 1990. (C.A.).

[34] *United Scientific Holdings* v. *Burnley Council* [1978] A.C. 904 at 946 (H.L.).

[35] *Rickards* v. *Oppenheim* [1950] 1 K.B. 616 at 624 (C.A.). Thus a subsequent strike may not excuse the contractor, *ibid.*

[36] *Felton* v. *Wharrie* (1906) H.B.C. (4th ed.), Vol. 2, p. 398 (C.A.); *Rickards* v. *Oppenheim* [1950] 1 K.B. 616 (C.A.); *United Scientific Holdings* v. *Burnley Council* [1978] A.C. 904 (H.L.).

[37] *British Holdings plc.* v. *Quadrex* [1989] 3 W.L.R. 723 (C.A.).

[38] *Ibid.*

[39] *Raineri* v. *Miles* [1981] A.C. 1050 (H.L.).

Contractual notices.   There is a distinction between:

(1) obligations for whose performance time is of the essence as discussed above and

(2) rights whose enforcement may depend on taking certain steps at strict times.

Building contracts often enable the contractor, the employer or the architect to serve notices and for resulting rights to depend on those notices. It is a question of construction whether strict compliance with any stipulated time provision for serving such notices is necessary to secure the resulting rights. If it is, the rights will be lost if the time for service is not strictly observed.[40]

B. Liquidated Damages

1. Generally

The parties often agree that a liquidated (*i.e.* fixed and agreed) sum shall be paid as damages for some breach of a contract. A typical clause provides that if the contractor shall fail to complete by a date stipulated in the contract, or any extended date, he shall pay or allow the employer to deduct liquidated damages at the rate of £x per day or week for the period during which the works are uncompleted.[41] Such a clause may result in a considerable saving of costs, because it often arises that "although undoubtedly there is damage the nature of the damage is such that proof of it is extremely complex, difficult and expensive."[42] Where there is such a clause and the contractor has failed to complete to time, he is *prima facie* liable to a claim for the liquidated damages either by way of action or by deduction (if there is an express power) or by a set-off. There can be no inquiry into the actual loss suffered. But he may have a defence to the claim[43] either by proving that the agreed sum is a penalty, or by showing the existence of one of the other matters set out below. If he establishes such a defence it may still leave the employer the right to pursue a claim for unliquidated damages (*i.e.* an ordinary claim for damages) for delay.[44] No general rule can be stated as to the date from which such unliquidated damages are recoverable. This depends upon the contract, the particular defence established and the circumstances. Where the employer causes

---

[40] Analogous cases are those relating to rent review clauses in leases, *e.g. Weller* v. *Akehurst* [1981] 3 All E.R. 411. For the notices provisions of the Standard Form of Building Contract, see Chap. 18.

[41] *cf.* clause 24 of the Standard Form of Building Contract.

[42] *Clydebank Engineering Co.* v. *Don Jose Yzquierdo y Castaneda* [1905] A.C. 6 at 11 (H.L.).

[43] Where the employer has set up a claim to deduct liquidated damages as a defence, the contractor will plead the matters discussed in Part B, Section 2 of this chapter by way of reply to defence or possibly by an amendment of his claim. For the approach to the construction of liquidated damages clauses see "*Contra proferentem* rule" at p. 43.

[44] See *Peak Construction* v. *McKinney Foundations* (1970) 69 L.G.R. 1 at 11, 16 (C.A.) also at 1 B.L.R. 111 at 121, 126; *cf. Arnhold* v. *Att.-Gen. of Hong Kong* (1989) 47 B.L.R. 129 (Hong Kong High Court)—clause providing for liquidated damages at two rates, a minimum and maximum, held void for uncertainty but employer could claim general damages; *Philips Hong Kong* v. *Att.-Gen. of Hong Kong* (1990) 50 B.L.R. 122 (Hong Kong High Court).

delay,[45] damages are not, it is submitted, in any event recoverable from a date earlier than that when the works could have been completed but for such delay, but it is not clear whether the delay sets time at large so that the works do not have to be completed before a reasonable time has elapsed.[46]

Exhaustive remedy?   Subject to defences discussed below, the nature and effect of a liquidated damages clause depends on its construction. Some such clauses provide an exhaustive remedy for the breach or breaches with which they deal so that the injured party cannot choose to claim general damages instead. The effect of such a clause, therefore, is to limit the defendant's liability.[47]

In *Cellulose Acetate* v. *Widnes Foundry*,[48] a contract for delivery and erection of an acetone recovery plant provided that the contractors should pay by way of penalty £20 for every week that completion was later than a stipulated time. Completion was 30 weeks late and the contractors were held liable for £600 and not a greater actual loss. In *Temloc* v. *Errill Properties*,[49] the parties provided in the Appendix of a 1980 Standard Form of Building Contract against clause 24.2 that liquidated damages for delay should be "£ nil." It was held that on a proper construction of the contract the parties had agreed that there should be no damages for delayed completion. It was said that completing the relevant part of the Appendix of this form of contract constituted an exhaustive agreement of the damages which were, or were not, to be payable. It was not open to the employer to claim general damages instead.

It is suggested that in building contracts at least a clause providing for payment by the contractor of liquidated damages for delay will normally operate as a limitation of the contractor's liability.[50] The question tends to be

---

[45] See p. 231.

[46] See *Trollope & Colls Ltd.* v. *N.W. Metropolitan Regional Hospital Board* [1973] 1 W.L.R. 601 at 607 (H.L.) where the majority of the House of Lords said that Lord Denning had been wrong when, in the Court of Appeal, he had said that *Dodd* v. *Churton* [1897] 1 Q.B. 562 (C.A.) established that time became at large. The House did not comment on *Wells* v. *Army & Navy Co-operative Society Ltd.* (1902) H.B.C. 346 (C.A.) or *Peak Construction* v. *McKinney Foundations* (1970) 69 L.G.R. 1 (C.A.) also at 1 B.L.R. 111 which were cited to the House in argument in support of the same proposition. See also the discussion in *Bilton* v. *Greater London Council* (1981) 17 B.L.R. 1 (C.A.) where the point was however not decided—the actual decision was upheld on appeal at (1982) 20 B.L.R. 1 (H.L.).

[47] *cf. Elsley* v. *J. G. Collins* (1978) 83 D.L.R. 1 at 14 *et seq.* (Canadian Supreme Court). In some charterparties, there may be circumstances where a demurrage (or liquidated damages) clause is not an exhaustive remedy for a breach giving rise to losses of more than one character—see *Reidar* v. *Arcos* [1927] 1 K.B. 352 (C.A.); *Total Transport* v. *Amoco Transport Co.* [1985] 1 Lloyd's Rep. 423.

[48] [1933] A.C. 20 (H.L.).

[49] (1987) 39 B.L.R. 30 (C.A.) *cf. M. J. Gleeson* v. *Taylor Woodrow Construction* (1989) 49 B.L.R. 95.

[50] There are charterparty cases which suggest that the plaintiff may have a choice either to sue under the liquidated damages clause or to ignore it and claim general damages without limitation—see, *e.g. Wall* v. *Rederiaktiebolaget* [1915] 3 K.B. 66 approved in *Watts* v. *Mitsui* [1917] A.C. 227 at 246 (H.L.); but see Lord Finlay at 235—"If this clause had appeared for the first time I think it might have been construed as imposing a limitation on the damages to be recovered, but the penalty clause is an old one with a settled meaning. ...." See also *Jobson* v. *Johnson* [1989] 1 W.L.R. 1026 (C.A.). See generally A. H. Hudson, "Penalties Limiting Damages" (1985) 101 L.Q.R. 480.

confused with a related but different question where the agreed sum is an unenforceable penalty.[51]

> "In many cases a man before entering into a contract wishes to know for what he is to be liable if he breaks it, and so he agrees a sum payable by him in that event. That obviously has nothing to do with figures fixed *in terrorem*."[52]

Both cases mentioned in the previous paragraph concerned sums which were clearly less than an estimate of likely loss,[53] although the decision in *Temloc* v. *Errill Properties* would have been the same if a substantial rate for liquidated damages had been entered into the Appendix.[54] It is suggested that there is no difference in principle where the rate is not obviously less than an estimate of likely loss. Unless the express words of the contract show that the employer does have a choice, where a liquidated damages clause is not a penalty and is enforceable, it should be construed as a mutual covenant binding both parties.

2. Defences to Claim for Liquidated Damages

(a) *Agreed sum is a penalty*

If the agreed sum, whatever it is called in the contract, is a penalty it will not be enforced by the courts.[55] The onus of showing that the clause is a penalty clause lies upon the party who is sued upon it.[56] It is sometimes a matter of some difficulty to determine whether agreed damages are, in the particular circumstances of the case, penalties or liquidated damages, but the principles applied by the courts are well established.

> "The classic form of penalty clause is one which provides that upon breach of a primary obligation under the contract a secondary obligation shall arise on the part of the party in breach which does not represent a genuine pre-estimate of any loss likely to be sustained by him as the result of the breach of primary obligation but is substantially in excess of that sum."[57]

Lord Dunedin's propositions. The principles were summarised in Lord Dunedin's speech to the House of Lords in *Dunlop Ltd.* v. *New Garage Co. Ltd.*[58]

---

[51] This is discussed separately below.

[52] Scrutton L.J. in *Widnes Foundry* v. *Cellulose Acetate* [1931] 2 K.B. 393 (C.A.)—the case referred to in the previous paragraph of the text in the Court of Appeal.

[53] *cf.* Scrutton L.J. in *Widnes Foundry* v. *Cellulose Acetate* [1931] 2 K.B. 393 at 407 (C.A.)—"I find great difficulty in saying that as estimate less than the actual loss can ever be a penalty *in terrorem*."

[54] See Nourse L.J. at 39.

[55] *Watts, Watts & Co. Ltd.* v. *Mitsui & Co. Ltd.* [1917] A.C. 227 (H.L.); *cf. Jobson* v. *Johnson* [1989] 1 W.L.R. 1026 (C.A.).

[56] *Robophone Facilities* v. *Blank* [1966] 1 W.L.R. 1428 at 1447 (C.A.). This case is also interesting for Diplock L.J.'s discussion at 1447 *et seq.* of the relationship between a liquidated damages clause and the second limb of the rule in *Hadley* v. *Baxendale* (1854) 9 Exch. 341.

[57] Lord Diplock in *Scandinavian Trading* v. *Flota Ecuatoriana* [1983] 2 A.C. 694 at 702 (H.L.).

[58] [1915] A.C. 79 at 86 (H.L.).

The relevant extracts will be set out in the text followed by discussion on the application of the principles to building contracts.

"*1. Though the parties to a contract who use the words 'penalty' or 'liquidated damages' may prima facie be supposed to mean what they say, yet the expression used is not conclusive. The court must find out whether the payment stipulated is in truth a penalty or liquidated damages. . . .*"

There have been several building contract cases in which an agreed sum has been held to be liquidated damages although termed a "penalty,"[59] and vice versa.[60]

"*2. The essence of a penalty is a payment of money stipulated as in terrorem of the offending party; the essence of liquidated damages is a genuine covenanted pre-estimate of damage.*"[61]

The principle is not limited to sums of money. It can also apply to a clause requiring a transfer of property as a penalty.[62] But an agreed sum may not be a genuine pre-estimate yet not be a penalty. This arises where a party is unwilling to run the risk of paying the heavy damages which might result from his breach, and therefore deliberately limits his liability to a smaller sum than that which might be awarded as unliquidated damages.[63] A stipulation for immediate repayment of a loan and all other monies due to the lender if the borrower failed to make instalment repayments on the due dates was held not to be a penalty.[64]

"*3. The question whether a sum stipulated is penalty or liquidated damages is a question of construction to be decided upon the terms and inherent circumstances of each particular contract, judged of as at the time of the making of the contract, not as at the time of the breach.*"[65]

"*4. To assist this task of construction various tests have been suggested, which if applicable to the case under consideration may prove helpful, or even conclusive. Such are: (a) It will be held to be a penalty if the sum stipulated for is extravagant and unconscionable in amount in comparison with the greatest loss that could conceivably be proved to have followed from the breach.*"[66]

---

[59] *e.g. Ranger* v. *G.W. Railway* (1854) 5 H.L.C. 72 (H.L.); *Crux* v. *Aldred* (1866) 14 W.R. 656; *Re White* (1901) 17 T.L.R. 461 (D.C.); *Clydebank, etc., Co.* v. *Yzquierdo, etc.* [1905] A.C. 6 (H.L.).

[60] *e.g. Re Newman* (1876) 4 Ch.D. 724 (C.A.); *Public Works Commissioner* v. *Hills* [1906] A.C. 368 (P.C.).

[61] Citing *Clydebank, etc., Co.* v. *Yzquierdo, etc.* [1905] A.C. 6 (H.L.); *cf. Photo Production* v. *Securicor* [1980] A.C. 827 at 850 (H.L.).

[62] *Jobson* v. *Johnson* [1989] 1 W.L.R. 1026 at 1034 (C.A.).

[63] *Cellulose Acetate* v. *Widnes Foundry* [1933] A.C. 20 (H.L.); *cf. Suisse Atlantique, etc.* v. *N.V. Rotterdamsche Kolen Centrale* [1967] 1 A.C. 361 at 421 (H.L.); see also "Exhaustive remedy?" at p. 223.

[64] *The Angelic Star* [1988] 1 Lloyd's Rep. 122 at 125.

[65] Citing *Public Works Commissioner* v. *Hills* [1906] A.C. 368 (P.C.) and *Webster* v. *Bosanquet* [1912] A.C. 394 (P.C.); *cf. Jobson* v. *Johnson* [1989] 1 W.L.R. 1026 at 1033 (C.A.).

[66] Citing *Clydebank, etc., Co.* v. *Yzquierdo, etc.* [1905] A.C. 6 (H.L.).

In practice this is probably the most important test to be applied. Lord Halsbury in the *Clydebank* case[67] indicates the approach:

> "if you agreed to build a house in a year, and agreed that if you did not build the house for £50, you were to pay a million of money as a penalty, the extravagance of that would become at once apparent. Between such an extreme case as I have supposed and other cases, a great deal must depend on the nature of the transaction—the thing to be done, the loss likely to accrue to the person who is endeavouring to enforce the performance of the contract, and so forth."

In considering the question the unequal financial position of the parties is irrelevant. "The word unconscionable . . . does not bring in at all the idea of an unconscionable bargain. It is merely a synonym for something which is extravagant and exorbitant."[68] Also irrelevant is any question of disproportion between the amount of the contract sum and the agreed sum payable on breach.[69] This principle might apply, for example, where building works are required for an important exhibition. In such a case a proper sum for liquidated damages might be so high that after the running of quite a short period of delay it might exceed the contract sum.

> *"(b) It will be held to be a penalty if the breach consists only in not paying a sum of money, and the sum stipulated is a sum greater than the sum which ought to have been paid.[70] This though one of the most ancient instances is truly a corollary to the last test. . . ."*

This test is based on the principle that because the exact amount of the loss is known a greater sum payable cannot be a genuine pre-estimate of the loss.[71]

> *"(c) There is a presumption (but no more) that it is penalty when 'a single lump sum is made payable by way of compensation, on the occurrence of one or more or all of several events, some of which may occasion serious and others but trifling damage.'"[72]*

An example of this principle arose where, in addition to the usual payment of £x per week for delay, there was also a provision that in case the contract should not be in all things duly performed by the contractors they should pay to the employers £1,000 as liquidated damages. It was held that the latter sum was a penalty.[73] But where it was provided that in default of completion by the

---

[67] [1905] A.C. 6 at 10 (H.L.); *cf. Export Credits Guarantee Dept.* v. *Universal Oil* [1983] 1 W.L.R. 399 (H.L.).

[68] Lord Wright M.R. in *Imperial Tobacco Co.* v. *Parslay* [1936] 2 All E.R. 515 at 521. See also *Robert Stewart & Sons Ltd.* v. *Carapanayoti* [1962] 1 W.L.R. 34, 40; Lord Radcliffe in *Bridge* v. *Campbell Discount Co. Ltd.* [1962] A.C. 600 at 626 (H.L.)—"the courts of equity never undertook to serve as a general adjuster of men's bargains."

[69] *Ibid.*

[70] Citing *Kemble* v. *Farren* (1829) 6 Bing. 141.

[71] *Kemble* v. *Farren* (1829) 6 Bing. 141.

[72] Citing Lord Watson in *Lord Elphinstone* v. *Monkland Iron & Coal Co.* (1886) 11 App.Cas. 332 (H.L.); *cf. Lombard plc.* v. *Butterworth* [1987] Q.B. 527 at 540 *et seq.* (C.A.).

[73] *Re Newman ex p. Capper* (1876) 4 Ch.D. 724 (C.A.); see also *Cooden Engineering Co. Ltd.* v. *Stanford* [1953] 1 Q.B. 86 at 98 (C.A.).

specified date the contractor should forfeit and pay the sum of £100 and £5 for every seven days of delay it was held that as these sums were payable on a single event only they were liquidated damages.[74]

Sectional completion and partial possession. Difficulties can arise where a single sum is stipulated for liquidated damages but the works are to be completed in sections at different times or where the employer takes possession of part of the works before completion of the whole. The principle under discussion is relevant so that, unless there are effective provisions for dividing the single sum between the sections or reducing it in proportion to the part taken into possession, a claim for liquidated damages will fail. Such claims have been held to fail where:

(1) there were no effective provisions for sectional completion[75];

(2) in a local authority housing contract a provision to reduce the damages upon partial possession was held to be inconsistent with liquidated damages expressed in the form "at the rate of £20 per week for each uncompleted dwelling"[76]; and

(3) in a contract for two houses where part of a single sum for liquidated damages was claimed for late completion of one of the houses but there was no contractual machinery to effect the reduction.[77]

"*On the other hand*:

(d) It is no obstacle to the sum stipulated being a genuine pre-estimate of damage, that the consequences of the breach are such as to make precise pre-estimation almost an impossibility. On the contrary, that is just the situation when it is probable that pre-estimated damage was the true bargain between the parties."[78]

Forfeiture clauses.   Forfeiture clauses are fairly common in building contracts and take a number of forms. Commonly, for instance, an employer is empowered to determine the contract or the contractor's employment under it if the contractor defaults in specified respects and the clause provides consequences following the determination which can include forfeiture of, for example, plant on site.[79] Such clauses can raise two related but rather different questions, *viz.* first whether the contractor could claim relief against forfeiture, and secondly whether the clause itself is a penalty clause which the

---

[74] *Law* v. *Redditch Local Board* [1892] 1 Q.B. 127 (C.A.); *cf. Pye* v. *British Automobile Commercial Syndicate* [1906] 1 K.B. 425. For a hire case, see *Robophone Facilities Ltd.* v. *Blank* [1966] 1 W.L.R. 1428 (C.A.).

[75] *M. J. Gleeson* v. *London Borough of Hillingdon* (1970) 215 E.G. 165; *Bruno Zorno (Builders)* v. *Beechcroft Developments* (1990) 6 Const.L.J. 132. There is now a Sectional Completion Supplement to the Standard Form of Building Contract.

[76] *Bramall & Ogden* v. *Sheffield City Council* (1983) 29 B.L.R. 73—what the judge described (at 88) as a "very technical" argument succeeded upon an application of the *contra proferentem* rule—see p. 43.

[77] *Stanor Electric* v. *R. Mansell* (1988) C.I.L.L. 399.

[78] Citing the *Clydebank* case, Lord Halsbury; *Webster* v. *Bosanquet*, Lord Mersey.

[79] See, *e.g.* clause 27 of the Standard Form of Building Contract and clause 63 of the I.C.E. Conditions at pp. 588 and 912 respectively.

court will not enforce.[80] The first of these questions is considered in Chapter 10.[81]

Forfeiture clauses as penalties.   Some forfeiture clauses have been held to be unenforceable as penalties.[82] In *Ranger* v. *G.W. Railway*,[83] for example, there was a clause providing that upon forfeiture the contractor was to receive no further payment, that all moneys then due or to become due to him and all tools and materials on the works were to become the property of the employer, and the contractor was to make up any deficiency in the cost of completion.[84] This clause was held to impose a penalty, and Lord Cranworth, referring to the cost to the employers of completion, said[85] that "the amount of their damage was capable of exact admeasurement"; the employers were entitled to recoup themselves out of the property seized to the extent of their loss and no further.

A clause purporting to forfeit retention money upon default is open to the objection that it may be a penalty, for the amount of the retention money increases with no relation to the cost of completion, and in the normal course increases as the cost of completion decreases.[86] A clause forfeiting only the unfixed materials on the site is not open to the same objections, for the amount of materials at any one time is likely to be reasonably constant except that towards completion it will decrease.[87]

In one case it was provided that upon forfeiture for the contractor's default the amount of money already paid to the contractor[88] should be considered the full value of the works which had been executed up to that time and that materials should be forfeited without any further payment. The provision was held to be enforceable although the contractor had not become entitled to any payment for work done at the time of forfeiture.[89]

Set-off clauses.   Clauses providing expressly for a right of set-off are common. They are enforceable provided they do not amount to a penalty. Thus a contractor relied on a clause in a sub-contract to withhold money from a sub-contractor.[90] Part of the clause said: ". . . if the sub-contractor fails to

---

[80] See *Jobson* v. *Johnson* [1989] 1 W.L.R. 1026 at 1041 (C.A.).

[81] See "Relief against forfeiture" at p. 241.

[82] See generally Hugh Beale, "Penalties in Termination Provisions" (1988) 104 L.Q.R. 355.

[83] (1854) 5 H.L.C. 72 (H.L.).

[84] There was also a clause providing for specified sums increasing each week to be paid as "penalties in case of delay." This was held to provide for liquidated damages.

[85] *Ibid.* at 108.

[86] See *Public Works Commissioner* v. *Hills* [1906] A.C. 368 (P.C.); *Walker* v. *L. & N.W. Railway* (1876) 1 C.P.D. 518 at 532; *cf. Roach* v. *G.W. Railway* (1841) 10 L.J.Q.B. 89; *Tooth* v. *Hallett* (1869) L.R. 4 Ch.App. 242; *Bridge* v. *Campbell Discount Co. Ltd.* [1962] A.C. 600 (H.L.).

[87] See *Re Garrud, ex p. Newitt* (1881) 16 Ch.D. 522 (C.A.). For vesting clauses operating upon forfeiture, see p. 244, noting that there is an implied right of revesting in respect of unused materials.

[88] There was an express provision for payment by instalments.

[89] *Davies* v. *Swansea Corporation* (1853) 8 Exch. 808.

[90] *Modern Engineering (Bristol) Ltd.* v. *Gilbert Ash (Northern) Ltd.* [1974] A.C. 689 (H.L.); *cf. The Fanti and Padre Island* [1989] 1 Lloyd's Rep. 239 (C.A.). For set-off generally, see p. 438.

comply with any of the conditions of this sub-contract the contractor reserves the right to suspend or withhold payment. . . ." This was unenforceable as a penalty because large sums of money could be withheld for trivial breaches.[91]

A clause is not a penalty clause if it provides for payment of money upon the happening of a specified event which is not a breach of a contractual duty owed by the payer to the payee.[92] The court will not in such a case relieve a party from the consequences of an onerous or commercially imprudent bargain.[93] If a sum of money is payable, not in respect of any breach of contract, but by one of the parties when he exercises a contractual right under the contract, then no question of penalty of liquidated damages arises.[94] But it is not clear whether equity can intervene to relieve against payment of that sum of money where it is such that it would he held to be a penalty if it were payable upon breach of the contract.[95]

Damages where the agreed sum is a penalty.[96]   Where the agreed sum is a penalty the employer has an option. He may either rely on his claim for the penalty, in which case he cannot recover more than the actual loss which he proves up to the amount of the penalty, or he can ignore the penalty and sue for unliquidated damages.[97] The effect, of course, is the same unless the law is that by following the latter course he is entitled to damages if he proves them in excess of the penalty. Cases are rare since it is inherently unlikely that an employer could prove both:

(1) that the agreed sum was so great that it was not a genuine pre-estimate of the loss; and

(2) that he has as a result of the breach suffered loss greater than the penalty.[98]

There is authority in charterparty cases suggesting that a plaintiff can recover more than the agreed sum if it is held to be a penalty.[99] On the other

---

[91] *Ibid.* at 698, 703, 711, 723. The case does not embody "any significant extension of the penalty area"—Slade L.J. in *Export Credits Guarantee Dept.* v. *Universal Oil Products* [1983] 1 Lloyd's Rep. 448 at 459 (C.A.) affirmed [1983] 1 W.L.R. 399 (H.L.).

[92] *Export Credits Guarantee Dept.* v. *Universal Oil* [1983] 1 W.L.R. 399 at 402 (H.L.).

[93] *Ibid.* at 403.

[94] *Associated Distributors Ltd.* v. *Hall* [1938] 2 K.B. 83; considered in *Bridge* v. *Campbell Discount Co. Ltd.* [1962] A.C. 600 (H.L.), where two of their lordships accepted this principle, two did not and the fifth left the matter open. In any event their lordships' views were *obiter*.

[95] See *Bridge* v. *Campbell Discount Co. Ltd.* [1962] A.C. 600 (H.L.) where their lordships considered the matter *obiter* and differed in their views in the same manner as set out in the last footnote; see also *Stockloser* v. *Johnson* [1954] 1 Q.B. 476 (C.A.); *Phonographic Equipment (1958) Ltd.* v. *Muslu* [1961] 1 W.L.R. 1379 (C.A.).

[96] See also "Damages where employer causes delay" at p. 233.

[97] *Watts* v. *Mitsui* [1917] A.C. 227 (H.L.); *Feather & Co.* v. *Keighley Corp.* (1953) 52 L.G.R. 30 at 33; but see *Cellulose Acetate Ltd.* v. *Widnes Foundry (1925) Ltd.* [1933] A.C. 20 at 25 (H.L.).

[98] *cf.* the *Cellulose Acetate Ltd.* v. *Widnes Foundry (1925) Ltd.* [1933] A.C. 20 (H.L.). See further an article 91 L.Q.R. 25.

[99] See *Wall* v. *Rederiaktiebolaget* [1915] 3 K.B. 66 approved in *Watts* v. *Mitsui* [1917] A.C. 227 at 246 (H.L.); see also *Jobson* v. *Johnson* [1989] 1 W.L.R. 1026 (C.A.). The law was so stated in the 4th edition of this book (although it was modified in the First Supplement) by reference also to *Feather & Co.* v. *Keighley Corporation* (1953) 52 L.G.R. 30 at 33 but this is thought to be a somewhat special case of limited application.

hand there are a number of judicial indications to the contrary.[1] It is suggested that the charterparty cases are special to the clauses in question,[2] and that in building contracts the question is open. It is submitted that it would be inequitable to permit an employer to impose an excessive liquidated damages clause *in terrorem* and then to avoid its effect in order to recover more. Further, where the nature of the clause is usually, as is suggested above, to limit the contractor's liability, there is every reason why the contractor should not be denied that limitation simply because the employer's estimate of his loss was not genuine.[3]

(b) *Omission of date in contract*

There must be a date from which liquidated damages can run and if the date is omitted from a written contract the court will not fix a date from conflicting oral evidence.[4]

(c) *Waiver*

There may be an express or implied waiver by the employer. An express undertaking not to enforce the clause at all, or to extend the time from which liquidated damages are to run, is, it is submitted binding notwithstanding the absence of consideration.[5] Waiver may be implied from circumstances, *e.g.* if the contract provides that the liquidated damages are to be deducted from time to time as progress payments are made and the employer fails to deduct them, he may have no right to deduct them from payments subsequently becoming due. But in the absence of words indicating the contrary, where, after there has been delay, payment of the contract price is made in full, this in itself does not operate as a bar to the recovery of liquidated damages.[6]

(d) *Final certificate*

Where the architect's decision is final and he has power to extend the time and to take into account in his final certificate any liquidated damages due, then he will be presumed to have extended the time for completion unless it is proved

---

[1] See *McGregor on Damages* (15th ed.), footnotes to para. 449; see also *Elsley* v. *J. G. Collins Insurance* (1978) 83 D.L.R. (3d) 1 at 14 *et seq.* (Canadian Supreme Court); *Rapid Building* v. *Ealing Family Housing* (1984) 29 B.L.R. 5 at 20 (C.A.); *Jobson* v. *Johnson* [1989] 1 W.L.R. 1026 at 1033H (C.A.); perhaps also *Beckham* v. *Drake* (1849) 2 H.L.Cas. 579 at 622, 645.

[2] See Lord Finlay in *Watts* v. *Mitsui* [1917] A.C. 227 at 235 (H.L.); and see above under "Exhaustive remedy?"

[3] The view preferred in the text has strong support from *Elsley* v. *J. G. Collins Insurance* (1978) 83 D.L.R. (3d) 1 at 14 *et seq.* (Canadian Supreme Court). *McGregor on Damages* (15th ed.), para. 449 comes to the opposite conclusion.

[4] *Kemp* v. *Rose* (1858) 1 Giff. 258 at 266; see pp. 34 and 561.

[5] See p. 264.

[6] *Clydebank, etc., Co.* v. *Yzquierdo etc.* [1905] A.C. 6 (H.L.).

or admitted[7] that the matter has not been determined by him, or was not expressly or impliedly within his jurisdiction.[8] But the architect's final certificate certifying the amount due to the contractor in settlement of the contract does not estop the employer from bringing an action for liquidated damages if the contract did not give the architect power to deal with liquidated damages.[9]

(e) *Employer causing delay*

If the employer prevents the completion of the works in any way, as, for example, by failing to give possession of the site[10] or to provide plans at the proper time,[11] or by interfering improperly through his agent in the carrying out of the works,[12] or by ordering extras which necessarily delay the works,[13] or by failing to deliver components he is bound to provide,[14] or by delay in giving essential instructions,[15] the general rule is that he loses the right to claim liquidated damages for non-completion to time, for he "cannot insist on a condition if it is his own fault that the condition has not been fulfilled."[16] The rule probably applies even if the contractor has by his own delays disabled himself from completing by the due date.[17] If the prevention occurs after the contractual completion date when the contractor is already in delay, the employer may be able to recover liquidated damages up to the date of prevention but not beyond.[18] There are two exceptions to the general rule, the first to be mentioned being of limited, and the second of general application.

---

[7] See *Jones* v. *St. John's College, Oxford* (1870) L.R. 6 Q.B. 115.

[8] Phillimore J. in *British Thomson-Houston Co.* v. *West* (1903) 19 T.L.R. 493 at 494, approving passage from H.B.C. (2nd ed.), Vol. 1, p. 332.

[9] *British Thomson-Houston Co.* v. *West* (1903) 19 T.L.R. 493. See also p. 110.

[10] *Holme* v. *Guppy* (1838) 3 M. & W. 387; *Felton* v. *Wharrie* (1906) H.B.C. (4th ed.), Vol. 2, p. 398 (C.A.); *Rapid Building* v. *Ealing Family Housing* (1984) 29 B.L.R. 5 (C.A.).

[11] *e.g. Roberts* v. *Bury Commissioners* (1870) L.R. 5 C.P. 310.

[12] *e.g. Russell* v. *Sa da Bandeira* (1862) 13 C.B. (N.S.) 149.

[13] *e.g. Dodd* v. *Churton* [1897] 1 Q.B. 562 (C.A.); *cf. Astilleros Canarios* v. *Cape Hatteras* [1982] 1 Lloyd's Rep. 518 at 526.

[14] *Perini Pacific* v. *Greater Vancouver Sewerage and Drainage District* (1966) 57 D.L.R. (2d) 307 (British Columbia Court of Appeal).

[15] *Peak Construction (Liverpool) Ltd.* v. *McKinney Foundations Ltd.* (1971) 69 L.G.R. 1 (C.A.) also 1 B.L.R. 111.

[16] *Amalgamated Building Contractors Ltd.* v. *Waltham Holy Cross Urban District Council* [1952] 2 All E.R. 452 at 455 (C.A.); *Wells* v. *Army & Navy Co-operative Society* (1902) H.B.C. (4th ed.), Vol. 2, p. 346 at 354 (C.A.); *Trollope & Colls Ltd.* v. *N.W. Metropolitan Regional Hospital Board* [1973] 1 W.L.R. 601 at 607 (H.L.); *Bilton* v. *Greater London Council* (1982) 20 B.L.R. 1 at 13 (H.L.); *S.M.K. Cabinets* v. *Hili Modern Electrics* [1984] V.R. 391 (Victoria Full Supreme Court). For a discussion of the date from which any claim for unliquidated damages runs, see p. 222.

[17] See the convincing analysis in *S.M.K. Cabinets* v. *Hili Modern Electrics* [1984] V.R. 391 at 398 *et seq.* (Victoria Full Supreme Court) citing among others a number of English authorities; *cf. Astilleros Canarios* v. *Cape Hatteras* [1982] 1 Lloyd's Rep. 518 at 526, Staughton J. doubting indications to the contrary in *Perini Pacific* v. *Greater Vancouver Sewerage and Drainage District* (1966) 57 D.L.R. (2d) 307 at 319 (British Columbia C.A.).

[18] See *S.M.K. Cabinets* v. *Hili Modern Electrics* [1984] V.R. 391 at 398 *et seq.* (Victoria Full Supreme Court). The question might be complicated if an architect's certificate was a condition precedent to the right to recover liquidated damages.

Extras ordered under absolute contract. The wording of the contract may be such that the contractor binds himself absolutely to complete the contract work with extras within the stipulated time, subject to payment of liquidated damages in default, even though extras may be ordered and no extension of time is granted. Such a contract, though it is very onerous and the contractor may have committed himself to an impossibility, will be enforced provided the extras were such as were contemplated by the contract.[19] But if there is any ambiguity in the contract the courts will not construe it so as to impose such an unreasonable obligation on the contractor and will give effect to the general rule stated above.[20] A provision that the ordering of extras is not to "vitiate" the contract or "is not to vitiate the contract or the claim for penalties" is not sufficient to impose this absolute obligation on the contractor.[21]

Extension of time for employer's delay. If the employer or his architect makes a valid extension of time in respect of the delay which he has caused, a new date is set for completion and, subject to any further extension or special defences raised by the contractor, liquidated damages will be payable from that extended date in the event of non-completion. There must be an express contractual power to make the extension and the employer cannot for his own benefit purport to extend the time because of his own delay if there is no express power in the contract.[22] Any purported extension must comply strictly with the provisions of the contract, and where the extension is for the employer's benefit and the contract was imposed by him on the contractor it will, if it is ambiguous, be construed against the employer.[23] Where delay is solely caused by the employer, then unless clear words are used, a power to extend time because of the employer's delay cannot, it seems, be exercised retrospectively.[24]

---

[19] *Jones* v. *St. John's College, Oxford* (1870) L.R. 6 Q.B. 115; *Tew* v. *Newbold-on-Avon United District School Board* (1884) 1 Cab. & El. 260; *Sattin* v. *Poole* (1901) H.B.C. (4th ed.), Vol. 2, p. 306 (D.C.).

[20] *Dodd* v. *Churton* [1897] 1 Q.B. 562 (C.A.); *Wells* v. *Army & Navy Co-Operative Society* (1902) H.B.C. (4th ed.), Vol. 2, p. 346 (C.A.).

[21] *Ibid.*

[22] *Dodd* v. *Churton* [1897] 1 Q.B. 562 (C.A.).

[23] *Miller* v. *L.C.C.* (1934) 50 T.L.R. 479, 482; *Peak Construction (Liverpool) Ltd.* v. *McKinney Foundations Ltd.* (1971) 69 L.G.R. 1 (C.A.). *cf. Tersons Ltd.* v. *Stevenage Development Corporation* [1963] 2 Lloyd's Rep. 333 at 368 (C.A.). See p. 43.

[24] *Amalgamated Building Contractors Ltd.* v. *Waltham Holy Cross Urban District Council* [1952] 2 All E.R. 452 at 455 (C.A.); *Miller* v. *L.C.C.* (1934) 50 T.L.R. 479. The point is not free from doubt for in *Sattin* v. *Poole* (1901) H.B.C. (4th ed.), Vol. 2, p. 306, referred to with approval in the *Amalgamated Building Contractors* case, an extension was granted after completion to a date in the past and the contractor was not permitted to adduce evidence to show that the delay was caused by the employer. But the contractor had specifically asked the architect to extend the time after he had completed the works, and it was not argued that the architect lacked the power to grant the extension. In *Miller's* case an extension made after completion because of extras ordered by the employer was held to be invalid, but Denning L.J. in the *Amalgamated Building Contractors* case (at 455) said that he regarded *Miller's* case as turning on the very special wording of the contract. For an example of clear words, see clause 25 of the Standard Form of Building Contract.

Damages where employer causes delay.   Where the right to claim liquidated damages is lost because the employer causes delay the contractor is
obliged to complete within a reasonable time[25] and the employer is entitled to
claim unliquidated damages if the contractor fails to do so.[26] It is thought that
where the cause of the unenforceability of the liquidated damages provision is
the employer's act, the Court would not permit the employer to recover greater
damages than the liquidated damages which would, if enforceable, have been
payable.[27]

(f) *Breach of condition precedent by employer*

The contract may provide that some condition precedent must be fulfilled
before the employer can claim liquidated damages. Thus in the Standard
Form of Building Contract, the architect's certificate under clause 24 is such a
condition precedent.[28] Similarly, where a contract imposes a duty on the
architect to extend the time and he fails to perform that duty in accordance
with the contract the employer is unable to claim liquidated damages.[29]

(g) *Extension of time*

It is common to provide an express power[30] for the extension of the time for
completion and if an extension has been granted it operates wholly or partially
as a defence to a claim for liquidated damages from the original completion
date. The type of events for which provision is made falls under two heads,[31]
viz:

(1) delay caused by the employer, considered above; and
(2) delay not caused by the employer, *e.g.* strikes, force majeure,[32] shortage
     of materials and labour and other events which though they may cause
     unavoidable delay do not, or might not, excuse the contractor.[33]

If there is no express power to extend time for a delay which is not the fault of
the employer, the contractor takes the risk of that delay and will not avoid
liquidated damages.[34]

---

[25] *I.e* time is at large—see p. 231.

[26] *Rapid Building* v. *Ealing Family Housing* (1984) 29 B.L.R. 5 at 16, 19 (C.A.).

[27] The point was argued but not decided in *Rapid Building* v. *Ealing Family Housing* (1984) 29 B.L.R.
    5 (C.A.). See also "Damages where the agreed sum is a penalty" at p. 229.

[28] *Amalgamated Building Contractors* case at 454; *cf. A. Bell & Son* v. *C.B.F. Residential Care* (1989) 46
    B.L.R. 102. See also commentary to clause 24 at p. 563.

[29] *Ibid.*; *cf.* clause 25 of the Standard Form of Building Contract.

[30] *cf. Bilton* v. *Greater London Council* (1982) 20 B.L.R. 1 at 14 (H.L.).

[31] *cf. Henry Boot* v. *Central Lancashire New Town* (1980) 15 B.L.R. 1 at 12.

[32] For meaning, see p. 576; *cf. Bilton* v. *Greater London Council* (1982) 20 B.L.R. 1 at 14 (H.L.).

[33] For excuses for non-completion, see Chap. 6. In the Standard Form of Building Contract,
    clauses 25.4.5, 25.4.6 and 25.4.8 correspond roughly with (1) in the text, and the other
    sub-clauses correspond with (2).

[34] *Bilton* v. *Greater London Council* (1982) 20 B.L.R. 1 at 13 *et seq.* (H.L.), where the withdrawal of a
    nominated sub-contractor was held not to be the "fault" of the employer.

Compliance with contract. Extensions of time for delay whether caused by the employer[35] or not[36] must comply with the terms of the contract unless one of the parties waives a condition inserted for his benefit.

Retrospective extension—not employer's delay. It is clearly desirable that when possible an extension of time should be granted to a date in the future so that the contractor can plan his work accordingly, and where the delay is caused by the employer an extension can frequently only be granted to a future date[37]; but where the delay is not caused by the employer and an extension is for the benefit of the contractor the position is different. This is illustrated by the facts of *Amalgamated Building Contractors Co. Ltd.* v. *Waltham Holy Cross Urban District Council.*[38] The contractors were liable under a modified R.I.B.A. form, 1939 edition, to complete the works by February 7, 1949. On January 19, 1949, the contractors applied for a 12-month extension because of labour and materials difficulties.[39] The architect did not reply beyond a formal acknowledgment.[40] The work was completed on August 28, 1950, and on December 20, 1950, the architect wrote to the contractors stating that he had decided that "an addition of 15 weeks bringing the completion date to May 23, 1949, would be a fair and reasonable extension."[41] He also wrote to the employers certifying in accordance with the contract. If the architect's extension had been invalid the employers could not have claimed liquidated damages at all, but it was held that it was valid. Denning L.J. said that this was a case where the cause of delay operated partially but not wholly, every day, until the works were completed. It must follow that an architect could not decide the length of the extension until after completion; therefore the parties must have intended that he could in such circumstances grant an extension retrospectively. And the same principle would apply:

> "where the contractors, near the end of the work, have overrun the contract time for six months without legitimate excuse ... Now suppose ... a strike occurs and lasts a month. The contractors can get an extension of time for that month. The architect can clearly issue a certificate which will operate

---

[35] See p. 231.

[36] See *Sattin* v. *Poole* (1901) H.B.C. (4th ed.), Vol. 2, p. 306 at 314, construing a clause indistinguishable (*Amalgamated Building Contractors Ltd.* v. *Waltham Holy Cross Urban District Council* [1952] 2 All E.R. 452 at 455 (C.A.)) from clause 18 of the R.I.B.A. form (1939 edition).

[37] See p. 231.

[38] [1952] 2 All E.R. 452 at 454 (C.A.).

[39] Invoking clause 18(ix), the equivalent of clause 25.4.10 in the Standard Form of Building Contract.

[40] It was suggested by Denning L.J. at 455 that if the contractors were dissatisfied they should have asked for arbitration. In the unmodified Standard Form of Building Contract this could not have been opened until after the completion of the works unless the employers consented— see now clause 41.3 of the 1980 Form. In any event without co-operation arbitration is rarely quick.

[41] The court rejected a submission that this letter was too informal.

retrospectively. He extends the time by one month from the original completion date, and the extended time will obviously be a date which is past."[42]

The wording of the contract may indicate that the extension of time must be granted before completion whether the delay is caused by the employer or not. Thus in *Miller* v. *L.C.C.*[43] the architect had the power to grant an extension, and "to assign such other time or times for completion as to him may seem reasonable." It was held that these words were not apt to refer to the fixing of a date *ex post facto*, and that a purported extension made after completion was invalid, and this though the power of extending could be exercised "prospectively or retrospectively," for "retrospectively" referred to after the causes of delay and not to after completion.[44]

Extension and contractor's claim for damages.   Where the contractor has a claim for damages against the employer for the latter's delay an extension of time does not, in the absence of express words, release the claim.[45]

(h) *Rescission or determination*

If the contract is brought to an end by determination or otherwise, then prima facie all future obligations cease and no claim can be made for liquidated damages accruing after determination.[46] But there may be some special clause which has the effect of keeping the provision for payment of liquidated damages alive although the work has been taken out of the hands of the contractor.[47]

---

[42] Denning L.J. in *Amalgamated Building Contractors Ltd.* v. *Waltham Holy Cross Urban District Council* [1952] 2 All E.R. 452 at 454 (C.A.).

[43] (1934) 50 T.L.R. 479.

[44] The delay was caused by the employer but the case was distinguished by Denning L.J. in the *Amalgamated Building Contractors Ltd.* v. *Waltham Holy Cross Urban District Council* [1952] 2 All E.R. 452 at 454 (C.A.) primarily because of the wording of the clause referred to in the text.

[45] *Trollope & Colls* v. *Singer* (1913) H.B.C. (4th ed.), Vol. 1, p. 849, and see *Roberts* v. *Bury Commissioners* (1870) L.R. 5 C.P. 310 at 327.

[46] See *Ex p. Sir W. Hart Dyke, re Morrish* (1882) 22 Ch.D. 410 (C.A.) (forfeiture of a lease); *British Glanzstoff Manufacturing Co. Ltd.* v. *General Accident, etc., Ltd.* [1913] A.C. 143 (H.L.); *Suisse Atlantique, etc.* v. *N.V. Rotterdamsche Kolen Centrale* [1967] 1 A.C. 361 at 398 (H.L.), and see generally pp. 236 *et seq. cf. Wood* v. *Tendring Rural Sanitary Authority* (1886) 3 T.L.R. 272 (D.C.).

[47] See *Re Yeadon Waterworks Co. & Wright* (1895) 72 L.T. 832 (C.A.). In such a case there is no determination of the contract but only a forfeiture of certain rights; see p. 237.

DEFAULT OF THE PARTIES—VARIOUS MATTERS

1. Forfeiture Clauses

The contractor has a licence to occupy the site for the purposes of the contract.[1] If the employer revokes the licence before completion, thus preventing the contractor carrying out the work, there is prima facie a repudiation by the employer.[2] To justify his act he must show either that there was a repudiation by the contractor which he has accepted,[3] or that he has acted under an express power of the contract contained in what is sometimes called a forfeiture clause.

---

[1] *Joshua Henshaw & Sons* v. *Rochdale Corporation* [1944] K.B. 381 (C.A.); *Hounslow London Borough Council* v. *Twickenham Garden Developments* [1971] Ch. 233, where Megarry J., in a judgment discussed at p. 270, considered the nature of the contractor's licence under the Standard Form of Building Contract; *cf. Surrey Heath Borough Council* v. *Lovell Construction* (1988) 42 B.L.R. 25 at 51.

[2] See p. 156.

[3] See pp. 153 *et seq.* and see especially "Repudiation and contractual determination clauses" at p. 153.

(a) *The nature of forfeiture clauses*

"Forfeiture clause" is a loose term used to describe a clause in a written building contract giving the employer the right upon the happening of an event to determine the contract or the contractor's employment under it, or to eject the contractor from the site, or otherwise to take the work substantially out of his hands.[4] The right may be stated to arise upon the happening of any event,[5] provided there is no illegality, and the clause is not void because it is contrary to the policy of the law, *e.g.* that materials should be forfeited on bankruptcy.[6] So far as the right arises on bankruptcy, it is discussed in Section 5 of Chapter 15. Examples of other events upon which the right can arise are[7] not proceeding with the works to the satisfaction of the architect,[8] not proceeding with due diligence,[9] not completing to time,[10] and not complying with the architect's orders.[11] Events which give rise to a contractual right to determine may or may not also amount to repudiation.[12] It is thought that the court would not normally exercise its equitable jurisdiction to grant relief against forfeiture where a party operates or purports to operate a forfeiture clause in a building contract.[13]

(b) *The mode of forfeiture*

Compliance with the contract. The requirements of the contract must be properly complied with, for the courts construe forfeiture clauses strictly,[14] and a wrongful forfeiture by the employer or his agent normally amounts to a repudiation on the part of the employer.[15] There must be some definite

---

[4] In this sense clause 27 of the Standard Form of Building Contract is a forfeiture clause although the word "forfeiture" is never used. Note that clause 28 gives the contractor the right of bringing his employment to an end upon the happening of certain events. For commentary on these clauses, see pp. 590 *et seq.*

[5] *Davies* v. *Swansea Corporation* (1853) 22 L.J. Ex. 297.

[6] See p. 379.

[7] For a longer list, see H.B.C. (7th ed.), p. 404.

[8] *Davies* v. *Swansea Corporation* (1853) 22 L.J. Ex. 297.

[9] *Roberts* v. *Bury Commissioners* (1870) L.R. 5 C.P. 310; *Canterbury Pipe Lines* v. *Christchurch Drainage* (1979) 16 B.L.R. 76 (New Zealand Court of Appeal).

[10] *Marsden* v. *Sambell* (1880) 43 L.T. 120.

[11] *Hunt* v. *S.E. Railway* (1875) 45 L.J.Q.B. 87; *Canterbury Pipe Lines* v. *Christchurch Drainage* (1979) 16 B.L.R. 76 (New Zealand Court of Appeal).

[12] See "Repudiation and contractual determination clauses" at p. 153.

[13] See "Relief against forfeiture" at p. 241. This is a different question from whether an injunction will issue to enforce or restrain a forfeiture as to which see "Injunction to enforce disputed forfeiture" at p. 270.

[14] *Roberts* v. *Bury Commissioners* (1870) L.R. 5 C.P. 310 at 326; in *Hill* v. *London Borough of Camden* (1980) 18 B.L.R. 31 at 47 (C.A.) the court did not welcome a "blatantly formalistic point" taken to defeat a determination; see also *Goodwin & Sons* v. *Fawcett* (1965) 195 E.G. 27; *cf. Eriksson* v. *Whalley* [1971] 1 N.S.W.L.R. 397; *Central Provident* v. *Ho Bock Kee* (1981) 17 B.L.R. 21 (Singapore Court of Appeal).

[15] *Lodder* v. *Slowey* [1904] A.C. 442 (P.C.), and see p. 156 for repudiation, and p. 207 for the contractor's claim for damages.

unqualified act showing that the power has been exercised, although writing or other formality is not necessary unless expressly required.[16] The contract may require a certain notice to be given, and that such notice must set out the default complained of.[17] In appropriate circumstanced the notice may be of a general character and need not necessarily refer to the number of the clause which is being invoked, provided that there is no doubt that it is exercising or purporting to exercise the contractual power of determination.[18] But it is obviously preferable to state explicitly the clause relied on and to follow its actual wording as closely as possible. It seems that if a material statement in such a notice is made recklessly, without an honest belief in its truth, the notice is a nullity.[19] Forfeiture in reliance on such a notice would be ineffective and would normally amount to repudiation by the employer.

Ascertainment of the event. Where the architect has the power to ascertain whether the event giving rise to the right to forfeit has arisen, his decision can only be attacked in those circumstances, described in Chapter 5,[20] where his certificates can be attacked.[21] If the contract gives the employer the right to ascertain whether the event has arisen, his determination must, in the absence of words to the contrary, be reasonable.[22] But the contract may make it clear that he is entitled to exercise a right of forfeiture when, in his opinion, whether reasonable or not, the event, such as delay, has arisen.[23] It may be reasonable for a main contractor, himself under onerous obligations to complete, to forfeit a sub-contract, where the exercise of a similar power by the employer would be unreasonable.[24] Where a Standard Form of Building Contract provided that the contractor should not give a notice determining his employment "unreasonably or vexatiously," it was held that the test of reasonableness was that of a reasonable contractor, circumstanced in all respects as was the contractor at

---

[16] *Drew* v. *Josolyne* (1887) 14 Q.B.D. 590 at 597 (C.A.); see also *Marsden* v. *Sambell* (1880) 43 L.T. 120 where it was held to be no exercise of a right of forfeiture by the employer merely sending an agent "to keep an eye" on houses being built. For a sale of land case, see *Aquis Estates Ltd.* v. *Minton* [1975] 1 W.L.R. 1452 (C.A.).

[17] See *Pauling* v. *Dover Corporation* (1855) 24 L.J. Ex. 128; *cf. Boot & Sons Ltd.* v. *Uttoxeter Urban District Council* (1924) 88 J.P. 118 (C.A.).

[18] *Supamarl* v. *Federated Homes* (1981) 9 Con.L.R. 25 at 30; *cf. Hounslow London Borough Council* v. *Twickenham Garden Developments* [1971] Ch. 233 at 264; *Architectural Installation Services* v. *James Gibbons Windows* (1989) 46 B.L.R. 91 at 97.

[19] See *Earl of Stradbroke* v. *Mitchell, The Times*, October 4, 1990 (C.A.)—a case concerning a notice to quit served under the Agricultural Holdings Act 1986.

[20] See p. 110.

[21] See *Northampton Gas Light Co.* v. *Parnell* (1855) 15 C.B. 630 where the architects' decision was not conclusive.

[22] *Stadhard* v. *Lee* (1863) 3 B. & S. 364; see p. 98.

[23] *Stadhard* v. *Lee* (1863) 3 B. & S. 364; *cf. Diggle* v. *Ogston Motor Co.* (1915) 112 L.T. 1029; *Loke Hong Kee* v. *United Overseas Land* (1982) 23 B.L.R. 35 (P.C.) where a determination clause was construed so that the opinion of the architect that the progress of the works was unsatisfactory was not subject to review by the arbitrator. The function of the arbitrator was limited to deciding whether as a matter of fact the opinion was given and was bona fide (at 46).

[24] *Stadhard* v. *Lee* (1863) 3 B. & S. 364.

the time when he gave the notice to determine. "Vexatiously" connotes an ulterior motive to oppress, harass or annoy.[25]

Time of forfeiture. When an event occurs which gives rise to the right to forfeit, the power of forfeiture must be exercised within a reasonable time or the employer will be deemed to have waived his right unless the event is a continuing breach of contract.[26] Where the contract provides for termination of the contract by a warning notice followed by a termination notice and two notices have been served, a party can only rely on that provision if an ordinary commercial businessman can see that there is a sensible connection between the two notices both in content and in time.[27] And the employer cannot exercise his right if the rights of third parties have intervened, or if he has treated the contract as subsisting.[28] But he can forfeit if a fresh event arises.[29]

Where the contract provides for completion by a certain date and also provides for forfeiture for delay, and the completion date has passed, it is a question of construction whether the forfeiture clause for delay can still be enforced. Thus where the object of the clause was to enable the architect to "have the means of requiring the works to be proceeded with in such a manner and at such a rate of progress as to ensure their completion at the time stipulated" it was held that the clause did not apply after the completion date.[30] But in another contract where the clause provided "for the execution of the work with due diligence and as much expedition as the surveyor shall require," it was held that the clause was as much applicable to the fulfilment of the contract within a reasonable time as to its completion by the contract date. Therefore a forfeiture under the terms of the clause was valid although the original date of completion had been ignored by the parties.[31] It should be noted that many contracts provide for the extension of the original completion date.[32]

(c) *Employer's default*

Forfeiture by the employer is wrongful if he or his agents have, in breach of a

---

[25] *John Jarvis* v. *Rockdale Housing Association* (1986) 36 B.L.R. 48 at 68 (C.A.); see also the commentary on clauses 27 and 28 of the Standard Form of Building Contract at pp. 590 *et seq.*

[26] *Marsden* v. *Sambell* (1880) 43 L.T. 120; *Aquis Estates Ltd.* v. *Minton* [1975] 1 W.L.R. 1452 (C.A.); *cf. Mvita Construction* v. *Tanzania Harbours Authority* (1988) 46 B.L.R. 19 at 30, 31 (Tanzanian Court of Appeal) citing this passage in the 4th edition of this book.

[27] *Architectural Installation Services* v. *James Gibbons Windows* (1989) 46 B.L.R. 91 at 98.

[28] *Marsden* v. *Sambell* (1880) 43 L.T. 120 at 122; *Re Garrud, ex p. Newitt* (1881) 16 Ch.D. 522 at 533 (C.A.); *Platt* v. *Parker* (1886) 2 T.L.R. 786 at 787 (C.A.); *cf. Hughes* v. *Metropolitan Railway* (1877) 2 App.Cas. 439 (H.L.); *Tool Metal Manufacturing Co. Ltd.* v. *Tungsten Electric Co. Ltd.* [1955] 1 W.L.R. 761 (H.L.); *Australian Blue Metal Ltd.* v. *Hughes* [1963] A.C. 74 (P.C.); *Alan (W. J.) & Co.* v. *El Nasr Co.* [1972] 2 Q.B. 189 (C.A.); *Woodhouse A.C.* v. *Nigerian Produce Co.* [1972] A.C. 741 (H.L.); *Bremer Handelsgesellschaft* v. *Finagrain* [1981] 2 Lloyd's Rep. 259 at 263 (C.A.).

[29] *Stevens* v. *Taylor* (1860) 2 F. & F. 419; *Re Garrud, ex p. Newitt* (1881) 16 Ch.D. 522 (C.A.).

[30] *Walker* v. *L. & N.W. Railway* (1876) 1 C.P.D. 518 at 530.

[31] *Joshua Henshaw & Sons* v. *Rochdale Corporation* [1944] K.B. 381 (C.A.); *cf. Canterbury Pipe Lines* v. *Christchurch Drainage* (1979) 16 B.L.R. 76 at 108 *et seq.* (New Zealand Court of Appeal).

[32] See p. 233.

contractual duty owed to the contractor,[33] been the means of bringing about the event which gave rise to the right to forfeit,[34] *e.g.* where delay by the contractor was caused by the wrongful failure of the architect to give proper plans,[35] or by the wrongful and improper withholding of a certificate by the architect.[36]

(d) *Effect of forfeiture*

The parties may agree that any consequences may follow the exercise of a right of forfeiture,[37] provided there is no illegality, nor fraud on the bankruptcy law,[38] and the clause is not so onerous that it will not be enforced on the grounds that it is a penalty.[39] The employer is usually given the right to take possession of the site and complete the works.[40] In addition there is frequently a clause vesting the property in unfixed materials, and perhaps plant, in the employer,[41] or there may be merely a right to seize the materials[42] or hold them by way of lien[43] until they are built into the works, or there may be clauses giving the employer rights to use the contractor's plant and materials.[44] Some of these matters are considered further in the next section.

Bills of sale. The ordinary forfeiture clause is not within the Bills of Sale Acts 1878 and 1882. The contract in which it is contained does not therefore require to be registered under the Acts.[45]

Employer's duty to account. When an employer in exercise of his rights under a forfeiture clause enters and completes the work and uses the contractor's materials or plant, or holds retention money due to the contractor, he must, subject to the provisions of the contract, account to the contractor, *i.e.* show that the materials and plant and money were expended reasonably.[46] But

---

[33] *Cheall* v. *A.P.E.X.* [1983] 2 A.C. 180 at 189 (H.L.); *cf. Thompson* v. *ASDA-MFI Group* [1988] Ch. 241.

[34] *Roberts* v. *Bury Commissioners* (1870) L.R. 5 C.P. 310; *New Zealand Shipping Co. Ltd.* v. *Ateliers de France* [1919] A.C. 1 (H.L.); *Alghussein Establishment* v. *Eton College* [1988] 1 W.L.R. 587 (H.L.).

[35] *Roberts* v. *Bury Commissioners* (1870) L.R. 5 C.P. 310; *cf. Stevens* v. *Taylor* (1860) 2 F. & F. 419.

[36] *Smith* v. *Howden Union* (1890) H.B.C. (4th ed.), Vol. 2, p. 156. For certificates generally, see Chap. 5.

[37] *Davies* v. *Swansea Corporation* (1853) 22 L.J. Ex. 297.

[38] See pp. 379 *et seq.*

[39] See p. 224 and *cf. Modern Engineering* v. *Gilbert-Ash* [1974] A.C. 689 at 698, 704, 711 (H.L.). See also "Forfeiture clauses as penalties" at p. 228.

[40] For a comprehensive list of clauses which had then come before the courts, see H.B.C. (7th ed.), p. 432.

[41] See further p. 244.

[42] See *Baker* v. *Gray* (1856) 25 L.J.C.P. 161.

[43] See *Re Waugh, ex p. Dickin* (1876) 4 Ch.D. 524.

[44] See *Hawthorn* v. *Newcastle, etc., Railway* (1840) 3 Q.B. 734n.; *Re Winters, ex p. Bolland* (1878) 8 Ch.D. 225.

[45] *Brown* v. *Bateman* (1867) L.R. 2 C.P. 272; *Re Garrud, ex p. Newitt* (1881) 16 Ch.D. 522 (C.A.).

[46] *Ranger* v. *G.W. Railway* (1854) 5 H.L.C. 72 (H.L.).

the court would, it seems, in principle, make full allowance for extra cost caused by the disruption and delay occasioned by the contractor's default.[47]

Employer's claim for damages. Where the employer determines the contract under a forfeiture clause because of some breach of contract by the contractor, the employer's right to damages depends upon the wording of the contract. He may not be entitled to the enhanced cost of completing by another contractor if the breach for which he determined the contract did not amount to a repudiation and the contract does not so provide.[48]

Relief against forfeiture.[49] In some instances, notably with forfeiture clauses in leases for non-payment of rent, the court has an equitable jurisdiction to grant relief against forfeiture. This is usually on condition that the defendant pays an appropriate sum of money with interest and costs.[50] It is thought most unlikely that the court would ever grant this remedy to relieve a contractor from the consequences of a forfeiture clause in a building contract.[51]

Injunctions to enforce or restrain forfeiture. These are discussed in Section 6 of Chapter 11 at page 270.

2. Materials and Plant

(a) *Ownership of materials and plant*

Materials brought onto the site by the contractor remain his property, in the absence of a provision to the contrary, until they become affixed to the land, *i.e.* are built into the works,[52] whereupon they become the property of the owner of the freehold.[53] If the employer has an estate or interest less than the freehold, he enjoys the property during such estate or interest.[54] In the case of ships the

---

[47] *cf. Dunkirk Colliery Co.* v. *Lever* (1878) 9 Ch.D. 20 at 25 (C.A.); see also *Fulton* v. *Dornwell* (1885) 4 N.Z.L.R. 207; *Dillon* v. *Jack* (1903) 23 N.Z.L.R. 547.

[48] *Feather* v. *Keighley Corporation* (1953) 52 L.G.R. 30, see further p. 155. The express words of the clause often give him the right to recover such costs. See also "Repudiation and contractual determination clauses" at p. 153.

[49] See also "Forfeiture clauses as penalties" at p. 228.

[50] See, *e.g. Jobson* v. *Johnson* [1989] 1 W.L.R. 1026 at 1041 (C.A.).

[51] See by analogy *Scandinavian Trading* v. *Flota Ecuatoriana* [1983] 2 A.C. 694 (H.L.) where such relief was held inappropriate in the case of a withdrawal clause under a time charterparty for practical reasons and because it was a contract for services for which specific performance would not be granted; *Sport International* v. *Inter-Footwear* [1984] 1 W.L.R. 776 (H.L.); *cf. B.I.C.C.* v. *Burndy Corporation* [1985] Ch. 232 (C.A.); *The Fanti and Padre Island* [1989] 1 Lloyd's Rep. 239 (C.A.) where Saville J. had held at first instance that the doctrine of relief against forfeiture was inapplicable to a commercial contract; *cf.* however *Hounslow L.B.C.* v. *Twickenham Garden Developments* [1971] Ch. 233.

[52] *Tripp* v. *Armitage* (1839) 4 M. & W. 687; *cf. Dawber Williamson* v. *Humberside County Council* (1979) 14 B.L.R. 70; *Hanson* v. *Rapid Civil Engineering* (1987) 38 B.L.R. 106.

[53] *Elwes* v. *Maw* (1802) 3 East 38.

[54] *Ibid.*

property passes when the materials are fixed, "or, in a reasonable sense, made part of the corpus."[55]

When the property has passed, the contractor cannot, without an express right remove the materials even though the employer may have severed them and they are no longer fixed,[56] but if he is under an obligation to keep the property in repair for a certain period then it seems that he will have an implied right to remove and replace defective materials during the period.[57]

Where there is a clause providing for the certification of the amount payable to the contractor in respect of materials upon their delivery, it appears that the property passes upon the making of the relevant certificate even though the materials are not fixed.[58]

In the case of plant erected for the purposes of the work and attached to the land so that technically it is fixed, there is sometimes an express provision for its removal by the contractor. But in any event it is submitted that, by analogy with so-called trade fixtures in the law of landlord and tenant,[59] it would not pass to the freeholder. If the property in such plant has, by express agreement, passed to the employer, it is implied that upon completion it revests in the contractor and can be removed.[60] In the absence of express agreement to the contrary it seems that hoardings erected by the contractor remain his property so that he can let them for advertising.[61]

Retention of title clauses.[62] Under contracts for the sale of goods, the legal property in specific or ascertained goods is transferred to the buyer at such time as the parties to the contract intend it to be transferred, regard being had to the terms of the contract, the conduct of the parties and the circumstances of the case.[63] Where suppliers contract to supply materials for building contracts, unless the contract expressly stipulates otherwise, the property will usually pass not later than the time when they are delivered.[64] A clause in a contract for the sale of building materials, providing for the full legal ownership in the materials to remain with the seller until payment is made may be effective

---

[55] *Seath* v. *Moore* (1886) 11 App.Cas. 350 at 381 (H.L.); for other cases on ships, see *Re Salmon and Woods, ex p. Gould* (1885) 2 Morr.Bkptcy.Cas. 137; *Reid* v. *Macbeth & Gray* [1904] A.C. 223 (H.L.); *Re Blyth Shipbuilding, etc., Co. Ltd.* [1926] Ch. 494 (C.A.). *cf. McDougall* v. *Aeromarine Ltd.* [1958] 1 W.L.R. 1126.

[56] *Lyde* v. *Russell* (1830) 1 B. & Ad. 394.

[57] *Appleby* v. *Myers* (1867) L.R. 2 C.P. 651 at 659.

[58] *Banbury, etc., Railway* v. *Daniel* (1884) 54 L.J.Ch. 265. For the passing of property in contracts for the sale of goods, see s.17 of the Sale of Goods Act 1979. For an example between contractor and supplier, see *Pritchett, etc., Co. Ltd.* v. *Currie* [1916] 2 Ch. 515 (C.A.).

[59] See Woodfall's *Landlord and Tenant* (28th ed.), paras. 1–1554–1–1556.

[60] *Hart* v. *Porthgain Harbour Co. Ltd.* [1903] 1 Ch. 690.

[61] *Partington Advertising Co.* v. *Willing & Co.* (1896) 12 T.L.R. 176.

[62] See generally, G. Antoinette Williams, "Reservation of Title in the Construction Industry: Who wants it?—Some Economic Perspectives on Risk-Allocation" (1987) 3 Const.L.J. 252.

[63] s.17 of the Sale of Goods Act 1979; *cf. McEntire* v. *Crossley Brothers* [1895] A.C. 457 (H.L.).

[64] See s.18 of the Sale of Goods Act 1979. Under the rule in this section, the property may pass earlier than upon delivery.

against a liquidator or trustee.[65] But such a clause may not effectively extend beyond the time when the materials are incorporated into the works,[66] and the clause on its true construction may create a registrable charge so that attempts to acquire rights over the finished product including any proceeds of sale may be ineffective for want of registration under section 395 of the Companies Act 1985.[67] Where, however, there are permitted sub-sales of unaltered materials, a clause retaining title and making the purchaser trustee for the seller of the materials or the proceeds of their sub-sale may be effective.[68] The abolition under the Insolvency Act 1986 of the doctrine of reputed ownership[69] may have removed one potential obstacle to the effectiveness of retention of title clauses.

A clause in a main contract, stipulating that the property in unfixed materials was to pass to the employer when their value had been included in an interim certificate under which the contractor had received payment, was held ineffective to transfer to the employer the property in a sub-contractor's materials where the property in them had not passed from the sub-contractor to the contractor. A clause in the sub-contract that the sub-contractor was deemed to have notice of all the provisions of the main contract did not operate to make the main contract clause part of the sub-contract.[70] If, however, the materials are supplied under a contract of sale, rather than a contract for work and materials,[71] the employer may claim that he has acquired a good title to them under section 25(1) of the Sale of Goods Act 1979. Such a claim would in principle succeed where the contractor, having possession of the materials with the consent of the seller, delivers or transfers them to the employer who receives them in good faith without notice that the seller has retained the property in them.[72]

---

[65] *Aluminium Industrie Vaassen* v. *Romalpa Aluminium* [1976] 1 W.L.R. 676 (C.A.); *John Snow* v. *Woodcroft* (1985) B.C.L.C. 54; *cf. Armour* v. *Thyssen Edelstahlwerke A.G.* [1990] 3 W.L.R. 810 (H.L.(Sc.)).

[66] See *Borden (U.K.)* v. *Scottish Timber* [1981] Ch. 25 (C.A.); *cf. Hendy Lennox* v. *Grahame Puttick* [1984] 1 W.L.R. 485, where engines incorporated without change into generating sets remained the seller's property until the generating sets became the property of sub-buyers; *Re Andrabell Ltd.* [1984] 3 All E.R. 407.

[67] *In re Bond Worth Ltd.* [1980] Ch. 228; *In re Peachdart* [1984] Ch. 131; *Clough Mill Ltd.* v. *Martin* [1984] 1 W.L.R. 1067; *Pfeiffer G.m.b.H.* v. *Arbuthnot Factors* [1988] 1 W.L.R. 150; *cf. Borden (U.K.) Scottish Timber* [1981] Ch. 25 at 42 (C.A.). For the characteristics of a charge, see *In re George Inglefield* [1933] Ch. 1 at 27 (C.A.). s.395 of the Companies Act 1985 will be amended when ss.93–107 of the Companies Act 1989 are brought into force. The section which will then render an unregistered charge void will be amended s.399 of the Companies Act 1985 and there will be other changes, *e.g.* in amended ss.404 and 405.

[68] *Aluminium Industrie Vaassen* v. *Romalpa Aluminium* [1976] 1 W.L.R. 676 (C.A.) applying *In re Hallett's Estate* (1880) 13 Ch.D. 696 (C.A.); *cf. In re Bond Worth Ltd.* [1980] Ch. 228.

[69] See "Vesting of property" at p. 244.

[70] *Dawber Williamson* v. *Humberside County Council* (1979) 14 B.L.R. 70; *cf. Hanson* v. *Rapid Civil Engineering* (1987) 38 B.L.R. 106; see also clause 16 of the Standard Form of Building Contract and in particular "Passing of property" at p. 526.

[71] The relevant point is that the Sale of Goods Act 1979 applies to the former but not the latter—see s.1(1) of that Act.

[72] See *Archivent* v. *Strathclyde Regional Council* (1984) 27 B.L.R. 98 (Court of Session—Outer House); *Four Point Garage* v. *Carter* [1985] 3 All E.R. 12; *cf. Hanson* v. *Rapid Civil Engineering* (1987) 38

(b) *Vesting clauses*

It is common to have a clause which purports to vest materials and sometimes plant in the employer before they are fixed.[73] The principal objects of such a clause are to provide a security to the employer for money advanced and to enable the employer to obtain the speedy completion of the works by another contractor in the event of the original contractor's default, by providing materials and plant on the site ready to use free from the claims of the original contractor, and his creditors, or his trustee in bankruptcy or liquidator. Whether or not the clause achieves its purpose depends upon the words used.[74] If the formula used is "the materials shall become and be,"[75] or "be and become"[76] the property of the employer, then normally "the clause means what it says, operates according to its tenor, and effectively transfers the title."[77] If, on the other hand, words like "considered to be,"[78] or "deemed to be" (the property of the employer) are used, the clause may be ineffective to achieve its purpose and the property may remain in the contractor.[79] Even so the contract must, it is submitted, be read as a whole to ascertain the intention of the parties.

In one case although the materials had become vested in the employer they were subject to such rights on the part of the contractor that they could not be seized by the sheriff under an execution upon a judgment against the employer.[80]

Where the materials and plant have vested in the employer there are normally implied rights on the part of the contractor to the use of the materials and plant for the purposes of the contract,[81] and to the revesting and removal of unused materials and plant upon completion.[82] Further the contractor may have a right and perhaps an obligation to replace defective materials.[83]

Bills of sale. The ordinary vesting clause does not operate as a bill of sale.[84]

B.L.R. 106, where there was held to have been no sale or disposition transferring the materials to the employer.

[73] See, *e.g.* clause 16 of the Standard Form of Building Contract discussed at p. 525.

[74] *Bennett, etc., Ltd.* v. *Sugar City* [1951] A.C. 786 (P.C.).

[75] *Ibid.*

[76] See *Reeves* v. *Barlow* (1884) 12 Q.B.D. 436 (C.A.).

[77] Lord Reid in *Bennett, etc., Ltd.* v. *Sugar City* [1951] A.C. 786 at 814 (P.C.). The clause is not effective if it contravenes the principles of the bankruptcy law, see p. 379.

[78] See *Re Keen, ex p. Collins* [1902] 1 K.B. 555; *cf. Brown* v. *Bateman* (1867) L.R. 2 C.P. 272; *Hart* v. *Porthgain Harbour Co. Ltd.* [1903] 1 Ch. 690.

[79] *Bennett, etc., Ltd.* v. *Sugar City* [1951] A.C. 786 at 814 (P.C.); *cf. Re Winter, ex p. Bolland* (1878) 8 Ch.D. 225.

[80] *Beeston* v. *Marriott* (1863) 8 L.T. 690.

[81] *Bennett, etc., Ltd.* v. *Sugar City* [1951] A.C. 786 (P.C.). For an express right, see *Beeston* v. *Marriott* (1863) 8 L.T. 690.

[82] *Hart* v. *Porthgain Harbour Co. Ltd.* [1903] 1 Ch. 690.

[83] *Appleby* v. *Myers* (1867) L.R. 2 C.P. 651.

[84] *Brown* v. *Bateman* (1867) L.R. 2 C.P. 272; *Re Garrud, ex p. Newitt* (1881) 16 Ch.D. 522 (C.A.). See p. 240.

Vesting clause operating on bankruptcy. Such a clause is prima facie void.[85]

3. Lien

A lien in the broad sense of a right of one party to retain the property of the other frequently arises under a building contract. It may be express[86] or implied.[87] An implied lien over unfixed materials may arise in favour of the employer where he has advanced money to the contractor on the security of such materials.[88] Where there is an express provision for a lien on unfixed materials to arise in favour of the employer upon giving notice to the contractor, the right to the lien is lost if before the notice is given the materials have been seized by the sheriff under a *fi. fa.*[89] A lien is ordinarily effective against a receiver of a company,[90] but so far as a right of lien may arise upon the bankruptcy of the contractor, it is on general principles void as against his trustee in bankruptcy.[91]

4. Defects and Maintenance Clauses

There is frequently a clause in building contracts which provides that the contractor shall make good defects, or repair or maintain the works for a certain period after completion. This period is sometimes referred to as the "defects liability period" or "maintenance period." As a security for the contractor's observance of his obligations, part of the contract sum, termed retention money, is usually retained by the employer until the end of the period, and is not released until the architect gives a certificate evidencing his satisfaction that the works accord with the contract.[92]

(a) *Meaning of terms*

The nature and extent of the obligations of the contractor, and the rights of the employer vary according to the terms of each contract, but in general an

---

[85] See p. 379.

[86] See *Banbury, etc., Railway* v. *Daniel* (1884) 54 L.J.Ch. 265. *cf. Poulton* v. *Wilson* (1858) 1 F. & F. 403.

[87] *Tripp* v. *Armitage* (1839) 4 M. & W. 687; *Re Waugh, ex p. Dickin* (1876) 4 Ch.D. 524. There is no statutory lien on land in favour of contractors as in some jurisdictions, *e.g.* Ontario: Construction Lien legislation.

[88] *Ibid.*

[89] *Byford* v. *Russell* [1907] 2 K.B. 522 (D.C.).

[90] *George Barker (Transport) Ltd.* v. *Eynon* [1974] 1 W.L.R. 462 (C.A.).

[91] See p. 379.

[92] See *National Coal Board* v. *William Neill* [1985] Q.B. 300 at 321; and see clause 17 of the Standard Form of Building Contract discussed on p. 528. For certificates, see Chap. 5.

obligation to maintain the works imposes a wider duty than one merely to make good defects, and extends to matters of wear and tear, whereas a defects clause does not.[93] An obligation to repair the works may include the rebuilding of parts destroyed by flood or fire,[94] but, subject to express terms, if substantially the whole of the works is destroyed the contract is frustrated and the liability ceases.[95] Under a repairing clause the contractor has ordinarily an implied right, if he thinks it necessary for its fulfilment, to replace parts of the works,[96] though the extent of any duty of replacement must depend, it is submitted, on the nature of the works, the degree to which he had the right of selecting materials or design, and whether there is also an express clause, *e.g.* in an engineering contract, to keep in working order.[97]

(b) *Investigation for defects*

The nature and extent of the investigations which the employer should carry out if he is to obtain the full benefit of a defects clause depends upon the circumstances of each case and on the wording of the clause. In a contract to construct sewers the contractor undertook to maintain and keep them in proper working order for three months after completion, and to amend and make good all defects which should appear within that period. After two months a stoppage occurred in a sewer, but the cause, the extensive failure to concrete bends properly, was not discovered until after the end of the three months. It was held that the employer was entitled under the clause to recover the cost of making good the defective work.[98] In a contract to construct a road the contractor was liable to make good bad work discovered within five years. Just before the expiry of the period the employer discovered by means of trial borings that the concrete was defective and not in accordance with the contract. Further investigations after the expiry of the period showed similar defects in many other parts of the road, but it was held that the employer was limited to a claim for the defects actually discovered within the five years.[99]

(c) *Notice is required*

If the contractor is not in possession of the site then in the absence of express

<hr>

[93] *Sevenoaks, etc., Railway* v. *London, Chatham, etc., Railway* (1879) 11 Ch.D. 625.

[94] *Brecknock and Abergavenny Canal Navigation* v. *Pritchard* (1796) 6 Term Rep. 750. For some assistance see *Smith & Snipes Hall Farm Ltd.* v. *River Douglas Catchment Board* [1949] 2 K.B. 500 (C.A.).

[95] *Appleby* v. *Myers* (1867) L.R. 2 C.P. 651; see further p. 139.

[96] *Appleby* v. *Myers* (1867) L.R. 2 C.P. 651.

[97] As in *Appleby* v. *Myers* (1867) L.R. 2 C.P. 651. Some assistance may be gained from the construction of repairing covenants in leases, see *Proudfoot* v. *Hart* (1890) 25 Q.B.D. 42 (C.A.); *Lurcott* v. *Wakely* [1911] 1 K.B. 905 (C.A.); *Post Office* v. *Aquarius Properties* [1987] 1 All E.R. 1055 (C.A.) and the cases there considered. See further Woodfall's *Landlord and Tenant* (28th ed.), Chap. 13, Section 1.

[98] *Cunliffe* v. *The Hampton Wick Local Board* (1893) 9 T.L.R. 378, H.B.C. (4th ed.), Vol. 2, p. 250 (C.A.).

[99] *Marsden Urban District Council* v. *Sharp* (1931) 47 T.L.R. 549; affd. 48 T.L.R. 23 (C.A.) and explained by Diplock L.J. in *Hancock* v. *Brazier, B. W. (Anerley) Ltd.* [1966] 2 All E.R. 1. For the alternative claim in damages, see below.

terms to the contrary, notice of the defects is, it seems, necessary before he can become liable and if the employer without giving notice to the contractor amends defects himself he cannot rely on the defects clause as against the contractor.[1] "The reason of the thing is this, that, where there is knowledge in the one party and not in the other there notice is necessary."[2] It has not been decided what the position would be if the contractor is not given notice but has actual knowledge. His liability in such a case would depend on the wording of the contract, *e.g.* the contract may make the giving of notice a condition precedent to the contractor's liability. If the contractor knows of the defect and states that he will not carry out his obligation or disables himself from carrying it out, he may, it seems, be liable despite the absence of notice.[3]

(d) *Alternative claim in damages*

The contractor's liability in damages is not removed by the existence of a defects clause except by clear words,[4] so that in the absence of such words the clause confers an additional right and does not operate to exclude the contractor's liability for breach of contract.[5] Clear words in this context usually require the kind of architect's binding and conclusive certificate referred to under the next heading. It is a matter of construction in each case whether a term relating to defects and headed "Guarantee" is an exclusion clause to be construed against the contractor or confers an additional right and is therefore to be construed like any other term.[6] But it is thought that most defects liability clauses will be construed to give the contractor the right, as well as to impose the obligation, to remedy defects which come within the clause. If the employer fails to give notice, or otherwise to avail himself of a defects clause and brings a claim for damages he may, on the principle of mitigation of loss,[7] be liable to some reduction in the damages which would ordinarily be awarded. He may not be able to recover more than the amount that it would have cost the contractor to perform his obligation.[8]

(e) *Liability after expiry of period*

In the absence of words to the contrary, the contractor's liability for not

---

[1] *London and S.W. Railway* v. *Flower* (1875) 1 C.P.D. 77.

[2] *Ibid.* Brett J. at 85. This principle has been often applied in the law of landlord and tenant, see, *e.g. McCarrick* v. *Liverpool Corporation* [1947] A.C. 219.

[3] *Johnstone* v. *Milling* (1886) 16 Q.B.D. 460 (C.A.) (landlord and tenant).

[4] *Hancock* v. *Brazier (Anerley) Ltd.* [1966] 1 W.L.R. 1317 (C.A.); see also *Billyack* v. *Leyland Construction Co. Ltd.* [1968] 1 W.L.R. 471; *H.W. Nevill (Sunblest)* v. *William Press & Son* (1981) 20 B.L.R. 78 at 88; *cf. National Coal Board* v. *William Neill* [1985] Q.B. 300 at 321.

[5] *Ibid.*

[6] *Adams* v. *Richardson & Starling Ltd.* [1969] 1 W.L.R. 1645 at 1653 (C.A.). For exclusion clauses, see p. 63 and for the effect of the Unfair Contract Terms Act 1977, see p. 66.

[7] *cf. National Coal Board* v. *William Neill* [1985] Q.B. 300 at 321. For mitigation, see p. 190 and for the position under the Standard Form of Building Contract, see p. 531.

[8] See *William Tomkinson* v. *Parochial Church Council of St. Michael* (1990) 6 Const.L.J. 319.

completing the works in accordance with the contract continues until barred by the Limitation Act 1980 and thus extends for the period of six years for a simple contract, and 12 years for a deed, from the date when the cause of action against him arose.[9] A cause of action for ordinary failure to build in accordance with the contract normally arises at practical completion. A cause of action for failure to comply with defects liability obligations normally arises at such later date after practical completion as the contract prescribes for carrying out those obligations.[10] If defects are concealed by the contractor, this may result in an extension of the limitation period.[11] A contractor may be liable under the express terms of a guarantee, warranty or indemnity for many years.[12]

Where there is a defects clause and at the end of the defects liability period a binding and conclusive final certificate of satisfaction is given by the architect then, in the absence of fraud or other special circumstances,[13] the contractor's liability in contract for any defects which may appear thereafter comes to an end,[14] and this notwithstanding that the certificate may have been granted after the commencement of legal proceedings in respect of the defects in question.[15]

5. Guarantees and Bonds

(a) *Guarantees*

A contract of guarantee is a promise to answer for the debt, default or miscarriage of another.[16] An ancillary contract of guarantee or suretyship is frequently entered into as a form of security against the default of one of the parties to the contract or of a person concerned with it. The person giving the guarantee is termed a surety.[17] The surety may guarantee performance by the

---

[9] See Chap. 15, Section 3. The limitation periods in the text do not relate to liability for death or personal injuries. Note that in *Cunliffe* v. *Hampton Wick Local Board* (1893) 9 T.L.R. 378, H.B.C. (4th ed.), Vol. 2, p. 250 (C.A.), it was held that completion of "the several works" meant "the whole works" and not each section thereof.

[10] *cf. Bellway (South East)* v. *Holley* (1984) 28 B.L.R. 139—a decision under a N.H.B.C. House Purchaser's Agreement.

[11] See p. 369.

[12] See, *e.g. Adams* v. *Richardson & Starling Ltd.* [1969] 1 W.L.R. 1645 (C.A.) where the period was 10 years. For liability under an indemnity in relation to limitation, see p. 371.

[13] See Chap. 5.

[14] See "Binding and conclusive certificates" at p. 106.

[15] *Kaye (P. & M.) Ltd.* v. *Hosier & Dickinson* [1972] 1 W.L.R. 147 (H.L) discussed at pp. 108 and 531 in relation to the Standard Form of Building Contract, noting that the question whether the contractor can be liable for consequential losses arising from defects appearing before the certificate may arise under other contracts.

[16] See Statute of Frauds 1677, s.4. The term is not used here in the sense of a guarantee or warranty by a person of his own performance, as to which see p. 130. For the requirement for guarantees to be in writing, see "Contracts of suretyship and guarantee" at p. 27. For "guarantees" as exclusion clauses, consider the Unfair Contract Terms Act 1977 discussed at p. 66.

[17] For a general account of the law of guarantees and suretyship, see *Chitty* (26th ed.), Vol. 2, Chap. 12; *Rowlatt on Principal and Surety* (4th ed.) esp. pp. 225–228.

contractor, payment by the employer, or the fidelity of the architect or any other person connected with the contract who may have responsibility for money. The wording of the principal contract may be such that the obtaining of a surety, or sureties, may be a condition precedent to the right to call for payment.[18]

The ordinary rule is that a surety who discharges the debt is entitled to be indemnified by the debtor but a person who discharges a debt without request from the debtor and under no necessity so to do ordinarily has no right to such indemnity.[19]

Liability of the surety. The liability of the surety depends upon the wording of the contract in each case.[20] In the absence of some special provision a surety for performance by the contractor is not liable for the repayment of loans made by the employer to enable the contractor to complete, of which loans the surety had no knowledge.[21] A surety for performance by the contractor is normally liable for loss due to the contractor's fraud.[22]

Discharge of the surety. Completion or release[23] of the promise guaranteed discharges the surety from further obligation.[24] In a guarantee of completion by the contractor, it seems that completion in fact discharges the surety unless the contract of guarantee expressly requires certificated completion.[25]

Repudiation. An innocent party who accepts the repudiation[26] of his contract by the party whose obligation is guaranteed does not thereby release the surety.[27] Thus a surety guaranteed payment of £40,000 payable by instalments. The debtor defaulted in payment and the creditor accepted his default as a repudiation of the contract at a time when there was £14,000 which had not yet fallen due for payment. It was held that the surety was liable for the total sum due under the contract including the sums not yet payable at the time of acceptance of repudiation.[28]

Fraud. A certificate of completion obtained by the fraud of the contractor does not discharge a surety for completion, because fraud is one of the acts

---

[18] See *Roberts* v. *Brett* (1865) 11 H.L.Cas. 337 (H.L.).
[19] *Owen* v. *Tate* [1976] 1 Q.B. 402 (C.A.), discussed 92 L.Q.R. 188.
[20] *Lewis* v. *Hoare* (1881) 44 L.T. 66 (H.L.). Note what is said below about the specially favoured position of a surety.
[21] *Trade Indemnity Co.* v. *Workington Harbour and Dock Board* [1937] A.C. 1 (H.L.).
[22] *Kingston-upon-Hull Corporation* v. *Harding* [1892] 2 Q.B. 494 (C.A.).
[23] See *Commercial Bank of Tasmania* v. *Jones* [1893] A.C. 313 (P.C.).
[24] *Lewis* v. *Hoare* (1881) 44 L.T. 66 (H.L.).
[25] *Ibid.*
[26] See p. 151.
[27] *Lep Air Services Ltd.* v. *Rolloswin Ltd.* [1973] A.C. 331 (H.l.); *cf. Re Amalgamated Investment and Property Co.* [1985] Ch. 349 at 389 *et seq.*
[28] *Lep Air Services Ltd.* v. *Rolloswin Ltd.* [1973] A.C. 331 (H.L.); *cf. Hyundai Heavy Industries* v. *Papadopoulos* [1980] 1 W.L.R. 1129 (H.L.).

against which the surety has guaranteed, at any rate if it was guaranteed that the work should be "well and truly" done.[29] Neither in such a case does payment of retention money to the contractor discharge the surety, nor failure by the employer to exercise an option of superintendence.[30] But it seems that if there is a duty to superintend, and the fraud is permitted because of failure to perform that duty, the surety is discharged.[31] The surety must be immediately informed of the discovery of any fraud or dishonesty.[32]

Invalid payment. A surety for payment is not discharged if the payment made can be set aside by process of law, as, *e.g.* a payment in fraud of creditors under the bankruptcy law.[33]

Non-disclosure. In some cases a surety may be discharged because of the failure of the person for whose benefit the guarantee is made to disclose some fact affecting the obligation. There is not, as in a contract of insurance, a general duty to disclose all material facts which might affect the mind of the surety, *i.e.* contracts of suretyship are not contracts *uberrimae fidei*[34] but there may be special circumstances which require some disclosure to be made.[35] It has been said that dislosure is necessary if "there is anything that might not naturally be expected to take place between the parties"[36] (referring to the contract of which an obligation is guaranteed). The duty depends upon the particular circumstances of each transaction.[37] Thus a surety for performance was released where the employer had not disclosed that the works were to be executed under the joint supervision of his own surveyor and the surveyor of an undisclosed third party.[38] Where there was a fidelity guarantee, an employer did not disclose to the surety that a servant had previously been dishonest, the surety having no knowledge of this dishonesty. It was held that the employer could not enforce the guarantee upon the subsequent dishonesty of the servant.[39] But in a guarantee of performance by a contractor who was to carry out certain harbour works, a surety could not escape liability because of undisclosed difficulties of terrain, where the building contract had expressly warned the contractor to make all proper inspections of the site himself.[40]

---

[29] *Kingston-upon-Hull Corporation* v. *Harding* [1892] 2 Q.B. 494 (C.A.)—defective work deliberately covered up on approach of clerk of works; discovered after completion and full payment.

[30] *Ibid.*

[31] *Ibid.*

[32] *Phillips* v. *Foxall* (1872) L.R. 7 Q.B. 666.

[33] *Petty* v. *Cooke* (1871) L.R. 6 Q.B. 790.

[34] *Seaton* v. *Heath* [1899] 1 Q.B. 782, 792 (C.A.); reversed on another point [1900] A.C. 135 (H.L.); *Provident Accident & White Cross Insurance Co. Ltd.* v. *Dahne and White* [1937] 2 All E.R. 255.

[35] *Ibid; cf. Toronto Dominion Bank* v. *Rooke* (1984) 49 B.C.L.R. 168 (British Columbia Court of Appeal); see also *Chitty on Contracts* (26th ed.), Vol. 2, para. 5024.

[36] Lord Campbell in *Hamilton* v. *Watson* (1845) 12 Cl. & F. 109, 119 (H.L.).

[37] Lord Atkin in *Trade Indemnity Co.* v. *Workington Harbour & Dock Board* [1937] A.C. 1 at 17 (H.L.).

[38] *Stiff* v. *Eastbourne Local Board* (1869) 20 L.T. 339; Contrast *Russell* v. *Trickett* (1865) 13 L.T. 280.

[39] *London General Omnibus Co. Ltd.* v. *Holloway* [1912] 2 K.B. 72 (C.A.).

[40] *Trade Indemnity Co.* v. *Workington Harbour & Dock Board* [1937] A.C. 1 (H.L.).

Conduct to prejudice of surety (laches). "A surety is undoubtedly and not unjustly the object of some favour both at law and in equity, and . . . is not to be prejudiced by any dealings without his consent between the secured creditor and the principal debtor."[41] Conduct which prejudices the surety's position may discharge the surety's obligation.[42] But "mere omission on the part of the employer, mere passive acquiescence in acts which are improper on the part of the employer, will not release the surety. If there be an omission to do some act which the employer has contracted with the surety to do, or to preserve some security to the benefit of which the surety is entitled, the case is different."[43] Merely irregular conduct on the part of the creditor, even if prejudicial to the interests of the surety, does not discharge the surety. But there may be particular circumstances in which the surety may be discharged, as if the creditor acts in bad faith towards him or is guilty of concealment amounting to misrepresentation or causes or connives at the default by the principal debtor.[44]

Thus a mere failure to exercise an option to superintend on the part of the employer did not release the surety,[45] although it seems that if there had been a duty to superintend and the loss had resulted through failure to exercise that duty the surety would have been released.[46] Similarly a surety will be released from loss resulting from fire if the employer has not carried out a duty to insure the works against fire.[47] In the case of a fidelity guarantee the surety must be immediately informed in the event of any dishonesty on the part of the person whose fidelity is guaranteed.[48]

The release of a co-surety discharges the other sureties to the extent of the contribution which would have been paid by the released surety.[49]

Material alteration in contract. Any material alteration of the obligation guaranteed releases the surety.[50] Thus extending the time for performance releases a surety for completion,[51] unless there is an express provision for the extension of time as, *e.g.* in clause 25 of the Standard Form of Building Contract.[52] It is submitted that on general principles a material variation of

---

[41] Lord Selborne in *Re Sherry* (1884) 25 Ch.D. 692 at 703 (C.A.); *National Bank of Nigeria Ltd.* v. *Oba M. S. Awolesi* [1964] 1 W.L.R. 1311 (P.C.).

[42] *Kingston-upon-Hull Corporation* v. *Harding* [1892] 2 Q.B. 494 (C.A.).

[43] *Ibid.* Bowen L.J. at 508. For failure to give notice to the surety of the contractors' default as expressly required by a bond, see *Clyde Bank, etc., Trustees* v. *Fidelity & Deposit Co. of Maryland* 1916 S.C. (H.L.) 69.

[44] See *Bank of India* v. *Patel* [1983] 2 Lloyd's Rep. 298 at 302 (C.A.) upholding Bingham J. at [1982] 1 Lloyd's Rep. 506 at 515.

[45] *Kingston-upon-Hull Corporation* v. *Harding* [1892] 2 Q.B. 494 (C.A.).

[46] *Ibid.*

[47] *Watts* v. *Shuttleworth* (1861) 7 H. & N. 353.

[48] *Phillips* v. *Foxall* (1872) L.R. 7 Q.B. 666.

[49] *Re Wolmershausen* (1890) 62 L.T. 541.

[50] See cases cited below and *National Bank of Nigeria Ltd.* v. *Oba M. S. Awolesi* [1964] 1 W.L.R. 1311 (P.C.); *Bank of India* v. *Patel* [1982] 1 Lloyd's Rep. 506 at 515 upheld at [1983] 2 Lloyd's Rep. 298 at 302 (C.A.).

[51] *Rees* v. *Berrington* (1795) 2 Ves.Jun. 540; *Harrison* v. *Seymour* (1866) L.R. 1 C.P. 518.

[52] See *Greenwood* v. *Francis* [1899] 1 Q.B. 312 (C.A.). See also p. 567.

the contract works, not within the scope of a clause permitting the ordering of variations, discharges the surety. The same result follows if there is an over-payment, as when retention money is prematurely advanced to the contractor, for the surety loses the strong inducement which otherwise would have operated on the contractor's mind to induce him to finish on time.[53] But the surety is not released if the retention money was obtained by fraud.[54] Where a building contract provided for the final determination of all questions by the employer's architect, but the parties chose to go to arbitration it was held that the surety was not liable to pay the costs of the arbitration.[55]

(b) *Bonds*

Bonds are archaic and, it is suggested, thoroughly undesirable in that they are frequently expressed in outmoded language and create obligations whose legal interpretation may be unclear. "I may be allowed to remark that it is difficult to understand why businessmen persist in entering upon considerable obligations in old-fashioned forms of contract which do not adequately express the true transaction."[56] There is no difficulty in principle in composing guarantees in clear modern language to effect the intended relationships and obligations.[57] The old practice nevertheless persists especially with international contracts.

A bond is a promise by deed whereby the person giving the promise (the obligor or bondsman) promises to pay another person (the obligee) a sum of money.[58] In the construction industry, the most common kind of bond is a performance bond entered into by a bank or insurance company at the behest of the contractor and in favour of the employer. In substance, the bondsman guarantees the contractor's performance up to a stated amount and he is liable if the contractor fails to perform his contract to the extent of his non-performance up to the stated amount. Enforcing the bondsman's liability is colloquially referred to as "calling the bond." The bank or insurance company makes a charge to the contractor for giving the bond and will almost invariably obtain a counter-indemnity from the contractor or a parent or associated company.[59] The requirement to procure a bond may be a stipulation of the construction contract which, subject to express words, may or may not be a

---

[53] *General Steam Navigation Co.* v. *Rolt* (1858) 6 C.B.(N.S.) 550 at 595.

[54] *Kingston-upon-Hull Corporation* v. *Harding* [1892] 2 Q.B. 494 (C.A.).

[55] *Hoole Urban District Council* v. *Fidelity & Deposit Co. of Maryland* [1916] 2 K.B. 568 (C.A.).

[56] Lord Atkin in *Trade Indemnity* v. *Workington Harbour and Dock Board* [1937] A.C. 1 at 17 (H.L.); *cf.* *Tins Industrial Co.* v. *Kono Insurance* (1987) 42 B.L.R. 110 at 119, 120 (Hong Kong Court of Appeal).

[57] The I.C.C. publish Uniform Rules and Model Forms for Contract Guarantees.

[58] See *Halsbury* (4th ed.), Vol. 12, para. 1385.

[59] Without an express counter-indemnity, the bondsman may not be able to recover from the party on whose behalf the bond was issued—see *Travel & General Insurance* v. *Barron, The Times,* November 25, 1988.

condition.[60] Where the bondsman is to be approved by the employer, it may be implied that such approval will not be unreasonably withheld.[61]

Conditional bonds.   A conditional bond is one which is expressed to be "conditioned" upon a particular event or events and commonly upon the satisfactory performance of the contractor. The employer's right to recover from the bondsman depends on the construction of the bond. If in substance it guarantees the contractor's performance, the employer has to establish damages occasioned by the breach or breaches of conditions and, if he succeeds, he recovers the amount of the damages proved.[62] It is thought that the position then is either that the judgment remains as security for the recovery of damages for other future breaches not sustained at the date of the commencement of the first action, or that the employer can bring a second action for such future breaches up to the balance of the amount of the bond remaining from the first recovery.[63] Other forms of bond may be conditional on facts or events other than the contractor's performance, so that, if the relevant facts or events are established, the beneficiary can recover without proving loss.[64] Where a condition of notification in writing of non-performance had not been fulfilled, the employer did not recover when the contractor subsequently failed to complete and went into liquidation.[65]

---

[60] See *State Trading Corporation of India* v. *Golodetz* [1989] 2 Lloyd's Rep. 277 (C.A.). For conditions, see "Breach of condition" and subsequent paras. at p. 147.

[61] *Arbiter Investments* v. *Wiltshier* (1987) 14 Con.L.R. 16 (Note); *cf.* generally *Convent Hospital* v. *Eberlin & Partners* (1988) 14 Con.L.R. 1.

[62] See *Nene Housing Society* v. *The National Westminster Bank* (1980) 16 B.L.R. 22; *Tins Industrial Co.* v. *Kono Insurance* (1987) 42 B.L.R. 110 (Hong Kong Court of Appeal).

[63] See *Workington Harbour & Dock Board* v. *Trade Indemnity Co. Ltd. (No. 2)* [1938] 2 All E.R. 101 at 105 (H.L.). This case was decided at a time when the Statute [1697] 8 & 9 William III, c. 11 was in force. (The statute is sometimes confusingly called the Breaches of Bonds Act 1696, although its first seven sections were not concerned with bonds. The confusion with the dates arises from the contemporary dating system whereby the New Year then conventionally started on March 25—see G. M. Trevelyan, *England under Queen Anne*, Vol. 1, p. viii.) The statute was repealed under a general repealing act in 1948. The passage in Lord Atkin's opinion at [1938] 2 All E.R. 105 D–F follows the language of s.8 of the statute closely and is probably stating a statutory, not a common law, position—*cf.* Slesser L.J. in the Court of Appeal at [1937] 3 All E.R. 146. The first supplement to the 4th edition of this book said, in effect, that the passage in Lord Atkin's opinion was no longer the law as it turned on a repealed statute. The Court of Appeal of Hong Kong did not agree with this in *Tins Industrial Co.* v. *Kono Insurance* (1987) 42 B.L.R. 110 at 118 for the reasons there given. The present editor considers that the requirement to establish both breach by the contractor and loss by the employer is a matter of general law and construction not dependent on statute; that the passage in Lord Atkin's opinion, although it reads as a statement of general law not dependent on statute, is in fact a statement of statutory law now repealed; and that, although it is unlikely to have been the intention of Parliament to change the law by a general repealing act, the *procedural* consequences of a judgment may have derived only from the statute. It is noted, however, that the procedural consequences were expressed in the statute to occur only "if judgment shall be given for the plaintiff on a demurrer, or by confession, or *nihil dicit.*" Accordingly the second alternative in this sentence in the text is, with caution, preferred as the present state of the law.

[64] See, *e.g. Esal Commodities* v. *Oriental Credit* [1985] 2 Lloyd's Rep. 546 (C.A.); *Siporex Trade* v. *Banque Indosuez* [1986] 2 Lloyd's Rep. 146; *cf. State Trading Corporation of India* v. *E.D. & F. Man* (1981) Comm.L.R. 235 (C.A.).

[65] *Clydebank and District Water Trustees* v. *Fidelity and Deposit Co. of Maryland* [1916] S.C.(H.L.) 69.

"On demand bonds."　　These are unconditional bonds obliging the bonds-man to pay simply on demand.[66] Problems that they raise include whether an employer who calls an on demand bond has to account for the amount received, and if so to whom and upon what legal principle.

In *Edward Owen* v. *Barclays Bank*,[67] contractors agreed with Libyan customers to supply and erect glass houses in Libya. There was to be a performance guarantee for 10 per cent. of the contract price. The guarantee, given by an English bank, was payable "on demand without proof or conditions." There was no evidence of any default or breach of contract on the part of the contractor. It was held that, subject only to proof of fraud on the part of the employer, the bond could be enforced with the result that the contractor became liable upon his indemnity to the English bank. Lord Denning said that, in so far as such bond was enforceable without any breach at all, it bore the colour of a discount which the contractor, if he were wise, would take into account when quoting his price. "These performance guarantees are virtually promissory notes payable on demand."[68] In the absence of fraud, the court will normally not grant an injunction restraining the enforcement of an on demand bond, but the underlying contract cannot be entirely ignored. If the contractor had lawfully avoided the underlying contract or there was a failure of its consideration, the court might prevent a call on the bond.[69]

Although the reference to a discount in *Edward Owen* v. *Barclays Bank*[70] suggests that the employer would not be obliged to account, the decision concerned whether the bondsman had to pay, and did not address questions of subsequent account. It is submitted that, where in relation to a building contract a contractor has at the request of the employer procured an unconditional bond, the court may depending on all the circumstances be able to imply into the building contract a term that the employer should account to the contractor for the proceeds of the bond. There may in some circumstances alternatively be a collateral contract to equivalent effect.[71] If this were correct, where the employer's loss was either nil or less than the amount recovered

---

[66] It is not understood why contractors ever agree to procure such bonds other than a belief that they will not obtain the contract if they do not.

[67] [1978] Q.B. 159 (C.A.).

[68] Lord Denning at 170; *cf. General Surety & Guarantee Co.* v. *Francis Parker* (1977) 6 B.L.R. 16; *Howe Richardson Scale* v. *Polimex-Cekop* [1978] 1 Lloyd's Rep. 161 (C.A.); *Wood Hall Ltd.* v. *The Pipeline Authority* (1979) 53 A.L.J.R. 487 (High Court of Australia); *United Trading Corporation* v. *Allied Arab Bank* [1985] 2 Lloyd's Rep. 554 at 558 (C.A.).

[69] *Potton Homes* v. *Coleman Contractors* (1984) 28 B.L.R. 19 (C.A.); *cf. Howe Richardson Scale* v. *Polimex-Cekop* [1978] 1 Lloyd's Rep. 161 (C.A.); *Intraco* v. *Notis Shipping* [1981] 2 Lloyd's Rep. 256 (C.A.); *State Trading Corporation of India* v. *E.D. & F. Man* (1981) Comm.L.R. 235 (C.A.); *Bolvinter Oil* v. *Chase Manhattan Bank* [1984] 1 Lloyd's Rep. 251 (C.A.); *G.K.N. Contractors* v. *Lloyds Bank* (1985) 30 B.L.R. 48 (C.A.); *Tukan Timber* v. *Barclays Bank* [1987] 1 Lloyd's Rep. 171.

[70] [1978] Q.B. 159 (C.A.).

[71] It is thought that an implied term or collateral contract might more readily be found in building contracts than in contracts of sale. In building contracts, an on demand bond is more likely to be seen as intended as a security for performance than as a discount.

under the bond, the contractor would be entitled to recover in part or in whole.[72]

Release by employer. Some bonds are expressly for fixed periods and others come to an end at stated times, *e.g.* on a particular date or at practical completion. Subject to the express provisions such as these, it is submitted that the typical bond guaranteeing performance of the contract according to its conditions extends to any latent defects for which the contractor may be liable in accordance with those conditions. The bondsman's liability therefore does not determine upon completion of the works save in so far as the contractor's obligations end at that stage. Further, it is not thought that there is any implied right to require the employer to release the bondsman upon completion of the works.

6. Liability to Third Parties

The carrying out of building operations may involve one of the parties in liability in tort to a third party for injury to his person or property. The possible heads of liability may include trespass,[73] nuisance, disturbance of easements, negligence, liability under the rule in *Rylands* v. *Fletcher*,[74] and liability to persons coming upon dangerous premises. Negligence is discussed in Chapter 7, otherwise for the nature of these torts reference must be made to one of the standard works.[75] In this section it is proposed to deal only with the question of who is liable for the torts committed, and to give a short account of certain aspects of the law of nuisance and trespass as they particularly apply to demolition and construction operations.

(a) *Who is liable*

Contractor. It is a general principal that a person is always liable for any tort he commits.[76] The contractor therefore can always be sued for torts which he has committed even though the employer may also be liable.[77] The contractor is also liable for the torts of his servants committed in the course of their

---

[72] Although the bond money itself will not have been paid by the contractor, it may readily be taken that he or his counter-indemnifier will have eventually provided its value.

[73] See, *e.g. London and Manchester Assurance* v. *O. and H. Construction* (1990) 6 Const.L.J. 155.

[74] (1866) L.R. 3 H.L. 330 (H.L.); see also *Ryeford Homes* v. *Sevenoaks District Council* (1990) 6 Const. L.J. 170.

[75] *e.g. Salmond* (19th ed.); *Winfield and Jolowicz* (13th ed.); *Clerk and Lindsell* (16th ed.); *Gale on Easements* (15th ed.).

[76] See *Dalton* v. *Angus* (1881) 6 App.Cas. 740 at 831 (H.L.).

[77] *Ibid.* For the extent of a contractor's potential liability in negligence to persons with whom he is not in contract, see generally Chap. 7. For the possible liability of a contractor to an adjoining owner for damage done by vandals and the like, see *Smith* v. *Littlewoods* [1987] A.C. 241 (H.L.); *cf. P. Perl (Exporters)* v. *Camden London Borough Council* [1984] Q.B. 342 (C.A.); *King* v. *Liverpool City Council* [1986] 1 W.L.R. 890 (C.A.); and *cf. Ward* v. *Cannock Chase District Council* [1986] Ch. 546.

employment,[78] but so far as torts are committed by sub-contractors or their servants, the contractor is only liable in the same manner and to the same extent as the employer is liable for the contractor's torts.[79] Normally, it seems, the contractor does not owe a duty other than in contract to supervise his sub-contractors.[80]

Employer.   The general rule is that a person is not responsible for the torts of an independent contractor.[81] Thus an employer, who engaged a contractor whom he reasonably believed to be competent, to fell a tree on his land, was held not liable when the negligent felling of the trees caused telephone wires to fall across a highway so that the plaintiff was injured avoiding the anticipated consequences of an approaching car striking the wires.[82] But there are certain important qualifications and exceptions to this rule so that in practice the employer can frequently be sued for a tort committed by the contractor. Thus he is liable:

(1) Where the result of building operations is to cause damage or loss to a third party and the employer does not impose on the contractor the duty of avoiding such damage or loss.[83]

(2) Where the carrying out of the work gives rise to some duty which the employer himself owes to the plaintiff,[84] for "a person causing something to be done, the doing of which casts on him a duty, cannot escape from the responsibility attaching on him of seeing that duty performed by delegating it to a contractor. He may bargain with the contractor that he shall perform the duty and stipulate for an indemnity from him if it is not performed, but he cannot thereby relieve himself from liability to those injured by the failure to perform it."[85] Whenever the work "of

---

[78] See, *e.g. Salmond* (19th ed.), para. 172.

[79] *D. & F. Estates* v. *The Church Commissioners* [1989] A.C. 177 at 208 *et seq.* (H.L.); *cf. Padbury* v. *Holliday & Greenwood Ltd.* (1912) 28 T.L.R. 494 (C.A.), and see p. 295. The contractor may expressly agree to indemnify the employer against claims arising out of the execution of the works, see p. 543, and *cf.* clause 20 of the Standard Form of Building Contract.

[80] See *D. & F. Estates* v. *The Church Commissioners* [1989] A.C. 177 at 208 *et seq.* (H.L.) and see also the decision in the Court of Appeal at (1987) 36 B.L.R. 72; *cf.* however *Linge* v. *Grayston Scaffolding* (1983) 133 N.L.J. 829 where a main contractor was held liable (with others) for personal injury to an employee of scaffolding sub-contractors.

[81] *Dalton* v. *Angus* (1881) 6 App.Cas. 740 at 829 (H.L.); *D. & F. Estates* v. *The Church Commissioners* [1989] A.C. 177 at 208 (H.L.); *cf. Honeywill & Stein* v. *Larkin Bros.* [1934] 1 K.B. 191 (C.A.); *Salsbury* v. *Woodland* [1970] 1 Q.B. 324 (C.A.). The term "independent contractor" is used in contrast with "servant" for whose torts he is liable. The architect in the ordinary professional position is an independent contractor: *A.M.F. International Ltd.* v. *Magnet Bowling Ltd.* [1968] 1 W.L.R. 1028.

[82] *Salsbury* v. *Woodland* [1970] 1 Q.B. 324 (C.A.).

[83] *Robinson* v. *Beaconsfield Rural District Council* [1911] 2 Ch. 188 (C.A.). (Contract for removal of sewage but no provision for its disposal; employer liable for contractor's trespass with sewage.)

[84] *Salsbury* v. *Woodland* [1970] 1 Q.B. 324 at 347 (C.A.).

[85] Lord Blackburn in *Dalton* v. *Angus* (1881) 6 App.Cas. 740 at 829 (H.L.); *Hughes* v. *Percival* (1883) 8 App.Cas. 443 at 446 (H.L.). For the statutory right of contribution or indemnity, see Civil Liability (Contribution) Act 1978 which enables contribution to be recovered from any other person liable in respect of the same damage, whatever the legal basis of his liability whether tort, breach of contract, breach of trust or otherwise.

its very nature involves a risk of damage to a third party" the employer is liable.[86] Examples of the application of this principle making the employer liable are where the contractor interfered with the right of support of an adjoining building[87]; where the works caused much dust and noise[88]; where extra hazardous techniques were used[89]; where electrical installations were so negligently carried out that a house caught fire damaging adjoining property[90]; and where persons on the highway were injured by the negligence of independent contractors.[91] The employer's liability for injuries to visitors to the site caused by its dangerous condition resulting from the works carried out by the contractor is governed by the Occupiers' Liability Acts 1957 and 1984.[92]

(3) Where fire is negligently caused on the site by the contractor in performance of the contract and spreads, causing damage.[93]

The employer is not liable for the casual or collateral negligence of the contractor or his servants.[94] The application of this principle is not always easy but an example occurred where the servant of sub-contractors, employed to insert metallic casements, left a tool on a sill and the wind blew the casement knocking off the tool which injured the plaintiff. It was held that the main contractor was not liable.[95]

(b) *Nuisance from building operations*

Building operations often substantially interfere with adjoining owners' enjoyment of their property because of noise, dust and perhaps vibration. Such matters in some circumstances might be held to be a nuisance and form grounds for an injunction prohibiting their continuance, or an action for

---

[86] Romer L.J. in *Matania* v. *National Provincial Bank Ltd. and Elevenist Syndicate* [1936] 2 All E.R. 633 at 648 (C.A.).

[87] *Bower* v. *Peate* (1876) 1 Q.B.D. 321; *Dalton* v. *Angus* (1881) 6 App.Cas. 740 (H.L.); see also "Easements" at p. 259.

[88] *Matania* v. *National Provincial Bank Ltd. and Elevenist Syndicate* [1936] 2 All E.R. 633 (C.A.); *Andreae* v. *Selfridge & Co. Ltd.* [1938] Ch. 1 (C.A.). See also Pt. III of the Control of Pollution Act 1974 and in particular ss.60 and 61 (discussed at p. 365) for control of noise on construction sites.

[89] *Honeywill & Stein* v. *Larkin Bros.* [1934] 1 K.B. 191 (C.A.) (open magnesium flash near curtains); *The Pass of Ballater* [1942] P. 112 (oxy-acetylene burner in confined space where danger of petrol fumes).

[90] *Spicer* v. *Smee* [1946] 1 All E.R. 489 where Atkinson J. stated that the employer was always liable for a nuisance created by his independent contractor applying dictum of Scrutton L.J. *Job Edwards Ltd.* v. *Birmingham Navigations* [1924] 1 K.B. 341 at 355 (C.A.).

[91] *Tarry* v. *Ashton* (1876) 1 Q.B.D. 314; *Penny* v. *Wimbledon Urban District Council* [1899] 2 Q.B. 72 (C.A.); *Holliday* v. *National Telephone Co.* [1899] 2 Q.B. 392 (C.A.).

[92] See esp. s.2(4)(b).

[93] *Balfour* v. *Barty-King* [1957] 1 Q.B. 496 (C.A.); *Emanuel (H. & N.) Ltd.* v. *G.L.C.* [1971] 2 All E.R. 835 (C.A.); see also *Goldman* v. *Hargrave* [1967] 1 A.C. 645 (P.C.); *Mason* v. *Levy Auto, etc., Ltd.* [1967] 2 Q.B. 530; *cf. Smith* v. *Littlewoods* [1987] A.C. 241 (H.L.) for damage to adjoining property by fire caused by vandal third parties.

[94] *Penny* v. *Wimbledon Urban District Council* [1899] 2 Q.B. 72 at 78.

[95] *Padbury* v. *Holliday* (1912) 28 T.L.R. 494 (C.A.). *cf. Holliday* v. *National Telephone Co.* [1899] 2 Q.B. 392 and see *Salmond* (19th ed.), p. 551.

damages, or both.[96] If this were the result of ordinary building operations "the business of life could not be carried on,"[97] for old buildings could not be pulled down and new erected in their place. But the law takes a common-sense view of the matter and if:

"operations ... such as demolition and building ... are reasonably carried on and all proper and reasonable steps are taken to ensure that no undue inconvenience is caused to neighbours whether from noise, dust, or other reasons, the neighbours must put up with it."[98]

The duty to minimise inconvenience.   "Those who say that their interference with the comfort of their neighbours is justified ... are under a specific duty ... to use reasonable and proper care and skill. It is not a correct attitude to say: 'We will go on and do what we like until somebody complains.' That is not their duty to their neighbours. Their duty is to take proper precautions, and to see that the nuisance is reduced to a minimum. It is no answer for them to say: 'But this would mean that we should have to do the work more slowly than we would like to do it, or it would involve putting us to some extra expense.' All those questions are matters of common sense and degree and quite clearly it would be unreasonable to expect people to conduct their work so slowly or expensively, for the purpose of preventing a transient inconvenience that the cost and trouble would be prohibitive. It is all a question of fact and degree. ... The use of reasonable care and skill in connection with matters of this kind may take various forms. It may take the form of restricting the hours during which work is to be done; it may take the form of limiting the amount of a particular type of work which is being done simultaneously within a particular area; it may take the form of using proper scientific means of avoiding inconvenience."[99]

Where no steps at all were taken to avoid inconvenience the employer[1] was held liable in damages for nuisance.[2] The measure of damages was held[3] to be not all the loss suffered, £4,000, as a result of the building operations, but that part of the loss and inconvenience attributable to the failure to take proper precautions as defined above, £1,000. Damages were awarded against an employer where part of a building was being altered and no steps were taken to minimise the nuisance, although sheets would have reduced the dust and other working arrangements might have reduced the loss caused to the adjoining occupier (a singing instructor) by the noise.[4]

---

[96] See generally *Salmond*, Chap. 4.
[97] Vaughan Williams J. in *Harrison* v. *Southwark & Vauxhall Water Co.* [1891] 2 Ch. 409 at 413.
[98] Sir Wilfrid Greene M.R. in *Andreae* v. *Selfridge & Co. Ltd.* [1938] Ch. 1 at 5 (C.A.).
[99] Sir Wilfrid Greene M.R. in *Andreae* v. *Selfridge & Co. Ltd.* [1938] Ch. 1 at 9 *et seq.* (C.A.).
[1] This is one of the cases where the employer is liable for the actions of the contractor, see above.
[2] *Andreae* v. *Selfridge & Co. Ltd.* [1938] Ch. 1 (C.A.). See also *Hoare* v. *McAlpine* [1923] 1 Ch. 167.
[3] By the Court of Appeal reducing the damages originally awarded.
[4] *Matania* v. *National Provincial Bank Ltd. and Elevenist Syndicate* (1936) 155 L.T. 74 (C.A.).

Easements. Building operations may infringe a variety of easements including rights of light, air and drainage, rights of way and rights of support.[5] In particular where a right of support is established,[6] withdrawal of support, as for instance by excavating beside or beneath neighbouring foundations, will almost always give rise to liability of both the contractor and the employer, and the employer will in this instance be liable for negligence by his contractor.[7]

> "He is not in the actual position of being responsible for injury, no matter how occasioned, but he must be vigilant and careful, for he is liable for injuries to his neighbour caused by any want of prudence and precaution, even though it may be *culpa levissima*."[8]

"Those who engage in operations inherently dangerous must take precautions which are not required of persons engaged in the ordinary routine of daily life."[9] In an appropriate case, disturbance of an easement will be restrained by injunction, and normally a plaintiff who has a seriously arguable case will not be required to take the risk of applying for an interlocutory injunction before proceeding to a full trial.[10]

Tower cranes. The jib of a modern tower crane travels through a wide area of air space. Without a licence from the adjoining owner, the incursion of the jib of a tower crane into his air space is a trespass and in an appropriate case the court will grant an injunction to restrain such an incursion without proof of actual loss.[11] In one case, the injunction was suspended for a period to enable the defendants to complete the building,[12] but such a suspension has been regarded as incorrect in the absence of special circumstances.[13] In practice, therefore, it will, normally be necessary to obtain a licence.

---

[5] For easements generally, see *Gale on Easements* (15th ed.).

[6] For the acquisition of rights of support, see *Gale on Easements* (15th ed.), Chap. 10.

[7] *Dalton* v. *Angus* (1881) 6 App.Cas. 740 at 829 (H.L.); *Bower* v. *Peate* (1876) 1 Q.B.D. 321.

[8] Lord FitzGerald in *Hughes* v. *Percival* (1883) 8 App.Cas. 443 at 455 (H.L.).

[9] Lord Macmillan in *Glasgow Corporation* v. *Muir* [1943] A.C. 448 at 456 (H.L.); *cf. I.B.A.* v. *E.M.I. and B.I.C.C.* (1980) 14 B.L.R. 1 at 28 where Lord Edmund-Davies said that risks might be so manifest and substantial and their elimination so difficult to ensure with reasonable certainty that the only proper course would be to abandon the project altogether.

[10] *Oxy Electric* v. *Zainuddin, The Times*, June 28, 1990—the risk arises from the usual undertaking as to damages which a plaintiff seeking an interlocutory injunction is obliged to give; *cp. Blue Town Investments* v. *Higgs and Hill* [1990] 1 W.L.R. 696, where a plaintiff's claim in a right of light case, which was extremely unlikely to succeed, was struck out when the plaintiff was not prepared to apply for an interlocutory injunction and give an undertaking in damages. For recent noise cases, see *Lloyds Bank* v. *Guardian Assurance* (1986) 35 B.L.R. 34 (C.A.); *City of London Corporation* v. *Bovis Construction* (1988) 49 B.L.R. 1 (C.A.). See also Pt. III of the Control of Pollution Act 1974 discussed at p. 365. For injunctions, see further p. 270.

[11] *Anchor Brewhouse Developments* v. *Berkley House* (1987) 38 B.L.R. 82; *cf. Kelsen* v. *The Imperial Tobacco Co. Ltd.* [1957] 2 Q.B. 334; *London and Manchester Assurance* v. *O. and H. Construction* (1990) 6 Const.L.J. 155. For a comprehensive review, see A. J. Wait, "Oversailing Tower Cranes: Problems of Trespass" (1989) 5 Const.L.J. 117.

[12] *Woollerton & Wilson Ltd.* v. *Richard Costain Ltd.* [1970] 1 W.L.R. 411.

[13] *Anchor Brewhouse Developments* v. *Berkley House* (1987) 38 B.L.R. 82; *Patel* v. *W.H. Smith (Eziot) Ltd.* [1987] 1 W.L.R. 853 (C.A.); *cf. Charrington* v. *Simons & Co. Ltd.* [1971] 1 W.L.R. 598 (C.A.); *John Trenberth* v. *National Westminster Bank* (1980) 39 P. & C.R. 104.

7. Contractor's Duty of Care towards Employer

Such a duty may arise in tort or by statute or as an implied term of the contract. Two instances are discussed below. In every case the effect of any express clause in the contract dealing with the matter must be considered.

Employer's visits to site. If the contractor knows that the employer is going to walk about on the site, it is his duty to make the site reasonably safe.[14] Further a contractor, who is aware of a danger or has reasonable grounds to believe that it exists, and knows or has reasonable grounds to believe that the employer may come into the vicinity of the danger and the risk is one against which in the circumstances he may reasonably be expected to offer some protection, owes the employer a duty to take such care as is reasonable in all the circumstances to see that the employer does not suffer injury by reason of the danger.[15]

The employer has no implied contractual right to enter the site at any time without the contractor's knowledge, and to expect to find the site ready and safe for his visit.[16] If the employer does enter the site without warning and without the knowledge of the contractor it seems that he does so at his own risk,[17] so that where an employer in such circumstances trod on an unsafe plank and fell and was injured, he was unable to recover damages from the contractor.[18]

Theft of employer's property. Arising out of the contractual relationship between the parties is a duty on the part of the contractor to take reasonable care with regard to the state of the employer's house if he leaves it empty during the performance of his work.[19]

8. Claim for Breach of Confidence

Persons involved in building contracts may have a remedy in respect of the unauthorised use or disclosure of confidential matter. It may arise in contract for "if two parties make a contract, under which one of them obtains for the purpose of the contract or in connection with it some confidential matter, then,

---

[14] *Nabarro* v. *Cope & Co.* [1938] 4 All E.R. 565 at 569; Occupiers Liability Act 1957, s.2.

[15] See s.1 of the Occupiers' Liability Act 1984; *cf. White* v. *St. Albans City and District Council, The Times,* March 3, 1990 (C.A.).

[16] *Nabarro* v. *Cope & Co.* [1938] 4 All E.R. 565 at 568.

[17] See n. 14 above.

[18] *Nabarro* v. *Cope & Co.* [1938] 4 All E.R. 565. It is thought that the result would be the same today under the Occupiers' Liability Act 1957, but see now s.1 of the Occupiers' Liability Act 1984, whose rules are in place of the rule of the common law for persons other than visitors.

[19] *Stansbie* v. *Troman* [1948] 2 K.B. 48 (C.A.)—decorator left alone in house goes out leaving it with catch of Yale lock fastened back; liable for theft while absent; *cf. Smith* v. *Littlewoods* [1987] A.C. 241 at 264 (H.L.).

even though the contract is silent on the matter of confidence, the law will imply an obligation to treat that confidential matter in a confidential way, as one of the implied terms of the contract."[20] But remedies under this head are not limited to those for breach of contract. Thus where the plaintiff, in the course of negotiations with the defendant where no contract resulted disclosed certain methods of manufacture which the defendant subsequently used, it was held that the plaintiff had a claim in damages,[21] the measure being analogous to that in tort.[22] In a suitable case an injunction can be obtained.[23] The remedies are not confined to commercial or domestic secrets but extend also to public secrets.[24] The claim is additional to any which may exist for breach of copyright or analogous statutory rights.[25]

---

[20] Lord Greene M.R. in *Saltman Engineering Co. Ltd.* v. *Campbell Engineering Co. Ltd.* (1948) [1963] 3 All E.R. 413 at 414 (C.A.); *cf. Fraser* v. *Thames Television* [1984] Q.B. 44 at 58 *et seq.* For an example of an express clause, see clause 5.7 of the Standard Form of Building Contract.

[21] *Seager* v. *Copydex Ltd.* [1967] 1 W.L.R. 923 (C.A.).

[22] *Seager* v. *Copydex Ltd.* (*No. 2*) [1969] 1 W.L.R. 809 (C.A.); *cp. Dowson & Mason* v. *Potter* [1986] 1 W.L.R. 1419 (C.A.).

[23] *Peter Pan Manufacturing Corporation* v. *Corsets Silhouette Ltd.* [1963] 3 All E.R. 402; *Att.-Gen.* v. *Jonathan Cape Ltd.* [1976] Q.B. 752; *Att.-Gen.* v. *Guardian Newspapers* (*No. 2*) [1990] A.C. 109 (H.L.).

[24] *Att.-Gen.* v. *Jonathan Cape Ltd.* [1976] Q.B. 752; *Att.-Gen.* v. *Guardian Newspapers* (*No. 2*) [1990] A.C. 109 (H.L.).

[25] See p. 337.

CHAPTER 11

VARIOUS EQUITABLE DOCTRINES AND REMEDIES

1. Estoppel

Estoppel is an equitable doctrine. Where it applies, usually as a defence,[1] a party is prevented (or estopped) from successfully asserting what would or might otherwise be his legal rights. In many instances it is the approximate legal equivalent of colloquial expressions such as: "you can't now just turn round and say that." Estoppel is a large subject and an outline only is given here.[2] For building contract purposes, it is appropriate to consider:

(1) estoppel by representation;
(2) estoppel by convention; and
(3) promissory estoppel.[3]

Estoppel by representation. If a party makes a representation with the intention and effect of inducing another party to alter his position to his detriment in reliance on the representation, the party making the representation may be estopped from relying on facts which are at variance with the representation.[4] The representation must be a representation of fact or of an existing state of mind or belief and not a future promise.[5] It must be unambiguous and unequivocal.[6] It may be by words or by acts or conduct including,

---

[1] *Combe* v. *Combe* [1951] 2 K.B. 215 (C.A.); *Syros Shipping* v. *Elaghill Trading* [1980] 2 Lloyd's Rep. 390; *cf. Amalgamated Property Co.* v. *Texas Bank* [1982] Q.B. 85 at 130 (C.A.). In certain circumstances, in relation to land, estoppel may lead to the creation of a proprietary interest, *Crabb* v. *Arun District Council* [1976] Ch. 179 (C.A.).

[2] For a full account, see, *e.g. Halsbury*, Vol. 16, paras. 1501 *et seq.*; Spencer Bower and Turner, *Estoppel by Representation* (3rd ed.).

[3] See also estoppel by deed, discussed at p. 59.

[4] See, *e.g. Greenwood* v. *Martins Bank* [1933] A.C. 51 at 57 (H.L.); *Hopgood* v. *Brown* [1955] 1 W.L.R. 215 at 224 (C.A.); *cf. Avon County Council* v. *Howlett* [1983] 1 W.L.R. 605 (C.A.). For a building contract case where a plea of estoppel failed because the relevant party did not act to their detriment on the strength of the representation, see *Whittal Builders* v. *Chester-le-Street District Council* (1987) 40 B.L.R. 82 at 89.

[5] *Nippon Menkwa Kabushiki Kaisha* v. *Dawsons Bank* (1935) Lloyd's L.L.R. 147 at 151 (P.C.); *Argy Trading* v. *Lapid Developments* [1977] 1 Lloyd's Rep. 67 at 76.

[6] *Woodhouse Ltd.* v. *Nigerian Produce Ltd.* [1972] A.C. 741 at 755, 768, 771 (H.L.); *Low* v. *Bouverie* [1891] 3 Ch. 82 at 106 (C.A.).

where there is a duty to speak or act, by silence or inaction.[7] Where the negligent designer of a bungalow gave reassuring advice to the plaintiff owner about internal cracks which had appeared within the limitation period, he was held to be estopped from relying on evidence that the plaintiff's cause of action had accrued more than six years before the commencement of her subsequent action.[8]

Estoppel by convention. Where parties have acted upon a common assumption of fact or law on the basis of which they have regulated their subsequent dealings, they will be estopped from subsequently denying that the assumption is true if it would be unjust or unconscionable to permit them to resile from it.[9]

Promissory estoppel. Where a party has made an unequivocal promise or representation to another party that he will not enforce his strict legal rights and the promise or representation is intended to be relied on and is in fact relied on, the first party may be estopped from successfully asserting his strict legal rights if it would be unconscionable or unjust to allow him to do so.[10]

> "It is the first principle upon which all Courts of Equity proceed, that if parties who have entered into definite and distinct terms involving certain legal results ... afterwards by their own act and with their own consent enter upon a course of negotiation which has the effect of leading one of the parties to suppose that the strict rights arising under the contract will not be enforced, or will be kept in suspense, or held in abeyance, the person who otherwise might have enforced those rights will not be allowed to enforce them where it would be inequitable having regard to the dealings which have thus taken place between the parties."[11]

---

[7] *Greenwood* v. *Martins Bank* [1933] A.C. 51 at 57 (H.L.); *Spiro* v. *Lintern* [1973] 1 W.L.R. 1002 at 1010 (C.A.); *cf. Meng Leong* v. *Jip Hong* [1985] A.C. 511 (P.C.).

[8] *Kaliszewska* v. *John Clague and Partners* (1984) 1 Const. L.J. 137.

[9] *Norwegian American Cruises* v. *Paul Mundy* [1988] 2 Lloyd's Rep. 343 (C.A.); *cf. Amalgamated Property Co.* v. *Texas Bank* [1982] Q.B. 85 at 122, 126, 130 (C.A.); *Keen* v. *Holland* [1984] 1 W.L.R. 251 (C.A.); *K. Locumal & Sons* v. *Lotte Shipping* [1985] 2 Lloyd's Rep. 28 (C.A.); *Government of Swaziland* v. *Leila Maritime* [1985] 2 Lloyd's Rep. 172 at 178; *Troop* v. *Gibson* (1986) 277 E.G. 1134 (C.A.). For a building contract case where a plea of estoppel by convention succeeded, see *Whittal Builders* v. *Chester-le-Street District Council* (1987) 40 B.L.R. 82 at 89. See also "Agreed factual assumption" at p. 38.

[10] *Hughes* v. *Metropolitan Railway Co.* (1877) 2 App.Cas. 439 (H.L.); *Birmingham and District Land* v. *London and North Western Railway* (1888) 40 Ch.D. 268 (C.A.); *Central London Property Trust Ltd.* v. *High Trees House Ltd.* [1947] K.B. 130; *Combe* v. *Combe* [1951] 2 K.B. 215 (C.A.); *Woodhouse Ltd.* v. *Nigerian Produce Ltd.* [1972] A.C. 741 (H.L.); *Peter Cremer* v. *Granaria B.V.* [1981] 2 Lloyd's Rep. 583 at 587; *Societe Italo-Belge* v. *Palm and Vegetable Oils* [1981] 2 Lloyd's Rep. 695; *cf. Crabb* v. *Arun District Council* [1976] Ch. 179 (C.A.); *Att.-Gen. of Hong Kong* v. *Humphreys Estate* [1987] A.C. 114 (P.C.); *Taylor Fashions* v. *Liverpool Victoria Friendly Society* [1981] Q.B. 133 (Note); *Habib Bank Ltd.* v. *Habib Bank A.G.* [1981] 1 W.L.R. 1265 at 1285 (C.A.).

[11] Lord Cairns L.C. in *Hughes* v. *Metropolitan Railway Co.* (1877) 2 App.Cas. 439 at 448 (H.L.); *cf. Tool Metal Manufacturing Co. Ltd.* v. *Tungsten Electric Co. Ltd.* [1955] 1 W.L.R. 761 (H.L.); *Scandinavian Trading* v. *Flota Ecuatorina* [1983] Q.B. 529 at 534 unaffected by the decision of the House of Lords at [1983] 2 A.C. 694 (H.L.); for a building contract application, see *Rees & Kirby* v. *Swansea City Council* (1985) 30 B.L.R. 1 at 21 (C.A.).

The promisor can resile from his promise on giving reasonable notice giving the promisee a reasonable opportunity of resuming his position and the promise only becomes final and irrevocable if the promisee cannot resume his position.[12] The promise need not be supported by consideration.[13]

2. Waiver

Waiver is related to, if not a species of, estoppel. A party to a contract may act so as to show that he does not intend to enforce a contractual right or require performance of a contractual obligation. By so acting, he may by waiver lose the right or cease to be entitled to the performance either temporarily or permanently. "It is always open to a party to waive a condition which is inserted for his benefit."[14] In building contracts, waiver is often asserted and sometimes upheld where contractual time limits are allowed to be exceeded or where requirements for written notices are not insisted on.[15] A breach of contract may be waived, as may a right to effect a contractual determination or to accept a repudiation.[16]

"In order to constitute a waiver there must be conduct which leads the other party reasonably to believe that the strict legal rights will not be insisted upon. The whole essence of waiver is that there must be conduct which evinces an intention to affect the legal relations of the parties. If that cannot properly be inferred, there is no waiver."[17] If, in a contract where time is of the essence, the defendant:

> "led the plaintiffs to believe that he would not insist on the stipulation as to time, and that, if they carried out the work, he would accept it, and they did it, he could not afterwards set up the stipulation as to time against them. . . . By his conduct he evinced an intention to affect their legal relations. He made, in effect, a promise not to insist on his strict legal rights. That promise was intended to be acted on, and was in fact acted on. He cannot afterwards go back on it."[18]

If a waiver is supported by consideration, it is contractually binding and new rights and obligations arise.[19] If a waiver is not supported by consideration, it

---

[12] *Ajayi* v. *R. T. Briscoe (Nigeria) Ltd.* [1964] 1 W.L.R. 1326 (P.C.).

[13] See *China-Pacific S.A.* v. *Food Corporation of India* [1981] Q.B. 403 at 429 (C.A.), the passage being unaffected by the decision of the House of Lords at [1982] A.C. 939 (H.L.).

[14] Denning L.J. in *Hoenig* v. *Isaacs* [1952] 2 All E.R. 176 at 181 (C.A.).

[15] See *Lickiss* v. *Milestone Motor Policies* [1966] 2 All E.R. 972 at 975 (C.A.); *cf. Rees & Kirby* v. *Swansea City Council* (1985) 30 B.L.R. 1 at 21 (C.A.), see also cases cited in *Chitty* (26th ed.), para. 1617.

[16] For repudiation generally, see p. 146 and in particular "Repudiation and contractual determination clauses" at p. 153.

[17] Denning L.J. in *Charles Rickards* v. *Oppenheim* [1950] 1 K.B. 616 at 626 (C.A.).

[18] *Ibid.* at 623.

[19] See "Variation and Rescission" below.

may not irrevocably alter the rights of the parties, but the waiver may be retracted for the future at least on reasonable notice.[20]

Waiver by the employer.   In an entire contract, if the contractor tenders work as being in fulfilment of the contract and the employer enters into possession and uses the building, he may depending on the circumstances waive his right to insist on entire performance as a condition of payment.[21] But the employer does not waive his claim for damages for defective work merely by occupying and using the contract works,[22] nor by paying money on account,[23] nor in full,[24] nor by suffering judgment for the whole contract sum to be entered against him.[25]

Waiver by contractor.   If the employer delays the works or otherwise commits a breach of contract while the work is being carried out the contractor does not waive a claim for damages merely by continuing with the work.[26]

Waiver by architect.   An architect or engineer has no implied authority from the building owner to vary or waive the terms of a building contract.[27]

3. Variation and Rescission

Parties may by mutual agreement vary the terms of an existing agreement and it is a good excuse to an allegation of non-performance to prove that the obligation has been performed according to a varied agreement. Such an agreement in effect discharges the original agreement and replaces it with the varied agreement. The agreement varying the original agreement must normally be supported by consideration.[28]

Variation of the contract works is usually governed by express terms and has been considered in Chapter 4.

---

[20] *Charles Rickards* v. *Oppenheim* [1950] 1 K.B. 616 (C.A.); *cf. Tool Metal Manufacturing Co.* v. *Tungsten Electrical Co.* [1955] 1 W.L.R. 761 (H.L.); *Woodhouse A.C.* v. *Nigerian Produce Co.* [1972] A.C. 741 at 757 (H.L.); *Alan & Co.* v. *El Nasr Co.* [1972] 2 Q.B. 189 (C.A.).

[21] See *Hoenig* v. *Isaacs* [1952] 2 All E.R. 176 at 181 (C.A.). For entire contracts, see p. 70.

[22] *Dakin* v. *Lee* [1916] 1 K.B. 566 (C.A.).

[23] *Cooper* v. *Uttoxeter Burial Board* (1864) 11 L.T. 565.

[24] *Davis* v. *Hedges* (1871) L.R. 6 Q.B. 687, unless paid under a binding and conclusive certificate. See p. 106.

[25] *Mondel* v. *Steel* (1841) 8 M. & W. 858; *Davis* v. *Hedges* (1871) L.R. 6 Q.B. 687; *Chell Engineering* v. *Unit Tool Co.* [1950] 1 All E.R. 378 (C.A.), and see Chap. 17 at p. 464. Payment or judgment may be evidence of satisfaction, although not a waiver. It may be advisable to state that they are without prejudice to a claim for defects.

[26] *Lawson* v. *Wallasey Local Board* (1883) 48 L.T. 507 (C.A.).

[27] *Toepfer* v. *Warinco* [1978] 2 Lloyd's Rep. 569 at 577; see also "The architect's authority as agent" at p. 305 and particularly "Variations" at p. 306.

[28] See *Williams* v. *Roffey Brothers* [1990] 2 W.L.R. 1153 (C.A.) and see generally *Chitty* (26th ed.), Vol. I, paras. 1599 *et seq.*; *cf.* Denning L.J. in *Rickards* v. *Oppenheim* [1950] 1 K.B. 616 at 623 (C.A.). For release of money due, see *Foakes* v. *Beer* (1884) 9 App.Cas. 605 (H.L.); *D. & C. Builders Ltd.* v. *Rees* [1966] 2 Q.B. 617 (C.A.).

Rescission by agreement.   The parties may have mutually agreed to rescind the contract and treat it as at an end.

4. Rectification

After a written contract has been entered into one of the parties may discover that it does not correctly set out his intention. He may find, for example, that a price or a period of time is wrong. He can approach the other party and ask him to agree that the contract shall be altered so as to correct the mistake. Alternatively he may be able to rely on an express term for the rectification of certain errors.[29] If he is unable to reach such an agreement or rely on a contractual right he may have grounds for seeking the discretionary[30] remedy of rectification.

Common mistake.   "Rectification is a remedy which is available where parties to a contract, intending to reproduce in a more formal document the terms of an agreement upon which they are already *ad idem*, use, in that document, words which are inapt to record the true agreement reached between them. The formal document may then be rectified so as to conform with the true agreement which it was intended to reproduce and enforced in its rectified form."[31]

The party seeking rectification must produce "convincing proof"[32] that there was a common intention, of which there was some outward expression of accord, in regard to a particular provision or aspect of the agreement continuing up to the moment of execution of the document which intention, by a mistake, the document failed to express.[33] He must also show that the instrument, if rectified as claimed, would accurately represent the true agreement between the parties at the time of its execution.[34] He does not have to show that there was before the execution of the document a binding and conclusive contract.[35] Where two persons have agreed expressly upon the meaning of a

---

[29] *e.g.* clause 2.2.2.2 of the Standard Form of Building Contract.

[30] See *Whiteside* v. *Whiteside* [1950] Ch. 65 at 71 (C.A.). The discretion is not exercised arbitrarily. If the plaintiff proves his case in accordance with the principles set out in the text, rectification will ordinarily be granted unless he is guilty of conduct such as delay or acquiescence which is a ground for refusing relief or there are some special circumstances such as arose in the *Whiteside* case in connection with tax considerations in a family matter. On the discretion of the court in equitable matters generally see the standard textbooks such as *Snell* or *Hanbury*. For fundamental mistake avoiding the contract at common law, for other equitable powers of the court not amounting to rectification and for mistake as to the nature of a document, see p. 12.

[31] Lord Diplock in *American Airlines Inc.* v. *Hope* [1974] 2 Lloyd's Rep. 301 at 307 (H.L.); see also *Re Butlin's Settlement Trusts* [1976] 1 Ch. 251 at 260.

[32] *Joscelyne* v. *Nissen* [1970] 2 Q.B. 86 at 98 (C.A.); *Ernest Scragg & Sons Ltd.* v. *Perseverance Banking Ltd.* [1973] 2 Lloyd's Rep. 101 at 104 (C.A.); *cf. ibid.* at 103 "satisfied beyond reasonable doubt"; *Thomas Bates Ltd.* v. *Wyndham's Ltd.* [1981] 1 W.L.R. 505 at 514 (C.A.).

[33] *Joscelyne* v. *Nissen* [1970] 2 Q.B. 86 (C.A.); *The "Nai Genova"* [1984] 1 Lloyd's Rep. 353 at 359 (C.A.).

[34] *The "Nai Genova"* [1984] 1 Lloyd's Rep. 353 (C.A.).

[35] *Joscelyne* v. *Nissen* [1970] 2 Q.B. 86 (C.A.).

particular phrase but do not record the definition in the contract itself, if one of them seeks to enforce the agreement on the basis of some other meaning he can be prevented by an action for rectification.[36]

Unilateral mistake.   If one party makes a mistake in expressing the contract and the other party has no knowledge of that mistake rectification is not granted. Where the other party at the time of the contract knows of and takes advantage of the mistake rectification is granted.[37] For a claim for rectification in these circumstances to succeed, it must be shown, firstly, that one party was mistaken as to the contents of the document; secondly, that the other party had actual knowledge of the mistake on the part of the first party; thirdly, that the other party did not draw the first party's attention to the mistake; and fourthly, that the mistake was one calculated to benefit the second party. In these circumstances, it is inequitable to allow the second party to resist rectification on the ground that the mistake was not a mutual mistake.[38]

In *Roberts & Co. Ltd.* v. *Leicestershire County Council*[39] the plaintiffs submitted a tender which specified a period for completion of 18 months. The defendants wrote stating that the tender was accepted and that a formal contract would shortly be submitted for execution. The contract was sent to the plaintiffs who sealed it believing the completion period to be 18 months. In fact they had failed to notice that the period inserted by the defendants was 30 months. Before the defendants sealed the contract there were two meetings by the end of the second of which the defendants must have known that the plaintiffs believed the period to be 18 months. However, the defendants sealed the contract without ever telling the plaintiffs of their mistake. It was held that, although the plaintiffs could not have rectification on the ground that there was a mistake in expressing a common intention, they were entitled to rectification on the ground that the defendants were prevented or estopped by their conduct from saying that there was no such mistake. It appears that the basis of the court's approach is that the plaintiff in such circumstances must prove conduct of the defendant such as to make it inequitable that he should be allowed to object to the rectification of the document.[40]

A typical case where rectification will not be granted is where a contractor makes arithmetical errors, operating against his interest in the tender, which are incorporated in the contract price without either party being aware of the errors before the contract is signed.[41]

---

[36] Megaw J. in *London Weekend Television Ltd.* v. *Harris and Griffith* (1969) 113 S.J. 222, referred to in *Joscelyne* v. *Nissen* [1970] 2 Q.B. 86 at 98 (C.A.).

[37] *Riverlate Properties Ltd.* v. *Paul* [1975] Ch. 133 (C.A.).

[38] *Thomas Bates Ltd.* v. *Wyndham's Ltd.* [1981] 1 W.L.R. 505 at 516 (C.A.); *The "Nai Genova"* [1984] 1 Lloyd's Rep. 353 at 360 *et seq.* (C.A.). For a case where a claim for rectification of this kind failed, see *Ishag* v. *Allied Bank* [1981] 1 Lloyd's Rep. 92 at 96.

[39] [1961] Ch. 555.

[40] *Thomas Bates Ltd.* v. *Wyndham's Ltd.* [1981] 1 W.L.R. 505 at 515 (C.A.).

[41] *Riverlate Properties Ltd.* v. *Paul* [1975] Ch. 133 (C.A.); *Ewing & Lawson* v. *Hanbury & Co.* (1900) 16 T.L.R. 140; *Kinlen* v. *Ennis Urban District Council* [1916] 2 I.R. 299, 309 (H.L.); *cf. Webster* v. *Cecil* (1861) 30 Beav. 62.

Arbitrators.[42]   Although an arbitrator does not have power to make a binding award as to the initial existence of the agreement from which his jurisdiction derives,[43] he may have jurisdiction to grant rectification of the agreement if the terms of the arbitration agreement are construed to be wide enough. In *Ashville Investments* v. *Elmer Construction*,[44] the Court of Appeal held that a claim for rectification was within the jurisdiction of an arbitrator appointed under clause 35 of the 1963 Standard Form of Building Contract.[45] But the claim for rectification was not a dispute or difference "as to the construction of this contract."[46] Claims for rectification do not arise "under" a principal contract,[47] but rectification will be within the scope of an arbitration clause which empowers the arbitrator to decide disputes "arising out of" the contract.[48] It is not clear whether, where the initial existence of the agreement is not in doubt, an arbitrator would have power to entertain a claim for rectification of the arbitration clause itself.[49]

Checking the bills of quantities.   It is common practice for the employer or his agent, *e.g.* the quantity surveyor, to check the calculations in the priced bills of quantities of the successful tenderer before a contract is finally concluded. If the employer discovers arithmetical errors[50] operating against the contractor's interest but these errors remain and are incorporated into the contract price, is the contractor entitled to rectification? The answer requires the application of the principles set out above to the facts of each case, but as a guide the following approach is suggested:

(1)   If the errors are clearly brought to the attention of the contractor and he decides to keep to his tender price and conditions, there cannot be rectification as there is no mistake.

(2)   If, in addition to the facts in (i) above, the parties agree upon some alteration in the tender price or upon some other alteration in the suggested terms of contract, *e.g.* as to calculation of prices for variations

---

[42] For Arbitration generally, see Chap. 16.

[43] *Heyman* v. *Darwins* [1942] A.C. 356 at 366 (H.L.); *Ashville Investments* v. *Elmer Construction* [1989] Q.B. 488 (C.A.). See also p. 387.

[44] [1989] Q.B. 488 (C.A.). See also the cases referred to in the judgments in the *Ashville Investments* case and also *Overseas Union Mutual* v. *A.A. Mutual* [1988] 2 Lloyd's Rep. 63 at 70.

[45] *cf. Kathmer Investments* v. *Woolworths* [1970] 2 S.A.L.R. 498 (Supreme Court of South Africa). For the equivalent clause in the 1980 Standard Form of Building Contract, see clause 41.4 at p. 674 where there is an express power to rectify the contract so that it accurately reflects the true agreement between the parties.

[46] *Ashville Investments* v. *Elmer Contractors* [1989] Q.B. 488 at 503 (C.A.).

[47] *Ibid.* at 502 (C.A.); *Fillite* v. *Aqua-Lift* (1989) 45 B.L.R. 27 (C.A.).

[48] See *Ethiopian Oilseeds* v. *Rio del Mar* [1990] 1 Lloyd's Rep. 86.

[49] It is suggested that he would not. See May L.J. in *Ashville Investments* v. *Elmer Contractors* [1989] Q.B. 488 at 499 (C.A.) suggesting that in some cases an arbitrator should not be invited to adjudicate upon his own jurisdiction.

[50] See *A Code of Procedure for Single Stage Selective Tendering* (April 1989) obtainable from the National Joint Consultative Committee for Building for the recommended procedure.

but by mistake the contract does not express these agreed alterations, then upon the agreement being clearly proved there can be rectification.[51]

(3) If errors are not brought to the attention of the contractor and he, ignorant of them, signs the contract, proof of these facts alone does not, it is submitted, give the contractor grounds for rectification,[52] but if the contractor proves clearly[53] that at the time of entering into the contract he believed the contract price to consist of the true totals of the properly calculated prices in the bills and that the employer at that time knew of the contractor's belief there can be rectification.[54]

5. Specific Performance

Specific performance is a decree issued by the court ordering the defendant to perform his promise. It is an equitable remedy granted by the court in its discretion, such discretion being exercised according to well-established principles. Thus the court will not grant a decree where the common law remedy of damages will adequately compensate the plaintiff, nor where the court cannot properly supervise performance. For these reasons "it is settled that, as a general rule, the court will not compel the building of houses."[55] Thus the court does not often order specific performance of a contract to build or do repairs but it has jurisdiction to do so and sometimes does.[56]

Building agreement. Where there is a purchase or lease of land and a agreement to carry out building works forms part of the consideration on one side or the other the court will order specific performance of the agreement to build if the following conditions are satisfied:

(1) "that the building work . . . is defined by contract; that is to say that the particulars of the work are so far definitely ascertained that the court can sufficiently see what is the exact nature of the work of which it is asked to order the performance."[57]

(2) "that the plaintiff has a substantial interest in having the contract

---

[51] See *Carlton Contractors* v. *Bexley Corp.* (1962) 60 L.G.R. 331.

[52] Neither do they give him a right to damages in fraud, see *Dutton* v. *Louth Corp.* (1955) unreported except in (1955) 116 E.G. 128 (C.A.), discussed at p. 124. For the importance of the distinction between lump sum contracts and measure and value contracts, see pp. 69 and 77. For the effect of pricing errors on valuation of variations, see p. 86. For misrepresentation, see pp. 120 *et seq.*

[53] For the standard of proof, see p. 266.

[54] See *Riverlate Properties Ltd.* v. *Paul* [1975] Ch. 133 (C.A.); *Thomas Bates Ltd.* v. *Wyndham's Ltd.* [1981] 1 W.L.R. 505 at 516 (C.A.); *The "Nai Genova"* [1984] 1 Lloyd's Rep. 353 at 360 *et seq.* (C.A.).

[55] Sir G. Mellish L.J. in *Wilkinson* v. *Clements* (1872) L.R. 8 Ch. 96 at 112.

[56] *Price* v. *Strange* [1978] 1 Ch. 337 at 359 (C.A.); *cf. Hounslow London Borough Council* v. *Twickenham Garden Developments* [1971] Ch. 233 at 251.

[57] Romer L.J. in *Wolverhampton Corp.* v. *Emmons* [1901] 1 K.B. 515 at 525 (C.A.). See also *Molyneux* v. *Richard* [1906] 1 Ch. 34.

performed which is of such a nature that he cannot adequately be compensated for breach of the contract by damages."[58]

(3) "that the defendant is in possession of the land on which the work is contracted to be done."[59]

Building contract—special circumstances. It is suggested that there may be special circumstances, even in the case of the ordinary building contract where there is no element of a transaction in land, where specific performance would be granted. The works would have to be exactly defined,[60] the defendant capable of carrying them out and damages an inadequate remedy. The position might arise in relation to specialised works when no other contractor is available to perform them.[61]

6. Injunction

The equitable remedy of an injunction ordering a person to do something or restraining him from continuing a wrong is not normally granted in building contracts as between employer and contractor for the same reasons that a decree of specific performance is not granted.[62] On the other hand, injunctions are sometimes granted to third parties to restrain trespass[63] or nuisance caused by building operations.[64]

Injunction to enforce disputed forfeiture. In *Hounslow London Borough Council* v. *Twickenham Garden Developments*,[65] Megarry J. refused an injunction whose effect would have been to exclude the contractor from the site. Notice of determination had been served under clause 25(1) of the 1963 Standard Form of Building Contract based on the alleged failure of the contractor "to proceed regularly and diligently with the works." The allegation was hotly disputed by the contractor and there were affidavits before the court upon the issues of fact. It was held that the case fell considerably short of any standard upon which it

---

[58] *Ibid.*

[59] Farwell J. in *Carpenters Estates Ltd.* v. *Davies* [1940] Ch. 160 at 164, extending the words of Romer L.J. in the *Wolverhampton* case, who said "that the defendant has by the contract obtained possession of land."

[60] See cases cited above; *Morris* v. *Redland Brick Ltd.* [1970] A.C. 652 (H.L.); *Jeune* v. *Queens Cross Properties Ltd.* [1974] 1 Ch. 97—order requiring landlord to reinstate stone balcony.

[61] *cf. Sky Petroleum Ltd.* v. *VIP Petroleum Ltd.* [1974] 1 W.L.R. 576—contract for supply of petrol enforced at time when other supplies might not be available.

[62] For the principles upon which mandatory injunctions are granted, see *Morris* v. *Redland Brick Ltd.* [1970] A.C. 652 (H.L.); *cf. Leakey* v. *National Trust* [1978] Q.B. 849 at 869; *Taylor Woodrow Construction* v. *Charcon Structure* (1982) 7 Con. L.R. 1 (C.A.); *London and Manchester Assurance* v. *O. and H. Construction* (1990) 6 Const. L.J. 155. For injunctions generally, see the notes to R.S.C., Ord. 29, r. 1 in the Supreme Court Practice 1991. For *Mareva* injunctions to prevent the dissipation of assets, see the Supreme Court Practice 1991 at 29/1/20 *et seq.*

[63] See *London and Manchester Assurance* v. *O. and H. Construction* (1990) 6 Const. L.J. 155.

[64] See generally "Nuisance from building operations" at p. 257.

[65] [1971] Ch. 233; *cf. Verrall* v. *Great Yarmouth Borough Council* [1981] Q.B. 202 (C.A.).

would be safe to grant an interlocutory injunction for "what is involved is the application of an uncertain concept to disputed facts."[66] Despite the importance to the Borough on social grounds of securing due completion of the works there was a contract in existence and the contractors were not to be stripped of their rights under it however desirable that might be for the Borough. An earier Irish case[67] was distinguished upon the ground that there the engineer's certificate of default had been conclusive whereas in the instant case the architect's opinion was not.[68]

The *Hounslow* case was decided at a time when it was generally accepted that before a plaintiff could obtain an interim injunction he had to show a *prima facie* case in his favour.[69] Subsequently the House of Lords in *American Cyanamid Co.* v. *Ethicon Ltd.*[70] held that there is no such rule and that it is sufficient in the first instance for the plaintiff to show that there is a serious issue to be tried. The court then considers damages. If they are an adequate remedy for the plaintiff an injunction is not granted. If they are inadequate and the defendant would be protected against the effect of an injunction by the plaintiff's undertaking as to damages[71] then it becomes a question of the balance of convenience whether or not an injunction should be granted. The court takes into account the parties' ability to pay damages.[72]

Having regard to the *Cyanamid* case, it is submitted that, on the facts in the *Hounslow* case, and assuming that all contractual requirements as to notices and the like have been complied with, an injunction would now be granted.[73] The contractor would be protected by the undertaking in damages. The injunction would enable the employer to complete his project. Where an employer had served notice under clause 63 of the I.C.E. Conditions (5th edition) expelling the contractor from the site, the contractor who challenged the contractual effectiveness of the expulsion failed to obtain an injunction restraining its implementation. It was held that the balance of convenience

---

[66] *Hounslow London Borough Council* v. *Twickenham Garden Developments* [1971] Ch. 233 at 269.

[67] *Cork Corporation* v. *Rooney* (1881) 7 L.R.Ir. 191.

[68] The *Hounslow* case was not followed in *Mayfield Holdings* v. *Moana Reef* [1973] 1 N.Z.L.R. 309, Supreme Court, Auckland. In a New South Wales case after disputes arose, the owner secured possession of the site and wrote revoking the contractor's licence to be upon the site. Notice of arbitration was given. It was held that, on the assumption that the revocation was wrongful, an injunction would not be granted to the builder since damages would be a sufficient remedy— *Graham H. Roberts Pty. Ltd.* v. *Naurbeth Investments Pty. Ltd.* [1974] 1 N.S.W.L.R. 93.

[69] See *Fellowes* v. *Fisher* [1976] Q.B. 122 (C.A.).

[70] [1975] A.C. 396; *cf. Garden Cottage Foods* v. *Milk Marketing Board* [1984] A.C. 130 (H.L.).

[71] The plaintiff as a condition of obtaining an interim injunction has to give an undertaking to pay to the defendant his damages suffered by the grant of the injunction if the defendant ultimately succeeds. See para. 29/1/12 of the Supreme Court Practice 1991, and for the position of the Crown see *Hoffman-La Roche (F.) & Co. A.G.* v. *Secretary of State for Trade and Industry* [1975] A.C. 295 (H.L.).

[72] *American Cyanamid Co.* v. *Ethicon Ltd.* [1975] A.C. 396; *Fellowes* v. *Fisher* [1976] Q.B. 122 (C.A.); *Hubbard* v. *Pitt* [1976] Q.B. 142 (C.A.).

[73] In *American Cyanamid Co.* v. *Ethicon Ltd.* [1975] A.C. 396 the *status quo* was protected by the grant of an interim injunction and that would not be the instant case. Nevertheless, it is thought that the principle stated in the text would apply; *cf. Surrey Heath Borough Council* v. *Lovell Construction* (1988) 42 B.L.R. 25 at 51.

strongly favoured the court supporting the Engineer's decision.[74] The position might be different if it appears that the employer is, or might be, unable to fulfil his undertaking in damages. But even here it does seem a strong step to maintain the contractor in possession for an indefinite period. This achieves a kind of contractor's lien on land such as exists by statute in some jurisdictions,[75] but not in England and Wales.

No injunction restraining forfeiture.   It is thought that the *American Cyanamid* case does not affect the principle that in the ordinary case the contractor cannot obtain an injunction restraining forfeiture by the employer, because this would be equivalent to ordering specific performance of the contract and the court does not normally grant this remedy in the case of a building contract.[76] The contractor can be adequately compensated in damages for any wrongful forfeiture.[77]

Injunction in aid of the criminal law.   There is jurisdiction to grant such an injunction but it is invoked exceptionally and with great caution. But the court may, for instance, grant an injunction to restrain contravention of the Control of Pollution Act 1974 by excessive noise on a building site where the inference is that unlawful operations would continue unless and until effectively restrained by the law and that nothing short of an injunction would be effective.[78]

---

[74] *Tara Civil Engineering* v. *Moorfield Developments* (1989) 46 B.L.R. 72; *cf. Att.-Gen. of Hong Kong* v. *Ko Hon Mau* (1988) 44 B.L.R. 144 (Hong Kong Court of Appeal).

[75] *e.g.* Ontario: Construction Lien legislation.

[76] *Garrett* v. *Banstead and Epsom Downs Railway* (1864) 12 L.T. 654; *Munro* v. *Wivenhoe, etc., Railway* (1865) 12 L.T. 655; *Tara Civil Engineering* v. *Moorfield Developments* (1989) 46 B.L.R. 72; *cf. Foster & Dicksee* v. *Hastings Corporation* (1903) 87 L.T. 736—interim injunction granted pending arbitration on whether forfeiture justified; *Garrett* v. *Salisbury, etc., Railway* (1866) L.R. 2 Eq. 358.

[77] *Munro* v. *Wivenhoe, etc., Railway* (1865) 12 L.T. 655 at 657, and see the cases cited in n. 72 above. For the measure of damages, see p. 207.

[78] *City of London Corporation* v. *Bovis Construction* (1988) 49 B.L.R. 1 (C.A.).

CHAPTER 12

ASSIGNMENTS, SUBSTITUTED CONTRACTS AND SUB-CONTRACTS

1. Assignments

In considering assignments it is essential to distinguish between the benefit and the burden of a contract. In the normal building contract the burden on the contractor is the duty to complete the works, and his benefit is the right to receive the contract money when it falls due. The burden on the employer is the duty to pay such money, and the benefit is the right to have the works completed.

(a) *Assignment by contractor of burden*

It is a general principle that the burden of a contract cannot be assigned without the consent of the other party. Therefore the contractor cannot assign his liability to complete.[1] "A debtor cannot relieve himself of his liability to his creditor by assigning the burden of the obligation to someone else. This can only be brought about by the consent of all three, and involves the release of the original debtor."[2] In substance, therefore, there has to be a novation.

---

[1] *Nokes* v. *Doncaster Amalgamated Collieries Ltd.* [1940] A.C. 1014 (H.L.).
[2] Collins M.R. in *Tolhurst* v. *Associated Portland Cement* [1902] 2 K.B. 660 at 668 (C.A.).

Novation.   A novation is a tripartite agreement by which an existing contract between A and B is discharged and a fresh contract is made between A and C usually on the same terms as the first contract. If by agreement with the employer the contractor ceases to be liable and a fresh contractor takes his place, there is a novation and not an assignment.[3] Thus there is a novation where the contractor is a firm but a limited company is formed which takes over the contractor's business and the employer accepts the company in place of the original firm.[4]

Vicarious performance.   In some cases a contractor is entitled to secure the vicarious performance of his obligations while remaining liable for non-performance himself.[5] The leading case is *British Waggon Co. v. Lea.*[6] The Parkgate Co., which was under a contract to Lea to keep certain railway wagons in repair for a number of years, went into liquidation[7] and assigned its contract (*i.e.* both benefit and burden) to the British Waggon Co. It was held that Lea could not refuse to accept performance of the contract by the British Waggon Co. This case has been explained by Lord Simon in the House of Lords where he said[8]:

> "I may add that a possible confusion may arise from the use of the word 'assignability' in discussing some of the cases usually cited on this subject. Thus in *British Waggon Co. v. Lea* the real point of the decision was that the contract which the Parkgate company had made with Lea for the repair of certain wagons did not call for the repairs being necessarily effected by the Parkgate company itself, but could be adequately performed by the Parkgate company arranging with the British Waggon company that the latter should execute the repairs. Such a result does not depend on assignment at all. It depends on the view that the contract of repair was duly discharged by the Parkgate company by getting the repairs satisfactorily effected by a third party. In other words, the contract bound the Parkgate company to produce a result, not necessarily by its own efforts, but, if it preferred, by vicarious performance through a sub-contract or otherwise."

It is a matter of construction of the contract whether or not the contractor has the right of securing vicarious performance.[9] He has the right where it is a matter of indifference whose hand should do the work,[10] as in the *British*

---

[3] See *Commercial Bank of Tasmania v. Jones* [1893] A.C. 313 (P.C.); see also *Chatsworth Investments Ltd. v. Cussins (Contractors) Ltd.* [1969] 1 W.L.R. 1 at 4, 6 (C.A.).

[4] As in *Chandler Bros. v. Boswell* [1936] 3 All E.R. 179 at 183 (C.A.).

[5] *Nokes v. Doncaster Amalgamated Collieries Ltd.* [1940] A.C. 1014 (H.L.); *Davies v. Collins* [1945] 1 All E.R. 247 at 249 (C.A.). For a shipbuilding case see *The "Diana Prosperity"* [1976] 2 Lloyd's Rep. 60 (C.A.) upheld on appeal at [1976] 1 W.L.R. 989 (H.L.).

[6] (1880) 5 Q.B.D. 149 (D.C.).

[7] It was not dissolved at the time of trial. See Cockburn C.J. at 151.

[8] *Nokes v. Doncaster Amalgamated Collieries Ltd.* [1940] A.C. 1014 at 1019 (H.L.).

[9] *Davies v. Collins* [1945] 1 All E.R. 247 at 249 (C.A.); and see *Tolhurst v. Associated Portland Cement Manufacturers Ltd.* [1903] A.C. 414 (H.L.), explained at 1020 of *Nokes'* case by Lord Simon.

[10] *Davies v. Collins* [1945] 1 All E.R. 247 (C.A.).

Waggon case, where the repairs were "a rough description of work which ordinary workmen conversant with the business would be perfectly able to execute."[11] If the employer acquiesces in vicarious performance he may lose the right to any objection he might otherwise possess.[12]

The contractor does not have the right of performing by another if, either there is a prohibition in the contract,[13] or there is some personal element in his obligation. The contract can be personal in this sense if it was made with the contractor because of his skill or special knowledge,[14] or because of his personality or character.[15] A contract to build a lighthouse was held to be personal,[16] and clearly most contracts of a specialist nature are personal. It is submitted that with large contracts involving great experience of site management and the appointment of men to positions of authority and other managerial duties, the administrative duties of the main contractor are personal.[17]

(b) *Assignment by contractor of benefit*

It is common for a contractor to assign the retention money or other sums due under the contract in order to secure advances from merchants, bankers and others. The assent of the employer to such assignments is not necessary and if after notice he ignores the assignment and pays the money to the contractor he will have to pay the money again to the assignee.[18] If, however, the contract under which the money is payable expressly prohibits the assignment of the right to receive it, any purported assignment will be invalid and the assignee cannot enforce a claim for such monies against the employer.[19]

Such assignments may be legal or equitable. The main difference is that under a legal assignment the assignee can sue in his own name for the money assigned, whereas under an equitable assignment the assignee must sue in the name of the assignor or, if he refuses to be joined as plaintiff, must add him as defendant. The difference is therefore in the main a matter of procedure.[20] It

---

[11] *British Waggon Co.* v. *Lea* at 153.

[12] *Falle* v. *Le Sueur & Le Huguel* (1859) 12 Moore P.C.C. 501 (P.C.).

[13] See, *e.g.* clause 19 of the Standard Form of Building Contract at p. 536.

[14] *Robson* v. *Drummond* (1831) 2 B. & Ad. 303 (an extreme case; see *British Waggon Co.* v. *Lea* (1880) 5 Q.B.D. 149 at 153); *Wentworth* v. *Cock* (1839) 10 A. & E. 42 at 45; *Knight* v. *Burgess* (1864) 33 L.J.Ch. 727; *Johnson* v. *Raylton* (1881) 7 Q.B.D. 438 (C.A.); *Davies* v. *Collins* [1945] 1 All E.R. 247 (C.A.); *Edwards* v. *Newland & Co.* [1950] 2 K.B. 534 (C.A.); *Kollerich* v. *State Trading* [1980] 2 Lloyd's Rep. 32 (C.A.).

[15] See *Kemp* v. *Baerselman* [1906] 2 K.B. 604 (C.A.); *Cooper* v. *Micklefield Coal & Lime Co.* (1912) 107 L.T. 457.

[16] *Anon.*, cited by Patteson J. in *Wentworth* v. *Cock* (1839) 10 A. & E. 42 at 45.

[17] *cf. Edwards* v. *Newland & Co.* [1950] 2 K.B. 534 at 542 (C.A.).

[18] *Brice* v. *Bannister* (1878) 3 Q.B.D. 569 (C.A.). This applies whether the assignment is legal or equitable. For a discussion of clause 19 of the Standard Form of Building Contract, see p. 538; *cf. Farley* v. *Housing and Commercial Developments* (1984) 26 B.L.R. 66 for the position where the contractor becomes insolvent and goes into liquidation.

[19] *Helstan Securities Ltd.* v. *Herts County Council* [1978] 3 All E.R. 262.

[20] *Tolhurst* v. *Associated Portland Cement Manufacturers Ltd.* [1903] A.C. 414 (H.L.). For procedure when seeking summary judgment on an assignment, see *Les Fils Dreyfus, etc.* v. *Clarke* [1958] 1 W.L.R. 300 (C.A.).

seems, however, that if an equitable assignee commences an action without joining the assignor, the action is not a nullity, although the equitable assignee cannot recover damages or a perpetual injunction until the assignor has been joined and the action will be stayed pending joinder.[21] The court can overlook non-joinder of the assignor, if no objection is taken,[22] but if any objection is raised it will dismiss the claim of an equitable assignee who does not bring the assignor before the court.[23]

An assignment of part of a debt or legal thing in action is merely an equitable assignment and is not effective to transfer the legal right.[24] If the assignor of part of a debt sues his debtor for the debt, he must join the assignee in the proceedings before he can recover the debt or even that part of it which was not assigned.[25]

Legal assignment.   A legal assignment derives its authority from section 136 of the Law of Property Act 1925. It must be absolute,[26] in writing, and express notice in writing[27] of the assignment must be given to the debtor.[28] In such a case the assignee can sue in his own name for the debt or thing in action assigned and has all legal and other remedies for the same and can give a good discharge without the concurrence of the assignor.[29]

An assignment of retention money or instalments earned, but not payable at the date of assignment, is absolute and within the section.[30] An assignment of unearned instalments is good in equity, and may, if it is of a definite sum, be good at law.[31]

A mortgage of all moneys due or to become due by way of security for advances is absolute and within the section.[32] In such a case there will either be

---

[21] *Weddell* v. *Pearce & Major* [1988] Ch. 26. This could affect questions of limitation as it did in *Weddell's* case.

[22] *Brandt's Sons & Co.* v. *Dunlop Rubber Co.* [1905] A.C. 454 (H.L.); *cf. Central Insurance* v. *Seacalf Shipping* [1983] 2 Lloyd's Rep. 25 at 34 (C.A.).

[23] *William* v. *Atlantic Assurance Co. Ltd.* [1933] 1 K.B. 81 (C.A.).

[24] *Ibid.*

[25] *Walter & Sullivan Ltd.* v. *J. Murphy & Sons Ltd.* [1955] 2 Q.B. 584 (C.A.).

[26] For an example of an assignment which was not absolute, see *The Halcyon the Great* [1984] 1 Lloyd's Rep. 283.

[27] See, *e.g. Gatoil Anstalt* v. *Omennial* [1980] 2 Lloyd's Rep. 489 for a case where a suspensory notice was held not to be within the section.

[28] s.136(1)—"Any absolute assignment by writing under the hand of the assignor (not purporting to be by way of charge only) of any debt or any other legal thing in action, of which express notice in writing has been given to the debtor, trustee or other person from whom the assignor would have been entitled to receive or claim such debt or thing in action, is effectual in law ...."

[29] *Ibid.*

[30] *G. & T. Earle (1925) Ltd.* v. *Hemsworth Rural District Council* (1928) 140 L.T. 69 (C.A.).

[31] *G. & T. Earle (1925) Ltd.* v. *Hemsworth Rural District Council* (1928) 140 L.T. 69 at 71 (C.A.); *Walker* v. *Bradford Old Bank* (1884) 12 Q.B.D. 511; *Jones* v. *Humphreys* [1902] 1 K.B. 10 at 13; *Re Tout and Finch* [1954] 1 W.L.R. 178; *cf. Brice* v. *Bannister* (1878) 3 Q.B.D. 569 (C.A.); *Durham Bros.* v. *Robertson* [1898] 1 Q.B. 765 (C.A.); *Drew* v. *Josolyne* (1887) 18 Q.B.D. 590 (C.A.); *Rayack Construction* v. *Lampeter Meat* (1979) 12 B.L.R. 30; *Re Arthur Sanders Ltd.* (1981) 17 B.L.R. 125; *cf. Re Jartay Developments Ltd.* (1982) 22 B.L.R. 134.

[32] *Tancred* v. *Delagoa Bay, etc., Railway* (1889) 23 Q.B.D. 239.

an express right of redemption by the mortgagor[33] (*i.e.* the contractor), or such a right will be implied by equity.[34] But where contractors charged the sum of £1,080 due to them under a contract as security for advances until such advances were repaid, this was held to be a conditional assignment and not within the section, though it was a good equitable assignment.[35]

The assignment of part of an entire debt is not within the section. Therefore if no provision is made in the contract for the payment of instalments or for retention money the contractor cannot make a legal assignment of part of the contract sum.[36]

Equitable assignment. An equitable assignment usually arises where there is a clear intention to assign a debt or other thing in action but one of the requirements of section 136 of the Law of Property Act 1925 has not been satisfied. Except that an equitable assignment of an equitable interest must be in writing,[37] no particular form is required provided the meaning is clear,[38] and a clearly defined fund is specified.[39] Thus it was held that clause 11(h) of the former Standard Form of Sub-contract[40] operated as a valid equitable assignment to the sub-contractor of that part of the retention money held by the employer under the main contract which was due to the sub-contractor under the sub-contractor thereby creating a trust in favour of the sub-contractor.[41] And a letter by the main contractor (a limited company) to the employer directing him to pay direct to the sub-contractor a sum of money out of the next certificate to be issued was held to be a valid equitable assignment, and not void as against the receiver of the debenture-holders of the main contractor as being an unregistered charge within the meaning of section 79[42] of the Companies Act 1929.[43]

---

[33] *Ibid.*

[34] As in *Hughes* v. *Pump House Hotel Co.* [1902] 2 K.B. 190 (C.A.).

[35] *Durham Bros.* v. *Robertson* [1898] 1 Q.B. 765 (C.A.).

[36] *Williams* v. *Atlantic Assurance Co.* [1933] 1 K.B. 81 (C.A.), though it would be good as an equitable assignment.

[37] See s.53(1)(c) of the Law of Property Act 1925.

[38] *Brandt's Sons & Co.* v. *Dunlop Rubber Co.* [1905] A.C. 454 at 462 (H.L.); *cf. Re McArdle* [1951] Ch. 669 (C.A.); *South East Thames R.H.A.* v. *Lovell* (1985) 32 B.L.R. 127 at 134 *cf. Kijowski* v. *New Capital Properties* (1987) 15 Con. L.R. 1 at 8.

[39] *Percival* v. *Dunn* (1885) 29 Ch.D. 128; *cf. Re Warren, ex p. Wheeler* [1938] Ch. 725 (D.C.).

[40] Reproduced in the 4th ed. of this book at p. 591.

[41] *Re Tout and Finch* [1954] 1 W.L.R. 178; *Rayack Construction* v. *Lampeter Meat* (1979) 12 B.L.R. 30; *Re Arthur Sanders Ltd.* (1981) 17 B.L.R. 125; *cf. Re Jartay Developments Ltd.* (1982) 22 B.L.R. 134. See now clause 21.9 of NSC/4 at p. 752. For the possible effect of *British Eagle Ltd.* v. *Air France* [1975] 1 W.L.R. 758 (H.L.) (discussed at p. 381) on cases such as these, see *Re Arthur Sanders Ltd.* (1981) 17 B.L.R. 125 at 140; see also *Carreras Rothmans* v. *Freeman Mathews* [1985] Ch. 207. It seems that an equitable assignment creating a trust is to be distinguished from one creating a charge which could be void if unregistered—see below.

[42] Now s.395 of the Companies Act 1985 for which see n. 46 below.

[43] *Ashby Warner & Co. Ltd.* v. *Simmons* (1936) 155 L.T. 371 (C.A.); *cf. Re Kent & Sussex Sawmills Ltd.* [1947] Ch. 177; *Walter & Sullivan Ltd.* v. *Murphy & Sons Ltd.* [1955] 2 Q.B. 584 (C.A.); In *Re Welsh Irish Ferries Ltd.* [1986] Ch. 471; *Annangel Glory* v. *M. Goldodetz* [1988] 1 Lloyd's Rep. 45; and see *Chitty* (26th ed.), paras. 1398 and 1401.

An equitable assignment can be of future property,[44] and it need not be absolute but may be by way of a charge.[45] But a charge within section 396 of the Companies Act 1985 created by a company will be void against the liquidator and any creditor of the company if it is not duly registered.[46]

Notice to the employer. Written notice to the debtor of the assignment is necessary to perfect a legal assignment.[47] Such assignment is complete from the date on which the notice is received by the debtor.[48] It should bring to the notice of the debtor with reasonable certainty the fact of the assignment so as to prevent him paying the debt to the original creditor.[49]

Notice to the debtor is not essential to an equitable assignment but is advisable for several reasons. The assignee is bound by any payments the debtor makes to the assignor without notice of the assignment,[50] and by the rule in *Dearle* v. *Hall*[51] the priority of an assignment against other assignees depends not upon the dates of the assignment but upon the order of giving notice to the debtor.[52] An equitable assignee of a contractual option who has not given notice to the grantor of the option cannot exercise the option in his own name so as to bind the grantor.[53]

Consideration. Consideration is not necessary to support a legal assignment,[54] nor an equitable assignment which is absolute and of an existing debt.[55] Where an equitable assignment is conditional or by way of charge or of future property, consideration is, it seems, necessary.[56]

Subject to equities. An assignee, whether legal or equitable, takes subject to equities. This means "subject to all rights of set-off and other defences which

---

[44] *Tailby* v. *The Official Receiver* (1888) 13 App.Cas. 523 at 546 (H.L.); *Re Tout and Finch* [1954] 1 W.L.R. 178; *cf. Annangel Glory* v. *M. Golodetz* [1988] 1 Lloyd's Rep. 45 at 49.

[45] As in *Durham Bros.* v. *Robertson* [1898] 1 Q.B. 765 (C.A.). For what was intended in a charge on "retention money," see *West Yorkshire Bank Ltd.* v. *Isherwood Bros. Ltd.* (1912) 28 T.L.R. 593.

[46] s.395 of the Companies Act 1985. This section will be amended when ss.93–107 of the Companies Act 1989 are brought into force. The section which will then render an unregistered charge void will be amended s.399 of the Companies Act 1985 and there will be other changes, *e.g.* in amended ss.404 and 405.

[47] See above.

[48] *Holt* v. *Heatherfield Trust Ltd.* [1942] 2 K.B. 1.

[49] *Van Lynn Developments Ltd.* v. *Pelias Construction Co. Ltd.* [1969] 1 Q.B. 607, 613, 615 (C.A.); see also *W. F. Harrison & Co. Ltd.* v. *Burke* [1956] 1 W.L.R. 419 (C.A.).

[50] *Stocks* v. *Dobson* (1853) 4 De G.M. & G. 11.

[51] (1828) 3 Russ. 1; *cf. Ellerman Lines* v. *Lancaster Maritime* [1980] 2 Lloyd's Rep. 497 at 503; *Rhodes* v. *Allied Dunbar* [1987] 1 W.L.R. 1703 at 1708 reversed on appeal on another point at [1989] 1 W.L.R. 800 (C.A.) and see 806.

[52] *cf. Pfeiffer G.m.b.H.* v. *Arbuthnot Factors* [1988] 1 W.L.R. 150 at 163; *The Attika Hope* [1988] 1 Lloyd's Rep. 439.

[53] *Warner Bros. Records Inc.* v. *Rollgreen Ltd.* [1976] Q.B. 430 (C.A.). See, however, *Chitty* (26th ed.), Vol. 1, p. 865, n. 28.

[54] *Re Westerton* [1919] 2 Ch. 104.

[55] *Holt* v. *Heatherfield Trust Ltd.* [1942] 2 K.B. 1; *Re McArdle* [1951] Ch. 669 at 674 (C.A.).

[56] *Holt* v. *Heatherfield Trust Ltd.* [1942] 2 K.B. 1; *Re McArdle* [1951] Ch. 669 (C.A.).

were available against the assignor."[57] Thus the assignee of moneys due under the contract takes subject to any claim by the employer arising out of the contract such as for defective work or for damages for delay.[58] Other applications of the principle are given below.

The only exception to the rule that the assignee takes subject to equities is "that after notice of an assignment of a chose in action,[59] the debtor cannot by payment or otherwise do anything to take away or diminish the rights of the assignee as they stood at the time of the notice."[60] Where, after notice, the employer advanced money to the contractor to enable him to complete, it was held that such advance could not be set off against the moneys assigned and he must pay the assignee.[61] It has been held that an employer could not set off a claim under a new contract with the contractor entered into after the notice of assignment, even though the new contract came into existence as the result of the exercise of an option in the original contract.[62] It was further held that although the employer, by an express clause in the original contract, was empowered to deduct or set off damages due from the contractor to the employer against any money due from the employer to the contractor, this did not enable him to set off claims arising out of concurrent and separate contracts.[63]

Certified completion.   If the building contract requires a certificate of completion before the final balance is payable an assignee is in no better position than the contractor, and cannot therefore recover payment until the certificate has been issued.[64]

Forfeiture.   An assignee takes subject to any right of the employer to forfeit or determine the contract, and if upon such forfeiture or determination the money assigned ceased to be payable by the employer the assignee will have no claim against the employer,[65] although he may, according to the terms of the assignment, have a claim for damages against the contractor.[66]

Fraud.   Where a certificate for payment was obtained by fraud between the contractor and the architect, it was held that the assignees of retention moneys

---

[57] James L.J. in *Roxburghe* v. *Cox* (1881) 17 Ch.D. 520 at 526 (C.A.). But this does not include rights against an intermediate assignee—*Banco Central* v. *Lingoss & Falce* [1980] 2 Lloyd's Rep. 266.

[58] *Young* v. *Kitchin* (1878) 3 Ex.D. 127; *Newfoundland Govt.* v. *Newfoundland Railway* (1888) 13 App.Cas. 199 (P.C.); *cf. Bank of Boston* v. *European Grain* [1989] A.C. 1056 at 1109 (H.L.).

[59] *I.e.* a debt or thing in action.

[60] James L.J. in *Roxburghe* v. *Cox* (1881) 17 Ch.D. 520 at 526 (C.A.).

[61] *Brice* v. *Bannister* (1878) 3 Q.B.D. 569 (C.A.).

[62] *Re Asphaltic Wood Pavement Co., ex p. Lee and Chapman* (1885) 30 Ch.D. 216 (C.A.). This is of particular significance in insolvency: see Insolvency Act 1986, s.323; *National Westminster Bank Ltd.* v. *Halesowen, etc., Ltd.* [1972] A.C. 785 esp. at 821 (H.L.); *cf. Willment Brothers* v. *North West Thames R.H.A.* (1984) 26 B.L.R. 51 (C.A.).

[63] *Re Asphaltic Wood Pavement Co., ex p. Lee and Chapman* (1885) 30 Ch.D. 216 (C.A.).

[64] Lord Blackburn in *Lewis* v. *Hoare* (1881) 44 L.T. 66 at 67 (H.L.).

[65] *Tooth* v. *Hallett* (1869) L.R. 4 Ch.App. 242; *Drew* v. *Josolyne* (1887) 18 Q.B.D. 590 (C.A.).

[66] See *Humphreys* v. *James* (1850) 20 L.J. Ex. 88.

due on the certificate, although innocent of the fraud, were in no better position than the contractor and the fraud was a good defence against them.[67] If the contract was induced by a fraudulent misrepresentation the employer can rescind the contract or set up the fraud as a defence to a claim by an assignee, but he cannot set off against an innocent assignee a claim for damages for the tort of deceit, for this is a personal claim against the wrongdoer.[68]

Employer cannot counterclaim. The employer's right against the assignee is limited to a set-off up to the amount of the claim. He cannot go beyond this and counterclaim against the assignee.[69]

Arbitration clause. Unless the subject-matter of the contract is such that it cannot be assigned,[70] it seems that the assignee of moneys due can enforce, and will be subject to, an arbitration clause in the contract.[71]

Rival claims. If there are rival claims to moneys due under the contract, either between assignor and assignee, or as a result of claims such as that of a trustee in bankruptcy, the employer should call upon the claimants to interplead, *i.e.* to commence a form of proceeding to determine to whom the money should be paid.[72] If the employer does this he will pay the right claimant and can normally recover his costs out of the moneys assigned. If he does not take this course and chooses to pay the wrong person he will have to pay twice over and may have to pay the costs of the successful claimant.[73]

(c) *Assignment by employer of burden*

The employer cannot without the contractor's assent assign the burden of the contract, *i.e.* the liability to pay the contract moneys.[74] If the contractor's

---

[67] *Wakefield and Barnsley Banking Co.* v. *Normanton Local Board* (1881) 44 L.T. 697 (C.A.).

[68] *Stoddart* v. *Union Trust Ltd.* [1912] 1 K.B. 181 at 194 (C.A.). See commentary on this case in *Chitty* (26th ed.), para. 1428.

[69] *Young* v. *Kitchin* (1878) 3 Ex.D. 127; *Newfoundland Government* v. *Newfoundland Railway* (1888) 13 App.Cas. 199 (P.C.).

[70] See p. 275. See also *Glegg* v. *Bromley* [1912] 3 K.B. 474 (C.A.); *Compania Colombiana de Seguras* v. *Pacific Steam Navigation Co.* [1965] 1 Q.B. 101.

[71] *Shayler* v. *Woolf* [1946] Ch. 320 at 323 (C.A.); confining statement of Wright J. in *Cottage Club Estates Ltd.* v. *Woodside Estates Co. (Amersham) Ltd.* [1928] 2 K.B. 463 to its particular facts. See also *Aspell* v. *Seymour* [1929] W.N. 152 (C.A.); *Rumput (Panama)* v. *Islamic Republic of Iran Shipping Lines* [1984] 2 Lloyd's Rep. 259 for a case under s.1 of the Arbitration Act 1975; Mustill & Boyd, *Commercial Arbitration* (2nd ed.), pp. 137 *et seq.*

[72] s.136(1) of the Law of Property Act 1925; this, it seems, applies only to legal assignments, but apart from the section the employer has a right to call for an interpleader issue where the assignment is equitable: R.S.C., Ord. 17; and see, *e.g.* *Drew* v. *Josolyne* (1887) 18 Q.B.D. 590 (C.A.).

[73] *G. & T. Earle (1925) Ltd.* v. *Hemsworth Rural District Council* (1928) 140 L.T. 69 at 71 (C.A.). For an example in a company liquidation of a summons to determine the issue in the Chancery Division, see *Re Tout and Finch* [1954] 1 W.L.R. 178.

[74] *Tolhurst* v. *Associated Cement Ltd.* [1903] A.C. 414 (H.L.).

consent is obtained there is a novation, and the original employer is released and a new one takes his place.[75]

(d) *Assignment by employer of benefit*

An employer can assign his rights under the contract provided that there is nothing of a personal nature about the rights,[76] and provided that the assignment in question is not precluded by the terms of the contract.[77]

Assignment of causes of action.   It is a fundamental principle of English law that a person cannot assign a bare right to litigate, and such purported assignments are void. This may occur where it is likely that the assignee may make a profit out of the litigation.[78] But if, looking at the totality of the transaction, the assignment is of a property right or interest, or if the assignee has a genuine commercial interest in taking the assignment and in enforcing it for his own benefit, there is no reason why the assignment should be struck down as an assignment of a bare cause of action.[79] It is thought that assignees of causes of action in building contract cases of the kind discussed below usually do have a sufficient genuine commercial interest.[80]

Assignment of warranties.   Modern developers often dispose of newly built properties to purchasers who want also to acquire the benefit of contractual rights which the developer has against builders, consultants or others. The various legal schemes for achieving this are complicated. One means often considered is for the developer to assign his contractual rights to the purchaser. Is this effective and, if it is, what losses can the assignee recover? Usually the sale will have been for full value and the main question is whether the defendant could successfully assert that, since the assignor has suffered no loss, the assignee has no more than a nominal claim. Put another way, can an assignee of contractual rights successfully attach his own losses to the assigned right? The answer may not be the same for both legal and equitable assignees.[81]

---

[75] *Commercial Bank of Tasmania* v. *Jones* [1893] A.C. 313 (P.C.).

[76] *Kemp* v. *Baerselman* [1906] 2 K.B. 604 (C.A.); *Cooper* v. *Micklefield Coal & Lime Co.* (1912) 107 L.T. 457; *Tolhurst* v. *Associated Cement Ltd.* [1903] A.C. 414 (H.L.).

[77] See *Helstan Securities Ltd.* v. *Herts County Council* [1978] 3 All E.R. 262.

[78] *Trendtex Trading* v. *Credit Suisse* [1982] A.C. 679 (H.L.); *cf. South East Thames R.H.A.* v. *Lovell* (1985) 32 B.L.R. 127 at 139.

[79] *Trendtex Trading* v. *Credit Suisse* [1982] A.C. 679 at 703 (H.L.); *Brownton* v. *Edward Moore Inbucom* [1985] 3 All E.R. 499 (C.A.); *cf. The Kelo* [1985] 2 Lloyd's Rep. 85 at 89.

[80] *cf. South East Thames R.H.A.* v. *Lovell* (1985) 32 B.L.R. 127; *Pickering* v. *Sogex Services* (1982) 20 B.L.R. 71.

[81] This may be of particular significance with large developments where the developer sells to more than one purchaser, since the assignment of part of a right can only be an equitable assignment—see p. 277.

There is no clear authority for assigned *contractual* rights.[82] It is submitted that, in principle, where there is a legal assignment of the benefit of a contractual promise, the assignee can claim such categories of loss as the assignor could have claimed but for the assignment, this question to be determined by the application of normal *Hadley* v. *Baxendale*[83] principles. If this is correct, the assignee can claim the cost of rectifying defects to the building caused by breach of the assigned right and may be able to claim other losses provided that they are of a class of loss which the assignor could have claimed. It is further submitted, but with caution, that the same principle can apply to an equitable assignment of the benefit of a contractual promise. It may be that the assignee of a tortious right can recover no more than the assignor's loss.[84]

2. Substituted Contracts

If by agreement or because of forfeiture a new contractor is substituted for the original it is a question of construction how far the new contractor is subject to the liabilities of the original contractor. If the contract between the new contractor and the employer expressly or impliedly incorporates or refers to the original contract both contracts must be read together.[85] Thus a new contractor has been held liable in liquidated damages for delay caused by the original contractor.[86] In another case, where the events were similar, but the contracts were different, it was held that the liquidated damages clause

---

[82] The nearest case is perhaps *Dawson* v. *Great Northern and City Railway* [1905] 1 K.B. 260 (C.A.)—a claim for statutory compensation—and it is thought that this case, esp. at 272 *et seq.*, supports the proposition stated in the text. The assignee plaintiff recovered the reinstatement cost for structural damage on the basis that the assignment did not place any greater burden on the defendants than if the claim had been made by the assignor. She did not recover for damage to her trade stock because she could not recover a greater amount of compensation than the assignor could have recovered. The proposition is also implicitly supported in the result by the majority decision in *Tolhurst* v. *Associated Portland Cement* [1903] A.C. 414 (H.L.)—see especially Lord Lindley at 423, "The Imperial Company could not by alienation or otherwise increase the burdens which Mr. Tolhurst undertook to bear. But this is the only limit which I can find in the present case." *cf. Cromlech Property Co.* v. *Costain Construction* (1986) 10 Con. L.R. 110. See also John Cartwright, "The Assignment of Collateral Warranties" (1990) 6 Const. L.J. at 14. See for assigned rights in *tort, Cole-Hamilton* v. *Boyd* [1963] S.C. (H.L.) 1; *Perry* v. *Tendring District Council* (1984) 30 B.L.R. 118 at 143; *R. L. Polk* v. *Edwin Hill & Partners* (1988) 41 B.L.R. 84; *cf. J. E. Warner* v. *Basildon Development Corporation* (1989) C.I.L.L. 484; s.3 of the Latent Damage Act 1986; G. Robertson, "Defective Premises and Subsequent Purchasers" (1983) 99 L.Q.R. at 559.
[83] (1854) 9 Ex. 341 and see pp. 186 *et seq.*
[84] See the tort cases referred to in n. 82 above. The problem is substantially affected by the effect on tortious claims of recent decisions culminating in *D. & F. Estates* v. *Church Commissioners* [1989] A.C. 177 (H.L.)—see generally Chap. 7. In tort, damage is an essential ingredient of the cause of action (as it is not in contract). Put simply, it is thought that an assignee could not attach his own injuries to an assignor's personal injury cause of action and that the same principle may apply to other sustainable claims in tort.
[85] *cf. Vigers, Sons & Co.* v. *Swindell* [1939] 3 All E.R. 590 at 594.
[86] *Re Yeadon Waterworks Co.* v. *Wright* (1895) 72 L.T. 832 (C.A.). The wording of both contracts should be carefully studied.

applied only where the original contractor completed, and that the new contractor was not liable.[87]

When a new contractor is to take over uncompleted building works it is advisable to draw up a schedule showing exactly the work already carried out, including any authorised alterations, and specifying any defects. Preferably such schedule should be agreed and signed by the new contractor.

3. Sub-contractors

(a) *Liability for sub-contractors*

The contractor, in the ordinary case and subject to any term to the contrary,[88] is liable to the employer for any default by the sub-contractor in carrying out the terms of the main contract, for the contractor is merely securing the vicarious performance of his own obligations.[89]

"Or other approved." It has been held that a contractor who was required to obtain stone from "the X Co. or other approved firm" was not entitled to extra payment when the employer refused permission to obtain cheaper stone from a supplier other than the X Co. The words "or other approved firm" were said to add nothing to the rights of the contractor. The employer's architect was not bound to act reasonably in withholding his consent for another firm, and did not have to give reasons for withholding such consent.[90] The principle that the architect, providing that he is acting honestly, has an absolute right to require performance by the named firm is, it is submitted, not confined to the use of materials.

(b) *Relationship between sub-contractors and employer*[91]

A sub-contractor who has entered into a contract with the main contractor to which the employer is not a party has no cause of action against the employer for the price of work done or goods supplied under his contract,[92] unless he sues under a valid assignment.[93] Neither has he any lien on goods supplied, the

---

[87] *British Glanzstoff Manufacturing Co. Ltd.* v. *General Accident, etc., Corporation Ltd.* 1912 S.C. 591; affd. [1913] A.C. 143 (H.L.); *Wood* v. *Tendring Rural Sanitary Authority* (1886) 3 T.L.R. 272.

[88] *e.g.* clause 25.4.7 of the Standard Form of Building Contract—extension of time for delay on the part of nominated sub-contractors and nominated suppliers—see p. 569.

[89] See p. 274. For the default of nominated sub-contractors and nominated suppliers, see pp. 289 *et seq.*

[90] *Leedsford Ltd.* v. *Bradford Corp.* (1956) 24 B.L.R. 45 (C.A.), following *Tredegar (Viscount)* v. *Harwood* [1929] A.C. 72 (H.L.); *cf.* on the question of reasonableness *Hang Wah Investment* v. *Att.-Gen. of Hong Kong* [1981] 1 W.L.R. 1141 (P.C.).

[91] See generally G. N. Prentice, "Remedies of Building Sub-Contractors against Employers" (1983) 46 M.L.R. 409.

[92] *Hampton* v. *Glamorgan County Council* [1917] A.C. 13 (H.L.); *Vigers, Sons & Co. Ltd.* v. *Swindell* [1939] 3 All E.R. 590; *cf. W.H.T.S.O.* v. *Haden Young* (1987) 37 B.L.R. 130 at 139.

[93] See above.

property in which has passed to the main contractor.[94] Conversely the employer normally has no claim in contract against a sub-contractor unless he can rely on a collateral warranty, and the employer may acquire no property in a sub-contractor's goods even though he has paid the main contractor for them if the property has not passed to the main contractor under the sub-contractor.[95]

Collateral warranty.   If a sub-contractor or supplier warrants the quality of his work or goods, as the case may be, in consideration of the employer causing the contractor to enter into a contract with the sub-contractor or supplier, the employer can sue the sub-contractor or supplier for loss caused by breach of that warranty.[96]

In *Shanklin Pier Ltd.* v. *Detel Products* the plaintiffs were owners of a pier which they wished to have repaired and repainted, and for this purpose had engaged a contractor and had specified the use of bituminous paint. The defendants then warranted to the plaintiffs that their paint would be suitable for repainting the pier, would give a surface impervious to rust and would have a life of seven to ten years. In reliance on this warranty the plaintiffs instructed the contractor to place an order for, and to use, the defendants' paint in lieu of the bituminous paint. The defendants' paint was a complete failure, and the plaintiffs recovered damages from the defendants[97] for breach of the warranty referred to, although the contract for the sale of the paint was between the defendants and the contractor.

A warranty can be given in respect of time, design or other matters and can be expressed in a formal document.[98]

Claim in negligence by employer.   An employer may in certain circumstances have a claim in negligence against a sub-contractor (a) for physical

---

[94] *Pritchett, etc., Co. Ltd.* v. *Currie* [1916] 2 Ch. 515 (C.A.), distinguishing and doubting *Bellamy* v. *Davey* [1891] 3 Ch. 540. There is nothing in English law which corresponds to the mechanics lien legislation in relation to building works which exists in some other common law jurisdictions. It is a matter, at least for discussion, whether there should be.

[95] *Dawber Williamson* v. *Humberside County Council* (1979) 14 B.L.R. 70; *cp. Archivent* v. *Strathclyde Regional Council* (1984) 27 B.L.R. 98 (Court of Session). Generally and subject to express terms, the property in a sub-contractor's materials passes when they are fixed or when they are paid for. See also clause 21.2.4 of NSC/4 at p. 749 and "Retention of title clauses" at p. 242.

[96] *Shanklin Pier Ltd.* v. *Detel Products* [1951] 2 K.B. 854; *Andrews* v. *Hopkinson* [1957] 1 Q.B. 229; *Yeoman Credit Ltd.* v. *Odgers* [1962] 1 W.L.R. 215 at 222 (C.A.); *Wells* (*Merstham*) *Ltd.* v. *Buckland Sand & Silica Ltd.* [1965] 2 Q.B. 170; *Bickerton Ltd.* v. *N.W. Hospital Board* [1969] 1 All E.R. 977, 982, 995 (C.A.); *Esso Petroleum Co. Ltd.* v. *Mardon* [1976] Q.B. 801 (C.A.); *Greater London Council* v. *Ryarsh Brick Co.* (1985) 4 Con. L.R. 85; *cf. Kleinworth Benson* v. *Malaysia Mining* [1989] 1 W.L.R. 379 (C.A.). See also Prof. Wedderburn [1959] C.L.J. 58. For collateral warranties generally see p. 130.

[97] The plaintiffs may not have been able to recover damages from the contractors; see pp. 53 *et seq.* For a case where an assurance by a sub-contractor designer was not intended as a warranty although it was a negligent misstatement, see *I.B.A.* v. *E.M.I. and B.I.C.C.* (1980) 14 B.L.R. 1 (H.L.).

[98] See, *e.g.* the forms at pp. 793 and 805.

injury to his person or property other than property which is the product of the negligence,[99] and (b) for negligent advice.[1]

Direct payment clause.   The main contract may provide for direct payment by the employer to the sub-contractor in the event of the main contractor's default.[2] In the absence of an express provision the employer has no such right,[3] and to be effective the words of the contract must be clear.[4] Such a clause is for the benefit of the employer as it encourages specialists to tender at reasonable prices knowing that they have a good chance of being paid.[5] It has never been held that such a clause creates a contractual relationship between employer and a specialist contractor to whom payment can be made under the clause.[6] Neither has it been held to raise the implication of a trust.[7] The right of the employer to pay direct is, it seems, good as against the main contractor's trustee in bankruptcy or liquidator[8] where the employer continues the contract.

Orders by employer.   If the employer gives a direct order to a sub-contractor to carry out work or deliver goods he may make himself liable to the sub-contractor on an express or implied promise to pay the sub-contractor.[9]

Orders by architect.   An architect has no implied authority to contract on behalf of the employer, and in the absence of express authority any attempt he makes to bind the employer is not effective unless the employer with full knowledge of all the facts ratifies the architect's act.[10] In *Vigers* v. *Swindell* the main contract was in the then current R.I.B.A. form which included a provision for direct payment to sub-contractors,[11] but which expressly provided that the exercise of this right did not create privity of contract between the employer and the sub-contractor. The main contractor went into liquidation and T became the new contractor as a result of a letter from the architect

---

[99] See generally Chap. 7, Section 2.
[1] See "Specialist sub-contractors" at p. 178.
[2] See, *e.g.* clause 35.13.5 of the Standard Form of Building Contract.
[3] *Re Holt, ex p. Gray* (1888) 58 L.J.Q.B. 5.
[4] *Milestone* v. *Yates* [1938] 2 All E.R. 439.
[5] *Re Wilkinson, ex p. Fowler* [1905] 2 K.B. 713.
[6] *cf. Hobbs* v. *Turner* (1902) 18 T.L.R. 235 (C.A.); *Milestone* v. *Yates* [1938] 2 All E.R. 439; *Vigers, Sons & Co. Ltd.* v. *Swindell* [1939] 3 All E.R. 590.
[7] *cf.* clause 27(f) of the 1963 Standard Form of Building Contract. There is no equivalent clause in the 1980 Form.
[8] *Re Wilkinson, ex p. Fowler* [1905] 2 K.B. 713; *Re Tout and Finch Ltd.* [1954] 1 W.L.R. 178; For the possible effect of *British Eagle Ltd.* v. *Air France* [1975] 1 W.L.R. 758 (H.L.) (discussed p. 381) on cases such as these, see *Re Arthur Sanders Ltd.* (1981) 17 B.L.R. 125 at 140 and see also *Carreras Rothmans* v. *Freeman Mathews* [1985] Ch. 207.
[9] *Dixon* v. *Hatfield* (1825) 2 Bing. 439; *Smith* v. *Rudhall* (1862) 3 F. & F. 143; *cf. Lakeman* v. *Mountstephen* (1874) L.R. 7 H.L. 17 (H.L.). See further p. 27.
[10] *Vigers, Sons & Co. Ltd.* v. *Swindell* [1939] 3 All E.R. 590; *Ashwell & Nesbitt Ltd.* v. *Allen & Co.* (1912) H.B.C. (4th ed.), Vol. 2, p. 462 (C.A.). See p. 305.
[11] Clause 15(b) of the 1931 edition of the R.I.B.A. form.

stating, "you yourself will be taking on this contract." The employer, S, knew
of this and at the architect's request signed a mandate to her bank authorising
it to pay T, "or such nominated sub-contractors as appear on the certificates
signed by the architect." Certain sub-contractors, V & Co., then carried out
work and the architect purported to pledge S's credit to V & Co. for the cost of
the work. S did not know before the work was finished that the architect had
pledged her credit. It was held that V & Co. could not recover from S, for the
new contract with T was on the same terms as the original contract. The
architect had no authority to pledge S's credit, and had not been given
authority by the mandate to the bank to pay sub-contractors, for this was
referable to the provision for direct payment, in the original contract. Neither
had S, with knowledge of the facts, ratified the architect's unauthorised act.[12]

Production of main contract. Where the sub-contractor claims that he is
entitled to payment from the employer for work extra to the main contract he
may, in addition to proving a contract with the employer, have to produce the
main contract, if it was in writing, to show that it did not include the work for
which the claim is made.[13]

(c) *Prime cost and provisional sums*

It is common to describe the sums that the contractor is to pay for the work of
sub-contractors as prime cost sums or provisional sums.[14] The contractor is
usually only entitled to charge the employer the net sums expended plus a very
small percentage[15] and therefore a favourable contract with the sub-contractor
is for the employer's benefit. For this reason it was once thought that there was
a presumption in such cases that the contractor was acting as agent on behalf
of the employer in making such contracts.[16] But it has now been clearly stated
by the House of Lords that no inference is to be drawn from the inclusion of a
provisional sum for certain goods in a lump sum contract, that the contractor
is ordering the goods as agent of the employer.[17] In the special circumstances of
one case in which there was an option for either the contractor or the employer
to pay provisional sums to the specialists, it was held that the employer was
liable.[18]

---

[12] *Vigers, Sons & Co. Ltd.* v. *Swindell* [1939] 3 All E.R. 590. In such a case the sub-contractor may
have a remedy against the architect. See p. 306.

[13] See *Eccles* v. *Southern* (1861) 3 F. & F. 142.

[14] See also p. 86.

[15] *cf.* clauses 35, 36 and 30.6.1.2 of the Standard Form of Building Contract.

[16] *Crittall Manufacturing Co.* v. *London County Council* (1910) 75 J.P. 203.

[17] *Hampton* v. *Glamorgan County Council* [1917] A.C. 13 at 22 (H.L.), overruling *Crittall's* case and
distinguishing *Hobbs* v. *Turner* (1902) 18 T.L.R. 235 (C.A.). *Young* v. *White* (1911) 28 T.L.R. 87,
which followed *Crittall's* case, will not, it is submitted, be followed; see *Hampton's* case at 17. See
also *Ramsden & Carr* v. *Chessum & Sons* (1913) 110 L.T. 274 (H.L.); *Bickerton, T.A. & Son Ltd.* v.
North West Regional Hospital Board [1970] 1 W.L.R. 607 at 615 (H.L.).

[18] *Hobbs* v. *Turner* (1902) 18 T.L.R. 235 (C.A.). See the remarks of Lord Haldane in *Hampton's* case
at 20 at 21. See also *Milestone* v. *Yates* [1938] 2 All E.R. 439.

4. Nominated Sub-contractors and Nominated Suppliers

It is frequently provided in the main contract that the employer may nominate sub-contractors. It is then the normal practice for the architect to negotiate with the sub-contractor and settle the terms of his sub-contract without prior consultation with the main contractor, merely informing him of the terms of the proposed sub-contract at the time of nomination.[19] In such a case the architect does not act as the agent of the employer,[20] therefore, the contractor has, apart from any express term in the main contract, no cause of action against the employer in respect of any delay or default on the part of the nominated sub-contractor.[21]

(a) *Delay in nomination*

If there is delay in making a nomination the contractor may have claims for extra time and payment against the employer.[22] The money claim may arise either as a claim for damages for breach of an express or implied term,[23] or for reimbursement under the express terms of the contract.[24] If a nominated sub-contractor withdraws, delay in making a timeous nomination of a new sub-contractor may have an equivalent result, although delay caused by the first nominated sub-contractor's withdrawal is the main contractor's risk.[25]

(b) *Problems inherent in nomination*

The system is an ingenious attempt to give the employer the benefit of two opposing concepts. Theoretically it enables him to have all the advantages of choosing his own specialist contractor and of bargaining with him for his price and the terms of his contract and for the performance of services, such as detailed technical design, which an architect cannot carry out, but avoids the disadvantages of a multiplicity of direct contracts. The achievement of these objects at first sight appears incompatible.[26] The result has been, particularly in those common form contracts where contractors were party to the drafting, provisions which are sometimes incomplete or unsatisfactory,[27] or otherwise at least complex.[28] Further, perhaps influenced to some extent by the suggestion

---

[19] See, *e.g.* the procedure in *Gloucestershire County Council* v. *Richardson* [1969] 1 A.C. 480 (H.L.) referred to at p. 55.

[20] *Mitchell* v. *Guildford Union (Guardians of)* (1903) 68 J.P. 84; *Leslie & Co. Ltd.* v. *Managers of Metropolitan Asylums District* (1901) 68 J.P. 86 (C.A.).

[21] *Ibid.* See also p. 52.

[22] *cf. Percy Bilton* v. *Greater London Council* [1982] 1 W.L.R. 794 (H.L.).

[23] See p. 51.

[24] Under the Standard Form of Building Contract there is a contractual right to payment and, it seems, a right to damages—see clauses 5 and 26 at pp. 498 and 580.

[25] *Percy Bilton* v. *Greater London Council* [1982] 1 W.L.R. 794 (H.L.).

[26] See the remarks of Lord Reid in *Bickerton* v. *North West Metropolitan Regional Hospital Board* [1970] 1 W.L.R. 607 at 611 (H.L.).

[27] See, *e.g.* the 1963 Standard Form of Building Contract, clauses 11, 27, 28, 30.

[28] See the 1980 Standard Form of Building Contract, clauses 35 and 36.

that it seems unjust in the absence of clear language to make a contractor liable for a nominated sub-contractor over whose activities he has such little control,[29] the court has, in a number of cases,[30] refused to hold a contractor liable for the default of a nominated sub-contractor or supplier even though it has sometimes left the employer without apparent remedy.[31] The system of nomination tends to give rise to difficulties and obscurities,[32] and problems frequently require a consideration of the terms of the main contract, of the sub-contract in question and of the surrounding circumstances, including in particular those relating to the actual nomination.

(c) *Express terms of main contract*

These must be considered first. Those relating to the Standard Form of Building Contract and the I.C.E. Conditions are discussed at pages 636 and 901 respectively. The Government form of contract (Form GC/Works 1 (3rd edition) December 1989) contains in clause 31(2)[33] what is, presumably, intended to be an unqualified guarantee by the contractor of the performance of nominated sub-contractors and suppliers.

Description of work in main contract. The traditional method, and that contemplated by the Standard Form of Building Contract,[34] is to give little description of the sub-contract works, but to include an item such as "P.C. Sum for steelwork to be supplied and erected by a nominated sub-contractor, £x." Therefore, at the time of entering into the contract there is an estimate of price and description of the type of work to be ordered but not of the works themselves. Subsequently, when the nomination is made the description of the works becomes known. At this stage, by necessary implication, it is submitted, such description defines the work as between employer and contractor. But a distinction must be drawn between the description of the work and the terms of the sub-contract subject to which it is to be carried out. There is, it is submitted, ordinarily no necessity[35] to imply that the terms of the sub-contract become terms of the main contract. In *Gloucestershire County Council* v. *Richardson*,[36] the

---

[29] See *Bickerton* v. *North West Metropolitan Regional Hospital Board* [1970] 1 W.L.R. 607 (H.L.).

[30] *Gloucestershire County Council* v. *Richardson* [1969] 1 A.C. 480 (H.L.), discussed at p. 55; *Bickerton's* case, discussed at p. 293; *Fairclough Building* v. *Rhuddlan Borough Council* (1985) 30 B.L.R. 26 (C.A.); *John Jarvis* v. *Rockdale Housing Association* (1986) 36 B.L.R. 48 (C.A.).

[31] *cf.* however *Percy Bilton* v. *Greater London Council* [1982] 1 W.L.R. 794 (H.L.).

[32] See, *e.g. M. Harrison* v. *Leeds City Council* (1980) 14 B.L.R. 118; *Holland Hannen & Cubitts* v. *W.H.T.S.O.* (1981) 18 B.L.R. 80; *John Laing* v. *County and District Properties* (1982) 23 B.L.R. 1.

[33] Referred to (in an earlier version) in *Gloucestershire County Council* v. *Richardson* in the Court of Appeal [1967] 3 All E.R. 458 at 473, but never tested in any reported case.

[34] See clause 35, and see Standard Method of Measurement of Building Works: 7th ed.—A51 Nominated sub-contractors.

[35] See p. 46.

[36] [1969] 1 A.C. 480 (H.L.)—see p. 55.

main contract was in the R.I.B.A. form (1939 edition). The House of Lords rejected an argument that the contractor was liable to the employer for latent defects in components delivered by a nominated supplier. The contractor's liability to the employer was limited to the same extent as the nominated supplier's liability to the contractor was limited under the express terms of the sub-contract which the contractor had been directed to enter into.

Description of sub-contract works written into main contract. This is sometimes done. Its advantages are that it avoids argument as to the description of the sub-contract work and it enables the contractor to know the work to be carried out at the time when he tenders instead of after the contract has been agreed. But problems of construction may arise. Thus the description of the sub-contract works may include an obligation to design. This may be express, *e.g.* to design, supply and erect a certain plant, or implied, *e.g.* to provide a heating system which will satisfy a certain defined performance specification. Are these design obligations undertaken by the contractor? Ordinarily it is thought that they are, but it is necessary to consider all the terms of the contract. Thus where the Standard Form of Building Contract is used it is not clear beyond argument that, without amendment of the conditions of contract,[37] such a description as that given above of the sub-contract works written into the bills of quantities or specification as the case may be, necessarily imposes the obligation of design upon the contractor.

I.B.A. v. E.M.I. and B.I.C.C.[38] was a case where a description of the sub-contract work was written into the main contract. Upon the particular terms of the main contract (not in common form) it was held that the main contractor had accepted liability for the sub-contractor's design of the works. On the facts it was found that this design was negligently carried out, so that it was not necessary to consider whether the liability for design went further and extended to a warranty of fitness for purpose. But the House seemed to take the view that it was an absolute liability for fitness for purpose and was not limited to that of due care.[39]

(d) Implied terms of main contract[40]

The contractor is ordinarily as liable for performance by his sub-contractor as by himself.[41] But the fact of and the circumstances surrounding nomination and the words of the main contract may bring about a departure, to greater or lesser degree, from the contractor's usual implied obligations. The problems are often difficult and vary according to the particular main contract and the circumstances, but an approach is suggested below.

---

[37] See clause 14 of the Standard Form of Building Contract, and discussion at p. 524.
[38] (1980) 14 B.L.R. 1 (H.L.).
[39] See esp. at 26, 44 and 47.
[40] For implied terms generally, see pp. 45 *et seq.*
[41] See p. 283.

Time.   Nomination does not, it is submitted, affect the contractor's liability for delay unless the terms of the main contract[42] or the surrounding circumstances show an intention to exclude such liability.[43]

Materials—patent defects.   There is, it is submitted, an implied term of the main contract that materials or goods supplied by nominated suppliers or used by nominated sub-contractors will not contain defects that reasonable inspection by the contractor would disclose, unless the express terms of the main contract or the surrounding circumstances show an intention to exclude such term.[44] The requisite standard of inspection will vary according to the terms of the main contract and the surrounding circumstances.

Materials—latent defects.   There is an implied term of the main contract that the materials or goods to be supplied by nominated suppliers or used by nominated sub-contractors will be of good quality, unless the express terms of the main contract or the surrounding circumstances show an intention to exclude such term. This term makes the contractor liable for latent defects even where the exercise of all proper skill and care on his part at the time of delivery or fixing would not have disclosed such defects. An instruction to place a sub-contract upon terms which limit the contractor's right of recourse may exclude the term. Other circumstances which, in the case of the delivery of a completed component, may assist the court to find an intention to exclude the term are if the design, choice of materials, specification, quality and price were fixed without reference to the contractor and there was no right to object to the nomination or to insist on an indemnity from the supplier.[45]

Design of materials.   In so far as the contractor is liable for the quality of materials, he is liable for any selection of the constituent parts of the materials and other acts by the sub-contractor or supplier which, in one sense of the term, may be considered as design. Such liability is of particular significance where the materials are made-up components such as concrete columns or beams.[46]

Workmanship.   It is, it is submitted, a question of construction in each case to determine whether the nomination of a sub-contractor excludes or reduces

---

[42] *e.g.* clause 25.4.7 of the Standard Form of Building Contract, discussed at p. 578; *cf. Percy Bilton v. Greater London Council* [1982] 1 W.L.R. 794 (H.L.); *Fairclough Building v. Rhuddlan Borough Council* (1985) 30 B.L.R. 26 (C.A.); *cp. H. Fairweather v. London Borough of Wandsworth* (1987) 39 B.L.R. 106.

[43] An analogy can be made with liability for defects in materials, see below.

[44] See *Young & Marten Ltd. v. McManus Childs Ltd.* [1969] 1 A.C. 454 (H.L.); *Gloucestershire County Council v. Richardson* [1969] 1 A.C. 480 (H.L.); *Norta v. John Sisk* (1976) 14 B.L.R. 49 at 57 (Irish High Court); *cf. I.B.A. v. E.M.I. and B.I.C.C.* (1980) 14 B.L.R. 1 at 45 (H.L.). See also "Design" below.

[45] *Ibid.*

[46] As in *Gloucestershire County Council v. Richardson* [1969] 1 A.C. 480 (H.L.) where the exact proportions of the mix of the concrete were left to the decision of the supplier and the defect in the columns was due to an excess of a chemical in the mix.

the main contractor's liability for the workmanship of the sub-contractor which would exist if the sub-contractor had not been nominated.[47]

Fitness for purpose.   Where the employer has not relied on the contractor's skill and judgment in the selection of a nominated sub-contractor or nominated supplier, or the work or materials they are to carry out or supply, a term that such work or materials will be reasonably fit for their purpose is not normally implied, unless the express terms of the main contract[48] or the surrounding circumstances show that the parties intended the contractor to accept such liability.[49]

The practical significance of this principle is great and frequently does not seem to be appreciated. It means that under the ordinary procedures of nomination currently in use the employer has no remedy against the contractor if, for example, tiles, bricks, windows, mechanical plant, heating or air conditioning systems or other specially designed aspects of the works, the subject of nomination, are of good quality but unfit for their purpose. Even an employer using the Government form of contract[50] has, it seems, no remedy where the contractor has supplied what he was told to supply or the sub-contractor has built what was agreed to be built.

Partial reliance upon the contractor's skill and judgment is sufficient to give rise to the warranty of fitness for purpose on the part of the contractor so as to make him responsible for the sub-contractor, at any rate in respect of that area where there has been such partial reliance.[51] But to be effective partial reliance must be such as to constitute a substantial and effective, inducement to the employer to enter into the main contract.[52]

Design.   Where there is no description of the sub-contract works in the main contract, and no express obligation to design on the part of the contractor, his liability, if any, for design by a nominated sub-contractor, must arise as an implied term of the main contract.[53] It is thought that the court would not easily find that it was necessary to imply a term, in such circumstances, that the contractor was, in effect, guaranteeing any design work carried out by the

---

[47] See *Norta* v. *John Sisk* (1976) 14 B.L.R. 49 at 57 (Irish High Court); *cf. I.B.A.* v. *E.M.I. and B.I.C.C.* (1980) 14 B.L.R. 1 at 45 (H.L.); *Rumbelows Ltd.* v. *A.M.K.* (1980) 19 B.L.R. 25; and see by analogy the cases dealing with materials and fitness for purpose; see also p. 53.

[48] See *I.B.A.* v. *E.M.I. and B.I.C.C.* (1980) 14 B.L.R. 1 (H.L.).

[49] *Young & Marten Ltd.* v. *McManus Childs Ltd.* [1969] 1 A.C. 454 (H.L.); *Gloucestershire County Council* v. *Richardson* [1969] 1 A.C. 480 (H.L.); *Norta* v. *John Sisk* (1976) 14 B.L.R. 49 (Irish Supreme Court); *cf. I.B.A.* v. *E.M.I. and B.I.C.C.* (1980) 14 B.L.R. 1 at 45 (H.L.); *Comyn Ching* v. *Oriental Tube* (1981) 17 B.L.R. 47 and 81 (C.A.); *University of Warwick* v. *Sir Robert McAlpine* (1988) 42 B.L.R. 1 unaffected on this point by the unreported decision of Court of Appeal on 4.4.90; see also generally p. 53.

[50] See p. 288.

[51] See *Cammell Laird* v. *Manganese Bronze* [1934] A.C. 402 (H.L.).

[52] *Medway Oil and Storage* v. *Silica Gel Corporation* (1928) 33 Com.Cas. (H.L.). 195.

[53] For implication of terms, see pp. 45 *et seq.* For how far the employer has a remedy against his architect when the R.I.B.A. Architect's Appointment, clauses 3.6, 3.8 and 3.9 apply, see p. 960.

nominated sub-contractor. It might more readily listen to such an argument where the contractor had accepted a nomination of a sub-contractor and the sub-contract contained an express duty to design.[54] But even here the position cannot be approached as one of general principle and must depend upon the particular circumstances. In one case a nominated sub-contractor had accepted the obligation both of supplying windows and designing them. The design was defective and work was held up while the problems were solved. It was held that the architect, either under the express terms or of the ordinary implied term on the part of the employer to do all things necessary to enable the contractor to carry out and complete the works, should have issued an instruction requiring a variation of the design of the windows so as to enable the works to be carried out and completed.[55]

Installation or shop drawings. Nominated sub-contractors are often required to produce "installation drawings" or "shop drawings." The status of such drawings is unclear both factually and in law. The are usually based upon and contrasted with "design drawings" themselves usually produced by consultants. Irrespective of the label given to various drawings, factual questions can arise whether installation or shop drawings contain part of the design or whether they are in effect part of the sub-contractor's work.[56] It is then a question of law, depending on the express and implied terms of the particular contract, whether the main contractor is responsible for such design as the drawings contain. Consultants' design drawings are sometimes said to contain the "design intent" and it is thought that, in so far as further drawings or specification are necessary to develop that design intent into something that can be built, the further drawings will be part of the design.[57] There is, however, undoubtedly a blurred borderline between design and workmanship. For example, a carpenter choosing a suitable nail in a sense makes a design choice. But such a choice would usually be regarded as a normal incident of good workmanship.

Where under the terms of the sub-contract a nominated sub-contractor was obliged to produce installation drawings in good time to meet an agreed programme, it was held that the main contractor had an equivalent obligation and that the employer was not in breach of a main contract term to provide necessary drawings in due time if the sub-contractor failed to produce the drawings on time.[58]

Guarantee. A nominated sub-contractor or nominated supplier may give a guarantee or warranty to the contractor. Although every case requires consid-

---

[54] See discussion of the position under the Standard Form of Building Contract at p. 636.
[55] *Holland Hannen & Cubitts* v. *W.H.T.S.O.* (1981) 18 B.L.R. 80.
[56] *cf. H. Fairweather* v. *London Borough of Wandsworth* (1987) 39 B.L.R. 106 at 116.
[57] This accords with the decision in Issue 1 in *Holland Hannen & Cubitts* v. *W.H.T.S.O.* (1981) 18 B.L.R. 80 at 114.
[58] *H. Fairweather* v. *London Borough of Wandsworth* (1987) 39 B.L.R. 106.

eration it is thought that the courts will ordinarily refuse to imply that the guarantee or warranty is part of the main contract. The result is that it cannot be enforced by the employer and is of no value to the employer.

(e) *Repudiation by nominated sub-contractor*

In *Bickerton* v. *N.W. Metropolitan Regional Hospital Board*[59] the contract was the 1963 edition of the R.I.B.A. Form of Contract. S Ltd. were nominated to provide the heating system. Before they had carried out any substantial part of the work, they went into voluntary liquidation and the liquidator refused to complete the sub-contract. The contractor's contentions that he was entitled to a renomination and to damages for delay awaiting such renomination and that he was not liable to reimburse the employer for the expenditure incurred in completing the sub-contract works over and above the original sub-contract price were upheld by the House of Lords. The contract did not deal expressly with the points. The chief factor influencing the House seems to have been that by the terms of the main contract the contractor had neither the duty nor the right to carry out any of the work the subject-matter of the P.C. sum in the Bills and which it was stated by the contract had to be carried out by a nominated sub-contractor.[60] Although the contractor was ultimately responsible for the nominated sub-contractor, such responsibility could not exist, and the contract could not be completed, unless there was a nominated sub-contractor in existence. Therefore if the first fell out another must be nominated.[61] But under the pre-1980 JCT Standard Form of Building Contract, so long as the first sub-contract subsisted, the main contractor was responsible for its administration including any decision whether to determine the sub-contractor's employment for default. The architect had no power, duty or right to give instructions to the main contractor either to determine or not to determine the sub-contract.[62]

In *Percy Bilton* v. *Greater London Council*,[63] it was held, again under the 1963 edition of the R.I.B.A. Form of Contract, that the main contractor took the risk of delay directly caused by the withdrawal of a nominated sub-contractor. Delay resulting from complete withdrawal did not come within clause 23(g), which entitled the contractor to an extension of time for delay on the part of a nominated sub-contractor. But the employer was obliged, upon the withdrawal of a nominated sub-contractor, to renominate within a reasonable time

---

[59] [1970] 1 W.L.R. 607 (H.L.).
[60] The current version of the Standard Form of Building Contract is unchanged in this respect, see p. 636.
[61] The *Bickerton* case was distinguished and not followed in *City of Adelaide* v. *Jennings Industries* (1985) 1 Const L.J. 197 (Australian High Court) on the basis that the R.A.I.A. Form of Contract was significantly different from the R.I.B.A. Form.
[62] *James Longley* v. *Borough of Reigate* (1982) 22 B.L.R. 31 (C.A.). For the position under the 1980 Standard Form of Building Contract, see clause 35.24 at p. 633; see also clause 59 of the I.C.E. Conditions at p. 898.
[63] [1982] 1 W.L.R. 794 (H.L.).

and failure to do so was a breach of contract. Under a pre-1980 JCT Standard Form of Building Contract, the contractor was held entitled to reject as invalid an instruction nominating sub-contractors who would not complete within the time allowed under the main contract.[64]

Such an instruction was also invalid if the proposed new sub-contract did not include work necessary to remedy defects left in the first sub-contractor's work.[65]

While *Bickerton's* case and those which followed it turned upon the express words of the main contract, the principle that certain work is reserved to be carried out by a nominated sub-contractor is to be found in other forms of contract and the decisions may, therefore, wholly or partly apply. The I.C.E. Conditions deal elaborately with the position.[66] The effect of clause 63(7) of Government form of contract (Form GC/Works/1, 3rd edition) has yet to be tested in court.

(f) *Protection of employer*

As will have appeared above, the system of nomination of sub-contractors may result in the employer in some cases having no remedy in contract against the contractor for defaults which may cause great loss and leave him with no remedy at all unless he can find that, fortuitously, there was an informal collateral warranty[67] given by the sub-contractor, or he can persuade the court to find that he has a remedy in negligence against the sub-contractor.[68] The best protection against this position is to avoid nomination. The nomination provisions of the 1980 Standard Form of Building Contract have clarified some former problems, but they are complicated. The reasons advanced in favour of nomination are that it gives the employer the choice of a specialist contractor, it enables him to obtain the best price for specialist works and it enables him to have the advantage of design work which his professional advisers cannot carry out. None of these arguments are valid save the first. Even here the employer can issue a list of sub-contractors any one of whom he will approve. The rest is a matter of tendering procedure. Nomination can be avoided if specialist works are described in terms of performance specification and the main contractors invited to tender are given sufficient time to make their own inquiries among specialist sub-contractors. If there is a competition among main contractors it will reflect any competition among specialist sub-contrac-

---

[64] *Fairclough Building* v. *Rhuddlan Borough Council* (1985) 30 B.L.R. 26 (C.A.); see also *Percy Bilton* v. *Greater London Council* (1981) 17 B.L.R. 1 at 18 (C.A.) and [1982] 1 W.L.R. 794 at 802 (H.L.); *cf. Trollope & Colls* v. *North West Metropolitan Regional Hospital Board* [1973] 1 W.L.R. 601 (H.L.). It is thought that this ground of invalidity applies equally to an original nomination and to a renomination.

[65] *Fairclough Building* v. *Rhuddlan Borough Council* (1985) 30 B.L.R. 26 (C.A.).

[66] See p. 898.

[67] See p. 130. In some cases the employer may have a remedy against his architect or other professional adviser, see Chap. 12.

[68] See Chap. 7.

tors. As regards the total time, there should be no difference. Instead of the architect spending months in negotiation with prospective nominated sub-contractors before sending out the invitation to tender the same period will be absorbed by the main contractor. As regards detailed design, if the specialist sub-contractors are not prepared to do this for nothing in the hope of getting the work, one of them can be employed on a separate contract to carry out the design.

If there must be nominations then it would appear (although it has never been tested) that the rigorous provisions of the Government form of contract would avoid most legal problems in that they appear to have the intention of putting all the risks, save lack of fitness for purpose, upon the contractor. Presumably the pricing of government tenders (by contractors who remain solvent) reflects this acceptance of risks.

A palliative is, while retaining the nomination system, to enter into formal collateral contracts[69] between the employer and the sub-contractors or suppliers. Depending on the wording of the collateral contracts, and the solvency of the sub-contractors or suppliers if and when the contractors have to be enforced, this procedure is of value.

Writing the description of the sub-contract works into the main contract sometimes assists[70] but the effect depends upon the particular words of the main contract.[71] Using the JCT Intermediate Form of Building Contract with its simpler provisions for Named Sub-contractors may also be considered.

A further possibility is to enter into direct contracts with specalist contractors. Various committees over the past 40 years have decried this procedure without seeming to understand the defects of the modern system of nomination. If the contractual arrangements are carefully prepared, and the employer engages an administrative contractor to co-ordinate the various direct contracts and the administration is skilfully and conscientiously carried out this procedure is probably no worse and could well be better than the present system of nomination.

5. Relationship Between Sub-contractor and Main Contractor

The relationship between a sub-contractor and the main contractor depends upon the construction of the sub-contract.[72] The Standard Form of Sub-contract for use where the sub-contractor is nominated under the Standard

---

[69] For forms and a commentary see pp. 798 and 805.

[70] See p. 289.

[71] For the position where the Standard Form of Building Contract is used, see p. 636.

[72] For the implication of a duty to supply necessary equipment in a labour only sub-contract, see *Quinn* v. *Burch Bros. (Builders) Ltd.* [1966] 2 Q.B. 370 (C.A.). For duties as regards safety, see *Sims* v. *Foster Wheeler Ltd.* [1966] 1 W.L.R. 769 (C.A.). For the tests whether an orally engaged person is a sub-contractor or an employee, see *Ferguson* v. *John Dawson & Partners (Contractors) Ltd.* [1976] 1 W.L.R. 1213 (C.A.); *cf. Calder* v. *H. Kitson Vickers* [1988] I.C.R. 232 (C.A.).

Form of Building Contract, is available and is printed with a commentary at page 699. There are also available Standard Forms of Sub-contract where the sub-contractor is not nominated. The ordinary rules of construction of contracts apply,[73] and much of the law set out earlier as between contractor and employer applies, with such modifications as the context makes necessary. In a case where the contractor forfeited a sub-contract for delay the court took into account the contractor's onerous position under the main contract.[74]

Incorporation of terms. Where the parties do not sign a formal sub-contract they sometimes seek to incorporate terms of contract. This is satisfactory provided the essential terms of the sub-contract are agreed and the words relied on as having the effect of incorporation are clear. An example of a form of words which caused some argument was where an order form was expressed to be "in full accordance with the appropriate form for nominated sub-contractors (R.I.B.A. 1965 ed.)." After considering expert evidence that this would be understood in the trade to be a reference to the former "Green Form" of nominated sub-contract,[75] the court held that these words did incorporate the Green Form including the arbitration agreement which it contains and, there being a dispute, granted a stay of proceedings.[76]

Incorporation of main contract terms. The parties sometimes seek to incorporate the main contract or some of it. This is inherently likely to cause problems having regard to the difference of subject-matter and is not to be recommended. If such incorporation is attempted each contract must be construed according to its own words, but there are some reported cases which may be of some assistance. Thus it was agreed that "the terms of payment for the work ... shall be exactly the same as those set forth in clause 30 of the [main] ... contract."[77] Clause 30 provided for the retention of money up to an amount exceeding the sum payable under the sub-contract, and for the repayment of such fund by certain sums at the end of various periods. It was held that effect could be given to the sub-contract clause on the basis that there should be a retention fund, and repayments in the same proportion that the sub-contract sum bore to the main contract sum. In another case[78] the main contract empowered the employer to order the contractor to remove a sub-contractor guilty of delay. The sub-contract contained a recital to the effect that the sub-contractor agreed to carry out the work in accordance with the terms of the main contract. It dealt expressly with many of the matters in the

---

[73] See pp. 33 *et seq.*
[74] *Stadhard* v. *Lee* (1863) 3 B. & S. 364, referred to at pp. 98 and 238.
[75] Reproduced in the 4th edition of this book at p. 576.
[76] *Modern Building Wales Ltd.* v. *Limmer & Trinidad Co. Ltd.* [1975] 1 W.L.R. 1281 (C.A.); *cf. Petrofina* v. *Magnaload* (1983) 25 B.L.R. 37 at 46; contrast *City of Manchester* v. *Fram Gerrard* (1974) 6 B.L.R. 70 at 94. See p. 398 for stay of proceedings under s.4 of the Arbitration Act 1950.
[77] *Geary, Walker & Co. Ltd.* v. *W. Lawrence & Son* (1906) H.B.C. (4th ed.), Vol. 2, p. 382 (C.A.).
[78] *Chandler Bros. Ltd.* v. *Boswell* [1936] 3 All E.R. 179 (C.A.).

main contract but not with the power to order the removal of the sub-contractor. The main contractor upon the order of the employer removed the sub-contractor for delay, and upon the latter's action for breach of contract it was held: (1) that the sub-contract was not frustrated[79] when the employer ordered the sub-contractor's removal; (2) that the removal clause in the main contract was not imported into the sub-contract by the recital which only meant that the sub-contractor "was to provide work of the quality and with the dispatch which was stipulated for in the head contract."[80] Therefore as the sub-contractor had not be guilty of such delay as to show an intention to repudiate the contract[81] the main contractor was in breach of the sub-contract.

In *Brightside Kilpatrick* v. *Mitchell Construction (1973) Ltd.*,[82] the main contractor's order to the sub-contractor referred to the conditions relating to the sub-contract "being those embodied in R.I.B.A. as above." The court, after referring to the difficulty of construing the words, held that their effect was that the sub-contractual relationship should be such as to be consistent with all those terms in the head contract that specifically dealt with matters relating to sub-contractors. This in turn led to a consideration of clause 27 of the 1963 R.I.B.A. contract and to the ruling that it was necessary to read into the contractual relationship between the contractor and the sub-contractor what would have been agreed between them in any formal contract had they entered into a contract in the former "Green Form" of nominated sub-contract.[83]

Sub-contractor's access to site.　The extent and times of such access may be the subject of express terms. Otherwise it is likely to be implied that the sub-contractor will have such reasonable access as will enable him properly to perform his sub-contract obligations. In a case where access was stopped for three months as a consequence of picketing arising out of a strike, it was held, on the construction of a provision requiring the contractor to afford access to the sub-contractor, that there was no breach of contract by the contractor.[84]

Set-off.　There are no special rules as to set-off applicable to building contracts and, in particular, to sub-contracts. Thus if, for example, a contractor is liable to pay a nominated sub-contractor money upon the direction of the architect, but satisfies the court that there is a triable issue whether he has a cross-claim for delay, he is entitled to leave to defend upon an application for summary judgment.[85] Some forms of sub-contract have elaborate provisions

---

[79] See p. 134 for frustration.
[80] Greer L.J. in *Chandler Bros. Ltd.* v. *Boswell* [1936] 3 All E.R. 179 at 185 (C.A.).
[81] *Ibid.*
[82] [1975] 2 Lloyd's Rep. 493 (C.A.).
[83] *cf. Sauter Automation* v. *Goodman* (1986) 34 B.L.R. 81 at 88; *Martin Grant* v. *Sir Lindsay Parkinson* (1984) 29 B.L.R. 31 at 38 (C.A.); see also "Battle of forms" at p. 19; see n. 75 above for the Green Form.
[84] *L.R.E. Engineering Services* v. *Otto Simon Carves* (1981) 24 B.L.R. 127.
[85] *Modern Engineering* v. *Gilbert-Ash* [1974] A.C. 689 (H.L.). For summary judgment, see p. 441. For set-off, see p. 438.

seeking to exclude or limit- the contractor's right of set-off against sums otherwise payable to the sub-contractor.[86] In construing such provisions, the court starts with the presumption that neither party intends to abandon any remedies, such as the right of set-off, arising by operation of law and clear express words must be used in order to rebut this presumption.[87]

Certificate condition precedent. The terms of the sub-contract may make the certificate of the architect given under the main contract a condition precedent to payment under the sub-contract.[88] Some sub-contracts contain "pay when paid" clauses stipulating in effect that the sub-contractor's right to payment does not arise until the main contractor is himself paid the relevant sum by the employer. There is, it seems, no reason in principle why such clauses, properly drafted, should not be effective.[89]

Damages. The principles upon which damages are awarded between the parties to a sub-contract are those set out in Chapter 8. The second limb of the rule in *Hadley* v. *Baxendale*[90] has particular application as the sub-contractor frequently knows of the losses the contractor is likely to suffer as a result of his default.[91] Thus he will be liable for the amount of liquidated damages payable as a result of his delay if he has notice of such liability in the main contract.[92] He will not be liable if he does not have notice, as the liability to pay liquidated damages is not a natural consequence of delay,[93] but he will be liable for such damages as he should, as a businessman in the trade have contemplated as a serious possibility (or not unlikely)[94] to result from his breach,[95] and such damages may in many cases be no less than the liquidated damages payable under the main contract.[96] If the contractor has settled a claim by the employer arising out of the sub-contractor's default the amount of the settlement is admissible prima facie evidence of the amount of the loss caused by the

---

[86] See, *e.g.* clauses 23 and 24 of NSC/4 at p. 760.
[87] *Modern Engineering* v. *Gilbert-Ash* [1974] A.C. 689 at 717 (H.L.); *cf. Mottram Consultants* v. *Bernard Sunley* [1975] 2 Lloyd's Rep. 197 at 205 (H.L.); *NEI-Thompson* v. *Wimpey Construction* (1987) 39 B.L.R. 65 at 72 (C.A.); *Acsim (Southern)* v. *Danish Contracting* (1989) 47 B.L.R. 55 (C.A.); *Mellowes P.P.G.* v. *Snelling Construction* (1989) 49 B.L.R. 109. For a full discussion of the set-off clauses of NSC/4, see p. 764.
[88] See *Dunlop & Ranken Ltd.* v. *Hendall* [1957] 1 W.L.R. 1102; see also *A. Davies & Co. (Shopfitters)* v. *William Old* (1969) 113 S.J. 262.
[89] *cf. Firma C-Trade* v. *Newcastle Protection and Indemnity* [1990] 3 W.L.R. 78 (H.L.).
[90] (1854) 9 Ex. 341 and see p. 187.
[91] See, *e.g. Hydraulic Engineering Co. Ltd.* v. *McHaffie* (1878) 4 Q.B.D. 670.
[92] *Ibid.* See, *e.g.* the fourth recital of NSC/4 at p. 700; but see also clause 25.4.7 of the Standard Form of Building Contract for delay on the part of nominated sub-contractors.
[93] *Ibid.*; *Elbinger Actien-Gesellschaft, etc.* v. *Armstrong* (1874) L.R. 9 Q.B. 473. For a clause limiting the sub-contractor's liability, see *Prince of Wales Dock Co.* v. *Fownes Forge Co.* (1904) 90 L.T. 527 (C.A.); *cf. Saint Line Ltd.* v. *Richardsons* [1940] 2 K.B. 99.
[94] *Koufos* v. *Czarnikow Ltd.* [1969] 1 A.C. 350 at 383 (H.L.).
[95] *Victoria Laundry Ltd.* v. *Newman Ltd.* [1949] 2 K.B. 528 (C.A.) and see generally p. 187.
[96] Liquidated damages in main contracts are frequently modest in relation to possible losses. In any event the contractor's own losses are often heavy so that the sub-contractor's total liability is usually greater than the liquidated damages in the main contract.

sub-contractor, but not of his liability.[97] And if the contractor has to pay damages to a plaintiff arising out of the sub-contractor's breach which he would not have had to pay if there had been no breach, the contractor's right to damages from the sub-contractor for that breach is not affected by the fact that the plaintiff recovered against the contractor and another defendant; and that on an apportionment between the contractor and the other defendant under the Law Reform (Married Women and Tortfeasors) Act 1935 the contractor was held to be partly to blame.[98] But so far as the contractor relies on an express indemnity in the sub-contractor he may fail completely if the loss was partly caused by himself.[99]

Inaccurate statements. The general principles are set out in Chapter 7 and in particular under "Contractor's pre-contract information" at page 178.

---

[97] *Biggin & Co. Ltd.* v. *Permanite Ltd.* [1951] 2 K.B. 314 (C.A.); *Fletcher & Stewart* v. *Peter Jay & Partners* (1976) 17 B.L.R. 38 (C.A.); *Comyn Ching* v. *Oriental Tube* (1979) 17 B.L.R. 47 (C.A.); see also "Sums paid in settlement of third party claims" at p. 200.

[98] *Sims* v. *Foster Wheeler Ltd.* [1966] 1 W.L.R. 769 (C.A.). For liability of persons in respect of the same damage, see the Civil Liability (Contribution) Act 1978 and "Statutory contribution" at p. 192.

[99] *A.M.F. International Ltd.* v. *Magnet Bowling Ltd.* [1968] 1 W.L.R. 1028 applying *Walters* v. *Whessoe* [1968] 2 All E.R. 816n. (C.A.); *Smith* v. *South Wales Switchgear* [1978] 1 W.L.R. 165 (H.L.); see also p. 60.

CHAPTER 13

ARCHITECTS, ENGINEERS AND SURVEYORS

1. Meaning and Use of the term "Architect"

"An 'architect' is one who possesses, with due regard to aesthetic as well as practical considerations, adequate skill and knowledge to enable him (i) to originate, (ii) to design and plan, (iii) to arrange for and supervise the erection of such buildings or other works calling for skill and design in planning as he might, in the course of his business, reasonably be asked to carry out or in respect of which he offers his services as a specialist."[1]

The use of the term architect is now, in general, restricted to architects registered under statutory provisions.

---

[1] This is the final sentence of the test applied by the tribunal set up under the Architects Registration Act 1938, s.2, in deciding whether a person was an architect practising on July 29, 1938, and was cited without disapproval in *R. v. Architects' Registration Tribunal, ex p. Jaggar* [1945] 2 All E.R. 131 at 134.

2. Registration[2]

Use of title "architect."   A person is prohibited from practising or carrying on business under any name, style or title containing the word "architect"[3] unless he is a person registered in the Register of Architects.[4]

" 'Practising' . . . means: Holding out for reward to act in a professional capacity in activities which form at least a material part of his business. A man is not practising who operates incidentally, occasionally, in an administrative capacity only, or in pursuit of a hobby."[5]

A person is not treated as not practising by reason only that he is in the employment of another person.[6] The prohibition does not affect the use of the designation "Naval Architect," "Landscape Architect," or "Golf-Course Architect," or the validity of any building contract in customary form.[7]

A body corporate, firm or partnership may carry on business under the style or title of architect if the business of the body corporate, firm or partnership so far as it relates to architecture is under the control and management of a superintendent who is a registered person and who does not act at the same time in a similar capacity for any other body corporate, firm or partnership; and if in every premises where such business is carried on and is not personally conducted by the superintendent such business is bona fide conducted under the direction of the superintendent by an assistant who is a registered person.[8]

Contravention of these provisions is a criminal offence, the person guilty being liable to be fined.[9] It would follow that, presumably, such a person could not sue for fees for work carried out while he was contravening the Acts.[10]

The Architects' Registration Council.   This is a statutory corporation one of whose duties is the maintenance of the Register of Architects.[11] It must also appoint annually a Board of Architectural Education, an Admission Committee,[12] and a Discipline Committee.[13]

---

[2] For an account of registration and of the professional conduct of an architect, see Rimmer's *The Law relating to the Architect* (2nd ed., 1964), Chap. 7.

[3] See *Jacobowitz* v. *Wicks* [1956] Crim.L.R. 697 (D.C.); use of letters "Dip. Ing. Arch." not an offence.

[4] Architects Registration Act 1938, s.1(1). This Act together with the Architects (Registration) Act 1931 and the Architects Registration (Amendment) Act 1969, may be cited together as the Architects Registration Acts 1931–1969 (s.4 of the 1969 Act).

[5] This is the other sentence of the test referred to in n. 1 above.

[6] Architects Registration Act 1938, s.4(2).

[7] *Ibid.* s.1(1), proviso.

[8] Architects (Registration) Act 1931, s.17.

[9] Architects Registration Act 1938, s.3; for certain special defences, see the proviso to s.3. See also Rimmer, *op. cit.* p. 191.

[10] See "Illegality" at p. 141. It has been held, upon similar legislation in Singapore, that a person could not sue for fees for work carried out while he was contravening the Acts—*Raymond Banham* v. *Consolidated Hotels Ltd.* (1976) *Malayan Law Journal* 5.

[11] Architects (Registration) Act 1931, s.3(3).

[12] *Ibid.* s.5(1).

[13] *Ibid.* s.7(2).

The right to be registered. A person who makes an application to the Registration Council in the prescribed manner and pays the prescribed fee[14] is entitled to be registered if the Council is satisfied on a report of the Admission Committee that he is an architect member of the Royal Academy or of the Royal Scottish Academy, or that he has passed any examination in architecture which is for the time being recognised by the Council or that he possesses the prescribed qualifications.[15]

European qualifications. A qualified national of a Member State of the European Community may apply for registration and is entitled to be registered if he satisfies the qualification requirements and pays the prescribed fee.[16] An architect established in another Member State of the European Community may practise or carry on business under the title "architect" while visiting the United Kingdom without being registered under the Act if he is enrolled on a list of visiting EEC architects.[17]

Removal of names from register. If a registered person is convicted of a criminal offence or if the Discipline Committee, after an inquiry, report to the Council that the person has been guilty of conduct disgraceful[18] to him in his capacity as an architect, the Council may cause his name to be removed from the register and he is then, during such period as the Council determine, disqualified for registration under the Acts.[19] Written notice served by registered post of a proposed inquiry must be served on the person concerned and he is entitled upon application to be heard by the Discipline Committee in person or by counsel or a solicitor.[20] Where the Council intends to remove the name of any person from the register for a criminal offence or professional misconduct a written notice must first be served on him by registered letter, and, on an application being made by that person in the prescribed manner within three months from the date of the service of the notice, the Council must consider any representations with regard to the matter which may be made by

---

[14] Prescribed means prescribed by regulations made under the Act. The regulations can be obtained from the Council—Architects (Registration) Act 1931, s.15.

[15] 1931 Act, s.6(1); the qualifying examinations and prescribed qualifications are set out in regulations which can be obtained from Council, 1931 Act, s.15.

[16] Architects (Registration) Act 1931, s.6A as inserted by Architects' Qualifications (EEC Recognition) Order 1987 (S.I. 1987 No. 1824 and further amended by S.I. 1988 No. 2241). The qualifications are as stated in the section and as listed in the Fourth and Fifth Schedules. Relevant Directives are 85/384/EEC, 85/614/EEC and 86/17/EEC.

[17] Architects Registration Act 1938, s.1A as inserted by Architect's Qualifications (EEC Recognition) Order 1987 (S.I. 1987 No. 1824 and further amended by S.I. 1988 No. 2241).

[18] For a discussion of the meaning of "disgraceful," see *Hughes* v. *Architects' Registration Council* [1957] 2 Q.B. 550 (D.C.). See also *Marten* v. *Royal College of Veterinary Surgeons' Disciplinary Committee* [1966] 1 Q.B. 1 (D.C.); *Lawther* v. *Royal College of Veterinary Surgeons* [1968] 1 W.L.R. 1441 (P.C.); *Le Scroog* v. *Optical Council* [1982] 1 W.L.R. 1238 (P.C.). For the Architects' Registration Council Code of Professional Conduct, apply to the Council.

[19] Architects (Registration) Act 1931, s.7(1).

[20] *Ibid.* s.7(4). Service may be by recorded delivery: Recorded Delivery Service Act 1962, s.1 and Sched. 1.

him to the Council either in person or by counsel or by a solicitor.[21] The Council may at any time, either of their own motion or on the application of the person concerned, cause his name to be restored to the register.[22]

For the purpose of maintaining the register the Council may at any time by notice in writing served on any registered person inquire if such person has changed his regular business address, and if no answer is received within six months from the sending of such notice, the Council must send to the said person a further notice by post as a registered letter, and if no answer is received within three months from the sending of such further notice, the Council may remove the name of such person from the register.[23]

Where the Council has removed the name of any person from the register, other than in consequence of his death, they must forthwith serve written notice by registered post on that person and where they have determined that there shall be a period of disqualification the determination must be specified in the notice.[24]

Any person aggrieved by the removal of his name from the register, or by a determination of the Council that he be disqualified for registration during any period, may, within three months from the date on which notice of the removal or determination was served on him, appeal to the High Court against the removal or determination, and on any such appeal the court may give such directions in the matter as they think proper and the order of the court is final.[25]

Trade Descriptions Act 1968.   A false statement by a person that he was an architect was held to be an offence under this Act.[26]

3. The Position of the Architect

(a) *The contract with the employer*

The contract may come into existence as the result of an individual agreement or a competition. The normal rules of formation of contract apply.[27] If there is a competition, the rules of entry and its announcement must be studied to see what is the entitlement of the winner[28] and whether the organisers make a definite promise to employ the successful or best competitor.[29] Contracts need

---

[21] *Ibid.* s.7(5).

[22] *Ibid.* s.7(1).

[23] *Ibid.* s.11.

[24] *Ibid.* s.8.

[25] *Ibid.* s.9; the appeal is to a divisional court. For procedure see R.S.C., Ords. 55 and 94, r. 6. See also *Hughes* v. *Architects' Registration Council* [1957] 2 Q.B. 550 (D.C.).

[26] *R.* v. *Breeze* [1973] 1 W.L.R. 994 (C.A., Crim. Div.).

[27] See Chap. 2.

[28] See *Jepson & Partners* v. *Severn Trent Water Authority* (1982) 20 B.L.R. 53 (C.A.).

[29] *cf. Rooke* v. *Dawson* [1895] 1 Ch. 480; *Carlill* v. *Carbolic Smokeball Co.* [1893] 1 Q.B. 256 (C.A.); *Harvela Investments* v. *Royal Trust Company* [1985] Ch. 103 (C.A.). The R.I.B.A. has special rules for architectural competitions.

not be in writing[30] and it is still the practice for much work to be carried out without any formal agreement, leaving the law to supply the necessary terms by implication.[31] It should be remembered in this context that what architects may take for granted or regard as customary may be quite unfamiliar to many of their clients. A written contract of engagement is desirable for all but the simplest commissions. As a minimum, it should clearly define the responsibilities undertaken by the architect and their timing, his fees and when they are to be paid, and the extent to which he is to be responsible for design, specification, supervision or other activities which may be undertaken by others. The R.I.B.A. publish a standard form of "Architect's Appointment" some of whose more important clauses are intended to limit the architect's liability.[32]

Limited companies performing architect's duties. The R.I.B.A. Code of Professional Conduct does not now prohibit a member from engaging in activities as a proprietor or director of a limited company provided that his conduct complies with the Principles of the Code and the Rules applying to his circumstances. Provided that there is no contravention of the Architects Registration Acts,[33] there is nothing to prevent limited companies performing architectural services, and many do, with or without building the works as well.[34] Often they employ architects as employees. Any claim against such companies for breach of contract is governed by the ordinary rules.

The architect's duty to act fairly. The architect is engaged by the employer to act as his agent for the purpose of securing the completion of the works in an economical and efficient manner. He must perform these duties properly and if he fails to do so may be liable to the employer in damages. But in performing them he must act fairly and professionally in applying the terms of the building contract. Formerly it was thought that this gave rise to a "dual capacity" as agent and as quasi-arbitrator.[35] It has now been settled by the House of Lords that an architect acting under the ordinary building contract is the employer's agent throughout notwithstanding that in the administration of the contract he has to act in a fair and professional manner.[36]

---

[30] See "Formalities of contract" at p. 26.

[31] For general principles as to implication of terms, see p. 45, and for the approach of the courts to the duties of architects see this section of this chapter.

[32] See, *e.g.* clauses 3.6, 3.8 and 3.9 and *cf. Investors in Industry* v. *South Bedfordshire District Council* (1985) 32 B.L.R. 1 at 36 *et seq.* (C.A.). The form is printed at p. 950. It was first published in June 1982 and there have been subsequent amendments. It replaced the former R.I.B.A. Conditions of Engagement printed in the 4th edition of this book.

[33] See p. 301.

[34] Design and build contracts are discussed at p. 6.

[35] *cf. Palacath* v. *Flanagan* [1985] 2 All E.R. 161.

[36] *Sutcliffe* v. *Thackrah* [1974] A.C. 727 (H.L.); *cf. Arenson* v. *Arenson* [1977] A.C. 405 (H.L.); *London Borough of Merton* v. *Leach* (1985) 32 B.L.R. 51 at 77 *et seq.*; *Pacific Associates* v. *Baxter* [1990] Q.B. 993 (C.A.); *cf. Canterbury Pipe Lines* v. *Christchurch Drainage* (1979) 16 B.L.R. 76 (New Zealand Court of Appeal). See also *Lubenham* v. *South Pembrokeshire District Council* (1986) 33 B.L.R. 39 at 52 (C.A.) reciting submissions by counsel with apparent approval. See also "Professional independence" at p. 114.

(b) *The architect's authority as agent*

An architect's authority is strictly limited by the terms of his employment.[37] His authority as agent[38] is a question in each case, but it is possible to consider how far for certain matters which have come before the courts he has an implied authority from his position as architect.

Tenders. An architect engaged "to originate ... design and ... arrange for the erection of buildings"[39] has, it is submitted, implied authority to invite tenders, but he may not, except perhaps in special circumstances, have implied authority to employ a quantity surveyor to prepare bills of quantities.[40] The invitation to tender may contain a specification, plans, drawings and bills of quantities. There is no implied warranty that the statements in these documents are accurate,[41] and the architect has no implied authority to warrant their accuracy.[42] If he does so and the contractor is put to extra cost as a result, the employer is not, in the absence of fraud, liable for breach of warranty unless he knew of or ratified the architect's statement,[43] although the contractor may have a remedy against the architect.[44] Further, if the architect was acting within his ostensible authority in making the statements the contractor may have a remedy against the employer for innocent misrepresentation or negligent misstatement.[45]

Contracts. In the absence of some express power acceptance should be by the employer. It seems reasonably clear that an architect engaged for the purposes referred to in the last paragraph has no implied power to bind the employer by acceptance of a tender,[46] and he cannot without authority pledge

---

[37] *Fredk, Betts Ltd.* v. *Pickfords Ltd.* [1906] 2 Ch. 87 at 95; and see cases cited below. For a statement of the law applicable in considering whether there is an agency relationship, see *Garnac Grain Co. Inc.* v. *H. M. F. Faure & Fairclough* [1968] A.C. 1130 at 1137 (H.L.); *cf. Freeman & Lockyer* v. *Buckhurst Park Properties* [1964] 2 Q.B. 480 especially at 502 *et seq.* (C.A.)—a case about a claim *by* architects.

[38] For agency generally, see *Bowstead on Agency* (15th ed.), and *Chitty* (26th ed.), Vol. 2, Chap. 1.

[39] See definition cited at p. 300.

[40] See *Antisell* v. *Doyle* (1899) 2 I.R. 275 (Irish Q.B.D.), the majority holding that there was then no customary authority in Ireland for an architect to engage a quantity surveyor. Certain older English authorities are referred to. Sir P. O'Brien L.C.J. dissented to the effect that, if the employer impliedly or expressly authorised the architect to invite tenders, she impliedly authorised the engagement of a quantity surveyor. For the position where the R.I.B.A. Architect's Appointment applies see clause 3.5 at p. 960. For quantity surveyors, see p. 343.

[41] See p. 132.

[42] *Scrivener* v. *Pask* (1865) L.R. 1 C.P. 715.

[43] *Ibid.*

[44] See below.

[45] See p. 120 *et seq.*; *cp.* however *Kooragang* v. *Richardson & Wrench* [1982] A.C. 462 (P.C.).

[46] See *Vigers, Sons & Co. Ltd.* v. *Swindell* [1939] 3 All E.R. 590; and *cf.* estate agent cases such as *Hamer* v. *Sharp* (1874) L.R. 19 Eq. 108; *Keen* v. *Mear* (1920) 89 L.J.Ch. 513. A local authority architect may have authority as an official: *Roberts & Co. Ltd.* v. *Leicestershire C.C.* [1961] Ch. 55; *Carlton Contractors* v. *Bexley Corporation* (1962) 106 S.J. 391; *cp. North West Leicestershire D.C.* v. *East Midlands Housing Association* [1981] 1 W.L.R. 1396 (C.A.).

the employer's credit.[47] A chartered civil engineer who accepted a quotation without disclosing that he was acting as agent for a client was held personally liable on the ensuing contract.[48] It was not sufficient to avoid liability that he had written on his firm's professional notepaper and that it was apparent that he was acting in a professional capacity.

Supervision.   It is part of the normal duties of the architect to supervise the work and there is implied such authority as is necessary to ensure that the work is carried out according to the terms of the contract.[49]

Variations.   The architect has no implied authority to vary the works or to order extras,[50] or to order as extras works impliedly included in the work for which the contract sum is payable.[51] A contract between employer and contractor giving the employer's architect power to order variations constitutes express authority to do so, but such an express power must be exercised within the scope of the contract.[52] An architect cannot, without the employer's knowledge or consent, bind the employer by a promise that a condition of the contract will be waived.[53]

Arrangements with adjoining owners.   An architect employed merely to superintend the construction of works has no implied power to agree with adjoining owners to vary the works in such a way as to affect the rights of his employer.[54]

Employed architect.   Where the architect is an employee of the employer he has that authority which the employer holds him out as having by virtue of his position and the particular facts, so that in some cases his authority may be greater than that of an architect engaged as an independent person.[55]

(c) *Excess of authority by architect*

Position of the employer.   If the architect exceeds the authority of his employment, the employer is not liable for his acts unless there is apparent or

---

[47] *Vigers, Sons & Co. Ltd.* v. *Swindell* [1939] 3 All E.R. 590.

[48] *Sika Contracts* v. *Gill and Closeglen Properties* (1978) 9 B.L.R. 11.

[49] *R.* v. *Peto* (1826) 1 Y. & J. 37; *Kimberley* v. *Dick* (1871) L.R. 13 Eq. 1; *Brodie* v. *Cardiff Corporation* [1919] A.C. 337 at 351 (H.L.).

[50] *Cooper* v. *Langdon* (1841) 9 M. & W. 60.

[51] See p. 88.

[52] See p. 88. For an emergency, see p. 90 and, where the R.I.B.A. Architect's Appointment applies see clause 3.3 at p. 960.

[53] *Sharpe* v. *San Paulo Railway* (1873) 8 Ch.App. 597; *Toepfer* v. *Warinco* [1978] 2 Lloyd's Rep. 569 at 577.

[54] *Fredk. Betts Ltd.* v. *Pickfords Ltd.* [1906] 2 Ch. 87.

[55] *Roberts & Co. Ltd.* v. *Leicestershire County Council* [1961] Ch. 55; *Carlton Contractors* v. *Bexley Corporation* (1962) 106 S.J. 391; *cp. North West Leicestershire District Council* v. *East Midlands Housing Association* [1981] 1 W.L.R. 1396 (C.A.).

ostensible authority so that the employer is prevented from denying the authority of his architect[56] or unless the employer subsequently ratifies the architect's acts.

An example of agency by estoppel would arise if E has appointed A to be his architect with express authority to order goods on his behalf, and A has given several orders to S, a supplier. If E then withdraws his authority from A and fails to notify S, he is liable to S on any contracts which A purports to make on his behalf.[57] This principle only applies if the person dealing with the alleged agent had no notice of the lack of authority, and the burden of proof is on such person to prove the agency, or that the alleged principal is estopped from disputing it.[58]

The employer can subsequently ratify an unauthorised contract of the architect provided it was professedly made on his behalf, even though he was not named,[59] and the contract was within the powers of the employer to make,[60] and the employer was in existence at the time when the contract was made.[61] The last question may arise where a promoter of a company purports to make contracts on behalf of a company which has not yet been formed.[62]

If an agent contracts subject to ratification by his principal there is no concluded contract until ratification is obtained, and accordingly it seems that if the person who has entered into such "contract" with the agent withdraws from it before ratification it cannot be ratified so as to bring a binding contract into existence.[63]

The employer is only bound by the ratification of a contract if at the time of ratification he had full knowledge of all the material facts, or there was an intention to ratify the contract whatever it may have been.[64]

---

[56] See *Pole* v. *Leask* (1863) 33 L.J.Ch. 155. See also *Ismail* v. *Polish Ocean Lines* [1976] Q.B. 893 at 903 (C.A.) and see *Bowstead on Agency* (15th ed.), p. 290 and *Chitty* (26th ed.), Vol. 2, para. 2545 on the relationship between apparent or ostensible authority and estoppel. For cases where the agent is fraudulent, see *Lloyd* v. *Grace, Smith & Co.* [1912] A.C. 716 (H.L.); *Armagas* v. *Mundogas* [1986] A.C. 717 (H.L.). For directors of companies, see s.35 of the Companies Act 1985.

[57] *Summers* v. *Solomon* (1857) 26 L.J.Q.B. 301; *Scarf* v. *Jardine* (1882) 7 App.Cas. 345 at 349 (H.L.); *Watteau* v. *Fenwick* [1893] 1 Q.B. 346; *cf. Rockland Industries* v. *Amerada Minerals* (1980) 108 D.L.R. (3d) 513 (Supreme Court of Canada).

[58] *Pole* v. *Leask* (1863) 33 L.J.Ch. 155 at 162.

[59] *Keighley, Maxsted & Co.* v. *Durant* [1901] A.C. 240 (H.L.); see also *Warehousing & Forwarding Co., etc., Ltd.* v. *Jafferali & Sons Ltd.* [1964] A.C. 1 (P.C.).

[60] *Ashbury Railway* v. *Riche* (1875) L.R. 7 H.L. 653 (H.L.); *cf. Bedford Insurance* v. *Instituto de Resseguros* [1985] Q.B. 966.

[61] *Kelner* v. *Baxter* (1866) L.R. 2 C.P. 174.

[62] For personal liability of promoters, see Companies Act 1985, s.36(4) (formerly s.9(2) of the European Communities Act 1972) and *Halsbury* (4th ed.), Vol. 7, para. 51; *cf. Phonogram* v. *Lane* [1982] Q.B. 938 (C.A.).

[63] *Warehousing & Forwarding Co., etc., Ltd.* v. *Jafferali & Sons Ltd.* [1964] A.C. 1 at 9 (P.C.). The point is difficult, see *Bolton Partners* v. *Lambert* (1889) 41 Ch.D. 295 (C.A.) apparently to the opposite effect, but distinguished and doubted in subsequent cases referred to in *Warehousing* v. *Jafferali.* See further *Chitty* (26th ed.), Vol. 2, para. 2524.

[64] *Bowstead on Agency* (15th ed.), Art. 16, p. 64 and see *Vigers* v. *Swindell* [1939] 3 All E.R. 590, the facts of which are set out at p. 285.

Position of the architect.   The architect may be liable in an action for breach of warranty of authority at the suit of the contractor or other person who has suffered loss as a result of the architect exceeding his authority. The principle upon which the action is based is:

> "that where a person by asserting that he has the authority of the principal induces another person to enter into any transaction which he would not have entered into but for that assertion, and the assertion turns out to be untrue, to the injury of the person to whom it is made, it must be taken that the person making it undertook that it was true and he is liable personally for the damage that has occurred."[65]

The liability arises:

> "(a) if he has been fraudulent, (b) if he has without fraud untruly represented that he had authority when he had not, and (c) also where he innocently represents that he has authority where the fact is either, (1) that he never had authority or (2) that his original authority has ceased by reason of facts of which he has not knowledge or means of knowledge."[66]

Thus the architect might be liable where, without his knowledge, his authority has ceased by reason of the employer's death.[67] He cannot be liable if the other party was aware of his lack of authority,[68] so that where there is a written contract, such as the Standard Form of Building Contract, it is difficult for a contractor to succeed in an action for breach of warranty of authority on some matter arising out of the contract, for he has notice of the extent of the architect's authority. The same principle would apply to a sub-contractor under a sub-contract whereby he is expressed to have notice of the terms of the main contract.[69]

Damages.   The starting point in considering the measure of damages in an action for breach of warranty of authority is to compare the plaintiff's position before the representation of authority with his position brought about by the representation.[70] Damages normally include the loss on any contract which cannot be enforced for the want of authority, and may include the costs of unsuccessful proceedings to enforce the contract against the alleged principal.[71] If there is doubt about an agent's authority it may be advisable, before

---

[65] Lord Esher M.R. in *Firbank's Executors* v. *Humphreys* (1886) 18 Q.B.D. 54 at 60 (C.A.). See also *Randell* v. *Trimen* (1856) 18 C.B. 786; *Collen* v. *Wright* (1857) 8 E. & B. 647.

[66] Buckley L.J. in *Yonge* v. *Toynbee* [1910] 1 K.B. 215 at 227 (C.A.).

[67] *Yonge* v. *Toynbee* [1910] 1 K.B. 215 (C.A.).

[68] *Halbot* v. *Lens* [1901] 1 Ch. 344.

[69] See the fourth recital to the Articles of Agreement of the Standard Form of Sub-contract at p. 700.

[70] *Doyle* v. *Olby (Ironmongers) Ltd.* [1969] 2 Q.B. 158 at 167 (C.A.); *Esso* v. *Mardon* [1976] Q.B. 801 (C.A.); *Archer* v. *Brown* [1985] Q.B. 401; *Smith Kline & French Laboratories* v. *Long* (1989) 1 W.L.R. 1 (C.A.).

[71] *Randell* v. *Trimen* (1856) 18 C.B. 786; *Simons* v. *Patchett* (1857) 7 E. & B. 568; *Collen* v. *Wright* (1857) 8 E. & B. 647; *V/O Rasnoimport* v. *Guthrie & Co.* [1966] 1 Lloyd's Rep. 1.

suing the principal, to give notice to the agent that such proceedings will be at his cost if they fail for lack of authority.[72] The date for assessing the loss may be the date when it was accepted or adjudged that the agent had no authority.[73]

(d) *Architect's personal liability on contracts*

The general rule is that an agent is not personally liable on contracts entered into on behalf of a disclosed principal, but in certain circumstances the architect may find himself liable on contracts made on behalf of his employer. This liability must be distinguished from that discussed in the last subsection which arises not on the original contract but on an implied warranty that the architect had authority to make it.

The architect is personally liable where he contracts on behalf of the employer but without disclosing the existence of a principal.[74] In such a case the contract may be enforced either against the architect or, upon discovering his existence, against the employer.[75] And the architect may make himself personally liable if he signs a contract in his own name without excluding his liability.[76] Thus an architect was held personally liable at the suit of a subcontractor where he had signed an order in this manner although earlier correspondence had referred to the existence of his clients and the judge considered that the main contractor was the person who ultimately ought to find the money.[77]

(e) *Fraudulent misrepresentation*

An architect who makes a fraudulent misrepresentation,[78] intending it to be acted upon, is liable in damages for the tort of deceit at the suit of the person who acted upon the statement and suffered loss, and it is no excuse that he merely acted as the agent of his employer, for "all persons directly concerned in the commission of a fraud are to be treated as principals ... The contract of agency or of service cannot impose any obligation on the agent or servant to commit or assist in the committing of a fraud."[79]

The employer is liable for his own fraudulent misrepresentations, and for any fraud committed by the architect in the execution of his authority,[80] even

---

[72] As in *Collen* v. *Wright* (1857) 8 E. & B. 647.

[73] See *Suleman* v. *Shahsavari* [1988] 1 W.L.R. 1181.

[74] See *Bowstead on Agency* (15th ed.); *cf. Sika Contracts* v. *Gill and Closeglen Properties* (1978) 9 B.L.R. 11.

[75] *Ibid.*

[76] See *Bowstead*, Art. 118; *Beigtheil & Young* v. *Stewart* (1900) 16 T.L.R. 177; *cf. Himley Brick Co.* v. *Lamb & Sons' The Guardian,* January 16, 1962—no contract where suppliers at architect's request "reserved" bricks.

[77] *Beigtheil & Young* v. *Stewart* (1900) 16 T.L.R. 177, Bigham J. See also "Contracts" at p. 305.

[78] See p. 122 for the elements of fraud.

[79] Lord Westbury in *Cullen* v. *Thomson's Trustees & Kerr* (1862) 4 Macq. 424 at 432.

[80] *Lloyd* v. *Grace, Smith & Co.* [1912] A.C. 716 (H.L.); *Uxbridge Permanent Benefit Building Society* v. *Pickard* [1939] 2 K.B. 248 (C.A.); *United Bank of Kuwait* v. *Hammoud* [1988] 1 W.L.R. 1051 (C.A.); see also *Briess* v. *Woolley* [1954] A.C. 333 (H.L.).

though it is done for the benefit of the architect,[81] and even though the employer is innocent.[82] But the employer would not be liable for his agent's deceit where the agent was not authorised to do what he was purporting to do, where what he was purporting to do was not within the class of acts that an agent in his position is usually authorised to do and when the employer had done nothing to represent that the agent was so authorised, the third party's belief that the agent was authorised being derived solely from reliance on the agent himself.[83] In *Pearson* v. *Dublin Corporation* it was held that a clause providing that the contractors must not rely on any representation would not protect the employer from an action for the fraudulent misrepresentation of his engineers, but a passage from Lord Loreburn's speech suggested that it might be possible by apt and express clauses in special circumstances for an employer to guard himself from liability for the fraud of his agents.[84]

Fraud involves dishonesty, and the employer cannot be liable for his architect's misrepresentation if neither of them had a guilty mind; "you cannot add an innocent state of mind to an innocent state of mind and get as a result a dishonest state of mind."[85] So if the architect were innocently to make statements about the contract works or the site and the employer knew of facts which rendered those statements untrue but had neither authorised the architect to make the statements nor hoped, nor suspected that he would make them,[86] nor knew he had made them, then there could be no fraud.[87] There would be fraud so as to make the employer liable if he had deliberately employed the architect hoping that he would, innocently, make the false statements.[88]

A contract may be rescinded for fraud on the part of an undisclosed principal.[89]

(f) *Misconduct as agent*

Bribes and secret commissions.   Any secret dealing which might tend to prevent an agent performing his duties faithfully to his principal is presumed by the law to be corrupt.[90] Criminal liability can arise both in respect of the

---

[81] *Ibid.*

[82] *Pearson* v. *Dublin Corporation* [1907] A.C. 351 (H.L.); as explained in *Armstrong* v. *Strain* [1952] 1 K.B. 232 at 258 (C.A.). See p. 122 for the facts of *Pearson's* case.

[83] *Armagas* v. *Mundogas* [1986] A.C. 717 (H.L.); *cf. Kooragang Investments* v. *Richardson & Wrench* [1982] A.C. 462 (P.C.).

[84] For the passage in extenso, see p. 123. See also *Tullis* v. *Jacson* [1892] 3 Ch. 441, discussed at p. 115.

[85] Devlin J. in *Armstrong* v. *Strain* [1951] 1 T.L.R. 856 at 872, referred to with approval in the Court of Appeal [1952] 1 K.B. 232 at 246.

[86] *cf. Ludgater* v. *Love* (1881) 44 L.T. 694 (C.A.).

[87] *Armstrong* v. *Strain* [1952] 1 K.B. 232 (C.A.).

[88] *cf. Ludgater* v. *Love* (1881) 44 L.T. 694 (C.A.).

[89] *Garnac Grain Co. Inc.* v. *H. M. F. Faure & Fairclough Ltd.* [1965] 1 All E.R. 47, overruled on different points [1966] 1 Q.B. 650 (C.A.); [1968] A.C. 1130 (H.L.). For rescission, see "Innocent misrepresentation" at p. 120.

[90] *Harrington* v. *Victoria Graving Dock Co.* (1878) 3 Q.B.D. 549; *Shipway* v. *Broadwood* [1899] 1 Q.B. 369 (C.A.); *cf. Logicrose* v. *Southend Football Club* [1988] 1 W.L.R. 1256; *cf.* also s.2 of the Prevention of Corruption Act 1916.

agents of private principals and of public bodies.[91] Quite apart from criminal liability, any secret dealing between the architect and the contractor, or other person, is a fraud on the employer, and entitles him to dismiss the architect,[92] and recover any money paid by way of bribe or secret commission.[93] Further, the employer may rescind the contract between himself and the contractor or other person concerned,[94] and if he has suffered loss he can recover damages from the architect and the contractor or other person.[95]

The Privy Council has held that a plaintiff, as against the briber and the agent bribed, has alternative remedies:

(1) for money had and received under which he can recover the amount of the bribe;

(2) for damages for fraud, under which he can recover the amount of the actual loss sustained in consequence of his entering into the transaction in respect of which the bribe was given;

and is bound to elect, at the time when judgment is to be entered, between the claim for the bribe and the claim for damages.[96] There are separate causes of action against the briber and the agent bribed but satisfaction of judgment against one of them constitutes satisfaction *pro tanto* of the claim against the other.[97]

The court will not listen to evidence of a custom to pay secret commissions,[98] but an agent accused of accepting a secret commission may be able to show that his principal must have been aware that he had received a commission.[99]

It was, apparently at one time the practice in some cases for the architect to charge the contractor with the cost of taking out the quantities or measuring up deviations. Unless the architect accounts fully to the employer for any sums received, or makes it clear to the employer that he will receive such sums, giving their amount,[1] this procedure would seem to be a fraud on the employer, coming within the principles stated above.

---

[91] See Public Bodies Corrupt Practices Act 1889, s.1, Prevention of Corruption Act 1906, ss.1 and 2(1) and Prevention of Corruption Act 1916, s.2. The Housing Corporation and Housing for Wales are public bodies for these purposes—see the Housing Associations Act 1985, s.74 and Sched. 6, para. 1(2) and the Housing Act 1988, s.46(2) and Sched. 5, para. 1(2). For the relevant law see *Archbold* (43rd ed.), para. 27–157, p. 2646.

[92] *Temperley* v. *Blackrod Manufacturing Co. Ltd.* (1907) 71 J.P. 341.

[93] *Grant* v. *Gold Exploration, etc., Syndicate* [1900] 1 Q.B. 233.

[94] *Panama & South Pacific Telegraph Co.* v. *India Rubber, etc., Co.* (1875) L.R. 10 Ch.App. 515; *Logicrose* v. *Southend Football Club* [1988] 1 W.L.R. 1256.

[95] *Salford Corporation* v. *Lever* [1891] 1 Q.B. 168 (C.A.); *Mahesan* v. *Malaysia Housing Society* [1979] A.C. 374 (P.C.).

[96] *Mahesan* v. *Malaysia Housing Society* [1979] A.C. 374 (P.C.); *cf. Armagas* v. *Mundogas* [1986] A.C. 717 (H.L.); *Logicrose* v. *Southend Football Club* [1988] 1 W.L.R. 1256.

[97] *Mahesan* v. *Malaysia Housing Society* [1979] A.C. 374 (P.C.) citing *United Australia* v. *Barclays Bank* [1941] A.C. 1 (H.L.).

[98] *Bulfield* v. *Fournier* (1894) 11 T.L.R. 62; affd. 11 T.L.R. 282 (C.A.).

[99] *Holden* v. *Webber* (1860) 29 Beav. 117.

[1] See *Dunne* v. *English* (1874) L.R. 18 Eq. 524.

Conflict of duty and interest. An agent must not put his personal interest in conflict with his duty towards his principal.[2] Thus where a surveyor who had been engaged to supervise certain work to be carried out by a building company[3] subsequently became managing director of that company, it was said that this was a breach of duty going to the root of his contract with the employer making him liable to dismissal without, it seems, any right to payment for the work he had done, his contract being entire.[4]

The employer may waive his rights in respect of his agent's breach of duty. Thus if he engages an agent with full knowledge of circumstances which give rise to a conflict between the agent's duty and his interest, or continues to employ him without protest after discovery of such circumstances, he waives his right to rely on the breach of duty.[5]

(g) *The architect's duties to the employer*

The architect must serve the employer faithfully as his agent.[6] Further, by holding himself out as an architect, he impliedly warrants that he possesses the requisite ability and skill.[7] Consequently if he fails to exercise such skill he is liable in damages if any loss is suffered, and may not be able to recover his fees.

The degree of skill required. An architect's liability is not, in the ordinary case, absolute in the sense that he is liable whenever loss results from his acts.[8] It must be shown that he has been negligent, *i.e.* that he has failed to exercise the standard of care required, and that the negligence complained of is a matter of substance.[9]

> "Where you get a situation which involves the use of some special skill or competence, then the test as to whether there has been negligence or not is ... the standard of the ordinary skilled man exercising and professing to have that special skill."[10]

---

[2] *Bank of Upper Canada* v. *Bradshaw* (1867) 1 L.R.P.C. 479 at 489 (P.C.); *Thornton Hall* v. *Wembley Electrical Appliances* [1947] 2 All E.R. 630 (C.A.); *Logicrose* v. *Southend Football Club* [1988] 1 W.L.R. 1256; *cf.* s.21 of the Estate Agents Act 1979 for the obligation of estate agents to disclose personal interests.

[3] And thus for present purposes was in the same position as an architect.

[4] *Thornton Hall* v. *Wembley Electrical Appliances* [1947] 2 All E.R. 630 at 634 (C.A.). For entire contracts, see p. 70.

[5] *Thornton Hall* v. *Wembley Electrical Appliances* [1947] 2 All E.R. 630 (C.A.); *cf. N.Z. Netherlands Society* v. *Kuys* [1973] 1 W.L.R. 1126 (P.C.).

[6] See above and generally, *Bowstead on Agency* (15th ed.).

[7] *Harmer* v. *Cornelius* (1858) 5 C.B.(N.S.) 236 at 246; see also *Jones* v. *Manchester Corporation* [1952] 2 Q.B. 852 at 876 (C.A.).

[8] See *Greaves & Co. Ltd.* v. *Baynham Meikle* [1975] 1 W.L.R. 1905 (C.A.) discussed below; *George Hawkins* v. *Chrysler (UK)* (1986) 38 B.L.R. 36 (C.A.); *cp. I.B.A.* v. *E.M.I. and B.I.C.C.* (1980) 14 B.L.R. 1 (H.L.); *Holland Hannen & Cubitts* v. *W.H.T.S.O.* (1985) 35 B.L.R. 1 (C.A.). See also clause 3.1 of the R.I.B.A. Architect's Appointment at p. 960.

[9] *Cotton* v. *Wallis* [1955] 1 W.L.R. 1168 (C.A.); a difficult case discussed further at p. 486.

[10] McNair J. in *Bolam* v. *Friern Hospital Management Committee* [1957] 1 W.L.R. 582 at 586 approved in *Whitehouse* v. *Jordan* [1981] 1 W.L.R. 246 (H.L.); *Chin Keow* v. *Government of Malaysia* [1967] 1 W.L.R. 813 (P.C.); *cf. Lanphier* v. *Phipos* (1831) 8 C. & P. 475 at 479; *Chapman* v. *Walton* (1833) 10 Bing. 57 at 63; *Slater* v. *Baker* (1767) 2 Wils. 359.

This test, frequently applied in cases of medical negligence, applies to all professions or callings which require special skill, knowledge or experience.[11] "The law does not require of a professional man that he be a paragon, combining the qualities of polymath and prophet."[12] It seems surprisingly that the standard required may not be higher where the client deliberately obtains and pays for someone with specially high skills.[13]

Thus, unless there are special circumstances, the normal measure of an architect's skill is that of ordinarily skilled architects.[14] An error of judgment may or may not amount to negligence.[15] If the majority of architects would, under the circumstances, have done the same thing this normally provides a good defence, for "a defendant charged with negligence can clear himself if he shows that he acted in accord with general and approved practice."[16] Where there is no one accepted practice, he will not be negligent if he acted in accordance with a practice accepted as proper by a responsible body of architects,[17] even if another body of competent professional opinion considered the practice wrong.[18]

If a course proposed by the architect is in accordance with competent practice but has risks, it is thought that the ordinarily competent architect ought normally to warn his client of the risks.[19] If the possibility of danger emerging is reasonably apparent, then to take no precautions is negligence even though others in like circumstances have in the past not taken proper precautions.[20] Thus if the nature of the contract clearly imposes a duty on the

---

[11] *Gold* v. *Haringey Health Authority* [1988] Q.B. 481 at 489 (C.A.); *cf. Luxmoore-May* v. *Messenger May Baverstock* [1990] 1 W.L.R. 1009 at 1020 (C.A.).

[12] Bingham L.J. (dissenting on the facts) in *Eckersley* v. *Binnie* (1988) 18 Con. L.R. 1 at 80 (C.A.); *cf.* "It is easy and tempting to impose too high a standard in order to see that the innocent victims of the disaster are compensated by the defendants' insurance." *Ibid.* at 81.

[13] *George Wimpey* v. *Poole* (1984) 27 B.L.R. 58 at 76 *et seq.*; *cf. Argyll (Duchess of)* v. *Beuselinck* [1972] 2 Lloyd's Rep. 172 at 183; *Greaves & Co. Ltd.* v. *Baynham Meikle* [1975] 1 W.L.R. 1905 (C.A.) discussed below; *Wilsher* v. *Essex A.H.A.* [1987] Q.B. 730 (C.A.).

[14] For a detailed example of the application of this test, see *Holland Hannen & Cubitts* v. *W.H.T.S.O.* (1981) 18 B.L.R. 80 at 126.

[15] *Whitehouse* v. *Jordan* [1981] 1 W.L.R. 246 (H.L.).

[16] Maugham L.J. in *Marshall* v. *Lindsey County Council* [1935] 1 K.B. 516 at 540 (C.A.), cited by Lord Porter in *Whiteford* v. *Hunter* [1950] W.N. 553 (H.L.). For an example of the application of this principle, see *Perry* v. *Tendring District Council* (1984) 30 B.L.R. 118 at 145.

[17] See *Bolam* v. *Friern Hospital Committee* [1957] 1 W.L.R. 582; *Cotton* v. *Wallis* [1955] 1 W.L.R. 1168 (C.A.); *Hasker* v. *Hall* (1958) (unreported) but noted at length in the R.I.B.A. Journal, October 1958; *Chin Keow* v. *Govt. of Malaysia* [1967] 1 W.L.R. 813 (P.C.); *Gold* v. *Haringey Health Authority* [1988] Q.B. 481 (C.A.). For the meaning of "faulty design" in an insurance policy, see *Manufacturers Mutual Insurance Ltd.* v. *Queensland Government Railways* [1969] 1 Lloyd's Rep. 214 (Australian High Court—fault in operation, not in preparation).

[18] *Maynard* v. *West Midlands R.H.A.* [1984] 1 W.L.R. 634 (H.L.); *cf. Hospitals for Sick Children* v. *McLaughlin & Harvey* (1990) 19 Con. L.R. 25 and (1990) 6 Const. L.J. 245.

[19] *cp. Sidaway* v. *Governors of Bethlem Royal Hospital* [1985] A.C. 871 (H.L.).

[20] *Savory & Co.* v. *Lloyds Bank Ltd.* [1932] 2 K.B. 122 at 136 (C.A.); *Markland* v. *Manchester Corporation* [1934] 1 K.B. 566; affd. [1936] A.C. 360 (H.L.). *cf. Marfani & Co. Ltd.* v. *Midland Bank Ltd.* [1968] 1 W.L.R. 956 at 972, 975, 980 (C.A.); *Investors in Industry* v. *South Bedfordshire District Council* (1985) 32 B.L.R. 1 at 37 (C.A.); *Nye Saunders & Partners* v. *Alan E. Bristow* (1987) 37 B.L.R. 92 (C.A.). See also p. 323.

architect, such as inspecting the work of one contractor before it is covered up by another contractor's work, then it is not sufficient that he has done what was customary if he fails to inspect.[21] But if an architect, out of the ordinary course, is employed upon a novel process, of which he does not profess experience, then its failure may be consistent with proper skill on his part.[22] He may profess experience by not refusing the job and not warning the client of his inexperience.[23] "The graver the foreseeable consequences of failure to take care, the greater the necessity for special circumspection . . . The law requires even pioneers to be prudent."[24]

State of the art.   Architects are not judged by hindsight.[25] What may subsequently be negligent, after warning of a risk in a publication likely to be read in the profession, may not have been negligent in the light of ordinary professional knowledge at the time of the act or omission complained of.[26]

Warranty of fitness.   A designer can, by contract, enter into a duty beyond that of using skill and care in his design.[27] He may do this either expressly or, in particular circumstances it may be implied that he has warranted that he will achieve a certain result. Thus in *Greaves & Co.* v. *Baynham Meikle*[28] "package deal" contractors undertook to the employer to produce a warehouse the first floor of which would be suitable for the use of stacker trucks. They engaged the defendants, who were structural engineers, as experts to carry out the design. In all the circumstances it was held that the defendants were liable in damages for designing a floor which failed because they had impliedly warranted that the floor would be reasonably fit for the purpose for which they knew it was required.[29] The Court of Appeal emphasised that it was not laying down any general principle as to the obligations and liabilities of professional men. "It is not open to this court, except where there are special facts and special circumstances, to extend the responsibilities of a professional man beyond the duty to exercise all reasonable skill and care in conformity with the usual standards of his profession."[30]

---

[21] *Jameson* v. *Simon* (1899) 1 F. (Ct. of Sess.) 1211 at 1222. This is a Scottish case with the work carried out by various individual contractors, and therefore requiring a higher degree of supervision than in the usual English contract where there is only one contractor. The defendant was held liable although he had followed the custom of local architects.

[22] *Turner* v. *Garland & Christopher* (1853) H.B.C. (4th ed.), Vol. 2, p. 2 at 3 cited with approval in *I.B.A.* v. *E.M.I. and B.I.C.C.* (1980) 14 B.L.R. 1 at 28 (H.L.); *cf. Wilsher* v. *Essex A.H.A.* [1987] Q.B. 730 at 749 (C.A.).

[23] *Moresk Cleaners Ltd.* v. *Hicks* [1966] 2 Lloyd's Rep. 338, discussed below.

[24] Lord Edmund-Davies in *I.B.A.* v. *E.M.I. and B.I.C.C.* (1980) 14 B.L.R. 1 at 28 (H.L.).

[25] *George Wimpey* v. *D. V. Poole* (1984) 27 B.L.R. 58 at 78; *Eckersley* v. *Binnie* (1988) 18 Con. L.R. 1 at 80 (C.A.); *cf. Kensington, etc., Health Authority* v. *Wettern Composites* (1984) 31 B.L.R. 57 at 74; *Luxmoore-May* v. *Messenger May Baverstock* [1990] 1 W.L.R. 1009 at 1020 (C.A.).

[26] *Roe* v. *Minister of Health* [1954] 2 Q.B. 66 (C.A.).

[27] *cf. I.B.A.* v. *E.M.I. and B.I.C.C.* (1980) 14 B.L.R. 1 (H.L.).

[28] [1975] 1 W.L.R. 1095 (C.A.). For package deals or "design and build" contracts, see p. 6.

[29] *cf. Holland Hannen & Cubitts* v. *W.H.T.S.O.* (1985) 35 B.L.R. 1 (C.A.).

[30] Neill L.J. in *Goerge Hawkins* v. *Chrysler (U.K.)* (1986) 38 B.L.R. 36 at 55 (C.A.); *cp. Eyre* v. *Measday* [1986] 1 All E.R. 488 (C.A.); *Thake* v. *Maurice* [1986] Q.B. 644 (C.A.)—both medical cases.

Expert evidence. Where a building, of ordinary description, of which an architect has had abundant experience, proves a failure that is evidence of want of skill or attention.[31] There may also be cases where it can be concluded without expert evidence that some action by an architect was so obviously necessary that no reasonably prudent architect would fail to take it.[32] But in most cases expert evidence from an equivalently qualified architect is necessary to prove negligence.[33] Evidence from other professionals is unlikely to be sufficient.[34]

Delegation of duties. On the principles stated in Chapter 12, the contract with the architect is personal in the sense that he cannot arrange for the general performance of his duties by another person.[35] The essential characteristic of the duty is that, if it is not performed, it is not a defence for the architect to show that he delegated its performance to a person whom he reasonably believed to be competent to perform it.[36]

In *Moresk Cleaners Ltd.* v. *Hicks*,[37] an architect was engaged to draw up plans, specification and contracts for building an extension to the plaintiff's laundry. The work involved the design of a reinforced concrete structure on a sloping site. The architect knew of a contractor whose partners were qualified engineers, and he invited the contractor to design and build the structure. After erection it became defective because of negligent design in that, *inter alia*, purlins were not strong enough and portal frames should have been, but were not, tied together. It was contended for the architect that he was entitled to delegate certain specialist design tasks to qualified specialist sub-contractors, and, alternatively, that he was acting as agent for the employer to employ the contractor to design the structure. These arguments were rejected and it was said[38]:

---

[31] Erle J. in *Turner* v. *Garland & Christopher* (1853) H.B.C. (4th ed.), Vol. 2, p. 2.

[32] See *Sidaway* v. *Governors of Bethlem Royal Hospital* [1985] A.C. 871 at 900 (H.L.); but *cp. Nye Saunders & Partners* v. *Alan E. Bristow* (1987) 37 B.L.R. 92 at 108 (C.A.).

[33] *Worboys* v. *Acme Investment Ltd.* (1969) 4 B.L.R. 133 at 139 (C.A.); *Investors in Industry* v. *South Bedfordshire D.C.* (1985) 32 B.L.R. 1 at 38 (C.A.); *cf. Chin Keow* v. *Government of Malaysia* [1967] 1 W.L.R. 813 at 817 (P.C.)—there may be a danger that expert evidence will introduce a standard higher than that required by law—and contrast *Midland Bank* v. *Hett, Stubbs and Kemp* [1979] Ch. 384 at 402; *University of Glasgow* v. *Whitfield and Laing* (1988) 42 B.L.R. 66 at 79. For general observations on experts' reports, see *University of Warwick* v. *Sir Robert McAlpine* (1988) 42 B.L.R. 1 at 22—these referred to as "illuminating" in the Court of Appeal (unreported) April 4, 1990.

[34] See *Investors in Industry* v. *South Bedfordshire District Council* (1985) 32 B.L.R. 1 at 39 (C.A.).

[35] See p. 274; *Hemming* v. *Hale* (1859) 7 C.B.(N.S.) 487 at 498; *Stubbs* v. *Holywell Railway* (1867) L.R. 2 Ex. 311. For analogous problems in the law of master and servant, see *Davie* v. *New Merton Board Mills* [1959] A.C. 604 (H.L.); shipowners, see *Riverstone Meat Co. Pty. Ltd.* v. *Lancashire Shipping Co. Ltd.* [1961] A.C. 807 (H.L.); estate agents, see *McCann (John) & Co.* v. *Pow* [1974] 1 W.L.R. 1643 (C.A.).

[36] See *McDermid* v. *Nash Dredging* [1987] A.C. 906 at 919 (H.L.); *cf. Luxmoore-May* v. *Messenger May Baverstock* [1990] 1 W.L.R. 1009 at 1021 (C.A.).

[37] [1966] 2 Lloyd's Rep. 338. See also *Sealand of the Pacific* v. *McHaffie* (1975) 51 D.L.R. (3d) 702, British Columbia C.A.—architect negligent who relied on recommendation of suitability of materials by supplier.

[38] At 342. See also *Hedley Byrne* v. *Heller & Partners* [1964] A.C. 465 at 486 (H.L.).

"... if a building owner entrusts the task of designing a building to an architect he is entitled to look to that architect to see that the building is properly designed. The architect has no power whatever to delegate his duty to anybody else, certainly not to a contractor ... If the defendant was not able, because this form of reinforced concrete was a comparatively new form of construction, to design it himself, he had three courses open to him. One was to say: 'This is not my field.' The second was to go to the client, the building owner, and say: 'This reinforced concrete is out of my line. I would like you to employ a structural engineer to deal with this aspect of the matter.' Or he can, while retaining responsibility for the design, himself seek the advice and assistance of a structural engineer, paying for his service out of his own pocket but having at any rate the satisfaction of knowing that if he acts upon that advice and it turns out to be wrong, the person whom he employed to give the advice will owe the same duty to him as he, the architect, owes to the building owner."[39]

In *London Borough of Merton* v. *Lowe*,[40] the defendants were engaged as architect to design and supervise the erection of a new indoor swimming pool which they designed with suspended ceiling rendered with a coat of "Pyrok," a proprietary product. Pyrok were nominated as sub-contractors. Eventually it was established that "Pyrok" was unsuitable for its purpose and it was suggested that the architects were responsible for the faulty design of the mix used by Pyrok. The *Moresk Cleaners* case was distinguished on the grounds that there the architect had virtually handed over to another the whole task of design. Here Pyrok were nominated sub-contractors employed for a specialised task using their own proprietary materials. In view of successful work done elsewhere the architect's decision to use Pyrok was reasonable and no witness was called to suggest that it was not reasonable.[41]

The terms of employment of the architect must be considered in each case. Bearing in mind that normally the architect is responsible for the design of the building as a whole and "very much the captain of the ship,"[42] it must be a question of construction whether the employer has expressly or impliedly agreed that the architect is not to be responsible for duties ordinarily entrusted to him.[43] One matter which the court may take into account is whether the employer has a remedy against the nominated sub-contractor or other person relied on by the architect as performing such duties,[44] for it is thought that the

---

[39] *cf. Sealand of the Pacific* v. *McHaffie* (1974) 2 B.L.R. 74 (British Columbia C.A.); *Richard Roberts* v. *Douglas Smith Stimson* (1988) 46 B.L.R. 50 at 66; *Eames* v. *North Hertfordshire District Council* (1980) 18 B.L.R. 50 at 70.

[40] (1981) 18 B.L.R. 130 (C.A.).

[41] *Ibid.* at 148.

[42] H.H. Judge Smout Q.C. in *Kensington, etc., Health Authority* v. *Wettern Composites* (1984) 31 B.L.R. 57 at 74.

[43] Consider the R.I.B.A. Architect's Appointment printed at p. 950 and referred to in the next paragraph.

[44] See "Protection of employer" at p. 294.

court would be unwilling, unless compelled to do so, to find that the employer had no remedy against anyone for bad design.

Where the R.I.B.A. Architect's Appointment is used, clauses 3.6, 3.8 and 3.9 provide in effect that the architect is not to be responsible for work, including design work, done by consultants or specialist contractors, subcontractors or suppliers, nor for the contractor's operational methods.[45] These clauses:

> "clearly contemplate that where a particular part of the work ... involves specialist knowledge or skill beyond that which an architect of ordinary competence may reasonably be expected to possess, the architect is at liberty to recommend to his client that a reputable independent consultant, who appears to have the relevant specialist knowledge or skill, shall be appointed by the client to perform this task. If following such a recommendation a consultant with these qualifications is appointed, the architect will normally carry no legal responsibility for the work to be done by the expert which is beyond the capability of an architect of ordinary competence; in relation to the work allotted to the expert, the architect's legal responsibility will normally be confined to directing and coordinating the expert's work in the whole. However, this is subject to one important qualification. If any danger or problem arises in connection with the work allotted to the expert, of which an architect of ordinary competence reasonably ought to be aware and reasonably could be expected to warn the client, despite the employment of the expert, and despite what the expert says or does about it, the duty of the architect [is] to warn the client."[46]

Where it is known that the contract between the employer and the contractor will contain provision for measurement by a skilled quantity surveyor an architect is not, it is submitted, in the ordinary case in breach of duty to the employer if he relies on such measurements,[47] provided, it seems, that the measurements are not grossly wrong.[48] But where an architect was held under a duty to warn about possible inflation when giving an estimate of cost, he was held not to have discharged that duty by consulting a quantity surveyor to prepare a schedule of cost.[49]

(h) *Architects' duties in detail*

The detailed duties of an architect must depend upon the application of the general principles stated above to the particular facts of the case, including any

---

[45] See p. 960.

[46] Slade L.J. in *Investors in Industry* v. *South Bedfordshire District Council* (1985) 32 B.L.R. 1 at 37 (C.A.) speaking of similar clauses in the former R.I.B.A. Conditions of Engagement.

[47] See *Clemence* v. *Clarke* (1880) H.B.C. (4th ed.), Vol. 2, p. 54 at 58 (C.A.); *R. B. Burden Ltd.* v. *Swansea Corporation* [1957] 1 W.L.R. 1167 (H.L.); both are cases on the architect's duty as certifier (see pp. 100 *et seq.*).

[48] *Priestley* v. *Stone* (1888) H.B.C. (4th ed.), Vol. 2, p. 134 at 142 (C.A.).

[49] *Nye Saunders* v. *Alan E. Bristow* (1987) 37 B.L.R. 92 (C.A.).

special terms.[50] So far as these duties are based upon what a competent experienced architect would do in the circumstances, they are a proper subject for a member of that profession rather than for a lawyer. To give some guidance there is first set out the list of duties suggested by Hudson, himself a practising architect as well as a lawyer. Although the last edition of *Hudson's Building Contracts* edited by Hudson was published in 1926, it is thought that the list remains fairly comprehensive. There is further discussion in the paragraphs which follow.

Hudson's list of duties[51]

"(i) To advise and consult with the employer (not as a lawyer) as to any limitation which may exist as to the use of the land to be built on, either (*inter alia*) by restrictive covenants or by the rights of adjoining owners or the public over the land, or by statutes[52] and by-laws affecting the works to be executed.[53]

(ii) To examine the site, sub-soil and surroundings.[54]

(iii) To consult with and advise the employer as to the proposed work.

(iv) To prepare sketch plans and a specification having regard to all the conditions which exist and to submit them to the employer for approval,[55] with an estimate of the probable cost, if requested.[56]

(v) To elaborate and, if necessary, modify or amend the sketch plans as he may be instructed and prepare working drawings and a specification or specifications.

(vi) To consult with and advise the employer as to obtaining tenders, whether by invitation or by advertisement, and as to the necessity or otherwise of employing a quantity surveyor.[57] (Engineers do not so often employ a quantity surveyor.)

(vii) To supply the builder with copies of the contract drawings and specification, supply such further drawings and give such instructions as may be necessary, supervise the work, and see that the contractor performs the contract, and advise the employer if he commits any serious breach thereof.[58]

(viii) To perform his duties to his employer as defined by any contract with his employer or by the contract with the builder, and generally to act as the employer's agent in all matters connected with the work and the contract, except where otherwise prescribed by the contract with the builder, as, for

---

[50] *e.g.* R.I.B.A. Architect's Appointment—see pp. 950 *et seq.*
[51] At p. 9 of the 7th ed. The footnotes have been inserted.
[52] *e.g.* town and country planning legislation.
[53] See "Law and practice" below.
[54] See "Examination of site" below.
[55] For the position where the employer does not approve, see p. 333.
[56] See "Estimates" and "Plans, drawings, specifications and quantities" below.
[57] See p. 343.
[58] For supervision, see p. 323.

instance, in cases where he has under the contract to act as arbitrator or quasi-arbitrator."[59]

Law and practice. An architect's duties are comparable, in some aspects, to those of ecclesiastical surveyors, of whom it has been said that, they "could not be expected to supply minute and accurate knowledge of the law; but we think under the circumstances they might properly be required to know the general rules applicable to the valuation of ecclesiastical property."[60] An architect must have sufficient knowledge of those principles of law relevant to his professional practice in order reasonably to protect his client from damage and loss. This may mean that in particular cases he should advise his client that he knows little or nothing of the relevant law and that the client should obtain legal advice.[61]

The law of which an architect should know the general rules includes, it is submitted, all statutes and by-laws affecting the building, the main principles of town and country planning law, and private rights likely to affect the works. He should also, it is thought, have a general knowledge of the law as applied to the more important clauses, at least, of standard forms of building contract particularly if he is to act as architect under such a contract. If his working drawings, plans or directions result in a building which contravenes the by-laws or building regulations which apply to it,[62] this is, it is submitted, some but not conclusive,[63] evidence of breach of duty. It would appear to be part of his duty to keep himself informed of recent relevant changes in the law, including important decisions.[64]

An architect who relied on the interpretation by the local authority of certain planning legislation, as a result of which his clients suffered loss was held not to have been negligent. The case concerned a difficult point of law, and it was reasonable in the circumstances to rely on the planning authority. The view which he had accepted was one widely held to be correct by others in property development, including a senior employee of the plaintiffs.[65]

Examination of site. It is part of the general duties of the architect to examine the site to ascertain whether it is suitable for the work to be carried out.[66] He must not rely on what he is told by a third person,[67] nor by a former

---

[59] The term "quasi-arbitrator" is now no longer used, see at p. 114.
[60] Jervis C.J. in *Jenkins* v. *Betham* (1855) 15 C.B. 168 at 189.
[61] See Gibson J. in *B.L. Holdings* v. *Wood* (1978) 10 B.L.R. 48 at 70—the decision overruled on appeal at (1979) 12 B.L.R. 1 (C.A.) but not, it is thought, so as to impugn the passage indicated.
[62] See *Townsends (Builders)* v. *Cinema News* [1959] 1 W.L.R. 119 (C.A.) and more fully reported at (1958) 20 B.L.R. 118 (C.A.), discussed at pp. 143 and 180.
[63] Even counsel may be wrong in giving legal advice but "not negligent, just mistaken, as any lawyer and judge might be"—Lawton J. in *Cook* v. *S.* [1966] 1 W.L.R. 635 at 641; *cf. Whitehouse* v. *Jordan* [1981] 1 W.L.R. 246 at 257 (H.L.).
[64] See *Lee* v. *Walker* (1872) L.R. 7 C.P. 121 (patent agent). Generally for the duty to keep up to date, see *Roe* v. *Minister of Health* [1954] 2 Q.B. 66 (C.A.).
[65] *B.L. Holdings* v. *Wood* (1979) 12 B.L.R. 1 (C.A.); *cf. Dunlop* v. *Woollahra Municipal Council* [1982] A.C. 158 (P.C.)—advice by solicitor on a finely balanced point of law not negligent.
[66] *Moneypenny* v. *Hartland* (1826) 2 C. & P. 378; *Columbus Co.* v. *Clowes* [1903] 1 K.B. 244.
[67] *Columbus Co.* v. *Clowes* [1903] 1 K.B. 244.

agent of the employer.[68] It would appear also to be part of his duty to observe whether there are obvious rights of way, light[69] or other private rights which might be affected by the proposed works. If the works require a site or soil investigation, as in very many instances they will, it is the architect's duty to recommend such an investigation and to seek his client's authority to arrange it.[70] The investigation or other considerations may result in the need for a structural engineer or other specialist to design suitable foundations,[71] and the architect should so advise if he does not himself have the necessary skill.

Estimates.   If the architect is asked for an estimate of the cost of the proposed work he should give an honest and careful estimate,[72] which should normally consider and if necessary warn about the possibility of inflation.[73] He should not enter into a firm undertaking that the estimate will not be exceeded, unless he discloses this to the contractor before the building contract is entered into; failure to disclose disqualifies him from carrying out his independent duties under the contract.[74]

Plans, drawings, specifications and quantities.   By analogy with the duty of a valuer it seems to be no excuse where the plans and drawings are defective that he has shown them to the employer and told him to examine them for himself.[75] But clients who were experienced property developers and passed plans showing no downstairs lavatories in a speculative housing development were held to be not entitled subsequently to complain of their absence.[76] If the architect's plans involve a trespass he may be personally liable to an adjoining owner for a trespass so caused.[77] The quantities are usually taken out by the client's quantity surveyor, but, if the architect takes them out himself or has a quantity surveyor do the work for him, he is liable for loss caused by errors due to negligence.[78] If the architect were to accept from

---

[68] *Moneypenny* v. *Hartland* (1826) 2 C. & P. 378.
[69] See, *e.g. Armitage* v. *Palmer* [1960] C.L.Y. 326 (C.A.).
[70] See *Eames* v. *North Hertfordshire District Council* (1980) 18 B.L.R. 50 at 70.
[71] *cf. Kaliszewska* v. *John Clague & Partners* (1984) 5 Con. L.R. 62; *Balcombe* v. *Wards Construction* (1981) 259 E.G. 765.
[72] *Moneypenny* v. *Hartland* (1826) 2 C. & P. 378; for the position when his estimate is substantially less than the lowest tender, see p. 333.
[73] *Nye Saunders* v. *Alan E. Bristow* (1987) 37 B.L.R. 92 (C.A.).
[74] *Kimberley* v. *Dick* (1871) L.R. 13 Eq. 1; *Kemp* v. *Rose* (1858) 1 Giff. 258; see p. 115.
[75] *Smith* v. *Barton* (1866) 15 L.T. 294; *cf. Holland Hannen & Cubitts* v. *W.H.T.S.O.* (1985) 35 B.L.R. 1 at 20 (C.A.).
[76] *Worboys* v. *Acme Investments* (1969) 4 B.L.R. 136 (C.A.).
[77] *Monks* v. *Dillon* (1882) 12 L.R.Ir. 321. For examples of trespass from works of construction, see *Kelson* v. *Imperial Tobacco* [1957] 2 Q.B. 334—advertising sign; *Armstrong* v. *Sheppard & Short* [1959] 2 Q.B. 384—sewer, discharge of effluent; *Woolerton and Wilson* v. *Richard Costain* [1970] 1 W.L.R. 411—crane jib. See also "Nuisance from building operations" at p. 257.
[78] *M'Connell* v. *Kilgallen* (1878) 2 L.R.Ir. 119 at 121. See also *Young* v. *Blake* (1887) H.B.C. (4th ed.), Vol. 2, p. 110; *Lansdowne* v. *Somerville* (1862) 3 F. & F. 236; *Nye Saunders* v. *Alan E. Bristow* (1987) 37 B.L.R. 92 (C.A.) For quantity surveyors, see p. 343.

the client's quantity surveyor quantities which were grossly wrong he might be liable to the employer for negligence if loss resulted.[79]

Design.   The usual standard of duty is that of reasonable care, but in special circumstances it may be implied that the architect has warranted that his design will be suitable for the purpose required by his client.[80] The architect cannot delegate his duty without his client's consent.[81] His duties do not end when work starts. He "is under a continuing duty to check that his design will work in practice and to correct any errors which may emerge."[82] The duty continues to completion[83] and may continue to the issue of a final certificate[84] although the action which the architect should take may vary according to the time when the error is discovered. The subsequent discovery of a design error does not necessarily mean that the architect's original design was negligent.[85]

R.I.B.A. Architect's Appointment.[86]   Where the architect's engagement is to provide all the services in Part 1, he is expressly obliged, by clause 1.4, to advise on the need for other consultants' services and on the scope of those services. At the detailed design stage, he is obliged, by clause 1.13, to develop the scheme design with other appointed consultants. He is obviously responsible for his own design, but he also has to "co-ordinate any design work done by consultants, specialist contractors, sub-contractors and suppliers." By clause 3.6, the client is to hold each consultant, and not the architect, responsible for the work entrusted to that consultant. By clause 3.8, the client is to hold any specialist contractor, sub-contractor or supplier, and not the architect, responsible for any design work entrusted to them. By clauses 3.7 and 3.8, the architect has the authority (and, it is thought, the responsibility) to co-ordinate and integrate consultants' and specialists' designs into the overall design. He may also, it is thought, be responsible for architectural features or consequences of a consultant's or specialist's design.[87]

If there is negligent design by directly appointed consultants or a directly appointed specialist contractor, the employer will normally have a remedy for breach of contract. The employer may possibly have a remedy in tort against a sub-contractor who carries out design,[88] but this will only be so in special

---

[79] Lord Esher M.R. in *Priestley* v. *Stone* (1888) H.B.C. (4th ed.), Vol. 2, p. 134 at 142 (C.A.); 4 T.L.R. 730; *cf. Nye Saunders* v. *Alan E. Bristow* (1987) 37 B.L.R. 92 (C.A.).

[80] See "The degree of skill required" and "Warranty of fitness" at pp. 312 and 314.

[81] See "Delegation of duties" at p. 315.

[82] *Brickfield Properties Ltd.* v. *Newton* [1971] 1 W.L.R. 862 at 873 (C.A.); *London Borough of Merton* v. *Lowe* (1981) 18 B.L.R. 130 (C.A.); *Chelmsford District Council* v. *Evers* (1983) 25 B.L.R. 99.

[83] *Chelmsford District Council* v. *Evers* (1983) 25 B.L.R. 99.

[84] *London Borough of Merton* v. *Lowe* (1981) 18 B.L.R. 130 (C.A.); *cf. Eckersley* v. *Binney* (1988) 18 Con. L.R. 1 at 67 (C.A.) for keeping abreast of developing knowledge after completion.

[85] *London Borough of Merton* v. *Lowe* (1981) 18 B.L.R. 130 at 148 (C.A.); see also "State of the art" at p. 314.

[86] This is printed at p. 950.

[87] *cf. Holland Hannen & Cubitts* v. *W.H.T.S.O.* (1985) 35 B.L.R. 1 (C.A.) where a majority held that an engineer advising on the structure of a hospital floor was not responsible for its appearance.

[88] See p. 178.

circumstances where the employer has positively relied on the sub-contractor for advice.[89] The employer ordinarily has no claim for such design against the main contractor,[90] although this will depend on the terms of the main contract and on whether the employer relevantly relied on the main contractor.[91] There is a serious danger, therefore, that if no further steps were taken the employer would be without remedy in many cases for loss caused by detailed design carried out by specialist sub-contractors or suppliers. The JCT publish forms of direct agreement between employer and sub-contractor and a warranty for suppliers which give the employer a remedy in contract for negligent design.[92] It is thought that an architect, who relied upon clause 3.8 of the R.I.B.A. Architect's Appointment to escape liability for a specialist's design, might be found to be in breach of duty to his client if he had failed to recommend the use of the form of agreement between sub-contractor and employer or the warranty as the case may be and had taken no other suitable step to protect his client's interests.

Inquiries as to materials.   An architect may be in breach of duty to his client if he fails to make proper inquiries about the suitability of materials but merely relies upon the recommendation or expertise of a supplier.[93] But where an engineer selected shower room tiles which turned out to be slippery after careful investigation of R.I.B.A. product data sheets and trade brochures and after consulting with an experienced specialist flooring firm, he was held on the facts not to have been negligent.[94]

Advising on the contract.   Some clients are very familiar with forms of contract, but others are not. At least for those clients who are not, it is suggested that the architect has a duty to give general advice.[95] Standard forms of contract have advantages and disadvantages and different forms are obviously more suitable for different types and sizes of contract. Specially drafted contracts are sometimes appropriate. The architect's general advice should include practical guidance on the advantages and disadvantages and on the

---

[89] See *University of Warwick* v. *Sir Robert McAlpine* unreported, C.A., April 4, 1990, reversing the factual decision of Garland J. on this issue at (1988) 42 B.L.R. 1.

[90] See discussion of position under the Standard Form of Building Contract at p. 637. See also *Holland Hannen & Cubitts* v. *W.H.T.S.O.* (1980) 18 B.L.R. 80; *University of Warwick* v. *Sir Robert McAlpine* (1988) 42 B.L.R. 1.

[91] See *University of Warwick* v. *Sir Robert McAlpine* (1988) 42 B.L.R. 1; *cf. I.B.A.* v. *E.M.I. and B.I.C.C.* (1980) 14 B.L.R. 1 (H.L.).

[92] Printed and discussed in Chap. 20.

[93] See *Sealand of the Pacific* v. *Robert C. McHaffie* (1974) 51 D.L.R. (3d) 702, British Columbia C.A.; *Richard Roberts* v. *Douglas Smith Stimson* (1988) 46 B.L.R. 50. Consider also *Clay* v. *Crump (A.J.) & Sons Ltd.* [1964] 1 Q.B. 533 at 559 (C.A.). For an example where the architect should have made inquiries of a design by nominated sub-contractors, see *Holland Hannen & Cubitts* v. *W.H.T.S.O.* (1981) 18 B.L.R. 89 at 127.

[94] *George Hawkins* v. *Chrysler (U.K.)* (1986) 38 B.L.R. 36 (C.A.).

[95] *cf.* clause 1.20 of the R.I.B.A. Architect's Appointment at p. 554 and see also "Law and practice" at p. 319.

requirements and common pitfalls[96] of the suggested form of contract. He should, it is thought, have regard to the likelihood of a particular event occurring and the losses which might result when carrying out the project in question. If, for example, interference with the works causing a suspension or delay is reasonably foreseeable as liable to occur then it may well be that he should draw this to his client's attention and perhaps suggest that appropriate amendments to the form should be considered. If nominated sub-contractors and nominated suppliers are to be engaged, he should, it is thought, ordinarily recommend the use of the form of agreement between the sub-contractor and the employer and, in some cases, of the warranty by a nominated supplier.[97] Insurance almost always requires particular consideration.

He should certainly see that all necessary blanks and appendices[98] in the form of contract are duly completed, that the contract is in form complete and that the contract documents are clearly identified. If the contract is made by exchange of correspondence without a formal contract document, he should see that all essential terms are unambiguously agreed.[99] He should consider recommending that the contract should be a deed[1] to secure the longer 12-year limitation period.[2] But he should be cautious about giving advice on specifically legal points and should consider recommending that the client takes separate legal advice. He should be particularly cautious about drafting contracts himself or recommending amendments to standard forms and should usually in this respect either take legal advice himself or see that the client does so.

Failure to take such steps as are referred to in the preceding two paragraphs may furnish some prima facie evidence of negligence, but each case would depend on its own facts.

Recommending contractors. It may, by analogy with estate agents letting houses,[3] be the duty of the architect, in recommending contractors, to make inquiries as to their solvency and capabilities. An architect who recommended two builders as "very reliable" was held liable for negligent misrepresentation when the chosen builder proved to be very unreliable.[4] In some cases it may be the duty of the architect to obtain competitive tenders but, in the absence of evidence of loss, damages for breach will be nominal.[5]

Supervision

"It can be said that when a person engages an architect in relation to the

---

[96] See, *e.g.* that illustrated by *Temloc* v. *Errill Properties* (1987) 39 B.L.R. 30 (C.A.).
[97] See n. 92 above.
[98] See, *e.g. Temloc* v. *Errill Properties* (1987) 39 B.L.R. 30 (C.A.).
[99] See "Essential terms" and "Certainty of terms" at pp. 20 and 22 respectively.
[1] See "Deeds" at p. 27.
[2] For limitation, see pp. 366 *et seq.*
[3] See *Heys* v. *Tindall* (1861) 1 B. & S. 296.
[4] *Valerie Pratt* v. *George J. Hill* (1987) 38 B.L.R. 25 (C.A.)—the finding of the Official Referee to this effect not being challenged on appeal.
[5] See *Hutchinson* v. *Harris* (1978) 10 B.L.R. 19 at 24 (C.A.).

building of a house, he is entitled to expect that the architect will perform his duties in such a manner as to safeguard his interests and that he will do all that is reasonably within his power to ensure that the work is properly and expeditiously carried out, so as to achieve the end result as contemplated by the contract. In particular the building owner is entitled to expect his architect so to administer the contract and supervise the work, as to ensure, as far as is reasonably possible, that the quality of work matches up to the standard contemplated."[6]

The quality of the contractor's work is the responsibility of the architect both generally and for the purpose of interim certificates. The architect must give such reasonable supervision to the works as enables him to give an honest certificate that the work has been properly carried out.[7] He is not required personally to measure or check every detail, but should check substantial and important matters, such as, for example, the bottoming of a cement floor, especially if failure to do so will result in the work being covered up and therefore not being capable of inspection at a later stage.[8] It has been held on particular facts that, following the key setting out, there was no duty on the architect to see that proper setting out was maintained.[9] It is for the architect to tell the quantity surveyor, if there is one, about defects for which allowance should be made in the measurement and valuation for interim certificates. But prolonged and detailed inspection and measurement at interim stage is impractical and not to be expected.[10]

"As is well-known, the architect is not permanently on the site but appears at intervals, it may be of a week or a fortnight, and he has, of course, to inspect the progress of the work. When he arrives on the site there may be many very important matters with which he has to deal: the work may be getting behind hand through labour troubles; some of the suppliers of materials or the sub-contractors may be lagging; there may be physical trouble on the site itself, such as, for example, finding an unexpected amount of underground water. All these are matters which may call for important decisions by the architect. He may in such circumstances think that he knows the builder sufficiently well and can rely upon him to carry out a good job[11]; that it is more important that he should deal with urgent

---

[6] H.H. Judge Stabb Q.C. in *Sutcliffe* v. *Chippendale & Edmondson* (1971) 18 B.L.R. 149 at 162—the case which on a different point became in the House of Lords *Sutcliffe* v. *Thackrah* [1974] A.C. 727 (H.L.). For the supervision to be expected from a consulting engineer, see *Oldschool* v. *Gleeson* (1976) 4 B.L.R. 105 at 123; *Kensington, etc., Health Authority* v. *Wettern Composites* (1984) 31 B.L.R. 57 at 82.

[7] *Jameson* v. *Simon* (1899) 1 F. (Ct. of Sess.) 1211; *Rogers* v. *James* (1891) 8 T.L.R. 67; H.B.C. (4th ed.), Vol. 2, p. 172 (C.A.); *Cotton* v. *Wallis* [1955] 1 W.L.R. 1168 (C.A.).

[8] *Jameson* v. *Simon* (1899) 1 F. (Ct. of Sess.) 1211; see also *Florida Hotels Pty.* v. *Mayo* (1965) 113 C.L.R. 588 (Aust.); but note R.I.B.A. Architect's Appointment clauses 1.22 and 3.10–3.12 at pp. 954 and 961.

[9] *Gray* v. *T. P. Bennett & Son* (1987) 43 B.L.R. 63 at 82.

[10] *Sutcliffe* v.*Chippendale & Edmondson* (1971) 18 B.L.R. 149 at 165.

[11] *cf. Sutcliffe* v. *Chippendale & Edmondson* (1971) 18 B.L.R. 149 at 162.

matters on the site than that he should make a minute inspection on the site to see that the builder is complying with the specifications laid down by him ... It by no means follows that, in failing to discover a defect which a reasonable examination should have disclosed, in fact the architect was necessarily thereby in breach of his duty to the building owner so as to be liable in an action for negligence. It may well be that the omission of the architect to find the defects was due to no more than an error of judgment,[12] or was a deliberately calculated risk which, in all the circumstances of the case, was reasonable and proper."[13]

Before suing the architect for negligence in supervision or certification, the employer does not have to prove the builder's inability to pay. He can proceed, if he wishes, solely against the architect. "No doubt the builder is also liable. It is a case of concurrent breaches of contract producing the same damage. In my judgment the plaintiff has an action against both, although she cannot obtain damages twice over."[14]

It may be that the standard of care required in supervision before giving his final certificate is higher where that certificate is binding on the employer[15] than where it can be appealed against to an arbitrator or the court.[16]

It seems that, if the building contract requires the contractor to complete the works to the architect's reasonable satisfaction, the architect is, subject to clear language in the contract to the contrary, entitled to have regard to the amount of the price and is not in breach of duty to the employer for permitting a lower standard of work where the price is low than one would expect where the price is high.[17] Certain minimum standards are, however, obviously required whatever the price.

R.I.B.A. Architect's Appointment.[18]   By clause 3.10, the architect is obliged to:

"visit the site at intervals appropriate to the stage of construction to inspect the progress and quality of the works and to determine that they are being

---

[12] *cf.* now *Whitehouse* v. *Jordan* [1981] 1 W.L.R. 246 (H.L.)—an error of judgment may or may not be negligent.

[13] Lord Upjohn in *East Ham Corporation* v. *Bernard Sunley* [1966] A.C. 406 at 443 (H.L.). The discussion was concerned with the meaning of "reasonable examination" in clause 24 of the 1939 R.I.B.A. form (revised 1950).

[14] H.H. Judge Fay, Q.C. in *Hutchinson* v. *Harris* (1978) 10 B.L.R. 22; *cf. London Borough of Merton* v. *Lowe* (1981) 18 B.L.R. 130 at 145 (C.A.).

[15] See *London Borough of Merton* v. *Lowe* (1981) 18 B.L.R. 130 (C.A.). *cf.* commentary to clause 2 of the Standard Form of Building Contract at p. 486.

[16] See "Crouch" at p. 389.

[17] *Cotton* v. *Wallis* [1955] 1 W.L.R. 1168 (C.A.) discussed at p. 486. The Court of Appeal by a majority upheld the finding of the county court judge that an architect who passed some trifling defects but nothing "rank bad" was not guilty of negligence; *Davis* v. *Afa-Minerva* [1974] 2 Lloyd's Rep. 27 at 31; *cf. Photo Production* v. *Securicor* [1980] A.C. 827 (H.L.) where the court took price into account in construing an exclusion clause in a contract to provide night security.

[18] See p. 950.

executed generally in accordance with the contract documents. The architect will not be required to make frequent or constant inspections."[19]

Clause 3.9 provides that the client will hold the contractor, not the architect, responsible for the contractor's operational methods and for the proper execution of the works. It is thought that the intention is to make it clear that the architect is not warranting compliance by the contractor with the building contract but that, read in the light of other clauses, it is not intended to exempt the architect from a duty of care in supervising the contractor.

By clause 3.11, "where frequent or constant inspection is required a clerk or clerks of works will be employed. They may be employed either by the client or by the architect and will in either event be under the architect's direction or control." By clause 3.12, "where frequent or constant inspection by the architect is agreed to be necessary, a resident architect may be appointed by the architect on a part or full time basis." It is thought that it is part of an architect's duty to advise the client when a clerk of works and a resident architect should be appointed. If a clerk of works or resident architect is employed by the architect, he will normally be liable for their negligence.[20]

Clerk of works. The duties of supervision where there is a clerk of works require special consideration. His powers and duties as between himself and the contractor depend upon the terms of the building contract. In *Leicester Board of Guardians* v. *Trollope* the building contract provided that he was to "be considered and act solely as the inspector and assistant of the architect."[21] It was said that the clerk of works was appointed to protect the interests of the employer against the contractor mainly because the architect could not be there all the time,[22] and that when a clerk of works is employed the architect is responsible to see that his design is carried out, but is entitled to leave the supervision of matters of detail to the clerk of works.[23] In that case an architect was held liable in damages where dry rot resulted from a failure to carry out the design of the lower floor. A series of concrete blocks had to be made, and the architect admitted that he had not checked whether they were made properly or not. It was said that "if the architect had taken steps to see that the first block was all right and he had then told the clerk of works that the work in the others was to be carried out in the same way, I would have been inclined to hold that the architect had done his duty."[24] The case is of interest because it

---

[19] See also clause 1.22.

[20] *cf.* clauses 2.37 and 4.13 which appear to provide that a clerk of works or resident architect employed by the architect are expected to be paid for by the client at hourly rates in addition to any percentage fee.

[21] *Leicester Board of Guardians* v. *Trollope* (1911) 75 J.P. 197; H.B.C. (4th ed.), Vol. 2, p. 419; the contract was described by Channell J. as of the usual character. *cf.* clause 12 of the Standard Form of Building Contract and clause 3.11 of the R.I.B.A. Architect's Appointment at pp. 513 and 961 respectively.

[22] Channell J. in *Leicester Board of Guardians* v. *Trollope* (1911) 75 J.P. 197; H.B.C. (4th ed.), Vol. 2, p. 419 at 423.

[23] *Ibid.*; see also *Lee* v. *Bateman (Lord)*, *The Times*, October 31, 1893.

[24] *Leicester Board of Guardians* v. *Trollope* (1911) 75 J.P. 197; H.B.C. (4th ed.), Vol. 2, p. 419 at 200 of the J.P. Report; *cf. Gray* v. *T. P. Bennett & Son* (1987) 43 B.L.R. 63 at 82.

was alleged that the deviation from the design was due to the fraud of the clerk of works, and it was held that even if this were so the architect could still be liable.[25] If an architect acquiesces in the appointment and carrying out of his duties by an incompetent clerk of works, he cannot afterwards set up such incompetence as a defence.[26]

Clerk of works as agent.   The clerk of works "has been aptly described as the Regimental Sergeant-Major. It is accepted that he acts as the eyes and ears of the architects, and has a responsibility to keep the architects informed as to what is or is not happening on site."[27] But the terms of the building contract usually give him very limited powers as agent and do not appoint him as agent for the architect to give instructions on his behalf.[28] Despite this, architects sometimes encourage the clerk of works to act as their agents, in particular in the giving of "site instructions." This procedure can lead to confusion and to claims for damages for delay by the contractor unless the parties carefully agree upon the status to be accorded to the clerk of works, his exact degree of authority and the procedure to be followed, such agreement to take effect by way of variation of the contract.

Clerk of works' manual.[29]   The R.I.B.A. and the Institute of Clerks of Works have collaborated to produce this manual. It is specifically directed to the position and duties of the clerk of works when the Standard Form of Building Contract is used, but it is thought that it is of general importance as stating the modern view of the clerk of works.

Liability of and for clerk of works to others.   By analogy with the duties owed by architects, the clerk of works is under a duty of care to the employer by virtue of his engagement. Conversely an employer has been held vicariously liable for the negligence of his clerk of works and, where the architect was also negligent, on the facts of that case their respective liabilities were held to be 20 per cent. and 80 per cent., so that the employer's claim against the architect was reduced by 20 per cent.[30] It is now questionable whether a clerk of works would be liable in tort to third parties, except perhaps where exceptionally his want of care caused personal injury or physical damage.[31]

---

[25] *Ibid.* Note that one of the grounds of this part of the decision was that the fraud, if any, was perpetrated by the clerk of works in his own interest and not in the interest of his employer. Since the decision in *Lloyd* v. *Grace, Smith & Co.* [1912] A.C. 716 (H.L.), this part of the judgment cannot be supported on this ground—see further "Fraudulent misrepresentation" at p. 122. But it may be that it is part of the architect's duty to take reasonable care to guard against fraud by the clerk of works.

[26] *Saunders & Collard* v. *Broadstairs Local Board* (1890) H.B.C. (4th ed.), Vol. 2, p. 164 (D.C.); *cf. Valerie Pratt* v. *George J. Hill* (1987) 38 B.L.R. 25 (C.A.).

[27] H.H. Judge Smout Q.C. in *Kensington, etc., Health Authority* v. *Wettern Composites* (1984) 31 B.L.R. 57 at 85.

[28] See his position under clause 12 of the Standard Form of Building Contract and for further discussion see p. 514.

[29] R.I.B.A. Publications Ltd. (2nd ed., 1984).

[30] *Kensington, etc., Health Authority* v. *Wettern Composites* (1984) 31 B.L.R. 57 at 87.

[31] See Chap. 7 generally and see p. 165 for position of architects.

Certificates.   In *Sutcliffe* v. *Thackrah* the official referee held[32] that an architect had, in the circumstances, been negligent in issuing an interim certificate for an excessive sum of money. The employer paid the amount certified. The contractor went into liquidation and the employer lost the money. Reluctantly, the Court of Appeal, taking the view that it was bound by an earlier decision,[33] held that the architect could not be liable for damages because he was performing his special function as a certifier. The House of Lords unanimously allowed the appeal[34] and thereby settled that an architect owes a duty of care towards his client in the performance of all his duties, including those of certifying, and is not entitled to any special exemption. In certifying, the architect has to "act in a fair and unbiased manner and it must therefore be implicit in the owner's contract with the architect that he shall not only exercise due care and skill but also reach such decisions fairly, holding the balance between the client and the contractor."[35] There was nothing incompatible between being fair and being careful. At the same time the House emphasised that proving negligence against an architect for over-certification may often be difficult. An architect, like other professional men, can be wrong without being negligent.

The architect's liability extends both to interim and final certificates[36] and indeed to all his functions under the contract. It has been held that an architect's fees were not liable to abatement where the employer had recovered damages against the architect for her negligent supervision and certification.[37]

It is accepted law that judges and arbitrators are entitled to immunity from actions for negligence in respect of the performance of their duties[38] but this does not apply to certifiers. It seems that there might be circumstances where there is in effect an arbitration, although not one that is within the provisions of the Arbitration Acts.[39] For this to arise there must have been a submission either of a specific dispute or of present points of difference or of defined differences that may in the future arise and an agreement that the decision will be binding.[40] These circumstances do not apply to the role of the architect under the Standard Form of Building Contract or ordinary forms of building

---

[32] Reported at first instance as *Sutcliffe* v. *Chippendale and Edmondson* (1971) 18 B.L.R. 157.

[33] *Chambers* v. *Goldthorpe* [1901] 1 K.B. 624 at 638 (C.A.). For other cases which dealt with the point, see the report of *Sutcliffe* v. *Thackrah* and pp. 225–227 of the 3rd ed. of this book.

[34] [1974] A.C. 727 (H.L.)—overruling *Chambers* v. *Goldthorpe* [1901] 1 K.B. 624 (C.A.) and distinguishing cases which appeared to follow it.

[35] *Ibid.* Lord Reid at 737; *cf. London Borough of Merton* v. *Leach* (1985) 32 B.L.R. 51 at 78; *Lubenham* v. *South Pembrokeshire District Council* (1986) 33 B.L.R. 36 at 52 *et seq.* (C.A.). The test of fairness is objective—see *Canterbury Pipe Lines* v. *Christchurch Drainage* (1979) 16 B.L.R. 76 at 97 *et seq.* (New Zealand Court of Appeal).

[36] See *London Borough of Merton* v. *Lowe* (1981) 18 B.L.R. 130 (C.A.).

[37] *Hutchinson* v. *Harris* (1978) 10 B.L.R. 19 (C.A.).

[38] *Sutcliffe* v. *Thackrah* [1974] A.C. 727 at 744, 753, 754, 757 (H.L.) and see p. 385.

[39] See Chap. 16.

[40] *Sutcliffe* v. *Thackrah* [1974] A.C. 727 at 752 (H.L.).

contract. It is possible that they arise in respect of the engineer giving his decision under clause 66 of the I.C.E. Conditions of Contract.[41]

(i) *Breach of architect's duties to employer*

Breach of the architect's duties to the employer may consist in misconduct in his position as agent or in failure to exercise the requisite skill of an architect.[42] Either breach, if so serious as to go to the root of his contract with the employer,[43] renders him liable to be dismissed,[44] and he may not be able to recover his fees if his work is useless or results in a loss to the employer.[45] He will be liable in an action for damages for loss suffered, the measure of damages being calculated upon the principles set out in Chapter 8, so that in some cases damages may greatly exceed the claim for fees.[46] The employer may either bring a separate action, or counterclaim to the architect's action for fees.[47] As with any breach of contract the employer must act reasonably and keep his loss resulting from the architect's breach of duty to the minimum. Thus, for example, if the plans are found to be wrong because of the architect's failure to measure the site properly the employer must normally give him the opportunity of making the plans good, and if he does not will only be awarded nominal damages.[48] But where a design was found to be defective after work had begun and the work had to be completed to a new design, the plaintiff recovered the cost of completing the works in accordance with the new design, less an allowance for the additional costs had the new design been incorporated originally.[49]

Unauthorised sub-contracting. Breach by an architect of his duty of personal performance[50] does not of itself amount to a total failure of consideration so as to entitle the employer to the return of fees paid for work carried out. Damages, other than nominal,[51] are only recoverable to the extent that actual loss is proved.[52] If the architect is a person of fame such loss may, it is

---

[41] See the wording of clause 66 of both the 1955 and 1973 editions and consider *Monmouth County Council.* v. *Costelloe & Kemple* (1965) L.G.R. 429 (C.A.).

[42] See p. 312.

[43] See p. 146.

[44] See *Harmer* v. *Cornelius* (1858) 5 C.B. (N.S.) 236; *Duncan* v. *Blundell* (1820) 3 Stark. 6; *Thornton Hall* v. *Wembley Electrical Appliances* [1947] 2 All E.R. 630 (C.A.).

[45] *Moneypenny* v. *Hartland* (1826) 2 C. & P. 378; *cf. Hutchinson* v. *Harris* (1978) 10 B.L.R. 24 (C.A.); see also p. 333.

[46] See *Saunders & Collard* v. *Broadstairs Local Board* (1890) H.B.C. (4th ed.), Vol. 2, p. 164. In *Florida Hotels Pty.* v. *Mayo* (1965) 113 C.L.R. 588 (Aust.) the architect was held liable for damages paid by the employer to a workman for injuries caused by the architect's negligence in supervision of the works.

[47] See, *e.g. Rogers* v. *James* (1891) H.B.C. (4th ed.), Vol. 2, p. 172 (C.A.).

[48] *Columbus Co.* v. *Clowes* [1903] 1 K.B. 244.

[49] *Bevan Investments* v. *Blackhall & Struthers* (1977) 11 B.L.R. 78 (New Zealand Court of Appeal).

[50] See p. 275.

[51] See p. 185.

[52] *Hamlyn Construction Co. Ltd.* v. *Air Couriers* [1968] 1 Lloyd's Rep. 395.

submitted, be capable of proof. Further, if the unauthorised sub-contracting is discovered, the employer can, it is submitted, require the architect to resume personal performance and failure to do so may well, it is thought, amount to a repudiation by the architect of his contract of employment with the employer rendering him liable to dismissal.

Negligent survey.[53]   Where an architect or surveyor is engaged to survey and report upon the condition of a property by an intending purchaser who acts on the report and purchases, the measure of damages arising from a negligent survey is normally the difference in value between the property as it was reported to be and its value in the condition in which it in fact was.[54] The difference may be less than the cost of amending the defects negligently omitted from the report,[55] but may be equivalent to the cost of repair.[56] Exceptionally the measure of damages may be the cost of repair.[57] Certain consequential losses may be recoverable in addition to the difference in value.[58] At least where the normal measure of damage applies, the plaintiff's cause of action accrues for limitation purposes at the date when he acts upon the negligent report or survey.[59] But where a surveyor carries out a negligent valuation for a prospective mortgagee who advances money on the faith of the valuation but otherwise would not have done so, the correct measure of damages is the whole loss that the mortgagee has suffered as a result of entering into the transaction, including unpaid interest, expenses and disbursements as well as the principal sum advanced, calculated by reference to the date when the actual loss was incurred.[60]

Liability in tort.   An architect's potential liability in tort is discussed in Chapter 7 in particular under "Negligent instructions" at page 165, "Professional negligence" at page 172 and "Consultants" at page 180.

Limitation of actions—contract.   Actions against the architect in contract must be commenced within six years of the date on which the cause of action

---

[53] See also "Building Society valuations" at p. 181.
[54] *Phillips* v. *Ward* [1956] 1 W.L.R. 471 (C.A.); *Ford* v. *White & Co.* [1964] 1 W.L.R. 885; *Simple Simon Catering* v. *Binstock Miller* (1973) 228 E.G. 527 (C.A.); *Perry* v. *Sidney Phillips & Son* [1982] 1 W.L.R. 1297 (C.A.); *County Personnel* v. *Alan R. Pulver* [1987] 1 W.L.R. 916 at 925 (C.A.).
[55] *Ibid.*
[56] *Steward* v. *Rapley* [1989] 1 E.G.L.R. 159 (C.A.).
[57] See *Hipkins* v. *Jack Cotton Partnership* [1989] 2 E.G.L.R. 157; *cf. Broadoak Properties* v. *Young & White* [1989] 1 E.G.L.R. 263 at 267. See also "Defective work" at p. 202.
[58] See *Perry* v. *Sidney Phillips & Son* [1982] 1 W.L.R. 1297 (C.A.)—inconvenience; *Treml* v. *Ernest W. Gibson & Partners* (1984) 272 E.G. 68—cost of temporary works to make building safe and other losses; *Broadoak Properties* v. *Young & White* [1989] 1 E.G.L.R. 263 at 267—investigation costs. See also "Inconvenience discomfort and distress" at p. 205.
[59] *Secretary of State for the Environment* v. *Essex Goodman & Suggitt* [1986] 1 W.L.R. 1432. This was a claim in tort by a client who also had a contract with the surveyors, and it is suggested under "Professional negligence" at p. 172 that such a claim needs reconsideration. For limitation generally, see p. 366.
[60] *Baxter* v. *F. W. Gapp & Co.* [1939] 2 K.B. 271 (C.A.); *Swingcastle* v. *Gibson* [1990] 1 W.L.R. 1223 (C.A.); *cf. London and South of England Building Society* v. *Stone* [1983] 1 W.L.R. 1242 (C.A.). Note that leave to appeal to the House of Lords was granted in *Swingcastle* v. *Gibson*.

accrued, or 12 years if his engagement is by deed.[61] Time runs, it is submitted, from the date of breach of duty and not from its discovery,[62] unless the employer can rely on the provisions of the Limitation Act 1980 relating to fraud, deliberate concealment or mistake.[63]

When does the cause of action arise? This depends on the terms of the contract. Where an architect was engaged to prepare plans and perform the duties of supervision required by the R.I.B.A. Form of Building Contract it was said that the correct approach was that "a claim against an architect for negligence in the design of a building raises a cause of action different from that of negligence in supervising its erection in purported compliance with that design."[64] Upon this approach where the design was carried out outside the limitation period a claim for defective design is prima facie barred notwithstanding that supervision by the architect was carried out within the period. But in such a case a claim may arise under a separate cause of action which arose after the design was originally carried out in respect of a breach of the architect's "continuing duty to check that his design will work in practice and to correct any errors which may emerge."[65] A somewhat different view has been expressed by the Full Court of South Australia which suggested that where there is the usual engagement of an architect to design and supervise there is an entire contract "to see the business through" so that a claim for damages for defective design work carried out more than six years (or 12 years as the case may be) before issue of the writ would not be barred if performance of any of the architect's duties, such as those relating to supervision, was carried out within the period of six years.[66]

It is thought that, when the R.I.B.A. Architect's Appointment[67] is the basis of the contract, causes of action can accrue from time to time as various duties are, or should have been, performed.

Limitation of actions—tort.   Subject to the provisions of the Limitation Act 1980 as to fraud, deliberate concealment and mistake, actions must be commenced within six years of the cause of action accruing.[68] If the liability of the architect is in the tort of negligence the cause of action does not accrue until there has been both the breach of duty and damage to the plaintiff. Considerations relating to limitation where the claim is in negligence are discussed in

---

[61] Limitation Act 1980, ss.5 and 8. See also s.10 for claims for contribution. See generally "Contract" at p. 366.

[62] See *Gibbs* v. *Guild* (1881) 8 Q.B.D. 296 at 302; *Cartledge* v. *Jopling* (*E. & Sons*) *Ltd.* [1963] A.C. 758 at 782 (H.L.); *Bagot* v. *Stevens Scanlan & Co. Ltd.* [1966] 1 Q.B. 197.

[63] s.32 of the Limitation Act 1980.

[64] *Brickfield Properties Ltd.* v. *Newton* [1971] 1 W.L.R. 862 at 869 (C.A.).

[65] *Brickfield Properties Ltd.* v. *Newton* [1971] 1 W.L.R. 862 at 873 (C.A.); *London Borough of Merton* v. *Lowe* (1981) 18 B.L.R. 130 (C.A.); *Chelmsford District Council* v. *Evers* (1983) 25 B.L.R. 99; *cf. Steamship Mutual* v. *Trollope & Colls* (1986) 33 B.L.R. 77 (C.A.).

[66] *Edelman* v. *Boehm* (1964) S.A.L.J. (South Australia Full Court); *cf. Chelmsford District Council* v. *Evers* (1983) 25 B.L.R. 99 at 106.

[67] See p. 950.

[68] Limitation Act 1980, ss.2 and 32.

Section 3 of Chapter 15 particularly under "Tort" at page 367 and "Latent Damage" at page 368.

(j) *Duration of architect's duties*

Completion of works.   In the normal course, if the architect is employed to arrange for and supervise the building of a complete works, then in the absence of express terms to the contrary,[69] he has the right and duty to act as architect until completion of the works, and if the employer wrongfully dismisses him, the architect can recover damages for breach of contract,[70] or possibly a reasonable sum for the work he has carried out.[71] In the normal course there is an implied term that the employer will not prevent the architect from earning his remuneration.[72]

Termination or resignation.   The contract between architect and employer frequently provides that the engagement of the architect may be terminated at any time by either party upon giving reasonable notice.[73] In the absence of a provision for earlier termination an architect who gives up his duties without the employer's consent before the completion of a whole work which he has undertaken is in breach of contract and prima facie is not entitled to his fees.[74]

Death.   The services of the architect are personal and his death therefore brings his contractual duties to an end.[75] The architect's personal representatives can, subject to the effect of the Law Reform (Frustrated Contracts) Act 1943,[76] recover money earned by the architect and payable at the time of his death, and are not limited to a claim for a reasonable sum if instalments were payable under the contract.[77] The death of the employer does not normally bring the contract between himself and the architect to an end.[78]

Bankruptcy.   Upon the bankruptcy of the architect the benefit and burden of his contract with the employer do not, it is submitted, vest in his trustee in

---

[69] See, *e.g.* if they apply, clauses 3.21–3.23 of the R.I.B.A. Architect's Appointment at p. 962.

[70] *Thomas* v. *Hammersmith Borough Council* [1938] 3 All E.R. 203 (C.A.). *Edwin Hill & Partners* v. *Leakcliffe Properties* (1984) 29 B.L.R. 43 at 68; *cf. Rutledge* v. *Farnham Local Board of Health* (1861) 2 F. & F. 406. It is doubtful whether an architect can insist on completing and charging for plans—see "Acceptance of repudiation" at p. 151.

[71] *Elkington* v. *Wandsworth Corporation* (1924) 41 T.L.R. 76. See however the view expressed under "Work partly carried out" at p. 207.

[72] Slesser L.J. in *Thomas* v. *Hammersmith Borough Council* [1938] 3 All E.R. 203 (C.A.).

[73] See, *e.g.* R.I.B.A. Architect's Appointment, clause 3.23.

[74] See *Cutter* v. *Powell* (1795) 2 Smith's Leading Cases 1, and other cases discussed in Chap. 4; see also for repudiation, p. 146.

[75] See also R.I.B.A. Architect's Appointment, clause 3.24.

[76] See p. 140.

[77] *Stubbs* v. *Holywell Railway* (1867) L.R. 2 Ex. 311.

[78] *Davison* v. *Reeves* (1892) 8 T.L.R. 391.

bankruptcy because the architect's duties are personal. The contract therefore continues and the architect can sue for his fees although his trustee in bankruptcy can intervene in the action and claim the proceeds.[79]

(k) *Remuneration*

Employer liable.   The architect must in the absence of express terms look to the person who employed him for payment.[80]

The right to remuneration.   There is a presumption that an architect is entitled to be paid something for his work for, "generally speaking, people who do work for others expect to be paid for it."[81] If there is an agreement for employment and the employer is to fix the amount, the employed person may, it seems, obtain a reasonable payment.[82] Where sketch plans and probationary drawings are sent in by way of tender, or subject to approval, and they are not accepted or approved the architect is not, it seems, entitled to be paid for such work,[83] unless there is an express or implied agreement to pay.[84]

Estimates.   Where an architect prepares plans and drawings and from them gives an estimate of the probable cost, he may not be able to recover any remuneration if the lowest tender is substantially higher than the estimate and the employer therefore refuses to carry on with the project.[85] In the absence of an express term,[86] it is a question whether, in all the circumstances, it is an implied condition of the architect's employment that the works should be capable of being executed at or reasonably near the estimated cost.[87] Where there is such an implied condition, and the tenders are too high, the employer must act reasonably to mitigate his loss so far as possible.[88] Thus it may be that

---

[79] *Emden* v. *Carte* (1881) 17 Ch.D. 169 at 768 (C.A.); *Bailey* v. *Thurston* [1903] 1 K.B. 137 (C.A.).

[80] *Locke* v. *Morter* (1885) 2 T.L.R. 121.

[81] Maule J. in *Moffat* v. *Laurie* (1855) 15 C.B. 583; *Landless* v. *Wilson* (1880) 8 R. (Ct. of Sess.) 289.

[82] *Byrant* v. *Flight* (1839) 5 M. & W. 114; *Bird* v. *McGaheg* (1849) 2 C. & K. 707; *cf. Kofi Sunkersette Obu* v. *A. Strauss & Co. Ltd.* [1951] A.C. 243 (P.C.).

[83] *Moffat* v. *Dickson* (1853) 13 C.B. 543; *Moffat* v. *Laurie* (1855) 15 C.B. 583; *cf. Jepson* v. *Severn Trent Water Authority* (1982) 20 B.L.R. 53 (C.A.).

[84] See *Moffat* v. *Dickson* (1853) 13 C.B. 543 at 575; and see "Costs of tendering" at p. 13. Where the R.I.B.A. Architect's Appointment applies there are express provisions for payment according to the stage of work reached. See also *Mander Raikes & Marshall* v. *Severn-Trent Water Authority* (1980) 16 B.L.R. 39; *National Coal Board* v. *Leonard & Partners* (1985) 31 B.L.R. 117— upheld on appeal on July 16, 1986 (unreported).

[85] See *Nelson* v. *Spooner* (1861) 2 F. & F. 613; *Burr* v. *Ridout, The Times,* February 22, 1893; *cf. Nye Saunders* v. *Alan E. Bristow* (1987) 37 B.L.R. 117 (C.A.).

[86] See, *e.g.* R.I.B.A. Architect's Appointment at p. 950—see esp. clauses 1.1, 1.8, 1.14 and 3.6. It is a difficult question of construction what effect those conditions would have in engagements to which they apply where the abandonment of the project is due to a faulty estimate of the architect.

[87] *Nelson* v. *Spooner* (1861) 2 F. & F. 613; for the duty of the architect in giving an estimate, see *Moneypenny* v. *Hartland* (1826) 2 C. & P. 378; *Nye Saunders* v. *Alan E. Bristow* (1987) 37 B.L.R. 117 (C.A.); see also *Hunt* v. *Wimbledon Local Board* (1878) 4 C.P.D. 48.

[88] See p. 190.

the employer can substantially achieve his desired object despite reductions in the work to be done. In such a case it seems that he should give the architect the opportunity of altering his plans so as to effect the reductions.[89]

When right to remuneration arises.   It is a question in each case whether the architect must complete his whole task before he has the right to call for payment of his services,[90] or whether he is entitled to be paid for what he actually does,[91] or at various stages of his work.[92]

Amount of remuneration.   An express agreement may govern the amount of the remuneration. In the absence of such an agreement the architect is entitled to a reasonable sum, the amount of which is a question of fact.[93] A reasonable sum is not recoverable where an express agreement for payment exists. Thus in *Gilbert & Partners* v. *Knight*[94] a surveyor agreed to prepare drawings, arrange tenders and supervise works of alteration, the cost of which he estimated at roughly £600, for a fee of £30. The employer ordered extra work which brought the total cost to £2,283 but the surveyor did not, while the work was going on, tell the employer that he would require further fees, and was held to be bound by the existing agreement to perform services for £30 and could not recover a reasonable sum on a new implied contract.

Implication of R.I.B.A. scale.   The R.I.B.A. scale, first issued in 1872, and now incorporated as percentage fee scales in the R.I.B.A. Architect's Appointment,[95] is based on a percentage of the cost of the works. Various attempts have been made to persuade the courts that the percentage charges from time to time set out in the scale are customary and reasonable, and should therefore, in the absence of express agreement, be payable automatically. The argument has in the past been rejected[96] on the ground that the architect was only entitled to charge for work he had actually carried out.[97] However, in *Whipham* v. *Everitt*,[98] where no building contract was placed because the tenders were

---

[89] See *Columbus* v. *Clowes* [1903] 1 K.B. 244 at 247; for the authority of the architect to employ a quantity surveyor to reduce the quantities, see p. 344.

[90] See *Cutter* v. *Powell* (1795) 2 Smith's Leading Cases 1, and see generally Chap.4.

[91] See *Appleby* v. *Myers* (1867) L.R. 2 C.P. 651 at 660.

[92] See, *e.g.* R.I.B.A. Architect's Appointment at p. 950.

[93] *Byrant* v. *Flight* (1839) 5 M. & W. 114. See also *Way* v. *Latilla* [1937] 32 All E.R. 759 (H.L.) for the position where there has been inconclusive negotiations as to fees.

[94] [1968] 2 All E.R. 248 (C.A.).

[95] See p. 950.

[96] *Gwyther* v. *Gaze* (1875) H.B.C. (4th ed.), Vol. 2, p. 34; *Bury* v. *Ridout*, *The Times*, February 22, 1893; *Farthing* v. *Tomkins* (1893) 9 T.L.R. 566; and see *Elkington* v. *Wandsworth Corporation* (1925) 41 T.L.R. 76. See the 4th ed. of this book at p. 222 for the court's reluctance to imply a term that Ryde's scale of charges for the valuation of land should be used.

[97] See Lord Coleridge in *Farthing* v. *Tomkins* (1893) 9 T.L.R. 566, objecting that where the work was abandoned, a scale charge would be unfair because it included supervision not carried out. This objection has now been met—see, *e.g.* clause 4.28 of the R.I.B.A. Architect's Appointment at p. 968.

[98] *The Times*, March 22, 1900.

too high, certain eminent architects were called to prove that it was customary in such a case for the architect to be paid for the plans and preliminary work on the percentage basis set out in the R.I.B.A. scale. It was held by Kennedy J. that the architect was entitled to a reasonable remuneration, and that, although the R.I.B.A. scale was not binding in law because it was not a custom of so universal an application as to be an implied term of every contract, nevertheless it was right to take into consideration the practice adopted by the large proportion of the profession, as shown by the rules drawn up by the Council of the R.I.B.A. for the guidance of the members of the profession.

The architect may be able to prove that his particular employer was, in the circumstances of the case, well acquainted with the R.I.B.A. scale and a custom to pay according to the scale, and that he must therefore be taken to have contracted on that basis.[99] In a case concerning copyright where both parties were familiar with the former R.I.B.A. Conditions of Engagement it was said that, they "may be assumed to have had regard to them,"[1] and the court looked at the Conditions to assist in the determination of the issue.

Assessment of reasonable sum.   A reasonable sum for the services of the architect will vary according to the circumstances of each case, and its amount is a question of fact in each case.[2] In *Brewin* v. *Chamberlain*,[3] Birkett J. had to consider what sum was payable under the then R.I.B.A. scale of charges for partial services. The relevant clause merely directed that the charge was on a *quantum meruit* and gave no guide as to how it was to be ascertained save that it was subject to a maximum of one-sixth of the percentage charge for complete services. The principles applied by Birkett J. are, therefore, of general application to claims on a *quantum meruit*. It was contended on behalf of the employer that the charge should be assessed on a time basis,[4] and on behalf of the architect that it should be assessed on a percentage basis. It was held that the time spent, and the fact that the maximum recoverable was expressed to be a percentage, were only two of the relevant factors, neither of which was dominant. Other relevant factors were that the work was not a straight forward ordinary task; that the drawings prepared were of great merit; that the architect was a person of standing[5] and had considerable experience; and the amount and nature of the work which was involved, including such matters as interviews with the authorities and correspondence, as well as the work of preparing the drawings.

---

[99] *Buckland and Garrard* v. *Pawson & Co.* (1890) 6 T.L.R. 421; *cf.* Lawton L.J. in *Sidney Kaye, Eric Firmin & Partners* v. *Bronesky* (1973) 4 B.L.R. 1 at 7 (C.A.). See also the Scottish case of *Wilkie* v. *Scottish Aviation Ltd.* 1956 S. C. 198.
[1] *Stovin-Bradford* v. *Volpoint Properties Ltd.* [1971] 1 Ch. 1007 at 1014 (C.A.). For copyright, see p. 337.
[2] *Bird* v. *McGaheg* (1849) 2 C. & K. 707.
[3] Only reported by way of an excerpt from the judgment in Rimmer's *Law relating to the Architect* (2nd ed.), p. 304.
[4] See now clauses 4.24–4.27 of the R.I.B.A. Architect's Appointment at p. 968.
[5] See also *Bird* v. *McGaheg* (1849) 2 C. & K. 707.

(l) *The architect's lien*

Where an architect or surveyor has been employed to carry out a specific work such as preparing plans or a survey, his right to payment, in the absence of express terms, arises as soon as he has done the work satisfactorily and has given his employer a reasonable opportunity of ascertaining whether it has been properly done.[6] Thereafter he may retain the plans or survey until he is paid and does not lose his right of subsequently suing for a reasonable price because he has demanded a sum in excess of a reasonable price.[7] An employer who brings proceedings for the recovery of such documents may obtain them by paying into court the amount claimed as fees to abide the event of the action.[8] The court has no jurisdiction on such an application to assess the value of the claim for fees or to rule on the validity of the claim to retain the documents.[9]

Discovery and inspection. The benefit of a professional man's lien may be lost if his client, in legal proceedings, can obtain inspection of the documents with the consequent right to copy them. Where accountants claimed a lien on documents, but had counterclaimed for the payment of the balance of their fees and the amount of such fees was in issue, it was held that the plaintiffs, their clients, were entitled to inspection of the documents.[10]

(m) *Property in plans and other documents*

Property in plans. In the ordinary building contract the property in the plans and drawings prepared for and used in the works passes to the employer on payment of the remumeration provided under the contract, and any custom to the effect that the architect is allowed to retain the plans is unreasonable and will not be enforced.[11]

Property in documents prepared as agent. "If an agent brings into existence certain documents while in the employment of his principal, they are the principal's documents and the principal can claim that the agent should hand them over."[12] It seems that such documents include communications with the contractor, sub-contractors, local authorities and others on behalf of the employer.[13]

---

[6] *Hughes* v. *Lenny* (1839) 5 M. & W. 183 at 191.
[7] *Ibid.*
[8] R.S.C., Ord. 29, r. 6.
[9] See *Segbedzi* v. *Glah* (1989) N.L.J. 1303 (C.A.) following *Gebruder Naf* v. *Ploton* (1890) 25 Q.B.D. 13 (C. A.).
[10] *Woodworth* v. *Conroy* [1976] Q.B. 884 (C.A.).
[11] *Gibbon* v. *Pease* [1905] 1 K.B. 810 at 813 (C.A.), applying *Ebdy* v. *M'Gowan* (1870) H.B.C. (4th ed.), Vol. 2, p. 9.
[12] MacKinnon L.J. in *Leicester County Council* v. *Micheal Faraday & Partners Ltd.* [1941] 2 K.B. 205 at 216 (C.A.).
[13] *Beresford (Lady)* v. *Driver* (1852) 22 L.J. Ch. 407.

Property in documents prepared as professional man.   Documents prepared by the architect as a professional man for his own assistance in carrying out his expert work, are not "documents brought into existence by an agent on behalf of his principal, and therefore they cannot be said to be the property of the principal."[14] Thus the employer is not, in the absence of express agreement, entitled to demand memoranda, calculations, draft plans and other documents which the architect has prepared to assist him in carrying out his duties.[15]

(n) *Copyright in plans and design*

Apart from any express term,[16] "the architect owns the copyright in the plans and also in the design embodied in the owner's building. The building owner may not therefore reproduce the plans or repeat the design in a new building without the architect's express or implied consent."[17] The protection is afforded by the Copyright, Designs and Patents Act 1988 and includes literary work and artistic work.[18] Artistic work includes paintings, drawings, diagrams, plans, engravings and photographs irrespective of artistic quality, and works of architecture being either buildings or models for buildings.[19] The blueprint of a new shop front has been held to be an original literary work, and therefore an unauthorised copying was a breach of copyright.[20] Copyright in a literary or artistic work normally expires at the end of the period of 50 years from the end of the calendar year in which the author dies.[21]

The case of *Meikle* v. *Maufe*[22] raised points of considerable interest. In 1912 H employed X, an architect, to erect certain buildings to be used as furniture

---

[14] MacKinnon L.J. in *Leicester County Council* v. *Micheal Faraday & Partners Ltd.* [1941] 2 K.B. 205 at 216 (C.A.).

[15] *Leicester County Council* v. *Micheal Faraday & Partners Ltd.* [1941] 2 K.B. 205 (C.A.); *London School Board* v. *Northcroft* (1889) H.B.C. (4th ed.), Vol. 2, p. 147; see also *Chantrey Martin* v. *Martin* [1953] 2 Q.B. 286 (C.A.).

[16] See, *e.g.* clauses 3.15–3.18 of the R.I.B.A. Architect's Appointment at p. 961.

[17] Uthwatt J. in *Meikle* v. *Maufe* [1941] 3 All E.R. 144 at 152; *cf. Stovin-Bradford* v. *Volpoint Ltd.* [1981] Ch. 1007 (C.A.); there is no infringement by reconstructing the original building—s.65 of the Copyright, Designs and Patents Act 1988; *cf. Hunter* v. *Fitzroy Robinson* & Partners (1977) 10 B.L.R. 84. The law of copyright and its allied subjects is complex. Only the briefest introduction is given here. See further Copinger and Skone James, *Law of Copyright*; Russell-Clarke, *Copyright and Industrial Designs*; Morris Quest, *Design* (1987); Rimmer's *Law relating to the Architect* (2nd ed.), Chap. 5. For breach of confidence, see p. 260.

[18] ss.1, 3 and 4 of the Copyright, Designs and Patents Act 1988. For a recent Australian decision, see *Ownit Homes Pty. Ltd.* v. *D. and F. Mancuso Investments Pty. Ltd.* (1989) 5 B.C.L. 64 and (1990) 6 Const. L.J. 161 (Australian Federal Court).

[19] s.4 of the Copyright, Designs and Patents Act 1988; for design documents or models recording or embodying a design for anything other than an artistic work, see s.51 of the 1988 Act and the new unregistered design right provided by Pt. III of the Act.

[20] *Chabot* v. *Davies* [1936] 3 All E.R. 221.

[21] s.12 of the Copyright, Designs and Patents Act 1988; see ss.10 and 12(4) for the joint authorship, and s.11(2) for the position where the author is in the employment of another under a contract of service; *Sterling Engineering Co.* v. *Patchett* [1955] A.C. 534 (H.L.).

[22] [1941] 3 All E.R. 144. It is thought that the substance of this decision is unaffected by the Copyright, Designs and Patients Act 1988, but all cases decided before the Act must be read with and subject to the Act.

showrooms. There were no express terms of engagement, and the possibility of extending the building southward was discussed. In 1935 H employed M, an architect, to extend the building southward. The extended facade consisted of repetitions, with minor alterations, of the design of the original facade, and the interior was reproduced to a substantial degree. Y, the owner of the copyright originally vested in X, brought proceedings for breach of copyright, and various arguments were raised by way of defence. It was said that there could be no separate copyright in a building as distinct from the copyright in the plans on which the building was based; alternatively, that if there was a separate copyright in the building then it was vested in the builder, and further that it was an implied term of the contract of engagement in 1912 that the employer could reproduce the design in an extension southwards. All these arguments were rejected, and it was held that the architect owned the copyright of the design embodied in the building as well as the plans.[23] Uthwatt J. referred to a feature of the architect's copyright—"apart from some express or implied bargain to the contrary, the architect is free, if so minded, to repeat the building for another owner."[24]

Licence to reproduce. This can be by express agreement,[25] or it can arise either from conduct as where the architect issues plans to the contractor for use in the erection of the building, or from the application of the ordinary rules relating to the implication of terms[26] into the contract between architect and employer. Copyright is transmissible by assignment in writing, by testamentary disposition or by operation of law, as personal or moveable property.[27]

Partial services by architect. The R.I.B.A. Architect's Appointment provides expressly in clauses 3.17 and 3.18 for the client's entitlement to reproduce the architect's design where the architect has not completed and been paid for the detailed design and production information. Where there is no such express agreement and the architect's engagement is terminated before completion of his services, the question whether any, and is so what, licence is to be implied must depend upon the express terms and the surrounding circumstances in each case.[28] In one case,[29] the architect was engaged to prepare plans suitable for obtaining full planning approval. He did this and charged the full scale fee applicable for work to that stage. Subsequently the owner sold the land and handed over the plans which were used by the builder.

---

[23] See quotation above. For the measure of damages, see below.
[24] At p. 152; see now generally ss.16 and 17 of the Copyright, Designs and Patents Act 1988.
[25] See, *e.g.* clauses 3.15–3.18 of the R.I.B.A. Architect's Appointment at p. 961. See also ss.90(4) and 92 of the Copyright, Designs and Patents Act 1988.
[26] *cf. Blair* v. *Osborne & Tomkins* [1971] 2 Q.B. 78 (C.A.); *Hunter* v. *Fitzroy Robinson & Partners* (1977) 10 B.L.R. 84. For the implication of terms, see pp. 45 *et seq.*
[27] See s.90 of the Copyright, Designs and Patents Act 1988.
[28] See *Stovin-Bradford* v. *Volpoint Ltd.* [1971] Ch. 1007 (C.A.).
[29] *Blair* v. *Osborne & Tomkins* [1971] 2 Q.B. 78 (C.A.).

It was held that there was no breach of copyright because the architect had granted an implied licence to the owner.[30] In another case[31] the architect again agreed to carry out certain design work with a view to obtaining planning approval. Both parties were familiar with the then R.I.B.A. scale of fees. They agreed upon a fee of 100 guineas which was nominal in comparison with the full stage payment. It was held that, while it was necessarily implied that the architect licensed the owners to make use of the drawings for the purpose of obtaining planning permission, there was no implication, in the circumstances, of a licence to use the drawings for erecting a building. It seems, from the cases just referred to, that the implied licence, if any, will only take effect from the time of payment (or, probably, tender of payment) by the client.[32]

Remedies for breach of copyright.   The main remedies are damages, and, in appropriate cases, an injunction to restrain the breach.[33] Where, however, the defendant did not know, and had no reason to believe, that copyright subsisted in the work, the plaintiff is not entitled to damages, but this is without prejudice to any other remedy.[34] If the infringement of copyright is flagrant, the court may award such additional damages as the justice of the case may require.[35] Formerly an injunction could not be obtained if building had commenced.[36]

Measure of damages.   Damages are to a certain extent at large,[37] but a sound basis from which to begin their assessment is the sum that "might fairly have been charged for a licence to use the copyright for the purpose for which it is used."[38] In *Meikle* v. *Maufe* a comparatively small sum was awarded on the grounds that:

(1)   the original design was such that the only market for it was its repetition in an extension of the original building;

(2)   the plaintiff, although the person in whom the copyright was now

---

[30]   *cf. Hunter* v. *Fitzroy Robinson & Partners* (1977) 10 B.L.R. 84.

[31]   *Stovin-Bradford* v. *Volpoint Properties Ltd.* [1971] 1 Ch. 1007 (C.A.).

[32]   The case of *Tingay* v. *Harris* [1967] 2 Q.B. 327 (C.A.) may be referred to on the point but is probably of no assistance. Lord Denning, in *Blair* v. *Osborne & Tomkins* [1971] 2 Q.B. 78 at 85 (C.A.) approaches the matter on the basis that the licence only takes effect on payment.

[33]   See the Copyright, Designs and Patents Act 1988, s.96; *cf. Hunter* v. *Fitzroy Robinson & Partners* (1977) 10 B.L.R. 84—injunction refused; *High Mark* v. *Patco Malaysia* (1984) 28 B.L.R. 129 (Malaya High Court)—injunction granted.

[34]   s.97(1) of the Copyright, Designs and Patents Act 1988.

[35]   s.97(2) of the Copyright, Designs and Patents Act 1988; *Williams* v. *Settle* [1960] 1 W.L.R. 1072 (C.A.).

[36]   Copyright Act 1956, s.17(4) repealed by s.303 and Sched. 8 of the Copyright, Designs and Patents Act 1988.

[37]   *Chabot* v. *Davies* [1936] 3 All E.R. 221; *Meikle* v. *Maufe* [1941] 3 All E.R. 144 at 153. This means that the judge has a certain discretion and is not necessarily limited to pecuniary loss actually proved. For damages generally, see Chap. 8.

[38]   Uthwatt J. in *Meikle* v. *Maufe* [1941] 3 All E.R. 144 at 53 Referring to *Chabot* v. *Davies* where this was the basis upon which damages were assessed; *Stovin-Bradford* v. *Volpoint Properties Ltd.* [1971] 1 Ch. 1007 (C.A.); *Hunter* v. *Fitzroy Robinson & Partners* (1977) 10 B.L.R. 84 at 94.

vested, was not himself personally responsible for the original design; and

(3) that when the defendant, before undertaking the work, informed the plaintiff of his intention to do so, the plaintiff wrote to him wishing him well.

This was not a licence, but the "defendant may well be forgiven for thinking that, *qua* Meikle,[39] Maufe had a free hand so far as the artistic necessities of the building required him to follow the original design."[40]

(o) *Architect's duties to contractor and others*[41]

Negligent certificate.   If the employer suffers loss the architect is liable.[42] But it now seems unlikely that a contractor or sub-contractor working under a normal modern building contract could successfully bring a claim in tort against the architect for negligent certification.[43] The leading case is *Pacific Associates* v. *Baxter*[44] in which a contractor claimed damages for economic loss against the engineer alleging negligent certification and breach of the duty to act fairly and impartially in administering the contract. The contract with the employer contained an arbitration clause and a disclaimer under which the defendants were not themselves to be held liable to the plaintiffs for any acts or omissions under the contract. The Court of Appeal upheld the judge's decision striking out the claim as disclosing no reasonable cause of action. The court reviewed dicta in the House of Lords[45] and decisions at first instance[46] suggesting that architects or engineers might owe contractors a duty of care of the kind alleged, but concluded that there was no basis on which a duty of care to prevent economic loss could be imposed on the engineer in favour of the contractor. The conclusion depends on elements of the modern law relating to negligence and economic loss discussed in Chapter 7 and particularly on the contractual structure of the relationship between employer, contractor and engineer. The existence of the arbitration clause enabling the contractor to challenge certificates was important if not decisive.[47] "It will be rare in these

---

[39] The plaintiff

[40] *Meikle* v. *Maufe* [1941] 3 All E.R. 144 at 155.

[41] This includes liability in tort generally, as to which see a standard textbook such as *Salmond* or *Clerk & Lindsell.*

[42] See p. 328.

[43] The upheaval of the law of negligence discussed in Chap. 7 is too recent to be confident about this.

[44] [1990] Q.B. 993 (C.A.).

[45] *Sutcliffe* v. *Thackrah* [1974] A.C. 727 at 736, 744 (H.L.); *Arenson* v. *Arenson* [1977] A.C. 405 at 438 (H.L.).

[46] *Lubenham* v. *South Pembrokeshire District Council* (unreported) H.H. Judge Newey Q.C. May 26, 1983, but reported in the Court of Appeal essentially on other topics at (1986) 33 B.L.R. 36 (C.A.); *Shui On Construction* v. *Shui Kay* (1985) 4 Const.L.J. 305 (Hong Kong Supreme Court); *Michael Salliss* v. *Calil* (1988) 4 Const.L.J. 125.

[47] See Purchas L.J. at 1024, Ralph Gibson L.J. at 1028/9, Russell L.J. at 1037; *cf. Lubenham* v. *South Pembrokeshire District Council* (1986) 33 B.L.R. 36 at 58 (C.A.) for a parallel decision.

days for a contract for engineering works of any substance in which a consulting engineer is appointed not to have an arbitration clause."[48] It is thought that the decision of the majority at least would have been the same even without the disclaimer.[49] Although it might be argued that the decision turns on its own facts, it is thought that it is of general application and that the first instance decisions should be taken to be wrongly decided.[50]

It remains possible that an architect or engineer might be liable to a contractor for negligent certification if there were no arbitration clause,[51] or for the tort of procuring a breach of contract if he interfered with the contractor's rights by deliberately misapplying the contractual provisions with the intention of depriving the contractor of the larger sums to which he would otherwise be entitled.[52]

Negligent misstatements.   The possibility that an architect might be liable to a contractor for negligent misstatement is discussed in Chapter 7 in particular under "Consultants" at page 180. See also "Negligent instructions" at page 165.

Fraud.   The architect is liable to the contractor for a fraudulent misrepresentation upon which the contractor has relied and thereby suffered damage;[53] and he is liable to the contractor for any refusal to certify or incorrect certification which is fraudulent and collusive or corrupt.[54]

Breach of warranty of authority.   This has been discussed on page 308.

Breach of statutory duty in connection with the provision of dwellings.   This could arise under the Defective Premises Act 1972 and is discussed at page 362.

4. Engineers and Others

Meaning of term "engineer."   No exact definition can be given of the term

---

[48] Purchas L.J. at 1024.
[49] See Purchas L.J. at 1023, Ralph Gibson L.J. at 1030, Russell L.J. at 1037; *cf.* Russell L.J. at 1038.
[50] See *Pacific Associates* v. *Baxter* [1990] Q.B. 993 at 1019B and 1020C (C.A.); *cf. Leon Engineering & Construction* v. *Ka Duk Investments* (1989) 47 B.L.R. 139 (Hong Kong High Court).
[51] See *Pacific Associates* v. *Baxter* [1990] Q.B. 993 at 1024 (C.A.).
[52] *Lubenham* v. *South Pembrokeshire District Council* (1986) 33 B.L.R. 36 at 74 (C.A.). For a review of Canadian authorities, see John R. Singleton, "The Consultants' Liability to the Builder" (1986) 2 Const.L.J. 87.
[53] See p. 122.
[54] *Ludbrook* v. *Barrett* (1877) 46 L.J. Q.B. 798; *Stevenson* v. *Watson* (1879) 4 C.P.D. 148; *Priestley* v. *Stone* (1888) 4 T.L.R. 730; H.B.C. (4th ed.), Vol. 2, p. 134 (C.A.); *Re De Morgan Snell & Co.* (1892) H.B.C. (4th ed.), Vol. 2, p. 185 (C.A.); *cf. Lubenham* v. *South Pembrokeshire District Council* (1986) 33 B.L.R. 36 at 74 (C.A.).

"engineer." It is sometimes used to describe a person who undertakes to carry out engineering and constructional works, but such a person is a contractor in the sense in which that term is used in this book. The term "engineer" is here used to describe one who, in relation to engineering or constructional works, carries out duties analogous to those carried out by an architect in a building contract. Such engineers frequently specialise and are usually members of some professional body, but the law does not require registration or qualification before a person can practise as an engineer, or term himself "engineer."

Consulting engineer. In large modern building contracts, there is frequently a team of consultants led by the architect. Such a team usually includes a structural engineer, frequently also a mechanical and electrical (or services) engineer and sometimes other engineers as well. These engineers often have specific contractual functions to be found in the mass of contract documents, but usually do not have wide contractual administrative powers such as building contracts usually give to the architect and engineering contracts to the engineer.

Resident engineer. In large contracts, or overseas contracts, there is sometimes appointed, in addition to a chief engineer, a resident engineer[55] who, as his name suggests, stays continuously on the site while the works are being carried out.

Other persons in the position of an architect. There are many contracts in which, although the term "architect" is never used, much of the law relating to architects, save registration,[56] applies. This arises where, in a contract for work and labour, there is a person placed in the position of exercising the duties of an architect. The most common example is the engineer in an engineering contract.[57] But he may be termed a surveyor,[58] a contract administrator,[59] a clerk of works,[60] a supervising officer,[61] a director of works,[62] or whatever else the parties choose to call him.

---

[55] *cf.* clause 1(1)(d) of the I.C.E. Conditions at p. 813.

[56] See p. 301.

[57] *e.g.* the I.C.E. Conditions.

[58] *e.g. Panamena* v. *Leyland* [1947] A.C. 428 (H.L.).

[59] See Arts. 3B of the 1980 Standard Form of Building Contract at p. 474 and the JCT Agreement for Minor Building Works.

[60] *e.g. Jones* v. *St. John's College* (1870) L.R. 6 Q.B. 115. Note that this is quite contrary to the usual meaning given to the term. See p. 326.

[61] *e.g. A. E. Farr Ltd.* v. *The Admiralty* [1953] 1 W.L.R. 965, a contract using Form CCC/Wks/1 General Conditions of Government Contracts.

[62] *e.g. Perini Corporation* v. *Commonwealth of Australia* (1969) 12 B.L.R. 82 (New South Wales Supreme Court).

5. Quantity Surveyors

(a) *Their duties generally*

A quantity surveyor's duties in a building contract include, "taking out in detail the measurements and quantities from plans prepared by an architect, for the purpose of enabling builders to calculate the amounts for which they would execute the plans."[63] His duties may also include other works of measurement such as taking measurements for the purpose of certificates[64] and preparing a bill of variations. He is normally employed by the employer to whom he owes a duty of care. The extent of his authority, which can be given in a number of ways, may derive from or be limited by the express terms of the building contract.[65]

In some cases a quantity surveyor may be employed by the contractor as, for example, where he is engaged by the contractor to take out quantities for the purposes of tender where quantities do not form part of the contract. The building contract may show that in regard to some matters he is intended to exercise his judgment fairly and professionally[66] as between the parties.

Qualification or registration is not required by law before a person can practise as a quantity surveyor, but there are certain well-known professional bodies to one of which most quantity surveyors belong.

(b) *Architect's authority to engage quantity surveyor*

If the employer himself engages the quantity surveyor he is, of course, liable to pay him. But sometimes the architect engages a quantity surveyor. If the employer knows that work is being done which normally involves the employment of a quantity surveyor, he may be taken to have tacitly assented to such employment, or, in any event, he may subsequently ratify it.[67] Otherwise the architect's authority to do this may be express[68] or implied.

To take out quantities for tender. An architect's authority to engage a quantity surveyor has been implied where the employer has authorised the architect to obtain tenders, and such tenders could only be obtained if quantities were prepared and issued,[69] but in modern conditions no useful rule of

---

[63] Morris J. in *Taylor* v. *Hall* (1870) I.R. 4 C.L. 467 at 476. Note that the reference was to a "building surveyor," but obviously referred to a "quantity surveyor" as that term is generally understood.
[64] *cf. Sutcliffe* v. *Chippendale & Edmondson* (1971) 18 B.L.R. 149 at 165—the case which on a different point became in the House of Lords *Sutcliffe* v. *Thackrah* [1974] A.C. 727 (H.L.).
[65] See *John Laing* v. *County and District Properties* (1982) 23 B.L.R. 1 at 13.
[66] See *Sutcliffe* v. *Thackrah* [1974] A.C. 727 (H.L.).
[67] *Evans* v. *Carte* (1881) H.B.C. (4th ed.), Vol. 2, p. 78 at 80 (D.C.). For the requisites of ratification, see p. 307.
[68] See, *e.g.* clauses 2.45 and 3.5 of the R.I.B.A. Architect's Appointment at pp. 959 *et seq.*
[69] *Waghorn* v. *Wimbledon Local Board* (1877) H.B.C. (4th ed.), Vol. 2, p. 52; see also *Gwyther* v. *Gaze* (1875) H.B.C. (4th ed.), Vol. 2, p. 34; *Moon* v. *Witney Union* (1837) 3 Bing.N.C. 814.

general application can, it is submitted, be stated. No authority to engage a quantity surveyor is implied where the employer's building plans are still inchoate and no definite order to proceed has been given to the architect.[70]

Reducing tenders.   The invitation to tender may result in tenders which are higher than the amount which the employer is prepared to expend. In such a case the plans, specification and bills of quantities are sometimes altered for the purpose of obtaining smaller tenders. It is doubtful whether the architect has any implied authority to employ a quantity surveyor for this purpose.[71] There would certainly seem to be no grounds for implying such an authority where the tenders are higher than expected because of some error or mis-calculation on the part of the architect.[72]

Measuring variations.   If by the building contract a quantity surveyor has to measure variations, then, in principle, it seems that the architect has implied authority to employ a quantity surveyor. If the contract merely provides that additions or deductions shall be ascertained and valued and the contract price adjusted, with no provision for the employment of a quantity surveyor, then it seems that it is the duty of the architect to measure,[73] and he would therefore have no implied authority to employ a quantity surveyor. In such a case the architect's right to be paid by the employer depends upon the contract, but he cannot in default of payment by the employer recover from the contractor.[74] If the contract is one of some magnitude then, even in the absence of any express provisions, the architect may by custom have authority to call in a quantity surveyor to measure.[75] There are no modern cases reported dealing with such a custom.

(c) *Duties to employer*

The quantity surveyor, like any professional man, owes a duty to the person by whom he is employed to carry out his work with proper care. The standard of care owed may be ascertained by reference to the same principles as those governing the architect's duties.[76] In general the test is whether he has failed to

---

[70] *Knox & Robb* v. *The Scottish Garden Suburb Co. Ltd.*, 1913 S.C. 872. See also *Antisell* v. *Doyle* [1899] 2 I.R. 275; *Nye Saunders* v. *Alan E. Bristow* (1987) 37 B.L.R. 92 (C.A.). For breach of warranty of authority, see p. 308.

[71] *Evans* v. *Carte* (1881) H.B.C. (4th ed.), Vol. 2, p. 78.

[72] See p. 333.

[73] *cf. Beattie* v. *Gilroy* (1882) 10 R. (Ct. of Sess.) 226.

[74] *Locke* v. *Morter* (1885) 2 T.L.R. 121.

[75] *Birdseye* v. *Dover Harbour Commissioners* (1881) H.B.C. (4th ed.), Vol. 2, p. 76; *cf. Plimsaul* v. *Kilmorey (Lord)* (1884) 1 T.L.R. 48. In *Birdseye's* case the total amount of the works was about £4,000, and the custom proved applied to works over £2,000. To allow for inflation an appropriate multiplier would have to be aplied to arrive at a comparable figure for today. Even so it must not be assumed that the court would, as a matter of course, find such a custom proved. For proof of custom, see p. 37.

[76] See p. 312.

take the care of an ordinarily competent quantity surveyor in the circumstances. Where the employer suffered a loss of £118 in a £12,000 contract because of an arithmetical error in the surveyor's accounts, it was held not to be negligence, for the error was due to the slip of a competent clerk who normally carried out his duties properly.[77] Negligence on the part of the surveyor makes him liable in damages upon the principles which apply to architects.[78]

Lithography.   The surveyor, as agent, must not make any secret commissions.[79] If he employs his own lithographer for making copies of the bills of quantities, it seems that he is entitled to retain any small cash discount, but should give the employer the benefit of any commission or trade discount.[80]

Checking bills of quantities.   The surveyor frequently checks bills of quantities submitted for tender for errors. It was said that if he discovers errors of substance operating against the interest of the contractor he is under a moral but not a legal duty to inform the contractor[81] and by so doing is not, it is submitted, in breach of duty to the employer. The N.J.C.C. Code of Procedure for Single Stage Selective Tendering (April 1989) provides that the quantity surveyor should examine priced bills of quantities submitted by tenderers in order to detect any errors in the tender. Where errors are found, the tenderer should be given an opportunity of withdrawing or amending his tender.[82] If these procedures are expressly incorporated as part of the tender documents, there is probably a contractual obligation binding the employer to follow this procedure.

(d) *Remuneration*

Amount.   The amount of the remuneration may be expressly agreed. Failing such agreement the surveyor is entitled to a reasonable sum for his services. The amount of such sum is a question of fact in each case, and the courts do not automatically award payment at the scale rates laid down by the main professional institutions.[83] It has been held that a custom that a surveyor should be paid 2½ per cent. on the lowest tender when no tender was accepted was unreasonable, and 1½ per cent. was awarded.[84]

Payment by employer, architect or contractor.   In the normal modern building contract the quantity surveyor is employed by the employer, and

---

[77] *London School Board* v. *Northcroft* (1889) H.B.C.) (4th ed.), Vol. 2, p. 147.
[78] See pp. 340 *et seq.*
[79] See p. 310.
[80] *London School Board* v. *Northcroft* (1889) H.B.C. (4th ed.), Vol. 2, p. 147.
[81] See *Dutton* v. *Louth Corporation* (1955) 116 E.G. 128 (C.A.). See also p. 268.
[82] See para. 6 of the Code of Procedure.
[83] See cases cited at p. 334 upon implication of the R.I.B.A. scale
[84] *Gwyther* v. *Gaze* (1875) H.B.C. (4th ed.), Vol. 2, p. 34, Quain J.

prima facie in such a case the employer is liable to pay him.[85] Where the employment is by the architect on behalf of the employer it must have been authorised or subsequently ratified or acquiesced in.[86] If the architect has personally employed the quantity surveyor for his own purposes[87] then he and not the employer is liable. He may also be liable in an action for breach of warranty of authority.[88] In the past certain difficulties arose from the fact that building contracts often used to provide that the contractor should pay the surveyor's charges out of money to be paid to the contractor under the building contract, but this is no longer the practice.[89]

(e) *Duties to contractor and others*

The position is analogous to that of the architect discussed at page 340.

---

[85] *Waghorn* v. *Wimbledon Local Board* (1877) H.B.C. (4th ed.), Vol. 2, p. 52; *Priestly* v. *Stone* (1888) 4 T.L.R. 730; H.B.C. (4th ed.), Vol. 2, p. 134 (C.A.).

[86] See p. 307.

[87] *e.g. Plimsaul* v. *Kilmorey (Lord)* (1884) 1 T.L.R. 48.

[88] See p. 308.

[89] The old law arising from this practice was discussed in the 4th edition of this book at pp. 231 *et seq.*

CHAPTER 14

THE EUROPEAN ECONOMIC COMMUNITY

Introduction. The law of the European Economic Community has potentially far-reaching implications for the construction industry. The Treaty of Rome envisages, for example, freedom of movement of labour, services and goods.[1] The scope of this chapter is limited to four areas of particular importance[2]:

(1) jurisdiction;
(2) product liability;
(3) restrictive agreements and competition;
(4) procurement.

1. Jurisdiction

The Civil Jurisdiction and Judgments Act 1982. This Act came into force in the United Kingdom on January 1, 1987.[3] By section 2(1) the Act gave effect as part of the national law to the 1968 Brussels Convention on Jurisdiction and the Enforcement of Judgments in Civil and Commercial Matters.[4] Although not strictly an item of EEC legislation,[5] the parties to the Convention are all member states of the Community[6] and the European Court of Justice has jurisdiction to give rulings on the interpretation of the Convention.[7] In

---

[1] Treaty Establishing the European Economic Community as Amended by subsequent Treaties. Rome, March 25, 1957.

[2] See generally Hartley, *The Foundations of European Community Law* (2nd ed.); Wyatt and Dashwood, *The Substantive Law of the EEC* (2nd ed.); Kapetyn and van Themaat, *Introduction to the Law of the European Communities* (2nd ed.).

[3] For more detailed discussion of the Act, see Dicey & Morris, *The Conflict of Laws* (11th ed.); O'Malley and Layton, *European Civil Practice* (1989); Kaye, *Civil Jurisdiction and Enforcement of Foreign Judgments*.

[4] The Convention forms an Appendix to the Act.

[5] See Treaty of Rome, Art. 189.

[6] The parties to the Convention are Belgium, the Federal Republic of Germany, France, Italy, Luxembourg, the Netherlands, Denmark, the Republic of Ireland, the United Kingdom and Greece; see also Treaty of Rome, Art. 220.

[7] The 1971 Protocol on the interpretation of the Convention of September 27, 1968, on Jurisdiction and the Enforcement of Judgments in Civil and Commercial Matters.

interpreting the Convention, the United Kingdom Courts are expressly entitled to consider three reports on the Convention and the Accession Convention, namely reports by Mr. P. Jenard, by Professor Peter Schlosser and by Professors Evrigenis and Kerameus.[8]

The Convention sets out uniform rules for the jurisdiction of national courts and the enforcement of judgments. The Act makes similar provision for the different jurisdictions within the United Kingdom.[9] Where the Act gives jurisdiction to the English High Court, leave is no longer required to serve process out of the jurisdiction.[10]

Civil and commercial matters.   The scope of the application of the Convention is limited to civil and commercial matters of an international nature.[11] The concept of civil and commercial matters is not dependent on classifications in domestic law but is to be given an independent Convention meaning.[12] The Convention expressly does not apply to administrative matters. It is not clear whether it applies to public works contracts, such as a contract with a public body for the construction of a hospital or a road. On this point, the Schlosser report[13] explains that the French legal system has a concept of the administrative contract which would include such public works contracts, whereas in Germany such works are carried out on the basis of private law. It is thought that it is more in keeping with the objectives and scheme of the Convention for such contracts to be treated as civil and commercial matters.[14]

Jurisdiction.   The basic principle of the Convention is that a party is generally to be sued in the courts of its domicile.[15] By Articles 52 and 53 of the Convention, a party's domicile is to be determined largely by national law, and sections 41–46 of the 1982 Act deal with domicile in the United Kingdom. The Convention provides optional additional bases of jurisdiction and permits parties to agree in writing the court which is to have jurisdiction. A party may also submit to a court's jurisdiction.[16] In some cases the Convention prescribes an exclusive basis of jurisdiction.[17] Articles 21–23 contain rules for resolving conflicts of jurisdiction.

---

[8] See s.3(3) of the Act as amended by the Civil Jurisdiction and Judgments Act 1982 (Amendment) Order 1989 (S.I. 1989 No. 1346), Art. 8.

[9] Sched. 4.

[10] See R.S.C., Ord. 11(2).

[11] Art. 1 of the Convention and para. 4 of its Preamble. Other treaties of similar scope are the Hague Conventions on Service Abroad of Judicial and Extrajudicial Documents in Civil or Commercial Matters (1965) and on the Taking of Evidence Abroad in Civil or Commercial Matters (1970).

[12] See *LTU Lufttransportunternehmen GmbH & Co. KG* v. *Eurocontrol* (1976) E.C.R. 1541; *Netherlands* v. *Rüffer* (1980) E.C.R. 3807.

[13] See para. 26.

[14] *cf.* the approach in the *Eurocontrol* case (1976) E.C.R. 1541 at 1551.

[15] See Art. 2; *cf. In Re Harrods* (*Buenos Aires*) *Ltd.*, *The Times*, January 11, 1991 (C.A.).

[16] See Arts. 5–6A, 17 and 18.

[17] See Art. 16.

Contract. Under Article 5(1) of the Convention, in matters relating to a contract, a person domiciled in a Contracting State may be sued in another Contracting State in the courts for the place of performance of the obligation in question. The parties may agree the place of performance.[18] Otherwise, how a national court decides whether it has jurisdiction under this Article involves a sequence of complex questions.[19] The Court must decide where the place of performance of the obligation in question is according to the law applicable to that obligation, the applicable law being found by the Court's own rules as to conflict of laws.[20] The leading case on what is the relevant obligation for this purpose is *Shevanai* v. *Kreischer*,[21] which concerned an architect's claim for fees. The European Court of Justice held that the relevant obligation was that which formed the actual basis of the legal proceedings, *i.e.* the obligation to pay the fees rather than the obligation to do work.

A national Court may have jurisdiction under Article 5 even where the existence of the contract is disputed.[22] It is thought that quasi-contractual claims, such as a claim on a *quantum meruit*, are probably within the scope of Article 5(1).[23]

Tort. Under Article 5(3) of the Convention, in a claim based on tort, delict or quasi-delict, a person domiciled in a Contracting State may be sued in another Contracting State in the courts for the place where the harmful event occurred. The Convention only addresses the question of jurisdiction and does not determine what law the national Court with jurisdiction applies in finding whether tortious liability exists. It is suggested that the Convention leaves the national Court to apply its own rules of conficts of laws.

The place where the harmful event occurred may be either where the damage occurred or where the event occurred which gave rise to the damage.[24] Where a claim is one for negligent misstatement,[25] it is submitted that the place where damage occurs may be the place where the negligent misstatement was either received or relied on or where either physical damage occurs or the relevant economic loss is suffered.[26]

---

[18] *Zelger* v. *Salinitri* (1980) E.C.R. 89.
[19] The questions are clearly set out in O'Malley, para. 17.03.
[20] *Industrie Tessili Italiana Como* v. *Dunlop A.G.* (1976) E.C.R. 1473.
[21] (1987) 3 C.M.L.R. 782. See also *Medway Packaging* v. *Meurer, Financial Times*, October 20, 1989.
[22] *Effer Sp A* v. *Kantner* (1982) E.C.R. 825. Compare *Tesam Distribution* v. *Schuh Mode Team GmbH*, [1989] L.S.Gaz., December 20, 38 (C.A.)—Plaintiffs had to establish that there was a serious question as to the existence of the contract which called for a trial; *cf. Finnish Insurance Co.* v. *Protective Insurance Co.* [1990] 2 W.L.R. 914—a case concerning R.S.C., Ord. 11, service out of the jurisdiction with leave where the plaintiffs sought a declaration that there was no contract between them and the defendants.
[23] Art. 5(1) might well be wide enough to cover a claim for payment for work done in anticipation of a contract being entered into as in *Marston* v. *Kigass* (1989) 46 B.L.R. 109.
[24] Dicey & Morris, r. 29(3); *Bier* v. *Mines de Potasse d'Alsace* (1976) E.C.R. 1735, [1978] Q.B. 708.
[25] See p. 174.
[26] Contrast *Rüffer* (1980) E.C.R. 3807 at 3836. See *Minster Investments* v. *Hyundai Precision Industry Co.* [1988] 2 Lloyd's Rep. 621—the place where the harmful event occurred was England where there was receipt of the negligently produced certificate which the plaintiffs were intended to and did rely on.

Co-defendants, third party proceedings and counterclaims. Article 6 of the Convention is of particular importance to the kind of multi-party dispute which is common in the building industry. It provides that a person domiciled in a Contracting State may also be sued, where he is one of a number of defendants, in the courts for the place where any one of them is domiciled, provided that there is a link between the claims made against each of the defendants.[27] Such a person may be sued as a third party in an action on a warranty or guarantee, or in any other third-party proceedings, in the court seised of the original proceedings, unless these were instituted solely with the object of removing him from the jurisdiction of the court which would be competent in his case. A counterclaim arising from the same contract or facts on which the original claim was based may be brought in the court in which the original claim is pending.

Lis pendens. Articles 21–23 of the Convention variously require a national Court to decline jurisdiction or permit it to stay proceedings where parties seek to invoke the jurisdiction of different Courts in the same or related actions.

Arbitration.   Arbitration is expressly excluded from the scope of the Convention. Thus it is thought that the Convention would not apply to proceedings to enforce an award or dismiss an arbitrator or extend his powers.[28] It is an open question whether the Convention applies in cases where the parties have agreed to refer disputes to arbitration but have not done so, or where the validity of an agreement to arbitrate is in issue.[29]

Recognition and enforcement of judgments.   Article 26 provides for a judgment given in a Contracting State to be recognised in the other Contracting States without any special procedure being required.[30] There are certain exceptions in Article 27. Article 31 provides that a judgment given in one Contracting State and enforceable in that State shall be enforced in another Contracting State when, on application of an interested party, an order for enforcement has been issued there. The procedure for making application is governed by the law of the State in which enforcement is sought.[31] Under Article 51, a settlement which has been approved by a court in the course of proceedings and is enforceable in the State in which it was concluded shall be enforceable in the State in which enforcement is sought under the same conditions as "authentic instruments."[32]

---

[27] *Kalfelis* v. *Schröder, Münchmeyer, Hengst & Co., The Times,* October 5, 1988.

[28] See Jenard Report, Chap. III and Schlosser Report, paras. 63–65.

[29] See O'Malley, paras. 14.32–14.33 and *Marc Rich & Co.* v. *Societa Italiana Impianti* [1989] 1 Lloyd's Rep. 548.

[30] The simplicity of the improved rights of enforcement of judgments is an important factor to take into account in deciding whether to order security for costs against a plaintiff resident in a State which is a party to the Convention—*De Bry* v. *Fitzgerald* [1990] 1 W.L.R. 552 (C.A.). For security for costs, see p. 454.

[31] See Art. 33 and see also Arts. 46–48.

[32] "Authentic instruments" are documents formally drawn up and registered and they must satisfy the conditions necessary to establish their authenticity in the State of origin—see Art. 50.

2. Product Liability

Consumer Protection Act 1987.   This Act was passed in order to implement Council Directive No. 85/374 dated July 25, 1985.[33] The Directive forms an Appendix to the Act but does not form part of the Act, although it can be used as an aid to construction.[34]

Part I of the Act provides for liability for damage caused by defective products. Where damage is caused wholly or partly by a defect in a product, the producer is liable for the damage. An importer in the course of business into a member state of the European Community may also be liable. So also in certain circumstances may a supplier.[35] The Act constitutes as a supply of goods the performance of any contract by the erection of any building or structure on any land in so far as it involves the provision of any goods by means of their incorporation into the building, structure or works.[36] Damage means death or personal injury or any loss of or damage to any property including land ordinarily and in fact mainly intended for private use, occupation or consumption. It does not include damage to the product itself.[37] There is a defect in a product if the safety of the product is not such as persons generally are entitled to expect and safety relates to risks of damage to property as well as risks of death or personal injury.[38] There are certain statutory defences including a "development risks defence" defence.[39] Section 6(4) of the Act has the effect of permitting contributory negligence to be a partial or complete defence. Liability under the Act may not be limited or excluded by any contract term, by any notice or by any other provision.[40] There are special limitation provisions applicable to claims under the Consumer Protection Act 1987.[41]

Accordingly, there may be liability under the Act if defects in goods supplied as part of construction works cause death, personal injury or damage to private property. The liability is unexplored judicially, but it might in certain circumstances be a rather wider liability than that now available under a negligence claim.[42]

Measure of damages.   The Act does not deal specifically with the measure of damages recoverable. Since there is no liability without damage to persons

---

[33] Pt. I of the Act with which this section of this chapter deals was brought into force on March 1, 1988.

[34] s.1(1).

[35] Consumer Protection Act 1987, s.2; "product" includes any goods or electricity—see s.1(2).

[36] *Ibid.* s.46(3).

[37] *Ibid.* s.5.

[38] *Ibid.* s.3.

[39] See *ibid.* s.4 generally and in particular s.4(1)(e).

[40] *Ibid.* s.7.

[41] See the Limitation Act 1980, s.11A as enacted by s.6(6) and Sched. 1 of the Consumer Protection Act 1987.

[42] For negligence, see Chap. 7.

or property other than the thing itself, it seems likely that the damages recoverable are limited to compensating the plaintiff for the injury or damage to property caused and would not extend to the cost of repairing the defective product or compensating the plaintiff for its loss in value.

3. Restrictive Agreements and Competition

Introduction. Contractors have, it seems, often entered into agreements, formal or informal, with other contractors restricting their prices or otherwise limiting their freedom to tender in a freely competitive manner. It is now also becoming common for contractors to enter into joint ventures with their competitors to perform a specific contract, or to set up an enterprise specialising in a particular field of the construction industry. The integration of the European market has also encouraged non-United Kingdom contractors to enter into arrangements with local contractors as an effective means of expanding their operations into the United Kingdom.

Any agreement of these types may distort competition. Both United Kingdom and EEC law operate to protect and encourage the operation of such competition. Any business operating in the United Kingdom may be subject to the domestic law on this subject, or the competition law of the European Community derived from Articles 85–90 of the Treaty of Rome.

Under United Kingdom law restrictive agreements or arrangements were solely governed by the common law before 1956. These agreements may now be registrable under the Restrictive Trade Practices Act 1976 and important consequences flow from registration, or the failure to register. As a result of section 2 of the European Communities Act 1972 these agreements may also be subject to the provisions of the Treaty of Rome which are effective in the United Kingdom. A brief account is given below. For these purposes the most important provisions are Articles 85 and 86.[43]

Contractor's position at common law. Agreements between contractors limiting their rights to tender are in restraint of trade.[44] They are prima facie invalid, but if supported by consideration will be enforced by the courts if they are reasonable both in the interests of the parties and of the public. It is a question for the court in each case to decide whether such a contract is reasonable, but in considering what is reasonable between the parties the law "regards the parties as the best judges of what is reasonable as between

---

[43] For further references see *Chitty on Contracts* (26th ed., 1989); Green, *Commercial Agreements and Competition Law, Practice and Procedure in the U.K. and EEC* (1986); Bellamy & Child, *Common Market Law of Competition* (3rd ed., 1977); Allan & Hogan, *Competition Laws of United Kingdom and Republic of Ireland*; Goyder, *EEC Competition Law* (1989).

[44] For the principle, see *Nordenfelt* v. *Maxim Nordenfelt Co.* [1894] A.C. 535 at 565 (H.L.); *Esso Petroleum Co.* v. *Harpers Garage (Stourport)* [1968] A.C. 269 (H.L.). For a detailed discussion of the whole subject, see Wilberforce, Campbell and Elles, *Restrictive Trade Practices and Monopolies* (2nd ed., 1966) and supplement.

themselves."[45] There is no reported case of an agreement between contractors restricting their right to tender being held to be unreasonable, although price fixing and marketing arrangements in other branches of trade and industry have from time to time been held to be unreasonable.[46] There is apparently no case reported in which an agreement reasonable in the interests of the parties has been held to be unenforceable because it is unreasonable in the interests of the public.[47] An agreement between two contractors that one should not tender has been enforced.[48]

Employer's position at common law.   An employer whose interests are adversely affected because of a restrictive tendering agreement is unlikely to have any effective remedy at common law,[49] unless he has previously taken from a contractor a warranty not to enter into such an agreement and can prove a breach of it.

The Restrictive Trade Practices Act 1976.[50]   This statute makes registrable a wide range of agreements under which specified restrictions are accepted by two or more parties in respect of the supply of goods[51] or services[52] and also in respect of the construction or carrying out of buildings, structures and other works by contractors.[53] The term "agreement" includes an arrangement not intended to be legally enforceable and the term "restriction" includes any negative obligation, whether express or implied, and whether absolute or not.[54] The restrictions specified include those relating to prices, terms and conditions,[55] quantities and descriptions, processes and the persons or classes

---

[45] *North Western Salt Co.* v. *Electrolytic Alkali Co.* [1914] A.C. 461 at 471 (H.L.).

[46] *e.g. Urmston* v. *Whitelegg* (1891) 7 T.L.R. 295 (C.A.); *Evans* v. *Heathcote* [1918] 1 K.B. 418 (C.A.); *McEllistrim* v. *Ballymacelligott Co-op Society* [1919] A.C. 548 (H.L.).

[47] *cf. Att.-Gen. of Australia* v. *Adelaide Steamship Co.* [1913] A.C. 781 at 796 (P.C.).

[48] *Metcalf* v. *Bouck* (1871) 25 L.T. 539; *Jones* v. *North* (1875) L.R. 19 Eq. 426; *cf. Rawlings* v. *General Trading Co.* [1921] 1 K.B. 635 (C.A.)—knock-out agreement at auction not illegal. Now subject to the Auctions (Bidding Agreements) Act 1927 and the Auctions (Bidding Agreements) Act 1969.

[49] Conspiracy is a form of action which comes to mind but it will fail if the defendants show that their predominant object was to further or protect their interests—see *Mogul Steamship Co.* v. *McGregor Gow & Co.* [1892] A.C. 25 (H.L.); *Crofter Hand Woven Harris Tweed Co.* v. *Veitch* [1942] A.C. 435 (H.L.); *Byrne* v. *Kinematograph Renters Society* [1958] 1 W.L.R. 762. There is no building contract case reported in which this form of action against contractors has been attempted.

[50] Only the briefest introduction is given here. Earlier legislation governing restrictive trade practices has now been consolidated in the Restrictive Trade Practices Act 1976 and the Restrictive Practices Court Act 1976. Both Acts are consolidating Acts although there has been substantial rewording and rearrangement. References are to the Restrictive Trade Practices Act 1976 unless otherwise stated. For loan finances and credit facilities, see the Restrictive Trade Practices Act 1977.

[51] ss.1(1) and 6(1). For restriction of price maintenance on goods, see the Resale Prices Act 1964.

[52] ss.1(1) and 11; Restrictive Trade Practices (Services) Order 1976. (S.I. 1976 No. 98).

[53] s.43(3).

[54] s.43(1).

[55] See *Re Birmingham Association of Building Trades Employers' Agreement* [1963] 1 W.L.R. 484—agreement that members shall press for inclusion of R.I.B.A. form; *Re Electrical Installations Agreement* [1970] 1 W.L.R. 1391—agreement between seven electrical contractors not to tender until after discussions registrable; *Re Building Employers Confederation's Application* [1985] I.C.R. 167.

of persons to, for or from whom or the areas or places in which goods are to be supplied or acquired or works carried out.[56] Certain information agreements are also registrable.[57] The agreements must in due course be proved to the satisfaction of the Restrictive Practices Court not to be contrary to the public interest. If they are found to be contrary to the public interest they become void and the court can prevent their enforcement.[58] If the agreements are not registered in accordance with the Acts they are void and unenforceable.[59]

Restrictions are deemed to be contrary to the public interest unless the court is satisfied of certain matters.[60] The result is, to take one example, that an agreement as to the adjusting of tender prices is registrable and it is most unlikely that the Restrictive Practices Court would be satisfied that it was not contrary to the public interest. An agreement between a few contractors made *ad hoc* for one occasion is, it is submitted, registrable.

The Competition Act 1980.   This statute was enacted to fill the substantial gaps left by the previous legislation. It introduced a new procedure, involving a preliminary investigation by the Director General of Fair Trading and, if appropriate, a reference to the Monopolies and Mergers Commission, for the control of "anti-competitive practices."[61] Where the Director General makes an investigation and finds that it is appropriate to make a reference he may accept from the persons concerned undertakings to vary or terminate the relevant practice instead of making the reference. If a reference is made and the Monopolies and Mergers Commission identifies an anti-competitive practice that operated or may be expected to operate against the public interest the Commission may recommend appropriate remedial action. The Secretary of State for Trade and Industry may act on that report by prohibiting any such anti-competitive practice.[62]

Remedies of employer by reason of the Acts.   Any person affected by a breach of the duty to register an agreement can bring an action for breach of that duty.[63] It seems therefore that, where an employer enters into a contract and then discovers that the price has been increased or the terms of the contract are adverse to his interests by reason of an unregistered but registrable agreement, he has a remedy in damages[64] against the persons who should have registered.

---

[56] ss.6(1), 11 and 43(3).
[57] ss.7 and 12; Restrictive Trade Practices (Information Agreements) Order 1969 (S.I. 1696 No. 1842).
[58] ss.1(3), 2 and 35.
[59] s.35(1).
[60] ss.10, 19 and 31(9).
[61] Definition of "anti-competitive practice" is provided in the Competition Act 1980, s.2.
[62] See the Competition Act 1980, ss.5–10.
[63] s.35(2) of the 1976 Act.
[64] Or, in the appropriate case, a set-off, see p. 438.

An injunction has been granted restraining persons from giving effect to an agreement interfering with the plaintiffs' trade, which the court was satisfied would be held to be void by the Restrictive Trade Practices Court.[65]

EEC competition law.　Article 85(1) of the Treaty of Rome prohibits all agreements between undertakings, decisions by associations of undertakings and concerted practices which may affect trade between Member States and which have as their object the prevention, restriction or distortion of competition within the common market. Any price fixing arrangement, or agreement to co-ordinate competitive behaviour which has an affect upon trade between Member States is likely to fall within this Article. Article 85(2) provides that any prohibited agreement is automatically void. Such an agreement is, therefore, unenforceable.[66]

The requirement that trade between Member States must be affected for EEC law to apply is widely construed. The requirement will be satisfied by the existence of an actual or potential effect, direct or indirect on the normal pattern of trade across borders within the EEC.[67] A potential effect on trade between Member States may be found even though the conduct takes place in only one Member State, when such conduct may deflect trade from the channels that it might otherwise follow.[68]

Article 86 prohibits "abuse" of "a dominant position" in a "substantial part" of the EEC. An enterprise is considered dominant if it is able to prevent effective competition or has the capacity to act, to an appreciable extent, independently of its competitors, suppliers and customers.[69] The Commission has found that suppliers of certain categories of construction materials enjoy such a dominant position,[70] but it is not thought that any contractors have been found to enjoy such a position. A collective dominant position can exist where two or more companies act jointly.[71]

The Commission of the European Communities has the power to issue a "negative clearance" where it finds no violation of Articles 85(1) or 86 or to grant an "exemption" pursuant to Article 85(3) declaring Article 85(1) inapplicable. The granting of individual exemptions under Article 85(3) on the application of one or more of the parties to an agreement is an important part of the Commission's activity in the competition field. The Commission is

---

[65] *Brekkes Ltd.* v. *Cattel* [1972] Ch. 105.

[66] The doctrine of severance is, however, applicable so that objectionable provisions may, in appropriate circumstances, be severed from the agreement leaving the remainder in effect—see, *e.g. Chemidus Wavin Ltd.* v. *Société pour la Transformation et L'Exploitation des Resines Industrielles S.A.* [1978] 3 C.M.L.R. 514 (C.A.).

[67] *Bureau National Interprofessionnel du Cognac* v. *Clair*, Case 123/83 [1985] E.C.R. 391.

[68] *Vereeniging van Cementhandelaren* v. *Commission*, Case 8/72 [1972] E.C.R. 977.

[69] *United Brands Co.* v. *Commission*, Case 27/76 [1978] E.C.R. 207.

[70] For example, in *BPB Industries plc*, O.J. No. L10, January 1, 1989, p. 50, the Commission found that BPB enjoyed a dominant position in the supply of plasterboard in Great Britain and the Island of Ireland. This decision is the subject of an appeal.

[71] *Italian Flat Glass*, O.J. No. L33, February 4, 1989, p. 44.

355

entitled to grant an exemption upon finding that all four conditions specified in Article 85(3) have been satisfied. There are a few instances of contractors applying for such individual exemption or for negative clearance for their activities.[72]

Remedies of an employer for violation of EEC competition law. It seems likely, although it is not decided, that Articles 85 and 86 may give rise to a cause of action in damages or for an injunction at the suit of a party injured by the abusive conduct of a dominant undertaking or the operation of a prohibited agreement. Both articles have, in the parlance of Community law, "direct effect" and create individual rights enforceable in national courts.[73] Two English decisions are now taken to indicate that, in principle, a right of action for damages exists in English law under Article 86 on the basis of breach of statutory duty.[74] It would seem that Article 85(1) should also, therefore, give rise to an action in damages even though this would lead to the anomalous result that conduct of a kind which would rarely be actionable in damages under United Kingdom domestic law would be actionable in damages under Community law. The right to damages would, as a consequence, turn on whether some actual or potential effect on inter-State trade could be made out. It is not even clear who would be entitled to bring such an action.

In principle, an injunction should also be available to prevent the continuation of a breach of Article 85(1) or Article 86 at the suit of an individual injured by that breach, on the basis of the normal principles relating to injunctions.[75]

It seems, therefore, that an employer may recover damages if he has suffered or is continuing to suffer loss by virtue of any action by contractors which violates Articles 85(1) or Article 86 and which also affects inter-State trade. A national price-fixing or tender allocation cartel might fall foul of these provisions.

Reform of law on restrictive trade practices. The Government has announced proposals for wide ranging reform of the law on restrictive trade

---

[72] See, *e.g. Eurotunnel*, O.J. No. L311, November 17, 1988, p. 36—a negative clearance was granted by the Commission for the construction contract for the Channel Tunnel between Eurotunnel and a consortium of eight contractors, and the "maître d'oeuvre" contract between Eurotunnel and four firms of construction professionals; *FIEC/CEETB*, 18th Report on Competition Policy, para. 60—the applicants sought exemption for an agreement for the standardisation of tender procedures for the provision of specialist equipment by sub-contractors to building contractors and negative clearance was granted after amendments had been made to the agreement on the basis of the Commission's suggestions.

[73] *Belgische Radio en Televisie* v. *SV SABAM*, Case 127/73 [1974] E.C.R. 51.

[74] *Garden Cottage Foods* v. *Milk Marketing Board* [1984] A.C. 10 (H.L.) which was only an interlocutory decision; *Bourgoin* v. *Ministry of Agriculture* [1986] Q.B. 716 (C.A.), which was primarily a decision on Art. 30.

[75] In *Cutsforth* v. *Mansfield Inns* [1986] 1 W.L.R. 558 suppliers of amusement machines obtained an injunction restraining a brewery company from excluding them from the brewery's tied houses on the basis of Art. 85(1) and subsidiary Community legislation.

practices in a White Paper.[76] The new legislation would replace the Restrictive Trade Practices Act 1976 and probably also the Resale Prices Act 1964 with a new law which will prohibit agreements or concerted practices which have the object or effect of restricting or distorting competition in the United Kingdom or in a part of the United Kingdom. The new law would be very similar to the law under Article 85 of the Treaty of Rome, subject to certain alterations which the Government believes may improve its operation. There will, of course, be no requirement that conduct should affect trade between Member States in order to fall within the scope of the proposed legislation.

4. Procurement

Prohibition of contracting restrictions. The economic system established by the Community is based on four "freedoms." These are the free movement of legal and natural persons,[77] the freedom to provide services,[78] the free movement of capital[79] and the free movement of goods.[80] The principle of free movement of goods has been most extensively applied and prohibits all quantitative restrictions on trade between Member States and all measures having equivalent effect.[81]

The unqualified application of these freedoms ought to lead to an uninhibited trade in construction services and materials throughout the Community, so that contractors should be able to compete without restriction to carry out works in any Member State. However, there has been a number of obstacles, some of which are now being resolved by technical harmonisation.[82] One of the principal difficulties has been a persistent national and even local preference in the procurement policies of central and local government authorities throughout the Community.

In recent years prospective contractors and suppliers have brought actions against authorities which let contracts in such a way as to discriminate in favour of their own nationals. These actions have primarily been brought under Article 30 of the Treaty of Rome and the principle of non-discrimination expressed in Article 7.

In *The Commission of the European Communities* v. *Ireland*,[83] the European Court of Justice found that a refusal by Irish authorities to check whether products

---

[76] "Opening Markets: New Policy on Restrictive Trade Practices" (Cmnd. 727, July 1989).

[77] Arts. 52–58 of the Treaty of Rome.

[78] Arts. 59–66 of the Treaty of Rome.

[79] Arts. 67–73 of the Treaty of Rome.

[80] Arts. 30–37 of the Treaty of Rome.

[81] See Art. 30. This is subject to the exceptions set out in the succeeding Articles, in particular Art. 36.

[82] See, *e.g.* Council Directive 89/106 on the approximation of laws, regulations and administrative provisions of the Member States relating to construction products. O.J. No. L40, February 11, 1989, p. 12.

[83] (1988) 44 B.L.R. 1—Case 45/87R [1988] E.C.R. 4929. This is commonly called the *Dundalk case.*

conforming to national or international standards recognised in other Member States offered guarantees of safety and suitability equivalent to those offered by the relevant Irish standard was incompatible with Article 30 and incapable of any justification in Community law. As a result of the refusal to make such checks, a tenderer could only secure the contract by using Irish materials. A restriction on trade between Member States will be a breach of Article 30 even if nationals of the State which has restricted trade will also be affected. Thus the Court of Justice found that a requirement imposed by Italian legislation that local authorities should obtain at least 30 per cent. of their supplies from companies established in the Mezzogiorno region was incompatible with Article 30 and incapable of justification.[84] The Court found that this was discrimination against products from other Member States. Such discrimination on a national basis is a sufficient, but not a necessary, criterion for infringement of Article 30.[85]

Recovery of damages in English courts.   It seems that it is not possible to recover damages in an English court for a breach of Article 30 for losses such as tender costs incurred in preparing a tender for a contract wrongfully let to a local contractor. Although damages are apparently recoverable in a national court for breaches of Articles 85 and 86,[86] it seems that a breach of Article 30 by a state-imposed prohibition or restriction does not give rise to liability in damages for the benefit of private individuals in English law.[87] This extends to administrative acts in the sphere of public law as well as legislative and quasi-legislative acts. It is undecided whether damages might be available for an act by an individual.[88]

It is possible, however, that an aggrieved tenderer might recover damages if he were to demonstrate that a public body (which should be taken to mean any body whose decisions are subject to judicial review) was guilty of misfeasance in public office. The elements of misfeasance are that the public body should have committed an *ultra vires* act with intent to injure the plaintiff or with knowledge of the illegality of the act. It seems that it may be sufficient if the defendant knows that the act in question is invalid and that it is not necessary to prove an intention to harm the plaintiff as long as that harm was a foreseeable result of the act.[89]

---

[84] *Du Pont de Nemours Italiana SpA* v. *Unità Sanitaria Locale no. 2 di Carrara* Case C–21/88 (unreported).

[85] See also *Gebroeders Beentjes B.V.* v. *Staat der Nederlanden* Case 31/87 (unreported); *Rush Portuguesa Lda.* v. *Office Nationale D'Immigration* Case C–113/89 (unreported).

[86] *Garden Cottage Foods* v. *Milk Marketing Board* [1984] A.C. 130 (H.L.); *cf.* "Remedies of an Employer for violation of EEC competition law" at p. 356.

[87] See *Bourgoin* v. *Ministry of Agriculture* [1986] Q.B. 716 (C.A.); *An Bord Bainne Co-operative* v. *Milk Marketing Board* [1988] 1 C.M.L.R. 605 (C.A.); Collins, *European Community Law in the United Kingdom* (4th ed., 1990).

[88] It is not clear whether as a matter of Community law Arts. 30–36 apply against individuals—see Gormley, *Prohibiting Restrictions on Trade within the EEC* (1985), pp. 259–262.

[89] See *Bourgoin* v. *Ministry of Agriculture* [1986] Q.B. 716 (C.A.).

Procurement legislation. The Community has consistently regarded restrictions on contracting as of considerable significance and has produced a growing body of legislation controlling the tender process for increasing categories of contracts.

In the United Kingdom, the only legislative controls on the competitive process have been in local government legislation. The Local Government Act 1972 provides that local authorities should set out formal contracting procedures which would usually involve competitive tender.[90] The Local Government Act 1988 expressly requires authorities to give reasons for their procurement decisions and prohibits contract awards based on certain non-commercial grounds.[91]

The Community legislation controlling procurement practices has until recently been confined to government contracts outside the so-called excluded sectors of water, energy, transport and supply contracts for telecommunications.[92] All the relevant legislative measures lay down certain general requirements, *viz.*:

(a) the basic principles of Article 7 of the Treaty of Rome that discrimination on grounds of nationality is prohibited and of Article 59 that persons established in one Member State should be free to provide services in another Member State are both reiterated.[93]

(b) contracts above a certain value must be advertised by specific procedures.

(c) tenders must be published in the Official Journal of the European Communities in the prescribed form within a specified time limit.

(d) the use of Community standards is promoted.

(e) contracting authorities may use open or restricted procedures in the award of public contracts, but contracts may only be negotiated with single tenderers in specific circumstances.

(f) notices of the award of contracts must be published.

(g) contracts must be awarded to the lowest or most economically advantageous tenderer.[94]

(h) records of compliance must be kept by the contracting authority.

The legislation sets out detailed provisions to implement these principles. There are, however, important differences between the legislation applying to

---

[90] s.135 of the Local Government Act 1972.

[91] ss.17–22 and Sched. 2 of the Local Government Act 1988.

[92] See Directive 71/305, O.J. No. L195, August 16, 1971, p. 5, on works contracts last amended by Directive 89/440, O.J. No. L210, July 21, 1989, p. 1; Directive 77/62, O.J. No. L13, January 1, 1977, p. 1 on supplies last amended by Directive 88/295, O.J. No. L127, May 5, 1988, p. 1; Directive 89/665, O.J. No. L395, December 30, 1989, p. 33 on enforcement.

[93] See *SA Transporoute et Travaux* v. *Minister of Public Works* Case 76/81 [1982] E.C.R. 417.

[94] For the procedure to be adopted for abnormally low tenders, see *SA Transporoute et Travaux* v. *Minister of Public Works* Case 76/81 [1982] E.C.R. 417.

different categories of contract.[95] A Directive has also been adopted which will apply comparable provisions to works and supplies contracts entered into by utilities in the water, energy, transport and telecommunications sectors.[96] The system will apply to contracting authorities regardless of whether they are privately or publicly owned. The Directive must be implemented in the Member States by January 1, 1993.

The Commission is expected to publish a proposal for a similar Directive applying to public service contracts in the near future. It is also believed to be preparing a draft proposal for a Directive applying to services in the utilities sector.

Implementation in England and Wales. In England and Wales, the various directives have in the past been implemented by way of Government circular.[97] There is considerable doubt whether this is satisfactory and United Kingdom legislation is now in preparation which will implement Directives 71/305 and 77/62 as amended.

Remedies. The European Court of Justice has held that the public works Directive 71/305 is capable of having direct effect in Member States after the date for its implementation without any implementing national legislation.[98] In *The Commission of the European Communities* v. *Italian Republic*,[99] the European Court of Justice granted interim measures to a tenderer requiring the Italian government to suspend a tender for a public contract until the hearing to determine whether the tender had been carried out lawfully. However, the only remedy for breach of any such directly effective directive in English law is through judicial review of the award of the contract. Damages may be awarded in an application for judicial review if damages are claimed in the original application, but such awards are rare. The usual remedy is an injunction or a declaration.[1]

In the public works and supplies sectors, provision for remedies will be made by the implementation of Directive 89/665. This directive is to be

---

[95] See E.C. Commission, "Guide to the Community Rules on Open Government Procurement" O.J. No. C358, December 31, 1989, p. 1; Marks, "The Community Law on the Procurement of Public Works and its Application to the U.K." (1989) I.C.L.R. 424; André-Dumont and Shelowitz, "The Amendment of July 18, 1989 of EEC Directive 71/305 and Co-ordination of National Procedures in the Countries of the European Community" (1990) I.C.L.R. 5; Heiermann, "The E.C. Directive concerning Co-ordination of Procedures for the Award of Public Works Contracts" (1990) I.C.L.R. 76; Boncompagni, "The Main Features of the Community Directives 89/440/EEC and 88/245/EEC" (1990) I.C.L.R. 225; Gormley, "Some Reflections of Public Procurement," *European Business Law Review*, November 1990.

[96] Not yet published.

[97] For example, Joint Circular Department of the Environment and Welsh Office 109/73, May 11, 1973, and Joint Circular Department of the Environment and Welsh Office 81/78, June 28, 1978 concerning Directive 71/305 and Directive 77/62 respectively.

[98] *Gebroeders Beentjes B.V.* v. *Staat der Nederlanden* Case 31/87 (unreported).

[99] Case 194/88–R (unreported).

[1] See House of Lords Select Committee on European Communities, Report on Compliance with Public Procurement Directives (1988) H.L. 72, para. 14.

implemented by December 1, 1991 and the necessary United Kingdom legislation is in preparation. The Commission has also published a proposal for a remedies Directive applicable in the utilities sectors.[2]

---

[2] O.J. No. C216, August 31, 1990, p. 8.

CHAPTER 15

VARIOUS LEGISLATION

1. The Defective Premises Act 1972

The Defective Premises Act 1972, which came into operation on January 1, 1974, imposes duties upon persons taking on work for or in connection with the provision of a dwelling.[1] The liability extends to contract work, work done without a contract but in circumstances where a *quantum meruit* may be claimed, to work done voluntarily, and to cases in which a building owner does the work himself.[2] The duties are additional to any duty otherwise owed[3] and cannot be excluded or restricted.[4] Thus it is still necessary to consider the position in contract and in tort[5] and under section 38 of the Building Act 1984.[6] Breach of the duty imposed by the statute gives rise, it is submitted, to a claim for damages at the suit of a person to whom the duty is owed and who has suffered damage by reason of the breach.[7] The Act does not apply to the repair or enlargement of a dwelling nor in certain circumstances where there is an "approved scheme."[8] For a period until 1979, the National House-Building Council's schemes were approved schemes for the purposes of section 2 of the Act. But the last such scheme came to an end on March 31, 1979, thus

---

[1] For a discussion of the Act and its origins, see *D. & F. Estates* v. *Church Commissioners* [1989] A.C. 177 at 193 *et seq.* (H.L.); *cf. Murphy* v. *Brentwood District Council* [1990] 3 W.L.R. 414 (H.L.) for the Act's significance in relation to liabilities in negligence.

[2] *Alexander* v. *Mercouris* [1979] 1 W.L.R. 1270 at 1273 (C.A.).

[3] s. 6(2). For a highly critical article by J. R. Spencer see [1974] C.L.J. 307.

[4] s.6(3).

[5] See Chap. 7.

[6] See Section 4 of this chapter.

[7] This is not expressed in the statute but arises from the general principles relating to actions for breach of statutory duty. See Salmond and Heuston, *Torts* (19th ed.), pp. 273 *et seq.*

[8] See ss.1(1) and 2(2).

removing a major potential restriction on the operation of the Act.[9] The Act had no retrospective effect, so persons who had taken on work before the Act came into force owed no duty to the plaintiffs under the statute.[10]

The duty to build dwellings properly.   Section 1(1) of the Act provides:

"A person taking on work for or in connection with the provision of a dwelling (whether the dwelling is provided by the erection or by the conversion or enlargement of a building) owes a duty—

> *(a) if the dwelling is provided to the order of any person, to that person; and*
> *(b) without prejudice to paragraph (a) above, to every person who acquires an interest (whether legal or equitable) in the dwelling;*

to see that the work which he takes on is done in a workmanlike or, as the case may be, professional manner, with proper materials and so that as regards that work the dwelling will be fit for habitation when completed."

The standard to be achieved corresponds substantially with that required by the usual implied terms upon sale of a house in the course of erection.[11] It is a question in each case whether a person has taken on work within the meaning of the Act. Thus ordinarily it will include the main contractor and any professional person, such as an architect, engineer or quantity surveyor and any sub-contractor specifically employed on or in connection with the provision of the dwelling. But, it seems, other persons may be liable. Thus a person, not a qualified architect, who provides plans for the dwelling is, it is submitted, within the section, and so also is a supplier who makes up some component specifically for the dwelling in question. How far other suppliers who provide such goods as boilers suitable for use in dwellings to a builder can be liable must depend upon the application of the section to the facts of a particular case. It is not clear whether a local authority performing its duties under the Building Regulations can ever come within the section.[12]

A person within the section doing professional work has to do it in a professional manner. It is thought that all persons coming within the section are under a strict duty to fulfil its requirements, and that it would not be a defence to show that the work was done with proper care.

Defence of "Instructions."   Section 1(2) and (3) of the Act provide:

---

[9] See s.2(1) and the House-building Standards (Approved Scheme, etc.) Orders 1973 (S.I. 1973 No. 1843), 1975 (S.I. 1975 No. 1462), 1977 (S.I. 1977 No. 642) and 1979 (S.I. 1979 No. 381). The 1979 Order was ineffective since the documents with the numbers referred to in it were never published. Other schemes can be approved under the Act. For the position where there is compulsory acquisition, see s.2(7).

[10] *Alexander* v. *Mercouris* [1979] 1 W.L.R. 1270 (C.A.); *Rimmer* v. *Liverpool City Council* [1985] Q.B. 1 at 7 (C.A.).

[11] See p. 57.

[12] See also s.1(4) discussed below. For local authorities' liability as landlords to tenants under s.4 of the Act, see, *e.g. Rimmer* v. *Liverpool City Council* [1985] Q.B. 1 at 10 (C.A.); *McDonagh* v. *Kent Area Health Authority* (1984) 134 N.L.J. 567; *Smith* v. *Metropolitan Council* (1982) 44 P. & C.R. 171 (C.A.).

"(2) *A person who takes on any such work for another on terms that he is to do it in accordance with instructions given by or on behalf of that other shall, to the extent to which he does it properly in accordance with those instructions, be treated for the purposes of this section as discharging the duty imposed on him by subsection (1) above except where he owes a duty to that other to warn him of any defects in the instructions and fails to discharge that duty.*

(3) A person shall not be treated for the purposes of subsection (2) above as having given instructions for the doing of work merely because he has agreed to the work being done in a specified manner, with specified materials or to a specified design."

There is no definition of the word "instructions" and it is difficult to understand its ambit. Subsection (3) helps in that it contrasts a mere agreement that work shall be done in a specified way with the giving of instructions. At least it seems fairly clear that a person in the position of the purchaser in *Lynch* v. *Thorne*[13] would ordinarily have a remedy under the Act. At the other end of the spectrum a contractor performing work under the Standard Form of Building Contract according to architect's instructions or in accordance with the contract documents is, it is submitted, and subject to the exception as to warning,[14] entitled to the defence provided by subsection (2). Between these extremes it must be a question in each case whether the communication relied on is an instruction or a mere agreement.

The Act does not itself impose a duty of warning and presumably does not refer to a mere moral duty. The result is, it is thought, that the exception as to a duty to warn must refer to a duty arising in contract or conceivably in tort.[15] The extent of an express or implied duty to warn arising under the Standard Form of Building Contract is discussed at page 476.

Persons owing the duty.   Section 1(4) of the Act provides:

"*A person who—*
   (a) *in the course of a business which consists of or includes providing or arranging for the provision of dwellings or installations in dwellings; or*
   (b) *in the exercise of a power of making such provision or arrangements conferred by or by virtue of any enactment;*
arranges for another to take on work for or in connection with the provision of a dwelling shall be treated for the purposes of this section as included among the persons who have taken on the work."

This includes the person often termed "the developer" within the ambit of those who take on work.

Limitation of actions.   Section 1(5) of the Act provides that any cause of action for breach of the duty imposed by the section shall be deemed for

---

[13] [1956] 1 W.L.R. 303 (C.A.), discussed at p. 58.
[14] See below.
[15] See Chap. 7.

limitation purposes to have accrued at the time when the dwelling was completed. If after that time a person who has done work for or in connection with the provision of the dwelling does further work to rectify the work he has already done, any such cause of action in respect of that further work is deemed to have accrued at the time when the further work was finished.[16]

This provides a limitation period which would usually start at a date different from that relevant to a claim in tort.[17]

Continuing duty upon disposal of premises. Section 3 of the Act imposes a continuing duty of care upon persons who have carried out works of construction, repair, maintenance or demolition upon premises after they have disposed of them. There are exceptions to the duty.[18]

Measure of damages. This is not dealt with by the Act. It is thought unlikely that the intention is to exclude economic loss as now understood from damages recoverable under the Act,[19] since the owner of the dwelling can obviously recover the cost of repairing defects in the dwelling resulting from the breach of statutory duty. It is not clear whether consequential economic loss is recoverable.[20]

2. Control of Pollution Act 1974

Noise on construction sites.[21] Part III of the Control of Pollution Act 1974 concerns noise. There are general provisions for summary proceedings to prevent noise amounting to a nuisance.[22] Additionally there are specific provisions for control of noise on construction sites. The local authority is empowered to serve a notice imposing requirements as to the way in which construction works are to be carried out. Notices may in particular specify the plant or machinery which is or is not to be used, the hours during which the works may be carried out and the level of noise which may be emitted. There is a right of appeal to a magistrates' court. A person who contravenes any requirement of the notice without reasonable excuse is guilty of an offence.[23] But there is nothing in the Act which prevents the High Court from imposing by injunction an embargo which is more extensive than that prescribed by a notice under the Act.[24]

---

[16] For limitation generally, see Section 3 of this chapter.

[17] See *Rimmer* v. *Liverpool City Council* [1985] Q.B. 1 at 15 (C.A.).

[18] See also p. 57. The matter is dealt with summarily as it is more suitable to a work on torts; see, *e.g.* Salmond and Heuston, *Torts* (19th ed.), pp. 333 *et seq.*

[19] See "Economic loss" at p. 165.

[20] See "Consequential economic loss" at p. 166.

[21] See generally A. J. Waite "Statutory Controls on Construction Site Noise" (1990) 6 Const.L.J. 97.

[22] See ss.58 and 59 of the Control of Pollution Act 1974.

[23] s.60 of the Control of Pollution Act 1974.

[24] See *Lloyds Bank* v. *Guardian Assurance* (1986) 35 B.L.R. 34 (C.A.); *cf. City of London Corporation* v. *Bovis Construction* (1988) 49 B.L.R. 1 (C.A.).

There are provisions for a person intending to carry out construction work to apply to the local authority for consent, which the local authority may give subject to conditions or limitations. Again there is a right of appeal to a magistrates' court. A person who knowingly carries out works or permits works to be carried out in contravention of any such condition is guilty of an offence.[25] There are also provisions regulating the level of noise which is acceptable emanating from new buildings to which a noise abatement order will apply.[26]

3. Limitation Act 1980 and Latent Damage Act 1986

The Limitation Act 1980 imposes limits of time within which actions must be brought or they become barred. The Act must be referred to for its full effect and in particular there are special provisions for personal injuries which are not discussed in this book.[27] There are ordinary time limits which are in certain instances subject to extension or exclusion.[28] There are important differences between claims in contract and claims in tort. The Act bars a plaintiff's remedy not his cause of action and a defence of limitation must be specifically pleaded.[29] If a defence of limitation is raised, it is initially for the plaintiff to show that his cause of action accrued within the limitation period. If he does so, the burden passes to the defendants to show that the apparent accrual of a cause of action is misleading and that in reality it accrued at an earlier date.[30]

At present an action in the High Court is brought for limitation purposes when the writ is issued.[31] Issuing but not serving a protective writ may not be regarded with judicial favour.[32] A set-off or counterclaim is deemed to have commenced on the same date as the original action.[33]

Contract. The ordinary time limit for an action founded on simple contract is six years from the date on which the cause of action accrues,[34] or 12 years for

---

[25] s.61 of the Control of Pollution Act 1974.

[26] s.67 of the Control of Pollution Act 1974.

[27] For architects and professional men see p. 330.

[28] See s.1 of the Limitation Act 1980. The main extensions and exclusions relevant to building contracts are discussed under "Latent damage," "Fraud, concealment or mistake" and "Claims for contribution" below. See also "Indemnities" below.

[29] *Ronex Properties* v. *John Laing Construction* [1983] Q.B. 398 (C.A.); *Ketteman* v. *Hansel Properties* [1987] A.C. 189 (H.L.); R.S.C., Ord. 18 r. 8(1).

[30] *Cartledge* v. *Jopling* [1962] 1 Q.B. 189 (C.A.) upheld at [1963] A.C. 758 at 784 (H.L.); *London Congregational Union* v. *Harriss* [1988] 1 All E.R. 15 (C.A.); *cf. Perry* v. *Tendring District Council* (1984) 30 B.L.R. 118 at 141.

[31] For third party proceedings, see s.35 of the Limitation Act 1980 and see also "Arbitration" below.

[32] See *Steamship Mutual* v. *Trollope & Colls* (1986) 33 B.L.R. 77 (C.A.). Note also that the period for which a writ is valid for service in the first instance has now been reduced to four months—see amended R.S.C., Ord. 6, r. 8(1).

[33] s.35 of the Limitation Act 1980.

[34] s.5 of the Limitation Act 1980.

a contract by deed.[35] Time runs from the date of breach and not from its discovery.[36] If a person liable or accountable for a debt or other liquidated pecuniary claim acknowledges the claim in writing or makes any payment in respect of it, the right is treated as having accrued on and not before the date of the acknowledgement or payment.[37]

Where a contractor is liable under an entire contract to complete works, the limitation period for defects runs, it is submitted, from the date of completion or purported completion, and not from any earlier date when that part of the works, the subject-matter of the defects, was carried out. It is thought that this also applies to a contract where payment is by instalments but the contractor's obligation is to carry out *and complete* the works. For breaches by the employer, time runs from the breach, so that, for example, if drawings and instructions are not supplied at the proper time, it runs, it is submitted, from the date when they should have been supplied. A set-off which is a defence to the claim cannot be defeated by a period of limitation not applicable to the claim.[38]

Tort. The ordinary time limit for an action founded on tort is six years from the date on which the cause of action accrues.[39] It seems that the same time limit applies to an action for breach of statutory duty.[40] For negligence claims, where damage is an essential ingredient, the cause of action accrues when the damage occurs.[41] It does not accrue when the negligent act is committed if damage does not then also occur. Nor does the cause of action accrue when the damage is discovered or should with reasonable diligence have been discovered.[42]

The damage which is necessary to found an action in negligence is normally actual physical injury to person or property other than property which is the product of the negligence.[43] In most instances there will be no difficulty in determining when such damage occurs. Cases on this topic decided before the counter-revolution referred to in the opening paragraph of Chapter 7 are thought to be obsolete (if not wrongly decided), unless perhaps they remain relevant either to claims in tort for professional negligence, or unless the

---

[35] s.8 of the Limitation Act 1980.
[36] *Gibbs* v. *Guild* (1881) 8 Q.B.D. 296 at 302; *Cartledge* v. *Jopling* (*E. & Sons*) *Ltd.* [1963] A.C. 758 at 782 (H.L.); *Bagot* v. *Stevens Scanlan & Co. Ltd.* [1966] 1 Q.B. 197.
[37] See ss.29, 30 and 31 of the Limitation Act 1980.
[38] *Henriksens Rederi A/S* v. *Rolimpex* [1974] 1 Q.B. 233 (C.A.); see also *Tersons* v. *Alec Colman Investments* (1973) 225 E.G. 230 (C.A.).
[39] s.2 of the Limitation Act 1980.
[40] See "Limitation of actions" at p. 364 for the time limit for a claim under the Defective Premises Act 1972.
[41] See *Pirelli* v. *Oscar Faber & Partners* [1983] 2 A.C. 1 (H.L.). This is subject to ss.14A and 14B of the Limitation Act 1980 and the Latent Damage Act 1986—see below.
[42] *Pirelli* v. *Oscar Faber & Partners* [1983] 2 A.C. 1 (H.L.).
[43] See generally Chap. 7.

"complex structure theory" can found a negligence claim where the damage is other than catastrophic.[44]

A cause of action for negligent misstatement or advice may accrue when the plaintiff acts on the statement or advice to his potential future detriment even if the actual financial loss occurs at a later date,[45] but it is a question of fact in each case when the damage occurs.[46] A cause of action against a surveyor for a negligent survey has been held to arise when the plaintiff relies on the survey report by committing himself to acquiring the property.[47] If the result of a negligent misstatement is physical damage, it seems that the cause of action accrues when that damage occurs.[48]

Latent damage.   The Latent Damage Act 1986 amended the Limitation Act 1980 in the light of dissatisfaction resulting from *Pirelli* v. *Oscar Faber & Partners*.[49] It had there been held that the date of accrual of a cause of action in tort caused by the negligent design or construction of a building was the date when the damage came into existence, and not the date when the damage was discovered or could with reasonable diligence have been discovered. The amendments effected by the Act extend the limitation period, for claims in tort but not in contract,[50] by three years starting from the date when the plaintiff had both the knowledge required for bringing an action for damages in respect of the relevant damage and a right to bring such an action. There is an overriding time limit for actions for negligence (other than for personal injury) of 15 years from the act of negligence to which the damage is alleged to be attributed.[51] Difficulties were also appreciated with successive owners, to

---

[44] For "Professional negligence," see p. 172 where it is suggested that the law needs reconsideration. The "complex structure theory" was mooted in *D. & F. Estates* v. *Church Commissioners* [1989] A.C. 177 (H.L.) and considered in *Murphy* v. *Brentwood District Council* [1990] 3 W.L.R. 414 (H.L.) and is discussed under "Other property" at p. 164. The "obsolete" cases include *Dove* v. *Banhams Patent Locks* [1983] 1 W.L.R. 1436; *Tozer Kemsley* v. *J. Jarvis & Sons* (1983) 4 Con.L.R. 24; *Chelmsford District Council* v. *Evers* (1983) 25 B.L.R. 99; *Kensington and Chelsea* v. *Wettern Composites* (1984) 31 B.L.R. 57; *London Borough of Bromley* v. *Rush & Tompkins* (1985) 35 B.L.R. 94; *Ketteman* v. *Hansel Properties* [1987] A.C. 189 (H.L.); *London Congregational Union* v. *Harriss* [1988] 1 All E.R. 15 (C.A.); *University of Glasgow* v. *Whitfield* (1988) 42 B.L.R. 66; numerous cases against local authorities directly based upon *Anns* v. *Merton London Borough Council* [1978] A.C. 728 (H.L) and now overruled by *Murphy* v. *Brentwood District Council* [1990] 2 W.L.R. 414 (H.L.).

[45] See *Forster* v. *Outred & Co.* [1982] 1 W.L.R. 86 (C.A.); *D. W. Moore & Co.* v. *Ferrier* [1988] 1 W.L.R. 267 (C.A.); *Bell* v. *Peter Browne & Co.* [1990] 3 W.L.R. 510 (C. A.); *cf. Midland Bank Trust Co.* v. *Hett, Stubbs & Kemp* [1979] Ch. 384; *Iron Trade Mutual Insurance* v. *J. K. Buckenham* [1990] 1 All E.R. 808.

[46] *D. W. Moore & Co* v. *Ferrier* [1988] 1 W.L.R. 267 (C.A.).

[47] *Secretary of State for the Environment* v. *Essex Goodman & Suggitt* [1986] 1 W.L.R. 1432. This was a claim in tort by a client who also had a contract with the surveyors, and it is suggested under "Professional negligence" at p. 172 that such a claim needs reconsideration.

[48] See *Pirelli* v. *Oscar Faber & Partners* [1983] 2 A.C. 1 (H.L.); *cf. Dove* v. *Banhams Patent Locks* [1983] 1 W.L.R. 1436.

[49] [1983] 2 A.C. 1 (H.L.).

[50] *Iron Trade Mutual Insurance* v. *J. K. Buckenham* [1990] 1 All E.R. 808.

[51] See ss.14A and 14B of the Limitation Act 1980 as amended. The sections do not apply if there is deliberate concealment within s.32(1)(b) of the 1980 Act—see s.32(5).

whom the Latent Damage Act in certain circumstances gives a fresh cause of action.[52]

The Latent Damage Act was passed upon an understanding of the law before the counter-revolution referred to in the opening paragraph of Chapter 7. It now seems that the main provisions will have little effect in building contract cases, since the kind of damage with which it was intended to deal is damage for which there is now no cause of action, *i.e.* damage to the building itself and damage which, once it becomes known, is irrecoverable economic loss.[53] The Act is capable of applying to claims for negligent misstatement or advice where the plaintiff was for a time unaware of the fact or consequences of the defendant's negligence.[54] It could apply generally to claims for professional negligence, but would not do so if the views expressed under "Professional negligence" at page 172 are correct.[55] It might also apply if the "complex structure theory" can found a negligence claim where the damage is other than catastrophic.[56] One incidental consequence of the Act in the present state of the law is to impose an overriding time limit of 15 years for negligence claims other than those for personal injury irrespective, it seems, of latent damage.

Consumer Protection Act 1987.   There are special limitation provisions for actions for damages by virtue of Part I of the Consumer Protection Act 1987.[57]

Fraud, concealment or mistake.   Section 32 of the Limitation Act 1980 provides that where the action is based upon the fraud of the defendant, or any fact relevant to the plaintiff's right of action has been deliberately concealed from him by the defendant, or the action is for relief from the consequence of a mistake, the period of limitation does not begin to run until the plaintiff has discovered the fraud, concealment or mistake or could with reasonable diligence have discovered it.[58] The deliberate commission of a breach of duty in circumstances in which it is unlikely to be discovered for some time amounts to deliberate concealment of the facts involved in that breach of duty.[59]

The statutory provisions relating to deliberate concealment were a reformulation of provisions in section 26 of the Limitation Act 1939, which referred to a cause of action being "concealed by the fraud" of the defendant. This had been interpreted by the court in terms of the 1980 reformulation.[60] Thus in *Clark* v.

---

[52] See s.3 of the Latent Damage Act; *Perry* v. *Tendring District Council* (1984) 30 B.L.R. 118.
[53] See generally Chap. 7.
[54] See *Iron Trade Mutual Insurance* v. *J. K. Buckenham* [1990] 1 All E.R. 808; *Bell* v. *Peter Browne & Co.* [1990] 2 W.L.R. 510 (C.A.).
[55] See however *Iron Trade Mutual Insurance* v. *J. K. Buckenham* [1990] 1 All E.R. 808.
[56] See "Other property" at p. 164.
[57] s.11A of the Limitation Act 1980 as inserted by s.6(6) and Sched. 1 of the Consumer Protection Act 1987. See "Product liability" at p. 351.
[58] For reasonable diligence, see *Peco Arts* v. *Hazlitt Gallery* [1983] 1 W.L.R. 1315—a case of mistake.
[59] s.32(2) of the Limitation Act 1980.
[60] See *King* v. *Victor Parsons & Co.* [1973] 1 W.L.R. 29 (C.A.).

Woor,[61] the plaintiffs, who knew nothing of building and had no architect or other person to supervise the works, relied on the defendant, a builder, to treat them in a decent, honest way in building them a house with best Dorking bricks. The defendant, an experienced bricklayer, could not get Dorking bricks and substituted without the plaintiffs' knowledge Ockley bricks containing a substantial portion of seconds which failed after eight years. It was held that there was that special relationship between the parties which brought the defendant's behaviour within the meaning of fraud as it was used in the 1939 Act so that the plaintiffs were not barred by expiry of time.

These principles were subsequently developed in the Court of Appeal. Thus, it was said that "if a builder does his work badly, so that it is likely to give rise to trouble thereafter, and then covers up his bad work so that it is not discovered for some years, then he cannot rely on the statute as a bar to the claim.[62] The concealment must be deliberate or reckless "like the man who turns a blind eye."[63] But mere shoddy or incompetent work which was subsequently covered up in the due succession of building work was not sufficient. The conscience of the defendant had to be affected so that it was unconscionable for the defendant to proceed with the work without putting it right.[64] It was not sufficient, in the absence of very special circumstances, that the defendant ought to have known the fact or facts which constituted the cause of action against him, if he did not have actual knowledge.[65] But knowledge could be inferred from the evidence.[66] The mere existence of professional supervision and inspection on behalf of the employer did not prevent an issue of fact arising whether there had been fraudulent concealment.[67]

In a case decided under the 1980 Act, a contractor hacked back concrete nibs supposed to support brickwork and took deliberate steps to conceal what was going on from the architect, engineer and clerk of works. The contractor was held to have deliberately concealed facts relevant to the plaintiff employer's right of action so as to postpone the start of the limitation period until the time when a bulge in the brickwork resulting from the hacking was discovered.[68] In another case, there was an equivalent finding in relation to defective joists, lack of bedding for drains and defective foundations.[69] But an architect who, in designing foundations for a bungalow, deliberately rejected current wisdom as idealistic and took a risk which he could not rationally

---

[61] [1965] 1 W.L.R. 650.
[62] *Applegate* v. *Moss* [1971] 1 Q.B. 406 at 413 (C.A.), where it was held that a developer was liable for the fraud of his contractor.
[63] *King* v. *Victor Parsons & Co.* [1973] 1 W.L.R. 29 at 34 (C.A.).
[64] *William Hill Organisation* v. *Bernard Sunley & Sons* (1982) 22 B.L.R. 1 (C.A.); *cf. London Borough of Lewisham* v. *Leslie & Co.* (1978) 12 B.L.R. 22 (C.A.).
[65] *King* v. *Victor Parsons & Co.* [1973] 1 W.L.R. 29 at 36 (C.A.).
[66] *Ibid.*
[67] *London Borough of Lewisham* v. *Leslie & Co.* (1978) 12 B.L.R. 22 (C.A.); *cf. William Hill Organisation* v. *Bernard Sunley & Sons* (1982) 22 B.L.R. 1 (C.A.).
[68] *Gray* v. *T. P. Bennett & Son* (1987) 43 B.L.R. 63.
[69] *Kijowski* v. *New Capital Properties* (1987) 15 Con.L.R. 1—this is, however, in other respects an "obsolete" case in the terms of n. 44 above.

justify was held to have made an "honest blunder" and not to have been guilty of deliberate concealment.[70]

Indemnities.[71]   Where there is an obligation to indemnify against loss, the cause of action does not arise until the loss has been established,[72] so that the limitation period runs from the date when the liability or loss indemnified against is established or incurred.[73] This may be after the expiry of the ordinary limitation period.

Claims for contribution.   Claims to recover contribution under section 1 of the Civil Liability (Contribution) Act 1978 are barred after two years from the date on which the right to contribution accrues. Such a right accrues when a judgment is given or an arbitration award made for the relevant damage against the person claiming contribution or, if there is no judgment or award, on the date when he agrees with the recipient the amount to be paid.[74]

Amendments.[75]   Amendments to add or substitute a new claim[76] may only be made after the expiry of a relevant limitation period if the new cause of action arises out of the same or substantially the same facts as are already in issue in the original action.[77] Such an amendment ordinarily takes effect from the date of the original document which it amends, but the court may exceptionally allow an amendment on terms, such as that it shall take effect from a specified later date.[78] Whether or not a proposed amendment would introduce a new claim is a mixed question of fact and law and a matter of degree. Whether or not a new cause of action arises out of the same or substantially the same facts is also a question of degree.[79] In a case where an original claim alleged defects in an airconditioning system, leave to amend after the expiry of the limitation period to add claims alleging defects in the walls of the same

---

[70] *Kaliszewska* v. *John Clague & Partners* (1984) 5 Con.L.R.

[71] For indemnities generally, see p. 62.

[72] *Collinge* v. *Hayward* (1839) 9 Ad. & El. 633 and other cases cited in *Halsbury* (4th ed.), Vol. 20, para. 315; *County & District Properties* v. *C. Jenner & Son Ltd.* [1976] 2 Lloyd's Rep. 728.

[73] *R. & H. Green & Silley Wier* v. *British Railways Board* (1980) 17 B.L.R. 94; *Telfair Shipping Corporation* v. *Inersea Carriers* [1985] 1 W.L.R. 553; *cf. National House-Building Council* v. *Fraser* (1982) 22 B.L.R. 143.

[74] s.10 of the Limitation Act 1980.

[75] For amendments generally, see R.S.C., Ord. 20 and the notes in the Supreme Court Practice 1991.

[76] See "Causes of action" at p. 431.

[77] s.35(3), (4) and (5) of the Limitation Act 1980 in effect adopting the narrower approach of Edmund Davies and Cross L. JJ. in *Brickfield Properties* v. *Newton* [1971] 1 W.L.R. 862 at 879 and 881 (C.A.); R.S.C., Ord. 20, r. 5(5).

[78] *Liverpool Roman Catholic Archdiocesan Trustees* v. *Gibberd* (1986) 7 Con.L.R. 113 exercising powers in R.S.C., Ord. 20 rule 8; *cf. Tilcon* v. *Land and Real Estate Investments* [1987] 1 W.L.R. 46 (C.A.).

[79] *Steamship Mutual* v. *Trollope & Colls* (1986) 33 B.L.R. 77 (C.A.) considering *Conquer* v. *Boot* [1928] 2 K.B. 336 (C.A.), *Brickfield Properties* v. *Newton* [1971] 1 W.L.R. 862 (C.A.), *Idyll* v. *Dineman Davison* (1971) 1 Const.L.J. 294 (C.A.) and *Circle Thirty-Three Housing Trust* v. *Fairview Estates* (1984) 8 Con.L.R. 1 (C.A.).

building was refused.[80] Leave to amend may be refused if allowing the amendment would cause injustice.[81]

A new party may be added or substituted if this is necessary for the determination of the original action.[82] If this occurs, time ceases to run against the new party from the date of joinder which will normally be the date when the new defendant is served.[83]

Arbitration.   The Limitation Act 1980 and any other limitation enactments apply to arbitrations as they apply to actions in the High Court.[84] For limitation purposes an arbitration is treated as being commenced when one party serves on the other a notice requiring him to appoint or agree to the appointment of an arbitrator or requiring the dispute to be referred to a person named or designated in the agreement. There are provisions for serving the notice.[85] A notice of arbitration is thus an important document for limitation purposes and care should be taken with its drafting and service. The time limit for an action to enforce an arbitrator's award is six years from the date of failure to honour the award.[86]

4. Building Act 1984 and the Building Regulations[87]

The Public Health Acts 1875 and 1936 enabled local authorities to make by-laws regulating the construction of buildings. There were model by-laws which many local authorities adopted with or without changes or additions. The Public Health Act 1961 provided for the replacement of local building by-laws by the Building Regulations which, when they came into force in 1966, applied throughout England and Wales with the exception of Inner London for which the London Building Acts remained in force. The current consolidating statute is the Building Act 1984 and the current Building Regulations are the Building Regulations 1985[88] (which came into force on November 11, 1985) and the Building Regulations (Amendment) Regulations 1989[89] (which came into force on April 1, 1990). The Public Health Act 1936 remains in force in relation to drains and sewers. Certain buildings are or may be exempt from the Building Regulations,[90] and a requirement of the Building Regulations may be relaxed or dispensed with upon application to the Secretary of State.[91]

---

[80] *Steamship Mutual* v. *Trollope & Colls* (1986) 33 B.L.R. 77 (C.A.).
[81] *Woodspring District Council* v. *J. A. Venn Ltd.* (1985) 5 Con.L.R. 54.
[82] s.35(5) of the Limitation Act 1980.
[83] *Ketteman* v. *Hansel Properties* [1987] A.C. 189 (H.L.).
[84] s.34(1) of the Limitation Act 1980.
[85] s.34(3) and (4) of the Limitation Act 1980.
[86] s.7 of the Limitation Act 1980; *Agromet Motoimport* v. *Maulden Engineering* [1985] 1 W.L.R. 762.
[87] See generally Knight's *Building Control Law* and Knight's *Building Regulations*; Powell-Smith and Billington, *The Building Regulations* (7th ed.).
[88] S.I. 1985 No. 1065. See also Karen Gough, "The Building Regulations 1985: Something New or More of the Same?" (1986) 2 Const.L.J. 262.
[89] S.I. 1989 No. 1119.
[90] ss.3–5 inclusive of the Building Act 1984.
[91] ss.8–11 inclusive of the Building Act 1984.

Inner London has now largely been brought within the national system,[92] but certain provisions of the London Building Acts remain in force.[93] Additionally the provisions of Part VI of the London Building Acts (Amendment) Act 1939 relating to the rights of building and adjoining owners and comprising the procedure for settling difference by the award of three (if necessary) surveyors remain in force.

For the purpose of providing practical guidance with respect to the requirements of any provision of Building Regulations, there is provision for approved documents.[94] A failure to comply with an approved document does not of itself render a person liable to civil or criminal proceedings, but compliance or otherwise with an approved document may be relied on as tending to negative or establish liability.[95]

Passing or rejection of plans. Where plans of any proposed work are deposited, it is generally the duty of the local authority to pass the plans unless they are defective or show that the proposed work would contravene any of the Building Regulations. If they are so defective, the local authority may reject them or pass them conditionally by request or consent in writing. Where deposited plans are accompanied by a certificate of compliance given by an approved person and prescribed evidence that an approved scheme applies or of prescribed insurance, the local authority may not generally reject the plans on the ground of non-compliance with the Building Regulations.[96]

Supervision. Where the work is to be supervised by the local authority, there is a prescribed system for giving notices to the local authority at certain stages of the construction so that inspections may be made.[97] There is a parallel system in Part II of the Building Act 1984 for supervision of building works by approved inspectors such as N.H.B.C. Building Control Services Limited, a wholly owned subsidiary of the N.H.B.C.[98]

Contravention. A person contravening the Building Regulations is liable on summary conviction to a fine not exceeding level 5 on the standard scale

---

[92] See the Building Regulations (Inner London) Regulations 1985 and 1987 (S.I. 1985 No. 1936 and S.I. 1987 No. 798).

[93] For details, see Knight's *Building Control Law*, pp. 280 *et seq.*

[94] s.6 of the Building Act 1984.

[95] s.7 of the Building Act 1984.

[96] s.16 of the Building Act 1984. For approval of persons and schemes, see s.17. See John Dyson Q.C. and John Bishop, "The Potential Liability of Local Authorities and 'Approved Inspectors' after *Peabody* and the 1984 Act" (1985) 1 Const.L.J. 264.

[97] See Regulation 14. For a discussion of the practicalities of determining the legal meaning of expressions in the Building Regulations, see *Worlock* v. *SAWS* (1982) 22 B.L.R. 66 (C.A.), but note that this case generally must be read in the light of *Murphy* v. *Brentwood District Council* [1990] 3 W.L.R. 414 (H.L.).

[98] See *NHBC Building Control* v. *Sandwell Borough Council* (1990) 50 B.L.R. 101 (C.A.); see also John Dyson Q.C. and John Bishop, "The Potential Liability of Local Authorities and 'Approved Inspectors' after *Peabody* and the 1984 Act" (1985) 1 Const.L.J. 264. For a case on an earlier version of the N.H.B.C. scheme and still of some application see *Marchant* v. *Casewell & Redgrave and the N.H.B.R.C.* (1976) J.P.L. 752.

(currently £2000) and to a further fine not exceeding £50 for each day on which the default continues.[99] The local authority may by notice require removal or alteration of offending work, and this power does not affect the right of the local authority, the Attorney General or any other person to apply for an injunction for the removal or alteration of any work on the ground that it contravenes any regulation or any provision of the Act.[1]

Civil liability of builder.[2]   Section 38 of the Building Act 1984 provides that, subject to the provisions of the section, breach of a duty imposed by building regulations, shall, so far as it causes damage, be actionable except in so far as the regulations provide otherwise. There is provision for the regulations to provide prescribed defences. Liability does not arise until a regulation is made bringing the section into force and this had not yet been done.[3] It will be necessary to consider the regulations when they appear, in particular the prescribed defences but the effect could be to provide for a very wide range of matters for which civil proceedings can be brought. Actions under the Act may well effectively supersede those under the Defective Premises Act 1972 and must be considered in relation to actions for breach of contract.

Apart from potential statutory civil liability, a contractor who builds in contravention of the Building Regulations may, depending on its terms, be in breach of his contract with the employer. This might be so if there was an unqualified term, such as existed in early versions of the 1963 Standard Form of Building Contract, obliging the contractor to comply with statutory requirements.[4] If there is no such express term, a contravention of the Building Regulations might be strong evidence that the contractor was in breach of an express or implied obligation of good workmanship or, possibly, of fitness for purpose. The court might alternatively imply a term that the contractor would build lawfully in accordance with the Regulations.[5] Where the contractor builds in accordance with the contractual design but in contravention of the Building Regulations, his liability may turn on whether he was aware of the contravention.[6] Where such a contravention is inadvertent, the 1980 Standard Form of Building Contract provides that the contractor is not to be liable to the Employer.[7] Contravention of the Building Regulations may be evidence of

---

[99] s.35 of the Building Act 1984.
[1] s.36 of the Building Act 1984 and, for injunctions, s.36(6); *cf. Gouriet* v. *Union of Post Office Workers* [1978] A.C. 435 (H.L.); *Ashby* v. *Ebdon* [1985] Ch. 394.
[2] See generally Donald Keating Q.C., "Breach of Building Regulations" by (1984) 1 Const.L.J. 87, but disregard the passage headed "Tortious liability" in the light of *Murphy* v. *Brentwood District Council* [1990] 3 W.L.R. 414 (H.L.).
[3] The section came into force for the purpose only of enabling regulations to be made on December 1, 1984—see s.134 of the Act.
[4] See *Townsend (Builders)* v. *Cinema News* [1959] 1 W.L.R. 119 (C.A.) more fully reported at 20 B.L.R. 118 (C.A.); *Acrecrest* v. *Hattrell* [1983] Q.B. 260 at 267 (C.A.); *Equitable Debenture Assets Corporation* v. *William Moss* (1984) 2 Con.L.R. 1.
[5] See also "Effect of Building Regulations" at p. 87.
[6] See *Equitable Debenture Assets Corporation* v. *William Moss* (1984) 2 Con.L.R. 1.
[7] See clause 6.1.5 at p. 502.

want of care by the contractor but, apart from contract, the builder of a house or other structure is liable at common law for negligence only where actual damage, either to person or property other than the building or structure itself, results from carelessness on his part in the course of construction.[8]

Breach of statutory duty.[9] Although section 38(3) of the Building Act 1984 appears to contemplate the possibility at least of an actionable breach of duty apart from the section, it appears that there is no common law liability for breach of statutory duty (as distinct from the limited liability in negligence referred to above) independent from that potentially available under section 38 of the Act.[10] "[T]here is nothing in the terms or purpose of the statutory provisions which support the creation of a private law right of action for breach of statutory duty."[11] It is thought that the very existence of section 38 is against such an independent right of action.

Liability of local authority. A local authority is not generally liable either to an original or subsequent owner for the cost of repairing a building which is defective in breach of the Building Regulations.[12] The approval of plans and the inspection of a building in the course of construction by the local authority in performance of their statutory function do not introduce the principle of reliance by a subsequent purchaser sufficient to found a duty of care.[13] It is an open question whether a local authority might be liable in negligence for

---

[8] *D. & F. Estates* v. *Church Commissioners* [1989] A.C. 177 (H.L.). For a fuller account, see generally Chap. 7. See also the Consumer Protection Act 1987 discussed in Chap. 14, Section 2.

[9] See generally R. A. Buckley, "Liability in Tort for Breach of Statutory Duty" (1984) 100 L.Q.R. 204.

[10] This is still not absolutely clear. The state of the law before *Murphy* v. *Brentwood District Council* [1990] 3 W.L.R. 414 (H.L.), quoted in the next sentence of the text, on whether breach of the Building Regulations *per se* gave rise to a liability in damages was reviewed in *Perry* v. *Tendring District Council* (1984) 30 B.L.R. 118 where it was held on conflicting authority that it did not. The reference in *Perry* to *Taylor Woodrow Construction* v. *Charcon Structure* is now at (1982) 7 Con.L.R. 1 at 12 (C.A.). See also *Dorset Yacht Co.* v. *Home Office* [1970] A.C. 1004 at 1030 (H.L.); *D. & F. Estates* v. *Church Commissioners* [1989] A.C. 177 at 214A (H.L.) where Lord Oliver seems to contemplate the possibility of an independant claim for breach of statutory duty; *Acrecrest* v. *Hattrell* [1983] Q.B. 260 at 267 (C.A.); and see generally *Lonrho* v. *Shell Petroleum* [1982] A.C. 173 (H.L.).

[11] Lord Oliver in *Murphy* v. *Brentwood District Council* [1990] 3 W.L.R. 414 at 449 (H.L.). This sentence is prefaced by the words "*ex hypothesi*," but it is not entirely clear what this refers to. See also his reference to claim for breach of statutory duty at 443, and see Lord Mackay L.C. at 419 and Lord Bridge at 441.

[12] *Murphy* v. *Brentwood District Council* [1990] 3 W.L.R. 414 (H.L.) departing from *Anns* v. *Merton London Borough Council* [1978] A.C. 728 (H.L.) and overruling *Dutton* v. *Bognor Regis Urban District Council* [1972] 1 Q.B. 373 (C.A.); *cf. Peabody Donation Fund* v. *Sir Lindsay Parkinson* [1985] A.C. 210 (H.L.). *Murphy* does not explicitly deal with original owners, but in the absence of a sufficient contract with the local authority to support a claim, it is thought that their position is the same as that of subsequent owners. See further Chap. 7 generally and in particular "Local authorities" at p. 168.

[13] See *Murphy* v. *Brentwood District Council* [1990] 3 W.L.R. 414 at 441, 443 (H.L.).

carelessly passing defective plans or for careless inspection of building works if this causes physical damage to person or property.[14]

5. Insolvency Act 1986

(a) *Insolvency generally*

The term insolvency is used here to cover bankruptcy and the winding up of insolvent companies both of which are now mainly covered by the Insolvency Act 1986. This Act repealed and replaced the Bankruptcy Act 1914 and consolidated with modifications certain provisions of the Insolvency Act 1985 and the Companies Act 1985. In general the same rules apply to personal and corporate insolvency but there are certain differences some of which are referred to below. No exposition is given of bankruptcy or winding up in general, for which reference should be made to the standard textbooks,[15] but attention is drawn here to some matters particularly relevant to building contracts.

Upon insolvency, subject to provisions as to preferential payments, the insolvent's liabilities are paid in full unless the assets are insufficient to meet them, in which case the liabilities abate in equal proportions between themselves.[16] "A man is not allowed, by a stipulation with a creditor, to provide for a different distribution of his effects in the event of bankruptcy from that which the law provides."[17] The court will not give effect to such a stipulation even where it is part of arrangements and the parties "had good business reasons for entering into them and did not direct their minds to the question how the arrangements might be affected by the insolvency of one or more of the parties."[18]

Control by the court.   Every bankruptcy is under the general control of the court and the court has full power, subject to the provisions of the Insolvency Act 1986, to decide all questions of priorities and all other questions, whether of law or fact, arising in any bankruptcy.[19]

---

[14] The builder is liable in negligence for physical injury to person or property caused by his carelessness—see, *e.g.* Lord Keith in *Murphy* v. *Brentwood District Council* [1990] 2 W.L.R. 414 at 424 (H.L.)—the liability of the local authority is not greater than that of the builder but it may not be co-extensive. In *Murphy*, the local authority appear to have conceded a limited duty of care, but Lord Mackay L.C. (at 419), Lord Keith (at 425) and Lord Jauncey (at 451) all reserved the question.

[15] *e.g. Williams and Hunter on Bankruptcy*; *Muir Hunter on Personal Insolvency*; *Buckley on Companies*; *Palmer's Company Law.*

[16] See ss.107 and 328(3) of the Insolvency Act 1986 and 4.181 of the Insolvency Rules 1986.

[17] James L.J. in *Ex p. Mackay* (1873) 8 Ch.App. 643 at 647 applied to companies in *British Eagle* v. *Air France* [1975] 1 W.L.R. 758 (H.L.).

[18] See *British Eagle* v. *Air France* [1975] 1 W.L.R. 758 at 780 (H.L.); *cf.* however "Equitable assignment" at p. 277.

[19] s.363(1) of the Insolvency Act 1986.

This power, in its former statutory form, was exercised where, after the contractor's bankruptcy, direct payment of a provisional sum was made to a subcontractor upon the latter giving the employer an indemnity against any claim by the contractor's trustee. There was apparently no express right of direct payment. The contractor's trustee applied to the architect for a certificate for the amount of the provisional sum and it was refused. It was held that the court had jurisdiction to order the architect to make such a certificate, and an order was made leaving the subcontractor to prove in the bankruptcy.[20] There is no comparable express general power on a winding up,[21] but on these facts, the court could, it is thought, declare that the payment was not in accordance with the contract and require the employer to account to the liquidator for the sum paid.

Vesting of property.   All the property belonging to or vested in a bankrupt at the commencement of the bankruptcy vests in his trustee in bankruptcy to be distributed among his creditors.[22] The bankruptcy commences on the day on which the order is made and continues until the individual is discharged.[23] The trustee may also claim for the bankrupt's estate property which has been acquired by, or has devolved upon, the bankrupt after the commencement of the bankruptcy.[24] The former provisions of s.38(c) of the Bankruptcy Act 1914 relating to reputed ownership are not reproduced in the Insolvency Act 1986 and the doctrine is accordingly abolished.[25]

In a winding up, there is no automatic vesting of the property. The liquidator takes the company's property into his custody or under his control unless there is an order of the court vesting the property in the liquidator.[26]

Stay of proceedings—winding up by the court.   "When a winding-up order has been made or a provisional liquidator has been appointed, no action or proceedings shall be proceeded with or commenced against the company or its property, except by leave of the court and subject to such terms as the court may impose."[27]

(b) *Insolvency of contractor*

Upon the contractor's bankruptcy the benefit and burden of the contract

---

[20] *Re Holt, ex p. Gray* (1888) 58 L.J.Q.B. 5 (D.C.).
[21] See ss.147–160 of the Insolvency Act 1986.
[22] See s.283 of the Insolvency Act 1986 which defines the bankrupt's estate and s.306 for vesting in the trustee immediately on his appointment taking effect. For definition of property, see s.463.
[23] See s.278 of the Insolvency Act 1986; see also s.284 for restrictions on dispositions between the day of the presentation of the petition and the vesting.
[24] See s.307 of the Insolvency Act 1986.
[25] See *Muir Hunter on Personal Insolvency*, para. 3–145. A discussion on reputed ownership relating in particular to unfixed materials in building contracts appeared at p. 191 of the 4th edition of this book to which reference can, if necessary, be made.
[26] See ss.144 and 145 of the Insolvency Act 1986.
[27] s.130(2) of the Insolvency Act 1986. See generally ss.117–160.

passes, subject to the effect of any valid forfeiture clause, to his trustee in bankruptcy unless the contract is personal. In the latter case the trustee cannot complete, but if the contractor completes, the contract moneys are payable to, and recoverable by, the contractor's trustee.[28] In a winding up the contract remains vested in the company and the liquidator may "carry on the business of the company so far as may be necessary for its beneficial winding up."[29]

Disclaimer. The trustee has a power to disclaim any onerous property including any unprofitable contract.[30] There is no longer a specific time limit for the exercise of this power[31] but any person interested may apply in writing to the trustee requiring him to decide whether he will disclaim or not and if he does not give a notice of disclaimer within 28 days or such further time as the court may allow[32] he will be deemed to have adopted the contract.[33] The effect of disclaimer is to bring the contract to an end from the date of disclaimer and the employer can thereupon prove in the bankruptcy for his prospective loss.[34] The liquidator has a similar power to disclaim.[35] There are special provisions relating to disclaimer of leaseholds and dwelling houses.[36]

Completion. If the trustee or liquidator adopts the contract and decides to complete, he steps into the shoes of the contractor and takes the contract and the contractor's property subject to the rights of the employer unless they contravene the bankruptcy law.[37] Thus if the trustee in completing is guilty of delay or other default giving rise to a right of forfeiture, the right can be validly exercised against him.[38]

The trustee when completing becomes personally liable on the contract.[39] The liquidator is not normally personally liable.[40]

---

[28] *Emden* v. *Carte* (1881) 17 Ch.D. 768 (C.A.).

[29] Insolvency Act 1986, ss.165(3) and 167(1) and Sched. 4, Pt. II; *cf.* for the trustee's powers, s.314 and Sched. 5. In carrying on the business the liquidator is not ordinarily personally responsible: *Stead Hazel* v. *Cooper* [1933] 1 K.B. 840; neither is a receiver if he does not enter into any new contract, but he is liable upon any new contract: Insolvency Act 1986, s.37; *Re Mack Trucks (Britain) Ltd.* [1967] 1 All E.R. 977.

[30] Insolvency Act 1986, s.315; *Re Bastable* [1901] 2 K.B. 518 (C.A.); *cf.* for receivers *Freevale* v. *Metrostore Holdings* [1984] Ch. 199.

[31] Formerly the disclaimer had to be within 12 months of the trustee's appointment or within 12 months of knowledge of the contract if it does not come within his knowledge within a month of his appointment—s.54 of the Bankruptcy Act 1914 (repealed).

[32] For extension of time limits, see s.376 of the Insolvency Act 1986.

[33] s.316 of the Insolvency Act 1986.

[34] s.315(3) and (5) of the Insolvency Act 1986; see further *Williams on Bankruptcy.*

[35] s.178 of the Insolvency Act 1986.

[36] ss.179, 317 and 318 of the Insolvency Act 1986.

[37] *Re Garrud, ex p. Newitt* (1881) 16 Ch.D. 522 at 531 (C.A.); *Bendall* v. *McWhirter* [1952] 2 Q.B. 466 at 487 (C.A.).

[38] *Re Keen, ex p. Collins* [1902] 1 K.B. 555 (D.C.); see also *Re Waugh* (1876) 4 Ch.D. 524; *Re Garrud, ex p. Newitt* (1881) 16 Ch.D. 522 (C.A.).

[39] *Titterton* v. *Cooper* (1882) 9 Q.B.D. 473 (C.A.). He has a right to recoup himself from the assets of the estate. For the liability of a debenture-holder's receiver for a defendant's costs of an action continued by the receiver after a compulsory winding-up order had been made, see *Bacal Contracting* v. *Modern Engineering* [1980] 2 All E.R. 645.

[40] See n. 29 above.

Where there is a provision which by its nature cannot be performed by the trustee or by the company, as where a company in liquidation was under an obligation to keep the works in repair for 15 years, the court may presume that the obligation cannot be carried out and allow the employer to prove his prospective damages.[41] These damages may be set off against payments and retention money due to the contractor upon completion.[42]

The trustee may, with the sanction of the creditors' committee, refer any dispute to arbitration.[43] The liquidator in a voluntary winding up may do so without sanction but in a winding up by the court requires the sanction of the court or of the liquidation committee.[44]

Mutual dealings.   If the employer is in possession of retention money or otherwise owes money to the contractor he can, subject to the provisions of the Insolvency Act 1986, set off against it any claims he proves against the contractor.[45] The statutory set-off, which is mandatory,[46] is not limited to dealings arising out of contract and can extend to taxes where a rebate is due.[47] It also extends to claims in contract for unliquidated damages.[48] But where money is held for a special or specific purpose inconsistent with the right of set-off the provisions do not apply. This arose where an employer under a building contract held retention money as trustee for nominated subcontractors.[49]

Forfeiture, lien and seizure clauses.   Most contracts contain clauses purporting to give the employer certain rights upon the bankruptcy or winding up of the contractor. These clauses are not effective if they are contrary to the principles of the bankruptcy law. Thus a provision that upon the contractor's bankruptcy unfixed materials or plant should be forfeited and vest in the employer is void, for an agreement that, "upon a man's becoming bankrupt, that which was his property up to the date of the bankruptcy should go over to someone else and be taken away from his creditors, is void as being a violation

---

[41] *Re Asphaltic Wood Pavement Co., ex p. Lee and Chapman* (1885) 30 Ch.D. 216 (C.A.).

[42] *Ibid.; cf. Willment Brothers* v. *North West Thames R.H.A.* (1984) 26 B.L.R. 51 (C.A.); see further "Mutual dealings" below.

[43] s.314 and Sched. 5, Pt. I of the Insolvency Act 1986.

[44] ss.165(3) and 167(1) and Sched. 4 of the Insolvency Act 1986.

[45] For mutual credit and set-off see s.323 of the Insolvency Act 1986 for bankruptcy and for companies r. 4.90 of the Insolvency Rules 1986—see s.411 of the Insolvency Act 1986; see, *e.g. Re Asphaltic Co., ex p. Lee & Chapman* (1885) 30 Ch.D. 216 (C.A.); *National Westminster Bank Ltd.* v. *Halesowen Presswork* [1972] A.C. 785 (H.L.) for an important review of cases under s.31 of the Bankruptcy Act 1914; *Willment Brothers* v. *North West Thames R.H.A.* (1984) 26 B.L.R. 51 (C.A.); *Farley* v. *Housing and Commercial Developments* (1984) 26 B.L.R. 66.

[46] *National Westminster Bank Ltd.* v. *Halesowen Presswork* [1972] A.C. 785 (H.L.).

[47] *Re D. H. Curtis (Builders) Ltd.* [1978] Ch. 162; *Re Cushla Ltd.* [1979] 2 All E.R. 415.

[48] *Peat* v. *Jones & Co.* (1881) 8 Q.B.D. 147 (C.A.); *cf. Re Islington Metal and Plating Works* [1983] 2 All E.R. 218.

[49] *Re Arthur Sanders Ltd.* (1981) 17 B.L.R. 125 applying *National Westminster Bank Ltd.* v. *Halesowen Presswork* [1972] A.C. 785 (H.L.).

of the bankrupt law."[50] For the same reason it seems that a right of lien on
unfixed materials, the property of the contractor, arising on his bankruptcy is
void. But if the property in the materials or plant is already vested in the
employer at the time of bankruptcy a right of seizure effective on the bankruptcy is good.[51] And if a right of forfeiture or lien is enforceable upon
bankruptcy and other events, and is exercised because of some other event
such as delay, the forfeiture or lien is good even though the contractor has
become bankrupt, provided the employer at the time of enforcing his right had
no notice of any available act of bankruptcy committed before the contract was
entered into.[52]

A forfeiture clause operating upon the contractor's bankruptcy and not
purporting to transfer any of the contractor's property is, it seems, valid and
enforceable although it may prevent the contractor's trustee from completing
the contract.[53]

The position of sub-contractors. A sub-contractor[54] must prove in the
bankruptcy or winding up for any debts due to him from the contractor. He
has no lien or charge on money due to the contractor from the employer in
respect of work carried out on goods supplied,[55] but if he still retains the
property in goods supplied he can sometimes retain the goods as against the
trustee.[56] If there is a clause in the contract providing that the employer may, if
the contractor delays payment to the sub-contractor, pay the sub-contractor
direct such a power is not annulled or revoked by the bankruptcy or winding
up of the contractor and a sub-contractor can be paid in full in priority to the

---

[50] James L.J. in *Re Harrison, ex p. Jay* (1880) 14 Ch.D. 19 at 25 (C.A.); *Re Walker, ex p. Barter* (1884)
26 Ch.D. 510 (C.A.). The clause is void as against the trustee, but was said by Cotton L.J. in *Re
Harrison* at p. 26 to be good as between the parties.
[51] *Re Walker, ex p. Barter* (1884) 26 Ch.D. 510 (C.A.).
[52] *Re Waugh, ex p. Dickin* (1876) Ch.D. 524; *cf.* Insolvency Act 1986 s.284(4). Acts of bankruptcy
have no reference to companies.
[53] *cf. Re Walker, ex p. Barter* (1884) 26 Ch.D. 510 (C.A.); *New Zealand Shipping Co.* v. *Ateliers de France*
[1919] 1 A.C. 1 at 13 (H.L.); Woodfall, *The Law of Landlord and Tenant* (28th ed.), para. 1–1786
for the operation of forfeiture clauses in leases which frequently provide for re-entry in the case
of the lessee's bankruptcy.
[54] This includes a person supplying goods under a contract with the contractor, sometimes
referred to as a supplier or "nominated supplier." See, *e.g.* clause 36 of the Standard Form of
Building Contract at p. 652.
[55] *Pritchett, etc., Co. Ltd.* v. *Currie* [1916] 2 Ch. 515 (C.A.), doubting *Bellamy* v. *Davey* [1891] 3 Ch.
540.
[56] See "Retention of title clauses" at p. 242. *cf. Re Fox, ex p. the Oundle and Thrapston Rural District
Council* [1948] 1 Ch. 407 (D.C.)—a decision under the now abolished doctrine of reputed
ownership (see "Vesting of property" above).

trustee.[57] "Wages" payable under a labour only sub-contract were not preferential debts under section 319(4) of the Companies Act 1948.[58]

Retention of title clauses. Such clauses are discussed in Section 2 of Chapter 10.[59] Their application usually becomes critical where one relevant party is insolvent.

Assignees. Subject to the effect of the provisions of the Insolvency Act 1986,[60] the assignee of money earned by the contractor at the date of his bankruptcy may have the right to payment of such money when it accrues due in priority to the trustee in bankruptcy,[61] and even though by completing under the original contract the trustee has perfected the title of the assignee to the money.[62] In such a case the right of the assignee to payment is not defeated merely because the trustee has expended his own money in completing.[63] But a charge within section 396 of the Companies Act 1985 created by a company is void against the liquidator and any creditor of the company unless it is duly registered.[64]

An assignment of money to be earned after bankruptcy is bad as against the trustee, for it is an "established principle of bankruptcy law that it is impossible to assign the profits of a business earned after the bankruptcy."[65]

Where the money assigned is not recoverable by the assignee because of the contractor's bankruptcy he can, if he has a provable bankruptcy debt,[66] prove his claim in the contractor's bankruptcy.

---

[57] *Re Wilkinson, ex p. Fowler* [1905] 2 K.B. 713; *Re Tout and Finch* [1954] 1 W.L.R. 178. For the possible effect of *British Eagle Ltd.* v. *Air France* [1975] 1 W.L.R. 758 (H.L.) on cases such as these, see *Re Arthur Sanders Ltd.* (1981) 17 B.L.R. 125 at 140 and also *Carreras Rothmans* v. *Freeman Matthews* [1985] Ch. 207. See also p. 629, and clause 35.13 of the Standard Form of Building Contract, and see p. 277 for equitable assignment of retention moneys.

[58] *Re C. W. & A. C. Hughes Ltd.* [1966] 1 W.L.R. 1369. s.319(4) of the Companies Act 1948 became s.614 and Schedule 19 of the Companies Act 1985 which was repealed but not replaced by the Insolvency Act 1986.

[59] See "Retention of title clauses" at p. 242.

[60] See, *e.g.* ss.339 and 340 of the Insolvency Act 1986 relating to transactions at an undervalue and preferences.

[61] *Drew* v. *Josolyne* (1887) 18 Q.B.D. 590 (C.A.); *Re Davis & Co., ex p. Rawlings* (1888) 22 Q.B.D. 193 (C.A.); *Re Tout and Finch* [1954] 1 W.L.R. 178; *Re Warren, ex p. Wheeler* [1938] Ch. 725 (D.C.); see also cases in n. 57 above.

[62] *Re Toward, ex p. Moss* (1884) L.R. 14 Q.B.D. 318 (C.A.); *Re Asphaltic Wood Pavement Co., ex p. Lee and Chapman* (1885) 30 Ch.D. 216 (C.A.); *Drew* v. *Josolyne* (1887) 18 Q.B.D. 590 (C.A.); *Re Tout and Finch* [1954] 1 W.L.R. 178 but see n. 57 above.

[63] *Re Asphaltic Wood Pavement Co., ex p. Lee and Chapman* (1885) 30 Ch.D. 216 (C.A.); *Drew* v. *Josolyne* (1887) 18 Q.B.D. 590 (C.A.).

[64] s.395 of the Companies Act 1985. This section will be amended when ss.93–107 of the Companies Act 1989 are brought into force. The section which will then render an unregistered charge void will be amended s.399 of the Companies Act 1985 and there will be other changes, *e.g.* in amended ss.404 and 405.

[65] Wynn-Parry J. in *Re Tout and Finch* [1954] 1 W.L.R. 178; *Re Jones, ex p. Nichols* (1883) 22 Ch.D. 782 (C.A.); *Wilmot* v. *Alton* [1897] 1 Q.B. 17 (C.A.). The principle applies to the winding up of an insolvent company—see *Re Tout and Finch.*

[66] See s.382 of the Insolvency Act 1986 and *Muir Hunter on Personal Insolvency*, pp. 3220–3222.

Arbitration clauses—bankruptcy.   Where the trustee has adopted a contract which contains a term referring any differences arising thereout or in connection therewith to arbitration, such term is enforceable by or against him.[67] Even when there has been no adoption, if the contractor had become a party to an arbitration agreement[68] before the commencement of his bankruptcy the court has a discretion upon the application of the trustee with the consent of the creditors' committee, or upon the application of any other party to the agreement, to make an order that the matter be determined by arbitration.[69]

(c) *Insolvency of employer*

Upon the bankruptcy or winding up of the employer the position is governed by the ordinary law of bankruptcy and winding up. See the matters discussed above in relation to the contractor, of which disclaimer is probably the most important.

If the contract requires the contractor to give credit for materials supplied or for work and labour he has, it seems, upon the employer's bankruptcy, the right to refuse further performance without payment.[70]

In a liquidation the contractor cannot claim as owner of materials incorporated in the building, but only as an unsecured creditor.[71]

---

[67] Arbitration Act 1950, s.3(1). For arbitration generally, see Chap. 16.
[68] For meaning, see p. 384.
[69] Arbitration Act 1950, s.3(2).
[70] *Re Edwards, ex p. Chalmers* (1873) L.R. 8 Ch. 289; *Re Sneezum, ex p. Davis* (1876) 3 Ch.D. 463 at 473.
[71] *Re Yorkshire Joinery Co.* (1967) 111 S.J. 701. See also p. 241.

CHAPTER 16

ARBITRATION

1. Introduction

"Arbitration is usually no more and no less than litigation in the private sector. The arbitrator is called upon to find the facts, apply the law and grant relief to one or other or both of the parties."[1]

The settlement of disputes arising out of building contracts by arbitration, rather than by the ordinary courts, is common practice. The advantages of this procedure are that, where the substantial questions are matters of fact, a final and conclusive decision can be obtained in a manner which theoretically is quicker and cheaper[2] than the ordinary processes of law. In particular the appointment as arbitrator of a person experienced in building matters such as an architect or engineer may shorten proceedings as he will have personal knowledge, which he is entitled to use,[3] of customs and technical terms and processes. Although in general arbitrators are obliged to receive all relevant evidence, in practice the amount of evidence required to prove a case before a professionally or technically qualified arbitrator may be materially less than in proceedings in court where the role of the judge is to find strictly on the

---

[1] Sir John Donaldson M.R. in *Northern Regional Health Authority* v. *Derek Crouch* [1984] Q.B. 644 at 670 (C.A.).

[2] *cf. Antaios Compania* v. *Salen A.B.* [1985] A.C. 191 at 208 (H.L.). But arbitrations are regrettably sometimes longer and dearer. One attraction of arbitrations is that they are private. See also "Arbitration procedure" at p. 403.

[3] *Mediterranean and Eastern Export Co. Ltd.* v. *Fortress Fabrics (Manchester) Ltd.* [1948] 2 All E.R. 186 (C.A.). He must not, however, make use of special personal expertise material to the dispute without disclosing his knowledge or view to the parties and giving them a proper opportunity to deal with it—see *Fox* v. *P.G. Wellfair Ltd.* [1981] 2 Lloyd's Rep. 514 (C.A.).

evidence before him.[4] The courts are no longer jealous of the jurisdiction of arbitrators and the modern tendency is, more especially in commercial arbitrations, to endeavour to uphold the awards of the skilled persons that the parties themselves have selected to decide the question at issue between them.[5]

English arbitrations are regulated by the Arbitration Act 1950 as amended by the Arbitration Act 1979.[6] The Arbitration Act 1975 applies to arbitration agreements which are not "domestic" in particular where there is an application to stay court proceedings.[7]

This chapter deals with some parts of the law of arbitration which more particularly affect building contracts. For an account of arbitration procedure, the powers of the arbitrator, admissibility of evidence, costs, the arbitrator's remuneration and other general matters, reference must be made to one of the standard works such as Mustill & Boyd, *Commercial Arbitration.*[8]

2. What is an Arbitration Agreement?

The statutory definition.   For the purposes of the Arbitration Act 1950 an arbitration agreement is a "written agreement to submit present or future differences to arbitration, whether an arbitrator is named therein or not."[9] Such an agreement is governed by the Act. The parties can agree orally to the settlement of disputes by arbitration, but oral agreements are not governed by the Act and are subject to many disadvantages. For example, the arbitrator's authority is revocable at any time before the award is made, and an award is not enforceable under the provisions of the Act.[10] An implied arbitration agreement cannot be a written agreement within the statutory definition,[11] but it is possible that an *ad hoc* extension of jurisdiction deriving from a written submission may come within the Act.[12] Arbitration agreements should therefore be in writing.

---

[4] *Metropolitan Tunnel and Public Works Ltd.* v. *London Electric Railway* [1926] Ch. 371 (C.A.). Note that the litigant before an arbitrator must often necessarily be ignorant of the extent of the arbitrator's technical knowledge on any particular item and how far, therefore, evidence on that item is necessary. But the arbitrator must give the parties an opportunity to deal with matters which might affect his decision—*Thomas Borthwick (Glasgow) Ltd.* v. *Faure Fairclough Ltd.* [1968] 1 Lloyd's Rep. 16; *Micklewright* v. *Mullock* (1974) 232 E.G. 237.

[5] Lord Goddard C.J. in *Mediterranean and Eastern Export Co. Ltd.* v. *Fortress Fabrics (Manchester) Ltd.* [1948] 2 All E.R. 186 at 189 (C.A.). See also the general policy of the 1979 Arbitration Act towards appeals from arbitrators discussed below. In City of London commercial arbitrations (*cf.* R.S.C., Ord. 72, r. 1(2)), it is common for procedures, by agreement, to be simpler and rely more upon the trade or business knowledge of the arbitrator than is usual in building disputes.

[6] The Report of the Mustill Committee (1989) recommended that new legislation should set out the essential principles of the existing law in a more comprehensive and logical way.

[7] See "The Right to Insist on Arbitration" at p. 397.

[8] All references in this chapter to Mustill & Boyd are to the 2nd ed. (1989). Much of the next chapter also applies to arbitrations.

[9] Arbitration Act 1950, s.32. For non-domestic arbitration agreements and certain foreign awards, see the Arbitration Act 1975 where in s.7(1) there is a somewhat different definition.

[10] See Mustill & Boyd, *Commercial Arbitration*, p. 6.

[11] *Blue Circle Industries* v. *Holland Dredging* (1987) 37 B.L.R. 40 at 50 (C.A.).

[12] See *Higgs & Hill* v. *Campbell Denis* (1982) 28 B.L.R. 47 at 68, 69 and 74. The point was taken and in the result (but without detailed reasons) apparently decided according to the text.

A distinction is sometimes made between a "submission," *i.e.* the actual submission of a particular, existing dispute or disputes, and an "agreement to refer," *i.e.* an agreement to refer future disputes, if they arise, to arbitration.[13] Both these terms are comprised in the statutory definition. Thus both the arbitration clause in the Standard Form of Building Contract, and a written agreement to submit an existing dispute arising out of an oral contract are arbitration agreements for the purposes of the Act.

An arbitrator is not liable in damages for negligence in performing his judicial duties.[14] When the House of Lords considered the extent of this judicial immunity, Lord Morris said:

"There may be circumstances in which what is in effect an arbitration is not one that is within the provisions of the Arbitration Act. The expression quasi-arbitrator should only be used in that connection. A person will only be an arbitrator or quasi-arbitrator if there is a submission to him either of a specific dispute or of present points of difference or of defined differences that may in the future arise and if there is agreement that his decision will be binding."[15]

The difference between arbitration and certification.   Where clear words are used referring disputes or differences to arbitration,[16] the court will have little difficulty in deciding that there is an arbitration agreement. But sometimes a difficult question of construction arises. The intention of the parties is the test. If the intention is that differences should be settled by a judicial inquiry worked out in a judicial manner upon evidence submitted, the case is one of arbitration.[17] If, on the other hand, a person is appointed "to ascertain some matter for the purpose of preventing differences from arising, not of settling them when they have arisen,"[18] this is a mere valuation, or, where the matter to be ascertained is to be stated in a certificate, a certification.[19] Intermediate between the case where a full judicial inquiry into a

---

[13] *Ibid.*

[14] *Sutcliffe* v. *Thackrah* [1974] A.C. 727, 736, 744, 753, 754, 758 (H.L.). In the subsequent decision of the House of Lords in *Arenson* v. *Arenson* [1977] A.C. 405 there are passages (at 430, 431, 440, 442) which indicate that the matter is not concluded, but it is submitted that the balance of judicial view supports the passage in the text, and that if there is any personal liability on the part of an arbitrator it does not arise out of mere negligence in the performance of his judicial duties but in respect of such matters as impropriety going beyond mere negligence or some deliberate non-performance of his duties causing loss to the parties.

[15] *Sutcliffe* v. *Thackrah* [1974] A.C. 727 at 752 (H.L.); see also *Arenson* v. *Arenson* [1977] A.C. 405 at 424, 429 (H.L.); *Palacath* v. *Flanagan* [1985] 2 All E.R. 161 at 164.

[16] *e.g.* Standard Form of Building Contract, clause 41. See *Jowett* v. *Neath Rural District Council* (1916) 80 J.P.J. 207; *Hobbs Padgett & Co.* v. *Kirkland* (1969) 113 S.J. 832 (C.A.), "suitable arbitration clause," valid agreement.

[17] Lord Esher M.R. in *Re Carus-Wilson and Greene* (1886) 18 Q.B.D. 7 at 9 (C.A.); see also Arbitration Act 1950, s.32; *Sutcliffe* v. *Thackrah* [1974] A.C. 727 (H.L.).

[18] Lord Esher M.R. in *Re Carus-Wilson and Greene* (1886) 18 Q.B.D. 7 (C.A.).

[19] *Ibid.*; *Northampton Gas Light Co.* v. *Parnell* (1855) 24 L.J.C.P. 60; *Scott* v. *Liverpool Corp.* (1858) 28 L.J.Ch. 230; *Wadsworth* v. *Smith* (1871) L.R. 6 Q.B. 332; *Kennedy Ltd.* v. *Barrow-in-Furness Corp.* (1909) H.B.C. (4th ed.), Vol. 2, p. 411 (C.A.); *Finnegan* v. *Allen* [1943] K.B. 425 at 436 (C.A.). See also *Arenson* v. *Arenson* [1977] A.C. 405 (H.L.).

dispute is intended and that where a third person is to give a decision merely to prevent a dispute arising is the case where:

"though a person is appointed to settle disputes that have arisen, still it is not intended that he shall be bound to hear evidence or arguments. In such cases it may often be difficult to say whether he is intended to be an arbitrator or to exercise some function other than that of an arbitrator. Such cases must be determined each according to its particular circumstances."[20]

Prima facie if a person is appointed to decide a matter solely by using his own eyes, knowledge and skill, he is a valuer or certifier and not an arbitrator for the purposes of the Arbitration Act.[21] But the parties may by clear words select as an arbitrator a person skilled in the trade intending that he shall decide disputes using his own skill and knowledge of the trade generally.[22] If the court finds that this was their intention the arbitrator's award will be upheld although no evidence was put before him.[23] The intention will not be presumed if the arbitrator selected is not an expert,[24] and in any event the arbitrator must hear the evidence of any party who puts in a claim to be heard.[25]

It has been held in the case of valuers that, if it appears that an arbitration was not intended, the mere fact that evidence is heard by a valuer,[26] or that an umpire is appointed,[27] or that valuers are termed arbitrators with power to appoint an umpire does not turn a valuation into an arbitration."[28]

The granting of certificates in a building contract is not an arbitration for the purposes of the Arbitration Act,[29] unless express words show that the certificates were intended to be given only after arbitration proceedings.[30] An engineer has been held not to be an arbitrator although he was termed "the exclusive judge" of a very wide range of matters arising under the contract and it was provided that his certificates should have the force and effect of awards.[31] Difficulties of terminology have arisen because a certifier must frequently act fairly and impartially in applying the terms of the contract.[32] He

---

[20] Lord Esher M.R. in *Re Carus-Wilson and Greene* (1886) 18 Q.B.D. 7 (C.A.).

[21] *Re Dawdy* (1885) 15 Q.B.D. 426 (C.A.); *Wadsworth* v. *Smith* (1871) L.R. 6 Q.B. 332.

[22] *Mediterranean, etc., Ltd.* v. *Fortress Fabrics Ltd.* [1948] 2 All E.R. 186 (C.A.); *Eads* v. *Williams* (1854) 24 L.J.Ch. 531. Note that it is misconduct for the arbitrator to use knowledge of special facts such as that one of the parties was bankrupt, acquired elsewhere than in the arbitration proceedings before him: *Owen* v. *Nicholl* [1948] 1 All E.R. 707 (C.A.). See also *Thomas Borthwick (Glasgow) Ltd.* v. *Faure Fairclough Ltd.* [1968] 1 Lloyd's Rep. 16 at 29. And see "Misconduct" at p. 411.

[23] *Ibid.*

[24] *Mediterranean, etc., Ltd.* v. *Fortress Fabrics Ltd.* [1948] 2 All E.R. 186 (C.A.).

[25] *Re Maunder* (1883) 49 L.T. 535; *cf. Johnston* v. *Cheape* (1817) 5 Dow 247.

[26] *Re Dawdy* (1885) 15 Q.B.D. 426 (C.A.).

[27] *Re Carus-Wilson and Greene* (1886) 18 Q.B.D. 7 (C.A.); *Re Hammond and Waterton* (1890) 62 L.T. 808.

[28] *Ibid.*

[29] *Sutcliffe* v. *Thackrah* [1974] A.C. 727 (H.L.).

[30] See cases cited at n. 19 above; *cf. Eaglesham* v. *McMaster* [1920] 2 K.B. 169.

[31] *Kennedy Ltd.* v. *Barrow-in-Furness Corp.* (1909) H.B.C. (4th ed.), Vol. 2, p. 411 (C.A.).

[32] See *Sutcliffe* v. *Thackrah* [1974] A.C. 727 (H.L.) discussed at p. 114. See also Chap. 5 "Professional independence" at p. 114.

has sometimes in the past been referred to as a quasi-arbitrator or even an arbitrator,[33] but these terms should no longer be used for a person performing the usual duties of a certifier.[34]

3. Jurisdiction of the Arbitrator

"A non-statutory arbitrator derives his jurisdiction from the agreement of the parties at whose instance he is appointed. He has such jurisdiction as they agree to give him and none that they do not. The only inherent limitation is that he cannot make a binding award as to the initial existence of the agreement from which his jurisdiction is said to derive."[35]

The extent of the arbitrator's jurisdiction depends upon the proper construction of the agreement in each case and in all the circumstances,[36] there being a presumption that the parties intended that all disputes arising from a particular transaction should be determined by the same tribunal.[37] An arbitrator may be empowered by the terms of the arbitration agreement to grant wider relief than might be available in court.[38] The arbitrator under an ordinary clause can decide questions of law such as the construction of the contract, including the implication of customs.[39] Without sufficient express agreement of all relevant parties, an arbitrator appointed under two or more references does not have jurisdiction to hear disputes to be determined in each of the references concurrently however convenient that might be and however closely related the disputes.[40]

Where an arbitration agreement incorporates one of a variety of institutional arbitration rules,[41] the arbitrator will have the powers conferred by those rules which may also affect his jurisdiction.[42]

---

[33] See, *e.g. Hickman & Co.* v. *Roberts* [1913] A.C. 229 (H.L.).

[34] *Sutcliffe* v. *Thackrah* [1974] A.C. 727 at 752 (H.L.).

[35] Bingham L.J. in *Ashville Investments* v. *Elmer Contractors* [1989] Q.B. 488 at 506 (C.A.); see also May L.J. at *ibid.* 495.

[36] *Heyman* v. *Darwins Ltd.* [1942] A.C. 356 at 360 (H.L.); *Ashville Investments* v. *Elmer Contractors* [1989] Q.B. 488 at 506 (C.A.); *cf. Northern Regional Health Authority* v. *Derek Crouch* [1984] Q.B. 644 at 660 (C.A.).

[37] See *Ashville Investments* v. *Elmer Contractors* [1989] Q.B. 488 at 502 (C.A.); *Ethiopian Oilseeds* v. *Rio del Mar* [1990] 1 Lloyd's Rep. 86 at 97.

[38] See *Northern Regional Health Authority* v. *Derek Crouch* [1984] Q.B. 644 (C.A.); *cf. Ashville Investments* v. *Elmer Contractors* [1989] Q.B. 488 at 495 (C.A.). See also "Crouch" at p. 389.

[39] *Produce Brokers Co.* v. *Olympia Oil and Cake Co.* [1916] 1 A.C. 314 (H.L.); *Re Hohenzollern, etc., and City of London Corp.* (1886) 54 L.T. 596; H.B.C. (4th ed.), Vol. 2, p. 100 (C.A.). This may be a ground for refusing a stay—see "Point of law" at p. 400.

[40] *Oxford Shipping* v. *Nippon Yusen Kaisha* [1984] 2 Lloyd's Rep. 373. See also pp. 675 and 777 for discussion of clause 41 of the Standard Form of Building Contract and clause 38 of the Standard Form of Sub-Contract. For a case where the court appointed the same arbitrator for two disputes under s.10 of the Arbitration Act 1950, the parties consenting to a means of returning to court for the appointment of another arbitrator if disadvantages resulted—see *Abu Dhabi Gas* v. *Eastern Bechtel* [1982] 2 Lloyd's Rep. 425 (C.A.).

[41] See those set out in Appendix 4 of Mustill & Boyd, *Commercial Arbitration* (2nd ed.), pp. 743 *et seq.* They include the ICC Rules—discussed at p. 416—and the I.C.E. Arbitration Procedure (1983).

[42] See, *e.g. Dalmia* v. *National Bank* [1978] 2 Lloyd's Rep. 223 at 284 (C.A.).

Where the agreement is to refer disputes or differences which have arisen "in respect of," or "with regard to," or "under,"[43] or "out of"[44] the contract, or where similar words are used, then prima facie it will give the arbitrator jurisdiction to decide all allegations of breach of the contract by either party,[45] and possibly allegations of tort closely connected with the allegations of breach of contract.[46] In *Ashville Investments* v. *Elmer Contractors*,[47] the Court of Appeal distinguished earlier authorities[48] in holding that the jurisdiction of an arbitrator empowered to determine disputes "as to any matter or thing of whatsoever nature arising ... in connection with" a 1963 Standard Form of Building Contract extended to claims for rectification of the agreement for mistake and for misrepresentation or negligent misstatement.[49] But the claim for rectification was not a dispute or difference "as to the construction of this contract."[50] Nor do claims for rectification, misrepresentation, negligent misrepresentation or a claim under a collateral contract arise "under" a principal contract.[51]

Repudiation, frustration, and void contracts. It was at one time thought that the jurisdiction of an arbitrator under an ordinary arbitration agreement did not extend to questions of whether the contract had been repudiated,[52] but the House of Lords in *Heyman* v. *Darwins Ltd.*[53] finally settled that an arbitrator appointed under a clause such as those referred to in the preceding two paragraphs has jurisdiction to decide whether a contract has been repudiated by one of the parties. Where one party accepts the other's repudiation, he is released from further performance of primary obligations, but the contract itself is not rescinded and the arbitration clause normally survives.[54] Such a clause is also effective where it is alleged that some supervening event has

---

[43] *Heyman* v. *Darwins Ltd.* [1942] A.C. 356 at 366 (H.L.); *Produce Brokers Co. Ltd.* v. *Olympia Oil & Cake Co. Ltd.* [1916] 1 A.C. 314 (H.L.); *Re Hohenzollern, etc., and City of London Corp.* (1886) 54 L.T. 596; H.B.C. (4th ed.), Vol. 2, p. 100 (C.A.).

[44] *Union of India* v. *Aaby's Rederi A/S* [1975] A.C. 797 (H.L.).

[45] See authorities in nts. 43 and 44; *cf.* also *The Antonis P. Lemos* [1985] A.C. 711 at 727 (H.L.).

[46] *Astro Vencedor S.A.* v. *Mabanaft* [1971] 2 Q.B. 588 (C.A.).

[47] [1989] Q.B. 488 (C.A.); *cf. Ethiopian Oilseeds* v. *Rio del Mar* [1990] 1 Lloyd's Rep. 86.

[48] *Printing Machinery* v. *Linotype and Machinery* [1912] 1 Ch. 566; *Monro* v. *Bognor Urban District Council* [1915] 3 K.B. 167 (C.A.); *Crane* v. *Hegeman-Harris* [1939] 4 All E.R. 68 (C.A.).

[49] The court additionally did not follow *obiter dicta* of Purchas L.J. in *Blue Circle Industries* v. *Holland Dredging* (1987) 37 B.L.R. 40 at 53 (C.A.) considering similar words in clause 66 of the I.C.E. Conditions (5th ed.). For rectification, see p. 266 esp. "Arbitrators" at p. 268.

[50] *Ashville Investments* v. *Elmer Contractors* [1989] Q.B. 488 at 503 (C.A.).

[51] *Ashville Investments* v. *Elmer Contractors* [1989] Q.B. 488 at 502 (C.A.); *Fillite* v. *Aqua-Lift* (1989) 45 B.L.R. 27 (C.A.).

[52] See *Hirji Mulji* v. *Cheong Yue Steamship Co.* [1926] A.C. 497 (P.C.); and for a building contract case, see Moulton L.J. in *Kennedy Ltd.* v. *Barrow-in-Furness Corp.* (1909) H.B.C. (4th ed.), Vol. 2, p. 411 at 415 (C.A.).

[53] [1942] A.C. 356 (H.L.); *Bloemen (F.J.) Pty. Ltd.* v. *Gold Coast City Council* [1973] A.C. 115 at 126 (P.C.).

[54] *Heyman* v. *Darwins Ltd.* [1942] A.C. 356 at 399 (H.L.); *cf. Photo Production* v. *Securicor* [1980] A.C. 827 and see "Acceptance of repudiation" at p. 151.

frustrated a contract,[55] whether partly executed or wholly executory (*i.e.* where no step has been taken towards its performance) at the date of the event.[56] But

> "if the dispute is whether the contract which contains the clause has ever been entered into at all, that issue cannot go to arbitration under the clause, for the party who denies that he has ever entered into the contract is thereby denying that he has ever joined in the submission. Similarly, if one party to the alleged contract is contending that it is void *ab initio* (because, for example, the making of such a contract is illegal), the arbitration clause cannot operate for on this view the clause itself also is void."[57]

Where an agreement refers disputes "arising out of" the contract the arbitrator has power not merely to determine whether the contract is frustrated but also to decide what is due to the parties upon such frustration.[58]

Fraud. By express words the parties can agree to submit questions of fraudulent misrepresentation to the arbitrator,[59] but in the absence of express words it seems that the ordinary clause does not extend to allegations of fraudulent misrepresentation rendering a contract voidable.[60] An arbitrator will, however, normally have jurisdiction to consider allegations of fraud in the performance of the contract unless the court exercises its power under section 24(2) of the Arbitration Act 1950 to give leave to revoke his authority.[61]

"Crouch." In *Northern Regional Health Authority* v. *Derek Crouch*,[62] the Court of Appeal considered the comparative powers of an arbitrator and the court where the arbitration clause of a 1963 Standard Form of Building Contract empowered the arbitrator "to open up, review and revise any certificate, opinion, decision ... as if no such certificate, opinion, decision, ... had been

---

[55] *Heyman* v. *Darwins Ltd.* [1942] A.C. 356 at 366 (H.L.); *Gibraltar (Govt. of)* v. *Kenney* [1956] 2 Q.B. 410. For frustration generally, see p. 134.

[56] *Kruse* v. *Questier & Co. Ltd.* [1953] 1 Q.B. 669.

[57] Lord Simon in *Heyman* v. *Darwins Ltd.* [1942] A.C. 356 at 366 (H.L.); see also *Toller* v. *Law Accident Ins. Soc. Ltd.* [1936] 2 All E.R. 952 (C.A.); *The Tradesman* [1962] 1 W.L.R. 61.

[58] *Gibraltar (Govt. of)* v. *Kenney* [1956] 2 Q.B. 410. Whether the arbitrator has such a power where "under" is used has not been decided, but probably he has: see *Union of India* v. *Aaby's Rederi A/S* [1975] A.C. 797 (H.L.) disapproving dicta by Lord Porter in *Heyman* v. *Darwins Ltd.* [1942] A.C. 356 at 398 (H.L.), and by Sellers L.J. in *Gibraltar (Govt. of)* v. *Kenney* to the effect that "arising out of" was wider than "under." See also *Fillite* v. *Aqua-Lift* (1989) 45 B.L.R. 27 (C.A.).

[59] Lord Porter in *Heyman* v. *Darwins Ltd.* [1942] A.C. 356 at 392 (H.L.).

[60] *Monro* v. *Bognor Urban District Council* [1915] 3 K.B. 167; *Heyman* v. *Darwins Ltd.* [1942] A.C. 356 (H.L.); *cf. Belcher* v. *Roedean School, etc., Ltd.* (1901) 85 L.T. 468; *Earl of Stradbroke* v. *Mitchell, The Times*, October 4, 1990 (C.A.). An allegation of fraud may in any event be a ground for refusing a stay of proceedings. See p. 401.

[61] The fact that the court's power to give leave to revoke is discretionary indicates that an arbitrator's jurisdiction can otherwise exist. *Cf. Yeu Shing Construction* v. *Att.-Gen. of Hong Kong* (1988) 40 B.L.R. 131 (Hong Kong High Court). For revocation see p. 409.

[62] [1984] Q.B. 644 (C.A.). See generally Karen Gough and Roger Dyer, "*Crouch* in Perspective" (1985) 1 Const.L.J. 333; and for a highly critical discussion, see I. N. Duncan Wallace Q.C., "Construction Contracts: The Architect, the Arbitrator and the Courts" (1986) 2 Const.L.J. 13.

given." The question was whether, if disputes were to be determined in court,[63] the court had equivalent powers. It was held that the court did not have such powers.[64]

"The limit of the court's jurisdiction would be to declare inoperative any certificate or opinion given by the architect if the architect had no power to give such certificate or opinion or had otherwise erred in law. The court could not (as the arbitrator could) substitute its discretion for that of the architect."[65]

But it seems that the court would have or assume the powers of an arbitrator if the arbitration machinery breaks down or is incapable of operating.[66] It seems further that the court does have power to deal with cases which do not require revision of an architect's certificate or decision,[67] and that it can determine the rights of the parties where a certificate is inconclusive in determining those rights.[68]

It is, it is submitted, debateable whether the *Crouch* decision:

(1) turned on the construction of the particular arbitration clause; or
(2) decides more generally that, where there is an arbitration clause whatever its terms, the court does not have power to substitute its discretion for that of the architect whereas the arbitrator does; or
(3) that some architect's certificates in some building contracts cannot be revised by the court and cannot be revised at all unless under the terms of an appropriate arbitration clause.

On one interpretation, the *Crouch* decision itself is in favour of the first view,[69] as is a subsequent decision of the Court of Appeal,[70] where it was held that the arbitration clause in a JCT Agreement for Minor Building Works was not a

---

[63] As by agreement between the parties, or where a defendant made no application to stay proceedings begun in court, or where the court had in its discretion refused a stay—see pp. 397 *et seq.*

[64] Distinguishing *Neale* v. *Richardson* [1938] 1 All E.R. 753; following a dictum of Lord Wilberforce in *P. & M. Kaye* v. *Hosier & Dickinson* [1972] 1 W.L.R. 146 at 158 (H.L.); not following a dictum of Lord Pearson in *East Ham Corporation* v. *Bernard Sunley* [1966] A.C. 406 at 447 (H.L.).

[65] Browne-Wilkinson L.J. at 667—where he also implies that the arbitrator would have "a right to modify contractual rights." It is submitted that, taken literally, this could be misleading. The arbitrator has power to revise architect's certificates, etc., but that is implementing the parties' contractual rights which remain unmodified; *cf.* on this point *Partington & Son* v. *Tameside* (1985) 32 B.L.R. 150 at 165.

[66] *Ibid.* at 668; *Sudbrook Trading Estate* v. *Eggleton* [1983] A.C. 444 (H.L.); *cf. Reed* v. *Van Der Vorm* (1985) 35 B.L.R. 136.

[67] See, *e.g. Finnegan* v. *Sheffield City Council* (1988) 43 B.L.R. 124.

[68] *Rapid Building* v. *Ealing Family Housing* (1984) 29 B.L.R. 5 at 14 (C.A.).

[69] "It [the arbitration clause] is, however, a rather special clause" and ". . . special powers given to the arbitrator . . ."—Sir John Donaldson M.R. at 670 and 672 respectively. See also s.43A of the Supreme Court Act 1981 as inserted by s.100 of the Courts and Legal Services Act 1990, referred to below.

[70] *Benstrete Construction* v. *Angus Hill* most fully reported at (1988) 4 Const.L.J. 114 (C.A.). It seems that in truth there was no *Crouch* point in issue in *Benstrete* at all, as the counterclaim for defects was not dependant on revising any certificate or decision of the architect.

clause of the kind to which the *Crouch* decision applies.[71] On another interpretation, the *Crouch* decision is in favour of the second view as is at least one other decision of the Court of Appeal.[72] There are at least three first instance decisions in favour of either the second or the third view.[73] It is submitted that the question generally should turn on:

(1) what powers the court intrinsically has; and
(2) the construction of the contract.

It is suggested that the court's power to make declarations, if no other, is sufficient for all cases where an architect's certificate or decision is not by contract immutable. In the absence of express words, the existence of an arbitration clause will usually indicate that the parties did not intend certificates to be immutable and the court will, it is submitted, have jurisdiction unless, as in *Crouch* itself, the terms of the arbitration clause itself show that only the arbitrator was to have the relevant power.

It is possible that strictly the decision in *Crouch* may be *obiter*[74] and the point is in any event open in the House of Lords.[75] It has, however, been applied generally,[76] though not universally.[77] The point may not, however, be taken to the House of Lords since section 100 of the Courts and Legal Services Act 1990 now provides[78] that the High Court may exercise specific powers conferred on an arbitrator by an arbitration agreement if all parties to the agreement agree. If all parties to the proceedings do not agree, the court will not have the statutory power and the House of Lords would no doubt take notice of the fact that Parliament had legislated on an apparent assumption that the court did not otherwise have such power.

---

[71] H.H. Judge Smout Q.C. had decided otherwise in *Oram Builders* v. *Pemberton* (1985) 29 B.L.R. 23. The decision in *Benstrete* is very short, given without argument and without reference to *Oram Builders*.

[72] See *Ashville Investments* v. *Elmer Contractors* [1989] Q.B. 488 at 495, 503, 507 (C.A.).

[73] *Oram Builders* v. *Pemberton* (1985) 29 B.L.R. 23; *Reed* v. *Van der Vorm* (1985) 35 B.L.R. 136; *Finnegan* v. *Sheffield City Council* (1988) 43 B.L.R. 124. Clause 41.4 of the 1980 Standard Form of Building Contract empowers the arbitrator "to rectify the Contract so that it accurately reflects the true agreement made by the Employer and the Contractor"—see p. 674. Does this mean that the court has no such power under this form of contract? For rectification generally, see p. 266 and for an arbitrator's powers of rectification generally, see p. 268.

[74] See Dunn L.J. at 663 and generally; *cf. Reed* v. *Van der Vorm* (1985) 35 B.L.R. 136 at 144; *Partington & Son* v. *Tameside* (1985) 32 B.L.R. 150.

[75] Relevant previous authority or dicta are in *Robins* v. *Goddard* [1905] 1 K.B. 294 (C.A.); *Neale* v. *Richardson* [1938] 1 All E.R. 753 (C.A.); *Prestige* v. *Brettell* [1938] 4 All E.R. 346 (C.A.); *East Ham Corporation* v. *Bernard Sunley* [1966] A.C. 406 at 424, 432, 434, 447 (H.L.); *Kaye (P. & M.)* v. *Hosier & Dickinson* [1972] 1 W.L.R. 146 at 157 (H.L.); *Modern Engineering* v. *Gilbert-Ash* [1974] A.C. 689 at 720 (H.L.).

[76] See, *e.g. Douglas Construction* v. *W.H.T.S.O.* (1985) 31 B.L.R. 88.

[77] See *Partington & Son* v. *Tameside* (1985) 32 B.L.R. 150; see also for a robust criticism, I. N. Duncan Wallace Q.C., "Construction Contracts: The Architect, the Arbitrator and the Courts" (1986) 2 Const.L.J. 13.

[78] As an inserted s.43A of the Supreme Court Act 1981.

Overlap with court proceedings. There is no inherent objection to an action and an arbitration proceeding side by side.[79] An arbitrator is entitled to refuse to decide any issue which overlaps with court proceedings and he is usually in the best position to decide whether such an overlap exists.[80] The court, it seems, should reciprocate.[81] But "it is well settled that the court has jurisdiction to restrain an arbitrator from deciding issues which are being litigated before the court."[82]

Official referee as arbitrator. By section 11 of the Arbitration Act 1950,[83] an official referee[84] may, if in all the circumstances he thinks fit and subject to permission from the Lord Chief Justice, accept appointment as sole arbitrator by or by virtue of an arbitration agreement.

Challenge to arbitrator's jurisdiction. Where the scope of the arbitration clause is in dispute, then in the absence of express language,[85] the arbitrator's decision as to the extent of his own jurisdiction is not final,[86] and an arbitrator cannot decide whether a condition precedent to his jurisdiction has been fulfilled.[87] Thus where a building contract provided that a "reference . . . shall not be opened until after the completion . . . of the works," and a reference was opened before completion it was held that the award was bad. "If one thing is quite plain, it is that an arbitrator cannot give himself jurisdiction by deciding in his favour some preliminary point upon which his jurisdiction depends."[88] But it seems that, if the parties make a sufficiently formal *ad hoc* submission to the arbitrator to determine his jurisdiction, his determination may be binding.[89]

If the arbitrator's jurisdiction is challenged he should not refuse to act until it has been determined by some court which has power to determine it finally.

---

[79] *Lloyd* v. *Wright* [1983] Q.B. 1065 (C.A.); *Northern Regional Health Authority* v. *Derek Crouch* [1984] Q.B. 644 at 660 (C.A.); *Douglas Construction* v. *W.H.T.S.O.* (1985) 31 B.L.R. 88.

[80] *Northern Regional Health Authority* v. *Derek Crouch* [1984] Q.B. 644 at 666 (C.A.).

[81] *Ibid.* at 669.

[82] *Ibid.* at 673; see also "Injunction to restrain arbitration proceedings" at p. 410.

[83] As amended by s.84 of the Courts and Legal Services Act 1990. The former unamended s.11 gave parties greater opportunity to appoint Official Referees as arbitrators, but surprisingly the opportunity was rarely taken. For a case where the procedure for making an application was discussed, see *Wimpey Construction* v. *Civil and Public Services Association* (1988) 5 Const. L.J. 162; *cf.* R.S.C., Ord. 36, r. 5(2).

[84] For official referees, see p. 422.

[85] *e.g. Willesford* v. *Watson* (1873) L.R. 8 Ch.App. 473. See cases cited in next three notes. See *Dalmia* v. *National Bank* [1978] 2 Lloyd's Rep. 223 at 284 (C.A.) for the extent of an arbitrator's jurisdiction under the ICC Rules, as to which see further at p. 416.

[86] *Pethick Bros.* v. *Metropolitan Water Board* (1911) H.B.C. (4th ed.), Vol. 2, p. 456 (C.A.); *May* v. *Mills* (1914) 30 T.L.R. 287; *Smith* v. *Martin* [1925] 1 K.B. 745; 94 L.J.K.B. 645 (C.A.).

[87] *Ibid.*

[88] Bankes L.J. in *Smith* v. *Martin* (1925) 94 L.J.K.B. 645 at 646 (C.A.). See also *Getreide-Import-Gessellschaft m.b.H.* v. *Contimar S.A. Cia, etc.* [1953] 1 W.L.R. 793 (C.A.); *Christopher Brown Ltd.* v. *Genossenschaft Oesterreichischer, etc.* [1954] 1 Q.B. 8; *Willcock* v. *Pickfords* [1979] 1 Lloyd's Rep. 244 (C.A.); *Hyundai Engineering* v. *Active Building* (1988) 45 B.L.R. 62 at 70.

[89] *Higgs & Hill* v. *Campbell Denis* (1982) 28 B.L.R. 47.

He should inquire into the merits of the issue to satisfy himself as a preliminary matter whether he ought to get on with the arbitration or not, and if it becomes abundantly clear to him that he has no jurisdiction then he might well take the view that he should not go on with the hearing at all.[90]

Extras.   Where the contract contains power to order extras, it is submitted that the ordinary arbitration clause covers disputes about such extras,[91] but the arbitration clause may expressly or by implication exclude certain matters, such as extras, from the jurisdiction of the arbitrator.[92]

Certificates.   The jurisdiction of the arbitrator to decide whether a certificate was wrongly withheld, or to open up a certificate, has been considered in Chapter 5.[93]

4. Disqualification for Bias

"The Court will set aside as void an award made by a tribunal which is infected by the appearance of a real likelihood of bias . . . if a reasonable and fair-minded person sitting in Court and knowing all the relevant facts would have a reasonable suspicion that a fair trial for the applicant was not possible."[94]

The case more often advanced is "imputed bias,"[95] although *a fortiori* sufficient actual bias obviously also has the same result.

The architect as arbitrator.   The architect under the contract has frequently in past years been appointed arbitrator under an arbitration clause in the contract. It has been said that this places him in a position "invoking and possibly involving on occasions considerable trouble."[96] It has often resulted in contractors opposing an application for a stay of proceedings,[97] or otherwise attacking the arbitration upon the grounds that the architect has an interest in the outcome of the proceedings and is therefore disqualified. The principles

---

[90] Devlin J. in *Christopher Brown Ltd.* v. *Genossenschaft Oesterreichischer, etc.* [1954] 1 Q.B. 8 at 12, 13; *cf. Northern Regional Health Authority* v. *Derek Crouch* [1984] Q.B. 644 at 674 (C.A.).

[91] *Heyman* v. *Darwins Ltd.* [1942] A.C. 356 (H.L.); *Union of India* v. *Aaby's (E.B.) Rederi A/S* [1975] A.C. 797 (H.L.). *Laidlaw* v. *Hastings Pier Co.* (1874) H.B.C. (4th ed.), Vol. 2, p. 13; *cf. Pashby* v. *Birmingham Corp.* (1856) 18 C.B. 2.

[92] *Re Meadows and Kenworthy* (1896) H.B.C. (4th ed.), Vol. 2, p. 265 (C.A.), affd. (H.L.); *Taylor* v. *Western Valleys Sewerage Board* (1911) 75 J.P. 409 (C.A.); *Pashby* v. *Birmingham Corp.* (1856) 18 C.B. 2.

[93] See pp. 105 and 117. For the Standard Form of Building Contract, see Chap. 18.

[94] Leggatt J. in *Cook International* v. *B. V. Handel* [1985] 2 Lloyd's Rep. 225 at 231. See also the cases cited in the judgment in that case and *cf. R.* v. *Mulvihill* [1990] 1 W.L.R. 438 (C.A.).

[95] See, *e.g. Bremer* v. *Ets. Soules* [1985] 2 Lloyd's Rep. 199 at 201 (C.A.); *Hagop Ardahalian* v. *Unifert International* [1984] 2 Lloyd's Rep. 84 at 89 (C.A.).

[96] Lord Shaw of Dunfermline in *Bristol Corp.* v. *Aird* [1913] A.C. 241 at 252 (H.L.).

[97] See p. 397 for stay proceedings.

upon which the courts decide whether an architect is disqualified have been stated by the courts, and an account follows, but it must be read subject to the effect of section 24 of the Arbitration Act 1950, discussed below.[98] This section makes it unlikely that parties will appoint the architect (or engineer in an engineering contract) as arbitrator. But they may. In any event there may remain a person who can be termed a quasi-arbitrator,[99] and it is submitted that the law set out below applies also to such a person.

Interests which have not disqualified. Parties to an arbitration are normally entitled to an unbiased arbitrator with no interest in the result of the proceedings.[1] Where the architect under a contract is appointed arbitrator for that contract he is interested to the extent that he is employed and paid by one of the parties to the dispute,[2] and is probably further interested in that in his capacity as agent for the employer he may have given orders relating to the matter in dispute, or have already expressed a strong view on the subject, and may even "be judge, so to speak, in his own quarrel."[3] Such interests have been held not to be sufficient in themselves to disqualify the architect from acting as arbitrator.[4] It has been held that the contractor must show, if not that the architect is biased, that at least there is a probability that he would be biased.[5] The basis of these decisions was that "the court ... ought to hold that nothing known at the time of the contract, nothing fairly to be expected from the position of the engineer when he becomes arbitrator, can be alleged as a ground why it should not keep the parties to their bargain."[6] It has further been held that the architect was not disqualified because he owned shares in the employer company, when the contractor knew or must be taken to have known of his ownership,[7] nor because in his capacity as agent he had previously expressed in strong language a derogatory view of a claim put forward by the contractor in the arbitration.[8]

---

[98] For the hybrid position of the engineer under clause 66 of the I.C.E. Conditions, see pp. 924 *et seq.*

[99] See passage from *Sutcliffe* v. *Thackrah* [1974] A.C. 727 at 752 (H.L.) set out at p. 385.

[1] See Mustill & Boyd, *Commercial Arbitration* (2nd ed.), pp. 249 *et seq.*

[2] See *Eckersley* v. *Mersey Docks and Harbour Board* [1894] 2 Q.B. 667 (C.A.).

[3] Bowen L.J. in *Jackson* v. *Barry Railway* [1893] 1 Ch. 238 at 247 (C.A.); *cf. Canterbury Pipe Lines* v. *Christchurch Drainage* (1979) 16 B.L.R. 76 at 111 (New Zealand Court of Appeal).

[4] *Ibid.*; *Ives and Barker* v. *Willians* [1894] 2 Ch. 478 (C.A.); *Eckersley* v. *Mersey Docks and Harbour Board* [1894] 2 Q.B. 667 (C.A.).

[5] See n. 101 above.

[6] Lord Moulton in *Bristol Corp.* v. *Aird* [1913] A.C. 241 at 258 (H.L.); but *cf.* Arbitration Act 1950, s.24(1). The engineer in the passage cited was in the position of an architect.

[7] *Ranger* v. *G.W. Railway* (1854) 5 H.L.C. 72 (H.L.); *cf. Sellar* v. *Highland Railway*, 1919 S.C.(H.L.) 19. In *Panamena, etc.* v. *Fredk. Leyland & Co.* [1947] A.C. 428 (H.L.) a certifier was not disqualified merely because be was president of the employer company. Note that s.24(1) of the Arbitration Act 1950 could not apply because the certifier was not an arbitrator for the purpose of the Act.

[8] *Scott* v. *Carluke Local Authority* (1879) 6 R. 616; *Cross* v. *Leeds Corp.* (1902) H.B.C. (4th ed.), Vol. 2, p. 339 (C.A.). These cases were referred to with approval by the House of Lords in *Panamena, etc.* v. *Fredk. Leyland & Co.* [1947] A.C. 428 (H.L.) as showing what conduct would not disqualify a certifier.

Where, unknown to one of the parties, the other party at the time of the reference owed the arbitrator money this was held to be not sufficient reason for setting aside the award.[9] But the court will look more narrowly at the circumstances to see whether the arbitrator has acted improperly, and may find that a large advance of money by the arbitrator to one of the parties has disqualified him.[10]

Where, after the submission of a dispute between the contractor and the employer to the architect as arbitrator, the contractor's assignee commenced proceedings against the architect alleging fraudulent misrepresentation by the architect, and then applied for revocation of the submission on the ground that the architect was disqualified, his application was refused.[11]

Interests which disqualify. In general any interest of the architect which makes him so biased, or puts him in such a position that he cannot give substantial justice disqualifies him from acting as arbitrator.[12] Thus although vigorous actions and expressions of opinion in his capacity as agent may not disqualify him, if a matter at issue involves the architect's professional reputation and capacity the court may in its discretion refuse a stay of proceedings[13] (*i.e.* refuse to enforce the arbitration).[14] And where the dispute is such that it is difficult to see how the matter can properly be dealt with without the cross-examination of the architect in respect of duties performed as agent, it is obviously impossible to permit the architect to act as arbitrator.[15]

A secret interest[16] or fraud or collusion or failure to keep an independent attitude will disqualify.[17] So also will gifts or hospitality if they have the effect of influencing the architect's mind, but not otherwise.[18]

Arbitration Act 1950, s.24(1). Section 24(1) is as follows:

"*Where an agreement between any parties provides that disputes which may arise in the future[19] between them shall be referred to an arbitrator named or designated in the*

---

[9] *Morgan* v. *Morgan* (1832) 2 L.J. Ex. 56; *cf. Cook International* v. *B.V. Handel* [1985] 2 Lloyd's Rep. 225 where an arbitrator and the umpire were employees of subsidiaries of creditors of one of the parties; *Bremer* v. *Ets. Soules* [1985] 2 Lloyd's Rep. 199 (C.A.); *Hagop Ardahalian* v. *Unifert International* [1984] 2 Lloyd's Rep. 84 (C.A.).

[10] *Malmesbury Railway* v. *Budd* (1876) 2 Ch.D. 113.

[11] *Belcher* v. *Roedean School* (1901) 85 L.T. 468 (C.A.).

[12] *Bristol Corp.* v. *Aird* [1913] A.C. 241 (H.L.); *cf. Tracomin* v. *Gibbs* [1985] 1 Lloyd's Rep. 587—a case under s.23(1) of the 1950 Act.

[13] See *Nuttall* v. *Manchester Corp.* (1892) 8 T.L.R. 513 and (1892) H.B.C. (4th ed.), Vol. 2, p. 203 (D.C.); *cf. Re Donkin and Leeds, etc., Canal Co.* (1893) 9 T.L.R. 192; H.B.C. (4th ed.), Vol. 2, p. 239 (D.C.).

[14] See p. 400.

[15] *Freeman* v. *Chester* [1911] 1 K.B. 783 at 790 (C.A.); *Bristol Corp.* v. *Aird* [1913] A.C. 241 (H.L.); *Blackwell* v. *Derby Corp.* (1909) 75 J.P. 129; H.B.C. (4th ed.), Vol. 2, p. 401 (C.A.).

[16] See *Kimberley* v. *Dick* (1871) L.R. 13 Eq. 1—firm undertaking to employer that cost should not exceed certain amount.

[17] *Hickman* v. *Roberts* [1913] A.C. 229 (H.L.); see also p. 115.

[18] *Re Hopper* (1867) L.R. 2 Q.B. 367; *Moseley* v. *Simpson* (1873) L.R. 16 Eq. 226; *Re Maunder* (1883) 49 L.T. 535.

[19] See *Yeu Shing Construction* v. *Att.-Gen. of Hong Kong* (1988) 40 B.L.R. 131 (Hong Kong High Court)—a decision on the Hong Kong equivalent of s.24(2) where there is similar wording.

agreement, and after a dispute has arisen any party applies, on the ground that the arbitrator so named or designated is not or may not be impartial, for leave to revoke the authority of the arbitrator or for an injunction to restrain any other party or the arbitrator from proceeding with the arbitration, it shall not be a ground for refusing the application that the said party at the time when he made the agreement knew, or ought to have known, that the arbitrator, by reason of his relation towards any other party to the agreement or of his connection with the subject referred, might not be capable of impartiality."

Where by virtue of the section the court has power to order that an arbitration agreement shall cease to have effect, or to give leave to revoke the authority of an arbitrator, it may refuse to stay proceedings brought in breach of the agreement.[20]

There have been no decisions upon the meaning of section 24(1)[21] but its words seem to be peculiarly apt to govern the position of an architect to a building contract who is appointed arbitrator of future disputes. It should be noted that it only applies to arbitrators and does not apply to a certifier performing those parts of his duties where he has to act fairly in applying the terms of the contract.[22]

5. Ousting the Jurisdiction of the Court

Subject to section 3 of the Arbitration Act 1979,[23] an arbitration agreement ousting the court's jurisdiction entirely is contrary to public policy and void.[24] Thus although the arbitrator's decision on fact is final, an agreement not to have any "recourse at all to the courts in case of error of law" is void.[25] But a provision making the arbitrator's award a condition precedent to the right to bring an action on the contract is good,[26] for the parties can agree that no action can be brought in a court of law until the amount of the liability has been settled by arbitration.[27] Further a clause providing that arbitration must

---

[20] s.24(3); *cf. Kruger Townswear Ltd.* v. *Northern Assurance Co. Ltd.* [1953] 1 W.L.R. 1049 (D.C.).

[21] First enacted as s.14(1), Arbitration Act 1934. But see the New Zealand case of *Canterbury Pipe Lines* v. *Att.-Gen.* [1961] N.Z.L.R. 785, where the engineer was the arbitrator and a stay (see p. 397) was refused.

[22] See p. 385.

[23] This section provides in certain circumstances (and subject to s.4) that parties may enter into an "exclusion agreement" effective to exclude recourse to the court under ss.1 and 2 of the Act. *cf. Pioneer Shipping* v. *B.T.P. Tioxide* [1982] A.C. 724 at 740 (H.L.) and see "Appeals to the High Court" at p. 412.

[24] *Scott* v. *Avery* (1856) 5 H.L.C. 811 (H.L.); *Doleman* v. *Ossett* [1912] 3 K.B. 257 (C.A.); *Lee* v. *The Showmen's Guild* [1952] 2 Q.B. 329 (C.A.); *cf. Lloyd* v. *Wright* [1983] Q.B. 1065 at 1072 (C.A.); *World Pride Shipping* v. *Daiichi Chuo* [1984] 2 Lloyd's Rep. 489 at 496.

[25] Denning L.J. in *Lee* v. *The Showmen's Guild* [1952] 2 Q.B. 329 at 342 (C.A.); *Czarnikow & Co.* v. *Roth* [1922] 2 K.B. 478 (C.A.); *cf.* Lord Roskill in *Antaios Compania* v. *Salen A.B.* [1985] A.C. 191 at 209 (H.L.)—"the additional, albeit not unrestricted autonomy of arbitral tribunals which the [Arbitration Act 1979] was designed to establish."

[26] *Scott* v. *Avery* (1856) 5 H.L.C. 811 (H.L.).

[27] *Czarnikow & Co.* v. *Roth* [1922] 2 K.B. 478 at 489 (C.A.); *Heyman* v. *Darwins Ltd.* [1942] A.C. 366 at 377 (H.L.).

commence within a limited time or not at all and that thereafter the claim will be barred is good.[28] Both these types of clause, respectively known as *Scott v. Avery* and *Atlantic Shipping* clauses, may be varied by the court in its limited discretion.[29]

An arbitration clause which purported to free the arbitrator to decide without regard to the law and according, for example, to his own notions of what would be fair would not be a valid arbitration clause.[30] But where a contract provided that arbitrators were "not bound by the strict rules of law, but shall settle any difference referred to them according to an equitable rather than a strictly legal interpretation of the provisions of this agreement," it was held that this did not oust the jurisdiction of the courts.[31] The clause would enable the arbitrators "to view the matter more leniently and having regard more generally to commercial considerations than would be done if the matter were heard in court."[32]

6. The Right to Insist on Arbitration

Apart from special cases where provision is made by statute,[33] the right to arbitration arises by agreement. Breach of the arbitration agreement gives rise to an action for damages, but unless costs have been thrown away it is difficult to prove any loss,[34] therefore "the appropriate remedy for breach of the agreement to arbitrate is not damages, but its enforcement."[35] This is achieved not by an order for specific performance, but by obtaining an order under section 4 of the Arbitration Act 1950 staying the legal proceedings while arbitration takes place.[36] For an agreement which is not "a domestic arbitration agreement,"[37] the court has a similar jurisdiction under section 1 of the Arbitration Act 1975. Under the 1950 Act, the court has a discretion, discussed below, to make an order staying the proceedings.[38] Under the 1975 Act, there is no discretion if the statutory conditions are fulfilled.[39]

---

[28] *Atlantic Shipping and Trading Co.* v. *Louis Dreyfus & Co.* [1922] A.C. 250.
[29] Arbitration Act 1950, ss.25(4), 27; see *Dennehy* v. *Bellamy* [1938] 2 All E.R. 262; *Hookway & Co.* v. *Hooper & Co.* [1950] 2 All E.R. 842 (C.A.); *Liberian Shipping Corp.* v. *A. King & Sons Ltd.* [1967] 2 Q.B. 86 (C.A.); *Nea Agrex S.A.* v. *Baltic Shipping Co. Ltd.* [1976] Q.B. 933 (C.A.).
[30] *Home and Overseas Insurance* v. *Mentor Insurance* [1990] 1 W.L.R. 153 at 161 (C.A.).
[31] *Eagle Star Insurance* v. *Yuval Insurance* [1978] 1 Lloyd's Rep. 357 at 362 (C.A.); *cf.* the "honourable engagement" abitration clause in *Home and Overseas Insurance* v. *Mentor Insurance* [1990] 1 W.L.R. 153 (C.A.).
[32] *Eagle Star Insurance* v. *Yuval Insurance* [1978] 1 Lloyd's Rep. 357 at 363 (C.A.).
[33] This does not apply to building contracts as such.
[34] *Doleman & Sons* v. *Ossett Corp.* [1912] 3 K.B. 257 at 268 (C.A.).
[35] Lord Macmillan in *Heyman* v. *Darwins Ltd.* [1942] A.C. 356 at 374 (H.L).
[36] See n. 34 above.
[37] As defined in s.1(4) of the Arbitration Act 1975.
[38] The discretion does not, of course, arise if on examination there is no relevant arbitration clause—see, *e.g. Lakers Mechanical* v. *Boskalis Westminster Construction* (1989) 5 Const.L.J. 139.
[39] See s.1(1) of the 1975 Act; *Associated Bulk Carriers* v. *Koch Shipping* [1978] 1 Lloyd's Rep. 24 (C.A.); *Paczy* v. *Haendler* [1981] 1 Lloyd's Rep. 302 (C.A.); *A and B* v. *C and D* [1982] 1 Lloyd's Rep. 166 at 172.

Section 4(1) of the Arbitration Act 1950 provides:

"*If any party to an arbitration agreement, or any person claiming through or under him, commences any legal proceedings in any court against any other party to the agreement, or any person claiming through or under him, in respect of any matter agreed to be referred, any party to those legal proceedings may at any time after appearance, and before delivering any pleadings or taking any other steps in the proceedings,[40] apply to that court to stay the proceedings, and that court or a judge thereof, if satisfied that there is no sufficient reason why the matter should not be referred in accordance with the agreement, and that the applicant was, at the time when the proceedings were commenced, and still remains, ready and willing to do all things necessary to the proper conduct of the arbitration, may make an order staying the proceedings.*"

The court's discretion under section 4. Even where the various conditions of section 4 are complied with the court has a discretion whether or not to grant a stay and declines to fetter its discretion by laying down any fixed rules on which it will exercise it.[41] But where there is a valid arbitration agreement[42] it has a strong bias in favour of enforcing that agreement by granting a stay,[43] and the onus on an application for a stay is upon the person opposing the stay.[44] Although these principles are applied in every case some guidance can be obtained on the manner in which the court exercises its discretion in particular cases.

Conduct of the defendant. The defendant's conduct relating to the right to arbitration is a factor relevant to the exercise of the court's discretion, as where the court inferred that the defendants' object had been to delay payment and that their motive for applying for a stay was to create further delay.[45]

---

[40] "A 'step in the proceedings' must be one which impliedly affirms the correctness of the proceedings and the willingness of the defendant to go along with a determination by the Courts of law instead of arbitration"—Lord Denning M.R. in *Eagle Star Insurance* v. *Yuval Insurance* [1978] 1 Lloyd's Rep. 357 at 361 (C.A.). See generally Mustill & Boyd, *Commercial Arbitration* (2nd ed.), pp. 472–473. For the position where the plaintiff takes out a summons under R.S.C., Ord. 14, for leave to sign final judgment, see *Pitchers Ltd.* v. *Plaza (Queensbury) Ltd.* [1940] 1 All E.R. 151 (C.A.); *Turner & Goudy* v. *McConnell* (1985) 30 B.L.R. 108 (C.A.).

[41] *Czarnikow* v. *Roth, Schmidt & Co.* [1922] 2 K.B. 478 at 488 (C.A.). See also *Kaye (P. & M.) Ltd.* v. *Hosier & Dickinson Ltd.* [1972] 1 W.L.R. 146 at 152 (H.L.); *Fakes* v. *Taylor Woodrow Construction Ltd.* [1973] 1 Q.B. 436 (C.A.).

[42] Where the matter is in dispute, the court determines it on the application to stay, *Modern Buildings Ltd.* v. *Limmer and Trinidad Co. Ltd.* [1975] 1 W.L.R. 1281 (C.A.).

[43] *Bristol Corp.* v. *Aird* [1913] A.C. 241 at 258–259 (H.L.); *Metropolitan Tunnel Works Ltd.* v. *London Electric Railway* [1926] Ch. 371 (C.A.); *W. Bruce Ltd.* v. *Strong* [1951] 2 K.B. 447 at 457 (C.A.); *Schindler Lifts* v. *Shui On Construction* (1984) 29 B.L.R. 95 at 105 (Hong Kong Court of Appeal).

[44] *Heyman* v. *Darwins Ltd.* [1942] A.C. 356 at 388 (H.L.); *Metropolitan Tunnel Works Ltd.* v. *London Electric Railway* [1926] Ch. 371 (C.A.); *Willesford* v. *Watson* (1873) L.R. 8 Ch.App. 473.

[45] *Croudace* v. *London Borough of Lambeth* (1986) 33 B.L.R. 20 at 36 (C.A.).

No dispute.   If there is no dispute or difference within the meaning of the arbitration agreement a stay will not be granted.[46] A creditor does not have to go to arbitration to collect an undisputed debt.[47] A stay is very commonly refused on the basis that there is no dispute where the plaintiff establishes that he is entitled to summary judgment under R.S.C., Order 14.[48] If part of a claim is indisputably due, judgment may be given for that part leaving the balance, where there is a dispute, to go to arbitration.[49] The court also has jurisdiction first to order an interim payment under R.S.C., Order 29 before granting a stay for the balance of the claim,[50] and has the further power to impose conditions if it decides to grant a stay.[51] A defendant opposing an application for summary judgment who wishes to enforce the arbitration agreement has to apply for a stay at the same time to avoid taking a step in the proceedings.[52]

In building contracts cases, applications under Order 14 and Order 29 (or both) are habitually made where, for instance, a contractor seeks payment on an architect's certificate and considers that the employer has no sustainable ground for not honouring it. Normally the payment of an interim certificate is not a condition precedent to the right to arbitrate.[53]

Where "Crouch" considerations apply.[54]   Where the party applying for a stay claims relief which the arbitrator has power to grant but the court does

---

[46] *London & N.W. & G.W. Railway* v. *Billington Ltd.* [1899] A.C. 79 (H.L.); *Nova (Jersey) Knit Ltd.* v. *Kammgarn Spinnerei GmbH* [1977] 1 W.L.R. 713 (H.L.); the dispute does not, however, have to be in existence at the time when the proceedings were commenced—*Croudace* v. *London Borough of Lambeth* (1986) 33 B.L.R. 20 (C.A.); *cf. Peter Leung Construction* v. *Tai Poon* (1985) 1 Const.L.J. 299 (Hong Kong Court of Appeal) deciding otherwise.

[47] *London & N.W. Railway* v. *Jones* [1915] 2 K.B. 35 at 38.

[48] For examples, see *Ellis Mechanical Services* v. *Wates Construction* [1978] 1 Lloyd's Rep. 33 (Note) (C.A.) and (1976) 2 B.L.R. 57; *C. M. Pillings* v. *Kent Investments* (1985) 30 B.L.R. 80 (C.A.); *Croudace* v. *London Borough of Lambeth* (1986) 33 B.L.R. 20 at 36 (C.A.); *Chatbrown* v. *Alfred McAlpine* (1986) 35 B.L.R. 44 (C.A.); *Imodco* v. *Wimpey and Taylor Woodrow* (1987) 40 B.L.R. 1 (C.A.). Contrast *Hayter* v. *Nelson, The Times*, March 3, 1990, where, under s.1 of the 1975 Act, Saville J. granted a stay in face of an Ord. 14 application. He held the modern view to be that there was no good reason why the courts should strive to take matters out of the hands of the tribunal into which the parties had by agreement undertaken to place them, and that if the claimant could persuade the tribunal that there was no defence there was no good reason why the tribunal could not resolve the dispute in his favour without any delay at all. This is not in line with Court of Appeal or Official Referees' practice in building contract cases, but s.4 of the 1950 Act and s.1 of the 1975 Act may possibly differ in this respect. *cf. Ellerine Brothers* v. *Klinger* [1982] 1 W.L.R. 1375 (C.A.). For Summary judgment generally, see p. 441.

[49] *Ellis Mechanical Services* v. *Wates Construction* [1978] 1 Lloyd's Rep. 33 (Note) and (1976) 2 B.L.R. 57 (C.A.). The position is different under the Arbitration Act 1975—*Associated Bulk Carriers Ltd.* v. *Koch Shipping Inc.* [1978] 1 Lloyd's Rep. 24 (C.A.).

[50] *Imodco* v. *Wimpey and Taylor Woodrow* (1987) 40 B.L.R. 1 (C.A.). For interim payments, see p. 443.

[51] *C. M. Pillings* v. *Kent Investments* (1985) 30 B.L.R. 80 (C.A.).

[52] See n. 40 above.

[53] *Modern Engineering* v. *Gilbert-Ash* [1974] A.C. 689 (H.L.); *C. M. Pillings* v. *Kent Investments* (1985) 30 B.L.R. 80 (C.A.).

[54] See p. 389 for consideration of *Northern Regional Health Authority* v. *Derek Crouch* [1984] Q.B. 644 (C.A.).

not, the view expressed in the *Crouch* case "will virtually give any party a right of veto on any attempt to bypass the arbitration clauses."[55]

Architect's certificate condition precedent.   The contract may be such as to prevent the person applying for a stay from saying that there was a dispute because he does not have an architect's certificate in his favour. In *Brightside Kilpatrick* v. *Mitchell Construction (1973)*,[56] the point arose in relation to the Standard Form of Sub-contract. The Court of Appeal held that the contractor could not say that there was a dispute in respect of his claim for loss caused by the sub-contractor's delay because he did not have in his favour the architect's certificate required by the contract. The court distinguished, and expressed no views upon, the case of *Ramac* v. *Lesser*[57] where the Standard Form of Building Contract was used and at the time of issue of the writ the architect had issued a certificate for payment which deducted liquidated damages although he had not certified under clause 22.[58] It was admitted that the clause 22 certificate was a condition precedent to the right to deduct liquidated damages.[59] Forbes J. held that a dispute or difference arose the minute the plaintiffs refused to accept that there was only the balance due to them on the certificate for payment and granted a stay. There is a difference of wording in the two contracts and the circumstances of the two cases are different, but it is difficult to see why the reasoning of the Court of Appeal does not apply to the absence of a clause 22 certificate.

Disqualification of the arbitrator.   The stay will be refused.[60]

Void or illegal contracts.   A stay will not be granted to an applicant who alleges that the contract was void *ab initio*, as *e.g.* for illegality, or that he never entered into the contract at all.[61]

Point of law.   Where the only point alleged is one of law such as the construction of a contract not involving the meaning of technical terms, the court may refuse a stay as the matter "will only come back to the court on a case stated,"[62] but the party opposing the stay must still discharge the burden

---

[55] Sir John Donaldson M.R. [1984] Q.B. 644 at 675 (C.A.); but see "Overlap with court proceedings" at p. 392.

[56] [1975] 2 Lloyd's Rep. 493 (C.A.).

[57] [1975] 2 Lloyd's Rep. 431.

[58] If the requisite certificate is issued after the writ but before the hearing the defendant can rely upon it to resist summary judgment. See *Ramac's* case at p. 432 and R.S.C., Ord. 18, r. 9.

[59] See p. 563.

[60] *Bristol Corp.* v. *Aird* [1913] A.C. 241 (H.L.); Arbitration Act 1950, s.24(3). For disqualification see p. 393.

[61] *Heyman* v. *Darwins Ltd.* [1942] A.C. 356 at 366 (H.L.). See further p. 388.

[62] Lord Parker in *Bristol Corp.* v. *Aird* [1913] A.C. 241 at 262 (H.L.). A case stated was a means of appeal from an arbitrator's decision before the Arbitration Act 1979. See now "Appeals to the High Court" at p. 412.

of showing why he should not be bound by his agreement.[63] And where technical terms, or words used in a technical sense, are to be found in a contract, such as a building contract, and the parties have chosen as arbitrator an expert in the trade with personal knowledge of the meaning of the terms used, a stay will probably be granted.[64]

Fraud or misconduct of one of the parties alleged.   Where a dispute involves the question whether a party has been guilty of fraud the court has an express statutory power to refuse a stay.[65] It still has a discretion and one factor it might take into account would be an express agreement to submit questions of fraud to arbitration.[66] It has been said that "where the party charged with the fraud desires it ... it is almost a matter of course to refuse the reference,"[67] but there must have been raised a concrete and specific issue of fraud, and the fraud relied on must be fraud by the party opposing the stay.[68] The court is inclined to refuse a stay where allegations of incompetence, negligence and impropriety are made so that a man's professional reputation is at stake.[69] One factor considered by the court where charges of fraud or misconduct such as negligence are made is that there is no appeal from a reference upon the finding of fact.[70] In cases of this kind an appellate court may vary the decision of the court of first instance where that court in exercising its discretion did not take into account all the relevant factors.[71]

Expiry of time for arbitration.   It is not a sufficient ground for refusing a stay that the party applying for the stay relies on an *Atlantic Shipping* clause[72] to allege that the arbitration is out of time.[73]

Delay in reaching arbitration.   Sub-contracts sometimes provide (usually subject to exceptions) that without the consent of the parties arbitration

---

[63] *Metropolitan Works Ltd.* v. *London Electric Railway* [1926] Ch. 371 (C.A.). See also *Heyman* v. *Darwins Ltd.* [1942] A.C. 356 at 369, 389 (H.L.) and Mustill & Boyd, *Commercial Arbitration* (2nd ed.), p. 477. For a building contract case where a stay would have been refused on this ground, see *Lakers Mechanical Services* v. *Boskalis Westminster* (1989) 5 Const.L.J. 139 at 147.

[64] *Ibid.*; *cf. Archital Luxfer* v. *A. J. Dunning* (1987) 47 B.L.R. 1 at 10 (C.A.).

[65] Arbitration Act 1950, s.24(2) and (3); *cf. Earl of Stradbroke* v. *Mitchell, The Times*, October 4, 1990 (C.A.). See also "Revocation of arbitrator's authority" at p. 409.

[66] See *Heyman* v. *Darwins Ltd.* [1942] A.C. 356 at 392 (H.L.).

[67] Jessel M.R. in *Russell* v. *Russell* (1880) 14 Ch.D. 471 at 477.

[68] *Camilla Cotton Co.* v. *Granadex* [1973] 2 Lloyd's Rep. 10 at 16 (H.L.); *Cunningham-Reid* v. *Buchanan-Jardine* [1988] 1 W.L.R. 678 (C.A.).

[69] *Turner* v. *Fenton* [1982] 1 W.L.R. 52; *cf. Charles Osenton* v. *Johnston* [1942] A.C. 130 (H.L.); *Radford* v. *Hair* [1971] Ch. 758.

[70] *Charles Osenton & Co* v. *Johnston* [1942] A.C. 130 (H.L.); *Simplicity Products Ltd.* v. *Domestic Installations Ltd.* [1973] 1 W.L.R. 837 (C.A.)—whether there should be a reference to the Official Referee—but the principle applies, it is thought, to arbitrations. The provisions for appeals from Official Referees has since been changed—see R.S.C., Ord. 58, r. 4(1) as amended with effect from October 1, 1988. There can now be an appeal on a question of fact with leave.

[71] *Ibid.* See also as to discretion *Birkett* v. *James* [1978] A.C. 297 (H.L.).

[72] See p. 397.

[73] *Bruce* v. *Strong* [1951] 2 K.B. 447 (C.A.); *cf. The Jemrix* [1981] 2 Lloyd's Rep. 544.

cannot commence until the completion or abandonment of the main contract works.[74] It is possible that, if the main contractor refuses to give his consent, thus delaying the hearing of the dispute, the courts would refuse a stay.[75]

More than two parties. In *Taunton-Collins* v. *Cromie*,[76] the employer sued his architect for bad design and lack of proper supervision of his house and was met with a defence putting the blame for some of the matters alleged upon the contractor. The contract between the employer and the contractor contained an arbitration clause. The refusal of an application for a stay on behalf of the contractor was upheld[77] on the grounds that if there were two proceedings before different tribunals in respect of the matters in question there would be delay, extra cost, procedural difficulties, and the danger of inconsistent findings of fact.[78] The principle of the decision applies, it is submitted, where a plaintiff has proper[79] grounds for joining two or more defendants initially, or where one of the parties to an arbitration agreement reasonably intends to join a third party. The principle does not apply where the application to stay is under section 1 of the 1975 Act because the court has no discretion to refuse a stay once it is shown that the claim falls within the scope of the clause.[80] The Arbitration Act 1950 makes no provision for proceedings between more than two parties.[81] The parties concerned may overcome this by agreement[82] but such agreements are often difficult to make and, if made, to give effect to, as an arbitrator lacks the wide powers possessed by the court in third party proceedings.[83]

---

[74] See, *e.g.* clause 38.3 of NSC/4 at p. 776.

[75] See Lord Salmon in *Gilbert Ash Ltd.* v. *Modern Engineering (Bristol) Ltd.* [1974] A.C. 689 at 726 (H.L.). In the unreported case of *Mitchell Construction Ltd.* v. *East Anglian Regional Hospital Board*, decided in 1966, where the 1957 revision of the R.I.B.A. Form limited arbitration as to the validity of determination until after completion, save with the consent of the parties, and the employer refused consent, Goff J., after considering evidence, granted a stay.

[76] [1964] 1 W.L.R. 633 (C.A.).

[77] Distinguishing *Bruce* v. *Strong* [1951] 2 K.B. 447 (C.A.); applying *Halifax Overseas Freighters Ltd.* v. *Rasmo Export* [1958] 2 Lloyd's Rep. 146. See also *Berkshire Housing* v. *Fitt* (1979) 15 B.L.R. 27 (C.A.); *Bulk Oil* v. *Trans-Asiatic Oil* [1973] 1 Lloyd's Rep. 129 at 137. See also "Where 'Crouch' considerations apply" at p. 399.

[78] These considerations may not be sufficient to get an arbitration stopped once it has been commenced, see *City Centre Properties (I.T.C. Pensions) Ltd.* v. *Matthew Hall & Co. Ltd.* [1969] 1 W.L.R. 772 (C.A.); *Property Investments* v. *Byfield Building Services* (1985) 31 B.L.R. 47; *cf. Abu Dhabi Gas* v. *Eastern Bechtel* [1982] 2 Lloyd's Rep. 425 (C.A.). See also p. 409.

[79] See Pearson L.J. in *Taunton-Collins* v. *Cromie* [1964] 1 W.L.R. 633 at 637 (C.A.).

[80] *A and B* v. *C and D* [1982] 1 Lloyd's Rep. 166 at 172.

[81] The inability to join a third party is "a fact of life in a great many international and domestic arbitrations"—Steyn J. in *Property Investments* v. *Byfield Building Services* (1985) 31 B.L.R. 47 at 56. Compare the position in Hong Kong where the Arbitration Ordinance (Cap. 341) does give the court power to consolidate arbitrations.

[82] *Ibid.*

[83] See R.S.C., Ord. 16, r. 4. The arbitrator's only effective power is, on the application of one of the parties, to give a notice marked "peremptory" of his intention to proceed *ex parte* if one of the parties does not attend, see *Bremer Vulcan* v. *South India Shipping* [1981] A.C. 909 at 986, 987 (H.L.) and see "Section 5 of the Arbitration Act 1979" at p. 405.

Part only of dispute referable.   Where part of the dispute lies outside the jurisdiction of the arbitrator the court may, if it is convenient, sever the dispute and grant a stay only in respect of that part referable.[84] If the matter cannot be split and a substantial part of the dispute is outside the arbitration agreement a stay will be refused.[85] If only a trifling and subordinate part of the dispute is outside the agreement a stay will not be refused.[86]

Expense of reference.   The plaintiff's poverty, if it is such as to preclude him from litigating or arbitrating without legal aid,[87] can be material but is not decisive.[88] It has been held not to be a ground for refusing a stay that the poverty of a litigant would cause him hardship in arbitration proceedings whereas in proceedings in the High Court he could sue as a poor person.[89] But it seems that, if the plaintiff can show that the probabilities point to his poverty being caused by the very breaches of contract by the defendant of which he complains, a stay will be refused.[90]

Where no stay granted.   Where no stay is granted, or where proceedings are allowed to continue without an application for a stay being made, "the private tribunal of the parties, [*i.e.* arbitrator or umpire] if it has ever come into existence, is *functus officio*,[91] and an award made by the arbitrator after the commencement of the action is invalid and affords no defence to the action.[92]

7. Arbitration Procedure

Some arbitrations are very long and costly.[92a] This can be commercially unsatisfactory and may lead to injustice where one party has a longer pocket than the other.[93] It does not appear that the High Court rules of procedure,

---

[84] *Ives & Barker* v. *Willans* [1894] 2 Ch. 478 at 489 (C.A.); *Bristol Corp.* v. *Aird* [1913] A.C. 261 (H.L.). See also *Bulk Oil Co.* v. *Trans-Asiatic Oil* [1973] 1 Lloyd's Rep. 129.

[85] *Turnock* v. *Sartoris* (1889) 43 Ch.D. 150 (C.A.).

[86] *Ives & Barker* v. *Willans* [1894] 2 Ch. 478 at 489 (C.A.).

[87] Legal aid is available for litigation but not currently for arbitration.

[88] *Goodman* v. *Winchester Railway* [1985] 1 W.L.R. 141 (C.A.). For applications to stay non-domestic arbitrations under s.1 of the Arbitration Act 1975, where there is no discretion if the statutory conditions are met, the plaintiff's financial position is, it seems, immaterial—see *Paczy* v. *Haendler* [1981] 1 Lloyd's Rep. 302 (C.A.).

[89] *Smith* v. *Pearl Assurance Co.* [1939] 1 All E.R. 95 (C.A.). The poor person procedure has since been replaced by legislation now consolidated in the Legal Aid Act 1974. Legal aid is still not available for arbitrations.

[90] *Fakes* v. *Taylor Woodrow Ltd.* [1973] Q.B. 436 (C.A.); *Goodman* v. *Winchester Railway* [1985] 1 W.L.R. 141 at 147 (C.A.).

[91] *Doleman* v. *Ossett Corp.* [1912] 3 K.B. 257 at 269 (C.A.), distinguished by the House of Lords in *Kaye (P. & M.) Ltd.* v. *Hosier & Dickinson Ltd.* [1972] 1 W.L.R. 146 holding that the court would not go behind an architect's certificate issued after service of a writ in so far as the certificate was expressed to be "conclusive evidence in any proceedings." See further at p. 618.

[92] *Ibid.* See however "Overlap with court proceedings" at p. 392.

[92a] For arbitrators' fees, see *K/S Norjave* v. *Hyundai Heavy Industries, The Times,* November 8, 1990.

[93] *cf.* Lawton L.J. in *Ellis* v. *Wates Construction* [1978] 1 Lloyd's Rep. 33 at 36 (Note) and (1976) 2 B.L.R. 57 at 64 (C.A.).

applicable in the Queen's Bench Division, with their emphasis upon oral evidence, have been developed for the speedy determination of complex and detailed building disputes. Sometimes they are quite inappropriate.

Suggestions for an approach to procedure include that the arbitrator should be encouraged to read the papers before the hearing and that oral evidence should be confined to those matters where it is really necessary.[94] Massive further and better particulars should be discouraged. In a complex case, pleadings are nearly always necessary. So also is discovery. It is suggested that thereafter the parties prepare and exchange witness statements and written opening submissions with full references to all the documents or parts of documents upon which they wish to rely. Such statements are to be taken as evidence on which the arbitrator can act, provided that either party may give notice of a requirement to cross-examine. The right to supplement witness statements is probably necessary, although it requires control by the arbitrator or much of the point of the procedure will be lost. At the hearing, as well as dealing with the oral evidence, if any, the advocates would enlarge upon their opening submissions. Final submissions should be encouraged to be in writing with, if necessary, an adjournment for their proper preparation. Something on these lines if carefully followed ought to result in a saving of time and cost.

The problem is to introduce and enforce such procedure. An express agreement between the parties empowering the arbitrator to make such orders removes doubt as to their validity. In the absence of such an agreement, it is not clear how far the arbitrator can go, although the ordinary position is that he is "master of the procedure to be followed in the arbitration ... he has a complete discretion to determine how the arbitration is to be conducted ... so long as the procedure he adopts does not offend the rules of natural justice."[95] However, in most building contract arbitrations at least, unless the parties agree otherwise the arbitrator is required to adopt an adversarial procedure giving each party a full opportunity to present their case at an oral hearing at which each party must have the opportunity to be present with advisers, including legal advisers who may act as advocates, and witnesses.[96]

Arbitrators have wide powers under section 12(1) of the Arbitration Act 1950[97] which sets out specific contractual obligations which the parties assume to one another in the procedure to be followed in the arbitration unless a contrary intention is expressed.[98] There is also a general requirement to "do all

---

[94] But arbitrators must act fairly in this respect—see *Carlisle Place* v. *Wimpey* (1980) 15 B.L.R. 109 at 116.

[95] Lord Diplock in *Bremer Vulkan* v. *South India Shipping* [1981] A.C. 909 at 985 (H.L.); *cf. Carlisle Place* v. *Wimpey* [1980] 15 B.L.R. 109 at 116.

[96] *Town & City Properties* v. *Wiltshier* (1988) 44 B.L.R. 114—H.H. Sir William Stabb Q.C. adopting a passage in Mustill & Boyd, *Commercial Arbitration* (1st ed.), p. 261. See now Mustill & Boyd, *Commercial Arbitration* (2nd ed.), pp. 289 and 302.

[97] See also s.12(6) of the 1950 Act (as amended by s.103 of the Courts and Legal Services Act 1990) for powers of the court.

[98] Where the arbitration agreement incorporates one of the institutional Arbitration Rules—see, *e.g.* those in Appendix 4 to Mustill & Boyd, *Commercial Arbitration* (2nd ed.)—the arbitrator will have the powers specified in the Rules.

other things which during the proceedings on the reference the arbitrator or umpire may require."[99] An arbitrator may make a peremptory direction requiring the claimant to give proper particulars of his claims within a limited time failing which the arbitrator will proceed to a hearing at which the claimant, if he appears, is debarred from tendering evidence of any claim of which he had not given the required particulars. Further, the arbitrator can make a peremptory order requiring the parties to appear at a time and place fixed for the hearing, and if one of them does not appear the arbitrator can proceed in his absence.[1]

> "In requiring particular steps to be taken by any party he [the arbitrator] is entitled to act not only on the application of a party to the arbitration but also on his own initiative; but he is not under any duty to do the latter, for in the absence of any application he is justified in assuming that both parties are satisfied with the way in which the proceedings leading up to his making an award are progressing."[2]

Section 5 of the Arbitration Act 1979. This section to some extent supplements an arbitrator's under-defined powers at common law to make peremptory orders to secure timely compliance with his procedural orders. Upon application to the High Court by the arbitrator or any party to the reference, the court has power to make an order under section 5, whereupon the arbitrator has power, subject to the terms of the order, "to continue with the reference in default of appearance or of any other act by one of the parties in like manner as a judge of the High Court might continue with proceedings" in such circumstances.[3] The operation of this salutary, if cumbersome, procedure is unclear in detail.[4]

Dismissal for want of prosecution. The court has power in certain circumstances to dismiss an action for want of prosecution,[5] but formerly an arbitrator did not have an equivalent power,[6] other than upon application to the court under section 5 of the Arbitration Act 1979 as discussed above. Further, since arbitration was consensual and both parties had a mutual obligation to progress the proceedings,[7] an injunction would not be granted by the court restraining the continuance of an arbitration merely because there had been shown to be inordinate and inexcusable delay on the part of the

---

[99] *cf. Bremer Vulcan* v. *South India Shipping* [1981] A.C. 909 at 986 (H.L.).
[1] *Ibid.* at 986, 987.
[2] *Ibid.* at 984.
[3] *cf. Bremer Vulcan* v. *South India Shipping* [1981] A.C. 909 at 987 (H.L.).
[4] For a discussion, see Mustill & Body, *Commercial Arbitration* (2nd ed.), pp. 539 *et seq.*
[5] See p. 436.
[6] *Bremer Vulcan* v. *South India Shipping* [1981] A.C. 909 (H.L.); *Crawford* v. *Prowting Ltd.* [1973] Q.B. 1.
[7] *Bremer Vulcan* v. *South India Shipping* [1981] A.C. 909 (H.L.); *Paal Wilson* v. *Partenreederei Hannah Blumenthal* [1983] 1 A.C. 854 (H.L.).

claimant.[8] Before the 1979 Act, the remedy of a party prejudiced by delay was, it seems, to apply to the arbitrator to fix a date for the hearing,[9] and for the arbitrator to proceed, if necessary, *ex parte*. After the 1979 Act, the section 5 procedure was not regarded as satisfactory and there were attempts to alleviate a plainly unsatisfactory state of the law by invoking principles of repudiation, frustration and abandonment.[10]

However, by section 13A of the Arbitration Act 1950 as inserted by section 102 of the Courts and Legal Services Act 1990, it is provided that, unless a contrary intention is expressed in the arbitration agreement, an arbitrator now does have power to dismiss a claim where there has been inordinate and inexcusable delay on the part of the claimant and where in consequence there is or is likely to be serious prejudice to the respondent or a substantial risk that it is not possible to have a fair resolution of the issues. The section is not yet in force. There are no statutory transitional provisions so that it is not clear whether the section applies to arbitrations already started when the provision comes into force. The language of the section suggests that it does.[11]

Offer to protect costs. The approximate effect of a payment into court under R.S.C., Order 22[12] can be achieved in arbitration proceedings by a suitably worded letter making an offer of settlement on terms that the letter is not to be disclosed to the arbitrator before all issues of liability and debt or damages are determined and costs come to be considered.[13] The offer should state that it is intended to have the effect of a payment into court.[14] It should say whether or not it includes interest. Normally it should include interest.[15] It should offer to pay costs up to the time of an acceptance within 21 days of the offer (in order to preserve the analogy with payment-in), but should not perhaps otherwise make payment of the sum offered conditional upon acceptance within a particular time. The reason for this would be that if an offer of payment is withdrawn before trial the judge may ignore it when considering costs.[16] If the offer does not stipulate a time for acceptance, it is likely,

---

[8] *Ibid.*

[9] *Crawford* v. *Prowting Ltd.* [1973] Q.B. 1.

[10] See, *e.g. Andre et Compagnie* v. *Marine Transocean* [1981] Q.B. 694 (C.A.); *Paal Wilson* v. *Partenreederei Hannah Blumenthal* [1983] 1 A.C. 854 (H.L.); *Allied Marine* v. *Vale Do Rio Doce* [1985] 1 W.L.R. 925 (C.A.); *The Agrabele* [1987] 2 Lloyd's Rep. 223 (C.A.); *Food Corporation of India* [1988] 1 W.L.R. 603 (H.L.). There is a number of other cases and see also Mustill & Boyd, *Commercial Arbitration* (2nd ed.), pp. 504 *et seq.*

[11] For a consideration of whether statutory provisions have retrospective effect, see *Halsbury*, Vol. 44, paras. 921 *et seq.* and in particular 922 and 925.

[12] See p. 458 and esp. "Written offers" at p. 462.

[13] *Tramountana Armadora* v. *Atlantic Shipping* [1978] 1 Lloyd's Rep. 391; *Archital Luxfer* v. *Henry Boot* [1981] 1 Lloyd's Rep. 642; *cf. Calderbank* v. *Calderbank* [1976] Fam. 93 at 106 (C.A); *Cutts* v. *Head* [1984] Ch. 290 (C.A.); R.S.C., Ord. 22, r. 14.

[14] See *Dineen* v. *Walpole* [1969] 1 Lloyd's Rep. 261 at 263 (C.A.).

[15] See "Interest" at p. 451.

[16] See *The Toni* [1974] 1 Lloyd's Rep. 489 (C.A.); *cf. Garner* v. *Cleggs* [1983] 1 W.L.R. 862 (C.A.); *Huron Liberian Co.* v. *Rheinoel* [1985] 2 Lloyd's Rep. 58.

depending on its terms and all the circumstances, to be construed as being open for a reasonable time. While a reasonable time may be held to have expired before the making of an award, at the very latest it would be held to have expired when an award is made.[17] It is thought, however, that an offer could validly and more closely simulate the effect of a payment into court if it stipulated that it was open for acceptance for 21 days from its receipt and that thereafter acceptance was to be conditional on the recipient agreeing to pay the offeror's subsequent costs or on an application being made to the arbitrator in respect of those costs. Where there is a counterclaim the offer should, by analogy with the rules, state whether it is intended to take into account and satisfy the counterclaim.[18] The claimant can make an offer in respect of the counterclaim.

Such an offer is sometimes called a "sealed offer" from the practice of handing the arbitrator a sealed envelope containing the offer. This has the disadvantage that it may inferentially tell the arbitrator that an offer of some kind has been made.[19] It is also thought to be unnecessary. At the end of the hearing, the arbitrator should be asked, without the existence of the offer being disclosed, to defer consideration of costs until he has made his award on all other issues. As he can ordinarily make only one final award this requires that his award on liability and debt or damages will be an interim award.[20] Costs are usually of such importance and the issues relating to them are sometimes so complex that this procedure is frequently and conveniently followed even if there is no offer to be taken into account. A request to follow this procedure should not, therefore, cause the arbitrator to think that an offer has necessarily been made.

An arbitrator has the same discretion as to costs as a High Court judge,[21] and the effect of such an offer on costs should in substance be the same as that of a payment into court. On being informed of the offer at the appropriate time, the arbitrator's approach is to ask himself whether the claimant achieved more by rejecting the offer and going on with the arbitration than he would have achieved if he had accepted the offer.[22]

Interim awards. Unless a contrary intention is expressed in the arbitration agreement, an arbitrator has power to make an interim award,[23] which may be made subject to any proper condition.[24] In building contract arbitrations, interim awards are often made upon preliminary issues. It is thought that there is no reason in principle why an arbitrator might not make an interim

---

[17] *Krupp Handel* v. *Intermare Transport* [1986] 1 Lloyd's Rep. 176.

[18] See "Counterclaim" at p. 461.

[19] See *Tramountana Armadora* v. *Atlantic Shipping* [1978] 1 Lloyd's Rep. 391; *cf. Huron Liberian Co.* v. *Rheinoel* [1985] 2 Lloyd's Rep. 58.

[20] See *M.F. King (Holdings)* v. *Thomas McKenna* (1990) 6 Const.L.J. 229.

[21] *Cutts* v. *Head* [1984] Ch. 290 at 309 (C.A.).

[22] *Tramountana Armadora* v. *Atlantic Shipping* [1978] 1 Lloyd's Rep. 391.

[23] s.14 of the Arbitration Act 1950.

[24] *Japan Line* v. *Aggeliki Charis* [1980] 1 Lloyd's Rep. 288 (C.A.).

award in circumstances where the court would give summary judgment under R.S.C., Order 14 and upon equivalent affidavit evidence. But he can only do this in exceptional circumstances where he can properly find that he is not satisfied that any defences advanced are made in good faith or on reasonable grounds.[25] All awards which are not final awards are interim awards and interim awards which are in effect final except as to costs or interest are frequently made where the parties need to know the substantive result before ancillary questions are argued.[26] Once an arbitrator has made a valid interim award on an issue, he is *functus officio* in relation to that part of his mandate which comprised the issue and the award creates an issue estoppel between the parties, crystalising the relationship between them in relation to that issue.[27]

Interest.   Arbitrators normally have power, equivalent to the court's power, to award interest[28] and to be exercised on equivalent principles.[29]

8. Control by the Court

Although the arbitrator's decision as to fact is final, the court retains control over arbitration agreements and references, and a party who considers that there has been some irregularity or other special reason may invoke its assistance.[30] For a full account reference should be made to Mustill & Boyd, *Commercial Arbitration.*[31] There follows an outline as a guide with particular reference to building contracts.

Appointment of arbitrator.   The court has power in certain circumstances to appoint an arbitrator.[32]

---

[25] See *S.L. Sethia Liners* v. *Naviagro Maritime* [1981] 1 Lloyd's Rep. 18 at 25 *et seq.*; *The Modern Trading Co.* v. *Swale Building and Construction* (1990) 6 Const.L.J. 251; see also "No dispute" at p. 399.

[26] *Cf. M.F. King (Holdings)* v. *Thomas McKenna* (1990) 6 Const.L.J. 229.

[27] *London Borough of Islington* v. *Turriff Construction* (unreported) March 16, 1990 (C.A.).

[28] See s.19A of the Arbitration Act 1950 as inserted by s.15(6) of the Administration of Justice Act 1982; *Food Corporation of India* v. *Marastro Compania* [1987] 1 W.L.R. 134 (C.A.); *Chandris* v. *Isbrandtsen-Moller Co. Inc.* [1951] 1 K.B. 240 (C.A.).

[29] See "Discretionary interest" at p. 451.

[30] The court's power of control over arbitrators is statutory and mainly contained in the Arbitration Acts 1950 and 1979; it has no inherent power, *Exormisis S.A.* v. *Oonsoo* [1975] 1 Lloyd's Rep. 432. See R.S.C., Ord. 73 for Rules of Court relating to the exercise of the powers discussed in this section.

[31] (2nd ed.), Chaps. 29–37.

[32] Arbitration Act 1950, s.10 as amended by s.6(3) and 6(4) of the Arbitration Act 1979; see also s.25; *cf. Mayer Newman* v. *Al Ferro Commodities, The Times,* April 9, 1990 (C.A.). The addition of s.10(2) by s.6(4) of the 1979 Act was to deal with the problem raised in *National Enterprises Ltd.* v. *Racal Communications Ltd.* [1975] Ch. 397 (C.A.).

Extension of time.   Section 27 of the Arbitration Act 1950[33] gives the court a discretion, where there would otherwise be undue hardship,[34] to extend a contractual time for starting arbitration proceedings if doing so will prevent a claim becoming time-barred.[35] The section can apply, for instance, to the time limit in clause 66 of the I.C.E. Conditions.[36] It can apply notwithstanding that the arbitrator may also have jurisdiction to extend time under the terms of the arbitration agreement.[37]

Clause 30 of the Standard Form of Building Contract provides that a final certificate shall be conclusive evidence that the contract has been properly performed except for matters in respect of which arbitration proceedings have been commenced not later than 28 days after the final certificate has been issued.[38] In *Emson Contractors* v. *Protea Estates*,[39] an application under section 27 for an extension of time failed on the ground that on the facts there was no undue hardship. It was apparently assumed that section 27 in principle applied to the clause in question. There may, however, arguably be a distinction between a clause, such as clause 30, providing that in certain circumstances a final certificate shall be conclusive evidence of certain facts and a clause, such as clause 30 is not, barring arbitration unless it is started within a stipulated time. On one view, section 27 would not apply to the first of these and it is perhaps questionable whether an extension of time under section 27 could alter the parties stipulated contractual rights.[40]

Revocation of arbitrator's authority.   By section 1 of the Arbitration Act 1950, the authority of the arbitrator is, unless the agreement expresses a contrary intention, irrevocable except by leave of the court. The power of the court under section 24(1) of the Arbitration Act 1950 to revoke the authority of the arbitrator for want of impartiality has been considered above. By section 24(2) of the Act, where the arbitration agreement concerns disputes which may arise in the future,[41] the court may give leave to revoke the arbitrator's

---

[33] For its history, see *Ch. E. Rolimpex* v. *Avra Shipping* [1973] 2 Lloyd's Rep. 226 at 229 and *Comdel Commodities* v. *Siporex* [1990] 3 W.L.R. 1 (H.L.). It seems that the court's jurisdiction under s.27 may not be excluded by contract—see *Comdel Commodities* v. *Siporex* [1989] 2 Lloyd's Rep. 13 (C.A.); [1990] 3 W.L.R. 1 (H.L.).

[34] See, *e.g. Libra Shipping* v. *Northern Sales* [1981] 1 Lloyd's Rep. 273 esp. at 280 (C.A.) and the cases there cited; *Comdel Commodities* v. *Siporex* [1989] 2 Lloyd's Rep. 13 at 23 (C.A.); [1990] 3 W.L.R. 1 (H.L.).

[35] See *Babanaft International* v. *Avanti Petroleum* [1982] 1 W.L.R. 871 at 885 (C.A.). It does not apply to extend any other time limits—*ibid.*; *cf. Jadranska Plovidba* v. *Oleagine* [1984] 1 W.L.R. 300 (C.A.).

[36] See p. 921 and *cf. International Tank and Pipe* v. *Kuwait Aviation* [1975] Q.B. 224 (C.A.)—a decision on a substantially similar clause in the F.I.D.I.C. Conditions.

[37] *Comdel Commodities* v. *Siporex* [1990] 3 W.L.R. 1 (H.L.).

[38] See p. 610.

[39] (1987) 39 B.L.R. 126.

[40] *Consolidated Investment* v. *Saponaria* [1978] 1 W.L.R. 986 (C.A.) and *Comdel Commodities* v. *Siporex* [1990] 3 W.L.R. 1 (H.L.) are perhaps against this view and *cf. Sioux Inc.* v. *China Salvage Co.* [1980] 1 W.L.R. 996 (C.A.); but see *Babanaft International* v. *Avant Petroleum* [1982] 1 W.L.R. 871 at 885 (C.A.).

[41] See *Yeu Shing Construction* v. *Att.-Gen. of Hong Kong* (1988) 40 B.L.R. 131 (Hong Kong High Court).

authority where a dispute involves a concrete and specific issue whether any party has been guilty of fraud.[42] The court has a discretion which it will normally exercise where a party charged with substantial fraud desires it.[43] Subject to these provisions and other specific provisions discussed below under which the court can control arbitrations, the court's general discretion to give leave to revoke is only exercised in wholly exceptional circumstances such as fundamentally imperil the fair and proper functioning of the arbitral process.[44] Convenience will never warrant an order under section 1 of the 1950 Act.[45] The discretion is not merely the converse of that exercised under section 4.[46]

Injunction to restrain arbitration proceedings.[47]   There is power to restrain arbitration proceedings when, exceptionally perhaps, there has been a repudiatory breach of an arbitration agreement[48] and the innocent party has elected to treat the contract as at an end.[49] There is power to restrain arbitration proceedings where an action has been brought impeaching the document containing the arbitration agreement,[50] or where the arbitrator has no jurisdiction to hear the claims in question.[51] The court may also grant an injunction where there are effective concurrent court proceedings which ought alone to proceed.[52] In such a case, the considerations are whether a stay of the reference would cause injustice to the claimant and whether continuance of the reference would be oppressive or vexatious to the respondent or an abuse of the process

---

[42] *Kruger Townswear Ltd.* v. *Northern Ass. Co.* [1953] 1 W.L.R. 1049 (D.C.); *Camilla Cotton Oil* v. *Granadex* [1976] 2 Lloyd's Rep. 10 at 16 (H.L.); *Ashville Investments* v. *Elmer Contractors* [1989] Q.B. 488 at 501, 506, 517 (C.A.).

[43] *Russell* v. *Russell* (1880) 14 Ch.D. 471; *Camilla Cotton Oil* v. *Granadex* [1976] 2 Lloyd's Rep. 10 (H.L.); *Cunningham-Reid* v. *Buchanan-Jardine* [1988] 1 W.L.R. 678 (C.A.); *cf. Yeu Shing Construction* v. *Att.-Gen. of Hong Kong* (1988) 40 B.L.R. 131 (Hong Kong High Court). See also "Fraud or misconduct of one of the parties alleged" at p. 401.

[44] *Property Investments* v. *Byfield Building Services* (1985) 31 B.L.R. 47; *City Centre Properties (I.T.C. Pensions) Ltd.* v. *Matthew Hall & Co. Ltd.* [1969] 1 W.L.R. 772 (C.A.); *cf. Scott* v. *Van Sandau* (1841) 1 Q.B. 102 at 110; *James* v. *James* (1889) 22 Q.B.D. 669 at 674 (D.C.); affd. 23 Q.B.D. 12 (C.A.); *Belcher* v. *Roedean School* (1901) 85 L.T. 468 (C.A.); *Stockport* v. *O'Reilly* [1983] 2 Lloyd's Rep. 70. "Section 1 must be construed as a provision which was intended to make it more difficult to remove arbitrators."—Steyn J. in *Property Investments* case at 54.

[45] *Property Investments* v. *Byfield Building Services* (1985) 31 B.L.R. 47 at 56.

[46] *City Centre Properties (I.T.C. Pensions) Ltd.* v. *Matthew Hall & Co. Ltd.* [1969] 1 W.L.R. 772 (C.A.). For s.4, see p. 397.

[47] See also "Overlap with court proceedings" at p. 392.

[48] N.B. this is not the same as a repudiation of an agreement containing an arbitration clause where the arbitration clause normally survives acceptance of repudiation—see *Heyman* v. *Darwins* [1942] A.C. 356 (H.L.); see also p. 151.

[49] *Bremer Vulcan* v. *South India Shipping* [1981] A.C. 909 (H.L.); *cf. Turriff* v. *Richards & Wallington* (1981) 18 B.L.R. 13; *Compagnie Europeene* v. *Tradax* [1986] 2 Lloyd's Rep. 301; *The Choko Star* [1987] 1 Lloyd's Rep. 508 (C.A.). See also "Dismissal for want of prosecution" at p. 405.

[50] *Kitts* v. *Moore* [1895] 1 Q.B. 253 (C.A.); *Bremer Vulcan* v. *South India Shipping* [1981] A.C. 909 at 981 (H.L.).

[51] *Siporex* v. *Comdel* [1986] 2 Lloyd's Rep. 428.

[52] *Northern Regional Health Authority* v. *Derek Crouch* [1984] Q.B. 644 at 673 (C.A.) where the application failed on the facts.

of the court.[53] The power to grant an injunction restraining arbitration is analogous to that of revoking the arbitrator's authority and is in effect the converse of granting a stay. It is a power which the court in practice uses sparingly.

Declaration as to arbitrator's jurisdiction.   The court has jurisdiction to grant such a declaration.[54]

Misconduct.   If an arbitrator has misconducted himself or the proceedings, the court may remove him or set an award aside.[55] Where misconduct on the part of the arbitrator is alleged an application for his removal is the correct course. If the application is granted the court has power to appoint a fresh arbitrator.[56] The test of misconduct, which does not necessarily involve moral turpitude, is whether there exist grounds from which a reasonable person would think that there was a real likelihood that the arbitrator could not, or would not, fairly determine the issue in question on the evidence and arguments to be adduced before him.[57]

An arbitrator's duty is to decide the matter which is submitted to him in accordance with the agreement under which he was appointed and he also has a duty to act fairly between the parties.[58] However informal an arbitration may be, the fundamental rules underlying the administration of all justice must always be applied.[59] Both sides must be heard, each in the presence of the other. The arbitrator must not permit one side to use means of influencing the conduct and decisions of the arbitrator, which means are not known to the other side.[60] In building contract disputes, an arbitrator has been removed:

(1) who made interim award on a point of law without hearing one of the parties, on the basis that he misconducted the proceedings in breach of natural justice[61];

---

[53] *Compagnie Nouvelle France* v. *Compagnie Navale Afrique* [1966] 1 Lloyd's Rep. 477 at 487 (C.A.); *Northern Regional Health Authority* v. *Derek Crouch* [1984] Q.B. 644 at 659 (C.A.).

[54] *Gibraltar (Govt. of)* v. *Kenney* [1956] 2 Q.B. 410; *Japan Line* v. *Aggeliki Charis* [1980] 1 Lloyd's Rep. 288 (C.A.); *cf. Metal Scrap Trade Corporation* v. *Kate Shipping* [1990] 1 W.L.R. 115 (H.L.); an analogous method is to proceed by way of a construction summons; see, *e.g. A. E. Farr Ltd.* v. *Ministry of Transport* [1960] 1 W.L.R. 956.

[55] Arbitration Act 1950, s.23. For a case discussing misconduct, see *Prod-export* v. *Man (E. D. & F.)* [1973] 1 Q.B. 389—error of law (or fact) not in itself misconduct, although illegality is. See also *GKN Centrax Gears Ltd.* v. *Matbro Ltd.* [1976] 2 Lloyd's Rep. 555 (C.A.). For a case with a full review of authorities, see *Turner (East Asia)* v. *Builders Federal* (1988) 42 B.L.R. 122 at 145 (Singapore High Court).

[56] Arbitration Act 1950, s.25.

[57] *Hagop Ardahalion* v. *Unifert International* [1984] 2 Lloyd's Rep. 84 at 89 (C.A.); *cf. Modern Engineering* v. *Miskin* [1981] 1 Lloyd's Rep. 135; *Asia Construction* v. *Crown Pacific* (1988) 44 B.L.R. 135 (Hong Kong High Court).

[58] See *Carlisle Place* v. *Wimpey* (1980) 15 B.L.R. 109 at 116; *cf. Ashville Investments* v. *Elmer Contractors* [1988] 3 W.L.R. 687 at 874 (C.A.); *Morgan Grenfell* v. *Seven Seas Dredging* (1989) 49 B.L.R. 31.

[59] *Maltin* v. *Donne* (1980) 15 B.L.R. 61 at 75.

[60] *Harvey* v. *Shelton* (1844) 7 Beav. 455 at 462.

[61] *Modern Engineering (Bristol)* v. *C. Miskin & Son* [1981] 1 Lloyd's Rep. 135 (C.A.); *cf. Pratt* v. *Swanmore Builders* [1980] 2 Lloyd's Rep. 504.

411

(2) who failed to give the claimants an opportunity to deal with the arbitrator's own special knowledge relating to the facts[62];

(3) who, in face of protests from one party, dispensed with an adversarial hearing in favour of meetings between himself and the parties' technical representatives and then issued a 70 page "Preliminary View" containing specific findings, although he did give the parties a nominal opportunity to make further submissions[63];

(4) who determined a preliminary issue without a proper hearing and then adopted the stance that what he did was fit and proper.[64]

An arbitrator would have been removed, had he not resigned, where in another action against a party to the arbitration he had appeared to be participating in the instructions of counsel for the other party.[65] An arbitrator's award was set aside where he received a prejudicial document from one party but refused to let the other party have a copy of it.[66]

On the other hand, the court does not generally interfere with procedural orders made in the course of an arbitration.[67] An arbitrator in a dispute where 83 roofs were alleged to be defective was held to have acted within his jurisdiction in ordering that liability should be determined by reference to a maximum of 25 of the roofs while leaving open a possibility that application might be made for evidence of additional defects in other roofs to be received.[68]

Removal of arbitrator for delay. An application can be made under section 13(3) of the Arbitration Act 1950 to remove an arbitrator who fails to use all reasonable dispatch.[69]

Preservation of status quo. The court has power to order the detention, preservation or inspection of property as to which any question may arise in the reference.[70]

Appeals to the High Court. Before the enactment of the Arbitration Act 1979, arbitrators' decisions on points of law could be reviewed by the High Court by means of the statement of a special case.[71] This procedure was

---

[62] *Fox* v. *P. G. Wellfair Ltd.* [1981] 2 Lloyd's Rep. 514 (C.A.).

[63] *Town & City Properties* v. *Wiltshier* (1988) 44 B.L.R. 109.

[64] *Asia Construction* v. *Crown Pacific* (1988) 44 B.L.R. 135 (Hong Kong High Court).

[65] *Tracomin* v. *Gibbs* [1985] 1 Lloyd's Rep. 586. See also "Disqualification for bias" at p. 393.

[66] *Maltin* v. *Donne* (1980) 15 B.L.R. 61; *cf. Brown* v. *CBS (Contractors)* [1987] 1 Lloyd's Rep. 279.

[67] See *Carlisle Place* v. *Wimpey* (1980) 15 B.L.R. 109 at 116; *cf. Stockport* v. *O'Reilly* [1983] 2 Lloyd's Rep. 70 at 78.

[68] *Ibid.*

[69] *cf. Pratt* v. *Swanmore Builders* [1980] 2 Lloyd's Rep. 504 at 512.

[70] Arbitration Act 1950, s.12(6)(g). For other powers of the court in relation to the reference, see this section of the Act generally. Thus for an order for security for costs, see *Bilcon Ltd.* v. *Fegmay Investments Ltd.* [1966] 2 Q.B. 221; *cf. Bank Mellat* v. *Helliniki Techniki* [1984] Q.B. 291 (C.A.).

[71] See the 4th edition of this book at p. 247 for a discussion of the procedure. See also generally article by Anthony Thornton, "Appeals in Construction Arbitrations" (1984–5) 1 Const.L.J. 103.

abolished by the 1979 Act[72] and replaced by a system of appeal to the High Court which, as applied, promotes greater finality in arbitral awards.[73] Parties may enter into an agreement in writing excluding the right of appeal.[74]

Under section 1(2) of the Arbitration Act 1979, appeals are possible on any question of law arising out of an award with the consent of all the other parties to the reference,[75] or with leave of the court.[76] The High Court shall not grant leave unless it considers that, having regard to all the circumstances, the determination of the question of law could substantially affect the rights of one or more of the parties.[77] For the purpose of applications for leave to appeal, arbitrators are normally asked to give reasons for their award and the court may order an arbitrator to state reasons where he has not sufficiently done so, provided normally that one of the parties asked him to do so before the award was made.[78] Applications for leave to appeal may be transferred to an Official Referee where this is appropriate, as it may be in a dispute concerning a building contract.[79] The principles upon which leave to appeal should be granted or refused are exactly the same in construction cases as in any other case.[80]

Leave to appeal is granted sparingly. The court has a discretion for whose exercise there are guidelines.[81] In "one-off cases" where the question of law is one which is unlikely to recur, leave is not normally given unless it is apparent to the judge upon a mere perusal of the reasoned award itself and with only brief oral argument[82] that the arbitrator was obviously wrong.[83] "Does it

---

[72] See s.1(1). See also s.2 for the limited possibility of determination by the court of a preliminary point of law.

[73] *Pioneer Shipping* v. *B.T.P. Tioxide* [1982] A.C. 724 at 742 (H.L.); *Antaios Compania* v. *Salen A.B.* [1985] A.C. 191 at 203 (H.L.); *Ipswich Borough Council* v. *Fisons* [1990] Ch. 709 at 722 (C.A.).

[74] See s.3(1); *cf. Arab African Energy* v. *Olieprodukten Nederland* [1983] 2 Lloyd's Rep. 419; *Marine Contractors* v. *Shell Petroleum* [1984] 2 Lloyd's Rep. 77 (C.A.)—both cases concerning Art. 24 of the ICC Rules of Arbitration. For arbitration under the ICC Rules, see p. 416.

[75] See s.1(3)(a)—such consent is rarely forthcoming after an award, but *cf. Ipswich Borough Council* v. *Fisons* [1990] Ch. 709 at 722 (C.A.).

[76] See s.1(3)(b). See also s.1(6A) and (7) for appeals to the Court of Appeal and *cf. Antaios Compania* v. *Salen A.B.* [1985] A.C. 191 at 205 (H.L.); *F. G. Whitley* v. *Clwyd County Council* (1982) 22 B.L.R. 48 (C.A.); *Geogas SA* v. *Trammo Gas, The Times,* November 26, 1990 (C.A.).

[77] See s.1(4).

[78] See s.1(5) and (6); *cf. Granges Aluminium* v. *Cleveland Bridge and Engineering, The Times,* May 15, 1990 (C.A.)—power to order further *additional* reasons should be exercised as sparingly as possible.

[79] *Tate & Lyle* v. *Davy McKee* [1990] Q.B. 1068 (C.A.).

[80] *Higgs & Hill* v. *University of London* (1983) 24 B.L.R. 139 at 148; *cf. Ipswich Borough Council* v. *Fisons* [1990] Ch. 709 (C.A.).

[81] See *Aden Refinery* v. *Ugland Management* [1987] Q.B. 650 at 667 (C.A.). In Hong Kong, where the legislation is similar but not identical, the approach is somewhat different—see *P.T. Dover Chemical* v. *Lee Chang Yung Chemical* (unreported) March 20, 1990 (Hong Kong Court of Appeal).

[82] *Ipswich Borough Council* v. *Fisons* [1990] Ch. 709 at 721 (C.A.).

[83] *Pioneer Shipping* v. *B.T.P. Tioxide* [1982] A.C. 724 at 742 (H.L.); *Antaios Compania* v. *Salen A.B.* [1985] A.C. 191 at 207 (H.L.); *Seaworld Ocean Line* v. *Catseye Maritime* [1989] 1 Lloyd's Rep. 30 at 32. For a building contract case where leave was refused, see *F. G. Whitley* v. *Clwyd County Council* (1982) 22 B.L.R. 48 (C.A.).

appear upon perusal of the award either that the arbitrator misdirected himself in law or that his decision was such that no reasonable arbitrator could reach?"[84] Where questions of the construction of contracts in standard terms are concerned, leave to appeal is rather more likely to be granted since it is in the public interest that the meaning of such contracts should be clear and certain. But leave is not given in these cases unless there is a strong prima facie case that the arbitrator's construction is wrong.[85] This applies even when there are conflicting judicial *obiter dicta*, although leave should be given if there are conflicting judicial decisions.[86] Where the events to which the standard clause falls to be applied are "one-off" events, stricter criteria are applied.[87] The standard term contract approach may well be appropriate to decisions which will have a recurring effect between the parties[88] and also to awards which raise questions of law of general importance which do not concern standard term contracts, especially where there is little or no direct authority.[89]

Remitting award.   The court has a discretionary power, upon application being made in accordance with Rules of the Supreme Court, to remit the matters referred or any of them to the reconsideration of the arbitrator or umpire.[90] This power was formerly available where there was an error of fact or law on the face of the award,[91] but that jurisdiction was abolished by section 1(1) of the Arbitration Act 1979. Circumstances where the power to remit is still available include:

(1) where the arbitrator has made an error which amounts to misconduct but which does not justify his removal. An example would be where he had failed to grant relief which he ought to have granted[92];

---

[84] Lord Diplock in *Pioneer Shipping* v. *B.T.P. Tioxide* [1982] A.C. 724 at 744 (H.L.); *cf.* Lord Diplock in *Antaios Compania* v. *Salen A.B.* [1985] A.C. 191 at 206 (H.L.)—was the arbitrator "so obviously wrong as to preclude the possibility that he might be right?"; *Bramall & Ogden* v. *Sheffield City Council* (1983) 29 B.L.R. 73 at 84—was the arbitrator's decision "perverse"?

[85] *Pioneer Shipping* v. *B.T.P. Tioxide* [1982] A.C. 724 at 743 (H.L.); *cf. Ipswich Borough Council* v. *Fisons* [1990] Ch. 709 at 723 (C.A.). For building contract examples of the application of this guideline, see *E. R. Dyer* v. *Simon Build/Peter Lind* (1982) 23 B.L.R. 23 (leave refused); *Anglian Water* v. *R.D.L. Contracting* (1988) 43 B.L.R. 98 (leave granted).

[86] *Antaios Compania* v. *Salen A.B.* [1985] A.C. 191 at 203 (H.L.).

[87] *Pioneer Shipping* v. *B.T.P. Tioxide* [1982] A.C. 724 at 743 (H.L.); *cf. Boskalis Westminster* v. *Liverpool City Council* (1983) 24 B.L.R. 83.

[88] *e.g.* rent review decisions—see *Ipswich Borough Council* v. *Fisons* [1990] Ch. 709 (C.A.).

[89] See *Bulk Oil* v. *Sun International* [1984] 1 W.L.R. 147 (C.A.); *Aden Refinery* v. *Ugland Management* [1987] Q.B. 650 at 661, 668 (C.A.); *Glenlion Construction* v. *The Guinness Trust* (1987) 39 B.L.R. 89. In Hong Kong, the approach to granting leave to appeal is rather different because local conditions are different and there are differences in the legislation—see *P.T. Dover Chemical* v. *Lee Chang Yung* (unreported) March 20, 1990 (Hong Kong Court of Appeal).

[90] Arbitration Act 1950, s.22(1); R.S.C., Ord. 75. For the court's discretion see *Universal Cargo Carriers Corp.* v. *Citati* [1957] 1 W.L.R. 979 (C.A.).

[91] See the 4th edition of this book at p. 248.

[92] See, *e.g. Wildhandel N.V.* v. *Tucker & Cross* [1976] 1 Lloyd's Rep. 341—arbitrator's failure to award interest where he had sufficient material before him to do so. For an arbitrator's power to award interest, see s.19A of the Arbitration Act 1950 as inserted by s.15(6) of the Administration of Justice Act 1982.

(2) where the arbitrator admits a mistake[93];

(3) where the court is satisfied that there is a real risk that the result of a procedural error is that there may be a substantial injustice if the error were to remain uncorrected[94];

(4) where the arbitrator has made an insupportable costs order,[95] but "it is of the utmost importance that an arbitrator's discretion as to costs is not interfered with save in plain cases."[96] An award was remitted to an arbitrator for reconsideration when he made an unusual award as to costs without giving his reasons.[97] The award could be justified in certain circumstances. If it could not have been justified at all according to the principles governing the exercise of discretion as to costs[98] it would have been set aside as to costs.[99]

Refusal to enforce award.   An award may be enforced by leave of the High Court or a judge thereof in the same manner as a judgment or order.[1] Alternatively an action may be brought on the award.[2] The former is the ordinary procedure where there is an arbitration agreement within the meaning of the Arbitration Act 1950.[3] An action to enforce an award is an independent cause of action accruing for limitation purposes upon failure to honour the award.[4] If there has been no application for leave to appeal or to remit or set it aside the award,[5] it is final and binding upon the parties[6] and leave will be given to enforce the award "unless there is real ground for doubting the validity of the award."[7] An action on the award is necessary where leave is refused, and is necessary, or to be advised, in certain other circumstances.[8]

---

[93] See, *e.g. Mutual Shipping* v. *Bayshore Shipping* [1985] 1 W.L.R. 625 (C.A.).

[94] *London Borough of Islington* v. *Turriff Construction* (unreported), March 16, 1990 (C.A.) citing *Societe Franco-Tunisienne* v. *Government of Ceylon* [1959] 1 W.L.R. 787 (C.A.); *Harrison* v. *Thompson* [1989] 1 W.L.R. 1325; *M.F. King (Holdings)* v. *Thomas McKenna* (1990) 6 Const.L.J. 229.

[95] See *The Ios I* [1987] 1 Lloyd's Rep. 321.

[96] Parker J. in *Higgs & Hill* v. *University of London* (1983) 24 B.L.R. 139 at 153; *cf. Thyssen (Great Britain)* v. *Borough Council of Afan* (1978) 15 B.L.R. 98 (C.A.); *Argolis Shipping* v. *Midwest Steel* [1982] 2 Lloyd's Rep. 594.

[97] *Centrala Morska* v. *Cia Nacional* [1975] 2 Lloyd's Rep. 69; *cf. Archital Luxfer* v. *Henry Boot* [1981] 1 Lloyd's Rep. 642.

[98] See p. 455.

[99] *The Erich Schroeder* [1974] 1 Lloyd's Rep. 192; see also *Pepys* v. *L.T.E.* [1975] 1 W.L.R. 234 (C.A.)—a Lands Tribunal case, but applying general principles.

[1] Arbitration Act 1950, s.26(1). For enforcement by the County Court of awards not exceeding the County Court jurisdiction, see s.26(2) as added by the Administration of Justice Act 1977, s.17(2).

[2] See Mustill & Boyd, *Commercial Arbitration* (2nd ed.), pp. 417 *et seq.*

[3] For meaning, see p. 384.

[4] *Agromet* v. *Maulden Engineering* [1985] 1 W.L.R. 762. See also s.7 of the Limitation Act 1980.

[5] R.S.C., Ord. 73, r. 5 prescribes a time limit of 21 days after the award is made or published for such applications.

[6] Arbitration Act 1950, s.16.

[7] *Middlemiss & Gould* v. *Hartlepool Corporation* [1972] 1 W.L.R. 1643 at 1647 (C.A.). See also *Hall & Wodehouse Ltd.* v. *Panorama Ltd.* [1974] 2 Lloyd's Rep. 413 (C.A.).

[8] See Mustill & Boyd, *Commercial Arbitration* (2nd ed.), p. 417.

9. Arbitration under ICC Rules

International commercial disputes, in particular international construction contract disputes, are difficult to resolve not least because parties are reluctant to have their disputes adjudicated in the courts of a country other than their own and with whose law and practice they are unfamiliar. Accordingly international construction contracts usually contain an arbitration clause and these often provide for arbitration under the ICC Arbitration Rules.[9]

The ICC Court of Arbitration was established in 1923 as an international arbitration body attached to the International Chamber of Commerce. Its headquarters are in Paris. Around 40 nationalities are represented on the Court itself. Its staff is multinational and there are National Committees of the ICC in many countries. An ICC arbitration may have arbitrators of any nationality, sitting in any place and using any language. The Court of Arbitration itself does not settle disputes, but it appoints, or confirms the appointment of arbitrators,[10] and supervises the adminstration of the arbitration. The Court fixes the place of the arbitration unless the parties agree where it is to be.[11] The Court scrutinises the form of Terms of Reference and Awards,[12] sees that time limits are, so far as possible, adhered to and sees that the parties provide for the costs of running the arbitration. The perceived international acceptability of its system greatly helps parties to achieve awards which are not only accepted but, generally speaking, enforceable.[13]

Appointment of arbitrators.[14]   Disputes may be settled by a sole arbitrator or by three arbitrators.[15] Where the parties have not agreed on the number of arbitrators, the Court appoints a sole arbitrator unless it appears to the Court that the dispute is such as to warrant the appointment of three arbitrators. A sole arbitrator may be appointed by agreement of the parties confirmed by the Court or, if the parties fail to agree, by the Court. Where the dispute is to be referred to three arbitrators, each party nominates one arbitrator. The third arbitrator, who acts as chairman, is appointed by the Court unless the parties have provided for him to be agreed upon by the two nominees and they do so

---

[9] *cf. Bank Mellat* v. *Helliniki Techniki* [1984] Q.B. 291 at 314 (C.A.). The ICC Rules are reproduced in Appendix 4 to Mustill & Boyd, *Commercial Arbitration* (2nd ed.). There is a standard ICC arbitration clause recommended by the ICC in various languages at p. 745 of Mustill & Boyd. The Rules also provide for optional conciliation. See Art. 7 of the Rules for circumstances in which an arbitration cannot proceed.

[10] See Art. 2 of the ICC Rules.

[11] See Art. 11 of the ICC Rules.

[12] See *Bank Mellat* v. *GAA Development* [1988] 2 Lloyd's Rep. 44 at 48.

[13] Often by means of the 1958 New York Convention on the Recognition and Enforcement of Foreign Arbitral Awards or, where this has not been adopted, the 1927 Geneva Convention on the Execution of Foreign Arbitral Awards. The Arbitration Act 1975 gives effect to the New York Convention. See also Art. 26 of the ICC Rules.

[14] See Art. 2 of the ICC Rules.

[15] Where appropriate, references in the text of this section to "the arbitrator" includes reference to a triumvirate.

agree within a time limit fixed by the parties. In nominating a sole arbitrator or chairman, the Court consults with an appropriate National Committee and usually chooses someone from a country other than those of which the parties are nationals. Every arbitrator must be and remain independent of the parties and arbitrators may be challenged and, if the Court upholds the challenge, replaced for lack of independence or otherwise. The parties are entitled to an impartial and fair consideration and resolution by the arbitrators, acting together, of all issues in the case.[16] An arbitrator may also be replaced on the ground that he is not fulfilling his functions in accordance with the Rules or within the prescribed time limits. The Court's reasons for its decisions in relation to the appointment, confirmation, challenge or replacement of arbitrators are not communicated and such decisions are final.

Pleadings.[17]   The Rules provide for a Request for Arbitration by the Claimant and for an Answer to the Request and, if appropriate, a Counterclaim by the Defendant within 30 days of his receiving the Request subject to extension in exceptional circumstances. The Claimant may file a Reply within 30 days of his receiving the Counterclaim. All these documents are sent to the Secretariat of the Court. If a party challenges the existence or validity of the agreement to arbitrate and the Court is satisfied of the prima facie existence of such an agreement, the arbitration may proceed and any decision as to the arbitrator's jurisdiction is taken by him.[18] It is at this stage that the Secretariat transmits the file to the arbitrator, subject to an advance payment by the parties in equal shares of a sum to cover the costs of the arbitration. The arbitrator may only proceed on those claims for which the advance on costs has been duly paid.[19] A party to an ICC arbitration agreement who was financially unable to pay his share of the advance failed to resist an application under section 1(1) of the Arbitration Act 1975 to stay proceedings which he had started in the High Court and for which he had obtained a legal aid certificate with a nil contribution.[20]

Terms of Reference.[21]   Before proceeding with the preparation of the case, the arbitrator has to draw up Terms of Reference containing, in addition to formal matters, a summary of the parties' respective claims and a definition of the issues, with particulars of procedural rules and such other particulars as may be required to make the arbitral award enforceable in law. The requirement for such Terms of Reference is sometimes thought by English lawyers familiar with English pleading practice to be an unnecessary addition to the Request for Arbitration and the Answer, but adherence to the procedure is

---

[16] *Bank Mellat* v. *GAA Development* [1988] 2 Lloyd's Rep. 44 at 50.
[17] See Arts. 3–6 inclusive of the ICC Rules.
[18] See Art. 8 of the ICC Rules; *Dalmia* v. *National Bank* [1978] 2 Lloyd's Rep. 223 at 284 (C.A.).
[19] See Arts. 9 and 10 of the ICC Rules.
[20] *Paczy* v. *Haendler* [1981] 1 Lloyd's Rep. 302 (C.A.).
[21] See Arts. 9 and 13 of the ICC Rules.

required by the Court and may be essential to ensure that the arbitral award is eventually enforceable. In addition, a Terms of Reference meeting or hearing usually achieves better definition of the issues and is often useful to sort out procedural matters generally. Since the parties may subsequently make new claims or counterclaims before the arbitrator provided that they are within the limits fixed by the Terms of Reference or a rider to that document signed by the parties,[22] the Terms of Reference themselves should be drawn sufficiently widely to encompass the possible addition of amended claims and counterclaims.

Proper law.   The parties are free to agree the law to be applied by the arbitrator to the merits of the dispute and this will often appear in the arbitration agreement. If the parties do not so agree, the arbitrator applies "the law designated as the proper law by the rule of conflict which he deems appropriate."[23] This delphic provision appears to mean that the arbitrator has to decide a system of law on the basis of which he is to decide the law to apply to the merits of the dispute, and on the basis of that system he then decides which law to apply to the merits of the dispute. In practice, he will probably choose the law of the country with which the contract has the closest connection which is likely to be the country where the works are situated.[24]

Procedural law.   The parties may, without infringing the agreement to arbitrate, apply to any competent judicial authority for "interim or conservatory measures."[25] Procedural rules are those resulting from the ICC Rules themselves and, where these are silent, any rules which the parties themselves, or failing them the arbitrator, may settle.[26] In practice, this normally means that, subject to the ICC Rules, the arbitrator is in charge of his own procedure. Otherwise where an ICC arbitration takes place in England, the procedural law governing the arbitration will be English law[27] and the Rules do not expressly or by necessary implication exclude all applications to the English court. The English court will, for instance, entertain in appropriate circumstances an application to remove an arbitrator or set aside his award for misconduct under section 23 of the Arbitration Act 1950,[28] or an application

---

[22] See Art. 16 of the ICC Rules.

[23] Art. 13.3 of the ICC Rules.

[24] For the English law on what is the proper law of a contract, see generally Dicey & Morris, *The Conflict of Laws*, (11th ed.).

[25] See Art. 8.5 of the ICC Rules. If the arbitration is taking place in England, the English court is a competent judicial authority. For "interim or conservatory measures," see *Bank Mellat* v. *Helliniki Techniki* [1984] Q.B. 291 at 305 (C.A.).

[26] Art. 11 of the ICC Rules.

[27] *Whitworth Street Estates* v. *James Miller & Partners* [1970] A.C. 583 (H.L.); *Bank Mellat* v. *Helliniki Techniki* [1984] Q.B. 291 at 301 (C.A.); *cf. Dalmia* v. *National Bank* [1978] 2 Lloyd's Rep. 223 (C.A.). Where the arbitration takes place in a country other than England, the procedural law of the arbitration will be determined by the law of that country. English decisions referred to in this Section will not, of course, necessarily be followed in other jurisdictions.

[28] See *Bank Mellat* v. *Helliniki Techniki* [1984] Q.B. 291 at 305 (C.A.); *Bank Mellat* v. *GAA Development* [1988] 2 Lloyd's Rep. 44 where the application failed on the merits.

under section 26(1) of the Act for leave to enforce an award.[29] But the ICC Rules are intended to provide a self-sufficient code, and it seems that such applications are unlikely to succeed at least where the parties to the arbitration have little or no connection with England. In one such case, an application by a party to an ICC arbitration for an order for security for costs under section 12(6)(a) of the Arbitration Act 1950 failed on the ground that it was inconsistent with the scheme and spirit of the ICC Rules.[30] The court's decision whether or not to make a discretionary order will always take account of the terms of the parties' contract.[31]

The proceedings. The arbitrator has to establish the facts "by all appropriate means." He has power to appoint one or more experts. He is obliged to hold a hearing in the parties' presence unless they request him to decide the case on the relevant documents alone. The hearing is in private unless the parties and the arbitrator agree that persons not involved in the proceedings may be admitted.[32]

The Award. The arbitrator has power to make an award by consent,[33] and also a "partial award"[34] which in England at least appears to be the same as an interim award.[35] Where there are three arbitrators, the award is if necessary by a majority or, if there is no majority, by the chairman.[36] The award has to fix the costs of the arbitration.[37] There is a time limit of six months from the operative signature of the Terms of Reference for the arbitrator to render his award to the Court for scrutiny. The Court has power to extend this time and does so in appropriate cases, but in general ICC arbitrations proceed rather more quickly than equivalent English domestic arbitrations.[38] The award is deemed to be made at the place of arbitration on the date when it is signed by the arbitrator.[39]

The arbitral award is final and the parties are deemed to have undertaken to carry out the resulting award without delay and to have waived their right to any form of appeal in so far as such waiver can be validly made.[40] An application for leave to appeal under section 1 of the Arbitration Act 1979 will

---

[29] *Bank Mellat* v. *GAA Development* [1988] 2 Lloyd's Rep. 44.
[30] *Bank Mellat* v. *Helliniki Techniki* [1984] Q.B. 291 (C.A.).
[31] *Ibid.* at 303 (C.A.).
[32] Arts. 14 and 15 of the ICC Rules.
[33] Art. 17 of the ICC Rules.
[34] Art. 21 of the ICC Rules.
[35] See *Marine Contractors* v. *Shell Petroleum* [1984] 2 Lloyd's Rep. 77 (C.A.) where the arbitrator had made an interim award deciding certain preliminary issues and the Court of Appeal rejected a construction of the Rules to the effect that there was no power to make an award which was not enforceable in money terms. For interim awards in English arbitrations, see p. 407.
[36] Art. 19 of the ICC Rules.
[37] Art. 20 of the ICC Rules.
[38] Arts. 18 and 21 of the ICC Rules.
[39] Art. 22 of the ICC Rules.
[40] Art. 24 of the ICC Rules.

normally fail *in limine* on account of this provision which applies also to partial awards as discussed above.[41] Merely asking the arbitrator for reasons does not amount to a waiver of the exclusion agreement.[42]

---

[41] See *Marine Contractors* v. *Shell Petroleum* [1984] 2 Lloyd's Rep. 77 (C.A.); *Arab African Energy* v. *Olie producten Nederland* [1983] 2 Lloyd's Rep. 419, where a telex provision for arbitration "according ICC rules" was held to be a sufficient agreement in writing excluding the right of appeal under s.3(1) of the Arbitration Act 1979. See generally "Appeals to the High Court" at p. 412.

[42] *Marine Contractors* v. *Shell Petroleum* [1984] 2 Lloyd's Rep. 77 (C.A.).

CHAPTER 17

LITIGATION

1. Features of Building Contract Litigation

There is no special procedure laid down by the rules for building contract disputes, and any such dispute may follow its own particular course, but there are some features which so frequently recur in disputes of fact over building contracts that they are to some extent characteristic. They are as follows[1]:

(1) the contract may show that the architect's certificate is intended to be a condition precedent to the right to bring an action, or when given is binding and conclusive as between the parties unless it can be reviewed or set aside.[2]

---

[1] Unless otherwise expressly stated High Court practice and procedure and the Rules of the Supreme Court are referred to, although most of the subject matter of this chapter applies in principle to county court litigation.

[2] See generally Chap. 5.

(2) the contract may contain a clause referring disputes to an arbitrator in which case if one party commences proceedings in a court of law the other can usually obtain a stay of the proceedings.[3] If there is a formal hearing by the arbitrator much of what is said in this chapter about practice and pleading will apply to the arbitration proceedings.

(3) the technical nature of disputes often gives rise to a reference to an official referee or an arbitrator.

(4) the special form of pleading known as a Scott or official referee's schedule is frequently used in detailed disputes of fact.

(5) costs tend to be high even when the amount in issue is small.

(6) a set-off or counterclaim is common and may give rise to various difficult questions.

(7) the number of parties tends to be high and the litigation in consequence to be complicated.

2. Official Referees

An official referee is a Circuit judge, deputy Circuit judge or recorder nominated by the Lord Chancellor to deal with official referees' business.[4] Official referees' business includes cases which involve a prolonged examination of documents or accounts, or a technical scientific or local investigation, or for which trial by an official referee is desirable in the interests of one or more of the parties on grounds of expedition, economy or convenience or otherwise.[5] Actions may now be started as official referees' business or they may be transferred.[6] An order for a reference may be made by the court of its own motion at any time and may be made at trial. Alternatively it may be made upon application at any time before trial. Orders are commonly made by the master at the close of pleadings upon the summons for directions and in some cases upon a summons under Order 14 where leave to defend is granted, *e.g.* where there is a claim for work done and an affidavit by the defendant alleging defective workmanship. Official referees have essentially the same powers as High Court judges.[7] They may hold trials at any convenient place.[8]

---

[3] See "The Right to Insist on Arbitration" at p. 397.
[4] s.68(1)(a) of the Supreme Court Act 1981 as amended by s.59 of the Administration of Justice Act 1982. See also R.S.C., Ord. 1, r. 4(1).
[5] See R.S.C., Ord. 36, r. 1.
[6] See R.S.C., Ord. 36, r. 2 and 3. Matters transferred can include applications for leave to appeal under s.1 of the Arbitration Act 1979—see *Tate & Lyle* v. *Davy McKee* [1990] Q.B. 1068 (C.A.); see also "Appeals to the High Court" at p. 412.
[7] R.S.C., Ord. 36, r. 4.
[8] R.S.C., Ord. 36, r. 5.

A majority of building contract actions in the High Court is tried by official referees.[9] In London, judges nominated to deal with official referees business sit full time in courts in St Dunstan's House, Fetter Lane. Outside London, there are nominated judges at various centres. Official referees may also in certain circumstances accept appointments as arbitrators.[10]

Practice. Official referees' business in London is allocated to particular official referees in rotation.[11] The allocated judge then deals personally with interlocutory applications as well as the trial. The plaintiff has to make an application for directions within 14 days of the defendant giving notice of intention to defend or of the date of the order transferring the case.[12] The powers and duties to give directions include those provided by the rules upon a summons for directions,[13] but official referees habitually give special directions aimed at organising the complexities of the case before trial so that it may be tried as efficiently as possible.[14] Such directions include, where appropriate, ordering a Scott or official referee's schedule,[15] directing issues to be tried[16] and giving directions relating to witness statements and expert evidence.[17] It may also be necessary to order a view.[18] The application for directions is usually adjourned at the first hearing and may be restored before trial for further directions. There is an increasing practice to restore it as a pre-trial review about six weeks before the hearing.

Appeals from official referees. Subject to section 18 of the Supreme Court Act 1981,[19] an appeal lies to the Court of Appeal from a decision of an official referee on a question of law and, with the leave of the official referee or

---

[9] For official referees' practice generally, see the commentary to R.S.C., Ord. 36 in the Supreme Court Practice 1991; H.H. Edgar Fay Q.C. *Official Referees' Business* (2nd ed.); H.H. Judge Newey Q.C., *Official Referees' Courts—Practice and Procedure*; H.H. Judge Fox-Andrews Q.C., "Practice Today in the Official Referees' Courts" (1989) 5 Const.L.J. 246; H.H. Judge Newey Q.C., "The Preparation and Presentation of Cases in the Official Referees' Courts" (1990) 6 Const.L.J. 216.

[10] See "Official referee as arbitrator" at p. 392.

[11] R.S.C., Ord. 36, r. 5(3).

[12] R.S.C., Ord. 36, r. 6(1).

[13] See R.S.C., Ord. 36, r. 6(4).

[14] See further Practice Direction (Official Referee: Procedure) at [1968] 1 W.L.R. 1425, most of which essentially still applies; para. 36/1–9/21 in the Supreme Court Practice 1991. One London official referee has as an experiment sophisticated video equipment in court which enables drawings, plans and photographs to be displayed on monitors. Witnesses are thereby able to refer to such technical documents much more easily.

[15] See p. 446.

[16] See "Preliminary point" at p. 435.

[17] See pp. 426 *et seq.*

[18] See p. 435.

[19] This section, which prohibits or restricts certain classes of appeal to the Court of Appeal, applies to official referees—see R.S.C., Ord. 58, r. 4 and *Giles (Electrical Engineers)* v. *Plessey Communications* [1985] 1 W.L.R. 243 (Practice Note) given under the former Ord. 58, r. 4, but still, it is thought, applicable. In particular, leave is required for appeals from any interlocutory order or judgment, as to which, see R.S.C., Ord. 59, r. 1A and the commentary in the Supreme Court Practice 1991.

the Court of Appeal, on any question of fact.[20] Formerly there was no right of appeal on questions of fact except from a decision relevant to a charge of fraud or breach of professional duty,[21] and this sometimes influenced a decision whether to transfer a case to an official referee or not.[22] It seems that the only principle upon which an official referee can decide whether to grant leave to appeal from himself on a question of fact is whether he thinks that the appeal would have any real prospect of success.[23] But official referees may perhaps for historical reasons more readily be persuaded to give leave where they have found facts amounting to fraud or breach of professional duty.

Inquiry and report. The court may, subject to any right to a trial with a jury,[24] refer to an official referee for inquiry and report any question or issue of fact arising in any cause or matter other than a criminal proceeding by the Crown.[25]

3. County Court Jurisdiction

The ordinary court of first instance for substantial building contract disputes is the High Court, but some disputes may be decided in the county' courts where the costs are less and the procedure is speedier.

County Courts have jurisdiction to hear and determine actions founded on contract or tort where the debt, demand, or damage claimed does not exceed the County Court limit.[26] A plaintiff who has a cause of action for more than the County Court limit may abandon the excess so as to give the court jurisdiction.[27] The parties may by a written memorandum give a County

---

[20] See R.S.C., Ord. 58, r. 4 as amended by R.S.C. (Amendment No. 2) 1988 (S.I. 1988 No. 1340) with effect from October 1, 1988. There may also be appeals, usually only with leave of the official referee, as to costs only. For the difference between fact and law, see *Instrumatic Ltd.* v. *Supabrase Ltd.* [1969] 1 W.L.R. 519 (C.A.); *Peak Construction (Liverpool) Ltd.* v. *McKinney Foundations Ltd.* (1971) 69 L.G.R. 1 at 8, 13 (C.A.) applying *Edwards* v. *Bairstow* [1956] A.C. 14 (H.L.).

[21] For the application of the former rule to building contract cases, see *Moody* v. *Ellis* (1983) 26 B.L.R. 39 (C.A.); *Hubert C. Leach* v. *Norman Crossley & Partners* (1984) 30 B.L.R. 95 at 106 (C.A.); *cf. Lubenham* v. *South Pembrokeshire District Council* (1986) 33 B.L.R. 39 at 48 (C.A.); *Greater Nottingham Co-operative* v. *Cementation Piling* [1989] Q.B. 71 (C.A.).

[22] See, *e.g. Simplicity Products Co.* v. *Domestic Installations Co. Ltd.* [1973] 1 W.L.R. 837 (C.A.); *Scarborough Rural District Council* v. *Moore* (1968) 112 S.J. 986 (C.A.).

[23] *Hoskisson* v. *Moody Homes* (1989) 46 B.L.R. 81.

[24] See R.S.C., Ord. 33, r. 5. Trial by jury is very unusual in civil actions; see *Williams* v. *Beesley* [1973] 1 W.L.R. 1295 (H.L.).

[25] R.S.C., Ord. 36, r. 8. There may also in certain circumstances be trials before or inquiries by special referees or masters—see R.S.C., Ord. 36, r. 10 and 11.

[26] s.15 of the County Courts Act 1984. The current limit is £5000—see County Courts Jurisdiction Order 1981 (S.I. 1981 No. 1123)—but will almost certainly soon be raised. See "Courts and Legal Services Act" below. See s.69(8) of the County Courts Act 1984 for the exclusion of statutory interest from a determination whether an amount exceeds the county court limit. See also "Transfer from High Court to County Court" below and "Recovery of small sums" at p. 456.

[27] s.17 of the County Courts Act 1984.

Court jurisdiction to hear and determine certain High Court matters.[28] County Courts have unlimited jurisdiction to try counterclaims unless a successful application has been made to transfer the matter to the High Court.[29]

Transfer from High Court to County Court.   Section 40 of the County Courts Act 1984 empowers the High Court, either on its own motion or on the application of any party, to order the transfer of the whole or any part of High Court proceedings to a County Court.[30] The power may be exercised where the parties consent, where the amount in issue is, or is likely to be, within the County Court limit, or where "the High Court considers that the proceedings are not likely to raise any important question of law or fact and are suitable for determination by a County Court."[31] If proceedings are transferred, the County Court may award any relief, including any amount of damages, which could have been awarded in the High Court.[32] It is thought that building cases which are likely to be lengthy or to involve complicated matters of fact upon which expert evidence is necessary are unlikely to be transferred other than by consent, nor cases where the amount in dispute exceeds £20,000, nor where professional negligence is alleged.[33]

Transfer from County Court to High Court.   The High Court may order transfer if it "thinks it desirable that the proceedings, or any part of them, should be heard and determined in the High Court."[34] The County Court may order transfer if the court considers that some important question of law or fact is likely to arise, if a party is likely to recover more than the County Court limit, or if a defendant's set-off or counterclaim involves matters beyond the jurisdiction of the County Court.[35]

Courts and Legal Services Act.   Section 1 of the Courts and Legal Services Act 1990, when it comes into force, will give the Lord Chancellor wide powers to make orders conferring jurisdiction on County Courts and allocating proceedings to the High Court or to County Courts. Section 2 of the Act amends section 40 of the County Courts Act 1984 and subjects section 41 of the 1984 Act to section 1 of the 1990 Act.

4. Preparation for Trial

This section deals with some of the more important matters that must be

---

[28] s.18 of the County Courts Act 1984.

[29] s.43 of the County Courts Act 1984; *cf. Hardwicke* v. *Gilroy* [1944] K.B. 460 (C.A.).

[30] The question of such possible transfer must be considered on the hearing of the summons for directions—see R.S.C., Ord. 25, r. 3(c). See also "Courts and Legal Services Act" below.

[31] The quotation is from s.40(1)(d).

[32] s.40(10) of the County Courts Act 1984.

[33] See Practice Statement (Listings), *The Times,* January 1, 1988 and commentary at 25/8/2 in the Supreme Court Practice 1991.

[34] s.41 of the County Courts Act 1984. See also "Courts and Legal Services Act" below.

[35] s.42 of the County Courts Act 1984.

considered in the preparation and course of a building contract dispute, and must be read with other sections of this chapter, in particular with Section 10 dealing with costs.[36]

(a) *Preparation of evidence*

Early and thorough preparation of evidence is advisable. Important questions include how it is proposed to prove basic facts and whether one or more expert witnesses will be necessary and, if so, who they should be. Detailed consideration also needs to be given to documents. There is now a welcome tendency to discourage allowing litigants unlimited time and unlimited scope to conduct their cases in the way which seems best to them. This results not infrequently in torrents of words, written and oral which are oppressive. The remedy lies in the judge taking time to read in advance pleadings, documents and proofs of witnesses, certified by counsel as necessary, and short skeleton arguments, and then, after a short discussion in open court, limiting the time and scope of oral evidence and oral argument.[37] This means that meticulous preparation is essential.

Witness statements. It remains a principle of English procedure that the primary means of proving facts is by oral evidence. But in building contract litigation the mutual disclosure before trial of witness statements is now regarded as normal[38] and, if the procedure is properly followed, much time and expense may thereby be saved. Order 38, rule 2A provides that the court may direct any party to serve on the other parties written statements of the oral evidence which the party intends to lead on any issues of fact to be decided at the trial.[39] There are consequent limitations on the oral evidence that may be called. But normally, if the witness is not called, no other party may put the statement in evidence at trial. The statement remains privileged and confidential until either the witness makes the statement public by verifying it on oath in the witness box or the party who served the statement waives the privilege. Privilege will be waived if parts of the statement are put to an opposing witness in cross-examination.[40]

Expert witnesses. When it becomes apparent that a dispute on detailed questions of fact is inevitable, each party should at an early stage select the

---

[36] See generally H.H. Judge Newey Q.C., "The Preparation and Presentation of Cases in the Official Referees' Courts" (1990) 6 Const.L.J. 216.

[37] See Lord Templeman in *Banque Keyser Ullmann* v. *Skandia (U.K.) Insurance* [1990] 3 W.L.R. 364 at 380 (H.L.).

[38] *cf. Richard Saunders* v. *Eastglen, The Times,* July 28, 1989.

[39] See generally R.S.C., Ord. 38, r. 2A and the commentary in the Supreme Court Practice 1991. The rule, which in English litigation originated with official referees, now applies to all divisions of the High Court, the suggestions of Garland J. in *University of Warwick* v. *Sir Robert McAlpine* (1988) 42 B.L.R. 1 at 24 having been put into effect. See also Practice Direction (Chancery Summons for Directions) [1989] 1 W.L.R. 133; s.5 of the Courts and Legal Services Act 1990.

[40] See *Fairfield-Mabey* v. *Shell* [1989] 1 All E.R. 576; see also *John Mowlem* v. *Liberal Jewish Synagogue* unreported, H.H. Judge Bowsher Q.C., March 27, 1990.

main expert witness on whom he intends to rely. "An expert may be qualified by skill and experience, as well as by professional qualifications."[41] The expert should be given the pleadings, if any, and all the contractual documents or, if the contract is oral, he should be furnished with a written version, giving the fullest possible detail, of the material interviews. An inspection of the site should be arranged, the other party being notified so that he may arrange his inspection at or about the same time. As a result of his observations and his study of the contract, the witness should draw up a detailed report in writing. He should endeavour to make as fair and impartial an appraisal as possible, remembering that an over-optimistic report will probably increase his client's costs in that reasonable offers of settlement may be refused, or too small a sum of money may be paid into court.[42]

The details of the report must vary according to the nature of the dispute. In a claim for a reasonable sum, for example, each item must be described and valued and a note made of the basis of the valuation, *e.g.* measurements, labour rates, the cost of materials and percentage additions for profits and overheads.[43]

In a claim for variations where he values according to principles stated in the contract the witness should refer to the particular clause, or sub-clause upon which he relies.[44] In a defects case the defects must be described in detail, and either a blank space left after each item for the insertion of the estimated cost of rectification by a contractor, or the witness should give his own estimate making a note of the basis of his valuation. The aim should be to provide a report from which both a Scott schedule and a proof of evidence can be prepared.

The expense of preparing a report such as that suggested may be consider-able.[45] Its great advantage is that it enables the party's legal advisers to attempt a reasonably accurate appraisal of the situation at an early stage in the proceedings, and thus be in a position to advise whether a settlement should be sought, or a sum of money should be paid into, or taken out of, court. Moreover, if the matter does come to trial (this may well be one or two years (or more) after the commencement of proceedings) the main witness is able before trial to read through his own detailed contemporaneous account instead of having to attempt a reconstruction of the processes of thought that led him to general conclusions at some considerable time in the past. When in the witness-box he can refer to his notes made at the time of his inspection to refresh his memory, and in certain circumstances the notes can become admissible as evidence.[46]

---

[41] Lloyd J. in *James Longley* v. *South West Regional Health Authority* (1983) 25 B.L.R. 56 at 62.

[42] See p. 458.

[43] See further "Assessment of a reasonable sum" at p. 80.

[44] *e.g.* Standard Form of Building Contract, clause 13.

[45] As to whether expert's fees properly incurred are recoverable as costs or damages, see "Cost of reports" at p. 200.

[46] Civil Evidence Act 1968, Pt. I; R.S.C., Ord. 38, Pt. III; for restrictions upon adducing expert evidence, see Civil Evidence Act 1972; R.S.C., Ord. 38, Pt. IV and p. 428.

Photographs or video recordings can sometimes be very useful. They should be taken under the supervision of the main expert witness and the photographer should keep a note of the date and, where it may be material, the time of day and lighting conditions. In some cases it may be desirable to make a small sketch plan showing the relative positions of the camera and the subject-matter, and of the latter to the whole works.

Experts' reports. In building contract cases, the court invariably orders the substance of expert evidence to be disclosed before trial.[47] It may also be desirable for the delivery of experts' reports in reply and the court may direct experts to meet "without prejudice" in order to identify those parts of their evidence which are in issue.[48] Where such a meeting takes place, the experts may prepare a joint statement or report. If there is no joint written report recording the precise nature and extent of agreement, all discussions including any "agreements" are privileged. An expert in these circumstances has no implied or ostensible authority to agree facts orally or in any form other than the joint statement or report envisaged by the direction.[49] It is questionable whether the expert derives authority to make *any* agreement binding his client from the mere fact that the court has given a direction, although he may have a greater actual authority.[50] There may be difficulties if further meetings are directed to take place after a trial has begun.[51] Where a party calls his expert, a report disclosed pursuant to the rules may be put in evidence at the beginning of his evidence in chief.[52] Such a report may also be put in by any other party thus making that report part of the evidence of the party putting it in.[53]

An expert expresses opinions upon facts agreed, proved or to be proved. He can additionally give factual evidence of matters of which he has first hand knowledge, but he cannot give hearsay evidence of primary facts,[54] unless it is admissible under the provisions of the Civil Evidence Acts 1968 and 1972.

"Once the primary facts on which their opinion is based have been proved by admissible evidence, [experts] are entitled to draw on the work of others

---

[47] See R.S.C., Ord. 38, r. 35–44, in particular rule 37. See also *Ollett* v. *Bristol Aerojet* [1979] 1 W.L.R. 1197 (Practice Note); *Derby & Co.* v. *Weldon (No. 9)*, *The Times*, November 9, 1990 (C.A.). The rules apply regardless of whether the export witness is an independent witness, an "in house" expert, or one of the parties—see *Shell Pensions Trust* v. *Pell Frischmann* [1986] 2 All E.R. 911.

[48] See *University of Warwick* v. *Sir Robert McAlpine* (1988) 42 B.L.R. 1 at 23; R.S.C., Ord. 38, r. 38.

[49] *Carnell Computer Technology* v. *Unipart Group* (1988) 45 B.L.R. 100; *cf. Richard Roberts Holdings* v. *Douglas Smith Stimson* (1989) 47 B.L.R. 113; *Murray Pipework* v. *U.I.E. Scotland Ltd.* (1988) 6 Const.L.J. 56; see also article by John Bray, Andrew Burr and Rowan Planterose, "The Law and Practice of 'without prejudice' Meetings" (1990) 6 Const.L.J. 23.

[50] See *Richard Roberts Holdings* v. *Douglas Smith Stimson* (1989) 47 B.L.R. 113 at 125.

[51] See *Richard Roberts Holdings* v. *Douglas Smith Stimson* (1989) 47 B.L.R. 113.

[52] R.S.C., Ord. 38, r. 43.

[53] See R.S.C., Ord. 38, r. 42.

[54] *English Exporters* v. *Eldonwall Ltd.* [1973] 1 Ch. 415 at 421. There is a regrettable tendency for expert reports in building contract litigation to contain inordinately long statements of hearsay fact coupled with inadmissible *factual* opinion. This should be avoided. *cf.* however *James Longley* v. *South West Regional Health Authority* (1983) 25 B.L.R. 56 at 63.

as part of the process of arriving at their conclusion. However, where they have done so, they should refer to this material in their evidence so that the cogency and probative value of their conclusion can be tested and evaluated by reference to it."[55]

The work of others can include statistical material lying within the field of the expert's expertise of the accuracy of which he has no personal knowledge, but which he has no reason to doubt.[56]

"While some degree of consultation between experts and legal advisers is entirely proper, it is necessary that expert evidence presented to the court should be, and should be seen to be, the independent product of the expert, uninfluenced as to form or content by the exigencies of litigation."[57] An expert should not enter into the arena in order to advocate his client's case,[58] and it seems that his report should contain his complete opinion and not merely selected parts of it which may be favourable to his client.[59] If a report contains evidence or expertise contributed by some person other than the apparent author, that person and his contribution should be identified so that at the very least he can be tendered for cross-examination. But this does not apply to the leader of a team of investigators or laboratory research assistants under the leader's direction and control.[60]

Documents.[61]   Much evidence is given by or by reference to documents, often without scrupulous regard to the rules of evidence relating to documents.[62] In practice this is usually unobjectionable and a convenient means of covering historical ground in evidence. Documents may be referred to to refresh a witness' memory, to prove statements made adverse to the interest of a writer who is a party to the proceedings, to enable factual inferences to be drawn when asserted facts are not rebutted, to establish the fact that the document was written when it was and, it is thought, to narrate uncontroversial facts.

It is essential that legible and clearly paginated bundles of documents are agreed and prepared in a form which will enable the judge, counsel and witnesses to find particular documents easily and without delay. It is equally

---

[55] Kerr L.J. in *R. v. Abadom* [1983] 1 W.L.R. 126 (C.A.).

[56] *Ibid.* The court certified that a point of law of general public importance was involved, but the House of Lords dismissed a petition for leave to appeal—[1983] 1 W.L.R. 405 (H.L.).

[57] *Whitehouse* v. *Jordan* [1981] 1 W.L.R. 246 at 256, 268 (H.L.). For the criticisms made by Lord Denning in the same case in the Court of Appeal, where the lawyers had "doctored" an expert's report by blocking out a couple of lines, see [1980] 1 All E.R. 650 at 655.

[58] Garland J. in *University of Warwick* v. *Sir Robert McAlpine* (1988) 42 B.L.R. 1 at 22; for the position where an expert inadvertently advised both sides, see *Harmony Shipping Co.* v. *Saudi Europe* [1979] 1 W.L.R. 1380 (C.A.).

[59] See *Kenning* v. *Eve Construction* [1989] 1 W.L.R. 1189—a decision under R.S.C., Ord. 25, r. 8(1)(b) in a personal injury action, but see *Derby & Co.* v. *Weldon (No. 9)*, *The Times*, November 9, 1990 (C.A.).

[60] *University of Warwick* v. *Sir Robert McAlpine* (1988) 42 B.L.R. 1 at 23.

[61] See also "Discovery" at p. 433.

[62] For such rules, see standard text books such as *Phipson on Evidence* (14th ed., 1990).

essential that in large cases the bulk of documents to be used in court is reduced to reasonable proportions by careful selection. Unthinking use of the photocopying machine is a waste of paper, time and money. The main agreed bundles should be provided to the court well in advance of the trial. Granted that judicial reading time may thereby be somewhat increased, the net saving in time and the attendance of the parties and their various advisers can be great.[63]

(b) *Pleadings*

Building contracts are contracts for work and labour, or for work and labour and materials supplied. Precedents for ordinary pleadings are not given in this book but can be found under these headings in other works.[64] The special form of pleading called a Scott or official referee's schedule and its relationship to the ordinary pleadings are discussed in Section 8 of this chapter.[65]

In drafting pleadings a defendant who has a cross-claim against the plaintiff should consider whether to advance it as a set-off or a counterclaim or both as set-off and counterclaim and whether any advantage as to costs or otherwise may be gained by the form of pleading employed.[66]

Particulars tend to become more and more voluminous in building contract proceedings, but issues must be properly and accurately defined and lengthy particulars are often unavoidable. They should nearly always be pressed for at an appropriately early stage bearing in mind that sometimes discovery can reduce the need for or length of particulars. It is now required that when particulars are given pursuant to a request or order, the request or order shall be incorporated with the particulars.[67] Voluntary particulars are to be placed immediately after the pleading to which they relate.[68] In appropriate cases, there can be a mutual agreement or direction for their delivery either as part of an official referee's schedule, or in a form suitable for inclusion in such a schedule.[69] Particulars may be ordered to be given in the form which is most convenient to both parties as, for example, and in a suitable case, by means of a scale plan.[70] The general rule is that a party need not, and ought not, to plead to particulars,[71] but this rule is often not followed in the official referee's court,

---

[63] *cf.* Garland J. in *University of Warwick* v. *Sir Robert McAlpine* (1988) 42 B.L.R. 1 at 24; *Banque Keyser Ullmann* v. *Skandia (U.K.) Insurance* [1990] 3 W.L.R. 364 at 380 (H.L.).

[64] *e.g.* Bullen & Leake and Jacob's Precedents of Pleadings; Atkins Court Forms for High Court pleadings; Butterworths County Court Precedents and Pleadings.

[65] See generally *Liverpool Archdiocesan Trustee* v. *Gibberd* (1987) 7 Con.L.R. 113 at 125.

[66] See p. 438.

[67] R.S.C., Ord. 18, r. 12.

[68] R.S.C., Ord. 34, r. 3(2).

[69] See also "Composite claims" at p. 216.

[70] *Tarbox* v. *St. Pancras Borough Council* [1952] 1 All E.R. 1306 (C.A.). See generally as to particulars R.S.C., Ord. 18, r. 12.

[71] *Pinson* v. *Lloyds & National Provincial Foreign Bank Ltd.* [1941] 2 K.B. 72 (C.A.); *Chapple* v. *E.T.U.* [1961] 1 W.L.R. 1290.

particularly when an official referee's schedule is ordered. Damages which are not the necessary and immediate consequence of a breach must be pleaded.[72]

Causes of action. "A cause of action is simply a factual situation the existence of which entitles one person to obtain from the court a remedy against another person."[73] Typically there is a contract imposing an obligation and facts constituting breach of that obligation or giving rise to a claim under it. In general, it will usually be a sensible practical expedient to include all known claims arising out of the same contract in the same proceedings, not least because "it is a well settled rule of law that damages resulting from one and the same cause of action must be assessed and recovered once for all."[74] Additionally problems arise if a party seeks to add new causes of action by amendment after the limitation period has expired.[75] An employer therefore should make a careful examination and include all the defects, for instance, in one claim. If he is sued for the balance of the contract price and is apprehensive lest all the defects have not yet manifested themselves, his correct course is to pay the claim and bring a separate action for the defects at a later stage,[76] unless the terms of the contract show that various defects or classes of defects such as latent defects are intended to give rise to separate causes of action.[77]

"Two actions may be brought in respect of the same facts where those facts give rise to two distinct causes of action,"[78] as, for example, where they result in injury to a man's property and injury to his person.[79] Whether there is a new cause of action in any circumstances is a mixed question of law and fact.[80] A contract may give rise to several causes of action.[81] But in *Conquer* v. *Boot*[82] an

---

[72] *Perestrello Ltd.* v. *United Paint Co. Ltd.* [1969] 1 W.L.R. 570 (C.A.); *Domsalla* v. *Barr* [1969] 1 W.L.R. 630 (C.A.).

[73] Diplock L.J. in *Letang* v. *Cooper* [1965] 1 Q.B. 232 at 242 (C.A.).

[74] Bowen L.J. in *Brunsden* v. *Humphrey* (1884) 14 Q.B.D. 141 at 147 (C.A.). The rule applies also to arbitrations—*Telfair Shipping* v. *Inersea Carriers* [1983] 2 Lloyd's Rep. 351.

[75] See *Steamship Mutual* v. *Trollope & Colls* (1986) 33 B.L.R. 77 (C.A.); and see generally "Amendments" at p. 371. A new cause of action has to be raised by amendment and cannot be raised by way of particulars—*Liverpool Archdiocesan Trustee* v. *Gibberd* (1987) 7 Con.L.R. 113.

[76] *Davis* v. *Hedges* (1871) L.R. 6 Q.B. 687.

[77] *cf.* clause 30(7) of the 1963 Standard Form of Building Contract in versions preceding the 1976 revision.

[78] Bowen L.J. in *Brunsden* v. *Humphrey* (1884) 14 Q.B.D. 141 at 146 (C.A.).

[79] *Brunsden* v. *Humphrey* (1884) 14 Q.B.D. 141 (C.A.); see also *Overstone Ltd.* v. *Shipway* [1962] 1 W.L.R. 118 (C.A.)—a hire-purchase case. *cf. Cahoon* v. *Franks* (1967) 63 D.L.R. (2d) 274 (Canadian Supreme Court); Griffiths L.J. in *Buckland* v. *Palmer* [1984] 1 W.L.R. 1109 at 1116 (C.A.).

[80] *Steamship Mutual* v. *Trollope & Colls* (1986) 33 B.L.R. 77 at 99 (C.A.).

[81] *Conquer* v. *Boot* [1928] 2 K.B. 336 at 339 (D.C.); *Telfair Shipping* v. *Inersea Carriers* [1983] 2 Lloyd's Rep. 351; *cf. Bovis Construction (South Eastern) Ltd.* v. *Greater London Council* (unreported) May 28, 1985 (C.A.) where it was held that the words "cause of action" in R.S.C., Ord. 22, r. 1(5) must be read in a broad sense as embracing an identifiable monetary claim which the plaintiff seeks to advance even though it may comprise a number of causes of action. The case concerned a building contractor's claim under various heads and the strict approach may have been that each individual variation or instruction gave rise to a separate cause of action; *cf. Letang* v. *Cooper* [1965] 1 Q.B. 232 at 242 (C.A.).

[82] [1928] 2 K.B. 336 (D.C.).

employer claimed and recovered £24 damages for breach of contract to complete a bungalow "in a good and workmanlike manner." Ten months later he made an identical claim save that the words "and with proper materials" were added and recovered a further £81 damages. On appeal it was held that the second judgment must be quashed as the matter was *res judicata*, Sankey L.J. saying, "So far as the claim is concerned it appears to me to be identical in both places—namely, a claim for breach of contract to complete the bungalow in a good and workmanlike manner."[83] By contrast in *Steamship Mutual* v. *Trollope & Colls*,[84] it was held that a claim for a defective airconditioning system and a claim for defective brickwork in the same building constructed under the same contract were different causes of action for the purposes of section 35 of the Limitation Act 1980.[85] It seems that claims against an architect for negligent design and negligent supervision are separate causes of action.[86]

The National House-Building Council's Scheme relating to the construction of dwellings[87] envisages serial arbitration, so that a claimant may bring more than one arbitration for alleged defects.[88] But plaintiffs whose claim for defects in a bungalow had failed in an arbitration under a National House-Builders Registration Council's agreement were held to be disentitled from bringing a claim for the same defects in an action for breach of the antecedent building contract. In so far as the builder's obligations under each contract differed, the higher standard was provided under the second contract. The plaintiffs could not pursue the same claim under the first contract as had been unsuccessfully arbitrated under the second contract.[89]

The court will not set aside an arbitrator's award because he gives effect to a trade custom that a party may from time to time refer different disputes arising out of the same contract to arbitration.[90]

Where a contract sum is payable by instalments, each instalment may be sued for as it falls due and the contractor may in proper cases seek summary judgment under Order 14.[91] An amendment of the pleadings cannot be granted so as to include a claim for an instalment falling due after proceedings have been commenced.[92]

---

[83] *Ibid.* at 340; see also *H. E. Daniels Ltd.* v. *Carmel Exporters and Importers Ltd.* [1953] 2 Q.B. 242; s.35 of the County Courts Act 1984. For the application of the doctrine to issues, see *Carl Zeiss Stiftung* v. *Rayner & Keeler Ltd.* (*No. 2*) [1967] 1 A.C. 853 (H.L.); *Khan* v. *Goleccha International* [1980] 1 W.L.R. 1482; *The Sennar* (*No. 2*) [1985] 1 W.L.R. 490 (H.L.).

[84] (1986) 33 B.L.R. 77 (C.A.).

[85] *cf. Idyll Ltd.* v. *Dinerman Davison* (1971) 1 Const.L.J. 294 (C.A.).

[86] *Brickfield Properties* v. *Newton* [1971] 1 W.L.R. 862 (C.A.).

[87] See p. 362.

[88] *Purser & Co.* (*Hillingdon*) v. *Jackson* [1977] Q.B. 166.

[89] *Willday* v. *Taylor* (1976) 241 E.G. 835 (C.A.).

[90] *Brian Smith Ltd.* v. *Wheatsheaf Mills Ltd.* [1939] 2 K.B. 302.

[91] *Workman, Clark & Co. Ltd.* v. *Lloyd Brazileno* [1908] 1 K.B. 968 (C.A.).

[92] *Eshelby* v. *Federated European Bank Ltd.* [1932] 1 K.B. 423 (C.A.); *cf. Tilcon* v. *Land and Real Estate Investments* [1987] 1 W.L.R. 46 (C.A.).

(c) *Discovery*

Discovery is the process by which each party lists "the documents which are or have been in their possession, custody or power relating to the matters in question in the action."[93] The documents are then made available for inspection in so far as they are not privileged from production. No complete account of this process is given here, but certain points of particular importance to building contract litigation are made.[94]

In building contract litigation, discovery is often lengthy, tedious and expensive, resulting in an unwieldy mass of duplicated paper. But the requirement to disclose all documents which are relevant frequently makes this unavoidable. There are many cases where discovery is quite essential to a party's case. For example, in claims for a reasonable sum for cost plus profit early discovery may be very important to the employer, for the contractor's wage sheets and invoices for materials used will often show the employer the strength of the case he has to meet. Documents in the possession, custody or power of a defendant which came into existence for the purposes of an arbitration between the defendant and a third party, being relevant to issues in an action between a plaintiff and the defendant, were ordered to be disclosed to the plaintiff.[95]

Legal professional privilege.   In brief, this protects from disclosure:

(1) confidential communications between a client and his solicitor acting in his professional capacity for the purpose of obtaining legal advice;

(2) communications between a solicitor and a non-professional agent or third party after litigation is contemplated and with a view to its conduct; and

(3) communications between a client and a non-professional agent or third party whose dominant objective purpose was to use it or its contents in order to obtain legal advice or to conduct or aid in the conduct of litigation.[96]

An insured's report to insurers under the terms of a professional indemnity policy was held to be privileged under the third of these categories.[97] Privileged documents disclosed or acquired by mistake may be recoverable if privilege has not been waived.[98] Disclosure may be ordered notwithstanding a claim for

---

[93] R.S.C., Ord. 24, r. 1(1).

[94] See in elaboration R.S.C., Ord. 24 and the commentary in the Supreme Court Practice 1991; see also "Documents" at p. 429.

[95] *Shearson Lehman Hutton* v. *Maclaine Watson* [1988] 1 W.L.R. 946; *cf. Lorne Stewart* v. *William Sindall* (1986) 35 B.L.R. 109 and see n. 94 above.

[96] *Waugh* v. *British Railways Board* [1980] A.C. 521 (H.L.); *Guinness Peat* v. *Fitzroy Robinson* [1987] 1 W.L.R. 1027 (C.A.).

[97] *Guinness Peat* v. *Fitzroy Robinson* [1987] 1 W.L.R. 1027 (C.A.).

[98] See, *e.g. English and American Insurance* v. *Herbert Smith & Co.* (1987) 137 N.L.J. 148; *Guinness Peat* v. *Fitzroy Robinson* [1987] 1 W.L.R. 1027 (C.A.); *C. H. Beazer* v. *C.J. Associates* (1985) 4 Con.L.R. 93; *Derby & Co.* v. *Weldon (No. 8)*, *The Times*, August 29, 1990 (C.A.).

legal professional privilege if the plaintiff establishes a strong prima facie case of relevant fraud. But such disclosure would not extend to documents brought into existence for the dominant purpose of being used in pending or contemplated legal proceedings.[99]

"Without prejudice" communications. Communications between parties to litigation with a view to resolving their disputes are inadmissible in evidence. The rule is founded upon the public policy of encouraging litigants to settle their differences rather than litigate them to a finish.[1]

> "The rule applies to exclude all negotiations genuinely aimed at settlement whether oral or in writing from being given in evidence. . . . the application of the rule is not dependent upon the use of the phrase 'without prejudice' and if it is clear from the surrounding circumstances that the parties were seeking to compromise the action, evidence of the content of those negotiations will, as a general rule, not be admissible at the trial."[2]

Privilege only arises if there is a dispute or negotiation,[3] and a "without prejudice" letter asserting a party's rights but not amounting to an offer to negotiate was held not to be privileged and was admissible in evidence.[4]

If there is an issue whether or not the negotiations resulted in an agreed settlement, or as to the terms of such a settlement, the "without prejudice" material will be admissible for the purpose of deciding that issue.[5] But admissions made with a genuine intention to reach a settlement with a different party in the same litigation are inadmissible whether or not settlement was reached with that party and are further inadmissible in any subsequent litigation connected with the same subject matter.[6] Although it is thought that privilege attaching to bilateral negotiations cannot be unilaterally withdrawn, privilege can be withdrawn by agreement,[7] and a "without prejudice" offer can usually be restated as an open offer by omitting reference to privileged communications.

---

[99] *Derby & Co.* v. *Weldon (No. 7)* [1990] 1 W.L.R. 1156; *cf. Finers* v. *Miro, The Times*, September 9, 1990 (C.A.).

[1] *Rush & Tompkins* v. *Greater London Council* [1989] A.C. 1280 at 1299 (H.L.); *Cutts* v. *Head* [1984] Ch. 290 at 306 (C.A.); *South Shropshire District Council* v. *Amos* [1986] 1 W.L.R. 1271 (C.A.); *cf. Simaan General Contracting* v. *Pilkington Glass* [1987] 1 W.L.R. 516 for the inadmissibility of "without prejudice" negotiations on an application for security for costs. See also "Written offers" at p. 462.

[2] Lord Griffiths in *Rush & Tompkins* v. *Greater London Council* [1989] A.C. 1280 at 1299 (H.L.); *cf. Walker* v. *Wilsher* (1889) 23 Q.B.D. 335 (C.A.); *Stotesbury* v. *Turner* [1943] K.B. 370; for without prejudice discussions between experts under R.S.C., Ord. 38, r. 38, see "Expert reports" at p. 428.

[3] *Re Daintrey* [1893] 2 Q.B. 116 at 119 (D.C.).

[4] *Buckinghamshire County Council* v. *Moran* [1990] Ch. 623 (C.A.).

[5] *Rush & Tompkins* v. *Greater London Council* [1989] A.C. 1280 at 1300 (H.L.); *Tomlin* v. *Standard Telephones & Cables Ltd.* [1969] 1 W.L.R. 1378 (C.A.).

[6] *Ibid.; cf. Lorne Stewart* v. *William Sindall* (1986) 35 B.L.R. 109—it is an open question whether the "name borrowing" aspect of this case would now distinguish it from the *Rush & Tompkins* decision.

[7] See *Blow* v. *Norfolk County Council* [1966] 3 All E.R. 579 (C.A.).

(d) *Preliminary Point*

"Where there is a point of law which, if decided in one way, is going to be decisive of the litigation, advantage ought to be taken of the facilities afforded by the rules of court to have it disposed of at the close of pleadings or very shortly afterwards."[8] But this course "frequently adds to the difficulties of courts of appeal and tends to increase the cost and time of legal proceedings. If this practice cannot be confined to cases where the facts are complicated and the legal issue short and easily decided, cases outside this guiding principle should at least be exceptional."[9]

The determination of a preliminary point of law is to be distinguished from the trial of preliminary issues of mixed fact and law which is often ordered in building contract litigation.[10] Careful thought is required before applying for such an order lest issues apparently separate are in reality so intermingled as to make the order inappropriate. Official referees sometimes divide very complicated cases into a number of sub-trials.[11]

(e) *Plans, photographs, models, mechanically recorded evidence*

Unless at or before the trial the court or a judge for special reasons otherwise orders or directs, no plan, photograph or model is receivable in evidence at the trial of an action unless at least 10 days before the commencement of the trial the parties, other than the party producing it, have been given an opportunity to inspect it and to agree to the admission thereof without further proof.[12] The court may exceptionally direct non-disclosure where the bona fides of a party is in issue.[13] Mechanically recorded evidence is admissible.[14]

(f) *View*

A view is sometimes helpful. "Where the matter for decision is one of ordinary common sense the judge of fact is entitled to form his own judgment on the real

---

[8] Romer L.J. in *Everett* v. *Ribbands* [1952] 2 Q.B. 198 at 206 (C.A.); applied in *Carl Zeiss Stiftung* v. *Herbert Smith & Co.* [1969] 1 Ch. 93 (C.A.). See Ord. 18, r. 11; Ord. 33, r. 3 and 4 and their notes in Supreme Court Practice 1991. See also *Gold* v. *Patman & Fotheringham Ltd.* [1958] 2 All E.R. 497 at 503 (C.A.); *Nissan* v. *Att.-Gen.* [1968] 1 Q.B. 286 (C.A.) (decisive of part only of litigation); *Goodchild* v. *Greatness Timber Co. Ltd.* [1968] 2 Q.B. 372 (C.A.); *Warner Bros. Records Inc.* v. *Rollgreen Ltd.* [1976] Q.B. 430 (C.A.).

[9] Lord Wilberforce in *Tilling* v. *Whiteman* [1980] A.C. 1 at 18 (H.L.).

[10] See R.S.C., Ord. 33, r. 3 and, for example, *Gloucestershire County Council* v. *Richardson* [1969] 1 A.C. 480 (H.L.).

[11] See, *e.g. Holland Hannen & Cubitts* v. *W.H.T.S.O.* (1981) 18 B.L.R. 80 at 90—the first sub-trial; *cf. Holland Hannen & Cubitts* v. *W.H.T.S.O.* (1985) 35 B.L.R. 1 (C.A.)—an appeal on issues arising from a partial settlement during a second sub-trial.

[12] Ord. 38, r. 5.

[13] See *McGuinness* v. *Kellogg Co.* [1988] 1 W.L.R. 913 (C.A.)—a film taken by a private inquiry agent on behalf of defendants in a personal injury action seeking to establish that the plaintiff was malingering.

[14] *The Statue of Liberty* [1968] 2 All E.R. 195.

evidence of a view just as much as on the oral evidence of witnesses,"[15] although "there may, of course, be cases in which the matter falls to be decided on technical evidence, and where a view will not be of any assistance, except no doubt as a substitute for a plan or photograph."[16] In any event each party must be given an opportunity of being present,[17] and it is undesirable for the judge even to have a "a mere look" without previously informing the parties.[18] It is a matter of discretion for the judge to decide whether or not to have a view.[19] What is derived from the view is part of the evidence and the view should take place at or before the conclusion of the evidence.[20]

(g) *Various interlocutory matters*

The provisions of Order 25 and a summons for directions in blank should be studied and all possible applications made on the first hearing of the summons for directions.

It may be desirable to join sub-contractors or others as third parties,[21] and in some cases, to apply for detention, preservation or inspection of property.[22]

The court can appoint a court expert,[23] or order trial with assessors,[24] or, in the Chancery Division, obtain the assistance of experts.[25]

Delay in proceedings.[26]   In recent years the courts have shown a greater willingness than in the past to strike out cases for delay, and the relevant principles have been authoritatively stated by the House of Lords in *Birkett* v. *James*.[27] Where, as will ordinarily be so, the limitation period has expired,[28] the order is "Draconian ... and will not be lightly made."[29] The court must be satisfied either:

(1) that the default has been intentional and contumelious; or
(2) (a) that there has been inordinate and inexcusable delay; and
    (b) that such delay will give rise to a substantial risk that it is not possible to have a fair trial, or is likely to cause serious prejudice to

---

[15] Denning L.J. in *Buckingham* v. *Daily News Ltd.* [1956] 2 Q.B. 534 at 551 (C.A.).
[16] *Ibid.* Parker L.J. at 550.
[17] *Goold* v. *Evans* [1951] 2 T.L.R. 1189.
[18] *Salsbury* v. *Woodland* [1970] 1 Q.B. 324 (C.A.); *cf. Parry* v. *Boyle* (1987) R.T.R. 282 (Q.B.D.).
[19] R.S.C., Ord. 35, r. 8(1); *Tito* v. *Waddell* [1975] 1 W.L.R. 1303.
[20] See *Parry* v. *Boyle* (1987) R.T.R. 282 (Q.B.D.).
[21] See R.S.C., Ord. 16, generally. For the position where there is an arbitration agreement with one but not with all the parties, see p. 402.
[22] See R.S.C., Ord. 29, r. 2 and 3; s.33 of the Supreme Court Act 1981.
[23] R.S.C., Ord. 40; see notes in Supreme Court Practice 1991.
[24] R.S.C., Ord. 33, r. 6.
[25] R.S.C., Ord. 32, r. 16.
[26] For delay in arbitrations, see "Dismissal for want of prosecution" at p. 405.
[27] [1978] A.C. 297 (H.L.).
[28] *Birkett* v. *James* [1978] A.C. 297 (H.L.); *cf. Barclays Bank* v. *Miller* [1990] 1 W.L.R. 343 (C.A.)—action dismissed where it was open to doubt and serious argument whether a fresh action would be statute-barred.
[29] *Allen* v. *Sir Alfred McAlpine & Sons Ltd.* [1968] 2 Q.B. 229 at 259 (C.A.).

the defendants, either as between themselves and the plaintiff, or between each other, or between them and a third party.[30]

The fact that the plaintiff may or may not have an alternative remedy against his solicitor is not a relevant consideration in deciding whether or not to dismiss an action for want of prosecution.[31]

Except where the plaintiff's conduct is contumelious, the power to dismiss an action for want of prosecution is not normally exercised within the currency of the limitation period, since the plaintiff would normally be entitled to issue a fresh writ for the same cause of action.[32] But disobedience to a peremptory order of the court generally amounts to "contumelious" conduct attracting the sanction that the plaintiff's action may be dismissed.[33] If it is, it seems that the court has a discretion to strike out a second action as an abuse of the process of the court even if the second action is started within the limitation period."[34]

Up to the expiry of the statutory limitation period, a plaintiff has a legal right to start an action.[35]

"To justify dismissal for want of prosecution some prejudice to the defendant additional to that inevitably flowing from the plaintiff's tardiness in issuing his writ must be shown to have resulted from his subsequent delay (beyond the period allowed by rules of court) in proceeding promptly with the successive steps in the action. The additional prejudice need not be great compared with that which may have already been caused by the time elapsed before the writ was issued; but it must be more than minimal; and the delay in taking a step in the action if it is to qualify as inordinate as well as prejudicial must exceed the period allowed by rules of court for taking that step."[36]

Prejudice may be of varying kinds and it is not confined to prejudice affecting the actual conduct of the trial.[37] But the mere fact of the anxiety that accompanies any litigation is unlikely by itself to be sufficient prejudice to justify striking out an action.[38]

---

[30] *Birkett* v. *James* [1978] A.C. 297 (H.L.); *Department of Transport* v. *Chris Smaller* [1989] A.C. 1197 at 1203 (H.L.).

[31] *Ibid.*

[32] *Birkett* v. *James* [1978] A.C. 297 (H.L.).

[33] *Tolley* v. *Morris* [1979] 1 W.L.R. 592 at 603 (H.L.).

[34] *Janov* v. *Morris* [1981] 1 W.L.R. 1389 (C.A.) considering *Tolley* v. *Morris* [1979] 1 W.L.R. 592 (H.L.); *cf. Cromlech Property Company* v. *Costain Construction* (1986) 10 Con.L.R. 110 where there was delay but no contumelious default.

[35] *Birkett* v. *James* [1978] A.C. 297 at 323 (H.L.).

[36] Lord Diplock in *Birkett* v. *James* [1978] A.C. 297 at 323 (H.L.); see also Lord Salmon at 331.

[37] *Department of Transport* v. *Chris Smaller* [1989] A.C. 1197 at 1209 (H.L.); *cf. Hayes* v. *Bowman* [1989] 1 W.L.R. 456 (C.A.). For building contract cases, see *Electricity Supply Nominees* v. *Longstaff and Shaw* (1986) 3 Const.L.J. 145 (C.A.); *City of Westminster* v. *Clifford Culpin & Partners* (1987) 4 Const.L.J. 141 (C.A.); *Lowfield Distribution* v. *Modern Engineering* (1988) 15 Con.L.R. 27; these cases now to be read in the light of *Department of Transport* v. *Chris Smaller* [1989] A.C. 1197 (H.L.).

[38] *Department of Transport* v. *Chris Smaller* [1989] A.C. 1197 (H.L.) expressing caution about decisions such as Lord Denning in *Biss* v. *Lambeth Health Authority* [1978] 1 W.L.R. 382 at 389 (C.A.).

Both the claim and counterclaim may be dismissed if plaintiff and defendant have been guilty of delay.[39] Periods of time bear a different complexion in cases of magnitude and complexity than they do in simple accident cases,[40] but building cases are not exempt from the Rules of the Supreme Court.[41]

(h) *Settlement of actions*

In settling an action the parties should decide whether they wish to be able to refer the action back to the court or whether they are content to rely upon the terms of the settlement as a contract and, if necessary, bring fresh proceedings for any breach of such contract.[42] Interest which might be awarded under section 35A of the Supreme Court Act 1981,[43] if the matter proceeded to judgment, should be taken into account. Breach of a valid compromise does not revive the original claims. The remedy is to sue for breach of the compromise agreement.[44]

5. Set-off and Counterclaim

Where a defendant has a cross-claim against the plaintiff he may be able to set this up in diminution of the plaintiff's claim, *i.e.* plead a set-off, or he may counterclaim[45] or he may both set off and counterclaim.[46]

Distinction between set-off and counterclaim. A set-off is a defence[47] and as such can be used only "as a shield, not as a sword."[48] Consequently a defendant must counterclaim if he hopes to obtain more on his cross-claim than the plaintiff will obtain on his claim, or if the defendant desires to be in a position to continue his cross-claim in the same proceedings although the plaintiff's claim is discontinued. A cross-claim by a defendant can always be made the subject of a counterclaim but not necessarily of a set-off, and it is sometimes difficult to decide whether a cross-claim can be set off.

The principles which determine whether a cross-claim can be set off were discussed in *Hanak* v. *Green*,[49] and in short the position is that there may be:

---

[39] *Zimmer Orthopaedic* v. *Zimmer Manufacturing Co.* [1968] 1 W.L.R. 1349 (C.A.).

[40] *City General Insurance Co. Ltd.* v. *Robert Bradford & Co. Ltd.* [1970] 1 Lloyd's Rep. 520 at 523 (C.A.).

[41] *Renown Investments Ltd.* v. *Shepherd Ltd., The Times,* November 11, 1976 (C.A.).

[42] See *Green* v. *Rozen* [1955] 1 W.L.R. 741 for a most useful discussion by Slade J. of various ways of settling actions. See also the *Encyclopaedia of Court Forms* (2nd ed.), Vol. 12, title "Compromise and Settlement" where there is a discussion of and precedents for 16 methods of settlement.

[43] See p. 451.

[44] *Supamarl* v. *Federated Homes* (1981) 9 Con.L.R. 25.

[45] R.S.C., Ord. 15, r. 2; *cf. C.S.I. International* v. *Archway Personnel* [1980] 1 W.L.R. 1069 (C.A.).

[46] R.S.C., Ord. 18, r. 17.

[47] *Hanak* v. *Green* [1958] 2 Q.B. 9 at 26 (C.A.); *Modern Engineering (Bristol) Ltd.* v. *Gilbert Ash (Northern) Ltd.* [1974] A.C. 689 (H.L.). See also *Henriksens A/S* v. *Rolimpex T.H.Z.* [1974] 1 Q.B. 233 (C.A.).

[48] Cockburn C.J. in *Stooke* v. *Taylor* (1880) 5 Q.B.D. 569 at 575 (D.C.).

[49] [1958] 2 Q.B. 9 (C.A.). All previous decisions should be read in the light of *Hanak* v. *Green*. See also *Hale* v. *Victoria Plumbing Co. Ltd.* [1966] 2 Q.B. 746 (C.A.).

(1) a set-off of mutual debts;

(2) in certain cases a setting up of matters of complaint which, if established, reduce or even extinguish the claim—this is referred to below as "abatement";

(3) reliance upon equitable set-off and reliance upon matters of equity which formerly might have called for injunction or prohibition.[50]

To this may be added:

(4) contractual set-off, and

(5) statutory set-off.

Abatement.[51]   With building contracts, "it is competent for the defendant, ... not to set off, by a proceeding in the nature of a cross action, the amount of damages which he has sustained by breach of the contract, but simply to defend himself by shewing how much less the subject matter of the action was worth, by reason of the breach."[52]

> "This is a remedy which the common law provides for breaches of warranty in contracts for sale of goods and for work and labour. It is restricted to contracts of these types. It is available as of right to a party to such a contract. It does not lie within the discretion of the court to withhold it. It is independent of the doctrine of 'equitable set-off' ..."[53]

Thus where there is a claim on a lump sum contract and the defendant alleges that there are defects he may either set off his loss in diminution of the claim, or he may counterclaim for damages.[54]

Equitable set-off.   The scope of the right of equitable set-off is fairly wide. The test whether a cross-claim can be relied on as an equitable set-off is whether it is so closely connected with the claim that it would be manifestly unjust to allow the claim without taking into account the cross-claim.[55] It is not

---

[50] *Hanak* v. *Green* [1958] 2 Q.B. 9 at 23 (C.A.), Morris L.J., in whose judgment are given examples of each class of set-off. The judgment contains a "masterly account of the doctrine of equitable set-off"—see Lord Diplock in *Modern Engineering* v. *Gilbert-Ash* [1974] A.C. 689 at 717 (H.L.); *cf.* *Federal Commerce* v. *Molena Alpha* [1978] Q.B. 927 (C.A.); *B.I.C.C.* v. *Burndy Corporation* [1985] Ch. 232 (C.A.); *Bank of Boston* v. *European Grain* [1989] A.C. 1056 at 1101 (H.L.).

[51] See, *e.g.* *Aries Tanker* v. *Total Transport* [1977] 1 W.L.R. 185 at 190 (H.L.); *Cathery* v. *Lithodomus* (1987) 41 B.L.R. 76 at 82 (C.A.). Abatement is sometimes referred to as "legal set-off" but this can be misleading—see *Acsim (Southern)* v. *Danish Contracting* (1989) 47 B.L.R. 55 (C.A.).

[52] *Mondel* v. *Steel* (1841) 8 M. & W. 858 at 871 cited by Lord Diplock in *Modern Engineering* v. *Gilbert-Ash* [1974] A.C. 689 at 717 (H.L.).

[53] Lord Diplock in *Modern Engineering* v. *Gilbert-Ash* [1974] A.C. 689 at 717 (H.L.); *cf.* s.53(1)(a) of the Sale of Goods Act 1979.

[54] *Hoenig* v. *Isaacs* [1952] 2 All E.R. 176 at 181 (C.A.), and see p. 73; *Modern Engineering* v. *Gilbert-Ash* [1974] A.C. 689 (H.L.); *Aries Tanker* v. *Total Transport* [1977] 1 W.L.R. 185 at 190, 194 (H.L.); *Acsim (Southern)* v. *Danish Contracting* (1989) 47 B.L.R. 55 at 70, 79, 80 (C.A.).

[55] *Dole Dried Fruit* v. *Trustin Kerwood*, *The Independent*, May 22, 1990; *Hanak* v. *Green* [1958] 2 Q.B. 9 at 24, 31 (C.A.). See also *Henriksens A/S* v. *Rolimpex T.H.Z.* [1974] 1 Q.B. 233 at 248, 252 (C.A.); *Federal Commerce* v. *Molena Alpha* [1978] Q.B. 927 at 974 (C.A.); *Cathery* v. *Lithodomus* (1987) 41 B.L.R. 76 at 82 (C.A.); *Guinness plc* v. *Saunders* [1988] 1 W.L.R. 863 at 870 (C.A.).

necessary that the subject matter of the cross-claim should actually serve to reduce or diminish the claim itself: that is the test for abatement or legal set-off as discussed above.[56] In *Hanak* v. *Green* the employer claimed damages for failure to complete properly. Against this the contractor was held entitled to set off a claim on a *quantum meruit* for extra work done outside the contract, loss caused by the employer's refusal to admit the contractor's workmen and damages for trespass to tools. Liquidated damages not exceeding the amount of the claim and arising under the same contract can normally be set off against the claim.

Contractual set-off. Parties may provide for set-off or deduction by contract and they frequently do this in building contracts. Where provision is made for deduction of cross-claims arising out of the same contract, the deduction would often be available any way as abatement or equitable set-off. But it seems that an employer cannot set off a claim arising under another unconnected contract with the same contractor unless he has been given express power by the contract upon which the contractor claims,[57] or there are special circumstances sufficiently connecting the two claims to sustain an equitable set-off. If there is such an express power, it will be effective according to its construction.[58]

Statutory set-off. Rights of set-off may arise under statute, as for instance under section 323 of the Insolvency Act 1986.[59]

Exclusion of right of set-off. The parties may by agreement limit or exclude their rights to set-off.

> "It is, of course, open to the parties to a contract ... for work and labour ... to exclude by express agreement a remedy for its breach which would otherwise arise by operation of law .... But in construing such a contract one starts with the presumption that neither party intends to abandon any remedies for its breach arising by operation of law, and clear express words must be used in order to rebut this presumption."[60]

In *Mottram Consultants* v. *Sunley*,[61] the House of Lords by a majority held that on the particular contract in question the right of set-off had been excluded. The

---

[56] *Dole Dried Fruit* v. *Trustin Kerwood, The Independent*, May 22, 1990.

[57] *Re Asphaltic Wood Payment Co., ex p. Lee and Chapman* (1885) 30 Ch.D. 216 (C.A.); *Ellis Mechanical* v. *Wates Construction* [1978] 1 Lloyd's Rep. 33 (C.A.); *cf. Small* v. *Middlesex Real Estates Ltd.* [1921] W.N. 245.

[58] For a clause considered to be effective under both heads considered in the text, see *Modern Engineering* v. *Gilbert-Ash* [1974] A.C. 689 at 698, 704, 711 (H.L.). A distinct earlier part of the same clause was considered to be an unenforceable penalty. For an example of a clause effecting a contractual set-off in a commercial contract, see *Federal Commerce* v. *Molena Alpha* [1978] Q.B. 927 (C.A.).

[59] See "Mutual Dealings" at p. 379 and the cases there cited.

[60] Lord Diplock in *Modern Engineering* v. *Gilbert-Ash* [1974] A.C. 689 at 717 (H.L.); *cf. C. M. Pillings* v. *Kent Investments* (1985) 30 B.L.R. 80 at 92 (C.A.); *Sonat Offshore* v. *Amerada Hess* (1987) 39 B.L.R. 1 and 21 (C.A.); *N.E.I. Thompson* v. *Wimpey Construction* (1987) 39 B.L.R. 65 (C.A.).

[61] [1975] 2 Lloyd's Rep. 197 (H.L.).

decision of the majority seems to have been materially affected by the special circumstance that there was a contract in being which the parties altered in such a way as to show an intention that a set-off should not be allowed.[62] Some standard forms of sub-contract contain elaborate provisions which seek to regulate and limit the contractor's right to set-off cross-claims against sums due for payment to the sub-contractor.[63] Such a clause, effective in some respects, has been construed as not preventing reliance on the remedy of abatement.[64]

6. Summary Judgment and Interim Payment

It has been said that one demerit of our system of justice is that because of our rules of procedure an arbitration under a building contract of some size is likely to take years; cases go to an arbitrator or an official referee and drag on and on and the cash flow is held up so that in the end there is some kind of compromise, very often not based on the merits of the case but on the economic situation of one of the parties.[65] In a proper case where one of the parties is entitled to money this result can be avoided by the application of the procedure for obtaining summary judgment under R.S.C., Order 14 or for interim payment under R.S.C., Order 29.

Summary judgment. This is available where there is no defence to the claim, or no defence to that part of the claim for which summary judgment is sought. It enables the plaintiff in such a case or a defendant on his counter-claim, upon summons supported by affidavit, to obtain judgment summarily without having to await trial.[66] The terms of Order 14 and the notes in the Supreme Court Practice should be consulted. Here there are discussed certain matters of particular interest in building disputes.

Degree of Proof of indebtedness required. This has been expressed in various ways. Thus the sum claimed or a definable and quantified part of it must be "indisputably due," or it must be "as plain as could be" that the sum is due, or it must be established "on the evidence beyond reasonable doubt."[67]

---

[62] The majority expressly applied that reasoning in the *Modern Engineering* case and it is submitted that there is no clash between the two decisions. *cf.* the vigorous dissenting opinion of Lord Salmon in the *Mottram* case, in particular at p. 215 where he expressed his opinion that the effect of the majority view would be to depart from what was decided by the House in the *Modern Engineering* case. The *Modern Engineering* case is now accepted as definitive. *cf. N.E.I. Thompson* v. *Wimpey Construction* (1987) 39 B.L.R. 65 (C.A.).

[63] See the discussion of clauses 23 and 24 of the Standard Form of Nominated Sub-contract at p. 764 and *cf. Chatbrown* v. *Alfred McAlpine Construction* (1986) 35 B.L.R. 44 (C.A.); *B.W.P. (Architectural)* v. *Beaver* (1988) 42 B.L.R. 86.

[64] *Acsim (Southern)* v. *Danish Contracting* (1989) 47 B.L.R. 55 (C.A.); *cf. Mellowes PPG* v. *Snelling Construction* (1989) 49 B.L.R. 109.

[65] Lawton L.J. in *Ellis Mechanical* v. *Wates Construction* [1978] 1 Lloyd's Rep. 33 at 36 (C.A.).

[66] See R.S.C., Ord. 14, r. 1 and 5; C.C.R., Ord. 9, r. 4.

[67] See judgments in the *Ellis* case; *Associated Bulk Carriers* v. *Koch Shipping* [1978] 1 Lloyd's Rep. 24 (C.A.). See also notes in the Supreme Court Practice.

441

"Order 14 is for clear cases, that is, cases in which there is no serious material factual dispute...."[68] The court arrives at its decision after considering the evidence served on behalf of the plaintiff and any evidence served on behalf of the defendant. The plaintiff does not get his judgment and the defendant will have leave to defend if it is shown that "there is an issue or question in dispute which ought to be tried or that there ought for some other reason to be a trial of the claim or part...."[69] The court may grant conditional leave to defend.[70] The court applies the same test in deciding whether leave to defend should be given as it does in deciding whether there is a dispute to be referred to arbitration and a stay of proceedings under section 4 of the Arbitration Act 1950.[71] There can be summary judgment for part of a claim and leave to defend or a stay of proceedings for arbitration for the remainder.[72]

Evidence upon an application for summary judgment. Every case turns upon its facts but excellent evidence is either an admission by the defendant, or his authorised agent, or a certificate by the defendant's architect or engineer, which is a special and formal kind of admission. When evidence of this nature is established the court usually requires cogent evidence from the defendant before it grants leave to defend. A set-off[73] can be a sufficient defence to a claim for summary judgment for a sum otherwise due.[74] But where for instance a defendant seeks to set-off a counterclaim for unliquidated damages for defects or delay against a sum due upon an architect's certificate, merely to allege the existence of defects in the works, or a claim for damages for delay without in each case giving some reasonable amount of detail and of quantification is unlikely to result in leave to defend.[75] Neither, it seems, will the court accept bare allegations, without satisfactory supporting evidence, that a certificate is not in accordance with the contract or that, for example, extras, part of the subject matter of the claim, were not sanctioned in writing.[76] It is the practice to allow additional evidence on appeal, even in the Court of Appeal on special grounds.[77]

Points of law. Where the defendant raises an arguable point of law, the current practice in England is that the court will nevertheless give summary

---

[68] Bingham L.J. in *Crown House Engineering* v. *Amec Projects* (1989) 48 B.L.R. 32 at 56 (C.A.).

[69] R.S.C., Ord. 14, r. 3.

[70] See R.S.C., Ord. 14, r. 4 and para. 14/3–4/15 of the Supreme Court Practice 1991.

[71] For stay of proceedings where there is an arbitration agreement, see p. 397.

[72] See, *e.g. Archital Luxfer* v. *A. J. Dunning* (1987) 47 B.L.R. 1 (C.A.).

[73] For set-off see p. 438.

[74] See, *e.g. C. M. Pillings* v. *Kent Investments* (1985) 30 B.L.R. 80 (C.A.); *cf. Shanning International* v. *George Wimpey* [1989] 1 W.L.R. 981 (C.A.); *Rosehaugh Stanhope* v. *Redpath Dorman Long* (1990) 50 B.L.R. 69 (C.A.).

[75] *Dawnays Ltd.* v. *Minter, F. G. Ltd.* [1971] 1 W.L.R. 1205 (C.A.), not overruled on this point in *Modern Engineering (Bristol) Ltd.* v. *Gilbert-Ash Ltd.* [1974] A.C. 689 at 713 (H.L.), *Kilby & Gayford Ltd.* v. *Selincourt Ltd.* (1973) 229 E.G. 1343 (C.A.).

[76] *Kilby & Gayford Ltd.* v. *Selincourt Ltd.* (1973) 229 E.G. 1343 (C.A.).

[77] See, *e.g. Kiu May Construction* v. *Wai Cheong* (1983) 29 B.L.R. 137 (Hong Kong High Court); R.S.C., Ord. 59, r. 10(2) and see paras. 59/10/7 *et seq.* of the Supreme Court Practice 1991.

judgment if it concludes, without reference to contested facts, that the defence advanced, though arguable, is bad. The existence of an arbitration clause makes no difference.[78] But if the point of law relied on by the defendant raises a serious question to be tried which calls for detailed argument and mature consideration, the point is not suitable to be dealt with in summary proceedings.[79] Order 14 is suitable for "no more than a crisp legal question, as well decided summarily as otherwise."[80] If the defence raises an arguable issue which is a mixed question of fact and law, leave to defend may be granted.[81]

Stay of execution.   The court has power to order a stay of execution of a judgment pending the determination of a cross-claim,[82] but will not normally do so where there is no defence because the parties have by contract excluded set-off.[83]

Interim payment.   The court has no inherent power to order an interim payment on account of damages expected to be recovered.[84] But there is now statutory power to order an interim payment on account of any damages, debt or other sum (excluding costs) which a defendant may in future be held liable to pay.[85] Applications for interim payment are often coupled with applications for summary judgment. "Order 29 rule 12 enables the court to order payment to a plaintiff to the extent that a claim, although not actually admitted, can scarcely be effectively denied."[86] The main circumstances relevant to building disputes where the court may exercise this power are if:

(1) the defendant has admitted liability for the plaintiff's damages,

(2) the plaintiff has obtained judgment for damages to be assessed,[87] and

---

[78] *Chatbrown* v. *Alfred McAlpine* (1986) 35 B.L.R. 44 (C.A.); *Ellis Mechanical* v. *Wates Construction* [1978] 1 Lloyd's Rep. 33 (Note) (C.A.); *Verrall* v. *Great Yarmouth Borough Council* [1981] Q.B. 202 at 215, 218 (C.A.); *Imodoco* v. *Wimpey and Taylor Woodrow* (1987) 40 B.L.R. 1 (C.A.); *cf. Sethia Liners* v. *State Trading Corporation of India* [1985] 1 W.L.R. 1398 (C.A.); *Forestal Mimosa* v. *Oriental Credit* [1986] 1 Lloyd's Rep. 329 (C.A.). The practice in Hong Kong may be somewhat different—see *Schindler Lifts* v. *Shui On Construction* (1984) 29 B.L.R. 95 (Hong Kong Court of Appeal).

[79] *Home and Overseas Insurance* v. *Mentor Insurance* [1989] 1 Lloyd's Rep. 473 at 484 (C.A.); *cf. British Holdings* v. *Quadrex* [1989] Q.B. 842 at 867 (C.A.); *R. G. Carter Ltd.* v. *Clarke* [1990] 1 W.L.R. 578 at 584 (C.A.); *John Mowlem* v. *Carlton Gate Development* (1990) 6 Const.L.J. 298.

[80] Bingham L.J. in *Crown House Engineering* v. *Amec Projects* (1989) 48 B.L.R. 32 at 57 (C.A.).

[81] *Archital Luxfer* v. *A. J. Dunning* (1987) 47 B.L.R. 1 (C.A.); *cf.* May L.J. at 10 who suggests that points of law amenable to the effects of special expertise might be left to an arbitrator.

[82] See R.S.C., Ord. 14, r. 3(2) where there is a counterclaim proceeding in court and R.S.C., Ord. 47, r. 1(a) where a cross-claim goes to arbitration.

[83] *Tubeworkers* v. *Tilbury Construction* (1985) 30 B.L.R. 67 (C.A.); *cf. Burnet* v. *Francis Industries* [1987] 1 W.L.R. 802 (C.A.); *Canada Enterprises* v. *MacNab Distilleries* [1987] 1 W.L.R. 813 (C.A.).

[84] *Moore* v. *Assignment Courier Ltd.* [1977] 1 W.L.R. 638 (C.A.); *Felix* v. *Shiva* [1983] Q.B. 82 (C.A.).

[85] s.32 of the Supreme Court Act 1981 and R.S.C., Ord. 29, Pt. II; *Schott Kem Ltd.* v. *Bentley* [1990] 3 W.L.R. 397 at 404 *et seq.* (C.A.). For a discussion of the amount of interim payments, see *Newport (Essex) Engineering* v. *Press & Shear Machinery* (1981) 24 B.L.R. 71 at 76 (C.A.).

[86] Bingham L.J. in *Crown House Engineering* v. *Amec Projects* (1989) 48 B.L.R. 32 at 57 (C.A.).

[87] For an example under this head, see *Croudace* v. *London Borough of Lambeth* (1986) 33 B.L.R. 20 (C.A.).

(3) the court is satisfied that, if the action proceeded to trial, the plaintiff would obtain judgment for a substantial amount.[88]

There is jurisdiction to order an interim payment even though the action is to be stayed to enable a dispute between the parties to be referred to arbitration.[89]

Under the third of the heads referred to above, there is a two stage approach. In the first stage, the court has to be satisfied that if the action proceeded to trial the plaintiff would obtain judgment for a substantial sum taking into consideration the likelihood of a set-off or other defence succeeding. Only if the court is satisfied at the first stage does it then proceed to consider at the second stage whether in the exercise of its discretion, it should order an interim payment and of what amount.[90] The burden of proof at the first stage is the civil burden on the balance of probabilities, but it is high.[91] The burden is not discharged where unconditional leave to defend has been granted, but it may be discharged where the court has granted conditional leave to defend in circumstances where it doubted the genuineness of the defence.[92]

7. Contractor's "Claims"

There is a tendency for contractors, or surveyors on their behalf, to spend much time in the preparation of claims for payment. The subject is dealt with briefly here because it is closely related to, and not infrequently results in, litigation. Claims prepared without a careful consideration of the legal principles upon which they may be based are usually a waste of time of both the person who prepares them and him who is asked to read them. Further, the form in which a claim is presented can provide a discipline for the person who prepares it, so as to ensure that he obtains and sets out the necessary information and by so doing assists the person who reads it to see whether, and to what extent, if any, there are grounds for payment.

Meaning and nature of "claims."   No exact meaning can be given to the term. It is used here to describe an application for payment by the contractor arising other than under the ordinary provisions for payment of the measured value of the work. A claim in this sense can arise either as a legally enforceable claim or *ex gratia*. Legally enforceable claims comprise rights to payment

---

[88] R.S.C., Ord. 29, r. 11(1) and 12(1)(c). See also R.S.C., Ord. 29, r. 12 generally.
[89] *Imodco* v. *Wimpey and Taylor Woodrow* (1987) 40 B.L.R. 1 (C.A.).
[90] *Shanning International* v. *George Wimpey* [1989] 1 W.L.R. 981 (C.A.). The court may also take account of a counterclaim which, though not available as a set-off, may nevertheless result in a balance judgment at trial—see *Smallman Construction* v. *Redpath Dorman Long* (1988) 47 B.L.R. 15 (C.A.).
[91] *Shearson Lehman* v. *Maclaine Watson & Co.* [1987] 1 W.L.R. 480 at 489 (C.A.); *British Holdings* v. *Quadrex* [1989] Q.B. 842 at 863 (C.A.); *cf. Brian Breeze* v. *McKennon & Son* (1985) 32 B.L.R. 41 (C.A.); *Imodco* v. *Wimpey and Taylor Woodrow* (1987) 40 B.L.R. 1 (C.A.).
[92] *British Holdings* v. *Quadrex* [1989] Q.B. 842 (C.A.); and see generally *Schott Kem Ltd.* v. *Bentley* [1990] 3 W.L.R. 397 at 404 *et seq.* (C.A.).

arising under the contract, claims for damages for breach of contract and occasionally under some other head of law, *e.g.* in tort or for breach of copyright or for misrepresentation.

Preparing the claim.   No useful general comment can be made upon the preparation of claims for *ex gratia* payments save to say that where they are made pursuant to some statement of principle accepted by the employer some of the suggestions below may be usefully adapted to bring the claim within the principles. What follows refers to the preparation of a claim enforceable in law.

The claim should be prepared from the beginning with litigation (which includes arbitration) in mind. This is for two reasons. The first is because the sanction for non-payment of a claim is that litigation will follow and if it is a good claim in law, the employer will have to pay the costs and interest as well as whatever is due on the claim. The claim document should therefore be such as to persuade him of the likelihood of this result if he does not pay. The second reason is that if litigation does follow it saves both time and money if the claims document has been so prepared that it can be used as, or form the basis for, the contractor's detailed pleading.[93] In particular the person preparing the claim should have in mind that if there is litigation the contractor is likely to be required to set out most of the material necessary to establish his right to payment in schedule form.[94] Therefore, whether or not the claim is originally prepared as a schedule it is usually prudent to assemble the material in such a way that it can be easily translated into a schedule. As an example, consider a claim made under clause 26.2.1 of the Standard Form of Building Contract for many cases of late delivery of drawings. It is necessary for each case to state (a) the date when the contractor specifically applied in writing for the drawing, (b) the due time when he should have received it, (c) the date when he actually received it, (d) the written application for direct loss of expense and (e) sufficient information and details of such loss or expense.

In all cases the ground in law relied on should be stated. If it is made under a clause of the contract, give its number. If it is made under an implied term, set out the term and the reasons for the implication. If it is a claim for breach, state the term of which it is alleged there is a breach and set out the facts relied on as constituting the breach. If it is a variation, describe it and refer to the relevant order. In all cases refer to relevant documents. The loss or other monetary claim should be stated showing how it is calculated and why it was caused by the ground relied on. Where the claim is made under various alternatives in law, say so. Thus, where the Standard Form of Building Contract is used there may be a claim for late delivery of drawings. Such a claim is ordinarily made for damages for breach of clause 5.4, or alternatively under clause. 26.2.1.

General words intended to arouse sympathy or other emotion favourable to the contractor's interest should be used sparingly lest they excite a suspicion

---

[93] For the recovery of the cost of work done by a claims' consultant, see *James Longley* v. *South West Regional Health Authority* (1983) 25 B.L.R. 56.
[94] See next section and in particular p. 449. See also "Composite claims" at p. 216.

that the contractor really thinks his claim is founded in mercy and not in law. Further, it is rarely useful to say that the contractor has suffered loss due to causes outside his control or which he did not reasonably anticipate. It is elementary law[95] that such factors are not grounds in law for extra payment unless, which is rare, they are expressly so made.[96] If this is put forward as the sole ground of a claim the reader may well assume that there is no other ground.

8. Scott or Official Referee's Schedule

The object of this document, widely used before official referees and in building contract arbitrations, is to define and state the issues clearly by assembling all the relevant allegations and defences or admissions in tabular form. If carefully drawn it will prevent confusion arising from the necessity of referring to two or three documents for one matter of detail, and it will save valuable time and energy at trial. Moreover, when it has been completed the parties may find that over a large number of small issues there is so little difference between them that they can be settled, thus reducing the dispute to a few substantial matters.

Settling the headings. There is no set form prescribed by rules nor even by the textbooks, but the forms suggested below should be found adequate for most purposes. They can, if necessary, be adapted in accordance with common sense in order to present the issues in any particular case as clearly and conveniently as possible. It is often desirable for the headings of the various columns to be settled before the official referee at the hearing of the summons for directions.[97] The parties can then explain what the issues are and suggest the appropriate headings. If the parties cannot agree, the official referee will determine what they should be. The schedule either is ordered to be or is adapted from a pleading. The rules for pleadings apply generally,[98] but with such modifications as the official referee or arbitrator may order or approve. In particular, the essence of an official referee's schedule is that a defendant *is* required to plead systematically to particulars, otherwise the issues could not sensibly be defined.

---

[95] See Chaps. 4, 5 and 8.
[96] For an example where they are material in a claim under a contract, see I.C.E. Conditions, clause 12.
[97] There is no summons for directions as such in an arbitration, but a preliminary meeting between the arbitrator and the legal representatives of the parties is usually arranged to settle the issues and deal with the matters ordinarily dealt with on a summons for directions.
[98] See R.S.C., Ord. 18, and p. 430.

Form 1. Defects alleged by employer

Serial No.	Contract Work	DEFENDANT'S		PLAINTIFF'S		Official Referee's Comments	
		Com-ments	Estimate of Loss	Com-ments	Estimate of Loss		
1	2	3	4	5	6	7	8

Generally. This form is suited to a dispute arising out of a lump sum contract where there has been substantial completion,[99] and the defendant (the employer) admits the claim subject to his counterclaim or set-off for defects and omissions.[1] The defendant will normally draft the first four columns and then submit the schedule to the plaintiff (the contractor) for his comments. Alternatively if the plaintiff has already delivered a reply dealing with the defendant's particulars the defendant can set out the relevant parts of the reply in column 5.

Column 1. Serial numbers should be inserted here for reference purposes. If items in the specification or bills of quantities are numbered the item number should appear in column 2.

Column 2. This sets out what the employer alleges should have been done to comply with the contract. If the contract is to do work according to a specification or bills of quantities it should refer to the relevant item. If the work is a variation, it should state what ought to have been done as a variation, giving particulars both of the original work, and of any variation order. If the quality of the work was not specified it should set out what ought to have been done in order to complete the work in accordance with the implied terms.[2]

Column 3. This sets out the defects alleged.

Column 4. This column sets out the amount of the defendant's claim. In the ordinary lump sum contract the measure of his claim is the difference in value between the work as done and the work as it should have been done to comply with the contract, and this is usually calculated by the cost of rectification, *i.e.* the cost of making the defective work correspond with the quality and quantity of work required by the contract.[3] If all the items are calculated on this basis the headings of columns 4 and 6 can be altered to "Cost to Rectify." If the damages claimed are the difference in value between the work as it is and as it ought to have been, it may be advisable to write "diminution of value" or

---

[99] See Chap. 4.
[1] See *Hoenig* v. *Isaacs* [1952] 2 All E.R. 176 at 181 (C.A.).
[2] See p. 52.
[3] See "Defective work" at p. 202.

otherwise to indicate that the cost of rectification is not being claimed. If there is a dispute about the principle by which the defendant's claim should be calculated, column 4 can be subdivided and figures inserted in each subdivision, it being stated that the lesser sum is claimed as an alternative. It may then be sensible to take the issue as a point of principle in the main pleadings and perhaps for it to be determined as a preliminary issue.[4]

Column 5. In this column the plaintiff sets up his defence to the claim admitting, not admitting, or denying the allegations of defects or raising an objection in point of law.[5] He may admit that the work was carried out as alleged, but say that it was done in pursuance of a variation order, giving particulars, or he may plead an architect's final certificate, or waiver or some special defence under the contract. Such defences may again be determined as one or more preliminary issues. If such a plea has been set out in full earlier in the schedule or in the body of the pleadings it is sufficient to refer back.

Column 6. Upon ordinary principles of pleading the plaintiff need insert nothing in this column.[6] But the object of the schedule is to gather together before trial in one document all the relevant contentions of the parties. In practice therefore a sum is usually inserted although there may have been a denial of liability in the previous column, the effect being of a plea in the alternative that, "if, which is denied, the plaintiff is liable, the amount recoverable is £x." The advantage of this course is that it shows to what extent the parties are at issue over damages.

Columns 7 and 8. These columns are inserted for the use of the official referee.

Form 2. Defects alleged: third parties or more than one defendant

The form will be as Form 1, save that special directions may have been given by the court[7] or official referee and extra columns must usually be added for each party interested in the allegations. In some cases it may be unnecessary to insert a column for a particular party. This may arise where, for example, a main contractor has made it clear that he will at trial confine himself to the issue of a claim for an indemnity or contribution from a sub-contractor who has carried out the allegedly defective work. In such a case the main contractor and the sub-contractor may have agreed between themselves, with a view to saving costs, that only the latter should plead to the defects and call evidence about the defects.

---

[4] See "Preliminary point" at p. 435.
[5] See notes to Ord. 18, r. 13 in Supreme Court Practice 1991.
[6] See R.S.C., Ord. 18, r. 13(4).
[7] See R.S.C., Ord. 16, r. 4(4) for third party directions. See p. 402 for the absence of such power on the part of an arbitrator.

Form 3. Extras: claim by contractor

Serial No.	Extra work carried out	PLAINTIFF'S		DEFENDANT'S		Official Referee's Comments	
		Comments	Price	Comments	Price		
1	2	3	4	5	6	7	8

Generally.   This form is suitable for a dispute where the contractor is the plaintiff and has issued a claim for extras, and he will normally first draft columns 1 to 4.[8]

Column 2. This sets out the work alleged to have been done.

Column 3. This deals by way of reply with any special defence raised in the pleadings such as absence of an order, or of an order in writing,[9] giving where appropriate particulars of the order or other matters relied on. It may also deal by way of reply with any allegations of defective work raised by the defendant.[10]

Column 5. The defendant (employer) sets up his defence in the usual way giving particulars of any defects upon which he relies by way of set-off in diminution of the price claimed. Where the plaintiff is claiming a reasonable sum and the defendant alleges that the sum claimed is excessive and unreasonable there is authority stating that the defendant need not give particulars of what he alleges to be a reasonable sum.[11] In practice it is usually desirable that the defendant should give such particulars and the official referees usually order them to be given.[12]

Counterclaim.   If the defendant has a counterclaim he should, after completing columns 5 and 6, prepare a separate schedule headed "Counterclaim." This will be as in Form 1 save that the serial numbers will be continued from the schedule for the claim. The plaintiff will complete the counterclaim schedule in the usual way.

Form 4. Reasonable sum: claim by contractor

Form 3 can be adapted by heading column 2 "Work carried out." The

---

[8] Subject to what follows, the comments for Form 1 apply with the necessary modifications.
[9] See p. 91 (contractual requirement of order in writing).
[10] See below.
[11] *James* v. *Radnor County Council* (1890) 6 T.L.R. 240 (C.A.).
[12] See para. 18/12/29 of the Supreme Court Practice 1991.

content of the columns will vary considerably according to the nature of the issues. Thus if the amount of the work is agreed, the only dispute being the pricing, column 2 may consist of summaries of costs, *e.g.* "Plasterer: 24 hrs. at £5.25 per hour."

Form 5. Schedule contract: claim by contractor

Form 3 can be adapted. In column 3 the contractor should state which part of the contract schedule he relies on. If it provides for varying percentage additions columns 3 and 4 can be adapted as follows:

PLAINTIFF'S			
Comments	Net Cost	Percentage Increase	Price Claimed
3	4	5	6

It will be a question in each case whether the next two columns should be correspondingly adapted, or whether it is sufficient for the defendant to set out his allegations as comments and the amount he considers should be paid under "price."

In many cases the official referee may direct that a formal schedule is unnecessary and that it is sufficient if the plaintiff supplies lists of labour and materials.[13]

Cost plus profit contract. In a cost plus profit contract where the only issue is the amount claimed by the contractor, a schedule is unnecessary unless its preparation has been directed by the official referee or the arbitrator. All that is normally required are two lists:

(1) A clear summary of the time sheets showing the time spent by each class of labour or by each workman, the rates actually paid, insurances, etc.
(2) A list of materials used upon the work setting out the actual cost and giving references to invoices, receipts and other documents.

Form 6. Contractors "claims"[14]

Form 3 can be adapted. The nature of the claim, (*i.e.* whether it is for payment under one of the terms of the contract or for damages for breach of contract,[15] or, unusually, for some other cause of action), will suggest the

---

[13] See below.
[14] For the meaning given to this term, see p. 444.
[15] For damages, see p. 206.

nature of the headings. Examples are given at page 445 for a claim for late issue of drawings where the Standard Form of Building Contract is used.[16]

Sometimes it is found convenient to use a chart to supplement or even instead of a schedule. This may arise where, for example, there is a contract programme[17] and the claim is for delay in the issue of drawings or instructions. If the programme is in, or capable of being expressed in, traditional bar-chart form it will set out the periods within which various activities were to be carried out. The contractor can insert, in a colour different from that in the original bars, the periods within which the works were in fact carried out. He then inserts for each activity the date when he alleges he should have received the necessary instruction or drawing referring to any relevant applications for information, and the date or dates when he in fact received them. When they were received over a long period and in various ways, *e.g.* by formal instruction, by letter, by the so-called "site instruction," by oral instruction confirmed in writing or simply by oral instruction, it may be convenient to use a code in order to save space and for clarity.

Damages. They are frequently in issue and their determination may require long and detailed inquiry. This is greatly assisted by full and detailed particulars supported by reference to the documents which will be relied on. Reference should be made to the heading "Employer's breach of contract" at page 206 for assistance in formulating the claim. No general rule can be stated for the use of a schedule or headings. Sometimes a schedule is not appropriate at all. In other cases it may be useful but the headings may have to be varied from time to time within the schedule according to the various heads of damage alleged. In all cases there should be a sufficient pleading of the casual connection between the quantum of damages claimed and the breach alleged, or the term of the contract under which the claim arises or other allegation of liability.

9. Interest

Discretionary interest.[18] Under section 35A of the Supreme Court Act 1981,[19] in proceedings before the High Court for the recovery of a debt or damages there may be included in any sum for which judgment is given simple interest on all or any part of the debt or damages. Interest may also be awarded

---

[16] For a discussion of claims for loss and expense and for damages arising under the Standard Form of Building Contract, see pp. 582 *et seq.*

[17] As, *e.g.* in accordance with clause 14 of the I.C.E. Conditions or agreed at the beginning of the contract with the architect where the Standard Form of Building Contract is used.

[18] See also "Interest for non-payment of money" and subsequent paragraphs at p. 213; for interest in relation to payments into court, see "Interest" at p. 461.

[19] See s.69 of the County Courts Act 1984 for equivalent provisions in the county court. Arbitrators also normally have power to award interest—see s.19A of the Arbitration Act 1950 as amended by s.15(6) of the Administration of Justice Act 1982.

where payment is made before judgment.[20] Interest may not be awarded on a debt for any period during which, for whatever reason, interest already runs.[21] This would be so, for instance, if a contract provided for interest to be payable at a stated rate if a certificate was not honoured within the stipulated period.[22]

All claims for interest must be pleaded in prescribed form.[23] There should be an explicit statement that interest is claimed under section 35A of the Supreme Court Act 1981 to distinguish the claim from one which might arise under other statutes or under contract.[24] Income tax is deductible from interest awarded under the Act.[25]

Interest ordinarily awarded. Although an award of interest is discretionary, there is a "well recognised rule of practice . . . that prima facie the losing party should be ordered to pay interest at a reasonable rate running from the date when the amount or amounts due should reasonably have been paid."[26] The general principle is that, unless there are special considerations affecting the particular case, interest is awarded on sums recovered so that the successful party should be compensated by the losing party for having kept him out of money to which he was entitled at or before the commencement of the proceedings.[27] An arbitrator who failed to follow the ordinary practice as to interest was held to be guilty of technical misconduct and the award was remitted to him.[28] Interest can be awarded upon summary judgment.[29] Interest can be awarded upon a sum allowed by the court under the Law Reform (Frustrated Contracts) Act 1943.[30] It is, however, inappropriate to award interest on moderate global sums awarded as damages for disappointment and inconvenience.[31]

Period for award of interest. The maximum period for calculating an award of interest is that between the date when the cause of action arose and

---

[20] See s.35A of the Act; *Edmunds* v. *Lloyds Italico* [1986] 1 W.L.R. 492 (C.A.).

[21] s.35A(4) of the Supreme Court Act 1981; *cf. Bushwall Properties Ltd.* v. *Vortex Properties Ltd.* [1975] 1 W.L.R. 1649 at 1660—reversed on other points at [1976] 1 W.L.R. 591 (C.A.).

[22] See, *e.g.* clause 60(7) of the I.C.E. Conditions at p. 906.

[23] R.S.C., Ord. 18, r. 8(4); Practice Note [1983] 1 W.L.R. 377.

[24] See para. 18/8/10 of the Supreme Court Practice 1991.

[25] *Riches* v. *Westminster Bank Ltd.* [1947] A.C. 390 (H.L.).

[26] *Panchaud Freres S.A.* v. *Pagnan and Fratelli* [1974] 1 Lloyd's Rep. 394 at 409, Kerr J.; see also in the Court of Appeal 411 at 414.

[27] *Cremer* v. *General Carriers S.A.* [1974] 1 W.L.R. 341 at 355. See also *Riches* v. *Westminster Bank Ltd.* [1947] A.C. 390 at 397 (H.L.). For the position where the successful party has received insurance money, see *Harbutt's "Plasticine"* v. *Wayne Tank & Pump Co.* [1970] 1 Q.B. 447 (C.A.); *Cousins (H.) & Co.* v. *D. & C. Carriers* [1971] 2 Q.B. 230 (C.A.); *Metal Box* v. *Currys* [1988] 1 W.L.R. 175.

[28] *Van der Zuden, P.J., Wildhandel, N.V.* v. *Tucker & Cross* [1976] 1 Lloyd's Rep. 341.

[29] *Gardner Steel Ltd.* v. *Sheffield Bros.* [1978] 1 W.L.R. 916 (C.A.); *cf. Wallersteiner* v. *Moir (No. 2)* [1975] Q.B. 373 at 387 (C.A.).

[30] *B.P. Explorations Ltd.* v. *Hunt (No. 2)* [1983] 2 A.C. 352 (H.L.).

[31] *Saunders* v. *Edwards* [1987] 1 W.L.R. 1116 (C.A.). See "Inconvenience, discomfort and distress" at p. 205.

the date of judgment or payment before judgment respectively.[32] In deciding the period for which interest should be awarded all the circumstances of the case should be taken into account. Where, for instance, the plaintiff is responsible for unjustifiable delay in bringing the action to trial the period for calculating interest may be reduced.[33] But it is not:

"a proper exercise of discretion to refuse to award interest against a party who has been held liable for damages for breach of contract on the ground that the successful party has been guilty of delay, unless and until an opportunity has been given to that party to show whether indeed he has been guilty of delay...."[34]

Rate of interest awarded. It is usual in building contract cases to award interest at a commercial rate.

"I feel satisfied that in commercial cases the interest is intended to reflect the rate at which the plaintiff would have had to borrow money to supply the place of that which was withheld. I am also satisfied that one should not look at any special position in which the plaintiff may have been:... The correct thing to do is to take the rate at which plaintiffs in general could borrow money. This does not, however, to my mind mean that you exclude entirely all attributes of the plaintiff other than that he is a plaintiff.... I think that it would always be right to look at the rate at which plaintiffs with the general attributes of the actual plaintiff... could borrow money as a guide to the appropriate interest rate."[35]

The rate of interest awarded to established companies is commonly assessed at bank base rate or minimum lending rate plus 1 per cent.[36] An adjustment is sometimes made if the plaintiff has saved tax as a result of the defendant's breach.[37]

Interest on judgment debts. Under section 17 of the Judgments Act 1838, every judgment debt carries interest at a prescribed rate from the time of entering up the judgment.[38] Where judgment is entered on liability with

---

[32] See s.35A of the Supreme Court Act 1981. For a discussion, see *B.P. Exploration Co.* v. *Hunt* (*No. 2*) [1979] 1 W.L.R. 783 at 845 *et seq.*

[33] *Birkett* v. *Hayes* [1982] 1 W.L.R. 816 at 825 (C.A.); *Metal Box* v. *Currys Ltd.* [1988] 1 W.L.R. 175; *Spittle* v. *Bunney* [1988] 1 W.L.R. 847 (C.A.); *cf. Wright* v. *British Railways Board* [1983] 2 A.C. 773 at 779 (H.L.).

[34] *Panchaud Freres S.A.* v. *R. Pagnan and Fratelli* [1974] 1 Lloyd's Rep. 394 at 414 (C.A.).

[35] Forbes J. in *Tate & Lyle* v. *Greater London Council* [1982] 1 W.L.R. 149 at 154.

[36] See *B.P. Exploration Co.* v. *Hunt* (*No. 2*) [1979] 1 W.L.R. 783 at 849; *Tate & Lyle* v. *Greater London Council* [1982] 1 W.L.R. 149 at 154; *Polish Steamship* v. *Atlantic Maritime* [1985] Q.B. 41 at 66 (C.A.); *Metal Box* v. *Currys* [1988] 1 W.L.R. 175 at 182. For interest in personal injury cases, see *Jefford* v. *Gee* [1970] 2 Q.B. 130 (C.A.); *Wright* v. *British Railways Board* [1983] 2 A.C. 773 (H.L.).

[37] See *Tate & Lyle* v. *Greater London Council* [1982] 1 W.L.R. 149 at 156.

[38] See generally para. 42/1/12 of the Supreme Court Practice 1991. The prescribed rate is currently 15 per cent.—Judgment Debts (Rate of Interest) Order 1985 (S.I. 1985 No. 437).

quantum to be decided at a later date, this statutory interest runs from the date of the judgment which quantifies or records the damages payable.[39]

10. Costs

Costs in building contract cases may be heavy. The pleadings are often long and involved, interlocutory applications are frequently necessary, hearings tend to be lengthy and expert witnesses are usually employed. In an arbitration, the arbitrator's fees and expenses are substantial. In the result the total costs may exceed the sum in dispute, and it is therefore important at all stages of the proceedings to have the question of costs well in mind. It is proposed here to deal with some of those matters which most frequently affect costs.[40]

Security for costs. In certain circumstances the defendant may apply for security for costs,[41] and the court has the same power to order security for costs in relation to an arbitration as it has for an action in the High Court.[42] The main possibilities relevant to building contract litigation are:

(1) where the plaintiff is ordinarily resident out of the jurisdiction[43]; and
(2) where the plaintiff is a limited company which may be unable to pay the defendant's costs if the defence is successful.[44]

A counterclaiming defendant may be treated as a plaintiff for these purposes if in substance he has taken up a position of plaintiff irrespective of his defence to the original action.[45] This would not be so where the defendant's counterclaim, even if it exceeded the claim, was pleaded as a set-off to the claim and was in substance advanced as a defence.[46] An order may be varied or set aside if there has been a subsequent material change of circumstances.[47]

---

[39] *Thomas* v. *Bunn* [1991] 2 W.L.R. 27 (H.L.).
[40] For a full account, see Supreme Court Practice 1991 in particular R.S.C., Ord. 62 and the notes thereto, and for county courts, see The County Court Practice. For litigants in person, see the Litigants in Person (Costs and Expenses) Act 1975; R.S.C. Ord. 62, r. 18; *Hart* v. *Aga Khan Foundation* [1984] 1 W.L.R. 994 (C.A.); *The Law Society* v. *Persaud, The Times*, May 5, 1990.
[41] See R.S.C., Ord. 23, and, for limited companies, s.726(1) of the Companies Act 1985.
[42] s.12(6)(a) of the Arbitration Act 1950.
[43] R.S.C., Ord. 23, r. 1(1). The simplicity of the improved rights of enforcement of judgments under the Convention on Jurisdiction and the Enforcement of Foreign Judgments 1968 is an important factor to take into account in deciding whether to order security for costs against a plaintiff resident in a State which is a party to the Convention—*De Bry* v. *Fitzgerald* [1990] 1 W.L.R. 552 (C.A.) and see "Recognition and Enforcement of Judgments" at p. 350; *cf. Thune* v. *London Properties* [1990] 1 W.L.R. 562 (C.A.). R.S.C., Ord. 23, r. 1(1)(a) does not discriminate on the ground of nationality contrary to Art. 7 of the EEC Treaty—*Berkeley Administration* v. *McClelland* [1990] 2 W.L.R. 1021 (C.A.).
[44] s.726(1) of the Companies Act 1985.
[45] *Neck* v. *Taylor* [1893] 1 Q.B. 560 (C.A.); *New Fenix Compagnie* v. *General Accident* [1911] 2 K.B. 619 (C.A.).
[46] *Cathery* v. *Lithodomus* (1987) 41 B.L.R. 76 (C.A.); *cf. Sloyan* v. *Brothers of Christian Instruction* [1974] 3 All E.R. 715.
[47] *Gordano Building Contractors* v. *Burgess* [1988] 1 W.L.R. 890 (C.A.).

Section 726(1) of the Companies Act 1985 provides that where a limited company is plaintiff in an action or other legal proceedings, the court may, if it appears by credible testimony[48] that there is reason to believe that the company will be unable to pay the defendant's costs if successful in his defence, require sufficient security to be given for those costs, and may stay all proceedings until the security is given. The leading case is *Sir Lindsay Parkinson & Co.* v. *Triplan*,[49] where the Court of Appeal held that the court has a discretion whether or not to order security for costs and gave instances of circumstances which may be relevant to the exercise of the discretion. These include:

"whether the company's claim is bona fide and not a sham and whether the company has a reasonably good prospect of success. Again [the court] will consider whether there is an admission by the defendants on the pleadings or elsewhere that money is due.[50] If there was a payment into court of a substantial sum of money ... that, too, would count. The court might also consider whether the application for security was being used oppressively[51]—so as to try to stifle a genuine claim. It would also consider whether the company's want of means had been brought about by any conduct by the defendants, such as delay in payment or delay in doing their part of the work."[52]

The application in that case also failed because it was made very late. But an impecunious company should not be allowed to put unfair pressure on a more prosperous company.[53]

Although the plaintiff company's prospects of success may be a relevant factor, parties should not seek to investigate in detail the likelihood of success in the action,[54] and it may indeed not be possible to do so.[55]

(a) *Costs are discretionary*

Costs are in the discretion of the trial judge subject to rules of court.[56]

---

[48] For building cases where there was no sufficient such credible testimony, see *Cheffick* v. *J.D.M. Associates* (1988) 43 B.L.R. 52 (C.A.); *Kim Barker Ltd.* v. *Aegon Insurance*, *The Times*, October 9, 1989 (C.A.).

[49] [1973] Q.B. 609 (C.A.).

[50] But "without prejudice" discussions are inadmissible—*Simaan General Contracting* v. *Pilkington Glass* [1987] 1 W.L.R. 516; *cf.* "Without prejudice" communications" at p. 434.

[51] *cf. Cheffick* v. *J.D.M. Associates* (1988) 43 B.L.R. 52 (C.A.); *Aquila Design* v. *Cornhill Insurance* [1988] B.C.L.C. 134 (C.A.).

[52] Lord Denning M.R. in *Sir Lindsay Parkinson & Co.* v. *Triplan* [1973] Q.B. 609 at 626 (C.A.).

[53] *Pearson* v. *Naydler* [1977] 1 W.L.R. 899.

[54] *Porzelack K.G.* v. *Porzelack (U.K.)* [1987] 1 W.L.R. 420; *Trident International* v. *Manchester Ship Canal* [1990] B.C.L.C. 263 (C.A.).

[55] See *Cheffick* v. *J.D.M. Associates* (1988) 43 B.L.R. 52 (C.A.).

[56] s.51(1) of the Supreme Court Act 1981; R.S.C., Ord. 62, r. 2(4); Ord. 38, r. 1(2) of the County Court Rules; *Donald Campbell & Co.* v. *Pollak* [1927] A.C. 732 at 811 (H.L.); *Aiden Shipping* v. *Interbulk* [1986] A.C. 965 (H.L.).

Arbitrators have an equivalent discretion to be exercised on equivalent principles.[57] In general and subject to certain special rules, costs follow the event,[58] that is to say, a successful party is awarded the costs unless there has been something in the nature of misconduct on his part.[59] There is no appeal to the Court of Appeal on costs only unless the trial judge has given leave,[60] except where the overriding or only matter taken into account by the judge in exercising his discretion was wrong.[61]

Two defendants. If a plaintiff reasonably joins two defendants in the alternative and succeeds against one, the court in its discretion may order the unsuccessful defendant to pay the costs of the successful defendant; the order may be for payment direct by one defendant to the other (a "Sanderson" order),[62] or for payment to the plaintiff against whom an order for payment of costs in favour of the successful defendant is made (a "Bullock" order).[63]

Third parties. The court should normally order the defendant to pay the costs of a successful third party.[64] But when a defendant has reasonably joined a third party, an unsuccessul plaintiff can, in the exercise of the court's discretion, be ordered to pay the third party's costs, either by adding them to the costs he has to pay to the defendant or direct to the third party.[65]

(b) *Recovery of small sums*

A plaintiff may, if he wishes, commence proceedings in the High Court to recover sums within the jurisdiction of the County Court, but he is

---

[57] *Dineen* v. *Walpole* [1969] 1 Lloyd's Rep. 261 (C.A.) distinguishing *Perry* v. *Stopher* [1959] 1 W.L.R. 415 (C.A.). See also *The Erich Schroeder* [1974] 1 Lloyd's Rep. 192; *Centrala Morska* v. *Cia Nacional* [1975] 2 Lloyd's Rep. 69—case remitted for reconsideration by arbitrator who had not given costs to the apparently successful party; *cf. Tramountana Armadora* v. *Atlantic Shipping* [1978] 1 Lloyd's Rep. 391; *Thyssen* v. *Borough Council of Afan* (1978) 15 B.L.R. 98 (C.A.); *Archital Luxfer* v. *Henry Boot* [1981] 1 Lloyd's Rep. 642; *James Allen* v. *London Export Corporation* [1981] 2 Lloyd's Rep. 632.

[58] R.S.C., Ord. 62, r. 3(3); *cf. The Aghios Nicolaos* [1980] 1 Lloyd's Rep. 17 (C.A.); *Alltrans Express* v. *C.V.A. Holdings* [1984] 1 W.L.R. 394 at 403 (C.A.)—defendant awarded costs where plaintiff recovered nominal damages but there was no payment into court; *Lipkin Gorman* v. *Karpnale* [1989] 1 W.L.R. 1340 at 1389 (C.A.).

[59] *Ibid.; Donald Campbell & Co. Ltd.* v. *Pollak* [1927] A.C. 732 at 811, 812 (H.L.); *Unimarine* v. *Canadian Transport* [1982] 1 Lloyd's Rep. 484 at 489; *cf.* R.S.C., Ord. 62, r. 6.

[60] s.18(1)(f) of the Supreme Court Act 1981.

[61] See *Smiths Ltd.* v. *Middleton* [1986] 1 W.L.R. 598 (C.A.); *cf. Alltrans Express* v. *C.V.A. Holdings* [1984] 1 W.L.R. 394 at 403 (C.A.).

[62] *Sanderson* v. *Blyth Theatre Company* [1903] 2 K.B. 533 (C.A.).

[63] *Bullock* v. *London General Omnibus Company* [1907] 1 K.B. 264 (C.A.); *cf. Goldsworthy* v. *Brickell* [1987] Ch. 378 at 418 (C.A.); *Mayer* v. *Harte* [1960] 1 W.L.R. 770 (C.A.); see also para. 62/2/46 of Supreme Court Practice 1991.

[64] *Johnson* v. *Ribbins* [1977] 1 W.L.R. 1458 at 1464 (C.A.).

[65] *Edginton* v. *Clark* [1964] 1 Q.B. 367 (C.A.); see also para. 62/2/85 of the Supreme Court Practice 1991; *L. E. Cattan Ltd.* v. *Michaelides & Co.* [1958] 1 W.L.R. 117 for observations on the position where there are "string" contracts with more than three parties involved.

discouraged from claiming less than £3,000 by the risk of being penalised in costs unless there are special circumstances.[66] Such actions, among others, may in any event be transferred to the County Court,[67] in which event costs are in the discretion of the court to which the proceedings are transferred.[68]

Where an action founded on contract or tort is commenced in the High Court which could have been commenced in the County Court and the plaintiff recovers less than £3,000, he is normally entitled only to County Court costs, and if he recovers less than £600 he is normally not entitled to any costs.[69] This does not, however, affect any question as to costs if it appears to the High Court that there was reasonable ground for supposing the amount recoverable in respect of the plaintiff's claim to be in excess of the amount recoverable in an action commenced in the County Court.[70] And the court may order costs either on the High Court scale or on a County Court scale if satisfied:

(1) that there was sufficient reason for bringing the action in the High Court[71]; or
(2) that the defendant or one of the defendants objected to the transfer of the action to a County Court.[72]

Further, where the claim is for a debt or liquidated demand only for £600 or upwards, and there is no defence, fixed High Court costs may in certain circumstances be awarded.[73] The provisions do not apply to counterclaims. Therefore, where a plaintiff commences proceedings in the High Court and the defendant succeeds on a counterclaim for however small an amount, the defendant has his costs on the High Court scale.[74]

The test whether an action could have been commenced in a County Court is, in money claims, whether the amount recovered on the claim, not the amount claimed on the writ, is within the jurisdiction of the County Court.[75] Thus the provisions will operate if the defendant by way of his defence reduces the amount claimed so as to bring it within the limit. A set-off is a defence and if

---

[66] Case suitable for Ord. 14 procedure used habitually to be brought in the High Court, but summary judgment is now also available in the County Court—see Ord. 9, r. 14 and Ord. 24, r. 1 of the County Court Rules. See also "Courts and Legal Services Act" at p. 425.
[67] See "Transfer from High Court to County Court" at p. 425.
[68] See s.45 of the County Courts Act 1984.
[69] See ss.19 and 20 of the County Courts Act 1984. See also "Courts and Legal Services Act" at p. 425.
[70] s.19(2) of the County Courts Act 1984.
[71] For an example, see *Columbus* v. *Clowes* [1903] 1 K.B. 244, referred to at p. 329.
[72] s.19(3) of the County Courts Act 1984.
[73] R.S.C., Ord. 62, App. 3. Money due as an instalment is a debt or liquidated demand—*Workman, Clark & Co. Ltd.* v. *Lloyd Brazileno* [1908] 1 K.B. 968 (C.A.).
[74] *Blake* v. *Appleyard* (1878) 3 Ex.D. 195; *Amon* v. *Bobbett* (1889) 22 Q.B.D. 543 (C.A.). When faced with this prospect a payment in by the plaintiff should be considered (see below) or, possibly, a written offer (see p. 462).
[75] *Lovejoy* v. *Cole* [1894] 2 Q.B. 861 (D.C.); *Solomon* v. *Mulliner* [1901] 1 K.B. 76 (C.A.).

established may have this effect,[76] but a counterclaim is a cross-action and does not operate to reduce the claim to within the limit.[77]

(c) *Notice to admit facts*

A notice to admit specific facts[78] may save costs. If the party on whom the notice was served neglects or refuses to admit the facts he must normally pay the costs of proving the facts whatever the result of the case.[79] It is relevant to consider whether a failure to admit the facts in the notice was reasonable. But the costs penalty will normally be imposed where a party fails to admit facts which it is highly probable will be proved and which could not be contested.[80]

(d) *Admissions on summons for directions*

At the hearing of the summons, the official referee or master must endeavour to secure that the parties make all admissions and all agreements as to the conduct of the proceedings which ought reasonably to be made by them and may cause the order on the summons to record any admissions or agreements so made and (with a view to such special order, if any, as to costs as may be just being made at the trial) any refusal to make any admission or agreement.[81]

Judgment can be signed if there is a clear admission,[82] although an application under R.S.C., Order 14 for summary judgment may sometimes be more appropriate.[83]

(e) *Payment into court*

In any action for a debt or damages the defendant may at any time after appearance, upon notice to the plaintiff in a prescribed form (No. 23 in Appendix A of the Rules), pay into court a sum of money in satisfaction of the claim or, where two or more causes of action are joined in one action, a sum or sums of money in satisfaction of any or all of the causes of action.[84] The amount

---

[76] *Lovejoy* v. *Cole* [1894] 2 Q.B. 861 (D.C.); *Solomon* v. *Mulliner* [1901] 1 K.B. 76 (C.A.), disapproving *Goldhill* v. *Clarke* (1893) 68 L.T. 414. These cases were decided upon s.57 of the County Courts Act 1888, where the wording was somewhat different. See also s.15(3) of the County Courts Act 1984.

[77] *Chell Engineering* v. *Unit Tool & Engineering Co.* [1950] 1 All E.R. 378 (C.A.). The distinction between a set-off and a counterclaim is discussed on p. 438.

[78] See R.S.C., Ord. 27, r. 2.

[79] R.S.C., Ord. 62, r. 6(7).

[80] *Baden, Delvaux and Lecuit* v. *Societe General* [1983] Com.L.R. 88 upheld on appeal [1985] B.C.L.C. 258 (C.A.).

[81] R.S.C., Ord. 25, r. 4; for official referees, see R.S.C., Ord. 36, r. 6(4).

[82] *Technistudy Ltd.* v. *Kelland* [1976] 1 W.L.R. 1042 (C.A.).

[83] *Ibid.* 1046; for summary judgment, see p. 441.

[84] R.S.C., Ord. 22, r. 1(1), (2). See the text of the rule, and notes in Supreme Court Practice 1991 for the plea of tender. For the position where two or more causes of action are joined in the action, see further, Ord. 22, r. 1(4), (5). For the right to sign judgment under Ord. 27, r. 3 on admissions, although there has been payment in under Ord. 22, r. 1, see *Lancashire Welders Ltd.* v. *Harland & Wolff Ltd.* [1950] 2 All E.R. 1096 (C.A.).

paid in can be increased.[85] In the event of the defendant's insolvency, the plaintiff is a secured creditor to the extent of the money in court.[86]

A plaintiff or other person made defendant to a counterclaim may pay money into court in the same manner as a defendant, the rules applying with the necessary modifications.[87]

Taking money out—before trial.   Within 21 days after receipt of the notice of payment into court or, where more than one payment has been made, within 21 days after receipt of the notice of the last payment but, in any case, before the trial or hearing of the action begins, the plaintiff may, by giving notice in the prescribed form, accept the sum or sums paid in satisfaction of his claim, or of the cause or causes of action to which the sum or sums relate.[88] If the money is paid in less than 21 days before the trial, the plaintiff has the lesser period in which to accept it.[89] If the plaintiff has taken out the sum in satisfaction of his claim or if he accepts a sum or sums in respect of one or more specified causes of action and gives notice that he abandons the other cause or causes of action, he may, unless the court otherwise orders, tax and recover his costs down to the date of giving notice of acceptance.[90] All further proceedings in respect of the causes of action to which the acceptance relates are stayed including those against another defendant sued jointly with or in the alternative to the defendant making the payment.[91] But acceptance of money paid in by one defendant does not debar the plaintiff from proceeding against another defendant where the claims against each are separate causes of action.[92] He cannot, however, recover more than the total sum due and the sum accepted from the defendant who paid into court may have to be attributed to one or more claims against the other defendant.[93]

Taking money out—at trial.   Where after the trial or hearing of an action has begun money is paid into court or money in court is increased, the plaintiff may accept the money within two days after receipt of the notice of payment or further payment but in any case before the judge begins to deliver judgment,[94] but is not entitled to tax his costs,[95] so that the question of costs will have to be dealt with by the judge in his discretion.

---

[85] R.S.C., Ord. 22, r. 1(3). For withdrawal of the money where there is a change of circumstances, see *Peal Furniture Co. Ltd.* v. *Adrian Share (Interiors) Ltd.* [1977] 1 W.L.R. 464 (C.A.).

[86] *W. A. Sherratt* v. *John Bromley* [1985] Q.B. 1038 (C.A.).

[87] R.S.C., Ord. 22, r. 6.

[88] R.S.C., Ord. 22, r. 3(1). The text is a summary and the rule itself should be referred to. For the position where there is a counterclaim, see p. 463.

[89] *King* v. *Weston-Howell* [1989] 1 W.L.R. 579 at 584 (C.A.).

[90] R.S.C., Ord. 62, r. 5(4); *Hudson* v. *Elmbridge Borough Council, The Times,* November 29, 1990 (C.A.).

[91] R.S.C., Ord. 22, r. 3(4).

[92] *Townsend* v. *Stone Toms* [1981] 1 W.L.R. 1153 (C.A.).

[93] See *Townsend* v. *Stone Toms* (1984) 27 B.L.R. 26 (C.A.).

[94] R.S.C., Ord. 22, r. 3(2).

[95] R.S.C., Ord. 22, r. 4(3); Ord. 62, r. 9(b).

Order for payment out.   If money is not taken out in accordance with the rules it can only be taken out pursuant to an order of the court made at any time before, at or after trial[96] and the court can,[97] and, it seems, normally will, upon making such order,[98] give the defendant the costs after payment in. Ordinarily, no application to take money out while the trial is proceeding should be made without the consent of the defendant.[99]

Failure to take money out—costs.   The court in exercising the discretion as to costs must, to the extent, if any, appropriate in the circumstances, take into account any payment into court and its amount.[1] If the plaintiff does not take the money out and recovers more than the sum paid in, the position is unaffected by the payment in save that at the conclusion of the trial the plaintiff must ask for an order for the money to be paid out.[2] If the plaintiff recovers a sum which is no more than the amount paid in and liability was admitted so that the only issue was quantum, the defendant is the successful party after payment in and is normally granted the costs after the date of payment in, and the plaintiff the costs before payment in.[3] Where liability is denied so that there are two distinct issues:

(1) liability;
(2) quantum;

and the plaintiff recovers no more than the amount paid in the plaintiff was formerly sometimes granted the costs of the issue upon which he had succeeded, *i.e.* liability, and the costs before payment in, and the defendant, the costs incurred after payment in on the issue of damages.[4] But now the costs on both issues after payment in are normally awarded to the defendant,[5] for "a payment into court is an offer to dispose of the action and, if accepted, prevents all further costs. A plaintiff who continues an action after payment in takes a risk and cannot normally complain if he has to pay all the costs which his acceptance of the offer would have avoided."[6]

---

[96] R.S.C., Ord. 22, r. 5.
[97] *Associated Recordings (Sales)* v. *Thomson Newspapers* (1967) 111 S.J. 376 (C.A.).
[98] *The Katcher 1 (No. 2)* [1968] 3 All E.R. 350 at 555; *Gaskins* v. *British Aluminium Co. Ltd.* [1976] Q.B. 524 at 530 (C.A.).
[99] *Gaskins* v. *British Aluminium Co. Ltd.* [1976] Q.B. 524 (C.A.). See also para. 22/5/2 of the Supreme Court Practice 1991 and see below "Non-disclosure of payment into court."
[1] R.S.C., Ord. 62, r. 9(b).
[2] See R.S.C., Ord. 22, r. 5.
[3] See R.S.C., Ord. 62, r. 9(b); para. 22/5/4 of the Supreme Court Practice 1991; *Findlay* v. *Railway Executive* [1950] 2 All E.R. 969 (C.A.). The matter is still within the discretion of the trial judge, but he must exercise his discretion judicially (*ibid.*). See also *Wagman* v. *Vare Motors* [1959] 1 W.L.R. 853 (C.A.); *Smiths Ltd.* v. *Middleton* [1986] 1 W.L.R. 598 (C.A.).
[4] *Wagstaffe* v. *Bentley* [1902] 1 K.B. 124 (C.A.); *Fitzgerald* v. *Thomas Tilling Ltd.* (1907) 96 L.T. 718 (C.A.); *Willcox* v. *Kettell* [1937] 1 All E.R. 222. But see *British Railways Board* v. *Jenkinson* [1968] C.L.Y. 3074 (C.A.).
[5] *Hultquist* v. *Universal, etc., Engineering Co. Ltd.* [1960] 2 Q.B. 467 (C.A.). See also para. 22/5/4 of the Supreme Court Practice 1991.
[6] *Ibid.* at 481, Sellers L.J.

Although prima facie the plaintiff has 21 days in which to accept the money paid into court,[7] a payment into court made less that 21 days before trial is not ineffective and is to be taken into account when the court exercises its discretion as to costs.[8]

Amendment after payment in.   A payment in relates only to the causes of action pleaded at the date of payment in.[9] If the amendment does not alter the causes of action relied on but only facts or figures it seems that, while the particular circumstances must be considered,[10] the usual approach is to look at the case as pleaded at the time of payment in.[11]

Non-disclosure of payment into court.   The fact that a payment of money into court has been made must not be disclosed on the pleadings, or at trial, until all questions of liability and of debt or damages have been decided.[12]

Assessment of amount.   The amount of money to be paid into court should be carefully assessed.[13] When a figure has been arrived at it may be thought advisable to add a substantial percentage to allow for the hazards of litigation.

Interest.[14]   For the purposes of payments into court, the plaintiff's cause of action for debt or damages is construed as including such interest as might be included in the judgment whether under section 35A of the Supreme Court Act 1981 or otherwise.[15] Payments into court should therefore generally include interest and the question whether an amount recovered on a judgment exceeds a payment into court has to be determined by reference to a notional interest calculation at the date of the payment into court.[16]

Set-off not relied on as counterclaim.[17]   The defendant should first assess the amount to be paid in as if there were no set-off, then deduct the amount he expects to establish on the set-off and pay in the balance.

Counterclaim.   If the defendant makes a counterclaim against the plaintiff for a debt or damages he must by his notice of payment state, if it be the case, that in making the payment he has taken into account and intends to satisfy:

---

[7] See above.

[8] *King* v. *Weston-Howell* [1989] 1 W.L.R. 579 (C.A.); *cf.* the slightly earlier decision in *Togo Amusements* v. *Estonian Shipping* [1989] 1 Lloyd's Rep. 542 (C.A.).

[9] *Tingay* v. *Harris* [1967] 2 Q.B. 327 (C.A.) decided on County Court Rules which then differed from the current Ord. 22, but the principle applies. For this purpose an amendment does not relate back to the date of issue of the writ as it normally does for purposes of the Limitation Act 1980—see "Amendments" at p. 371.

[10] See *The Katcher 1 (No. 2)* [1968] 3 All E.R. 350 at 356.

[11] *Cheeseman* v. *Bowaters Ltd.* [1971] 1 W.L.R. 1773 at 1778 (C.A.).

[12] R.S.C., Ord. 22, r. 7. *Gaskins* v. *British Aluminium Ltd.* [1976] Q.B. 524 (C.A.). The rule does not apply where there is a defence of tender before action.

[13] See generally "Preparation of evidence" at p. 426.

[14] For interest generally, see p. 451.

[15] See R.S.C., Ord. 22, r. 1(8).

[16] See para. 22/1/11 of the Supreme Court Practice 1991.

[17] For the distinction, see p. 438, and see Ord. 18, r. 17.

(1) the cause of action in respect of which he counterclaims; or
(2) where two or more causes of action are joined in the counterclaim, all those causes of action or, if not all, which of them.[18]

Thus in effect he must elect whether he offers up his cross-claim in satisfaction or whether he wishes to retain it and pay in only on the claim so that if the money is taken out he can still proceed with his counterclaim.[19] If the defendant states by his notice that he takes into account and satisfies his counterclaim and the plaintiff accepts the money paid into court, the defendant is entitled without order to the costs of the counterclaim up to the time when the defendant receives the notice of acceptance by the plaintiff of the money paid into court.[20]

Parties liable to contribution.   The provisions as to payment in only apply as between plaintiffs and defendants, but R.S.C., Order 16, rule 10(1), enables a third party[21] or joint tortfeasor who may be liable to another party to contribute towards any debt or damages recovered by the plaintiff, to make (without prejudice to his defence) a written offer to that party reserving the right to bring the offer to the attention of the judge. The offer must not be brought to the attention of the judge until all questions of liability and debt or damages have been decided. The judge must take the offer into account in exercising his discretion as to costs.[22] Where there is a split trial of liability and quantum and the issue of liability has been tried and the costs of that issue fall to be decided, any party may bring to the attention of the judge the fact that a written offer has or has not been made and the date (but not the amount) of the offer.[23]

(f) *Written offers*[24]

"Payment into court is not the only method a defendant may have to save costs."[25] Firstly, he may make an open offer. Secondly, although an ordinary "without prejudice" offer is inadmissible and cannot be referred to,[26] a party to proceedings may at any time make a written offer to any other party which is expressed to be "without prejudice save as to costs" and which relates to any issue in the proceedings.[27] As with a payment into court, the fact that such an offer has been made may not be communicated to the court until the question of costs falls to be decided. Then the court takes it into account, but the court may not take such an offer into account if, at the time it was made, the party

---

[18] R.S.C., Ord. 22, r. 2; see also Ord. 22, r. 3(5).
[19] See *Martin French* v. *Kingswood Hill Ltd.* [1961] 1 Q.B. 96 (C.A.) and the discussion at para. 22/2/1 of The Supreme Court Practice 1991.
[20] R.S.C., Ord. 62, r. 5(6).
[21] See also *Bates* v. *Burchell* [1884] W.N. 108.
[22] R.S.C., Ord. 62, r. 9(a).
[23] R.S.C., Ord. 16, r. 10(2).
[24] See also "Offer to protect costs" at p. 406.
[25] *Martin French* v. *Kingswood Hill Ltd.* [1961] 1 Q.B. 96 at 104 (C.A.).
[26] See "Without prejudice" communications at p. 434.
[27] R.S.C., Ord. 22, r. 14.

making it could have protected his position as to costs by means of a payment into court.[28] Thus, for example, such a letter may be appropriate where what is in issue is not liability but the proportions of contribution to liability where a defence of contributory negligence is raised. But it cannot be relied on in a simple money claim. There a payment in must be made to achieve costs protection.[29]

(g) *Costs where there are cross-claims*

Where there are cross-claims[30] the court has a very wide discretion as to costs,[31] and will look to the substance of the matter and not be enslaved by the pleadings,[32] but it seems likely that the court's discretion will be influenced to some extent by whether the defendant succeeds upon a set-off or a counter-claim which is not or cannot be set off. Thus a set-off may reduce a plaintiff's claim to a sum which does not normally carry costs,[33] while if the defendant's claim was a counterclaim a "usual order" (see below) may be made, or a sum of money which he has paid into court may be inadequate to secure him the costs of the claim.[34] Where a defendant is liable to the plaintiff on the plaintiff's claim but can rely by way of defence on matters which indicate that had he brought a counterclaim he would have been entitled in law to recover from the plaintiff the sum claimed against him by the plaintiff, there is a circuity of action, and the defendant has not only a valid counterclaim but a valid defence to the claim.[35] It seems that a cross-claim not the subject of a set-off will be ignored in considering the amount of any security for costs to be ordered to be given by the plaintiff where such order is appropriate.[36]

Costs where counterclaim.   Where there is a claim and counterclaim and both parties are successful it has been said that the usual and convenient order is judgment for the plaintiff for £x on the claim with costs, and for the defendant £y on the counterclaim with costs.[37] But frequently this order should

---

[28] R.S.C. Ord. 22, r. 14(2); Ord. 62, r. 9(d).

[29] See *Cutts* v. *Head* [1984] Ch. 290 at 310, 312 (C.A.); *cf. Corby District Council* v. *Holst & Co.* [1985] 1 W.L.R. 427 (C.A.). Both cases were before the introduction of R.S.C., Ord. 22, r. 14.

[30] See "Set-off and counterclaim" at p. 438.

[31] *Childs* v. *Blacker* [1954] 2 All E.R. 243 at 245, *sub nom. Childs* v. *Gibson* [1954] 1 W.L.R. 809 (C.A.); see also paras. 15/2/7 and 15/2/8 of the Supreme Court Practice 1991.

[32] *N.V. Amsterdamsche Lucifersfabrieken* v. *H. & H. Trading Agencies Ltd.* [1940] 1 All E.R. 587 at 590 (C.A.).

[33] See "Recovery of small sums" at p. 456. In the county court it can affect the scale of costs, see, *e.g. Hanak* v. *Green* [1958] 2 Q.B. 9 (C.A.).

[34] See *Chell Engineering Ltd.* v. *Unit Tool, etc., Ltd.* [1950] 1 All E.R. 378 (C.A.) decided before R.S.C., Ord. 22, r. 2, was introduced (see "Counterclaim" at p. 461) but the principle applies, it is thought, where the defendant does not take into account and satisfy his counterclaim, although the relationship of the rule to set off is not altogether clear.

[35] *Post Office* v. *Hampshire County Council* [1980] Q.B. 124 at 136 (C.A.).

[36] *Sloyan, T. & Sons Ltd.* v. *Brothers of Christian Instruction* [1974] 3 All E.R. 715; *cf. Cathery* v. *Lithodomus* (1987) 41 B.L.R. 76 (C.A.). See "Security for costs" at p. 454.

[37] Singleton L.J. in the *Chell Engineering Ltd.* v. *Unit Tool, etc., Ltd.* [1950] 1 All E.R. 378 at 382 (C.A.); see also *Medway Oil and Storage Co.* v. *Continental Contractors Ltd.* [1929] A.C. 88 (H.L.); *Millican* v. *Tucker* [1980] 1 W.L.R. 640 (C.A.); *R. & T. Thew* v. *Reeves* [1982] Q.B. 172 (C.A.).

not be made,[38] for in "most of these cases it is desirable that a judge should consider whether a special order should be made as to costs because the issues are often very much interlocked, and the usual order . . . does not always give a just result,"[39] and "where the counterclaim amounts to an equitable set-off,[40] it is only right that the judge should deal with the claim and cross-claim as one."[41] The nature of a special order is within the judge's discretion, but one method is "to say that the plaintiff or the defendant is to have his costs less, perhaps, some small proportion."[42]

Admission of claim. Where the defendant by his defence admits the claim, and the action is fought solely upon his counterclaim upon which he is successful, an order frequently made[43] is that the defendant has the general costs of the action after delivery of defence, and the plaintiff has the costs of the action up to the time of such delivery, and thereafter only the costs of setting down for trial.[44] In a defects case the employer is not bound to set off the defects in diminution of the claim. He may pay or admit the claim and bring a separate cross-action.[45] It seems to follow that by admitting the claim he is in no way estopped from setting up the defects on the counterclaim. If he is successful on his counterclaim for however small a sum he is normally awarded High Court costs where the claim was commenced in the High Court[46] and he is therefore in a very strong position. Where such an admission is made it becomes particularly important for the plaintiff to consider whether he ought to pay money into court in satisfaction of the counterclaim, and, if the amount remaining in dispute in respect of the counterclaim does not exceed

---

[38] *Childs* v. *Blacker* [1954] 2 All E.R. 243 *sub nom. Childs* v. *Gibson* [1954] 1 W.L.R. 809 (C.A.).

[39] Denning L.J. in the *Chell Engineering Ltd.* v. *Unit Tool, etc., Ltd.* [1950] 1 All E.R. 378 at 383 (C.A.) approved by the Court of Appeal in *Childs* v. *Blacker* [1954] 2 All E.R. 243 *sub nom. Childs* v. *Gibson* [1954] 1 W.L.R. 809 (C.A.); see also *Cullinane* v. *British Rema* [1953] 2 All E.R. 1257 at 1271 (C.A.).

[40] See below.

[41] Parker L.J. in *Baylis Baxter Ltd.* v. *Sabath* [1958] 1 W.L.R. 529 at 538 (C.A.); *cf. Box* v. *Midland Bank* [1981] 1 Lloyd's Rep. 434 (C.A.); *Archital Luxfer* v. *Henry Boot Construction* [1981] 1 Lloyd's Rep. 642 at 650.

[42] Lord Goddard C.J. in *Childs* v. *Blacker* [1954] 2 All E.R. 243 at 245, *sub nom. Childs* v. *Gibson* [1954] 1 W.L.R. 809 (C.A.). It was said (at p. 244) that *Chell Engineering Ltd.* v. *Unit Tool, etc., Ltd.* [1950] 1 All E.R. 378 (C.A.) dealt only with the application of the County Courts Act 1934.

[43] The judge has a complete discretion to make a different order: *Nicholson* v. *Little* [1956] 1 W.L.R. 829 (C.A.), but note that in this case (a county court appeal) the defendant claimed to set off his counterclaim not an admission at all in the sense that judgment could have been signed on it under Ord. 27, r. 3, in High Court proceedings. See also *Proctor & Lavender* v. *G. T. Crouch* (1966) 110 S.J. 273; where claim admitted subject to set-off and counterclaim and plaintiffs awarded half costs. For application for stay of execution, see R.S.C., Ord. 47, r. 1.

[44] *N.V. Amsterdamsche, etc.* v. *H. & H., etc., Ltd.* [1940] 1 All E.R. 587 (C.A.); *Childs* v. *Blacker* [1954] 2 All E.R. 243 *sub nom. Childs* v. *Gibson* [1954] 1 W.L.R. 809 (C.A.); *cf. Nicholson* v. *Little* [1956] 1 W.L.R. 829 (C.A.).

[45] *Davis* v. *Hedges* (1871) L.R. 6 Q.B. 687; *Moss* v. *L. & N.W. Railway* (1874) 22 W.R. 532; *cf.* R.S.C., Ord. 15, r. 2(1) and (3).

[46] See p. 457.

£5,000, whether he should apply for the transfer of the counterclaim to a County Court.[47]

Admission of the claim in a defects case simplifies the whole proceedings. At trial the defendant opens the case and affirmative evidence is given at once of the alleged defective work.

---

[47] See s.40(1)(c) of the County Courts Act 1984 and see also p. 425.

CHAPTER 18

THE JCT STANDARD FORM OF BUILDING CONTRACT (1980 EDITION)

Introduction

A document termed "the Standard Form of Building Contract" is issued by the Joint Contracts Tribunal. This body is neither statutory nor government sponsored. Its constituent bodies are the following: Royal Institute of British Architects; Building Employers Confederation; Royal Institution of Chartered Surveyors; Association of County Councils; Association of Metropolitan Authorities; Association of District Councils; Confederation of Associations of Specialist Engineering Contractors; Federation of Associations of Specialists and Sub-Contractors; Association of Consulting Engineers; British Property Federation; Scottish Building Contract Committee. The copyright is vested in R.I.B.A. Publications Limited and the form is printed here by kind permission. It is the document which, subject to revisions from time to time, was long known as "the R.I.B.A. Contract" but its current title reflects the fact that the R.I.B.A. is now only one of the many bodies which sponsor it. The correct expression is now "JCT Form." It is in extensive use both privately and in contracts with Local and Public Authorities.

History of Form. In view of the complexity of rights and liabilities in building contracts it has long been thought desirable to use a standard (or common) form acceptable to the parties concerned, thus avoiding the expense and hazards of special Contracts. Towards the end of the nineteenth century a Standard Form was apparently in fairly common use.[1] It seems that later versions of this Form were issued towards the end of the nineteenth century and successive versions have been issued in 1909, 1931, 1939, 1963 and 1980. Revision of the Standard Form is made by the Joint Contracts Tribunal and this body also issues from time to time "Practice Notes."

Six variants. There are variants of the Standard Form of Building Contract as follows:

(i) Form for use by Local Authorities where quantities form part of the Contract.
(ii) As (i) where quantities do not form part of the Contract.

---

[1] See *Clemence* v. *Clarke* (1880) H.B.C. (4th ed.), Vol. 2, p. 54. The form is set out in H.B.C. (3rd ed.), Vol. 2, p. 630.

(iii) Form for private use where quantities form part of the Contract.

(iv) As (iii) where quantities do not form part of the Contract.

(v) and (vi) As for (i) and (iii) but for use with Bills of Approximate Quantities.

Nature of the Standard Form of Building Contract. Each of the variants (i)–(iv) of the Standard Form of Building Contract creates a lump sum contract, that is to say, a contract to complete a whole work for a lump sum.[2] Thus in essence it does not differ from an oral contract to reglaze a window for £5. There is a single lump sum agreed to be payable by the Employer for the completion of a defined whole work by the Contractor. But whereas the law will imply many of the terms of the oral reglazing contract, the Form provides in its Conditions an elaborate code of private law[3] which deals with most of the problems which might arise, and the court's function is usually confined to construing those Conditions, *i.e.* to discovering the intention of the parties as expressed in the Conditions. The problems of the Form are therefore, in the main, problems of construction. The general law becomes of importance only insofar as it assists in the solution of those problems, or fills the gaps left unfilled by the Conditions of the Standard Form, or overrides or controls those Conditions as, for example, in matters of bankruptcy law. Where the court has once decided the meaning of words in the Form, it follows its previous decisions[4] but great care must be taken when reading a decision on a version of the Form earlier than that under consideration lest the revision makes the decision no longer applicable.

The variants (i)–(iv) of the Form do not differ in principle but the description of the contract work is very exact where quantities form part of the contract[5] and may be less exact where they do not.[6] The Forms for the use of Local Authorities do not differ in substance from the Forms for Private Use but contain certain provisions necessary to accord with Local Government Law and Practice.

Forms (v) and (vi) are adaptations respectively of Forms (i) and (iii) for use when the quantities in the Bills are approximate and are all to be remeasured.

For a further introduction to some of the main features of the Form, see commentary to the Articles of Agreement.

The 1980 Form. The 1980 Form is a new document. However, as appears below, many of the clauses and much of the drafting are very much the same as in the 1963 edition. The most immediately apparent differences are the

---

[2] See generally p. 81.

[3] The R.I.B.A. Form was judicially likened to a legislative code: see Denning L.J. in *Amalgamated Building Contractors Ltd.* v. *Waltham Holy Cross Urban District Council* [1952] 2 All E.R. 452 at 453 (C.A.).

[4] *cf. Milestone & Sons* v. *Yates Brewery* [1938] 2 All E.R. 439 at 444.

[5] Variants (i) and (iii) above.

[6] Variants (ii) and (iv) above.

adoption of decimal numbering and the way in which nomination is dealt with. The clauses relating to nomination appear separately in Part II of the Form and have to be read for their full understanding with the various Sub-Contract documents prepared by the Tribunal.

Related documents under the 1980 Form.   The 1980 Form brought into existence an elaborate scheme of contractual documents for nomination of Sub-Contractors and Suppliers:

(1) JCT Standard Form of Nominated Sub-Contract Tender and Agreement—Tender NSC/1.
(2) JCT Standard Form of Employer/Nominated Sub-Contractor Agreement—Agreement NSC/2.
(3) Agreement NSC/2 adapted for use when the alternative method of nomination used under clauses 35.5.1.2, 35.11 and 35.12 of the Main Contract—Agreement NSC/2a.
(4) Standard Form for Nomination of a Sub-Contractor where Tender NSC/1 has been used—Nomination NSC/3.
(5) JCT Standard Form of Sub-Contract for Sub-Contractors who have tendered on NSC/1 and executed Agreement NSC/2 and have been nominated by Nomination NSC/3—Sub-Contract NSC/4.
(6) Sub-Contract NSC/4 adapted for use where NSC/1, Agreement NSC/2 and Nomination NSC/3 have not been used—Sub-Contract NSC/4a.
(7) Forms for Nomination of Suppliers—TNS/1: Tender and TNS/2: Warranty.

Amendments to Form.   The 1980 Form has been amended on nine occasions since its publication. Some of the amendments are intended to improve the drafting. Others are to take account of decisions on the Form or developments in the general law. Others, again, are of considerable importance, particularly the 1987 Amendments. All amendments of significance are discussed below. Great care must be taken when using any particular contract or the commentary below to see which amendments have been applied to the Contract in question. These are shown on the front and back of the Form. Assistance can be obtained by reading the 1980 Form in the light of the list of amendments issued by the Joint Contracts Tribunal. These are summarised below.

The version of the 1980 Form reproduced in this book is that printed in 1988 and incorporating Amendments up to and including Amendment 6. The text of Amendments 7, 8 and 9 is printed after the main text and commentary at page 688.

Amendment 1 issued in January 1984

Clause 19.4. "Sub-letting—determination of employment of Domestic Sub-Contractor"—existing text deleted and new clause 19.4 inserted.

Amendment 2 issued in November 1986, "Insurance and Related Liability Provisions"

1. **Article 5.2.2.** "Whether a determination under clause 22C.4.3.1 will be just and equitable, or," inserted as 2nd item.
2. **Article 5.2.3, line 2.** After "Contractor" insert "under clause 18.1 or clause 23.3.2 in regard to a withholding of consent by the Contractor."
3. **Clause 1.3 Definitions.** "Clause 22 Perils" deleted and "All Risks Insurance," "Excepted Risks," "Joint Names Policy," "Site Materials," "Specified Perils" inserted.
4. **Clause 18.** "Partial Possession" deleted, entirely new clause inserted.
5. **Clause 19A.3.** Deleted. Clauses 19A.4, 19A.5, 19A.6, 19A.7 and 19A.8 renumbered as 19A.3, 19A.4, 19A.5, 19A.6 and 19A.7 respectively.
6. **Clause 20.** Deleted. New clause inserted.
7. **Clause 21.** Deleted. New clause inserted.
8. **Additional clause 22.** Inserted.
9. **Clauses 22A, 22B, 22C.** Deleted and new clauses inserted.
10. **Additional clause 22D.** Inserted.
11. **Additional Subclause 23.3.** Inserted.
12. **Clause 25.4.3.** "Specified Perils" substituted for "Clause 22 Perils."
13. **Clause 28.1.3.2.** "Specified Perils" substituted for "Clause 22 Perils."
14. **Clause 30.3.9.** "Specified Perils" substituted for "Clause 22 Perils."
15. **Clause 30.4.1.2.** "18.1.2" deleted, "18.1.1" inserted.
16. **Clause 30.4.1.3.** "18.1.2," "18.1.3" deleted, "18.1.1" and "18.1.2" inserted.

Amendment 3 issued in March 1987

Applied to the Without Quantities version only.

Amendment 4 issued in July 1987, "Miscellaneous Amendments"

1. **Articles 3A, 3B.** "The Contract Administrator" replaced "Supervising Officer" (and throughout the Form).
2. **Articles 3, 4.** Amended.
3. **Article 5.** Redrafted.
4. **Clause 1.3.** "Date of Tender" deleted, "Base Date" substituted.
5. **Clause 2.3.5.** "The Numbered Documents" added.
6. **Clause 7.** Redrafted.
7. **Clause 8.1.** Redrafted.
8. **Clause 11.** Additional sentence inserted.
9. **Clause 13.1.2.** Redrafted.
10. **Clause 13.4.1.** Second paragraph numbered.
11. **Clause 13.5.5.** Redrafted.
12. **Clause 17.2.** Redrafted.
13. **Clause 19.1.** New Clause 19.1.2 inserted.

14. **Clause 19.5.2.** Amended.
15. **Clauses 21.1.1.2, 21.1.2, 21.1.3.** Amended.
16. **Clause 23.1.** New Clause 23.1.2 inserted.
17. **Clause 25.3.1.** New paragraph inserted.
18. **Clause 25.3.2.** Amended.
19. **Clause 25.3.3.** Redrafted.
20. **Clause 26.4.1.** Amended.
21. **Clause 27.1.3.** Amended—Insolvency Act.
22. **Clause 28.1.3.** New clause 28.1.3.5 inserted.
23. **Clause 28.1.4.** Amended—Insolvency Act.
24. **Clause 28.1.3.4.** Amended.
25. **Clause 28A.** New clause "Determination by Employer or Contractor" inserted.
26. **Clause 30.2.** Amended.
27. **Clause 30.6.2.1.** Amended.
28. **Clause 30.6.1.1.** Amended.
29. **Clause 30.6.12.** Redrafted.
30. **Clause 30.8.** Redrafted.
31. **Clause 30.9.** Clauses 30.9.1.3 and 30.9.1.4 added.
32. **Clause 35.13.6.** New clause inserted.
33. **Clause 35.24.** New clause 35.24.4 inserted—subsequent clauses renumbered.
34. **Clause 35.24.7.** Renumbered as 35.24.8 and redrafted.
35. **Clause 35.24.9.** New clause inserted.
36. **Clause 36.4.3.** Redrafted.
37. **Clause 36.4.8.** Redrafted as 36.4.8.1 and 36.4.8.2.
38. **Clause 38.6.4 and clause 39.7.4.** New definition wage-fixing body inserted.
39. **Clause 40.4.** Deleted.
40. **Clauses 41.1 to 41.7.** New Part 4 "Arbitration" inserted.
41. **Appendix.** Amended.

Amendment 5 issued in January 1988

Part 1: New clauses 1.4   (**1.5** in Without Quantities version) and **8.2.2.**
Part 2: Revised clause 8.4.   (Code of Practice referred to in this clause inserted following clause 41).

Amendment 6 issued in July 1988

1. **Clause 41 "Settlement of disputes—Arbitration."** Revised.
2. **Clause 19A "Fair Wages."** Deleted.

Amendment 7 issued in July 1988 (With Quantities Version only)

Amendments to take account of 7th edition of Standard Method of Measurement:

1. **Clause 1.3 Definitions.** "Approximate Quantity," "Provisional sum" added.
2. **Clause 2.2.2.** Redrafted.
3. **Clause 13.4.1.** Redrafted.
4. **Clauses 13.5.1, 13.5.3.3 and 13.5.5.** Redrafted.
5. **Clause 25.4.5.1 and 25.4.6.** Redrafted.
6. **Clause 25.4.14.** New Relevant Event added.
7. **Clauses 26.2.1 and 26.2.7.** Redrafted.
8. **Clause 26.2.8.** New matter added.
9. **Clause 30.6.2.** Redrafted.

Amendment 8 issued in April 1989. Amendments to VAT provisions.

1. **Clause 15.** Drafting revised.
2. **Clause 1A.** Added to Supplemental Provisions (the VAT Agreement).

Amendment 9 issued in July 1990

1. **Clause 1.3.** Redrafted.
2. **Clause 2.1** Redrafted.
3. **Clause 8.** New clauses 8.1.3. and 8.5 inserted.
4. **Clause 19.2.** Redrafted.
5. **Clause 19.5.** Redrafted.
6. **Clause 22C.1.** New footnote.
7. **Clause 24.** Clauses 24.1. and 24.2.1 redrafted and new clause 24.2.3 inserted.

Criticisms of Standard Form. The 1963 Form was subject to numerous, strongly expressed criticisms, judicial[7] and otherwise.[8] These criticisms may be summarised as including the following principal heads of complaint:

(1) the Form was unnecessarily long, complex and obscure;
(2) it failed, despite its length and complexity, to deal adequately or at all with problems which occurred frequently in practice;
(3) from a commercial point of view, it placed nearly all of the risk of the unforeseen upon the Employer;
(4) it was based upon an illusory lump sum in that the price was in fact adjustable in myriad situations, usually to the benefit of the Contractor.

However, the 1963 Form had its defenders. The view was expressed that it worked well enough in practice.[9]

---

[7] *e.g.* Edmund Davies L.J. in *English Industrial Estates* v. *Wimpey* [1973] 1 Lloyds Rep. 118 at 126—"... the farrago of obscurities...."

[8] See the work of Professor Duncan Wallace Q.C. *passim.* A convenient starting point is his *Construction Contracts: Principles and Policies in Tort and Contract* (1986), Chap. 29—"A Criticism of the 1963 R.I.B.A. Joint Contracts Tribunal Contracts."

[9] *Modern Engineering (Bristol)* v. *Gilbert Ash (Northern)* [1974] A.C. 689 at 726 (H.L.).

The publication of the 1980 Form did not meet with universal acclaim. On the one hand, it was said that the 1980 Form reproduced the major problems and failings of the 1963 Form, exemplifying "the resistance to change of the U.K. standard forms, and in particular the R.I.B.A./JCT group of contracts."[10] On the other hand, Contractors and Employers found such novelty as it contained difficult to deal with. In the result, many continued to use the 1963 Form after 1980. Equally, from 1984 onwards many made use of the new Intermediate Form of Building Contract. This was intended for use for "works of simple content" but has in fact been employed extensively for substantial construction projects.

However, it is thought that after a hesitant start, the 1980 Form is now in widespread use and working satisfactorily. It should be noted that the Amendments to it summarised above are of great significance. The Joint Contracts Tribunal has shown itself willing to move quickly in order to remedy drafting defects revealed by decided cases or otherwise. Moreover, the 1987 Amendments (which are discussed in detail below) have done much to redress the balance between Employer and Contractor.[11]

It is thought that the policy of the 1980 Form, namely a lump sum price adjustable in defined circumstances, represents a fair attempt at risk allocation between Contractor and Employer. The alternative policy of requiring Contractors to accept most of the risk of unforeseen contingencies at tender stage would be likely to result in tenders at higher rates or widespread insolvency among Contractors. Neither of these would be in the long term interests of Employers. So, with all its faults, it is thought that the extensive use of the Standard Form will continue.

Scope of chapter. The Form for the use of Local Authorities where quantities form part of the contract is printed with a commentary.[12] The other variants are not printed, but the commentary refers to the major differences.

Commentary appears after most clauses intended, not as a paraphrase of the Form, but as an aid to the reading of its text. Footnotes forming part of the published text of the forms are generally indicated by lower case letters in square brackets as in the published text. The editor's footnotes to the commentary are indicated by numerals.

Reference to parts of this book dealing with the subject matter of the various clauses may be facilitated by the use of the footnotes to this chapter, the index and the table of references to the Standard Form at the front of the book.

The practice notes issued by the Joint Contracts Tribunal are not printed.

---

[10] Professor Duncan Wallace, *Construction Contracts: Principles and Policies in Tort and Contract*, p. 499.
[11] For an appreciation of the 1980 Form, and a consideration of the 1987 Amendments, see Donald Keating Q.C., "The Making of a Standard Form—Alwyn Waters Memorial Lecture."
[12] Note that this is the version published in 1988 incorporating Amendments up to and including Amendment 6.

Articles of Agreement

made the . . . . day of . . . . 19 . . . .
between . . . .
(hereinafter called "the Employer") of the one part and
. . . .
of (or whose registered office is situated at) . . . .
. . . .
(hereinafter called "the Contractor") [a] of the other part.

Whereas

First
the Employer is desirous of [b] . . . .
. . . .
. . . .
(hereinafter called "the Works") at . . . .
. . . .
and has caused Drawings and Bills of Quantities showing and describing the work to be
done to be prepared by or under the direction of
. . . .

Second
the Contractor has supplied the Employer with a fully priced copy of the said Bills of
Quantities (which copy is hereinafter referred to as "the Contract Bills").

Third
the said Drawings numbered . . . .
. . . .
(hereinafter referred to as "the Contract Drawings") and the Contract Bills have been
signed by or on behalf of the parties hereto;

Fourth
the status of the Employer, for the purposes of the statutory tax deduction scheme
under the Finance (No. 2) Act, 1975, as at the Base Date is stated in the Appendix;

Now it is hereby agreed as follows

Article 1
For the consideration hereinafter mentioned the Contractor will upon and subject to
the Contract Documents carry out and complete the Works shown upon, described by
or referred to in those Documents.

Article 2
The Employer will pay to the contractor the sum of . . . .

---

[a] *Where the Contractor is not a limited liability company incorporated under the Companies Acts, see Footnote
[v] to clause 35.13.5 4.4.*
[b] *State nature of intended works.*

.... (£ ....)

(hereinafter referred to as "the Contract Sum") or such other sum as shall become payable hereunder at the times and in the manner specified in the Conditions.

Article 3A [c] [d]

The term "the Architect" in the Conditions shall mean the said

....

of ....

or, in the event of his death or ceasing to be the Architect for the purpose of this Contract, such other person as the Employer shall nominate within a reasonable time but in any case no later than 21 days after such death or cessation for that purpose, *not being a person to whom the Contractor no later than 7 days after such nomination shall object for reasons considered to be sufficient by an Arbitrator appointed in accordance with article 5.* [e] Provided always that no person subsequently appointed to be the Architect under this Contract shall be entitled to disregard or overrule any certificate or opinion or decision or approval or instruction given or expressed by the Architect for the time being.

Article 3B [c] [d]

The term "the Contract Administrator" in the Conditions shall mean the said

....

of ....

or, in the event of his death or ceasing to be the Contract Administrator for the purpose of this Contract, such other person as the Employer shall nominate within a reasonable time but in any case no later than 21 days after such death or cessation for that purpose, *not being a person to whom the Contractor no later than 7 days after such nomination shall object for reasons considered to be sufficient by an Arbitrator appointed in accordance with article 5.* [e] Provided always that no person subsequently appointed to be the Contract Administrator under this Contract shall be entitled to disregard or overrule any certificate or opinion or decision or approval or instruction given or expressed by the Contract Administrator for the time being.

Article 4 [d]

The Term "the Quantity Surveyor" in the Conditions shall mean

....

of ....

or, in the event of his death or ceasing to be the Quantity Surveyor for the purpose of this Contract, such other person as the Employer shall nominate within a reasonable time but in any case no later than 21 days after such death or cessation for that purpose, *not being a person to whom the Contractor no later than 7 days after such nomination shall object for reasons considered to be sufficient by an Arbitrator appointed in accordance with article 5.* [e]

---

[c] *Article 3A is applicable where the person concerned is entitled to the use of the name "Architect" under and in accordance with the Architects Registration Acts, 1931 to 1969. Article 3B is applicable in all other cases. Therefore complete whichever is appropriate and delete the alternative. Where article 3A is completed the expression "the Contract Administrator" shall be deemed to have been deleted throughout the Conditions. Where article 3B is completed the expression "Architect" shall be deemed to have been deleted throughout the Conditions.*

[d] *In cases where the Works are to be carried out under the direction of officials of the Local Authority, insert the names of such officials as are to perform the respective functions of the "Architect/the Contract Administrator" and the "Quantity Surveyor" under this Contract.*

[e] *Strike out words in italics in cases where "the Architect," "the Contract Administrator" or "the Quantity Surveyor" is an official of the Local Authority.*

Article 5

If any dispute or difference as to the construction of this contract or any matter or thing of whatsoever nature arising thereunder or in connection therewith shall arise between the Employer or the Architect/the Contract Administrator on his behalf and the Contractor either during the progress or after the completion or abandonment of the Works or after the determination of the employment of the Contractor, except under clause 31 (*statutory tax deduction scheme*) to the extent provided on clause 31.9 or under clause 3 of the VAT Agreement, it shall be and is hereby referred to arbitration in accordance with clause 41.

Attestation[g]

Articles of Agreement

Derivation. The Articles of Agreement are derived from the Articles in the 1963 Form. Article 5 is derived from part of clause 35 of the 1963 Form, the Arbitration clause.

The Recitals. The passages beginning "Whereas" are recitals. For the construction of recitals, see page 59.

The Fourth Recital was introduced by the 1980 Form. It provides for it to be stated in the Appendix whether the Employer is or is not a "Contractor" for the purposes of the Finance (No. 2) Act 1975. See clause 31.

The operative part of the agreement. This begins with the words "Now it is hereby agreed as follows."

Articles 1 and 2. Some of the main features of the contract appear from this part of the Articles of Agreement. Thus:

(a) It is a lump sum contract. A lump sum contract is a contract to complete the whole work[13] for a lump sum. The whole work to be performed is that the Contractor must "upon and subject to the Contract Documents carry out and complete the Works shown upon, described by or referred to in those documents." The Contract Documents are defined by clause 2.1 of the Conditions as the Contract Drawings, the Contract Bills, the Articles of Agreement, the Conditions and the Appendix. From this definition important results follow as to the nature of extra work.[14] The lump sum payable is the stated sum "or such other sum as shall become payable hereunder at the times and in the manner specified in the Conditions." The manner of payment[15] is upon the

---

[13] See p. 81.
[14] See p. 477.
[15] Apart from the special case of determination—see clauses 27, 28 and 28A.
[f] *Not used.*
[g] *This page should be completed with the appropriate attestation clause.*

Architects' Certificates issued in accordance with and at the times stated in clause 30. The "other sum" may arise by adjustment of the original Contract Sum under many clauses.[16] To be distinguished from such adjustments are the express contractual rights for the Employer to make certain deductions from sums certified for payment.[17]

(b) The right to payment. There is a right to be paid instalments of the Contract Sum adjusted as may be necessary upon Architects' Certificates issued in accordance with clause 30. This is not, therefore, an entire contract in the sense in which the term has been used in certain textbooks because entire completion by the Contractor is not a condition precedent to the right to call for and receive any payment. However, entire completion of the Works[18] is, it is submitted, a condition precedent to the right to the Certificate under clause 30.8 and hence to the release of the residue of the Contract Sum then retained in accordance with clause 30.2.

(c) Design obligations. The general approach of the contract is that the Architect designs, and communicates his design to the Contractor who must carry it out but does not accept liability for its fitness for any particular purpose. But the Contractor cannot be indifferent to matters of design for the following reasons:

(1) frequently the Drawings or Bills expressly impose some design responsibility on the Contractor or a Nominated Sub-Contractor[19];

(2) the Contractor's express or implied duties as to workmanship and the supply of materials may import some element of design responsibility[20];

(3) the duty of conforming to Building Regulations and the like makes it necessary for the Contractor to give some consideration to whether the Works as designed by the Architect are in accordance with statutory requirements[21];

(4) There are express duties under clause 2.3 upon the Contractor to bring the Architect's attention any discrepancy in or divergence between the documents there set out, and under clause 6.1.2 any divergence be-

---

[16] *e.g.* clauses 2.2.2.2 (correction of errors in items in Contract Bills); 13.3, 13.4, 13.5 (Variations, provisional sum work); 17.2, 17.3 (defects); 26.1 (loss and expense); 30.6 (prime cost, provisional sums); 34.3 (antiquities); 37–40 in various alternatives (fluctuations). For a full list, see clause 30.6.2

[17] *e.g.* under clauses 4.1.2 (default); 21.1.3 (insurance); 22.A.2 (insurance); 24 (liquidated damages); 35.13 (direct payment to Nominated Sub-Contractor).

[18] *cf. Hoenig* v. *Isaacs* [1952] 2 All E.R. 176 at 181 (C.A). For a discussion of entire contracts, see p. 70.

[19] For Nominated Sub-Contractors, see clause 35. For the relationship between the Bills and the Conditions, see clause 2.2.1.

[20] See clause 8. See also "Warranties of fitness for purpose and good quality" at p. 53.

[21] See clause 6. See also p. 372.

tween the Statutory Requirements and design documents. A Contractor in breach of these duties may be unable to recover loss and expense under clauses 26.1 and may, in certain circumstances, be liable in damages. The duties imposed by clauses 2.3 and 6.1.2 arise only if the Contractor "shall find" a discrepancy or divergence. It seems clear therefore that a Contractor is under no duty positively to search for errors in the Architect's design or the Quantity Surveyor's taking off. But considerable losses can be caused if an obvious error of design goes unnoticed until much work has been done and demolition eventually has to take place with, perhaps, consequential delays. It is an implied term of the contract that the Contractor in his workmanship will use the proper skill to be expected of a Contractor.[22] It is suggested that a Contractor who fails to observe errors which ought to have been obvious to him as the Contractor in the circumstances and exercising such proper skill cannot take advantage of such failure.[23]

(e) The nature of extra work. The amount of work for which the Contract Sum is payable is defined in exact terms and not by a broad description.[24] The Contractor does not undertake for the Contract Sum to build a house or factory but to complete certain exactly stated quantities of work. He must carry out greater quantities if required to do so by the Architect (clause 4) but in general is entitled to be paid extra for them. The Contractor must bear losses from his faulty pricing unless there is a proper case for the Court or Arbitrator to grant rectification,[25] and many of the risks of an unanticipated expense fall on the Contractor, but the risk of extra cost resulting from faulty description or measurement of the Works is in general borne by the Employer. This appears from reference to the following:

(i) *the Contract Bills.* These, subject to clause 8, describe the quality and quantity of work included in the Contract Sum (clause 14.1). If more work is required to complete the Works, the Contractor is entitled to be paid for it as a variation, provided he can bring his claim within clause 13.

(ii) *Drawings, instructions and documents.* For the Contractor's duty if he finds any discrepancy or divergence see clause 2.3. The Architect must issue an Instruction in regard thereto (clause 2.3). If an Instruction involves more or less work than that set out in the Contract Bills, it will be treated as a variation and increase or decrease the Contract Sum as the case may be (clauses 2.2, 2.3, 4, 13) and may entitle the Contractor to recover loss and expense under clause 26.2.3.

(iii) *Architect's satisfaction.* See clause 2.1 for where the quality and standards

---

[22] For the proper skill of a Contractor, see p. 52.
[23] See further commentary on clause 6 at p. 503.
[24] For exactly defined contracts generally, see p. 83.
[25] For rectification, see p. 266.

of materials or workmanship may have to be to the reasonable satisfaction of the Architect.[26] But it is submitted that any discretion vested in the Architect by these words cannot enlarge the obligations expressly undertaken by the Contractor as to the description of the Works.[27] The result is that, if the Architect requires a higher quality or standard than that provided for in a description in the Bills, it is a Variation (see also clause 13.1.2).

(iv) *Variations.* The Architect has a very wide power to give Instructions requiring Variations (clause 13.2) but the Contractor has, in addition to the right to payment of the costs of the Variations, valuable, although carefully limited, rights to recovery of loss and expense in which he is involved by carrying out such Variations (clause 26.2.7).

(f) Unanticipated loss or expense.   The Contractor may find as the Works proceed that he is suffering some loss or expense which he did not anticipate at the time of entering into the contract. The general rule is that the Contractor's undertaking to complete the Works requires that he must bear such loss or expense himself, but there are important exceptions to the rule which can arise under one or more of the following heads:

   (i) The express provisions for adjustment of the Contract Sum (see commentary to clause 30 at page 610);
  (ii) The express provisions for determination of the Contractor's employment (see clauses 22C.4.3, 27, 28A and 32);
 (iii) A claim for damages for the Employer's breach of contract or breach of collateral warranty, misrepresentation or misstatement[28];
  (iv) A right to treat the contract as at an end by reason of the Employer's repudiation or misrepresentation[29];
   (v) Frustration. Frustration is discussed at page 134. Note in particular *Davis Contractors* v. *Fareham Urban District Council* which illustrates the difficulty of attempting to rely on frustration.[30] Although the form of contract differed, the principle applies.

For the right in certain cases to an extension of time, see clause 25 and for the right, where there is a suspension of the Works, to determine the Contractor's employment, see clause 27. For fire, storm, etc., see clause 22. For the dis-

---

[26] For comments on the effects of these words in an earlier version of the Standard Form of Building Contract, see *P. & M. Kaye Ltd.* v. *Hosier & Dickinson Ltd.* [1972] 1 W.L.R. 146 at 168 (H.L.).

[27] See *Cammell Laird* v. *Manganese Bronze* [1934] A.C. 402 at 433 (H.L.); *Minster Trust* v. *Traps Tractors* [1954] 1 W.L.R. 963 at 974; *Cotton* v. *Wallis* [1955] 1 W.L.R. 1168 (C.A.) but note comment on this case at p. 486. See also clauses 2.2 and 8.

[28] See generally pp. 124 and 130.

[29] See generally pp. 120 and 156.

[30] *Davis Contractors* v. *Fareham Urban District Council* [1956] A.C. 696 (H.L.). For a recent illustration of the difficulties, see *Wates Ltd.* v. *Greater London Council* (1983) 25 B.L.R. 1 (C.A.).

covery of antiquities, see clause 34. For increases in prices, see clauses 37–40, and for war, see clauses 32 and 33.

Articles 3 and 4.   For the position of the Architect generally, see page 303, and for duties of the Quantity Surveyor, see page 343.

Architect/Contract Administrator.   The reason for the two terms appears from the footnote. No contractual difference follows from the use of the term "Contract Administrator" and all references in the commentary to Architect include Contract Administrator. The term "Contract Administrator" was introduced into the 1980 Form by Amendment 4 issued in July 1987. It is now used throughout the contract in place of the former term "Supervising Officer."

Architect and Quantity Surveyor same person.   The contract contemplates two persons, but sometimes one is named as performing both offices. In such a case, if the person named becomes unable to perform the duties of Quantity Surveyor, it seems that the Employer is entitled to appoint another person as Quantity Surveyor.[31] Further, even if different persons are appointed as Architect and Quantity Surveyor respectively, the Architect is, it seems, entitled to consult an independent surveyor with regard to a valuation.[32]

No Architect appointed.   If the parties enter into a contract in this form agreeing that no Architect shall in fact be appointed, many of the clauses are nonsense and cannot be of any effect. It is thought, however, that the court would not say that the contract was void but would enforce it as an ordinary lump sum contract ignoring those clauses which depend for their effect upon the act or decision of the Architect.[33]

Amendments to Articles 3 and 4.   By Amendment 4 dated July 1987 the term "Contract Administrator" was introduced into the Articles and throughout the contract. The provisions relating to the death of the Architect or his ceasing to be Architect for the purpose of his contract were varied somewhat. The Employer is now required to nominate a new Architect "within a reasonable time but in any case no later than 21 days after such death or cessation." The Contractor is now required to make any objection to such renomination "no later than 7 days after such nomination."

Article 5.   This is derived from clause 35 of the 1963 Form. The original version of the 1980 Form set out all the arbitration provisions in Article 5.

---

[31] See *Burden* v. *Swansea Corporation* [1957] 1 W.L.R. 1167 (H.L.).
[32] See *Burden* v. *Swansea Corporation* in the Court of Appeal, (1956) 54 L.G.R. 161 at 167, 168 (C.A.). The point was not dealt with in the House of Lords and the case was decided in the 1939 Form, but the principle, it is thought, applies.
[33] *cf. Nicolene* v. *Simmonds* [1953] 1 Q.B. 543 at 551, discussed at p. 22.

However by Amendment 4 dated July 1987 a new clause 41 was introduced into the 1980 Form. This clause now contains the detailed arbitration provisions. This amendment also introduced the words "or after the determination of the employment of the Contractor" so as to make it clear that the right to arbitrate is not lost by the determination of the employment of the Contractor. The terms of the Article as to the matters which fall within the arbitration provisions of the Contract are very wide. For a consideration of arbitration generally, see Chapter 16. For consideration of the scope and mechanics of arbitration under the 1980 Form, see clause 41 and its commentary at page 675.

Without Quantities version.   In general terms the difference is as follows:

(a) Bills of Quantities in the With Quantities versions describe the work for which the Contract Sum is payable, and provide the basis for the measurement and valuation of variations. In the Without Quantities version, the Bills of Quantities are replaced by the Specification and the Schedule of Rates.

(b) In the Without Quantities version, the Contract Drawings and Specification describe the quality and quantity of the work included in the Contract Sum (clause 14.1). Any Bills of Quantities or other statements as to quantities of work which may have been supplied to the Contractor do not form part of the contract (clause 14.3). Two important results follow:

(i) *Meaning of extra work.* There is no required standard method for the preparation of Contract Drawings and Specification. They may be in great detail so that they describe the work for which the Contract Sum is payable in exact terms, or they may be lacking in detail and describe the Works for which the Contract Sum is payable in wide terms. The latter class of Contract Drawings and Specification invites disputes as to whether work is contract work or extra work. There is greater opportunity than with the With Quantities version for the Employer to say that, although some item may not be expressly shown or described in the Contract Documents, it is nevertheless impliedly included in the work for which the original Contract Sum is payable and therefore not extra work.[34]

(ii) *Errors in estimates.* By virtue of clause 14.2 the Contractor must bear the loss flowing from any error, arithmetical or otherwise, in pricing the Contract Sum. However, this is subject to the provisions of clause 2.2.2 of the contract which provides that, if in the Contract Drawings and/or the Specification there is any error in description or in quantity or omission of items, then such error or omission shall be corrected and such correction shall be treated as if it were a variation required by the instruction of the Architect under clause 13.2.

(c) Variations are priced by reference to the Schedule of Rates (clause 13).

---

[34] See p. 81.

THE CONDITIONS

PART 1: GENERAL

1. Interpretation, definitions, etc.

1.1 Unless otherwise specifically stated a reference in the articles of Agreement, the Conditions or the Appendix to any clause means that clause of the Conditions.

1.2 The Articles of Agreement, the Conditions and the Appendix are to be read as a whole and the effect or operation of any article or clause in the Conditions or item in or entry in the Appendix must therefore unless otherwise specifically stated be read subject to any relevant qualification or modification in any other article or any of the clauses in the Conditions or item in or entry in the Appendix.

1.3 Unless the context otherwise requires or the Articles or the Conditions or an item in or entry in the Appendix specifically otherwise provides, the following words and phrases in the Articles of Agreement, the Conditions and the Appendix shall have the meanings given below or as ascribed in the article, clause or Appendix item to which reference is made:

Word or phrase	*Meaning*
All Risks Insurance:	see **clause 22.2.**
Appendix:	the Appendix to the Conditions as completed by the parties.
Arbitrator:	the person appointed under **clause 41** to be the Arbitrator.
Articles or Articles of Agreement:	the Articles of Agreement to which the Conditions are annexed, and references to any recital are to the recitals set out before the Articles.
Architect:	the person entitled to the use of the name "Architect" and named in **article 3A** or any successor duly appointed under **article 3A** or otherwise agreed as the person to be the Architect.
Base Date:	the date stated in the Appendix.
Certificate of Completion of Making Good Defects:	see **clause 17.4**.
Completion Date:	the Date for Completion as fixed and stated in the Appendix or any date fixed under either **clause 25** or **33.1.3.**
Conditions:	the clauses 1 to 37 and 41 and either clause 38 or 39 or 40, and the Supplemental Provisions ("the VAT Agreement") annexed to the Articles of Agreement.
Contract Administrator:	the person named in **article 3B** or any successor duly appointed under **article 3B** or otherwise agreed as the person to be the Contract Administrator.
Contractor:	the person named as Contractor in the Articles of Agreement.
Contract Bills:	the Bills of Quantities referred to in the **First recital** which have been priced by the Contractor and signed by or on behalf of the parties to this Contract.
Contract Documents:	see **clause 2.1**.
Contract Drawings:	the Drawings referred to in the **First recital** which have been signed by or on behalf of the parties to this Contract.

Word or phrase	*Meaning*
Contract Sum:	the sum named in **article 2** but subject to **clause 15.2**.
Date for Completion:	the date fixed and stated in the Appendix.
Date of Possession:	the date stated in the Appendix under the reference to **clause 23.1**.
Defects Liability Period:	the period named in the Appendix under the reference to **clause 17.2**.
Domestic Sub-Contractor:	see **clause 19.2**.
Employer:	the person named as Employer in the Articles of Agreement.
Excepted Risks:	ionising radiations or contamination by radioactivity from any nuclear fuel or from any nuclear waste from the combustion of nuclear fuel, radioactive toxic explosive or other hazardous properties of any explosive nuclear assembly or nuclear component thereof, pressure waves caused by aircraft or other aerial devices travelling at sonic or supersonic speeds.
Final Certificate:	the certificate to which **clause 30.8** refers.
Interim Certificate:	any one of the certificates to which **clauses 30.1** and **30.7** and the entry in the **Appendix** under the reference to **clause 30.1.3** refers.
Joint Names Policy:	a policy of insurance which includes the Contractor and the Employer as the insured.
Nominated Sub-Contractor:	see **clause 35.1**.
Nominated Sub-Contract Documents: Tender NSC/1 Agreement NSC/2 Agreement NSC/2a Nomination NSC/3 Sub-Contract NSC/4 Sub-Contract NSC/4a	see **clause 35.3**.
Nominated Supplier:	see **clause 36.1.1**.
Numbered Documents:	any Document referred to in the first recital in any Sub-Contract with a Nominated Sub-Contractor.
Period of Final Measurement and Valuation:	the period named in the **Appendix** under the reference to **clause 30.6.1.2**.
Period of Interim Certificates:	the period named in the **Appendix** under the reference to **clause 30.1.3**.
person:	an individual, firm (partnership) or body corporate.
Practical Completion:	see **clause 17.1**.
Quantity Surveyor:	the person named in **article 4** or any successor duly appointed under **article 4** or otherwise agreed as the person to be the Quantity Surveyor.
Relevant Event:	any one of the events set out in **clause 25.4**.
Retention:	see **clause 30.2**.
Retention Percentage:	see **clause 30.4.1.1** and any entry in the Appendix under the reference to **clause 30.4.1.1**.
Site Materials:	see **clause 22.2**.
Specified Perils:	fire, lightning, explosion, storm, tempest, flood, bursting or overflowing of water tanks, apparatus or pipes, earthquake, aircraft and other aerial devices or articles dropped therefrom, riot and civil commotion, but excluding Excepted Risks.

Word or phrase	*Meaning*
Statutory Requirements:	see **clause 6.1.1**.
Sub-Contract:	the sub-contractual rights and obligations of the Contractor and a Nominated Sub-Contractor as set out in the Sub-Contract Documents as defined in Sub-Contract NSC/4 or NSC/4a.
Valuation:	see **clause 13.4.1.1**.
Variation:	see **clause 13.1**.
VAT Agreement:	see **clause 15.1**.
Works:	the works briefly described in the **First recital** and shown and described in the Contract Drawings and in the Contract Bills.

1.4 Notwithstanding any obligation of the Architect/the Contract Administrator to the Employer and whether or not the Employer appoints a clerk of works, the Contractor shall remain wholly responsible for carrying out and completing the Works in all respects in accordance with clause 2.1, whether or not the Architect/the Contract Administrator or the clerk of works, if appointed, at any time goes on to the Works or to any workshop or other place where work is being prepared to inspect the same or otherwise, or the Architect/the Contract Administrator includes the value of any work, materials or goods in a certificate for payment, save as provided in clause 30.9.1.1 with regard to the conclusiveness of the Final Certificate.

Clause 1: interpretation, definitions, etc.

This interpretation and definition clause was introduced as a new clause to the 1980 Form. Apart from the word "person" and the phrase "provisional sum," all defined words or phrases are given initial capital letters throughout the contract. Most of the words or phrases defined in clause 1.3 appeared in the 1963 Form with the same meanings. The principal defined expressions which were new to the original version of the 1980 Form are: "Domestic Sub-Contractor," "Nominated Sub-Contract Documents" and "Relevant Event." The definition of "Variation" which appeared in clause 11(2) of the 1963 Form has been enlarged in substance in clause 13.1 of the 1980 Form.[35]

Amendments.   Clause 1.3 has been amended in the following respects since the publication of the 1980 Form:

(1) by Amendment 2 dated November 1986, the expression "Clause 22 Perils" was deleted. New expressions "Specified Perils" and "Excepted Risk" in substance cover the same ground as the expression "Clause 22 Perils." By this Amendment, the following additional expressions relating to insurance have been introduced: "All Risks Insurance," "Joint Names Policy," "Site Materials."

---

[35] See commentary to clause 13 at p. 517.

(2) by Amendment 4 dated July 1987, the expression "Contract Administrator" was introduced in place of "Supervising Officer" and the expression "Base Date" was substituted for "Date of Tender."

(3) by Amendment 7 dated July 1988, the expressions "Approximate Quantity" and "provisional sum" were added to clause 1.3.

(4) by Amendment 9 dated July 1990, the definition of "Contract Documents" was transferred to Clause 1.3 and Clause 2.1 consequentially reworded. The definition of Works was reworded to make it clear that they include not only the works shown upon the Contract Documents but also any change made to the Works in accordance with the Conditions.

Clause 1.4 is a new sub-clause introduced by Amendment 5 dated January 1988. The Guidance Note issued with this new sub-clause states that it is intended to make clear:

(a) that the Architect is not, under the Standard Form, made responsible for the supervision of the works which the Contractor is to carry out and complete; and

(b) that nothing in the Conditions of the Standard Form makes the contractor other than responsible for carrying out and completing the Works as stated in clause 2.1.

It does not appear that this is a change of substance since the responsibility of the Contractor under clause 2.1 to carry out and complete the Works is clear.

2. Contractor's obligations

2.1 The Contractor shall upon and subject to the Conditions carry out and complete the Works shown upon the Contract Drawings and described by or referred to in the Contract Bills and in the Articles of Agreement, the Conditions and the Appendix (which Drawings, Bills, Articles of Agreement, Conditions and Appendix are in this Contract referred to collectively as "the Contract Documents") in compliance therewith, using materials and workmanship of the quality and standards therein specified, provided that where and to the extent that approval of the quality of materials or of the standards of workmanship is a matter for the opinion of the Architect/the Contract Administrator, such quality and standards shall be to the reasonable satisfaction of the Architect/the Contract Administrator.

2.2 .1 Nothing contained in the Contract Bills shall override or modify the application or interpretation of that which is contained in the Articles of Agreement, the Conditions or the Appendix.

.2 Subject always to clause 2.2.1.:

.2.1 the Contract Bills, unless otherwise specifically stated therein in respect of any specified item or items, are to have been prepared in accordance with the Standard Method of Measurement of Building Works, 6th Edition published by the Royal Institution of Chartered Surveyors and the Building Employers Confederation;

.2.2 if in the Contract Bills there is any departure from the method of preparation referred to in clause 2.2.2.1 or any error in description or in quantity or omission

484

of items, then such departure or error or omission shall not vitiate this Contract but the departure or error or omission shall be corrected and such correction shall be treated as if it were a Variation required by an instruction of the Architect/the Contract Administrator under clause 13.2.

2.3 If the Contractor shall find any discrepancy in or divergence between any two or more of the following documents, including a divergence between parts of any one of them or between documents of the same description, namely:

.1 the Contract Drawings,
.2 the Contract Bills,
.3 any instruction issued by the Architect/the Contract Administrator under the Conditions (save insofar as any such instruction requires a Variation in accordance with the provisions of clause 13.2) and
.4 any drawings or documents issued by the Architect/the Contract Administrator under clause 5.3.1.1, 5.4 or 7,
.5 the Numbered Documents,

he shall immediately give to the Architect/the Contract Administrator a written notice specifying the discrepancy or divergence, and the Architect/the Contract Administrator shall issue instructions in regard thereto.

Clause 2: Contractor's obligations

Derivation. Clauses 2.1 and 2.3 reproduce with minor drafting amendments clause 1 of the 1963 Form 1976 Revision. Clause 2.2 is derived from part of clause 12 of the 1963 Form.

Amendments. Clause 2.1 was redrafted by Amendment 9 dated July 1990 to take account of the transfer of the definition of "Contract Documents" to clause 1.3.

Clause 2.2.2 was amended by Amendment 7 dated July 1988. This has the effect that:

(1) the reference to the Standard Method of Measurement is updated to the 7th edition;
(2) the word "information" has been included to follow General Rule 10.3 of the Standard Method of Measurement 7th edition which sets out in paragraphs 10.3(a)–(d) what information has to be provided in respect of a provisional sum for defined work.

Clause 2.3.5 was added by Amendment 4 dated July 1987. This introduces a reference to the Numbered Documents which are defined in clause 1.3 as "any Document referred to in the First Recital in any Sub-Contract with a Nominated Sub-Contractor."

The Contractor's obligations. Clause 2.1 provides a general description of the Contractor's obligations. Clause 2.2 specifies how the Contract Bills should be prepared and their relationship with the Articles, Conditions and Appendix. Clause 2.3 deals with discrepancies in or divergences between documents. Clauses 2.1 and 2.3 should be read in conjunction with clause 4 dealing with Architect's Instructions.

Clause 2.1. *"Such quality and standards shall be to the reasonable satisfaction of the Architect."*

The words "to the reasonable satisfaction of the Architect" as used in this Form have a special meaning as applying only to that class of materials or workmanship referred to in clauses 2.1, 8.1 and 30.9.1.1 where the Architect's decision as expressed in his Final Certificate is conclusive. Whether or not the relevant quality or standards come within this class is a question of construction. As examples, consider: "finished to the Architect's approval" and "to the standards of BSS No. . . ." (with no reference to the Architect). The first example, it is suggested, comes within clause 30.9.1.1, the second does not. Between these examples it is a question of fact and degree but, having regard to the importance of the result, it is thought that a clear intention must be apparent to bring the materials or workmanship within the class where quality or standards are to be to the reasonable satisfaction of the Architect. The Contract Bills are the prime documents (see clauses 2.2 and 8.1), but they may show that it is necessary to refer to the Contract Drawings. Documents or evidence outside the Contract Documents cannot, it is submitted, be referred to unless they can be relied on in support of a collateral warranty or agreement.[36] The question whether the Architect ought reasonably to be satisfied can, it is thought, be challenged either by the Contractor or the Employer before the Arbitrator, provided that the procedure required by clauses 30.9.3 and 41 is followed.

Effect of price. When considering whether he is reasonably satisfied, can the Architect take into account whether the price is high or low in comparison with the work to be done? The case of *Cotton* v. *Wallis*[37] seems to suggest that he can, and that in particular he can allow a certain tolerance where the price is low even though the Bills of Quantities expressly state, "the whole of the materials and workmanship is to be the best of their respective kinds . . . ." But *Cotton* v. *Wallis* is not, it is submitted, a binding authority upon the construction of the Contract in disputes between Employer and Contractor[38] and does not affect the well settled rule that extrinsic evidence may not normally be

---

[36] For collateral warranties, see p. 130. For a discussion of the limit of the Architect's power when considering whether he is reasonably satisfied, see p. 98.

[37] [1955] 1 W.L.R. 1168 (C.A.); see also p. 58.

[38] Because the issue was whether the Architect as a professional man had been guilty of such a dereliction of duty to his client, the Employer, as to make him guilty of negligence. It was not, and was not argued as, a dispute between the Employer and the Contractor as to the construction of the building contract—the 1939 edition of the R.I.B.A. Form, pre-1957 Version. Presumably for this reason evidence of whether the price was high or low was, it seems, admitted without objection and in the Court of Appeal it was "conceded that . . . one could not leave out of account altogether the price at which the work was to be done"—[1955] 1 W.L.R. 1168 at 1175.

adduced to add to, vary, modify or contradict the written terms of the document.[39] It is submitted that, if this rule is applied to a dispute between the Employer and the Contractor where the Contract Bills use the words quoted above, it results in the exclusion of evidence as to the nature of the price.[40] Nevertheless, until the point is directly decided, *Cotton* v. *Wallis* is the only authority on the question. It is therefore suggested that the Architect, in deciding whether he is reasonably satisfied as to quality or standards, should first consider carefully the express terms of the Contract, in particular the Contract Bills. If, then, he is still left in doubt, he may as a last resort and, always provided that it is not contrary to any express term, consider whether the Contract Sum is high or low.

Effect of Architect's Inspection. The Contractor cannot rely on lack of inspection by the Architect, or the clerk of works if there is one, as an excuse for not complying with the Contract.[41] Can the Contractor rely, and if so, to what extent, upon an Architect's inspection as evidence of compliance with the Contract? No general answer can be given. The facts and the Contract Documents must be considered in each case. An example is suggested. Say the Contract Bills require the finish of an item to be that of a sample to be approved by the Architect, and the Architect approves a sample. Thereafter it is submitted, he cannot, without requiring a variation, demand a higher standard. Neither, it is submitted, can the Arbitrator substitute a different standard from that approved by the Architect. The reason is that the Architect's approval completes the description of the quality of the Works required by the contract. Where there is no comparable Bill item, approval by the Architect, or even lack of comment by the Architect as to work offered as finished, may be greater or less evidence of compliance with the Contract, but such action or inaction by the Architect does not ordinarily, it is submitted, prevent the Arbitrator as a matter of law deciding whether the offered finish complied with the Contract.

Clause 2.3. " ... *any discrepancy in* ..."

If the Contractor fails to give notice upon finding a discrepancy or divergence and carries out work shown for example on the Contract Drawings but not described in the Contract Bills, he may lose rights to extra payment (clause 13); to extension of time (clause 25.4.5); and to loss and expense (clause 26.2.3). For a discussion of how far the Contractor is under a duty to look out for discrepancies or divergences, see commentary to the Articles of Agreement at page 476. If there is no breach of such duty and the Contractor only finds the

---

[39] For the rules about extrinsic evidence, see p. 34.

[40] *cf.* the dissenting judgment of Denning L.J. in *Cotton* v. *Wallis* [1955] 1 W.L.R. 1168 at 1170 (C.A.).

[41] *East Ham Corporation* v. *Bernard Sunley & Sons Ltd.* [1966] A.C. 406 (H.L.); *AMF International* v. *Magnet Bowling* [1968] 1 W.L.R. 1028 at 1053; *Sutcliffe* v. *Chippendale & Edmonson* (1971) 18 B.L.R. 149 at 162 *et seq.*

discrepancy or divergence after the work has been carried out, an adjustment must be made under clauses 13.2, 13.4 and 14.2 and the Contractor is entitled to any loss and expense in which he has been involved under clause 26.2.3.

Clause 2.2.1. *"nothing contained in the Contract Bills shall override or modify the application or interpretation of that which is contained in the Articles of Agreement, the Conditions or the Appendix."*

These words are of considerable importance. They may have an effect different from the ordinary rule that written words (*i.e.* the Bills) prevail over printed words (*i.e.* the Conditions).[42] Clause 2.2.1 is derived, as noted above, from clause 12 of the 1963 Form. However, the 1963 Form provided that "nothing contained in the Contract Bills shall override, modify or *affect in any way whatsoever* ... these Conditions." The italicised words have been deleted from the 1980 Form. Authorities decided under pre-1980 Contracts held that provisions in the Bills affecting matters dealt with in the Conditions such as insurance,[43] nomination of Sub-Contractors,[44] or partial possession[45] had to be disregarded.

The words now omitted were considered by Stephenson L.J. in *English Industrial Estates* v. *Wimpey.*[46] His construction was that insofar as the Bills dealt with matters covered by the Conditions they had no effect on the printed Conditions. It is thought that, under the present wording, the court is entitled to look at the Bills and to give effect to them to the extent that the Bills supplement the Conditions. Insofar as the Bills purport to override or modify the Articles of Agreement, the Conditions or the Appendix, they continue to have no effect.

A further difference between clause 2.2.1 and clause 12(1) of the 1963 Form is that the former clause 12(1) provided that "the quality and quantity of the work included in the Contract Sum shall be deemed to be that which is set out in the Contract Bills ... but save as aforesaid nothing contained in the Contract Bills shall override etc." In the 1980 Form, clause 2.2.1 provides without qualification that "nothing contained in the Contract Bills shall override etc." Reference to the "quality and quantity of the work" now appears separately at clause 14.1. It is therefore not wholly clear whether the provision in clause 2.2.1 remains subject to the proviso that it does not apply to the quality and quantity of the work set out in the Contract Bills. It is thought that the 1980 Form assumes that matters of quality and quantity will for practical purposes not feature in the Articles of Agreement, the Conditions or the Appendix other than by reference to the Bills[47] so that clause 2.2.1 would not

---

[42] For the principle, see p. 42.

[43] *Gold* v. *Patman & Fotheringham* [1958] 1 W.L.R. 697 at 701 (C.A).

[44] *Bickerton* v. *North West Metropolitan Regional Hospital Board* [1970] 1 W.L.R. 607 at 617.

[45] *English Industrial Estates* v. *Wimpey* [1973] 1 Lloyd's Rep. 118 (C.A.); *cf. Gleeson* v. *Hillingdon London Borough* (1970) 215 E.G. 165.

[46] [1973] 1 Lloyd's Rep. 118 at 127 *et seq.* (C.A.).

[47] See, *e.g.* clauses 2.1 and 8.1.

normally be called into play. If exceptionally, as for example by an amendment to the Conditions,[48] there were provisions relating to quality or quantity in the Conditions, a difficult question of construction would arise. If then there were no other decisive factor, it is thought that the provisions in the Conditions would prevail by virtue of clause 2.2.1.

Even under the pre-1980 wording, the court was able to give effect to the Contract Bills in a number of circumstances:

(1) in *AMF International* v. *Magnet Bowling*,[49] the contract was in the 1939 Form. Clause 14 made the Contractor liable for injury to property in words substantially similar to those of clause 20.2 of the 1980 Form. The Bills contained certain items expressly requiring the Contractor to protect all work and materials. Equipment stored in a partially completed part of the Works was damaged by a flood. It was held that clause 10 (the then equivalent of clause 12 in the 1963 Conditions) did not prevent the court from giving full effect to these items in the Bills so that the Contractor was liable.

(2) In *English Industrial Estates* v. *Wimpey*,[50] the Court of Appeal held that special provisions in the Bills of Quantities could not be used for the purpose of interpreting the Contract but were of help in order to follow what was going on.

(3) In *Henry Boot* v. *Central Lancashire New Town Development Corporation*,[51] the Contract Bills contained provisional sums for work to be executed by certain statutory undertakers but also stated that such sums were to be expended under the direct order of the Employer. Various services were constructed by statutory undertakers engaged directly by the employer. The court held that the phrase "quality and quantity of the work included in the Contract Sum" was wide enough for it to look at the Bills and to find that the relevant work, although formally included in the contract, was in reality excluded when the contract was read as a whole.

(4) In *Moody* v. *Ellis*,[52] the Court of Appeal indicated that a provision in the Bills, by which the contractor was to be responsible for the execution of Works in conformity with a programme agreed with the Architect, did not override, modify or affect the Conditions in any way. There was no reason why this provision should not take effect as part of the Building Contract in the ordinary way.

Amendment of Form. Although the provisions of the pre-1980 clause have been modified, it is still necessary to amend the Form itself if the parties wish to have special terms on any matters dealt with in the Conditions, and certainly

---

[48] See "Amendment of Form" below.
[49] [1968] 1 W.L.R. 1028.
[50] [1973] 1 Lloyd's Rep. 118 (C.A.).
[51] (1980) 15 B.L.R. 1.
[52] (1983) 26 B.L.R. 39 (C.A.).

insofar as they wish to override or modify the Conditions. It is not sufficient to say, for instance, in the Contract Bills that the Articles of Agreement and Conditions will be in the Standard Form "with certain amendments and additional clauses as set out in the bill."[53] Various methods of amendment may be used. One is to follow the procedure very common in engineering contracts of having special conditions. Another, where the amendments are contained in the Preliminary Bill is expressly to write in a reference to that Bill in the Articles of Agreement and in clause 1 which defines the Contract Documents. The greatest care should, however, always be taken to ensure that *ad hoc* amendments do not have unintended consequences.

Clause 2.2.2.1. *"the Contract Bills, unless otherwise specifically stated ..."*

Unless otherwise specifically stated in respect of any specified item or items, the Contract Bills are to have been prepared in accordance with the Standard Method of Measurement. If they have not been so prepared, there is an error which must be corrected and the correction is deemed to be a variation required by the Architect (clause 2.2.2.2.). For example, if there is no provision in the Contract Bills for excavation in rock but in carrying out the Works it becomes clear that such excavation is necessary then, it is submitted, the Bills must be corrected by inserting an item for excavation in rock and the Contractor will be entitled to extra payment under clause 13.2 and, where appropriate, clause 26.1.[54]

Clause 2.2.2.1. *"... in respect of any specified item ..."*

It is a question of construction of the Contract Bills in question whether or not adequate notice is given of any particular departure from the principles of the Standard Method, but it is thought that general statements at the beginning of the Bill such as, "any departure from the Standard Method of Measurement must be accepted" are not sufficient.

Clause 2.2.2.2. *"any error in description ... of items ... shall be corrected ..."*

Errors can arise from discrepancies between Contract Drawings and Contract Bills, from mathematical errors of measurement and from failure to prepare the Contract Bills in accordance with the Standard Method.[55] Such failure may be due to facts unknown to the parties at the time of making the contract, *e.g.* the presence of rock. The result is to place upon the Employer many of the risks relating to the soil which would otherwise be upon the Contractor.[56]

Remeasurement. Correction of the Bills is effected by inserting or deleting items as the case may be, or remeasuring items wrongly described, and valuing

---

[53] See *Gleeson* v. *Hillingdon London Borough* (1970) 215 E.G. 165.
[54] See *Bryant* v. *Birmingham H.S.F.* [1938] 1 All E.R. 503 where the Contract was the 1931 edition of the R.I.B.A. Form and the clause corresponding to clause 12 was somewhat different.
[55] See above.
[56] See clause 2.3 and pp. 134 and 478.

in accordance with clause 13.2 and, where appropriate, 26.1. If items in or sections of the Contract Bills are marked "provisional," it is submitted that this operates as an agreement that such items or sections will be remeasured in any event. In some cases there may be a dispute as to the existence of an error, which dispute can only be resolved on a remeasurement. It is thought that there is an implied term that either party may require remeasurement of a disputed item or items but must act reasonably in the exercise of such right, so that if he unreasonably puts the other party to the expense of remeasurement he may be liable to that other party for such expense. There is always remeasurement where the form for use with Approximate Quantities is used.

3.   Contract Sum—additions or deductions—adjustment—Interim Certificates

Where in the Conditions it is provided that an amount is to be added to or deducted from the Contract Sum or dealt with by adjustment of the Contract Sum then as soon as such amount is ascertained in whole or in part such amount shall be taken into account in the computation of the next Interim Certificate following such whole or partial ascertainment.

Clause 3: Contract Sum—additions or deductions—adjustment— Interim Certificates

This clause, which is new to the 1980 Form, provides for changes in the amount to be paid to the Contractor to be taken into account in the computation of Interim Certificates. In practice, this will mainly apply to the valuation of Variations (clause 13.7) and the ascertainment of loss and expense (clause 26.5). See also clauses 30.6.2.5 and 30.6.2.16.

4.   Architect's/Contract Administrator's instructions

4.1   .1   The Contractor shall forthwith comply with all instructions issued to him by the Architect/the Contract Administrator in regard to any matter in respect of which the Architect/the Contract Administrator is expressly empowered by the Conditions to issue instructions; save that where such instruction is one requiring a Variation within the meaning of clause 13.1.2 the Contractor need not comply to the extent that he makes reasonable objection in writing to the Architect/the Contract Administrator to such compliance.

.2   If within 7 days after receipt of a written notice from the Architect/the Contract Administrator requiring compliance with an instruction the Contractor does not comply therewith, then the Employer may employ and pay other persons to execute any work whatsoever which may be necessary to give effect to such instruction; and all costs incurred in connection with such employment may be deducted by him from any monies due or to become due to the Contractor under this Contract or may be recoverable from the Contractor by the Employer as a debt.

4.2   Upon receipt of what purports to be an instruction issued to him by the Architect/the Contract Administrator the Contractor may request the Architect/the Contract Administrator to specify in writing the provision of the Conditions which empowers the issue of the said instruction. The Architect/the Contract Administrator shall forthwith comply with any such request, and if the Contractor shall thereafter comply with the said instruction (neither party before such compliance having given to the other a written request to concur in the appointment of an Arbitrator under clause 41 in order that it may be decided whether the provision specified by the Architect/the Contract Administrator empowers the issue of the said instruction), then the issue of the same shall be deemed for all the purposes of this Contract to have been empowered by the provision of the Conditions specified by the Architect/the Contract Administrator in answer to the Contractor's request.

4.3 .1 All instructions issued by the Architect/the Contract Administrator shall be issued in writing.

.2 If the Architect/the Contract Administrator purports to issue an instruction otherwise than in writing it shall be of no immediate effect, but shall be confirmed in writing by the Contractor to the Architect/the Contract Administrator within 7 days, and if not dissented from in writing by the Architect/the Contract Administrator to the Contractor within 7 days from receipt of the Contractor's confirmation shall take effect as from the expiration of the latter said 7 days. Provided always:

.2.1 that if the Architect/the Contract Administrator within 7 days of giving such an instruction otherwise than in writing shall himself confirm the same in writing, then the Contractor shall not be obliged to confirm as aforesaid, and the said instruction shall take effect as from the date of the Architect's/the Contract Administrator's confirmation; and

.2.2 that if neither the Contractor nor the Architect/the Contract Administrator shall confirm such an instruction in the manner and at the time aforesaid but the Contractor shall nevertheless comply with the same, then the Architect/the Contract Administrator may confirm the same in writing at any time prior to the issue of the Final Certificate, and the said instruction shall thereupon be deemed to have taken effect on the date on which it was issued otherwise than in writing by the Architect/ the Contract Administrator.

Clause 4: Architect's/Contract Administrator's instructions

Derivation. This clause is substantially the same as clause 2 of the 1963 Form.

Scheme of clause. The clause provides for compliance with Architect's instructions (clause 4.1); testing the validity of Architect's instructions (clause 4.2); the mode of Architect's instructions (clause 4.3).

The position of the Architect. The general position is that "it is the function and the right of the [Contractor] to carry out his own building operation as he thinks fit."[57] The Architect has no authority to tell the

---

[57] See *Clayton* v. *Woodman & Sons Ltd.* [1962] 1 W.L.R. 585 at 593 (C.A.), a decision in a personal injury case on the 1939 edition of the R.I.B.A. Form where, arguably, the Architect's authority was wider because of his power to give "directions." See also *AMF International* v. *Magnet Bowling* [1968] 1 W.L.R. 1028 at 1046, 1053.

Contractor how to do the Works. However, it is submitted that the Contract Drawings and Contract Bills must be read to consider whether in respect of any particular item a right to require work to be done in a certain way is reserved to the Architect. The function and right of the Contractor discussed in the preceding sentences is further emphasised by clause 1.4 of the 1980 Form, discussed above, which makes it clear that "the Contractor shall remain wholly responsible for carrying out and completing the Works in all respects in accordance with clause 2.1" and that his responsibility in that regard is not in any way diluted by the presence or involvement of the Architect or the clerk of works.

The Architect has ample power to vary the Works, but, it is submitted, he has no authority to vary or to waive[58] the conditions of the contract[59] nor to vary the whole nature of the Works, for example, to change works designed as a single dwelling house into a complex block of flats. He probably cannot omit work in order to have it carried out by another Contractor.[60] He cannot nominate a Sub-Contractor or supplier save in accordance with the provisions of clauses 35 and 36. For Variations generally, see clause 13.

The Architect's duty to act fairly and professionally. The parties contract on the understanding that in all matters where the Architect has to apply his professional skill, he will act in a fair and unbiased manner in applying the terms of the contract. This is not limited to the issue of Certificates but applies to every function where he has to form a professional opinion upon matters which would affect the amount paid to (or to be deducted from) the Contractor.[61] The duty of fairness does not have the effect, as was long thought to be the position, of making him a quasi-arbitrator, *i.e.* a person with most of the attributes of an arbitrator although not formally appointed as such.[62] There is, it is submitted, an implied term[63] that the Employer will not so act as to disqualify the Architect. It is a question in each case depending on the nature of the employer's act, and its effect, whether the breach of the term amounts to a repudiation of the Contract.[64] Interference with or obstruction by the Employer in the issue of a Certificate is a ground for determination by the Contractor under clause 28.1.2.[65]

---

[58] For waiver see p. 264.

[59] *Sharpe* v. *San Paulo Railway* (1873) L.R. 8 Ch.App. 597.

[60] See "Omissions" at p. 86.

[61] For a general discussion of these principles, see "Disqualification of the certifier" at p. 114. See also p. 621 for the effect of disqualification under the Standard Form.

[62] See p. 114.

[63] For implication of terms, see p. 45.

[64] For repudiation generally, see p. 146.

[65] For the position of the Architect under the 1963 Form, including the question of the implication of terms, see *London Borough of Merton* v. *Leach* (1985) 32 B.L.R. 51. The court considered that his position was not affected by *Derek Crouch Construction* v. *North Western Regional Health Authority* [1984] Q.B. 644 (C.A.). For general discussions of *Merton* v. *Leach* see p. 500 and of *Crouch* see p. 389; *cf. Sutcliffe* v. *Thackrah* (1974) A.C. 727 at 730 (H.L.); *Partington & Son* v. *Tameside M.B.C.* (1985) 32 B.L.R. 150.

Architect's Certificates.   One of the features of the contract is the number of different certificates which the Architect can or must issue under various clauses, thus: of Practical Completion (17.1); of Completion of Making Good Defects (17.4); Frost Damage (17.5); Partial Possession (18.1); Liquidated Damages (24); Loss and Expense upon determination (27.4.4); Interim Certificates for Payment (30.1); Final Certificate (30.8); Failure to complete by a Nominated Sub-Contractor (35.15).

Clause 4.1.1.   *"The Contractor shall forthwith comply with all instructions . . ."*
   Failure to comply with a valid instruction is a breach of contract which can have serious consequences. Under this clause, if the non-compliance continues for 7 days after written notice from the Architect, the Employer may employ others to give effect to the instruction and recover the cost from the Contractor. If the failure to comply causes delay, there is a liability in liquidated damages (clause 24), and failure to comply with an instruction can be an element in a default giving rise to a right on the part of the Employer to determine the Contractor's employment (see clause 27.1.3). The Contractor is not in breach of contract if he fails to comply with what purports to be an instruction but is not authorised by the conditions. Clause 4.2 gives the Contractor a method of challenging such a purported instruction and there can be immediate arbitration upon the dispute (clauses 4.2. and 41). Clause 4.2 does not, it is submitted, entitle the Contractor to refuse to comply with what is subsequently determined to have been a valid instruction. It is therefore prudent for the Contractor to comply with the purported instruction which he challenges, having first made the request referred to in clause 4.2. If the Arbitrator should subsequently find in the Contractor's favour, the Contractor is, it is submitted, entitled to a reasonable sum for complying with the purported instructions.[66]

Clause 4.1.1.   *". . . is expressly empowered by the Conditions to issue instructions . . ."*
   The power arises under the following clauses:

2.3	Discrepancies
6.1.3	Statutory Requirements
7.	Errors in setting out
8.3	Opening up and testing
8.4	Work not in accordance with the Contract
8.5	Exclusion of persons employed
12.	Confirmed clerk of work's Directions
13.2	Variations
13.3	Provisional Sums
17.2, 17.3	Defects

---

[66] See *Molloy* v. *Liebe* (1910) 102 *Law Times* 616 and cases cited at p. 92. It is useful although not, it is thought, essential for the Contractor complying with the purported instruction, after making his request under the sub-clause, to say that his compliance is without prejudice to his contentions.

23.2	Postponement
32.2, 33.1.2	War
34.2	Antiquities
35.5.2, 35.8, 35.10.2, 35.11.2, 35.18.1.1, 35.23, 35.24.6.1, 35.24.6.3 and 35.25	Nominated Sub-Contractors
36.2	Nominated Suppliers.

Clause 4.1.1. *". . . save that where such instruction is one requiring a variation within the meaning of clause 13.1.2 the Contractor need not comply to the extent that he makes reasonable objection . . ."*

Clause 13.1.2 of the 1980 Form as amended introduced a new class of variation, whereby the Architect is empowered to issue instructions imposing or altering obligations or restrictions imposed by the Employer in regard to access to or use of the site, limitations of working space or working hours and the execution or completion of the work in any specific order. By virtue of clause 4.1.1, the Contractor is not absolutely obliged to comply with this class of variation instruction. He need not do so to the extent that he makes reasonable objection. A dispute under this provision may be determined by immediate arbitration under clause 41.3.3. It is not easy to suggest any general principle by which such a dispute should be determined. A relevant consideration will be that the Contractor is entitled to additional payment for the variation under clause 13.4 and 26.2.7 (loss and expense). It is suggested that special facts personal to the Contractor may establish a reasonable objection under this clause. He might, for instance, show that he was already committed to another subsequent contract, the performance of which would be seriously prejudiced if his working hours were limited. On the other hand, circumstances can readily be envisaged when, for example, restrictions on access or limitations of working hours were legally unavoidable. This might occur if the Employer, contrary to expectation, failed to obtain the grant of a right of way over an adjoining owner's land, or if the court granted to an adjoining owner an injunction restraining noisy building operations outside certain limited hours. In these examples, under the 1963 Form, the Employer might have been in breach of contract and if there was delay, might have lost his right to claim liquidated damages for non-completion to time. The new class of variation instruction may serve to eliminate these consequences. It is suggested that a Contractor could not sustain a reasonable objection on the ground that he would prefer the Employer to be in breach of contract and to lose his rights to liquidated damages.

Clause 4.1.2. *"If within 7 days . . . the Contractor does not comply . . ."*
Instructions to which this provision may particularly be applied are those to open up or to test (clause 8.3), to remove defective work, materials or goods (clause 8.4.1) or to make good defects during the Defects Liability Period (clause 17.3). The power under this clause should be compared with the right of determination under clause 27.1.3 which can apply if "works are materially affected" and the other conditions of clause 27.1 are fulfilled.

Clause 4.2. *". . . what purports to be an instruction . . ."*
See page 495.

Orders by Employer personally.   The Contract makes no provision for any order by the Employer himself. It is thought, therefore, that such an order would amount only to an offer by the Employer to enter into a separate contract for the work in question, which offer the Contractor need not accept. If the Contractor does accept the offer, it is prudent to confirm it in writing both to the Employer and to the Architect. The parties may find it convenient to agree that the order shall be treated as if it were an instruction under the appropriate clause so that the difficulties which might otherwise arise are avoided.

Reasonableness of instructions.   Should instructions be limited to a reasonable number and issued at reasonable times? The court or the Arbitrator, it is submitted, in the absence of words importing an absolute discretion, readily implies a duty to act reasonably, and such a duty may be implied in this Contract.[67] But in considering what is reasonable the court would have regard to all the circumstances including the terms of the Contract. Thus, for example, in considering whether the Architect is acting reasonably in the number and time of instructions requiring variations the court will consider the provisions for altering contract rates under clause 13.5 and the right to loss or expense under clause 26.1 so that a very large number of variations ordered at different times might not be unreasonable under this contract although they might be unreasonable under a different Contract with less provision for financial compensation to the Contractor.

Clause 4.3.   Clause 4.3.1 states the general intention, namely, that instructions should be in writing. Clause 4.3.2 recognises the practice that in fact oral instructions are sometimes given. In the 1963 Form the expression used was "instruction issued orally." In the 1980 Form the expression is "an instruction otherwise than in writing." It is difficult to think, in practice, of an instruction which could be given otherwise than in writing but not orally. It is therefore thought that there is no practical distinction between these expressions. Throughout this commentary reference is made to oral instructions as being synonymous with instructions otherwise than in writing.

---

[67] See also p. 48.

Oral instructions.   The Contractor cannot ignore an oral instruction. He must confirm it within 7 days and, if it is not dissented from in writing by the Architect, must comply with it at the expiry of 7 days from receipt by the Architect of his, the Contractor's, confirmation. Meanwhile the Architect himself may confirm it within 7 days of giving it (clause 4.3.2.1). The Contractor is at risk if before the expiry of the period of 7 days from receipt by the Architect of his, the Contractor's, confirmation he carries out an oral instruction which has not been confirmed by the Architect. He must rely upon the Architect in the exercise of his discretion subsequently to confirm under clause 4.3.2.2. If the Architect refuses to do so, then, it is submitted, the Arbitrator has jurisdiction to exercise the discretion to confirm the instruction and to make an award as if there had been such confirmation (clause 41.4).

Urgent oral instruction.   In a case where an oral instruction is urgent and cannot await the processes of clause 4.3, what should the Contractor do? It is suggested that when receiving such oral instruction he obtains from the Architect a request to comply with it forthwith and an undertaking to confirm in writing. The Contractor should then as soon as possible confirm in writing to the Architect the instruction, request and undertaking. If the Architect contests the confirmation the Contractor can go to arbitration and if he satisfies the Arbitrator of the fact that there was such instruction, request and undertaking the Arbitrator should, it is submitted, make an award as if the instruction had been confirmed in writing in accordance with clause 4.3.2.2. For the position where there is an emergency compliance with Statutory Requirements, see clause 6.1.4.1.

Form of instruction.   Instructions do not have to be in any particular form, although to avoid disputes, it is good practice to use a common form such as that issued by the R.I.B.A. If this is not used, the Architect should use clear words. Vague words can provoke an argument as to what was intended, *e.g.* where there is a permission or a suggestion.

Site Meeting Minutes.   If site meeting minutes are kept and distributed, questions sometimes arise as to their effect, if any, under clause 4. This varies according to the circumstances and any agreement between the parties. If they are prepared and sent out by the Architect they will normally operate as confirmation under clause 4.3.2. If they are prepared by the Contractor and sent to the Architect, they are prima facie only confirmation by the Contractor required by clause 4.3.2 and do not take effect until 7 days from their receipt or earlier confirmation in writing by the Architect. For the purposes of clause 4.3.2 it is therefore better for Site Meeting Minutes to be prepared and issued promptly by the Architect.

Position of clerk of works.   See clause 12 and its commentary.

Work done without any instruction. The provisions for confirmation do not apply and prima facie the Contractor cannot recover extra payment. There could, however, be two exceptions:

(1) Under clause 2.2.2.2, where the Contractor, after he has carried out work in accordance with the Drawings, finds that the quantities exceed those in the Contract Bills;

(2) Under clause 13.2 where the Architect has a discretion to sanction in writing a variation made by the Contractor otherwise than pursuant to an instruction of the Architect. For the exercise of that discretion see commentary to clause 13.

Oral instructions as defence. In *G. Bilton & Sons* v. *Mason*,[68] it was held that compliance with the Architect's oral instructions, unconfirmed in writing, to vary the Contract, was a defence to a claim by the Employer for damages for breach of contract, where the breach alleged was that the Contractor had complied with those instructions and not with the original Contract.[69]

5.   Contract Documents—other documents—issue of certificates

5.1   The Contract Drawings and the Contract Bills shall remain in the custody of the Employer so as to be available at all reasonable times for the inspection of the Contractor.

5.2   Immediately after the execution of this Contract the Architect/the Contract Administrator without charge to the Contractor shall provide him (unless he shall have been previously so provided) with:

.1   one copy certified on behalf of the Employer of the Contract Documents;
.2   two further copies of the Contract Drawings; and
.3   two copies of the unpriced Bills of Quantities.

5.3   .1   So soon as is possible after the execution of this Contract:

.1.1   the Architect/the Contract Administrator without charge to the Contractor shall provide him (unless he shall have been previously so provided) with 2 copies of any descriptive schedules or other like documents necessary for use in carrying out the Works; and

.1.2   the Contractor without charge to the Employer shall provide the Architect/the Contract Administrator (unless he shall have been previously so provided) with 2 copies of his master programme for the execution of the Works and within 14 days of any decision by the Architect/the Contract Administrator under clause 25.3.1 or 33.1.3 with 2 copies of any amendments and revisions to take account of that decision.[h]

.2   Nothing contained in the descriptive schedules or other like documents referred to in clause 5.3.1.1 (nor in the master programme for the execution of the Works or

---

[68] (1957) (unreported) Sir Walker Carter, Q.C., Official Referee.
[69] The contract was in the 1939 R.I.B.A. Form but the principle applies, it is submitted, to the current Form.
[h] *To be deleted if no master programme is required.*

any amendment to that programme or revision therein referred to in clause 5.3.1.2) shall impose any obligation beyond those imposed by the Contract Documents.[i]

5.4   As and when from time to time may be necessary the Architect/the Contract Administrator without charge to the Contractor shall provide him with 2 copies of such further drawings or details as are reasonably necessary either to explain and amplify the Contract Drawings or to enable the Contractor to carry out and complete the Works in accordance with the Conditions.

5.5   The Contractor shall keep one copy of the Contract Drawings, one copy of the unpriced Bills of Quantities, one copy of the descriptive schedules or other like documents referred to in clause 5.3.1.1, one copy of the master programme referred to in clause 5.3.1.2 (unless clause 5.3.1.2 has been deleted) and one copy of the drawings and details referred to in clause 5.4 upon the Works so as to be available to the Architect/the Contract Administrator or his representative at all reasonable times.

5.6   Upon final payment under clause 30.8 the Contractor shall if so requested by the Architect/the Contract Administrator forthwith return to him all drawings, details, descriptive schedules and other documents of a like nature which bear the name of the Architect/the Contract Administrator.

5.7   None of the documents mentioned in clause 5 shall be used by the Contractor for any purpose other than this Contract, and neither the Employer, the Architect/the Contract Administrator nor the Quantity Surveyor shall divulge or use except for the purposes of this Contract any of the rates or prices in the Contract Bills.

5.8   Except where otherwise specifically so provided any certificate to be issued by the Architect/the Contract Administrator under the Conditions shall be issued to the Employer, and immediately upon the issue of any such certificate the Architect/the Contract Administrator shall send a duplicate copy thereof to the Contractor.

Clause 5: Contract Documents—other documents—issue of certificates

Derivation.   Clause 5 is, with one significant addition and two administrative changes, substantially the same as clause 3 of the 1963 Form. The significant addition is the reference to the master programme discussed below. The two administrative alterations are that the Contract Bills and Contract Drawings are to be in the custody of the Employer instead of the Architect, and that the Contractor is now entitled to receive a certified copy of all the Contract Documents.

Scheme of clause.   This clause deals with various matters relating to the provision, custody and use of documents connected with the carrying out of the Works. In considering it, reference should also be made to the Articles of Agreement, clause 2.1 (Contractor's obligations), clause 2.3 (Notification of discrepancies), clause 7 (Accurately dimensioned drawings for setting out)

---

[i] *Words in parentheses to be deleted if no master programme is required.*

and clauses 8.1 and 14 (Contract Bills). Note that, although the Side Note to this clause is "Contract Documents," they are in fact defined in clause 2.1.

Clause 5.3.1.1. "... *2 copies of any descriptive schedules or other like documents* ..."

The descriptive schedules and other like documents are intended to be for the assistance of the Contractor and are, or should be, prepared from the Contract Documents, *i.e.* Contract Drawings and the Contract Bills.

Clause 5.3.1.2. "*the Contractor ... shall provide the Architect ... with 2 copies of his master programme* ..."

The reference in the Conditions to a master programme is optional, the footnotes indicating that it can be deleted. If the reference is included, the master programme is nevertheless not a Contract Document and does not add to the Contractor's obligation (see clause 5.3.2). It should be noted that there is an express provision requiring the Contractor, if necessary, to amend or revise the master programme each time the Architect fixes a new completion date under clauses 25.3.1 or 33.1.3 to take account of that decision. The Contractor then has to provide the Architect with two copies of the amendments and revisions within 14 days.

Clause 5.4. "*As and when from time to time may be necessary* ..."

This clause read with clauses 25.4.6 and 26.2.1 recognises that the Contract Documents are frequently not adequate to enable the work to be carried out. Necessary drawings and details should, it is submitted, be furnished at times which will enable the Contractor to comply with his duties as to progress required by clause 23. Clause 3(4) of the 1963 Form, which is materially identical to clause 5.4 of the 1980 Form, was considered by Vinelott J. in *London Borough of Merton* v. *Leach*.[70] He held that in relation to clause 3(4) it must have been in the contemplation of the parties when making the contract that the Architect would act with reasonable diligence and would use reasonable skill and care in providing the information required by that clause. He also held that clause 3(4) did not exclude an implied term that "the Architect would provide the Contractor correct information concerning the works."[71]

For the delay in delivery of instructions and drawings there is an express contractual right under clause 26.2.1 to recover loss and expense subject to fulfilment of certain conditions appearing in the clause. This right is expressed to be without prejudice to any other rights and remedies which the Contractor may possess (clause 26.6). The Contractor may therefore claim damages for breach of clause 5.4 or of the implied term set out above. But he will ordinarily only claim damages if he cannot satisfy the requirements of a claim under clause 26.2.1. This is because is it is usually more convenient to recover on a certificate issued under the terms of the Contract than to seek damages for

---

[70] (1985) 32 B.L.R. 51.
[71] *Ibid.* at 81 *et seq.*

breach of the Contract, and because a Contractor who cannot prove compliance with the requirements of clause 26.2.1 may find it difficult to establish his loss as a matter of evidence and to defeat allegations of failure to mitigate his loss, or that the loss is too remote.[72]

Consultants' drawings. The Contract makes no provision for the position of consultants although it is common for them to design much of the structural work and specialist services. They act, it is submitted, as agents for the Architect and, as between Contractor and Employer, their delay is the Architect's delay.

Nominated Sub-Contractors' Drawings. Nominated Sub-Contractors sometimes have to supply Drawings to enable the Contractor to carry out work not to be performed by themselves. Delay in the provision of their Drawings is discussed in the commentary to clause 35. The application of clause 3(4) of the 1963 Form, which is materially identical to clause 5.4 of the 1980 Form, to such drawings was considered in *H. Fairweather & Co.* v. *London Borough of Wandsworth*.[73] On appeal from the Arbitrator one question posed for the Court was whether the Arbitrator was correct in law in finding that Drawings produced by Nominated Sub-Contractors were not within the ambit of clause 3(4). It was held that, since the Nominated Sub-Contractors were obliged under the terms of the Sub-Contract to produce various Drawings in good time to meet the agreed programme of the work, it necessarily followed that the Contractors had a similar obligation to the Employer. It further followed that the failure of the Nominated Sub-Contractors to supply the Drawings could not amount to a breach by the Employer of clause 3(4) nor, without fault on the part of the Employer, could it result in liability to the Main Contractors for the delay.

Clause 5.6. "*... the Contractor shall if so requested, ... return ... all drawings ...*"
For property in the plans, the Architect's lien and his copyright, see pages 336 *et seq.* For remedies for breach of confidence, see page 260.

Without quantities version. There are many differences to allow for the significance of the Specification as a Contract Document. For the general effect, see the commentary to the Articles of Agreement.

6. Statutory obligations, notices, fees and charges

6.1 .1 Subject to clause 6.1.5 the Contractor shall comply with, and give all notices

---

[72] For damages generally, see Chap. 8; for Contractors' claims, see p. 444; see also commentary to clause 26.
[73] (1987) 39 B.L.R. 106.

required by, any Act of Parliament, any instrument, rule or order made under any Act of Parliament, or any regulation or byelaw of any local authority or of any statutory undertaker which has any jurisdiction with regard to the Works or with whose systems the same are or will be connected (all requirements to be so complied with being referred to in the Conditions as "the Statutory Requirements").

.2   If the Contractor shall find any divergence between the Statutory Requirements and all or any of the documents referred to in clause 2.3 or between the Statutory Requirements and any instruction of the Architect/the Contract Administrator requiring a Variation issued in accordance with clause 13.2, he shall immediately give to the Architect/the Contract Administrator a written notice specifying the divergence.

.3   If the Contractor gives notice under clause 6.1.2 or if the Architect/the Contract Administrator shall otherwise discover or receive notice of a divergence between the Statutory Requirements and all or any of the documents referred to in clause 2.3 or between the Statutory Requirements and any instruction requiring a Variation issued in accordance with clause 13.2, the Architect/the Contract Administrator shall within 7 days of the discovery or receipt of a notice issue instructions in relation to the divergence. If and insofar as the instructions require the Works to be varied, they shall be treated as if they were Architect's/Contract Administrator's instructions requiring a Variation issued in accordance with clause 13.2.

.4.1   If in any emergency compliance with clause 6.1.1 requires the Contractor to supply materials or execute work before receiving instructions under clause 6.1.3 the Contractor shall supply such limited materials and execute such limited work as are reasonably necessary to secure immediate compliance with the Statutory Requirements.

.4.2   The Contractor shall forthwith inform the Architect/the Contract Administrator of the emergency and of the steps that he is taking under clause 6.1.4.1.

.4.3   Work executed and materials supplied by the Contractor under clause 6.1.4.1 shall be treated as if they had been executed and supplied pursuant to an Architect's/a Contract Administrator's instruction requiring a Variation issued in accordance with clause 13.2 provided that the emergency arose because of a divergence between the Statutory Requirements and all or any of the documents referred to in clause 2.3 or between the Statutory Requirements and any instruction requiring a Variation issued in accordance with clause 13.2, and the Contractor has complied with clause 6.1.4.2.

.5   Provided that the Contractor complies with clause 6.1.2, the Contractor shall not be liable to the Employer under this Contract if the Works do not comply with the Statutory Requirements where and to the extent that such non-compliance of the Works results from the Contractor having carried out work in accordance with the documents referred to in clause 2.3 or with any instruction requiring a Variation issued by the Architect/the Contract Administrator in accordance with clause 13.2.

6.2   The Contractor shall pay and indemnify the Employer against liability in respect of any fees or charges (including any rates or taxes) legally demandable under any Act of Parliament, any instrument, rule or order made under any Act of Parliament, or any regulation or byelaw of any local authority or of any statutory undertaker in respect of the Works. The amount of any such fees or charges (including any rates or taxes other than value added tax) shall be added to the Contract Sum unless they:

.1   arise in respect of work executed or materials or goods supplied by a local authority or statutory undertaker as a Nominated Sub-Contractor or as a Nominated Supplier; or

.2   are priced in the Contract Bills; or

.3   are stated by way of a provisional sum in the Contract Bills.

6.3   The provisions of clauses 19 and 35 shall not apply to the execution of part of the Works by a local authority or a statutory undertaker executing such work solely in pursuance of its statutory obligations and such bodies shall not be Sub-Contractors within the terms of this Contract.

Clause 6—statutory obligations, notice, fees and charges

Derivation.   Clause 6 is substantially the same as clause 4 of the 1963 Form save for certain modifications which now appear at clause 6.3.

Clause 6.1.1.   "*... shall comply with ...*"

Provided that he has the requisite knowledge (see below) the Contractor has, it is submitted, both to comply with and give statutory notices, and also, to comply with relevant Statutory Requirements including the Building Regulations. It seems that a flagrant breach of the Building Regulations or the like, apparent in the Contract Documents, may make the contract illegal.[74]

Losses caused by non-compliance with Statutory Requirements. Clauses 6.1.2. and 6.1.3 set out a clear procedure to be followed if the Contractor finds a divergence from Statutory Requirements. There is a useful provision for emergency compliance with Statutory Requirements (clause 6.1.4.1). Clause 6.1.5 qualifies clause 6.1.1 and operates as a valuable protection to the Contractor who either gives the requisite notice to the Architect under clause 6.1.2 or has not found any divergence between Statutory Requirements and the Contract Documents or Variation instructions. For a discussion of whether clause 6.1.5 protects a Contractor who negligently fails to observe a divergence, see page 487. In any claim for breach of contract by the Employer, damages require careful consideration having regard to the Contractor's right to be paid for work required to comply with Statutory Requirements.

Contractor's Claim against Architect.   In certain circumstances where the Contractor is liable for non-compliance with Statutory Requirements to the Employer, he may have a claim against the Architect where he can show a breach of a duty of care owed to him by the Architect. For a discussion of whether a duty of care is owed by the Architect to the Contractor and the scope of the duty, see page 340.

Unauthorised Variation.   If the Contractor at the request of a local official or for some other reason makes a variation in order to comply with Statutory

---

[74] For illegality, see p. 141.

Requirements without following the procedure of this clause and it is not an emergency, he is in breach of contract and prima facie loses any rights under clause 13 to extra payment, under clause 25 to extension of time and under clause 26 to loss or expense. The Architect can, however, in his discretion sanction a variation under clause 13.2.[75] In certain special circumstances, where the Contractor has had to pay money which the Employer is legally liable to pay, the Contractor may be able to recover such money in a claim in restitution.[76]

Major alteration necessary.   If a major and extensive alteration is necessary to comply with a Statutory Requirement, it is possible that in certain circumstances the Employer might be able to say that the contract is frustrated.[77] Subject to this, if there is a delay the Contractor may be able to found a determination on lack of instructions (clause 28.1.3.3) or postponement of work (clauses 23.2 and 28.1.3.1).

Clause 6.2.   "*... rates ...*"

The general principle is that building sites themselves are not to be treated as rateable hereditaments while the work of building is in progress.[78] The stage at which the works become rateable has been considered in a number of authorities.[79] Builders' huts and sheds erected on the site may have a sufficient degree of permanency to become rateable.[80] It is a question of fact and degree in each case whether such huts and sheds have this degree of permanency.[81] It should be noted that these principles derive from cases decided under the General Rate Act 1967. The system of Non-Domestic Rating has been significantly altered by the Local Government Finance Act 1988. However, the definition of "hereditament" and the test whether a hereditament is occupied or not have not been changed by the 1988 Act.[82] The Act confers powers upon the Secretary of State to make regulations causing certain descriptions of unoccupied hereditaments to be liable to Non-Domestic Rating.[83] No such regulation has so far been made.

---

[75] For the exercise of that discretion see commentary to clause 13.2.

[76] See discussion in *Owen* v. *Tate* [1976] Q.B. 402 (C.A.).

[77] The Contractor will not usually object to the alteration because of his rights under clauses 13, 25 and 26. Neither will he plead frustration because of his much better position under clause 28. For frustation generally, see p. 134.

[78] See *London County Council* v. *Wilkins* [1957] A.C. 362 at 380 (H.L.); *Dick Hampton (Earthmoving) Ltd.* v. *Lewis* [1976] Q.B. 254 (C.A.); *Makins* v. *Elson* [1977] 1 W.L.R. 221.

[79] See *Ravenseft Properties* v. *Newham London Borough Council* [1976] Q.B. 464 (C.A.); *Post Office* v. *Nottingham City Council* [1976] 1 W.L.R. 624 (C.A.); *Tower Hamlets London Borough Council* v. *St. Katharine by the Tower Ltd.* (1982) 80 L.G.R. 843; *Hailbury Investments* v. *Westminster City Council* [1986] 1 W.L.R. 1232 (H.L.); *London Merchant Securities* v. *Islington London Borough Council* [1988] A.C. 303 (H.L.).

[80] See *London County Council* v. *Wilkins* [1957] A.C. 362 (H.L.).

[81] Various temporary structures used for offices, stores and a canteen on site for 18 months were held to be rateable.

[82] See ss.64(1) and 65(2).

[83] s.45(1)(d).

Clause 6.3.   This sub-clause deals with such matters as the provision by local authorities of crossovers from a site to the highway. The sub-clause makes it clear that a local authority or a statutory undertaker executing part of the Works "solely in pursuance of its statutory obligation" is not to be regarded as a Domestic Sub-Contractor or a Nominated Sub-Contractor. Extension of time for delay by a statutory undertaker is dealt with by clause 25.4.11. It should be noted that the word "solely" does not appear in clause 25.4.11.[84]

7.   Levels and setting out of the Works

The Architect/The Contract Administrator shall determine any levels which may be required for the execution of the Works, and shall provide the Contractor by way of accurately dimensioned drawings with such information as shall enable the Contractor to set out the Works at ground level. The Contractor shall be responsible for, and shall, at no cost to the Employer, amend any errors arising from his own inaccurate setting out. With the consent of the Employer the Architect/the Contract Administrator may instruct that such errors shall not be amended and an appropriate deduction for such errors not required to be amended shall be made from the Contract Sum.

Clause 7—Levels and setting out of the Works

Derivation.   The original version of this clause was substantially the same as clause 5 of the 1963 Form.

"*. . . such information . . .*"

It is thought that the Contractor is entitled to an indemnity from the Employer in respect of claims made against him by an adjoining owner for trespass, committed by the Contractor in reliance upon faulty information furnished by the Architect.[85]

"*The Contractor shall be responsible for, and shall, at no cost to the Employer, amend any errors arising from his own inaccurate setting out.*"

The equivalent sentence in the 1963 Form and in the original version of the 1980 Form read that "unless the Architect/Supervising Officer shall otherwise instruct, in which case the Contract Sum shall be adjusted accordingly, the Contractor shall be responsible for and shall entirely at his own cost amend any errors arising from his own inaccurate setting out." These words apparently gave the Architect a discretion to issue an instruction which could result in the Employer becoming liable to bear the cost of amending errors due to the Contractor's inaccurate setting out. The words were deleted and the last two sentences of clause 7 inserted by Amendment 4 dated July 1987. This amendment appears substantially to limit the scope of the Architect's discretion. He may allow such errors to remain without amendment. However, if

---

[84] See *Henry Boot* v. *Central Lancashire Development Corporation* (1980) 15 B.L.R. 1 discussed in commentary to clause 25 at p. 579. Note also that there is no equivalent provision for payment of loss and expense under clause 26.1.

[85] See *Kirby* v. *Chessum & Sons Ltd.* (1914) 79 J.P. 81 (C.A.).

the Architect so decides, an appropriate deduction from the Contract Sum must be made.

8. **Materials, goods and workmanship to conform to description, testing and inspection**

8.1   .1   All materials and goods shall, so far as procurable, be of the kinds and standards described in the Contract Bills, provided that materials and goods shall be to the reasonable satisfaction of the Architect/the Contract Administrator where and to the extent that this is required in accordance with clause 2.1.

.2   All workmanship shall be of the standards described in the Contract Bills, or, to the extent that no such standards are described in the Contract Bills, shall be of a standard appropriate to the Works, provided that workmanship shall be to the reasonable satisfaction of the Architect/the Contract Administrator where and to the extent that this is required in accordance with clause 2.1.

8.2   .1   The Contractor shall upon the request of the Architect/the Contract Administrator provide him with vouchers to prove that the materials and goods comply with clause 8.1.

.2   In respect of any materials, goods or workmanship, as comprised in executed work, which are to be to the reasonable satisfaction of the Architect/the Contract Administrator in accordance with clause 2.1, the Architect/the Contract Administrator shall express any dissatisfaction within a reasonable time from the execution of the unsatisfactory work.

8.3   The Architect/The Contract Administrator may issue instructions requiring the Contractor to open up for inspection any work covered up or to arrange for or carry out any test of any materials or goods (whether or not already incorporated in the Works) or of any executed work, and the cost of such opening up or testing (together with the cost of making good in consequence thereof) shall be added to the Contract Sum unless provided for in the Contract Bills or unless the inspection or test shows that the materials, goods or work are not in accordance with this Contract.

8.4   If any work, materials or goods are not in accordance with this Contract the Architect/the Contract Administrator without prejudice to the generality of his powers, may:

.1   issue instructions in regard to the removal from the site of all or any of such work, materials or goods; and/or

.2   after consultation with the Contractor (who shall immediately consult with any relevant Nominated Sub-Contractor) and with the agreement of the Employer, allow all or any of such work, materials or goods to remain and confirm this in writing to the Contractor (which shall not be construed as a Variation) and where so allowed and confirmed an appropriate deduction shall be made in the adjustment of the Contract Sum; and/or

.3   after consultation with the Contractor (who shall immediately consult with any relevant Nominated Sub-Contractor) issue such instructions requiring a Variation as are reasonably necessary as a consequence of such an instruction under clause 8.4.1 or such confirmation under clause 8.4.2 and to the extent that such instructions are so necessary and notwithstanding clauses 13.4, 25 and 26 no addition to the Contract Sum shall be made and no extension of time shall be given; and/or

.4   having had due regard to the Code of Practice appended to these Conditions (*following clause 41*), issue such instructions under clause 8.3 to open up for inspection or to test as are reasonable in all the circumstances to establish to the

506

reasonable satisfaction of the Architect/the Contract Administrator the likelihood or extent, as appropriate to the circumstances, of any further similar non-compliance. To the extent that such instructions are so reasonable, whatever the results of the opening up for inspection or test, and notwithstanding clauses 8.3 and 26 no addition to the Contract Sum shall be made. Clause 25.4.5.2 shall apply unless as stated therein the inspection or test showed that the work, materials or goods were not in accordance with this Contract.

8.5   The Architect/The Contract Administrator may (but not unreasonably or vexatiously) issue instructions requiring the exclusion from the Works of any person employed thereon.

Clause 8: Materials, goods and workmanship

Derivation.   Clause 8 is substantially derived from clause 6 of the 1963 Form.

Amendments.   The 1980 Form has been amended in the following respects:

(1) clause 8.1 was redrafted by Amendment 4 issued in July 1987;
(2) clauses 8.2 and 8.4 were revised by Amendment 5 issued in January 1988.
(3) new clauses 8.1.3 and 8.5 were inserted by Amendment 9 issued in July 1990.

These amendments are of significance and are discussed below.

Scheme of clause.   This clause defines the kinds and standards of materials, goods and workmanship. It gives the Architect certain important powers relating to inspection and testing and to work not in accordance with the Contract. It should be read with clauses 2 and 4 and their commentaries.

Clause 8.1.   *Amendments*
   Clause 6(1) of the 1963 Form and the original version of clause 8.1 of the 1980 form provided that "all materials, goods and workmanship shall so far as procurable be of the respective kinds and standards described in the Contract Bills." By Amendment 4 issued in July 1987, clause 8.1 has been divided into two sub-clauses. Clause 8.1.1 deals with materials and goods and 8.1.2 deals with workmanship.

Clause 8.1.1.   The position as to materials and goods is now as follows:

(1) to the extent that clause 2.1 applies,[86] the materials and goods are required to be to the reasonable satisfaction of the Architect;
(2) to the extent that standards are described in the Contract Bills, the materials and goods must be of those standards;

---

[86] See p. 486.

(3) to the extent that the standards are not expressly described in the Contract Bills, the ordinary implied duties of the Contractor as to materials and goods apply[87];

(4) the obligation of the Contractor is limited by the phrase "... so far as procurable." It is submitted that there is an implied duty upon the Contractor who seeks to rely on these words to notify the Architect before supplying materials or goods not of the kinds or standards described in the Contract Bills.

Clause 8.1.2. The position as to workmanship is now as follows:

(1) to the extent that clause 2.1 applies, workmanship is required to be to the reasonable satisfaction of the Architect;

(2) to the extent that standards are described in the Contract Bills, workmanship must be of those standards;

(3) to the extent that standards are not described in the Contract Bills, workmanship must "be of a standard appropriate to the Works." It is probable that this phrase does no more than make express the usual implied duty of the Contractor as to workmanship.[88] However, the words "appropriate to the Works" appear to mean that, in assessing whether the Contractor has complied with his duty, the nature, quality and scale of the work must be taken into account;

(4) the qualification "so far as procurable" does not appear. The deletion of these words has the effect, it is submitted, that it is no defence for a Contractor whose workmanship is criticised to show that he was unable to recruit the necessary skilled workmen.

In the Without Quantities version, "Specification" appears in place of "Contract Bills."

Clause 8.1.3. A new clause 8.1.3. was inserted by Amendment 9 issued in July 1990 to provide expressly what would in any event be implied, namely that all works should be carried out in a proper and workmanlike manner. Consequentially, the new clause 8.5 provides for the Architect to deal with failure to comply with clause 8.1.3.

Clause 8.2. *Amendments*

Clause 8.2.1 substantially reproduces clause 6(2) of the 1963 Form, and is the same as the unamended version of clause 8.2 in the 1980 Form. Clause 8.2.2 was inserted by Amendment 5 issued in January 1988 and requires the Architect to express dissatisfaction in relation to executed work to which clause 2.1 applies within a reasonable time from the execution of the unsatisfactory work.

---

[87] See p. 53.
[88] See p. 52.

Clause 8.3.   *". . . the cost of such opening up . . ."*

The Contractor has a right to extension of time (under clause 25.4.5.2) and to loss and expense additional to such cost (under clause 26.2.2) for delay or disturbance of the regular progress of the works due to an unjustified order to open up or test. The right to loss and expense is qualified by clause 8.4.4 (see below).

The meaning of "executed work" is, it is submitted, a question of fact and degree in each case. The Architect does not have to order a test under clause 8.3 before issuing instructions under clause 8.4.1.

Clause 8.4.   *Amendments*

Clause 8.4.1 is substantially the same as clause 6(4) in the 1963 Form and clause 8.4 in the original version of the 1980 Form. Clauses 8.4.2, 8.4.3 and 8.4.4 were inserted by Amendment 5 dated January 1988.

Clause 8.4.1.   *". . . removal from the site . . ."*

The Architect no doubt has the power to issue instructions to remove defective works even without this clause.[89] The power under clause 8.4 is "without prejudice to the generality of his powers." Even where materials or workmanship are not required to be to the Architect's reasonable satisfaction under clause 2.1, the duty to complete the works requires the Contractor to replace defective work with work which is in accordance with the Contract.

The form of an instruction to remove defective work under clause 6(4) of the 1963 Form was considered in *Holland Hannen & Cubitts* v. *W.H.T.S.O.*[90] The court considered that the power was simply to instruct the removal of work and that therefore a notice containing a statement that certain work was unsatisfactory which did not require the removal of anything at all was not a valid notice.

Damages.   Work may during the construction period not conform to the Contract requirements. If the Architect orders its removal, and it is satisfactorily removed and replaced before completion, does the Employer have a remedy in damages for this temporary disconformity? Lord Diplock in *Kaye (P. and M.)* v. *Hosier & Dickinson*[91] suggested that there was no such remedy. However, it has since been questioned whether this suggestion was intended to be of universal application.[92]

---

[89] See *Modern Engineering (Bristol) Ltd.* v. *Gilbert-Ash* [1974] A.C. 689 at 710 (H.L.) *per* Viscount Dilhorne.

[90] (1981) 18 B.L.R. 80. This case went to the Court of Appeal—see (1985) 35 B.L.R. 1—but this point was not argued.

[91] [1972] 1 W.L.R. 146 at 165 (H.L.).

[92] *Lintest Builders* v. *Roberts* (1980) 13 B.L.R. 38 at 44 (C.A.), Roskill L.J.; *William Tomkinson* v. *Parochial Church Council of St. Michael* (1990) 6 Const. L.J. 319; *cf. Surrey Heath Borough Council* v. *Lovell Construction* (1988) 42 B.L.R. 25—point not argued on appeal.

(1) before acting under clause 8.4.2 the Architect is required both to consult the Contractor and to obtain the agreement of the Employer;
(2) the Architect must confirm in writing to the Contractor what non-conforming work he is allowing to remain;
(3) in respect of that work "an appropriate deduction shall be made in the adjustment of the Contract Sum." The amount of the deduction is a matter for the Quantity Surveyor: see clause 30.6.1.2.2.

Clause 8.4.3. Alternatively or additionally to his powers under clause 8.4.1 to order removal and under clause 8.4.2 to allow non-conforming work to remain, the Architect may issue such Variation instructions "as are reasonably necessary." Note that:

(1) before issuing such instructions, the Architect must consult the Contractor;
(2) provided that (a) such consultation has taken place; *and* (b) the instructions are "reasonably necessary," the Contractor is nct entitled either to additional remuneration under clause 13 nor to extension of time under clause 25 nor to loss and expense under clause 26.[93]

Clause 8.4.4. This should be read in conjunction with clause 8.3. The Architect can issue instructions to open up or test by one of two routes, namely (a) clause 8.3 and (b) clause 8.3 *via* clause 8.4.4. By route (a), the Architect may issue such instructions without first having discovered non-conforming work. However, if the test does not show non-conforming work, the Contractor is entitled to the cost of such opening up or testing together with loss and expense under clause 26.2.2. By route (b):

(1) non-conforming work must first have been discovered;
(2) the Architect must have had due regard to the Code of Practice[94];
(3) the Architect may issue "such instructions ... as are reasonable in all the circumstances to establish to (his) reasonable satisfaction ... the likelihood or extent ... of any further non-compliance."

Payment. Provided that the instruction is properly issued under clauses 8.4.4 and 8.3, even if the inspection shows that the work conforms to the Contract, the Contractor is entitled neither to the cost of such inspection nor to loss and expense under clause 26. He is however entitled to an extension of time under clause 25.4.5.2. unless the inspection or test showed non-conforming work. If, on the other hand, the instruction does not comply with clause

---

[93] This provision would appear to deal with the problem exemplified by *Simplex* v. *The Borough of St. Pancras* (1958) 14 B.L.R. 80. In that case the Contractor proposed alternative works in substitution for those which had proved defective. The Architect approved the proposal. Edmund Davies J. held that there was thereby a variation for which the Contractors were entitled to additional remuneration.
[94] Reproduced at p. 681.

loss and expense under clause 26. He is however entitled to an extension of time under clause 25.4.5.2. unless the inspection or test showed non-conforming work. If, on the other hand, the instruction does not comply with clause 8.4.4, it is treated as if it were an instruction via route (1). The Contractor has the rights to reimbursement of cost and loss and expense set out above.

Arbitration.   A dispute or difference arising out of clause 8.4 is now listed in clause 41.3.3 as one on which arbitration can be opened before Practical Completion. Clause 41.4 provides that "a decision of the Architect . . . to issue instructions pursuant to clause 8.4.1" is excepted from the Arbitrator's scope of review. It is submitted that the effect of this is that all of the decisions and instructions of the Architect under clause 8.4 are open to review by the Arbitrator save that his decision to order removal of non-conforming work may not be so reviewed. The Arbitrator certainly has power to review the Architect's conclusion as to non-conformity.

Nominated Sub-Contractors.   The powers conferred by clause 8.4 clearly apply to the work of Nominated Sub-Contractors. The opening words of the clause indicate that it applies to "any work" and the Contractor is required under clauses 8.4.2 and 8.4.3 to "consult with any relevant Nominated Sub-Contractor."[95] The instruction is issued to the Contractor who transmits it to the Nominated Sub-Contractor. If the latter fails to comply, the Architect can reduce the sum which he would otherwise direct the Contractor as due under clause 35.13, and, if necessary, advise the Employer of his remedy under clause 4.1.2. The cost so expended can be deducted from monies which would become due to the Contractor and which would otherwise be directed to be paid to the Nominated Sub-Contractor.

Renomination.   A renomination is necessary if the Contractor informs the Architect that in his opinion the Nominated Sub-Contractor has refused or neglected after notice to remove defective work.[96] A new provision for renomination was introduced at clause 35.24.5 by Amendment 5 issued January 1988 in circumstances where the Architect has required "work properly executed" to be taken down under, *inter alia*, clause 8.4 and the Contractor requires the Nominated Sub-Contractor to re-execute the work but this is refused. It is thought that the Employer cannot validly determine the employment of the Contractor under clause 27.1.3 on the basis of the failure or refusal of a Nominated Sub-Contractor to remove defective work. Such a failure or refusal entitles the Contractor to renomination if the procedure of clause 35.24 is followed.[97]

---

[95] See also clauses 35.24.1 and 25.24.5 relating to renomination. In *Fairclough Building* v. *Rhuddlan Borough Council* (1985) 30 B.L.R. 26 at 44 (C.A.), the Court of Appeal accepted without deciding that clause 6(4) of the 1963 Form applied to Nominated Sub-Contract work "although in our view this is not necessarily so."

[96] See clause 35.24.1 and clause 29.1.3 of NSC/4.

[97] *cf. John Jarvis* v. *Rockdale Housing Association* (1986) 36 B.L.R. 48 (C.A.).

Clause 8.5.   This new clause, inserted by Amendment 9 issued in July 1990, provides for the Architect to deal with non-compliance with clause 8.1.3. He may issue such instructions as are reasonably necessary as a result of such non-compliance. These instructions may require a Variation or otherwise (*e.g.* merely to proceed in future in accordance with clause 8.1.3). However, the Contractor is not entitled to additional payment, extension of time or loss and expense for complying with such instruction. By Amendment to clause 41.3.3 a dispute under clause 8.5 may be arbitrated before Practical Completion.

9.   Royalties and patent rights

9.1   All royalties or other sums payable in respect of the supply and use in carrying out the Works as described by or referred to in the Contract Bills of any patented articles, processes or inventions shall be deemed to have been included in the Contract Sum, and the Contractor shall indemnify the Employer from and against all claims, proceedings, damage, costs and expense which may be brought or made against the Employer or to which he may be put by reason of the Contractor infringing or being held to have infringed any patent rights in relation to any such articles, processes or inventions.

9.2   Provided that where in compliance with Architect's/Contract Administrator's instructions the Contractor shall supply and use in carrying out the Works any patented articles, processes or inventions, the Contractor shall not be liable in respect of any infringement or alleged infringement of any patent rights in relation to any such articles, processes or inventions and all royalties damages or other monies which the Contractor may be liable to pay to the persons entitled to such patent rights shall be added to the Contract Sum.

Clause 9: Royalties and patent rights

Clause 9 reproduces clause 7 of the 1963 Form.

10.   Person-in-charge

The Contractor shall constantly keep upon the Works a competent person-in-charge and any instructions given to him by the Architect/the Contract Administrator or directions given to him by the clerk of works in accordance with clause 12 shall be deemed to have been issued to the Contractor.

Clause 10: Person-in-charge

Derivation.   This clause is substantially derived from clause 8 of the 1963 Form. There are two changes of detail. First, the phrase "person-in-charge" is substituted for "foreman-in-charge" in the 1963 Form. Secondly, the person-in-charge is additionally required to receive "directions given to him by the clerk of works in accordance with clause 12."[98]

---

[98] See clause and commentary at p. 514.

General.   The person-in-charge is the Contractor's agent to receive instructions and directions. To avoid confusion he should be named and his role within the Contractor's organisation identified. For the procedure relating to instructions, see clauses 2 and 4 and their commentary.

11. Access for Architect/Contract Administrator to the Works

The Architect/The Contract Administrator and his representatives shall at all reasonable times have access to the Works and to the workshops or other places of the Contractor where work is being prepared for this Contract, and when work is to be so prepared in workshops or other places of a Domestic Sub-Contractor or a Nominated Sub-Contractor the Contractor shall by a term in the sub-contract so far as possible secure a similar right of access to those workshops or places for the Architect/the Contract Administrator and his representatives and shall do all things reasonably necessary to make such right effective. Access in accordance with clause 11 may be subject to such reasonable restrictions of the Contractor or any Domestic Sub-Contractor or any Nominated Sub-Contractor as are necessary to protect any proprietary right of the Contractor or of any Domestic or Nominated Sub-Contractor in the work referred to in clause 11.

Clause 11:   Access for Architect/Contract Administrator to the Works

Derivation.   Clause 11 is substantially the same as clause 9 of the 1963 Form.

Amendments.   The first sentence of clause 11 allowing "such reasonable restrictions ... (on the right of access) ... as are necessary to protect any proprietary right ..." was introduced by Amendment 4 issued in July 1987.

Generally.   "*... a term in the sub-contract ...*"
See, *e.g.* clause 25 of Form NSC/4.

12. Clerk of works

The Employer shall be entitled to appoint a clerk of works whose duty shall be to act solely as inspector on behalf of the Employer under the directions of the Architect/the Contract Administrator and the Contractor shall afford every reasonable facility for the performance of that duty. If any direction is given to the Contractor by the clerk of works the same shall be of no effect unless given in regard to a matter in respect of which the Architect/the Contract Administrator is expressly empowered by the Conditions to issue instructions and unless confirmed in writing by the Architect/the Contract Administrator within 2 working days of such direction being given. If any such direction is so given and confirmed then as from the date of issue of that confirmation it shall be deemed to be an Architect's/a Contract Administrator's instruction.

Clause 12:   Clerk of works.

Derivation.   Clause 12 is substantially the same as clause 10 of the 1963 Form.

Generally.   This clause and these notes should be read with the discussion of the position of clerks of works generally at page 326. The clerk of works is not the Architect's agent to give instructions. For the effect of inspections by the Architect or clerk of works see commentary to clause 2.

". . . solely as inspector . . ."

The import of these words was considered in *Kensington & Chelsea Westminster A.H.A.* v. *Wettern Composites.*[99] The plaintiffs' claim was for negligence by architects and engineers in the construction of a building. Such negligence was established. The Judge also considered that the plaintiffs' clerk of works had been negligent and that this materially contributed to the damage suffered. He applied the general rule that the burden of proof rests on the general employer to shift his prima facie responsibility for the negligence of a servant engaged and paid by him. He considered that there was a strong inference that the clerk of works was acting as servant of the Employer, *inter alia*, because of the words "solely as inspector on behalf of the Employer under the direction of the Architect." There was no evidence to displace the inference that the Employer was vicariously liable for the clerk of works and the plaintiffs' damages were accordingly reduced by 20 per cent.

"If any direction . . ."

This provision recognises that in practice a clerk of works in the course of his inspection makes comments which in ordinary language amount to "directions" and is an attempt to deal with difficulties which can then arise. When such a direction is given, *e.g.* for the removal of materials alleged to be defective, the Contractor, can, if he is so minded, do nothing and ignore the direction unless and until confirmed by the Architect. In practice the prudent Contractor in any case where he considers a direction involves a variation or extra cost for which he wishes to claim will inform the Architect immediately and seek his instructions.

Sanctioning by Architect of Variation.   The Architect has power under clause 13.2 to sanction a Variation made otherwise than pursuant to a direction of the Architect. This power can, it is submitted, be used where the clerk of works in a case of urgency has directed the Contractor to carry out some variation and the Contractor has complied with the direction without awaiting confirmation and it was reasonable in the circumstances for the Contractor to carry out the variation. If the Architect refuses to exercise the power under clause 13.2 the Contractor can go to arbitration and seek an award for the cost of the variation.[1]

---

[99] (1984) 31 B.L.R. 57 also reported at [1985] 1 All E.R. 346 but not on this point.
[1] See clause 41.4.

"... *expressly empowered* ..."

For instructions by the Architect see clauses 2 and 4 and their commentary and in particular the commentary to clause 4.1.1 for the Architect's powers to issue instructions.

13. Variations and provisional sums

13.1 The term "Variation" as used in the Conditions means:

.1 "the alteration or modification of the design, quality or quantity of the Works as shown upon the Contract Drawings and described by or referred to in the Contract Bills; including

.1.1 the addition, omission or substitution of any work,

.1.2 the alteration of the kind or standard of any of the materials or goods to be used in the Works,

.1.3 the removal from the site of any work executed or materials or goods brought thereon by the Contractor for the purposes of the Works other than work materials or goods which are not in accordance with this Contract;

.2 the imposition by the Employer of any obligations or restrictions in regard to the matters set out in clauses 13.1.2.1 to 13.1.2.4 or the addition to or alteration or omission of any such obligations or restrictions so imposed or imposed by the Employer in the Contract Bills in regard to:

.2.1 access to the site or use of any specific parts of the site;

.2.2 limitations of working space;

.2.3 limitations of working hours;

.2.4 the execution or completion of the work in any specific order;

but excludes

.3 nomination of a Sub-Contractor to supply and fix materials or goods or to execute work of which the measured quantities have been set out and priced by the Contractor in the Contract Bills for supply and fixing or execution by the Contractor.

13.2 The Architect/The Contract Administrator may, subject to the Contractor's right of reasonable objection set out in clause 4.1.1, issue instructions requiring a Variation and he may sanction in writing any Variation made by the Contractor otherwise than pursuant to an instruction of the Architect/the Contract Administrator. No Variation required by the Architect/the Contract Administrator or subsequently sanctioned by him shall vitiate this Contract.

13.3 The Architect/The Contract Administrator shall issue instructions in regard to:

.1 the expenditure of provisional sums included in the Contract Bills; [*j*] and

.2 the expenditure of provisional sums included in a Sub-Contract.

13.4 .1.1 Subject to clause 13.4.1.2 all Variations required by the Architect/the Contract Administrator or subsequently sanctioned by him in writing and all work

---

[*j*] *If the Architect/the Contract Administrator nominates a Sub-Contractor or Supplier by any instructions under clause 13.3.1, then the provisions of Part 2 of the Conditions apply to such nominations.*

executed by the Contractor in accordance with instructions by the Architect/the Contract Administrator as to the expenditure of provisional sums which are included in the Contract Bills shall be valued by the Quantity Surveyor and such Valuation (in the Conditions called "the Valuation") shall, unless otherwise agreed by the Employer and the Contractor, be made in accordance with the provisions of clause 13.5.

.1.2 The valuation of Variations to the Sub-Contract Works executed by a Nominated Sub-Contractor in accordance with instructions of the Architect/the Contract Administrator and of all instructions issued under clause 13.3.2 shall (unless otherwise agreed by the Contractor and the Nominated Sub-Contractor concerned with the approval of the Employer) be made in accordance with the relevant provisions of Sub-Contract NSC/4 or NSC/4a as applicable.

.2 Where under the instruction of the Architect/the Contract Administrator as to the expenditure of a provisional sum a prime cost sum arises and the Contractor under clause 35.2 tenders for the work covered by that prime cost sum and that tender is accepted by or on behalf of the Employer, that work shall be valued in accordance with the accepted tender of the Contractor and shall not be included in the Valuation of the instruction of the Architect/the Contract Administrator in regard to the expenditure of the provisional sum.

13.5 .1 To the extent that the Valuation relates to the execution of additional or substituted work which can properly be valued by measurement such work shall be measured and shall be valued in accordance with the following rules:

.1.1 where the work is of similar character to, is executed under similar conditions as, and does not significantly change the quantity of, work set out in the Contract Bills the rates and prices for the work so set out shall determine the Valuation;

.1.2 where the work is of similar character to work set out in the Contract Bills but is not executed under similar conditions thereto and/or significantly changes the quantity thereof, the rates and prices for the work so set out shall be the basis for determining the valuation and the valuation shall include a fair allowance for such difference in conditions and/or quantity;

.1.3 where the work is not of similar character to work set out in the Contract Bills the work shall be valued at fair rates and prices.

.2 To the extent that the Valuation relates to the omission of work set out in the Contract Bills the rates and prices for such work therein set out shall determine the valuation of the work omitted.

.3 In any valuation of work under clauses 13.5.1 and 13.5.2:

.3.1 measurement shall be in accordance with the same principles as those governing the preparation of the Contract Bills as referred to in clause 2.2.2.1;

.3.2 allowance shall be made for any percentage or lump sum adjustments in the Contract Bills; and

.3.3 allowance, where appropriate, shall be made for any addition to or reduction of preliminary items of the type referred to in the Standard Method of Measurement, 6th Edition, Section B (Preliminaries).

.4 To the extent that the Valuation relates to the execution of additional or substituted work which cannot properly be valued by measurement the Valuation shall comprise:

.4.1 the prime cost of such work (calculated in accordance with the "Definition of Prime Cost of Daywork carried out under a Building Contract" issued by the Royal Institution of Chartered Surveyors and the Building Employers Confederation which was current at the Base Date) together with percentage additions to

516

each section of the prime cost at the rates set out by the Contractor in the Contract Bills; or

.4.2   where the work is within the province of any specialist trade and the said Institution and the appropriate [k] body representing the employers in that trade have agreed and issued a definition of prime cost of daywork, the prime cost of such work calculated in accordance with that definition which was current at the Base Date together with percentage additions on the prime cost at the rates set out by the Contractor in the Contract Bills.

Provided that in any case vouchers specifying the time daily spent upon the work, the workmen's names, the plant and the materials employed shall be delivered for verification to the Architect/the Contract Administrator or his authorised representative not later than the end of the week following that in which the work has been executed.

.5   If compliance with any instruction requiring a Variation or any instruction as to the expenditure of a provisional sum substantially changes the conditions under which any other work is executed, then such other work shall be treated as if it had been the subject of an instruction of the Architect/the Contract Administrator requiring a Variation under clause 13.2 which shall be valued in accordance with the provisions of clause 13.

.6   To the extent that the Valuation does not relate to the execution of additional or substituted work or the omission of work or to the extent that the valuation of any work or liabilities directly associated with a Variation cannot reasonably be effected in the Valuation by the application of clauses 13.5.1 to .5 a fair valuation thereof shall be made.

Provided that no allowance shall be made under clause 13.5 for any effect upon the regular progress of the Works or for any other direct loss and/or expense for which the Contractor would be reimbursed by payment under any other provision in the Conditions.

3.6   Where it is necessary to measure work for the purpose of the Valuation the Quantity Surveyor shall give to the Contractor an opportunity of being present at the time of such measurement and of taking such notes and measurements as the Contractor may require.

3.7   Effect shall be given to a Valuation under clause 13.5 by addition to or deduction from the Contract Sum.

Clause 13: Variations and provisional sums

Derivation.   Clause 13 is generally derived from clause 11 of the 1963 Form, but it has been completely redrafted and there are a number of significant changes of substance. Clause 13.1.1 is derived from clause 11(2). Clause 13.1.2 introduces a new class of variation and the text of clause 13.1.3 is new. Clause 13.2 reproduces clause 11(1). Clause 13.3 is derived in part from clause 11(3), but the former reference to Prime Cost Sums is omitted, nomination of Sub-Contractors and Suppliers being dealt with in Part 2 of the 1980 contract.

---

[k] *There are three Definitions to which clause 13.5.4.2 refers namely those agreed between the Royal Institution and the Electrical Contractors Association, the Royal Institution and the Electrical Contractors Association of Scotland and the Royal Institution and the Heating and Ventilating Contractors Association.*

Clauses 13.4 and 13.5 are derived from clause 11(4), but they are redrafted and expanded. Clause 13.6 is an isolated provision extracted in substance from clause 11(4). Clause 13.7 (read with clause 3) reproduces the substance of clause 11(5). It is important to note that clause 11(6) of the 1963 Form, which provided for direct loss and/or expense caused by Variations, no longer appears in the new clause 13. It has been transferred to the new clause 26 (see clause 26.2.7) and it is now made clear that the claim only arises where the regular progress of the Works is affected. Cases arising under the former clause 11(6) are discussed, where relevant, in the context of clause 26.

Amendments.   Clauses 13.1.2, 13.2, 13.4 and 13.5.5 were redrafted by Amendment 4 issued in July 1987. Except for the amendment to clause 13.1.2 discussed below, these amendments are drafting amendments only. Amendment 7 issued July 1988 made important changes to clauses 13.4 and 13.5, including the insertion of new sub-clauses 13.5.1.4 and 13.5.1.5. These are discussed below.

Scheme of clause.   The clause generally provides for: the definition of the term Variation (clause 13.1); the ordering or sanctioning of Variations (clause 13.2); instructions in regard to provisional sums (clause 13.3); the Valuation of Variations and provisional sum work (clause 13.4); rules for Valuation (clause 13.5); giving effect to such Valuations (clause 13.7).

Without Quantities Version.   For the general position, see commentary to Articles of Agreement. For the Schedule of Rates which is the basic document for pricing Variations, see clause 5.3.1.3 observing that it has to be furnished by the Contractor so soon as is possible after the execution of the Contract. In practice it is prudent to insist upon its production before the execution of the Contract so that the Employer may know, before signing the Contract, the rates proposed to be charged for Variations. The definition of the term "Variation" is not easy to follow. It seems to say that if the Contractor has to do something which is not shown both on the Drawings and described by or referred to in the Specification, then it is a Variation. Compare this with clause 14.1 which states that the quality and quantity of the work included in the Contract Sum is deemed to be that which is shown on the Drawings or described in the Specification. This suggests that the Contractor is not entitled to extra payment if the work appears in either document, and it is submitted that this is the intention and that clause 2.2.2 which provides for correction of errors in the Drawings and/or Specification should be read in this way.

Clause 13.1.   *"The term 'Variation' ..."*
This sub-clause contains the definition of Variation. For the Contract Drawings and the Contract Bills, see clause 2.1. For the kind or standard of materials or goods, see clause 8.1.1. For removal from the site of work,

materials or goods, see clause 8.4.1. For the effect of authority to depart from the specified method of construction to assist the Contractor, see page 89.

Clause 13.1.2. This clause of the 1980 Form introduced a new class of Variation. The Architect may now issue instructions either imposing obligations or restrictions or changing obligations or restrictions imposed in the Contract Bills in regard to access to or use of the site, limitations of working space or working hours and the execution or completion of the work in any specific order. The power to impose such obligations or restrictions where none is mentioned in the Contract Bills was conferred by Amendment 4 issued in July 1987. Under the 1963 Contract some at least of these changes could not, it is thought, be made on behalf of the Employer within the terms of the contract, although limitation of working hours and delay in the execution or completion of work could be achieved by means of a postponement instruction under clause 21(2).[2] The Contractor can make "reasonable objection" to such instruction (see commentary to clause 4). The new provisions are useful to enable employers to accommodate practical difficulties without being in breach of contract and to enable contractors to be paid for what in practice may be unavoidable restrictions. Clause 13 does not deal specifically with the valuation of this class of Variation, but it can be accommodated, if nowhere else, by clauses 13.5.5, 13.5.6 and 26.2.7.

Clause 13.1.3. This exclusion should be read with clause 35, where the ambit of nomination is somewhat enlarged.

Clause 13.2.[3] "... *subject to the Contractor's right of reasonable objection set out in clause 4.1.1 ...*"
This is an amendment inserted by Amendment 4 issued in July 1987. This simply makes clear what is in any event the case under clause 4.1.1.

Clause 13.2. "... *he may sanction in writing any Variation ...*"
For instructions generally, see clauses 2 and 4 and their commentary, particularly at page 494. These words give the Architect a discretion to sanction a Variation although the ordinary procedure has not been followed and even, apparently, where there was no order or request at all for the Variation to be carried out.[4] There is no express guidance as to the exercise of the discretion. It is submitted that the test is whether in all the circumstances it is reasonable to exercise it. Matters which might be taken into account include the interests of each of the parties, the reason why the Variation was carried out, the nature and extent of the Variation and the reason why the ordinary

---

[2] See *Harrison* v. *Leeds* (1980) 14 B.L.R. 118.
[3] Clause 13.2. For consideration of the relationship between the Contractor's obligation to insure and his entitlement to certain Variation instructions, see *Higgs & Hill* v. *University of London* (1983) 24 B.L.R. 139.
[4] See "Work done without request" at p. 89.

procedure was not followed.[5] The power to sanction is not limited to claims for extra payment by the Contractor but includes an unauthorised departure from the contract work not involving extra cost, and omissions which result in a reduction of the Contract Sum.[6] The Architect's discretion is subject to arbitration (see clause 41).

Deemed Variation under clause 2.2.2.2.[7]   This requires, it is thought, neither an instruction nor a sanctioning in writing. But note the Contractor's duty to give notice upon finding a discrepancy between the Contract Drawings and the Contract Bills (clause 2.3 and its commentary), breach of which makes him liable, it is submitted, for any loss thereby suffered, *e.g.* because it deprives the Architect of the opportunity to require a Variation minimising the financial result of the discrepancy.

Clause 13.2.   *"No Variation . . . shall vitiate this Contract."*
It is submitted that the intention is that the ordering of substantial Variations does not entitle the Contractor either to rescind the contract and refuse to do further work or to have the completed work measured and paid for on a *quantum merit* and not in accordance with the terms of the contract.[8] Despite the width of the words, it is submitted that there must be some limit to the nature and extent of the Variations which can be ordered.[9] For the pricing of the Variations not of similar character or not executed under similar conditions to work in the Contract Bills, see clauses 13.5.1.2 and 13.5.1.3. For the position where omissions substantially vary the Conditions under which any remaining items of work are carried out, see clause 13.5.5.

Variations after Practical Completion.   It is submitted that the Architect cannot issue instructions requiring a Variation after Practical Completion,[10] so that if thereafter the Employer wishes them to be executed, they should be the subject of a separate agreement.

Clause 13.3.   Clause 13.3 applies only to provisional sums. The awkwardly placed provisions in clause 11(3) or the 1963 Form about Prime Cost Sums are removed, nomination being dealt with in Part 2 of the 1980 Form. The term "provisional sum" is now defined at clause 1.3 of the 1980 Form, such

---

[5] For variations ordered by the Employer personally, see p. 496.
[6] See *H. Fairweather & Co.* v. *Wandsworth* (1987) 39 B.L.R. 106 at 107, 111, 120–123.
[7] See p. 490.
[8] Substantially similar words have been judicially considered but the points at issue and the wording of the contracts were such as to afford but small assistance in the construction of the Standard Form of Building Contract. See *Dodd* v. *Churton* [1897] 1 Q.B. 562 (C.A.); *Wells* v. *Army & Navy Co-op. Society* (1902) 86 L.J. 764 referred to at p. 231. For "*quantum meruit,*" see p. 78.
[9] See commentary to clauses 2 and 4, in particular "Reasonableness of instructions" at p. 496.
[10] The Works are complete and the procedure for final adjustment of the Contract Sum begins, see clause 17.1 and 30.6.

definition having been inserted by Amendment 7 issued in July 1988. Reference should be made to the footnotes to clause 1.3 which set out the definitions of "a provisional sum for defined work" and "a provisional sum for undefined work" in the Standard Method of Measurement 7th edition. A provisional sum included in the Contract Bills can still be converted into a Prime Cost Sum to enable the Architect to make a nomination (see clauses 35.1.2 and 36.1.1.2). Clause 13.3.2 is a clause enabling the Architect to issue instructions in regard to the expenditure of provisional sums included in a Nominated Sub-Contract. This power could not be found explicitly in the 1963 Contract, although it is a power which Architects often purported to exercise. Careful reference to clauses 35.1.2 and 36.1.1.2 shows that the power to convert a provisional sum into a Prime Cost Sum does not extend to provisional sums included in a Nominated Sub-Contract.

Clause 13.4. *Amendments*

This clause was redrafted into two sub-clauses by Amendment 4 issued in July 1987. The effect of Amendment 7 issued in July 1988 is to extend the ambit of the Valuation rules under clause 13.5 to the execution of work for which an Approximate Quantity is included in the Contract Bills. The Architect is not required to give a specific instruction in regard to the execution of such work.

Clause 13.4. *"the Valuation"*

In *Burden Ltd.* v. *Swansea Corporation*[11] Lord Radcliffe said, referring to a Contract not materially different from the Standard Form:

"Generally speaking, I regard the surveyor as the person charged with the duty of valuing the contractors' work and advising the architect as to the allowance of their claims for payment, interim and final. But I do not see anything in the contract which suggests the Architect is bound to accept the surveyor's opinions or valuations when he exercises his own function of certifying sums for payment. At that point the Architect remains master in his own field."

The Surveyor must, subject to any special agreement, value in accordance with the rules of clause 13.5. It is submitted that the Architect must give proper consideration to such a valuation.

Clause 13.4. *". . . unless otherwise agreed . . ."*

The agreement can, it is submitted, have been made or be made, at any time. If a price is quoted by the Contractor, it is desirable to agree whether or not it includes any claim for loss or expense under clause 26.1 and is otherwise inclusive of all "claims." Under clause 13.4.1.1 any such agreement must be made by the Employer and the Contractor. Under clause 13.4.1.2 any such

---

[11] [1957] 1 W.L.R. 1167 at 1173 (H.L.).

agreement is to be made by the Contractor and the Nominated Sub-Contractor concerned with the approval of the Employer.

Pricing errors in Contract Bills.   Opportunity for errors can arise in writing down the unit price, the extension of that price and the casting up and carrying forward of the extended prices. Unless there is a case for rectification of prices,[12] both parties are bound by these errors in the carrying out of the original contract work.[13] But must the errors be taken into account in pricing Variations where there was no express agreement to do so operating as an additional term of the Contract, and the parties cannot agree upon a special method under the provisions of the clause? Consider the following: the Contractor in error inserts a unit price of £50 instead of £500 and the total of his prices (excluding preliminary items, prime cost and provisional sums) is stated to be £10,000. If he had written down £500, the total would have been £10,450. If five further units of the item are required by way of Variation, must he carry them out for five times £50 thus multiplying the effect of his error? It is thought that, having regard to clause 14.2, the Contractor is bound by his £50 for the purposes of valuation under clauses 13.5.1.1 and 13.5.1.2, but that the Employer is not entitled to say that prices for Variations shall be deemed to be reduced by 45/1045.[14] Further, it is submitted, the Contractor cannot recover the difference between £50 and his intended price of £500 per unit as "loss or expense" under clause 26.1. Conversely, if the Contractor had written £500 when he intended £50 he obtains the benefit of his error.

Clause 13.4.1.2.   This is new to the 1980 Form and provides for the valuation of Nominated Sub-Contract Variations and work executed pursuant to provisional sums included in a Nominated Sub-Contract. The 1963 contract did not contain equivalent explicit provisions, although the effect of clause 30(5)(c) of the 1963 Form was probably in substance the same.[15]

Clause 13.5.1.   This sub-clause was significantly amended by Amendment 7 issued in July 1988. The effect of the amendment is that Rules 13.5.1.1 to 13.5.1.3 refer to the Valuation of additional or substituted work. The additional Rules 13.5.1.4 and 13.5.1.5 refer to the Valuation of work for which an Approximate Quantity is included in the Contract Bills where the work is not altered or modified other than in quantity. The first consideration for Valuation of additional or substituted work is, as in the 1963 Form, whether the work is of a similar character to and executed under similar conditions as work

---

[12] For rectification, see p. 266; see also the words of clause 14.2.
[13] See clause 14 but the principle would, as a matter of construction apply, it is submitted, even without clause 14.2. Note that the provision for correction in clause 2.2.2.2 is for items and not prices.
[14] See discussion at p. 86.
[15] See Amendment 7 issued July 1988 for the Nominated Sub-Contracts NSC/4 and NSC/4A for the rules for the valuation of the work referred to in clause 13.4.1.2.

set out in the Contract Bills. These are alternative considerations. It is sufficient to establish either to obtain the Valuation. Similar conditions might, it is suggested, include physical site conditions such as wet compared with dry, high compared with low, confined space compared with ample working space and winter working compared with summer working where the Contract Documents show that the Bill prices were based on summer working. The 1980 Form introduces a new explicit consideration of whether a Variation significantly changes the quantity of the work.

Clause 13.5.3.   This provides explicitly that measurement shall, subject to clause 2.2.2.1, be in accordance with the principles of the Standard Method of Measurement, that allowance shall be made for a percentage or lump sum adjustment and that an appropriate allowance shall be made for preliminaries. The proviso to clause 13.5.3.3 was introduced by Amendment 7 issued July 1988. This is to give contractual effect to the statement in the 7th edition of the Standard Method of Measurement that where a provisional sum for defined work is given in the Contract Bills the Contractor will be "deemed to have made due allowance in ... pricing preliminaries." If however a provisional sum for defined work is the subject of a Variation instruction under clause 13.2 or is corrected under clause 2.2.2.2 and the correction in consequence is treated as if it were a Variation, the valuation of that Variation may include an allowance, where appropriate, for any addition to or reduction of preliminary items.

Clause 13.5.5.   This provides for other Contract Work to be treated for Valuation purposes as if it were varied work, if compliance with a Variation instruction or an instruction as to the expenditure of a provisional sum or the execution of work for which an approximate quantity is included in the Contract Bills substantially changes the conditions under which the work is executed. The references to defined and undefined work and to approximate quantity were introduced by Amendment 7 issued July 1988.[16]

14.   Contract Sum

14.1   The quality and quantity of the work included in the Contract Sum shall be deemed to be that which is set out in the Contract Bills.

14.2   The Contract Sum shall not be adjusted or altered in any way whatsoever otherwise than in accordance with the express provisions of the Conditions, and subject to clause 2.2.2.2 any error whether of arithmetic or not in the computation of the Contract Sum shall be deemed to have been accepted by the parties hereto.

---

[16] As to clause 13.1.1.3, note the provisions of clause 8.4.3 in relation to instructions issued where work, materials or goods are not in accordance with the contract.

Clause 14: Contract Sum

Derivation. Clause 14.1 reproduces the first words of clause 12 of the 1963 Form. The balance of that clause has been transferred to clause 2.2 of the 1980 Form. Clause 14.2 substantially reproduces clause 13 of the 1963 Form.

Clause 14.1. *"The quality and quantity . . ."*
  This clause defines the work for which the Contract Sum is payable. On the importance of these words in defining the Contractor's obligation, see the commentary to the Articles of Agreement, in particular, as to the nature of extra work.[17] For the kinds and standards of materials, goods and workmanship, see clause 8.1. For the Without Quantities Version see commentary to Articles of Agreement and to clause 13. Clause 14.1 should be read in conjunction with clause 2.2.2.2 which provides for the correction of errors in items but not prices in the Contract Bills.

Clause 14.2. *"The Contract Sum shall not be adjusted . . ."*
  Unless there is a case for the equitable remedy of rectification,[18] the parties are bound by any errors incorporated into the Contract Sum. For the question whether pricing errors affect the pricing of variations, see commentary to clause 13. For the correction of items (not prices) in the Contract Bills, see clause 2.2.2 and its commentary.

15. Value added tax—supplemental provisions

15.1 In clause 15 and in the supplemental provisions pursuant hereto (hereinafter called the "VAT Agreement") "tax" means the value added tax introduced by the Finance Act 1972 which is under the care and management of the Commissioners of Customs and Excise (hereinafter and in the VAT Agreement called "the Commissioners").

15.2 Any reference in the Conditions to "Contract Sum" shall be regarded as such Sum exclusive of any tax and recovery by the Contractor from the Employer of tax properly chargeable by the Commissioners on the Contractor under or by virtue of the Finance Act 1972 or any amendment or re-enactment thereof on the supply of goods and services under this Contract shall be under the provisions of clause 15 and of the VAT Agreement.

15.3 To the extent that after the Base Date the supply of goods and services to the Employer becomes exempt from the tax there shall be paid to the Contractor an amount equal to the loss of credit (input tax) on the supply to the Contractor of goods and services which contribute exclusively to the Works.

---

[17] On p. 477.
[18] See p. 266.

Clause 15: Value added tax—supplemental provisions

Derivation. Clause 15 is substantially the same as clause 13A of the 1963 Form.

Generally. In the 1980 Form, Value Added Tax is dealt with by means of supplemental provisions substantially similar to the former Supplemental Agreement under the 1963 Form. The parties are not, however, required to execute a separate agreement. For the supplemental provisions, see page 684.

16. **Materials and goods unfixed or off-site**

16.1 Unfixed materials and goods delivered to, placed on or adjacent to the Works and intended therefor shall not be removed except for use upon the Works unless the Architect/the Contract Administrator has consented in writing to such removal which consent shall not be unreasonably withheld. Where the value of any such materials or goods has in accordance with clause 30.2 been included in any Interim Certificate under which the amount properly due to the Contractor has been paid by the Employer, such materials and goods shall become the property of the Employer, but, subject to clause 22B or 22C (if applicable), the Contractor shall remain responsible for loss or damage to the same.

16.2 Where the value of any materials or goods intended for the Works and stored off-site has in accordance with clause 30.3 been included in any Interim Certificate under which the amount properly due to the Contractor has been paid by the Employer, such materials and goods shall become the property of the Employer and thereafter the Contractor shall not, except for use upon the Works, remove or cause or permit the same to be moved or removed from the premises where they are, but the Contractor shall nevertheless be responsible for any loss thereof or damage thereto and for the cost of storage, handling and insurance of the same until such time as they are delivered to and placed on or adjacent to the Works whereupon the provisions of clause 16.1 (except the words "Where the value" to the words "the property of the Employer, but,") shall apply thereto.

Clause 16: Materials and goods unfixed or off-site

Derivation. Clause 16 is substantially the same as clause 14 of the 1963 Form.

Generally. This clause is of a kind sometimes termed a "vesting clause"[19] and is of particular importance in the event of the Contractor's default or insolvency.[20]

---

[19] For ownership of materials and vesting clauses generally, see pp. 241 *et seq.*
[20] For insolvency generally, see p. 376 and for default and insolvency of the Contractor, see p. 377.

Clause 16.1. *"Unfixed materials ... shall not be removed ..."*

A lien[21] is created in favour of the Employer even before certification under clause 30.2. The effect of these words in the 1963 Form was considered in the Scottish case of *Archivent* v. *Strathclyde Regional Council*.[22] The plaintiffs sold materials to Main Contractors. The contract of sale contained an effective retention of title clause. The value of the materials was contained in an Interim Certificate which was duly paid by the defendant employers. The Main Contractors became insolvent and did not pay the plaintiffs. The court held that the Main Contractors had conferred a good title on the employers by virtue of section 25(1) of the Sale of Goods Act 1979. In so holding the court rejected an argument advanced by the plaintiffs that, by virtue of clause 14(1) of the 1963 Form, the Main Contractors never came into possession of the materials but always held them for the Employers. The proper analysis of the clause was held to be that the Main Contractors were in possession of the materials prior to delivering them to the Employers. The restriction upon removal in the clause was not inconsistent with possession. It is submitted that this analysis is correct and likely to be followed by an English court.

Passing of property. The property in materials built into the works normally passes to the owner of the land whether paid for or not.[23] The clear intention of this clause is that the property in materials and goods should pass to the Employer upon payment of the Certificate which includes the value of such materials and goods. However, this intention must be set against the general principle *"Nemo dat quod non habet."* The point was considered in *Dawber Williamson* v. *Humberside County Council*.[24] The plaintiffs were Sub-Contractors to supply and fix roof covering under the pre-1980 Non-Nominated Standard Form of Sub-Contract. Clause 1 of the Sub-Contract provided that the plaintiffs were deemed to have notice of all provisions of the Main Contract (which was in the 1963 Form). However, the Sub-Contract made no provision for the passing of property in unfixed materials. The plaintiffs delivered materials to site and they were certified and paid by the defendant employers. The main contractors went into liquidation without paying the plaintiffs. It was held that title in the materials had not passed to the main contractors by reason of any provisions in the Sub-Contract and that clause 1(1) of the Sub-Contract did not operate to make clause 14 of the Main Contract part of the Sub-Contract.

It followed that clause 14(1) of the Main Contract was ineffective to transfer title to the defendant employers because it would only transfer property in the materials if the Main Contractors had a good title to them. The particular problem encountered in *Dawber Williamson* has now been dealt with by an amendment to clause 19.4 of the 1980 Form (see below) in relation to Domestic

---

[21] For meaning see p. 379.
[22] (1984) 27 B.L.R. 98.
[23] See generally "Retention of title clauses" at p. 242.
[24] (1979) 14 B.L.R. 70.

Sub-Contracts.[25] However, the general principle remains valid, namely that property will only pass under clause 16.1 in circumstances where the Contractor himself has acquired a good title either by payment or by a provision in the Sub-Contract or by reliance upon provisions of the Sale of Goods Act 1979 where relevant.

Passing of risk.   Both before and after certification the risk remains with the Contractor.

Clause 16.2.   *"... in accordance with clause 30.3 ..."*
The Architect is bound to certify for materials and goods properly and not prematurely delivered to or adjacent to the Works (clause 30.2.1.2). He has a discretion whether to certify for materials and goods before delivery (clause 30.3). For a discussion of the problems arising from certification of goods and materials not on the site and of the provisions of clause 30.3, see commentary to clause 30 at page 610.

17.   Practical Completion and Defects Liability

17.1   When in the opinion of the Architect/the Contract Administrator Practical Completion of the Works is achieved, he shall forthwith issue a certificate to that effect and Practical Completion of the Works shall be deemed for all the purposes of this Contract to have taken place on the day named in such certificate.

17.2   Any defects, shrinkages or other faults which shall appear within the Defects Liability Period and which are due to materials or workmanship not in accordance with this Contract or to frost occurring before Practical Completion of the Works, shall be specified by the Architect/the Contract Administrator in a schedule of defects which he shall deliver to the Contractor as an instruction of the Architect/the Contract Administrator not later than 14 days after the expiration of the said Defects Liability Period, and within a reasonable time after receipt of such schedule the defects, shrinkages, and other faults therein specified shall be made good by the Contractor at no cost to the Employer unless the Architect/the Contract Administrator with the consent of the Employer shall otherwise instruct; and if the Architect/the Contract Administrator does so otherwise instruct then an appropriate deduction in respect of any such defects, shrinkages or other faults not made good shall be made from the Contract Sum.

17.3   Notwithstanding clause 17.2 the Architect/the Contract Administrator may whenever he considers it necessary so to do, issue instructions requiring any defect, shrinkage or other fault which shall appear within the Defects Liability Period and which is due to materials or workmanship not in accordance with this Contract or to frost occurring before Practical Completion of the Works, to be made good, and the Contractor shall within a reasonable time after receipt of such instructions comply with the same and at no cost to the Employer unless the Architect/the Contract Administrator with the consent of the Employer shall otherwise instruct; and if the Architect/the Contract

---

[25] See also new clauses 21.2.4.1–21.2.4.4 inserted into NSC/4 by Amendment 2 issued January 1984, discussed at p. 755.

Administrator does so otherwise instruct then an appropriate deduction in respect of any such defects, shrinkages or other faults not made good shall be made from the Contract Sum. Provided that no such instructions shall be issued after delivery of a schedule of defects or after 14 days from the expiration of the Defects Liability Period.

17.4 When in the opinion of the Architect/the Contract Administrator any defects, shrinkages or other faults which he may have required to be made good under clauses 17.2 and 17.3 shall have been made good he shall issue a certificate to that effect, and completion of making good defects shall be deemed for all the purposes of this Contract to have taken place on the day named in such certificate (the "Certificate of Completion of Making Good Defects").

17.5 In no case shall the Contractor be required to make good at his own cost any damage by frost which may appear after Practical Completion, unless the Architect/the Contract Administrator shall certify that such damage is due to injury which took place before Practical Completion.

Clause 17: Practical Completion and Defects Liability

Derivation.　Clause 17 is derived from clause 15 of the 1963 Form.

Amendments.　Clauses 17.2 and 17.3 were redrafted by Amendment 4 issued in July 1987. These amendments, which are for clarification, are discussed below.

Scheme of clause.　The clause provides for a Certificate of Practical Completion (clause 17.1), a schedule of defects (clause 17.2), instructions requiring the making good of particular defects (clause 17.3), a Certificate of Completion of Making Good Defects (clause 17.4) and damage by frost (clause 17.5).

For the Contractor's obligations generally, see clause 2. For standards of materials, goods and workmanship, see clause 8.1. For the way in which the provisions of this clause fit into the Final Account procedure, see commentary to clause 30. For a discussion of defects clauses generally, see page 245.

Clause 17.1.　*"When ... Practical Completion of the Works is achieved ..."*
Practical Completion is perhaps easier to recognise than to define. No clear answer emerges from the authorities as to the meaning of the term. The authorities are themselves limited to dicta in two decisions of the House of Lords[26] and one decision at first instance.[27] It is submitted that the following is the correct analysis:

(1) The Works can be practically complete notwithstanding that there are latent defects;

---

[26] *Jarvis & Sons* v. *Westminster Corporation* [1970] 1 W.L.R. 637 at 646, Viscount Dilhorne; *P. & M. Kaye* v. *Hosier & Dickinson* [1972] 1 W.L.R. 146 at 165, Lord Diplock.
[27] *H. W. Nevill (Sunblest)* v. *William Press* (1981) 20 B.L.R. 78.

(2) A Certificate of Practical Completion may not be issued if there are patent defects. The Defects Liability Period is provided in order to enable defects not apparent at the date of Practical Completion to be remedied.[28]

(3) Practical Completion means the completion of all the construction work that has to be done.[29]

(4) However, the Architect is given a discretion under clause 17.1 to certify Practical Completion where there are very minor items of work left incomplete, on *"de minimis"* principles.[30]

This discretion of the Architect is to be exercised with caution. He should obtain a written acknowledgement from the Contractor of the items of work left incomplete and an undertaking to complete them. The Architect should satisfy himself that the retention money will cover both the cost of completing such items and the likely cost of attending to remedial works. He should also be satisfied that there is no likelihood of the Employer suffering loss due to interference with his use of the Works while the items are completed. See commentary to clause 23 for the relationship of Practical Completion to liability for liquidated damages.

Clause 17.1. *"... a certificate to that effect ..."*

No particular form is specified, but the certificate should be clear and definite. The R.I.B.A. makes available a common form certificate for use under this clause.

Clause 17.1. *"... for all the purposes of this Contract ..."*

These are to fix the dates: for the commencement of the Defects Liability Period (clauses 17.2, 17.3 and Appendix), upon which the Employer may assign the right to bring proceedings in his name (clause 19.1.2), for the commencement of the Contractor's liability for damage to the Works (clause 20.3), for the release of the obligation to insure under clause 22, for the release of the first moiety of retention (clause 30.4.1.2 read with clause 17), for the release of the whole retention (clause 30.4.1.3 read with clause 17.4) and for the commencement of the period of the final adjustment of the Contract Sum under clause 30.6.

Clause 17.2. *"... defects, shrinkages or other faults ..."*

Excluding frost damage, which is dealt with separately below, defects, including shrinkage or other faults, must be due to "materials or workmanship not in accordance with this Contract...." Thus the failure of the Architect's design of the Works,[31] or the unsuitability for their purpose of goods and

---

[28] See *Jarvis & Sons* v. *Westminster Corporation* [1970] 1 W.L.R. 637 at 646–647 and *H. W. Nevill (Sunblest)* v. *William Press* (1981) 20 B.L.R. 78 at 87.

[29] See *Jarvis & Sons* v. *Westminster Corporation* [1970] 1 W.L.R. 637 at 646.

[30] *H. W. Nevill (Sunblest)* v. *William Press* (1981) 20 B.L.R. 78 at 87.

[31] See p. 476 for a discussion of the extent of the Contractor's design responsibility.

materials which are of good quality and exactly described in the Contract Bills or as required by an instruction of, or sanctioned in writing by the Architect,[32] are not defects. For materials or goods not "procurable," see clause 8.1.1. For defects in the work of Nominated Sub-Contractors and the goods of Nominated Suppliers, see commentary to clauses 35 and 36. For limitation of the Contractor's liability where final payment is made to a Nominated Sub-Contractor, see clause 35.18. For the effect, if any, of price see commentary to clause 2. For the effect of inspections of the Architect or the clerk of works, see commentary to clause 2. There is no reference to "goods" in this clause although there is such a reference elsewhere (*e.g.* clause 8). It is submitted that "materials" here is used to include goods.[33] Either party can, subject to clauses 30.8 and 30.9, challenge the Architect's decisions on what is or is not a defect, see clause 41.

Clause 17.2. "... *defects ... which shall appear* ..."
These words support the construction of the phrase Practical Completion set out above, namely that a certificate of Practical Completion may not be issued where there are patent defects. Should a certificate nonetheless be issued, it is submitted that defects outstanding at the date of Practical Completion could be dealt with within clause 17. The Contractor who had taken the benefit of the first moiety of retention would be estopped from denying that clause 17 applied to such defects.

Clause 17.2. "... *frost* ..."
The Contractor is liable to make good at his own cost damage by frost which appears within the Defects Liability Period but only if the Architect certifies that such damage is due to injury which took place before Practical Completion (clause 17.5). It is thought that an example of the Contractor's liability might arise where concrete is injured by frost while being laid, but the damage does not appear until the Defects Liability Period and the Architect gives his certificate under clause 17.5.

Clause 17.2. "... *a schedule of defects* ..."
Compare clause 17.3 which is supplementary to clause 17.2 and which is in substantially similar terms save that it empowers the Architect to issue instructions requiring the making good of defects appearing within the Defects Liability Period "whenever he considers it necessary." Thus, very broadly, clause 17.3 provides for instructions for making good defects from time to time during the Defects Liability Period and clause 17.2 for a schedule of defects at the end of the period.

---

[32] See clauses 2, 4, 8.1, 12 and 13. See also *Young & Marten Ltd.* v. *McManus Childs Ltd.* [1969] 1 A.C. 454 (H.L.); *Gloucestershire County Council* v. *Richardson* [1969] 1 A.C. 480 (H.L.); *Cotton* v. *Wallis* [1955] 1 W.L.R. 1168 (C.A.).
[33] Under the Sale of Goods Act 1979, "goods" includes materials.

Clause 17.2. "*... at no cost to the Employer ... deduction ... from the Contract Sum.*"

These words were inserted by Amendment 4 issued July 1987. The former wording suggested that the Architect might issue an instruction resulting in the Employer having to bear the cost of the Contractor making good his own defects. The new wording makes it clear that there are two alternatives only, *viz*: either the Contractor makes good the defects at no cost to the Employer, or the Architect instructs that the defects should not be made good, but an appropriate deduction for such defects is made from the Contract Sum.

Clause 17.3. "*... at no cost to the Employer ... deduction ... from the Contract Sum.*"

See commentary to clause 17.2 above. These words were inserted by Amendment 4 issued July 1987.

Clause 17.4. "*When ... defects ... shall have been made good he shall issue a certificate to that effect ...*"

Contractual remedies for breach. The second half of the retention is not released until this certificate is given (clause 30.4.1.3). The issue of the Final Certificate, with the protection it affords the Contractor (see clause 30.9.1), may be delayed by the absence of this certificate (clause 30.8). For breach of an instruction under clause 17.3, a notice under clause 4.1.2 may be given and upon non-compliance others can be employed to do the work necessary and the cost deducted from the retention. It is not clear whether the power of determination under clause 27.1.3 can be exercised after Practical Completion, but having regard to the other remedies available, it is unlikely, in ordinary circumstances, to be necessary to attempt such a serious step.

Damages for breach. Clause 17 imposes a liability and gives a right to make good defects.[34] It does not exclude a claim for damages in respect of those breaches. It is no more than a simple mechanism for dealing with such breaches, but is not to be construed as depriving the injured party of his other rights. Such damages include damage for consequential loss.[35] However, it is thought that failure by the Employer/Architect to make use of the provisions of the clause may put the Employer at some risk as to costs and may affect the amount of damages recoverable.[36] Thus insofar as the diminution in value of the Works exceeds the cost of rectification, the Employer cannot recover such excess if he has not given the Contractor an opportunity of remedying the defects under clause 17.[37] Conversely, if the Contractor fails to comply with the

---

[34] *Kaye (P. & M.)* v. *Hosier & Dickinson* [1972] 1 W.L.R. 147 at 166 (H.L.); see generally "Alternative claim in damages" at p. 247.
[35] *H. W. Nevill (Sunblest)* v. *William Press & Son* (1981) 20 B.L.R. 78.
[36] For damages generally see Chap. 8.
[37] *Kaye (P. & M.)* v. *Hosier & Dickinson* [1972] 1 W.L.R. 147 at 163.

Architect's requirements, the Employer can recover the cost of remedying defects though such cost is greater than the diminution in value of such unremedied defects.[38]

Effect of the certificate.   The Certificate of Completion of Making Good Defects is some, but not conclusive, evidence of the completion of the Works in accordance with the Contract and of the making good of defects (clause 30.10). For the effect of the Final Certificate see clause 30.9 and its commentary.

Irremediable Breach.   The Architect may include a defect in an instruction or the schedule, but then find on representation by the Contractor that it cannot be remedied, or cannot be remedied except at unreasonable cost. In such circumstances he has a discretion under clauses 17.2 and 17.3 to issue the certificate and to make an appropriate deduction in the amount certified for payment, the deduction being the amount by which the Works are reduced in value by reason of the unremedied defect. However, if approval of the quality of any materials or the standards of any workmanship is a matter for his opinion, he should not issue a Final Certificate (see clauses 2.1 and 30.9 and their commentary).

Defects after certificate.   If defects appear after the Certificate of Completion of Making Good Defects is issued under clause 17.4, the Architect has no power to issue any further instructions but can adjust any further certificate. The amount of the adjustment is, it is submitted, assessed by the cost of rectification or, where the breach is irremediable, the diminution in value of the Works. It should not, it is submitted, include any deduction for consequential loss, this being the subject matter of a claim for damages by the Employer. Insofar as such defects, as they appear, evidence a breach of contract by the Contractor, the usual rules as to damages, including those relating to mitigation, apply so that ordinarily the Employer should give the Contractor an opportunity of remedying the defects if it is reasonable to do so. For defects appearing after the issue of the Final Certificate, see clause 30 and its commentary.

Clause 17.4.   *"... for all the purposes of this Contract ..."*
See clause 30.4.1.3 for the release of second half of retention and clause 30.8 for timing of issue of Final Certificate.

18.   Partial possession by Employer

18.1   If at any time or times before the date of issue by the Architect/the Contract Administrator of the certificate of Practical Completion the Employer wishes to take

---

[38] *Ibid.*

possession of any part or parts of the Works and the consent of the Contractor (which consent shall not be unreasonably withheld) has been obtained, then notwithstanding anything expressed or implied elsewhere in this Contract, the Employer may take possession thereof. The Architect/The Contract Administrator shall thereupon issue to the Contractor on behalf of the Employer a written statement identifying the part or parts of the Works taken into possession and giving the date when the Employer took possession (in clauses 18, 20.3, 22.3.1 and 22C.1 referred to as "the relevant part" and "the relevant date" respectively).

.1 For the purposes of clauses 17.2, 17.3, 17.5 and 30.4.1.2 Practical Completion of the relevant part shall be deemed to have occurred and the Defects Liability Period in respect of the relevant part shall be deemed to have commenced on the relevant date.

.2 When in the opinion of the Architect/the Contract Administrator any defects, shrinkages or other faults in the relevant part which he may have required to be made good under clause 17.2 or clause 17.3 shall have been made good he shall issue a certificate to that effect.

.3 As from the relevant date the obligation of the Contractor under clause 22A or of the Employer under clause 22B.1 or clause 22C.2 whichever is applicable to insure shall terminate in respect of the relevant part but not further or otherwise; and where clause 22C applies the obligation of the Employer to insure under clause 22C.1 shall from the relevant date include the relevant part.

.4 In lieu of any sum to be paid or allowed by the Contractor under clause 24 in respect of any period during which the Works may remain incomplete occurring after the relevant date there shall be paid or allowed such sum as bears the same ratio to the sum which would be paid or allowed apart from the provisions of clause 18 as the Contract Sum less the amount contained therein in respect of the relevant part bears to the Contract Sum.

Clause 18: Partial possession by Employer

Derivation.   Clause 18 of the original 1980 Form was substantially the same as clause 16 of the 1963 Form with the omission of the former clause 16(f) rendered unnecessary by the new clause 30.4. However, by Amendment 2 issued in November 1986 clause 18 was deleted and a new clause 18 inserted. The derivation of the present provisions is as follows:

— clause 18.1 is a substantially redrafted version of clause 18.1 (original) and the introductory part of clause 16 (1963 Form);

— clause 18.1.1 (original) relating to Certificate of Value, the equivalent of clause 16(a) of the 1963 Form, has been deleted;

— clause 18.1.1 of the amended Form is a redrafted version of clause 18.1.2 (original) and clause 16(b) (1963 Form);

— clause 18.1.2 of the amended Form is materially identical to clause 18.1.3 (original) and clause 16(c) (1963);

— clause 18.1.3 of the amended Form is a substantially redrafted version of clause 18.1.4 (original) and clause 16(d) (1963);

— clause 18.1.4 of the amended Form is a redrafted version of clause 18.1.5 (original) and clause 16(e) (1963).

Scheme of clause.   The clause provides for the Employer with the consent of the Contractor to take possession of part or parts of the Works before the

Works are completed, and for the application to each part of provisions for Practical Completion, defects, insurance and liquidated damages analogous to those which apply to the whole. Clause 18 should be read with clause 17.

Clause 18.1. *Amendments*

The effect of the amendments[39] was:

(1) to clarify that the reference to Practical Completion was to the date of issue of the Certificate of Practical Completion;

(2) to provide that the consent of the Contractor to the Employer taking possession should not be unreasonably withheld;

(3) to replace the former Certificate of Value with a written statement identifying the relevant part and the relevant date.

Clause 18.1. *"If . . . the Employer wishes to take possession . . ."*

The Employer is not bound to take possession of a completed part of the Works. But it is thought that where liquidated damages are running, an Employer who, in all the circumstances, was unreasonable in refusing the Contractor's offer of possession of a completed part of the Works might be subject to a proportional reduction in liquidated damages for failing to mitigate his loss.

Sectional completion. It is well settled that this clause does not provide for sectional completion.[40] This remains so, it is submitted, even if provisions in the Contract Bills set out that the work is to be completed and handed over in sections. The basis of this submission is the words of clause 2.2.1 "Nothing contained in the Contract Bills shall override or modify. . . ."[41] Clearly, sectional completion amounts to a substantial modification of the Conditions.

If a contract providing for sectional completion is required, the Form itself must be amended. A Sectional Completion Supplement is published by the Joint Contracts Tribunal for this purpose. An alternative, but much less desirable course, is to state the parts of the Works, the dates when they are to be completed and the amount of liquidated damages for each part and to use general words indicating that the Contract must be read as if the necessary consequential amendments had been made. If this latter course is adopted, the likelihood of unintended complications of construction is great.

Use but not possession of part. Where the parties intend that the Employer shall have use of some parts of the Works not amounting to possession, it is again desirable that they should amend the Form. This point was considered in the context of the 1963 Form in *English Industrial Estates* v.

---

[39] See above.

[40] *Gleeson Ltd.* v. *Hillingdon, London Borough of* (1970) 215 E.G. 165; *Bramall and Ogden* v. *Sheffield City Council* (1983) 29 B.L.R. 73.

[41] Discussed at p. 488.

Wimpey.[42] Provisions in the Bills envisaged such use. The majority of the Court of Appeal, applying clause 12 of the 1963 Form,[43] held that they could not look at the Bills to construe the contract but only "in order to follow exactly what was going on."[44] It is suggested that, by virtue of the deletion of the words "or affect in any way whatsoever ..." from clause 2.2, it is now permissible to consider such provisions in the Bills. They deal with a matter not provided for at all in the Conditions and thus would be purely supplementary (see commentary to clause 2.2). However, the more prudent and less confusing course is to amend the Form by providing that the relevant items in the Bills are expressly made part of the Contract. Care must be taken to deal with the various consequential matters including, in particular, those relating to insurance.

Clause 18.1.   *"... a written statement ..."*

This is a useful innovation. Under the former provisions the Certificate of Value could be given up to seven days from the date of taking possession. The effect of the new provision is that:

(1) the statement must be issued "thereupon" *i.e.*, it is submitted, at the time of or very shortly after the taking of possession. This should leave the parties in no doubt that the various consequences of taking possession have come into effect;

(2) there is now some formality evidencing the transfer of possession;

(3) the statement must identify the relevant part rather than its value;

(4) the statement must give the relevant date;

(5) the terms "the relevant part" and "the relevant date" are now used throughout the insurance clauses of the Form.

Clauses 18.1.3.   The insurance part of this clause has been amended. The effect is that:

(1) the obligation to insure, either of Contractor or Employer, "shall terminate" in respect of the relevant part, rather than, as formerly, be reduced in value "by the full value of the relevant part." This amendment is consequential upon the introduction of the written statement in place of the former Certificate of Value, but makes no substantive change;

(2) the relevant part is no longer "at the sole risk of the Employer." Where clause 22C applies (Insurance of Works in or extensions to existing structures), the obligation of the Employer to insure under clause 22C "shall from the relevant date include the relevant part."

However, it seems that where the Works consist of the erection of new buildings, so that clause 22C does not apply *and* clause 18 has been operated,

---

[42] [1973] 1 Lloyd's Rep. 118 (C.A.).

[43] Clause 2.2 of the present Form but with significantly different wording—see p. 488.

[44] *English Industrial Estates* v. *Wimpey* [1973] 1 Lloyd's Rep. 118 at 126, 128 (C.A.).

then the Contractor is liable as from the relevant date to indemnify the Employer against damage to the relevant part and to take out and maintain insurance against such liability (see clauses 20.2, 20.3.2 and 21.1.1).

Clause 18.1.4. The materially identical provisions of clause 16(e) of the 1963 Form were considered in *Bramall & Ogden* v. *Sheffield City Council*.[45] In a local authority housing contract, the Appendix provided for liquidated damages "at the rate of £20 per week for each uncompleted dwelling." Dwellings were taken over by the Employer as they were completed. The arbitrator found that dwellings were completed late. It was held on appeal from the arbitrator that the Employer was not entitled to claim or deduct liquidated damages. The basis of the decision was that the contract did not provide for Sectional Completion, that since the Employer had taken possession of some dwellings they were operating under clause 16(e), but that clause 16(e) was not consistent with the liquidated damages as set out in the Appendix. The inconsistency was that the provision for liquidated damages in the Appendix did not allow for the calculation required by clause 16(e). The clause provided for a reduced sum to be payable after taking partial possession for the period during which the Works (*i.e.* all the work that had to be completed under the Contract) remained incomplete. The inconsistency would only be resolved if the Contract were to provide, as this Contract did not, for sectional completion of those parts taken over, to which specific liquidated damages provisions would be applied.[46]

19.   Assignment and Sub-Contracts

19.1 .1   Neither the Employer nor the Contractor shall, without the written consent of the other, assign this Contract.

.2   Where clause 19.1 .2 is stated in the Appendix to apply then, in the event of transfer by the Employer of his freehold or leasehold interest in, or of a grant by the Employer of a leasehold interest in, the whole of the premises comprising the Works, the Employer may at any time after Practical Completion of the Works assign to any such transferee or lessee the right to bring proceedings in the name of the Employer (whether by arbitration or litigation) to enforce any of the terms of this contract made for the benefit of the Employer hereunder. The assignee shall be estopped from disputing any enforceable agreements reached between the Employer and the Contractor and which arise out of and relate to this Contract (whether or not they are or appear to be a derogation from the right assigned) and made prior to the date of any assignment.

19.2   The Contractor shall not without the written consent of the Architect/the Contract Administrator (which consent shall not be unreasonably withheld) sub-let any portion of the Works. A person to whom the Contractor sub-lets any portion of the Works other

---

[45] (1983) 29 B.L.R. 73.

[46] See also *Bruno Zorno (Builders)* v. *Beechcroft Developments* (1990) 6 Const. L.J. 132.

than a Nominated Sub-Contractor is in this Contract referred to as a "Domestic Sub-Contractor."

19.3 .1 Where the Contract Bills provide that certain work measured or otherwise described in those Bills and priced by the Contractor must be carried out by persons named in a list in or annexed to the Contract Bills, and selected therefrom by and at the sole discretion of the Contractor the provisions of clause 19.3 shall apply in respect of that list.

.2.1 The list referred to in clause 19.3.1 must comprise not less than three persons. Either the Employer (or the Architect/the Contract Administrator on his behalf) or the Contractor shall be entitled with the consent of the other, which consent shall not be unreasonably withheld, to add [*l*] additional persons to the list at any time prior to the execution of a binding sub-contract agreement.

.2.2 If at anytime prior to the execution of a binding sub-contract agreement and for whatever reason less than three persons named in the list are able and willing to carry out the relevant work then

either the Employer and the Contractor shall by agreement (which agreement shall not be unreasonably withheld) add [*l*] the names of other persons so that the list comprises not less than three such persons

or the work shall be carried out by the Contractor who may sub-let to a Domestic Sub-Contractor in accordance with clause 19.2.

.3 A person selected by the Contractor under clause 19.3 from the aforesaid list shall be a Domestic Sub-Contractor.

19.4 It shall be a condition in any sub-letting to which clause 19.2 or 19.3 refers that:

.1 the employment of the Domestic Sub-Contractor under the Sub-Contract shall determine immediately upon the determination (for any reason) of the Contractor's employment under this Contract; and

.2 the Sub-Contract shall provide that

.2.1 Subject to clause 16.1 of these Conditions (in clauses 19.4.2.2 to .4 called "the Main Contract Conditions"), unfixed materials and goods delivered to, placed on or adjacent to the Works by the Sub-Contractor and intended therefor shall not be removed except for use on the Works unless the Contractor has consented in writing to such removal, which consent shall not be unreasonably withheld.

.2.2 Where, in accordance with clause 30.2 of the Main Contract Conditions, the value of any such materials or goods shall have been included in any Interim Certificate under which the amount properly due to the Contractor shall have been discharged by the Employer in favour of the Contractor, such materials or goods shall be and become the property of the Employer and the Sub-Contractor shall not deny that such materials or goods are and have become the property of the Employer.

.2.3 Provided that if the Main Contractor shall pay the Sub-Contractor for any such materials or goods before the value therefor has, in accordance with clause 30.2 of the Main Contract Conditions, been included in any Interim Certificate under which the amount properly due to the Contractor has been discharged by the Employer in favour of the Contractor, such materials or goods shall upon such payment by the Main Contractor be and become the property of the Main Contractor.

[*l*] *Any such addition must be initialled by or on behalf of the parties.*

537

.2.4 The operation of clause 19.4.2.1 to .3 hereof shall be without prejudice to any property in any materials or goods passing to the Contractor as provided in clause 30.3.5 of the Main Contract Conditions (off-site materials or goods).

19.5 .1 The provisions of this Contract relating to Nominated Sub-Contractors are set out in Part 2 of the Conditions.

.2 Subject to clause 35.2 the Contractor is not himself required, unless otherwise agreed, to supply and fix materials or goods or to execute work which is to be carried out by a Nominated Sub-Contractor.

Clause 19: Assignment and Sub-Contracts

Derivation. Clauses 19.1, 19.2 and 19.4 are derived from clause 17 of the 1963 Form. Clauses 19.3 and 19.5 were new to the original 1980 Form.

Amendments. Amendments have been made as follows:

— by Amendment 1 issued in January 1984, clause 19.4 of the original 1980 Form was renumbered 19.4.1 and a new sub-clause 19.4.2 was inserted;
— by Amendment 4 issued in July 1987:
  — clause 19.1 was renumbered 19.1.1 and a new sub-clause 19.1.2 inserted;
  — clause 19.5.2 was slightly redrafted.
— by Amendment 9 issued in July 1990, clauses 19.2 and 19.5 were slightly redrafted. These amendments make express what is in any event implied, namely that, save as otherwise expressed in the Conditions in respect of Nominated Sub-Contractors, the Contractor remains wholly responsible for carrying out and completing the Works in all respects in accordance with Clause 2.1, notwithstanding either sub-letting to a Domestic Sub-Contractor or nomination.

These Amendments are significant and they are discussed below.

Generally. This clause provides for a qualified prohibition on assignment by either party and for a system of Domestic, *i.e.* non-Nominated, Sub-Contracting. Breach of the provisions of clause 19 is a ground for determination by the Employer under clause 27.1.4.

Clause 19.1. *"Neither the Employer nor the Contractor ..."*
Note that all versions of the 1980 Form now prohibit the Employer, as well as the Contractor, from assigning the Contract without written consent.

Clause 19.1. *"... assign ..."*
Since the prohibition is imposed upon both parties, it is thought that the word is likely to be construed in the strict sense of assigning the benefit of the

Contract,[47] rather than in the sense of merely an injunction against securing the vicarious performance by another of duties under the Contract.[48] It would follow that consent is required to an assignment by the Contractor of monies to be received under the Contract. So far as the clause refers to assignment of the burden of the Contract, it appears to be unnecessary since the burden of a contract cannot be assigned without the consent of the other party anyway.[49]

Clause 19.1.2. This new sub-clause was inserted by Amendment 4 issued July 1987. It qualifies the prohibition upon assignment to meet the practice of some employers who transfer an interest in the building immediately upon Practical Completion. However, this right is extremely limited. Note that:

(1) such assignment may only be made after Practical Completion;
(2) it is not the benefit of the Contract that may be assigned but only "the right to bring proceedings in the name of the Employer," so that it is more akin to a contractual right of subrogation than an assignment proper;
(3) the proceedings are themselves limited to proceedings "to enforce any of the terms of this Contract made for the benefit of the Employer hereunder." It is likely that the sub-clause is intended to permit what is in effect an equitable assignment of the right to bring proceedings and the final sentence of the sub-clause approximates to the principle that assignments are subject to equities.[50] If this is the effect, then the assignee is nevertheless on the wording of the sub-clause limited to claiming the *employer's* losses.[51] It is possible that the use of the words "to enforce," and the omission of any reference to a right to obtain damages for breach of the contract, show an intention to restrict the proceedings to specific performance or other proceedings to compel the Contractor to carry out his contractual obligations. It is not easy in practice to conceive what contractual obligations of the Contractor might be specifically enforced after Practical Completion. For example, the obligation of the Contractor to make good defects under clause 17.2 cannot be intended, it is submitted, to be embraced by this new provision because of the general rule that a contract to carry out building works cannot be specifically enforced against the builder.[52]

---

[47] See *Helstan Securities Ltd.* v. *Hertfordshire County Council* [1978] 3 All E.R. 262. That case concerned I.C.E. Conditions, 4th edition, Condition 3 of which read "The Contractor shall not assign the Contract or any part thereof or any benefit or interest therein or thereunder without the written consent of the Employer." However, it is submitted that the reasoning of Croom-Johnson J. is wide enough to support the conclusion set out in the text.
[48] For assignment generally, see Chap. 12. For the difference between assignment and vicarious performance, see p. 274.
[49] See p. 273.
[50] See "Subject to equities" at p. 278.
[51] For the difficult general position in relation to ordinary assignments, see "Assignment of warranties" at p. 281.
[52] See p. 269.

Clause 19.2. *"Domestic Sub-Contractor"*

This expression was introduced in the 1980 Form to refer to a person other than a Nominated Sub-Contractor to whom the Contractor sublets any portion of the Works. This encompasses, but is not limited to, a person selected under clause 19.3. The withholding of consent by the Architect to sub-letting is subject to the test of reasonableness and may be challenged in arbitration (see clause 41). Standard Forms of Domestic Sub-Contract have been published and are in widespread use under the style DOM/1 and DOM/2.

Clause 19.3. Under the 1963 Form, a practice not expressly provided for by the form grew up whereby the Contract Bills sometimes contained a provision specifying that certain work should be carried out by a single named Sub-Contractor. The Sub-Contractor was "specified" but not nominated within the meaning of clause 27 of the 1963 Form. This practice enabled the Employer to insist upon work being carried out by a particular specialist but without a nomination. However the practice of "specified Sub-Contractors" had a number of serious disadvantages from the point of view of the Employer. Firstly, the Contractor was not responsible for whether the "specified" Sub-Contractor's work was suitable for its purpose (because the choice of specialist was entirely the Employer's). Secondly, if the "specified" Sub-Contractor repudiated his Sub-Contract, it was probable that the Employer was obliged to provide a new Sub-Contractor by analogy with the principles applied in *Bickerton* v. *North West Metropolitan Regional Hospital Board*[53] in relation to Nominated Sub-Contractors. Further, if the Employer, or his agent, knew that the "specified" Sub-Contractor would only contract upon terms which excluded or severely limited his liability the Contractor might not even be responsible for latent defects in the quality of goods or materials used by the specified Sub-Contractor.[54]

The Scheme of clause 19.3. The Contract Bills may list not less than three persons from whom the Contractor must select at his sole discretion a Domestic Sub-Contractor to carry out work described in the Bills. Either party may with the consent of the other add to the list at any time before the execution of a binding Sub-Contract Agreement. Consent is not to be unreasonably withheld. If the number of persons on the list able and willing to carry out the relevant work falls below three, either the number must be made up to three by agreement, or the Contractor becomes free to carry out the work himself or (subject to clause 19.2) by a Domestic Sub-Contractor of his choice.

Advantages of this Scheme. Compared with the practice of "specified" Sub-Contractors, the procedure under clause 19.3 has a number of advantages. The Employer has a reasonable assurance that specialist work will be

---

[53] [1970] 1 W.L.R. 607 (H.L.).
[54] *Gloucestershire County Council* v. *Richardson* [1969] A.C. 480 (H.L.).

carried out by a competent specialist while avoiding the complications of nomination. The Contractor is not compelled to work with a Sub-Contractor not of his own choosing. The Contractor assumes full liability for the Sub-Contractor's performance so that he is liable for defects in workmanship or materials and for any delay that he causes. The Contractor is (probably) liable for the fitness for purpose of the Sub-Contractor's work because he chooses the Sub-Contractor at his sole discretion from a list to which he may himself add names. If the Sub-Contractor drops out, the Contractor must seek the consent of the Architect to a further sub-letting (clauses 19.2 and 19.3.3) but the Employer is not obliged to provide a new Sub-Contractor and the Contractor is liable for any extra costs caused by the default of the previous Sub-Contractor. It is submitted that the Contractor cannot escape liability for a latent defect in the quality of goods and materials used by the Sub-Contractor because of a limitation of liability in the Sub-Contractor's conditions of contract because he can select a Sub-Contractor who does not have such conditions. If all three have such conditions, the Contractor may add further persons to the list who do not have such conditions.[55]

Clause 19.4.   Sub-clause 19.4.2 was inserted by Amendment 1 issued in January 1984 and seeks to deal with the problem of unfixed materials and goods which arose in *Dawber Williamson* v. *Humberside County Council*.[56] Clause 19.4.2 makes it a condition of any sub-letting to a Domestic Sub-Contractor that the Sub-Contract shall provide that:

(1) unfixed materials and goods delivered to the Works shall not be removed except for use on the Works unless the Contractor has consented in writing (19.4.2.1);

(2) if the Main Contractor pays the Sub-Contractor for such materials and goods before their value has been certified and paid under the Main Contract, the materials and goods shall become the property of the Main Contractor (19.4.2.3);

(3) once the value of the materials and goods has been certified and paid under the Main Contract, such materials and goods shall be and become the property of the Employer and the Sub-Contractor shall not deny this fact (19.4.2.2).

These provisions remain provisions of the Main Contract. The Contractor binds himself *to the Employer* to enter into certain Sub-Contract conditions. That by itself is of no effect between the Contractor and the Domestic Sub-Contractor unless the Domestic Sub-Contract in fact contains these conditions. The conditions of the Domestic Sub-Contract require careful drafting to achieve the effect that property should pass not upon payment to the Sub-

---

[55] It is not clear what the position would be if all available persons have the same objectionable conditions, but see Chap. 14, Section 3.

[56] (1979) 14 B.L.R. 70; see also clause 16.1 and its commentary.

Contractor but upon payment being made to the Contractor.[57] If, however, the Contractor does not make a Sub-Contract whose terms satisfy clause 19.4, he will be in breach of contract to the Employer and liable in damages for any loss which the Employer suffers in consequence.

Clause 19.5.   The original version of clause 19.5.2 reflected the law as stated in *Bickerton* v. *North West Metropolitan Regional Hospital Board*[58] that, where a nomination had been made, the Contractor had neither right nor duty to carry out the work himself. This sub-clause was amended by Amendment 4 issued July 1987 by the insertion of the words "unless otherwise agreed." This enables the Contractor to carry out the work himself should he so agree with the Employer, presumably with the concurrence of the Architect. This agreement is not subject to any term as to reasonableness so that it would appear that the Contractor has an unfettered discretion to agree or not.

Summary of choice of Sub-Contractors.   In summary, therefore, under the 1980 Form there are only three methods available for choosing Sub-Contractors:

(1) sub-letting to a Domestic Sub-Contractor chosen entirely by the Contractor, but subject to the written consent of the Architect (clause 19.2);
(2) sub-letting to a Domestic Sub-Contractor chosen under the clause 19.3 procedure;
(3) where the Architect has "... reserved to himself the final selection and approval of the Sub-Contractor ...," the Sub-Contractor so nominated is a Nominated Sub-Contractor so that the full machinery of clause 35 comes into effect.[59]

It follows that the practice of "specified" Sub-Contractors has no place within the 1980 Form.

Clause 19A: Fair wages.   This clause formerly appeared in the Local Authorities edition only. It was deleted by Amendment 6 issued July 1988 because it could no longer be operated by virtue of the provisions of the Local Government Act 1988.

20.   Injury to persons and property and indemnity to Employer

20.1   The Contractor shall be liable for, and shall indemnify the Employer against, any expense, liability, loss, claim or proceedings whatsoever arising under any statute or at

---

[57] Note that the NFBTE/FASS/CASEC Domestic Sub-Contract DOM/1 seeks to achieve precisely this result—see clauses 21.4.5.1 to 21.4.5.4.
[58] [1970] 1 W.L.R. 607 (H.L.).
[59] See p. 626.

common law in respect of personal injury to or the death of any person whomsoever arising out of or in the course of or caused by the carrying out of the Works, except to the extent that the same is due to any act or neglect of the Employer or of any person for whom the Employer is responsible including the persons employed or otherwise engaged by the Employer to whom clause 29 refers.

20.2   The Contractor shall, subject to clause 20.3 and, where applicable, clause 22C.1, be liable for, and shall indemnify the Employer against, any expense, liability, loss, claim or proceedings in respect of any injury or damage whatsoever to any property real or personal in so far as such injury or damage arises out of or in the course of or by reason of the carrying out of the Works, and to the extent that the same is due to any negligence, breach of statutory duty, omission or default of the Contractor, his servants or agents or of any person employed or engaged upon or in connection with the Works or any part thereof, his servants or agents or of any other person who may properly be on the site upon or in connection with the Works or any part thereof, his servants or agents, other than the Employer or any person employed, engaged or authorised by him or by any local authority or statutory undertaker executing work solely in pursuance of its statutory rights or obligations.

20.3   .1   Subject to clause 20.3.2 the reference in clause 20.2 to "property real or personal," does not include the Works, work executed and/or Site Materials up to and including the date of issue of the certificate of Practical Completion or up to and including the date of determination of the employment of the Contractor (whether or not the validity of that determination is disputed) under clause 27 or clause 28 or clause 28A, where clause 22C applies, under clause 27 or clause 28 or clause 28A or clause 22C.4.3, whichever is the earlier.
        .2   If clause 18 has been operated then, in respect of the relevant part, and as from the relevant date such relevant part shall not be regarded as "the Works" or "work executed" for the purpose of clause 20.3.1.

Clause 20: Injury to persons and indemnity to Employer

Derivation.   The original version of clause 20 was substantially the same as clause 18 of the 1963 Form. Clauses 20.1 and 20.2 were substantially reworded and a new clause 20.3 introduced by Amendment 2 issued in November 1986. These amendments are important and difficult and are discussed below.

Generally.   Clauses 20.1 and 20.2 are indemnity clauses subject to exceptions. The principles relating to indemnity and exception clauses are well established and have been held to apply to these clauses.[60] Thus the indemnity part of the clause should be construed strictly and the Employer must show that the wording of the clause clearly renders the Contractor liable to indemnify him for the loss claimed. Insofar as the Contractor seeks to rely on an exception to a liability otherwise arising under the clause, he has to show that the exception is in plain words and covers his negligence and its consequences. It is inherently improbable that one party should intend to absolve the other

---

[60] See *City of Manchester* v. *Fram Gerrard* (1974) 6 B.L.R. 70, considering Clause 14(b) in the 1939 Form, the predecessor of Clause 20.2.

from the consequences of the other's negligence. If the words relied upon clearly exempt that party from the consequences of his own negligence, effect must be given to them. If there is no express reference to negligence, the Court must consider whether the words used are wide enough to cover the negligence sought to be exempted. Any doubt should be resolved against the party claiming exemption. If the words used are wide enough, the Court must then consider whether the head of damage may be based on some ground other than negligence which is not exempted and which is not fanciful or remote. If such a head of damage exists, it is fatal to the exemption.[61]

Clause 20.1. *"The Contractor shall be liable for ..."*
A wide liability is placed upon the Contractor. If an injured person sues the Employer[62] for an injury within the scope of this clause the Employer can join the Contractor as a third party to the action or bring separate proceedings against the Contractor on the indemnity.

Clause 20.1. *"... except to the extent that the same is due ..."*
These words were inserted in place of "unless due to ..." by Amendment 2 issued in November 1986. The effect of this change of wording, it is submitted, is that where loss is caused partly by the negligence of the Employer and partly by the Contractor, there will have to be an apportionment of liability. This is a useful clarification.

Clause 20.1. *"... any act or neglect ..."*
The exception does not, it is submitted, save the Contractor from liability to indemnify the Employer where the claim by the injured person arises out of a breach of statutory duty by the Employer not amounting to common law negligence.[63] This is especially so since breach of statutory duty is specifically mentioned, by amendment, in clause 20.2, so that its omission from clause 20.1 must be taken to be deliberate.

Clause 20.1. *"... including the persons ... clause 29 refers"*
These words of clarification were introduced by Amendment 2 issued November 1986.

Clause 20.2. *"... subject to ..., where applicable, clause 22C.1 ..."*
These words were introduced by Amendment 2 issued November 1986 in place of "except for such loss or damage as is at the sole risk of the Employer under clause 22B or 22C (if applicable)...." They present considerable diffi-

---

[61] See *Canada Steamship* v. *The King* [1952] A.C. 192 (P.C.); *The Raphael* [1982] 2 Lloyd's Rep. 42 (C.A.); see also generally Part B of Chap. 3.
[62] For the rights of third parties to sue Contractor or Employer, see pp. 255 *et seq.* For persons who come upon the site, see the Occupiers' Liability Acts 1957 and 1984.
[63] *Murfin* v. *United Steel Companies* [1957] 1 W.L.R. 104 (C.A.).

culties of construction. To understand this amendment it is necessary to consider clause 22C.1 and the cases decided in relation to the former wording.

Clause 22C.1 requires the Employer to take out a Joint Names Policy in respect of the existing structure, if the Works are alterations or extensions to existing structures, and in respect of the contents owned by the Employer or for which he is responsible. The Policy is to cover "... loss or damage due to one or more of the Specified Perils." This term is defined by clause 1.3. The Perils include some which might occur with or without the negligence of the Contractor (*e.g.* fire) and some which could not be caused by such negligence (*e.g.* lightning). The former wording was considered in *Scottish Special Housing Association* v. *Wimpey*,[64] where it was held that, on the true construction of clauses 18(2) and 20[C] of the 1963 form (materially identical with clause 20.2 and 22C of the original 1980 Form), it was intended that the Employer should bear the whole risk of damage by fire, including fire caused by the negligence of the Contractor. The opening words of clause 18(2) made it clear that the liability of the Contractor for damage to property caused by his negligence was subject to an exception, the ambit of the exception being found in clause 20[C]. Clause 20[C] provided that the existing structures were to be at the sole risk of the Employer as regards damage by, *inter alia*, fire. There was no difference in the obligation of the Employer to insure under clause 20[C] between perils that might or might not be due to the negligence of the Contractor. The obligation to insure was in quite general terms. The exception in the opening words only had meaning if it had the effect that certain damage caused by the negligence of the Contractor for which he would otherwise be liable is not to result in liability on his part. The nature of such damage appeared from clause 20[C] which referred in general terms to damage by fire to the existing structure. Thus it was intended that the Employer should bear the whole of risk of such damage.

At first sight and bearing in mind the general principles of construction set out above, especially the inherent improbability of the Employer absolving the Contractor from the consequences of his own negligence, it is arguable that the effect of the change of wording is that the Contractor is now to be liable for damage to the existing structure from a Specified Peril to the extent that it is due to his negligence. The clause no longer contains the word "except." The references to the sole risks of the Employer are deleted from both clause 20.1 and 22C.

It is thought, nevertheless, that the Employer continues to bear the whole risk of damage to the existing structures caused by Specified Perils, including damage caused by the negligence of the Contractor. The words "subject to ... clause 22C.1" must be intended to qualify the liability of the Contractor in

---

[64] [1986] 1 W.L.R. 995 (H.L.) approving *James Archdale* v. *Comservices* [1954] 1 W.L.R. 459 (C.A.); *cf. Coleman Street Properties* v. *Denco Miller* (1982) 31 B.L.R. 32. See generally J. Kodwo Bentil, "Liability for Fire Damage under the Standard Form of Building Contract" (1987) 3 Const. L.J. 83.

some way. The liability of the Contractor would otherwise be simply for damage to property to the extent that it was due to his negligence, etc.[65] Although clause 22C.1 is an insurance provision, these words must be intended to qualify the liability and not just the duty to insure in respect of the liability. Otherwise the words would appear in clause 21 which deals with the obligation to insure in respect of liability under clause 20. The qualification of liability cannot be in respect of Specified Perils which might occur (*e.g.* fire) or could only occur (*e.g.* storm) without the negligence of the Contractor, since the Contractor would not in any event be liable for such Perils under clause 20.2 which imposes liability only to the extent that the injury or damage is due to his negligence. The only remaining meaning to be given to these words is that they qualify the liability of the Contractor in respect of damage to the existing structures by Specified Perils due to his negligence.

Sub-Contractors. The position of a Sub-Contractor whose employee negligently set fire to an existing building and its extension where the Main Contract was in the 1963 Form was considered in *Norwich City Council* v. *Harvey*.[66] It was held that, although there was no direct contractual relationship between Employer and Sub-Contractor, since each had contracted on the basis that the Employer assumed the risk of damage by fire, there was no sufficiently close and direct relationship between them to impose on the Sub-Contractor a duty of care to the Employer in respect of such damage. It is thought that this remains the position with the amended wording.

The duration of the exemption. The Contractor continues to benefit from the exemptions from liability under clauses 20.1 and 20.2, notwithstanding destruction of the property or such negligence as would amount to a repudiatory breach of contract.[67]

Clause 20.2. "... *any property real or personal* ..."
     The Court of Appeal considered these words in *Surrey Heath Borough Council* v. *Lovell Construction*.[68] It was held that they include property which belonged to the Employer[69] and thus the Works. The effect of this decision is now negated as regards the Works by the new clause 20.3 (see below), but otherwise the decision remains an effective guide to the meaning of this phrase.

---

[65] For consideration of similar provisions in a non-standard form, see *Dorset County Council* v. *Southern Felt Roofing* (1989) 48 B.L.R. 96.
[66] [1989] 1 W.L.R. 828 (C.A.).
[67] *Photo Production* v. *Securicor* [1980] A.C. 827 (H.L.).
[68] (1990) 48 B.L.R. 108 (C.A.)—a decision on the identical provisions of clause 20.2 of the 1981 JCT with Contractor's Design Form.
[69] Disapproving *Tozer Kemsley* v. *Jarvis & Sons* (1983) 4 Con. L.R. 24, where clause 18(2) of the 1963 Form had been construed as applying only to the property of a third party.

Clause 20.2.   "*... to the extent that ...*"

These words were inserted by Amendment 2 issued in November 1986 in place of "provided always that...." The effect of this change of wording is to provide for an apportionment of liability where both Contractor and Employer are at fault.[70] The Employer must prove that the damage to property is due at least to some extent, to the Contractor's negligence, etc.

Clause 20.2.   "*... breach of statutory duty ...*"

These words were inserted by Amendment 2 issued in November 1986. Their effect is that breach of statutory duty not amounting to negligence is now within the scope of the liability.

Clause 20.2.   "*... default ...*"

This word in an earlier version of clause 20.2 was considered in *City of Manchester* v. *Fram Gerrard.*[71] It was held that default would be established if one of the persons covered by the clause either did not do what he ought to have done or did what he ought not to have done in all the circumstances, and provided that the conduct in question involved something in the nature of a breach of duty so as to be properly described as a default.

Clause 20.2.   "*... or of any person ... any other person who may properly be on the site ...*"

This wording, inserted by Amendment 2 issued in November 1986, for "or of any sub-contractor, his servants or agents" makes it clear that sub-subcontractors are within the scope of the liability.[72]

Clause 20.2.   "*... other than the Employer ... rights or obligations.*"

These words were added by Amendment 2 issued in November 1986. Some difficulty might arise as to the construction of the phrase "authorised by [the Employer]." For example, Domestic Sub-Contractors may only be engaged by the Contractor with the written consent of the Employer's agent, the Architect. Are they to be regarded as persons authorised by the Employer or as persons properly on the site in connection with the Works? It is thought that the intention must be that they are the latter but the point is not free from difficulty.

---

[70] This change of wording negates the effect of *A.M.F. International* v. *Magnet Bowling* [1968] W.L.R. 1028, which concerned clause 14(b) of the 1939 Form, materially identical with the unamended version of the clause 20.2. The plaintiff recovered damages against both employer and contractor for breach of duty under the Occupiers' Liability Act 1957, liability being apportioned between them. It was held that, as the employer's liability to the plaintiff was partly in respect of his negligence, he could not recover on the indemnity provided by the clause. Such a clause could not found a claim in respect of the employer's own negligence unless on its true construction it allowed such a claim by express words or necessary implication.

[71] (1974) 6 B.L.R. 70.

[72] Held not to be included on the former wording in *City of Manchester* v. *Fram Gerrard* (1974) 6 B.L.R. 70.

547

Clause 20.3. This was added by Amendment 2 issued in November 1986. The effect is that the liability under clause 20.2 does not extend to the Works, work executed and/or Site Materials up to the date of Practical Completion or determination, whichever is the earlier. However, if the Employer has taken partial possession under clause 18 then the relevant part becomes subject to the liability as from the relevant date.[73]

Summary. The Contractor is liable to indemnify the Employer in respect of the following classes of damage to property to the extent that it is due to his negligence, etc.:

(1) the property of third parties;
(2) damage to the relevant part from the relevant date (see clause 18);
(3) damage to the Works after Practical Completion;
(4) damage to existing structures and their contents not caused by a Specified Peril;
(5) damage to other property of the Employer.

21.   Insurance against injury to persons or property

21.1   .1.1   Without prejudice to his obligation to indemnify the Employer under clause 20 the Contractor shall take out and maintain insurance which shall comply with clause 21.1.1.2 in respect of claims arising out of his liability referred to in clauses 20.1 and 20.2.

.1.2   The insurance in respect of claims for personal injury to, or the death of any person under a contract of service or apprenticeship with the Contractor and arising out of and in the course of such person's employment, shall comply with the Employer's Liability (Compulsory Insurance) Act 1969 and any statutory orders made thereunder or any amendment or re-enactment thereof. For all other claims to which clause 21.1.1.1 applies the insurance cover shall be not less than the sum stated in the Appendix [*l.1*] for any one occurrence or series of occurrences arising out of one event.

.2   As and when he is reasonably required to do so by the Employer the Contractor shall send to the Architect/the Contract Administrator for inspection by the Employer documentary evidence that the insurances required by clause 21.1.1.1 have been taken out and are being maintained, but at any time the Employer may (but not unreasonably or vexatiously) require to have sent to the Architect/the Contract Administrator for inspection by the Employer the relevant policy or policies and the premium receipts therefor.

.3   If the Contractor defaults in taking out or in maintaining insurance as provided in clause 21.1.1.1 the Employer may himself insure against any liability or expense which he may incur arising out of such default and a sum or sums equivalent to the amount paid or payable by him in respect of premiums therefor may be deducted by him from any monies due or to become due to the Contractor under this Contract or such amount may be recoverable by the Employer from the Contractor as a debt.

---

[73] See commentary on clause 18 for these terms.

[*l.1*] *The Contractor or any sub-contractor may, if they so wish, insure for a sum greater than that stated in the Appendix.*

21.2 .1 Where it is stated in the Appendix that the insurance to which clause 21.2.1 refers may be required by the Employer the Contractor shall, if so instructed by the Architect/the Contract Administrator, take out and maintain a Joint Names Policy for such amount of indemnity as is stated in the Appendix in respect of any expense, liability, loss, claim or proceedings which the Employer may incur or sustain by reason of injury or damage to any property other than the Works and Site Materials caused by collapse, subsidence, heave, vibration, weakening or removal of support or lowering of ground water arising out of or in the course of or by reason of the carrying out of the Works excepting injury or damage:

   .1.1 for which the Contractor is liable under clause 20.2;
   .1.2 attributable to errors or omissions in the designing of the Works;
   .1.3 which can reasonably be foreseen to be inevitable having regard to the nature of the work to be executed or the manner of its execution;
   .1.4 which it is the responsibility of the Employer to insure under clause 22C.1 (if applicable);
   .1.5 arising from war risks or the Excepted Risks.

   .2 Any such insurance as is referred to in clause 21.2.1 shall be placed with insurers to be approved by the Employer, and the Contractor shall send to the Architect/the Contract Administrator for deposit with the Employer the policy or policies and the premium receipts therefor.

   .3 The amounts expended by the Contractor to take out and maintain the insurance referred to in clause 21.2.1 shall be added to the Contract Sum.

21.2 .4 If the Contractor defaults in taking out or in maintaining the Joint Names Policy as provided in clause 21.2.1 the Employer may himself insure against any risk in respect of which the default shall have occurred.

21.3 Notwithstanding the provisions of clauses 20.1, 20.2 and 21.1.1, the Contractor shall not be liable either to indemnify the Employer or to insure against any personal injury to or the death of any person or any damage, loss or injury caused to the Works or Site Materials, work executed, the site, or any property, by the effect of an Excepted Risk.

Clause 21: Insurance against injury to persons and property

Derivation. Clause 21 is derived from clauses 19 and 19A of the 1963 Form. It was amended by Amendment 2 issued in November 1986 and Amendment 4 issued in November 1987. These amendments, which are not of great importance, are noted below.

Generally. This clause should be read with clause 20 (indemnities) and clauses 22A-C (Insurance of the Works and existing structures).

Clause 21.1. The Contractor has to insure against his liabilities under clause 20 for injury to persons and property. Note that for claims, other than those to which the Employer's Liability (Compulsory Insurance) Act relates, the minimum insurance cover for any one occurrence or series of occurrences is that set out in the Appendix.

Clause 21.1 was redrafted without any changes of substance by Amendment 2 issued in November 1986. By Amendment 4 issued in July 1987 all references

549

to insurance by Sub-Contractors were deleted. This recognises the reality that many Sub-Contractors do not carry satisfactory liability insurance. The (Main) Contractor remains liable to the Employer to indemnify him against the negligence etc. of such Sub-Contractors and is obliged to obtain insurance cover to the sum stated in the Appendix.

Clause 21.2. The origin of this clause is the case of *Gold* v. *Patman & Fotheringham Ltd.*,[74] where adjoining owners in a crowded city area suffered damage to their property from the carrying out of contract works. There was no negligence on the part of the Contractor. The Employer sought to recover against the Contractor on the ground that a duty to insure, by implication, meant a duty to effect joint insurance. This contention was rejected. However, the extent of the exceptions set out in clauses 21.2.1.1 to 21.2.1.5 shows that the situations covered by this insurance are narrow in scope.

Clause 21.2 was amended by Amendment 2 issued in November 1986. The amendments were, in the main, consequential drafting amendments. There is one important administrative change. The original version of clause 21.2 provided for such insurance "where a provisional sum is included in the Contract Bills . . . ." Insurance Under clause 21.2 is now required when it is so stated in the Appendix.

Clause 19(2) in the 1963 Form, the predecessor of clause 21.2, was considered in *Higgs & Hill Building* v. *University of London*[75] on an application for leave to appeal under the Arbitration Act 1979. In order to reinstate a policy, insurers required different works from those provided for by the contract. The Arbitrator held that this work ought to have been the subject of a variation instruction. It was held that the Arbitrator was probably right "unless it can be said that the Contractor's obligation to insure obliged him to carry out at his own cost any and all works which insurers may require, notwithstanding that it is wholly additional to, or different from the agreed contract works. Such a proposition appears to me to be unsustainable."[76]

22. Insurance of the Works [m]

22.1 Clause 22A or clause 22B or clause 22C shall apply whichever clause is stated to apply in the Appendix.

---

[74] [1958] 1 W.L.R. 697 (C.A.).

[75] (1983) 24 B.L.R. 139.

[76] Parker J. (1983) 24 B.L.R. 139 at 150.

[m] *Clause 22A is applicable to the erection of new buildings where the Contractor is required to take out a Joint Names Policy for All Risks Insurance for the Works and clause 22B is applicable where the Employer has elected to take out such Joint Names Policy. Clause 22C is to be used for alterations of or extensions to existing structures under which the Employer is required to take out a Joint Names Policy for All Risks Insurance for the Works and also a Joint Names Policy to insure the existing structures and their contents owned by him or for which he is responsible against loss or damage thereto by the Specified Perils.*

22.2 In clauses 22A, 22B, 22C and, so far as relevant, in other clauses of the Conditions the following phrases shall have the meanings given below:

All Risks Insurance: [*n*]	insurance which provides cover against any physical loss or damage to work executed and Site Materials but excluding the cost necessary to repair, replace or rectify
	1 property which is defective due to
	.1 wear and tear,
	.2 obsolescence,
	.3 deterioration, rust or mildew;
All Risks Insurance: [*m.1*]	2 any work executed or any Site Materials lost or damaged as a result of its own defect in design, plan, specification, material or workmanship or any other work executed which is lost or damaged in consequence thereof where such work relied for its support or stability on such work which was defective;
	3 loss or damage caused by or arising from
	.1 any consequence of war, invasion, act of foreign enemy, hostilities (whether war be declared or not), civil war, rebellion, revolution, insurrection, military or usurped power, confiscation, commandeering, nationalisation or requisition or loss or destruction of or damage to any property by or under the order of any government *de jure* or *de facto* or public, municipal or local authority;
	.2 disappearance or shortage if such disappearance or shortage is only revealed when an inventory is made or is not traceable to an identifiable event;
	.3 an Excepted Risk (as defined in clause 1.3); and if the Contract is carried out in Northern Ireland
	.4 civil commotion;
	.5 any unlawful, wanton or malicious act committed maliciously by a person or persons acting on behalf of or in connection with an unlawful association; 'unlawful association' shall mean any organisation which is engaged in terrorism and includes an organisation which at any relevant time is a proscribed organisation within the

[*n*] *The definition of "All Risks Insurance" in clause 22.2 defines the risks for which insurance is required. Policies issued by insurers are not standardised and there will be some variation in the way the insurance for those risks is expressed. See also Practice Note 22 and Guide, Part A.*

[*m.1*] *In any policy for "All Risks Insurance" taken out under clauses 22A, 22B or 22C.2 cover should not be reduced by the terms of any exclusion written in the policy beyond the terms of paragraph 2; thus an exclusion in terms "This Policy excludes all loss or of damage to the property insured due to defective design, plan, specification, materials or workmanship" would not be in accordance with terms of those clauses and of the definition of "All Risks Insurance." Cover which goes beyond the terms of the exclusion in paragraph 2 may be available though not standard in all policies taken out to meet the obligation in clauses 22A, 22B or 22C.2 and leading insurers who underwrite "All Risks" cover for the Works have confirmed that where such improved cover is being given it will not be withdrawn as a consequence of the publication of the terms of the definition in clause 22.2 of "All Risks Insurance."*

	meaning of the Northern Ireland (Emergency Provisions) Act 1973; 'terrorism' means the use of violence for political ends and includes any use of violence for the purpose of putting the public or any section of the public in fear.
Site Materials:	all unfixed materials and goods delivered to, placed on or adjacent to the Works and intended for incorporation therein.

22.3 .1 The Contractor where clause 22A applies, and the Employer where either clause 22B or clause 22C applies shall ensure that the Joint Names Policy referred to in clause 22A.1 or clause 22A.3 or the Joint Names Policies referred to in clause 22B.1 or in clause 22C.1 and 22C.2 shall

> **either** provide for recognition of each Sub-Contractor nominated by the Architect/the Contract Administrator as an insured under the relevant Joint Names Policy
>
> **or** include a waiver by the relevant insurers of any right of subrogation which they may have against any such Nominated Sub-Contractor

in respect of loss or damage by the Specified Perils to the Works and Site Materials where clause 22A or clause 22B or clause 22C.2 applies and, where clause 22C.1 applies, in respect of loss or damage by the Specified Perils to the existing structures (which shall include from the relevant date any relevant part to which clause 18.1.3 refers) together with the contents thereof owned by the Employer or for which he is responsible; and that this recognition or waiver shall continue up to and including the date of issue of the certificate of practical completion of the Sub-Contract Works (as referred to in clause 14.2 of the Sub-Contract NSC/4 or NSC/4a) or the date of determination of the employment of the Contractor (whether or not the validity of that determination is contested) under clause 27 or clause 28 or clause 28A, or, where clause 22C applies, under clause 27 or clause 28 or clause 28A or clause 22C.4.3, whichever is the earlier. The provisions of clause 22.3.1 shall apply also in respect of any Joint Names Policy taken out by the Employer under clause 22A.2.

.2 Except in respect of the Joint Names Policy referred to in clause 22C.1 the provisions of clause 22.3.1 in regard to recognition or waiver shall apply to Domestic Sub-Contractors. Such recognition or waiver for Domestic Sub-Contractors shall continue up to and including the date of issue of any certificate or other document which states that the Domestic Sub-Contract Works are practically complete or the date of determination of the employment of the Contractor as referred to in clause 22.3.1 whichever is the earlier.

22A. **Erection of new buildings—All Risks Insurance of the Works by the Contractor** [*m*]

22A.1 The Contractor shall take out and maintain a Joint Names Policy for All Risks Insurance for cover no less than that defined in clause 22.2 [*n*] [*o.1*] for the full

---

[*o.1*] *In some cases it may not be possible for insurance to be taken out against certain of the risks covered by the definition of "All Risks Insurance." This matter should be arranged between the parties prior to entering into the Contract and either the definition of "All Risks Insurance" given in clause 22.2 amended or the risks actually covered should replace this definition; in the latter case clause 22A.1, clause 22A.3 or clause 22B.1 whichever is applicable, and other relevant clauses in which the definition "All Risks Insurance" is used should be amended to include the words used to replace this definition.*

reinstatement value of the Works (plus the percentage, if any, to cover professional fees stated in the Appendix) and shall (subject to clause 18.1 .3) maintain such Joint Names Policy up to and including the date of issue of the certificate of Practical Completion or up to and including the date of determination of the employment of the Contractor under clause 27 or clause 28 or clause 28A (whether or not the validity of that determination is contested) whichever is the earlier.

2A.2   The Joint Names Policy referred to in clause 22A.1 shall be taken out with insurers approved by the Employer and the Contractor shall send to the Architect/the Contract Administrator for deposit with the Employer that Policy and the premium receipt therefor and also any relevant endorsement or endorsements thereof as may be required to comply with the obligation to maintain that Policy set out in clause 22A.1 and the premium receipts therefor. If the Contractor defaults in taking out or in maintaining the Joint Names Policy as required by clauses 22A.1 and 22A.2 the Employer may himself take out and maintain a Joint Names Policy against any risk in respect of which the default shall have occurred and a sum or sums equivalent to the amount paid or payable by him in respect of premiums therefor may be deducted by him from any monies due or to become due to the Contractor under this Contract or such amount may be recoverable by the Employer from the Contractor as a debt.

2A.3   .1   If the Contractor independently of his obligations under this Contract maintains a policy of insurance which provides (*inter alia*) All Risks Insurance for cover no less than that defined in clause 22.2 for the full reinstatement value of the Works (plus the percentage, if any, to cover professional fees stated in the Appendix) then the maintenance by the Contractor of such policy shall, if the policy is a Joint Names Policy in respect of the aforesaid Works, be a discharge of the Contractor's obligation to take out and maintain a Joint Names Policy under clause 22A.1. If and so long as the Contractor is able to send to the Architect/the Contract Administrator for inspection by the Employer as and when he is reasonably required to do so by the Employer documentary evidence that such a policy is being maintained then the Contractor shall be discharged from his obligation under clause 22A.2 to deposit the policy and the premium receipt with the Employer but on any occasion the Employer may (but not unreasonably or vexatiously) require to have sent to the Architect/the Contract Administrator for inspection by the Employer the policy to which clause 22A.3.1 refers and the premium receipts therefor. The annual renewal date, as supplied by the Contractor, of the insurance referred to in clause 22A.3.1 is stated in the Appendix.
         .2   The provisions of clause 22A.2 shall apply in regard to any default in taking out or in maintaining insurance under clause 22A.3.1.

2A.4   .1   If any loss or damage affecting work executed or any part thereof or any Site Materials is occasioned by any one or more of the risks covered by the Joint Names Policy referred to in clause 22A.1 or clause 22A.2 or clause 22A.3 then, upon discovering the said loss or damage, the Contractor shall forthwith give notice in writing both to the Architect/the Contract Administrator and to the Employer of the extent, nature and location thereof.
         .2   The occurrence of such loss or damage shall be disregarded in computing any amounts payable to the Contractor under or by virtue of this Contract.
         .3   After any inspection required by the insurers in respect of a claim under the Joint Names Policy referred to in clause 22A.1 or clause 22A.2 or clause 22A.3 has been completed the Contractor with due diligence shall restore such work damaged, replace or repair any such Site Materials which have been lost or damaged, remove and dispose of any debris and proceed with the carrying out and completion of the Works.

.4 The Contractor, for himself and for all Nominated and Domestic Sub-Contractors who are, pursuant to clause 22.3, recognised as an insured under the Joint Names Policy referred to in clause 22A.1 or clause 22A.2 or clause 22A.3, shall authorise the insurers to pay all monies from such insurance in respect of the loss or damage referred to in clause 22A.4.1 to the Employer. The Employer shall pay all such monies (less only the percentage, if any, to cover professional fees stated in the Appendix) to the Contractor by instalments under certificates of the Architect/the Contract Administrator issued at the Period of Interim Certificates.

.5 The Contractor shall not be entitled to any payment in respect of the restoration, replacement or repair of such loss or damage and (when required) the removal and disposal of debris other than the monies received under the aforesaid insurance.

22B. **Erection of new buildings—All Risks Insurance of the Works by the Employer** [*m*]

22B.1 The Employer shall take out and maintain a Joint Names Policy for All Risks Insurance for cover no less than that defined in clause 22.2 [*n*] [*o.1*] for the full reinstatement value of the Works (plus the percentage, if any to cover professional fees stated in the Appendix) and shall (subject to clause 18.1.3) maintain such Joint Names Policy up to and including the date of issue of the certificate of Practical Completion or up to and including the date of determination of the employment of the Contractor under clause 27 or clause 28 or clause 28A (whether or not the validity of that determination is contested) whichever is the earlier.

22B.2 [Number not used]

22B.3 .1 If any loss or damage affecting work executed or any part thereof or any Site Materials is occasioned by any one or more of the risks covered by the Joint Names Policy referred to in clause 22B.1 then, upon discovering the said loss or damage, the Contractor shall forthwith give notice in writing both to the Architect/the Contract Administrator and to the Employer of the extent, nature and location thereof.

.2 The occurrence of such loss or damage shall be disregarded in computing any amounts payable to the Contractor under or by virtue of this Contract.

.3 After any inspection required by the insurers in respect of a claim under the Joint Names Policy referred to in clause 22B.1 has been completed the Contractor with due diligence shall restore such work damaged, replace or repair any such Site Materials which have been lost or damaged, remove and dispose of any debris and proceed with the carrying out and completion of the Works.

.4 The Contractor, for himself and for all Nominated and Domestic Sub-Contractors who are, pursuant to clause 22.3, recognised as an insured under the Joint Names Policy referred to in clause 22B.1, shall authorise the insurers to pay all monies from such insurance in respect of the loss or damage referred to in clause 22B.3.1 to the Employer.

.5 The restoration, replacement or repair of such loss or damage and (when required) the removal and disposal of debris shall be treated as if they were a Variation required by an instruction of the Architect/the Contract Administrator under clause 13.2.

2C. **Insurance of existing structures—Insurance of Works in or extensions to existing structures** [*m*]

2C.1 The Employer shall take out and maintain a Joint Names Policy in respect of the existing structures (which shall include from the relevant date any relevant part to which clause 18.1.3 refers) together with the contents thereof owned by him or for which he is responsible, for the full cost of reinstatement, repair or replacement of loss or damage due to one or more of the Specified Perils [*o.2*] up to and including the date of issue of the certificate of Practical Completion or up to and including the date of determination of the employment of the Contractor under clause 22C.4.3 or clause 27 or clause 28 or clause 28A (whether or not the validity of that determination is contested) whichever is the earlier. The Contractor, for himself and for all Nominated Sub-Contractors who are, pursuant to clause 22.3.1, recognised as an insured under the Joint Names Policy referred to in clause 22C.1 shall authorise the insurers to pay all monies from such insurance in respect of loss or damage to the Employer.

2C.2 The Employer shall take out and maintain a Joint Names Policy for All Risks Insurance for cover no less than that defined in clause 22.2 [*n*] [*o.2*] for the full reinstatement value of the Works (plus the percentage, if any, to cover professional fees stated in the Appendix) and shall (subject to clause 18.1.3) maintain such Joint Names Policy up to and including the date of issue of the certificate of Practical Completion or up to and including the date of determination of the employment of the Contractor under clause 22C.4.3 or clause 27 or clause 28 or clause 28A (whether or not the validity of that determination is contested) whichever is the earlier.

2C.3 [Number not used]

2C.4 If any loss or damage affecting work executed or any part thereof or any Site Materials is occasioned by any one or more of the risks covered by the Joint Names Policy referred to in clause 22C.2 then, upon discovering the said loss or damage, the Contractor shall forthwith give notice in writing both to the Architect/the Contract Administrator and to the Employer of the extent, nature and location thereof and

.1 the occurrence of such loss or damage shall be disregarded in computing any amounts payable to the Contractor under or by virtue of this Contract;

.2 the Contractor, for himself and for all Nominated and Domestic Sub-Contractors who are, pursuant to clause 22.3, recognised as an insured under the Joint Names Policy referred to in clause 22C.2, shall authorise the insurers to pay all monies from such insurance in respect of the loss or damage referred to in clause 22C.4 to the Employer;

.3.1 if it is just and equitable so to do the employment of the Contractor under this Contract may within 28 days of the occurrence of such loss or damage be determined at the option of either party by notice by registered post or recorded delivery from either party to the other. Within 7 days of receiving such a notice (but not thereafter) either party may give to the other a written request to concur in the appointment of an Arbitrator under clause 41 in order that it may be determined whether such determination will be just and equitable;

[*o.2*] *In some cases it may not be possible for insurance to be taken out against certain of the Specified Parts or the risks covered by the definition of "All Risks Insurance." This matter should be arranged between the parties prior to entering into the Contract and either the definition of Specified Perils and/or All Risks Insurance given in clauses 1.3 and 22.2 amended or the risks actually covered should replace the definition; in the latter case clause 22C.1 and/or clause 22C.2 and other relevant clauses in which the definitions "All Risks Insurance," and/or "Specified Perils" are used should be amended to include the words used to replace those definitions.*

.3.2   upon the giving or receiving by the Employer of such a notice of determination or, where a reference to arbitration is made as aforesaid, upon the Arbitrator upholding the notice of determination, the provisions of clause 28.2 (except clause 28.2.2.6) shall apply.

.4   If no notice of determination is served under clause 22C.4.3.1, or, where a reference to arbitration is made as aforesaid, if the Arbitrator decides against the notice of determination, then

.4.1   after any inspection required by the insurers in respect of a claim under the Joint Names Policy referred to in clause 22C.2 has been completed, the Contractor with due diligence shall restore such work damaged, replace or repair any such Site Materials which have been lost or damaged, remove and dispose of any debris and proceed with the carrying out and completion of the Works; and

.4.2   the restoration, replacement or repair of such loss or damage and (when required) the removal and disposal of debris shall be treated as if they were a Variation required by an instruction of the Architect/the Contract Administrator under clause 13.2.

22D.   Insurance for Employer's loss of liquidated damages—clause 25.4.3

22D.1   Where it is stated in the Appendix that the insurance to which clause 22D refers may be required by the Employer then forthwith after the Contract has been entered into the Architect/the Contract Administrator shall either inform the Contractor that no such insurance is required or shall instruct the Contractor to obtain a quotation for such insurance. This quotation shall be for an insurance on an agreed value basis [*o.3*] to be taken out and maintained by the Contractor until the date of Practical Completion and which will provide for payment to the Employer of a sum calculated by reference to clause 22D.3 in the event of loss or damage to the Works, work executed, Site Materials, temporary buildings, plant and equipment for use in connection with and on or adjacent to the Works by any one or more of the Specified Perils and which loss or damage results in the Architect/the Contract Administrator giving an extension of time under clause 25.3 in respect of the Relevant Event in clause 25.4.3. The Architect/the Contract Administrator shall obtain from the Employer any information which the Contractor reasonably requires to obtain such quotation. The Contractor shall send to the Architect/the Contract Administrator as soon as practicable the quotation which he has obtained and the Architect/the Contract Administrator shall thereafter instruct the Contractor whether or not the Employer wishes the Contractor to accept that quotation and such instruction shall not be unreasonably withheld or delayed. If the Contractor is instructed to accept the quotation the Contractor shall forthwith take out and maintain the relevant policy and send it to the Architect/the Contract Administrator for deposit with the Employer, together with the premium receipt therefor and also any relevant endorsement or endorsements thereof and the premium receipts therefor.

22D.2   The sum insured by the relevant policy shall be a sum calculated at the rate stated in the Appendix as liquidated and ascertained damages for the period of time stated in the Appendix.

[*o.3*] *The adoption of an agreed value is to avoid any dispute over the amount of the payment due under the insurance once the policy is issued. Insurers on receiving a proposal for the insurance to which clause 22D refers will normally reserve the right to be satisfied that the sum referred to in clause 22D.2 is not more than a genuine pre-estimate of the damages which the Employer considers, at the time he enters into the Contract, he will suffer as a result of any delay.*

2D.3 Payment in respect of this insurance shall be calculated at the rate referred to in clause 22D.2 (or any revised rate produced by the application of clause 18.1.4) for the period of any extension of time finally given by the Architect/the Contract Administrator as referred to in clause 22D.1 or for the period of time stated in the Appendix, whichever is the less.

2D.4 The amounts expended by the Contractor to take out and maintain the insurance referred to in clause 22D.1 shall be added to the Contract Sum. If the Contractor defaults in taking out or in maintaining the insurance referred to in clause 22D.1 the Employer may himself insure against any risk in respect of which the default shall have occurred.

Clauses 22–22D: Insurances

Derivation. The original version of clause 22 was substantially the same as clause 20 of the 1963 Form. The clause was substantially amended by Amendment 2 issued in November 1986.

Scheme of clauses. Clauses 22.1–22.3 deal with definitions and introductory matters. Clause 22A is applicable to the erection of new buildings where the Contractor is required to take out a Joint Names Policy for All Risks Insurance for the Works and clause 22B is applicable where the Employer has elected to take out such a Policy. Clause 22C is to be used for alterations of or extensions to existing structures under which the Employer is required to take out a Joint Names Policy to insure the existing structure and their contents against loss or damage thereto by the Specified Perils and a Joint Names Policy for All Risks Insurance for the Works. Clause 22D deals with the insurance of the Employers' loss of liquidated damages. These clauses should be read with clauses 20 and 21 and clause 25 (extension of time) is also material.

Clause 22. This introductory clause was added by Amendment 2 issued in November 1986. All Risks Insurance is defined as "insurance which provides cover against any physical loss or damage to work executed and Site Materials . . ." subject to certain exclusions.

Clause 22A.1. This sub-clause was significantly amended by Amendment 2 issued in November 1986. In the original version of the 1980 form, the obligation was to insure against loss or damage by the Clause 22 Perils. The obligation now is to take out and maintain a Policy for All Risks Insurance, as defined in clause 22.2. The last words of the sub-clause "or up to . . . whichever is the earlier" were also added by the amendment so that the obligation to insure ceases either upon Practical Completion or determination, whichever is the earlier.

Clause 22A.4. This sub-clause deals with the procedure where the Works suffer loss or damage. This was substantially amended by Amendment 2

557

issued in November 1986. This is of great importance because of the Contractor's entitlement to extension of time (clause 25.4.3) and the right of either party to determine (clause 28A.1.2). Under the former procedure, the Contractor's obligation to restore work damaged arose upon acceptance of a claim under clause 22A. The new procedure is that the Contractor is required to give written notice of the nature, extent and location of the loss or damage upon discovery (clause 22A.4.1); the occurrence of the loss or damage is to be disregarded in computing any amounts payable to the Contractor (22A.4.2); the obligation of the Contractor to restore now arises after inspection by the Insurers has been completed (22A.4.3), so that it arises at an earlier stage than formerly; and the Contractor is now required to authorise insurers to pay insurance monies direct to the Employer (22A.4.4).

Clause 22B. In the 1963 Form and in the original version of the 1980 Form, clause 22B provided that "All work . . . shall be at the sole risk of the Employer as regards loss or damage by the clause 22 Perils." In the Local Authorities version there was no obligation to insure but in the Private version there was. The effect of those words was that the Employer accepted liability for loss or damage caused by the clause 22 Perils even if caused by the Contractor's negligence (see commentary to clause 20) but damage to the Works due to theft or other risks not within the named contingencies was the liability of the Contractor.

The effect of the amendments is that the obligation to insure now extends to Local Authorities; the insurance is now against All Risks not just the Specified Perils; the obligation continues until Practical Completion or determination, whichever is the earlier; and damage to the Works or Site Materials is not the liability of the Contractor in any circumstance (see clause 20.3) save after Practical Completion or determination.

Clause 22C. Clause 22C.1 has been redrafted substantially. It formerly provided that "The existing structures . . . shall be at the sole risk of the Employer as regards loss or damage by the clause 22 Perils." The Employer is now required to take out and maintain a Joint Names Policy for loss or damage due to the Specified Perils. The effect of this change of wording does not, however, appear to be great. If the existing structures are damaged by a Specified Peril, such damage remains, it is thought, at the sole risk of the Employer whether or not caused by the negligence of the Contractor (see commentary to clause 20). If the existing structures are damaged by a peril that is not a Specified Peril (*e.g.* theft) that is at the risk of the Contractor until Practical Completion or determination to the extent that it is due to his negligence, etc.

"Specified Perils." Certain of the Perils have been considered by the court, as "storm, tempest, flood,"[77] "explosion"[78] and "bursting or overflowing of water tanks"[79];

Clause 22C.4.3.1. *"If it is just and equitable so to do . . ."*
This is a special provision for determination: see also clause 28A.1.2.

It was unsuccessfully argued that clause 20(C) of the 1963 Form required the Employer to indemnify the Contractor in respect of liability to third parties arising out of his negligence and to insure against such liability.[80] Clause 22C of the 1980 Form clearly does not impose any such obligation upon the Employer.

Clause 22D. This new sub-clause was inserted by Amendment 2 issued in November 1986. Where stated in the Appendix and subsequently required by the Architect, the Contractor is to take out insurance for the Employer's loss of liquidated damages in circumstances where loss and damage by one of the Specified Perils results in an extension of time under clause 25.3 and 25.4.3.

23.   **Date of Possession, completion and postponement**

23.1   .1   On the Date of Possession possession of the site shall be given to the Contractor who shall thereupon begin the Works, regularly and diligently proceed with the same and shall complete the same on or before the Completion Date.

.2   Where clause 23.1.2 is stated in the Appendix to apply the Employer may defer the giving of possession for a period not exceeding six weeks or such lesser period stated in the Appendix calculated from the Date of Possession.

23.2   The Architect/the Contract Administrator may issue instructions in regard to the postponement of any work to be executed under the provisions of this Contract.

23.3   .1   For the purposes of the Works insurances the Contractor shall retain possession of the site and the Works up to and including the date of issue of the certificate of Practical Completion, and, subject to clause 18, the Employer shall not be entitled to take possession of any part or parts of the Works until that date.

.2   Notwithstanding the provisions of clause 23.3.1 the Employer may, with the consent in writing of the Contractor, use or occupy the site or the Works or part thereof whether for the purposes of storage of his goods or otherwise before the date of issue of the certificate of Practical Completion by the Architect/the Contract Administrator. Before the Contractor shall give his consent to such use or occupation the Contractor or the Employer shall notify the insurers under clause 22A or

---

[77] *Oddy* v. *Phoenix Assurance* [1966] 1 Lloyd's Rep. 134; *S. & M. Hotels* v. *Legal & General Assurance* [1972] 1 Lloyd's Rep. 157; *Anderson* v. *Norwich Union* [1977] 1 Lloyd's Rep. 293; *Young* v. *Sun Alliance* [1976] 2 Lloyd's Rep. 189.

[78] *Commonwealth Smelting* v. *Guardian Royal Exchange* [1986] 1 Lloyd's Rep. 121.

[79] *Computer & Systems Engineering* v. *John Lelliott (Ilford) The Times*, May 23, 1989—a case on the orginal version of the 1980 Form.

[80] *Coleman Street Properties* v. *Denco Miller* (1982) 31 B.L.R. 32; *Aberdeen Harbour Board* v. *Heating Enterprises (Aberdeen)* (1988) 4 Const. L.J. 195, Court of Session (Outer House).

    clause 22B or clause 22C.2 and .4 whichever may be applicable and obtain
confirmation that such use or occupation will not prejudice the insurance. Subject
to such confirmation the consent of the Contractor shall not be unreasonably
withheld.

.3   Where clause 22A.2 or clause 22A.3 applies and the insurers in giving the confirmation referred to in clause 23.3.2 have made it a condition of such confirmation
that an additional premium is required the Contractor shall notify the Employer of
the amount of the additional premium. If the Employer continues to require use or
occupation under clause 23.3.2 the additional premium required shall be added to
the Contract Sum and the Contractor shall provide the Employer, if so requested,
with the additional premium receipt therefor.

Clause 23: Date of Possession, completion and postponement

Derivation.   Clause 23 is substantially derived from clause 21 of the 1963
Form. The clause was amended by Amendment 2 issued in November 1986
and Amendment 4 issued in July 1987.

Generally.   Clauses 23, 24 and 25 deal with time, liquidated damages and
extension of time and should be read together. For the recovery of loss or
expense in certain cases where the regular progress of the Works has been
materially affected, see clause 26.1. For determination for delay, see clauses 27
and 28. For time for completion generally, see page 218. For extension of time
clauses, see page 233. For liquidated damages generally, see page 222.

Sectional Completion.   These clauses only deal with the position where
there is one date for handing over the Site to the Contractor and one date for
completion of all the Works. Amendment is required if this is not intended.[81]

Clause 23.1.   "*... possession of the site ...*"

    "The contract necessarily requires the building owner to give the Contrac-
tor such possession, occupation or use as is necessary to enable him to perform
the contract...."[82] The phrase "possession of the site" was considered in
Whittal Builders v. *Chester Le Street D.C.*[83] in the context of clause 21 of the 1963
Form. It was held that the phrase meant possession of the whole site and that,
in giving piecemeal possession, the Employer was in breach of contract so as to
entitle the Contractor to damages. It is submitted, however, that possession of
the site will be a question of fact and degree in all the circumstances. Provided
that the Contractor has sufficient possession, in all the circumstances, to
enable him to perform, the Employer will not be in breach of contract.[84]

---

[81] See commentary to clause 18.

[82] *Hounslow London Borough* v. *Twickenham Garden Developments* [1971] Ch. 233 at 257. The decision
in this case is further discussed at p. 270 and, with reference to clause 27 (determination) at p.
590.

[83] (1987) 40 B.L.R. 82.

[84] For a Canadian case on possession of the site, see *The Queen* v. *Walter Cabott Construction* 21 B.L.R.
42. See also "Cooperation" at p. 48.

Clause 23.1. "... *regularly and diligently proceed with the same* ..."

Breach of this obligation is a ground for determination under clause 27.1.2. There has been some judicial interest on the meaning of these words.[85] The Contractor is required to provide to the Architect a master programme for the execution of the Works (see clause 5.3.1.2). Failure to comply with such a programme is not itself a breach of contract but it may be some evidence of failure to proceed regularly and diligently. The Contractor may be able to rebut the inference of breach by showing, *inter alia*, that he is entitled to an extension of time under clause 25, that delay is caused by some act of the Employer not within clause 25 or that some other programme which he is following is in compliance with the duty to proceed regularly and diligently.

Clause 23.1. "... *complete the same on or before the Completion Date.*"

The expression "Completion Date" is defined in clause 1.3 to include the effect of extensions of time. There is no reference to Practical Completion. However, it has been said that the obligation under clause 21 of the 1963 Form was "to complete the Works in the sense in which the words "practically completed" and "practical completion" are used in clauses 15 and 16...."[86]

Date omitted. If the Date for Completion is not inserted in the Appendix, liquidated damages are not payable.[87] In a proper case, if the date had been clearly agreed and was accidentally omitted the court would, it is thought, grant rectification and insert the date, but *Kemp* v. *Rose*[88] would have to be distinguished.

Earlier completion. The Contractor is entitled to complete before the contractual completion date, whether or not he has so programmed the Works. But there is no implied term in the Contract requiring the Employer so to perform the agreement as to enable the Contractor to complete before the contractual date. Such a term would require that the Contractor was both entitled and obliged to complete early which cannot be so.[89]

Clause 23.1.2. This sub-clause was inserted by Amendment 4 issued in July 1987. Where the sub-clause is stated in the Appendix to apply, the Employer may defer giving possession of the site for up to six weeks. Such deferment is not a breach of contract and does not disentitle the Employer from recovering liquidated damages. The Contractor is entitled to an extension of time under clauses 25.3 and 25.4.13, and to loss and expense under clause 26.1.

---

[85] *Hounslow London Borough* v. *Twickenham Garden Developments* [1971] Ch. 233 at 269.

[86] Salmon L. J. in *J. Jarvis & Sons* v. *City of Westminster* [1969] 1 W.L.R. 1448 at 1458 (C.A.); *cf. Kaye (P & M)* v. *Hosier & Dickinson* [1972] 1 W.L.R. 146 at 165 (H.L.); *H. W. Nevill (Sunblest)* v. *William Press & Son* (1981) 20 B.L.R. 78 at 87.

[87] *Kemp* v. *Rose* (1858) 1 Giff. 258 at 266.

[88] (1858) 1 Giff. 258.

[89] *Glenlion Construction* v. *The Guinness Trust* (1987) 39 B.L.R. 89; see also "Cooperation" at p. 48.

Where the sub-clause does not apply, delay by the Employer in giving possession prima facie disentitles the Employer from recovering liquidated damages,[90] but the Architect can, it is submitted, issue an instruction under clause 23.2 postponing the commencement of the Works. Such an instruction may entitle the Contractor to an extension of time under clause 25.4.5 and to loss and expense under clause 26.2.5. Postponement of commencement of the Works may give the Contractor a right of determination under clause 28.1.3.5. Where this may arise, the Architect should advise the Employer who may wish to make a special agreement with the Contractor to avoid the possibility of such determination.

Clause 23.2.   "*. . . the postponement of any work . . .*"
An instruction to postpone work leading to a suspension of the Works can be disastrous for the Employer. The Contractor may be able to determine under clause 28.1.3.1.[91] In any event he will usually have a claim to loss and/or expense under clause 26.2.5. Can the Contractor rely on such an instruction when it arose out of a defect in the Works or other matter for which he is responsible? *In Gloucestershire County Council* v. *Richardson* it was conceded in the Court of Appeal that he could not.[92] When the case went to the House of Lords[93] the concession was maintained but it appeared that some of their Lordships were not satisfied it was necessarily correct. The point must be regarded as open although, having regard to the care with which the courts approach determination clauses, it may well be that it was correct.

Nomination and Postponement.   In *Harrison* v. *Leeds City Council*,[94] the Court of Appeal held that a nomination requiring a Contractor to enter into a Sub-Contract, the terms of which contained a provision as to the Sub-Contract works which was inconsistent with the Main Contractor's programme and necessarily required part of the Main Contractor's work to be postponed operated as a postponement instruction under clause 21(2) of the 1963 Form with a right to loss and expense under clause 24(1)(e).

Clause 23.3.   This sub-clause was inserted by Amendment 2 issued in November 1986. It deals with insurance arrangements for use or occupation by the Employer prior to the date of Practical Completion.

---

[90] *Amalgamated Building Contractors* v. *Waltham Holy Cross U.D.C.* [1952] 2 All E.R. 452 at 455 (C.A.).
[91] See commentary at p. 600.
[92] [1967] 3 All E.R. 458 (C.A.).
[93] [1969] 1 A.C. 480 (H.L.). The Contract was in the 1939 edition, where the Contractor had an absolute right of determination and was not subject to the proviso of reasonableness.
[94] (1980) 14 B.L.R. 118 (C.A.).

24. Damages for non-completion

24.1 If the Contractor fails to complete the Works by the Completion Date then the Architect/the Contract Administrator shall issue a certificate to that effect.

24.2 .1 Subject to the issue of a certificate under clause 24.1 the Contractor shall, as the Employer may require in writing not later than the date of the Final Certificate, pay or allow to the Employer the whole or such part as may be specified in writing by the Employer of a sum calculated at the rate stated in the Appendix as liquidated and ascertained damages for the period between the Completion Date and the date of Practical Completion and the Employer may deduct the same from any monies due or to become due to the Contractor under this Contract (including any balance stated as due to the Contractor in the Final Certificate) or the Employer may recover the same from the Contractor as a debt.

.2 If, under clause 25.3.3, the Architect/the Contract Administrator fixes a later Completion Date the Employer shall pay or repay to the Contractor any amounts recovered allowed or paid under clause 24.2.1 for the period up to such later Completion Date.

Clause 24: Damages for non-completion

Derivation. This clause is derived from clause 22 of the 1963 Form. It differs from clause 22 in a number of important respects dealt with below.

Amendment. Clauses 24.1 and 24.2.1 were somewhat redrafted and a new clause 24.2.3 inserted by Amendment 9 issued in July 1990. These amendments are discussed below.

Contra proferentem? Clauses 23–25 are not, it is thought, to be construed against either party as they are part of a document prepared by bodies representative of each.[95]

Pre-conditions to liquidated damages. Before the Employer is entitled to liquidated damages there must be a failure by the Contractor to complete the Works by the Completion Date. The Architect must have performed his duties in regard to any necessary extension of time under clause 25 or 33.1.3, since the delay is a failure by the Contractor to complete the Works by the Completion Date, which is defined by clause 1.3 as the Date for Completion as fixed and stated in the Appendix or any date fixed under either clause 25 or 33.1.3. The Architect must issue a certificate under clause 24.1. The Employer must require the payment of liquidated damages in writing no later than the date of the Final Certificate.[96]

Liquidated and ascertained damages. For liquidated damages generally, see page 222. For the significance of the sum being a genuine pre-estimate of

---

[95] *Tersons Ltd.* v. *Stevenage Development Corporation* [1963] 2 Lloyd's Rep. 333 at 368 (C.A.); see also "Contra proferentem rule" at p. 43.

[96] See *A. Bell & Son* v. *C.B.F. Residential Care and Housing Association* (1989) 46 B.L.R. 102 at 107; *cf. Jarvis Brent* v. *Rowlinson Constructions* (1990) 6 Const. L.J. 292.

the damage likely to be suffered by non-completion, see page 224. For damages where the agreed sum is a penalty, see page 229. For a discussion of whether a liquidated damages clause operates to limit the Contractor's liability, see "Exhaustive remedy?" at page 223. It is thought that clause 24 in the 1980 Form does limit the Contractor's liability for damages for delay, but it does not affect any claim the Employer may have under the Contract or at common law for the costs of having the work completed or rectified by another Contractor. For damages where the employer causes delay, see page 231.

Clause 24.1. *". . . a certificate to that effect."*
The wording of the clause is mandatory, so that the Architect is obliged to issue the certificate irrespective of whether the Employer intends to operate clause 24.2.1.[97] The nature of the certificate under clause 24 is significantly different from that formerly issued under clause 22 of the 1963 Form. Clause 22 required a certificate of the Architect that "in his opinion [the Works] ought reasonably ... to have been completed" by the Date for Completion as extended. The giving of that certificate required, it is thought, the expression by the Architect of a judgment and opinion independent from and additional to that required of him in granting extensions of time. This opinion reflected the law as exemplified by *Peak Construction* v. *McKinney Foundations*[98] to the effect that liquidated damages are not payable under a building contract if the Employer causes delay to the completion of the Works in circumstances where the Contract does not provide for an extension of time for completion.[99] In those, and perhaps other circumstances, the Architect might conclude that he could not certify that the Contractor ought reasonably to have completed the Works by the extended completion date. Clause 24.1 provides for a certificate which requires no additional exercise of judgment by the Architect. It is a simple statement that the Contractor has failed to complete the Works by the Completion Date (as extended, if appropriate). The principle of law referred to above will, of course, still apply, although the additions to what are now referred to as "Relevant Events" in clause 25 may make it less likely that an Employer will lose his right to liquidated damages. Since, however, the giving of the certificate itself will no longer have the effect of applying the principle of law, it will be more necessary for Employers and their advisers to be aware of the principle of law. It is possible that Architects may owe some duty to their clients to inform them of events in the course of a contract to which the principle of law may apply. An awareness of this problem is particularly important when an Employer who fails to pay money certified relying on an unfounded right to liquidated damages may risk a determination by the Contractor under clause 28.1.1.

---

[97] See *A. Bell & Son* v. *C.B.F. Residential Care and Housing Association* (1989) 46 B.L.R. 102 at 107.
[98] (1970) 1 B.L.R. 111 (C.A.) also (1970) 69 L.G.R. 1.
[99] See "Employer causing delay" at p. 231.

The form of the certificate under clause 24. None is prescribed, but in each case it must be clear that there was an intention to issue the relevant document and that it in substance expressed what is required by clause 24.[1] The Court of Appeal has held that where a certificate issued under clause 22 of the 1963 Form was inconclusive in determining the rights of the parties, the Court had jurisdiction to determine such rights.[2]

More than one certificate. The procedure for damages for non-completion may now, as a result of Amendment 9 issued in July 1990, be summarised as follows:

(1) the Contractor fails to complete by the Completion Date;

(2) the Architect issues a Certificate of Non-Completion;

(3) once such a Certificate has been issued, the deduction or recovery of liquidated damages can be effected by the Employer. He does not have to wait until the total period of default is known.

(4) if, after the issue of a Cerfificate of Non-Completion, a new Completion Date is fixed, that cancels the Certificate.

(5) however, if the Contractor fails to complete by the new Completion Date, one or more further Certificates of Non-Completion must be issued. Steps (4) and (5) in the procedure are expressly inserted by the sentence added to clause 24.1 by Amendment 9, although this was probably in any event the position.

(6) the new clause 24.2.3 provides that, notwithstanding the issue of further Certificates of Non-Completion, an earlier requirement of the Employer that the Contractor pay or allow liquidated damages "shall remain effective unless withdrawn by the Employer." It is not clear what is intended by these words. It was thought, prior to the Amendment, that the notice under clause 24.2.1 in reliance upon a Certificate which was later superseded fell with that Certificate[3] and that a new notice was required. It may be that the intention is to protect the Employer against having to pay interest upon liquidated damages.[4] It is not clear whether the Employer must give fresh notice under clause 24.2.1. It is thought that the intention is probably that no such notice is required, but that the earlier notice stands as implicitly amended by the issue of the further Certificate. No doubt the prudent course is to give fresh notice for the avoidance of doubt.

---

[1] *Token Construction* v. *Charlton Estates* (1973) 1 B.L.R. 50 applying a passage from *Minster Trust Ltd.* v. *Traps Tractors Ltd.* [1954] 1 W.L.R. 963 at 982; see also *Crestar* v. *Carr* (1987) 37 B.L.R. 113. For a form of words held to be a sufficient extension in writing, see *Amalgamated Building Contractors* v. *Waltham Holy Cross U.D.C.* [1952] 2 All E.R. 452. See also "Form of certificate" at p. 111.

[2] *Rapid Building* v. *Ealing Family Housing* (1984) 29 B.L.R. 5 (C.A.) applying *Northern Regional Health Authority* v. *Derek Crouch Construction* (1984) Q.B. 644 (C.A.).

[3] See *A. Bell & Son* v. *C.B.F. Residential Care and Housing Association* (1989) 46 B.L.R. 102.

[4] See *Department of Environment for Northern Ireland* v. *Farrans* (1981) 19 B.L.R. 1 (Northern Ireland High Court); see also n. 10 below.

Is there a time limit for the issue of the certificate?   It seems clear that under the 1980 Form no valid certificate may be issued under clause 24.1 after the issue of the Final Certificate. By clause 24.2.1, the Employer may only make requirement in writing of the payment of liquidated damages not later than the date of the Final Certificate and under clause 30.9.1.3 the Final Certificate is now stated to be conclusive as to extensions of time.[5]

Clause 24.1 certificate and extensions of time.   The Architect cannot issue a certificate under clause 24.1 for a date which differs from the extended time under clauses 25 or 33.1.3. The intention of the certificate under clause 24.1 is to ensure that, before the Employer is entitled to liquidated damages, the Architect reviews all extensions of time. The Architect cannot by issuing a certificate under clause 24.1 alter or override his decisions under clause 25 extending time.

Clause 24.2.1.   "*. . . the Contractor shall . . . pay or allow . . .*"
The Employer can either sue for the liquidated damages or deduct them from money due under the Contract. In any claim by the Contractor against the Employer under another Contract, the Employer can counterclaim for liquidated damages due from the Contractor under this Contract but cannot, it is thought, set-off the liquidated damages against the claim.[6] Payment certificates should be for the full amount (see clause 30) and the Employer may deduct the liquidated damages from the amount so certified. The Employer does not waive his claim for liquidated damages by failure to deduct them from money due under the Contract but he may recover them from the Contractor as a debt.

Clause 24.2.1.   "*. . . the rate stated in the Appendix . . .*"
These words were considered in *Temloc* v. *Errill Properties*,[7] a case concerning the 1980 Form. The parties had entered "nil" in the Appendix against clause 24.2. The Court of Appeal held that the effect of this entry was that it had been agreed between the parties that there should be no damages for delayed completion. If clause 24 was incorporated in the Contract and the parties completed the relevant part of the Appendix, that constituted an exhaustive agreement as to damages for delay. No such damages were recoverable at common law on the basis of any implied term.[8]

---

[5] The view had in any event been expressed in relation to the 1963 Form (1972 Revision) that once the Architect has issued a Final Certificate, if no notice of arbitration had been given, the Architect was *functus officio* and precluded thereafter from issuing any valid certificate under clause 22—see *Fairweather* v. *Asden* (1979) 12 B.L.R. 40.
[6] See "Set-off and counterclaim" at p. 438 above and in particular "Contractual set-off" at p. 440.
[7] (1987) 39 B.L.R. 30 (C.A.).
[8] See also "Exhaustive remedy?" at p. 223.

Clause 24.2.1. "*... may deduct ... may recover ...*"

Clause 24.2.1 is expressed entirely in permissive terms. In contrast, although it was always open to an Employer under the 1963 Contract not to enforce, payment of liquidated damages, and although clause 22 gave the Employer a discretion whether to deduct liquidated damages from money due to the Contractor under the Contract, the language as to payment of liquidated damages was imperative.

Clause 24.2.2. This provision is necessary because clause 25.3.3 enables the Architect to review extensions of time previously granted and fix a later Completion Date.[9] The Employer is required, if necessary, to repay any liquidated damages deducted or received under clause 24.2.1. It seems that the contractor may be entitled in addition to interest on such repayment from the date of deduction or receipt.[10]

Liquidated damages and retention. For consideration of the inter-relationship of clause 24 and the obligation to set aside retention monies under clause 30, see *Henry Boot Building* v. *Croydon Hotel*.[11]

Sectional completion. For consideration of the inter-relationship between the provisions for partial possession and for liquidated damages, see *Bramall & Ogden* v. *Sheffield City Council*[12] discussed above in relation to clause 18.

25. **Extension of time** [*p*]

25.1 In clause 25 any reference to delay, notice or extension of time includes further delay, further notice or further extension of time.

25.2 .1.1 If and whenever it becomes reasonably apparent that the progress of the Works is being or is likely to be delayed the Contractor shall forthwith give written notice to the Architect/the Contract Administrator of the material circumstances including the cause or causes of the delay and identify in such notice any event which in his opinion is a Relevant Event.

.1.2 Where the material circumstances of which written notice has been given under clause 25.2.1.1 include reference to a Nominated Sub-Contractor, the Contractor

---

[9] See commentary to clause 25 below.

[10] See *Department of Environment for Northern Ireland* v. *Farrans* (1981) 19 B.L.R. 1 (Northern Ireland High Court). Interest was held to be payable on the basis that the Employer was in breach of contract in deducting liquidated damages in reliance on certificates which were subsequently vitiated. See the editorial comment at 19 B.L.R. 4 on this decision. It is arguable under the 1980 Form that an employer who deducts liquidated damages upon a proper operation of clause 24 is not in breach of contract if the Architect subsequently extends time under clause 25.3.3, and that clause 24.2.2 merely stipulates a contractual repayment without providing for interest.

[11] (1985) 36 B.L.R. 41 (C.A.).

[12] (1983) 29 B.L.R. 73.

[*p*] *See clauses 38.4.7, 39.5.7 and 40.7 (restriction of fluctuations or price adjustment during period where Contractor is in default over completion).*

shall forthwith send a copy of such written notice to the Nominated Sub-Contractor concerned.

.2 In respect of each and every Relevant Event identified in the notice given in accordance with clause 25.2.1.1 the Contractor shall if practicable in such notice, or otherwise in writing as soon as possible after such notice:

.2.1 give particulars of the expected effects thereof; and

.2.2 estimate the extent, if any, of the expected delay in the completion of the Works beyond the Completion Date resulting therefrom whether or not concurrently with delay resulting from any other Relevant Event and shall give such particulars and estimate to any Nominated Sub-Contractor to whom a copy of any written notice has been given under clause 25.2.1.2.

.3 The Contractor shall give such further written notices to the Architect/the Contract Administrator, and send a copy to any Nominated Sub-Contractor to whom a copy of any written notice has been given under clause 25.2.1.2, as may be reasonably necessary or as the Architect/the Contract Administrator may reasonably require for keeping up-to-date the particulars and estimate referred to in clauses 25.2.2.1 and 25.2.2.2 including any material change in such particulars or estimate.

25.3 .1 If, in the opinion of the Architect/the Contract Administrator, upon receipt of any notice, particulars and estimate under clauses 25.2.1.1 and 25.2.2,

.1.1 any of the events which are stated by the Contractor to be the cause of the delay is a Relevant Event and

.1.2 the completion of the Works is likely to be delayed thereby beyond the Completion Date
the Architect/the Contract Administrator shall in writing to the Contractor give an extension of time by fixing such later date as the Completion Date as he then estimates to be fair and reasonable. The Architect/The Contract Administrator shall, in fixing such new Completion Date, state:

.1.3 which of the Relevant Events he has taken into account and

.1.4 the extent, if any, to which he has had regard to any instruction under clause 13.2 requiring as a Variation the omission of any work issued since the fixing of the previous Completion Date,
and shall, if reasonably practicable having regard to the sufficiency of the aforesaid notice, particulars and estimates, fix such new Completion Date not later than 12 weeks from receipt of the notice and of reasonably sufficient particulars and estimate, or, where the period between receipt thereof and the Completion Date is less than 12 weeks, not later than the Completion Date.
If, in the opinion of the Architect/the Contract Administrator, upon receipt of any such notice, particulars and estimate it is not fair and reasonable to fix a later date as a new Completion Date, the Architect/the Contract Administrator shall if reasonably practicable having regard to the sufficiency of the aforesaid notice, particulars and estimate so notify the Contractor in writing not later than 12 weeks from receipt of the notice, particulars and estimate, or, where the period between receipt thereof and the Completion Date is less than 12 weeks, not later than the Completion Date.

.2 After the first exercise by the Architect/the Contract Administrator of his duty under clause 25.3.1 the Architect/the Contract Administrator may in writing fix a Completion Date earlier than that previously fixed under clause 25 if in his opinion the fixing of such earlier Completion Date is fair and reasonable having regard to the omission of any work or obligation instructed or sanctioned by the Architect/the Contract Administrator under clause 13 after the last occasion on which the Architect/the Contract Administrator fixed a new Completion Date.

.3   After the Completion Date, if this occurs before the date of Practical Completion, the Architect/the Contract Administrator may, and not later than the expiry of 12 weeks after the date of Practical Completion, shall in writing to the Contractor either

.3.1   fix a Completion Date later than that previously fixed if in his opinion the fixing of such later Completion Date is fair and reasonable having regard to any of the Relevant Events, whether upon reviewing a previous decision or otherwise and whether or not the Relevant Event has been specifically notified by the Contractor under clause 25.2.1.1; or

.3.2   fix a Completion Date earlier than that previously fixed under clause 25 if in his opinion the fixing of such earlier Completion Date is fair and reasonable having regard to the omission of any work or obligation instructed or sanctioned by the Architect/the Contract Administrator under clause 13 after the last occasion on which the Architect/the Contract Administrator fixed a new Completion Date; or

.3.3   confirm to the Contractor the Completion Date previously fixed.

.4   Provided always

.4.1   the Contractor shall use constantly his best endeavours to prevent delay in the progress of the Works, howsoever caused, and to prevent the completion of the Works being delayed or further delayed beyond the Completion Date;

.4.2   the Contractor shall do all that may reasonably be required to the satisfaction of the Architect/the Contract Administrator to proceed with the Works.

.5   The Architect/The Contract Administrator shall notify in writing to every Nominated Sub-Contractor each decision of the Architect/the Contract Administrator under clause 25.3 fixing a Completion Date.

.6   No decision of the Architect/the Contract Administrator under clause 25.3 shall fix a Completion Date earlier than the Date for Completion stated in the Appendix.

25.4   The following are the Relevant Events referred to in clause 25:

.1   force majeure;

.2   exceptionally adverse weather conditions;

.3   loss or damage occasioned by any one or more of the Specified Perils;

.4   civil commotion, local combination of workmen, strike or lock-out affecting any of the trades employed upon the Works or any of the trades engaged in the preparation, manufacture or transportation of any of the goods or materials required for the Works;

.5   compliance with the Architect's/the Contract Administrator's instructions

.5.1   under clauses 2.3, 13.2, 13.3, 23.2, 34, 35 or 36; or

.5.2   in regard to the opening up for inspection of any work covered up or the testing of any of the work, materials or goods in accordance with clause 8.3 (including making good in consequence of such opening up or testing) unless the inspection or test showed that the work, materials or goods were not in accordance with this Contract;

.6   the Contractor not having received in due time necessary instructions, drawings, details or levels from the Architect/the Contract Administrator for which he specifically applied in writing provided that such application was made on a date which having regard to the Completion Date was neither unreasonably distant from nor unreasonably close to the date on which it was necessary for him to receive the same;

.7   delay on the part of Nominated Sub-Contractors or Nominated Suppliers which the Contractor has taken all practicable steps to avoid or reduce;

.8.1   the execution of work not forming part of this Contract by the Employer himself or by persons employed or otherwise engaged by the Employer as referred to in clause 29 or the failure to execute such work;

.8.2   the supply by the Employer of materials and goods which the Employer has agreed to provide for the Works or the failure so to supply;

.9   the exercise after the Base Date by the United Kingdom Government of any statutory power which directly affects the execution of the Works by restricting the availability or use of labour which is essential to the proper carrying out of the Works or preventing the Contractor from, or delaying the Contractor in, securing such goods or materials or such fuel or energy as are essential to the proper carrying out of the Works;

.10.1   the Contractor's inability for reasons beyond his control and which he could not reasonably have foreseen at the Base Date to secure such labour as is essential to the proper carrying out of the Works; or

.10.2   the Contractor's inability for reasons beyond his control and which he could not reasonably have foreseen at the Base Date to secure such goods or materials as are essential to the proper carrying out of the Works;

.11   the carrying out by a local authority or statutory undertaker of work in pursuance of its statutory obligations in relation to the Works, or the failure to carry out such work;

.12   failure of the Employer to give in due time ingress to or egress from the site of the Works or any part thereof through or over any land, buildings, way or passage adjoining or connected with the site and in the possession and control of the Employer, in accordance with the Contract Bills and/or the Contract Drawings, after receipt by the Architect/the Contract Administrator of such notice, if any, as the Contractor is required to give, or failure of the Employer to give such ingress or egress as otherwise agreed between the Architect/the Contract Administrator and the Contractor;

.13   where clause 23.1.2 is stated in the Appendix to apply, the deferment by the Employer of giving possession of the site under clause 23.1.2.

Clause 25: Extension of time

Derivation.   Clause 25 is derived from clause 23 of the 1963 Form but there are major innovations in the 1980 Form which include the following:

(1)   clauses 25.2 and 25.3 contain elaborate new machinery for the notification of delay by the Contractor and the grant of extensions of time by the Architect;

(2)   the undesirable practice of Architects putting off granting extensions of time until the end of a long Contract or even until after Practical Completion is discouraged. Under clause 25.3.1 the Architect is now required to grant extensions of time not later than 12 weeks after receipt of the Contractor's notice or not later than the Completion Date if that is less than 12 weeks after receipt of the Contractor's notice;

(3)   There is now power in clause 25.3.2 for the Architect to reduce a previously granted extension of time if there is a subsequent variation instruction requiring an omission. However, there is no power to fix a Completion Date earlier than the Date for Completion originally stated in the Appendix (see clause 25.3.6);

(4) Under clause 25.3.3, the Architect is now required to deal comprehensively with extensions of time not later than 12 weeks after Practical Completion. In so doing, the Architect can grant further extensions of time both by reviewing previous decisions and by taking into account Relevant Events which have not been notified to him by the Contractor;

(5) Certain additional grounds for extension are included as Relevant Events in clause 25.4.

Amendments. Clause 25 was amended by Amendment 2 issued in November 1986, by Amendment 4 issued in July 1987 and by Amendment 7 issued July 1988. These Amendments principally relate to matters of detail and drafting and are not fundamental.

Scheme of clause. Clause 25.2 deals with the time for the giving of notice by the Contractor of the delay to progress and the contents of such notice. Clause 25.3 provides machinery for the Architect to fix and refix Completion Dates. Clause 25.4 sets out a list of Relevant Events, the occurrence of which may give rise to an extension of time.

Clause 25.2.1.1. "... *the progress of the Works is being or is likely to be delayed ...*"
Clause 23 of the 1963 Form required notice where "... the progress of the Works is delayed ...." These words were considered in *London Borough of Merton* v. *Leach*,[13] where it was held that a Contractor was not required under clause 23 to give notice of delay which would be caused by some expected future event however probable its occurrence, but that he was required to give notice if there would be inevitable delay because of events which had already happened. A clause 23 notice need not relate to future anticipated delay. In view of the change of wording in the 1980 Form, it would seem that the notice could now refer to future anticipated delay and to expected future events likely to give rise to such delay.

Clause 25.2.1.1. "... *the Contractor shall forthwith give written notice ...*"
Under the 1963 Form it was held that such notice was not a condition precedent to the performance by the Architect of his duties under the clause.[14] It seems that under the 1980 Form a notice may well be a condition precedent to the grant of extensions of time during the Contract Period and before Practical Completion (see clause 25.3.1). A notice is clearly not a condition precedent to the grant of an extension of time after Practical Completion (see clause 25.3.3.1).

The duty of the Architect in relation to extensions of time was discussed in *London Borough of Merton* v. *Leach*[15] especially in issues 6 and 14. Despite the

---

[13] (1985) 30 B.L.R. 51.
[14] *London Borough of Merton* v. *Leach* (1985) 30 B.L.R. 51.
[15] (1985) 30 B.L.R. 51.

changes made in the 1980 Form, it is thought that the discussion remains valid at least in relation to the grant of an extension of time after Practical Completion. It was held that, if the Architect was of the opinion that because of an event falling within clause 23, progress of the Works was likely to be delayed beyond the Completion Date, he must estimate the delay and make an appropriate extension of time. The Architect owed a duty both to the Employer and to the Contractor to do this. The Architect under the 1963 Form was under such a duty notwithstanding the failure of the Contractor to give notice. However, failure by the Contractor to give notice was a breach of contract and this breach could be taken into account by the Architect in making the extension of time. It is not clear how in practice the breach would be taken into account. It is submitted that in any event the Contractor must not benefit from his breach by receiving a greater extension than he would have received had the Architect upon notice at the proper time been able to avoid or reduce the delay by some instructions or reasonable requirement.

Clause 25.2.1.1. *". . . the material circumstances . . ."*
The Contractor is required to give notice of material circumstances, even if the cause of the delay is not a Relevant Event entitling him to an extension of time.

Clause 25.2.1.2. *". . . the Contractor shall . . . send . . . such written notice to the Nominated Sub-Contractor . . ."*
Here and in clause 25.2.2, the Contractor is now required to send a copy of his notices to any Nominated Sub-Contractor referred to in the notice.

Clause 25.2.2. *The contents of the notice.*
This clause requires the Contractor to give written particulars of the expected effects of Relevant Events delaying the Works, to estimate the expected delay and to keep the particulars and estimate up to date. It is no doubt implied that the Contractor shall furnish such information in these respects as the Architect reasonably requires so as to assist him in the performance of his duty in relation to extensions of time.[16]

Application for loss and expense. An extension of time relieves the Contractor from liability for liquidated damages but gives him no right to extra payment. The causes of delay in clauses 25.4.5, 25.4.6, 25.4.8, 25.4.12, 25.4.13 and 25.4.14 are however part of the grounds for recovery of loss and/or expense under clause 26.1. If the Contractor wishes to claim such loss and expense, he should make the appropriate applications or say that his notice of a cause of delay is also an application under clause 26.1. However, the grant of an extension of time under clause 25 is not a condition precedent to a right to direct loss and expense under clause 26.1.[17]

---

[16] See *London Borough of Merton* v. *Leach* (1985) 30 B.L.R. 51—issue 6.
[17] *Fairweather* v. *Wandsworth* (1987) 39 B.L.R. 106.

Clause 25.3.1. The Architect is required to give extensions of time, if in his opinion the completion of the Works is likely to be delayed beyond the Completion Date by one or more Relevant Events notified by the Contractor. The Architect has to state which Relevant Events he has taken into account and the extent to which he has operated clause 25.3.2. The Architect has to grant the extension of time not later than 12 weeks from the receipt of the Contractor's notice and of reasonably sufficient particulars and estimate, if it is "reasonably practicable having regard to the sufficiency of the aforesaid notice, particulars and estimates." It is thought that the notice, particulars and estimates will be "sufficient" if they comply with clauses 25.2.2.1 and 25.2.2.2. If this is correct, provided the Contractor gives the best particulars and estimates that he reasonably can, the Architect will not legitimately be able to delay granting an extension beyond the 12 weeks on the grounds that he cannot yet judge the effect that the cause of delay will have on the progress. The 12 week period for dealing with extensions of time is reduced if the Architect receives the Contractor's notices, particulars and estimates less than 12 weeks before the Completion Date. This means both that Contractors will want to give their notices before the Completion Date (they are of course obliged by clause 25.2.1.1 to give notice "forthwith"), and that Architects will have to deal before the Completion Date with all notices of Delay received by then. It is to be noted that the Completion Date is defined in clause 1.3 to vary as extensions of time are granted. Thus the requirement for the Architect to deal with notices of Delay "not later than the Completion Date" may occur more than once.

The final paragraph of clause 25.3.1 was introduced by Amendment 4 issued in July 1987. This provides for the Architect to notify the Contractor in writing where his decision is not to fix a later date as a new Completion Date.

Clause 25.3.1. "... *the opinion of the Architect* ..."

This opinion is subject to the jurisdiction of the Arbitrator. However, it should be noted that by clause 30.9.1.3, introduced by Amendment 4 issued in July 1987, the Final Certificate is conclusive evidence that all and only such extensions of time, if any, as are due under clause 25 have been given. The Architect has to decide whether the cause notified is a Relevant Event. There is no widely expressed general ground for extension of time (such as clause 44 of the I.C.E. Conditions).[18] In particular there is no general clause entitling the Architect to extend time for delay caused by the Employer. If there is such delay not falling within the Relevant Events, it will invalidate the provisions for liquidated damages and the Employer will have to prove general damages.[19]

---

[18] See p. 871.
[19] See "Employer causing delay" at p. 231.

Clause 25.3.1.2. "*... the completion of the Works is likely to be delayed thereby beyond the Completion Date ...*"

Notice must be given if the progress of the Works is or is likely to be delayed, but there is a right to an extension only if the completion of the Works is likely to be delayed. Thus, for example, the delay in the progress of the Works at an early stage, may, by the use of the Contractor's best endeavours, be reduced or eliminated.

Programme date earlier than Date for Completion. In such a case, there can be no extension of time when the completion of the Works will be delayed beyond the programme date but not beyond the Date for Completion. There may, however, in certain circumstances, be grounds for payment under clause 26.1.

Clause 25.3.1. "*... fair and reasonable ...*"

These words acknowledge that the period of extension can rarely be arrived at by simple process of arithmetic but has to be the result of a consideration of various factors which it is thought may include:

(1) The exact terms and application to the facts of the Relevant Event in question;

(2) The amount of the immediate delay in the progress of the Works;

(3) The effect of any causes of delay, *e.g.* inadequate supervision, which are not within clause 25;

(4) The effect of concurrent causes of delay, whether within clause 25 or not, and whether one of them is an effective, dominant cause of delay[20];

(5) The extent to which the Contractor has used his best endeavours to prevent delay and has done all that might reasonably be required to proceed with the Works (see the proviso at clause 25.3.4).

Clause 25.3.3. This provision requires the Architect in effect to reconsider and deal finally with the question of extension of time within a period of 12 weeks from the date of Practical Completion. The previous grants of extension of time can only be reduced if there have been omissions justifying a reduction since the last grant of an extension of time. Apart from this, the reconsideration can only operate to confirm the Completion Date previously fixed or grant further extensions of time. Two important innovations in the 1980 Form are that the Architect can:

(1) review previous decisions; and

(2) take into account Relevant Events which have not been specifically notified by the Contractor.

It is to be noted further that the operation of clause 25.3.3 may result in the repayment to the Contractor under clause 24.2.2 of liquidated damages paid by reference to a Completion Date previously fixed.[21]

---

[20] For concurrent causes, see p. 191.
[21] See commentary to clause 24.2.2 at p. 567.

It was sometimes argued in relation to clause 23 of the 1963 Form that a Variation Order issued after the current completion date (*i.e.* the Date for Completion as extended by awards of the architect up to the date of the Variation Order) was to be treated as an act of prevention by the Employer. The argument was that the words of clause 23 required the qualifying event to *cause* completion to overshoot the current date for completion, not merely to have the effect that completion was further postponed from a date already past. Thus a Variation Order after the current date for completion could not be a qualifying event since the date was already gone. The effect of such a Variation Order, on this argument, was to set time for completion at large and so prevent the Employer from recovering liquidated damages.[22]

Whether or not this argument was correct for the 1963 Form, it is thought that it does not apply to the 1980 Form. It may be that, in relation to the Contractor's applications under clause 25.2, the Architect is only able to award extensions where, in his opinion upon receipt of the Contractor's application, the completion of the Works is likely to be delayed thereby (*i.e.* by a Relevant Event) *beyond* the Completion Date—see clause 25.3.1.2—and it may be that he cannot be of this opinion if the Relevant Event occurs and is notified after the Completion Date. However, this is subject to clause 25.3.3, which requires the Architect to review extensions comprehensively after the Completion Date. He must then grant fair and reasonable extensions of time. It is thought that in doing so he must have regard to all Relevant Events without limitation of time. He is not restricted to a review of previous decisions or to matters notified by the Contractor. It is thought that this procedure entitled and obliges the Architect, where it is appropriate, to grant fair and reasonable further extensions for Variation Orders issued after the Completion Date.

Clause 25.3.4.   This proviso is an important qualification of the right to an extension of time. Thus, for example, in some cases it might be the Contractor's duty to reprogramme the Works either to prevent or to reduce delay. How far the Contractor must take other steps depends upon the circumstances of each case, but it is thought that the proviso does not contemplate the expenditure of substantial sums of money.

Clause 25.4.   The expression "Relevant Events" was introduced by the 1980 Form. Many of the events in question were derived from the causes of delay in clause 23 of the 1963 Form but there are three new provisions and some significant alterations or additions to the former provisions. Two further Relevant Events have since been added by amendment.

Striking out relevant events.   In the 1963 Form there was an express invitation to strike out one or more of the causes of delay. There is no such

---

[22] See "Employer causing delay" at p. 231.

express invitation in the 1980 Form, but the parties may agree to strike out one of the Relevant Events. They should not, however, do so without careful consideration since such an amendment may have unintended consequences, *e.g.* in relation to the Employer's ability to recover liquidated damages.

It seems that if the parties strike out one of the Relevant Events but leave them legible the Court can look at the clauses struck out in order to construe the agreement.[23] If the parties make the struck out parts wholly illegible, it is submitted that extrinsic evidence is not admissible to show what appears in the Standard Form and to assist the construction of the Agreement generally. It is thought that by such striking out, the parties have indicated their intention that they do not wish the struck out parts to be referred to. The matter is one of general application to any alteration or striking out of parts of the Form. There is no clear authority on the point.

Clause 25.4.1. *"force majeure"*

This is a term of foreign law which has been introduced into English Contracts.[24] A statement of its meaning in French law by Goirand, approved by McCardie J. in *Lebeaupin* v. *Crispin*[25] as applying to many English Contracts, says:

> *"Force majeure.* This term is used with reference to all circumstances independent of the will of man, and which it is not in his power to control ... thus, war, inundations and epidemics are cases of *force majeure*; it has even been decided that a strike of workmen constitutes a case of *force majeure.*"

Force majeure is wider in its meaning than the phrases *"vis major"* or the "Act of God"[26] and it has been said that "any direct legislative or administrative interference would of course come within the term: for example, an embargo"[27] but "a *"force majeure"* clause should be construed in each case with a close attention to the words which precede or follow it and with due regard to the nature and general terms of the contract. The effects of the clause may vary with each instrument."[28] Thus it is thought that in the Standard Form *force majeure* has a restricted meaning because matters such as war, strikes, fire, weather and Government action are expressly dealt with in the contract.

---

[23] See *Mottram Consultants Ltd.* v. *Bernard Sunley & Sons Ltd.* [1975] 2 Lloyd's Rep. 197 at 209 (H.L.) discussed at p. 36, noting that the striking out there was by way of a variation of a contract in being.

[24] *Lebeaupin* v. *Crispin* [1920] 2 K.B. 714 at 719; *cf. Hackney Borough Council* v. *Doré* [1922] 1 K.B. 431 (D.C.).

[25] *Lebeaupin* v. *Crispin* [1920] 2 K.B. 714 at 718; see also *Hong Guan & Co.* v. *R. Jumabhoy & Sons Ltd.* [1960] A.C. 684 at 700 (P.C.).

[26] *Lebeaupin* v. *Crispin* [1920] 2 K.B. 714; *Matsoukis* v. *Priestman* [1915] 1 K.B. 681.

[27] *Lebeaupin* v. *Crispin* [1920] 2 K.B. 714 at 719.

[28] *Lebeaupin* v. *Crispin* [1920] 2 K.B. 714 at 720; see also *Yrazu* v. *Astral Shipping Co.* (1904) 20 T.L.R. 153; *The Concadoro* [1916] 2 A.C. 199 (P.C.); *Re Podar Trading Co., etc.* [1949] 2 K.B. 277.

Clause 25.4.2. *"exceptionally adverse weather conditions"*
"Adverse" is substituted for "inclement" in the 1963 Form. Exceptional heat may now qualify as a Relevant Event. The former provision was considered in *Walter Lawrence* v. *Commercial Union Properties.*[29] It was held that the correct test to be applied by the Architect was whether the weather itself was exceptionally inclement so as to give rise to delay and not whether the amount of time lost was exceptional. The effect of the weather was to be assessed at the time the work was actually carried out and not when it was programmed to be carried out. It is thought that equivalent reasoning applies to the 1980 Form.

Clause 25.4.3. *"loss or damage occasioned by any one or more of the Specified Perils"*
These are defined by clause 1.3. Their ambit is very wide and their underlying causes may, in some instances, be due to acts of negligence by the Contractor.[30]

Clause 25.4.4. *"civil commotion . . ."*
In the construction of insurance policies these words have been used "to indicate a stage between a riot and civil war."[31]

Clause 25.4.5. *"Architect's . . . instructions . . . under clauses . . . 35 or 36 . . ."*
These are new grounds to the 1980 Form. They relate to instructions connected with nomination.[32] There is no corresponding new ground for loss and expense in clause 26. The Contractor, wishing to protect himself against loss and expense caused by late nomination must make a specific application in writing so as to bring himself within clause 26.2.1. If he does, these new grounds for extension of time become otiose because he can rely on clause 25.4.6. Whether or not he can refuse a late nomination is not clear.

Clause 25.4.6. *". . . in due time . . ."*
These words were considered in the context of materially identical provisions of clause 23(f) of the 1963 Form in *Percy Bilton* v. *Greater London Council.*[33] It was held that "in due time" means "in a reasonable time" not "in time to avoid delay."

Clause 25.4.6 and the Contractor's programme. In *London Borough of Merton* v. *Leach,*[34] it was an issue whether the Contractor's programme presented at the commencement of the Works could be a specific application for instructions within the meaning of clause 23(f) of the 1963 Form. It was held

---

[29] (1984) 4 Con. L.R. 37.
[30] See also commentary to clauses 20 and 22.
[31] *Levy* v. *Assicurazioni Generali* [1940] 3 All E.R. 427 at 437.
[32] See clauses 35.5.2, 35.7.1, 35.8, 35.10.2, 35.11.2, 35.18.1.1, 35.23, 35.24.4.1, 35.24.4.3, 35.25 and 36.2.
[33] [1982] 1 W.L.R. 794 (H.L.).
[34] (1985) 30 B.L.R. 51.

that a document which set out in diagrammatic form the planned programme for the work and indicated the dates by which instructions *etc.* were required could be a specific application so as to meet the requirements of clause 23(f). Such an application might be made at the commencement of the work for all the instructions which the Contractor could foresee would be required in the course of the Works provided that the date specified for delivery for each set of instructions met the requirement of not being unreasonably distant from nor unreasonably close to the relevant date. If the Works did not progress strictly according to plan, some modification might be required.

Clause 25.4.6 and Nominated Sub-Contractors.   In *Percy Bilton* v. *Greater London Council*,[35] the House of Lords held that the withdrawal of a Nominated Sub-Contractor did not come within clause 23 of the 1963 Form. Thus the Main Contractor took the risk of any delay caused by such withdrawal. Time did not become at large and the Date for Completion was unaffected. However, delay by the Employer in making a timeous renomination of a new Sub-Contractor did come within clause 23(f) so that, if there was such delay, the Contractor was entitled to an extension of time provided that he had made a specific application in writing for the renomination.

Clause 25.4.7.   *"delay on the part of Nominated Sub-Contractors or Nominated Suppliers ..."*
An extension of time on this ground deprives the Employer of remedy for such delay and neither the Contractor nor the Nominated Sub-Contractor or Supplier as the case may be has to pay the liquidated damages payable but for the extension. The cause of the delay is immaterial. It matters not whether it is due to sloth, the remedying of defects, bad luck or other cause.[36] The apparent injustice of this and the encouragement to delay has been much criticised. One remedy is not to nominate. Another is to strike out the sub-clause. The commercial problem which arises when the invitation to tender indicates that the sub-clause will be struck out is that careful Contractors either refuse to tender or demand a material increase in price.[37]

Delay after completion of sub-contract works.   This is not within clause 25.4.7. In *Jarvis* v. *Westminster Corporation*[38] Nominated Sub-Contractors carried out piling. They claimed to have completed their work. The Contractor accepted it as complete and so did the Architect despite his suspicions as to its quality. The Contractor proceeded to the next stage of the Works and while carrying them out discovered substantial defects in the piling. The Sub-Contractors returned to site and carried out extensive remedial work which

---

[35] [1982] 1 W.L.R. 794 (H.L.).
[36] *Jarvis J. & Sons Ltd.* v. *Westminster Corporation* [1970] 1 W.L.R. 637 (H.L.).
[37] For the protection of the Employer where there are nominations and the clause is retained, see p. 294.
[38] [1970] 1 W.L.R. 637 (H.L.).

caused a delay to the completion of the Main Contract Works of 21½ weeks. It was held that the Contractor was not entitled to an extension of time as the sub-clause was limited in its operation to the period when the Sub-Contractor was carrying out the Works and did not apply after purported completion of the Sub-Contract Works accepted by the Architect and the Contractor.

Contractor's losses. The Employer is not liable to the Contractor for losses caused by Nominated Sub-Contractors and Nominated Suppliers.[39]

Clause 25.4.8. The terminology of clause 29 of the 1963 Form ("... artists, tradesmen or others engaged by the Employer ...") has been changed in clause 29 of the 1980 Form and in the equivalent other clauses where the expression appears. It seems that, notwithstanding clause 25.4.11, statutory undertakers who install main services in a new development under direct contract arrangements with the Employer fall within clause 25.4.8.1.[40] The ground for extension of time under clause 25.4.8 is also a ground for loss and expense under clause 26.2.4.

Clause 25.4.9. This clause is new in the 1980 Form. It will tend to reduce the ambit of "*force majeure*" in clause 25.4.1.

Clause 25.4.10. "*... which he could not reasonably have foreseen ...*"
These words limit the effect of the sub-clause. Thus, for example, a Contractor is not entitled to an extension of time in respect of shortages of labour or materials which he could by reasonable enquiry have reasonably foreseen were likely to continue or to arise. To make clause 25.4.10.1 work, there must be some implication as to the rate of wages to be paid. It is submitted that it is such rate, including bonuses, as the parties must reasonably be taken to have foreseen at the time of the Contract as necessary to obtain labour for the Contract.

Clause 25.4.11. "*... in pursuance of its statutory obligations ...*"
Clause 23(1) of the 1963 Form, from which this provision is derived, was considered in *Henry Boot* v. *Central Lancashire Development Corporation*.[41] It was held that, where statutory undertakers were doing their work, not because of statutory obligations upon them so to do, but because they had contracted with the Employer, delay so occasioned fell within clause 23(h) (25.4.8.1) and not within clause 23(1) (25.4.11). If, however, without having a contract, the undertakers using statutory powers to fulfill statutory obligations come on the scene and hinder the Works and cause delay, the delay falls within clause 25.4.11. It follows that for most developments on any size, clause 25.4.11

---

[39] See pp. 289 *et seq.*
[40] See commentary to clause 25.4.11.
[41] (1980) 15 B.L.R. 1.

would in practice be of a limited application. Upon such developments, the authority usually enter into a Contract either with the Employer or the Contractor.[42] They will thus be carrying out work pursuant to their contract and not in pursuance of statutory obligations. If they are engaged by the Employer, clause 25.4.8.1 will apply. If they are engaged by the Contractor, their delay will be at the Contractor's risk unless they are nominated, in which case clause 25.4.7 might apply.

Clause 25.4.12.   *"failure of the Employer to give ... ingress to or egress from the site ..."*

This clause is new to the 1980 Form. It seems that clause 25.4.12 is not concerned with possession of the site itself but with access to it over other land in the possession and control of the Employer.

Clause 25.4.13.   This is a new Relevant Event introduced by Amendment 4 issued in July 1987. It is consequential upon the insertion of clause 23.1.2.[43] Thus, where clause 23.1.2 is stated in the Appendix to apply, the Contractor is entitled to an extension of time in relation to deferment under the clause. The Employer by such deferment is not in breach of the Contract and remains able to claim liquidated damages for delay.

Clause 25.4.14.   This is a new Relevant Event introduced by Amendment 7 issued in July 1988.

26.   **Loss and expense caused by matters materially affecting regular progress of the Works**

26.1   If the Contractor makes written application to the Architect/the Contract Administrator stating that he has incurred or is likely to incur direct loss and/or expense in the execution of this Contract for which he would not be reimbursed by a payment under any other provision in this Contract due to deferment of giving possession of the site under clause 23.1.2 where clause 23.1.2 is stated in the Appendix to be applicable or because the regular progress of the Works or of any part thereof has been or is likely to be materially affected by any one or more of the matters referred to in clause 26.2; and if and as soon as the Architect/the Contract Administrator is of the opinion that the direct loss and/or expense has been incurred or is likely to be incurred due to any such deferment of giving possession or that the regular progress of the Works or of any part thereof has been or is likely to be so materially affected as set out in the application of the Contractor then the Architect/the Contract Administrator from time to time thereafter shall ascertain, or shall instruct the Quantity Surveyor to ascertain, the amount of such loss and/or expense which has been or is being incurred by the Contractor; provided always that:
.1   the Contractor's application shall be made as soon as it has become, or should reasonably have become, apparent to him that the regular progress of the Works or of any part thereof has been or was likely to be affected as aforesaid, and

---

[42] Statutory undertakers statutory *obligations* are in general quite limited—see, *e.g.* s.16(1) of the Electricity Act 1989—duty to supply on request in certain specified circumstances.

[43] See clause 23.1.2 and its commentary at p. 561.

.2   the Contractor shall in support of his application submit to the Architect/the Contract Administrator upon request such information as should reasonably enable the Architect/the Contract Administrator to form an opinion as aforesaid, and

.3   the Contractor shall submit to the Architect/the Contract Administrator or to the Quantity Surveyor upon request such details of such loss and/or expense as are reasonably necessary for such ascertainment as aforesaid.

26.2   The following are the matters referred to in clause 26.1:

.1   the Contractor not having received in due time necessary instructions, drawings, details or levels from the Architect/the Contract Administrator for which he specifically applied in writing provided that such application was made on a date which having regard to the Completion Date was neither unreasonably distant from nor unreasonably close to the date on which it was necessary for him to receive the same;

.2   the opening up for inspection of any work covered up or the testing of any of the work, materials or goods in accordance with clause 8.3 (including making good in consequence of such opening up or testing), unless the inspection or test showed that the work, materials or goods were not in accordance with this Contract;

.3   any discrepancy in or divergence between the Contract Drawings and/or the Contract Bills and/or the Numbered Documents;

.4.1   the execution of work not forming part of this Contract by the Employer himself or by persons employed or otherwise engaged by the Employer as referred to in clause 29 or the failure to execute such work;

.4.2   the supply by the Employer of materials and goods which the Employer has agreed to provide for the Works or the failure so to supply;

.5   Architect's/Contract Administrator's instructions under clause 23.2 issued in regard to the postponement of any work to be executed under the provisions of this Contract;

.6   failure of the Employer to give in due time ingress to or egress from the site of the Works, or any part thereof through or over any land, buildings, way or passage adjoining or connected with the site and in the possession and control of the Employer, in accordance with the Contract Bills and/or the Contract Drawings, after receipt by the Architect/the Contract Administrator of such notice, if any, as the Contractor is required to give, or failure of the Employer to give such ingress or egress as otherwise agreed between the Architect/the Contract Administrator and the Contractor;

.7   Architect's/Contract Administrator's instructions issued under clause 13.2 requiring a Variation or under clause 13.3 in regard to the expenditure of provisional sums (other than work to which clause 13.4.2 refers).

26.3   If and to the extent that it is necessary for ascertainment under clause 26.1 of loss and/or expense the Architect/the Contract Administrator shall state in writing to the Contractor what extension of time, if any, has been made under clause 25 in respect of the Relevant Event or Events referred to in clause 25.4.5.1 (so far as that clause refers to clauses 2.3, 13.2, 13.3 and 23.2) and in clauses 25.4.5.2, 25.4.6, 25.4.8 and 25.4.12.

26.4   .1   The Contractor upon receipt of a written application properly made by a Nominated Sub-Contractor under clause 13.1 of Sub-Contract NSC/4 or NSC/4a as applicable shall pass to the Architect/the Contract Administrator a copy of that written application. If and as soon as the Architect/the Contract Administrator is of the opinion that the loss and/or expense to which the said clause 13.1 refers has been incurred or is likely to be incurred due to any deferment of the giving of possession where clause 23.1.2 is stated in the Appendix to apply or that the regular progress of the Sub-Contract Works or of any part thereof has been or is likely to be materially affected as referred to in clause 13.1 of Sub-Contract NSC/4 or NSC/4a and as set out in the application of the Nominated Sub-Contractor then the Architect/the Contract Administrator shall himself ascertain, or shall instruct the Quantity Surveyor to ascertain, the amount of loss and/or expense to which the said clause 13.1 refers.

.2   If and to the extent that it is necessary for the ascertainment of such loss and/or expense the Architect/the Contract Administrator shall state in writing to the Contractor with a copy to the Nominated Sub-Contractor concerned what was the length of the revision of the period or periods for completion of the Sub-Contract Works or of any part thereof to which he gave consent in respect of the Relevant Event or Events set out in clause 11.2.5.5.1 (so far as that clause refers to clauses 2.3, 13.2, 13.3 and 23.2 of the Main Contract Conditions), 11.2.5.5.2, 11.2.5.6, 11.2.5.8 and 11.2.5.12 of Sub-Contract NSC/4 or NSC/4a as applicable.

26.5   Any amount from time to time ascertained under clause 26 shall be added to the Contract Sum.

26.6   The provisions of clause 26 are without prejudice to any other rights and remedies which the Contractor may possess.

Clause 26: Loss and expense caused by matters materially affecting regular progress of the Works

Derivation.   Clause 26 is derived from clauses 11(6) and 24 of the 1963 Form. The 1980 provisions for loss and expense closely follow those of the 1963 Form in substance subject to certain drafting amendments. Clause 26 was amended by Amendment 4 issued in July 1987 and Amendment 7 issued in July 1988. These are consequential amendments and not of great significance.

Nature of clause.   During the carrying out of building contracts, particularly if they are complicated, it is common for Contractors to suffer, or to allege that they suffer, disturbance in the regular progress of the Works due to causes within the Employer's or the Architect's control. With highly paid staff and costly machines, such losses can be heavy. Clause 26 provides a right for the Contractor in certain carefully defined circumstances to obtain payment for some of the more common causes of disturbance of the Works by the ordinary certificate procedure of the Contract. Clause 26.6 preserves any other rights and remedies which the Contractor may possess including, in particular, his right to claim damages.[44]

Meaning of "direct loss and/or expense."   This was considered by the Court of Appeal in *F. G. Minter* v. *W.H.T.S.O.*[45] The court held that direct loss

---

[44] The nature of Contractors' "claims" generally is discussed at p. 444 with some comments upon the preparation of a claim under this sub-clause. The pleading of a claim and the calculation of losses are discussed at p. 445. See also "Claims under or for breach of the contract" at p. 209.

[45] (1980) 13 B.L.R. 1 (C.A.).

and/or expense is loss and expense which arises naturally and in the ordinary course of things, as comprised in the first limb in *Hadley* v. *Baxendale*.[46] The court approved the definition of "direct damage" in *Saint Line Ltd.* v. *Richardsons*[47] as ";that which flows naturally from the breach without other intervening cause and independently of special circumstances, whereas indirect damage does not so flow." It follows from the decision in *Minter* that the sole question which arises in relation to any head of claim put forward by a Contractor is whether such claim properly falls within the first limb in *Hadley* v. *Baxendale* so that it may be said to arise naturally and in the ordinary course of things. The use by Contractors and others of formulae cannot displace or detract from this principle.

Composite claims and concurrent causes.   These are both important for claims for direct loss and expense. For composite claims, see page 216. For concurrent causes, see page 191.

Prolongation costs: on site overheads.   A claim for delay is frequently quantified in whole or in part by extending for the period of delay those items in the Preliminary Bill, or elsewhere in the Contract Bills, the cost of which is affected by time.[48] It should be noted that ordinarily prolongation costs will only begin to be recoverable from the Completion Date. A provision either in the Bills or in the Contractor's Programme which provides for an earlier Completion Date but which does not form part of the Contract does not give rise to any time related contractual obligation. The Contractor cannot therefore claim prolongation costs commencing upon his programmed Completion Date if it is earlier than the Date for Completion stated in the Contract.[49]

Head office overheads.   Contractors' claims for direct loss and expense frequently include claims for Head Office overheads and loss of profit. These are discussed under the headings "Overheads," "Loss of profit" and "Hudson formula" at pages 210 *et seq.*

Loss of productivity or uneconomic working.   This is discussed at page 212.

Interest as direct loss and/or expense.   In *F. G. Minter* v. *W.H.T.S.O.*,[50] the Court of Appeal held that "direct loss and/or expense" in clauses 11 and 24(1) of the 1963 Form could include interest which the Contractor had paid on capital which he had borrowed as a result of the events specified in those

---

[46] (1854) 9 Ex. 341. See generally p. 186.
[47] [1940] 2 K.B. 99 at 103.
[48] See also "Increased preliminaries" at p. 209.
[49] *Glenlion Construction* v. *The Guinness Trust* (1987) 39 B.L.R. 89; *J. F. Finnegan* v. *Sheffield City Council* (1988) 43 B.L.R. 124.
[50] (1980) 13 B.L.R. 1 (C.A.).

clauses and interest which he had been prevented on earning as capital as a result of those events. In the ordinary course of things in the construction industry contractors who are required to finance particular operations will require to use capital. That capital will either have to be borrowed, thus incurring interest charges or may be available from the contractor's own resources, thus foregoing interest. It followed that whenever the carrying out of varied or delayed works involved the Contractor in laying out money which was not reimbursed by proper interim payments for the total value of the work properly executed as provided by clause 30, the amount paid or lost by obtaining the use of the necessary capital was part of the loss or expense which arose naturally and in the ordinary course of things. The historic common law hostility to awards of interest[51] was no bar to the recovering of such finance charges. Stephenson L.J. considered that in the context of the Standard Form the financing charges claimed were part of the direct loss and/or expense recoverable. Ackner L.J. put the matter on a slightly broader basis that what was here claimed was not interest on a debt but a debt which had as one of its constituent parts interest charges which had been incurred. In *Rees & Kirby* v. *Swansea City Council*,[52] the court further held that interest did not cease to be recoverable as direct loss and/or expense at Practical Completion and that compound interest with periodic rests was recoverable.[53]

Interest as damages. This is discussed generally at page 214. In *Department of Environment for Northern Ireland* v. *Farrans*,[54] the High Court of Northern Ireland awarded interest as damages[55] where an Employer under a 1963 Form was held liable to repay sums deducted as liquidated damages because the deductions were vitiated by subsequent clause 22 certificates.[56]

Clause 26.1. The limits to the recovery by the Contractor of direct loss and/or expense should be noted. The Contractor must make written application. The direct loss and/or expense must be an item for which the Contractor would not be reimbursed by a payment under any other provision in the Contract. He must incur it either due to deferment of giving possession of the site or because the regular progress of the Works is materially affected by the list of matters in clause 26.2.

---

[51] As, *e.g.* in *London Chatham & Dover Railway* v. *South East Railway* [1893] A.C. 249 (H.L.); see also "Interest as damages" at p. 214.

[52] (1985) 30 B.L.R. 1 (C.A.).

[53] See also "Direct loss and/or expense" at p. 582.

[54] (1981) 19 B.L.R. 1 (High Court of Northern Ireland).

[55] Following *Wadsworth* v. *Lydall* [1981] 1 W.L.R. 598 (C.A.); see also *Rees & Kirby* v. *Swansea City Council* (1985) 30 B.L.R. 1; *Farrans (Construction)* v. *Dunfermline District Council* (1988) 4 Const. L.J. 314.

[56] See commentary to clause 24.2.2 at p. 567.

Clause 26.1. *". . . written application . . ."*

The requirements of this application are set out in sub-clauses 26.1.1 to 26.1.3. The Contractor must make his application promptly. He must submit in support of it such information and details as are reasonably necessary.

The contents of the application. This was considered in *London Borough of Merton* v. *Leach*.[57] This was a case under the 1963 Form which set out the procedure much more shortly, but the decision should apply to the 1980 Form. Applications must be framed with sufficient particularity to enable the Architect to do what he is required to do. The application must be made within a reasonable time. It must not be made so late that the Architect can no longer form a competent opinion of the matters on which he is required to satisfy himself that the Contractor has suffered the loss and expense claimed. In considering whether the Contractor has acted reasonably, it must be borne in mind that the Architect is not a stranger to the claim and it is always open for the Architect to call for further information either before or in the course of investigating it.

Contents of the application: finance charges. If finance charges are claimed, the written application must make some reference to the fact that the Contractor has suffered loss and expense by reason of being kept out of his money, if it is to be read as relating to financing charges.[58] However, ". . . I do not consider that more than the most general reference is required, sufficient to give notice that the Contractor's application does include loss or expense incurred by him by reason of his being kept out of pocket in respect of the . . . relevant event."[59]

Clause 26.1. *". . . has incurred or is likely to incur . . ."*

These words were added in the 1980 Form in place of the wording of the 1963 Form ". . . has been involved in direct loss and/or expense . . . ." Under the 1963 Form, successive applications were necessary,[60] but they are no longer necessary under the 1980 Form.

Clause 26.1. *". . . for which he would not be reimbursed by a payment under any other provision . . ."*

When considering claims for direct loss and/or expense it is always necessary to look carefully at what the Contractor has recovered under clause 13.5. Even the Bill rate under sub-clause 13.5.1.1 ordinarily includes some element

---

[57] (1985) 32 B.L.R. 51—see Issues 7 and 8 at pp. 94–98.
[58] *Rees & Kirby* v. *Swansea City Council* (1985) 30 B.L.R. 1 (C.A.).
[59] Robert Goff L.J. in *Rees & Kirby* v. *Swansea City Council* (1985) 30 B.L.R. 1 at 20 (C.A.). Robert Goff L.J. indicated, *obiter*, that upon the revised wording of the 1980 Form (see below) there might be no need for express reference to interest as financing charges in a written application. Prudent contractors will, however, continue to include such a reference.
[60] *F. G. Minter* v. *W.H.T.S.O.* (1980) 13 B.L.R. 1 at 19 (C.A.).

for overheads and profit. The daywork rate includes a substantial element although one cannot say that payment at daywork rates automatically excludes any claim under clause 26.1.

Clause 26.1. *"... due to deferment of giving possession ..."*

The references to deferment of giving possession were introduced by Amendment 4 issued in July 1987. This is a new ground for loss and/or expense. It is consequential upon the new provisions of clause 23.1.2 discussed at page 561.

Clause 26.1. *"... the regular progress of the Works ..."*

See clause 23.1 and its commentary for the Contractor's duty to proceed regularly and diligently. An agreed programme of work is, it is submitted, some, but not conclusive, evidence of what regular progress should be. Where the programme date is earlier than the Date for Completion stated in the Contract, it may be that some direct loss and/or expense may be recoverable on the grounds of disruption. However, provided that the Contractor can still complete within the Contract Period, he cannot recover prolongation costs.[61]

Clause 26.1. *"... the Architect ... shall ascertain ..."*

These words place an important duty upon the Architect. The Contractor must, as required by clauses 26.1.1 to 26.1.3, provide sufficient information and details to enable the Architect to form the necessary opinion. However, once the Architect has formed an opinion favourable to the Contractor, it is his duty to ascertain or to instruct the Quantity Surveyor to ascertain the loss or expense suffered.[62] Failure by the Architect to take such steps as are necessary to enable the Contractor's claim for loss or expense to be ascertained, once the Contractor has supplied all necessary information, amounts to a breach of contract entitling the Contractor to damages if he can prove them.[63]

Clause 26.1. *"... the Architect ... shall instruct the Quantity Surveyor to ascertain ..."*

If the Architect so instructs the Quantity Surveyor, is he bound to carry the amount of such ascertainment into his Certificates or can he vary it? The matter is not clear. It is arguable from the wording of clause 26.5 that the Architect is bound by the Quantity Surveyor's ascertainment and that, if he disagrees with it, he must nevertheless include it in his Certificates and, as part of his duty to the Employer, advise that it can be challenged in arbitration proceedings. But it is usually accepted that the Architect can revise his own Certificates other than the Final Certificate, and it is difficult to see why he

---

[61] See *Glenlion Construction* v. *The Guinness Trust* (1987) 39 B.L.R. 89; *J. F. Finnegan Ltd.* v. *Sheffield City Council* (1988) 43 B.L.R. 124.
[62] See *London Borough of Merton* v. *Leach* (1985) 32 B.L.R. 51, issue 10, p. 103.
[63] *Croudace* v. *London Borough of Lambeth* (1986) 33 B.L.R. 20 (C.A.).

cannot also revise the Quantity Surveyor's ascertainment. In practice, unless the Surveyor can be shown to have gone wrong in principle, the amount of his ascertainment will be important evidence of the true amount.

Clause 26.2. The matters which may entitle the Contractor to be paid loss and expense are set out in clause 26.2. As with the 1963 Contract these reproduce some, but not all, of the "Relevant Events" in clause 25.4 which may give rise to an extension of time. Clauses 26.2.4 and 26.2.6 are new matters to the 1980 Form. The latter is in line with the introduction of clause 25.4.12 as a ground for extension of time.

Clause 26.2.1. This reproduces clause 25.4.6. See commentary to that clause and discussion in *London Borough of Merton* v. *Leach.*[64]

Clause 26.2.7. This is in substance the former clause 11(6) of the 1963 Form. Variations may give rise to loss and/or expense in that either the Contractor suffers delay before receiving an instruction requiring a Variation or the Contractor suffers a delay caused by the Variation. It is often, in practice, difficult to draw a precise distinction between these two causes of delay. The Contractor should set out the material facts in his application to the Architect and put his claim for delay on these two alternative grounds.

Clause 26.2.8. This is a new matter introduced by Amendment 7 issued in July 1988.

Clause 26.3. This is a new provision to the 1980 Form. It provides for the Architect to state in writing to the Contractor what extension of time he has made under clause 25 where that extension of time is necessary for ascertainment of loss and expense under clause 26.

Clause 26.4. This provides for applications for loss and expense made by Nominated Sub-Contractors.

Clause 26.6. "*. . . without prejudice to any other rights and remedies . . .*"
This provision in the 1963 Form was considered in *London Borough of Merton* v. *Leach,*[65] where it was held that the elaborate machinery of the Contract was not exhaustive of the Contractor's remedies. The Contractor retained an unfettered right to make a claim for damages as an alternative to and independent of a claim for direct loss and/or expense.[66] For the right of determination, see clause 28. For the right to treat the Contract as at an end because of a repudiation by the Employer, see commentary to clause 28. For a discussion of

---

[64] (1985) 32 B.L.R. 51, issue 5 at pp. 85 to 89.
[65] (1985) 32 B.L.R. 51, issue 11 at pp. 105 to 109.
[66] See also "Claims under or for breach of the contract" at p. 209.

a claim for damages or breach of the relevant terms of this Contract, additional to the rights to recover payment under the Contract, see commentary to clause 5.

27.   Determination by Employer

27.1   Without prejudice to any other rights or remedies which the Employer may possess, if the Contractor shall make default in any one or more of the following respects, that is to say:
.1   if without reasonable cause he wholly suspends the carrying out of the Works before completion thereof; or
.2   if he fails to proceed regularly and diligently with the Works; or
.3   if he refuses or neglects to comply with a written notice from the Architect/the Contract Administrator requiring him to remove defective work or improper materials or goods and by such refusal or neglect the Works are materially affected; or
.4   if he fails to comply with the provisions of clause 19 or 19A,
then the Architect/the Contract Administrator may give to him a notice by registered post or recorded delivery specifying the default. If the Contractor either shall continue such default for 14 days after receipt of such notice or shall at any time thereafter repeat such default (whether previously repeated or not), then the Employer may within 10 days after such continuance or repetition by notice by registered post or recorded delivery forthwith determine the employment of the Contractor under this Contract; provided that such notice shall not be given unreasonably or vexatiously.

27.2   In the event of the Contractor becoming bankrupt or making a composition or arrangement with his creditors or having a proposal in respect of his company for a voluntary arrangement for a composition of debts or scheme or arrangement approved in accordance with the Insolvency Act 1986, or having an application made under the Insolvency Act 1986 in respect of his company to the court for the appointment of an administrator, or having a winding up order made or (except for the purposes of amalgamation or reconstruction) a resolution for voluntary winding up passed or having a provisional liquidator, receiver or manager of his business or undertaking duly appointed, or having an administrative receiver, as defined in the Insolvency Act 1986, appointed, or having possession taken, by or on behalf of the holders of any debentures secured by a floating charge, of any property comprised in or subject to the floating charge, the employment of the Contractor under this Contract shall be forthwith automatically determined but the said employment may be reinstated and continued if the Employer and the Contractor, his trustee in bankruptcy, liquidator, provisional liquidator, receiver or manager as the case may be shall so agree.

27.3   The Employer shall be entitled to determine the employment of the Contractor under this or any other contract, if the Contractor shall have offered or given or agreed to give to any person any gift or consideration of any kind as an inducement or reward for doing or forbearing to do or for having done or forborne to do any action in relation to the obtaining or execution of this or any other contract with the Employer, or for showing or forbearing to show favour or disfavour to any person in relation to this or any other contract with the Employer, or if the like acts shall have been done by any person employed by the Contractor or acting on his behalf (whether with or without the knowledge of the Contractor), or if in relation to this or any other contract with the Employer the Contractor or any person employed by him or acting on his behalf shall have committed any offence under the Prevention of Corruption Acts, 1889 to 1916, or

588

shall have given any fee or reward the receipt of which is an offence under sub-section (2) of section 117 of the Local Government Act 1972 or any re-enactment thereof.

27.4   In the event of the employment of the Contractor under this Contract being determined under clauses 27.1, 27.2 or 27.3 and so long as it has not been reinstated and continued, the following shall be the respective rights and duties of the Employer and the Contractor:

.1   the Employer may employ and pay other persons to carry out and complete the Works and he or they may enter upon the Works and use all temporary buildings, plant, tools, equipment, goods and materials intended for, delivered to and placed on or adjacent to the Works, and may purchase all materials and goods necessary for the carrying out of completion of the Works;

.2.1   except where the determination occurs by reason of the bankruptcy of the Contractor or of him having a winding up order made or (other than for the purposes of amalgamation or reconstruction) a resolution for voluntary winding up passed, the Contractor shall if so required by the Employer or by the Architect/the Contract Administrator on behalf of the Employer within 14 days of the date of determination, assign to the Employer without payment the benefit of any agreement for the supply of materials or goods and/or for the execution of any work for the purposes of this Contract but on the terms that a supplier or sub-contractor shall be entitled to make any reasonable objection to any further assignment thereof by the Employer;

.2.2   unless the exception to the operation of clause 27.4.2.1 applies the Employer may pay any supplier or sub-contractor for any materials or goods delivered or works executed for the purposes of this Contract (whether before or after the date of determination) in so far as the price thereof has not already been paid by the Contractor. The Employer's rights under clause 27.4.2 are in addition to his obligation or discretion as the case may be to pay Nominated Sub-Contractors as provided in clause 35.13.5 and payments made under clause 27.4.2 may be deducted from any sum due or to become due to the Contractor or shall be recoverable from the Contractor by the Employer as a debt;

.3   the Contractor shall as and when required in writing by the Architect/the Contract Administrator so to do (but not before) remove from the Works any temporary buildings, plant, tools, equipment, goods and materials belonging to or hired by him. If within a reasonable time after any such requirement has been made the Contractor has not complied therewith, then the Employer may (but without being responsible for any loss or damage) remove and sell any such property of the Contractor, holding the proceeds less all costs incurred to the credit of the Contractor;

.4   the Contractor shall allow or pay to the Employer in the manner hereinafter appearing the amount of any direct loss and/or damage caused to the Employer by the determination. Until after completion of the Works under clause 27.4.1 the Employer shall not be bound by any provision of this Contract to make any further payment to the Contractor, but upon such completion and the verification within a reasonable time of the accounts therefor the Architect/the Contract Administrator shall certify the amount of expenses properly incurred by the Employer and the amount of any direct loss and/or damage caused to the Employer by the determination and, if such amounts when added to the monies paid to the Contractor before the date of determination exceed the total amount which would have been payable on due completion in accordance with this Contract, the difference shall be a debt payable to the Employer by the Contractor; and if the said amounts when added to the said monies be less than the said total amount, the difference shall be a debt payable by the Employer to the Contractor.

589

Clause 27: Determination by Employer

Derivation.   Clause 27 is substantially the same as clause 25 of the 1963 Form. It was amended by Amendment 4 issued in July 1987. These amendments are of detail only and not of great significance.

Outline of clause.   Clause 27 provides for the determination of the Contractor's employment by the Employer for certain specified defaults (clause 27.1), automatic determination upon bankruptcy, liquidation and other event symptomatic of insolvency (clause 27.2), determination for corruption (clause 27.3) and the effect of determination (clause 27.4).

This type of clause is often loosely described as a forfeiture clause. Such clauses are discussed generally at page 236. It is prudent to think carefully before using the clause because if it should turn out that the Employer was not entitled to stop the contract by treating the Contractor's employment as at an end, the Employer himself will ordinarily be guilty of repudiation and will be liable to the Contractor in damages.[67]

Performance bonds.   For consideration of the relationship between a performance bond and the terms of clause 25 of the 1963 Form, see *Nene Housing Society* v. *National Westminster Bank*.[68]

Interim injunction to remove Contractor.   It has been held that such an injunction would not be granted where the affidavits showed the allegations of fact upon which a determination was based were hotly disputed.[69] For a discussion of this case and the reasons for a submission that it would now no longer ordinarily be followed, see page 270.

Clause 27.1.   *Elements of a valid determination*
Forfeiture clauses are strictly construed and care must be taken to see that the terms of the contract are properly complied with.[70] The following is suggested as an introduction both for an Employer minded to determine and the Contractor considering whether he has a defence to a purported determination. Reference to the exact words of the clause must be made. The procedure is based on two notices[71] which have been termed "the Architect's Notice" and "the Employer's Notice."[72]

> *The First Notice.* Is the Contractor guilty of a default as specified in one of the sub-clauses 27.1.1–27.1.4? Does the Notice specify the default? Is it posted correctly?

---

[67] For repudiation generally, see p. 146.

[68] (1980) 16 B.L.R. 22. For bonds generally see p. 252.

[69] *Hounslow, London Borough Council* v. *Twickenham Garden Developments* (1971) Ch. 233.

[70] See generally "The mode of forfeiture" at p. 237.

[71] Save under clause 27.1.3 where there must additionally have been an earlier notice to remedy defects.

[72] *Hounslow, London Borough Council* v. *Twickenham Garden Developments* (1971) Ch. 233.

The Second Notice. Has the Contractor continued the default for a period of 14 days after receipt of the First Notice, or repeated such default at any time after the expiration of such period? Is the Second Notice given within 10 days of such continuance or repetition? Is it posted correctly? Is it given unreasonably or vexatiously?

Clause 27.1.   *"Without prejudice to any other rights or remedies . . ."*

It is clear that this express reservation to the Employer of any other rights or remedy preserves his normal rights at common law against the Contractor. If the Contractor's conduct can properly be interpreted as amounting to repudiation of the Contract, the Employer is entitled to treat the contract as at an end.[73] It follows that repudiatory conduct by the Contractor which does not constitute an event within clauses 27.1.1–27.1.4 nonetheless entitles the Employer to determine the Contract.

There may be a breach by the Contractor which both falls within clause 27.1 and constitutes repudiation.[74] An absolute refusal to carry out the Works or an abandonment of the Works before they are substantially completed, without any lawful excuse, is a repudiation.[75] But delay, bad work and unauthorised subletting are not breaches any one of which is automatically a repudiation (compare clauses 27.1.2, 27.1.3 and 27.1.4) although the effect of any such breach or more than one considered together may, in the circumstances, be repudiatory so as to entitle the Employer to treat the Contract as at an end.[76] If the Contractor is guilty of default which is both a repudiation and also an event which gives rise to a right of determination under clause 27.1, the Employer has, it is submitted, an option. He may either follow the procedure of clause 27.1 whereupon he will have the advantage of clause 27.4 or he may accept the repudiation and treat the Contract as at an end forthwith.[77] Immediate arbitration is available for disputes (see clause 41.3).

Clause 27.1.1.   *". . . without reasonable cause . . ."*

This provision under clause 25 of the 1963 Form was considered by the Court of Appeal in *Lubenham* v. *South Pembrokeshire District Council*.[78] The Architects issued Interim Certificates which were not correctly calculated in that they included unauthorised deductions for liquidated damages and defects. The Contractor thereupon withdrew labour from site. The Employer served 14-day default notices under the predecessor provisions in the 1963 Form of clause 27.1.1 and 27.1.2. Subsequently the Contractor's employment was determined. The Court of Appeal held that the Contracts had been

---

[73] *Sutcliffe* v. *Chippendale & Edmondson* (1971) 18 B.L.R. 149 at 160 to 162. This case subsequently went to the Court of Appeal and to the House of Lords but these issues were not argued there.
[74] For repudiation generally, see p. 146.
[75] See p. 153.
[76] See p. 154.
[77] See further "Repudiation and contractual determination clauses" at p. 153.
[78] (1986) 33 B.L.R. 39 (C.A.).

properly determined. The Employer was not obliged to pay more than the amount stated as due on the face of the Interim Certificate. Whatever the cause of the under-valuation, the proper remedy of the Contractor was to request the Architect to make an appropriate adjustment in another Certificate or to go to arbitration. In default of a new Certificate or arbitration, the Contractor had no right to sue for a higher sum than that stated to be due in the Certificate. The issue of the Certificate was a condition precedent to the right of the Contractor to be paid. The court further held that there was no necessity or scope for the implication of a term that if and when it became known to the Employer that the Architect was departing from his proper function, it was the Employer's duty to stop the Architect and tell the Architect what the function was. It follows that dissatisfaction on the part of the Contractor with Interim Certificates does not amount to reasonable cause within the meaning of clause 27.1.1.

Clause 27.1.2. *"... fails to proceed regularly and diligently with the Works ..."*

This ground of determination applies, it is submitted, after as well as before the Date for Completion is passed. For the Contractor's duty to proceed regularly and diligently, see clause 23.1 and its commentary.

Clause 27.1.3. *"... refuses or neglects to comply ... and ... the Works are materially affected ..."*

This sub-clause was amended by the removal of the word "persistently" before "neglects" by Amendment 4 issued in July 1987. It follows that, in principle, a single such neglect would entitle the Employer to determine. However, this is qualified by the proviso to clause 27.1 that notice of determination shall not be given unreasonably or vexatiously. It is thought that only in exceptional circumstances would the Employer be able to determine the contract validly for a single such neglect. It is arguable that this ground is only intended to be available before Practical Completion. For failure to comply with an instruction to remedy defects under clause 17, a less drastic remedy is available under clause 4.1.2. Note that for determination under this sub-clause there must be three Notices.

Clause 27.1.3 and Nominated Sub-Contractors. The Contractor has no right or duty to carry out the work of the Nominated Sub-Contractor,[79] and it may be argued that this sub-clause is not intended to apply. However, it can be said that the wording of this sub-clause is quite general and that by necessary implication the Contractor has power to remove the defective work of a Nominated Sub-Contractor who refuses to do so himself. This appears more likely to be the intention of the contract in view of the amendments to clause 8.4 (discussed at page 509) which refer in terms to Nominated Sub-Contractors in the context of work, materials or goods not being in accordance with the Contract.[80]

---

[79] See p. 293.
[80] cf. however *John Jarvis* v. *Rockdale Housing Association* (1986) 36 B.L.R. 48 (C.A.).

Clause 27.1. "*. . . determine the employment . . .*"

The contract is not determined, for on both sides important contractual rights and liabilities continue or arise.

Clause 27.1. "*. . . provided that such notice shall not be given unreasonably or vexatiously.*"

If so given it is, it is submitted, void. This proviso imposes an important limitation on the operation of the clause. What is unreasonable or vexatious depends upon the circumstances and may give rise to a lengthy investigation in subsequent proceedings. The identically worded proviso to clause 28.1 was considered by the Court of Appeal in *John Jarvis* v. *Rockdale Housing Association.*[81] "Unreasonably" was held to be "a general term which can include anything which can be objectively judged to be unreasonable." A notice would not be considered as given unreasonably unless it was one which no reasonable Contractor in the circumstances of the particular Contractor would have given. "Vexatiously" was said to connote "an ulterior motive to oppress, harass or annoy."[82]

Clause 27.2. This clause was somewhat redrafted by Amendment 4 issued in July 1987 to take account of the provisions of the Insolvency Act 1986.

Clause 27.2. "*. . . automatically determine . . .*"

Upon the happening of one of the events set out in clause 27.2, the employment of the Contractor is automatically determined and no notice or other formality is required. Nevertheless, as soon as the Employer discovers the event, if he wishes to take advantage of the clause[83] he is well advised to tell the Contractor, his trustee in bankruptcy, etc., that he relies on the clause. Otherwise if the Employer takes no step and permits the Works to continue, it may be said that the Employer has waived his rights under the clause, or, to use the words of the clause, that the employment of the Contractor, his trustee in bankruptcy, etc., has been "reinstated and continued."

Right to disclaim. The trustee in bankruptcy and liquidator have a statutory right to disclaim the contract if it is unprofitable, *i.e.* to bring the Contract to an end from the date of the disclaimer.[84] It is doubtful how far the provisions of clause 27.4 are good against a trustee in bankruptcy or liquidator who disclaims.[85]

---

[81] (1986) 36 B.L.R. 48 (C.A.).

[82] Bingham L.J. in *John Jarvis* v. *Rockdale Housing Association* (1986) 36 B.L.R. 48 at 68 (C.A.).

[83] In practice it is often to the advantage of both parties for the Contractor's trustee in bankruptcy, etc., to complete the contract.

[84] ss.178 and 315 of Insolvency Act 1986.

[85] See further "Insolvency of Contractor" at p. 377 and in particular "Disclaimer" and "Forfeiture, lien and seizure clauses." For the position as to materials upon bankruptcy or liquidation, see further commentary to clause 30 and "Retention of title clauses" at p. 242.

Clause 27.3. The provisions relating to corruption were introduced into the Private Version by Amendment 4 issued in July 1987. They had always formed part of the Local Authorities Edition.

Clause 27.4.1. *"... use all temporary buildings, plant, tools, ..."*
This does not bind a person not party to the contract, *e.g.* owners of cranes, scaffolding and other equipment who have hired it to the Contractor. See also clause 27.4.3.

Clause 27.4.2.2. *"unless the exception to the operation of clause 27.4.2.1 applies the Employer may pay any supplier or Sub-Contractor ..."*
This provision gives the Employer the right to pay any supplier or Sub-Contractor direct. Note that the Employer's discretion to pay suppliers or Sub-Contractors direct is excluded where the determination of the Contractor's employment occurred because of the Contractor's bankruptcy or liquidation. This reflects the view that the decisions in *Re. Wilkinson*[86] and *Re Tout and Finch*[87] have not survived the decision of the House of Lords in *British Eagle* v. *Air France.*[88]

Clause 27.4.4. *"Until after completion ... the Employer shall not be bound ... make any further payment ..."*
This extends, it is submitted, not only to work not certified, but to sums certified but not due for payment under clause 30.1 at the date of determination. It only applies if the Employer proceeds to complete.

Clause 27.4.4. *"... the Architect ... shall certify the amount of expenses properly incurred by the Employer and the amount of any direct loss and/or damage caused to the Employer by the determination ..."*
The Contractor has to allow or pay these sums subject to receiving a credit for what he would have been paid if the Contract had not been determined. There thus has to be taken a notional final account. Theoretically there could be something payable to the Contractor. In practice this is unlikely to happen because the Employer is entitled to the expenses of completing under clause 27.4.1 and, under the words "direct loss and/or damage" any damages which he has suffered by reason of the determination. This includes, it is submitted, damages for delay. Note the difference in the wording of "direct loss and/or damage" in this clause and "direct loss and/or expense" in clauses 26 and 34, the meaning of which is discussed in the commentary to clause 26. It appears that there is no difference in meaning between the two terms and that the word "expense" is avoided in clause 27 in order to keep quite distinct the two elements which go to make up the Architect's Certificate under clause 27.4.4

---

[86] [1905] 2 K.B. 713.
[87] [1954] 1 W.L.R. 178.
[88] [1975] 1 W.L.R. 758 (H.L.). These decisions are discussed further in the context of Clause 35.

as allowable or payable to the Employer subject to the credit in favour of the Contractor.[89]

It was held under the 1963 Form that the operation of clause 25(4)(d) created a contingent liability in favour of the Employer provable in the winding-up of the Contractor as a contingent debt or liability within section 30 of the Bankruptcy Act 1914 (now section 322 of the Insolvency Act 1986). The Employer had a statutory right under section 31 of the Bankruptcy Act 1914 (now section 323 of the Insolvency Act 1986) to set-off such contingent liabilities against sums otherwise due to the Contractor because the term "debt" in section 31 included a contingent liability and the building contract established that there had been mutual dealings between the parties within the meaning of section 31.[90]

28. Determination by Contractor

28.1 Without prejudice to any other rights and remedies which the Contractor may possess, if

.1 the Employer does not pay the amount properly due to the Contractor on any certificate (otherwise than as a result of the operation of the VAT Agreement) within 14 days from the issue of that certificate and continues such default for 7 days after receipt by registered post or recorded delivery of a notice from the Contractor stating that notice of determination under clause 28 will be served if payment is not made within 7 days from receipt thereof; or

.2 the Employer interferes with or obstructs the issue of any certificate due under this Contract; or

.3 the carrying out of the whole or substantially the whole of the uncompleted Works (other than the execution of work required under clause 17) is suspended for a continuous period of the length named in the Appendix by reason of:

.3.1 Architect's/Contract Administrator's instructions issued under clause 2.3, 13.2 or 23.2 unless caused by reason of some negligence or default of the Contractor, his servants or agents or of any person employed or engaged upon or in connection with the Works or any part thereof, his servants or agents other than a Nominated Sub-Contractor or the Employer or any person employed, engaged or authorised by the Employer or by any local authority or statutory undertaker executing work solely in pursuance of its statutory obligations; or

.3.2 the Contractor not having received in due time necessary instructions, drawings, details or levels from the Architect/the Contract Administrator for which he specifically applied in writing provided that such application was made on a date which having regard to the Completion Date was neither unreasonably distant from nor unreasonably close to the date on which it was necessary for him to receive the same; or

.3.3 delay in the execution of work not forming part of this Contract by the Employer himself or by persons employed or otherwise engaged by the Employer as referred to in clause 29 or the failure to execute such work or delay in the supply

---

[89] See *Wraight Ltd.* v. *P.H. & T. (Holdings) Ltd.* (1968) 13 B.L.R. 27 discussed at p. 601.

[90] *Willment Brothers* v. *North West Thames R.H.A.* (1984) 26 B.L.R. 51 (C.A.). See also "Mutual dealings" at p. 379.

by the Employer of materials and goods which the Employer has agreed to provide for the Works or the failure so to supply; or

.3.4 the opening up for inspection of any work covered up or the testing of any of the work, materials or goods in accordance with clause 8.3 (including making good in consequence of such opening up or testing), unless the inspection or test showed that the work, materials or goods were not in accordance with this Contract;

.3.5 failure of the Employer to give in due time ingress to or egress from the site of the Works or any part thereof through or over any land, buildings, way or passage adjoining or connected with the site and in the possession and control of the Employer, in accordance with the Contract Bills or the Contract Drawings, after receipt by the Architect/the Contract Administrator of such notice, if any, as the Contractor is required to give, or failure of the Employer to give such ingress or egress as otherwise agreed between the Architect/the Contract Administrator and the Contractor.

then the Contractor may thereupon by notice by registered post or recorded delivery to the Employer or the Architect/the Contract Administrator forthwith determine the employment of the Contractor under this Contract; provided that such notice shall not be given unreasonably or vexatiously.

28.2 Upon such determination, then without prejudice to the accrued rights or remedies of either party or to any liability of the classes mentioned in clause 20 which may accrue either before the Contractor or any Sub-Contractors shall have removed his or their temporary buildings, plant, tools, equipment, goods or materials or by reason of his or their so removing the same, the following shall be the respective rights and liabilities of the Contractor and the Employer:

.1 the Contractor shall with all reasonable dispatch and in such manner and with such precautions as will prevent injury, death or damage of the classes in respect of which before the date of determination he was liable to indemnify the Employer under clause 20 remove from the site all his temporary buildings, plant, tools, equipment, goods and materials and shall give facilities for his Sub-Contractors to do the same, but subject always to the provisions of clause 28.2.2.4;

.2 after taking into account amounts previously paid under this Contract the Contractor shall be paid by the Employer:

.2.1 the total value of work completed at the date of determination, such value to be computed as if it were a valuation in respect of the amounts to be stated as due in an Interim Certificate issued under clause 30.1 but after taking account of any amounts referred to in clauses 28.2.2.3 to .6;

.2.2 the total value of work begun and executed but not completed at the date of determination, the value being ascertained in accordance with clause 13.5 as if such work were a Variation required by the Architect/the Contract Administrator under clause 13.2 but after taking account of any amounts referred to in clauses 28.2.2.3 to .6;

.2.3 any sum ascertained in respect of direct loss and/or expense under clauses 26 and 34.3 (whether ascertained before or after the date of determination);

.2.4 the cost of materials or goods properly ordered for the Works for which the Contractor shall have paid or for which the Contractor is legally bound to pay, and on such payment by the Employer any materials or goods so paid for shall become the property of the Employer;

.2.5 the reasonable cost of removal under clause 28.2.1;

.2.6 any direct loss and/or damage caused to the Contractor or to any Nominated Sub-Contractor by the determination.

.3   The Employer shall inform the Contractor in writing which part or parts of the amount paid or payable under clause 28.2.2 is or are fairly and reasonably attributable to any Nominated Sub-Contractor and shall so inform each Nominated Sub-Contractor in writing.

Clause 28: Determination by Contractor

Derivation.   The original version of clause 28 is substantially the same as clause 26 of the 1963 Form. The clause was substantially amended by Amendment 4 issued in July 1987. The principal change was that suspension of the Works by reason of *force majeure*, or loss or damage to the Works occasioned by a specified peril or by reason of civil commotion were removed from clause 28. They are now to be found in the new clause 28A. Moreover, these grounds are now available for determination both to the Contractor and the Employer. Formerly such grounds were available to the Contractor only. It follows that the grounds in clause 28.1.3 are now confined to a suspension of the Works by reason of some fault on the part of the Employer. Suspension which is the fault of neither Contractor nor Employer is dealt with by clause 28A. There are also some more minor amendments to clause 28 which are discussed below.

Outline of clause.   The clause provides for the Contractor, without prejudice to any other rights and remedies he may possess,[91] determining his employment on certain specified grounds including the suspension of the work due to causes within the control of the Employer for a continuous period which the parties have stated in the Appendix. Clause 28.2 provides for the effect of such determination in terms which, in effect, indemnify the Contractor against loss. Immediate arbitration is available for disputes (see clause 41.3), but proceedings are not always quick. In the Private Version there is a further clause 28.1.4 entitling the Contractor to determine upon the Employer's bankruptcy or other event symptomatic of insolvency.

Nature of clause.   It should be compared with clause 27. It gives the Contractor the right upon the happening of events referred to and upon following the procedure set out to withdraw from the site and to have the benefit of the valuable provisions of clause 28.2. As with clause 27, if it is relied upon it must be properly and exactly complied with, for if the Contractor wrongfully withdraws permanently from the site, it is normally a repudiation of the contract by the Contractor which not only deprives him of the benefit of clause 28.2 but renders him liable in damages to the Employer.

Clause 28 events compared with repudiation.   For repudiation generally, see page 146 and see also commentary to clause 27.1 at page 590.

---

[91] For the meaning of this phrase, see *Sutcliffe* v. *Chippendale & Edmondson* (1971) 18 B.L.R. 149 at 160, discussed at p. 154.

Most of the clause 28 events would amount to breaches of contract by the Employer. However, they would not necessarily be repudiatory in effect. If, however, the event in clause 28.1 is also a repudiation, the Contractor has, it is submitted, an option either to determine under clause 28 or to accept the repudiation and treat the Contract as at an end and forthwith claim damages.[92] The rights under clause 28.2 are so extensive that it is usually in his interests to determine.

Determination of employment.   The Contract is not determined for on both sides important contractual rights and liabilities continue to arise.

Procedure.   The procedure is simpler than under clause 27.1 in that if one of the conditions in clause 28.1 is satisfied, only one notice is required. But the condition itself must be carefully studied, *e.g.* under clause 28.1.1 a prior written notice and a continuance thereafter of the default for 7 days is required, and under clause 28.1.3.2 prior written application and the expiry of due time is necessary.

Clause 28.1.1.   "*. . . the Employer does not pay the amount properly due to the Contractor on any certificate . . .*"

What is meant by "the amount properly due"? In the 1963 Form the equivalent expression was "the amount due." This expression was considered by the Court of Appeal in *Lubenham* v. *South Pembrokeshire District Council.*[93] The Court held that the amount due was the amount stated as due on the face of the Interim Certificate. This was so even if the Interim Certificate contained unauthorised deductions and even if the Employer knew that the Architect was departing from his function by making such unauthorised deductions. In those circumstances, the remedy of the Contractor was by means of arbitration.[94] It is thought that the introduction of the word "properly" may be of significance. It may now be that the first part of the clause 28.1.1 condition would be satisfied if a certificate contained an improper deduction on its face or possibly if such a deduction could be established by reference to accompanying explanatory documents. But the Contractor would have to establish what was "properly due" on the certificate in question, not some other certificate which he might argue the Architect could have issued. The first part of the condition would not, it is thought, be satisfied where the Architect's certificate, although low, was within the scope of the discretion entrusted to him by the Contract. The Contractor would have to show more than an undervaluation. He would have to show both that the certificate had been issued in a manner unauthorised by the Contract and that some particular amount other than the purported amount of the certificate was "the amount

---

[92] See further "Repudiation and contractual determination clauses" at p. 153.
[93] (1986) 33 B.L.R. 39 (C.A.).
[94] See also "Co-operation" at p. 48.

properly due" on the certificate. This will rarely be possible except where there is a palpably wrong deduction which the Employer nevertheless persists in adopting.

The Employer has express contractual rights to make deductions from sums certified for payments, for example, under clauses 4.1.2, 22A.2 and 24. Commenting on clause 26(1) of the 1963 Form it was said that the reference to "the amount due on any certificate" meant the amount due after deduction of any sums which the Employer was entitled under the Contract to deduct.[95] It is submitted that this remains so in the 1980 Form. Further, the Employer may have a right of set-off. There is no authority upon the question whether "the amount properly due" means the amount due after allowing for such set-off, but it is probable that it does. The introduction of the word "properly" makes it more likely that the Employer is entitled to rely upon a right of set-off.[96] In any event, if the Contractor knew of the Employer's claim to make such set-off and the claim was eventually established, the Arbitrator might well find that a Contractor who had given notice in such circumstances had given it unreasonably.

Clause 28.1.2. *"the Employer interferes with or obstructs the issue of any certificate"*

This includes the Employer "refusing to allow the architect to go on to the site for the purpose of giving his certificate, or directing the architect as to the amount for which he is to give his certificate or as to the decision which he should arrive at on some matter within the sphere of his independent duty."[97] For the Architect's duty to act fairly and professionally when certifying, see page 114.

Clause 28.1.3. This sub-clause was amended by Amendment 4 issued in July 1987. As previously noted, three causes of suspension were removed from this clause and inserted in the new clause 28A. There is consequential renumbering. Clause 28.1.3.5 is a new cause of suspension introduced by this amendment.

Clause 28.1.3. *". . . the length named in the Appendix . . ."*

The contract positively requires the insertion of such a period. It is suggested that the Architect should consider carefully with his client whether the period suggested in the Appendix of one month is adequate. For example, in a complex project a technical problem might arise making it necessary to suspend the Works whilst it is solved. One month's suspension might be wholly inadequate.

---

[95] *Modern Engineering (Bristol)* v. *Gilbert Ash (Northern)* [1974] A.C. 689 at 709 (H.L.).

[96] For set-off generally, see pp. 438 *et seq.*

[97] Lord Tucker in *Burden* v. *Swansea Corporation* [1957] 1 W.L.R. 1167 at 1180 (H.L.). This arose on the 1939 Form where the clause was confined to certificates of payment but where the principle was, it is submitted, the same.

Clause 28.1.3.1. *"... default ..."*

The meaning of this word was considered in the context of the predecessor provision to clause 20.2 in *City of Manchester* v. *Fram Gerrard*.[98] It was held that default would be established if either a person did not do what he ought to have done or did what he ought not to have done in all the circumstances and provided that the conduct in question involved something in the nature of a breach of duty so as to be properly describable as a default. It should be noted that breach of statutory duty is not referred to in this clause although, for example, it is specifically mentioned in clause 20.2. It is thought, therefore, that breach of statutory duty which does not amount to negligence does not come within this clause.

Clause 28.1.3.1. *"... his servants or agents ... statutory obligations"*

These words were introduced by Amendment 4 issued in July 1987. The original version of the sub-clause was considered by the Court of Appeal in *John Jarvis* v. *Rockdale Housing Association*.[99] The court held that the reference to the Contractor was to the Main Contractor and did not include Nominated Sub-Contractors. It now seems reasonably clear that this clause extends to all subcontractors except for Nominated Sub-Contractors and to all suppliers, whether nominated or not. This is subject to the question of what is meant by "authorised by the Employer" (see commentary to clause 20.2 above).

Clause 28.1.3.2. This ground of suspension is not subject to the qualification in clause 28.1.3.1 relating to the negligence or default of the Contractor (see above). In the appropriate case, therefore, the Architect will postpone the Works under clause 23.2 and not leave a negligent or defaulting Contractor the opportunity of determining under this sub-clause.

Clause 28.1.3.5. This is a new sub-clause introduced by Amendment 4 issued in July 1987. It corresponds to the Relevant Event relating to extension of time at clause 25.4.12 (see commentary above).

Clause 28.1. *"... by notice by registered post or recorded delivery ..."*

This phrase was considered by the Court of Appeal in the context of clause 26 of the 1963 Form in *J.M. Hill* v. *London Borough of Camden*.[1] The court held that the notice of Determination operates only from the time when it is received, not when it is posted.

Clause 28.1. *"... provided that such notice shall not be given unreasonably or vexatiously."*

The Court of Appeal has twice considered the meaning to be given to these words. In *J.M. Hill* v. *London Borough of Camden*,[2] the Employer contended that

---

[98] (1974) 6 B.L.R. 70.
[99] (1986) 36 B.L.R. 48 (C.A.).
[1] (1980) 18 B.L.R. 31 (C.A.).
[2] (1980) 18 B.L.R. 31 (C.A.).

the Contractor's determination was unreasonable or vexatious because the Contractor had withdrawn a substantial proportion of his workforce from the site before the relevant certificate became due for payment. This contention was rejected. Ormrod L.J., discussing the meaning of the term "unreasonably," said:

> "I imagine that it is meant to protect an Employer who is a day out of time in payment, or whose cheque is in the post, or perhaps because the Bank is closed; or there has been a delay in clearing the cheque or something ... accidental or purely incidental so that the court could see that the contractor was taking advantage of the other side in circumstances in which, from a business point of view, it would be totally unfair and almost smacking of sharp practice."[3]

In *John Jarvis* v. *Rockdale Housing Association*,[4] the court held that notice was not given unreasonably or vexatiously unless a reasonable Contractor, circumstanced in all respects as was the Contractor at the time when he gave the notice, would have thought that it was unreasonable or vexatious to give such a notice. "Vexatiously" was said to connote "an ulterior motive to oppress, harass or annoy."[5]

Clause 28.2.2. "... *after taking into account* ..."

The procedure under this subclause was considered by the Court of Appeal in the context of clause 26(2) of the 1963 Form in *Lintest Builders Ltd.* v. *Roberts*.[6] The Contractor determined under clause 26(1). The Employer alleged that some work was defective. The Contractor argued, in reliance upon certain dicta in *Kaye (P. & M.)* v. *Hosier & Dickinson*,[7] that any such defective work amounted only to a temporary disconformity entitling the Employer to purely nominal damages. This contention was rejected. The court held that the Employer acquired a right to have the defective work put right at the time the defective work was done. This was an accrued right within the terms of clause 26(2). Thus the reasonable cost of the necessary remedial works was to be taken into account when calculating sums due to the Contractor under clause 26(2).

Clause 28.2.6. "... *direct loss and/or damage* ..."

See commentary to clause 27. In *Wraight Ltd.* v. *P.H. & T. (Holdings) Ltd.*[8] Megaw J. rejected submissions that, because the clause could operate where there was no fault on the part of the Employer, the words were to have a limited effect different from their natural meaning. He held that the Contractor was

---

[3] (1980) 18 B.L.R. 31 at 49 (C.A.).
[4] (1986) 36 B.L.R. 48 (C.A.).
[5] Bingham L.J. in *John Jarvis* v. *Rockdale Housing Association* (1986) 36 B.L.R. 48 at 68 (C.A.).
[6] (1980) 13 B.L.R. 38; *cf. William Tomkinson* v. *Parochial Church Council of St. Michael* (1990) 6 Const. L.J. 319.
[7] (1972) 1 W.L.R. 146 at 165 (H.L.).
[8] (1968) 13 B.L.R. 27.

entitled to recover that which he would have obtained if the Contract had been fulfilled in terms of the picture visualised in advance but which he had not obtained and could not obtain because of the determination. Such entitlement included loss of profit even though the Contractor had only worked a few weeks out of a 60-week Contract when work was suspended due to unanticipated difficulties.

28A.   Determination by Employer or Contractor

28A.1   Without prejudice to any other rights or remedies which the Employer or the Contractor may possess, if the carrying out of the whole or substantially the whole of the uncompleted Works (other than the execution of work required under clause 17) is suspended for a continuous period of the length named in the Appendix by reason of:

.1   force majeure; or

.2   loss or damage to the Works occasioned by any one or more of the Specified Perils; or

.3   civil commotion

then the Employer or the Contractor may thereupon by notice by registered post or recorded delivery to the Contractor or to the Employer forthwith determine the employment of the Contractor under this Contract; provided that such notice shall not be given unreasonably or vexatiously.

28A.2   The Contractor shall not be entitled to give notice under clause 28A.1 where the loss or damage to the Works occasioned by the Specified Perils was caused by some negligence or default of the Contractor, his servants or agents or of any person employed or engaged upon or in connection with the Works or any part thereof, his servants or agents other than the Employer or any person employed, engaged or authorised by the Employer or by any local authority or statutory undertaker executing work solely in pursuance of its statutory obligations.

28A.3   Upon such determination under clause 28A.1 the provisions of clause 28.2 shall apply with the exception of clause 28.2.2.6.

Clause 28A: Determination by Employer or Contractor

Generally.   This is a new clause introduced into the Contract by Amendment 4 issued in July 1987. The grounds set out at clause 28A.1.1 to 28A.1.3 were formerly only grounds for determination open to the Contractor under clause 28 but not to the Employer under clause 27. The effect of this new clause is that these grounds for determination of the employment of the Contractor are now open both to the Contractor and to the Employer.

Clause 28A.1.   For the phrases "without prejudice to any other rights or remedies ...," "notice by registered post or recorded delivery ..." and "provided that such notice shall not be given unreasonably or vexatiously," see the commentary to clauses 27 and 28.

Clause 28A.1.1. For the meaning of *"force majeure,"* see commentary to clause 25.4.1. For "civil commotion," see commentary to clause 25.4.4.

Clause 28A.2. The right of the Contractor to determine where loss or damage to the Works was occasioned by any one or more of the Specified Perils was subject to the proviso, in the original version of the 1980 Form, "unless caused by the negligence of the Contractor, his servants or agents or of any Sub-Contractor, his servants or agents ...." It was unclear whether the negligence of Nominated Sub-Contractors and of sub-Sub-Contractors was included or not.[9] The wording is now apt to include sub-Sub-Contractors. It would appear, by virtue of the specific inclusion of Nominated Sub-Contractors in clause 28.1.3.1 but their exclusion here, that the Contractor is not entitled to give notice of determination where the loss or damage was caused by the negligence of a Nominated Sub-Contractor. However, there remains some difficulty as to the phrase "authorised by the Employer."[10]

Clause 28A.3. Upon determination under this clause the provisions of clause 28.2 apply except that the Contractor is not entitled to claim "direct loss and/or damage" under clause 28.2.2.6.

29.   Works by Employer or persons employed or engaged by Employer

29.1   Where the Contract Bills, in regard to any work not forming part of this Contract and which is to be carried out by the Employer himself or by persons employed or otherwise engaged by him, provide such information as is necessary to enable the Contractor to carry out and complete the Works in accordance with the Conditions, the Contractor shall permit the execution of such work.

29.2   Where the Contract Bills do not provide the information referred to in clause 29.1 and the Employer requires the execution of work not forming part of this Contract by the Employer himself or by persons employed or otherwise engaged by the Employer, then the Employer may, with the consent of the Contractor (which consent shall not be unreasonably withheld) arrange for the execution of such work.

29.3   Every person employed or otherwise engaged by the Employer as referred to in clauses 29.1 and 29.2 shall for the purpose of clause 20 be deemed to be a person for whom the Employer is responsible and not to be a Sub-Contractor.

Clause 29: Works by Employer or persons employed or engaged by the Employer

Derivation.   Clause 29 is derived from clause 29 of the 1963 Form. It is

---

[9] See *City of Manchester* v. *Fram Gerrard* (1974) 6 B.L.R. 70, discussed above in relation to clause 20.
[10] See commentary to clause 20.2.

substantially redrafted. The former expression "artists, tradesmen or others engaged by the Employer" was somewhat curious and was arguably open to a restrictive interpretation (although such an interpretation was in fact rejected by the Court in *Henry Boot* v. *Central Lancashire Development Corporation*).[11]

Outline of clause. Clause 29 applies to work to be carried out "by the Employer himself or by persons employed or otherwise engaged by him." The reference to work carried out by the "Employer himself" is an innovation in the 1980 Form. Clause 29 distinguishes between work by others which is sufficiently described in the Contract Bills to put the Contractor on notice when he is tendering (clause 29.1), and work by others which is not so described (clause 29.2). For delay or disruption caused by work the subject of clause 29, see clauses 25.4.8.1, 26.2.4.1 and 28.1.3.3.

Clause 29.1. The wording is wide enough to enable substantial works to be carried out by direct Contractors. Nomination under the 1980 Form involves a long cumbersome procedure which by inadvertence or bad luck may go wrong (see commentary to clause 35). Further, its legal consequences remain somewhat unsatisfactory even if success is achieved in complying with the terms of the Contract. One alternative to nomination is the "three persons" procedure (see clause 19.3 and its commentary). Another is to make direct contracts. This is at least worth considering where the Employer dislikes nomination under the Contract but cannot or does not wish to use the three persons procedure.

Clause 29.2. Where there is no sufficient description in the Bills, the Employer has no absolute right to interfere with the Contractor's work by having work which does not form part of the contract carried out. This can now only be done with the Contractor's consent. Consent is not to be unreasonably withheld. Immediate arbitration is not available for a dispute of this subject (see clause 41.3).

30.   Certificates and Payments

30.1   .1.1   The Architect/The Contract Administrator shall from time to time as provided in clause 30 issue Interim Certificates stating the amount due to the Contractor from the Employer and the Contractor shall be entitled to payment therefor within 14 days from the date of issue of each Interim Certificate. [*q*]

.1.2   Notwithstanding the fiduciary interest of the Employer in the Retention as stated in clause 30.5.1 the Employer is entitled to exercise any right under this Contract of deduction from monies due or to become due to the Contractor against any

---

[11] (1981) 15 B.L.R. 1.

[*q*] *This entitlement is subject to the various rights of deduction given to the Employer in the Conditions including any obligation to deduct under clause 31 and to the obligations of the parties under the VAT Agreement.*

amount so due under an Interim Certificate whether or not any Retention is included in that Interim Certificate by the operation of clause 30.4. Such deduction is subject to the restriction set out in clause 35.13.5.4.2.

.1.3   Where the Employer exercises any right under this Contract of deduction from monies due or to become due to the Contractor he shall inform the Contractor in writing of the reason for that deduction.

.2   Interim valuations shall be made by the Quantity Surveyor whenever the Architect/the Contract Administrator considers them to be necessary for the purpose of ascertaining the amount to be stated as due in an Interim Certificate. [*r*]

.3   Interim Certificates shall be issued at the Period of Interim Certificates specified in the Appendix up to and including the end of the period during which the Certificate of Practical Completion is issued. Thereafter Interim Certificates shall be issued as and when further amounts are ascertained as payable to the Contractor from the Employer and after the expiration of the Defects Liability Period named in the Appendix or upon the issue of the Certificate of Completion of Making Good Defects (whichever is the later) provided always that the Architect/the Contract Administrator shall not be required to issue an Interim Certificate within one calendar month of having issued a previous Interim Certificate.

30.2   The amount stated as due in an Interim Certificate, subject to any agreement between the parties as to stage payments, shall be the gross valuation as referred to in clause 30.2 less

any amount which may be deducted and retained by the Employer as provided in clause 30.4 (in the Conditions called "the Retention") and
the total amount stated as due in Interim Certificates previously issued under the Conditions.

The gross valuation shall be the total of the amounts referred to in clauses 30.2.1 and 30.2.2 less the total of the amounts referred to in clause 30.2.3 and applied up to and including a date not more than 7 days before the date of the Interim Certificate.

.1   There shall be included the following which are subject to Retention:

.1.1   the total value of the work properly executed by the Contractor including any work so executed to which clause 13.5 refers but excluding any restoration, replacement or repair of loss or damage and removal and disposal of debris which in clauses 22B.3.5 and 22C.4.4.2 are treated as if they were a variation, together with, where applicable, any adjustment of that value under clause 40;

.1.2   the total value of the materials and goods delivered to or adjacent to the Works for incorporation therein by the Contractor but not so incorporated, provided that the value of such materials and goods shall only be included as and from such times as they are reasonably, properly and not prematurely so delivered and are adequately protected against weather and other casualties;

.1.3   the total value of any materials or goods other than those to which clause 30.2.1.2 refers where the Architect/the Contract Administrator in the exercise of his discretion under clause 30.3 has decided that such total value shall be included in the amount stated as due in an Interim Certificate;

.1.4   the amounts referred to in clause 21.4.1 of Sub-Contract NSC/4 or NSC/4a as applicable in respect of each Nominated Sub-Contractor;

.1.5   the profit of the Contractor upon the total of the amounts referred to in clauses 30.2.1.4 and 30.2.2.5 less the total of the amount referred to in clause 30.2.3.2 at

---

[*r*] *Where formula adjustment under clause 40 applies see amendment set out in clause 40.2.*

the rates included in the Contract Bills, or, in the cases where the nomination arises from an instruction as to the expenditure of a provisional sum, at rates related thereto, or if none, at reasonable rates.

.2 There shall be included the following which are not subject to Retention:

.2.1 any amounts to be included in Interim Certificates in accordance with clause 3 as a result of payments made or costs incurred by the Contractor under clauses 6.2, 8.3, 9.2 and 21.2.3;

.2.2 any amounts ascertained under clause 26.1 or 34.3 or in respect of any restoration, replacement or repair of loss or damage and removal and disposal of debris which in clauses 22B.3.5 and 22C.4.4.2 are treated as if they were a Variation;

.2.3 any amount to which clause 35.17 refers;

.2.4 any amount payable to the Contractor under clause 38 or 39, if applicable;

.2.5 the amounts referred to in clause 21.4.2 of Sub-Contract NSC/4 or NSC/4a as applicable in respect of each Nominated Sub-Contractor.

.3 There shall be deducted the following which are not subject to Retention:

.3.1 any amount deductible under clause 7 or 8.4.2 or 17.2 or 17.3 or any amount allowable by the Contractor to the Employer under clause 38 or 39, if applicable;

.3.2 any amount referred to in clause 21.4.3 of Sub-Contract NSC/4 or NSC/4a as applicable in respect of each Nominated Sub-Contractor.

30.3 The amount stated as due in an Interim Certificate may in the discretion of the Architect/the Contract Administrator include the value of any materials or goods before delivery thereof to or adjacent to the Works (in clause 30.3 referred to as "the materials") provided that:

.1 the materials are intended for incorporation in the Works;

.2 nothing remains to be done to the materials to complete the same up to the point of their incorporation in the Works;

.3 the materials have been and are set apart at the premises where they have been manufactured or assembled or are stored, and have been clearly and visibly marked, individually or in sets, either by letters or figures or by reference to a pre-determined code, so as to identify:

.3.1 the Employer, where they are stored on the premises of the Contractor, and in any other case the person to whose order they are held; and

.3.2 their destination as the Works;

.4 where the materials were ordered from a supplier by the Contractor or by any sub-contractor, the contract for their supply is in writing and expressly provides that the property therein shall pass unconditionally to the Contractor or the sub-contractor (as the case may be) not later than the happening of the events set out in clauses 30.3.2 and 30.3.3;

.5 where the materials were ordered from a supplier by any sub-contractor, the relevant sub-contract between the Contractor and the sub-contractor is in writing and expressly provides that on the property in the materials passing to the sub-contractor the same shall immediately thereon pass to the Contractor;

.6 where the materials were manufactured or assembled by any sub-contractor, the sub-contract is in writing and expressly provides that the property in the materials shall pass unconditionally to the Contractor not later than the happening of the events set out in clauses 30.3.2 and 30.3.3;

.7 the materials are in accordance with this Contract;

.8 the Contractor provides the Architect/the Contract Administrator with reasonable proof that the property in the materials is in him and that the appropriate conditions set out in clauses 30.3.1 to .7 have been complied with;

.9   the Contractor provides the Architect/the Contract Administrator with reasonable proof that the materials are insured against loss or damage for their full value under a policy of insurance protecting the interests of the Employer and the Contractor in respect of the Specified Perils, during the period commencing with the transfer of property in the materials to the Contractor until they are delivered to, or adjacent to, the Works.

30.4   .1   The Retention which the Employer may deduct and retain as referred to in clause 30.2 shall be such percentage of the total amount included under clause 30.2.1 in any Interim Certificate as arises from the operation of the following rules:

.1.1   the percentage (in the Conditions and Appendix called "the Retention Percentage") deductible under clause 30.4.1.2 shall be 5 per cent. (unless a lower rate shall have been agreed between the parties and specified in the Appendix as the Retention Percentage); and the percentage deductible under clause 30.4.1.3 shall be one half of the Retention Percentage; [*s*]

.1.2   [*t*] the Retention Percentage may be deducted from so much of the said total amount as relates to:

work which has not reached Practical Completion (as referred to in clauses 17.1, 18.1.1 or 35.16); and
amounts in respect of the value of materials and goods included under clauses 30.2.1.2, 30.2.1.3 and 30.2.1.4 (so far as that clause relates to materials and goods as referred to in clause 21.4.1 of Sub-Contract NSC/4 or NSC/4a as applicable);

.1.3   [*t*] half the Retention Percentage may be deducted from so much of the said total amount as relates to work which has reached Practical Completion (as referred to in clauses 17.1, 18.1.1 or 35.16) but in respect of which a Certificate of Completion of Making Good Defects under clause 17.4 or a certificate under clause 18.1.2 or an Interim Certificate under clause 35.17, has not been issued.

.2   The Retention deducted from the value of work executed by the Contractor or any Nominated Sub-Contractor, and from the value of materials and goods intended for incorporation in the Works, but not so incorporated, and specified in the statements issued under clause 30.5.2.1, is hereinafter referred to as the "Contractor's retention" and the "Nominated Sub-Contract retention" respectively.

30.5   The Retention shall be subject to the following rules:

.1   the Employer's interest in the Retention is fiduciary as trustee for the Contractor and for any Nominated Sub-Contractor (but without obligation to invest);

.2.1   at the date of each Interim Certificate the Architect/the Contract Administrator shall prepare, or instruct the Quantity Surveyor to prepare, a statement specifying the Contractor's retention and the Nominated Sub-Contract retention for

---

[*s*] *Where the Employer at the tender stage estimates the Contract Sum to be £500,000 or over, the Retention Percentage should not be more than 3 per cent.*

[*t*] *By the operation of clauses 30.4.1.2 and 30.4.1.3 the Contractor will have released to him by the Employer upon payment of the next Interim Certificate after Practical Completion of the whole or part of the Works approximately one half of the Retention on the whole or the appropriate part; and upon payment of the next Interim Certificate after the expiration of the Defects Liability Period named in the Appendix, or after the issue of the Certificate of Completion of Making Good Defects, whichever is the later, the balance of the Retention on the whole or the appropriate part. When Retention is so included in Interim Certificates it becomes a "sum due" to the Contractor and therefore subject to the rights of the Employer to deduct therefrom in accordance with the rights of the Employer so to deduct as set out in the conditions.*

each Nominated Sub-Contractor deducted in arriving at the amount stated as due in such Interim Certificate;

.2.2 such statement shall be issued by the Architect/the Contract Administrator to the Employer, to the Contractor and to each Nominated Sub-Contractor whose work is referred to in the statement.

.3 [Number not used]

.4 Where the Employer exercises the right to deduct referred to in clause 30.1.1.2 against any Retention he shall inform the Contractor of the amount of that deduction from either the Contractor's retention or the Nominated Sub-Contract retention of any Nominated Sub-Contractor by reference to the latest statement issued under clause 30.5.2.1.

30.6 .1.1 Not later than 6 months after Practical Completion of the Works the Contractor shall provide the Architect/the Contract Administrator, or if so instructed by the Architect/the Contract Administrator, the Quantity Surveyor, with all documents necessary for the purposes of the adjustment of the Contract Sum including all documents relating to the accounts of Nominated Sub-Contractors and Nominated Suppliers.

.1.2 Not later than 3 months after receipt by the Architect/the Contract Administrator or by the Quantity Surveyor of the documents referred to in clause 30.6.11

.2.1 the Architect/the Contract Administrator, or, if the Architect/the Contract Administrator has so instructed, the Quantity Surveyor shall ascertain (unless previously ascertained) any loss and/or expense under clauses 26.1, 26.4.1 and 34.3, and

.2.2 the Quantity Surveyor shall prepare a statement of all adjustments to be made to the Contract Sum as referred to in clause 30.6.2 other than any to which clause 30.6.1.2.1 applies

and the Architect/the Contract Administrator shall forthwith send a copy of any ascertainment to which clause 30.6.1.2.1 refers and of the statement prepared in compliance with clause 30.6.1 .2.2 to the Contractor and the relevant extract therefrom to each Nominated Sub-Contractor.

.2 The Contract Sum shall be adjusted as follows:
There shall be deducted:

.2.1 all prime cost sums, all amounts in respect of Sub-Contractors named as referred to in clause 35.1, the certified value of any work by a Nominated Sub-Contractor, whose employment has been determined in accordance with clause 35.24, which was not in accordance with the relevant Sub-Contract but which has been paid or otherwise discharged by the Employer, and any Contractor's profit thereon included in the Contract Bills;

.2.2 all provisional sums and the value of all work described as provisional included in the Contract Bills;

.2.3 the amount of the valuation under clause 13.5.2 of items omitted in accordance with a Variation required by the Architect/the Contract Administrator under clause 13.2, or subsequently sanctioned by him in writing, together with the amount included in the Contract Bills for any other work as referred to in clause 13.5.5 which is to be valued under clause 13.5;

.2.4 any amount deducted or deductible under clause 7 or 8.4.2 or 17.2 or 17.3 or any amount allowed or allowable to the Employer under clause 38, 39 or 40, whichever is applicable;

.2.5 any other amount which is required by this Contract to be deducted from the Contract Sum.
There shall be added:

.2.6 the amounts of the Nominated Sub-Contract Sums or Tender Sums for all Nominated Sub-Contractors as finally adjusted or ascertained under all relevant provisions of Sub-Contract NSC/4 or NSC/4a as applicable;

.2.7 the tender sum (or such other sum as is appropriate in accordance with the terms of the tender as accepted by or on behalf of the Employer) for any work for which a tender made under clause 35.2 has been accepted;

.2.8 any amounts properly chargeable to the Employer in accordance with the nomination instruction of the Architect/the Contract Administrator in respect of materials or goods supplied by Nominated Suppliers; such amounts shall include the discount for cash of 5 per cent. referred to in clause 36 but shall exclude any value added tax which is treated, or is capable of being treated, as input tax (as referred to in the Finance Act 1972) by the Contractor;

.2.9 the profit of the Contractor upon the amounts referred to in clauses 30.6.2.6, 30.6.2.7 and 30.6.2.8 at the rates included in the Contract Bills or in the cases where the nomination arises from an instruction as to the expenditure of a provisional sum at rates related thereto or if none at reasonable rates;

.2.10 any amounts paid or payable by the Employer to the Contractor as a result of payments made or costs incurred by the Contractor under clauses 6.2, 8.3, 9.2 and 21.2.3;

.2.11 the amount of the Valuation under clause 13.5 of any Variation, including the valuation of other work, as referred to in clause 13.5.5, other than the amount of the valuation of any omission under clause 13.5.2;

.2.12 the amount of the Valuation of work executed by, or the amount of any disbursements by, the Contractor in accordance with instructions of the Architect/the Contract Administrator as to the expenditure of provisional sums included in the Contract Bills and of all work described as provisional included in the Contract Bills;

.2.13 any amount ascertained under clause 26.1 or 34.3;

.2.14 [Number not used]

.2.15 any amount paid or payable to the Contractor under clause 38, 39 or 40, whichever is applicable;

.2.16 any other amount which is required by this Contract to be added to the Contract Sum.

30.7 So soon as is practicable but not less than 28 days before the date of issue of the Final Certificate referred to in clause 30.8 and notwithstanding that a period of one month may not have elapsed since the issue of the previous Interim Certificate, the Architect/the Contract Administrator shall issue an Interim Certificate the gross valuation for which shall include the amounts of the Sub-Contract sums for all Nominated Sub-Contracts as finally adjusted or ascertained under all relevant provisions of Sub-Contract NSC/4 or NSC/4a as applicable.

30.8 The Architect/The Contract Administrator shall issue the Final Certificate (and inform each Nominated Sub-Contractor of the date of its issue) not later than 2 months after whichever of the following occurs last:

the end of the Defects Liability Period;

the date of issue of the Certificate of Completion of Making Good Defects under clause 17.4;

the date on which the Architect/the Contract Administrator sent a copy to the Contractor of any ascertainment to which clause 30.6.1.2.1 refers and of the statement prepared in compliance with clause 30.6.1.2.2. The Final Certificate shall state:

.1 the sum of the amounts already stated as due in Interim Certificates, and

.2 the Contract Sum adjusted as necessary in accordance with clause 30.6.2

and the difference (if any) between the two sums shall (without prejudice to the rights of the Contractor in respect of any Interim Certificates which have not been paid by the Employer) be expressed in the said Certificate as a balance due to the Contractor from the Employer or to the Employer from the Contractor as the case may be, and subject to any deductions authorised by the Conditions, the said balance shall as from the 28th day after the date of the said Certificate be a debt payable as the case may be by the Employer to the Contractor or by the Contractor to the Employer.

30.9 .1 Except as provided in clauses 30.9.2 and 30.9.3 (and save in respect of fraud),the Final Certificate shall have effect in any proceedings arising out of or in connection with this Contract (whether by arbitration under article 5 or otherwise) as

.1.1 conclusive evidence that where and to the extent that the quality of materials or the standard of workmanship are to be to the reasonable satisfaction of the Architect/the Contract Administrator the same are to such satisfaction, and

.1.2 conclusive evidence that any necessary effect has been given to all the terms of this Contract which require that an amount is to be added to or deducted from the Contract Sum or an adjustment is to be made of the Contract Sum save where there has been any accidental inclusion or exclusion of any work, materials, goods or figure in any computation or any arithmetical error in any computation, in which event the Final Certificate shall have effect as conclusive evidence as to all other computations and

.1.3 conclusive evidence that all and only such extensions of time, if any, as are due under clause 25 have been given, and

.1.4 conclusive evidence that the reimbursement of direct loss and/or expense, if any, to the Contractor pursuant to clause 26.1 is in final settlement of all and any claims which the Contractor has or may have arising out of the occurrence of any of the matters referred to in clause 26.2 whether such claim be for breach of contract, duty of care, statutory duty or otherwise.

.2 If any arbitration or other proceedings have been commenced by either party before the Final Certificate has been issued the Final Certificate shall have effect as conclusive evidence as provided in clause 30.9.1 after either:

.2.1 such proceedings have been concluded, whereupon the Final Certificate shall be subject to the terms of any award or judgment in or settlement of such proceedings, or

.2.2 a period of 12 months during which neither party has taken any further step in such proceedings, whereupon the Final Certificate shall be subject to any terms agreed in partial settlement,

whichever shall be the earlier.

.3 If any arbitration or other proceedings have been commenced by either party within 28 days after the Final Certificate has been issued, the Final Certificate shall have effect as conclusive evidence as provided in clause 30.9.1 save only in respect of all matters to which those proceedings relate.

30.10 Save as aforesaid no certificate of the Architect/the Contract Administrator shall of itself be conclusive evidence that any works, materials or goods to which it relates are in accordance with this Contract.

Clause 30: Certificates and Payments

Derivation. Clause 30 is substantially derived from clause 30 of the 1963 form. It was amended by Amendment 2 issued in November 1986, Amendment 4 issued in July 1987 and Amendment 7 issued in July 1988. The 1987 amendments are of great importance and are discussed in detail below.

Scheme of clause. Clause 30 provides for Interim Certificates and valuations (30.1); ascertainment of amounts due in Interim Certificates (30.2); certification of materials or goods before delivery to the Works (30.3); rules for ascertainment of Retention (30.4); rules on treatment of Retention (30.5); procedure for final adjustment of Contract Sum (30.6.1); items to be included in the adjustment of the Contract Sum (30.6.2); final adjustment of Nominated Sub-Contract Sums (30.7); issue of Final Certificate (30.8); effect of Final Certificate (30.9); effect of Interim Certificates (30.10).

For the position of the Architect as agent and his duty to act fairly and professionally, see commentary to clauses 2 and 4, and for his relationship to the Quantity Surveyor, see commentary to clause 13.[12]

Clause 30.4.1. *"... the Contractor shall be entitled to payment therefor ..."*
The meaning of these words was discussed by the Court of Appeal in *Lubenham* v. *South Pembrokeshire D.C.*[13] The court held that the words meant "the Contractor shall be entitled to payment of the sum stated in the Interim Certificates to be due to the Contractor from the Employer." The issue of a Certificate was held to be always a condition precedent to the right of the Contractor to be paid.[14] There are however limited circumstances in which a contractor may be able to recover without a certificate.[15] Immediate arbitration is available on the questions whether a certificate has been improperly withheld or is not in accordance with the Conditions.[16]

Clause 30.1.1.1. *"... within 14 days from the date of issue ..."*
Under the 1980 Form, the period for payment now runs from the issue of the Certificate for both the Local Authorities and the Private Version (see clause 5.8 of the Private Version).

Clause 30.1.1.2. *"... the Employer is entitled to exercise any right under this Contract of deduction ..."*

---

[12] For discussions of the Architect's certifying duties under earlier versions of this Form, see *East Ham Borough Council* v. *Bernard Sunley* [1966] A.C. 406 (H.L.)—1939 Form, pre-1957 revision; *Sutcliffe* v. *Chippendale & Edmondson* (1971) 18 B.L.R. 149 at 166—1963 Form; *Townsend* v. *Stone Toms* (1984) 27 B.L.R. 26 at 46, 54 (C.A.)—JCT Fixed Fee Form—provisions not materially different from 1963 Form.
[13] (1986) 33 B.L.R. 39 at 54, 55 (C.A.).
[14] For summary judgment on a certificate, see p. 442.
[15] These are discussed in the Section "Recovery of payment without certificate" at p. 103. It appears that the decision in *Panamena* v. *Leyland* [1947] A.C. 428 (H.L.) does not apply at least where there is a wide arbitration clause—see *Lubenham* v. *South Pembrokeshire District Council* (1986) 33 B.L.R. 39 at 58 (C.A.)—and thus will not normally apply to the 1980 Form.
[16] See clause 41.3.2. In practice, however, such arbitrations often take a long time to reach an award.

This is an express provision of the 1980 Form. Deduction from sums certified can be made under clauses 4.1.2 (non-compliance with Architect's instructions), 21.1.3 and 22A.2 (insurance premiums), 24.2.1 (liquidated damages), 27.4.2.2 (direct payment to Nominated Sub-Contractors), 35.2.4.6 (valid determination by Nominated Sub-Contractor). See also clause 35.13.5.3 (direct payment to Nominated Sub-Contractors).

Clause 30.1.1.3. *". . . shall inform the Contractor in writing of the reason for that deduction."*

This was a new provision introduced by the 1980 Form. It is thought that an otherwise valid deduction will not be invalidated if the Employer fails to inform the Contractor of the reason. It is further thought that, except where in special circumstances an estoppel arises, an Employer's statement of a reason for deduction which upon investigation is proved to be unsustainable will not invalidate a sustainable, but unstated, deduction. Since Interim Certificates are cumulative, the Employer will presumably have a periodic opportunity for restating any reason for deduction.

Clause 30.1.2. Where formula adjustment under clause 40 applies, this clause is amended as set out in clause 40.2 by the deletion of the words "whenever the Architect/the Contract Administrator considers them to be necessary."

Clause 30.2. This is a redrafted and expanded version of clause 30(2) of the 1963 Form. It should be read with clause 3. It gathers together explicitly all the elements of payment to be taken into account in Interim Certificates. The new clause also sets out those elements of payment which are subject to Retention and those which are not.

Clause 30.2.1. This lists the elements of payment which are subject to Retention. These are payments for measured work, variations and formula price adjustment (30.2.1.1), the value of on-site materials and goods (30.2.1.2); the value of off-site materials and goods in accordance with clause 30.3 (30.2.1.3), payments to Nominated Sub-Contractors which by virtue of clause 21.4 of NSC/4 or 4a are to be paid subject to Retention (30.2.1.4) and the Contractor's profit on Nominated Sub-Contractor's accounts (30.2.1.5).

Clause 30.2.1.1. *". . . properly executed . . ."*

The Architect should exclude work which is not properly executed from the value of the work which he certifies. Work properly executed does not include work which is defective at the date of issue of the Certificate but which it is expected that the Contractor will remedy. The Architect should keep the Quantity Surveyor continually informed of any defective work which he has observed.[17] The Architect should not certify works which he knows to be

---

[17] For authority for all these propositions, see *Sutcliffe* v. *Chippendale & Edmondson* (1971) 18 B.L.R. 149 at 166.

improperly executed but which he thinks may be remedied for a cost within the Retention. The provision of Retention is to protect the Employer against latent defects or non-completion.[18] For the meaning and use of the term "reasonable satisfaction" and the test to be applied by the Architect when certifying, see commentary to clause 2.

Clause 30.2.1.1. *"... but excluding ... as if they were a variation ..."*
These words were inserted by Amendment 4 issued in July 1987. Clause 30.2.2.2 has also been amended. The effect is that where such works are treated as a variation by virtue of clauses 22B.3.5 or 22C.4.4.2 they are not subject to Retention unless certified.

Clause 30.2.1.2. *"... delivered to or adjacent to the works ..."*
For the passing of property in unfixed materials which have been paid for, see clause 16.1.

Clause 30.2.2. This lists the elements of payment which are not subject to Retention. These are amounts to be taken into account in Interim Certificates in accordance with clause 30.3 (30.2.2.1), amounts ascertained for direct loss and/or expense or in respect of restoration, etc. (30.2.2.2), final payments to Nominated Sub-Contractors (30.2.2.3.), fluctuations other than formula price adjustments (30.2.2.4) and amounts payable to Nominated Sub-Contractors which by virtue of clause 21.4 of NSC/4 or 4a are not subject to Retention (30.2.2.5).

Clause 30.2.2.1. This sub-clause was amended by Amendment 4 issued in July 1987 to delete "22B and 22C." This is consequential upon the amendments relating to restoration, *etc.*

Clause 30.2.2.2. *"... or in respect of ... a Variation"*
These words were inserted by Amendment 4 issued in July 1987, as explained above.

Clause 30.2.3. This provides for various deductions not subject to Retention to be made from the gross valuation. These are amounts allowable by the Contractor to the Employer under the provisions for fluctuations (30.2.3.1) and amounts allowable by Nominated Sub-Contractors to the Contractor under clause 21.4.3 of NSC/4 or 4a (clause 30.2.3.2).

Clause 30.3. The Architect may be asked to exercise his discretion by the Contractor where, *e.g.* he supplies the goods or materials from his own factory, or by a Sub-Contractor or supplier. In the latter case the Contractor may ask the Architect not to exercise his discretion (see below). The Architect should,

---

[18] See *Townsend* v. *Stone Toms* (1984) 27 B.L.R. 26 at 54 (C.A.).

it is suggested, particularly bear in mind whether the Contractor and any Sub-Contractor or supplier are likely to remain solvent and not in default, and whether the detailed provisions 30.3.1–30.3.9 have been complied with. These provisions have been drafted in an attempt to deal with the problems which can arise. They should be read with clause 16.2.

Clause 30.3.3.   This clause is directed at the difficulties which can arise upon the insolvency of the Contractor. For a discussion of this topic, see "Vesting of property" at page 377.

Passing of property.   The property cannot pass from the Contractor to the Employer (see clause 16.2 and commentary to clause 16.1) unless it is already vested in the Contractor, hence sub-clauses 30.3.4, 30.3.5, 30.3.6 and 30.3.8.

Transfer of title to other persons.   A person buying in good faith and without notice of the previous passing of the property to the Employer from a supplier (including in the appropriate case the Contractor) who is left in possession of the goods or materials, can take a good title.[19] A bona fide purchaser from the Sheriff selling under a Writ of *fi. fa.* and where no claim has been made can acquire a good title.[20] In certain circumstances a Landlord can distrain on the materials or goods for unpaid rent.[21] Clause 30.3.1 is particularly aimed at these matters.

Defects after certification.   It is submitted that nothing in clause 30.2 affects the Architect's powers under clause 8.4 or otherwise.

The Contractor's objections to the exercise of the Architect's discretion under clause 30.3.

The materials and goods remain at the Contractor's risk (clause 16.2). If they are lost or damaged or by fraud or negligence disposed of by a Sub-Contractor or supplier, the Contractor is liable to replace them at his own cost. Further, he cannot recover any loss from the Employer due to any delay which might thereby arise and he may have to pay liquidated damages for such delay. If the Architect intends to certify at the request of a supplier or a Sub-Contractor, it is in the Contractor's interest to see that provisions 30.3.1 to 30.3.9 are enforced and that there is adequate insurance cover.

Clause 30.4.   In the 1980 Form Retention is no longer released by specific certificates for that purpose. Clause 30.4.2 provides for "Contractor's Retention" and "Nominated Sub-Contract Retention" to be separately specified.

---

[19] See Sale of Goods Act 1979, s.25(1); *cf. Archivent Sales* v. *Strathclyde Regional Council* (1984) 27 B.L.R. 98 (Court of Session (Outer House)). Much law is involved and reference should be made to the standard textbooks, *e.g.* Benjamin.

[20] See Bankruptcy and Deed of Arrangement Act 1913, s.15.

[21] See Woodfall, *Landlord and Tenant* (28th ed.), Chap. 9.

Practical Completion to Final Certificate. There is a detailed but clear procedure to be carried out which may be summarised as follows:

(1) Certificate of Practical Completion (clause 17.1), and at the same time;

(2) Release of first half of Retention (clause 30.4.1.2);

(3) Defects Liability Period begins and if none stated is six months from Practical Completion (clause 17.2, Appendix);

    (a) schedule of defects to be delivered not later than 14 days after expiration of Defects Liability Period (clause 17.2),

    (b) particular defects may be required to be made good before such schedule or such 14 days, whichever is the earlier (clause 17.3),

    (c) Certificate of Completion of Making Good Defects when in opinion of the Architect they have been made good (clause 17.3),

(4) Not later than 6 months after Practical Completion the Contractor must provide the Architect with all documents necessary for adjustment of the Contract Sum (clause 30.6.1.1);

(5) Not later than 3 months after receipt of such documents, the Architect must ascertain any loss and expense and the Quantity Surveyor must prepare a statement of all other adjustments to the Contract Sum (clause 30.6.1.2);

(6) The residue of Retention is released on Certificate of Completion of Making Good Defects (clause 30.4.1.3);

(7) Not less than 28 days before issue of the Final Certificate, the Architect must issue an Interim Certificate including a final adjustment or ascertainment of Nominated Sub-Contract sums;

(8) Final Certificate not later than two months after the latest of end of Defects Liability Period, Certificate of Completion of Making Good Defects under clause 17.4 and the date upon which the ascertainment under clause 30.6.1.2.1 and the statement under clause 30.6.1.2.2 are sent to the Contractor;

(9) There is a 28 day period from the issue of the Final Certificate for either party to challenge the Final Certificate by arbitration or other proceedings for the effect of which see clauses 30.9.2 and 30.9.3, discussed below.

Clause 30.5.1. "... *fiduciary as trustee* ..."

These words impose an obligation on the Employer to appropriate and set aside as a separate trust fund a sum equal to the Retention. This obligation will be enforced, if necessary, by the grant of a mandatory injunction.[22] Clause 30.5.3 of the Private Version makes explicit provision for this obligation. Once sums so set aside have become impressed with the trust, they remain subject to this trust whatever the fate of the Contractor's employment or of the Contract.[23] The effect is that upon the Employer's bankruptcy or liquidation the

---

[22] *Rayack* v. *Lampeter* (1979) 12 B.L.R. 30, approved in *Henry Boot Building* v. *Croydon Hotel* (1985) 36 B.L.R. 41 (C.A.).

[23] *Re Arthur Sanders Ltd.* (1981) 17 B.L.R. 125.

trustee in bankruptcy or liquidator holds the balance of the trust fund as trustee for the Contractor. However, if no such fund has been established at the date of liquidation, no mandatory injunction will be granted to create such a fund and the Contractor is merely an unsecured creditor.[24]

Clause 30.5.1. "... *trustee* ... *for any Nominated Sub-Contractor* ..."
In the 1963 Form the Employer was stated to be trustee for the Contractor, but no reference was made to the position of the Nominated Sub-Contractor (see clause 30(4)(a) 1963 Form). In a number of authorities it was held that the Contractor was in turn trustee for the Nominated Sub-Contractor in relation to his proportion of the Retention. This involved difficult questions of assignment.[25] The 1980 Form makes the Employer trustee directly for the Nominated Sub-Contractor who stands in exactly the same position, and has the same rights, as the Contractor.

Clause 30.5.3 (Private Version only). "*the Employer shall* ... *place the Retention in a separate banking account* ..."
This makes express the obligation to set aside a separate trust fund. It will be enforced, if necessary, by the grant of a mandatory injunction (see above).

Clause 30.5.4. "... *the right to deduct referred to in clause 30.1.1.2 against any Retention* ..."
Clause 30.1.1.2 expressly entitles the Employer to make deductions authorised by the Contract from amounts certified in Interim Certificates. This sub-clause further entitles the Employer to set these deductions against Retention. The equivalent provisions of the 1963 Form were considered in *Henry Boot Building* v. *Croydon Hotel.*[26] The Architect had issued a certificate of non-completion. The Employer deducted liquidated damages and set them against Retention. The Court of Appeal held that a mandatory injunction would not be granted to compel the Employer to set aside a trust fund at a time when the Employer was entitled to deduct a greater amount of liquidated damages because there was no subsisting obligation to set aside. This was so although there was a serious issue to be tried as to the validity of the certificates of non-completion.[27]

Clause 30.6.1. This sub-clause was substantially amended by Amendment 4 issued in July 1987. It provides a stricter timetable for the adjustment of the Contract Sum. The Contractor must now send all necessary documents not later than 6 months after Practical Completion rather than, as formerly, "within a reasonable time after Practical Completion." The revised clause

---

[24] *Re: Jartay Developments Ltd.* (1982) 22 B.L.R. 135.
[25] See Re *Tout & Finch* [1954] 1 W.L.R. 178 and *Re Arthur Sanders Ltd.* (1981) 17 B.L.R. 125.
[26] (1985) 36 B.L.R. 41 (C.A.).
[27] For a case decided in Hong Kong on mandatory injunctions and deductions, see *Concorde Construction Ltd.* v. *Colgan Co.* (1984) 29 B.L.R. 121 (Hong Kong High Court).

30.6.1.2 requires an ascertainment of all loss and expense and a statement of all adjustments of the Contract Sum to be sent to the Contractor not later than 3 months after receipt of the Contractor's final account documents rather than, as formerly, "within the period of Final Measurement and Valuation stated in the Appendix."

Clause 30.6.2. This clause sets out comprehensively all the deductions and additions to be made to the Contract Sum.

Clause 30.6.2.1. *". . . the certified value . . . discharged by the Employer . . ."*
These words were added by Amendment 4 issued in July 1987 to take account of the decision of the Court of Appeal in *Fairclough Building* v. *Rhuddlan B.C.*[28] They allow the Employer a credit for the amount paid to the Contractor for any work not in accordance with the Nominated Sub-Contract performed by a Nominated Sub-Contractor whose employment has been determined under clause 35.24.

Clause 30.7. This requires an Interim Certificate certifying final payment to Nominated Sub-Contractors to be issued not less than 28 days before the issue of the Final Certificate. The purpose is, it seems, to enable the provisions in clause 35.13.5 for direct payment by the Employer to Nominated Sub-Contractors to be operated if the Contractor fails to make final payment to Nominated Sub-Contractors. This will only be possible in practice to the extent that a net amount is certified in the Final Certificate as due to the Contractor which is sufficient to cover any amount which the Contractor may have failed to pay to Nominated Sub-Contractors.

Clause 30.8. This sub-clause was amended by Amendment 4 issued in July 1987. This is part of the stricter timetable. The Final Certificate[29] must be issued not later than 2 months after the occurrence of whichever of the three listed events occurs last. The former reference to the Period of Final Measurement and Valuation is deleted.

Clause 30.8. *". . . or to the Employer . . ."*
It is a useful feature of this Contract that the Final Certificate can be for the return of monies overpaid in earlier Certificates. However, the Architect is not entitled to retain a sum of money merely to ensure that there is something held in favour of the Employer until the Final Certificate. If he does so, the Contractor can go to immediate arbitration.

---

[28] (1985) 30 B.L.R. 26 (C.A.).
[29] For consideration of what amounts to a Final Certificate, see *London Borough of Merton* v. *Lowe* (1981) 18 B.L.R. 130 at 143–144 (C.A.).

Clause 30.9: Conclusive effect of Final Certificate.

This sub-clause is very important. The Final Certificate is conclusive in respect of some but not all matters which can arise out of the Contract. The conclusive effect of the Final Certificate is excluded or limited if the parties take certain steps. The matters upon which Final Certificate is conclusive are listed in clauses 30.9.1.1–30.9.1.4. Clauses 30.9.1.3 and 30.9.1.4 were added by Amendment 4 issued in July 1987.

Clause 30.9.1.1. *"... conclusive evidence ..."*

This means, it is submitted, that no evidence may be called to contradict or qualify in any way the Architect's decision as expressed in the Final Certificate.[30] Upon matters with which it deals, it is therefore as binding upon the parties on questions of fact as an Arbitrator's award.[31] It is not, however, an award[32] and is not subject to the Arbitration Acts 1950–1979.[33]

The conclusive effect as regards quality of materials and standard of workmanship applies only where those matters are to be to the reasonable satisfaction of the Architect (see commentary to clause 2). The words "and to the extent that" were added by Amendment 4 issued in July 1987 to follow more closely the drafting of the provision in clause 2.1.

Clause 30.9.1.3. The effect of this sub-clause is, it seems, that after the issue of the Final Certificate, no further extensions of time may be granted, and the Contractor cannot dispute the extensions already granted except in arbitration or proceedings commenced within the time limits prescribed (see clauses 30.9.2 and 30.9.3).

Clause 30.9.1.4. This is a very significant amendment. Under the 1963 Contract it was held that, notwithstanding the elaborate machinery of the Contract for loss and expense and certification, the Contractor might nevertheless recover sums by way of damages in respect of breaches of contract.[34] The effect of this new clause, it is submitted, is that the Contractor is conclusively bound by the Architect's Final Certificate as to loss and expense in respect of compensation for matters described in 26.2 under whatever legal formulation that compensation is sought, subject to clauses 30.9.2 and 30.9.3.

Steps which limit the conclusiveness of the Final Certificate. If no arbitration or other proceedings have been commenced by either party before the Final Certificate is issued (clause 30.9.2) or within 28 days after its issue (clause 30.9.3) the Final Certificate has the full conclusive effect given to it by

---

[30] *cf. Kerr* v. *John Mottram Ltd.* [1940] 1 Ch. 657 at 660; *Kaye (P. & M.)* v. *Hosier & Dickinson* [1972] 1 W.L.R. 146 at 169 (H.L.).

[31] See *Goodyear* v. *Weymouth Corp.* (1865) 35 L.J.C.P. 12 at 17.

[32] *Sutcliffe* v. *Thackrah* [1974] A.C. 727 (H.L.).

[33] For arbitration generally, see Chap. 16. For Architect's Certificates generally, see Chap. 5.

[34] *London Borough of Merton* v. *Leach* (1985) 32 B.L.R. 51, issue 11 at pp. 105–109.

clause 30.9.1. If arbitration or other proceedings were commenced by either party before its issue, then the conclusive effect of the Final Certificate is subject to clause 30.9.2. If clause 30.9.2.1 applies, the Certificate remains conclusive subject to "the terms of any award of judgment in or settlement of such proceedings." It will be most desirable that such award, judgment or settlement is a "speaking" award,[35] judgment or settlement in order to determine the remaining ambit of the conclusiveness of the Final Certificate. If clause 30.9.2.2 applies, then if there is "a period of 12 months during which neither party has taken any further steps in such proceedings" prima facie the full conclusive effect of the Final Certificate revives "subject to any terms agreed in partial settlement." The latter words are not easy to construe. Ordinarily one thinks of a matter as either being settled or not settled.[36] Perhaps what is intended is a reference to an agreement which does not dispose of the whole dispute but of some or all of the matters dealt with in the Final Certificate and that, for those matters, the Final Certificate ceases to have any effect.

Clause 30.9.3. *Proceedings commenced within 28 days after the Final Certificate*
The period of 28 days was substituted for 14 days by Amendment 4 issued in July 1987. The Final Certificate has its conclusive effect "save only in respect of all matters to which those proceedings relate." The document by which such proceedings are commenced will therefore be of the greatest importance. If sufficiently widely drawn it can deprive the Final Certificate of all conclusive effect. Proceedings are commenced in the High Court by the issue of a Writ and in arbitration by a written notice to refer to arbitration (see clause 41.1). In such a notice it will be particularly important to define the dispute which it is requested that the Arbitrator should deal with in terms wide enough to prevent the Claimant subsequently being hampered by the conclusive effect of the Certificate. Presumably if proceedings have been commenced upon a somewhat narrow ground before the Certificate is issued, there is nothing to prevent either party commencing further proceedings upon wider grounds within 28 days after the issue of the Final Certificate.

Powers of the court. For the question of whether a court has the same powers as the Arbitrator, see commentary to clause 41 and "Crouch" at page 389.

Written notice under clause 41.1. A party who wishes to rely upon arbitration proceedings to defeat or attack a Final Certificate should, preferably, follow the words of clause 41.1 closely so as to show that he is commencing arbitration proceedings and not merely threatening to commence them in the future. The meaning of the word "commence" in the context of clause

---

[35] *I.e.* it "speaks" on its face as to what it deals with. In the case of an award see further p. 413.
[36] For settlement of actions, see p. 438.

30.9.3 was considered in *Emson Contractors Protea Estates*.[37] It was held that it meant the date when one party either invited agreement to a named individual being designated Arbitrator or requested the other to concur in the appointment of an Arbitrator. As a matter of general principle, it seems that if a party uses less formal language than that used by the Contract but such as to indicate a clear requirement to refer the dispute to arbitration, this will be sufficient.[38] However, the party seeking arbitration should so far as possible follow the provisions of sections 34(3) and 34(4) of the Limitation Act 1980. Accordingly, the notice should (a) require the other party to agree to the appointment of an Arbitrator, (b) contain proper particulars of the disputes in respect of which the Arbitrator is to be appointed and (c) be served in one of the manners set out in section 34(4) of the Act.[39]

Extension of time for arbitration. For the question whether section 27 of the Arbitration Act 1950 applies to clause 30 of the 1980 Form, see "Extension of time" at page 409.

Attacking a Final Certificate. A party wishing to attack an allegation that a certificate is conclusive evidence upon certain matters within the meaning of clause 30.9.1 should consider one or more of the following:
  (1) commencing proceedings before or within 28 days after the issue of the Final Certificate (see above);
  (2) whether the matters fall within the express exception to the conclusive effect of the Certificate, *i.e.* fraud;
  (3) whether the point at issue is not within the range of matters upon which the Certificate is stated to be conclusive evidence. The range of matters upon which the Certificate is conclusive is now much wider than formerly by virtue of the amendments to clause 30.9.1 discussed above. However, it is clear that many matters remain outside the ambit of the Final Certificate. For example, materials and workmanship not required to be to the Architect's reasonable satisfaction (see above and commentary to clause 2.1);
  (4) that there was an irregularity in the giving of the Certificate so that it cannot be said to be the Certificate required by the contract in which case it will not be conclusive at all.[40] An example might be where the Architect delegated his whole function of certifying.[41] It is submitted that a mere delay in issuing the Final Certificate does not prevent it when issued from being conclusive;

---

[37] (1987) 39 B.L.R. 126.
[38] See *Nea Agrex S.A.* v. *Baltic Shipping* [1976] Q.B. 933 (C.A.); *cf. Surrendra Overseas Ltd.* v. *Government of Sri Lanka* [1977] 1 W.L.R. 565.
[39] *I.e.* by delivery to the other party or by leaving it at the usual or last known place of abode in England of the other party or by sending it by registered post or recorded delivery addressed to the other party at his last known place of abode.
[40] See generally p. 106.
[41] *C. F. Clemence* v. *Clarke* (1880) HBC (4th ed.), Vol. 2, pp. 54, 59. (C.A.); *Burden* v. *Swansea Corporation* [1957] 1 W.L.R. 1167 at 1173 (H.L.), cited at p. 599.

(5) that the Architect was disqualified at the time when he gave his Certificate, in which case the Certificate is of no effect.[42]

Claims by the Employer for consequential losses.   In *P. & M. Kaye* v. *Hosier & Dickinson*[43] a point arose in the House of Lords under a pre-1976 version of the 1963 Form which the majority of their Lordships refused to consider because it had not been argued in the courts below. Consequential loss, *i.e.* loss of profits due to defects in a warehouse, had been suffered by the Employer due to defects which appeared after Practical Completion but before the issue of the Final Certificate. Two meanings were put forward as to the effect of the Certificate. The first was that the whole series of building operations from beginning to end must have been deemed to have been duly carried out and completed so that any claim in respect of alleged past defects and their consequences was excluded. The second meaning was that everything which had to be done by way of building operations had now been done and all defects made good but there was no exclusion of claims in respect of alleged past defects and their consequences. Lord Diplock, contrary to the views of the majority, found it necessary to decide the point. He was in favour of the second meaning. The decision of the majority has been both followed and distinguished in cases under pre-1976 versions of the 1963 Form.[44] The question is one of construction. It is thought that clause 30.9.1.1 of the 1980 Form is to be construed in this respect in the same way as the pre-1976 version of the 1963 Form, although the scope of matters relating to materials and workmanship is more limited in the 1980 Form than it was in the pre-1976 versions of the 1963 Form.[45] If, therefore, the majority decision in *P. & M. Kaye* v. *Hosier & Dickinson* is properly distinguishable, an Employer's claim for consequential loss arising out of breaches of contract before the issue of the Final Certificate is not barred by the Final Certificate.

---

[42] See generally p. 114.

[43] [1972] 1 W.L.R. 146 (H.L.).

[44] See *Fairweather* v. *Asden Securities* (1979) 12 B.L.R. 40; *H. W. Nevill (Sunblest)* v. *Wm. Press* (1981) 20 B.L.R. 78; see further "When is a certificate binding and conclusive?" at p. 107.

[45] The pre–1976 version of the 1963 Form provided by clause 30(7) that the Final Certificate was conclusive evidence that "... the Works have been properly carried out and completed in accordance with the terms of this Contract." The 1976 amendments continued into clause 30.9.1.1 of the 1980 Form limit the range of materials and workmanship matters for which the Final Certificate is conclusive. However, the question posed by *P. & M. Kaye* v. *Hosier & Dickinson* continues to arise, although in a narrower form, *i.e.* does the issue of a Final Certificate provide conclusive evidence not only that the Architect is satisfied with the quality of materials or the standard of workmanship (where appropriate), but also that he has always been so satisfied so as to preclude claims by the Employer for damages for past defects which were corrected before the Final Certificate was issued?

31. **Finance (No. 2) Act 1975—statutory tax deduction scheme**

31.1 In this Condition "the Act" means the Finance (No. 2) Act 1975; "the Regulations" means the Income Tax (Sub-Contractors in the Construction Industry) Regulations 1975 S.I. No. 1960; "contractor" means a person who is a contractor for the purposes of the Act and the Regulations; "evidence" means such evidence as is required by the Regulations to be produced to a "contractor" for the verification of a "sub-contractor's" tax certificate; "statutory deduction" means the deduction referred to in S.69(4) of the Act or such other deduction as may be in force at the relevant time; " 'sub-contractor' " means a person who is a sub-contractor for the purposes of the Act and the Regulations; "tax certificate" is a certificate issuable under S.70 of the Act.

31.2 .1 Clauses 31 .3 to .9 shall not apply if, in the Appendix, the Employer is stated not to be a "contractor."

.2 If in the Appendix the words "is a 'contractor' " are deleted, nevertheless if, at any time up to the issue and payment of the Final Certificate, the Employer becomes such a "contractor," the Employer shall so inform the Contractor and the provisions of clause 31 shall immediately thereupon become operative.

31.3 .1 Not later than 21 days before the first payment under this Contract is due to the Contractor or after clause 31.2.2 has become operative the Contractor shall: either

.1.1 provide the Employer with the evidence that the Contractor is entitled to be paid without the statutory deduction; or

.1.2 inform the Employer in writing, and send a duplicate copy to the Architect/the Contract Administrator, that he is not entitled to be paid without the statutory deduction.

.2 If the Employer is not satisfied with the validity of the evidence submitted in accordance with clause 31.3.1.1, he shall within 14 days of the Contractor submitting such evidence notify the Contractor in writing that he intends to make the statutory deduction from payments due under this contract to the Contractor who is a "sub-contractor" and give his reasons for that decision. The employer shall at the same time comply with clause 31.6.1.

31.4 .1 Where clause 31.3.1.2 applies, the Contractor shall immediately inform the Employer if he obtains a tax certificate and thereupon clause 31.3.1.1 shall apply.

.2 If the period for which the tax certificate has been issued to the Contractor expires before the final payment is made to the Contractor under this Contract the Contractor shall not later than 28 days before the date of expiry: either

.2.1 provide the Employer with evidence that the Contractor from the said date of expiry is entitled to be paid for a further period without the statutory deduction in which case the provisions of clause 31.3.2 shall apply if the Employer is not satisfied with the evidence;
or

.2.2 inform the Employer in writing that he will not be entitled to be paid without the statutory deduction after the said date of expiry.

.3 The Contractor shall immediately inform the Employer in writing if his current tax certificate is cancelled and give the date of such cancellation.

31.5 The Employer shall, as a "contractor" in accordance with the Regulations, send promptly to the Inland Revenue any voucher which, in compliance with the Contractor's obligations as a "sub-contractor" under the Regulations, the Contractor gives to the Employer.

31.6 .1 If at any time the Employer is of the opinion (whether because of the information given under clause 31.3.1.2 or of the expiry or cancellation of the Contractor's tax certificate or otherwise) that he will be required by the Act to make a statutory deduction from any payment due to be made the Employer shall immediately so notify the Contractor in writing and require the Contractor to state not later than 7 days before each future payment becomes due (or within 10 days of such notification if that is later) the amount to be included in such payment which represents the direct cost to the Contractor and any other person of materials used or to be used in carrying out the Works.

.2 Where the Contractor complies with clause 31.6.1 he shall indemnify the Employer against loss or expense caused to the Employer by any incorrect statement of the amount of direct cost referred to in clause 31.6.1.

.3 Where the Contractor does not comply with clause 31.6.1 the employer shall be entitled to make a fair estimate of the amount of direct cost referred to in clause 31.6.1.

31.7 Where any error or omission has occurred in calculating or making the statutory deduction the Employer shall correct that error or omission by repayment to, or by deduction from payments to, the Contractor as the case may be subject only to any statutory obligation on the Employer not to make such correction.

31.8 If compliance with clause 31 involves the Employer or the Contractor in not complying with any other of the Conditions, then the provisions of clause 31 shall prevail.

31.9 The provisions of article 5 shall apply to any dispute or difference between the Employer or the Architect/the Contract Administrator on his behalf and the Contractor as to the operation of clause 31 except where the Act or the Regulations or any other Act of Parliament or statutory instrument, rule or order made under an Act of Parliament provide for some other method of resolving such dispute or difference.

Clause 31: Finance (No. 2) Act 1975—statutory tax deduction scheme
This clause, providing for statutory tax deduction under the Finance (No. 2) Act 1975, is substantially the same as clause 30B of the 1963 Form.

32. **Outbreak of hostilities** [*u*]

32.1 If during the currency of this Contract there shall be an outbreak of hostilities (whether war is declared or not) in which the United Kingdom shall be involved on a scale involving the general mobilisation of the armed forces of the Crown, then either the Employer or the Contractor may at any time by notice by registered post or recorded delivery to the other, forthwith determine the employment of the Contractor under this Contract:

.1 before the expiration of 28 days from the date on which the order is given for general mobilisation as aforesaid, or

.2 after Practical Completion of the Works unless the Works or any part thereof shall have sustained war damage as defined in clause 33.4.

[*u*] *The parties hereto in the event of the outbreak of hostilities may at any time by agreement between them make such further or other arrangements as they may think fit to meet the circumstances.*

32.2   The Architect/The Contract Administrator may within 14 days after notice under clause 32.1 shall have been given or received by the Employer issue instructions to the Contractor requiring the execution of such protective work as shall be specified therein and/or the continuation of the Works up to points of stoppage to be specified therein, and the Contractor shall comply with such instructions as if the notice of determination had not been given.

Provided that if the Contractor shall for reasons beyond his control be prevented from completing the work to which the said instructions relate within 3 months from the date on which the instructions were issued, he may abandon such work.

32.3   Upon the expiration of 14 days from the date on which a notice of determination shall have been given or received by the Employer under clause 32.1 or where works are required by the Architect/the Contract Administrator under clause 32.2 upon completion or abandonment as the case may be of any such works, the provisions of clause 28.2 (except clause 28.2.2.6) shall apply and the Contractor shall also be paid by the Employer the value of any work executed pursuant to instructions given under clause 32.2, the value being ascertained in accordance with clause 13.5 as if such work were a Variation required by an instruction of the Architect/the Contract Administrator under clause 13.2.

33.   War damage

33.1   In the event of the Works or any part thereof or any unfixed materials or goods intended for, delivered to and placed on or adjacent to the Works sustaining war damage as defined in clause 33.4 then notwithstanding anything expressed or implied elsewhere in this Contract:

.1   the occurrence of such war damage shall be disregarded in computing any amounts payable to the Contractor under or by virtue of this Contract;

.2   the Architect/the Contract Administrator may issue instructions requiring the Contractor to remove and/or dispose of any debris and/or damaged work and/or to execute such protective work as shall be specified;

.3   the Contractor shall reinstate or make good such war damage and shall proceed with the carrying out and completion of the Works, and the Architect/the Contract Administrator shall in writing fix such later Completion Date as, in his opinion, is fair and reasonable;

.4   the removal and disposal of debris or damaged work, the execution of protective works and the reinstatement and making good of such war damage shall be treated as if it were a Variation required by an instruction of the Architect/the Contract Administrator under clause 13.2.

33.2   If at any time after the occurrence of war damage as aforesaid either party serves notice of determination under clause 32, the expression "protective work" as used in clause 32 should in such case be deemed to include any matters in respect of which the Architect/ the Contract Administrator can issue instructions under clause 33.1.2 and any instructions issued under clause 33.1.2 prior to the date on which notice of determination is given or received by the Employer and which shall not then have been completely complied with shall be deemed to have been given under clause 32.2.

33.3   The Employer shall be entitled to any compensation which may at any time become payable out of monies provided by Parliament in respect of war damage sustained by the Works or any part thereof or any unfixed materials or goods intended for the Works which shall at any time have become the property of the Employer.

33.4 The expression "war damage" as used in clause 33 means war damage as defined by S.9 of the War Damage Act 1943 or any amendment or re-enactment thereof.

Clause 32: Outbreak of hostilities

Clause 33—War damage

Clauses 32 and 33 of the 1980 Form are substantially the same as clauses 32 and 33 in the 1963 Form.

For frustration, the effect of war and clauses of this kind, see generally page 134.

34. Antiquities

34.1 All fossils, antiquities and other objects of interest or value which may be found on the site or in excavating the same during the progress of the Works shall become the property of the Employer and upon discovery of such an object the Contractor shall forthwith:

.1 use his best endeavours not to disturb the object and shall cease work if and insofar as the continuance of work would endanger the object or prevent or impede its excavation or its removal;

.2 take all steps which may be necessary to preserve the object in the exact position and condition in which it was found; and

.3 inform the Architect/the Contract Administrator or the clerk of works of the discovery and precise location of the object.

34.2 The Architect/The Contract Administrator shall issue instructions in regard to what is to be done concerning an object reported by the Contractor under clause 34.1, and (without prejudice to the generality of his power) such instructions may require the Contractor to permit the examination, excavation or removal of the object by a third party. Any such third party shall for the purposes of clause 20 be deemed to be a person for whom the Employer is responsible and not to be a Sub-Contractor.

34.3 .1 If in the opinion of the Architect/the Contract Administrator compliance with the provisions of clause 34.1 or with an instruction issued under clause 34.2 has involved the Contractor in direct loss and/or expense for which he would not be reimbursed by a payment made under any other provision of this Contract then the Architect/the Contract Administrator shall himself ascertain or shall instruct the Quantity Surveyor to ascertain the amount of such loss and/or expense.

.2 If and to the extent that it is necessary for the ascertainment of such loss and/or expense the Architect/the Contract Administrator shall state in writing to the Contractor what extension of time, if any, has been made under clause 25 in respect of the Relevant Event referred to in clause 25.4.5.1 so far as that clause refers to clause 34.

.3 Any amount from time to time so ascertained shall be added to the Contract Sum.

Clause 34: Antiquities

Clause 34 is substantially the same as clause 34 of the 1963 Form, subject to the incorporation of certain drafting amendments to accord with provisions in clauses 25 and 26 of the 1980 Form as to extension of time and loss and/or expense.

Clause 34.3.1. *". . . direct loss and/or expense . . ."*

For other grounds for the recovery of loss and expense, see clause 26 and see its commentary for the meaning of these words.

PART 2: NOMINATED SUB-CONTRACTORS AND NOMINATED SUPPLIERS

NOMINATED SUB-CONTRACTORS

35.   **General**

35.1   Where

.1   in the Contract Bills; or

.2   in any instruction of the Architect/the Contract Administrator under clause 13.3 on the expenditure of a provisional sum included in the Contract Bills; or

.3   in any instruction of the Architect/the Contract Administrator under clause 13.2 requiring a Variation to the extent, but not further or otherwise,

.3.1   that it consists of work additional to that shown upon the Contract Drawings and described by or referred to in the Contract Bills and

.3.2   that any supply and fixing of materials or goods or any execution of work by a Nominated Sub-Contractor in connection with such additional work is of a similar kind to any supply and fixing of materials or the execution of work for which the Contract Bills provided that the Architect/the Contract Administrator would nominate a Sub-Contractor; or

.4   by agreement (which agreement shall not be unreasonably withheld) between the Contractor and the Architect/the Contract Administrator on behalf of the Employer

the Architect/the Contract Administrator has, whether by the use of a prime cost sum or by naming a Sub-Contractor, reserved to himself the final selection and approval of the Sub-Contractor to the Contractor who shall supply and fix any materials or goods or execute work, the Sub-Contractor so named or to be selected and approved shall be nominated in accordance with the provisions of clause 35 and a Sub-Contractor so nominated shall be a Nominated Sub-Contractor for all the purposes of this Contract. The provisions of clause 35.1 shall apply notwithstanding the provisions of Section B.9.1 of the Standard Method of Measurement, 6th Edition.

35.2   .1   Where the Contractor in the ordinary course of his business directly carries out works included in the Contract Bills and to which clause 35 applies, and where items of such works are set out in the Appendix and the Architect/the Contract Administrator is prepared to receive tenders from the Contractor for such items, then the Contractor shall be permitted to tender for the same or any of them but without prejudice to the Employer's right to reject the lowest or any tender. If the

626

Contractor's tender is accepted, he shall not sub-let the work to a Domestic Sub-Contractor without the consent of the Architect/the Contract Administrator. Provided that where an item for which the Architect/the Contract Administrator intends to nominate a Sub-Contractor is included in Architect's/Contract Administrator's instructions issued under clause 13.3 it shall be deemed for the purposes of clause 35.2.1 to have been included in the Contract Bills and the item of work to which it relates shall likewise be deemed to have been set out in the Appendix.

.2 It shall be a condition of any tender accepted under clause 35.2 that clause 13 shall apply in respect of the items of work included in the tender as if for the reference therein to the Contract Drawings and the Contract Bills there were references to the equivalent documents included in or referred to in the tender submitted under clause 35.2.

.3 None of the provisions of clause 35 other than clause 35.2 shall apply to works for which a tender of the Contractor is accepted under clause 35.2.

35.3 The following documents relating to Nominated Sub-Contractors (identified as under) are issued by the Joint Contracts Tribunal for the Standard Form of Building Contract and are referred to in the Conditions and in those documents:

Name of document	*Identification No.*
The JCT Standard Form of Nominated Sub-Contract Tender and Agreement	Tender NSC/1
The JCT Standard Form of Employer/Nominated Sub-Contractor Agreement	Agreement NSC/2
Agreement NSC/2 adapted for use where Tender NSC/1 has not been used	Agreement NSC/2a
The Standard Form for Nomination of a Sub-Contractor where NSC/1 has been used	Nomination NSC/3
The JCT Standard Form of Sub-Contract for Sub-Contractors who have tendered on Tender NSC/1 and executed Agreement NSC/2 and been nominated by Nomination NSC/3 under the Standard Form of Building Contract (clause 35.10.2)	Sub-Contract NSC/4
Sub-Contract NSC/4 adapted for use where Tender NSC/1 has not been used.	Sub-Contract NSC/4a

PROCEDURE FOR NOMINATION OF A SUB-CONTRACTOR

35.4 .1 No person against whom the Contractor makes a reasonable objection shall be a Nominated Sub-Contractor.

.2 Where the Tender NSC/1 and Agreement NSC/2 are used the Contractor shall make any such reasonable objection at the earliest practicable moment but in any case not later than the date when in accordance with clause 35.10.1 he sends the Tender NSC/1 to the Architect/the Contract Administrator.

.3 Where the Tender NSC/1 and Agreement NSC/2 are not used so that the provisions of clauses 35.11 and 35.12 apply the Contractor shall make any such reasonable objection at the earliest practicable moment but in any case not later than 7 days from receipt by him of the instruction of the Architect/the Contract Administrator under clause 35.11 nominating the Sub-Contractor.

35.5 .1.1 Tender NSC/1 and Agreement NSC/2 shall be used in respect of any part of the

Works for which a sub-contractor will be nominated by the Architect/the Contract Administrator unless clause 35.5.1.2 is operated.

.1.2   The Contract Bills, or any instruction under clause 13.2 requiring a Variation (including an instruction under clause 35.5.2) or under clause 13.3 on the expenditure of a provisional sum, may state that clauses 35.11 and 35.12 (Tender NSC/1 and Agreement NSC/2 not used) shall apply to any part of the Works for which a Sub-Contractor will be nominated by the Architect/the Contract Administrator; and where so stated the Contract Bills or the instruction shall also state whether or not the proposed Sub-Contractor has tendered, or has been or will be asked to tender on the basis that Agreement NSC/2a will be used.

.2   In respect of any part of the Works for which a Sub-Contractor will be nominated, the Architect/the Contract Administrator may issue an instruction substituting for the use of Tender NSC/1 and Agreement NSC/2, the application of the provisions of clauses 35.11 and 35.12 or substituting the use of Tender NSC/1 and Agreement NSC/2 for the application of clauses 35.11 and 35.12. Any such instruction shall be treated as if it were a Variation required by an instruction of the Architect/the Contract Administrator under clause 13.2. No such instruction may be issued after the Architect/the Contract Administrator has issued a preliminary notice of nomination under clause 35.7.1 or a nomination instruction under clause 35.11 in regard to any such part of the Works for which a Sub-Contractor will be nominated, save in any case where clause 35.23 or 35.24 is applicable.

Use of Tender NSC/1 and Agreement NSC/2

35.6   Unless clauses 35.11 and 35.12 apply only persons who have tendered on Tender NSC/1 and entered into Agreement NSC/2 may be nominated.

35.7   .1   Where under clause 35.6 a proposed Sub-Contractor has tendered on Tender NSC/1 and entered into Agreement NSC/2 the Architect/the Contract Administrator, before being empowered to issue an instruction as referred to in clause 35.10.2 nominating such proposed Sub-Contractor, shall send to the Contractor the tender of the proposed Sub-Contractor set out on the Tender NSC/1 duly completed, a copy of Agreement NSC/2 and a preliminary notice of nomination instructing the Contractor forthwith to settle with the proposed Sub-Contractor any of the Particular Conditions in Schedule 2 of the Tender NSC/1 which remain to be agreed.

.2   Upon receipt of the preliminary notice of nomination the Contractor shall forthwith proceed to settle with the proposed Sub-Contractor any of the Particular Conditions in Schedule 2 of the Tender NSC/1 which remain to be agreed.

35.8   If the Contractor is unable within 10 working days from receipt of the preliminary notice of nomination to reach agreement with the proposed Sub-Contractor the Contractor shall continue to comply with clause 35.7 but inform the Architect/the Contract Administrator in writing of the reasons for the inability to reach such agreement; and the Architect/the Contract Administrator shall issue such instructions as may be necessary.

35.9   If the proposed Sub-Contractor named in the Tender NSC/1 informs the Contractor that he is withdrawing his offer set out in that Tender the Contractor shall immediately inform the Architect/the Contract Administrator in writing and shall take no further action under clause 35.7 until the further instructions of the Architect/the Contract Administrator are received.

5.10   .1   Immediately upon settlement with the proposed Sub-Contractor under clause 35.7.2 the Contractor shall send the duly completed Tender NSC/1 (including the Particular Conditions at Schedule 2) to the Architect/the Contract Administrator.

       .2   Upon receipt thereof but not otherwise the Architect/the Contract Administrator shall forthwith issue an instruction to the Contractor (with a copy to the proposed Sub-Contractor) on Nomination NSC/3 nominating the proposed Sub-Contractor to supply and fix the materials or goods or to execute the work referred to in that Tender.

Tender NSC/1 and Agreement NSC/2 not used

5.11   Where clause 35.5.1.2 has been operated:

       .1   the Employer shall enter into Agreement NSC/2a with the proposed Sub-Contractor (unless the tender of the proposed Sub-Contractor referred to in clause 35.5.1.2 has been requested and submitted and approved on behalf of the Employer on the basis that Agreement NSC/2a shall not be entered into) and

       .2   the Architect/the Contract Administrator shall issue an instruction to the Contractor (with a copy to the proposed Sub-Contractor) nominating the proposed Sub-Contractor to supply and fix the materials or goods or to execute the work.

5.12   The Contractor shall proceed so as to conclude a Sub-Contract on Sub-Contract NSC/4a with the proposed Sub-Contractor within 14 days of the nomination instruction under clause 35.11.

PAYMENT OF NOMINATED SUB-CONTRACTOR

5.13   .1   The Architect/The Contract Administrator shall on the issue of each Interim Certificate:

       .1.1   direct the Contractor as to the amount of each interim or final payment to Nominated Sub-Contractors which is included in the amount stated as due in Interim Certificates and the amount of such interim or final payment shall be computed by the Architect/the Contract Administrator in accordance with the relevant provisions of Sub-Contract NSC/4 or NSC/4a as applicable; and

       .1.2   forthwith inform each Nominated Sub-Contractor of the amount of any interim or final payment directed in accordance with clause 35.13.1.1.

       .2   Each payment directed under clause 35.13.1.1 shall be duly discharged by the Contractor in accordance with Sub-Contract NSC/4 or NSC/4a as applicable.

       .3   Before the issue of each Interim Certificate (other than the first Interim Certificate) and of the Final Certificate the Contractor shall provide the Architect/the Contract Administrator with reasonable proof of the discharge referred to in clause 35.13.2.

       .4   If the Contractor is unable to provide the reasonable proof referred to in clause 35.13.2 because of some failure or omission of the Nominated Sub-Contractor to provide any document or other evidence to the Contractor which the Contractor may reasonably require and the Architect/the Contract Administrator is reasonably satisfied that this is the sole reason why reasonable proof is not furnished by the Contractor, the provisions of clause 35.13.5 shall not apply and the provisions of clause 35.13.3 shall be regarded as having been satisfied.

       .5.1   The Employer may, but where the Employer and the Nominated Sub-Contractor have executed Agreement NSC/2 or NSC/2a, shall, operate clauses 35.13.5.3 and .4.

.5.2   If the Contractor fails to provide reasonable proof under clause 35.13.3, the Architect/the Contract Administrator shall issue a certificate to that effect stating the amount in respect of which the Contractor has failed to provide such proof, and the Architect/the Contract Administrator shall issue a copy of the certificate to the Nominated Sub-Contractor concerned.

.5.3   Provided that the Architect/the Contract Administrator has issued the certificate under clause 35.13.5.2 and subject to clause 35.13.5.4, the amount of any future payment otherwise due to the Contractor under this Contract (after deducting any amounts due to the Employer from the Contractor under this Contract) shall be reduced by any amounts due to Nominated Sub-Contractors which the Contractor has failed to discharge (together with the amount of any value added tax which would have been due to the Nominated Sub-Contractor) and the Employer shall himself pay the same to the Nominated Sub-Contractor concerned. Provided that the Employer shall in no circumstances be obliged to pay amounts to Nominated Sub-Contractors in excess of amounts available for reduction as aforesaid

.5.4   The operation of clause 35.13.5.3 shall be subject to the following:

.5.4.1   where the Contractor would otherwise be entitled to payment of an amount stated as due in an Interim Certificate under clause 30, the reduction and payment to the Nominated Sub-Contractor referred to in clause 35.13.5.3 shall be made at the same time as the Employer pays the Contractor any balance due under clause 30 or, if there is no such balance, not later than the expiry of the period of 14 days within which the Contractor would otherwise be entitled to payment;

.5.4.2   where the sum due to the Contractor is the Retention or any part thereof, the reduction and payment to the Nominated Sub-Contractor referred to in clause 35.13.5.3 shall not exceed any part of the Contractor's retention (as defined in clause 30.4.2) which would otherwise be due for payment to the Contractor;

.5.4.3   where the Employer has to pay 2 or more Nominated Sub-Contractors but the amount due or to become due to the Contractor is insufficient to enable the Employer to pay the Nominated Sub-Contractors in full, the Employer shall apply the amount available pro rata to the amounts from time to time remaining undischarged by the Contractor or adopt such other method of apportionment as may appear to the Employer to be fair and reasonable having regard to all the relevant circumstances;

.5.4.4   clause 35.13.5.3 shall cease to have effect absolutely if at the date when the reduction and payment to the Nominated Sub-Contractor referred to in clause 35.13.5.3 would otherwise be made there is in existence

> either a Petition which has been presented to the Court for the winding up of the Contractor,
> or a resolution properly passed for the winding up of the Contractor other than for the purposes of amalgamation or reconstruction

whichever shall have first occurred. [*v*]

.6   Where, in accordance with clause 2.2 of Agreement NSC/2 or clause 1.2 of Agreement NSC/2a, the Employer, before the issue of an instruction nominating a Sub-Contractor, has paid to him an amount in respect of design work and/or materials or goods and/or fabrication which is/are included in the subject of the Sub-Contract Sum or Tender Sum:

[*v*] *Where the Contractor is a person subject to bankruptcy law and not the law relating to the insolvency of a company, clause 35.13.5.4.4 will require amendment to refer to the events on the happening of which bankruptcy occurs (see also Footnote [a]).*

.6.1   The Employer shall send to the Contractor the written statement of the Nominated Sub-Contractor of the amount to be credited to the Contractor, and

.6.2   The Employer may make deductions up to the amount of such credit from the amounts stated as due to the Contractor in any of the Interim Certificates which include amounts of interim or final payment to the Nominated Sub-Contractor; provided that the amounts so deducted from that stated as due in any one Interim Certificate shall not exceed the amount of payment to the Nominated Sub-Contractor included therein as directed by the Architect/the Contract Administrator.

EXTENSION OF PERIOD OR PERIODS FOR COMPLETION OF NOMINATED SUB-CONTRACT WORKS

5.14   .1   The Contractor shall not grant to any Nominated sub-Contractor any extension of the period or periods within which the Sub-Contract Works (or where the Sub-Contract Works are to be completed in parts any part thereof) are to be completed except in accordance with the relevant provisions of Sub-Contract NSC/4 or NSC/4a as applicable which requires the written consent of the Architect/the Contract Administrator to any such grant.

    .2   The Architect/The Contract Administrator shall operate the relevant provisions of Sub-Contract NSC/4 or NSC/4a as applicable upon receiving any notice particulars and estimate and a request from the Contractor and any Nominated Sub-Contractor for his written consent to an extension of the period or periods for the completion of the Sub-Contract Works or any part thereof as referred to in clause 11.2.2 of Sub-Contract NSC/4 or NSC/4a as applicable.

FAILURE TO COMPLETE NOMINATED SUB-CONTRACT WORKS

5.15   .1   If any Nominated Sub-Contractor fails to complete the Sub-Contract Works (or where the Sub-Contract Works are to be completed in parts any part thereof) within the period specified in the Sub-Contract or within any extended time granted by the Contractor with the written consent of the Architect/the Contract Administrator, and the Contractor so notifies the Architect/the Contract Administrator with a copy to the Nominated Sub-Contractor, then, provided that the Architect/the Contract Administrator is satisfied that clause 35.14 has been properly applied, the Architect/the Contract Administrator shall so certify in writing to the Contractor. Immediately upon the issue of such a certificate the Architect/the Contract Administrator shall send a duplicate thereof to the Nominated Sub-Contractor.

    .2   The certificate of the Architect/the Contract Administrator under clause 35.15.1 shall be issued not later than 2 months from the date of notification to the Architect/the Contract Administrator that the Nominated Sub-Contractor has failed to complete the Sub-Contract Works or any part thereof.

PRACTICAL COMPLETION OF NOMINATED SUB-CONTRACT WORKS

5.16   When in the opinion of the Architect/the Contract Administrator practical completion of the works executed by a Nominated Sub-Contractor is achieved he shall forthwith issue a certificate to that effect and Practical Completion of such Works for the purposes of clauses 35.16 to 35.19 or clause 18 shall be deemed to have taken place on the day named in such certificate, a duplicate copy of which shall be sent by the Architect/the Contract Administrator to the Nominated Sub-Contractor.

EARLY FINAL PAYMENT OF NOMINATED SUB-CONTRACTORS

35.17   Where the Agreement NSC/2 or NSC/2a has been entered into and provided that clause 5 of agreement NSC/2 or clause 4 of agreement NSC/2a remain in force unamended, then at any time after the day named in the certificate issued under clause 35.16 the Architect/the Contract Administrator may, and on the expiry of 12 months from the aforesaid day shall, issue an Interim Certificate the gross valuation for which shall include the amount of the relevant Sub-Contract Sum or Ascertained Final Sub-Contract Sum as finally adjusted or ascertained under the relevant provisions of Sub-Contract NSC/4 or NSC/4a as applicable; provided always that the Nominated Sub-Contractor:

.1   has in the opinion of the Architect/the Contract Administrator and the Contractor remedied any defects, shrinkages or other faults which have appeared and which the Nominated Sub-Contractor is bound to remedy under the Sub-Contract; and

.2   has sent through the Contractor to the Architect/the Contract Administrator or the Quantity Surveyor all documents necessary for the final adjustment of the Sub-Contract Sum or the computation of the Ascertained Final Sub-Contract Sum referred to in clause 35.17.

35.18   Upon due discharge by the Contractor to the Nominated Sub-Contractor ("the original Sub-Contractor") of the amount certified under clause 35.17 then:

.1.1   if the original Sub-Contractor fails to rectify any defect, shrinkage or other fault in the Sub-Contract works which he is bound to remedy under the Sub-Contract and which appears before the issue of the Final Certificate under clause 30.8 the Architect/the Contract Administrator shall in accordance with clause 35.24.4 issue an instruction nominating a person ("the substituted Sub-Contractor") to carry out such rectification work and all the provisions relating to Nominated Sub-Contractors in clause 35 shall apply to such further nomination;

.1.2   the Employer shall take such steps as may be reasonable to recover, under the Agreement NSC/2 or NSC/2a as applicable, from the original Sub-Contractor a sum equal to the Sub-Contract price of the substituted Sub-Contractor. The Contractor shall pay or allow to the Employer any difference between the amount so recovered by the Employer and the Sub-Contract price of the substituted Sub-Contractor provided that, before the further nomination has been made, the Contractor has agreed (which agreement shall not be unreasonably withheld) to the Sub-Contract price to be charged by the substituted Sub-Contractor.

.2   Nothing in clause 35.18 shall override or modify the provisions of clause 35.21.

35.19   Notwithstanding any final payment to a Nominated Sub-Contractor under the provisions of clause 35:

.1   until the date of Practical Completion of the Works or the date when the Employer takes possession of the Works, whichever first occurs, the Contractor shall be responsible for loss or damage to the Works, materials and goods for which a payment to which clause 35.17 refers has been made to the same extent but not further or otherwise than he is responsible for that part of the Works for which a payment as aforesaid has not been made;

.2   the provisions of clause 22A or 22B or 22C whichever is applicable shall remain in full force and effect.

POSITION OF EMPLOYER IN RELATION TO NOMINATED SUB-CONTRACTOR

5.20 Neither the existence nor the exercise of the powers in clause 35 nor anything else contained in the Conditions shall render the Employer in any way liable to any Nominated Sub-Contractor except by way and in the terms of the Agreement NSC/2 or NSC/2a as applicable.

CLAUSE 2 OF AGREEMENT NSC/2 OR CLAUSE 1 OF AGREEMENT NSC/2a-POSITION OF CONTRACTOR

5.21 Whether or not a Nominated Sub-Contractor is responsible to the Employer in the terms set out in clause 2 of the Agreement NSC/2 or clause 1 of the Agreement NSC/2a the Contractor shall not be responsible to the Employer in respect of any nominated Sub-Contract works for anything to which such terms relate. Nothing in clause 35.21 shall be construed so as to affect the obligations of the Contractor under this Contract in regard to the supply of workmanship, materials and goods.

RESTRICTIONS IN CONTRACTS OF SALE ETC.—LIMITATION OF LIABILITY OF NOMINATED SUB-CONTRACTORS

5.22 Where any liability of the Nominated Sub-Contractor to the Contractor is limited under the provisions of clause 2.3 of Sub-Contract NSC/4 or NSC/4a as applicable the liability of the Contractor to the Employer shall be limited to the same extent.

POSITION WHERE PROPOSED NOMINATION DOES NOT PROCEED FURTHER

5.23 The Architect/The Contract Administrator shall either issue an instruction under clause 13.2 requiring as a Variation the omission of the work for which the Architect/ the Contract Administrator intended to nominate a proposed Sub-Contractor or select another person to be nominated as a Sub-Contractor under the provisions of clause 35 if:

.1 the Contractor under clause 35.4 sustains a reasonable objection to a proposed Sub-Contractor; or

.2 where clauses 35.6 to 35.10 apply (use of Tender NSC/1), the proposed sub-contractor does not within a reasonable time settle and agree the Particular Conditions in Schedule 2 of the Tender NSC/1 when so requested by the Contractor on receipt of the Architect's/the Contract Administrator's preliminary notice of nomination under clause 35.7.1; or

.3 where clauses 35.11 and 35.12 apply (use of Sub-Contract NSC/4a), the proposed nominated sub-contractor without good cause fails within a reasonable time to enter into the Sub-Contract NSC/4a.

CIRCUMSTANCES WHERE RE-NOMINATION NECESSARY

5.24 If in respect of any Nominated Sub-Contract:

.1 the Contractor informs the Architect/the Contract Administrator that in the opinion of the Contractor the Nominated Sub-Contractor has made default in respect of any one or more of the matters referred to in clause 29.1.1 to .1.4 of

Sub-Contract NSC/4 or NSC/4a as applicable; and the Contractor has passed to the Architect/the Contract Administrator any observations of the Sub-Contractor in regard to the matters on which the Contractor considers the Sub-Contractor is in default; and the Architect/the Contract Administrator is reasonably of the opinion that the Sub-Contractor has made default; or

.2 the Nominated Sub-Contractor becomes bankrupt or makes a composition or arrangement with his creditors or has a proposal in respect of his company for a voluntary arrangement for a composition of debts or a scheme of arrangement approved in accordance with the Insolvency Act 1986 or has an application made under the Insolvency Act 1986 in respect of his company to the Court for the appointment of an administrator, or has a winding up order made or (except for the purposes of amalgamation or reconstruction) passes a resolution for voluntary winding up or a provisional liquidator or receiver or manager of the business or undertaking is duly appointed or has an administrative receiver, as defined in the Insolvency Act 1986, appointed, or possession is taken, by or on behalf of the holders of any debentures secured by a floating charge, of any property comprised in or subject to the floating charge; or

.3 the Nominated Sub-Contractor determines his employment under clause 30 of Sub-Contract NSC/4 or NSC/4a as applicable; or

.4 the Contractor has been required by the Employer to determine the employment of the Sub-Contractor under clause 29.3 of Sub-Contract NSC/4 or NSC/4a as applicable and has so determined that employment; or

.5 work properly executed or materials or goods properly fixed or supplied by the Nominated Sub-Contractor have to be taken down and/or re-executed or re-fixed or re-supplied ('work to be re-executed') as a result of compliance by the Contractor or by any other Nominated Sub-Contractor with any instruction or other exercise of a power of the Architect/the Contract Administrator under clauses 7 or 8.4 or 17.2 or 17.3 and the Nominated Sub-Contractor cannot be required under the Sub-Contract and does not agree to carry out the work to be re-executed;

then

.6 where clause 35.24.1 applies:

.6.1 the Architect/the Contract Administrator shall issue an instruction to the Contractor to give to the Sub-Contractor the notice specifying the default to which clause 29.1 of Sub-Contract NSC/4 or NSC/4a as applicable refers; and may in that instruction state that the Contractor must obtain a further instruction of the Architect/the Contract Administrator before determining the employment of the Sub-Contractor under clause 29.1 of Sub-Contract NSC/4 or NSC/4a as applicable; and

.6.2 the Contractor shall inform the Architect/the Contract Administrator whether, following the giving of that notice for which the Architect/the Contract Administrator has issued an instruction under clause 35.24.6.1, the employment of the Sub-Contractor has been determined by the Contractor under clause 29.1 of Sub-Contract NSC/4 or NSC/4a as applicable; or where the further instruction referred to in clause 35.24.6.1 has been given by the Architect/the Contract Administrator the Contractor shall confirm that the employment of the Sub-Contractor has been determined; then

.6.3 if the Contractor informs, or confirms to the Architect/the Contract Administrator that the employment of the Sub-Contractor has been so determined the Architect/the Contract Administrator shall make such further nomination of a Sub-Contractor in accordance with clause 35 as may be necessary to supply and fix the materials or goods or to execute the work and to make good or re-supply or re-execute as necessary any work executed by or any materials or goods supplied

634

by the Sub-Contractor whose employment has been determined which were not in accordance with the relevant Sub-Contract; provided that where the employment of the Nominated Sub-Contractor has been determined for the reasons referred to in clause 29.1.3 of Sub-Contract NSC/4 or NSC/4a as applicable, the Contractor shall agree (which agreement shall not be unreasonably withheld) the price to be charged by the substituted Sub-Contractor as provided in clause 35.1 8.1.

.7 Where clause 35.24.2 or clause 35.24.4 apply, the Architect/the Contract Administrator shall make such further nomination of a Sub-Contractor in accordance with clause 35 as may be necessary to supply and fix the materials or goods or to execute the work and to make good or re-supply or re-execute as necessary any work executed by or any materials or goods supplied by the Sub-Contractor whose employment has been determined which were not in accordance with the relevant Sub-Contract; provided that where a receiver or manager or administrative receiver or administrator of the business of the Nominated Sub-Contractor is appointed the Architect/the Contract Administrator may postpone the duty to make a further nomination as provided in clause 35.24.7 if there are reasonable grounds for supposing that the receiver or manager or administrative receiver or administrator is prepared to continue to carry out or fulfil the relevant Sub-Contract in a way that will not prejudice the interests of the Employer, the Contractor or any Sub-Contractor whether Nominated or Domestic engaged, or to be engaged, upon or in connection with the Works.

.8.1 Where clause 35.24.3 applies the Architect/the Contract Administrator shall make such further nomination of a Sub-Contractor in accordance with clause 35 as may be necessary to supply and fix the materials or goods or to execute the work and to make good or re-supply or re-execute as necessary any work executed by or any materials or goods supplied by the Sub-Contractor who has determined his employment which were not in accordance with the relevant Sub-Contract.

.8.2 Where clause 35.24.5 applies the Architect/the Contract Administrator shall make such further nomination of a Sub-Contractor in accordance with clause 35 as may be necessary to carry out the work to be re-executed referred to in clause 35.24.5.

.9 The amount properly payable to the Nominated Sub-Contractor under the Sub-Contract resulting from such further nomination under clause 35.24.6.3 or 35.24.7 shall be included in the amount stated as due in Interim Certificates and added to the Contract Sum. Where clauses 35.24.3 and 35.24.8.1 apply any extra amount, payable by the Employer in respect of the Sub-Contractor nominated under the further nomination over the price of the Nominated Sub-Contractor who has validly determined his employment under his Sub-Contract, and where clauses 35.24.5 and 35.24.8.2 apply the amount payable by the Employer, resulting from such further nomination may at the time or any time after such amount is certified in respect of the Sub-Contractor nominated under the further nomination be deducted by the Employer from monies due or to become due to the Contractor under this Contract or may be recoverable from the Contractor by the Employer as a debt.

.10 The Architect/The Contract Administrator shall make the further nomination of a Sub-Contractor as referred to in clauses 35.24.6.3, 35.24.7, 35.24.8.1 and 35.24.8.2 within a reasonable time, having regard to all the circumstances, after the obligation to make such further nomination has arisen.

DETERMINATION OR DETERMINATION OF EMPLOYMENT OF NOMINATED SUB-CONTRACTOR—ARCHITECT'S/CONTRACT AD-MINISTRATOR'S INSTRUCTIONS

35.25 The Contractor shall not determine any Nominated Sub-Contract by virtue of any right to which he may be or may become entitled without an instruction from the Architect/the Contract Administrator so to do.

35.26 Where the employment of the Nominated Sub-Contractor is determined under clause 29 of Sub-Contract NSC/4 or NSC/4a as applicable the Architect/the Contract Administrator shall direct the Contractor as to any amount included in the amount stated as due in an Interim Certificate in respect of the value of work executed or materials or goods supplied by the Nominated Sub-Contractor in accordance with clause 29.4 of that Sub-Contract.

Clause 35: Nominated Sub-Contractors

Derivation. In the 1963 Form, the principal clause dealing with Nominated Sub-Contractors was clause 27. Clause 35 of the 1980 Form sets out a completely new code in relation to nomination of Sub-Contractors. However, some material has been derived from clause 27 of the 1963 Form. Moreover, the basic concept of nomination remains unchanged.

Amendments. Clause 35 was amended by Amendment 4 issued in July 1987 and Amendment 5 issued in January 1988. The only amendments of consequence are to clause 35.24 dealing with renomination. These are discussed below.

The structure of nomination. In addition to clause 35 itself, clause 35.3 refers to other documents issued by the Joint Contracts Tribunal each of which is referred to in clause 35 and drafted to be used in conjunction with it. NSC/4 and 4a are alternative versions of a Standard Form of Nominated Sub-Contract. Use of one or other of these Standard Forms of Nominated Sub-Contract is obligatory. (If NSC/4 or NSC/4a are not used, the clauses relating to nomination of Sub-Contractors do not work.) These replace the former "Green Form" of Nominated Sub-Contract. The 1980 Form also introduced new alternative versions of a Standard Form of Employer/Nominated Sub-Contractor Agreement, Forms NSC/2 and NSC/2a. Although clause 35 recognises that NSC/2 or 2a may not be used (see clauses 35.5.1.2 and 35.11.1), there is a clear assumption that this will only rarely occur. If they are not used, the Employer loses the degree of protection of his interests which they are intended to achieve.

Assuming, therefore, that the expected procedure is followed and that one or other of the alternatives of the Standard Forms of Agreement and Sub-Contract are entered into, the following is a simplified summary of the resulting rights, obligations and relationships:

(1) the Architect is obliged to nominate Sub-Contractors where, in accor-

dance with clause 35.1, he has "reserved to himself the final selection and approval of the sub-contractor. . . ." The general principle discussed in *Bickerton* v. *N.W. Metropolitan Regional Hospital Board*[46] that the Contractor has neither the right nor the obligation to carry out such work himself, applies equally, so it seems, to the 1980 Contract.[47]

(2) subject to a right to make reasonable objection (clause 35.4), the Contractor is obliged to enter into Sub-Contract NSC/4 with a Nominated Sub-Contractor where the procedure in clauses 35.6 to 35.10 has been followed, or Sub-Contract NSC/4a where clauses 35.11 and 35.12 apply.

(3) the Nominated Sub-Contractor is entitled to interim and final payment in accordance with his Sub-Contract pursuant to Main Contract Interim Certificates (clauses 35.13.1 and 2). If the Contractor fails to discharge payments in accordance with clause 35.13.2, the Nominated Sub-Contractor is entitled, subject to certain limitations, to receive payment direct from the Employer, who makes an equivalent reduction of amounts due to the Contractor (clause 35.13.5 and clauses 7.1 and 6.1 of NSC/2 and 2a respectively).

(4) the nominated Sub-Contractor will be entitled to extensions of the period of completion of the Sub-Contract Works if the relevant provisions of NSC/4 or 4a apply.

(5) delay on the part of a Nominated Sub-Contractor entitles the Contractor to an extension of time under clause 25.4.7, and constitutes a breach by the Sub-Contractor of clause 3.4 or 2.4 of NSC/2 or 2a respectively entitling the Employer to damages.

(6) failure by the Nominated Sub-Contractor to complete the Sub-Contract Works within the period specified in the Sub-Contract, extended if appropriate, will entitle the Contractor to recover any loss or damage from the Sub-Contractor provided that he has obtained a certificate from the Architect under clause 35.15 of the Main Contract (clause 12.2 of NSC/4).

(7) the Contractor is ultimately responsible to the Employer for the Nominated Sub-Contractor's workmanship, materials and goods, the general law in this respect being preserved by clause 35.21.

(8) the Contractor is not responsible to the Employer for anything to which the terms of clause 2 or clause 1 of NSC/2 or 2a respectively relate (clause 35.21). The Contractor is thus not responsible for the design of the Sub-Contract Works, the selection of materials and goods for the Sub-Contract Works or for the satisfaction of any performance specification referred to in the description of the Sub-Contract Works.

---

[46] [1970] 1 W.L.R. 607 (H.L.).

[47] For further consideration and elucidation of the principles of *Bickerton* see: *Fairclough Building* v. *Rhuddlan B.C.* (1985) 30 B.L.R. 26 (C.A.). *Percy Bilton Ltd.* v. *Greater London Council* [1982] 1 W.L.R. 794 (H.L.) and *John Jarvis* v. *Rockdale Housing Association* (1986) 36 B.L.R. 48 (C.A.).

(9) if a nomination does not result in the making of a Nominated Sub-Contract, the Architect is obliged either to issue a Variation instruction omitting the work or to make a further nomination (clause 35.23).

(10) if a *Bickerton* situation arises,[48] and in certain other circumstances, the Architect is obliged to renominate (clause 35.24). The Architect is also obliged to renominate, if an original Nominated Sub-Contractor fails to rectify defects after Practical Completion which he is bound to remedy under the Sub-Contract (clause 35.18).

Default of Nominated Sub-Contractor—summary of Contractor's liability. The Nominated Sub-Contractor, despite the elaborate terms, remains a Sub-Contractor. The starting point is therefore that the Contractor is as responsible for his Sub-Contractor's default as he is for his own default. But the Contractor's liability is always subject to the terms of the Contract. The effect here is to diminish the Contractor's liability substantially and to leave the Employer's remedy for many defaults of the Nominated Sub-Contractor against the Nominated Sub-Contractor direct under NSC/2 or NSC/2a if one of them is used. But at least one potentially heavy liability remains with the Contractor. Very roughly and subject always to the detailed words of the Contract one can attempt a summary of the Contractor's liability for a Nominated Sub-Contractor's default thus:

(i) *No liability for his delay.* The Contractor has a right to an extension of time under clause 25.4.7 for such delay. Delay by a Nominated Sub-Contractor is not a ground upon which the Contractor can rely to determine his employment under clause 28 or to claim his losses from the Employer.[49] For delay causing a suspension of the Works, see commentary to clause 28. Authority by the Architect to depart from the specified method of construction in order to reduce loss being caused by a Nominated Sub-Contractor is not, it is submitted, a ground for additional payment unless it can be shown that there was an intention to issue an instruction requiring a Variation under clause 13.1.[50]

(ii) *No liability for the delay of the Nominated Sub-Contractor relating to drawings and information.* It is often necessary to obtain information from Nominated Sub-Contractors or proposed Nominated Sub-Contractors as to the details of their work to enable adequate instructions, details and drawings to be given to the Contractor. Failure to give such information may delay the progress of the Works. If the failure arises before nomination it will ordinarily give the Contractor a right to an extension of

---

[48] *Bickerton* v. *N.W. Metropolitan Regional Hospital Board* [1970] 1 W.L.R. 607 (H.L.). For further discussion of the decision in *Bickerton*, see pp. 293 and 648.

[49] See p. 595.

[50] See, for some assistance, *Kirk & Kirk Ltd.* v. *Croydon Corporation* (1956) J.P.L. 585; *Simplex Concrete Piles Ltd.* v. *St. Pancras Borough Council* (1958) 14 B.L.R. 80; *cf. Tharsis Sulphur & Copper Co.* v. *M'Elroy & Sons* (1878) 3 App. Cas. 1040 at 1053 (H.L.).

time under clause 25.4.6 if completion is delayed, and if he has suffered loss and expense, to payment under clause 26.2.1 or to claim damages for delay in the issue of drawings or instructions. After nomination the position is the same as regards delay generally by a Nominated Sub-Contractor, but the Contractor may be able to show that what appears, prima facie, to be delay by the Nominated Sub-Contractor is on the facts, delay by the Architect. Thus the Nominated Sub-Contractor may be delayed by lack of information by the Architect, or the Architect may have relied on the Nominated Sub-Contractor to provide the Contractor with information which he, the Architect, is under a duty to provide under clause 5.3. In such instances the Contractor can claim from the Employer under clause 26.2.1 or for breach of contract.

(iii) *No liability for his design.*[51] Clause 35.21 is explicit that the Contractor is not to be responsible for the Nominated Sub-Contractor's design.

(iv) *No liability for fitness for purpose.* It is in the nature of the system of nomination that there is no reliance upon the Contractor's skill and judgment. Therefore the Contractor is under no liability if the work, materials or equipment carried out and supplied by the Nominated Sub-Contractor are not fit for their purpose.[52]

(v) *No liability for his repudiation and the like* (subject to a restricted liability under clause 35.18.1.2).

(vi) *A liability for bad workmanship and materials* which in general (and subject as before to clause 35.18.1.2) only becomes enforceable after the issue of the Final Certificate under clause 30.8. In practice, and assuming that the Architect has properly performed his duty to the Employer to supervise, the liability is limited to latent defects, of which examples might be poor concrete in beams or missing fixings in cladding. The liability should therefore only rarely arise, but if it does, it may be very great. The effect is comparable to that of a guarantee of latent defects of workmanship and materials.

Guarantees. Unless this is written in to the Bills, in which case the clause 2.2 problems arise,[53] it is submitted that the court would not imply a term that the Contractor accepted liability for a guarantee given to him by the Sub-Contractor.[54] If this is correct the guarantee is of no value to the Employer. If a guarantee is required by the Employer he should obtain it direct from the Nominated Sub-Contractor and have it expressed to be given in consideration of nomination or alternatively pay a sum for it.

---

[51] See generally "Design" and "Installation or shop drawings" at pp. 291 *et seq.*

[52] See generally "Fitness for purpose of completed works" at p. 55 and "Fitness for purpose" at p. 291.

[53] See p. 488.

[54] For implication of terms generally, see pp. 45 *et seq.*

Clause 35.1. *The duty to nominate*

This arises where under clause 35.1 the Architect has reserved to himself the final selection and approval of a Sub-Contractor either by the use of a prime cost sum or by naming the Sub-Contractor. This may be done in the Contract Bills (clause 35.1.1); or by an instruction relating to a provisional sum included in the Contract Bills (clause 35.1.2); or by a Variation instruction instructing work similar to work for which the Contract Bills already provide for a nomination (clause 35.1.3); or by agreement (clause 35.1.4).

Delay in giving instructions. Delay by the Architect in giving instructions nominating a Sub-Contractor can give rise to claims for extensions of time under clause 25.4.6,[55] to loss or expense under clause 26.2.1 and probably to damages at common law.

Nomination of designer. The right of nomination is in respect of persons to supply and fix materials or goods or to execute work. It does not extend to persons who are to design and the Contractor can, it is submitted, refuse to accept a purported nomination of a person who is expressed to be required to carry out design work.

Clause 35.2. This clause is substantially the same as clause 27(g) of the 1963 Form.

PROCEDURE FOR NOMINATION

Clause 35.4.1. "*... reasonable objection ...*"

These words appeared in clause 27(a) of the 1963 Form. In *Bickerton* in the Court of Appeal[56] it was said that the Contractor cannot object merely because he considers the price is too low, and "[h]e has no right to object to any of the details in the specifications in the sub-contract, any more than to the sub-contract price. Provided the sub-contract conforms to the provisions of condition 27, his sole right or objection is to the person nominated."[57] No guidance is given as to the grounds which might be held to be reasonable, but it is suggested that they can include both the technical competence and financial ability of the proposed Nominated Sub-Contractor.

There is no equivalent in the 1980 Form of that part of Condition 27(a) of the 1963 Contract which followed the words "against whom the Contractor shall make reasonable objection," *i.e.* the model Sub-Contract clauses in Condition 27(a)(i)–(x) upon which the Contractor was entitled to insist as a

---

[55] *cf. Bilton Ltd.* v. *Greater London Council* [1982] 1 W.L.R. 794 (H.L.).

[56] [1969] 1 All E.R. 977 (C.A.).

[57] Sachs L.J. in *Bickerton* v. *N.W. Metropolitan Regional Hospital Board* [1969] 1 All E.R. 977 at 983 (C.A.).

condition of nomination. These are now unnecessary since it is obligatory to use Sub-Contract NSC/4 or NSC/4a.[58]

Clause 35.5.1. "*Tender NSC/1 and Agreement NSC/2 shall be used . . . unless clause 35.5.1.2 is operated*"

The effect of clause 35.5 is that the procedure and documents referred to in clauses 35.6–35.10 inclusive are obligatory unless either (a) the document which is the genesis of the nomination states that clauses 35.11 and 35.12 shall apply, or (b) the Architect issues an instruction under clause 35.5.2.

Clause 35.5.2. "*. . . the Architect . . . may issue an instruction substituting . . . any such instruction shall be treated as if it were a Variation . . .*"

The effect of this clause is that the Architect may by instruction substitute the procedure in clauses 35.6 to 35.10 inclusive for that in clauses 35.11 and 35.12 or vice versa. He cannot do so after he has issued a preliminary notice of nomination under clause 35.7.1 or a nomination instruction under clause 35.11 unless a further nomination or a renomination is necessary under clause 35.23 or 35.24. An instruction under clause 35.5.2 is to be treated as if it were a Variation. This presumably means that it is a Variation to which the valuation provisions of clauses 13.4 and 13.5 apply and to which the provisions of clause 25.4.5.1 for extension of time and clause 26.2.7 for loss and expense also apply.

The difference between the procedure in clauses 35.6–35.10 inclusive on the one hand and clauses 35.11 and 35.12 on the other. It is essentially a difference of procedure, not of substance. The Appendix to Sub-Contract NSC/4 provides for the completed tender (NSC/1) to be attached to the Sub-Contract. Sub-Contract NSC/4a has on the other hand an extensive Appendix of its own. But tender NSC/1 and the Appendix to Sub-Contract NSC/4a contain essentially the same material. The difference between the two procedures lies in the fact that clauses 35.6 to 35.10 inclusive embody a formal procedure whereby "the Particular Conditions" in Schedule 2 of tender NSC/1 are agreed between the Contractor and the Nominated Sub-Contractor before the formal nomination instruction is issued, whereas this is not so under clauses 35.11 and 35.12. The only differences between Agreement NSC/2 and NSC/2a are that NSC/2 contains (but NSC/2a does not) clause 1, dealing with the agreement between the Sub-Contractor and the Contractor of the Particular Conditions and clause 9 dealing with any conflict between the terms of the tender and the Agreement.

Clauses 35.6–35.10 inclusive. These clauses, which are annotated in detail below, set out a procedure leading to nomination after the Contractor

---

[58] In relation to clause 27(a) of the 1963 Form, it was held that a Contractor was entitled to refuse a nomination or a renomination of a Sub-Contractor who did not offer to complete his part of the work within the overall completion period for the Contract as a whole: see *Bilton Ltd.* v. *Greater London Council* [1982] 1 W.L.R. 794 and *Fairclough Building* v. *Rhuddlan Borough Council* (1985) 30 B.L.R. 26 (C.A.). These decisions are superseded by the fact that the Sub-Contractor must now enter into either Form NSC/4 or NSC/4a.

and proposed Sub-Contractor have agreed upon the "Particular Conditions in Schedule 2 of the tender NSC/1." These Conditions include many important matters, in particular the programme. The intention of the procedure set out in these clauses is, presumably, to provide for the problem which frequently arises in practice when there is a failure to agree promptly upon the terms of the Sub-Contract. This can lead to delay in nomination, disruption in the progress of the Works and delay in completion. Sometimes the Sub-Contract Works are started (and sometimes even completed) before the terms of the Sub-Contract have been agreed. The procedure set out here is, at first glance, attractive and clear. But there are, on examination, potential difficulties.

Clause 35.7.1. *"a preliminary notice of nomination instructing the Contractor forth-with to settle . . ."*

This is an instruction entitling the Contractor to an extension of time under clause 25 but lateness in giving it does not as such entitle the Contractor to loss and expense under clause 26. It is thought that it must be implied that the instruction must be given within such reasonable time as will enable the procedure contemplated by clauses 35.6–35.10 to be carried out. If this is correct, breach of the implied term gives rise to a right to damages.

Clause 35.7.2. *". . . the Contractor shall forthwith proceed to settle . . ."*

These words cannot be given their literal meaning. It takes two to make an agreement. Compare clause 1.1 of NSC/2 and see its commentary at page 801. Presumably the intention under clause 35.7.2 is that the Contractor shall enter into bona fide negotiations.

Clause 35.8. *"If the Contractor is unable . . . the Architect shall issue such instructions as may be necessary"*

What instructions does the Architect issue? He cannot instruct the Contractor to agree. By clause 4.1.1 the Architect can issue instructions where he is expressly empowered so to do. Upon the duty arising under clause 35.8 to issue instructions, the Architect might, for example, issue a Variation instruction under clause 13.2, a postponement instruction under clause 23.2 or a fresh preliminary notice of nomination under clause 35.7.1 insofar as the proposed Sub-Contractor has not within a reasonable time settled and agreed the conditions (see clause 35.23.2). Is the Architect expressly empowered by clause 35.8 to issue instructions independently of a power arising under other clauses? The answer is not clear. It may be that he can instruct the Contractor to continue negotiating. Subject to this it is thought that no power arises under clause 35.8 independently of other clauses.

Delay in agreeing a Sub-Contract. See clause 35.23.2 for the Architect's duty either to issue an instruction to omit or a fresh preliminary notice of nomination. There may be arguments of fact as to what is a reasonable time to settle and agree the Particular Conditions of the Sub-Contract. What of time and loss and expense? As to this, see commentary to clause 25. The Contractor is entitled to an extension of time under clause 25 if the completion of the Works is likely to be delayed by compliance with the Architect's instructions, but is not entitled to loss and expense under clause 26. The Architect's preliminary notice of nomination under clause 35.7.1 must have been given at a proper time (see above). If it was not, there is a claim for damages for breach of contract. Thereafter the Contractor is probably not entitled to loss and expense or damages during the period which is a reasonable time within which to settle and agree the Particular Conditions because he has accepted this risk (see clause 35.23.2). But presumably he is not to be taken as having accepted the risk of an indeterminate number of notices of nomination, or even, perhaps, more than one. How is the Contractor's loss dealt with? If he has specifically applied in writing for instructions, he will have a claim under clause 26.2.1, alternatively it may be that there is some kind of implied term.

Clauses 35.11 and 35.12. The alternative procedure under clauses 35.11 and 35.12 in effect requires the Contractor to agree with the Sub-Contractor those parts of the Appendix to NSC/4a which are the equivalent of the Particular Conditions in Schedule 2 of tender NSC/1 within 14 days of the nomination (see above). Presumably the intention in clause 35.12 is that the Contractor shall enter into bona fide negotiations and use his best endeavours to conclude a Sub-Contract. The relationship of clause 35.12 to clause 35.23.3 is not altogether clear. If the Contractor under clause 35.12 has to conclude a Sub-Contract within 14 days then, presumably, it is contemplated that if the proposed Nominated Sub-Contractor fails without good cause to enter into the Sub-Contract within 14 days, the reasonable time will have expired so that the Architect has to apply the provisions of clause 35.23. As to loss caused to the Contractor, see "Delay in agreeing a Sub-Contract" above.

PAYMENT OF NOMINATED SUB-CONTRACTOR

Clauses 35.13.1 and 35.13.2. *"The Architect ... shall ... direct the Contractor ... Each payment directed ... shall be duly discharged by the Contractor ..."*
These clauses, providing for certification in Interim Certificates and the discharge of sums due to Nominated Sub-Contractors, are in substance derived from clause 27(b) of the 1963 Form. Both the calculation of the amount due and its discharge by the Contractor are now expressly required to be made in accordance with the terms of the relevant Sub-Contract.

Clauses 35.13.3 to 35.13.5 inclusive. *Direct payment to Sub-Contractors*
These much expanded and redrafted clauses are derived from clause 27(c) of the 1963 Form. For direct payment clauses generally, see page 285. For the position of Sub-Contractors on insolvency, see page 380. Clause 35.13.3 now makes it obligatory for the Contractor to provide the Architect with reasonable proof that he has discharged all sums due to Nominated Sub-Contractors

643

under clause 35.13.2. This obligation arises before the issue of each Interim Certificate. Under clause 27(c) of the 1963 Form, the obligation to provide reasonable proof only arose upon request by the Architect. If the Contractor fails to provide reasonable proof of payment, the direct payment provisions of clause 35.13.5 apply. Where the Employer and the Nominated Sub-Contractor have executed Agreement NSC/2 or 2a, the Employer is obliged to operate the direct payment procedure both by virtue of clause 35.13.5.1 and clauses 7.1 and 6.1 of NSC/2 and 2a respectively. Direct payment is effected under clause 35.13.5.3 by reducing the amount of any future payment otherwise due to the Contractor by any amounts due to Nominated Sub-Contractors which the Contractor has failed to discharge. The Employer himself pays the Nominated Sub-Contractor direct, but is not obliged to make payments in excess of amounts due to the Contractor and available for reduction.

Clause 35.13.5.4 provides for the time when direct payment is to be made; for the direct payment against Retention not to exceed the Contractor's retention as defined in clause 30.4.2; for the division of an insufficient amount available for direct payments between two or more Nominated Sub-Contractors; and for the rights and obligations as to direct payment to cease upon the Contractor's insolvency. This last provision recognises the uncertainty of the law as to the effectiveness of direct payment clauses in cases of insolvency.[59] Clauses 7.2 and 6.2 of NSC/2 and 2a respectively provide for repayment by the Nominated Sub-Contractor to the Employer of direct payments made contrary to clause 35.13.5.4.4 in ignorance of the Contractor's insolvency. The operation of clause 35.13.5 is discretionary where the Employer and the Nominated Sub-Contractor have not executed Agreement NSC/2 or 2a. An example of the operation of the direct payment provisions is given in the commentary to clause 21 of NSC/4 at page 757.

Clause 35.13.6. This new sub-clause was inserted by Amendment 4 issued in July 1987. It should be read in conjunction with amendments to the Nominated Sub-Contracts and the Employer/Nominated Sub-Contractor Agreements. These amendments deal with payment by the Employer under the Agreements NSC/2 (clause 2) or NSC/2a (clause 1) to a Nominated Sub-Contractor before the nomination, and with the resultant credit for such payments due to the Employer.

Clauses 35.14 and 35.15. These clauses deal with extension of the period for completion of Nominated Sub-Contract Works and failure to complete Nominated Sub-Contract Works on time. They are derived from clause 27(d) of the 1963 Form. A Certificate of the Architect under clause 35.15.1 of the 1980 Form remains a condition precedent to the Contractor's right to claim loss or damage caused by the Nominated Sub-Contractor's failure to complete on time (see clause 12.2 of NSC/4 and its commentary at page 732). The

---

[59] See commentary to clause 27 at p. 594.

nature of the certificate to be issued by the Architect has, however, changed in line with the certificate now to be issued under clause 24 of the 1980 Form (see commentary to clause 24).

Clause 35.14.1. *"The Contractor shall not grant . . ."*

If the Contractor grants an extension in breach of this clause the Architect can, it is thought, take the breach and its effect, if any, into account in considering any extension of time under clause 25 for the Nominated Sub-Contractor's delay (see generally clause 25.4.6 and commentary to clause 25). Further, the Architect is, it appears, released from the duty of granting a Certificate under clause 35.15.1.

Clause 35.15.1. *". . . shall so certify in writing to the Contractor . . ."*

It has been held in relation to such a certificate under clause 27(d)(ii) of the 1963 Form that provided the date in the certificate was the same or later than the Sub-Contract completion date, as extended, the certificate was valid.[60]

Clause 35.16. *". . . practical completion of the works executed by a Nominated Sub-Contractor . . ."*

This provision, requiring the Architect to certify practical completion of works executed by a Nominated Sub-Contractor, in appropriate circumstances in advance of the Practical Completion of the Works under clause 17 or partial possession by the Employer under clause 18, is introduced as part of the machinery to enable final payment to be made to Nominated Sub-Contractors under clauses 35.17 to 35.19 inclusive.

Clauses 35.17 to 35.19 inclusive. *Early Final Payment of Nominated Sub-Contractors*

These clauses derive from clause 27(e) of the 1963 Form, but have been redrafted and much extended. They should be read with clauses 5 and 4 of NSC/2 and 2a respectively and clause 21.3.2 of NSC/4.

Under clause 27(e) of the 1963 Form, the making of early final payment to a Nominated Sub-Contractor was discretionary. Under clause 35.17 of the 1980 Form, it is obligatory on the expiry of 12 months from a certificate of Practical Completion under clause 35.16, where the terms of clause 35.17 are fulfilled. The operation of clause 35.17 is in particular conditional upon clauses 5 and 4 of NSC/2 and 2a respectively remaining in force unamended so that the Employer has, *inter alia*, a direct right of recovery against the Nominated Sub-Contractor for the purpose of clause 35.18.1.2. The Sub-Contractor's indemnity to the Contractor formerly required under clause 27(e) of the 1963 Form is now to be found in clause 21.3.2.2 of NSC/4.

Clause 27(e) of the 1963 form contained a provision that "upon such final payment the Contractor shall, save for latent defects, be discharged from all

---

[60] See *R. M. Douglas Ltd.* v. *C.E.D. Building Services* (1985) 1 Const. L.J. 232.

liability for the work, materials or goods executed or supplied by such Sub-Contractor under the Sub-Contract to which the payment relates." This does not appear in the 1980 Form. The position under the 1980 Form appears to be as follows:

(1) early final payment can only occur at a date after the Architect has certified practical completion of the Nominated Sub-Contract Works;

(2) such a certificate cannot be issued unless the Architect is satisfied that the Nominated Sub-Contract Works are complete and do not contain patent defects[61];

(3) the Contractor remains liable for latent defects appearing in the Nominated Sub-Contract Works before the issue of the Final Certificate to the extent and in the manner set out in clause 35.18.1;

(4) the Contractor is liable for patent defects if and only if the certificate under clause 35.16 is opened up and revised.

Clause 35.18 operates where a Nominated Sub-Contractor has received final payment and fails to rectify defects of workmanship or materials (see clause 35.18.2) which he is obliged to remedy under his Sub-Contract and which appeared before the issue of a Final Certificate. The Contractor is ultimately responsible for the failure of his Sub-Contractor, by virtue of clauses 17.2 and 17.3 of the Main Contract, but this responsibility is modified by two important qualifications. First, the Contractor is not obliged to remedy the defects himself. The Architect has to make a renomination to which the provisions of clause 35 are to apply, so that the Contractor is entitled to be paid by the Employer sums which are due to the substituted Sub-Contractor. Secondly, the onus is on the Employer, not the Contractor, to take reasonable steps to recover from the original Sub-Contractor a sum equal to the Sub-Contract price of the substituted Sub-Contractor under or as damages for breach of clauses 5.2 or 4.2 of NSC/2 or 2a respectively. It is only if the Employer fails to make full recovery from the original Sub-Contractor that the Contractor becomes responsible, and then only if he has agreed to the Sub-Contract price to be charged by the substituted Sub-Contractor. Before, therefore, the Contractor becomes liable, there may, in addition to arbitration between the Employer and Nominated Sub-Contractor, have to be arbitration between Employer and Contractor to determine whether the Contractor's withholding of agreement to the Sub-Contract Price was unreasonable. Compared to the position under the 1963 Form, the position under the 1980 Form is therefore very favourable to the Contractor.

It is submitted that the Contractor is liable in damages in respect of defects in the Sub-Contract works which appear after the issue of the Final Certificate save to the extent that the Final Certificate is conclusive.[62]

---

[61] See Clause 17 and its commentary for the meaning of "Practical Completion."
[62] See Clause 30 and its commentary.

POSITION OF EMPLOYER IN RELATION TO NOMINATED SUB-CONTRACTOR

Clause 35.20.   This clause is derived from clause 27(f) of the 1963 Form. It is probable that the words "Neither the existence nor . . ." both negative any trust, apart from that arising under clause 30.5.1, and also any actionable duty of care. The reference to agreement NSC/2 or NSC/2a is added, and the anticipated widespread use of these direct contracts between the Employer and the Nominated Sub-Contractors will result in a triangular contractual relationship between Employer, Contractor and Nominated Sub-Contractor (see commentary to clause 35.21).

Clause 35.21.   This important clause helps to clarify the nature of the triangular relationship referred to in the previous paragraph. The Contractor is responsible to the extent and at the time discussed above, for the quality of the workmanship, materials and goods of his Nominated Sub-Contractor, but any responsibility on his part to the Employer for the Sub-Contractor's design of the Sub-Contract Works, or the suitability of materials or goods selected by the Sub-Contractor, or the satisfaction of any performance specification or requirement referred to in the description of the Sub-Contract Works is expressly excluded. In general, therefore, design obligations and obligations as to the suitability of Sub-Contract materials do not travel on the lines of the triangle which link the Employer to the Contractor or the Contractor to the Sub-Contractor, and a nomination instruction which sought to impose such design obligations would be invalid.[63] Such obligations travel, if at all, on the line which links the Sub-Contractor directly with the Employer. It is for this reason essential that Employers should insist that all Nominated Sub-Contractors enter into Agreement NSC/2 or 2a. It is thought that Architects who fail to advise their clients to this effect would be in breach of their professional duty. The clause also highlights the increasing tendency for substantial elements of the detailed design of modern buildings to be carried out by Nominated Sub-Contractors.

Clause 35.22.   *"Where any liability . . . is limited . . ."*
This clause, which should be read with clause 2.3 of NSC/4 and compared with clause 36.5, states expressly what the majority of the House of Lords would not imply in *Gloucestershire County Council* v. *Richardson.*[64]

POSITION WHERE PROPOSED NOMINATION DOES NOT PROCEED FURTHER

Clause 35.23.   This provides what is to happen where the making of a

---

[63] See clause 35.1, where the Nominated Sub-Contractor is to "supply and fix any materials or goods or execute work," not to design.
[64] [1969] 1 A.C. 480; see also *Norta* v. *John Sisk* (1971) 14 B.L.R. 49 (Irish Supreme Court).

Nominated Sub-Contract is not achieved by the Contractor through no fault of his. The Architect can issue a Variation instruction omitting the work or he has to operate the procedure for nomination again. In either of these circumstances there may be delay and loss, as to which see commentary at page 582.

CIRCUMSTANCES WHERE RENOMINATION NECESSARY

Background. *Bickerton v. N.W. Metropolitan Regional Hospital Board*[65]

The position under the 1963 form where a nominated Sub-Contractor repudiated his Sub-Contract was considered by the House of Lords in *Bickerton*. It was held that where, in the course of, and before completion of, the Sub-Contract Works, a Nominated Sub-Contractor repudiates[66] his Sub-Contract, the Employer must, unless he omits the rest of the Sub-Contract Works, nominate a new Sub-Contractor, bearing any increased costs resulting from such renomination, and must pay damages to the Contractor for any delay suffered by the Contractor awaiting a renomination. ". . . if a Contractor wrongfully terminates the Sub-Contract—it may be because he thinks erroneously that the Sub-Contractor is in fundamental breach of the Sub-Contract . . . the Contractor would be in breach of his contract with the Employer. A new Sub-Contractor would have to be nominated. But the Contractor would have to pay damages for his breach of contract including any loss caused to the Employer by that breach."[67] It should be observed that the Employer's duty of renomination was said to arise upon repudiation and not liquidation as such. The decision in *Bickerton* left a number of matters unclear, including at what point the right of renomination arose, what terms were to be required of the new Sub-Contract and who was to bear the cost of putting right the first Nominated Sub-Contractor's defective work.

Clause 35.24 deals expressly with the problems arising out of the *Bickerton* case. The 1980 Form maintains the principle that, apart from the case where the departure of the Nominated Sub-Contractor from site is due to the defaults of the Contractor, the Employer bears the risks of the Nominated Sub-Contractor's default. Further, clause 35.24 increases the risks to the Employer. The exact effect of the decision in *Bickerton* was not wholly clear, but it seems that under the 1963 Form the Employer had to pay the costs of renomination only when the Nominated Sub-Contractor both repudiated the Contract and left the site. Now the position is different. The procedure is not limited to repudiation. The grounds appear in clause 29 of NSC/4. These include matters which at common law would amount to repudiation such as wholly suspending the Works without reasonable cause, matters which would not be held to be repudiation such as sub-letting any portion of the work without the

---

[65] [1970] 1 W.L.R. 607 (H.L.). See p. 293 for the facts of this case.
[66] Used as including both a refusal to carry out a contract and a breach of contract of such king as to entitle the innocent party to treat the contract as at an end. For a full discussion see pp. 146 *et seq.*
[67] *Bickerton v. N.W. Metropolitan Regional Hospital Board* [1970] 1 W.L.R. 607 at 613 (H.L.).

written consent of the Architect and other matters which may or may not be held to be a repudiation according to the circumstances. Reference should be made to clause 29 of NSC/4 and its commentary. When the Nominated Sub-Contractor stops work by reason of determination under clause 29 of NSC/4, the effect of clause 35.24 is that there has to be a renomination at the Employer's expense.

Scheme of clause 35.24.   Clauses 35.24.1 to 35.24.5 set out five circumstances where renomination is necessary. Clauses 35.24.6 to 35.24.8 set out the procedure for renomination. Clause 35.24.9 deals with the financial consequences of renomination. Clause 35.24.10 deals with the time for renomination.

Clause 35.24.1.   The operation of the determination provisions by the Contractor under NSC/4, and in consequence of the renomination provisions of clause 35.24 of the Main Contract depends upon the Architect forming the opinion that the Nominated Sub-Contractor has made default (clause 35.24.1), and the issuing of an instruction by the Architect to the Contractor to give notice (clause 35.24.6.1). It appears that, once the Architect has formed his opinion under clause 35.24.1, he has no discretion whether or not to issue the instruction under clause 35.24.6.1 but must issue such instruction. The Architect and Contractor may disagree. The Contractor may be of the opinion that the Nominated Sub-Contractor is not proceeding with the diligence required by clause 11.1 of NSC/4 and may wish to get rid of him because of the losses which he, the Contractor, is suffering. The Architect may disagree. The Contractor cannot, it seems, determine the Nominated Sub-Contractor's employment under clause 29 of NSC/4 without being instructed to do so by the Architect (see clause 35.24.6.1) and cannot determine the Nominated Sub-Contract without an Architect's instruction (see clause 35.25). Thus it appears that the Contractor must continue to employ the Nominated Sub-Contractor but can take the question of whether or not the Architect's opinion was reasonable to arbitration under Article 5 of the Articles of Agreement and clause 41.

Clause 35.24.4.   This is a new circumstance where renomination is necessary introduced by Amendment 4 issued in July 1987. It deals with the obligation to renominate where the Nominated Sub-Contractor's employment has been determined as a result of an instruction of the Employer due to "corruption."

Clause 35.24.5.   This is a further circumstance where renomination is necessary introduced by Amendment 5 issued in January 1988. It deals with the situation where work of a Nominated Sub-Contractor has to be taken down and re-executed as a result of compliance by the Contractor or another Nominated Sub-Contractor with the instructions issued by the Architect under clauses 7, 8.4, 17.2 or 17.3.

Clause 35.24.6. This sets out the procedure to be adopted where clause 35.24.1 applies. First, the Architect must issue an instruction to the Contractor to give a notice of default to the Sub-Contractor. Next, the Contractor must inform the Architect whether the Employment of the Sub-Contractor has been determined. Finally, if he is so informed, the Architect must make a renomination.

Clause 35.24.6.3. *"... and to make good ... with the relevant Sub-Contract ..."*
These words were inserted by Amendment 4 issued in July 1987. Identically worded provisions were inserted in clauses 35.24.7 and 35.24.8.1. These provide that the work for which a replacement Nominated Sub-Contractor has been appointed must include the putting right of work not in accordance with the Nominated Sub-Contract by the Sub-Contractor whose employment has been determined. These amendments were inserted because the Court of Appeal had held in *Fairclough Building* v. *Rhuddlan B.C.*[68] that a renomination was invalid where the proposed Nominated Sub-Contract did not include remedial work.

Clause 35.24.7. This sets out that the Architect shall make a renomination where clauses 35.24.2 (bankruptcy, etc., of Nominated Sub-Contractor) or 35.24.4 (corruption) apply.

Clause 35.24.8.1. This sets out the procedure for renomination where clause 35.24.3 (determination of employment by Nominated Sub-Contractor) applies.

Clause 35.24.8.2. This new sub-clause was introduced by Amendment 4 issued in July 1987 consequentially upon the new clause 35.24.5. Where clause 35.24.5 applies, the Architect must make a renomination to deal with the re-execution of work. This provision, for obvious reasons, does not include the provision relating to remedial works.

Clause 35.24.9. This sub-clause provides that amounts properly payable to a new Nominated Sub-Contractor under the renomination procedure shall be added to the Contract Sum. The words "where clause 35.24.3 ... by the Employer as a debt" were added by Amendment 4 issued in July 1987. Their effect is to confer upon the Employer a right of deduction in circumstances where the obligation to renominate arose due to default by the Contractor. Otherwise, the Employer has no such right of deduction. The Court of Appeal held in *Fairclough Building* v. *Rhuddlan B.C.*[69] that there was no basis upon which the Employer could charge the Contractor with the full cost of remedial work when the obligation to renominate included the obligation to include reme-

---

[68] (1985) 30 B.L.R. 26 (C.A.).
[69] (1985) 30 B.L.R. 26 (C.A.).

dial work in the works to be done by the renominated Sub-Contractor which the Contractor was neither obliged nor entitled to do.

Clause 35.24.10. This new sub-clause was inserted by Amendment 4 issued in July 1987. It makes express what was held to be implied in *Percy Bilton Ltd.* v. *G.L.C.*,[70] that the obligation to renominate was to be performed within a reasonable time.

Terms of the new Sub-Contract. These must be the same as the original Sub-Contract, namely NSC/4 or NSC/4a. Such terms must provide for the new Nominated Sub-Contractor to complete his part of the work within the overall completion period for the Main Contract as a whole.[71]

More than one renomination. The *Bickerton* principle and the express provisions of the Contract are not limited to one renomination. The Employer must supply an effective Nominated Sub-Contractor, or alternatively, omit the work.

Extension of time. Insofar as the completion of the Works is likely to be delayed as a result of the instruction issued under clause 35.24.6.1 and clause 35.24.6.2 then, presumably, the Contractor is entitled to an extension of time under clause 25.4.5.1. The question of whether the Contractor is entitled to loss and expense resulting from the interference with the progress of the work caused by the instruction to determine is not dealt with expressly. It is thought that the position is the same as under the 1963 Form, namely, that the Contractor is only entitled to extra payment if and insofar as he can prove a breach of the implied term to give instructions at reasonable times, alternatively to bring himself within the provisions of clause 26.2.1. Note that, in general, the Contractor is not entitled to an extension of time simply because the Nominated Sub-Contractor has dropped out.[72] Such extension of time must be founded either upon an instruction (under clause 25.4.5.1) or a delay in receipt of the necessary instructions (under clause 25.4.6).

Determination due to delay. If the Contractor has specifically applied in writing for a renomination and the Works are brought to a standstill for one month or whatever other period is inserted in the Appendix, can the Contractor serve notice of determination under clause 28? It appears that he can but it is thought that the court or an Arbitrator would look at the circumstances to consider whether the notice was given unreasonably and therefore was not effective.[73]

---

[70] [1982] 1 W.L.R. 794 (H.L.).

[71] See *Percy Bilton Ltd.* v. *Greater London Council* [1982] 1 W.L.R. 794 at 800C (H.L.).

[72] See *Percy Bilton Ltd.* v. *Greater London Council* [1982] 1 W.L.R. 794 (H.L.).

[73] See Clause 28.1.3.2 and also *Gloucestershire County Council* v. *Richardson* [1969] 1 A.C. 480 (H.L.) but noting that under the form of R.I.B.A. Contract there used the Contractor had an absolute right of determination and was not subject to the proviso of reasonableness.

36.   Nominated Suppliers

36.1   .1   In the Conditions "Nominated Supplier" means a supplier to the Contractor who is nominated by the Architect/the Contract Administrator in one of the following ways to supply materials or goods which are to be fixed by the Contractor:

.1.1   where a prime cost sum is included in the Contract Bills in respect of those materials or goods and the supplier is either named in the Contract Bills or subsequently named by the Architect/the Contract Administrator in an instruction issued under clause 36.2;

.1.2   where a provisional sum is included in the Contract Bills and in any instruction by the Architect/the Contract Administrator in regard to the expenditure of such sum the supply of materials or goods is made the subject of a prime cost sum and the supplier is named by the Architect/the Contract Administrator in that instruction or in an instruction issued under clause 36.2;

.1.3   where a provisional sum is included in the Contract Bills and in any instruction by the Architect/the Contract Administrator in regard to the expenditure of such a sum materials or goods are specified for which there is a sole source of supply in that there is only one supplier from whom the Contractor can obtain them, in which case the supply of materials or goods shall be made the subject of a prime cost sum in the instructions issued by the Architect/the Contract Administrator in regard to the expenditure of the provisional sum and the sole supplier shall be deemed to have been nominated by the Architect/the Contract Administrator;

.1.4   where the Architect/the Contract Administrator requires under clause 13.2, or subsequently sanctions, a Variation and specifies materials or goods for which there is a sole supplier as referred to in clause 36.1.1.3, in which case the supply of the materials or goods shall be made the subject of a prime cost sum in the instruction or written sanction issued by the Architect/the Contract Administrator under clause 13.2 and the sole supplier shall be deemed to have been nominated by the Architect/the Contract Administrator.

.2   In the Conditions the expression "Nominated Supplier" shall not apply to a supplier of materials or goods which are specified in the Contract Bills to be fixed by the Contractor unless such materials or goods are the subject of a prime cost sum in the Contract Bills, notwithstanding that the supplier has been named in the Contract Bills or that there is a sole supplier of such materials or goods as defined in clause 36.1.1.3.

36.2   The Architect/The Contract Administrator shall issue instructions for the purpose of nominating a supplier for any materials or goods in respect of which a prime cost sum is included in the Contract Bills or arises under clause 36.1.

36.3   .1   For the purposes of clause 30.6.2.8 the amounts "properly chargeable to the Employer in accordance with the nomination instruction of the Architect/the Contract Administrator" shall include the total amount paid or payable in respect of the materials or goods less any discount other than the discount referred to in clause 36.4.4, properly so chargeable to the Employer and shall include where applicable:

.1.1   any tax (other than any value added tax which is treated, or is capable of being treated, as input tax (as referred to in the Finance Act 1972) by the Contractor) or duty not otherwise recoverable under this Contract by whomsoever payable which is payable under or by virtue of any Act of Parliament on the import, purchase, sale, appropriation, processing, alteration, adapting for sale or use of the materials or goods to be supplied; and

.1.2   the net cost of appropriate packing, carriage and delivery after allowing for any credit for return of any packing to the supplier; and

652

.1.3 the amount of any price adjustment properly paid or payable to, or allowed or allowable by the supplier less any discount other than a case discount for payment in full within 30 days of the end of the month during which delivery is made.

.2 Where in the opinion of the Architect/the Contract Administrator the Contractor properly incurs expense, which would not be reimbursed under clause 36.3.1 or otherwise under this Contract, in obtaining the materials or goods from the Nominated Supplier such expenses shall be added to the Contract Sum.

36.4 Save where the Architect/the Contract Administrator and the Contractor shall otherwise agree, the Architect/the Contract Administrator shall only nominate as a supplier a person who will enter into a contract of sale with the Contractor which provides, inter alia:

.1 that the materials or goods to be supplied shall be of the quality and standard specified provided that where and to the extent that approval of the quality of materials or of the standards of workmanship is a matter for the opinion of the Architect/the Contract Administrator, such quality and standards shall be to the reasonable satisfaction of the Architect/the Contract Administrator;

.2 that the Nominated Supplier shall make good by replacement or otherwise any defects in the materials or goods supplied which appear up to and including the last day of the Defects Liability Period under this Contract and shall bear any expenses reasonably incurred by the Contractor as a direct consequence of such defects provided that:

.2.1 where the materials or goods have been used or fixed such defects are not such that reasonable examination by the Contractor ought to have revealed them before using or fixing;

.2.2 such defects are due solely to defective workmanship or material in the materials or goods supplied and shall not have been caused by improper storage by the Contractor or by misuse or by any act or neglect of either the Contractor, the Architect/the Contract Administrator or the Employer or by any person or persons for whom they may be responsible or by any other person for whom the Nominated Supplier is not responsible;

.3 that delivery of the materials or goods supplied shall be commenced, carried out and completed in accordance with a delivery programme to be agreed between the Contractor and the Nominated Supplier including, to the extent agreed, the following grounds on which that programme may be varied:

force majeure; or
civil commotion, local combination of workmen, strike or lock-out; or
any instruction of the Architect/the Contract Administrator under clause 13.2 (Variations) or clause 13.3 (provisional sums); or
failure of the Architect/the Contract Administrator to supply to the Nominated Supplier within due time any necessary information for which he has specifically applied in writing on a date which was neither unreasonably distant from nor unreasonably close to the date on which it was necessary for him to receive the same; or
exceptionally adverse weather conditions

or, if no such programme is agreed, delivery shall be commenced, carried out and completed in accordance with the reasonable directions of the Contractor.

.4 that the Nominated Supplier shall allow the Contractor a discount for cash of 5 per cent. on all payments if the Contractor makes payment in full within 30 days of the end of the month during which delivery is made;

653

.5 that the Nominated Supplier shall not be obliged to make any delivery of materials or goods (except any which may have been paid for in full less only any discount for cash) after the determination (for any reason) of the Contractor's employment under this Contract;

.6 that full discharge by the Contractor in respect of payments for materials or goods supplied by the Nominated Supplier shall be effected within 30 days of the end of the month during which delivery is made less only a discount for cash of 5 per cent. if so paid;

.7 that the ownership of materials or goods shall pass to the Contractor upon delivery by the Nominated Supplier to or to the order of the Contractor, whether or not payment has been made in full;

.8.1 that in any dispute or difference between the Contractor and the Nominated Supplier which is referred to arbitration the Contractor and the Nominated Supplier agree and consent pursuant to Sections 1(3)(a) and 2(1)(b) of the Arbitration Act 1979 that either the Contractor or the Nominated Supplier
— may appeal to the High Court on any question of law arising out of an award made in the arbitration and
— may apply to the High Court to determine any question of law arising in the course of the arbitration;
and that the Contractor and the Nominated Supplier agree that the High Court should have jurisdiction to determine any such questions of law;

.8.2 that if any dispute or difference between the Contractor and the Nominated Supplier raises issues which are substantially the same as or are connected with issues raised in a related dispute between the Employer and the Contractor under this contract then, where clauses 41.2.1 and 41.2.2 apply, such dispute or difference shall be referred to the Arbitrator to be appointed pursuant to clause 41; that the Arbitrator shall have power to make such directions and all necessary awards in the same way as in the procedure of the High Court as to joining one or more defendants or joining co-defendants or third parties was available to the parties; that the agreement and consent referred to in clause 36.4.8.1 on appeals or applications to the High Court on any question of law shall apply to any question of law arising out of the awards of such arbitrator in respect of all related disputes referred to him or arising in the course of the reference of all the related disputes referred to him; and that in any case, subject to the agreement referred to in clause 36.4.8.1, the award of such Arbitrator shall be final and binding on the parties.

.9 that no provision in the contract of sale shall override, modify or affect in any way whatsoever the provisions in the contract of sale which are included therein to give effect to clauses 36.4.1 to 36.4.9 inclusive.

36.5 .1 Subject to clauses 36.5.2 and 36.5.3, where the said contract of sale between the Contractor and the Nominated Supplier in any way restricts, limits or excludes the liability of the Nominated Supplier to the Contractor in respect of materials or goods supplied or to be supplied, and the Architect/the Contract Administrator has specifically approved in writing the said restrictions, limitations or exclusions, the liability of the Contractor to the Employer in respect of the said materials or goods shall be restricted, limited or excluded to the same extent.

.2 The Contractor shall not be obliged to enter into a contract with the Nominated Supplier until the Architect/the Contract Administrator has specifically approved in writing the said restrictions, limitations or exclusions.

.3 Nothing in clause 36.5 shall be construed as enabling the Architect/the Contract Administrator to nominate a supplier otherwise than in accordance with the provisions stated in clause 36.4.

Clause 36: Nominated Suppliers

Derivation. Clause 36 is substantially derived from clause 28 of the 1963 Form. The structure of the clause is essentially unchanged. It was subject to certain relatively minor or consequential amendments by Amendment 4 issued in July 1987, discussed below.

Structure of clause. This clause provides for the definition of a Nominated Supplier (clause 36.1), Architect's Instructions for nominating Suppliers (clause 36.2), price (clause 36.3), the terms of the contract which should be used with the Nominated Supplier (clause 36.4) and approved limitation of the Contractor's liability (clause 36.5).

Comparison with Sub-Contractors nominated under clause 35. There is a difference of subject matter in that Nominated Suppliers do not fix. Further, the Contract does not attempt such elaborate regulation of matters affecting Nominated Suppliers as it does for Nominated Sub-Contractors. But there are substantial similarities as regards the liability of the Contractor for the default of the Nominated Suppliers. There is no right for the Contractor to make reasonable objection to a Nominated Supplier. There is no equivalent to clause 35.2 (Tender by Contractor), clause 35.13 (Direct Payment) or clauses 35.14, 35.15 (Delay).

Default of Nominated Supplier—Contractor's liability. The Contractor's liability is broadly similar to that for Nominated Sub-Contractors and reference should be made to the commentary to clause 35. This particularly applies to delay on the part of a Nominated Supplier, delay by the Nominated Supplier in giving information, fitness for purpose of the materials or goods to be supplied by the Nominated Supplier, design by the Nominated Supplier and guarantee by the Nominated Supplier. It seems that it is the Contractor's duty to make a reasonable inspection of materials or goods delivered by a Nominated Supplier and that if he accepts the goods with defects which a reasonable inspection using proper skill and care would have disclosed, he is liable to the Employer in respect of such defects.[74]

Defects of quality. Subject to clause 36.5, the Contractor is liable, it is submitted, for defects in the quality of the materials or goods delivered even though a reasonable inspection by him at the time of delivery of the goods or materials could not have disclosed such defects of quality.[75] This submission is based upon general principles as to liability of a Contractor for the supply of

---

[74] See *Young & Marten Ltd.* v. *McManus Childs Ltd.* [1969] 1 A.C. 454 (H.L.); *Gloucestershire County Council* v. *Richardson* [1969] 1 A.C. 480 (H.L.), discussed at p. 55. See also *I.B.A.* v. *E.M.I. and B.I.C.C.* (1980) 14 B.L.R. 1 (H.L.); *Rumbelows* v. *A.M.K.* (1980) 19 B.L.R. 25.
[75] *Ibid.*

goods discussed at page 53 and upon the effect of clause 36.5, which deals with the most important ground upon which the case of *Gloucestershire County Council v. Richardson*[76] was decided. The existence of the clause indicates that, where and to the extent that it does not operate, the Contractor is liable for quality defects in Nominated Suppliers' goods and materials.

Clause 36 does not deal with the possibility or necessity of renomination. It is thought that the reasoning in *Bickerton v. N.W. Metropolitan Regional Hospital Board*[77] still applies to a Nominated Supplier so that upon repudiation there must be a renomination. It should be noted, however, that clause 35 now deals expressly with the renomination of Sub-Contractors, so that a general argument might be advanced to the effect that the omission to deal with renomination in clause 36 by contrast means that renomination upon repudiation by the Nominated Supplier is not required. It is thought that this argument would not prevail, but in any event the argument would not be available in practice where it was a "sole supplier" who had repudiated. In these circumstances, a variation instruction would be necessary unless very exceptionally the contract was frustrated. Clause 36.1.1.4 might apply to such a Variation Instruction. It is thought also, that if there was repudiation by a sole supplier who came within clause 36.1.2 (as he was thus not a Nominated Supplier), a Variation Instruction would be necessary, and again clause 36.1.1.4 might apply. In these circumstances the second sole supplier would be a Nominated Supplier.

Clause 36.1.1. *"In the Conditions "Nominated Supplier" means …"*

The Architect's obligation under clause 36.2 to nominate a supplier is defined to arise in two types of circumstance namely:

(1) where a prime cost sum is either included in the Contract Bills or arises by an instruction converting a provisional sum into a prime cost sum; and

(2) where, either in an instruction in relation to a provisional sum or in a Variation instruction, the Architect specifies materials or goods for which there is a "sole supplier."

Clause 36.1.2 provides that a supplier of materials or goods which are specified in the Contract Bills to be fixed by the Contractor but for which there is no prime cost sum is not a Nominated Supplier, even if the supplier is named in the Contract Bills or is a sole supplier.

Clause 36.2. This clause contains the duty to nominate formerly to be found in the 1963 Form in clauses 11(3) and 28(b). See commentary to clause 35.

---

[76] See above.
[77] [1970] 1 W.L.R. 607 (H.L.).

Clause 36.3.1. "... *the total amount paid or payable* ..."

The Contractor is entitled to be paid under the Main Contract the total of all sums that he has to pay to the Nominated Supplier, but he is entitled to retain the 5 per cent. discount for cash referred to in clause 36.4.4, provided of course that he earns that discount. The amounts payable to the Nominated Supplier are expressed to include any tax (other than Value Added Tax), the cost of packing, carriage and delivery and the amount of any price adjustment.

Clause 36.3.2. This entitles the Contractor to be paid any other proper expense incurred in obtaining materials or goods from the Nominated Supplier which is not covered by clause 36.3.1.

Clause 36.4. This clause is an expanded version of the former clauses 28(b) and 28(c) in the 1963 Form. Clauses 36.4.7, 36.4.8 and 36.4.9 are new to the 1980 Form.

Clause 36.4. "... *the Architect* ... *shall only nominate* ..."

It is important to note that the sale contract provisions set out at clauses 36.4.1 to 36.4.9 can have no effect themselves upon any contract of sale. They must be given effect to and incorporated into the contract of sale before it is entered into.

Clause 36.4.3. This sub-clause was redrafted by Amendment 4 issued in July 1987. The material part of the amendment is to add the words from "including" to "exceptionally adverse weather conditions." This amendment sets out grounds for varying a delivery programme which may be included in the contract of sale without the risk of them being considered as constituting a breach of clause 36.4.9. Note that if the Nominated Supplier does vary his delivery programme in accordance with these provisions, the Contractor would be able to establish a Relevant Event in clause 25.4.7 in regard to any application for an extension of time.

Clause 36.4.7. See commentary to clause 16, and for an example of the position where the ownership did not pass before payment, see *Dawber Williamson Roofing* v. *Humberside C.C.*[78] there discussed. This decision is an illustration of the important general principle that provisions in the Main Contract have no effect upon any Sub-Contract unless and until they are expressly incorporated into the Sub-Contract.

Clause 36.4.8. This sub-clause accords with the provisions for multipartite arbitration in clause 41 (see commentary to clause 41). The sub-clause was amended by Amendment 4 issued in July 1987. The substance of this amendment is to provide that the provisions in the Contract of supply relating to

---

[78] (1979) 14 B.L.R. 70.

arbitration should include an agreement by the Contractor and the Nominated Supplier to consent to the jurisdiction of the High Court on appeals and applications relating to questions of law.

Clause 36.5: Exclusion clauses.   This clause is very important. Its existence shows, it is submitted, that, where there is no exclusion or limitation of liability to which this sub-clause applies, the Contractor is under a liability for latent defects in materials or goods supplied by a Nominated Supplier. Therefore he should read the offer of any proposed Nominated Supplier carefully. Such offers frequently contain exclusion clauses.[79] If the Contractor finds such a clause he can require the Architect specifically to approve it in writing. If the Architect gives such specific approval the Contractor is protected by having the benefit of an equivalent exclusion. If the Architect refuses to give the approval, the Contractor can reject the nomination. If the Contractor does not follow this procedure and enters into a contract of supply containing an exclusion clause without referring it to the Architect he is ordinarily, it is submitted, liable for losses suffered by the Employer due to latent defects which appear even though he, the Contractor, is subject to the exclusion clause as between himself and the Nominated Supplier. Early nomination is desirable. If the Architect is asked to approve an exclusion clause he can consult with the Employer and discuss the risks involved. If the nomination was not early, delay in consideration of the matter may give the Contractor a claim for loss and/or expense or damages and may delay completion.

Clause 36.5.3, which is new to the 1980 Form, will, it seems, restrict the possibility of having approved exclusion clauses in a Nominated Supplier's contract of supply. It is submitted, for example, that a clause which purported to limit the Nominated Supplier's liability for breach of a clause equivalent to clause 36.4.1 or clause 36.4.3 would contravene clause 36.5.3.

Nominated supplier warranty.   See Form TNS/2 reproduced at page 805.

PART 3: FLUCTUATIONS

37.   .1   Fluctuations shall be dealt with in accordance with whichever of the following alternatives[*w*]
clause 38; or
clause 39; or
clause 40[*y*]

---

[79] For exclusion clauses generally, see p. 63.

[*w*] *Clause 39 should be used where the parties have agreed to allow the labour and materials cost and tax fluctuations to which clause 39.1 to .3 refers. Alternatively, clause 40 should be used where the parties have agreed that fluctuations shall be dealt with by adjustment of the Contract Sum under the Price Adjustment Formulae for Building Contracts.*

[*y*] *Clause 40 is used where the parties have agreed that fluctuations shall be dealt with by adjustment of the Contract Sum under the Price Adjustment Formulae for Building Contracts.*

is identified in the Appendix. The provisions so identified shall be[x] deemed to be incorporated with the Conditions as executed by the parties hereto.

.2   Clause 38 shall apply where neither clause 39 nor 40 is identified in the Appendix.

Clause 38: Contributions, levy and tax fluctuations

Clause 39: Labour and materials cost and tax fluctuations

Clause 40: Use of price adjustment formulae

These clauses are published separately in "Fluctuation clauses for use with the Local Authorities Edition With, Without and With Approximate Quantities."

Clause 38—For use with the Local Authorities Edition With Quantities

38.   **Contribution, levy and tax fluctuations**

38.1   The Contract Sum shall be deemed to have been calculated in the manner set out below and shall be subject to adjustment in the events specified hereunder:

.1   The prices contained in the Contract Bills are based upon the types and rates of contribution, levy and tax payable by a person in his capacity as an employer and which at the Base Date are payable by the Contractor. A type and rate so payable are in clause 38.1.2 referred to as a "tender type" and "tender rate."

.2   If any of the tender rates other than a rate of levy payable by virtue of the Industrial Training Act 1964, is increased or decreased, or if a tender type ceases to be payable, or if a new type of contribution, levy or tax which is payable by a person in his capacity as an employer becomes payable after the Base Date, then in any such case the net amount of the difference between what the Contractor actually pays or will pay in respect of

.2.1   workpeople engaged upon or in connection with the Works either on or adjacent to the site, and

.2.2   workpeople directly employed by the Contractor who are engaged upon the production of materials or goods for use in or in connection with the Works and who operate neither on nor adjacent to the site and to the extent that they are so engaged

or because of his employment of such workpeople and what he would have paid had the alteration, cessation or new type of contribution, levy or tax not become effective, shall, as the case may be, be paid to or allowed by the Contractor.

.3   There shall be added, to the net amount paid to or allowed by the Contractor under clause 38.1.2, in respect of each person employed by the Contractor who is engaged upon or in connection with the Works either on or adjacent to the site and who is not within the definition of "workpeople" in clause 38.6.3 the same amount as is payable or allowable in respect of a craftsman under clause 38.1.2 or such proportion of that amount as reflects the time (measured in whole working days) that each such person is so employed.

.4   For the purposes of clause 38.1.3:

no period less than 2 whole working days in any week shall be taken into account and periods less than a whole working day shall not be aggregated to amount to a whole working day;

---

[x] *Notwithstanding the provisions of clause 37.1 on deemed incorporation the parties may nevertheless wish to incorporate the agreed alternative fluctuation provisions in the executed Contract.*

the phrase "the same amount as is payable or allowable in respect of a craftsman" shall refer to the amount in respect of a craftsman employed by the Contractor (or by any Domestic Sub-Contractor under a sub-contract to which clause 38.3 refers) under the rules or decisions or agreements of the National Joint Council for the Building Industry or other wage-fixing body and, where the aforesaid rules or decisions or agreements provide for more than one rate of wage emolument or other expense for a craftsman, shall refer to the amount in respect of a craftsman employed as aforesaid to whom the highest rate is applicable; and the phrase "employed by the Contractor" shall mean an employment to which the Income Tax (Employment) Regulations 1973 (the PAYE Regulations) under S.204 of the Income and Corporation Taxes Act 1970, apply.

.5 The prices contained in the Contract Bills are based upon the types and rates of refund of the contributions, levies and taxes payable by a person in his capacity as an employer and upon the types and rates of premium receivable by a person in his capacity as an employer being in each case types and rates which at the Base Date are receivable by the Contractor. Such a type and such a rate are in clause 38.1.6 referred to as a "tender type" and a "tender rate."

.6 If any of the tender rates is increased or decreased or if a tender type ceases to be payable or if a new type of refund of any contribution, levy or tax payable by a person in his capacity as an employer becomes receivable or if a new type of premium receivable by a person in his capacity as an employer becomes receivable after the Base Date, then in any such case the net amount of the difference between what the Contractor actually receives or will receive in respect of workpeople as referred to in clauses 38.1.2.1 and 38.1.2.2 or because of his employment of such workpeople and what he would have received had the alteration, cessation or new type of refund or premium not become effective, shall, as the case may be, be paid to or allowed by the Contractor.

.7 The references in clauses 38.1.5 and 38.1.6 to premiums shall be construed as meaning all payments howsoever they are described which are made under or by virtue of an Act of Parliament to a person in his capacity as an employer and which affect the cost to an employer of having persons in his employment.

.8 Where employer's contributions are payable by the Contractor in respect of workpeople as referred to in clauses 38.1.2.1 and 38.1.2.2 whose employment is contracted-out employment within the meaning of the Social Security Pensions Act 1975 the Contractor shall for the purpose of recovery or allowance under clause 38.1 be deemed to pay employer's contributions as if that employment were not contracted-out employment.

.9 The reference in clause 38.1 to contributions, levies and taxes shall be construed as meaning all impositions payable by a person in his capacity as an employer howsoever they are described and whoever the recipient which are imposed under or by virtue of an Act of Parliament and which affect the cost to an employer of having persons in his employment.

38.2 The Contract Sum shall be deemed to have been calculated in the manner set out below and shall be subject to adjustment in the events specified hereunder:

.1 The prices contained in the Contract Bills are based upon the types and rates of duty if any and tax if any (other than any value added tax which is treated, or is capable of being treated, as input tax (as referred to in the Finance Act 1972) by the Contractor) by whomsoever payable which at the Base Date are payable on the import, purchase, sale, appropriation, processing or use of the materials, goods, electricity and, where so specifically stated in the Contract Bills, fuels, specified in a list submitted by the Contractor and attached to the Contract Bills under or by virtue of any Act of Parliament. A type and a rate so payable are in clause 38.2.2 referred to as a "tender type" and a "tender rate."

.2 If in relation to any materials or goods specified as aforesaid, or any electricity or fuels specified as aforesaid and consumed on site for the execution of the Works including temporary site installations for those Works, a tender rate is increased or decreased, or a tender type ceases to be payable or a new type of duty or tax (other than any value added tax which is treated, or is capable of being treated as input tax (as referred to in the Finance Act 1972) by the Contractor) becomes payable on the import, purchase, sale, appropriation, processing or use of those materials, goods, electricity or fuels, after the Base Date then in any such case the net amount of the difference between what the Contractor actually pays in respect of those materials, goods, electricity or fuels and what he would have paid in respect of them had the alteration, cessation or imposition not occurred, shall, as the case may be, be paid to or allowed by the Contractor. In clause 38.2.2 the expression "a new type of duty or tax" includes an additional duty or tax and a duty or tax imposed in regard to specified materials, goods, electricity or fuels in respect of which no duty or tax whatever was previously payable (other than any value added tax which is treated, or is capable of being treated, as input tax (as referred to in the Finance Act 1972) by the Contractor).

38.3   Fluctuations—work sub-let—Domestic Sub-Contractors

.1 If the Contractor is obliged by clause 19.3, or shall decide subject to clause 19.2, to sub-let any portion of the Works to a Domestic Sub-Contractor he shall incorporate in the sub-contract provisions to the like effect as the provisions of
    clause 38 (excluding clause 38.3) including the percentage stated in the Appendix pursuant to clause 38.7
which are applicable for the purposes of this Contract.

.2 If the price payable under such a sub-contract as referred to in clause 38.3.1 is increased above or decreased below the price in such sub-contract by reason of the operation of the said incorporated provisions, then the net amount of such increase or decrease shall, as the case may be, be paid to or allowed by the Contractor under this Contract.

.4–.6   Provisions relating to clause 38

38.4   .1 The Contractor shall give a written notice to the Architect/the Contract Administrator of the occurrence of any of the events referred to in such of the following provisions as are applicable for the purposes of this Contract:

.1.1 clause 38.1.2;
.1.2 clause 38.1.6;
.1.3 clause 38.2.2;
.1.4 clause 38.3.2.

.2 Any notice required to be given under clause 38.4.1 shall be given within a reasonable time after the occurrence of the event to which the notice relates, and the giving of a written notice in that time shall be a condition precedent to any payment being made to the Contractor in respect of the event in question.

.3 The Quantity Surveyor and the Contractor may agree what shall be deemed for all the purposes of this Contract to be the net amount payable to or allowable by the Contractor in respect of the occurrence of any event such as is referred to in any of the provisions listed in clause 38.4.1.

.4 Any amount which from time to time becomes payable to or allowable by the Contractor by virtue of clauses 38.1 and .2 or clause 38.3 shall, as the case may be, be added to or deducted from:

.4.1 the Contract Sum; and

.4.2 any amounts payable to the Contractor and which are calculated in accordance with either clauses 28.2.2.1 or 28.2.2.2.

The addition or deduction to which clause 38.4.4 refers shall be subject to the provisions of clauses 38.4.5 to .4.7.

.5 As soon as is reasonably practicable the Contractor shall provide such evidence and computations as the Architect/the Contract Administrator or the Quantity Surveyor may reasonably require to enable the amount payable to or allowable by the Contractor by virtue of clauses 38.1 and .2 or clause 38.3 to be ascertained; and in the case of amounts payable to or allowable by the Contractor under clause 38.1.3 (or clause 38.3 for amounts payable to or allowable by the Domestic Sub-Contractor under provisions in the sub-contract to the like effect as clauses 38.1.3 and 38.1.4)—employees other than workpeople—such evidence shall include a certificate signed by or on behalf of the Contractor each week certifying the validity of the evidence reasonably required to ascertain such amounts.

.6 No addition to or deduction from the Contract Sum made by virtue of clause 38.4.4 shall alter in any way the amount of profit of the Contractor included in that Sum.

.7 Subject to the provisions of clause 38.4.8 no amount shall be added or deducted in the computation of the amount stated as due in an Interim Certificate or in the Final Certificate in respect of amounts otherwise payable to or allowable by the Contractor by virtue of clauses 38.1 and .2 or clause 38.3 if the event (as referred to in the provisions listed in clause 38.4.1) in respect of which the payment or allowance would be made occurs after the Completion Date.

.8 Clause 38.4.7 shall not be applied unless:

.8.1 the printed text of clause 25 is unamended and forms part of the Conditions; and

.8.2 the Architect/the Contract Administrator has, in respect of every written not-ification by the Contractor under clause 25, fixed or confirmed in writing such Completion Date as he considers to be in accordance with clause 25.

38.5 Clauses 38.1 to .3 shall not apply in respect of:

.1 work for which the Contractor is allowed daywork rates under clause 13.5.4;

.2 work executed or materials or goods supplied by any Nominated Sub-Contractor or Nominated Supplier (fluctuations in relation to Nominated Sub-Contractors and Nominated Suppliers shall be dealt with under any provision in relation thereto which may be included in the appropriate sub-contract or contract of sale);

.3 work executed by the Contractor for which a tender made under clause 35.2 has been accepted (fluctuations in relation to such work shall be dealt with under any provision in the accepted tender of the Contractor);

.4 changes in the rate of value added tax charged on the supply of goods or services by the Contractor to the Employer under this Contract.

38.6 In clause 38:

.1 the expression "the Base Date" means the Date stated in the Appendix;

.2 the expressions "materials" and "goods" include timber used in formwork but do not include other consumable stores, plant and machinery (save that electricity and, where specifically so stated in the Contract Bills, fuels are dealt with in clause 38.2);

.3 the expression "workpeople" means persons whose rates of wages and other emoluments (including holiday credits) are governed by the rules or decisions or agreements of the National Joint Council for the Building Industry or some other wage-fixing body for trades associated with the building industry;

.4 the expression "wage-fixing body" shall mean a body which lays down recognised terms and conditions of workers. For the purposes of clause 38 "recognised terms and conditions" means terms and conditions of workers in comparable employment in the trade or industry, or section of trade and industry, in which the employer in question is engaged, which have been settled by an agreement or award, to which the parties are employers' associations and independent trade unions which represent (generally, or in the district in question, as the case may be) a substantial proportion of the employers and of the workers in the trade, industry or section being workers of the description to which the agreement or award relates.

38.7 Percentage addition to fluctuation payments or allowances

.1 There shall be added to the amount paid to or allowed by the Contractor under:

.1.1 clause 38.1.2,
.1.2 clause 38.1.3,
.1.3 clause 38.1.6,
.1.4 clause 38.2.2

the percentage stated in the Appendix.

Clause 39—For use with the Local Authorities Edition With Quantities

39. Labour and materials cost and tax fluctuations

39.1 The Contract Sum shall be deemed to have been calculated in the manner set out below and shall be subject to adjustment in the events specified hereunder:

.1 The prices (including the cost of employer's liability insurance and of third party insurance) contained in the Contract Bills are based upon the rates of wages and the other emoluments and expenses (including holiday credits) which will be payable by the Contractor to or in respect of

.1.1 workpeople engaged upon or in connection with the Works either on or adjacent to the site, and

.1.2 workpeople directly employed by the Contractor who are engaged upon the production of materials or goods for use in or in connection with the Works and who operate neither on nor adjacent to the site and to the extent that they are so engaged

in accordance with:

.1.3 the rules or decisions of the National Joint Council for the Building Industry or other wage-fixing body which will be applicable to the Works and which have been promulgated at the Base Date; and

.1.4 any incentive scheme and/or productivity agreement under the provisions of Rule 1.16 or any successor to this Rule (Productivity Incentive Schemes and/or Productivity Agreements) of the Rules of the National Joint Council for the Building Industry (including the General Principles covering Incentive Schemes and/or Productivity Agreements published by the aforesaid Council to which

Rule 1.16 or any successor to this Rule refers) or provisions on incentive schemes and/or productivity agreements contained in the rules or decisions of some other wage-fixing body; and

.1.5 the terms of the Building and Civil Engineering Annual and Public Holidays Agreements (or the terms of agreements to similar effect in respect of workpeople whose rates of wages and other emoluments and expenses (including holiday credits) are in accordance with the rules or decisions of a wage-fixing body other than the National Joint Council for the Building Industry) which will be applicable to the Works and which have been promulgated at the Base Date;

and upon the rates or amounts of any contribution, levy or tax which will be payable by the Contractor in his capacity as an employer in respect of, or calculated by reference to, the rates of wages and other emoluments and expenses (including holiday credits) referred to herein.

.2 If any of the said rates of wages or other emoluments and expenses (including holiday credits) are increased or decreased by reason of any alteration in the said rules, decisions or agreements promulgated after the Base Date, then the net amount of the increase or decrease in wages or other emoluments and expenses (including holiday credits) together with the net amount of any consequential increase or decrease in the cost of employer's liability insurance, of third party insurance, and of any contribution, levy or tax payable by a person in his capacity as an employer shall, as the case may be, be paid to or allowed by the Contractor.

.3 There shall be added, to the net amount paid to or allowed by the Contractor under clause 39.1.2, in respect of each person employed by the Contractor who is engaged upon or in connection with the Works either on or adjacent to the site and who is not within the definition of "workpeople" in clause 39.7.3 the same amount as is payable or allowable in respect of a craftsman under clause 39.1.2 or such proportion of that amount as reflects the time (measured in whole working days) that each such person is so employed.

.4 For the purposes of clauses 39.1.3 and 39.2.3:

no period less than 2 whole days in any week shall be taken into account and periods less than a whole working day shall not be aggregated to amount to a whole working day;

the phrase "the same amount as is payable or allowable in respect of a craftsman" shall refer to the amount in respect of a craftsman employed by the Contractor (or by any Domestic Sub-Contractor under a sub-contract to which clause 39.4 refers) under the rules or decisions or agreements of the National Joint Council for the Building Industry or other wage-fixing body and, where the aforesaid rules or decisions or agreements provide for more than one rate of wage, emolument or other expenses for a craftsman, shall refer to the amount in respect of a craftsman employed as aforesaid to whom the highest rate is applicable; and

the phrase "employed by the Contractor" shall mean an employment to which the Income Tax (Employment) Regulations 1973 (the PAYE Regulations) under S.204 of the Income and Corporation Taxes Act 1970, apply.

.5 The prices contained in the Contract Bills are based upon:

the transport charges referred to in a basic transport charges list submitted by the Contractor and attached to the Contract Bills and incurred by the Contractor in respect of workpeople engaged in either of the capacities referred to in clauses 39.1.1.1 and 39.1.1.2; or

the reimbursement of fares which will be reimbursable by the Contractor to workpeople engaged in either of the capacities referred to in clauses 39.1.1.1 and 39 1.1.2 in accordance with the rules or decisions of the National Joint Council for the Building Industry which will be applicable to the Works and which have been promulgated at the Base Date or, in the case of workpeople so engaged whose rates of wages and other emoluments and expenses are governed by the rules or decisions of some wage-fixing body other than the National Joint Council for the Building Industry, in accordance with the rules or decisions of such other body which will be applicable and which have been promulgated as aforesaid.

.6   If:

.6.1   the amount of transport charges referred to in the basic transport charges list is increased or decreased after the Base Date; or

.6.2   the reimbursement of fares is increased or decreased by reason of any alteration in the said rules or decisions promulgated after the Base Date or by any actual increase or decrease in fares which takes effect after the Base Date,

then the net amount of that increase or decrease shall, as the case may be, be paid to or allowed by the Contractor.

39.2   The Contract Sum shall be deemed to have been calculated in the manner set out below and shall be subject to adjustment in the events specified hereunder:

.1   The prices contained in the Contract Bills are based upon the types and rates of contribution, levy and tax payable by a person in his capacity as an employer and which at the Base Date are payable by the Contractor. A type and a rate so payable are in clause 39.2.2 referred to as a "tender type" and a "tender rate."

.2   If any of the tender rates other than a rate of levy payable by virtue of the Industrial Training Act 1964, is increased or decreased or if a tender type ceases to be payable, or if a new type of contribution, levy or tax which is payable by a person in his capacity as an employer becomes payable after the Base Date, then in any such case the net amount of the difference between what the Contractor actually pays or will pay in respect of workpeople as referred to in clauses 39.1.1.1 and 39.1.1.2 or because of his employment of such workpeople and what he would have paid had the alteration, cessation or new type of contribution, levy or tax not become effective, shall, as the case may be, be paid to or allowed by the Contractor.

.3   There shall be added, to the net amount paid to or allowed by the Contractor under clause 39.2.2, in respect of each person employed by the Contractor who is engaged upon or in connection with the Works either on or adjacent to the site and who is not within the definition of "workpeople" in clause 39.7.3, the same amount as is payable or allowable in respect of a craftsman under clause 39.2.2 or such proportion of that amount as reflects the time (measured in whole working days) that each such person is so employed. The provisions of clause 39.1.4 shall apply to clause 39.2.3.

.4   The prices contained in the Contract Bills are based upon the type and rates of refund of the contributions, levies and taxes payable by a person in his capacity as an employer and upon the types and rates of premium receivable by a person in his capacity as an employer being in each case types and rates which at the Base Date are receivable by the Contractor. Such a type and such a rate are, in clause 39.2.5 referred to as a "tender type" and a "tender rate."

.5   If any of the tender rates is increased or decreased or if a tender type ceases to be payable or if a new type of refund of any contribution, levy or tax payable by a person in his capacity as an employer becomes receivable or if a new type of premium receivable by a person in his capacity as an employer becomes receivable after the Base Date, then in any such case the net amount of the difference between what the Contractor actually receives or will receive in respect of workpeople as referred to in clauses 39.1.1.1 and 39.1.1.2 or because of his employment of such workpeople, and what he would have received had the alteration, cessation or new type of refund or premium not become effective, shall, as the case may be, be paid to or allowed by the Contractor.

.6   The reference in clauses 39.2.4 and 39.2.5 to premiums shall be construed as meaning all payments howsoever they are described which are made under or by virtue of an Act of Parliament to a person in his capacity as an employer and which affect the cost to an employer of having persons in his employment.

.7   Where employer's contributions are payable by the Contractor in respect of workpeople as referred to in clauses 39.1.1.1 and 39.1.1.2 whose employment is contracted-out employment within the meaning of the Social Security Pensions Act 1975, the Contractor shall, subject to the proviso hereto, for the purpose of recovery or allowance under clause 39.2 be deemed to pay employer's contributions as if that employment were not contracted-out employment; provided that clause 39.2.7 shall not apply where the occupational pension scheme, by reference to membership of which the employment of workpeople is contracted-out employment, is established by the rules of the National Joint Council for the Building Industry or of some other wage-fixing body so that contributions to such occupational pension scheme are within the payment and allowance provisions of clause 39.1.

.8   The reference in clauses 39.2.1 to 39.2.5 and 39.2.7 to contributions, levies and taxes shall be construed as meaning all impositions payable by a person in his capacity as an employer howsoever they are described and whoever the recipient which are imposed under or by virtue of an Act of Parliament and which affect the cost to an employer of having persons in his employment.

39.3   The Contract Sum shall be deemed to have been calculated in the manner set out below and shall be subject to adjustment in the events specified hereunder:

.1   The prices contained in the Contract Bills are based upon the market prices of the materials, goods, electricity and, where specifically so stated in the Contract Bills, fuels, specified in a list submitted by the Contractor and attached to the Contract Bills, which were current at the Base Date. Such prices are hereinafter referred to as "basic prices" and the prices set out by the Contractor on the said list shall be deemed to be the basic prices of the specified materials, goods, electricity and fuels.

.2   If after the Base Date the market price of any of the materials or goods specified as aforesaid increases or decreases, or the market price of any electricity or fuels specified as aforesaid and consumed on site for the execution of the Works (including temporary site installations for those Works) increases or decreases, then the net amount of the difference between the basic price thereof and the market price payable by the Contractor and current when the materials, goods, electricity or fuels are bought shall, as the case may be, be paid to or allowed by the Contractor.

.3   The references in clauses 39.3.1 and 39.3.2 to "market prices" shall be construed as including any duty or tax (other than value added tax which is treated, or is capable of being treated as input tax (as referred to in the Finance Act 1972) by the Contractor) by whomsoever payable which is payable under or by virtue of any Act of Parliament on the import, purchase, sale, appropriation, processing or use of the materials, goods, electricity or fuels specified as aforesaid.

39.4   Fluctuations—work sub-let—Domestic Sub-Contractors

.1   If the Contractor is obliged by clause 19.3, or shall decide subject to clause 19.2, to sub-let any portion of the Works to a Domestic Sub-Contractor he shall incorporate in the sub-contract provisions to the like effect as the provisions of
        clause 39 (excluding clause 39.4) including the percentage stated in the Appendix pursuant to clause 39.8
    which are applicable for the purposes of this Contract.

.2   If the price payable under such a sub-contract as referred to in clause 39.4.1 is increased above or decreased below the price in such sub-contract by reason of the operation of the said incorporated provisions, then the net amount of such increase or decrease shall, as the case may be, be paid to or allowed by the Contractor under this Contract.

.5–7   **Provisions relating to clause 39**

39.5   .1   The Contractor shall give a written notice to the Architect/the Contract Administrator of the occurrence of any of the events referred to in such of the following
provisions as are applicable for the purposes of this Contract:

.1.1   clause 39.1.2;
.1.2   clause 39.1.6;
.1.3   clause 39.2.2;
.1.4   clause 39.2.5;
.1.5   clause 39.3.2;
.1.6   clause 39.4.2.

.2   Any notice required to be given by clause 39.5.1 shall be given within a reasonable
time after the occurrence of the event to which the notice relates and the giving of
written notice in that time shall be a condition precedent to any payment being
made to the Contractor in respect of the event in question.

.3   The Quantity Surveyor and the Contractor may agree what shall be deemed for all
the purposes of this Contract to be the net amount payable to or allowable by the
Contractor in respect of the occurrence of any event such as is referred to in any of
the provisions listed in clause 39.5.1.

.4   Any amount which from time to time becomes payable to or allowable by the
Contractor or by virtue of clause 39.1 to .3 or clause 39.4 shall, as the case may be,
be added to or from sum deducted from:

.4.1   the Contract Sum; and
.4.2   any amounts payable to the Contractor and which are calculated in accordance
with either clauses 28.2.2.1 or 28.2.2.2.

The addition or deduction to which clause 39.5.4 refers shall be subject to the
provisions of clauses 39.5.5 to .5.7.

.5   As soon as is reasonably practicable the Contractor shall provide such evidence
and computations as the Architect/the Contract Administrator or the Quantity
Surveyor may reasonably require to enable the amount payable to or allowable by
the Contractor by virtue of clauses 39.1 to .3 or clause 39.4 to be ascertained; and in
the case of amounts payable to or allowable by the Contractor under clause 39.1.3
(or clause 39.4 for amounts payable to or allowable by the Domestic Sub-Contractor under provisions in the sub-contract to the like effect as clauses 39.1.3 and
39.1.4)—employees other than workpeople—such evidence shall include a certificate signed by or on behalf of the Contractor each week certifying the validity of
the evidence reasonably required to ascertain such amounts.

.6   No addition to or deduction from the Contract Sum made by virtue of clause 39.5.4
shall alter in any way the amount of profit of the Contractor included in that Sum.

.7   Subject to the provisions of clause 39.5.8 no amount shall be added or deducted in
the computation of the amount stated as due in an Interim Certificate or in the
Final Certificate in respect of amounts otherwise payable to or allowable by the
Contractor by virtue of clauses 39.1 to .3 or clause 39.4 if the event (as referred to in
the provisions listed in clause 39.5.1) in respect of which the payment or allowance
would be made occurs after the Completion Date.

.8   Clause 39.5.7 shall not be applied unless:
.8.1   the printed text of clause 25 is unamended and forms part of the Conditions; and
.8.2   the Architect/the Contract Administrator has, in respect of every written notification by the Contractor under clause 25, fixed or confirmed in writing such
Completion Date as he considers to be in accordance with clause 25.

39.6   Clauses 39.1 to .4 shall not apply in respect of:

.1 work for which the Contractor is allowed daywork rates under clause 13.5.4;

.2 work executed or materials or goods supplied by any Nominated Sub-Contractor or Nominated Supplier (fluctuations in relation to Nominated Sub-Contractors and Nominated Suppliers shall be dealt with under any provision in relation thereto which may be included in the appropriate sub-contract or contract of sale);

.3 work executed by the Contractor for which a tender made under clause 35.2 has been accepted (fluctuations in relation to such works shall be dealt with under any provision in the accepted tender of the Contractor);

.4 changes in the rate of value added tax charged on the supply of goods or services by the Contractor to the Employer under this Contract.

39.7 In clause 39:

.1 the expression "the Base Date" means the Date stated in the Appendix;

.2 the expressions "materials" and "goods" include timber used in formwork but do not include other consumable stores, plant and machinery (save that electricity and, where specifically so stated in the Contract Bills, fuels are dealt with in clause 39.3),

.3 the expression "workpeople" means persons whose rates of wages and other emoluments (including holiday credits) are governed by the rules or decisions or agreements of the National Joint Council for the Building Industry or some other wage-fixing body for trades associated with the building industry;

.4 the expression "wage-fixing body" shall mean a body which lays down recognised terms and conditions of workers. For the purposes of clause 39 "recognised terms and conditions" means terms and conditions of workers in comparable employment in the trade or industry, or section of trade and industry, in which the employer in question is engaged, which have been settled by an agreement or award, to which the parties are employers' associations and independent trade unions which represent (generally, or in the district in question, as the case may be) a substantial proportion of the employers and of the workers in the trade, industry or section being workers of the description to which the agreement or award relates.

39.8 Percentage addition to fluctuation payments or allowances

.1 There shall be added to the amount paid to or allowed by the Contractor under:

.1.1 clause 39.1.2,

.1.2 clause 39.1.3,

.1.3 clause 39.1.6,

.1.4 clause 39.2.2,

.1.5 clause 39.2.5,

.1.6 clause 39.3.2

the percentage stated in the Appendix.

Clause 40—For use with the Local Authorities Edition with Quantities

40. Use of price adjustment formulae

.1.1 The Contract Sum shall be adjusted in accordance with the provisions of clause 40 and the Formula Rules current at the Base Date issued for use with clause 40 by the Joint Contracts Tribunal for the Standard Form of Building Contract (hereinafter called "the Formula Rules").

.1.2 Any adjustment under clause 40 shall be to sums exclusive of value added tax and nothing in clause 40 shall affect in any way the operation of clause 15 and the VAT Agreement.

.2 The Definitions in rule 3 of the Formula Rules shall apply to clause 40.

.3 The adjustment referred to in clause 40 shall be effected (after taking into account any Non-Adjustable Element) in all certificates for payment issued under the provisions of the Conditions.

.4 If any correction of amounts of adjustment under clause 40 included in previous certificates is required following any operation of rule 5 of the Formula Rules such correction shall be given effect in the next certificate for payment to be issued.

40.2 Interim valuations shall be made before the issue of each Interim Certificate and accordingly the words "whenever the Architect/the Contract Administrator considers them to be necessary" shall be deemed to have been deleted in clause 30.1.2.

40.3 For any article to which rule 4(ii) of the Formula Rules applies the Contractor shall insert in a list attached to the Contract Bills the market price of the article in sterling (that is the price delivered to the site) current at the Base Date. If after that Date the market price of the article inserted in the aforesaid list increases or decreases then the net amount of the difference between the cost of purchasing at the market price inserted in the aforesaid list and the market price payable by the Contractor and current when the article is bought shall, as the case may be, be paid to or allowed by the Contractor. The reference to "market price" in clause 40.3 shall be construed as including any duty or tax (other than any value added tax which is treated, or is capable of being treated, as input tax (as defined in the Finance Act 1972) by the Contractor) by whomsoever payable under or by virtue of any Act of Parliament on the import, purchase, sale, appropriation or use of the article specified as aforesaid.

40.4 [Number not used.]

40.5 The Quantity Surveyor and the Contractor may agree any alteration to the methods and procedures for ascertaining the amount of formula adjustment to be made under clause 40 and the amounts ascertained after the operation of such agreement shall be deemed for all the purposes of this Contract to be the amount of formula adjustment payable to or allowable by the Contractor in respect of the provisions of clause 40. Provided always:

.1 that no alteration to the methods and procedures shall be agreed as aforesaid unless it is reasonably expected that the amount of formula adjustment so ascertained will be the same or approximately the same as that ascertained in accordance with Part I or Part II of Section 2 of the Formula Rules whichever Part is stated to be applicable in the Contract Bills; and

.2 that any agreement under clause 40.5 shall not have any effect on the determination of any adjustment payable by the Contractor to any sub-contractor.

40.6 .1 If at any time prior to the issue of the Final Certificate under clause 30.8 formula adjustment is not possible because of delay in, or cessation of, the publication of the Monthly Bulletins, adjustment of the Contract Sum shall be made in each Interim Certificate during such period of delay on a fair and reasonable basis.

.2 If publication of the Monthly Bulletin is recommenced at any time prior to the issue of the Final Certificate under clause 30.8 the provisions of clause 40 and the Formula Rules shall apply for each Valuation Period as if no delay or cessation as aforesaid had occurred and the adjustment under clause 40 and the Formula Rules shall be substituted for any adjustment under clause 40.6.1.

.3 During any period of delay or cessation as aforesaid the Contractor and Employer shall operate such parts of clause 40 and the Formula Rules as will enable the amount of formula adjustment due to be readily calculated upon recommencement of publication of the Monthly Bulletins.

669

40.7 .1.1   If the Contractor fails to complete the Works by the Completion Date, formula adjustment of the Contract Sum under clause 40 shall be effected in all Interim Certificates issued after the aforesaid Completion Date by reference to the Index Numbers applicable to the Valuation Period in which the aforesaid Completion Date falls.

       .1.2   If for any reason the adjustment included in the amount certified in any Interim Certificate which is or has been issued after the aforesaid Completion Date is not in accordance with clause 40.7.1.1, such adjustment shall be corrected to comply with that clause.

       .2   Clause 40.7.1 shall not be applied unless:

       .2.1   the printed text of clause 25 is unamended and forms part of the Conditions; and

       .2.2   the Architect/the Contract Administrator has, in respect of every written notification by the Contractor under clause 25, fixed or confirmed in writing such Completion Date as he considers to be in accordance with clause 25.

Clause 37:   Fluctuations

The fluctuation clauses are now printed in a separate booklet. They may be incorporated in the Contract by reference by completing the appropriate part of the Appendix. If deletions are not made in the Appendix, clause 38 will apply.

Clauses 38 and 39:   Fluctuations Provisions

Derivation.   These clauses are derived from and in large measure reproduce clauses 31A–31E of the 1963 Form. Clauses 31A and 31B of the 1963 Form were different versions of basic fluctuations provisions. Clauses 31C, D and E applied as machinery if either clause 31A or clause 31B was chosen. Clause 38 is substantially derived from clause 31B and clauses 31C, D and E insofar as they applied to the former clause 31A.

Generally.   Clause 38 is a fluctuations clause providing for increases or decreases in statutory contributions, levies or taxes. Clause 39 is a fluctuations clause providing for increases or decreases in labour and materials costs as well as tax fluctuations.

As the term "fluctuations" suggest, these are "rise and fall" clauses. In practice, prices have risen and continue to rise. These clauses, if properly operated, provide a considerable measure of protection for the Contractor, but not an indemnity against increased costs. For example, they do not apply to increases in head office or administrative costs. They do not apply to consumable stores, plant and machinery other than timber used in formwork, electricity and fuels where so stated in the Contract Bills (see clause 39.7.3). For these reasons prudent Contractors incorporate an adjustment to their rates to allow for non-recoverable increases. Clauses 38.7 and 39.8 expressly allow for a percentage addition to fluctuation payments or allowances where so stated in the Appendix.

Scheme of clause 38.   Clauses 38.1.2 to 38.1.4 provide for alteration in the type and rates of statutory contributions, levies and taxes payable by a person in his capacity as Employer. Clauses 38.1.5 to 38.1.7 provide for alterations in statutory refunds or premiums receivable by a person in his capacity as Employer. Clause 38.2 provides for alterations in statutory duties or taxes affecting materials or goods specified in a list attached to the Contract Bills. Clause 38.3 requires the Contractor to incorporate relevant fluctuation clauses in Domestic Sub-Contracts. Clauses 38.4–38.6 deal with the procedure for fluctuations. The Contractor has to give written notice of any relevant alterations. There is machinery for adjustment of price. The clause is not to apply to dayworks or work executed by or materials supplied by Nominated Sub-Contractors or Nominated Suppliers. Clause 38.7 provide for the percentage addition.

Scheme of clause 39. Clause 39.1 provides for alterations in wages, emoluments and expenses. Clause 39.3 deals with alterations in market prices in materials and goods specified in a list attached to the Contract Bills, such alterations to include alteration of any statutory duty or tax. Clause 39.4 substantially reproduces clause 38.3. Clauses 39.5–39.7 reproduces the procedure at clauses 38.4–38.6. Clause 39.8 provides for the percentage addition.

Matters common to clauses 38 and 39

Definition of "workpeople": clauses 38.1.2, 38.1.3, 38.6.3 and 39.1.1, 39.1.3, 39.7.3.

In the 1963 Form the reference was to prices, etc., "payable by the Contractor to or in respect of workpeople . . . in accordance with the rules or decisions of the National Joint Council. . . ." In *J. Murphy & Sons* v. *London Borough of Southwark*,[80] the Court of Appeal held that this wording applied only to those workpeople directly employed whose rates of wages was governed by the N.J.C., *i.e.* not to self-employed labour. The effect of the new definition, it is submitted, is that it covers:

(1) workpeople directly employed whose rates of wages are governed by the N.J.C.;

(2) workpeople directly employed whose rates of wages are not so governed (by virtue of 38.1.3), but not self-employed labour.

The reference to "workpeople" and to the machinery for fixing their wages excludes, in general, from the operation of clauses 38 and 39, administrative staff. Further, head office staff are usually not within the words "workpeople engaged upon or in connection with the Works."

Electricity and fuels

Fluctuations are allowed for these: see clauses 38.2.1 and 39.3.2.

---

[80] (1982) 22 B.L.R. 41 (C.A.).

Notice condition precedent: clauses 38.4.2 and 39.5.2.

This is plain language. If the Contractor does not give notice within a reasonable time after the occurrence of the event to which it relates he is not, in ordinary circumstances, entitled to payment. What is reasonable is a question of fact but it is thought that a most important consideration is whether an opportunity to check the facts has been lost.

Agreement between Quantity Surveyor and Contractor: clauses 38.4.3 and 39.5.3.

The scope of this agreement was considered in *John Laing* v. *County and District*,[81] where it was held that this did not confer on the Quantity Surveyor authority to waive the Contractor's failure to comply with the requirement for written notice. The words should be construed as if the emphasis were on the words "net amount," *i.e.* to confer authority on the Quantity Surveyor to agree quantum only as opposed to liability. Looking at the words in the context of the Contract as a whole, the function and authority of the Quantity Surveyor is confined to measuring and quantifying.

Evidence

Clauses 38.4.5 and 39.5.5 require the Contractor to submit evidence and computations to the Architect or the Quantity Surveyor.

Contractor's default over completion

Clauses 38.4.7, 38.4.8, 39.5.7 and 39.5.8 were new to the 1980 Form. The effect is that if the printed text of clause 25 is unamended and if the Architect has properly operated clause 25, the Contractor will not be entitled to fluctuation payments for increases which occur after the Completion Date as extended.[82]

"Wage fixing body"

Note that a new definition of this term was inserted by Amendment 4 issued in July 1987 (clauses 38.6.4 and 39.7.4).

Clause 39.1.1.3. *"... which have been promulgated at the Base Date ..."*
The Contractor cannot claim an increase in respect of a wage award which becomes effective during the course of carrying out the Works but which had been promulgated at the Base Date. The Base Date is defined in the Appendix by insertion.

Clause 39.1.1.4. *"... any incentive scheme ..."*
This sub-clause provides for the terms of incentive schemes or productivity agreements included in the rules of wage fixing bodies to be taken into account.

---

[81] (1982) 23 B.L.R. 1.
[82] Thus avoiding the effect of *Peak Construction* v. *McKinney Foundations* (1970) 1 B.L.R. 114 at 125 (C.A.).

This takes account of the decision in *Sindall (William)* v. *N. W. Thames Regional Health Authority*.[83] The House of Lords there held that the increase in cost in operating a bonus scheme, based upon wage rates, where that scheme was voluntarily entered into by the Contractors was not an increase recoverable under the equivalent clause in the 1963 Form.

Clauses 39.1.5 and 39.1.6. Fluctuations are allowable for transport charges and fares.

Clause 40:   Price Adjustment Formulae

Derivation.   This clause, with other provisions elsewhere in the 1980 Form, substantially reproduces clause 31F of the 1963 Form introduced in March 1975. Those concerned with the detailed application of the clause should refer to the Formula Rules, which are published separately and not printed in this Book.

Clause 40.5.   This gives the Quantity Surveyor a carefully limited authority to agree variations of formula with the Contractor.

Clause 40.7.   This deals with the position where the Contractor is in delay: see commentary to clauses 38.4.7, 38.4.8, 39.5.7 and 39.5.8.

PART 4: SETTLEMENT OF DISPUTES—ARBITRATION

41.1   When the Employer or the Contractor require a dispute or difference as referred to in Article 5 including:
   any matter or thing left by this Contract to the discretion of the Architect/the Contract Administrator, or
   the withholding by the Architect/the Contract Administrator of any certificate to which the Contractor may claim to be entitled; or
   the adjustment of the Contract Sum under clause 30.6.2, or
   the rights and liabilities of the parties under clauses 27, 28, 32 or 33; or
   unreasonable withholding of consent or agreement by the Employer or the Architect/the Contract Administrator on his behalf or by the Contractor
to be referred to arbitration then either the Employer or the Contractor shall give written notice to the other to such effect and such dispute or difference shall be referred to the arbitration and final decision of a person to be agreed between the parties as the Arbitrator, or, upon failure so to agree within 14 days after the date of the aforesaid written notice, of a person to be appointed as the Arbitrator on the request of either the Employer or the Contractor by the person named in the Appendix.

41.2   .1   Provided that if the dispute or difference to be referred to arbitration under this Contract raises issues which are substantially the same as or connected with issues raised in a related dispute between:

---

[83] [1977] I.C.R. 294 (H.L.).

the Employer and Nominated Sub-Contractor under Agreement NSC/2 or NSC/2a as applicable, or

the Contractor and any Nominated Sub-Contractor under Sub-contract NSC/4 or NSC/4a as applicable, or

the Contractor and/or the Employer and any Nominated Supplier whose contract of sale with the Contractor provides for the matters referred to in clause 36.4.8.2,

and if the related dispute has already been referred for determination to an Arbitrator, the Employer and the Contractor hereby agree

that the dispute or difference under this Contract shall be referred to the Arbitrator appointed to determine the related dispute;

that the JCT Arbitration Rules applicable to the related dispute shall apply to the dispute under this Contract;

that such Arbitrator shall have power to make such directions and all necessary awards in the same way as if the procedure of the High Court as to joining one or more defendants or joining co-defendants or third parties was available to the parties and to him; and

that the agreement and consent referred to in clause 41.6 on appeals or applications to the High Court on any question of law shall apply to any question of law arising out of the awards of such arbitrator in respect of all related disputes referred to him or arising in the course of the reference of all the related disputes referred to him;

.2 save that the Employer or the Contractor may require the dispute or difference under this Contract to be referred to a different Arbitrator (to be appointed under this Contract) if either of them reasonably considers that the Arbitrator appointed to determine the related dispute is not appropriately qualified to determine the dispute or difference under this Contract.

.3 Clauses 41.2.1 and 41.2.2 shall apply unless in the Appendix the words "clauses 41.2.1 and 41.2.2 apply" have been deleted.

41.3 Such reference, except

.1 on article 3 or article 4; or

.2 on the questions

whether or not the issue of an instruction is empowered by the Conditions; or

whether or not a certificate has been improperly withheld; or

whether a certificate is not in accordance with the Conditions; or

whether a determination under clause 22C.4.3.1 will be just and equitable; or

.3 on any dispute or difference under clause 4.1 in regard to a reasonable objection by the Contractor under clause 8.4, under clause 18.1 or clause 23.3.2 in regard to withholding of consent by the Contractor, and clauses 25, 32 and 33,

shall not be opened until after Practical Completion or alleged Practical Completion of the Works or termination or alleged termination of the Contractor's employment under this Contract or abandonment of the Works, unless with the written consent of the Employer or the Architect/the Contract Administrator on his behalf and the Contractor.

41.4 Subject to the provisions of clauses 4.2, 30.9, 38.4.3, 39.5.3 and 40.5 the Arbitrator shall, without prejudice to the generality of his powers, have power to rectify the contract so that it accurately reflects the true agreement made by the Employer and the Contractor, to direct such measurements and/or valuations as may in his opinion be desirable in order to determine the rights of the parties and to ascertain and award any sum which ought to have been the subject of or included in any certificate and to open up, review and revise any certificate, opinion, decision (except, where clause 8.4 is relevant, a decision of the Architect/the Contract Administrator to issue instructions pursuant to clause 8.4.1), requirement or notice and to determine all matters in dispute which shall be submitted to him in the same manner as if no such certificate, opinion, decision, requirement or notice had been given.

41.5   Subject to clause 41.6 the award of such Arbitrator shall be final and binding on the parties.

41.6   The parties hereby agree and consent pursuant to Section 1(3)(a) and 2(1)(b) of the Arbitration Act, 1979, that either party
.1   may appeal to the High Court on any question of law arising out of an award made in an arbitration under this Arbitration Agreement; and
.2   may apply to the High Court to determine any question of law arising in the course of the reference;
and the parties agree that the High Court should have jurisdiction to determine any such question of law.

41.7   Whatever the nationality, residence or domicile of the Employer, the Contractor, any sub-contractor or supplier or the Arbitrator, and wherever the Works or any part thereof are situated, the law of England shall be the proper law of this Contract and in particular (but not so as to derogate from the generality of the foregoing) the provisions of the Arbitration Acts 1950 (notwithstanding anything in S.34 thereof) to 1979 shall apply to any arbitration under this Contract wherever the same, or any part of it, shall be conducted. [*y.2*]

41.8   If before making his final award the Arbitrator dies or otherwise ceases to act as the Arbitrator, the Employer and the Contractor shall forthwith appoint a further Arbitrator, or, upon failure so to appoint within 14 days of any such death or cessation, then either the Employer or the Contractor may request the person named in the Appendix to appoint such further Arbitrator. Provided that no such further Arbitrator shall be entitled to disregard any direction of the previous Arbitrator or to vary or revise any award of the previous Arbitrator except to the extent that the previous Arbitrator had power so to do under the JCT Arbitration Rules and/or with the agreement of the parties and/or by the operation of law.

41.9   The arbitration shall be conducted in accordance with the "JCT Arbitration Rules" current at the Base Date. [*y.3*] Provided that if any amendments to the Rules so current have been issued by the Joint Contracts Tribunal after the Base Date the Employer and the Contractor may, by a joint notice in writing to the Arbitrator, state that they wish the arbitration to be conducted in accordance with the JCT Arbitration Rules as so amended.

Clause 41 (and Article 5): Arbitration

Derivation.   In the original version of the 1980 Form, arbitration was dealt

---

[*y.2*] *Where the parties do not wish the proper law of the Contract to be the law of England appropriate amendments to clause 41.7 should be made. Where the Works are situated in Scotland then the forms issued by the Scottish Building Contract Committee which contain Scots proper law and arbitration provisions are the appropriate documents. It should be noted that the provisions of the Arbitration Acts 1950 to 1979 do not extend to Scotland.*

[*y.3*] *The JCT Arbitration Rules contain stricter time limits than those prescribed by some arbitration rules or those frequently observed in practice. The parties should note that a failure by a party or the agent of a party to comply with the time limits incorporated in these Rules may have adverse consequences.*

with exclusively by Article 5. This, in turn, substantially reproduced clause 35 of the 1963 Form with the significant addition that provision was made for multipartite arbitration.

However, by Amendment 4 issued in July 1987 the scheme was changed again. A new Part 4 of the Contract for settlement of disputes was introduced which set out in clause 41 the details of the arbitration procedures. Article 5 was, however, retained. Article 5, as amended, now briefly states that the method of settling disputes is to be by arbitration. The detailed provisions are transferred to clause 41. Article 5 and clause 41 are therefore dealt with together in this commentary.

The arbitration provisions have, in addition, been amended as to matters of detail by Amendment 2 issued in November 1986, Amendment 4 issued in July 1987, Amendment 5 issued in January 1988 and Amendment 6 issued in July 1988. These amendments are referred to below as appropriate.

Scope of arbitration provisions: the general law.   In order to determine the jurisdiction of the Arbitrator one must consider the terms of the arbitration clause and the contract of which it forms a part. However, there are certain general principles which apply to arbitration clauses including this one.

In summary,[84] an Arbitrator cannot make a binding award as to the initial existence of the Contract.[85] He cannot decide whether the contract was void *ab initio* for illegality[86] or some other reason, *e.g.* that the parties had never entered into a contract at all. He cannot make a binding decision as to the existence of facts said to found his jurisdiction.[87] An Arbitrator may rule, however, on the continued existence of the Contract because normally the arbitration clause survives the termination of the Contract.[88] He therefore generally has power to decide whether the Contract has been repudiated,[89] whether the Contract has been frustrated,[90] and whether one party is entitled to avoid the Contract on grounds of misrepresentation.[91]

Scope of Article 5.   The key words are "any dispute or difference as to the construction of this Contract or any matter or thing of whatsoever nature arising thereunder or in connection therewith." These words have been recently considered by the Court of Appeal in *Ashville Investments* v. *Elmer Contractors*.[92]

---

[84] For arbitration generally, see Chap. 16 and especially "Jurisdiction of the arbitrator" at p. 387.

[85] *Duke of Buccleuch* v. *Metropolitan Board of Works* (1870) L.R. 5 Exch. 221 at 222.

[86] *Heyman* v. *Darwins Ltd.* [1942] A.C. 356.

[87] See *Smith* v. *Martin* [1925] 1 K.B. 745 (C.A.). Building Contract provided that arbitration should not take place until after completion of the works. Held that the parties were not bound by the decision of the arbitrator that the works were completed (see also clause 41.3 discussed below).

[88] *Heyman* v. *Darwins Ltd.* [1942] A.C. 356.

[89] *Ibid.*

[90] *Ibid.*; see also *Kruse* v. *Questier & Co.* [1953] 1 Q.B. 669; *Government of Gibraltar* v. *Kenney* [1956] 2 Q.B. 410.

[91] See *Ashville Investments* v. *Elmer Contractors* [1989] 1 Q.B. 488 (C.A.), discussed below.

[92] [1989] 1 Q.B. 488 (C.A.).

Article 5. *"... as to the construction of this Contract ..."*

This establishes that any dispute concerning the interpretation of the Contract terms and documents is to be referred to arbitration.[93]

Article 5. *"... any matter ... arising thereunder ..."*

This provides for the reference to arbitration of all contractual claims arising under the Contract as executed. It does not cover claims in tort.[94]

Article 5. *"... any matter ... in connection therewith ..."*

These words are very wide. They cover misrepresentation and negligent misstatement. The Court of Appeal held that these were in connection with the contract because they were said to have induced it. Thus a dispute between the parties based upon an allegation of mistake at the time they entered into the Contract, and upon allegations of misrepresentation or negligent misstatement were within the scope of the clause.[95] Nothing in the clause precludes the Arbitrator from granting rectification[96] or awarding damages if such allegations are made out.

Article 5. *"... after the determination of the employment of the Contractor ..."*

These words were inserted by Amendment 4 issued in July 1987. Since, in any event, the arbitration provision survives the termination of the Contract, they appear to be unnecessary.

Article 5. *"... except ... VAT Agreement ..."*

As an exception to the very wide jurisdiction explained above, these matters are excluded.

Employer challenging architect. The Employer, as well as the Contractor, can ask the Arbitrator to review the Architect's decisions.[97]

Does the court have the arbitrator's powers? This important and difficult question arises from the Court of Appeal decision in *Northern Regional Health Authority* v. *Derek Crouch*,[98] and is discussed under the heading "Crouch" at page 389. On the authority of that case, subject to certain qualifications the court does not have power to "open up, review and revise any certificate, opinion, decision ..." of the Architect under the 1980 Form. The position will change somewhat when section 100 of the Courts and Legal Service Act 1990 comes into force.

---

[93] *Ibid.* at 508.
[94] *Ibid.* at 508.
[95] Distinguishing *Printing Machinery* v. *Linotype & Machinery* [1912] 1 Ch. 566; *Monro* v. *Bognor Urban District Council* [1915] 3 K.B. 167; *Crane* v. *Hegemann Harris Co. Inc.* [1939] 4 All E.R. 68; and not following dicta of Purchas L.J. in relation to I.C.E. Conditions in *Blue Circle Industries* v. *Holland Dredging Co.* (1987) 37 B.L.R. 40 (C.A.).
[96] See also clause 41.4.
[97] *Modern Engineering (Bristol)* v. *Gilbert-Ash (Northern)* [1974] AC 689 at 709 (H.L.).
[98] [1984] Q.B. 644 (C.A.).

Stay of court proceedings.   Where one party has commenced proceedings in court, if the other party wishes to arbitrate he can usually insist on arbitration by taking the appropriate steps to obtain a stay of the court proceedings. There are however exceptions.[99]

Clause 41.1.   The matters listed are substantially the same as those listed in clause 35 of the 1963 Form. They are, in any event, only examples of the very wide jurisdiction discussed above.

The clarification of the requirement for written notice to commence the arbitration was inserted by Amendment 6 issued in July 1988. For the degree of formality required of a notice for the purposes of clause 30.9, see clause 30.9 and its commentary.

Clause 41.2.   This substantially reproduces Articles 5.1.4 to 5.1.6 of the original version of the 1980 Form which introduced provisions for multipartite arbitrations.[1]

Amendments.   By Amendment 4 issued in July 1987 it was provided that the agreement of the parties to the jurisdiction of the High Court over questions of law (under clause 41.6) extended to multipartite arbitrations. By Amendment 6 issued in July 1988 it was provided that the JCT Arbitration Rules (as to which, see below) applicable to the related dispute should apply to the Main Contract dispute.

Scheme of sub-clause.   In addition to a dispute between the Employer and the Contractor, there may be a related dispute between either of them and a Nominated Sub-Contractor or Nominated Supplier. Agreements NSC/2 and 2a and Sub-Contracts NSC/4 and 4a all contain equivalent joinder provisions. All potential parties to multipartite arbitrations will thus have agreed in advance to the procedure and it is thought that this nexus of agreement would be regarded as effective in principle to overcome the difficulties discussed at page 402 between the parties referred to. These difficulties remain if it is sought to involve other parties. In multipartite arbitration the Arbitrator's powers of controlling the proceedings are particularly important.[2]

Clause 41.2.   "*... dispute or difference ...*"
It would appear that this will be held to mean a difference on a specific item or at least those grouped under a specific heading so that the courts would not regard a very long unrelated list of complaints as falling within the phrase.[3]

---

[99] See s.4 of the Arbitration Act 1950 and see generally "The right to insist on arbitration" at p. 397.

[1] For some assistance, see *Higgs & Hill Building* v. *Campbell Denis* (1982) 28 B.L.R. 47; *Multi Construction (Southern) Ltd.* v. *Stent Foundations Ltd.* (1988) 41 B.L.R. 98 (decisions on the not dissimilar clause 24 of the "Green Form"); and *Hyundai Engineering* v. *Active Building* (1988) 45 B.L.R. 62 (decision on clause in Form similar to clause 24).

[2] See p. 402.

[3] See *Hyundai Engineering* v. *Active Building* (1988) 45 B.L.R. 62.

Clause 41.1.   "... *issues which are substantially the same as or connected with* ..."

These words are wide. In view of the meaning given to the phrase "in connection therewith" in *Ashville Investments* v. *Elmer Contractors*,[4] it seems that similar considerations to those by which the Court determines under R.S.C., Order 16, rule 1 whether Third Party proceedings are appropriate should apply to determine whether there is a sufficient connection between the disputes for there to be multipartite arbitration proceedings.

Clause 41.2.   "... *if the related dispute has already been referred for determination* ..."

The scheme is that multipartite disputes are referred to the Arbitrator appointed to determine whichever of the related disputes is first referred to arbitration.

Clauses 41.2.2 and 41.2.3.   These provide that the parties may exclude the joinder provisions altogether and that either the Employer or the Contractor may require a dispute between them to be referred to a different Arbitrator if he considers that the Arbitrator appointed is not appropriately qualified.

Clause 41.3.   The embargo on arbitration prior to Practical Completion is important, but note the exceptions. These include the issue and amount of Interim Certificates and extensions of time under clause 25. With care a great range of matters may be brought within these exceptions. This is very important from the point of view of the Contractor in view of the decision of the Court of Appeal in *Lubenham* v. *South Pembrokeshire District Council*.[5]

The range of excepted matters has been still further extended by Amendments to include

(1) whether a determination under clause 22C.4.3.1 will be just and equitable (41.3.2 added by Amendment 2 issued in November 1986);

(2) the Contractor's obligation under clauses 4.1 and 8.4 (Amendment 5 issued in January 1988);

(3) the reasonableness of the Contractor in withholding consent under clauses 18.1 and 23.3.2 (Amendment 2).

Clause 41.4.   "... *have power to rectify* ..."

This express power was inserted by Amendment 6 issued in July 1988. The Arbitrator probably had such power in any event.[6]

---

[4] [1989] Q.B. 488 (C.A.) discussed at p. 388.

[5] (1986) 33 B.L.R. 39, discussed at p. 598 in relation to determination under clause 28 and at p. 611 in relation to recovery without a certificate under clause 30.

[6] *Ashville Investments Ltd.* v. *Elmer Contractors Ltd.* [1989] 1 Q.B. 488 (C.A.); see also "Arbitrators" at p. 268 and the intriguing question raised at n. 73 under "Crouch" at p. 391.

Clause 41.4. *"... to direct such measurements and/or valuations ..."*

When he so directs, the Arbitrator is not acting as an Arbitrator. But when the time comes to determine the rights of the parties arising from such measurements, he must act in a proper arbitral fashion and in accordance with the rules of natural justice.[7]

Clause 41.4. *"... to open up, review and revise any certificate, opinion ..."*

For general discussion of these words, see "Does the court have the Arbitrator's powers?" at page 677. Note that they give the Arbitrator power to open up, review or revise assessments made by the Quantity Surveyor under clause 26.1.[8]

Clause 41.4. *"... except ... pursuant to clause 8.4.1 ..."*

These words were inserted by Amendment 5 issued in January 1988. The intention, it seems, is that the decision of the Architect under clause 8.4 that work is non-conforming is open to review, but that his discretion to order removal of such work under clause 8.4.1, as opposed to deploying his alternative remedies, is not reviewable.

Clause 41.4. *"... requirement or notice ..."*

Insofar as the Conditions require the Contractor to take specified steps before the Architect is obliged to issue a certificate, form an opinion or make a decision, the Arbitrator cannot waive these requirements.[9]

Clause 41.6. This clause, by which the parties agree that the High Court shall have jurisdiction on questions of law under the Arbitration Act 1979, was inserted by Amendment 4 issued in July 1987.[10]

Clause 41.8. This clause, providing for the procedure in the event of the death of the Arbitrator before making his final award, was inserted by Amendment 6 issued in July 1988.

Clause 41.9. This new clause, inserted by Amendment 6 issued in July 1988, provides that the arbitration shall be conducted in accordance with the "JCT Arbitration Rules" current at the Base Date. These Rules are published separately and not reprinted in this book. They were operational as from 18th July 1988. Unless the parties otherwise consent, whatever the scope of the dispute, the Arbitrator is required to adopt an adversarial rather than inquisitorial procedure allowing each party to present its case in accordance with the rules of natural justice.[11]

---

[7] *Town & City Properties* v. *Wiltshier* (1988) 44 B.L.R. 109.

[8] *Moody* v. *Ellis* (1983) 26 B.L.R. 39 (C.A.).

[9] *London Borough of Merton* v. *Leach* (1985) 32 B.L.R. 51 at 113—Issue 15.

[10] For consideration of the Arbitration Act 1979, see generally Chap. 16 and in particular "Control by the Court" at p. 408.

[11] *Town & City Properties* v. *Wiltshier* (1988) 44 B.L.R. 109.

Code of Practice: referred to in clause 8.4.4

1. This is the Code of Practice referred to in clause 8.4.4. The purpose of the Code is to help in the fair and reasonable operation of the requirements of clause 8.4.4.

2. The Architect/The Contract Administrator and the Contractor should endeavour to agree the amount and method of opening up or testing but in any case in issuing his instructions pursuant to clause 8.4.4 the Architect/the Contract Administrator is required to consider the following criteria:
   .1 the need in the event of non-compliance to demonstrate at no cost to the Employer either that it is unique and not likely to occur in similar elements of the Works or alternatively the extent of any similar non-compliance in the Works already constructed or still to be constructed;
   .2 the need to discover whether any non-compliance in a primary structural element is a failure of workmanship and/or materials such that rigorous testing of similar elements must take place; or where the non-compliance is in a less significant element whether it is such as is to be statistically expected and can be simply repaired; or whether the non-compliance indicates an inherent weakness such as can only be found by selective testing the extent of which must depend upon the importance of any detail concerned;
   .3 the significance of the non-compliance having regard to the nature of the work in which it has occurred;
   .4 the consequence of any similar non-compliance on the safety of the building, its effect on users, adjoining property, the public, and compliance with any Statutory Requirements;
   .5 the level and standard of supervision and control of the Works by the Contractor;
   .6 the relevant records of the Contractor and where relevant of any sub-contractor resulting from the supervision and control referred to in paragraph 2.5 above or otherwise;
   .7 any Codes of Practice or similar advice issued by a responsible body which are applicable to the non-complying work, materials or goods;
   .8 any failure by the Contractor to carry out, or to secure the carrying out of any tests specified in the Contract Documents or in an instruction of the Architect/the Contract Administrator;
   .9 the reason for the non-compliance when this has been established;
   .10 any technical advice that the Contractor has obtained in respect of the non-complying work, materials or goods;
   .11 current recognised testing procedures;
   .12 the practicability of progressive testing in establishing whether any similar non-compliance is reasonably likely;
   .13 if alternative testing methods are available, the time required for and the consequential costs of such alternative testing methods;
   .14 any proposals of the Contractor;
   .15 any other relevant matters.

Appendix

Clause etc.

Statutory tax deduction scheme—Finance (No. 2) Act 1975	Fourth recital and 31	Employer at Base Date *is a 'contractor'/is not a 'contractor' for the purposes of the Act and the Regulations *(Delete as applicable)
Base Date	1.3	_____
Date for Completion	1.3	_____
Defects Liability Period (if none other stated is 6 months from the day named in the Certificate of Practical Completion of the Works)	17.2	_____
Assignment by Employer of benefits after Practical Completion	19.1.2	Clause 19.1.2* applies/does not apply *(Delete as applicable)
Insurance cover for any one occurrence or series of occurrences arising out of one event	21.1.1	£ _____
Insurance—liability of Employer	21.2.1	Insurance *may be required/is not required Amount of indemnity for any one occurrence or series of occurrences arising out of one event £ _____ [*y.1*] *(Delete as applicable)
Insurance of the Works—alternative clauses	22.1	*Clause 22A/Clause 22B/Clause 22C applies (See Footnote [*m*] to Clause 22) *(Delete as applicable)
Percentage to cover professional fees	*22A 22B.1 22C.2 *(Delete as applicable)	_____
Annual renewal date of insurance as supplied by Contractor	22A.3.1.	_____
Insurance for Employer's loss of liquidated damages—clause 25.4.3	22D	Insurance *may be required/is not required *(Delete as applicable)
	22D.2	Period of time
Date of Possession	23.1	_____
Deferment of the Date of Possession	23.1.2 25.4.13 26.1	Clause 23.1.2 *applies/does not apply Period of deferment if it is to be less than 6 weeks is _____ *(Delete as applicable)

[*y.1*] *If the indemnity is to be for an aggregate amount and not for any one occurrence or series of occurrences the entry should make this clear.*

Liquidated and ascertained damages	24.2	at the rate of £ —————— per —————

It is essential that periods be inserted since otherwise no period of delay would be prescribed.

Period of delay: [z.1]	28.1.3	—————————————
Period of delay: [z.2]	28A.1.1	
	28A.1.3	—————————————
Period of delay: [z.3]	28A.1.2	—————————————
Period of Interim Certificates (if none stated is one month)	30.1.3	—————————————
Retention Percentage (if less than 5 per cent.) [aa]	30.4.1.1	—————————————
Work reserved for Nominated Sub-Contractors for which the Contractor desires to tender	35.2	—————————————
Fluctuations: (if alternative required is not shown clause 38 shall apply)	37	clause 38 [cc] clause 39 clause 40
Percentage addition	38.7 or 39.8	—————————————
Formula Rules	40.1.1.1	
	rule 3	Base Month ————————————19————
	rule 3	Non-Adjustable Element ————— (not to exceed 10%)
	rules 10 and 30 (i)	Part I/Part II [dd] of Section 2 of the Formula Rules is to apply
Settlement of disputes—Arbitration—appointer (if no appointer is selected the appointer shall be the President or a Vice-President, Royal Institute of British Architects)	41.1	President or a Vice-President: *Royal Institute of British Architects *Royal Institution of Chartered Surveyors *Chartered Institute of Arbitrators *(Delete as applicable)
Settlement of disputes—Arbitration	41.2	Clauses 41.2.1 and 41.2.2 apply (See clause 41.2.3)

---

[z] *It is suggested that the periods should be:*

   z.1 one month.

   z.2 one month.

   z.3 three months.

[aa] *The percentage will be 5 per cent. unless a lower rate is specified here.*

[bb] *Not used.*

[cc] *Delete alternatives not used.*

[dd] *Strike out according to which method of formula adjustment (Part I—Work Category Method or Part II—Work Group Method) has been stated in the documents issued to tenderers.*

Appendix

Liquidated and ascertained damages.   For the significance of inserting "nil" in the Appendix, see *Temloc* v. *Errill Properties Ltd.*[12] discussed above at page 566 in relation to clause 24. For liquidated damages generally, see pages 222 *et seq*.

**Supplemental Provisions
(the VAT Agreement)**

The following are the supplemental provisions (the VAT Agreement) referred to in clause 15.1 of the Conditions:

1.   The Employer shall pay to the Contractor in the manner hereinafter set out any tax properly chargeable by the Commissioners on the Contractor on the supply to the Employer of any goods and services by the Contractor under this Contract. Supplies of goods and services under this Contract are supplies under a contract providing for periodical payment for such supplies within the meaning of Regulation 21(1) of the Value Added Tax (General) Regulations 1972 or any amendment or re-enactment thereof.

1.1   The Contractor shall not later than the date for the issue of each Interim Certificate and, unless the procedure set out in clause 1.3 of this Agreement shall have been completed, for the use of the Final Certificate give to the Employer a written provisional assessment of the respective values (less any Retention Percentage applicable thereto) of those supplies of goods and services for which the Certificate is being issued and which will be chargeable, at the relevant time of supply under Regulation 21(1)(a) of the Value Added Tax (General) Regulations 1972 on the Contractor at
.1   a zero rate of tax (Category (i)) and
.2   any rate or rates of tax other than zero (Category (ii)).
The Contractor shall also specify the rate or rates of tax which are chargeable on those supplies included in Category (ii), and shall state the grounds on which he considers such supplies are so chargeable.

1.2   .1   Upon receipt of such written provisional assessment the Employer, unless he has reasonable grounds for objection to that assessment, shall calculate the amount of tax due by applying the rate or rates of tax specified by the Contractor to the amount of the assessed value of those supplies included in Category (ii) of such assessment, and remit the calculated amount of such tax, together with the amount of the Certificate issued by the Architect/the Contract Administrator, to the Contractor within the period for payment of certificates set out in clause 30.1.1.1 of the Conditions.

1.2   .2   If the Employer has reasonable grounds for objection to the provisional assessment he shall within 3 working days of receipt of that assessment so notify the Contractor in writing setting out those grounds. The Contractor shall within 3 working days of

---

[12] (1987) 39 BLR 30 (C.A.).

receipt of the written notification of the Employer reply in writing to the Employer either that he withdraws the assessment in which case the Employer is released from his obligation under clause 1.2.1 of this Agreement or that he confirms the assessment. If the Contractor so confirms then the Contractor may treat any amount received from the Employer in respect of the value which the Contractor has stated to be chargeable on him at a rate or rates of tax other than zero as being inclusive of tax and issue an authenticated receipt under clause 1.4 of this Agreement.

1.3   .1   After the issue of the Certificate of Completion of Making Good Defects under clause 17.4 of the Conditions the Contractor shall as soon as he can finally so ascertain prepare a written final statement of the respective values of all supplies of goods and services for which certificates have been or will be issued which are chargeable on the Contractor at

   .1.1   a zero rate (Category (i)) and
   .1.2   any rate or rates of tax other than zero (Category (ii))

and shall issue such final statement to the Employer.
The Contractor shall also specify the rate or rates of tax which are chargeable on the value of those supplies included in Category (ii) and shall state the grounds on which he considers such supplies are so chargeable.
The Contractor shall also state the total amount of tax already received by the Contractor for which a receipt or receipts under clause 1.4 of this Agreement have been issued.

   .2   The statement under clause 1.3.1 of this Agreement may be issued either before or after the issue of the Final Certificate under clause 30.8 of the Conditions.

   .3   Upon receipt of the written final statement the Employer shall, subject to clause 3 of this Agreement, calculate the final amount of tax due by applying the rate or rates of tax specified by the Contractor to the value of those supplies included in Category (ii) of the statement and deducting therefrom the total amount of tax already received by the Contractor specified in the statement, and shall pay the balance of such tax to the Contractor within 28 days from receipt of the statement.

   .4   If the Employer finds that the total amount of tax specified in the final statement as already paid by him exceeds the amount of tax calculated under clause 1.3.3 of this Agreement the Employer shall so notify the Contractor who shall refund such excess to the Employer within 28 days of receipt of the notification, together with a receipt under clause 1.4 of this Agreement showing the correction of the amounts for which a receipt or receipts have previously been issued by the Contractor.

1.4   Upon receipt of any amount paid under certificates of the Architect/the Contract Administrator and any tax properly paid under the provisions of clause 1 of this Agreement the Contractor shall issue to the Employer a receipt of the kind referred to in Regulation 21(2) of the Value Added Tax (General) Regulations 1972 containing the particulars required under Regulation 9(1) of the aforesaid Regulations or any amendment or re-enactment thereof to be contained in a tax invoice.

2.1   If, when the Employer is obliged to make payment under clause 1.2 or 1.3 of this Agreement he is empowered under clause 24 of the Conditions to deduct any sum calculated at the rate stated in the Appendix as liquidated and ascertained damages from sums due or to become due to the Contractor under this Contract he shall disregard any such deduction in calculating the tax due on the value of goods and services supplied to which he is obliged to add tax under clause 1.2 or 1.3 of this Agreement.

2.2 The Contractor when ascertaining the respective values of any supplies of goods and services for which certificates have been or will be issued under the Conditions in order to prepare the final statement referred to in clause 1.3 of this Agreement shall disregard when stating such values any deduction by the Employer of any sum calculated at the rate stated in the Appendix as liquidated and ascertained damages under clause 24 of the Conditions.

3.1 If the Employer disagrees with the final statement issued by the Contractor under clause 1.3 of this Agreement he may but before any payment or refund becomes due under clause 1.3.3 or 1.3.4 of this Agreement request the Contractor to obtain the decision of the Commissioners on the tax properly chargeable on the Contractor for all supplies of goods and services under this Contract and the Contractor shall forthwith request the Commissioners for such decision. If the Employer disagrees with such decision then, provided the Employer indemnifies and at the option of the Contractor secures the Contractor against all costs and other expenses, the Contractor shall in accordance with the instructions of the Employer make all such appeals against the decision of the Commissioners as the Employer shall request. The Contractor shall account for any costs awarded in his favour in any appeals to which clause 3 of this Agreement applies.

3.2 Where, before any appeal from the decision of the Commissioners can proceed, the full amount of the tax alleged to be chargeable on the Contractor on the supply of goods and services under the Conditions must be paid or accounted for by the Contractor, the Employer shall pay to the Contractor the full amount of tax needed to comply with any such obligation.

3.3 Within 28 days of the final adjudication of an appeal (or of the date of the decision of the Commissioners if the Employer does not request the Contractor to refer such decision to appeal) the Employer or the Contractor, as the case may be, shall pay or refund to the other in accordance with such final adjudication any tax underpaid or overpaid, as the case may be, under the provisions of this Agreement and the provisions of clause 1.3.4 of this Agreement shall apply in regard to the provision of authenticated receipts.

4. Upon receipt by the Contractor from the Employer or by the Employer from the Contractor, as the case may be, of any payment under clause 1.3.3 or 1.3.4 of this Agreement or upon final adjudication of any appeal made in accordance with the provisions of clause 3 of this Agreement and any resultant payment or refund under clause 3.3 of this Agreement, the Employer shall be discharged from any further liability to pay tax to the Contractor in accordance with the VAT Agreement. Provided always that if after the date of discharge under clause 4 of this Agreement the Commissioners decide to correct the tax due from the Contractor on the supply to the Employer of any goods and services by the Contractor under this Contract the amount of any such correction shall be an additional payment by the Employer to the Contractor or by the Contractor to the Employer, as the case may be. The provisions of clause 3 of this Agreement in regard to disagreement with any decision of the Commissioners shall apply to any decision referred to in this proviso.

5. If any dispute or difference is referred to an Arbitrator appointed under article 5 or to a court then insofar as any payment awarded in such arbitration or court proceedings varies the amount certified for payment for goods or services supplied by the Contractor to the Employer under this Contract or is an amount which ought to have been so certified but was not so certified then the provisions of this Agreement shall so far as relevant and applicable apply to any such payments.

6.   The provisions of article 5 shall not apply to any matters to be dealt with under clause 3 of this Agreement.

7.   Notwithstanding any provisions to the contrary elsewhere in the Conditions the Employer shall not be obliged to make any further payment to the Contractor under the Conditions if the Contractor is in default in providing the receipt referred to in clause 1.4 of this Agreement. Provided that clause 7 of this Agreement shall only apply where:

    .1   the Employer can show that he requires such receipt to validate any claim for credit for tax paid or payable under this Agreement which the Employer is entitled to make to the Commissioners, and

    .2   the Employer has paid tax in accordance with the provisional assessment of the Contractor under clause 1 of this Agreement unless he has sustained a reasonable objection under clause 1.2 of this Agreement.

8.   Where clause 27.4 of the Conditions becomes operative there shall be added to the amount allowable or payable to the Employer in addition to the amounts certified by the Architect/the Contract Administrator any additional tax that the Employer has had to pay by reason of determination under clause 27 of the Conditions as compared with the tax the Employer would have paid if the determination had not occurred.

Supplemental Provisions (the VAT Agreement)

These Supplemental provisions are substantially the same as the Supplemental VAT Agreement in the 1963 Form.

Nature of VAT.   VAT is a tax introduced by the Finance Act 1972, as amended and extended by subsequent legislation, and in Orders and Regulations made under the Act. It is a substantial subject and it is not appropriate to deal with it as such here. Reference should be made to the relevant statutes, Orders and Regulations and textbooks thereon, and assistance can be gained from the literature issued by the Commissioners of Customs and Excise who are charged with the management of the tax. There is also Practice Note No. 6 issued by the Joint Contracts Tribunal. The tax is chargeable on the supply of all goods and services unless there is a specific provision to the contrary in the VAT legislation. Relief from VAT arises either by zero rating or because a person supplying exempt goods or services does not have to charge his customers' output tax.

Reason for Supplemental Provisions.   The Joint Contracts Tribunal decided, when VAT was introduced, that the Contract Sum should be exclusive of the tax. Hence there are these Supplemental Provisions to provide for the payment of whatever tax is payable by the Employer to the Contractor and for dealing with difficulties which may arise.

Zero rating.   For a full consideration, reference should be made to Schedule 5 Group 8 of the VAT Act 1983 as amended. As from April 1, 1989 the majority of work supplied by Contractors under this Form will be chargeable on the Contractor at the standard rate of tax. The supply of such services is zero rated if it is made in the course of construction of a building designed as one or more dwellings or intended for use solely for relevant residential purposes (*e.g.* an

Old Peoples' Home) or for a relevant charitable purpose. However, a person does not supply services in the course of the construction of the building if he carries out the conversion, reconstruction, alteration or enlargement of an existing building or constructs an extension or annex to an existing building, so that domestic alterations are chargeable on the Contractor at the standard rate of tax. Certain alteration works carried out to listed buildings are zero rated.

Supplemental Provisions.   If tax is chargeable it has to be charged upon each Interim Payment. Therefore the provisions allow for a provisional assessment and a final statement (clause 1). Liquidated damages are disregarded (clause 2). Provision is made in clause 3 for the Employer to challenge the tax claimed by the Contractor. Effectively he has to indemnify and pay for the litigation to be carried out in the name of the Contractor. The other clauses are ancillary. If there are problems in the Provisions it would be prudent to consult Practice Note No. 6.

Amendment.   The VAT Provisions were amended by Amendment 8 issued in April 1989.

Since the scope of zero rating is now very limited, it will be possible in a great number of building contracts for the Contractor to be aware at the outset of the Contract that all supplies thereunder will be standard rated. Therefore there will be a very considerable reduction in the need, as required hitherto, for each supply to be analysed by the Contractor into what proportion of that supply is chargeable on him at the standard rate and what proportion is chargeable on him at the zero rate.

A new clause 1A was therefore inserted into the Supplemental Provisions by Amendment 8. This provides an alternative system which is for use where the Appendix so states pursuant to an additional sentence in clause 15.2. Where clause 1A is operated, each Interim Certificate and the Final Certificate must have shown thereon an amount calculated at the rate of tax notified by the Contractor. In this way the Employer, where clause 1A applies, will receive Certificates which show the VAT exclusive amount as certified by the Architect and the amount of VAT chargeable. He thus pays one total sum and avoids the problem of the Contractor having to provide the Employer, once he is aware of the amount of the Certificate, with a provisional assessment of the value upon which VAT is due and the Employer having himself to calculate the amount of VAT. There are certain consequential amendments throughout the Supplemental Provisions.

Amendment 7
Issued July 1988

Alter the clauses shown below so that they stand part of the Conditions with the words ruled through deleted, the words underlined inserted, the two definitions inserted in clause 1.3 after the definition of "Appendix" and of "Practical Completion" respectively, and the footnote thereto which reproduces SMM 7 General Rules 10.1 to 10.6 inserted.

Sidenote	*Clause*		
Definitions	1.3	Approximate Quantity:	a quantity in the Contract Bills identified therein as an approximate quantity.*
		provisional sum:	includes a sum provided for work whether or not identified as being for defined or undefined work.*

*Footnote: General Rules 10.1 to 10.6 of the Standard Method of Measurement 7th Edition provide:

10.1
Where work can be described and given in items in accordance with these rules but the quantity of work required cannot be accurately determined, an estimate of the quantity shall be given and identified as an approximate quantity.

10.2
Where work cannot be described and given in items in accordance with these rules it shall be given as a Provisional Sum and identified as for either defined or undefined work as appropriate.

10.3
A Provisional Sum for defined work is a sum provided for work which is not completely designed but for which the following information shall be provided:
(a) The nature and construction of the work.
(b) A statement of how and where the work is fixed to the building and what other work is to be fixed thereto.
(c) A quantity or quantities which indicate the scope and extent of the work.
(d) Any specific limitations and the like identified in Section A35.

10.4
Where Provisional Sums are given for defined work the Contractor will be deemed to have made due allowance in programming, planning and pricing Preliminaries. Any such allowance will only be subject to adjustment in those circumstances where a variation in respect of other work measured in detail in accordance with the rules would give rise to adjustment.

10.5
A Provisional Sum for undefined work is a sum provided for work where the information required in accordance with rule 10.3 cannot be given.

10.6
Where Provisional Sums are given for undefined work the Contractor will be deemed not to have made any allowance in programming, planning and pricing Preliminaries.

2.2 .2 Subject always to clause 2.2.1:
.2.1 the Contract Bills, unless otherwise specifically stated therein in respect of any specified item or items, are to have been prepared in accordance with the Standard Method of Measurement of Building Works, ~~6th Edition~~ <u>7th Edition</u>, published by the Royal Institution of Chartered Surveyors and the Building Employers Confederation;

.2.2   if in the Contract Bills there is any departure from the method of preparation referred to in clause 2.2.2.1 or any error in description or in quantity or omission of items (including any error in or omission of information in any item which is the subject of a provisional sum for defined work*) then such departure or error or omission shall not vitiate this Contract but the departure or error or omission shall be corrected; where the description of a provisional sum for defined work* does not provide the information required by General Rule 10.3 in the Standard Method of Measurement the correction shall be made by correcting the description so that it does provide such information; any such correction under this clause 2.2.2.2 shall be treated as if it were a Variation required by an instruction of the Architect under clause 13.2.

*See footnote to clause 1.3 (Definitions)

13.4   .1.1   Subject to clause 13.4.1.2

all Variations required by the Architect or subsequently sanctioned by him in writing and all work executed by the Contractor in accordance with instructions by the Architect as to the expenditure of provisional sums which are included in the Contract Bills shall be valued by the Quantity Surveyor and all work executed by the Contractor for which an Approximate Quantity is included in the Contract Bills shall be measured and valued by the Quantity Surveyor

and such Valuation (in the Conditions called "the Valuation") shall, unless otherwise agreed by the Employer and the Contractor, be made in accordance with the provisions of clause 13.5.

.1.2   The valuation of Variations to the Sub-Contract Works executed by a Nominated Sub-Contractor in accordance with the instructions of the Architect and of all instructions issued under clause 13.3.2 and all work executed by a Nominated Sub-Contractor for which an Approximate Quantity is included in any bills of quantities included in the Numbered Documents shall (unless otherwise agreed by the Contractor and the Nominated Sub-Contractor concerned with the approval of the Employers be made in accordance with the relevant provisions of Sub-Contract NSC/4 or NSC/4a as applicable.

[clause 13.4.2 unchanged]

13.5   .1   To the extent that the Valuation relates to the execution of additional or substituted work which can properly be valued by measurement or to the execution of work for which an Approximate Quantity is included in the Contract Bills such work shall be measured and shall be valued in accordance with the following rules:

.1.1   where the additional or substituted work is of similar character to, is executed under similar conditions as, and does not significantly change the quantity of, work set out in the Contract Bills the rates and prices for the work so set out shall determine the Valuation;

.1.2   where the additional or substituted work is of similar character to work set out in the Contract Bills but is not executed under similar conditions thereto and/or significantly changes the quantity thereof, the rates and prices for the work so set out shall be the basis for determining the Valuation and the Valuation shall include a fair allowance for such difference in conditions and/or quantity;

.1.3   where the additional or substituted work is not of similar character to work set out in the Contract Bills the work shall be valued at fair rates and prices;

.1.4   where the Approximate Quantity is a reasonably accurate forecast of the quantity of work required the rate or price for the Approximate Quantity shall determine the Valuation;

.1.5   where the Approximate Quantity is not a reasonably accurate forecast of the
        quantity of work required the rate or price for that Approximate Quantity shall
        be the basis for determining the Valuation and the Valuation shall include a fair
        allowance for such difference in quantity.

[clauses 13.5.2, 13.5.3, 13.5.3.1 and 13.5.3.2 unchanged]

.3.3   allowance, where appropriate, shall be made for any addition to or reduction of
        preliminary items of the type referred to in the Standard Method of Measure-
        ment 6th Edition, Section B (Preliminaries) 7th Edition, Section A (Prelimin-
        aries/General Conditions); provided that no such allowance shall be made in
        respect of compliance with an Architect's instruction for the expenditure of a
        provisional sum for defined work.*

[clauses 13.5.4, 13.5.4.1 and 13.5.4.2 unchanged]

*See footnote to clause 1.3 (Definitions).

.5   If
        compliance with any instruction requiring a Variation or
        compliance with any instruction as to the expenditure of a provisional sum for
        undefined work* or
        compliance with any instruction as to the expenditure of a provisional sum for
        defined work* to the extent that the instruction for that work differs from the
        description given for such work in the Contract Bills or
        the execution of work for which an Approximate Quantity is included in the
        Contract Bills to such extent as the quantity is more or less than the quantity
        ascribed to that work in the Contract Bills
        substantially changes the conditions under which any other work is executed, then
        such other work shall be treated as if it had been the subject of an instruction of the
        Architect requiring a Variation under clause 13.2 which shall be valued in accor-
        dance with the provisions of clause 13.

[clause 13.5.6 and proviso to clause 13.5 unchanged]

*See footnote to clause 1.3 (Definitions).

25.4 The following are the Relevant Events referred to in clause 25:

[clauses 25.4.1 to 25.4.4 unchanged]

.5.1   under clause 2.3, 13.2, 13.3 (except compliance with an Architect's instruction
        for the expenditure of a provisional sum for defined work*) 23.2, 34, 35 or 36 or

[clause 25.4.5.2 unchanged]

.6   The Contractor not having received in due time necessary instructions (including
        those for or in regard to the expenditure of provisional sums), drawings, details or
        levels from the Architect for which he specifically applied in writing provided that
        such application was made on a date which having regard to the Completion Date
        was neither unreasonably distant from nor unreasonably close to the date on which
        it was necessary for him to receive the same;

[clauses 25.4.7 to 25.4.13 unchanged]

.14 by reason of the execution of work for which an Approximate Quantity is included in the Contract Bills which is not a reasonably accurate forecast of the quantity of work required.

*See footnote to clause 1.3 (Definitions).

The following are the matters referred to in clause 26.1.

26.2 .1 The Contractor not having received in due time necessary instructions (including those for or in regard to the expenditure of provisional sums), drawings, details or levels from the Architect for which he specifically applied in writing provided that such application was made on a date which having regard to the Completion Date was neither unreasonably distant from nor unreasonably close to the date on which it was necessary for him to receive the same;

[clauses 26.2.2 to 26.2.6 unchanged]

.7 Architect's instructions issued
under clause 13.2 requiring a Variation or
under clause 13.3 in regard to the expenditure of provisional sums (other than ~~work~~ instructions to which clause 13.4.2 refers or an instruction for the expenditure of a provisional sum for defined work*).
.8 the execution of work for which an Approximate Quantity is included in the Contract Bills which is not a reasonably accurate forecast of the quantity of work required.

*See footnote to clause 1.3 (Definitions)

30.6 .2 The Contract Sum shall be adjusted as follows:
There shall be deducted:
[clause 30.6.2.1 unchanged]
.2.2 all provisional sums and the value of all work ~~described as provisional~~ for which an Approximate Quantity is included in the contract Bills;

[clause 30.6.2.3 to 30.6.2.5 unchanged]

There shall be added:
[clauses 30.6.2.6 to 30.6.2.11 unchanged]

.2.12 the amount of the Valuation of work executed by, or the amount of any disbursements by, the Contractor in accordance with instructions of the Architect as to the expenditure of provisional sums included in the Contract Bills and of all work ~~described as provisional~~ for which an Approximate Quantity is included in the Contract Bills;

[clauses 30.6.2.13 to 30.6.2.16 unchanged]

Local Authorities versions only

If this amendment is used to amend a Local Authorities version of the Standard Form the term "the Architect/the Contract Administrator" shall be deemed to be substituted for the term "the Architect."

* * *

692

Amendment 8
Issued April 1989

1: Clause 15 Value added tax—supplemental provisions

15.2   At end **insert** additional sentence:

Clause 1A of the VAT Agreement shall only apply where so stated in the Appendix.[k.1]

Insert new Footnote:

[k.1] Clause 1A can only apply where the Contractor is satisfied at the date the Contract is entered into that his output tax on **all** supplies to the Employer under the Contract will be at either a positive or a zero rate of tax.

On and from April 1, 1989 the supply in respect of a building designed for a "relevant residential purpose" or for a "relevant charitable purpose" (as defined in the legislation which gives statutory effect to the VAT changes operative from April 1, 1989) is only zero rated if the person to whom the supply is made has given to the Contractor a certificate in statutory form: see the VAT leaflet 708 revised 1989. Where a contract supply is zero rated by certificate only the person holding the certificate (usually the Contractor) may zero rate his supply.

Consequential amendment

Appendix   After entry relating to "Date for Completion" **insert**:

VAT Agreement   15.2   Clause 1A of the VAT Agreement
*applies/does not apply [k.1]
*(Delete as applicable)

Insert new Footnote:

[k.1] Clause 1A can only apply where the Contractor is satisfied at the date the Contract is entered into that his output tax on **all** supplies to the Employer under the Contract will be at either a positive or a zero rate of tax.

On and from April 1, 1989 the supply in respect of a building designed for a "relevant residential purpose" or for a "relevant charitable purpose" (as defined in the legislation which gives statutory effect to the VAT changes operative from April 1, 1989) is only zero rated if the person to whom the supply is made has given to the Contractor a certificate in statutory form: see the VAT leaflet 708 revised 1989. Where a contract supply is zero rated by certificate only the person holding the certificate (usually the Contractor) may zero rate his supply.

This footnote repeats footnote [k.1] for clause 15.2.

2: Supplemental Provisions (the VAT Agreement)

After clause 1 **insert** additional clause 1A:

1A.1   Where it is stated in the Appendix pursuant to clause 15.2 of the Conditions that clause 1A of this Agreement applies clauses 1.1 to 1.2.2 inclusive hereof shall not apply unless and until any notice issued under clause 1A.4 hereof becomes effective or unless the Contractor fails to give the written notice required under clause 1A.2. Where clause 1A applies clauses 1 and 1.3 to 8 of this Agreement remain in full force and effect.

1A.2   Not later than 7 days before the date for the issue of the first Interim Certificate the Contractor shall give written notice to the Employer, with a copy to the Architect, of the rate of tax chargeable on the supply of goods and services for which Interim Certificates and the Final Certificate are to be issued. If the rate of tax so notified is varied under statute the Contractor shall, not later than 7 days after the date when such varied rate comes into effect, send to the Employer, with a copy to the Architect, the necessary amendment to the rate given in his written notice and that notice shall then take effect as so amended.

1A.3   For the purpose of complying with the VAT Agreement for the recovery by the Contractor, as stated in clause 15.2 of the Conditions, from the Employer of tax properly chargeable by the Commissioners on the Contractor, an amount calculated at the rate given in the aforesaid written notice (or, where relevant, amended written notice) shall be shown on each Interim Certificate issued by the Architect and, unless the procedure set out in clause 1.3 hereof shall have been completed, on the Final Certificate issued by the Architect. Such amount shall be paid by the Employer to the Contractor or by the Contractor to the Employer as the case may be within the period for payment of certificates set out in clause 30.1.1.1 (Interim Certificates) or clause 30.8 (Final Certificate) as applicable.

1A.4   Either the Employer or the Contractor may give written notice to the other, with a copy to the Architect, stating that with effect from the date of the notice clause 1A shall no longer apply. From that date the provisions of clause 1.1 to 1.2.2 inclusive hereof shall apply in place of clause 1A hereof.

        Consequential amendments

1.1   **Insert** at beginning: "Unless clause 1A applies."

1.3.1   At the beginning **insert** additional sentence:
Where Clause 1A is operated clause 1.3 only applies if no amount of tax pursuant to clause 1A.3 has been shown on the Final Certificate issued by the Architect.

1.4   Line 2, after "clause 1" **insert** "or clause 1A."

2   **Insert** new clause 2.3:

2.3   Where clause 1A is operated the Employer shall pay the tax to which that clause refers notwithstanding any deduction which the Employer may be empowered to make under clause 24 of the Conditions from the amount certified by the Architect in an Interim Certificate or from any balance certified by the Architect as due to the Contractor under the Final Certificate.

4   Line 2, after "or 1.3.4 of this Agreement" **insert** or where clause 1A of this Agreement is operated of any payment of the amount of tax shown upon the Final Certificate issued by the Architect.

7.2   **Redraft** as follows:
7.2   the Employer has

        paid tax in accordance with the provisional assessment of the Contractor under clause 1 of this Agreement unless he has sustained a reasonable objection under clause 1.2 of this Agreement; or

        paid tax in accordance with clause 1A of this Agreement.

Amendment 8

Statutory References

1 Lines 5 and 6 **delete** "Regulation 21(1) of the Value Added Tax (General) Regulations 1972" and **insert** "Regulation 26 of the Value Added Tax (General) Regulations 1985."

1.1 Lines 6 and 7 **delete** "Regulation 21(1)(a) of the Value Added Tax (General) Regulations 1972" and **insert** "Regulation 26 of the Value Added Tax (General) Regulations 1985."

1.4 Lines 3 and 4, **delete** "Regulation 21(2) of the Value Added Tax (General) Regulations 1972" and **insert** "Regulation 12(4) of the Value Added Tax (General) Regulations 1985,"
Line 4 **delete** "Regulation 9(1)" and **insert** "Regulation 13(1)"

Local Authorities versions only

If this Amendment is used to amend a Local Authorities version of the Standard Form the term "the Architect/the Contract Administrator" shall be deemed to be substituted for the term "the Architect."

Amendment 9
Issued July 1990

1: Clause 1.3 Definitions

With Quantities and With Approximate Quantities versions only

In the definition of "Contract Documents," **delete** "see **clause 2.1**" and **insert** "the Contract Drawings, the Contract Bills, the Articles of Agreement, the Conditions and the Appendix"

All Versions

In the definition of "Works" **delete** the meaning given and **insert** "the works briefly described in the **First recital** and shown upon, described by or referred to in the Contract Documents and including any changes made to these works in accordance with this Contract."

Consequential amendments

First recital
Delete "(hereinafter called 'the Works')"

5.5 Line 5 **delete** "Works" and **insert** "site"

8.5 Last line **delete** "Works" and **insert** "site"

10 First line **delete** "Works" and **insert** "site"

With Quantities versions

13.1.1 **Delete** "as shown upon the Contract Drawings and described by or referred to in the Contract Bills";

With Approximate Quantities versions

14.1.1 **Delete** "as shown upon the Contract Drawings and described by or referred to in the Contract Bills";

Without Quantities versions

13.1.1 **Delete** "as shown upon the Contract Drawings and described by or referred to in the Specification/Schedules of Work";

2: Clause 2.1 Contract Documents

With Quantities and With Approximate Quantities versions

Delete "The Contractor shall upon and subject to the Conditions carry out and complete the Works shown upon the Contract Drawings and described by or referred to in the Contract Bills and in the Articles of Agreement, the Conditions and the Appendix (which Drawings, Bills, Articles of Agreement, Conditions and Appendix are in this Contract referred to collectively as "the Contract Documents") in compliance therewith," and **insert** "The Contractor shall upon and subject to the Conditions carry out and complete the Works in compliance with the Contract Documents,"

Without Quantities versions

Delete "The Contractor shall upon and subject to the Conditions carry out and complete the Works shown upon the Contract Drawings and described by or referred to in the Specification/Schedules of Work and in the Articles of Agreement, the Conditions and the Appendix in compliance therewith," and **insert** "The Contractor shall upon and subject to the Conditions carry out and complete the Works in compliance with the Contract Documents,"

3: Clause 8 Materials, goods and workmanship to conform to description, testing and inspection

---

Clause heading
  Delete and **insert "Work, materials and goods."**

8.1   **Delete** side heading and **insert** "Kinds and standards etc."
      Insert as new clause 8.1.3:

   8.1.3   All work shall be carried out in a proper and workmanlike manner.

8.5   Re-number as "8.6"
      Insert as new clause 8.5:

Powers of Architect—non-compliance with clause 8.1.3

8.5   Where there is any failure to comply with clause 8.1.3 in regard to the carrying out of the work in a proper and workmanlike manner the Architect, without prejudice to the generality of his powers, may, after consultation with the Contractor (who shall immediately consult with any relevant Nominated Sub-Contractor), issue such instructions whether requiring a Variation or otherwise as are reasonably necessary as a consequence thereof. To the extent that such instructions are so necessary and notwithstanding clauses 13.4 and 25 and 26 no addition to the Contract Sum shall be made and no extension of time shall be given in respect of compliance by the Contractor with such instruction.

Consequential amendments

35.21   Final words **delete** "workmanship, materials and goods" and **insert** "work, materials and goods."

41.3.3   After "under clause 8.4," **insert** "under clause 8.5."

Correction

41.3.3   Amend to read: "on any dispute or difference under clause 4.1 in regard to a reasonable objection by the Contractor, under clause 8.4, under clause 8.5, under clause 18.1 or under clause 23.3.2 in regard to withholding of consent by the Contractor, and under clauses 25, 32 and 33."

4: Clause 19.2 Sub-letting—Domestic Sub-Contractors—Architect's consent

---

19.2   **Delete** existing text and **insert**:

19.2.1   A person to whom the Contractor sub-lets any portion of the Works other than a Nominated Sub-Contractor is in this Contract referred to as a "Domestic Sub-Contractor."

19.2.2   The Contractor shall not without the written consent of the Architect (which consent shall not be unreasonably withheld) sub-let any portion of the Works. The Contractor shall remain wholly responsible for carrying out and completing the Works in all respects in accordance with clause 2.1 notwithstanding the sub-letting of any portion of the Works.

5: Clause 19.5 Nominated Sub-Contractors

19.5.1   **Delete** existing text and **insert**:

19.5.1   The provisions of this Contract relating to Nominated Sub-Contractors are set out in Part 2 of the Conditions. Save as otherwise expressed in the Conditions the Contractor shall remain wholly responsible for carrying out and completing the Works in all respects in accordance with clause 2.1, notwithstanding the nomination of a sub-contractor to supply and fix materials or goods or to execute work.

6: Clause 22C.1 Existing structures and contents—Specified Perils—Employer to take out and maintain Joint Names Policy

---

Insert new Footnote reference at end of clause 22C.1: [*o.2A*]

After Footnote [*o.2*] **insert** an additional Footnote:

697

[*o.2A*] Some Employers e.g. tenants may not be able to fulfil the obligations in clause 22C.1. If so clause 22C.1 should be amended accordingly.

7: Clause 24 Damages for non-completion

24.1 **Insert** an additional sentence:

"In the event of a new Completion Date being fixed after the issue of such a certificate such fixing shall cancel that certificate and the Architect shall issue such further certificate under clause 24.1 as may be necessary."

24.2.1 Line 1, **delete** "issue of a certificate" and **insert** "issue of any certificate."

Line 3, after "allow to the Employer" **delete** "the whole or such part as may be specified in writing by the Employer of a sum calculated at the rate stated in the Appendix as liquidated and ascertained damages" and **insert** "liquidated and ascertained damages at the rate stated in the Appendix (or at such lesser rate as may be specified in writing by the Employer)."

The text of clause 24.2.1 as so amended is:

24.2.1 Subject to the issue of any certificate under clause 24.1 the Contractor shall, as the Employer may require in writing but not later than the date of the Final Certificate, pay or allow to the Employer liquidated and ascertained damages at the rate stated in the Appendix (or at such lesser rate as may be specified in writing by the Employer) for the period between the Completion Date and the date of Practical Completion and the Employer may deduct the same from any monies due or to become due to the Contractor under this Contract (including any balance stated as due to the Contractor in the Final Certificate) or the Employer may recover the same from the Contractor as a debt.

24.2 **Insert** an additional clause:

24.2.3 Notwithstanding the issue of any further certificate of the Architect under clause 24.1 any requirement of the Employer which has been previously stated in writing in accordance with clause 24.2.1 shall remain effective unless withdrawn by the Employer.

Correction

In clause 25.3.3, line 3, after "Practical Completion" **delete** the comma; after "shall" **insert** a comma.

Local Authorities Versions Only

In this Amendment 9 the term "the Architect" wherever appearing is deemed to have been delected and the term "the Architect/the Contract Administrator" is deemed to have been substituted.

CHAPTER 19

COMMENTARY ON JCT NOMINATED SUB-CONTRACT NSC/4

Introduction.   With their 1980 edition of the Standard Form of Building Contract, the Joint Contracts Tribunal published a series of new Nominated Sub-Contract Documents, and for the first time published Standard Forms of Nominated Sub-Contract. The basic form, for which there is a commentary below, is referred to as Sub-Contract NSC/4. There is an adapted version of the Sub-Contract, referred to as Sub-Contract NSC/4a. The circumstances in which each of these two forms of Sub-Contract are to be used are dealt with in clauses 35.4–35.12 inclusive of the Main Contract and a commentary on the differences between the two forms appears in the commentary to clause 35 of the Main Contract at page 636. NSC/4 is for use where the Sub-Contractor has tendered on Tender NSC/1, and the essential difference between NSC/4 and NSC/4a is that NSC/4a contains in its Appendix material which for NSC/4 will be found in Tender NSC/1.

These Sub-Contracts are the successors of the former "Green Form" of Nominated Sub-Contract. NSC/4 and 4a are drafted to complement the new Form of Main Contract. The "Green Form" should not be used with the 1980 Contract.

Amendments.   NSC/4 has been extensively amended as set out below.
  (1) Amendment 1 issued in April 1983;
  (2) Amendment 2 issued in January 1984;
  (3) Amendment 3 issued in November 1986;
  (4) Amendment 4 issued in July 1987;
  (5) Amendment 5 issued in January 1988;
  (6) Amendment 6 issued in July 1988;
  (7) Amendment 7 issued in July 1988;
  (8) Amendment 8 issued in April 1989.
  (9) Amendment 9 issued in July 1990.
These Amendments, in large part, are complementary to the Amendments to the Main Contract. The important Amendments are discussed below in relation to the relevant clauses. All references to Amendments are to Amendments to NSC/4 unless otherwise stated.

The version of NSC/4 reproduced in this book is that printed in 1988 and incorporating Amendments up to and including Amendment 5. The text of Amendments 6, 7, 8 and 9 is printed after the main text and commentary at page 779.

Articles of Sub-Contract Agreement

made the............... day of .... 19.....
Between

....
of (or whose registered office is situated at)

....
(hereinafter called "the Contractor") of the one part and

....
of (or whose registered office is situated at)

....
(hereinafter called "the Sub-Contractor") of the other part.

Whereas

First
the Sub-Contractor has submitted a tender on Tender NSC/1 for works (hereinafter
called "the Sub-Contract Works") referred to on page 1 thereof and described in
numbered documents annexed thereto (hereinafter called the "Numbered Documents") and which are to be executed as part of works (hereinafter called "the Works")
referred to in Schedule 1 of the tender and being carried out by the Contractor under a
contract as described by or referred to in Schedule 1 of the tender (hereinafter called
"the Main Contract") with
(name of Employer)

....
(hereinafter called "the Employer");

Second
the tender on Tender NSC/1 has been duly completed and signed which tender
(comprising page 1 and the numbered documents and the completed Schedules 1 and 2
thereof) is hereinafter called "the Tender";

Third
the Contractor has retained the original of the Tender and the Sub-Contractor and the
Employer each have a certified copy of the Tender and a further certified copy is
appended hereto;

Fourth
the Sub-Contractor has been given notice of the provisions of the Main Contract as set
out or referred to in Schedule 1 of the Tender except the detailed prices of the
Contractor included in schedules and bills of quantities;

Fifth
the Contractor and the Sub-Contractor by a signature on page 1 of the Tender have
agreed that the provisions of Sub-Contract NSC/4 shall apply unamended to the
Sub-Contract for the Sub-Contract Works;

Sixth
the Architect has nominated the Sub-Contractor in Nomination NSC/3;

Seventh
at the date of the Sub-Contract

700

(A) the Sub-Contractor is/is not [*a*] the user of a current sub-contractor's tax certificate under the provisions of the Finance (No.2) Act 1975 (hereinafter called "the Act") in one of the forms specified in Regulation 15 of the Income Tax (Sub-Contractors in the Construction Industry) Regulations, 1975 and the Schedule thereto (hereinafter called "the Regulations") or any re-enactment or amendment thereof;

(B) the Contractor is/is not [*a*] the user of a current sub-contractor's tax certificate under the Act and the Regulations;

(C) the Employer under the Main Contract is/is not [*a*] a "contractor" within the meaning of the Act and the Regulations.

Now it is hereby agreed as follows

Article 1

1.1 In accordance with the Tender the Sub-Contractor will carry out and complete the Sub-Contract Works.

Article 2

2.1 Where a Sub-Contract Sum is stated on page 1 of the Tender the Contractor will pay to the Sub-Contractor that Sub-Contract Sum or such other sum as shall become payable in accordance with the Sub-Contract.

2.2 Where a Tender Sum is stated on page 1 of the Tender the Contractor will pay to the Sub-Contractor such sum or sums as shall become payable in accordance with the Sub-Contract and the total of such sums is in Sub-Contract NSC/4 called "the Ascertained Final Sub-Contract Sum."

Article 3

3.1 If any dispute or difference, except a dispute or difference under clause 20A or clause 20B to the extent provided in clause 20A.8 or 20B.6, shall arise between the Contractor and Sub-Contractor, whether arising during the execution or after the completion or abandonment of the Sub-Contract Works or after the determination of the employment of the Sub-Contractor under Sub-Contract NSC/4 (whether by breach or in any other manner) it shall be and is hereby referred to arbitration in accordance with clause 38.

| **Attestation** | (A) | Signed by or on behalf of the Contractor in the presence of: [*b*] | _____ |
| | | Signed by or on behalf of the Sub-Contractor in the presence of: [*b*] | _____ |

[*a*] *Delete whichever alternative is not applicable: such deletion must follow the way in which the Tender, Schedule 1, item 10 and Schedule 2, item 7 have been completed unless the position as set out in the Tender has changed by the time NSC/4 is executed: in such circumstances the Seventh recital should be correctly completed and the Tender corrected so that the seventh recital and the Tender are not in conflict.*

[*b*] *Delete if Tender, Schedule 2, item 11 states that Sub-Contract NSC/4 is to be executed under seal and execute as provided in (B).*

(B)	The Common Seal of the Contractor was hereunto affixed in the presence of: [*c*]	(C.S.)
	The Common Seal of the Sub-Contractor was hereunto affixed in the presence of: [*c*]	(C.S.)

Recitals and Articles of Sub-Contract Agreement

The recitals.   The first six recitals essentially state that the procedure for nomination envisaged by clauses 35.4 to 35.10 inclusive of the Main Contract has taken place. [In NSC/4a, the first four recitals essentially state that the procedure for nomination envisaged by clauses 35.4, 35.5, 35.11 and 35.12 of the Main Contract has been operated].

Article 3: Arbitration.   In the original version of NSC/4, Article 3 contained all provisions for Arbitration. This was complementary to Article 5 of the Main Contract. However, by Amendment 4 issued in July 1987, Article 3 was completely redrafted. The effect is that the Article merely states shortly that the method of settling disputes is to be by arbitration. The detailed provisions relating to the appointment and powers of the Arbitrator were transferred to a new clause 38. This clause is discussed below.

1.   Interpretation, definitions, etc.

1.1   Unless otherwise specifically stated a reference in the Articles of Agreement or the Sub-Contract Conditions to any clause means that clause in the Sub-Contract Conditions.

1.2   Sub-Contract NSC/4 is to be read as a whole and the effect or operation of any recital, article or clause in Sub-Contract NSC/4 must therefore unless otherwise specifically stated be read subject to any relevant qualification or modification in any other recital, article or clause in Sub-Contract NSC/4.

1.3   Unless the context otherwise requires or Sub-Contract NSC/4 specifically otherwise provides, the following words and phrases shall have the meanings given below or as ascribed in the article, clause or other provision to which reference is made;

Word or phrase	*Meaning*
Agreement NSC/2:	the Employer/Nominated Sub-Contractor Agreement referred to in the Main Contract Conditions, **clause 35.3**.
Arbitrator:	the person appointed under **clause 38** to be the

[*c*] *Delete if Tender, Schedule 2, item 11 states that Sub-Contract NSC/4 is to be executed under seal and execute as provided in (A).*

	Arbitrator.
Architect:	the person named as the Architect/Contract Administrator in the **Tender, Schedule 1** or any successor appointed or otherwise agreed under the Main Contract Conditions.
Article or Articles of Sub-Contract Agreement:	the Articles of Sub-Contract Agreement in Sub-Contract NSC/4 to which the Sub-Contract Conditions are annexed and references to any recital are to the recitals set out before the Articles.
Ascertained Final Sub-Contract Sum:	see **article 2.2** and **clause 15.2**.
Base Date:	the date set out in the **Tender, Schedule 1, Appendix [A]** or **[B]** whichever is applicable.
Completion Date:	the Completion Date for the Main Contract as defined in **clause 1.3** of the Main Contract Conditions.
Contractor:	the person named as the Main Contractor in the **Tender, Schedule 1.**
Contract Bills:	the Bills of Quantities referred to in the Main Contract Conditions, **first recital** and **clause 1.3**.
Contract Drawings:	the drawings referred to in the Main Contract Conditions, **first recital** and **clause 1.3**.
Date for Completion:	the date stated in the completed Appendix of the Main Contract Conditions set out in the **Tender, Schedule 1, item 10**.
Employer:	the person with whom the Contractor has entered into the Main Contract.
Excepted Risks:	ionising radiations or contamination by radioactivity from any nuclear fuel or from any nuclear waste from the combustion of nuclear fuel, radioactive toxic explosive or other hazardous properties of any explosive nuclear assembly or nuclear component thereof, pressure waves caused by aircraft or other aerial devices travelling at sonic or supersonic speeds.
Joint Names Policy:	a policy of insurance which includes the Contractor and the Employer as the insured.
Main Contract:	the contract between the Contractor and the Employer as described by or referred to in the **Tender, Schedule 1**.
Main Contract Conditions:	the Articles of Agreement, Conditions and completed Appendix of the edition of the Standard Form of Building Contract identified in the **Tender, Schedule 1, items 5 and 10**.
Numbered Documents:	the documents referred to in the **First Recital**.
person:	an individual, firm (partnership) or body corporate.

703

Quantity Surveyor:	the person named as the Quantity Surveyor in the **Tender Schedule 1** or any successor appointed or otherwise agreed under the Main Contract Conditions.
Relevant Event:	see **clause 11.2.5**.
Site Materials:	all unfixed materials and goods delivered to, placed on or adjacent to the Works and intended for incorporation therein.
Specified Perils:	fire, lightning, explosion, storm, tempest, flood, bursting or overflowing of water tanks, apparatus or pipes, earthquake, aircraft and other aerial devices or articles dropped therefrom, riot and civil commotion but excluding Excepted Risks.
Sub-Contract:	the contractual rights and obligations of the Contractor and Sub-Contractor as set out in the Sub-Contract Documents.
Sub-Contract Conditions:	the Conditions in Sub-Contract NSC/4.
Sub-Contract Documents:	see **clause 2.1.1**.
Sub-Contract NSC/4:	the document referred to in the **Tender, Schedule 1, item 1,** comprising the Articles of Sub-Contract Agreement, the Sub-Contract Conditions annexed thereto and the Tender appended thereto.
Sub-Contract Sum:	the sum referred to in **clause 15.1**.
Sub-Contract Works:	the works referred to in the **Tender, page 1**, and described in the Numbered Documents annexed thereto to be executed as part of the Works.
Sub-Contractor:	the person named as the Sub-Contractor in the Tender and/or in the Articles of Sub-Contract Agreement.
Tender:	the duly completed and signed Tender NSC/1 (see **second recital** and **clause 2.1.1**).
Tender Sum:	the sum referred to in **clause 15.2**.
Terminal Dates:	see **clause 6.1.2**.
Variation:	where **clause 15.1** applies the term "Variation" means any of the following changes which are required by an instruction of the Architect:

.1 the alteration or modification of the design, quality or quantity of the Sub-Contract Works as shown in the Sub-Contract Documents including:

.1 the addition, omission or substitution or any work;

.2 the alteration of the kind or standard of any of the materials or goods to be used in the Sub-Contract Works;

704

  .3 the removal from the site of any work, materials or goods executed or brought thereon by the Sub-Contractor for the purposes of the Sub-Contract Works other than work, materials or goods which are not in accordance with the Sub-Contract.

 .2 the imposition by the Employer of any obligations or restrictions in regard to the matters set out in paragraphs .2.1 to .2.4 or the addition to or alteration or omission of any such obligations or restrictions so imposed or imposed by the Employer as set out or referred to in the **Tender, Schedule 1, item 13** in regard to:

  .1 access to the site or use of any specific parts of the site;

  .2 limitations of working space;

  .3 limitations of working hours;

  .4 the execution or completion of the work in any specific order.

where **clause 15.2** applies the term "Variation" has the same meaning but in lines 4 and 5 of this definition **delete** "design, quality or quantity" **insert** "design or quality".

Works: the main contract works referred to in the **Tender, Schedule 1, item 4** including the Sub-Contract Works.

1.4 Where in the Tender, Schedule 1, item 5 it is stated that the Sectional Completion Supplement (JCT Practice Note 1) applies to the Main Contract Conditions and the "Appendix (Sectional Completion Supplement)" and entries therein have been set out in the Tender, Schedule 1, item 10, Sub-Contract NSC/4 shall be deemed to incorporate the modifications set out in the NSC/4 Sectional Completion Supplement at pages 46.1 and 46.2 of this Sub-Contract.

Clause 1: Interpretation, definitions, etc.

This interpretation and definitions clause is the equivalent of clause 1 of the Main Contract. See commentary to that clause at page 483.

The definition of "Variation" is the same as that in clause 13 of the Main Contract, except that there is no equivalent in the Sub-Contract of the exclusion in clause 13.1.3. This definition was redrafted by Amendment 4 issued in July 1987 to make clear that where the Employer has not in the Contract or Sub-Contract Documents imposed any obligations or restrictions of the type identified in paragraph 2 of the definition, such obligations may nevertheless be imposed by a Variation instruction. This is complementary with the identical change to the Main Contract.

The following definitions were added by Amendment 3 issued in November 1986: Excepted Risks, Joint Names Policy, Site Materials, Specified Perils and

705

Terminal Dates. By Amendment 4 issued in July 1987 the Architect became defined as Architect/Contract Administrator and Date of Tender was changed to Base Date. By Amendment 9 issued in July 1990, the definition of Sub-Contract Works was redrafted to make clear that this term means not only the works referred to in the Tender, page 1 and described in the Numbered Documents but also any changes made thereto in accordance with the Sub-Contract Conditions.

In the Sub-Contract there is no power of nomination, but clause 2.3.1 contemplates that the Sub-Contractor may be required to enter into a sub-sub-contract or a contract of sale with a person or persons other than the Contractor.

Clause 1.4. The Sectional Completion Supplement is not reproduced in this book.

2. Sub-Contract Documents

2.1 .1 The Tender (comprising page 1 and the Numbered Documents annexed thereto and the completed Schedules 1 and 2 and any documents annexed thereto or referred to therein) and the Sub-Contract NSC/4 shall constitute the Sub-Contract Documents.

      .2 Nothing contained in any descriptive schedule or other like document issued in connection with and for use in carrying out the Sub-Contract Works shall impose any obligation beyond those imposed by the Sub-Contract Documents.

2.2 If any conflict appears between the terms of Sub-Contract NSC/4 and any other Sub-Contract Documents apart from the terms of the Main Contract as described by or referred to in the Tender, Schedule 1 the terms of Sub-Contract NSC/4 shall prevail. If any conflict appears between the terms of the Main Contract as described by or referred to in the Tender, Schedule 1 and the other Sub-Contract Documents, the terms of the Main Contract as so described or referred to shall prevail.

2.3 .1 If in the Sub-Contract Documents the Sub-Contractor is required to enter into a sub-contract or a contract of sale with a person or persons other than the Contractor, then clauses 2.3.2 to 2.3.4 shall apply.

      .2 If the said sub-sub-contract or contract of sale in any way restricts, limits or excludes the liability of the sub-sub-contractor or supplier in respect of work or services carried out or the goods or materials supplied then the Sub-Contractor shall forthwith inform the Contractor in writing of the restriction, limitation or exclusion who shall thereupon send a copy of such information to the Architect.

      .3 Where the Contractor, and the Architect through the Contractor, have specifically approved in writing the said restriction, limitation or exclusion, the liability of the Sub-Contractor to the Contractor in respect of the said work, services, materials or goods shall be restricted, limited or excluded to the same extent as the liability of the sub-sub-contractor or supplier to the Sub-Contractor is restricted, limited or excluded.

      .4 The Sub-Contractor shall not be obliged to enter into a sub-sub-contract or a contract of sale as aforesaid until the specific written approval referred to above has been obtained.

Clause 2: Sub-Contract Documents

Clause 2.1. The Sub-Contract Documents are the Tender, with its Schedules and documents annexed to it, and Sub-Contract NSC/4 itself. Tender NSC/1 contemplates that Drawings, Specifications, Bills of Quantities or a Schedule of Rates may be annexed to it, and, if they are, they will be Sub-Contract Documents. Clause 18 contains provisions if Bills of Quantities are a Sub-Contract Document.

Clause 2.2. *"If any conflict appears ..."*
With the exception of the terms of the Main Contract as described by or referred to in the Tender, NSC/4 is the prevailing document. The terms of the Main Contract as described by or referred to in the Tender are to prevail over other Sub-Contract Documents. It is unlikely that there will be any conflict between the terms of the Main Contract and NSC/4 itself, but the terms of the Main Contract might be differently described in, for example, the introduction to a Sub-Contract specification. Note that this clause does not refer to the terms of the Main Contract simpliciter, but to the terms of the Main Contract as described by or referred to in the Tender. Schedule 1 of Tender NSC/1 provides for extensive transcription of details of the terms of the Main Contract. If mistakes are made in this transcription, it seems that the mistakes will be perpetuated into the Sub-Contract, unless the Sub-Contract could be rectified.[1]

Clause 2.3.2. *"if the said sub-sub-contract or contract of sale ... restricts, limits or excludes the liability ..."*
This clause contemplates the possibility that the Sub-Contract Documents may require the Sub-Contractor to enter into a sub-Sub-Contract or a contract of sale with particular persons. The Sub-Contractor is not obliged to do so, where the sub-Sub-Contract or contract of sale contains terms restricting, limiting or excluding the liability of the sub-Sub-Contractor or the supplier, until the specific written approval of the Contractor and the Architect has been obtained. If that approval is obtained, the Sub-Contractor's own liability to the Contractor is to be equivalently restricted, limited or excluded. It is unclear how specific a requirement is needed in the Sub-Contract Documents for these provisions to apply. Reference to clauses 36.1 and 36.5 of the Main Contract might indicate that the specification of a "sole supplier" might be sufficient. It should, however, be noted that, if the construction of clause 36.5 of the Main Contract suggested in the commentary to clause 36 is correct, the Architect's power to approve restrictions, limitations or exclusions of liability is wider under clause 2.3 of NSC/4 than for Nominated Suppliers under clause 36.5 of the Main Contract.

---

[1] For rectification, see p. 266.

3. **Sub-Contract Sum—additions or deductions—computation of Ascertained Final Sub-Contract Sum**

Where in Sub-Contract NSC/4 it is provided that an amount is to be added to or subtracted from the Sub-Contract Sum or dealt with by adjustment of the Sub-Contract Sum or included in the computation of the Ascertained Final Sub-Contract Sum, then as soon as such amount is ascertained in whole or in part such ascertained amount shall be taken into account in the computation of the interim payment next following such whole or partial ascertainment.

Clause 3: Sub-Contract Sum—additions or deductions—computation of Ascertained Final Sub-Contract Sum

This clause is the Sub-Contract equivalent to clause 3 of the Main Contract. See commentary on that clause at page 491.

4. **Execution of the Sub-Contract Works—instructions of Architect—directions of Contractor**

4.1 .1 The Sub-Contractor shall carry out and complete the Sub-Contract Works in compliance with the Sub-Contract Documents and in conformity with all reasonable directions and requirements of the Contractor (so far as they may apply) regulating for the time being the due carrying out of the Works.

.2 All materials and goods shall, so far as procurable, be of the kinds and standards described in the Sub-Contract Documents provided that where and to the extent that approval of the quality and standards of materials and goods is a matter for the opinion of the Architect such quality and standards shall be to the reasonable satisfaction of the Architect.

.3 All workmanship shall be of the standards described in the Sub-Contract Documents, or, to the extent that no such standards are specified in the Sub-Contract Documents, shall be of a standard appropriate to the Sub-Contract Works provided that where and to the extent that approval of workmanship is a matter for the opinion of the Architect such workmanship shall be to the reasonable satisfaction of the Architect.

.4 The Sub-Contractor shall continually keep upon the Sub-Contract Works while such Sub-Contract Works are being executed a competent person-in-charge and any instruction of the Architect given to him by the Contractor, or any direction given to him by the Contractor, shall be deemed to have been issued to the Sub-Contractor.

.5 If the Sub-Contractor shall find any discrepancy in, or divergence between any two or more of, the documents referred to in clause 2.3 of the Main Contract Conditions, including a divergence between parts of any one of them or between documents of the same description, he shall immediately give to the Contractor a written notice specifying the discrepancy or divergence, and the Contractor shall forthwith send that notice to the Architect and request instructions under clause 2.3 of the Main Contract Conditions.

4.2 The Contractor shall forthwith issue to the Sub-Contractor any written instruction of the Architect issued under the Main Contract affecting the Sub-Contract Works (including the ordering of any Variation therein); and may issue any reasonable direction in writing to the Sub-Contractor in regard to the Sub-Contract Works.

Clause 4—Execution of the Sub-Contract Works

4.3 1. The Sub-Contractor shall forthwith comply with any instruction or direction referred to in clause 4.2 save that where such instruction is one requiring a Variation within the definition of "Variation" clause 1.3, paragraph .2, the Sub-Contractor need not comply to the extent that he makes reasonable objection in writing to such compliance. Upon receipt by the Contractor of any written objection by the Sub-Contractor, the Contractor shall thereupon submit that objection to the Architect.

.2.1 Where any work, materials or goods are not in accordance with this Sub-Contract ("non-complying work") and the provisions of clause 8.4 of the Main Contract Conditions ("Main Contract 8.4") are operated in respect of such non-complying work clauses 4.3.3, 4.3.4, 4.3.5 and 4.3.7 shall apply.
.2.2 Where the Architect consults with the Contractor as required by Main Contract 8.4 the Contractor shall immediately, as required by Main Contract 8.4.2 and 8.4.3, consult with the Sub-Contractor and report the outcome of such consultation to the Architect in writing with a copy of that report to the Sub-Contractor.

.3 The Sub-Contractor shall comply

.3.1 with any instructions under Main Contract 8.4.1 issued to the Sub-Contractor by the Contractor pursuant to clause 4.2; and
.3.2 with any instructions under Main Contract 8.4.3 issued to the Sub-Contractor by the Contractor pursuant to clause 4.2 requiring a Variation to the extent that they are reasonably necessary as a consequence of an instruction under Main Contract 8.4.1; and to the extent that such instructions are so necessary and notwithstanding clause 16 (*valuation of Variations and provisional sum work*) and clause 17 (*valuation of all work comprising the Sub-Contract Works*), clause 11.2 (*extension of Sub-Contract time*) and clause 13.1 (*matters affecting regular progress—direct loss and/or expense*) no adjustment shall be made to the Sub-Contract Sum or be included in the computation of the Ascertained Final Sub-Contract Sum and no extension of time shall be given.
.4.1 Where the Architect under Main Contract 8.4.2 allows all or any non-complying work to remain the Contractor shall so inform the Sub-Contractor in writing and an appropriate deduction shall be made from the Sub-Contract Sum or in the computation of the Ascertained Final Sub-Contract Sum.
.4.2 The Sub-Contractor shall comply with any instructions under Main Contract 8.4.3 issued to the Sub-Contractor by the Contractor pursuant to clause 4.2 requiring a Variation to the extent that they are reasonably necessary as a consequence of the Architect allowing all or any non-complying work to remain; and to the extent that such instructions are so necessary and notwithstanding clause 16 (*valuation of Variations and provisional sum work*) and clause 17 (*valuation of all work comprising the Sub-Contract Works*), clause 11.2 (*extension of Sub-Contract time*) and clause 13.1 (*matters affecting regular progress—direct loss and/or expense*) no adjustment shall be made to the Sub-Contract Sum or be included in the computation of the Ascertained Final Sub-Contract Sum and no extension of time shall be given.

.5 Where there is non-complying work the Sub-Contractor shall comply with such instructions issued by the Architect pursuant to Main Contract 8.4.4 and issued to the Sub-Contractor by the Contractor pursuant to clause 4.2 to open up for inspection or to test as are reasonable in all the circumstances to establish to the reasonable satisfaction of the Architect the likelihood or extent, as appropriate to the circumstances, of any further similar non-compliance. To the extent that such instructions are so reasonable, whatever the results of the opening up for inspection or test and notwithstanding clause 8.3 of the Main Contract Conditions and clause 13.1 (*matters affecting regular progress—direct loss and/or expense*), no addition

709

shall be made to the Sub-Contract Sum nor shall any monies be included in the computation of the Ascertained Final Sub-Contract Sum in respect of such instructions. Clause 11.2.5.5.2 shall apply unless as stated therein the inspection or test showed that the work, materials or goods were not in accordance with this Sub-Contract.

.6.1   Where compliance by the Contractor or by any other Nominated Sub-Contractor with any instruction or other exercise of a power of the Architect under Main Contract 8.4 necessarily results in work properly executed or materials or goods properly fixed or supplied under this Sub-Contract having to be taken down and/or re-executed or re-fixed or re-supplied, the Sub-Contractor shall, in accordance with directions, so take down and/or re-execute or re-fix or re-supply if the direction so to do is issued at any time before the date of practical completion of the Sub-Contract Works (as referred to in clause 14.2). A copy of such directions shall be sent forthwith by the Contractor to the Nominated Sub-Contractor in respect of whose non-complying work the Architect issued instructions or allowed non-complying work to remain under Main Contract 8.4.

.6.2   The Sub-Contractor shall be paid by the Contractor on the basis of a fair valuation for any taking down and/or re-execution or re-fixing or re-supply directed under clause 4.3.6.1 and which has been carried out by the Sub-Contractor and the provisions of clause 11.2 (*extension of Sub-Contract time*) and clause 13.2 (*matters affecting regular progress—direct loss and/or expense*) shall apply in respect of any compliance with directions to which clause 4.3.6.1 refers. The payment to which clause 4.3.6.2 refers shall be made by the Contractor within 14 days after the end of the month during which the taking down and/or re-execution or re-fixing or re-supply was carried out.

.7   The Sub-Contractor shall indemnify the Contractor in respect of any liability, and reimburse the Contractor for any costs, which the Contractor has incurred as a direct result of compliance by the Sub-Contractor with clauses 4.3.3 and/or 4.3.4 and/or 4.3.5 or arising out of the operation of clause 4.3.6 in other Nominated Sub-Contracts but only to the extent that such operation is a direct result of the provisions of Main Contract 8.4 being operated in respect of non-complying work.

4.4   If the Architect or Contractor purports to give any instruction or direction referred to in clause 4.2 otherwise than in writing to the Sub-Contractor or his person-in-charge then such instruction or direction shall be of no immediate effect but shall be confirmed in writing by the Sub-Contractor to the Contractor within 7 days and if not dissented from in writing by the Contractor within 7 days from the receipt of the Sub-Contractor's confirmation shall take effect as from the expiration of the latter said 7 days. Provided always:

.1   that if the Contractor within 7 days of such instruction or direction otherwise than in writing having been given shall himself confirm the same in writing, then the Sub-Contractor shall not be obliged to confirm as aforesaid and the said instruction or direction shall take effect as from the date of the Contractor's confirmation; and

.2   if neither the Contractor nor the Sub-Contractor shall confirm such an instruction or direction in the manner and at the time aforesaid but the Sub-Contractor shall nevertheless comply with the same, then the Contractor may confirm the same in writing (and must if the Architect has confirmed in writing in similar circumstances under the Main Contract) at any time prior to the final payment of the Sub-Contractor in accordance with Sub-Contract NSC/4 and the said instruction or direction shall thereupon be deemed to have taken effect on the date on which it was issued.

4.5   If within 7 days after receipt of a written notice from the Contractor requiring compliance with a direction of the Contractor the Sub-Contractor does not begin to comply therewith, then the Contractor may, if so permitted by the Architect, employ and pay other persons to comply with such direction and all costs incurred in connection with such employment may be deducted from any monies due or to become due to the Sub-Contractor under the Sub-Contract or shall be recoverable from the Sub-Contract as a debt.

4.6   Upon receipt of what purports to be an instruction of the Architect issued in writing by the Contractor to the Sub-Contractor, the Sub-Contractor may require the Contractor to request the Architect to specify in writing the provision of the Main Contract which empowers the issue of the said instruction. The Contractor shall forthwith comply with any such requirement and deliver to the Sub-Contractor a copy of the Architect's answer to the Contractor's request. If the Sub-Contractor shall thereafter comply with the said instruction then the issue of the same shall be deemed for all the purposes of the Sub-Contract to have been empowered by the provision of the Main Contract specified by the Architect in answer to the Contractor's request. Provided always that if before compliance the Sub-Contractor shall have made a written requirement to the Contractor to request the Employer to concur in the appointment of an Arbitrator under the Main Contract Conditions in order that it may be decided whether the provision specified by the Architect empowers the issue of the said instruction then, subject to the Sub-Contractor giving the Contractor such indemnity and security as the Contractor may reasonably require, the Contractor shall allow the Sub-Contractor to use the Contractor's name and if necessary will join with the Sub-Contractor in arbitration proceedings at the instigation of the Sub-Contractor to decide the matter as aforesaid.

Clause 4: Execution of Sub-Contract Works—instructions of Architect—directions of Contractor

Generally.   Clause 4 in substance reproduces in the Sub-Contract context equivalent provisions of the Main Contract as follows:

clauses 4.1.1 to 4.1.3 are the equivalent of Main Contract clauses 2.1 and 8.1;
clauses 4.1.4 and 4.3.5A are the equivalent of Main Contract clauses 8.1.3 and 8.5.
clause 4.1.5 is the equivalent of Main Contract clause 10;
clauses 4.2 to 4.5 inclusive are the equivalent of Main Contract clauses 4.1, 4.3 and 8.4;
clause 4.6 is the equivalent of Main Contract clause 4.2.

See the commentary on those Main Contract clauses and in particular see commentary to Main Contract clause 4 on the question of reasonable objection to a Variation instruction under clause 13.1.2 of the Main Contract.

Amendments.   Clauses 4.1 and 4.3 were substantially redrafted by Amendment 4 issued in July 1987, Amendment 5 issued in January 1988, and Amendment 9 issued in July 1990. The latter Amendment mirrors the redrafting of clause 8 of the Main Contract by Amendment 9.

Clause 4.1.   Clause 4.1.1 of the original version of NSC/4 has been divided by Amendment into three sub-clauses 4.1.1 to 4.1.3. These changes are

711

complementary to the redrafted clause 8.1 of the Main Contract. The requirement that all materials and goods should be of the kinds and standard
described in the Sub-Contract Documents is now qualified by the words "so
far as procurable" (clause 4.1.2). The requirement for workmanship is that it
should be "of a standard appropriate to the Sub-Contract Works" if no
standards are specified in the Sub-Contract Documents. Clause 4.1.2 is consequentially renumbered 4.1.4. Clause 4.1.5 is a new sub-clause providing a
procedure for notices to deal with discrepancies or divergencies between
documents.

Clause 4.1.4. This new clause, inserted by Amendment 9 issued in July
1990, makes express the implied obligation of the Sub-Contractor to carry out
work in a proper and workmanlike manner.

Clause 4.2. *"the Contractor ... may issue any reasonable direction ..."*
In addition to passing on to the Sub-Contractor Architect's instructions
issued under the Main Contract, the Contractor is entitled to issue "any
reasonable direction" to the Sub-Contractor. By Clause 4.3, the Sub-Contractor is required to comply with any such direction, and this is to be contrasted
with directions given to the Contractor by the clerk of works under clause 12 of
the Main Contract. See the commentary on Main Contract clause 12. The
subject matter of Main Contractor's "directions" must as a matter of construction be different from matters which can be the subject of Architect's instructions under the Main Contract. Thus, for example, it is submitted that orders
to remove defective work (see clause 8.4.1 of the Main Contract) or changes
coming within the expanded definition of Variations (see clause 13.1 of the
Main Contract and 1.3 of the Sub-Contract) cannot come within the ambit of
Main Contractor's "directions." For this reason, and because additionally the
Sub-Contract does not provide for any financial consequence of Main Contractor's directions, it seems that they will in practice be limited to matters
such as the general organisation of the site.

Clause 4.3. This clause was substantially amended by Amendment 5
issued in January 1988 to bring into the Sub-Contract the revised provisions of
clause 8.4 of the Main Contract about non-conforming work. For commentary
on these revised provisions, see commentary to clause 8.4.

Clause 4.3.5A. This new clause was inserted by Amendment 9 issued in
July 1990. It requires the Sub-Contractor to comply with any instruction
issued by the Architect under Main Contract Clause 8.5 in respect of non-
compliance with Clause 4.1.4. To the extent that such instructions are reasonably necessary in consequence of such non-compliance, the Sub-Contractor is
entitled neither to extension of time nor to additional remuneration. Note that:

(1) the indemnity provisions of Clause 4.3.7 apply also to any breach by the
    Sub-Contractor of the new obligation in Clause 4.1.4 and resultant
    compliance with an instruction pursuant to Main Contract Clause 8.5.

(2) an arbitration concerning a dispute under the new Clause 4.3.5A may be opened before Practical Completion.

Clause 4.6. " . . . *the Contractor shall allow the Sub-Contractor to use the Contractor's name* . . ."

Here, as in clauses 11.3 and 21.7 of the Sub-Contract, where the Sub-Contractor's rights or liabilities depend upon the operation of terms of the Main Contract, the Sub-Contract enables the Sub-Contractor, subject to suitable indemnity and security, to take arbitration proceedings under the Main Contract in the name of the Main Contractor. See also clause 22 of the Sub-Contract. It is thought that in principle this procedure, which is analogous to an insurer exercising by subrogation the rights of his insured, would be held to be effective. In practice, however, complications are likely to arise if, as may happen, the Contractor's own interest in the subject matter of the dispute is other than neutral.

An example of such problems is the case of *Lorne Stewart* v. *William Sindall*.[2] Lorne Stewart were Nominated Sub-Contractors to Sindall under the old "Green Form." Three arbitrations were commenced:

(1) a Main Contract arbitration between Sindall and the Employer;
(2) a "name borrowing" arbitration commenced by Lorne Stewart in the name of Sindall against the Employer;
(3) a Sub-Contract Arbitration between Lorne Stewart and Sindall.

Arbitration (1) was settled, but (2) and (3) remained active. Considerable difficulties arose in relation to discovery. It was held that there was an implied term of the Sub-Contract that: "[u]pon the sub-contractor exercising its right to use the main contractor's name in an arbitration against the employer, the main contractor will render to the sub-contractor such assistance and co-operation as may be necessary in order to enable the sub-contractor properly to conduct the said arbitration." In the name borrowing arbitration, it was held that the Arbitrator was entitled to order discovery against both Lorne Stewart and Sindall on the basis that this was effectively a tripartite arbitration agreement.[3]

It is to be hoped that the provisions for multipartite arbitrations to be found in clause 41 of the Main Contract and clause 38 of the Sub-Contract may help to reduce the procedural problems raised by Name Borrowing Arbitrations.

5.   Sub-Contractor's liability under incorporated provisions of the Main Contract

5.1   The Sub-Contractor shall:

---

[2] (1986) 35 B.L.R. 109.
[3] The Judge also reached conclusions in relation to the use that could be made of documents in one arbitration that were privileged in another arbitration. Those conclusions are now open to considerable doubt in view of the decision of the House of Lords in *Rush & Tompkins* v. *G.L.C.* [1989] A.C. 1280 (H.L.).

.1 observe, perform and comply with all the provisions of the Main Contract as described by or referred to in the Tender, Schedule 1 on the part of the Contractor to be observed, performed and complied with so far as they relate and apply to the Sub-Contract Works (or any portion of the same). Without prejudice to the generality of the foregoing, the Sub-Contractor shall observe, perform, and comply with the following provisions of the Main Contract Conditions: clauses 6, 7, 9, 16, 32, 33 and 34; and

.2 indemnify and save harmless the Contractor against and from:

.2.1 any breach, non-observance or non-performance by the Sub-Contractor or his servants or agents of any of the provisions of the Main Contract referred to in clause 5.1.1; and

.2.2 any act or omission of the Sub-Contractor or his servants or agents which involves the Contractor in any liability to the Employer under the provisions of the Main Contract referred to in clause 5.1.1.

5.2 Nothing contained in the Sub-Contract Documents shall be construed so as to impose any liability on the Sub-Contractor in respect of any act or omission or default on the part of the Employer, the Contractor, his other Sub-Contractors or their respective servants or agents nor (except by way of and in the terms of the Agreement NSC/2) create any privity of contract between the Sub-Contractor and the Employer or any other Sub-Contractor.

Clause 5: Sub-Contractor's liability under incorporated provisions of the Main Contract

Generally. This clause obliges the Sub-Contractor so to perform his obligations under the Sub-Contract that his performance shall *pro tanto* constitute performance of the Main Contractor's obligations under the Main Contract. The Sub-Contractor indemnifies the Main Contractor against failure to achieve such performance.

Clause 5.1. *"The Sub-Contractor shall . . . comply with all the provisions of the Main Contract . . ."*

Consistently with clause 2.2, it is the terms of the Main Contract as transcribed into Schedule 1 of the Tender that are to be complied with (see commentary to Sub-Contract clause 2). The Sub-Contractor does not, of course, become a party to the Main Contract (see clause 5.2), and his obligation to comply with the terms of the Main Contract, being an obligation to the Contractor, only extends so far as the provisions of the Main Contract relate and apply to the Sub-Contract Works. The second sentence of clause 5.1.1 refers to seven specific Main Contract clauses which the Sub-Contractor is to comply with. These are, it seems, given what might appear to be misleading prominence because they deal with matters which are not specifically dealt with elsewhere in the Sub-Contract.[4]

---

[4] For a case where the Court of Appeal considered the effect of incorporating terms of a Main Contract into a Sub-Contract, see *Brightside Kilpatrick* v. *Mitchell Construction (1973)* [1975] 2 Lloyd's Rep. 493 (C.A.).

Clause 5.1.2. *"The Sub-Contractor shall ... indemnify ... the Contractor ..."*

This important indemnity clause gives the Main Contractor rights in excess of the ordinary right to claim damages for breach of clause 5.1.1. In particular, the period of limitation may be extended.[5]

6.   Injury to persons and property—indemnity to Contractor

6.1   .1   In clauses 6 to 10 inclusive the phrase in column 1 shall have the meaning set out in column 2:

Column 1	**Column 2**
the Contractor or any person for whom the Contractor is responsible	the Contractor, his servants or agents or any person employed or engaged upon or in connection with the Works or any part thereof his servants or agents (other than the Sub-Contractor or any person for whom the Sub-Contractor is responsible), or any other person who may properly be on the site upon or in connection with the Works or any part thereof, his servants or agents; but such persons shall not include the Employer or any person employed, engaged or authorised by him or by any local authority or statutory undertaker executing work solely in pursuance of its statutory rights or obligations;
the Sub-Contractor or any person for whom the Sub-Contractor is responsible	the Sub-Contractor, his servants or agents, or any person employed or engaged by the Sub-Contractor upon or in connection with the Sub-Contract Works or any part thereof, his servants or agents or any other person who may properly be on the site upon or in connection with the Sub-Contract Works or any part thereof, his servants or agents; but such persons shall not include the Contractor or any person for whom the Contractor is responsible nor the Employer or any person employed, engaged or authorised by him or by any local authority or statutory undertaker executing work solely in pursuance of its statutory rights or obligations.

.2   The term "Terminal Dates" shall mean the dates identified in clause 6.4.

6.2   The Sub-Contractor shall be liable for, and shall indemnify the Contractor against, any expense, liability, loss, claim or proceedings whatsoever arising under any statute or at common law in respect of personal injury to or the death of any person whomsoever arising out of or in the course of or caused by the carrying out of the Sub-Contract Works except to the extent that the same is due to any act or neglect, breach of statutory duty, omission or default of the Contractor or any person for whom the Contractor is responsible or of the Employer or any person for whom the Employer is responsible including the persons employed or otherwise engaged by the Employer to whom clause 29 of the Main Contract Conditions refers or of any local authority or statutory undertaker executing work solely in pursuance of its statutory rights or obligations.

6.3   The Sub-Contractor shall, subject to clause 6.4 and where applicable clause 8C.1.1, be liable for, and shall indemnify the Contractor against, any expense, liability, loss, claim

---

[5] See p. 371.

715

or proceedings in respect of any injury or damage whatsoever to any property real or personal including the Works in so far as such injury or damage arises out of or in the course of or by reason of the carrying out of the Sub-Contract Works, and to the extent that the same is due to any negligence, breach of statutory duty, omission or default of the Sub-Contractor or any person for whom the Sub-Contractor is responsible.

6.4 The liability and indemnity to the Contractor referred to in clause 6.3 shall not include any liability or indemnity in respect of injury or damage to the Works and/or Site Materials (nor, where clause 8C applies, injury or damage to the existing structures and the contents thereof owned by the Employer or for which the Employer is responsible) by one or more of the Specified Perils, whether or not caused by the negligence, breach of statutory duty, omission or default of the Sub-Contractor or any person for whom the Sub-Contractor is responsible, for the period up to and including whichever of the following is the earlier date:

> the date of issue of the certificate of practical completion of the Sub-Contract Works (as referred to in clause 14.2) or
> the date of determination of the employment of the Contractor (whether or not the validity of that determination is contested) under clause 22C.4.3 (where applicable) or clause 27 or clause 28 of the Main Contract Conditions.

Clause 6: Injury to persons and property—indemnity to Contractor

Generally. This clause is the Sub-Contract equivalent of clause 20 of the Main Contract. See commentary on that clause at page 543. The clause was substantially amended by Amendment 3 issued in November 1986. This mirrors the insurance and liability amendments to the Main Contract.

Clause 6.2. This provides for the liability of and indemnity by the Sub-Contractor for personal injury or death. It contains materially identical amendments to those to clause 20.1 of the Main Contract.

Clauses 6.3 and 6.4. These clauses provide for liability and indemnity by the Sub-Contractor for damage to property. As amended, the provisions may be summarised as follows:

(1) The Sub-Contractor is liable to indemnify the Contractor in respect of any damage to any property including the Works to the extent that this is due to the negligence, etc., of the Sub-Contractor;

(2) However, this liability is qualified in two respects:

(a) the Sub-Contractor is not so liable for damage to the Works by a Specified Peril until the earlier of two dates, namely the Practical Completion of the Sub-Contract Works or the date of determination of the employment of the Contractor. These dates are known throughout the Sub-Contract as the "Terminal Dates";

(b) The liability is qualified by the words "subject to . . . where applicable clause 8C.1.1 . . . ." which refers to the insurance of existing structures required by clause 22C of the Main Contract. For the reasons given in the commentary to Main Contract clause 20, it is

716

thought that the Employer bears the sole risk of damage to existing structures by a Specified Peril.

7.   Insurance against injury to persons or property

7.1   Without prejudice to his obligation to indemnify the Contractor under clause 6, the Sub-Contractor shall take out and maintain insurance which shall comply with clause 7.2 in respect of claims arising out of his liability referred to in clauses 6.2 and 6.3 as modified by clause 6.4, except that the obligation of the Sub-Contractor to take out and maintain insurance in respect of his liability for injury or damage to property as stated in clause 6.3 shall not extend to taking out and maintaining insurance for injury and damage to the Sub-Contract Works by a risk other than a Specified Peril up to and including whichever is the earlier of the Terminal Dates.[d]

7.2   The insurance in respect of claims for personal injury to, or the death of any person under a contract of service or apprenticeship with the Sub-Contractor and arising out of and in the course of such person's employment, shall comply with the Employer's Liability (Compulsory Insurance) Act, 1969, and any statutory orders made thereunder or any amendment or re-enactment thereof. For all other claims to which clause 7.1 applies the insurance cover shall be not less than[e] the sum stated in the Sub-Contract Documents for any one occurrence or series of occurrences arising out of one event.

7.3   Notwithstanding the provisions of clauses 6.2, 6.3 and 7.1 the Sub-Contractor shall not be liable either to indemnify the Contractor or to insure against any personal injury to or the death of any person or any damage, loss or injury caused to the Works, work executed, Site Materials, the site or any property by the effect of an Excepted Risk.

Clause 7: Insurance against injury to person or property

This clause is the Sub-Contract equivalent of clause 21.1.1 of the Main Contract. See commentary on that clause at page 549. The Sub-Contract equivalent of clause 21.1.2 and 21.1.3 is at clause 9 of the Sub-Contract.

Clause 7 was amended by Amendment 3 issued in November 1986. These are essentially drafting amendments of no great consequence. The new clause 7.3 makes clear that the Sub-Contractor is not liable to indemnify the Contractor or to insure against injury to person or property by the effect of an Excepted Risk.

---

[d] *The Sub-Contractor has the benefit of the main contract works insurance for loss or damage by the Specified Perils to the Sub-Contract Works but not for other risks e.g. subsidence, impact, theft or vandalism. The insurance to which clause 7.1 refers in respect of injury or damage to property is a third party or public liability policy; such policy will not however give cover for any property such as the Sub-Contract Works while they are in the custody and control of the Sub-Contractor. For this reason the obligation to insure under clause 7.1 is modified by this sentence. As the Sub-Contractor is liable for those other risks if they cause loss or damage to the Sub-Contract Works he may well consider that he needs to take out a works insurance to provide such cover which he does not get under the main contract works insurance, See also footnote [f].*

[e] *The Sub-Contractor may, if he wishes, insure for a sum greater than that stated in the Sub-Contract Documents.*

8.   Loss or damage to the Works and to the Sub-Contract Works

8.1   Clause 8A shall apply where it is stated in the Sub-Contract Documents that clause 22A shall apply to the Main Contract; clause 8B shall apply where it is stated in those Documents that clause 22B shall apply to the Main Contract; clause 8C shall apply where it is stated in those Documents that clause 22C shall apply to the Main Contract.

8.2   The exception set out in clause 8A.2.1 or clause 8B.2.1 or clause 8C.2.1 whichever is applicable shall extend to any loss or damage for which either the Employer or the Contractor as Joint Insured under the Joint Names Policy referred to in clause 22A or clause 22B or clause 22C.2 of the Main Contract Conditions does not make a claim under that Policy or to the extent that no claim under that Policy can be made because of a condition therein that the insured shall bear the first part of any claim for loss or damage.

8.3   Nothing in clause 8A or clause 8B or clause 8C whichever is applicable shall in any way modify the Sub-Contractor's obligations in regard to defects in the Sub-Contract Works as set out in clauses 14.3 and 14.4.

8.4   Where the Sub-Contractor is, pursuant to clause 22.3 of the Main Contract Conditions, recognised as an insured under the Joint Names Policy referred to in clause 22A or clause 22B or clause 22C of the Main Contract Conditions, whichever is applicable to the Main Contract, the Sub-Contractor shall not object to the payment by the insurers under such Joint Names Policy to the Employer of any relevant insurance monies.

8.5   The occurrence of loss or damage affecting the Sub-Contract Works occasioned by one or more of the Specified Perils shall be disregarded in computing any amounts payable to the Sub-Contractor under or by virtue of this Sub-Contract.

[*f*] 8A.   Sub-Contract Works in New Buildings—Main Contract Conditions Clause 22A

8A.1   The Contractor shall, prior to the commencement of the Sub-Contract Works, ensure that the Joint Names Policy referred to in clause 22A of the Main Contract Conditions shall be so issued or so endorsed that, in respect of loss or damage by the Specified Perils to the Works and Site Materials insured thereunder, the Sub-Contractor is either recognised as an insured under the Joint Names Policy or the insurers waive any rights of subrogation they may have against the Sub-Contractor; and that this recognition or waiver shall continue up to and including whichever is the earlier of the Terminal Dates.

8A.2   .1   Before whichever is the earlier of the Terminal Dates the Sub-Contractor shall (subject to clause 8A.2.2) be responsible for the cost of restoration of Sub-Contract work lost or damaged, replacement or repair of Sub-Contract Site Materials and removal and disposal of any debris arising therefrom in accordance with clause 8A.3 except to the extent that the loss or damage to the Sub-Contract Works or Sub-Contract Site Materials is due to:

one or more of the Specified Perils (whether or not caused by the negligence, breach of statutory duty, omission or default of the Sub-Contractor or any person for whom the Sub-Contractor is responsible) or

---

[*f*] *The Sub-Contractor should consider whether he should take out insurance to cover any risks for which he is not covered under clause 8A.1 e.g. impact, subsidence, theft, vandalism.*

any negligence, breach of statutory duty, omission or default of the Contractor or any person for whom the Contractor is responsible or of the Employer or any person engaged, employed or authorised by him or by any local authority or statutory undertaker executing work solely in pursuance of its statutory rights or obligations.

.2   Where during the progress of the Sub-Contract Works sub-contract materials or goods have been fully, finally and properly incorporated into the Works before practical completion of the Sub-Contract Works, the Sub-Contractor shall be responsible, in respect of loss or damage to Sub-Contract work comprising the materials or goods so incorporated caused by the occurrence of a peril other than a Specified Peril, for the cost of restoration of such work lost or damaged and removal and disposal of any debris arising therefrom in accordance with clause 8A.3 but only to the extent that such loss or damage is caused by the negligence, breach of statutory duty, omission or default of the Sub-Contractor or any person for whom the Sub-Contractor is responsible.

8A.3   If before the earlier of the Terminal Dates any loss or damage affecting the Sub-Contract Works or Sub-Contract Site Materials is occasioned, whether by one or more of the Specified Perils or otherwise, then, upon discovering the loss or damage, the Sub-Contractor shall forthwith give notice in writing to the Contractor of the extent, nature and location thereof. The Sub-Contractor shall, in accordance with any instructions of the Architect or directions of the Contractor, with due diligence restore Sub-Contract work lost or damaged, replace or repair any Sub-Contract Site Materials which have been lost or damaged, remove and dispose of any debris arising therefrom and proceed with the carrying out and completion of the Sub-Contract Works.

8A.4   Where under clause 8A.2 the Sub-Contractor is not responsible for the cost of compliance with clause 8A.3, such compliance shall be treated as if it were a Variation required by an instruction of the Architect to which clause 4.2 refers and valued under clause 16 or clause 17 whichever is applicable. The amount of the valuation under clause 16 shall not be added to the Sub-Contract Sum and the amount of the valuation under clause 17 shall not be included in the gross valuation referred to in clause 21.4 but such amounts shall be paid by the Contractor to the Sub-Contractor or recoverable by the Sub-Contractor from the Contractor as a debt.

8A.5   On or after the earlier of the Terminal Dates the Sub-Contractor shall not be responsible for loss or damage to the Sub-Contract Works except to the extent of any loss or damage caused thereto by the negligence, breach of statutory duty, omission or default of the Sub-Contractor or any person for whom the Sub-Contractor is responsible.

8B.   Sub-Contract Works in new buildings—Main Contract Conditions clause 22B

8B.1   The Contractor shall, prior to the commencement of the Sub-Contract Works, ensure that the Employer arranges that the Joint Names Policy referred to in clause 22B.1 of the Main Contract Conditions shall be so issued or so endorsed that, in respect of loss or damage by the Specified Perils to the Works and Site Materials insured thereunder, the Sub-Contractor is either recognised as an insured under the Joint Names Policy or the insurers waive any rights of subrogation they may have against the Sub-Contractor;

[*f*]   *The Sub-Contractor should consider whether he should take out insurance to cover any risks for which he is not covered under clause 8B e.g. impact, subsidence, theft, vandalism.*

and that this recognition or waiver shall continue up to and including whichever is the earlier of the Terminal Dates.

8B.2 .1 Before whichever is the earlier of the Terminal Dates the Sub-Contractor shall (subject to clause 8B.2.2) be responsible for the cost of restoration of Sub-Contract work lost or damaged, replacement or repair of Sub-Contract Site Materials and removal and disposal of any debris arising therefrom in accordance with clause 8B.3 except to the extent that the loss or damage to the Sub-Contract Works or Sub-Contract Site Materials is due to:

one or more of the Specified Perils (whether or not caused by the negligence, breach of statutory duty, omission or default of the Sub-Contractor or any person for whom the Sub-Contractor is responsible) or

any negligence, breach of statutory duty, omission or default of the Contractor or any person for whom the Contractor is responsible or of the Employer or any person employed, engaged or authorised by him or by any local authority or statutory undertaker executing work solely in pursuance of its statutory rights or obligations.

.2 Where during the progress of the Sub-Contract Works sub-contract materials or goods have been fully, finally and properly incorporated into the Works before practical completion of the Sub-Contract Works, the Sub-Contractor shall be responsible, in respect of loss or damage to sub-contract work comprising the materials or goods so incorporated caused by the occurrence of a peril other than a Specified Peril, for the cost of restoration of such work lost or damaged and removal and disposal of any debris arising therefrom in accordance with clause 8B.3 but only to the extent that such loss or damage is caused by the negligence, breach of statutory duty, omission or default of the Sub-Contractor or any person for whom the Sub-Contractor is responsible.

8B.3 If before the earlier of the Terminal Dates any loss or damage affecting the Sub-Contract Works or Sub-Contract Site Materials is occasioned, whether by one or more of the Specified Perils or otherwise, then, upon discovering the loss or damage, the Sub-Contractor shall forthwith give notice in writing to the Contractor of the extent, nature and location thereof. The Sub-Contractor shall, in accordance with any instructions of the Architect or directions of the Contractor, with due diligence restore Sub-Contract work lost or damaged, replace or repair any Sub-Contract Site Materials which have been lost or damaged, remove and dispose of any debris arising therefrom and proceed with the carrying out and completion of the Sub-Contract Works.

8B.4 Where under clause 8B.2 the Sub-Contractor is not responsible for the cost of compliance with clause 8B.3, such compliance shall be treated as if it were a Variation required by an instruction of the Architect to which clause 4.2 refers and valued under clause 16 or clause 17 whichever is applicable.

8B.5 On or after the earlier of the Terminal Dates the Sub-Contractor shall not be responsible for loss or damage to the Sub-Contract Works except to the extent of any loss or damage caused thereto by the negligence, breach of statutory duty, omission or default of the Sub-Contractor or any person for whom the Sub-Contractor is responsible.

[*f*] 8C. Sub-Contract Works in existing structures—Main Contract Conditions clause 22C

8C.1 The Contractor shall, prior to the commencement of the Sub-Contract Works, ensure

---

[*f*] *The Sub-Contractor should consider whether he should take out insurance to cover any risks for which he is not covered under clause 8C.1.2 e.g. impact, subsidence, theft, vandalism.*

.1   that the Employer arranges that the Joint Names Policy referred to in clause 22C.1 of the perils Main Contract Conditions shall be so issued or so endorsed that, in respect of loss or damage by the Specified Perils to the existing structures and the contents thereof owned by the Employer or for which the Employer is responsible and which are insured thereunder, the Sub-Contractor is either recognised as an insured under the Joint Names Policy or the insurers waive any rights of subrogation they may have against the Sub-Contractor; and

.2   that the Employer arranges that the Joint Names Policy referred to in clause 22C.2 of the Main Contract Conditions shall be so issued or so endorsed that, in respect of loss or damage by the Specified Perils to the Works and Site Materials insured thereunder, the Sub-Contractor is either recognised as an insured under the Joint Names Policy or the insurers waive any rights of subrogation they may have against the Sub-Contractor; and

.3   that the recognition or waiver referred to in clauses 8C.1.1 and 8C.1.2 shall continue up to and including whichever is the earlier of the Terminal Dates.

8C.2   1.   Before whichever is the earlier of the Terminal Dates the Sub-Contractor shall (subject to clause 8C.2.2) be responsible for the cost of restoration of Sub-Contract work lost or works damaged, replacement or repair of Sub-Contract Site Materials and removal and disposal of any debris arising therefrom in accordance with clause 8C.3.3 except to the extent that the loss or damage to the Sub-Contract Works or Sub-Contract Site Materials is due to:

> one or more of the Specified Perils (whether or not caused by the negligence, breach of statutory duty, omission or default of the Sub-Contractor or any person for whom the Sub-Contractor is responsible) or
> any negligence, breach of statutory duty, omission or default of the Contractor or any person for whom the Contractor is responsible or of the Employer or any person employed, engaged or authorised by him or by any local authority or statutory undertaker executing work solely in pursuance of its statutory rights or obligations.

.2   Where during the progress of the Sub-Contract Works sub-contract materials or goods have been fully, finally and properly incorporated into the Works before practical completion of the Sub-Contract Works, the Sub-Contractor shall be responsible, in respect of loss or damage to Sub-Contract work comprising the materials or goods so incorporated caused by the occurrence of a peril other than a Specified Peril, for the cost of restoration of such work lost or damaged and removal and disposal of any debris arising therefrom in accordance with clause 8C.3.3 but only to the extent that such loss or damage is caused by the negligence, breach of statutory duty, omission or default of the Sub-Contractor or any person for whom the Sub-Contractor is responsible.

8C.3   1.   If before the earlier of the Terminal Dates any loss or damage affecting the Sub-Contract Works or Sub-Contract Site Materials is occasioned, whether by one or more of the Specified Perils or otherwise, then, upon discovering the loss or damage, the Sub-Contractor shall forthwith give notice in writing to the Contractor of the extent, nature and location thereof.

.2   If the occurrence of such loss or damage or any other loss or damage gives rise to a determination of the employment of the Contractor under clause 22C.4 of the Main Contract Conditions clause 31.2 shall apply as if the employment of the Contractor had been determined under clause 28 of the Main Contract Conditions but subject to the exception in regard to the application of clause 28.2.2.6 of the Main Contract Conditions referred to in clause 22C.4.3.2 of the Main Contract Conditions.

.3   If the employment of the Main Contractor is not determined under clause 22C.4 of the Main Contract Conditions the Sub-Contractor shall, in accordance with any instructions of the Architect or directions of the Contractor, with due diligence restore Sub-Contract work lost or damaged, replace or repair any Sub-Contract Site Materials which have been lost or damaged, remove and dispose of any debris arising therefrom and proceed with the carrying out and completion of the Sub-Contract Works.

8C.4 Where under clause 8C.2 the Sub-Contractor is not responsible for the cost of compliance with clause 8C.3.3 such compliance shall be treated as if it were a Variation required by an instruction of the Architect to which clause 4.2 refers and valued under clause 16 or clause 17 whichever is applicable.

8C.5 On or after the earlier of the Terminal Dates the Sub-Contractor shall not be responsible for loss or damage to the Sub-Contract Works except to the extent of any loss or damage caused thereto by the negligence, breach of statutory duty, omission or default of the Sub-Contractor or any person for whom the Sub-Contractor is responsible.

Clause 8: Loss or damage to the Works or the Sub-Contract Works

This clause deals with the application to the Sub-Contract of the provisions of clause 22 of the Main Contract, as amended. See commentary on that clause. The scheme in respect of loss or damage to Main Contract Works, including the Sub-Contract Works, and Site Materials and to existing structures and their contents may be summarised as follows:

(1) clause 8 follows the three alternative clauses 22A, 22B and 22C by providing that clauses 8A, 8B or 8C applies according to which of the three possible clauses are included in the Main Contract;

(2) each NSC possible clause requires the Contractor to obtain for the Nominated Sub-Contractor the benefit of the Joint Names Policy referred to in the relevant part of clause 22;

(3) the benefit which the Nominated Sub-Contractor obtains is in respect of loss or damage to the Main Contract Works and Site Materials, including Nominated Sub-Contract Works and Sub-Contract Site Materials, caused by Specified Perils;

(4) the duration of the benefit is up to the first of the "Terminal Dates" as to which see the commentary to Sub-Contract clause 6;

(5) up to the Terminal Dates, the Sub-Contractor is thus liable for loss to Nominated Sub-Contract Works and Site Materials except to the extent that this is due to a Specified Peril or to the negligence etc., of the Contractor or the Employer;

(6) up to the Terminal Dates, the Sub-Contractor is not liable for loss or damage by the Specified Perils to the Main Contract Works and Site Materials (other than the Nominated Sub-Contract Works and Site Materials) or to existing structures where clause 22C applies, however the loss or damage is caused;

(7) for any loss or damage up to the Terminal Dates caused by a risk other than a Specified Peril, the position is as follows:

(a) *to the Nominated Sub-Contract Works and Site Materials*—the Nominated Sub-Contractor is responsible unless the loss or damage was due to the Contractor's negligence etc., except that if Sub-Contract Materials or Goods have been finally incorporated into the Works, the Nominated Sub-Contractor is only liable if the loss is due to his own negligence;

(b) *to the Main Contract Works and Site Materials*—the Nominated Sub-Contractor is only responsible if the loss is due to his negligence, etc.

(c) *to the existing structures*—the Nominated Sub-Contractor is responsible if the loss is due to his negligence, etc.

(8) after the Terminal Dates, the Nominated Sub-Contractor is only liable for any loss to the Main Contract Works and Site Materials, including the practically completed Nominated Sub-Contract Works, and to existing structures if the loss is due to his own negligence.

The following general points should be noted:

(1) the references above to the negligence of the Contractor and the Sub-Contractor are, respectively, to "the Contractor or any person for whom the Contractor is responsible" and to "the Sub-Contractor or any person for whom the Sub-Contractor is responsible" (see Sub-Contract clause 6.1.1);

(2) the Specified Perils do not include a number of obvious risks such as theft and vandalism. The Sub-Contractor is not obliged to insure against such risks but would be wise to do so;

(3) clause 8 is not concerned with defects in the Sub-Contract Works (see clause 8.3);

(4) responsibility for the Sub-Contractor's plant, etc., is dealt with in clause 10.

9. Policies of Insurance—production—payment of premiums

9.1 The Sub-Contractor shall, as and when reasonably required to do so by the Contractor, produce documentary evidence showing that the insurance required under clause 7 has been taken out and is being maintained by the Sub-Contractor. On any occasion the Contractor may, but not unreasonably or vexatiously, require the Sub-Contractor to produce the relevant policy or policies and premium receipts therefor.

9.2 If the Sub-Contractor defaults in insuring as provided in clause 7 the Contractor may himself take out insurance against any liability or expense which he may incur arising out of such default and the premium for such insurance shall be paid by the Sub-Contractor to the Contractor or recoverable by the Contractor from the Sub-Contractor as a debt.

9.3 Except where the Main Contract Conditions include clause 22B or clause 22C of the Local Authorities version of the Standard Form[g] the Contractor shall, as and when

---

[g] *This exception is included because the Local Authorities version of the Standard Form does not provide any right for the Contractor to require the Employer to produce any documentary evidence or relevant policy or policies and premium receipts.*

reasonably required to do so by the Sub-Contractor, produce documentary evidence of compliance by the Contractor with the provisions of clause 8A.1 or clause 8B.1 or clause 8C.1 whichever is applicable and the Sub-Contractor may on any occasion, but not unreasonably or vexatiously, require the Contractor to produce the relevant policy or policies and premium receipts therefor.

9.4   If the Contractor defaults in compliance with clause 9.3 the Sub-Contractor may himself take out insurance against any liability or expense which he may incur arising out of such default and the premium for such insurance shall be paid by the Contractor to the Sub-Contractor or recoverable by the Sub-Contractor from the Contractor as a debt.

Clause 9: Policies of Insurance

This clause is the Sub-Contract equivalent of clauses 21.1.2 and 21.1.3 of the Main Contract. See also clause 7 and the commentary on clause 21 of the Main Contract. It was subject to certain drafting and procedural amendments by Amendment 3 issued in November 1986.

10.   **Sub-Contractor's plant etc.—responsibility of Contractor**

The Contractor shall only be responsible for any loss or damage to the plant, tools, equipment or other property belonging to or provided by the Sub-Contractor, his servants or agents and to any materials or goods of the Sub-Contractor which are not Sub-Contract Site Materials to the extent that such loss or damage is due to any negligence, breach of statutory duty, omission or default of the Contractor or any person for whom the Contractor is responsible.

Clause 10: Sub-Contractor's responsibility for his own plant, etc.

This was redrafted by Amendment 3 issued in November 1986. It now provides shortly that the Contractor should only be responsible for loss or damage to plant, etc., of the Sub-Contractor to the extent that such loss or damage is due to any negligence, etc., of the Contractor.

11.   **Sub-Contractor's obligation—carrying out and completion of Sub-Contract Works—extension of Sub-Contract time [h]**

11.1   The Sub-Contractor shall carry out and complete the Sub-Contract Works in accordance with the agreed programme details in the Tender, Schedule 2, item 1C, and reasonably in accordance with the progress of the Works but subject to receipt of the notice to commence work on site as detailed in the Tender, Schedule 2, item 1C, and to the operation of clause 11.2.

---

[h] *See clauses 35.4.7, 36.5.8 and 37.7 (restriction of fluctuations or price adjustments where Sub-Contractor is in default over completion).*

11.2 .1.1 If and whenever it becomes reasonably apparent that the commencement, progress or completion of the Sub-Contract Works or any part thereof is being or is likely to be delayed, the Sub-Contractor shall forthwith give written notice to the Contractor of the material circumstances including the cause or causes of the delay and identify in such notice any matter which in his opinion comes within clause 11.2.2.1. The Contractor shall forthwith inform the Architect of any written notice by the Sub-Contractor and submit to the Architect any written representations made to him by the Sub-Contractor as to such cause as aforesaid.

.1.2 In respect of each and every matter which comes within clause 11.2.2.1, and identified in the notice given in accordance with clause 11.2.1.1, the Sub-Contractor shall, if practicable in such notice, or otherwise in writing, as soon as possible after such notice:

.1.2.1 give particulars of the expected effects thereof; and

.1.2.2 estimate the extent, if any, of the expected delay in the completion of the Sub-Contract Works or any part thereof beyond the expiry of the period or periods stated in the Tender, Schedule 2, item 1C, or beyond the expiry of any extended period or periods previously fixed under clause 11 which results therefrom whether or not concurrently with delay resulting from any other matter which comes within clause 11.2.2.1; and

.1.2.3 the Sub-Contractor shall give such further written notices to the Contractor as may be reasonably necessary or as the Contractor may reasonably require for keeping up-to-date the particulars and estimate referred to in clause 11.2.1.2.1 and .2 including any material change in such particulars or estimate.

.1.3 The Contractor shall submit to the Architect the particulars and estimate referred to in clause 11.2.1.2.1 and .2 and the further notices referred to in clause 11.2.1.2.3 to the extent that such particulars and estimate have not been included in the notice given in accordance with clause 11.2.1.1 and shall, if so requested by the Sub-Contractor join with the Sub-Contractor in requesting the consent of the Architect under clause 35.14 of the Main Contract Conditions.

.2 If on receipt of any notice, particulars and estimate under clause 11.2.1 and of a request by the Contractor and the Sub-Contractor for his consent under clause 35.14 of the Main Contract Conditions the Architect is of the opinion that:

.2.1 any of the matters which are stated by the Sub-Contractor to be the cause of the delay is an act, omission or default of the Contractor, his servants or agents or his sub-contractors, their servants or agents (other than the Sub-Contractor, his servants or agents) or the occurrence of a Relevant Event; and

.2.2 the completion of the Sub-Contract Works or any part thereof is likely to be delayed thereby beyond the period or periods stated in the Tender, Schedule 2, item 1C, or any revised such period or periods

then the Contractor shall, with the written consent of the Architect, give in writing to the Sub-Contractor an extension of time by fixing such revised or further revised period or periods for the completion of the Sub-Contract Works or any part thereof as the Architect in his written consent then estimates to be fair and reasonable. The Contractor shall, in agreement with the Architect, when fixing such revised period or periods state:

.2.3 which of the matters, including any of the Relevant Events, referred to in clause 11.2.2.1 they have taken into account; and

.2.4 the extent, if any, to which the Architect, in giving his written consent, has had regard to any instructions under clause 13 of the Main Contract Conditions requiring the omission of any work or obligation or restriction since the previous fixing of any such revised period or periods for the completion of the Sub-Contract Works or any part thereof, and shall, if reasonably practicable having regard to the sufficiency of the aforesaid notice, particulars and estimate, fix such revised period or periods not later than 12 weeks from the receipt by the Contractor of the notice and of reasonably sufficient particulars and estimates, or, where the time between receipt thereof and the expiry of the period or periods for the completion of the Sub-Contract Works or any part thereof is less than 12 weeks, not later than the expiry of the aforesaid period or periods.

If, upon receipt of the aforesaid notice, particulars and estimate and request of the Contractor and the Sub-Contractor, the Architect is of the opinion that he is unable to give his written consent to any revision or further revision of the period or periods for completion of the Sub-Contract Works or any part thereof, the Architect shall so inform the Contractor who shall inform the Sub-Contractor of the opinion of the Architect not later than 12 weeks from the receipt by the Contractor of the aforesaid notice, particulars and estimate and request by the Sub-Contractor or, where the period of time between such receipt and the expiry of the period or periods for the completion of the Sub-Contract Works is less than 12 weeks, not later than the expiry of the aforesaid period or periods.

.3 After the first exercise by the Contractor of the duty under clause 11.2.2, the Contractor, with the written consent of the Architect, may in writing to the Sub-Contractor fix a period or periods for completion of the Sub-Contract Works or any part thereof shorter than that previously fixed under clause 11.2.2 if, in the opinion of the Architect, the fixing of such shorter period or periods is fair and reasonable having regard to any instructions issued under clause 13 of the Main Contract Conditions requiring the omission of any work or obligation or restriction where such issue is after the last occasion on which the Contractor with the consent of the Architect made a revision of the aforesaid period or periods.

.4 If the expiry of the period when the Sub-Contract Works should have been completed in accordance with the agreed programme details in the Tender, Schedule 2, item 1C, as revised by any operation of the provisions of clause 11, occurs before the date of practical completion of the Sub-Contract Works certified under clause 35.16 of the Main Contract Conditions the Contractor with the consent of the Architect, may
and
not later than the expiry of 12 weeks after the aforesaid date of practical completion of the Sub-Contract Works, the Contractor, with the consent of the Architect, shall either:

.1 fix such a period or periods for completion of the Sub-Contract Works or any part thereof longer than that previously fixed under clause 11.2 as the Architect in his written consent considers to be fair and reasonable having regard to any of the matters referred to in clause 11.2.2.1 whether upon reviewing a previous decision or otherwise and whether or not the matters referred to in clause 11.2.2.1 have been specifically notified by the Sub-Contractor under clause 11.2.1; or

.2 fix such a period or periods for completion of the Sub-Contract Works or any part thereof shorter than that previously fixed under clause 11.2 as the Architect in his written consent considers to be fair and reasonable having regard to any instruction issued under clause 13.2 of the Main Contract Conditions requiring as a Variation the omission of any work where such issue is after the last occasion on which the Contractor made a revision of the aforesaid period or periods; or

.3 confirm to the Sub-Contractor the period or periods for the completion of the Sub-Contract Works previously fixed.

Provided always the Sub-Contractor shall use constantly his best endeavours to prevent delay in the progress of the Sub-Contract Works, howsoever caused, and to prevent any such delay resulting in the completion of the Sub-Contract Works being delayed or further delayed beyond the period or periods for completion; and the Sub-Contractor shall do all that may reasonably be required to the satisfaction of the Architect and the Contractor to proceed with the Sub-Contract Works.

.5   The following are the Relevant Events referred to in clause 11.2.2.1:

.5.1   force majeure;

.5.2   exceptionally adverse weather conditions;

.5.3   loss or damage occasioned by any one or more of the Specified Perils;

.5.4   civil commotion, local combination of workmen, strike or lock-out affecting any of the trades employed upon the Works or any of the trades engaged in the preparation, manufacture or transportation of any of the goods or materials required for the Works;

.5.5   compliance by the Contractor and/or Sub-Contractor with the Architect's instructions:

.5.5.1   under clauses 2.3, 13.2, 13.3, 23.2, 34, 35 or 36 of the Main Contract Conditions, or

.5.5.2   in regard to the opening up for inspection of any work covered up or the testing of any of the work, materials or goods in accordance with clause 8.3 of the Main Contract Conditions (including making good in consequence of such opening up or testing) unless the inspection or test showed that the work, materials or goods were not in accordance with the Main Contract or the Sub-Contract as the case may be;

.5.6   the Contractor, or the Sub-Contractor through the Contractor, not having received in due time necessary instructions, drawings, details or levels from the Architect for which the Contractor or the Sub-Contractor, through the Contractor, specifically applied in writing provided that such application was made on a date which having regard to the Completion Date or the period or periods for the completion of the Sub-Contract Works was neither unreasonably distant from nor unreasonably close to the date on which it was necessary for the Contractor or the Sub-Contractor to receive the same;

.5.7   delay on the part of Nominated Sub-Contractors (other than the Sub-Contractor) or of Nominated Suppliers in respect of the Works which the Contractor has taken all practicable steps to avoid or reduce;

.5.8.1   the execution of work not forming part of the Main Contract by the Employer himself or by persons employed or otherwise engaged by the Employer as referred to in clause 28 of the Main Contract Conditions or the failure to execute such work;

.5.8.2   the supply by the Employer of materials and goods which the Employer has agreed to provide for the Works or the failure so to supply;

.5.9   the exercise after the Base Date by the United Kingdom Government of any statutory power which directly affects the execution of the Works by restricting the availability or use of labour which is essential to the proper carrying out of the Works, or preventing the Contractor or Sub-Contractor from, or delaying the Contractor or Sub-Contractor in, securing such goods or materials or such fuel or energy as are essential to the proper carrying out of the Works;

.5.10.1   the Contractor's or Sub-Contractor's inability for reasons beyond his control and which he could not reasonably have foreseen at the Base Date for the purposes of the Main Contract or the Sub-Contract as the case may be to secure such labour as is essential to the proper carrying out of the Works; or

.5.10.2   the Contractor's or Sub-Contractor's inability for reasons beyond his control and which he could not reasonably have foreseen at the Base Date for the purposes of the Main Contract or the Sub-Contract as the case may be to secure such goods or materials as are essential to the proper carrying out of the Works;

.5.11   the carrying out by a local authority or statutory undertaker of work in pursuance of its statutory obligations in relation to the Works, or the failure to carry out such work;

.5.12   failure of the Employer to give in due time ingress to or egress from the site of the Works or any part thereof through or over any land, buildings, way or passage adjoining or connected with the site and in the possession and control of the Employer, in accordance with the Contract Bills and/or the Contract Drawings, after receipt by the Architect of such notice, if any, as the Contractor is required to give, or failure of the Employer to give such ingress or egress as otherwise agreed between the Architect and the Contractor;

.5.13   the valid exercise by the Sub-Contractor of the right in clause 21.8 to suspend the further execution of the Sub-Contract Works;

.5.14   Where it is stated in the Tender, Schedule 1, item 10 that clause 23.1.2 of the Main Contract Conditions applies to the Main Contract, any deferment by the Employer in giving possession of the site of the Works to the Contractor.

11.3   If the Sub-Contractor shall feel aggrieved by:

a failure of the Architect to give the written consent referred to in clause 11.2.2; and/or

a failure of the Architect to give the written consent referred to in clause 11.2.2 within the period allowed in that clause; and/or

the terms of any written consent referred to in clause 11.2.2

then, subject to the Sub-Contractor giving the Contractor such indemnity and security as the Contractor may reasonably require, the Contractor shall allow the Sub-Contractor to use the Contractor's name and if necessary will join with the Sub-Contractor in arbitration proceedings at the instigation of the Sub-Contractor to decide the matter as aforesaid.

Clause 11: Sub-Contractor's obligation—carrying out and completion of Sub-Contract Works—extension of Sub-Contract time

Generally.   This clause is the Sub-Contract equivalent of clauses 23.1 and 25 of the Main Contract. See the commentary on those Main Contract clauses. There are certain differences between this clause and the Main Contract clauses as follows:

(1)   in clause 23.1 of the Main Contract, the Main Contractor is obliged to proceed "regularly and diligently." In clause 11.1 of the Sub-Contract, the Sub-Contractor is obliged to carry out and complete the Sub-Contract Works "in accordance with the agreed programme details . . . and reasonably in accordance with the progress of the Main Contract Works."[6]

---

[6] See commentary to clause 11.1.

(2) under clause 25.3.1 of the Main Contract, extensions of time are granted by the Architect. Under clause 11.2.2 of the Sub-Contract, extensions of time are granted by the Contractor, but with the written consent of the Architect. See clause 35.14 of the Main Contract, and see also commentary below.

(3) there are two grounds for extension of time in clause 11.2 of the Sub-Contract which do not appear in clause 25 of the Main Contract. These are:

   (a) "an act, omission or default of the Contractor ..." in clause 11.2.2.1, and

   (b) the additional Relevant Event in clause 11.2.5.13, *i.e.* the valid exercise by the Sub-Contractor of a right to suspend the Sub-Contract Works.

Clause 11.1. *"... in accordance with the agreed programme details in the Tender ..."*
One of the "Particular Conditions" in Schedule 2 of Tender NSC/1 which the Contractor and the Sub-Contractor are required to agree before an effective nomination can be made[7] is Item 1C—agreed programme details "including Sub-Contract Completion Date." (These words did not appear in the former "Green Form"). It may be anticipated, therefore, that a period for completion of the Sub-Contract and a Sub-Contract Completion Date will have been agreed. The Sub-Contractor is obliged to carry out the Sub-Contract Works "reasonably in accordance with the progress of the Main Contract Works" subject to extensions of time under clause 11.2. The express obligation which appeared in clause 8(a) of the former "Green Form" of Nominated Sub-Contract that the Sub-Contractor should proceed "with due expedition" is not perpetuated in NSC/4. Failure without reasonable cause "to proceed with the Sub-Contract Works in the manner provided in clause 11.1" is a ground for determination of the Sub-Contractor's employment under clause 29.1.

A distinction is to be drawn between an obligation to complete and an obligation to proceed at a particular speed or in a particular manner towards completion. Disputes often arise, especially on large building projects with many Sub-Contractors, about the speed or manner in which a Sub-Contractor is obliged or entitled to proceed. This occurs particularly where a Main Contractor's programme is dislocated by a variety of causes some or all of which may have nothing to do with the particular Sub-Contractor. Each such dispute will have its particular facts. Generally, however, it is submitted that upon the construction of this Sub-Contract or as a matter of necessary implication:

(1) the Sub-Contractor is both obliged and entitled to start his Sub-Contract Works at the time provided in the agreed programme details. If he

---

[7] See clauses 35.7.2 and 35.10.1 of the Main Contract and clause 1.1 of Agreement NSC/2.

fails to do so, having been given notice to commence work, he will be in breach of contract. If the Contractor is unable to permit him so to start, the Contractor will be in breach of contract.

(2) the Sub-Contractor, having started the Sub-Contract Works, is obliged and entitled to carry them out in accordance with the agreed programme detail and at such a pace as will enable him to complete in accordance with the agreed programme details. This obligation and right is qualified by the provisions in clause 11.2 for extensions of time, and further qualified to the extent that the Sub-Contractor is obliged to proceed "reasonably in accordance with the progress of the Main Contract Works." It is suggested that this last obligation presupposes that the Main Contract Works are proceeding "regularly and diligently" (see clause 23.1 of the Main Contract), and that it is not to be construed as obliging the Sub-Contractor to proceed without recompense in accordance with a Main Contract progress which is not in accordance with the agreed Sub-Contract programme details.

(3) if the Sub-Contractor fails to proceed in accordance with the obligations outlined in (2) above, he will be in breach of contract. If the Main Contractor is unable to permit the Sub-Contractor to proceed in accordance with the rights outlined in (2) above, he will be in breach of contract.

(4) some of the consequences of failures referred to in (1) and (3) above are dealt with in clause 13 of the Sub-Contract (see below).

(5) if the Sub-Contractor fails to complete the Sub-Contract Works in accordance with and subject to clause 11.1, he will be in breach of contract and is liable to the Contractor in damages. He will also be liable to the Employer under clause 3.4 of Agreement NSC/2.

Clause 11.2.2. "*. . . the Contractor shall, with the written consent of the Architect, give . . . an extension of time . . .*"

The scheme for granting extensions of time to the Sub-Contractor is essentially the same as that contained in clause 8(b) of the former "Green Form" of Nominated Sub-Contract. The Sub-Contractor gives notice of material circumstances (clause 11.2.1.1) and also gives the particulars and estimate required by clause 11.2.1.2. The Contractor submits these to the Architect with a request for the Architect's consent to an extension of time under clause 35.14 of the Main Contract. The Architect is then required by clause 35.14.2 of the Main Contract to express (or refuse to express) the opinion envisaged by clause 11.2.2 of the Sub-Contract, and, if appropriate, to estimate a fair and reasonable extension of time for the Sub-Contract Works and give his written consent to such an extension. The Contractor then gives the Sub-Contractor that extension. The Sub-Contractor must be notified where the Architect is of the opinion that he will not consent to the Contractor granting an extension of time to the Sub-Contractor (final paragraph of clause 11.2.2, added by Amendment 4 issued in July 1987).

730

Cumbersome though it may be, this machinery is in a sense straightforward. Nevertheless, there are practical difficulties and the granting of extensions of time to Nominated Sub-Contractors under clause 8(b) of the "Green Form" did not work well. This was for two principal reasons. First, as often as not, the Contractor has an interest not to promote a Sub-Contractor's request for extension. If the Sub-Contractor's ground for an extension is "an act, omission or default of the Contractor ... or his sub-contractors ..." (clause 11.2.2.1), the Contractor's interest is obvious. Even if the ground for extension is a Relevant Event under clause 11.2.5, the Contractor still has an interest, where the Main Contract is generally delayed, in denying his Sub-Contractors extensions of time, since by this means the Sub-Contractors may be liable to him for the delay. Secondly, Architects frequently do not know all the facts relevant to the grant or refusal of an extension of time for Sub-Contract Works. They usually do not see correspondence passing between the Contractor and the Sub-Contractor and often do not attend Sub-Contractors' site meetings. However, a close analysis of clause 11.2.2 indicates, it seems, that the decision whether or not to grant an extension of time for the Sub-Contract Works is in effect the Architect's alone. It is the Architect's opinion in the opening words of clause 11.2.2 that governs the giving of the extension and the Architect's estimate of a fair and reasonable extension that the Contractor is to grant. Although the Contractor has an executive function, he is not, it seems, required to exercise any judgment. There seems no reason why the difficulties in operating the Green Form should not apply to NSC/4.

Clause 11.2.5.13. *"the valid exercise by the Sub-Contractor of the right ... to suspend ..."*
Under Sub-Contract clause 21.8, the Sub-Contractor is in certain circumstances where he has not received payment entitled to suspend the further execution of the Sub-Contract Works. By clause 21.8.2 such a period of suspension is not a delay for which the Sub-Contractor is liable under the Sub-Contract, and in these circumstances is included as a Relevant Event which has no equivalent in the Main Contract.

Clause 11.2.5.14. *"... any deferment by the Employer in giving possession of the site ..."*
This is a new Relevant Event inserted by Amendment 4 issued in July 1987 to bring into the Sub-Contract the consequences of the inclusion in the Main Contract at clause 23.1 of a right for the Employer to defer the giving of possession of the site for a period not exceeding six weeks.

Clause 11.3. This clause enables the Sub-Contractor to take arbitration proceedings under the Main Contract in the Contractor's name, if he is aggrieved by the Architect's performance or non-performance of his functions under clause 11.2.2. For this form of proceeding, see commentary to Sub-Contract clause 4.

12. Failure of Sub-Contractor to complete on time

12.1 If the Sub-Contractor fails to complete the Sub-Contract Works (or any part thereof) within the period or periods for completion or any revised period or periods as provided in clause 11.2.2, the Contractor shall so notify the Architect and give to the Sub-Contractor a copy of such notification.

12.2 The Sub-Contractor shall pay or allow to the Contractor a sum equivalent to any loss or damage suffered or incurred by the Contractor and caused by the failure of the Sub-Contractor as aforesaid. Provided that the Contractor shall not be entitled so to claim unless the Architect in accordance with clause 35.15 of the Main Contract Conditions shall have issued to the Contractor (with a copy to the Sub-Contractor) a certificate in writing certifying any failure notified under clause 12.1.

Clause 12: Failure of Sub-Contractor to complete on time

Clause 12.2. *"The Sub-Contractor shall pay ... any loss or damage ..."*

This clause is the Sub-Contract equivalent of clause 24 of the Main Contract. In the Sub-Contract the Contractor's damages are not liquidated. A failure by the Sub-Contractor to complete on time will also give rise to a liability to the Employer under clause 3.4 of Agreement NSC/2.[8]

Clause 12.2. *"... the Contractor shall not be entitled so to claim unless the Architect ... shall have issued ... a certificate in writing certifying any failure notified under clause 12.1"*

The procedure relating to the certificate must be followed with some care. This matter has been before the courts on a number of occasions and the following propositions emerge:

(1) the certificate is a condition precedent to the Contractor's right to claim loss or damage for delay.[9]

(2) if there is no such certificate, the Contractor will not be entitled to set-off any claim for the Sub-Contractor's delay in completion against sums due to the Sub-Contractor (see clause 23.2.1).

(3) it follows that where the Contractor seeks to rely upon such a Certificate for the purposes of set-off, it must have been issued prior to the date upon which the monies claimed became due.[10]

(4) the certificate must be clear and unambiguous, stating as required that the Sub-Contract Works ought to have been completed within the specified time or extended period. A bald statement that the Sub-Contractor is in delay will not suffice.[11]

---

[8] See commentary to clause 3.4 of NSC/2 at p. 802.

[9] See *Brightside Kilpatrick* v. *Mitchell Construction (1973)* [1975] 2 Lloyd's Rep. 493 (C.A.).

[10] See *William Cox* v. *Fairclough Building* (1988) 16 Con. L.R. 7.

[11] See *Savage Brothers* v. *Shillington (Heating & Plumbing)* (1985) 5 Const.L.J. 295 (Northern Ireland High Court); *Pyrok* v. *Chee Tai* (1988) 41 B.L.R. 124 (Hong Kong Supreme Court). It is submitted that these cases were rightly decided and would be followed in England.

(5) in the absence of such a certificate, the Contractor is not entitled to claim damages for breach of some separate duty to proceed.[12]

(6) the Arbitrator cannot waive the requirement for a certificate.[13]

13. Matters affecting regular progress—direct loss and/or expense—Contractor's and Sub-Contractor's rights

13.1   .1   If the Sub-Contractor makes written application to the Contractor stating that he has incurred or is likely to incur direct loss and/or expense in the execution of the Sub-Contract for which he would not be reimbursed by a payment under any other provision in the Sub-Contract due to deferment of giving to the Contractor possession of the site of the Works where it is stated in the Tender, Schedule 1, item 10 that clause 23.1.2 of the Main Contract Conditions applies to the Main Contract or by reason of the regular progress of the Sub-Contract Works or of any part thereof having been or being likely to be materially affected by any one or more of the matters referred to in clause 13.1.2 the Contractor shall require the Architect to operate clause 26.4 of the Main Contract Conditions so that the amount of that direct loss and/or expense, if any, may be ascertained. Provided always that:

.1.1   the Sub-Contractor's application shall be made as soon as it has become, or should reasonably have become, apparent to him that the regular progress of the Sub-Contract Works or of any part thereof has been or was likely to be affected as aforesaid; and

.1.2   the Sub-Contractor shall submit to the Contractor such information in support of his application as the Contractor is requested by the Architect to obtain from the Sub-Contractor in order reasonably to enable the Architect to operate clause 26.4 of the Main Contract Conditions; and

.1.3   the Sub-Contractor shall submit to the Contractor such details of such loss and/or expense as the Contractor is requested by the Architect or the Quantity Surveyor to obtain from the Sub-Contractor in order reasonably to enable the ascertainment of that loss and/or expense under clause 26.4 or the Main Contract Conditions.

.2   The following are the matters referred to in clause 13.1.1.

.2.1   the Contractor, or the Sub-Contractor through the Contractor, not having received in due time necessary instructions, drawings, details or levels from the Architect for which the Contractor, or the Sub-Contractor through the Contractor, specifically applied in writing provided that such application was made on a date which having regard to the Completion Date or the period or periods for completion of the Sub-Contract Works was neither unreasonably distant from nor unreasonably close to the date on which it was necessary for the Contractor or the Sub-Contractor to receive the same; or

.2.2   the opening up for inspection of any work covered up or the testing of any of the work, materials or goods in accordance with clause 8.3 of the Main Contract Conditions (including making good in consequence of such opening up or testing), unless the inspection or test showed that the work, materials or goods

---

[12] *Savage Brothers* v. *Shillington (Heating & Plumbing)* (1985) 5 Const.L.J. 295 (Northern Ireland High Court).

[13] *Savage Brothers* v. *Shillington (Heating & Plumbing)* (1985) 5 Const.L.J. 295 (Northern Ireland High Court).

were not in accordance with the Main Contract or the Sub-Contract as the case may be; or

.2.3 any discrepancy in or divergence between the Contract Drawings and/or the Contract Bills and/or the Numbered Documents; or

.2.4 the execution of work not forming part of the Main Contract by the Employer himself or by persons employed or otherwise engaged by the Employer as referred to in clause 29 of the Main Contract Conditions or the failure to execute such work or the supply by the Employer of materials and goods which the Employer has agreed to provide for the Works or the failure so to supply; or

.2.5 Architect's instructions issued in regard to the postponement of any work to be executed under the provisions of the Main Contract or the Sub-Contract; or

.2.6 failure of the Employer to give in due time ingress to or egress from the site of the Works, or any part thereof through or over any land, buildings, way or passage adjoining or connected with the site and in the possession and control of the Employer, in accordance with the Contract Bills and/or the Contract Drawings, after receipt by the Architect of such notice, if any, as the Contractor is required to give or failure of the Employer to give such ingress or egress as otherwise agreed between the Architect and the Contractor; or

.2.7 Architect's instructions issued under clause 13.2 of the Main Contract Conditions requiring a Variation or under clause 13.3 of the Main Contract Conditions in regard to the expenditure of provisional sums (other than work to which clause 13.4.2 of the Main Contract Conditions refers).

.3 Any amount from time to time ascertained as a result of the operation of clause 13.1.1 shall be added to the Sub-Contract Sum or included in the calculation of the Ascertained Final Sub-Contract Sum.

.4 The Sub-Contractor shall comply with all directions of the Contractor which are reasonably necessary to enable the ascertainment which results from the operation of clause 13.1.1 to be carried out.

13.2 If the regular progress of the Sub-Contract Works (including any part thereof which is sub-contracted) is materially affected by any act, omission or default of the Contractor, his servants or agents, or any sub-contractor, his servants or agents or sub-sub-contractor (other than the Sub-Contractor, his servants or agents or sub-sub-contractors) employed by the Contractor on the Works, the Sub-Contractor shall within a reasonable time of such material effect becoming apparent give written notice thereof to the Contractor and the agreed amount of any direct loss and/or expense thereby caused to the Sub-Contractor shall be recoverable from the Contractor as a debt.

13.3 If the regular progress of the Works (including any part thereof which is sub-contracted) is materially affected by any act, omission or default of the Sub-Contractor, his servants or agents, or any sub-Sub-Contractor employed by the Sub-Contractor on the Sub-Contract Works, the Contractor shall within a reasonable time of such material effect becoming apparent give written notice thereof to the Sub-Contractor and the agreed amount of any direct loss and/or expense thereby caused to the Contractor (whether suffered or incurred by the Contractor or by Sub-Contractors employed by the Contractor on the Works from whom claims under similar provisions in the relevant Sub-Contracts have been agreed by the Contractor, Sub-Contractor and the Sub-Contractor) may be deducted from any monies due or to become due to the Sub-Contractor or may be recoverable from the Sub-Contractor as a debt.

13.4 The provisions of clause 13 are without prejudice to any other rights or remedies which the Contractor or Sub-Contractor may possess.

Clause 13: Matters affecting regular progress—direct loss and/or expense—Contractor's and Sub-Contractor's rights

Generally.   Clauses 13.1.1 and 13.1.2 are the Sub-Contract equivalent of clauses 26.1 and 26.2 of the Main Contract. See commentary on clause 26 of the Main Contract above and see in particular clauses 26.4.1 and 26.4.2 for the integration of Sub-Contractor's claims for loss and expense under clause 13.1 with the Main Contract machinery. By clause 21.4.2.2 of the Sub-Contract and clause 30.2.2.5 of the Main Contract, payments for Sub-Contractor's loss and expense are to be made in Interim Certificates and are not subject to Retention.

Clauses 13.2 and 13.3.   " *... the agreed amount of any direct loss and/or expense ...*"

These two clauses provide for the payment of loss and expense as between the Contractor and the Sub-Contractor where the Sub-Contract Works have been materially affected by an act, omission or default of the Contractor, or where the Works have been materially affected by an act, omission or default of the Sub-Contractor. Each clause blandly refers to the payment of "the agreed amount" of the loss and expense, but such matters are often not agreed. By virtue of clause 13.4 (and, it is submitted, in any event), agreement is not a prerequisite of ultimate recovery. Claims by the Contractor under clause 13.3 are affected by the provisions of clauses 23 and 24. Under clause 23.1, the Contractor has a right of set-off and deduction for agreed claims. For claims which are not agreed, the Contractor's right of set-off and deduction is circumscribed by the remainder of clause 23 and clause 24. Claims by the Sub-Contractor under clause 13.2 will have to be enforced, in the absence of agreement, by arbitration or litigation.

Clause 13.4.   This is the Sub-Contract equivalent of clause 26.6 of the Main Contract.

---

14.   Practical completion of Sub-Contract Works—liability for defects

14.1   If the Sub-Contractor notifies the Contractor in writing of the date when in the opinion of the Sub-Contractor the Sub-Contract Works will have reached practical completion the Contractor shall immediately pass to the Architect any such notification together with any observations thereon by the Contractor (a copy of which observations must immediately be sent by the Contractor to the Sub-Contractor).

14.2   Practical completion of the Sub-Contract Works shall be deemed to have taken place on the day named in the certificate of practical completion of the Sub-Contract Works issued by the Architect under clause 35.16 of the Main Contract Conditions or as provided in clause 18.1.1 of the Main Contract Conditions.

14.3   Subject to clause 18 of the Main Contract Conditions but without prejudice to the obligation of the Sub-Contractor to accept a similar liability to any liability of the Contractor under the Main Contract to remedy defects in the Sub-Contract Works, the Sub-Contractor shall be liable to make good at his own cost and in accordance with any instruction of the Architect or direction of the Contractor all defects, shrinkages and other faults in the Sub-Contract Works or in any part thereof considered necessary by reason of such defects, shrinkages or other faults being due to materials or work-manship not in accordance with the Sub-Contract or due to frost occurring before the date of practical completion of the Sub-Contract Works.

14.4 Where under clause 17.2 or clause 17.3 of the Main Contract Conditions an appro-priate deduction from the Contract Sum is made then to the extent that such deduction is relevant to the Sub-Contract Works a pro rata share of such appropriate deduction shall be borne by the Sub-Contractor; and such share may be deducted from any monies due or to become due to the Sub-Contractor or may be recoverable by the Contractor from the Sub-Contractor as a debt.

14.5 The Sub-Contractor upon practical completion of the Sub-Contract Works shall properly clear up and leave the Sub-Contract Works, and all areas made available to him for the purpose of executing them and, so far as used by him for that purpose, clean and tidy to the reasonable satisfaction of the Contractor.

Clause 14: Practical Completion of Sub-Contract Works—liability for defects.

This clause is the Sub-Contract equivalent of clause 17 of the Main Con-tract, but is drafted to recognise the possibility that the Sub-Contract Works may have reached Practical Completion before the Main Contract Works are practically complete. For clause 17 of the Main Contract see above. Clause 14.4 was redrafted by Amendment 4 issued in July 1987 to bring into the Sub-Contract the amendments to clauses 17.2 and 17.3 of the Main Contract. See also clause 18 of the Main Contract. The Architect's obligation to certify Practical Completion of works executed by a Nominated Sub-Contractor is contained in clause 35.16 of the Main Contract. Upon such certification, clauses 35.17 to 35.19 of the Main Contract come into operation. See also clause 5 of Agreement NSC/2.

15. **Price for Sub-Contract Works**

15.1 Where in the Tender the Sub-Contractor has quoted a VAT-exclusive Sub-Contract Sum the price for the Sub-Contract Works shall be the Sub-Contract Sum or such other sum as shall become payable in accordance with the Sub-Contract.

15.2 Where in the Tender the Sub-Contractor has quoted a VAT-exclusive Tender Sum subject to complete remeasurement the price for the Sub-Contract Works shall be such sum or sums as shall become payable in accordance with the Sub-Contract and the total of such sum or sums shall be the Ascertained Final Sub-Contract Sum.

Clause 15: Price for Sub-Contract Works

Tender NSC/1 provides for alternative forms of quotation. One is referred to as the "Sub-Contract Sum," the other as the "Tender Sum." Clauses 15.1 and 16 apply to the first alternative, which is essentially a lump sum quotation subject to adjustment for Variations and provisional sums only. Clauses 15.2 and 17 apply to the second alternative where the Sub-Contract Works are subject to complete remeasurement. For lump sum contracts generally, see page 69. For what constitutes extra work in a lump sum contract see page 81. For measurement and value contracts see page 85. VAT is dealt with in clause 19A.

16.   Valuation of Variations and provisional sum work

16.1   Where clause 15.1 applies, all Variations (including any sanctioned by the Architect in writing) and all work executed by the Sub-Contractor in accordance with the instructions of the Architect as to the expenditure of provisional sums included in the Sub-Contract Documents, shall be valued by the Quantity Surveyor and such valuation (in clause 16 called "the Valuation") shall (unless otherwise agreed by the Contractor and Sub-Contractor and approved by the Employer) be made in accordance with the provisions of clause 16.3.

16.2   Where the Sub-Contractor has included in the Tender a schedule of rates or prices for measured work and/or a schedule of daywork prices, such rates or prices shall be used in determining the Valuation—in substitution for any rates or prices or Daywork Definitions which would otherwise be applicable under the relevant provisions of clause 16.3.

16.3   .1   To the extent that the Valuation relates to the execution of additional or substituted work which can properly be valued by measurement such work shall be measured and shall be valued in accordance with the following rules:

    .1.1   where the work is of similar character to, is executed under similar conditions as, and does not significantly change the quantity of, work set out in bills of quantities and/or other documents comprised in the Sub-Contract Documents the rates and prices for the work so set out shall determine the Valuation;

    .1.2   where the work is of similar character to work set out in bills of quantities and/or other documents comprised in the Sub-Contract Documents but is not executed under similar conditions thereto and/or significantly changes the quantity thereof, the rates and prices for the work so set out shall be the basis for determining the Valuation and the Valuation shall include a fair allowance for such difference in conditions and/or quantity;

    .1.3   where the work is not of similar character to work set out in bills of quantities and/or other documents comprised in the Sub-Contract Documents the work shall be valued at fair rates and prices.

    .2   To the extent that the Valuation relates to the omission of work set out in bills of quantities and/or other documents comprised in the Sub-Contract Documents the rates and prices for such work therein set out shall determine the Valuation of the work omitted.

    .3   In any Valuation of work under clauses 16.3.1 and 16.3.2:

    .3.1   where bills of quantities are a Sub-Contract Document measurement shall be in accordance with the same principles as those governing the preparation of those bills of quantities as referred to in clause 18;

.3.2 allowance shall be made for any percentage or lump sum adjustments in bills of quantities and/or other documents comprised in the Sub-Contract Documents; and

.3.3 allowance, where appropriate, shall be made for any addition to or reduction of preliminary items of the type referred to in the Standard Method of Measurement 6th Edition, Section 8 (Preliminaries).

.4 To the extent that the Valuation relates to the execution of work which cannot properly be valued by measurement the Valuation shall comprise the prime cost of such work calculated in accordance with the Definition or Definitions of Prime Cost of Daywork identified on page 1 of the Tender together with percentage additions to each section of the prime cost at the rates set out by the Sub-Contractor in the Tender.

Provided that in any case vouchers specifying the time daily spent upon the work, the workmen's names, the plant and the materials employed shall be delivered for verification to the Contractor for transmission to the Architect or his authorised representative not later than the end of the week following that in which the work has been executed.

.5 To the extent that the Valuation does not relate to the execution of additional or substituted work or the omission of work or to the extent that the valuation of any work or liabilities directly associated with a Variation cannot reasonably be effected in the Valuation by the application of clauses 16.3.1 to .4 a fair valuation thereof shall be made.

Provided that no allowance shall be made under clause 16.3 for any effect upon the regular progress of the Sub-Contract Works or for any other direct loss and/or expense for which the Sub-Contractor would be reimbursed by payment under any other provision in the Sub-Contract.

16.4 Where it is necessary to measure work for the purpose of the Valuation the Contractor shall give to the Sub-Contractor an opportunity of being present at the time of such measurement and of taking such notes and measurements as the Sub-Contractor may require.

16.5 If compliance with any instruction requiring a Variation under clause 13.2 of the Main Contract Conditions or any instruction as to the expenditure of a provisional sum under clause 13.3 of the Main Contract Conditions substantially changes the conditions under which any part or parts of the Sub-Contract Works which are not the subject of the aforementioned instruction is executed, then such part or parts shall be treated as if it had been the subject of an instruction of the Architect requiring a Variation under clause 13.2 of the Main Contract Conditions which shall be valued in accordance with the provisions of clause 16.

16.6 Effect shall be given to a Valuation under clause 16.3 by addition to or deduction from the Sub-Contract Sum.

Clause 16: Valuation of Variations and provisional sum work

Generally. This clause provides for the valuation of Variations and provisional sum work where the Sub-Contract Works are not subject to complete remeasurement. See the commentary on clause 15 above. "Variations" are defined in clause 1.3 and the Sub-Contractor is obliged to comply with

Variation instructions issued under clause 13.2 of the Main Contract by virtue of clause 4.3 of the Sub-Contract. The Architect is obliged to issue instructions in regard to the expenditure of provisional sums included in a Sub-Contract by clause 13.3.2 of the Main Contract and clause 4.3 of the Sub-Contract applies equally to those instructions. The second paragraph of clause 13.4.1 of the Main Contract applies to the valuation of Variations and provisional sum work in the Sub-Contract, stating that the relevant provisions of the Sub-Contract shall apply.

Clause 16.1. *". . . such valuation . . . shall . . . be made in accordance with the provisions of Clause 16.3"*

Clause 16.3 is the Sub-Contract equivalent of clause 13.5 of the Main Contract (see its commentary above). Clause 16.3 is to be read subject to clause 16.2.

Clause 16.5. This sub-clause was formerly numbered 16.3.5 and was renumbered and redrafted by Amendment 4 issued in July 1987. The effect is that when Variations to the Main Contract Works affect the Sub-Contract Works, then such parts of the Nominated Sub-Contract Works shall be treated as if they were subject to Variation instructions and are to be valued in accordance with clause 16.

17.   Valuation of all work comprising the Sub-Contract Works

17.1   Where clause 15.2 applies all work executed by the Sub-Contractor in accordance with the Sub-Contract Documents and the instructions of the Architect, including any instruction requiring a Variation or in regard to the expenditure of a provisional sum included in the Sub-Contract Documents, shall be valued by the Quantity Surveyor and such valuation (in clause 17 called "the Valuation") shall (unless otherwise agreed by the Contractor and Sub-Contractor and approved by the Employer) be made in accordance with the provisions of clause 17.4.

17.2   Where it is necessary to measure work for the purpose of the Valuation the Contractor shall give to the Sub-Contractor an opportunity of being present at the time of such measurement and of taking such notes and measurements as the Sub-Contractor may require.

17.3   Where the Sub-Contractor has included in the Tender a schedule of rates or prices for measured work and/or a schedule of daywork prices, such rates or prices shall be used in determining the Valuation in substitution for any rates or prices or Daywork Definitions which would otherwise be applicable under the relevant provisions of clause 17.4.

17.4   .1   To the extent that the Valuation relates to the execution of work which can properly be valued by measurement such work shall be measured and shall be valued in accordance with the following rules:

.1.1   where the work is of similar character to, is executed under similar conditions as, and does not significantly change the quantity of, work set out in bills of quantities and/or other documents comprised in the Sub-Contract Documents the rates and prices for the work so set out shall determine the Valuation;

.1.2 where the work is of similar character to work set out in bills of quantities and/or other documents comprised in the Sub-Contract Documents but is not executed under similar conditions thereto and/or significantly changes the quantity thereof, the rates and prices for the work so set out shall be the basis for determining the Valuation and the Valuation shall include a fair allowance for such difference in conditions and/or quantity;

.1.3 where the work is not of similar character to work set out in bills of quantities and/or other documents comprised in the Sub-Contract Documents the work shall be valued at fair rates and prices.

.2 In any valuation of work under clause 17.4.1:

.2.1 where bills of quantities are a Sub-Contract Document measurement shall be in accordance with the same principles as those governing the preparation of those bills of quantities as referred to in clause 18;

.2.2 allowance shall be made for any percentage or lump sum adjustments in bills of quantities and/or other documents comprised in the Sub-Contract Documents; and

.2.3 any amounts priced in the Preliminaries section of the Sub-Contract Documents adjusted, where appropriate, to take into account any instructions of the Architect requiring a Variation or in regard to the expenditure of a provisional sum included in the Sub-Contract Documents, shall be included.

.3 To the extent that the Valuation relates to the execution of work which cannot properly be valued by measurement the Valuation shall comprise the prime cost of such work calculated in accordance with the Definition or Definitions of Prime Cost of Daywork identified on page 1 of the Tender together with percentage additions to each section of the prime cost at the rates set out by the Sub-Contractor in the Tender.

Provided that in any case vouchers specifying the time daily spent upon the work, the workmen's names, the plant and the materials employed shall be delivered for verification to the Contractor for transmission to the Architect or his authorised representative not later than the end of the weeks following that in which the work has been executed.

.4 If compliance with any instruction of the Architect requiring a Variation under clause 13.2 of the Main Contract Conditions or any instruction as to the expenditure of a provisional sum under clause 13.3 of the Main Contract Conditions or any instruction as a result of which work included in the Tender is not executed substantially changes the conditions under which any part or parts of the Sub-Contract Works which are not the subject of the aforementioned instruction is executed, then such part or parts shall be valued in accordance with the provisions of clause 17.4.1.2.

.5 To the extent that the Valuation of any instruction of the Architect requiring a Variation or any instruction as to the expenditure of a provisional sum does not relate to the execution of work or to the extent that the valuation of any work or liabilities directly associated with such Variation cannot reasonably be effected in the Valuation by the application of clause 17.4.1 to .4 a fair valuation thereof shall be made.

Provided that no allowance shall be made under clause 17.4 for any effect upon the regular progress of the Sub-Contract Works or for any other direct loss and/or expense for which the Sub-Contractor would be reimbursed by payment under any other provision in the Sub-Contract.

Clause 17: Valuation of all work comprising the Sub-Contract Work

This clause applies where there is to be complete remeasurement of the Sub-Contract Works (see commentary on clause 15). The scheme of the clause is similar to that of clause 16 and the rules for valuation in clause 17.4 are similar to those in clause 16.3. See the commentary on clause 16.

18.   Bills of quantities—Standard Method of Measurement

18.1   Subject always to clause 2.2, if bills of quantities are a Sub-Contract Document:

.1   such bills, unless otherwise specifically stated in respect of any specified item or items, are to have been prepared in accordance with the Standard Method of Measurement of Building Works, 6th Edition published by the Royal Institution of Chartered Surveyors and the National Federation of Building Trades Employers;

.2   if in the bills of quantities there is any departure from the method of preparation referred to in clause 18.1.1 or any error in description or in quantity or omission of items, then such departure or error shall not vitiate the Sub-Contract but the departure or error shall be corrected and such correction shall be treated as if it were a Variation required by an instruction of the Architect under clause 13.2 of the Main Contract Conditions;

.3   the quality and quantity of the work included in the Sub-Contract Sum or Tender Sum shall be deemed to be that which is set out in the bills of quantities.

Clause 18: Bills of Quantities—Standard Method of Measurement

Clauses 18.1.1 and 18.1.2 are the Sub-Contract equivalent of clauses 2.2.2.1 and 2.2.2.2 respectively of the Main Contract. Clause 18.1.3 is the Sub-Contract equivalent of clause 14.1 of the Main Contract. See commentaries to clauses 2 and 14 of the Main Contract. The introductory words to clause 18 recognise the possibility that Bills of Quantities may not be a Sub-Contract Document. The clause was amended by Amendment 7 issued in July 1988 to take account of the publication of the 7th edition of the Standard Method of Measurement which became operative on July 1, 1988. There are consequential and related Amendments to the following clauses of the Sub-Contract:

— clause 1.3: Definitions;
— clauses 11.2.5.5.1 and 11.2.5.6: redrafting of two Relevant Events;
— clauses 13.1.2.1, 13.1.2.7 and 13.1.2.8: redrafting of three Matters affecting regular progress of the Sub-Contract Works;
— clause 16.1: redrafting of provisions for valuation by Quantity Surveyor;
— clauses 16.3, 16.5 and 17.4: redrafting of Valuation Rules;
— clause 21.10.2: redrafting of items included in adjustment of Sub-Contract Sum.

The version of the Sub-Contract reproduced in this book does not incorporate these amendments, but they are set out separately at pages 779 *et seq.*

19A.   Value added tax

19A.1   .1   In this clause "tax" means the value added tax introduced by the Finance Act 1972, which is under the care and management of the Commissioners of Customs and Excise (hereinafter called "the Commissioners").

.2   To the extent that after the Base Date the supply of goods and services to the Contractor becomes exempt from the tax there shall be paid to the Sub-Contractor an amount equal to the loss of credit (input tax) on the supply to the Sub-Contractor of goods and services which contribute exclusively to the Sub-Contract Works.

19A.2   Any reference in the Sub-Contract to "Sub-Contract Sum," "Tender Sum" or "Ascertained Final Sub-Contract Sum" shall be regarded as such Sum exclusive of any tax and recovery by the Sub-Contractor from the Contractor of tax properly chargeable by the Commissioners on the Sub-Contractor under or by virtue of the Finance Act 1972, or any amendment or re-enactment thereof on the supply of goods and services under the Sub-Contract shall be under the provisions of clause 19A.

19A.3   Supplies of goods and services under the Sub-Contract are supplies under a contract providing for periodical payment for such supplies within the meaning of Regulation 21(1) of the Value Added Tax (General) Regulations 1872 or any amendment thereof.

19A.4   .1.1   The Contractor shall pay to the Sub-Contractor in the manner set out in clause 19A any tax chargeable by the Commissioners on the Sub-Contractor on the supply to the Contractor of any goods and services by the Sub-Contractor under the Sub-Contract.

.1.2   The Sub-Contractor shall, not later than 7 days before the date when payment is due to the Sub-Contractor under clause 21.3, give to the Contractor a written provisional assessment of the respective values (less the Retention and cash discount referred to in clause 21.3) of those supplies of goods and services for which payment is due as aforesaid and which will be chargeable at the relevant time of supply under the aforesaid Regulation 21(1) on the Sub-Contractor at

a zero rate of tax (category one)
and
any rate or rates of tax other than zero (category two).

The Sub-Contractor shall also specify the rate or rates of tax which are chargeable on those supplies included in category two and shall state the grounds on which he considers such supplies are so chargeable.

.2   The Contractor shall in relation to any amount payable in accordance with the provisions of clause 21 calculate, by applying the rate or rates of tax specified by the Sub-Contractor as applicable to the sub-contract supply, the tax properly chargeable on such supply and remit such tax to the Sub-Contractor within the period prescribed by clause 21.3 for the payment of the amount in relation to which the tax was calculated.

.3   Upon receipt of the amounts referred to in clause 21.3 and 19A.4.2 the Sub-Contractor shall immediately issue to the Contractor a receipt as referred to in Regulation 21 as aforesaid containing the particulars required under Regulation 9(1) of the Value Added Tax (General) Regulations 1972 or any amendment thereof.

.4   If the Sub-Contractor disallows any cash discount claimed by the Contractor under clause 21.3 and the Contractor pays the amount of such discount to the Sub-Contractor the provisions of clause 19A.4.2 shall not apply to such payment.

.5   If for any reason the amount paid under clause 19A.4.2 is not the amount of tax properly chargeable on the Sub-Contractor by the Commissioners, the Sub-Contractor shall notify the Contractor and the Contractor shall forthwith make any adjustment that may be necessary.

19A.5   Notwithstanding any provisions to the contrary elsewhere in the Sub-Contract, the Contractor, if he has not received from the Sub-Contractor, within 21 days of a payment to which clause 19A refers, any receipt or receipts due under clause 19A.4.3 may so notify the Sub-Contractor in writing and shall be entitled in that notice to state that he will withhold further payments to the Sub-Contractor unless the receipt or receipts outstanding as specified in the aforesaid written notice have been received before the next payment becomes due. If any payment to the Sub-Contract is withheld in accordance with clause 19A.5, such payment shall be released to the Sub-Contractor immediately upon receipt by the Contractor of the outstanding receipt or receipts as specified in the aforesaid written notice. Clause 19A.5 does not entitle the Contractor to withhold any payment due to the Sub-Contractor on any ground other than that specified in clause 19A.5.

] **19B.**   **Value Added Tax—Special Arrangement—VAT (General) Regulations 1972, Regulations 8(3) and 21**

19B.1   .1   In this clause "tax" means the value added tax introduced by the Finance Act 1972, which is under the care and management of the Commissioners of Customs and Excise (hereinafter called "the Commissioners").

.2   To the extent that after the Base Date the supply of goods and services to the Contractor becomes exempt from the tax there shall be paid to the Sub-Contractor an amount equal to the loss of credit (input tax) on the supply to the Sub-Contractor of goods and services which contribute exclusively to the Sub-Contract Works.

19B.2   Any reference in the Sub-Contract to "Sub-Contract Sum," "Tender Sum" or "Ascertained Final Sub-Contract Sum," shall be regarded as such Sum exclusive of any tax and recovery by the Sub-Contractor from the Contractor of tax properly chargeable by the Commissioners on the Sub-Contractor under or by virtue of the Finance Act 1972, or any amendment or re-enactment thereof on the supply of goods and services under the Sub-Contract shall be under the provisions of clause 19B.

19B.3   Supplies of goods and services under the Sub-Contract are supplies under a contract providing for periodical payment for such supplies within the meaning of Regulation 21(1) of the Value Added Tax (General) Regulations 1972 or any amendment thereof.

19B.4   .1.1   The Contractor shall pay to the Sub-Contractor in the manner set out in clause 19B any tax chargeable by the Commissioners on the Sub-Contractor on the supply to the Contractor of any goods and services by the Sub-Contractor under the Sub-Contract.

[*i*] *Clause 19B can only be used where the Contractor under the Value Added Tax (General) Regulations 1972, Regulation 8(3) has been allowed to prepare the tax documents in substitution for an authenticated receipt—issued by the Sub-Contractor under Regulation 21(2) of the above Regulations; and the Sub-Contractor has consented to the use of this method. Where clause 19B applies, clause 19A must be deleted and its deletion initialled by the parties. The Tender, Schedule 2, item 8 states whether clause 19A or 19B applies.*

.1.2　The Sub-Contractor shall, not later than 7 days before the date when payment is due to the Sub-Contractor under clause 21.3 give to the Contractor a written provisional assessment of the respective values (less the Retention and cash discount referred to in the aforesaid clause 21.3) of those supplies of goods and services for which payment is due as aforesaid and which will be chargeable at the relevant time of supply under the aforesaid Regulation 21(1) on the Sub-Contractor at

> a zero rate of tax (category one)
> and
> any rate or rates of tax other than zero (category two).

The Sub-Contractor shall also specify the rate or rates of tax which are chargeable on those supplies included in category two and shall state the grounds on which he considers such supplies are so chargeable.

.2　The Contractor shall in relation to any amount payable in accordance with the provisions of clause 21 calculate, by applying the rate or rates of tax specified by the Sub-Contractor as applicable to the sub-contract supply the tax properly chargeable on such supply, and remit such tax to the Sub-Contractor within the period prescribed by clause 21.3 for the payment of the amount in relation to which the tax was calculated.

.3　The Contractor shall together with the payment under clause 21.3 and the payment of tax under clause 19B.4.2 issue to the Sub-Contractor a document approved by the Commissioners under Regulation 8(3) of the Value Added Tax (General) Regulations 1972, and shall not insert in this document any date or other writing which purports to represent for any purposes whatsoever the time of supply in respect of which the Sub-Contractor becomes liable for tax (output tax) on the relevant supplies of goods and services to the Contractor. Without prejudice to the above obligation of the Contractor in relation to the time of supply by the Sub-Contractor, the Contractor shall insert in this document the date of despatch of the document to the Sub-Contractor. Provided always that the payment including tax referred to in the document (or reconciled with the actual payment received by the Sub-Contractor in accordance with clause 19B.4.2) has been received, the Sub-Contractor shall insert on this document in a space left thereon for this purpose by the Contractor the date of receipt of the document by the Sub-Contractor. If such payment has not been received the Sub-Contractor shall immediately reject the document and explain to the Contractor the reasons for such rejection.

.4　If the Sub-Contractor disallows any cash discount claimed by the Contractor under clause 21.3 and the Contractor pays the amount of such discount to the Sub-Contractor the provisions of clause 19B.4.2 and .3 shall not apply.

.5　If the payment received is different from that stated in the document issued by the Contractor to the Sub-Contractor, the Contractor shall issue with that document a reconciliation statement.

19B.5　If:

.1　at any time the Commissioners withdraw the approval referred to in clause 19B.4.3 (in which event the Contractor shall immediately so inform the Sub-Contractor in writing);
or

.2　the Sub-Contractor withdraws his consent to the procedure referred to in clause 19B.4.3 and so notifies the Commissioners and the Contractor in writing

then clause 19A shall be deemed to be incorporated in the Sub-Contract Conditions in respect of payment and tax thereon for any supplies of goods and services remaining to be supplied and/or paid for under the Sub-Contract.

B.6   Subject to clause 19B.5 the Sub-Contractor shall at no time in respect of supplies and goods and services under the Sub-Contract issue a document which is or purports to be an authenticated receipt within the meaning of Regulation 21(2) of the Value Added Tax (General) Regulations 1972.

B.7   It is hereby agreed and declared that in issuing any documents referred to in clause 19B the Contractor is not acting as agent for the Sub-Contractor.

Clauses 19A, 19B: Value Added Tax

Clause 19A is the Sub-Contract equivalent of clause 15 of the Main Contract and the Supplemental Provisions (the VAT Agreement). See their commentaries. Clause 19B is an alternative clause which can only be used where there is a special arrangement under the VAT (General) Regulations 1985, Regulations 12(3) and 26. The VAT provisions of the Sub-Contract were amended by Amendment 8 issued in April 1989. This Amendment was introduced because of major changes to the VAT status of supplies of goods and services which came into effect on April 1, 1989. A new alternative system (see new clauses 19A.5 and 19B.5) was introduced where the Sub-Contractor is satisfied at the date of the Sub-Contract that his output tax on all supplies will be either at the standard rate or at a zero rate.

A.   **Finance (No. 2) Act 1975—Tax Deduction Scheme** [j] [k]

A.1   In clause 20A and in clause 20B the Act means the Finance (No. 2) Act 1975 and the Regulations means the Income Tax (Sub-Contractors in the Construction Industry) Regulations 1975 S.1. No. 1960 or any re-enactment or amendment thereof.

A.2   .1   Subject to clause 20A.2.2:

     either
.1.1   the Sub-Contractor, not later than 21 days before the first payment is due to the Sub-Contractor, shall produce to the Contractor his current tax certificate issued to him under S.70 of the Act and the Contractor shall within 7 days of the date of such production confirm to the Sub-Contractor in writing such production and his satisfaction or non-satisfaction under Regulation 21(1)(a) of the Regulations;
     or
.1.2   at the sole option of the Sub-Contractor where the Sub-Contractor is a company which is the user of a tax certificate in the form numbered 714C in the Schedule to the Regulations, the Sub-Contractor, not later than 21 days before the first payment is due to the Sub-Contractor, shall lodge with the Contractor a document, as referred to in Regulation 22(1)(c) of the Regulations, referable to his current tax certificate, and the Contractor shall within 7 days of such production

---

[j] *For use where in the Seventh recital (A) the words "is not" have been deleted; see also Tender, Schedule 2, item 7. Clause 20B should be deleted where clause 20A applies.*

[k] *Where the Contractor operates with the permission of Inland Revenue the system of dealing with the Tax Deduction Scheme known as "self-vouchering," clause 20A is not applicable; and the Contractor and Nominated Sub-Contractor must make appropriate sub-contractual arrangements; see also Tender, Schedule 2, item 7.*

confirm to the Sub-Contractor in writing such production and that he has or has not reason to doubt the correctness of the information shown on the document under Regulation 22(1).

.2 Clause 20A.2.1 shall not apply where the Sub-Contractor has previously produced to the Contractor either the tax certificate referred to in clause 20A.2.1.1 or the document referred to in clause 20A.2.1.2 and the Contractor has previously expressed in writing to the Sub-Contractor either his satisfaction as referred to in Regulation 21(1)(a) of the Regulations or that he has no reason to doubt the correctness of the information shown on the document under Regulation 22(1), whichever is applicable.

.3 Where under clause 20A.2.1.2 the Sub-Contractor has produced to the Contractor the document referred to therein the Sub-Contractor shall notify the Contractor in writing of any change in the nominated bank account or accounts specified in that document.

.4 Where either production of the tax certificate and notification of satisfaction under clause 20A.2.1 or lodgement of the document and admission that the Contractor has no reason to doubt under clause 20A.2.1.2 have been made, payment under the Sub-Contract shall, subject to clause 20A.4, be made without the statutory deduction referred to in S.69(4) of the Act.

20A.3 .1 The Sub-Contractor shall immediately inform the Contractor in writing if the tax certificate produced by him or referred to in the document produced by him is withdrawn or cancelled and give the date of such withdrawal or cancellation.

.2 The Contractor shall immediately inform the Sub-Contractor of any change in the position stated in the Seventh recital (B) (or in the Tender, Schedule 2, item 7) in regard to the user by the Contractor of a sub-contractor's tax certificate or in the position stated in the Seventh recital (C) (or in the Tender, Schedule 1, item 10) as to whether the Employer is or is not a "contractor" within the meaning of the Act and the Regulations.

20A.4 .1 Where the tax certificate produced to the Contractor is in one of the forms numbered 714I or 714P in the Schedule to the Regulations the Sub-Contractor shall immediately upon receipt of any payment from which the deduction referred to in S.69(4) of the Act has not been made issue to the Contractor a voucher as required by Regulation 23(1) of the Regulations in the form numbered 715 in the aforesaid Schedule.

.2 Where the tax certificate produced to the Contractor is in the form numbered 714S in the Regulations, not later than 7 days before any payment under this Sub-Contract becomes due the Sub-Contractor shall inform the Contractor in writing of the amount to be included in such payment which represents the direct cost to the Sub-Contractor of materials used or to be used by the Sub-Contractor and give to the Contractor a special voucher as required by the Regulations in the form numbered 715S. Where the remainder of the payment as indicated by the voucher exceeds for payment during any one week £150 the Contractor will in accordance with the Regulations deduct the statutory rate of deduction for the time being in force from any excess.

.3 The Contractor shall immediately on receipt pass the voucher referred to in clause 20A.4.1 or clause 20A.4.2 as applicable to the Inland Revenue.

20A.5 .1 If at any time before a payment is due under the Sub-Contract the Contractor is required by the Act and the Regulations (whether by reason of expiry, withdrawal or cancellation of the Sub-Contractor's tax certificate or otherwise) to make the deduction referred to in S.69(4) of the Act the Contractor shall immediately notify the Sub-Contractor in writing and require him to state not later than 7 days before such payment becomes due (or, if the said notification is less than 7 days before the payment becomes due, within 10 days of such notification) the amount to be included in such payment which represents the direct cost to the Sub-Contractor of materials used or to be used by the Sub-Contractor.

   .2   Where the Sub-Contractor complies with clause 20A.5.1 he shall indemnify the Contractor against any loss or expense caused to the Contractor by any incorrect statement of the amount of direct cost referred to in clause 20A.5.1.

   .3   Where the Sub-Contractor does not comply with clause 20A.5.1 the Contractor shall be entitled to make a fair estimate of the amount of direct cost referred to in clause 20A.5.1 and calculate the deduction to be made under S.69(4) of the Act by taking into account the amount of that fair estimate.

A.6   Where any error or omission has occurred in calculating or making the deduction referred to in S.69(4) of the Act the Contractor shall correct that error or omission by repayment to, or by further deduction from payments to, the Sub-Contractor as the case may be, subject only to any statutory obligation on the Contractor not to make such correction.

A.7   If compliance with clause 20A involves the Contractor or the Sub-Contractor in not complying with any other provisions of the Sub-Contract, then the provisions of clause 20A shall prevail.

A.8   The provisions of Article 3 shall apply to any dispute or difference as to the operation of clause 20A except where the Act or the Regulations or any other Act of Parliament or statutory instrument rule or order made under an Act of Parliament provide for some other method of resolving such dispute or difference.

B.   **Finance (No. 2) Act 1975—Tax Deduction Scheme—Sub-Contractor not user of a current tax certificate [*l*]**

B.1   .1   Not later than 7 days before any payment under this Sub-Contract becomes due the Sub-Contractor shall inform the Contractor in writing of the amount to be included in such payment which represents the direct cost to the Sub-Contractor of materials used or to be used by the Sub-Contractor in order that the deduction referred to in S.69(4) of the Act can be made from that payment.

   .2   Where the Sub-Contractor complies with clause 20B.1.1 he shall indemnify the Contractor against any loss or expense caused to the Contractor by any incorrect statement of the amount of direct cost referred to in clause 20B.1.1.

   .3   Where the Sub-Contractor does not comply with clause 20B.1.1 the Contractor shall be entitled to make a fair estimate of the amount of direct cost referred to in clause 20B.1.1 and calculate the deduction to be made under S.69(4) of the Act by taking into account the amount of that fair estimate.

B.2   Where any error or omission has occurred in calculating or making the deduction referred in S.69(4) of the Act, the Contractor shall correct that error or omission by repayment to, or by further deduction from payments to, the Sub-Contractor as the case may be, subject only to any statutory obligation on the Contractor not to make such correction.

[*l*] *For use where in the Seventh recital (A) the word "is" has been deleted; see also Tender, Schedule 2, item 7. Clause 20A.2 to .8 should be deleted where clause 20B applies.*

20B.3 The Contractor shall immediately inform the Sub-Contractor of any change in the position stated in the Seventh recital (B) (or in the Tender, Schedule 2, item 7) in regard to the user by the Contractor of a sub-contractor's tax certificate or in the position stated in the Seventh recital (C) (or in the Tender, Schedule 1, item 10) as to whether the Employer is or is not a "contractor" within the meaning of the Act and the Regulations.

20B.4 If compliance with clause 20B involves the Contractor or the Sub-Contractor in not complying with any other provisions of the Sub-Contract, then the provisions of clause 20B shall prevail.

20B.5 If at any time up to and including the date when the last payment under the Sub-Contract is due to the Sub-Contractor the Sub-Contractor becomes the user of a current sub-contractor's tax certificate under the Act and Regulations, the Sub-Contractor shall immediately notify the Contractor in writing and clause 20A.2 to .8 of the Sub-Contract Conditions shall be reinstated from the date of such notification as if it had not been deleted and shall come into effect in substitution for clause 20B with the following amendment:
> clauses 20A.2.1.1 and 20A.2.1.2—
>
> **delete** "first payment"
> **insert** "first or next payment"

20B.6 The provisions of Article 3 shall apply to any dispute or difference as to the operation of clause 20B except where the Act or the Regulations or any other Act of Parliament or statutory instrument, rule or order made under an Act of Parliament provide for some other method or resolving such dispute or difference.

Clause 20A: Finance (No. 2) Act 1975—Tax Deduction Scheme

Clause 20B: Finance (No. 2) Act 1975—Tax Deduction Scheme—Sub-Contractor not user of current tax certificate.

These clauses are the Sub-Contract equivalent of clause 31 of the Main Contract. Clause 20A applies where the Sub-Contractor holds a current tax certificate, except that it is not appropriate where the Contractor operates with the permission of the Inland Revenue the system of dealing with the Tax Deduction Scheme known as "self-vouchering." By Amendment 4 issued in July 1987, a new clause 20A.4.2 was inserted (and the existing clause 20A.4.2 consequently redrafted and renumbered as 20A.4.3) to deal with the tax certificate under the statutory Tax Deductions Scheme in the Form numbered 714S which was introduced in December 1982. Clause 20B applies where the Sub-Contractor is not the holder of a current tax certificate. By clause 20B.5, if the Sub-Contractor obtained a tax certificate before the last payment under the Sub-Contract is due to him, clause 20A is reinstated.

21. Payment of Sub-Contractor

21.1 Interim payments and final payment shall be made to the Sub-Contractor in accordance with the provisions of clause 21.

Clause 21—Payment of Sub-Contractor

21.2 .1 Notwithstanding the requirement that the Architect shall issue Interim Certificates under clause 30 of the Main Contract Conditions, the Contractor shall, if so requested by the Sub-Contractor, make application to the Architect as to the matters referred to in clauses 30.2.1.4, 30.2.2.5 and 30.2.3.2 of the Main Contract Conditions.

.2 The Contractor shall include in or annex to any application under clause 21.2.1 any written representations of the Sub-Contractor which the Sub-Contractor wishes the Architect to consider including those referred to in clause 37.3.2.

.3 The Sub-Contractor shall observe any relevant conditions in clause 30.3 of the Main Contract Conditions before the Architect is empowered to include the value of any off-site materials or goods in Interim Certificates.

.4.1 Subject to clause 16.1 of the Main Contract Conditions, unfixed materials and goods delivered to, placed on or adjacent to the Works by the Sub-Contractor and intended therefor shall not be removed except for use on the Works unless the Contractor has consented in writing to such removal, which consent shall not be unreasonably withheld.

.4.2 Where, in accordance with clause 30.2 of the Main Contract Conditions, the value of any such materials or goods shall have been included in any Interim Certificate under which the amount properly due to the Contractor shall have been discharged by the Employer in favour of the Contractor, such materials or goods shall be and become the property of the Employer and the Sub-Contractor shall not deny that such materials or goods are and have become the property of the Employer. Provided always that the Architect shall in accordance with clause 35.13.1.2 of the Main Contract Conditions have informed the Sub-Contractor of the amount of any interim or final payment directed by the Architect in the Interim Certificate to which clause 21.2.4.2 refers.

.4.3 Provided also that if the Contractor shall pay the Sub-Contractor for any such materials or goods before the value therefor has, in accordance with clause 30.2 of the Main Contract Conditions, been included in any Interim Certificate under which the amount properly due to the Contractor has been discharged by the Employer in favour of the Contractor, such materials or goods shall upon such payment by the Contractor be and become the property of the Contractor.

.4.4 The operation of clauses 21.2.4.1 to 21.2.4.3 shall be without prejudice to any property in any materials or goods passing to the Contractor as provided in clause 30.3.5 of the Main Contract Conditions (*off-site materials or goods*).

21.3 .1.1 Within 17 days of the date of issue of an Interim Certificate (including the Interim Certificate referred to in clause 35.17 or clause 30.7 of the Main Contract Conditions) the Contractor shall notify to the Sub-Contractor the amount of the interim or final payment in respect of the Sub-Contract Works which, in accordance with clause 35.13.1 of the Main Contract Conditions, is included in the amount stated as due in the Interim Certificate. The Contractor shall duly discharge his obligation under clause 35.13.2 of the Main Contract Conditions and the Sub-Contract to make that payment within the aforementioned 17 days but less a cash discount of 2½ per cent. if discharge is so effected. Immediately upon discharge by the Contractor as aforesaid the Sub-Contractor shall supply the Contractor with written proof of such discharge so as to enable the Contractor to provide the Architect with the "reasonable proof" referred to in clause 35.13.3 of the Main Contract Conditions.[m]

.1.2 Where the Employer has exercised any right under the Main Contract to deduct from monies due to the Contractor and such deduction is in respect of some act or

---

[m] *Attention is directed to clause 23 and also to clause 20A or 20B which may be relevant to the due discharge by the Contractor to which clause 21.3.1.1 refers.*

749

default of the Sub-Contractor, his servants or agents the amount of such deduction may be deducted by the Contractor from any monies due or to become due under the Sub-Contract or may be recoverable by the Contractor from the Sub-Contractor as a debt.

.2.1 The Contractor shall only be under an obligation duly to discharge any amount certified in an Interim Certificate issued under clause 35.17 of the Main Contract Conditions provided the Sub-Contractor shall have entered into Agreement NSC/2 including clause 5 of that Agreement unamended in any way and such Agreement is in full force and effect;

.2.2 Where the Contractor is under an obligation duly to discharge any amount certified in an Interim Certificate issued under clause 35.17 of the Main Contract Conditions the Sub-Contractor upon such discharge hereby agrees to indemnify the Contractor in respect of any omission, fault or defect in the Sub-Contract Works caused by the Sub-Contractor, his servants or agents for which the Contractor may at any time become liable to the Employer but subject always to the terms of clause 35.19.1 of the Main Contract Conditions.

.3 Where, in accordance with clause 2.2 of Agreement NSC/2, the Employer, before the issue of an instruction nominating the Sub-Contractor, has paid to him an amount in respect of design work and/or materials or goods and/or fabrication which is/are included in the subject of the Sub-Contract Sum or Tender Sum and the Employer has made a deduction from the amount due to the Contractor in an Interim Certificate in accordance with clause 35.13.6 of the Main Contract Conditions, then, to the extent of the amount deducted by the Employer, the Contractor shall be deemed to have discharged the interim or final payment to the Sub-Contractor directed by the Architect as being included in the amount due in that Interim Certificate.

21.4 Subject to any agreement between the Sub-Contractor and the Architect as to stage payments, the amount of an interim payment to the Sub-Contractor which is included in the amount stated as due in an Interim Certificate and to which the provisions of clause 35.13 of the Main Contract Conditions apply shall be the gross valuation as referred to in clause 21.4 less

an amount equal to any amount which may be deducted and retained by the Employer as provided in clause 30.2 of the Main Contract Conditions (referred to in the Main Contract Conditions as "the Retention") in respect of the Sub-Contract Works; and

the total amount in respect of the Sub-Contract Works included in the total amount stated as due in Interim Certificates previously issued under the Main Contract Conditions.

The gross valuation shall be the total of the amounts referred to in clauses 21.4.1 and 21.4.2 less the total amount referred to in clause 21.4.3 as applied up to and including a date not more than 7 days before the date of the Interim Certificate as follows:

.1.1 the total value of the sub-contract work properly executed by the Sub-Contractor including any work so executed to which clause 16.1 refers but excluding any restoration, replacement or repair of loss or damage and removal and disposal of debris which in clauses 8B.4 and 8C.4 are treated as if they were a Variation, together with, where applicable, any adjustment of that total value under clause 37;

.1.2 the total value of the materials and goods delivered to or adjacent to the Works for incorporation therein by the Sub-Contractor but not so incorporated provided that the value of such materials and goods shall only be included as and from such times as they are reasonably, properly and not prematurely so delivered and are adequately protected against weather and other casualties;

.1.3   the total value of any materials or goods other than those to which clause 21.4.1.2 refers where the Architect in the exercise of his discretion under clause 30.3 of the Main Contract Conditions has decided that such total value shall be included in the amount stated as due in an Interim Certificate.

.2.1   any amount to be included in Interim Certificates in accordance with clause 3 as a result of payments made or costs incurred by the Sub-Contractor under clause 6 or 7 of the Main Contract Conditions as referred to in clause 5.1.1, and under clause 14.4;

.2.2   any amount ascertained as a result of the application of clause 13.1 or in respect of any restoration, replacement or repair of loss or damage and removal and disposal of debris which in clauses 8B.4 and 8C.4 are treated as if they were a Variation;

.2.3   any amount payable to the Sub-Contractor under clause 35 or 36, whichever is applicable;

.2.4   an amount equal to one thirty-ninth of the amounts referred to in clauses 21.4.2.1, 21.4.2.2 and 21.4.2.3.

.3   any amount deductible under clause 4.3.4.1 or 14.4 or any amount allowable by the Sub-Contractor to the Contractor under clause 35 or 36, whichever is applicable together with an amount equal to one thirty-ninth of that amount.

21.5   The Retention which the Employer may deduct and retain as referred to in clause 30.2 of the Main Contract Conditions and clause 21.4 is such percentage of the total amount included under clauses 21.4.1.1 to 21.4.1.3 in any Interim Certificate as arises from the operation of the rules set out in clause 30.4 of the Main Contract Conditions.

21.6   The Retention is subject to the rules set out in clause 30.5 of the Main Contract Conditions.

21.7   If the Sub-Contractor shall feel aggrieved by any amount certified by the Architect or by his failure to certify, then subject to the Sub-Contractor giving to the Contractor such indemnity and security as the Contractor shall reasonably require, the Contractor shall allow the Sub-Contractor to use the Contractor's name and if necessary will join with the Sub-Contractor in arbitration proceedings at the instigation of the Sub-Contractor in respect of the said matters complained of by the Sub-Contractor.

21.8   .1   If:

.1.1   subject to clause 23 the Contractor shall fail to discharge his obligation to make any payment to the Sub-Contractor as herein before provided; and

.1.2   the Employer has

either for any reason not operated the provisions of clause 35.13.5 of the Main Contract Conditions
or has operated those provisions but for any reason has not paid the Sub-Contractor direct the whole amount which the Contractor has failed to discharge,

within 35 days from the date of issue of the Interim Certificate in respect of which the Contractor has so failed to make proper discharge of his obligation in regard to payment of the Sub-Contractor,

then provided the Sub-Contractor shall have given 14 days' notice in writing to the Contractor and the Employer of his intention to suspend the further execution of the Sub-Contract Works, the Sub-Contractor may (but without prejudice to any other right or remedy) suspend the further execution of the Sub-Contract Works until such discharge or until such direct payment is made whichever first occurs.

751

.2   Such period of suspension shall not be deemed a delay for which the Sub-Contractor is liable under the Sub-Contract. The Contractor shall be liable to the Sub-Contractor for any loss, damage or expense caused to the Sub-Contractor by any suspension of the Sub-Contract Works under the provisions of clause 21.8.1. The right of the Sub-Contractor under clause 21.8.1 shall not be exercised unreasonably or vexatiously.

21.9   .1   The Contractor's interest in the Sub-Contractor's retention (as identified in the statement issued under clause 30.5.2 of the Main Contract Conditions and referred to in clause 21.6) is fiduciary as trustee for the Sub-Contractor (but without obligation to invest) and if the Contractor attempts or purports to mortgage or otherwise charge such interest or his interest in the whole of the amount retained as aforesaid (otherwise than by floating charge if the Contractor is a limited company) the Contractor shall thereupon immediately set aside in a separate bank account and become a trustee for the Sub-Contractor of a sum equivalent to the Sub-Contractor's retention as identified in the aforesaid statement; provided that upon payment of the same to the Sub-Contractor the amount due to the Sub-Contractor upon final payment under the Sub-Contract shall be reduced accordingly by the amount so paid.

.2   If any of the Sub-Contractor's retention is withheld by the Contractor after the period within which such retention should be discharged by the Contractor, the Contractor shall immediately upon the expiry of the aforesaid period place any such unpaid retention money in a separate trust account so identified as to make clear that the Contractor is the trustee for the Sub-Contractor of all such undischarged retention.

21.10   .1.1   Where clause 15.1 applies not later than 6 months after practical completion of the Sub-Contract Works the Sub-Contractor shall send to the Contractor or, if so instructed by him, to the Architect or the Quantity Surveyor, all documents necessary for the purpose of the adjustment of the Sub-Contract Sum.

.1.2   Not later than 3 months after receipt by the Contractor (or, if so instructed under clause 21.10.1.1, after receipt by the Architect or the Quantity Surveyor) of the documents referred to in clause 21.10.1.1 a statement of all adjustments to the Sub-Contract Sum to which clause 21.10.2 refers shall be prepared by the Architect or, if the Architect has so instructed, by the Quantity Surveyor and the Architect shall forthwith send a copy of the statement to the Contractor and the Sub-Contractor which shall be before the Architect certifies final payment for the Sub-Contract Works under clause 35.17 or clause 30.7 of the Main Contract Conditions.

.2   The Sub-Contract Sum shall be adjusted as follows.

There shall be deducted:

.2.1   all provisional sums and the value of all work described as provisional included in the Sub-Contract Documents;

.2.2   the amount of the valuation under clause 16.3.2 of items omitted in accordance with a Variation required by an instruction of the Architect or subsequently sanctioned by him in writing together with the amount of any other work included in the Sub-Contract Documents as referred to in clause 16.3.5 which is to be valued under clause 16.3;

.2.3   any amount deducted or deductible under clause 4.3.4.1 or 14.4 or any amount allowed to the Contractor under clause 35, 36 or 37, whichever is applicable, together with (except where clause 37 is applicable) an amount equal to one thirty-ninth of that amount;

.2.4   any other amount which is required by the Sub-Contract Documents to be deducted from the Sub-Contract Sum.

There shall be added:

.2.5　any amount paid or payable by the Contractor to the Sub-Contractor as a result of payments made or costs incurred by the Sub-Contractor under clause 6 or 7 of the Main Contract Conditions as referred to in clause 5.1.1 and under clause 14.4;

.2.6　the amount of the valuation under clause 16.3 of any Variation including the valuation of other work, as referred to in clause 16.3.5, under clause 16.3 other than the amount of the valuation of any omission under clause 16.3.2;

.2.7　the amount of the valuation of work executed by, or the amount of any disbursements made by, the Sub-Contractor in accordance with the instructions of the Architect as to the expenditure of provisional sums included in the Sub-Contract Documents, and of all work described as provisional included in the Sub-Contract Documents;

.2.8　any amount ascertained as a result of the application of clause 13.1;

.2.9　any amount paid or payable to the Sub-Contractor under clause 35, 36 or 37, whichever is applicable;

.2.10　any other amount which is required by the Sub-Contract to be added to the Sub-Contract Sum;

.2.11　an amount equal to one thirty-ninth of the amounts referred to in clauses 21.10.2.5, 21.10.2.8 and, where clause 35 or 36 applies, of the amount referred to in clause 21.10.2.8.

.11　.1　Where clause 15.2 applies, not later than 6 months after practical completion of the Sub-Contract Works the Sub-Contractor shall send to the Contractor or, if so instructed by him, to the Architect or the Quantity Surveyor, all documents necessary for the purpose of computing the Ascertained Final Sub-Contract Sum. Not later than 3 months after receipt by the Contractor (or, if so instructed under clause 21.11.1, after receipt by the Architect or the Quantity Surveyor) of the aforesaid documents a statement of the computation of the Ascertained Final Sub-Contract Sum to which clause 21.11.2 refers shall be prepared by the Architect or, if the Architect has so instructed, by the Quantity Surveyor, and the Architect shall forthwith send a copy of the statement to the Contractor and the Sub-Contractor which shall be before the Architect certifies final payment for the Sub-Contract Works under clause 35.17 or clause 30.7 of the Main Contract Conditions.

.2　The Ascertained Final Sub-Contact Sum shall be the aggregate of the following:

.2.1　any amount paid or payable by the Contractor to the Sub-Contractor as a result of payments made or costs incurred by the Sub-Contractor under clause 6 or 7 of the Main Contract Conditions as referred to in clause 5.1.1 and under clause 14.4;

.2.2　the amount of the Valuation under clause 17;

.2.3　any amount ascertained as a result of the application of clause 13.1;

.2.4　any amount deducted or deductible under clause 4.3.4.1 or 14.4 or any amount paid or payable to or allowed or allowable by the Sub-Contractor under clause 35, 36 or 37, whichever is applicable;

.2.5　any other amount which is required to be included or taken into account in computing the Ascertained Final Sub-Contract Sum;

.2.6　an amount equal to one thirty-ninth of the amounts referred to in clauses 21.11.2.1, 21.11.2.3 and 21.11.2.4 (so far as clause 21.11.2.4 refers to clauses 35 and 36).

.12　.1　Except as provided in clauses 21.12.2 and 21.12.3 (and save in respect of fraud) the Final Certificate issued under clause 30.8 of the Main Contract Conditions shall have effect in any proceedings arising out of or in connection with this Sub-Contract (whether by arbitration under Article 3 or otherwise) as

.1   conclusive evidence that where and to the extent that the quality of materials or goods or the standard of workmanship are to be to the reasonable satisfaction of the Architect the same are to such satisfaction, and

.2   conclusive evidence that any necessary effect has been given to all the terms of this Sub-Contract which require that an amount is to be added to or subtracted from the Sub-Contract Sum or included in the calculation of the Ascertained Final Sub-Contract Sum save where there has been any accidental inclusion or exclusion of any work, materials, goods or figure in any computation or any arithmetical error in any computation in which event the Final Certificate shall have effect as conclusive evidence as to all other computations, and

.3   conclusive evidence that all and only such extensions of time, if any, as are due under clause 11 have been given, and

.4   conclusive evidence that the reimbursement of direct loss and/or expense, if and to the Sub-Contractor pursuant to clause 13.1 is in final settlement of all or any claims which the Sub-Contractor has or may have arising out of the occurrence of any of the matters referred to in clause 13.1.2 whether such claim be for breach of contract, duty of care, statutory duty or otherwise.

.2 If any arbitration or other proceedings have been commenced by either party (or by the Employer and to which the Sub-Contractor is a party) before the Final Certificate under clause 30.8 of the Main Contract Conditions has been issued the Final Certificate shall have effect as conclusive evidence as provided in clause 21.12.1 after either:

.1   such proceedings have been concluded, whereupon the Final Certificate shall be subject to the terms of any award or judgment in or settlement of such proceedings,
   or

.2   a period of 12 months during which no party has taken any further steps in such proceedings, whereupon the Final Certificate shall be subject to any terms agreed in partial settlement

whichever shall be the earlier.

.3 If any arbitration or other proceedings have been commenced by either party (or by the Employer and to which the Sub-Contractor is a party) within 21 days after the Final Certificate under clause 30.8 of the Main Contract Conditions has been issued, the Final Certificate shall have effect as conclusive evidence as provided in clause 21.12.1 save only in respect of all matters to which those proceedings relate.

Clause 21: Payment of Sub-Contractor

Generally.   This clause deals with interim and final payments to the Sub-Contractor and should be read with clause 30 of the Main Contract. It also contains in clause 21.8 an important provision entitling the Sub-Contractor in certain circumstances where he has not been fully paid to suspend the further execution of the Sub-Contract Works (see commentary below).

Clause 21.2.1. "*... the Contractor shall, if so requested by the Sub-Contractor, make application to the Architect ...*"

Clause 30.2 of the Main Contract requires the Architect to include in Interim Certificates the amounts due to each Nominated Sub-Contractor under clause 21.4 of NSC/4 without application. It is, however, often convenient for the Nominated Sub-Contractor to inform the Architect of his understanding of his entitlement.

Clause 21.2.4.1 to 21.2.4.4. These sub-clauses were added by Amendment 2 issued in January 1984. They are directed to dealing with the problem exemplified by *Dawber Williamson Roofing* v. *Humberside County Council*[14] namely that provisions in the Main Contract for the passing of property from Contractor to Employer are of no effect in circumstances where the Contractor has not acquired a good title in materials or goods from his Sub-Contractor. The scheme of these sub-clauses is that:

(1) unfixed materials and goods delivered to the Works by the Sub-Contractor and intended therefor are not to be removed except for use on the Works unless the Contractor otherwise consents;

(2) where such materials and goods have been credited in an Interim Certificate under the Main Contract and the Certificate discharged "such materials or goods shall be and become the property of the Employer" and the Sub-Contractor is not to deny this fact;

(3) the latter provision is subject to two provisos:

    (a) the Architect must have informed the Sub-Contractor of the amount of the payment in the Interim Certificate;

    (b) if the Contractor has already paid the Sub-Contractor prior to the Interim Certificate, property passes to the Contractor on payment.

It is thought that these provisions are probably effective to pass title to the Employer and to protect him against the Contractor's liquidation. However, they will bear harshly upon the Sub-Contractor who has not been paid for certified materials or goods in circumstances where the Contractor has gone into liquidation.

Clause 21.3.1.1. "*Within 17 days of the date of issue of an Interim Certificate ... the Contractor ... shall duly discharge ...*"

Under clause 30.1.1.1 of the Main Contract, the Contractor is himself entitled to payment within 14 days from the date of issue of each Interim Certificate. Thus, in theory, the Main Contractor is not expected to fund payments to Nominated Sub-Contractors. The Sub-Contractor's entitlement to payment, however, is not dependent upon the Contractor himself receiving payment under the Main Contract. It is submitted that an amount due to a Nominated Sub-Contractor will be "duly discharged" by the valid exercise of a right of set-off under clause 23.[15]

---

[14] (1979) 12 B.L.R. 70; see discussion in the commentary to clause 16 of the Main Contract.
[15] See *Modern Engineering* v. *Gilbert-Ash* [1974] A.C. 689 at 708 (H.L.); *cf. Scobie & McIntosh* v. *Clayton Bowmore* (1990) 49 B.L.R. 119.

Clause 21.3.1.1. *". . . written proof of such discharge . . ."*
This is necessary for the operation of the direct payment provisions in clause 35.13.5 of the Main Contract.[16] An example of the operation of the direct payment provisions and of the Sub-Contractor's right to suspend the further execution of the Sub-Contract Works is given in the commentary to clause 21.8.

Clause 21.3.1.2. It is thought that the Contractor's right of deduction under this clause, where the Employer has exercised a right of deduction under the Main Contract for some act or default of the Sub-Contractor, is not a provision to which clause 23.2 applies.[16a]

Clause 21.3.2.1. This clause should be read with clauses 35.16–35.19 inclusive of the Main Contract and their commentaries.

Clause 21.3.3. This amendment should be read with the amendment to clause 35.13 of the Main Contract and Amendment 1 to NSC/2. It deals with the treatment of payments by the Employer under NSC/2 to a Nominated Sub-Contractor and with the resultant credit due to the Employer. The scheme is that:

    (1) such payments are ignored in computing the amounts stated as due in certificates issued to the Main Contractor;
    (2) deductions representing the credit are made by the Employer from the amounts stated as due to the Main Contractor in any Interim Certificate up to an amount not exceeding the total included in it for the relevant Nominated Sub-Contractor;
    (3) where the Employer has made such deductions the Main Contractor may make a deduction of the same amount from the amount directed for payment to the Nominated Sub-Contractor.

Clause 21.4. This clause is the Sub-Contract equivalent of clause 30.2 of the Main Contract (see commentary to Main Contract clause 30). Additionally, clauses 30.2.1.4, 30.2.2.5 and 30.2.3.3 of the Main Contract provide for the various amounts in clause 21.4 of the Sub-Contract to be taken into account in ascertaining the amounts due in Interim Certificates. The "one-thirty-ninth" referred to in clauses 21.4.2.4 and 21.4.3 represents the Main Contractor's cash discount of 2½ per cent. referred to in clause 21.3.1.1.

Clause 21.4.1.1. *". . . the total value of the Sub-Contract Works properly executed by the Sub-Contractor . . ."*
These words have been considered in the context of attempts by the Main Contractor to circumvent the very limited availability of the defence of set-off

---

[16] See commentary to Main Contract clause 35 and see also clause 7 of Agreement NSC/2.
[16a] See *Mellowes PPG* v. *Snelling Construction* (1989) 49 B.L.R. 109.

in this and similar forms of Sub-Contract (as to which see clause 23 and its commentary). The provisions of clause 23 do not deprive the Main Contractor of the opportunity to show that sums claimed are not in fact due either because the Sub-Contractor has sought to claim the value of work not in fact done, or because the sum claimed is calculated upon a mistaken basis as to the agreed price of the work done, or because part of the work done is worth less than the agreed price by reason of breach by the Sub-Contractor of the terms of the Sub-Contract. The Main Contractor is entitled to resist the claim by proving that the Sub-Contract Works are not properly executed and thus advancing the defence of abatement (as distinct from equitable set-off) which is not caught by the provisions of clause 23.[17]

Clauses 21.4.1.1 and 21.4.2.2. *". . . any restoration, replacement or repair . . . as if they were a Variation . . ."*
These words were added by Amendment 4 issued in July 1987 to bring into the Sub-Contract the equivalent amendments to clauses 30.2.1.1 and 30.2.2.2 of the Main Contract.

Clause 21.7. *"If the Sub-Contractor shall feel aggrieved . . ."*
This clause enables the Sub-Contractor to take proceedings in the name of the Main Contractor to enforce his rights to certification (see commentary to Sub-Contract clause 4).

Clause 21.8. *". . . the Sub-Contractor may . . . suspend . . ."*
The detailed operation of this clause may be illustrated by an example as follows:

October 1	—	the Architect issues Certificate No. 10 under clause 30.1.1.1 of the Main Contract, and directs the Contractor under clause 35.13.1.1 of the Main Contract that there is included £20,000 for a Nominated Sub-Contractor.
October 15	—	payment of Certificate No. 10 is due to the Main Contractor under clause 30.1.1.1 of the Main Contract.
October 18	—	payment is due to the Sub-Contractor under clause 35.13.2 of the Main Contract and clause 21.3.1.1 of

---

[17] See *Acsim (Southern)* v. *Danish Contracting* (1989) 47 B.L.R. 55 (C.A.) disapproving on this point *B.W.P. (Architectural)* v. *Beaver* (1988) 42 B.L.R. 86 where it had been held in the context of the simiar provisions of Form NAM/SC that Main Contractors were not entitled to allege that work to which the application related was not properly executed since that would have the effect of nullifying Condition 21 of that form (equivalent to Clause 23 of NSC/4) which contained the exclusive machinery by which a Contractor might challenge the Sub-Contractor's right to an interim payment of work not properly executed. For "Abatement" and "Equitable set-off" generally, see p. 439.

		the Sub-Contract. If payment is made, Sub-Contractor has to provide written proof "immediately" (clause 21.3.1.1 of the Sub-Contract).
Before November 1	—	Contractor has to provide Architect with reasonable proof of discharge under clause 35.13.3 of the Main Contract.
If he fails to do so November 1	—	Architect issues Certificate No. 11 for (say) £50,000. Architect certifies amount (£20,000) for which the Contractor has failed to provide reasonable proof (clause 35.13.5.2 of the Main Contract).
November 5	—	expiry of 35 day period in clause 21.8.1.2 of the Sub-Contract.
November 6	—	Sub-Contractor serves 14 day notice of intention to suspend under clause 21.8.1.2 of the Sub-Contract.
November 15	—	payment of Certificate No. 11 due. Employer pays Contractor £30,000 and Sub-Contractor £20,000.
November 20	—	expiry of Sub-Contractor's 14 day notice.

In this example, the Sub-Contractor cannot suspend because he was paid on November 15 before the expiry of his 14-day notice. If, however, either the Employer did not pay the Sub-Contractor or Certificate No. 11 was for less than £20,000 so that the Employer was not obliged to pay the whole of the £20,000 direct (see the proviso to clause 35.13.5.3 of the Main Contract), the Sub-Contractor may suspend the further execution of the Sub-Contract Works on November 21. The maximum period during which the Sub-Contractor is obliged under this procedure to continue to work without payment is 34 days (*i.e.* October 18–November 20). The right to suspend is, however, without prejudice to any other right or remedy. The valid exercise by the Sub-Contractor of his right to suspend is a Relevant Event under clause 11.2.5.13 of the Sub-Contract, and compare clause 29.1.1 under which a suspension without reasonable cause may lead to determination of the Sub-Contractor's employment.

Clause 21.8.2.   "*. . . shall not be exercised unreasonably or vexatiously.*"

For some assistance as to the meaning of this phrase, see commentary to Main Contract clauses 27 and 28. It is thought that the exercise of a right to suspend is generally less likely to be regarded as unreasonable or vexatious than the exercise of a right of determination.

Clause 21.9.   "*. . . the Sub-Contractor's retention . . .*"

For holding retention money "as trustee," see commentary to clause 30 of the Main Contract. The retention referred to in clause 21.9 is, of course, retention held by the Employer under clauses 30.4 and 30.5 of the Main Contract. The money is not expected to be in the hands of the Contractor other than for a brief period upon its release, and the Contractor is not normally required to set aside an identified fund for Nominated Sub-Contractor's retention. Where a Nominated Sub-Contract retention is released under the Main Contract, the Contractor will have to pay this to the Sub-Contractor under clause 21.3.1.1 of the Sub-Contract. He will have to make this payment even if the Employer has exercised a right of deduction to which clause 30.5.4 of the Main Contract applies, unless clause 21.3.1.2 also applies. Clause 21.9.2 recognises that the Contractor may have a valid right to withhold payment of retention under clause 23.2. In those circumstances, he has to set up a separate trust account pending a determination under clause 24.

Clauses 21.10 and 21.11.   These clauses are the Sub-Contract equivalent of clause 30.6 of the Main Contract and apply respectively where clause 15.1 and clause 15.2 apply (see commentary to Sub-Contract clause 15). Clauses 21.10 and 21.11 were amended by Amendment 4 issued in July 1987 to bring into the Sub-Contract the amendments to clause 30.6.1 of the Main Contract (as to which see commentary to clause 30 of the Main Contract). The intention is to provide a stricter timetable for the adjustment of the Main Contract Sum and the issue of the Final Certificate.

Clause 21.12.   *Effect of Final Certificate.*

This important clause was added by Amendment 4 issued in July 1987. Formerly, the Sub-Contract made no provision for the effect of the Final Certificate in relation to the Sub-Contract. This amendment has the result that the Final Certificate is of conclusive effect in any proceedings arising out of or in connection with the Sub-Contract in respect of the same matters, *mutatis mutandis*, as in the Main Contract. For consideration of the effect of the Final Certificate generally, see commentary to Main Contract clause 30.

As with the Main Contract, such effect is qualified where arbitration or other proceedings are commenced before or within 21 days after the issue of the Final Certificate, except that the equivalent period in Main Contract clause 30.9.3 is 28 days. The 7 day difference is presumably to enable the Contractor to start protective Main Contract proceedings in time upon receiving notice of arbitration from the Sub-Contractor. It follows that both the Contractor and the Sub-Contractor should carefully consider the terms and effect of the Final Certificate in respect of the matters listed at clause 21.12.1–21.12.4.

2.   Benefits under Main Contract

The Contractor will so far as he lawfully can at the request and cost, if any, of the Sub-Contractor obtain for him any rights or benefits of the Main Contract so far as the same are applicable to the Sub-Contract Works but not further or otherwise.

Clause 22: Benefits under Main Contract

This clause should be read with clauses 4.6, 11.3 and 21.7 and see commentary to clause 4.6. Under those clauses, the Sub-Contractor has an express right to take proceedings himself. There are other rights under the Main Contract for which the Sub-Contractor is not given an express right to take proceedings, *e.g.* under clause 13.1 of the Sub-Contract. The extent of the duty of the Contractor under clause 22 is not altogether clear. Presumably it requires him, for example, to arrange for meetings with the Architect or Employer, write letters and perhaps even, at the Sub-Contractor's expense, take legal advice upon matters under the Main Contract which may benefit the Nominated Sub-Contractor. Does it go beyond this? Having regard to the express words of clauses 4.6, 11.3 and 21.7, it may be difficult to say that it requires him to lend his name to arbitration proceedings. The Sub-Contractor may be dissatisfied with the certificate of the Architect under clause 35.15.1 or the Architect's opinion under clause 35.24.1 of the Main Contract. These are matters which probably do not arise for determination under the Arbitration provisions of the Sub-Contract.[18] In any event the Contractor's interest would be against lending his name to the Nominated Sub-Contractor. In these circumstances it may be that the best course for the Nominated Sub-Contractor is to bring proceedings against Employer, Architect and Main Contractor for a suitable declaration and other relief.

23. Contractor's right to set-off

23.1 The Contractor shall be entitled to deduct from any money (including any Sub-Contractor's retention, notwithstanding the fiduciary obligation of the Contractor under clause 21.9.1) otherwise due under the Sub-Contract any amount agreed by the Sub-Contractor as due to the Contractor, or finally awarded in arbitration or litigation in favour of the Contractor and which arises out of or under the Sub-Contract.

23.2 .1 Subject to clause 23.2.2, where the Contractor has claim for loss and/or expense and/or damage which he has suffered or incurred by reason of any breach of, or failure to observe the provisions of, the Sub-Contract by the Sub-Contractor (whether or not the Contractor may have further claims for loss and/or expense and/or damage by reason of any such breach or failure) the Contractor shall be entitled to set-off the amount of such loss and/or expense and/or damage so suffered or incurred against any money otherwise due under the Sub-Contract from the Contractor to the Sub-Contractor including any Sub-Contractor's retention notwithstanding the fiduciary obligation of the Contractor under clause 21.9.1. No loss and/or expense and/or damage suffered or incurred by the Contractor which relates to any delay in completion by the Sub-Contractor may be set-off under clause 23.2 unless the certificate of the Architect has been issued in accordance with clause 12.2 to the Contractor with a duplicate copy to the Sub-Contractor.

.2 No set-off under clause 23.2.1 may be made unless

such set-off has been quantified in detail and with reasonable accuracy by the Contractor;
and
the Contractor has given to the Sub-Contractor notice in writing specifying his intention to set-off the amount so quantified together with the details referred to

[18] See *Brightside Kilpatrick* v. *Mitchell Construction* [1975] 2 Lloyd's Rep. 493 at 497 (C.A.).

above and the grounds on which such set-off is claimed to be made. Such notice shall be given not less than 3 days before the date of issue of the Interim Certificate which includes, in the amount stated as due, an amount in respect of the Sub-Contractor and from which latter amount the Contractor intends to make the set-off

provided that such written notice shall not be binding insofar as the Contractor may amend it in preparing his pleadings for any arbitration pursuant to the notice of arbitration referred to in clause 24.1.1.1.

23.3   Any amount set off under the provisions of clause 23.2 is without prejudice to the rights of the Contractor or Sub-Contractor in any subsequent negotiations, arbitration proceedings or litigation to seek to vary the amount claimed and set off by the Contractor under clause 23.2.

23.4   The rights of the parties to the Sub-Contract in respect of set-off are fully set out in Sub-Contract NSC/4 and no other rights whatsoever shall be implied as terms of the Sub-Contract relating to set-off.

24.   **Contractor's claims not agreed by the Sub-Contractor—appointment of Adjudicator**

24.1   .1   If the Sub-Contractor, at the date of the written notice of the Contractor issued under clause 23.2.3, disagrees the amount (or any part thereof) specified in that notice which the Contractor intends to set off, the Sub-Contractor may, within 14 days of receipt by him of such notice, send to the Contractor by registered post or recorded delivery a written statement setting out the reasons for such disagreement and particulars of any counterclaim against the Contractor arising out of the Sub-Contract to which the Sub-Contractor considers he is entitled, provided always that he shall have quantified such counterclaim in detail and with reasonable accuracy (which statement and counterclaim if any, shall not however be binding insofar as the Sub-Contractor may amend it in preparing his pleadings for any arbitration pursuant to the notice of arbitration referred to in clause 24.1.1.1) and shall at the same time:

.1.1   give notice of arbitration under Article 3 to the Contractor; and

.1.2   request action by the Adjudicator in accordance with the right given in clause 24.1.2 (and immediately inform the Contractor of such request) and send to the Adjudicator by registered post or recorded delivery a copy of the aforesaid statement and the written notice of the Contractor to which that statement relates and the aforesaid counterclaim (if any) and brief particulars[n] of the Sub-Contract sufficient to identify for the Adjudicator the terms thereof and where relevant a copy of the certificate of the Architect referred to in clause 12.2.

.2   Subject to the provisions of clause 24 and of clauses 21.3 and 23 the Sub-Contractor shall be entitled to request the Adjudicator named in the Tender, Schedule 2, item 6 to act as the Adjudicator to decide those matters referable to the Adjudicator under the provisions of clause 24. If

an Adjudicator is not named in the Sub-Contract Documents; or

the Adjudicator so named is deceased or is otherwise unable or unwilling to act as the Adjudicator

---

[n] *If such brief particulars do not, in the Adjudicator's view, sufficiently identify the terms of the Sub-Contract he has power under clause 24.3.1, lines 8–10, to obtain further particulars.*

the Adjudicator shall be a person appointed by the Sub-Contractor from the list of Adjudicators maintained by the Building Employers Confederation [o]. Provided that no person shall be appointed, or if appointed shall act, as Adjudicator who has any interest in the Sub-Contract or the Main Contract of which the Sub-Contract is part or in other contracts or sub-contracts in which the Contractor or the Sub-Contractor is engaged unless the Contractor, Sub-Contractor and the Adjudicator so interested otherwise agree in writing within a reasonable time of the Adjudicator's interest becoming apparent.

24.2   Upon receipt of the aforesaid statement the Contractor may within 14 days from the date of such receipt send to the Adjudicator by registered post or recorded delivery a written statement with a copy to the Sub-Contractor setting out brief particulars of his defence to any counterclaim by the Sub-Contractor.

24.3   .1   If

no statement by the Contractor under clause 24.2 has been received by the Adjudicator within the time limit set out in clause 24.2, then within 7 days of expiry of that time limit, or
a statement by the Contractor under clause 24.2 has been received within that time, limit, then within 7 days of receipt by the Adjudicator of such statement,

the Adjudicator without requiring any further statements than those submitted to him under clause 24.1 and where relevant clause 24.2 (save only such further written statements as may appear to the Adjudicator to be necessary to clarify or explain any ambiguity in the written statements of either the Contractor or the Sub-Contractor) and without hearing the Contractor or Sub-Contractor in person, shall, subject to clause 24.3.2, in his absolute discretion and, without giving reasons, decide, in respect of the amount notified by the Contractor under clause 23.2.3, whether the whole or any part of such amount shall be dealt with as follows:

.1.1   shall be retained by the Contractor; or
.1.2   shall, pending arbitration, be deposited by the Contractor for security with the Trustee-Stakeholder named in the Sub-Contract Documents, or if no Trustee-Stakeholder is so named, with the Trustee-Stakeholder, being a deposit-taking Bank, selected by the Adjudicator; or
.1.3   shall be paid by the Contractor to the Sub-Contractor; or
.1.4   any combination of the courses of action set out in clauses 24.3.1.1, 24.3.1.2 and 24.3.1.3.

The Adjudicator's decision shall be binding upon the Contractor and the Sub-Contractor until the matters upon which he has given his decision have been settled by agreement or determined by an Arbitrator or the court.
.2   The Adjudicator shall reach such decision under clause 24.3.1 as he considers to be fair, reasonable and necessary in all the circumstances of the dispute as set out in the statements referred to in clauses 24.1 to .3, and such decision shall deal with the whole amount set off by the Contractor under clause 23.2.
.3   The Adjudicator shall immediately notify in writing the Contractor and the Sub-Contractor of his decision under clause 24.3.1.

---

[o] *While the Building Employers Confederation (BEC) takes all reasonable care to ensure that the persons entered in the list are appropriately qualified to settle sub-contract disputes of the kind referable to an Adjudicator the BEC offers no guarantee of any kind as to the compentence of those listed to discharge the duties of an Adjudicator.*

24.4 .1 Where any decision of the Adjudicator notified under clause 24.3.3 requires the Contractor to deposit an amount with the Trustee-Stakeholder, the Contractor shall thereupon pay such amount to the Trustee-Stakeholder to hold upon the terms hereinafter expressed provided that the Contractor shall not be obliged to pay a sum greater than the amount due from the Contractor under clause 21.3 in respect of which the Contractor has exercised the right of set-off referred to in clause 23.2.

.2 Where any decision of the Adjudicator notified under clause 24.3.3 requires the Contractor to pay an amount to the Sub-Contractor, such amount shall be paid by the Contractor immediately upon receipt of the decision of the Adjudicator but subject to the same proviso as set out in clause 24.4.1.

24.5 .1 The Trustee-Stakeholder shall hold any sum received under the provisions of clauses 24.3 and 24.4 in trust for the Contractor and Sub-Contractor until such time as:

.1.1 the Arbitrator appointed pursuant to the notice of arbitration given by the Sub-Contractor under clause 24.1.1.1; or

.1.2 the Contractor and Sub-Contractor in a joint letter signed by each of them or on their behalf,

shall otherwise direct and shall, in either of the above cases, forthwith dispose of the said sums as may be directed by the Arbitrator, or failing any direction by the Arbitrator, as the Contractor and Sub-Contractor shall jointly determine. The Trustee-Stakeholder shall deposit the sum received in a deposit account in the name of the Trustee-Stakeholder but shall add the interest to the sum deposited. The Trustee-Stakeholder shall be entitled to deduct his reasonable and proper charges from the sum deposited (including any interest added thereto). The Sub-Contractor shall notify the Trustee-Stakeholder of the name and address of the Adjudicator and Arbitrator referred to in clause 24.

.2 Where the Trustee-Stakeholder is a deposit-taking Bank then sums so received by it under the provisions of clauses 24.3 and 24.4 may, notwithstanding the trust imposed, be held by the Trustee-Stakeholder as an ordinary bank deposit to the credit of an account of the Bank as a Trustee-Stakeholder re the Contractor and Sub-Contractor referred to herein; and in respect of such deposit the Trustee-Stakeholder shall pay such usual interest which shall accrue to and form part of the deposit subject to the right of the Trustee-Stakeholder to deduct its reasonable and proper charges and any tax in respect of such interest from the sum deposited.

24.6 The Arbitrator appointed pursuant to the notice of arbitration given under clause 24.1.1.1 may be in his absolute discretion at any time before his final award on the application of either party vary or cancel the decision of the Adjudicator given under clause 24.3 if it appears just and reasonable to him so to do.

24.7 Any action taken by the Contractor under clause 23.2 and by the Sub-Contractor in respect of any counterclaim under clause 24.1.1 is without prejudice to similar action by the Contractor or Sub-Contractor as the case may be if and when further sums become due to the Sub-Contractor.

24.8 The fee of the Adjudicator shall be paid by the Sub-Contractor but the Arbitrator appointed pursuant to the notice of arbitration under clause 24.1.1.1 shall in his final award settle the responsibility of the Contractor or Sub-Contractor or both for payment of the fee or any part thereof and where relevant for the charges of the Trustee-Stakeholder or any part thereof.

Clause 23: Contractor's right to set-off

Clause 24: Contractor's claims not agreed by the Sub-Contractor—appointment of Adjudictor

Background These clauses reproduce with modifications clauses 13A and 13B of the former "Green Form" of Nominated Sub-Contract. The clauses were introduced in 1976 in response to developments in the law of set-off with particular reference to money due under Architect's Certificates in Building Contracts. The practical problem for the building industry lay in the varying results of applications for summary judgment[19] for money certified in Architect's certificates where payment was withheld in reliance on cross-claims usually for defects or delay. In the period after *Dawnays* v. *Minter*[20] and before *Modern Engineering (Bristol)* v. *Gilbert-Ash*,[21] summary judgment was given for sums that had been certified even in the face of the strongest (although disputed) cross-claim. After *Modern Engineering (Bristol)* v. *Gilbert-Ash*, it was possible at least that shadowy cross-claims might be dressed up to be sufficient to defeat an application for summary judgment. Neither of these extreme positions was regarded as satisfactory. The scheme of the clauses was to recognise that there was no special principle limiting the ordinary rules of set-off but that those rules could be modified by express agreement[22]; to give the Contractor a modified contractual right to set-off against sums certified as due to Nominated Sub-Contractors; but to discourage and in certain circumstances prevent the Contractor from unfairly holding on to money which he ought, broadly speaking, to pay to the Sub-Contractor. The machinery to achieve this is elaborate.

Scheme of Clause 23. The Contractor may set-off against any money otherwise due under the Sub-Contract:

(1) any amount agreed by the Sub-Contractor as due to the Contractor (23.1);
(2) any amount finally awarded in arbitration or litigation in favour of the Contractor and which arises out of or under the Sub-Contract (23.1);
(3) a claim for loss and/or expense as defined in clause 23.2.1 and subject to the notice provisions of clause 23.2.2.

Clause 23.3 provides consequentially that any amount set-off under clause 23.2 may subsequently be varied. Clause 23.4 seeks to exclude any implied right of set-off which is wider than that contained in clause 23.

---

[19] For summary judgment, see p. 441.
[20] [1971] 1 W.L.R. 1205 (C.A.).
[21] [1974] A.C. 689 (H.L.).
[22] For set-off, see p. 438.

Clause 23.1. *"... or finally awarded in arbitration or litigation ..."*

It is suggested that this refers to any amount for which the Contractor has obtained an enforceable award or judgment. It would not include a judgment under appeal where there was a stay of execution pending the appeal. It would include an amount for which the Contractor had himself obtained summary judgment.

Clause 23.2. This sub-clause was entirely redrafted by Amendment 4 issued in July 1987. The most material change is the rewording of the scope of what may be set-off. The original wording of clause 23.2 provided for the set-off of "any claim for loss and/or expense which has actually been incurred by the Contractor." This wording was considered in *Chatbrown Ltd.* v. *Alfred McAlpine.*[23] At first instance, the court was satisfied that some meaning should be attached to the word "actually." The word added emphasis to the fact that the loss and/or expense had been incurred and had a "temporal connotation."[24] The Court of Appeal approved this construction saying that "... it was not sufficient that a liability should have been incurred which would, or was liable to, lead to loss and/or damage in the future ... it was necessary that loss and/or expense should actually have been incurred prior to the notice...."[25]

The scope of the set-off is now defined as "... where the Contractor has a claim for loss and/or expense and/or damage which he has suffered or incurred ... the Contractor shall be entitled to set-off the amount of such loss and/or expense and/or damage so suffered or incurred...." "Suffered" is therefore now an alternative to "incurred." The word "actually" is deleted before "incurred." This new wording has not yet been judicially considered. It is thought that it is at least arguable that the scope of set-off is thereby widened to include the situation where the Contractor has incurred a present liability to suffer or incur loss and/or expense in the future.

Clause 23.2.1. *"... delay in completion ..."*

The proviso in the final sentence relates to the need for a certificate of the Architect as referred to in clause 12.2 (see commentary to that clause).

Clause 23.2.2. *"... notice in writing ..."*

The Contractor must give his notice 3 days before the date of issue of the relevant Interim Certificate. This period is to give the Sub-Contractor the opportunity to initiate the machinery of clause 24.[26]

---

[23] (1986) 7 Con. L.R. 131; (1986) 35 B.L.R. 44 (C.A.).

[24] (1986) 7 Con. L.R. 131 at 137.

[25] Kerr L.J. (1986) 35 B.L.R. 44 at 52 (C.A.).

[26] For some assistance on what may be held to be a sufficient notice for the purposes of clause 23, see *Archital Luxfer* v. *A. J. Dunning & Son* (1987) 47 B.L.R. 1 (C.A.).

Clause 23.4. *"the rights . . . in respect of set-off are fully set out . . . and no other rights whatsoever shall be implied . . ."*

For rights of set-off generally, see page 438. It is possible by contract to limit some or all of the rights of set-off which the law would otherwise recognise. *Modern Engineering (Bristol)* v. *Gilbert-Ash*[27] is an example of a case where the court considered whether contractual terms had effectively limited or excluded rights of set-off. The House of Lords held in that case that they had not. It is thought that this clause is effective to limit the parties' rights of set-off.

Stay of Execution. If the Sub-Contractor brings an application for summary judgment and the Contractor is unable to bring his counterclaim for loss and/or expense within the set-off provisions of clause 23, such counterclaim will not without more constitute "special circumstances" entitling the Contractor to a stay of execution within R.S.C., Order 47, rule 1(a). To hold otherwise would be to negate the contractual machinery.[28]

Clause 24.3. *". . . the Adjudicator . . . without hearing the Contractor or Sub-Contractor in person, shall . . . in his absolute discretion and, without giving reasons, decide . . ."*

The Adjudicator is not, it is submitted, an Arbitrator within the meaning of the Arbitration Acts 1950–1979.[29] The material upon which the Adjudicator has to reach his decision is limited to:

(1) the Contractor's notice under clause 23.2.3 specifying the grounds on which set-off is claimed;

(2) the Sub-Contractor's written statement under clause 24.1.1 setting out his reasons for disagreement and particulars of any counterclaim;

(3) brief particulars of the Sub-Contract;

(4) a copy of the Architect's Certificate under clause 12.2;

(5) the Contractor's written statement under clause 24.2 setting out brief particulars of his defence to any counterclaim by the Sub-Contractor; and

(6) any further written statements under clause 24.3.1 which the Adjudicator may consider necessary to clarify or explain any ambiguity.

The Adjudicator is forbidden to hear the Contractor or Sub-Contractor in person, has an "absolute discretion" and decides without giving reasons. Under clause 24.3.2 his discretion is to be such as "he considers to be fair, reasonable and necessary in all the circumstances of the dispute as set out in the statements." Under clause 24.3.1, his decision is binding until the dispute is settled by agreement or determined by an Arbitrator or the court. By clause

---

[27] [1974] A.C. 689 (H.L.).

[28] See *Tubeworkers* v. *Tilbury Construction* (1985) 30 B.L.R. 67 (C.A.).

[29] See p. 384 and in particular the section entitled "The difference between arbitration and certification" at p. 385.

24.1.1 the Sub-Contractor is required to give notice of arbitration at the same time as he requests action by the Adjudicator. The extent of the Adjudicator's powers of decision are contained in clause 24.3.1. These extend only to deciding the interim destination of the amount which the Contractor claims to be entitled to set-off against money otherwise due to the Sub-Contractor.

The Adjudicator has power only where a valid notice has been given by the Contractor and the Sub-Contractor disputes the amount specified by the Sub-Contractor in the notice. Where the notice itself has been impugned and not the amount in the notice, the Adjudicator has no powers.[30]

In these circumstances, it is submitted that the function of the Adjudicator is to achieve a rough, temporary settlement between the parties. He makes no decision as to their final rights and is not, it seems, obliged or able to reach his decision according to the strict legal rights of the parties (or at least what their strict legal rights would have been had they not made a contract which contained clause 24). Under clause 24.6, the discretion to decide the interim destination of the money in dispute passes to the Arbitrator upon his appointment. There is, therefore, in a sense a right of appeal from the Adjudicator to the Arbitrator, and it is submitted that on an application under clause 24.6 the Arbitrator would not be limited to considering the written material which under clause 24.3 is the Adjudicator's sole basis for decision. Unlike the Adjudicator's decision, a decision of the Arbitrator to vary or cancel the Adjudicator's decision would presumably be an interim award in the arbitration.

25. Right of Access of Contractor and Architect

The Contractor and the Architect and all persons duly authorised by either of them shall, but subject to such reasonable restrictions of the Sub-Contractor as are necessary to protect any proprietary right of the Sub-Contractor, at all reasonable times have access to any work which is being prepared for or will be utilised in the Sub-Contract Works unless the Architect shall certify in writing that the Sub-Contractor has reasonable grounds for refusing such access.

Clause 25: Right of Access of Contractor and Architect

This clause was redrafted by Amendment 4 issued in July 1987 in order to protect the proprietary interests of Sub-Contractors.

26. Assignment—sub-letting

26.1 The Sub-Contractor shall not without the written consent of the Architect and Contractor assign the Sub-Contract.

---

[30] See *Chatbrown Ltd.* v. *Alfred McAlpine* (1986) 7 Con. L.R. 131 at 134.

26.2 The Sub-Contractor shall not without the written consent of the Architect and Contractor (which consents shall not be unreasonably withheld) sub-let any portion of the Sub-Contract Works. In case of any difference of opinion on this issue between the Architect and the Contractor the opinion of the Architect shall prevail.

Clause 26: Assignment—sub-letting

This clause is the Sub-Contract equivalent of clauses 19.1 and 19.2 of the Main Contract.

An additional sentence was inserted into clause 26.2 by Amendment 9 issued in July 1990 to make clear that the Sub-Contractor is to remain wholly responsible for carrying out and completing the Sub-Contract Works in all respects in accordance with the Sub-Contract, notwithstanding any sub-letting.

27.   General attendance—other attendance, etc.

27.1   .1   General attendance shall be provided by the Contractor free of charge to the Sub-Contractor and shall be deemed to include only the use of the Contractor's temporary roads, pavings and paths, standing scaffolding, standing power operated hoisting plant, the provision of temporary lighting and water supplies, clearing away rubbish, provision of space for the Sub-Contractor's own offices and for the storage of his plant and materials and the use of mess rooms, sanitary accommodation and welfare facilities.

      .2   Without prejudice to the obligations set out in clause 27.1.1 the Sub-Contractor shall from time to time during the execution of the Sub-Contract Works clear away to a place provided on the site all rubbish resulting from his execution of the Sub-Contract Works and shall keep access to those Works clear at all times.

27.2 The Contractor shall provide, free of charge to the Sub-Contractor, the other items of attendance detailed in the Tender, Schedule 2, item 3.

27.3 Subject to clauses 27.1 and 27.2 the Sub-Contractor shall at his own expense provide, erect, maintain and subsequently remove all necessary workshops, sheds or other temporary buildings for his employees and workmen at or from such places on the site as the Contractor, subject to any reasonable objection by the Sub-Contractor, shall appoint and the Contractor agrees to give all reasonable facilities to the Sub-Contractor for such erection.

27.4 The Contractor, the Sub-Contractor, their employees and workmen respectively in common with all other persons having a like right shall for the purposes of the Works (but not further or otherwise) be entitled to use any erected scaffolding belonging to or provided by the Contractor or the Sub-Contractor as the case may be while it remains so erected upon the site. Provided that such user shall be on the express condition that no warranty or other liability on the part of the Contractor or the Sub-Contractor as the case may be or of their other sub-contractors shall be created or implied under the Sub-Contract in regard to the fitness, condition or suitability of the said scaffolding.

Clause 27: General Attendance—other attendance, etc.

The provisions for general attendance and other attendance follow the provi-

768

sions in the Standard Method of Measurement (7th edition), sections A42 and 51.

28.   Contractor and Sub-Contractor not to make wrongful use or interfere with the property of the other

The Contractor and the Sub-Contractor respectively and their respective servants or agents or sub-contractors shall not wrongfully use or interfere with the plant, ways, scaffolding, temporary works, appliances or other property belonging to or provided by the other of them or be guilty of any breach or infringement of any Act of Parliament or bye-law, regulations, order or rule made under the same or by any local or other public or competent authority; provided that nothing herein contained shall prejudice or limit the rights of the Contractor or of the Sub-Contractor in the carrying out of their respective statutory duties or contractual duties under the Sub-Contract or under the Main Contract.

Clause 28: Contractor and Sub-Contractor not to make wrongful use of or interfere with property of the other

No commentary.

29.   Determination of the employment of the Sub-Contractor by the Contractor

29.1   Without prejudice to any rights or remedies which the Contractor may possess, if the Sub-Contractor shall make default in any one or more of the following respects that is to say:

.1   if without reasonable cause he wholly suspends the carrying out of the Sub-Contract Works before completion thereof; or

.2   if without reasonable cause he fails to proceed with the Sub-Contract Works in the manner provided in clause 11.1; or

.3   if he refuses or neglects after notice in writing from the Contractor to remove defective work or improper materials or goods and by such refusal or neglect the Works are materially affected, or wrongfully fails to rectify defects, shrinkages or other faults in the Sub-Contract Works, which rectification is in accordance with his obligations under the Sub-Contract; or

.4   if he fails to comply with the provisions of either clause 26 or clause 32;

then the Contractor shall so inform the Architect and send to the Architect any written observation of the Sub-Contractor in regard to the default or defaults of which the Contractor is informing the Architect. If so instructed by the Architect under clause 35.24.4.1 of the Main Contract Conditions the Contractor shall issue a notice to the Sub-Contractor by registered post or recorded delivery specifying the default (and send a copy thereof by registered post or recorded delivery to the Architect). If the Sub-Contractor shall either continue such default for 14 days after receipt of such notice or shall at any time thereafter repeat such default (whether previously repeated or not), then the Contractor may (but subject where relevant to the further instruction of the Architect to which clause 35.24.4.1 of the Main Contract Conditions refers) within 10 days after such continuance or repetition by notice by registered post or recorded delivery forthwith determine the employment of the Sub-Contractor under the Sub-Contract; provided that such notice shall not be given unreasonably or vexatiously.

29.2   In the event of the Sub-Contractor becoming bankrupt or making a composition or arrangement with his creditors or having a proposal in respect of his company for a voluntary arrangement for a composition of debts or scheme of arrangement approved in accordance with the Insolvency Act 1986, or having an application made under the Insolvency Act 1986 in respect of his company to the court for the appointment of an administrator, or having a winding up order made or (other than for the purposes of amalgamation or reconstruction) having a resolution for voluntary winding up passed, or having a provisional liquidator, receiver or manager of his business or undertaking duly appointed or, having an administrative receiver, as defined in the Insolvency Act 1986, appointed, or having possession taken by or on behalf of the holders of any debentures secured by a floating charge, of any property comprised in or subject to the floating charge, the employment of the Sub-Contractor under the Sub-Contract shall forthwith automatically be determined. Such determination shall be without prejudice to any other rights or remedies of the Contractor.

29.3   If the Sub-Contractor or any person employed by the Sub-Contractor or acting on his behalf (whether with or without the knowledge of the Sub-Contractor)

.1   shall have offered or given or agreed to give to any person any gift or consideration of any kind as an inducement or reward for doing or forbearing to do or for having done or forborne to do any action in relation to the obtaining or execution of this or any other sub-contract with the Contractor where the Employer is the same Employer as named in the First recital, or for showing or forbearing to show any favour or disfavour to any person in relation to this or any other sub-contract where the Employer is the same Employer as named in the First recital; or

.2   in relation to this or any other sub-contract with the Contractor where the Employer is the same Employer as named in the First recital, shall have committed any offence under the Prevention of Corruption Acts, 1889 to 1916 or where the Employer is a local authority shall have given any fee or reward the receipt of which is an offence under sub-section (2) of Section 117 of the Local Government Act 1972 or any re-enactment thereof

then, if the Employer so requires, the Contractor shall determine the employment of the Sub-Contractor under this Sub-Contract or any other sub-contract referred to in clause 29.3.

29.4   In the event of the employment of the Sub-Contractor under the Sub-Contract being determined under clause 29.1 or 29.2 or 29.3 the following shall be the respective rights and duties of the Contractor and the Sub-Contractor:

.1   when the Employer through the Architect nominates a person to carry out and complete the Sub-Contract Works such person may enter upon the Sub-Contract Works and use all temporary buildings, plant, tools, equipment, goods and materials intended for, delivered to and placed on or adjacent to the Works, and may purchase all materials and goods necessary for the carrying out and completion of the Sub-Contract Works;

.2.1   except where the determination occurs by reason of the bankruptcy of the Sub-Contractor or of him having a winding up order made or (other than for the purposes of amalgamation or reconstruction) a resolution for voluntary winding up passed, the Sub-Contractor shall if so required by the Employer or by the Architect on behalf of the Employer and with the consent of the Contractor within 14 days of the date of determination, assign to the Contractor without payment the benefit of any agreement for the supply of materials or goods and/or for the execution of any work for the purposes of the Sub-Contract but on the terms that the supplier or sub-sub-contractor shall be entitled to make any reasonable objection to any further assignment thereof by the Contractor;

770

.2.2   unless the exception to the operation of clause 29.3.2.1 applies the Contractor, if so directed by the Architect, shall pay any supplier or sub-sub-contractor for any materials or goods delivered or works executed for the purposes of the Sub-Contract (whether before or after the determination) insofar as the price thereof has not already been paid by the Sub-Contractor;

.3   the Sub-Contractor shall as and when required by a direction of the Contractor or by an instruction of the Architect so to do (but not before) remove from the Works any temporary buildings, plant, tools, equipment, goods and materials belonging to or hired by him. If within a reasonable time after any such requirement has been made the Sub-Contractor has not complied therewith, then the Contractor may (but without being responsible for any loss or damage) remove and sell any such property of the Sub-Contractor holding the proceeds less all costs incurred to the credit of the Sub-Contractor.

29.5   The Sub-Contractor shall allow or pay to the Contractor in the manner hereinafter appearing the amount of any direct loss and/or damage caused to the Contractor by the determination. Until after completion of the Sub-Contract Works under clause 29.3.1 the Contractor shall not be bound by any provision of the Sub-Contract to make any further payment to the Sub-Contractor. Upon such completion the Sub-Contractor may apply to the Contractor who shall pass such application to the Architect who shall ascertain or instruct the Quantity Surveyor to ascertain the amount of expenses properly incurred by the Employer and the amount of direct loss and/or damage caused to the Employer by the determination; and shall issue an Interim Certificate certifying the value of any work executed or goods and materials supplied by the Sub-Contractor to the extent that their value has not been included in previous Interim Certificates; in paying that Certificate the Employer may deduct the amount of the expenses and direct loss and/or damage of the Employer as aforesaid. The Contractor in discharging his obligation to pay the Sub-Contractor such amount may deduct therefrom a cash discount of 2½ per cent. and, without prejudice to any other rights of the Contractor, the amount of any direct loss and/or damage caused to the Contractor by the determination.

Clause 29: Determination of the employment of the Sub-Contractor by the Contractor

This clause is the Sub-Contract equivalent of clause 27 of the Main Contract (see its commentary). It should also be noted that, under this clause and clause 35.24 of the Main Contract, the Contractor can only determine the employment of the Sub-Contractor under Sub-Contract clause 29.1 upon the instructions of the Architect. This is because, as between the Contractor and the Employer, the financial risk of determining the employment of the Sub-Contractor and the consequent renomination falls upon the Employer.[31] Under clause 35.24.6 of the Main Contract, the Employer bears the extra cost if the Contractor determines the Sub-Contractor's employment. Conversely, under clause 35.24.9, the Contractor bears the extra cost, if the Sub-Contractor determines his employment under clause 30 of the Sub-Contract.

There were the following minor amendments to clause 29 by Amendment 4 issued in July 1987:

---

[31] See the commentary on Main Contract clause 35.24.

(1) the deletion of the word "persistently" before "neglects ... to remove defective work" in clause 29.1.3;

(2) the redrafting of clause 29.2 to take account of the Insolvency Act 1986;

(3) the introduction of a new clause 29.3 right of determination on grounds of corruption by a Sub-Contractor. This applies whichever version of the Main Contract is used.

30.   Determination of employment under the Sub-Contract by the Sub-Contractor

30.1   Without prejudice to any other rights or remedies which the Sub-Contractor may possess if the Contractor shall make default (for which default a remedy under any other provisions of the Sub-Contract would not adequately recompense the Sub-Contractor) in any of the following respects:

.1.1   if without reasonable cause he wholly suspends the Works before completion; or

.1.2   if without reasonable cause he fails to proceed with the Works so that the reasonable progress of the Sub-Contract Works is seriously affected;

then the Sub-Contractor may issue to the Contractor a notice by registered post or recorded delivery (a copy of which must be sent at the same time to the Architect by registered post or recorded delivery) specifying the default. If the Contractor shall continue such default for 14 days after receipt of such notice or if the Contractor shall at any time thereafter repeat such default (whether previously repeated or not) the Sub-Contractor may thereupon by notice by registered post or recorded delivery determine the employment of the Sub-Contractor; provided that such notice shall not be given unreasonably or vexatiously.

30.2   Upon such determination, then without prejudice to the accrued rights or remedies of either party or to any liability of the classes mentioned in clause 6 which may accrue before the Sub-Contractor shall have removed his temporary buildings, plant, tools, equipment, goods or materials or by reason of his so removing the same, the respective rights and duties of the Sub-Contractor and Contractor shall be as follows:

.1   the Sub-Contractor shall with all reasonable dispatch and in such manner and with such precautions as will prevent injury, death or damage of the classes in respect of which he is liable to indemnify the Contractor under clause 6 remove from the site all his temporary buildings, plant, tools, equipment, goods or materials subject to the provisions of clause 30.2.2.4;

.2   after taking into account amounts previously paid under the Sub-Contract the Sub-Contractor shall be paid by the Contractor:

.2.1   the total value of work completed at the date of determination, such value to be ascertained in accordance with clause 21;

.2.2   the total value of work begun and executed but not completed at the date of determination, such value to be ascertained either under clause 16 as if it were a Valuation of a Variation (where clause 15.1 applies) or under clause 17 (where clause 15.2 applies);

.2.3   any sum ascertained in respect of direct loss and/or expense under clause 13.1 (whether ascertained before or after the date of determination);

.2.4   the cost of materials or goods properly ordered for the Sub-Contract Works (but not incorporated therein) for which the Sub-Contractor shall have paid or is legally bound to accept delivery and on such payment by the Contractor any materials or goods so paid for shall become the property of the Contractor;

.2.5   the reasonable cost of removal under clause 30.2.1;

.2.6 any direct loss and/or expense caused to the Sub-Contractor by the determination.

Clause 30: Determination of employment under the Sub-Contract by the Sub-Contractor.

This clause is the Sub-Contract equivalent of clause 28 of the Main Contract (see its commentary). Some of the grounds for determination which appear in clause 28 of the Main Contract do not have their equivalent in clause 30 of the Sub-Contract. Some of these are inappropriate to the relationship between the Contractor and the Sub-Contractor. Others are dealt with elsewhere in the Sub-Contract. In particular, clause 21.8 provides a remedy where the Sub-Contractor is not duly paid, and the effect of clause 31.1 is to effect a determination of the Sub-Contractor's employment upon the terms of clause 30.2 in the event of the Contractor's insolvency (see clause 27.2 of the Main Contract). For renomination where the Sub-Contractor determines his Employment under clause 30, see clause 35.24.3 and 35.24.8.1 of the Main Contract and the commentary to Sub-Contract clause 29.

31.   **Determination of the Contractor's employment under the Main Contract**

31.1   If the employment of the Contractor is determined under clause 27 of the Main Contract Conditions, then the employment of the Sub-Contractor under the Sub-Contract shall thereupon also determine and the provisions of clause 30.2 shall thereafter apply.

31.2   .1   If the employment of the Contractor is determined under clause 28 or clause 28A of the Main Contract Conditions then the employment of the Sub-Contractor under the Sub-Contract shall thereupon also determine. The entitlement of the Sub-Contractor to payment shall be the proportion fairly and reasonably attributable to the Sub-Contract Works of the amounts paid by the Employer under clause 28.2.2.1 to .5 of the Main Contract Conditions inclusive together with, where the determination is under clause 28 any amounts paid in respect of the Sub-Contractor under clause 28.2.2.6 of the Main Contract Conditions provided the Sub-Contractor shall have supplied to the Contractor all evidence reasonably necessary to establish the direct loss and/or damage caused to the Sub-Contractor by the determination as referred to in clause 28.2.2.6 of the Main Contract Conditions.

  .2   Nothing in clause 31.2.1 shall affect the entitlement of the Sub-Contractor to the proper operation of clause 21 in respect of the amount, included in the amount stated as due therein, in respect of the Sub-Contract Works in an Interim Certificate of the Architect whose date of issue was prior to the date of determination of the employment of the Contractor under clause 28 of the Main Contract Conditions.

Clause 31: Determination of the Contractor's employment under the Main Contract.

Under this clause, if the employment of the Contractor is determined under

773

either clause 27 or clause 28 of the Main Contract, the employment of the Sub-Contractor is also determined. If the Main Contractor's employment was determined under clause 27 of the Main Contract (*i.e.* by reason of his default), the consequences for the Sub-Contractor are as if he had determined his own employment under clause 30 of the Sub-Contract. If the Main Contractor's employment was determined under clause 28 of the Main Contract (*i.e.* by reason of events for which the Employer is responsible), then the Sub-Contractor participates in the consequences provided by clause 28 of the Main Contract. By virtue of Amendment 4 issued in July 1987, clause 31 now deals with additional clause 28A in the Main Contract under which either Employer or Contractor can determine the Contractor's employment for events which are the fault of neither. The position for the Sub-Contractor is as for determination under clause 28 except that he is not entitled to any direct loss or damage where the Contract is determined under clause 28A. The Sub-Contractor remains entitled under Sub-Contract clause 31.2.2, however, to be paid any amount included for him in an Interim Certificate issued before the date of determination.

Clause 32: Fair Wages

The text was deleted by Amendment 6 issued in July 1988 and replaced with the words "Number not used." This follows the deletion, in view of the provisions in the Local Government Act 1988, of the Fair Wages clause 19A in the Main Contract.

33.   **Strikes—loss or expense**

33.1   If the Works or the Sub-Contract Works are affected by a local combination of workmen, strike or lockout affecting any of the trades employed upon the Works or any of the trades engaged in the preparation, manufacture or transportation of any of the goods or materials required for the Works:

    .1   neither the Contractor nor the Sub-Contractor shall be entitled to make any claim upon the other for any loss and/or expense resulting from such action as aforesaid;

    .2   the Contractor shall take all reasonably practicable steps to keep the site open and available for the use of the Sub-Contractor;

    .3   the Sub-Contractor shall take all reasonably practicable steps to continue with the Sub-Contract Works.

33.2   Nothing in clause 33 shall affect any other right of the Contractor or Sub-Contractor under the Sub-Contract if such action as aforesaid occurs.

Clause 33: Strikes—loss or expense

The events with which this clause deals are Relevant Events under both clause 25.4.4 of the Main Contract and clause 11.2.5.4 of the Sub-Contract. They are thus events entitling the Main Contractor and the Sub-Contractor in appropriate circumstances to extensions of time. They are not, however, events which reappear in clause 26 of the Main Contract or clause 13.1 of the

Sub-Contract as entitling the Main Contractor or the Sub-Contractor to claim loss and expense, and it is thought, therefore, that clause 33.1.1 is strictly unnecessary.

34.   **Choice of fluctuation provisions—Tender, Schedule 1, item 2** [*p*]

34.1   Fluctuations shall be dealt with in accordance with whichever of the following alternatives:
        clause 35, or
        clause 36, or
        clause 37

is stated in the Tender, Schedule 1, item 2 as being applicable to the Sub-Contract. The provisions so stated shall be deemed to be incorporated with Sub-Contract NSC/4 as executed by the parties thereto. [*q*]

34.2   Clause 35 shall be used where neither clause 36 nor 37 is stated in the Tender, Schedule 1, item 2 as applicable to the Sub-Contract.

Note: Clauses 35, 36 and 37 are published separately in "Fluctuation Clauses for use with NSC/4 and NSC/4a."

Clause 34: Choice of fluctuation provisions—Tender, Schedule 1, item 2.

This clause is the Sub-Contract equivalent of clause 37 of the Main Contract (see its commentary).

Clauses 35, 36 and 37

These clauses, which are printed separately and not reproduced in this book, are the clauses referred to in clause 34 of the Sub-Contract and provide for fluctuation payments or formula price adjustment. They are the Sub-Contract equivalent of clauses 38, 39 and 40 of the Main Contract (see their commentary).

38.   **Settlement of disputes—Arbitration**

38.1   If a dispute or difference as referred to in Article 3 arises in regard to any matter or thing

---

[*p*] *Clause 36 should be used where the parties have agreed to allow the labour and materials cost and tax fluctuations to which clauses 36.1 to .3 refer, Alternatively clause 37 should be used where the parties have agreed that the Sub-Contract Sum or the Tender Sum shall be adjusted by the formula method under the JCT Sub-Contract/Works Contract Formula Rules.*

[*q*] *Notwithstanding the provisions of clause 34.1 on deemed incorporation the parties may nevertheless wish to incorporate the agreed alternative fluctuation provisions in the executed Sub-Contract.*

of whatsoever nature arising out of this Sub-Contract or in connection therewith, then either party shall give to the other notice in writing of such dispute or difference and such dispute or difference shall be referred to the arbitration and final decision of a person to be agreed between the parties to act as Arbitrator, or, failing such agreement within 14 days after either party has given to the other a written request to concur in the appointment of an Arbitrator, a person to be appointed on the request of either party by the person named in the Tender, Schedule 2.

38.2 .1 Provided that if the dispute or difference to be referred to arbitration under this Sub-Contract raises issues which are substantially the same as or connected with issues raised in a related dispute between

> the Contractor and the Employer under the Main Contract, or
> the Sub-Contractor and the Employer under Agreement NSC/2, or
> the Contractor and any other nominated sub-contractor under Sub-Contract NSC/4 or NSC/4a as applicable, or
> the Contractor and any Nominated Supplier whose contract of sale with the Contractor provides for the matters referred to in clause 36.4.8 of the Main Contract Conditions

and if the related dispute has already been referred for determination to an Arbitrator, the Contractor and the Sub-Contractor hereby agree that the dispute or difference under this Sub-Contract shall be referred to the Arbitrator appointed to determine the related dispute; such Arbitrator shall have power to make such directions and all necessary awards in the same way as if the procedure of the High Court as to joining one or more defendants or joining co-defendants or third parties was available to the parties and to him; and the agreement and consent referred to in clause 38.7 on appeals or applications to the High Court on any question of law shall apply to any question of law arising out of the awards of such Arbitrator in respect of all related disputes referred to him or arising in the course of the reference of all the related disputes referred to him.

.2 Save that the Contractor or the Sub-Contractor may require the dispute or difference under this Sub-Contract to be referred to a different Arbitrator (to be appointed under this Sub-Contract) if either of them reasonably considers that the Arbitrator appointed to determine the related dispute is not appropriately qualified to determine the dispute or difference under this Sub-Contract.

.3 Clauses 38.2.1 and 38.2.2 shall apply unless in the Tender, Schedule 1, item 10 the words "clauses 41.2.1 and 41.2.2 apply" have been deleted.

38.3 Such Arbitrator shall not without the written consent of the Contractor and the Sub-Contractor enter on the arbitration until after the practical completion or abandonment of the Works, except to arbitrate:

.1 whether a payment has been improperly withheld or is not in accordance with the Sub-Contract; or

.2 whether practical completion of the Sub-Contract Works shall be deemed to have taken place under clause 14.2; or

.3 in respect of a claim by the Contractor or counterclaim by the Sub-Contractor to which the provisions of clause 24 apply in which case the Arbitrator shall exercise his powers given to him in clause 24; or

.4 any matters in dispute under clause 4.3.1 in regard to reasonable objection by the Sub-Contractor or under clauses 4.3.2 to 4.3.7 inclusive or under clauses 11.2 and 11.3 as to extension of time.

38.4 In any such arbitration as is provided for in clause 38 any decision of the Architect which is final and binding on the Contractor under the Main Contract shall also be and be deemed to be final and binding between and upon the Contractor and the Sub-Contractor.

8.5   Subject to the provisions of clauses 4.6, 21.12, 35.4.3, 36.5.3, 37.5 and clause 30 of the Main Contract Conditions the Arbitrator shall, without prejudice to the generality of his powers, have power to direct such measurements and/or valuations as may in his opinion be desirable in order to determine the rights of the parties and to ascertain and award any sum which ought to have been the subject of or included in any certificate and to open up, review and revise any certificate, opinion, decision (except a decision of the Architect to issue instructions pursuant to clause 8.4.1 of the Main Contract Conditions and which instructions were issued to the Sub-Contractor as referred to in clause 4.3.3.1), requirement or notice and to determine all matters in dispute which shall be submitted to him in the same manner as if no such certificate, opinion, decision, requirement or notice had been given.

8.6   Subject to clause 38.7 the award of such Arbitrator shall be final and binding on the parties.

8.7   The parties hereby agree and consent pursuant to Sections 1(3)(a) and 2(1)(b) of the Arbitration Act 1979 that either party
    .1   may appeal to the High Court on any question of law arising out of an award made in an arbitration under this Arbitration Agreement and
    .2   may apply to the High Court to determine any question of law arising in the course of the reference;
and the parties agree that the High Court should have jurisdiction to determine any such questions of law.

8.8   Whatever the nationality, residence or domicile of the Employer, the Contractor, the Sub-Contractor, and any sub-contractor or supplier or the Arbitrator, and wherever the works or Sub-Contract Works, or any parts thereof, are situated, the law of England shall be the proper law applicable to the Sub-Contract and in particular (but not so as to derogate from the generality of the foregoing) the provisions of the Arbitration Acts 1950 (notwithstanding anything in Section 34 thereof) to 1979 shall apply to any arbitration under article 3 and clause 38 wherever the same, or any part of it, shall be conducted. [r]

Appendix (Third recital)

The completed Tender (NSC/1) or a certified copy thereof must be attached to the Sub-Contract.

Sectional Completion Supplement—see Clause 1.4

This is not reproduced in this book.

Clause 38: Settlement of disputes—Arbitration

Generally.   This clause, introduced by Amendment 4 issued in July 1987,

---

[r] *Where the parties do not wish the proper law of the Sub-Contract to be the law of England and/or do not wish the provisions of the Arbitration Acts 1950 to 1979 to apply to any arbitration under the Sub-Contract held under the procedural law of Scotland (or other country) appropriate amendments to clause 38.8 should be made.*

contains the detailed provisions for the arbitration which Article 3 prescribes as the method of settling disputes.[32] The scheme and wording of clause 38 closely follow clause 41 of the Main Contract, as to which see page 675.

Amendments.   Clause 38 has been amended in parallel with amendments to clause 41 of the Main Contract:

(i) *Amendment 4 issued in July 1987.* This introduced new provisions where the Parties are unable to agree on the appointment of an Arbitrator and a new clause 38.7 whereby the parties agree at the time of entering into the Sub-Contract that questions of law may be determined under the provisions of the Arbitration Act 1979.

(ii) *Amendment 6 issued in July 1988.* Clause 38.1 was redrafted to require either party to give to the other written notice when they require a dispute or difference to be referred to Arbitration. The new clause 38.9 provides for the situation where the Arbitrator dies or otherwise ceases to be Arbitrator before making a final Award. The new clause 38.10 provides for the arbitration to be conducted in accordance with the JCT Arbitration Rules.

Clause 38.2.   *Multipartite arbitrations*

The provisions for such arbitrations are optional in the Main Contract and by Sub-Contract clause 38.2.3 the choice made in the Main Contract determines whether clauses 38.2.1 and 38.2.2 apply.

Provisions for multipartite arbitrations have been considered in the context of clause 24 of the Green Form and similar provisions.[33] The following points emerge:

(1) such provisions on their proper construction contain not one but two separate unequivocal submissions to arbitration, the first comprising the reference of all disputes to Sub-Contract Arbitration subject only to the proviso (*i.e.* Article 3) and the second comprising all related disputes as defined to Main Contract Arbitration (*i.e.* clause 38.2);

(2) the first submission is the dominant one out of which the proviso is carved;

(3) in the sphere of building contracts, "dispute" in its natural meaning means a difference on a specific item or at least those grouped under a specific heading;

(4) the machinery contained in clause 38.2 does not come into play unless both conditions there set out are fulfilled;

(5) once the Sub-Contract dispute has been referred to the Arbitrator already appointed to deal with the related dispute, his authority cannot

---

[32] For arbitration generally, see Chap. 16.

[33] *Higgs & Hill Building* v. *Campbell Denis* (1982) 28 B.L.R. 47; *Hyundai Engineering* v. *Active Building* (1988) 45 B.L.R. 62; see also *Multi Construction* v. *Stent Foundations* (1988) 41 B.L.R. 98.

be revoked. There is then a single reference in which the Arbitrator must proceed to deal with both related disputes.

It is not, however, entirely clear who is to decide whether "the dispute or difference to be referred to arbitration under the Sub-Contract raises issues which are substantially the same as or connected with issues raised in a related dispute." In *Higgs & Hill Building* v. *Campbell Denis*,[34] where the related dispute was between Employer and Contractor under the Main Contract, it was suggested this was a matter for the judgment of the Main Contractor. However, in *Hyundai Engineering* v. *Active Building*,[35] the court directed that this question should be determined by the court. It is submitted that, in the event of disagreement whether a dispute is or is not properly related, it is the Court that should resolve such disagreement. It is thought that one party to a prospective arbitration cannot unilaterally determine finally whether the necessary conditions are fulfilled.[36]

Amendment 6
Issued July 1988

| 1 | Clause 32 | **Fair Wages** |

Delete text of clause and **insert** "Number not used."

Consequential amendment
Clause 29.1.4 **delete** "either clause 26 or clause 32" and **insert** "clause 26":

| 2 | Clause 38 | **Settlement of disputes—Arbitration** |

8.1 **delete** text and **insert:**

"When the Contractor or the Sub-Contractor require a dispute or difference as referred to in Article 3 as to the construction of this Sub-Contract or any matter or thing of whatsoever nature arising thereunder or in connection therewith to be referred to arbitration then either the Contractor or the Sub-Contractor shall give written notice to the other to such effect and such dispute or difference shall be referred to the arbitration and final decision of a person to be agreed between the parties as the Arbitrator or, upon failure so to agree within 14 days after the date of the aforesaid written notice of a person to be appointed as the Arbitrator on the request of either the Contractor or the Sub-Contractor by the person named in the (*for NSC/4*) Tender, Schedule 2 (*for NSC/4a*) Appendix part 13."

---

[34] (1982) 28 B.L.R. 47.
[35] (1988) 45 B.L.R. 62.
[36] For the possibility of the arbitrator determining the point, see "Challenge to arbitrator's jurisdiction" at p. 392.

38.2.1   Line 13 after "related dispute" **insert**:

"and the JCT Arbitration Rules applicable to the related dispute shall apply to the dispute under this Sub-Contract and that"

38.3   Line 2, after "practical completion" **insert:**

"or alleged practical completion of the Works or termination or alleged termination of the Sub-Contractor's employment under this Sub-Contract."

38.5   Line 3 after "power" **insert:**

"to rectify the Sub-Contract so that it accurately reflects the true agreement made by the Contractor and the Sub-Contractor."

38.8   Line 2, **delete** "and any" and **insert** "or any"; line 4 **delete** "the Sub-Contract" and **insert** "this Sub-Contract"; line 6, **delete** "Article 3 and clause 38" and **insert** "this Sub-Contract."

Delete footnote reference **"[r]"** and **insert** footnote reference **"[r.1]."**

Delete footnote **"[r]"** and **insert:**

"[r.1]   where the parties do not wish the proper law of the Sub-Contract to be the law of England appropriate amendments to clause 38.8 should be made. Where the works are situated in Scotland then the forms issued by the Scottish Building Contract Committee which contain Scots proper law and arbitration provisions are the appropriate documents it should be noted that the provisions of the Arbitration Acts 1950 to 1979 do not extend to Scotland."

Insert new clause 38.9:

"38.9   If before making his final award the Arbitrator dies or otherwise ceases to act as the Arbitrator, the Contractor and the Sub-Contractor shall forthwith appoint a further Arbitrator, or upon failure so to appoint within 14 days of any such death or cessation then either the Contractor or the Sub-Contractor may request the person named in the (for NSC/4) Tender, Schedule 2 (for NSC/4a) the Appendix part 13 to appoint such further Arbitrator. Provided that no such further Arbitrator shall be entitled to disregard any direction of the previous Arbitrator or to vary or revise any award of the previous Arbitrator except to the extent that the previous Arbitrator had power so to do under the JCT Arbitration Rules and/or with the agreement of the parties and/or by the operation of law."

Insert new clause 38.10:

"38.10   The arbitration shall be conducted in accordance with the JCT Arbitration Rules current at the Base Date **[r.2]** Provided that if any amendments to the Rules so current have been issued by the Joint Contracts Tribunal after the Base Date the Contractor and the Sub-Contractor may, by a joint notice in writing to the Arbitrator, state that they wish the arbitration to be conducted in accordance with the JCT Arbitration Rules as so amended."

Insert as footnote **[r.2]:**

"[r.2]   The JCT Arbitration Rules contain stricter time limits than those prescribed by some arbitration rules or those frequently observed in practice. The parties

780

should note that a failure by a party or the agent of a party to comply with the time limits incorporated in these Rules may have adverse consequences."

Amendment 7
Issued July 1988

Alter the clauses shown below so that they stand part of the Sub-Contract Conditions with the words ruled through deleted, the words underlined inserted, the two definitions inserted in clause 1.3 after the definition of "Appendix" and "person" respectively, and the footnote thereto which reproduces SMM 7 General Rules 10.1 to 10.6 inserted.

Definitions   1.3   Approximate Quantity: a quantity in any bills of quantities included in the Numbered Documents identified therein as an approximate quantity.*

provisional sum: includes, where bills of quantities are included in the Numbered Documents, a sum provided in those bills for work whether or not identified as being for defined or undefined work.*

*Footnote: General Rules 10.1 to 10.6 of the Standard Method of Measurement 7th Edition provide:

10.1
Where work can be described and given in items in accordance with these rules but the quantity of work required cannot be accurately determined, an estimate of the quantity shall be given and identified as an approximate quantity.

10.2
Where work cannot be described and given in items in accordance with these rules it shall be given as a Provisional Sum and identified as for either defined or undefined work as appropriate.

10.3
A Provisional Sum for defined work is a sum provided for work which is not completely designed but for which the following information shall be provided:
(a) The nature and construction of the work.

(b) A statement of how and where the work is fixed to the building and what other work is to be fixed thereto.
(c) A quantity or quantities which indicate the scope and extent of the work.
(d) Any specific limitations and the like identified in Section A35.

10.4
Where Provisional Sums are given for defined work the Contractor will be deemed to have made due allowance in programming, planning and pricing Preliminaries. Any such allowance will only be subject to adjustment in those circumstances where a variation in respect of other work measured in detail in accordance with the rules would give rise to adjustment.

10.5
A Provisional Sum for undefined work is a sum provided for work where the information required in accordance with rule 10.3 cannot be given.

10.6
Where Provisional Sums are given for undefined work the Contractor will be deemed not to have made any allowance in programming, planning and pricing Preliminaries.

11.2   .5   The following are the Relevant Events referred to in clauses 11.2.2.1:

[clauses 11.2.5.1 to 11.2.5.5 unchanged]

.5.5.1   under clause 2.3, 13.2, 13.3 (except where bills of quantities are included in the Numbered Documents, compliance with an Architect's instruction for the expenditure of a provisional sum for defined work*) 23.2, 34, 35 or 36 of the Main Contract Conditions or

[clause 11.2.5.5.2 unchanged]

.5.6   the Contractor, or the Sub-Contractor through the Contractor, not having received in due time necessary instructions (including those for or in regard to the expenditure of provisional sums), drawings, details or levels from the Architect for which the Contractor, or the Sub-Contractor through the Contractor, specifically applied in writing provided that such application was made on a date which having regard to the Completion Date or the period or periods for the completion of the Sub-Contract Works was neither unreasonably distant from nor unreasonably close to the date on which it was necessary for the Contractor or the Sub-Contractor to receive the same;

[clause 11.2.5.7 to 11.2.5.14 unchanged]

.5.15   where bills of quantities are included in the Numbered Documents by reason of the execution of work for which an Approximate Quantity is included in those bills which is not a reasonably accurate forecast of the quantity of work required.

* See footnote to clause 1.3 (Definitions)

[clause 13.1.1 unchanged]

13.1   .2   the following are the "matters" referred to in clause 13.1.1:

.2.1   the Contractor, or the Sub-Contractor through the Contractor, not having received in due time necessary instructions (including those for or in regard to the expenditure of provisional sums) drawings, details or levels from the Architect for which the Contractor, or the Sub-Contractor through the Contractor, specifically applied in writing provided that such application was made on a date which having regard to the Completion Date or the period or periods for completion of the Sub-Contract Works was neither unreasonably distant from nor unreasonably close to the date on which it was necessary for the Contractor or the Sub-Contractor to receive the same; or

[clauses 13.1.2.2 to 13.1.2.6 unchanged]

.2.7 Architect's instructions issued

under clause 13.2 of the Main Contract Conditions requiring a Variation or

under clause 13.3 of the Main Contract Conditions in regard to the expenditure of provisional sums (other than ~~work~~ instructions to which clause 13.4.2 of the Main Contract Conditions refers or where bills of quantities are included in the Numbered Documents, an instruction for the expenditure of a provisional sum for defined work*)

.2.8 where bills of quantities are included in the Numbered Documents the execution of work for which an Approximate Quantity is included in those bills which is not a reasonably accurate forecast of the quantity of work required.

* See footnote to clause 1.3 (Definitions)

16.1 Where clause 15.1 applies:

all Variations (including any sanctioned by the Architect in writing) and all work executed by the Sub-Contractor in accordance with the instructions of the Architect as to the expenditure of provisional sums included in the Sub-Contract Documents, shall be valued by the Quantity Surveyor and

all work executed by the Sub-Contractor for which an Approximate Quantity is included in any bills of quantities which are included in the Numbered Documents shall be measured and valued by the Quantity Surveyor

and such valuation (in clause 16 called "the Valuation") shall (unless otherwise agreed by the Contractor and Sub-Contractor and approved by the Employer) be made in accordance with the provisions of clause 16.3.

16.3 .1 To the extent that the Valuation relates to the execution of additional or substituted work which can properly be valued by measurement or where bills of quantities are included in the Numbered Documents to the execution of work for which an Approximate Quantity is included in those bills such work shall be measured and shall be valued in accordance with the following rules:

.1.1 where the additional or substituted work is of similar character to, is executed under similar conditions as, and does not significantly change the quantity of, work set out in bills of quantities and/or other documents comprised in the Sub-Contract Documents the rates and prices for the work so set out shall determine the Valuation;

.1.2 where the additional or substituted work is of similar character to work set out in bills of quantities and/or other documents comprised in the Sub-Contract Documents but is not executed under similar conditions thereto and/or significantly changes the quantity thereof, the rates and prices for the work so set out shall be the basis for determining the Valuation and the Valuation shall include a fair allowance for such difference in conditions and/or quantity,

.1.3 where the additional or substituted work is not of similar character to work set out in bills of quantities and/or other documents comprised in the Sub-Contract Documents the work shall be valued at fair rates and prices.

.1.4 where the Approximate Quantity is a reasonably accurate forecast of the quantity of work required the rate or price for that Approximate Quantity shall determine the Valuation;

.1.5 where the Approximate Quantity is not a reasonably accurate forecast of the quantity of work required the rate or price for that Approximate Quantity shall be the basis for determining the Valuation and the Valuation shall include a fair allowance for such difference in quantity.

[Clauses 16.3.2, 16.3.3, 16.3.3.1 and 16.3.3.2 unchanged]

.3.3   allowance, where appropriate, shall be made for any addition to or reduction of preliminary items of the type referred to in the Standard Method of Measurement ~~6th Edition, Section B (Preliminaries)~~ 7th Edition Section A (Preliminaries/General Conditions) provided that where bills of quantities are included in the Numbered Documents no such allowance shall be made in respect of compliance with an instruction of the Architect for the expenditure of a provisional sum for defined work*.

[clauses 16.3.4, 16.3.4.1, 16.3.4.2 and the Proviso, 16.3.5, and the Proviso to clause 16.3 unchanged]

16.5   If

compliance with any instruction requiring a Variation under clause 13.2 of the Main Contract Conditions or

compliance with any instruction as to the expenditure of a provisional sum under clause 13.3 of the Main Contract Conditions except where bills of quantities are included in the Numbered Documents a provisional sum for defined work* included in those bills other than to the extent that the instruction for that work differs from the description given for such work in the bills of quantities or

where bills of quantities are included in the Numbered Documents the execution of work for which an Approximate Quantity is included in those bills to such extent as the quantity is more or less than the quantity ascribed to that work in the bills of quantities

substantially changes the conditions under which any other part or parts of the Sub-Contract Works ~~which are not the subject of the aforementioned instruction~~ is executed, then such other part or parts shall be treated as if it had been the subject of an instruction of the Architect requiring a Variation under clause 13.2 of the Main Contract Conditions which shall be valued in accordance with the provisions of clause 16.

* See footnote to clause 1.3 (Definitions)

17.4   [clauses 17.4.1, 17.4.1.1, 17.4.1 2, 17.4.1.3, 17.4.2, 17.4.2.1, 17.4.2.2 unchanged]

.2.3   any amounts priced in the Preliminaries section of the Sub-Contract Documents adjusted, where appropriate, to take into account any instructions of the Architect requiring a Variation or in regard to the expenditure of a provisional sum included in the Sub-Contract Documents, shall be included provided that where bills of quantities are included in the Numbered Documents, no such allowance shall be made in respect of compliance with an instruction of the Architect for the expenditure of a provisional sum for defined work*.

[clauses 17.4.3, 17.4.3.1, 17.4.3.2 and the Proviso unchanged]

.4   If compliance with

any instruction requiring a Variation under clause 13.2 of the Main Contract Conditions or

any instruction as to the expenditure of a provisional sum under clause 13.3 of the Main Contract Conditions except, where bills of quantities are included in the Numbered Documents, a provisional sum for defined work* included in those bills other than to the extent that the instruction for that work differs from the description given for such work in the bills of quantities or

any instruction as a result of which work included in the Sub-Contract Documents is not executed

substantially changes the conditions under which any part or parts of the Sub-Contract Works which are not the subject of the aforementioned instruction is executed, then such other part or parts shall be valued in accordance with the provisions of clause 17.4.1.2.

[clause 17.4.5 and Proviso to clause 17.4 unchanged]

* See footnote to clause 1.3 (Definitions)

8.1   Subject always to clause 2.2, if bills of quantities are a Sub-Contract Document:

    .1   such bills, unless otherwise specifically stated therein in respect of any specified item or items, are to have been prepared in accordance with the Standard Method of Measurement of Building Works, 6th Edition 7th Edition published by the Royal Institution of Chartered Surveyors and the Building Employers Confederation;

    .2   if in the bills of quantities there is any departure from the method of preparation referred to in clause 18.1.1 or any error in description or in quantity or omission of items (including any error in or omission of information in any item which is the subject of a provisional sum for defined work*) then such departure or error or omission shall not vitiate this Sub-Contract but the departure or error or omission shall be corrected; where the description of a provisional sum for defined work* does not provide the information required by General Rule 10.3 in the Standard Method of Measurement the correction shall be made by correcting the description so that it does provide such information—any such correction under this clause 18.1.2 shall be treated as if it were a Variation required by an instruction of the Architect under clause 13.2 of the Main Contract Conditions.

[clause 18.1.3 unchanged]

* See footnote to clause 1.3 (Definitions)

10   .2   The Sub-Contract Sum shall be adjusted as follows:

There shall be deducted:

    .2.1   all provisional sums and the value of all work described as provisional included in the Sub-Contract Documents and, where bills of quantities are included in the Numbered Documents the value of all work for which an Approximate (Quantity is included in those bills.

clauses 21.10.2.2 to 21.10.2.4 unchanged]

There shall be added:

[clauses 21.10.2.5 and 21.10.2.6 unchanged]

.2.7   the amount of the Valuation of work executed by, or the amount of any dis-
bursement made by, the Sub-Contractor in accordance with instructions of the
Architect and of all work described as provisional included in the Sub-Contract
Documents and, where bills of quantities are included in the Numbered Documents, of all work for which an Approximate Quantity is included in those bills;

[clauses 21.10.2.8 to 21.10.2.11 unchanged]

*   *   *

Amendment 8
Issued April 1989

1	**Clause 19A**	**Value added tax**

19A.   .2   At end **insert** additional sentence:

"Clause 19A.5 shall only apply where so stated in the Tender Schedule 2, Item 8
(NSC/4) in Appendix part 5A (NSC/4a)"

.3   **Delete** "Regulation 21(1) of the Value Added Tax (General) Regulations 1972"
and **insert** "Regulation 26 of the Value Added Tax (General) Regulations 1985"

Re-number as follows:

existing	revised
19A.4.1.1	19A.4
19A.4.1.2	19A.6.1
19A.4.2	19A.6.2
19A.4.3	19A.7
19A.4.4	19A.8
19A.4.5	19A.9
19A.5	19A.10

Insert additional clause 19A.5:

19A.5.1   Where it is stated in the Tender Schedule 2, item 8 (NSC/4) in the
[h.1]   Appendix part 5A (NSC/4a) that clause 19A.5 applies, clauses 19A.6.1
and 19A.6.2 shall not apply unless and until any notice issued under clause
19A.5.4 hereof becomes effective or the Sub-Contractor fails to give the
written notice required under clause 19A.5.2. Where clause 19A.5 applies,
clauses 19A.1.1, 19A.1.2, 19A.2, 19A.3, 19A.4 and 19A.7 to 19A.10
remain in full force and effect.

19A.5.2   Not later than 14 days before the first payment under the Sub-Contract is
due to the Sub-Contractor, the Sub-Contractor shall give written notice to
the Contractor of the rate of tax chargeable on the supply of goods and
services for which interim and final payments are to be made. If the rate of

tax so notified is varied under statute the Sub-Contractor shall, not later than seven days after the date when such varied rate comes into effect, send to the Contractor the necessary amendment to the rate given in his written notice and that notice shall then take effect as so amended.

19A.5.3 For the purpose of complying with clause 19A.2 for the recovery by the Sub-Contractor from the Contractor of tax properly chargeable by the Commissioners on the Sub-Contractor, an amount calculated at the rate given in the aforesaid written notice (or, where relevant, amended written notice) shall be added to the amount of each interim payment and of the final payment to which clause 21 refers.

19A.5.4 Either the Contractor or the Sub-Contractor may give written notice to the other stating that with effect from the date of the notice, clause 19A.5 shall no longer apply. From that date the provisions of clauses 19A.6.1 and 19A.6.2 shall apply in place of clause 19A.5.

Footnote: [h.1] Clause 19A.5 can only apply where the Sub-Contractor is satisfied at the date the Sub-Contract is entered into that his output tax on **all** ~supplies to the Contractor under the Sub-Contract will be at either a positive or a zero rate of tax. Some supplies by the Contractor to the Employer are zero rated by a certificate in statutory form. Only the person holding the certificate, usually the Contractor, may zero rate his supply. Sub-contract supplies for a main contract zero rated by certificate are standard rated: see the VAT leaflet 708 revised 1989.

.6.1 **Insert** at the beginning:

"Unless clause 19A.5 applies"

(formerly 19A.4.1.2)

Line 6, **delete** "Regulation 21(1)" and **insert** "Regulation 26."

.7 Line 1, **delete** "and 19A.4.2" and **insert** "and in either clause 19A.5.3 or clause 19A.6.2 whichever is applicable"

(formerly 19A.4.3)

Line 2, **delete** "Regulation 21 as aforesaid" and **insert** "Regulation 12(4) of the Value Added Tax (General) Regulations 1985."

Lines 3 and 4, **delete** "Regulation 9(1) of the Value Added Tax (General) Regulations 1972" and **insert** "Regulations 13(1) of the Value Added Tax (General) Regulations 1985."

.8 Line 3, **delete** "clause 19A.4.2" and **insert** "either clause 19A.5.3 or clause 19A.6.2 whichever is applicable."

(formerly 19A.4.4)

.9 Line 1, **delete** "clause 19A.4.2" and **insert** "either clause 19A 5.3 or clause 19A.6.2 whichever is applicable."

(formerly 19A.4.5)

.10 Line 3, **delete** "19A.4.3" and **insert** "19A.7"

Lines 7, 9 and 11 **delete** "19A.5" and **insert** "19A.10."

(formerly 19A.5)

<table>
<tr><td>2</td><td>**Clause 19B**</td><td>**Value added tax—Special Arrangement—VAT (General) Regulations 1972, Regulations 8(3) and 21**</td></tr>
</table>

Delete statutory reference and **insert**: "—Value Added Tax Act 1983 s.5(4)—Value Added Tax (General) Regulations 1985, Regulations 12(3) and 26."

19B.   .2   At end **insert** "Clause 19B.5 shall only apply where so stated in the Tender Schedule 2 item 8 (NSC/4) in the Appendix, part 5A (NSC/4a)."

.3   Lines 2 and 3 **delete** "Regulations 21(1) of the Value Added Tax (General) Regulations 1972" and **insert** "Regulation 26 of the Value Added Tax (General) Regulations 1985."

Re-number as follows:

existing	revised
19B.4.1.1	19B.4
19B.4.1.2	19B.6.1
19B.4.2	19B.6.2
19B.4.3	19B.7.1
19B.4.4	19B.7.2
19B.4.5	19B.7.3
19B.5	19B.8
19B.5.1	19B.8.1
19B.5.2	19B.8.2
19B.6	19B.9
19B.7	19B.10

Insert additional clause 19B.5:

"19B.5.1   Where it is stated in the Tender Schedule 2, item 8 (NSC/4) in the
[i.1]   Appendix part 5A (NSC/4a) that clause 19B.5 applies, clauses 19B.6.1 and 19B.6.2 shall not apply unless and until any notice issued under clause 19B.5.4 hereof becomes effective or unless the Sub-Contractor fails to give the written notice required under clause 19B.5.2. Where clause 19A.5 applies, clauses 19B.1.1, 19B.1.2, 19B.2, 19B.3, 19B.4, 19B.7.1 to .7.3 and 19B.8 to 19B.10 remain in full force and effect.

.5.2   Not later than 14 days before the first payment under the Sub-Contract is due to the Sub-Contractor, the Sub-Contractor shall give written notice to the Contractor of the rate of tax chargeable on the supply of goods and services for which interim and final payments are to be made. If the rate of tax so notified is varied under statute the Sub-Contractor shall, not later than 7 days after the date when such varied rate comes into effect, send to the Contractor the necessary amendment to the rate given in his written notice and that notice shall then take effect as so amended.

.5.3   For the purpose of complying with clause 19B.2 for the recovery by the Sub-Contractor from the Contractor of tax properly chargeable by the Commission ers on the Sub-Contractor, an amount calculated at the rate given in the aforesaid written notice (or where relevant, amended written notice) shall be added to the amount of each interim payment and of the final payment to which clause 21 refers.

.5.4 Either the Contractor or the Sub-Contractor may give written notice to the other stating that with effect from the date of the notice clause 19B.5 shall no longer apply. From that date the provisions of clauses 19B.6.1 and 19B.6.2 shall apply in place of clause 19B.5.

Footnote: [i.1] Clause 19B.5 can only apply where the Sub-Contractor is satisfied at the date the Sub-Contractor is entered into that his output tax on all supplies to the Contractor under the Sub-Contract will be at either a positive or a zero rate of tax. Some supplies by the Contractor to the Employer are zero rated by a certificate in statutory form. Only the person holding the certificate, usually the Contractor, may zero rate his supply. Sub-contract supplies for a main contract zero rated by certificate are standard rated: see the VAT leaflet 708 revised 1989."

.6.1 **Insert** at the beginning "Unless clause 19B.5 applies"

(formerly 19B.4.1.2)

Line 6, **delete** "Regulation 21(1)" and **insert** "Regulation 26."

.7.1 Line 2, **delete** "clause 19B.4.2" and **insert** "clause 19B.5.3 or clause 19B.6.2, whichever is applicable."

(formerly 19B.4.3)

Lines 3 and 4, **delete** "Regulation 8(3) of the Value Added Tax (General) Regulations 1972" and **insert** "Regulations 12(3) and 26 of the Value Added Tax (General) Regulations, 1985."

Line 11, **delete** "19B.4.2" and **insert** "clause 19B.7.3."

.7.2 Line 3, **delete** "clause 19B.4.2 and .3" and **insert** "clause 19B.5.3 or clause 19B.6.2 whichever is applicable and clause 19B.7.1."

(formerly 19B.4.4)

.8.1 Line 1, **delete** "19B.4.3" and **insert** "19B.7.1."

(formerly 19B.5.1)

.8.2 Line 2, **delete** "19B.4.3" and **insert** "19B.7.1."

(formerly 19B.5.2)

.8 Line 6, after "then clause 19A" **insert** "(as amended by Amendment 8 issued April 1989)."

(formerly 19B.5)

.9 Line 1, **delete** "19B.5" and **insert** "19B.8."

Lines 3 and 4, **delete** "Regulation 21(2) of the Value Added Tax (General) Regulations 1972" and **insert** "Regulation 12(4) of the Value Added Tax (General) Regulations 1985."

(formerly 19B.6)

Footnote [i]   **Delete** "Value Added Tax (General) Regulations 1972 Regulations 8(3)" and **insert** "Value Added Tax (General) Regulations 1985 Regulations 12(3) and 26"; **delete** "Regulation 21(2)" and **insert** "Regulation 12(4)."

---

3   **Standard Form of Nominated Sub-Contract NSC/4a—Appendix**

Appendix   **Insert** additional part after part 5:

"part 5A

| Clause 19A | Value added tax |
| Clause 19B | |

clause *19A/19B will apply
clause 19A.5   *applies/does not apply
clause 19B.5   *applies/does not apply
(* *delete as applicable*)

**Amendment 9
Issued July 1990**

---

1   **Clause 1.3**   **Definitions**

NSC/4 only
In the definition of "Sub-Contract Documents" **delete** "see clause 2.1.1" and **insert**:

"The Tender (comprising page 1 and the Numbered Documents annexed thereto and the completed Schedules 1 and 2 and any documents annexed thereto or referred to therein) and the Sub-Contract NSC/4."

NSC/4a only
In the definition of "Sub-Contract Documents" **delete** "see **clause 2.1.1**" and **insert** a full stop.

In the definition of "Sub-Contract Works" **delete** the meaning given and **insert**:

NSC/4 only
"the works referred to in the **Tender, page 1** and described in the Numbered Documents annexed thereto to be executed as part of the Works and including any changes made to such works in accordance with this Sub-Contract."

NSC/4a only
"the works referred to in the Appendix, part 1 and described in the Numbered Documents to be executed as part of the Works including any changes made to such works in accordance with this Sub-Contract."

NSC/4 and NSC/4a
In the definition of "Variation" paragraph .1 **delete** "as shown in the Sub-Contract Documents."

NSC/4 and NSC/4a
In the definition of "Works" **insert** at end: "and including any changes made to such works in accordance with the Main Contract."

Consequential amendments

NSC/4 and NSC/4a
First recital: **delete** "(hereinafter called the "Sub-Contract Works.)"

NSC/4 and NSC/4a
Clause 2.1: **delete** clause 2.1.1; **re-number** clause 2.1.2 as "2.1." **Delete** side heading to clause 2.1.1 and insert as side heading to the re-numbered clause 2.1: "Documents other than Sub-Contract Documents."

2	**Clause 4**	**Execution of the Sub-Contract Works—instructions of Architect—directions of Contractor**

NSC/4 and NSC/4A
Re-number clause 4.1.4 as "4.1.5" and 4.1.5 as "4.1.6." **Insert** new sub-clause 4.1.4:

"4.1.4 All work shall be carried out in a proper and workmanlike manner."

Insert new clause 4.3.2.2:

"Where there is any failure to comply with clause 4.1.4 in regard to the carrying out of the Sub-Contract Works in a proper and workmanlike manner and the provisions of clause 8.5 of the Main Contract Conditions ('Main Contract 8.5') are operated in respect of such failure clauses 4.3.5A and 4.3.7 shall apply."

4.3.2.2: **re-number** as "4.3.2.3"; line 1 after "8.4" **insert** "and/or 8.5"; line 2 after "and 8.4.3" **insert** "and 8.5"

Insert new sub-clause 4.3.5A:

Work not carried out in a proper and workmanlike manner	4.3.5A	Where there is any failure to comply with clause 4.1.4 as referred to in clause 4.3.2.2 the Sub-Contractor shall comply with such instructions issued by the Architect pursuant to Main Contract 8.5 and issued to the Sub-Contractor pursuant to clause 4.2 whether requiring a Variation or otherwise to the extent that they are reasonably necessary as a consequence thereof; and to the extent that such instructions are so necessary and notwithstanding clause 16 (valuation of Variations and provisional sum work) and clause 17 (valuation of all work comprising the Sub-Contract Works), clause 11.2 (extension of sub-Contract time) and clause 13.1 (matters affecting

regular progress—direct loss and/or expense) no adjustment shall be made to the Sub-Contract Sum to be
included in the computation of the Ascertained Final
Sub-Contract Sum and no extension of time shall be given
in respect of compliance by the Sub-Contractor with such
instructions."

4.3.6.1
Line 2 after "8.4" **insert** "and/or 8.5."

Line 9 after "non-complying work" **insert** "or failure to carry out work in a proper and
workmanlike manner."

Line 10 after "8.4" **insert** "and/or 8.5."

4.3.7
Line 3 after "and/or 4.3.5" **insert** "and/or 4.3.5A." At end **insert** "or Main Contract
8.5 being operated in respect of the failure to carry out work in a proper and workmanlike manner."

---

3   **Clause 26.2**   **Sub-Contractors not to sub-let without Architect's
                                    and Contractor's consent**

Insert additional sentence: "The Sub-Contractor shall remain wholly responsible for
carrying out and completing the Sub-Contract Works in all respects in accordance with
the Sub-Contract notwithstanding the sub-letting of any portion of the Sub-Contract
Works."

CHAPTER 20

ANCILLARY STANDARD FORMS

In this Chapter, there are reproduced with commentary the JCT Standard Form of Employer/Nominated Sub-Contractor Agreement (NSC/2) and the JCT Nominated Supplier Warranty (TNS/2).

The version of NSC/2 printed below incorporates Amendment 1 issued in July 1987 and Amendment 2 issued in July 1988.

JCT STANDARD FORM OF EMPLOYER/NOMINATED SUB-CONTRACTOR AGREEMENT

Agreement between a Sub-Contractor to be nominated for Sub-Contract Work in accordance with clauses 35.6 to 35.10 of the Standard Form of Building Contract for a main contract and the Employer referred to in the main contract.

Main Contract Works: . . . .
Location: . . . .
Sub-Contract Works: . . . .

This Agreement

is made the . . . . day of . . . . 19. . . . .
between

. . . .
of or whose registered office is situated at

. . . .
(hereinafter called "the Employer") and

. . . .
of or whose registered office is situated at

. . . .
(hereinafter called "the Sub-Contractor").

Whereas

First
the Sub-Contractor has submitted a tender on Tender NSC/1 (hereinafter called "the Tender") on the terms and conditions in that Tender to carry out Works (referred to above and hereinafter called "the Sub-Contract Works") as part of the Main Contract Works referred to above to be or being carried out on the terms and conditions relating thereto referred to in Schedule 1 of the Tender (hereinafter called "the Main Contract");

Second
the Employer has appointed

. . . .
to be the Architect/the Contract Administrator for the purposes of the Main Contract and this Agreement (hereinafter called "the Architect/the Contract Administrator"

which expression as used in this Agreement shall include his successors validly appointed under the Main Contract or otherwise before the Main Contract is operative);

Third

the Architect/the Contract Administrator on behalf of the Employer has approved the Tender and intends that after agreement between the Contractor and Sub-Contractor on the Particular Conditions in Schedule 2 thereof an instruction on Nomination NSC/3 shall be issued to the Contractor for the Main Contract (hereinafter called "the Main Contractor") nominating the Sub-Contractor to carry out and complete the Sub-Contract Works on the terms and conditions of the Tender;

Fourth

nothing contained in this Agreement nor anything contained in the Tender is intended to render the Architect/the Contract Administrator in any way liable to the Sub-Contractor in relation to matters in the said Agreement and Tender.

Now it is hereby agreed

1.1 The Sub-Contractor shall, after the Architect/the Contract Administrator has issued his preliminary notice of nomination under clause 35.7.1 of the Main Contract Conditions, forthwith seek to settle with the Main Contractor the Particular Conditions in Schedule 2 of the Tender.

1.2 The Sub-Contractor shall, upon reaching agreement with the Main Contractor on the Particular Conditions in Schedule 2 of the Tender and after that Schedule is signed by or on behalf of the Sub-Contractor and the Main Contractor, immediately through the Main Contractor so inform the Architect/the Contract Administrator.

2.1 The Sub-Contractor warrants that he has exercised and will exercise all reasonable skill and care in

.1 the design of the Sub-Contract Works insofar as the Sub-Contract Works have been or will be designed by the Sub-Contractor; and

.2 the selection of materials and goods for the Sub-Contract Works insofar as such materials and goods have been or will be selected by the Sub-Contractor; and

.3 the satisfaction of any performance specification or requirement insofar as such performance specification or requirement is included or referred to in the description of the Sub-Contract Works included in or annexed to the Tender.

Nothing in clause 2.1 shall be construed so as to affect the obligations of the Sub-Contractor under Sub-Contractor NSC/4 in regard to the supply under the Sub-Contract of workmanship, materials and goods.

2.2 .1 If, after the date of this Agreement and before the issue by the Architect/the Contract Administrator of the instruction on Nomination NSC/3 under clause 35.10.2 of the Main Contract Conditions, the Architect/the Contract Administrator instructs in writing that the Sub-Contractor should proceed with

.1 the designing of, or

.2 the purchase under a contract of sale of materials or goods or the fabrication of components for

the Sub-Contract Works the Sub-Contractor shall forthwith comply with the instruction and the Employer shall make payment or reimbursement for such compliance in accordance with clauses 2.2.2 to 2.2.4.

.2 No payment or reimbursement referred to in clauses 2.2.3 and 2.2.4 shall be made after the issue of Nomination NSC/3 under clause 35.10.2 of the Main Contract Conditions except in respect of any design work properly carried out and/or materials or goods properly ordered under a contract of sale or components properly fabricated in compliance with an instruction under clause 2.2.1 but which are not used for the Sub-Contract Works by reason of some written decision against such use given by the Architect/the Contract Administrator before the issue of Nomination NSC/3 of the Main Contract Conditions.

.3 The Employer shall pay the Sub-Contractor the amount of any expense reasonably and properly incurred by the Sub-Contractor in carrying out work in the designing of the Sub-Contract Works and upon such payment the Employer may use that work for the purpose of the Sub-Contract Works but not further or otherwise.

.4 The Employer shall pay the Sub-Contractor for any component properly fabricated and shall reimburse the Sub-Contractor for any amounts properly due and paid by the Sub-Contractor under the contract of sale for materials or goods properly purchased by the Sub-Contractor for the Sub-Contract Works and upon such payment or reimbursement the materials and goods shall become the property of the Employer.

.5 If any payment or reimbursement has been made by the Employer under clauses 2.2.3 and 2.2.4 and the Sub-Contractor is subsequently nominated in Nomination NSC/3 issued under clause 35.10.2 of the Main Contract Conditions to execute the Sub-Contract Works the Sub-Contractor shall allow to the Main Contractor or, where clause 35.13.6 of the Main Contract Conditions is operated, to the Employer full credit for such payment or reimbursement in the discharge of the amount due in respect of the Sub-Contract Works and the Sub-Contractor shall provide the Employer with a written statement, in duplicate, of the amount so credited. Provided that no credit shall be so allowed in respect of payments or reimbursements made by the Employer for design work properly carried out and/or materials or goods properly purchased under a contract of sale and/or components properly fabricated in compliance with an instruction under clause 2.2.1 but which are not used by reason of some written decision against such use by the Architect/ the Contract Administrator before the issue of Nomination NSC/3 under clause 35.10.2 of the Main Contract Conditions.

3.1 The Sub-Contractor will not be liable under clauses 3.2, 3.3 or 3.4 until the Architect/ the Contract Administrator has issued his instruction on Nomination NSC/3 under clause 35.10.2 of the Main Contract Conditions nor in respect of any revised period of time for delay in carrying out or completing the Sub-Contract Works which the Sub-Contractor has been granted under clause 11.2 of Sub-Contract NSC/4.

3.2 The Sub-Contractor shall so supply the Architect/the Contract Administrator with information (including drawings) in accordance with the agreed programme details or at such time as the Architect/the Contract Administrator may reasonably require so that the Architect/the Contract Administrator will not be delayed in issuing necessary instructions or drawings under the Main Contract, for which delay the Main Contractor may have a valid claim to an extension of time for completion of the Main Contract Works by reason of the Relevant Event in clause 25.4.6 or a valid claim for direct loss and/or expense under clause 26.2.1 of the Main Contract Conditions.

3.3 The Sub-Contractor shall so perform his obligations under the Sub-Contract that the Architect/the Contract Administrator will not by reason of any default by the Sub-Contractor be under a duty to issue an instruction to determine the employment of the Sub-Contractor under clause 35.24 of the Main Contract Conditions provided that any suspension by the Sub-Contractor of further execution of the Sub-Contract Works under clause 21.8 of Sub-Contract NSC/4 shall not be regarded as a "default by the Sub-Contractor" as referred to in clause 3.3.

3.4 The Sub-Contractor shall so perform the Sub-Contract that the Contractor will not become entitled to an extension of time for completion of the Main Contract Works by reason of the Relevant Event in clause 25.4.7 of the Main Contract Conditions.

4. The Architect/The Contract Administrator shall operate the provisions of [*a*] clause 35.13.1 of the Main Contract Conditions.

5.1 The Architect/The Contract Administrator shall operate the provisions in [*b*] clauses 35.17 to 35.19 of the Main Contract Conditions.

5.2 After due discharge by the Contractor of a final payment under clause 35.17 of the Main Contract Conditions the Sub-Contractor shall rectify at his own cost (or if he fails so to rectify, shall be liable to the Employer for the costs referred to in clause 35.18 of the Main Contract Conditions) any omission, fault or defect in the Sub-Contract Works which the Sub-Contractor is bound to rectify under Sub-Contract NSC/4 after written notification thereof by the Architect/the Contract Administrator at anytime before the issue of the Final Certificate under clause 30.8 of the Main Contract Conditions.

5.3 After the issue of the Final Certificate under the Main Contract Conditions the Sub-Contractor shall in addition to such other responsibilities, if any, as he has under this Agreement, have the like responsibility to the Main Contractor and to the Employer for the Sub-Contract Works as the Main Contractor has to the Employer under the terms of the Main Contract relating to the obligations of the Contractor after the issue of the Final Certificate.

6. Where the Architect/the Contract Administrator has been under a duty under clause 35.24 of the Main Contract Conditions except as a result of the operation of clause 35.24.6 to issue an instruction to the Main Contractor making a further nomination in respect of the Sub-Contract Works, the Sub-Contractor shall indemnify the Employer against any direct loss and/or expense resulting from the exercise by the Architect/the Contract Administrator of that duty.

7.1 The Architect/The Contract Administrator and the Employer shall operate the provisions in regard to the payment of the Sub-Contractor in clause 35.13 of the Main Contract Conditions.

7.2 If, after paying any amount to the Sub-Contractor under clause 35.13.5.3 of the Main Contract Conditions, the Employer produces reasonable proof that there was in existence at the time of such payment a petition or resolution to which clause 35.13.5.4.4 of the Main Contract Conditions refers, the Sub-Contractor shall repay on demand such amount.

8. Where [*c*] clause 2.3 of Sub-Contract NSC/4 applies, the Sub-Contractor shall forth-

---

[*a*] *Note: Clause 35.13.1 requires that the Architect/the Contract Administrator, upon directing the Main Contractor as to the amount included in any Interim Certificates in respect of the value of the Nominated Sub-Contract Works issued under clause 30 of the Main Contract Conditions, shall forthwith inform the Sub-Contractor in writing of that amount.*

[*b*] *Note: Clause 35.17 deals with final payment by the Employer for Sub-Contract Works prior to the issue of the Final Certificate under the Main Contract Conditions.*

[*c*] *Note: Clause 2.3 deals with specified supplies and restrictions etc. in the contracts of sale for such supplies.*

with supply to the Contractor details of any restriction, limitation or exclusion to which that clause refers as soon as such details are known to the Sub-Contractor.

8A. Where clause 19.1.2 of the Main Contract applies then, in the event of transfer by the Employer of his freehold or leasehold interest in, or of a grant by the Employer of a leasehold interest in, the whole of the premises comprising the Works, the Employer may at any time after Practical Completion of the Works assign to any such transferee or lessee the right to bring proceedings in the name of the Employer (whether by arbitration or litigation) to enforce any of the terms of this Agreement made for the benefit of the Employer hereunder. The assignee shall be estopped from disputing any enforceable agreements reached between the Employer and the Sub-Contractor and which arise out of and relate to this Agreement (whether or not they are or appear to be a derogation from the rights assigned) and made prior to the date of any assignment.

9. If any conflict appears between the terms of the Tender and this Agreement, the terms of this Agreement shall prevail.

10.1 If any dispute or difference shall arise between the Employer or the Architect/the Contract Administrator on his behalf and the Sub-Contractor, either during the progress or after the completion or abandonment of the Works or after the determination or alleged determination of the employment of the Sub-Contractor, as to the construction of this Agreement or any matter or thing of whatsoever nature arising there under or in connection therewith it shall be and is hereby referred to arbitration. When the Employer or the Sub-Contractor require such dispute or difference to be referred to arbitration then either the Employer or the Sub-Contractor shall give written notice to the other to such effect and such dispute or difference shall be referred to the arbitration and final decision of a person to be agreed between the parties as the Arbitrator, or, upon failure so to agree within 14 days after the date of the aforesaid written notice, of a person to be appointed as the Arbitrator on the request of either the Employer or the Sub-Contractor by the person named in the Appendix of the Main Contract.

10.2 .1 Provided that if the dispute or difference to be referred to arbitration under this Agreement raises issues which are substantially the same as or connected with issues raised in a relation dispute between the Employer and the Contractor under the Main Contract or between the Sub-Contractor and the Contractor under Sub-Contract NSC/4 or NSC/4a or between the Employer and any other Nominated Sub-Contractor under Agreement NSC/2 or NSC/2a or between the Employer and any Nominated Supplier whose contract of sale with the Main Contractor provides for the matters referred to in clause 36.4.8 of the Main Contract Conditions, and if the related dispute has already been referred for determination to an Arbitrator, the Employer and the Sub-Contractor hereby agree that the dispute or difference under this Agreement shall be referred to the Arbitrator appointed to determine the related dispute; and the JCT Arbitration Rules applicable to the related dispute shall apply to the dispute under this Agreement; and such Arbitrator shall have power to make such directions and all necessary awards in the same way as if the procedure of the High Court as to joining one or more defendants or joining co-defendants or third parties was available to the parties and to him; and the agreement and consent referred to in clause 10.5 on appeals or applications to the High Court on any question of law shall apply to any question of law arising out of the awards of such Arbitrator in respect of all related disputes referred to him or arising in the course of the reference of all the related disputes referred to him.

.2 Save that the Employer or the Sub-Contractor may require the dispute or difference under this Agreement to be referred to a different Arbitrator (to be appointed under this Agreement) if either of them reasonably considers that the Arbitrator appointed to determine the related dispute is not appropriately qualified to determine the dispute or difference under this Agreement.

.3 Clauses 10.2.1 and 10.2.2 shall apply unless in the Appendix to the Main Contract Conditions the words "clauses 41.2.1 and 41.2.2 apply" have been deleted.

10.3 Such reference shall not be opened until after Practical Completion or alleged Practical Completion of the Main Contract Works or termination or alleged termination of the Contractor's employment under the Main Contract or abandonment of the Main Contract Works, unless with the written consent of the Employer or the Architect/the Contract Administrator on his behalf and the Sub-Contractor.

10.4 Subject to clause 10.5 the award of such Arbitrator shall be final and binding on the parties.

10.5 The parties hereby agree and consent pursuant to Sections 1(3)(a) and 2(1)(b) of the Arbitration Act 1979, that either party

.1 may appeal to the High Court on any such question of law arising out of an award made in an arbitration under this Arbitration Agreement and

.2 may apply to the High Court to determine any question of law arising in the course of the reference;

and the parties agree that the High Court should have jurisdiction to determine any such question of law.

10.6 Whatever the nationality, residence or domicile of the Employer, the Contractor, the Sub-Contractor or any sub-contractor or supplier or the Arbitrator, and wherever the Works or the Sub-Contract Works or any part thereof are situated, the law of England shall be the proper law of this Agreement and in particular (but not so as to derogate from the generality of the foregoing) the provisions of the Arbitration Acts 1950 (notwithstanding anything in S.34 thereof) to 1979 shall apply to any arbitration under this Agreement wherever the same, or any part of it, shall be conducted. [d]

10.7 If before making his final award the Arbitrator dies or otherwise ceases to act as the Arbitrator, the Employment and the Sub-Contractor shall forthwith appoint a further Arbitrator, or, upon failure so to appoint within 14 days of any such death or cessation, then either the Employer or the Sub-Contractor may request the person named in the Appendix of the Main Contract to appoint such further Arbitrator. Provided that no such further Arbitrator shall be entitled to disregard any direction of the previous Arbitrator or to vary or revise any award of the previous Arbitrator except to the extent that the previous Arbitrator had power so to do under the JCT Arbitration Rules and/or with the agreement of the parties and/or by the operation of law.

10.8 The arbitration shall be conducted in accordance with the "JCT Arbitration Rules" current at the Base Date stated in the Sub-Contract. [d.1] Provided that if any

---

[d] *Where the parties do not wish the proper law of this Agreement to be the law of England appropriate amendments to clause 10.6 should be made. Where the works are situated in Scotland then the forms issued by the Scottish Building Contract Committee which contain Scots proper law and arbitration provisions are the appropriate documents. It should be noted that the provisions of the Arbitration Acts 1950 to 1979 do not extend to Scotland.*

[d.1] *The JCT Arbitration Rules contain stricter time limits than those prescribed by some arbitration rules or those frequently observed in practice. The parties should note that a failure by a party or the agent of a party to comply with the time limits incorporated in these Rules may have adverse consequences.*

amendments to the Rules so current have been issued by the Joint Contracts Tribunal after the aforesaid Base Date the Employer and the Sub-Contractor may, by a joint notice in writing to the Arbitrator, state that they wish the arbitration to be conducted in accordance with the JCT Arbitration Rules as so amended.

Signed by or on behalf of the Sub-Contractor [*e.1*]

in the presence of:

Signed by or on behalf of the Employer [*e.1*]

in the presence of:

Signed, sealed and delivered by [*e.2*] The Common seal of [*e.3*]:

in the presence of [*e.2*]/was hereunto affixed in the presence of [*e.3*]:

Signed, sealed and delivered by [*e.2*]/The common seal of [*e.3*]:

in the presence of [*e.2*]/was hereunto affixed in the presence of [*e.3*]:

Commentary on JCT Standard Form of Employer/Nominated Sub-Contractor Agreement (Agreement NSC/2)

Introduction.   Recent developments in the law relating to liability in negligence for purely economic loss[1] make it highly desirable for Employers to enter into collateral contracts with Nominated Sub-Contractors. Without such a collateral agreement, there will, of course, be no contractual connection between Employer and Sub-Contractor. There is unlikely to be any liability in tort except for personal injury and certain limited classes of property damage.

Generally.   Agreement NSC/2 is derived from the 1973 R.I.B.A. Form of Agreement between Employer and Nominated Sub-Contractor. The Agreement is redrafted and there have been substantial additions of substance. It is one of the Agreements referred to in clause 35.3 of the Main Contract and is one of the two agreements provided as part of the procedure for the nomination of a Sub-Contractor set out in clauses 35.4–35.12 of the Main Contract. See in particular clauses 35.6–35.10 of the Main Contract.[2] The other Employer/ Nominated Sub-Contractor Agreement which the procedure for nomination provides for is Agreement NSC/2a (see clauses 35.11 and 35.12 of the Main Contract). Agreement NSC/2a is in substance the same as Agreement NSC/2 with differences to provide for the fact that, with NSC/2a, the Form of Tender NSC/1 will not have been used. Thus NSC/2a has different recitals and

---

[*e.1*] *For use if Agreement is executed under hand.*
[*e.2*] *For use if executed under seal by an individual or firm or unincorporated body.*
[*e.3*] *For use if executed under seal by a company or other body corporate.*
[1] See Chap. 7 and in particular "Specialist sub-contractors" at p. 178.
[2] See pp. 628 *et seq.* for these Main Contract clauses and their commentary.

clauses 1 and 9 of NSC/2 are omitted. For a commentary on the differences between the two agreements and procedures, see commentary to clause 35 of the Main Contract. The commentary below refers to Agreement NSC/2 unless there is a specific reference to NSC/2a.

Amendments.   Agreements NSC/2 was amended by Amendment 1 issued in July 1987 and Amendment 2 issued in July 1988. With one exception discussed below, these Amendments are not of great significance and may be summarised as follows:

(1) the term "the Contract Administrator" is used in place of "Supervising Officer" throughout the Agreement;
(2) drafting changes to clause 2.2;
(3) a new clause 8A, relating to assignment, discussed below;
(4) the Arbitration provisions in clause 10 have been amended consequentially upon the amendments to the Arbitration provisions of the Main Contract introduced by Amendments 4 and 6.

First Recital.   *"the Sub-Contractor has submitted a tender on Tender NSC/1 ... "*
This Tender has a section to insert details of the Main Contract Appendix and its entries. These entries include the Date for Completion and the rate of liquidated and ascertained damages. Provided these entries are properly made in the Tender, they will fix the Sub-Contractor with knowledge of the loss which the Employer will suffer by reason of the Sub-Contractor's default resulting in the Contractor obtaining an extension of time.[3] Therefore, ordinarily this will be the measure of damages payable by the Nominated Sub-Contractor for delay in breach of clause 3 of NSC/2, discussed below.

Third Recital.   *"the Architect ... has approved the Tender and intends ... "*
In order to achieve a nomination, the Architect will first have to send to the Contractor a preliminary notice of nomination under clause 35.7.1 of the Main Contract. This will not necessarily result in an effective nomination (see commentary to clause 35 of the Main Contract). It is clear, however, that in part, at least, Agreement NSC/2 will come into force between the Employer and the Sub-Contractor before a nomination is made. In this respect, it differs from the former Employer/Nominated Sub-Contractor Form of Agreement. There are obligations in NSC/2 which are intended to be binding and others which are contingently capable of being binding before nomination is effected. Clause 1 comes into the first of these categories: clause 2.2 comes into the second. It is thought that NSC/2 will become an effective agreement in law not later than the sending to the Contractor of the Architect's preliminary notice of

---

[3] For the significance of such knowledge, see "Principles upon which damages are awarded" at p. 185.

nomination. By doing this, the Architect as the Employer's agent provides, it is submitted, sufficient consideration to support a binding agreement with the Sub-Contractor. The Architect will no doubt also inform the Sub-Contractor that he has sent the preliminary notice thereby communicating acceptance of the Sub-Contractor's offer. The Recital refers to the Architect having approved the Tender, but it is thought that mere approval would not bind the Employer to continue with the nomination procedure.

For Agreement NSC/2a, where the Recitals are different and where there will be no preliminary notice of nomination, it is thought that the Agreement will come into force if the Architect instructs the Sub-Contractor under clause 1.2.1 of NSC/2a (which is clause 2.2.1 of NSC/2), or, if there is no such instruction, when the nomination is made under clause 35.11.2 of the Main Contract.

The discussion above supposes that the parties will not have actually executed the Form of Agreement in the period before an effective nomination instruction. In practice they probably will not do so, but of course, if they were to do so, the agreement would operate from the date of execution.

It should be noted that in any event, the Sub-Contractor's liability under clause 3 does not begin until a nomination instruction has been issued (see clause 3.1).

Fourth Recital. This is presumably intended to negative any personal liability in contract on the part of the Architect.[4] It may also be intended to prevent a duty of care arising as between Architect and Nominated Sub-Contractor in relation to the matters in the Agreement and Tender.

Clause 1.1. *"The Sub-Contractor shall ... forthwith seek to settle ..."*

It is thought that this clause obliges the Sub-Contractor to enter into bona fide negotiations. The Main Contractor has an equivalent obligation not expressed in exactly the same words in clause 35.7.2 of the Main Contract. This is not, it is submitted, an agreement to agree.[5] The Main Contractor and the proposed Sub-Contractor are each obliged to the Employer to negotiate with each other. If their negotiations do not produce agreement the Main Contract provides, in clauses 35.8 and 35.23, courses which the Architect can take so that the Main Contract can proceed. See also clause 2.2 of NSC/2 for a proposed Nominated Sub-Contractor's entitlement to payment irrespective of whether he is eventually nominated. For the position if the Main Contractor and the Sub-Contractor fail to reach agreement or if there is delay in reaching agreement, see clause 35.8 of the Main Contract and its commentary.

---

[4] See "Architect's personal liability on contracts" at p. 309.
[5] As to which see, *e.g. Courtney & Fairbairn* v. *Tolaini* [1975] 1 W.L.R. 297 at 301; see also "Contract to negotiate" at p. 24.

Clause 2.1. *"the Sub-Contractor warrants ..."*

The Sub-Contractor's warranty is substantially the same as that in A(1) of the former Employer/Nominated Sub-Contractor Agreement. The warranty is limited in two respects. Firstly, it is restricted to the exercise of all reasonable skill and care. There is no absolute warranty. Secondly, it is confined to the particular aspects of design, selection of materials and goods and satisfaction of performance specification set out at clauses 2.1.1 to 2.1.3.

Clause 2.2. *"If ... the Architect ... instructs ... that the Sub-Contractor should proceed ..."*

This useful clause enables the designing of the Sub-Contract Works and ordering materials or goods or fabrication of components to proceed before a formal nomination is made. This is often in practice desirable. The Employer becomes expressly liable to pay for the design work or the materials or goods (clauses 2.2.3 and 2.2.4). As between himself and the Nominated Sub-Contractor, the Architect has, it is submitted, ostensible authority to make the Employer liable. As between himself and the Employer, it is, at the least, a question of some doubt whether the Architect has implied authority to make the Employer liable.[6] The Architect would therefore be well advised to obtain the Employer's express agreement.

Clause 2.2.5 provides for payments made in advance of nomination to be allowed in full as credits after nomination against amounts due for the Sub-Contract Works. The proviso at the end of clause 2.2.5 was added by Amendment 1 issued in July 1987. The effect is that the Employer receives no credit for such payments where the design works or materials or goods are not in the event used by reason of some written decision against such use by the Architect. Again, the Architect will have to consider his position carefully *vis-à-vis* the Employer.

Clause 3. *Delay and non-performance by the Sub-Contractor*

After a nomination instruction has been issued, the Sub-Contractor becomes liable to the Employer for three specific aspects of his performance of the Sub-Contract Works. Each of these is subject to his entitlement to be granted an extension of time under clause 11.2 of NSC/4 (see clause 3.1). The three liabilities are:

(1) under clause 3.2, to supply the Sub-Contract design information to the Architect in due time so that necessary instructions or drawings are not delayed.

(2) under clause 3.3, to perform his Sub-Contract obligations so as not to cause a determination under clause 35.24 of the Main Contract.

(3) under clause 3.4, not to cause delay to the Main Contract Works.

---

[6] See "The Architect's authority as agent" at p. 305 and, where it applies, the Architect's appointment and in particular clause 3.2 at p. 821.

Provided that the Nominated Sub-Contractor is solvent when the liability is sought to be enforced, these are valuable rights. Breaches of the obligations arising under clauses 3.2, 3.3 and 3.4 are likely to cause the Employer loss which he cannot recover from the Contractor. The earlier Forms of Agreement of this kind contemplated the possibility of insurance by the Nominated Sub-Contractor against his liabilities. This has now gone. It is thought that in practice insurance for design can be obtained but not for bad work or delay. The prudent Employer might consider requiring the Nominated Sub-Contractor to insure and keep himself insured so far as he is able against his liabilities.

Clause 5.   *Final payment of Nominated Sub-Contractors*

This clause requires the Architect to operate the provisions for final payment of Nominated Sub-Contractors in clauses 35.17–35.19 of the Main Contract, and contains in clause 5.2 the obligation which forms the basis of clause 35.18.1.2 of the Main Contract. See the commentary on these clauses of the Main Contract.

Clause 6.   *"... the Sub-Contractor shall indemnify ..."*

This clause provides for the Sub-Contractor to become directly liable to the Employer if a renomination becomes necessary because of default by the Sub-Contractor. This is a potentially valuable and important addition to the liabilities undertaken by the Nominated Sub-Contractor towards the Employer under the previous Form of Agreement.

Clause 7.   *Payment to Sub-Contractor*

This clause obliges the Architect and the Employer to operate provisions for direct payment in clause 35.13 of the Main Contract. Unless the Employer and the Nominated Sub-Contractor have executed Agreement NSC/2 or NSC/2a, these provisions are optional for the Employer (see commentary to Main Contract clause 35.13).

The direct payment procedure is subject to a very important proviso which protects the interests of the Employer in the event of the Main Contractor's insolvency. This reflects the uncertainty in the law about the effectiveness of such direct payment provisions in the event of insolvency. The proviso has the result that the direct payment procedure ceases to have effect if there is in existence a winding-up petition or resolution to which Main Contract clause 35.13.5.4.4 refers. The Sub-Contractor is liable to repay any direct payments where they were made in ignorance of such petition or resolution.

Clause 8A: Assignment.   This is a new clause inserted by Amendment 1 issued in July 1987. It follows the insertion into the Main Contract of the new clause 19.1.2 introduced by Amendment 4 issued in July 1987 (see commentary to Main Contract clause 19). For the reasons set out in the commentary, the benefit to be assigned appears to be extremely limited.[7]

---

[7] See also "Assignment of warranties" at p. 281.

Clause 10. *Arbitration*

This arbitration clause is drafted to complement the provisions for arbitration in the Main Contract. See Article 5 and clause 41 of the Main Contract and the commentary to clause 41. Note in particular that the provisions for multipartite arbitration are optional in the Main Contract and that by clause 10.2.2 of Agreement NSC/2 the choice made in the Main Contract determines whether clauses 10.2.1 and 10.2.2 are to apply.

JCT STANDARD FORM OF WARRANTY BY A NOMINATED SUPPLIER (AGREEMENT TNS/2)

To the Employer:

named in our Tender dated

For:

(abbreviated description of goods/materials)

To be supplied to:

(job title)

1. Subject to the conditions stated in the above mentioned Tender (that no provision in this Warranty Agreement shall take effect unless and until the instruction nominating us, the order of the Main Contractor accepting the Tender and a copy of this Warranty Agreement signed by the Employer have been received by us) WE WARRANT in consideration of our being nominated in respect of the supply of the goods and/or materials to be supplied by us as a Nominated Supplier under the Standard Form of Building Contract referred to in the Tender and in accordance with the description, quantity and quality of the materials or goods and with the other terms and details set out in the Tender ("the supply") that:

1.1 We have exercised and will exercise all reasonable skill and care in:

   .1 the design of the supply insofar as the supply has been or will be designed by us; and

   .2 the selection of materials and goods for the supply insofar as such supply has been or Will be selected by us; and

   .3 the satisfaction of any performance specification or requirement insofar as such performance specification or requirement is included or referred to in the Tender as part of the description of the supply.

1.2 We will:

   .1 save insofar as we are delayed by:

   .1.1 force majeure; or

   .1.2 civil commotion, local combination of workmen, strike or lock-out; or

   .1.3 any instruction of the Architect/Supervising Officer under SFBC clause 13.2 (Variations) or clause 13.3 (provisional sums); or

   .1.4 failure of the Architect/Supervising Officer to supply to us within due time any necessary information for which we have specifically applied in writing on a date which was neither unreasonably distant from nor unreasonably close to the date on which it was necessary for us to receive the same

   so supply the Architect/Supervising Officer with such information as the Architect/Supervising Officer may reasonably require; and

805

.2   so supply the Contractor with such information as the Contractor may reasonably require in accordance with the arrangements in our contract of sale with the Contractor; and

.3   so commence and complete delivery of the supply in accordance with the arrangements in our contract of sale with the Contractor

that the Contractor shall not become entitled to an extension of time under SFBC clauses 25.4.6 or 25.4.7 of the Main Contract Conditions nor become entitled to be paid for direct loss and/or expense ascertained under SFBC clause 26.1 for the matters referred to in clause 26.2.1 of the Main Contract Conditions; and we will indemnify you to the extent but not further or otherwise that the Architect/Supervising Officer is obliged to give an extension of time so that the Employer is unable to recover damages under the Main Contractor for delays in completion, and/or pay an amount in respect of direct loss and/or expense as aforesaid because of any failure by us under clause 1.2.1 or 1.2.2 hereof.

2.   We have noted the amount of the liquidated and ascertained damages under the Main Contract, as stated in TNS Schedule 1, item 8.

3.   Nothing in the Tender is intended to or shall exclude or limit our liability for breach of the warranties set out above.

4.1   If at anytime any dispute or difference shall arise between the Employer or the Architect/Supervising Officer on his behalf and ourselves as to the construction of this Agreement or as to any matter or thing of whatsoever nature arising out of this Agreement or in connection therewith; then such dispute shall be and is hereby referred to the arbitration and final decision of a person to be agreed between the parties hereto, or, failing agreement within 14 days after either party has given to the other a written request to concur in the appointment of an arbitrator, a person to be appointed on the request of either party by the President or a Vice-President for the time being of the Royal Institute of British Architects.

4.2   .1   Provided that if the dispute or difference to be referred to arbitration under this Agreement raises issues which are substantially the same as or connected with issues raised in a related dispute between the Employer and the Contractor under the Main Contract or between a Nominated Sub-Contractor and the Contractor under Agreement NSC/4 or NSC/4a or between the Employer and any Nominated Sub-Contractor under Agreement NSC/2 or NSC/2a, or between the Employer and any other Nominated Supplier, and if the related dispute has also been referred for determination to an arbitrator, the Employer and ourselves hereby agree that the dispute or difference under this Agreement shall be referred to the arbitrator appointed to determine the related dispute; and such arbitrator shall have power to make such directions and all necessary awards in the same way as if the procedure of the High Court as to joining one or more of the defendants or joining co-defendants or third parties was available to the parties and to him.

.2   Save that the Employer or ourselves may require the dispute or difference under this Agreement to be referred to a different arbitrator (to be appointed under this Agreement) if either of us reasonably considers that the arbitrator appointed to determine the related dispute is not properly qualified to determine the dispute or difference under this Agreement.

4.3   Paragraphs 4.2.1 and 4.2.2 hereof shall apply unless in the Appendix to the Main Contract Conditions the words "Articles 5.1.4 and 5.1.5 apply" have been deleted.

4.4   The award of such arbitrator shall be final and binding on the parties.

Signature of Supplier: ....

Signature of Employer: ....

Commentary on JCT Standard Form of Warranty by a Nominated Supplier (Agreement TNS/2)

Preliminary Note.   The version of Agreement TNS/2 printed here is that first published in 1980. The Agreement is in the process of revision but the revised version has yet to be published.

History.   The R.I.B.A. in 1969 issued forms of warranty to be given respectively by Nominated Sub-Contractors and Nominated Suppliers in consideration of nomination. TNS/2 broadly follows the scheme of the 1969 form save that:

(1) the Performance Specification aspect of the warranty is diluted;
(2) optional provisions for a Performance Bond and/or insurance are removed;
(3) provision is made for arbitration, including multipartite arbitration.

Recital.   *"... our Tender dated ..."*
The Tender is to be made upon form TNS/1. This has a section to insert certain details of the Main Contract Appendix and its entries. These include the Completion Date of the Main Contract and the rate of liquidated and ascertained damages.
Provided these entries are properly made in the Tender, they together with Clause 2 of TNS/2 will fix the Supplier with knowledge of the loss which the Employer will suffer if the Supplier's default results in the Contractor obtaining an extension of time.[8] Therefore, ordinarily, this will be the measure of damages payable by the Nominated Supplier for delay in breach of clause 1.2 of TNS/2, discussed below.

Clause 1.   *"Subject to the Conditions stated in the above mentioned Tender ..."*
No provision of the Warranty Agreement is to take effect unless the Nominated Supplier has received (a) a copy of the Nomination instruction, (b) the Main Contractor's order accepting Tender TNS/1 and (c) a copy of TNS/2 signed by the Employer. This is in contrast with the position of the Nominated Sub-Contractor whereby in part, at least, Agreement NSC/2 will come into force between Employer and Sub-Contractor before a nomination is made.[9]

---

[8] For the significance of such knowledge, see "Principles upon which damages are awarded" at pp. 185 *et seq.*
[9] See clause 2.2 of NSC/2 and commentary at p. 802.

Clause 1.1. *"We have exercised and will exercise all reasonable skill and care ..."*
The warranty is limited in two respects. Firstly, it is restricted to the exercise of all reasonable skill and care. There is no absolute warranty. Under the 1969 Form of Warranty, the Supplier undertook an absolute obligation to comply with the Performance Specification. This was potentially a very heavy duty. Secondly, the warranty is confined to the particular aspects of design, selection of materials and goods and satisfaction of performance specification set out at clauses 2.1.1–2.1.3. Nonetheless, the warranties are potentially valuable.

Clause 1.2. *Delay and non-performance of the Supplier*
Once the Conditions stated in the Tender are satisfied, the Supplier becomes liable to the Employer for three specific aspects of his performance of the contract of sale. The three liabilities are:

(1) to supply the Architect with such information as he may reasonably require (clause 1.2.1);
(2) to supply the Contractor with such information as he may reasonably require in accordance with arrangements in the contract of sale (clause 1.2.2);
(3) to commence and complete delivery of the supply in accordance with the contract of sale (clause 1.2.3)

so that the Contractor is not entitled to an extension of time under clauses 25.4.6 or 25.4.7 of the Main Contract nor to loss and expense under clause 26.2.1.
The Supplier's liability is subject to the events mentioned at clauses 1.2.1.1–1.2.1.4. He is likely to be entitled to an extension of time under the contract of sale for these events (see clause 36.4.3 of the Main Contract).[10] If the Supplier fails to comply with clauses 1.2.1 or 1.2.2, he must indemnify the Employer against consequent loss of liquidated damages or payment of loss and expense. Provided that the Nominated Supplier is solvent when the liability is sought to be enforced, these are valuable rights. The prudent Employer might consider requiring the Supplier to insure himself so far as he was able against his liabilities. There was an optional provision in the 1969 form for insurance against liability for breach of the warranties now found at clause 1.1, but there is no such provision in TNS/2.

Clause 4. *Arbitration*
This Clause is drafted to complement the provisions for Arbitration in the Main Contract. See Article 5 and clause 41 of the Main Contract and their

---

[10] Clause 36.4 of the Main Contract requires the contract of sale between the Contractor and Nominated Supplier to contain certain provisions. Clause 36.4.3 requires a provision for a delivery programme. However, that programme may be varied on grounds which are identical with those set out in clauses 1.2.1.1 to 1.2.1.4 of TNS/2.

commentary. Note in particular that the provisions for multipartite arbitration are optional in the Main Contract and that by clause 4.3 of TNS/2 the choice made in the Main Contract determines whether clauses 4.2.1 and 4.2.2 are to apply.

Chapter 21

THE I.C.E. FORM OF CONTRACT—6TH EDITION 1991

A Standard Form of Civil Engineering Contract, commonly known as the I.C.E. Conditions of Contract, is issued under the sponsorship and approval of the Institution of Civil Engineers (I.C.E.), the Association of Consulting Engineers (A.C.E.) and the Federation of Civil Engineering Contractors (F.C.E.C.). The Form is used extensively in all types of civil engineering work, both by Private Employers and by Local and Central Government Departments.

This commentary deals with the 6th edition, published in 1991 and incorporating a variety of earlier revisions to the 5th edition made between 1973 and 1986. The 6th edition is more a revision than a new edition, because it follows the same format and clause numbering and many clauses are substantially unamended. The new edition is produced by the Conditions of Contract Standing Joint Committee, set up expressly to review the 5th edition. This commentary deals only with the Main Contract Conditions. The so-called I.C.E. Form of Sub-Contract is published by the F.C.E.C. and, while being intended for use with the I.C.E. Main Contract, it is a quite separate document.

The I.C.E. Conditions of Contract have a surprisingly short history as such. The 1st edition was issued in December 1945, followed by further editions in 1950, 1951 and 1955. During the next 18 years, there were attempts to produce a new edition containing radical revisions, but in the event the 5th edition of 1973 followed closely the format and much of the wording of the 4th edition. Despite much criticism, the 5th edition has proved remarkably popular with all sides of the industry. The fact that the document has survived virtually intact for 17 years amid the sea of change surrounding most other aspects of construction law is perhaps sufficient justification for adhering to the same format for the new edition.

Unlike the Standard Form of Building Contract,[1] the I.C.E. Conditions are published in one version only. The Institution of Civil Engineers has, however, in recent years embarked upon the production of alternative forms of Contract, aimed at specific types of project. Thus, a set of Conditions of Contract for Minor Works was produced in 1988 by the I.C.E. and approved by the same sponsoring bodies as those involved in the main I.C.E. Form. The Minor Works Form is published with notes for guidance which indicate that the Form is intended for use in simple and straightforward Contracts specifically limited to 6 months duration and £100,000 value. The Form has proved very popular

---

[1] See Chap. 18.

and is occasionally used for Contracts outside these limits. A notable feature of this form was the introduction of an optional conciliation procedure alongside a conventional arbitration clause (clause 11), an innovation which has now been introduced into the I.C.E. Main Contract Conditions.

The Institution of Civil Engineers is also considering introducing separate forms of Contract for maintenance works and for design and build Contracts. A further major departure from previous policy is the introduction of a "New Engineering Contract" which is intended to operate in a wide range of different Contract strategies (including cost reimbursable or target cost Contracts and Contracts including design).[2] Whatever new Forms may be produced, the 6th edition is an indication that the Institution of Civil Engineers will continue to promulgate these standard Main Contract Conditions for all conventional types of civil engineering Contract.

Nature of the I.C.E. Form.   The Form creates what is known as a "Measure and Value" or "Re-Measurement" Contract, by which the Employer undertakes to pay for the actual quantities of work executed. Prima facie, the work is to be paid for at the rates quoted, but the rates themselves are subject to adjustment depending upon the nature or the volumes of work executed. The Conditions of Contract also contain numerous provisions by which additional or adjusted payments may become due. The Contract contains a substantial body of administrative machinery, employing language which has been refined from time to time, but which remains rooted in the public authority Contracts which were the forerunners of the I.C.E. Conditions.[3] In large measure, the administrative machinery operates by placing wide discretionary powers on the Engineer. The Engineer's powers under the 4th edition of the I.C.E. Conditions have been referred to as "wide and arbitrary."[4] Under the present edition, the Engineer's powers are wider. The question whether and in what circumstances the Engineer is bound to exercise his powers requires particular consideration in the light of recent authorities.[5]

The policy of the I.C.E. in maintaining the clause numbering from earlier editions is to be welcomed. Generally, the document is clearly presented and well laid out, containing, as in previous editions, a table of contents and index to the Conditions. The Conditions are published together with a Form of Tender, Appendix, Form of Agreement and Form of Bond. Also provided is a copy of the I.C.E. Arbitration Procedure (1983) which is now normally mandatory under clause 66, the I.C.E. Conciliation Procedure and the Contract Price Fluctuation clauses. One clause which has been dropped is the

---

[2] See Barnes, "The Role of Contracts in Management": Proceedings of a Conference on Construction Contract Policy (Kings College, London, 1989).

[3] See generally Uff, "Origin and Development of Construction Contracts": Proceedings of a Conference on Construction Contract Policy (Kings College, London, 1989); and see H.B.C. (4th ed.), Vol. 2 for many examples of 19th-century Public Works Contracts.

[4] Buckley J. in *A.E. Farr* v. *Ministry of Transport* [1960] 1 W.L.R. 956 at 964.

[5] See clause 8(3): "Methods of Construction" and commentary to clause 51.

previous clause 71: *Metrication*, presumably in view of the now universal adoption of metric units in civil and structural engineering practice. The final clause (Special Conditions) is therefore renumbered 71.

The principal changes introduced in the 6th edition are the following:

(1) some altered and some new definitions are added in clause 1;

(2) under clause 2, provision is made for identifying a Chartered Engineer who is to act as the Engineer where the Contract identifies only a firm or company in this position;

(3) there are changes to the clauses dealing with assignment and sub-contracting and as to the supply of documents;

(4) the Contractor's duty when undertaking design is now provided for in clause 8;

(5) as regards claims for unforeseen conditions, clauses 11 and 12 contain some amendments, the most important of which is that the Employer is now deemed to have made available relevant information that he may have;

(6) there are amendments to the insurance and liability provisions in clauses 20–25;

(7) the provisions governing commencement and delays in clauses 41–46 have been revised and the liquidated damages clause (47) rewritten;

(8) in clause 49 (and elsewhere) references to "maintenance" have been dropped, and replaced by "defects correction";

(9) the provisions dealing with property in materials and plant (clause 53) have been extensively redrafted;

(10) clauses 59A, B and C have been simplified and consolidated into a single clause with the Main Contractor now taking an increased share of the risk in nomination;

(11) there are some changes in clause 60 relating to retention;

(12) clause 63 (formerly having a marginal note "Forfeiture") has been renamed "Determination of the Contractor's Employment" and the clause has been clarified to some extent;

(13) clause 66, which was substantially amended in 1985, has been further substantially amended and enlarged to incorporate some of the provisions introduced by the Minor Works Form[6] including optional conciliation.

CONDITIONS OF CONTRACT

DEFINITIONS AND INTERPRETATION

Definitions

1 (1) In the Contract (as hereinafter defined) the following words and expressions shall

---

[6] See p. 811.

have the meanings hereby assigned to them except where the context otherwise requires.

(a)　"Employer" means the person or persons firm company or other body named in the Appendix to the Form of Tender and includes the Employer's personal representatives successors and permitted assigns.

(b)　"Contractor" means the person or persons firm or company to whom the Contract has been awarded by the Employer and includes the Contractor's personal representatives successors and permitted assigns.

(c)　"Engineer" means the person firm or company appointed by the Employer to act as Engineer for the purposes of the Contract and named in the Appendix to the Form of Tender or such other person firm or company so appointed from time to time by the Employer and notified in writing as such to the Contractor.

(d)　"Engineer's Representative" means a person notified as such from time to time by the Engineer under clause 2(3)(a).

(e)　"Contract" means the Conditions of Contract Specification Drawings Bill of Quantities the Tender the written acceptance thereof and the Contract Agreement (if completed).

(f)　"Specification" means the specification referred to in the Tender and any modification thereof or addition thereto as may from time to time be furnished or approved in writing by the Engineer.

(g)　"Drawings" means the drawings referred to in the Specification and any modification of such drawings approved in writing by the Engineer and such other drawings as may from time to time be furnished or approved in writing by the Engineer.

(h)　"Bill of Quantities" means the priced and completed Bill of Quantities.

(i)　"Tender Total" means the total of the Bill of Quantities at the date of award of the Contract or in the absence of a Bill of Quantities the agreed estimated total value of the Works at that date.

(j)　"Contract Price" means the sum to be ascertained and paid in accordance with the provisions hereinafter contained for the construction and completion of the Works in accordance with the Contract.

(k)　"Prime Cost (PC) Item" means an item in the Contract which contains (either wholly or in part) a sum referred to as Prime Cost (PC) which will be used for the execution of work or the supply of goods materials or services for the Works.

(l)　"Provisional Sum" means a sum included and so designated in the Contract as a specific contingency for the execution of work or the supply of goods materials or services which may be used in whole or in part or not at all at the direction and discretion of the Engineer.

(m)　"Nominated Sub-contractor" means any merchant tradesman specialist or other person firm or company nominated in accordance with the Contract to be employed by the Contractor for the execution of work or supply of goods materials or services for which a Prime Cost has been inserted in the Contract or ordered by the Engineer to be employed by the Contractor to execute work or supply goods materials or services under a Provisional Sum.

(n)　"Permanent Works" means the permanent works to be constructed and completed in accordance with the Contract.

(o)　"Temporary Works" means all temporary works of every kind required in or about the construction and completion of the Works.

(p)　"Works" means the Permanent Works together with the Temporary Works.

(q)　"Works Commencement Date"—as defined in clause 41(1).

(r)　"Certificate of Substantial Completion" means a certificate issued under clause 48(2)(a) 48(3) or 48(4).

(s)　"Defects Correction Period" means that period stated in the Appendix to the Form of Tender calculated from the date on which the Contractor becomes entitled to a Certificate of Substantial Completion for the Works or any Section or part thereof.

(t)   "Defects Correction Certificate"—as defined in clause 61(1).

(u)   "Section" means a part of the Works separately identified in the Appendix to the Form of Tender.

(v)   "Site" means the lands and other places on under in or through which the Works are to be executed and any other lands or places provided by the Employer for the purposes of the Contract together with such other places as may be designated in the Contract or subsequently agreed by the Engineer as forming part of the Site.

(w)   "Contractors's Equipment" means all appliances or things of whatsoever nature required in or about the construction and completion of the Works but does not include materials or other things intended to form or forming part of the Permanent Works.

Singular and plural

(2)   Words importing the singular also include the plural and vice-versa where the context requires.

Headings and marginal notes

(3)   The headings and marginal notes in the Conditions of Contract shall not be deemed to be part thereof or be taken into consideration in the interpretation or construction thereof or of the Contract.

Clause references

(4)   All references herein to clauses are references to clauses numbered in the Conditions of Contract and not to those in any other document forming part of the Contract.

Cost

(5)   The word "cost" when used in the Conditions of Contract means all expenditure properly incurred or to be incurred whether on or off the Site including overhead finance and other charges properly allocatable thereto but does not include any allowance for profit.

Communications in writing

(6)   Communications which under the Contract are required to be "in writing" may be hand-written typewritten or printed and sent by hand post telex cable or facsimile.

Clause 1—Definitions and Interpretation

The definitions in sub-clause (1) are not of uniform importance; (a)–(c) are matters of identification; (d) needs to be read with clause 2(3); (e)–(h) are part of the defined structure of the Contract (see clause 5); (i) and (j) are convenient shorthand expressions which appear in other clauses (see, *e.g.* clause 10); (k),

(l) and (m) are an important part of the machinery of clauses 58 and 59; (n), (o) and (p) appear throughout the Conditions and occasionally give rise to problems of interpretation which are not wholly answered by the definitions; (q) notes the definition in clause 41(1); (r) links in with clause 48; (s) needs to be read into clause 49; (t) notes the definition in clause 61; (u) is a definition required under clauses 47, 48 and 49; (v) needs to be read into other clauses (*e.g.* clause 11(2)), and (w) likewise (*e.g.* clause 53).

Sub-clause (1)(c): Engineer.   Note that by clause 2(2), where the identified Engineer is a firm or company, the Contractor is to be notified of an individual Chartered Engineer who will act as the Engineer under the Contract.

Sub-clause (1)(d): Engineer's Representative.   See clause 2(3) and (4) for the powers of the Engineer's Representative, or other delegate of the Engineer.

Sub-clause (1)(e): Contract.   See clause 5 for the mutual effect of the Contract Documents. The Tender and the Contract Agreement may incorporate other documents which thereby become part of the Contract.

Sub-clause (1)(f), (g): Specification, drawings.   The references to modification or addition to these documents complement the powers of the Engineer to issue modified or further Drawings Specification or instructions under clause 7(1).

Sub-clause (1)(n), (o): Permanent Works, Temporary Works.   While the distinction may be of considerable importance (see clause 8(2)) it is far from clear. It is not clear that the two definitions are mutually exclusive, and there may well be items which could fall into both. Common examples are a cofferdam which is subsequently built into the permanent structure, or grouting around the periphery of a tunnel. The Standard Method of Measurement[7] does not clarify the matter. Where work which may be regarded as temporary is to be billed, the Contract should make clear that such work is to be regarded as Temporary Works for the purpose of responsibility.

Sub-clause (1)(s), (t): Defects correction.   This is identical with the former term "maintenance" appearing in clause 49 of the 5th edition.

Sub-clause (1)(v): Site.   References to the Site appear in clauses 11(1), 22(2), 32, 42, 53 and 54. It is often important to know what is and what is not within the term. The Contract contains no obligation on the Employer to provide land beyond what is necessary to make the work possible to perform. It is therefore of importance from the Contractor's point of view to have a

---

[7] The 2nd edition of the CESMM (see clause 57 below) states in Section 2 General Principles: "2.6 all work which is expressly required should be covered in the Bill of Quantities."

satisfactory definition. Uncertainty can arise in relation to land utilised by the Contractor not directly for execution of the works, but for ancillary purposes, *e.g.* a borrow pit for providing fill material. The definition still leaves it uncertain whether such locations are to be regarded as part of the Site, and by what criteria the Engineer should agree (or not) to extend the Site. The better course is to adopt as precise a definition as possible in the Contract.

Sub-clause (1)(w): Contractor's equipment. This is a new term replacing the former "Constructional Plant." The definition does not help to distinguish this term from "Temporary Works", nor does the definition of that term assist. Clauses 8(1) and 53(1) appear to draw such a distinction. Clause 21(1) (Insurance of Works, etc.) uses a different expression "plant and equipment."

Clause 1(5): Cost. The word "cost" appears extensively in the Conditions where provision is made for contractual claims.[8] The express inclusion of overheads does not limit the generality of the term. The words "properly incurred" do, however, impose a potential limit, as does the express exclusion of profit. An addition for profit is expressly permitted, *e.g.* under clause 12(6).

The definition expressly includes "finance ... charges properly allocatable." Such charges must be "incurred or to be incurred", indicating that there is no automatic right to interest, as under clause 60(7). Finance charges may run up to the date of certifying[9] it is thought, and need not be limited to simple interest.[10]

Clause 1(6): Communications in writing. This provision should be read with clause 68 (designating the address for service). The reference to modern electronic communications is useful, but it is still necessary for service to take place at the correct place.

ENGINEER AND ENGINEER'S REPRESENTATIVE

Duties and authority of Engineer

2 (1) (a) The Engineer shall carry out the duties specified in or necessarily to be implied from the Contract.
(b) The Engineer may exercise the authority specified in or necessarily to be implied from the Contract. If the Engineer is required under the terms of his appointment by the Employer to obtain the specific approval of the Employer before exercising any such authority particulars of such requirements shall be those set out in the Appendix to the Form of Tender. Any requisite approval shall be deemed to have been given by the Employer for any such authority exercised by the Engineer.

---

[8] See clauses 7(3), 12(3), 13(3), 14(6), 17, 27(6), 31(2), 36(2), (3), 38(2), 40(1), 42(1), 50.
[9] Compare *F.G. Minter* v. *W.H.T.S.O.* (1980) 13 B.L.R. 1 (C.A.); see also "Direct loss and/or expense" at p. 213.
[10] See *Rees &. Kirby* v. *Swansea City Council* (1985) 30 B.L.R. 1 (C.A.); see also "Simple or compound interest?" at p. 215.

(c) Except as expressly stated in the Contract the Engineer shall have no authority to amend the Terms and Conditions of the Contract nor to relieve the Contractor of any of his obligations under the Contract.

Named individual

(2) (a) Where the Engineer as defined in clause 1(1)(c) is not a single named Chartered Engineer the Engineer shall within 7 days of the award of the Contract and in any event before the Works Commencement Date notify to the Contractor in writing the name of the Chartered Engineer who will act on his behalf and assume the full responsibilities of the Engineer under the Contract.

(b) The Engineer shall thereafter in like manner notify the Contractor of any replacement of the named Chartered Engineer.

Engineer's Representative

(3) (a) The Engineer's Representative shall be responsible to the Engineer who shall notify his appointment to the Contractor in writing.

(b) The Engineer's Representative shall watch and supervise the construction and completion of the Works. He shall have no authority

(i) to relieve the Contractor of any of his duties or obligations under the Contract

nor except as expressly provided hereunder

(ii) to order any work involving delay or any extra payment by the Employer or

(iii) to make any variation of or in the Works.

Delegation by Engineer

(4) The Engineer may from time to time delegate to the Engineer's Representative or any other person responsible to the Engineer any of the duties and authorities vested in the Engineer and he may at any time revoke such delegation. Any such delegation

(a) shall be in writing and shall not take effect until such time as a copy thereof has been delivered to the Contractor or his agent appointed under clause 15(2)

(b) shall continue in force until such time as the Engineer shall notify the Contractor in writing that the same has been revoked

(c) shall not be given in respect of any decision to be taken or certificate to be issued under clauses 12(6) 44 46(3) 48 60(4) 61 63 or 66.

Assistants

(5) (a) The Engineer or the Engineer's Representative may appoint any number of persons to assist the Engineer's Representative in the carrying out of his duties under sub-clause (3)(b) or (4) of this clause. He shall notify to the Contractor the names duties and scope of authority of such persons.

(b) Such assistants shall have no authority to issue any instructions to the Contractor save insofar as such instructions may be necessary to enable them to carry out their duties and to secure their acceptance of materials and workmanship as being in accordance with the Contract. Any instructions given by an assistant for these purposes shall where appropriate be in writing and be deemed to have been given by the Engineer's Representative.

(c) If the Contractor is dissatisfied by reason of any instruction of any assistant of the Engineer's Representative appointed under sub-clause (5)(a) of this clause he shall be entitled to refer the matter to the Engineer's Representative who shall thereupon confirm reverse or vary such instruction.

Instructions

(6)   (a) Instructions given by the Engineer or by the Engineer's Representative exercising delegated duties and authorities under sub-clause (4) of this clause shall be in writing. Provided that if for any reason it is considered necessary to give any such instruction orally the Contractor shall comply with such instruction.
(b) Any such oral instruction shall be confirmed in writing by the Engineer or the Engineer's Representative as soon as is possible under the circumstances. Provided that if the Contractor shall confirm in writing any such oral instruction and such confirmation is not contradicted in writing by the Engineer or the Engineer's Representative forthwith it shall be deemed to be an instruction in writing by the Engineer.
(c) Upon the written request of the Contractor the Engineer or the Engineer's Representative exercising delegated duties or authorities under sub-clause (4) of this clause shall specify in writing under which of his duties and authorities any instruction is given.

Reference on dissatisfaction

(7)   If the Contractor is dissatisfied by reason of any act or instruction of the Engineer's Representative he shall be entitled to refer the matter to the Engineer for his decision.

Impartiality

(8)   The Engineer shall except in connection with matters requiring the specific approval of the Employer under sub-clause (1)(b) of this clause act impartially within the terms of the Contract having regard to all the circumstances.

Clause 2—Engineer and Engineer's Representative

The intention of this clause is to facilitate limited delegation of the powers of the Engineer. The clause is unnecessarily cumbersome for the matters it deals with. It appears to be drafted on the assumption the Engineer is a party to the Contract, which he is not. The provisions must, therefore, take effect as defining or limiting the rights of the parties in regard to actions of the Engineer.[11]

Clause 2(1)(b): Need for specific approval of the Employer.   This provision is borrowed from clause 2.1 of the F.I.D.I.C. Form of Contract. It is

---

[11] For the position of the Engineer, see generally *Sutcliffe* v. *Thackrah* [1974] A.C. 727 (H.L.); *Pacific Associates* v. *Baxter* [1990] Q.B. 993 (C.A.).

unlikely to be of much practical effect if the requirement for approval is not stated in the Appendix. Interference with the actions of the Engineer outside any stated limitation may give grounds for disqualification of the Engineer[12] or even termination of the Contract. Conversely, where restriction on the Engineer's independence is set out, the Contractor will have no ground for complaint if the Employer acts within such terms.

Clause 2(1)(c): No authority to relieve the Contractor. The Engineer would not normally have such authority unless it arises outside the Contract. This might otherwise be so where the Engineer is an Officer of a Local Authority Employer,[13] but this provision will negative any such authority.

Clause 2(2): Named Chartered Engineer to act. It is rare to have an individual named as Engineer: more often a partnership or limited company is named. The requirement for such a body to act through a named Chartered Engineer (who may be replaced where necessary) is obviously sensible, and represents what must frequently in fact happen.

Clause 2(3): Engineer's Representative. He is sometimes referred to as the Resident Engineer. Note the restriction in sub-clause (4)(c) on delegation of power to the Engineer's Representative. He may be given delegated power to order variations (clause 51) and to deal with all matters of account (clause 60) save for the Final Account. The title "Engineer's Representative" under the Contract is of little importance, since the power of delegation under sub-clause (4) may be exercised also in favour of "any other person responsible to the Engineer."

Appeals procedure. Sub-clause (5)(c) provides that, if the Contractor is dissatisfied with an instruction from an Assistant, he may refer the matter to the Engineer's Representative. Similarly, sub-clause (7) allows an appeal from the Engineer's Representative to the Engineer. Such references are distinct from the further reference of a dispute to the Engineer under clause 66.

Clause 2(8): Engineer to act impartially. This requirement appears (subject to sub-clause (1)(b)) to apply to all actions of the Engineer under the Contract. While impartiality may be appropriate to some actions (*e.g.* valuing the work or granting an extension of time) it is not appropriate when the Engineer is required to act in the Employer's interest (*e.g.* when deciding whether to instruct a variation). It is thought that the clause will have little effect other than to reinforce the need for the Engineer to act fairly where he is required to adjudicate between the parties.

---

[12] See p. 114.

[13] *Carlton Contractors* v. *Bexley Corporation* (1962) 60 L.G.R. 311; *Roberts & Co. Ltd.* v. *Leicestershire County Council* [1961] Ch. 555.

ASSIGNMENT AND SUB-CONTRACTING

Assignment

3   Neither the Employer nor the Contractor shall assign the Contract or any part thereof or any benefit or interest therein or thereunder without the prior written consent of the other party which consent shall not unreasonably be withheld.

Sub-contracting

4   (1)   The Contractor shall not Sub-Contract the whole of the Works without the prior written consent of the Employer.
(2)   Except where otherwise provided the Contractor may sub-contract any part of the Works or their design. The extent of the work to be Sub-Contracted and the name and address of the Sub-Contractor must be notified in writing to the Engineer prior to the Sub-Contractor's entry on to the Site or in the case of design on appointment.
(3)   The employment of labour-only Sub-Contractors does not require notification to the Engineer under sub-clause (2) of this clause.
(4)   The Contractor shall be and remain liable under the Contract for all work Sub-Contracted under this clause and for acts defaults or neglects of any Sub-Contractor his agents servants or workpeople.
(5)   The Engineer shall be at liberty after due warning in writing to require the Contractor to remove from the Works any Sub-Contractor who mis-conducts himself or is incompetent or negligent in the performance of his duties or fails to conform with any particular provisions with regard to safety which may be set out in the Contract or persists in any conduct which is prejudicial to safety or health and such Sub-Contractor shall not be again employed upon the Works without the permission of the Engineer.

Clauses 3 and 4: Assignment and Sub-Contracting

Clause 3: Assignment.   The prohibition on assignment applied, under the 5th edition, to the Contractor alone. Assignment by Employers is now perhaps as common as assignment by Contractors. Note that the embargo applies to "any benefit or interest", which includes money due under the Contract. Any purported assignment without consent is invalid.[14]

Clause 4: Sub-Contracting.   Sub-clause (1) prevents sub-contracting of the whole without consent, but there is no restriction on sub-contracting of parts of the works under sub-clause (2), subject to notifying the Engineer of the Sub-Contractors concerned.

Clause 4(4): Contractor liable for acts, defaults or neglects of any Sub-Contractor.   The Main Contractor would be liable for sub-contracted work in any event. These words are, however, wide enough to cover tortious acts of

---

[14] *Helstan Securities Ltd.* v. *Hertfordshire C.C.* [1978] 3 All E.R. 262. For assignment generally, see Chap. 12.

the Sub-Contractor, for which the Main Contractor may be held liable "under the Contract."[15]

CONTRACT DOCUMENTS

Documents mutually explanatory

5   The several documents forming the Contract are to be taken as mutually explanatory of one another and in case of ambiguities or discrepancies the same shall be explained and adjusted by the Engineer who shall thereupon issue to the Contractor appropriate instructions in writing which shall be regarded as instructions issued in accordance with clause 13.

Clause 5: Contract Documents

This clause avoids the type of problem which can arise when some documents are given precedence over others.[16] The requirement for all documents to be construed mutually will, it is submitted, override the principle of giving precedence to specially prepared documents as against printed forms.[17]

The documents forming the Contract consist of the Conditions, the Specification, the Drawings, the Bill of Quantities, the Tender and written acceptance thereof and the Contract Agreement (if completed)[18]; together with any modification to the Specification or Drawings[19] and any further documents that may be incorporated into the Contract. The task of mutual construction can pose particular problems where the parties incorporate correspondence and other documents in which views are expressed as to the proposed contract. In such a case, although full effect is to be given to all such documents, they must, it is submitted, be construed in the context of ascertaining the mutual intention of the parties at the date that the Contract is concluded.

"Ambiguities or discrepancies."   This clause is unique to I.C.E. Contracts and their derivatives.[20] Ordinarily, an ambiguity[21] or discrepancy will be resolved by the process of legal construction, if necessary on a reference to the Engineer under clause 66. It is thought that the words here need be given no wider meaning than "uncertainty" concerning the technical description of the works. This is plainly an area in which the Engineer needs to impose

---

[15] But there will be no general liability in tort: see *D. & F. Estates* v. *Church Commissioners* [1989] A.C. 177 (H.L.).

[16] See Standard Form of Building Contract 1980 edition, clauses 13 and 2.2.1; and see *English Industrial Estates* v. *Wimpey* [1973] 1 Lloyds Rep. 118 (C.A.).

[17] See *Robertson* v. *French* (1803) 4 East 130; *Glynn* v. *Margetson* [1893] A.C. 351 (H.L.) and Lord Denning M.R. in *English Industrial Estates* v. *Wimpey* [1973] 1 Lloyds Rep. 118 (C.A.).

[18] Clause 1(1)(e).

[19] Clause 1(1)(f) and (g), clause 7(1).

[20] It appears also in clause 5.2 of the F.I.D.I.C. Form of Contract.

[21] Note that the technical meaning of this term is a provision having two meanings.

certainty. Note that an instruction issued in accordance with clause 13 gives a right to payment under clause 13(3), but only for "cost beyond that reasonably to have been foreseen by an experienced contractor at the time of tender." Thus, if the discrepancy is reasonably plain, the Engineer may correct it without incurring liability on behalf of the Employer to pay.

SUPPLY OF DOCUMENTS

Supply of documents

6 (1)   Upon award of the Contract the following shall be furnished to the Contractor free of charge

> (a)   four copies of the Conditions of Contract Specification and (unpriced) bill of quantities and
> (b)   the number and type of copies as entered in the Appendix to the Form of Tender of all Drawings listed in the Specification.

(2)   Upon approval by the Engineer in accordance with clause 7(6) the Contractor shall supply to the Engineer four copies of all Drawings Specifications and other documents submitted by the Contractor. In addition the Contractor shall supply at the Employer's expense such further copies of such Drawings Specifications and other documents as the Engineer may request in writing for his use.

(3)   Copyright of all Drawings Specifications and the Bill of Quantities (except the pricing thereof) supplied by the Employer or the Engineer shall not pass to the Contractor but the Contractor may obtain or make at his own expense any further copies required by him for the purposes of the Contract. Similarly copyright of all documents supplied by the Contractor under clause 7(6) shall remain in the Contractor but the Employer and the Engineer shall have full power to reproduce and use the same for the purpose of completing operating maintaining and adjusting the Works.

Further Drawings Specifications and instructions

7 (1)   The Engineer shall from time to time during the progress of the Works supply to the Contractor such modified or further Drawings Specifications and instructions as shall in the Engineer's opinion be necessary for the purpose of the proper and adequate construction and completion of the Works and the Contractor shall carry out and be bound by the same.

If such Drawings Specifications or instructions require any variation to any part of the works the same shall be deemed to have been issued pursuant to clause 51.

Contractor to provide further documents

(2)   Where sub-clause (6) of this clause applies the Engineer may require the Contractor to supply such further documents as shall in the Engineer's opinion be necessary for the purpose of the proper and adequate construction completion and maintenance of the Works and when approved by the Engineer the Contractor shall carry out and be bound by the same.

Notice by Contractor

(3)   The Contractor shall give adequate notice in writing to the Engineer of any

further Drawing or Specification that the Contractor may require for the construction and completion of the Works or otherwise under the Contract.

Delay in issue

(4) (a) If by reason of any failure or inability of the Engineer to issue at a time reasonable in all the circumstances Drawings Specifications or instructions requested by the Contractor and considered necessary by the Engineer in accordance with sub-clause (1) of this clause the Contractor suffers delay or incurs cost then the Engineer shall take such delay into account in determining any extension of time to which the Contractor is entitled under clause 44 and the Contractor shall subject to clause 52(4) be paid in accordance with clause 60 the amount of such cost as may be reasonable.

(b) If the failure of the Engineer to issue any Drawing Specification or instruction is caused in whole or in part by the failure of the Contractor after due notice in writing to submit drawings specifications or other documents which he is required to submit under the Contract the Engineer shall take into account such failure by the Contractor in taking any action under sub-clause (4)(a) of this clause.

One copy of documents to be kept on Site

(5) One copy of the Drawings and Specification furnished to the Contractor as aforesaid and of all Drawings Specifications and other documents required to be provided by the Contractor under sub-clause (6) of this clause shall at all reasonable times be available on the Site for inspection and use by the Engineer and the Engineer's Representative and by any other person authorized by the Engineer in writing.

Permanent Works designed by Contractor

(6) Where the Contract expressly provides that part of the Permanent Works shall be designed by the Contractor he shall submit to the Engineer for approval

(a) such drawings specifications calculations and other information as shall be necessary to satisfy the Engineer as to the suitability and adequacy of the design and

(b) operation and maintenance manuals together with as completed drawings of that part of the Permanent Works in sufficient detail to enable the Employer to operate maintain dismantle reassemble and adjust the Permanent Works incorporating that design. No certificate under clause 48 covering any part of the Permanent Works designed by the Contractor shall be issued until manuals and drawings in such detail have been submitted to and approved by the Engineer.

Responsibility unaffected by approval

(7) Approval by the Engineer in accordance with sub-clause (6) of this clause shall not relieve the Contractor of any of his responsibilities under the Contract. The Engineer shall be responsible for the integration and co-ordination of the Contractor's design with the rest of the Works.

Clauses 6 and 7: Supply of documents

These clauses deal with the supply of Contract Documents upon the award of the Contract, and further documents that may from time to time become necessary. Clause 7 provides for additional payment in the event of delay in the provision of necessary information. Clause 7 has been enlarged to cover the mechanics of design work carried out by the Contractor. These provisions should be read with clauses 8(2) and 58(3).

Clause 7(1): *"Necessary for the purpose of the proper and adequate construction and completion of the Works."*

The question when further Drawings, Specifications or instructions are "necessary" requires reference to other provisions of the Contract, particularly clauses 8, 11, 13(2) and 14(9). *Prima facie*, the Contractor's entitlement under this clause is limited to those matters for which the Employer (or the Engineer) takes responsibility, *i.e.* the permanent works together with any temporary works designed by the Engineer, and any other matters for which the Employer is responsible.[22]

The Contract Drawings rarely contain sufficient particulars to construct the Works, and it is anticipated that they will be followed by more detailed drawings and schedules, *e.g.* detailing reinforced concrete work. In other cases, such as earthworks contracts, details of the construction will depend on materials that become available as a result of excavation. In all such cases it is anticipated that detailed instructions will be given in such time as will allow the Contractor to carry out the work within the Contract timescale.[23]

Clause 7(4): Late Instructions: notice by the Contractor.   The right to make a claim arises upon the Engineer's failure or inability to issue drawings, etc., "requested by the Contractor". The notice required by sub-clause (3) is, therefore, effectively a condition precedent. The notice under sub-clause (3) must be "adequate" and in writing, and the Engineer is then obliged to deliver the required information "at a time reasonable in all the circumstances." If the Contractor is unable to bring a claim under sub-clause (4), a claim for damages for breach of the primary obligation under clause 7(1) may be available.

Clause 7(6): Design by the Contractor.   Note that this applies only to design of the permanent works where there is express provision to this effect in the Contract.[24] The Contractor is not required to produce to the Engineer full working drawings, but only drawings and other information to satisfy the Engineer as to the suitability and adequacy of the design, together with operation and maintenance manuals and "as completed" drawings. The possibility of delay in provision of the Contractor's Drawings is noted under sub-clause (4)(b), where the Engineer may take such delay into account if it affects the Engineer's ability to issue details of his part of the design.

---

[22] See Notes on "Methods of Construction" under clause 8.

[23] For the Contractor's right to receive instructions generally, see *Neodox* v. *Swinton & Pendelbury B.C.* (1958) 5 B.L.R. 34; *London Borough of Merton* v. *Leach* (1985) 32 B.L.R. 51; and see also pp. 50 *et seq.*

[24] See clause 8(2) and 58(3).

Clause 7(7): Contractor's responsibility for design. This is unaffected by the Engineer's approval under sub-clause (6). The Contractor's responsibility is limited to the works that he designs, the Engineer remaining responsible for integration and co-ordination with the rest of the works. Note that, despite the reference in sub-clause (6)(a) to "suitability and adequacy", clause 8(2) requires the Contractor to exercise "reasonable skill, care and diligence."[25]

GENERAL OBLIGATIONS

Contractor's general responsibilities

8   (1)   The Contractor shall subject to the provisions of the Contract

      (a) construct and complete the Works and
      (b) provide all labour materials Contractor's Equipment Temporary Works transport to and from and in or about the Site and everything whether of a temporary or permanent nature required in and for such construction and completion so far as the necessity for providing the same is specified in or reasonably to be inferred from the Contract.

Design responsibility

(2)   The Contractor shall not be responsible for the design or specification of the Permanent Works or any part thereof (except as may be expressly provided in the Contract) or of any Temporary Works designed by the Engineer. The Contractor shall exercise all reasonable skill care and diligence in designing any part of the Permanent Works for which he is responsible.

Contractor responsible for safety of site operations

(3)   The Contractor shall take full responsibility for the adequacy stability and safety of all site operations and methods of construction.

Clause 8: General obligations

This clause has been rearranged, but is substantially the same as the clause appearing in the 5th edition, save for the express provision dealing with the Contractor's design responsibility.

Clause 8(1)(a) repeats the obligation set out in the Tender and in the Form of Agreement, to "construct and complete" the Works. There is no reference here, or elsewhere in the Contract to "maintenance." This term appeared extensively in the first five editions.[26] The term was capable of being misunderstood, and has now been recast as "defects correction."[27] References to

---

[25] But see commentary to clause 8(2).
[26] See clauses 8(1) and 49 of the 5th edition, 1973.
[27] The term is borrowed from the I.C.E. Minor Works Form of Contract.

maintenance are therefore omitted from the Contractor's general obligations. If the Contract requires the Contractor to maintain the Works during some period of their operation, express provisions should be made.

Clause 8(1)(b).   "*. . . so far as the necessity for providing the same is specified in or reasonably to be inferred from the Contract*"

These words probably add nothing to what would otherwise be the effect of the Contract.[28] The words quoted do not, it is submitted, override the limitation on the work which is taken to be included within the Contractor's prices by virtue of clauses 57 and 55(2).[29] This clause confirms the Contractor's obligation to carry out all such work,[30] subject to the possibility of extra payment.

Clause 8(2): Design responsibility.   "*. . . except as may be expressly provided in the Contract*"

It is reasonably plain that this refers to responsibility for the adequacy, and not mere provision of the design or specification. A requirement to carry out design may be contained in any part of the Contract documentation and difficult questions of construction may arise whether a particular requirement is sufficiently expressed. Where the Contractor in fact carries out the design of the permanent works, either by invitation or as part of an alternative tender, there will be no responsibility for such design unless the Contract contains wording sufficient to create such responsibility.[31] See also clause 58(3) as to design requirements under Provisional Sum or Prime Cost items.

Clause 8(2): Contractor to exercise reasonable skill.   The wording of the sub-clause is not wholly clear. The intention appears to be to limit the Contractor's design responsibility to one requiring proof of negligence.[32] However the wording is not sufficient to limit the Contractor's responsibility to make good any loss or damage to the Works, etc., under clause 20(3). The Contractor's design is not an excepted risk.[33] It is thought that an express requirement to produce a design fit for purpose would prevail over the apparent intention to limit the duty (see also clause 7(6) and (7)).

Clause 8(3): Safety of Site Operations.   The placing of contractual responsibility upon the Contractor will not affect liability under Part 1 of the Health and Safety at Work, etc., Act 1974.[34] The general duty under section 4

---

[28] See particularly the words of clause 13(1), the Tender and the Form of Agreement.
[29] See Commentary to these clauses.
[30] Subject to impossibility: see "Methods of construction" below.
[31] *cp.* "Suitability for purpose" at p. 8, "Fitness for purpose of completed works" at p. 55 and "Package deals" at p. 56.
[32] But see commentary to clause 58(3).
[33] See commentary to clauses 20 and 21.
[34] See particularly ss.4, 6 and 36.

of that Act applies to any person "who has, to any extent, control of premises" (which may include the Employer) and requires that the premises and any plant, etc., should be "safe and without risks to health." See also clauses 15 (Contractor's Superintendence) and 19 (Safety and Security) of this Contract.

Clause 8(3): Methods of Construction.   This provision is to be read with clauses 13(2) and 14(1), (6), (7) and (9). These provisions are substantially to the same effect as those under the 5th edition, where the effect of a Method Statement being bound into the Contract has been considered by the courts. In *Yorkshire Water Authority* v. *Sir Alfred McAlpine*,[35] Skinner J. held that, despite clause 8(3),[36] the incorporation of a Method Statement bound the Contractor to follow the specified method. If the Works then became impossible within the meaning of clause 13(1),[37] the Contractor became entitled to a Variation Order with consequent entitlement to payment pursuant to clauses 51 and 52. A distinction was drawn between a Method Statement bound into the Contract, and one submitted post-Contract pursuant to clause 14. In the latter case, clauses 8 and 14 preserved the Contractor's responsibility for the method. This case was followed by the Court of Appeal in *Holland Dredging* v. *Dredging & Construction Co.*,[38] where an incorporated Method Statement was held to impose a limit on what the Contractor had undertaken to do by restricting the sources of fill material. In consequence, work that had to be carried out beyond the limit imposed was held to be an extra.

These cases do not, it is submitted, affect the question of responsibility for the methods of construction. The judgment of Skinner J. includes the following passage:

> "*Clause 8(2) is only relevant in the context of the present agreement (and I emphasise those words "in the context of the present agreement") to such part of the method or programme as is submitted, or may be submitted, post-contractually under clause 14.*"[39]

In view of the finding that the Contractor was entitled to a Variation Order if work in accordance with the stipulated method became physically impossible (and not if otherwise), the suggested limit on the application of clause 8(2) is *obiter* and does not appear to have any compelling foundation. There is no reason in principle why the Contractor should not remain responsible for the method in the ordinary sense (being liable for the consequences if use of the method leads to damage or additional cost) while at the same time being entitled to a Variation Order when (but not before) continued use of the method becomes impossible. These distinctions may have important consequences.

---

[35] (1985) 32 B.L.R. 114.
[36] Equivalent to clause 8(2) of the 5th edition.
[37] Substantially the same as clause 13(1) of the 5th edition.
[38] (1987) 37 B.L.R. 1 (C.A.).
[39] (1985) 32 B.L.R. 114 at 126.

CONTRACT AGREEMENT

Contract Agreement

9 The Contractor shall if called upon so to do enter into and execute a Contract Agreement to be prepared at the cost of the Employer in the form annexed to these Conditions.

Clause 9: Contract Agreement

The Form of Agreement (see above) adds nothing to the obligations contained in other Contract Documents.[40] In order for this clause to be binding, there will already be a Contract in existence, formed by the written acceptance of the Form of Tender (see below). If the Form of Agreement is to contain any new terms, this clause amounts to an agreement to agree, unenforceable under English law, unless the new agreement was already in existence and known to the parties when the tender was accepted, in which case the parties may have bound themselves already to the additional terms. Fortunately, such problems rarely occur in practice. It is much more common for the parties to continue negotiating after the work has commenced, sometimes not reaching agreement by the date of completion. In such a case, this clause will be of no avail.

The principal difference between the Contract formed by acceptance of the tender and the written agreement, is that the latter may be made as a deed,[41] increasing the limitation period in Contract, for both parties, to 12 years.[42] Strictly, neither party can be bound to convert a simple Contract into a Deed, but this does not appear to create problems in practice. From the Contractor's point of view, the extended period of contractual liability may be regarded as a matter of some importance in the light of the retrenchment which has occurred in the law of tort.[43]

PERFORMANCE SECURITY

Performance security

10 (1) If the Contract requires the Contractor to provide security for the proper performance of the Contract he shall obtain and provide to the Employer such security in a sum not exceeding 10% of the Tender Total within 28 days of the award of the Contract. The security shall be provided by a body approved by the Employer and be in the Form of Bond annexed to these Conditions. The Contractor shall pay the cost of such security unless the Contract provides otherwise.

---

[40] See commentary to clause 5.

[41] Note that seals as such have been abolished by the Law of Property (Miscellaneous Provisions) Act 1989: a document may be made a deed by signing with a witness coupled with physical delivery of the document.

[42] s.8 of the Limitation Act 1980. See generally Chap. 15, Section 3.

[43] See generally Chap. 7.

Arbitration upon security

(2) For the purposes of the arbitration provisions in such security

(a) the Employer shall be deemed a party to the said security for the purpose of doing everything necessary to give effect to such provisions and

(b) any agreement decision award or other determination touching or concerning the relevant date for the discharge of such security shall be wholly without prejudice to the resolution or determination of any dispute or difference between the Employer and the Contractor under clause 66.

Clause 10: Performance Security. *"If the Contract requires ..."*

The Form of Tender, which will form part of the initial contract agreement, contains an undertaking "if required" to provide security for the due performance of the Contract; and the Form of Appendix provides for a statement whether security is required. For notes on the form of Bond annexed to the Conditions, see below. It is important to note that the Bond provides security only during and for a limited period after performance of the work. The principal protection which it affords is against failure to complete the works through insolvency or other default. It affords no effective protection against latent defects in the work.

Arbitration under the Bond. The subject matter of such arbitration is limited to the date of the Defects Correction Certificate, for the purpose of discharge of the security. Note that the parties to the Bond are the Contractor, the Surety and the Employer. An arbitration under the Bond will be separate and distinct from any dispute under the head Contract. Both the Bond (see above) and clause 10(2) provide that a decision concerning the Defects Correction Certificate for the purpose of the Bond is without prejudice to any dispute under the head Contract. These provisions do not, however, prevent the parties making an ad hoc agreement to consolidate the two related disputes or to be bound by one determination.

PROVISION AND INTERPRETATION OF INFORMATION

Provision and interpretation of information

11 (1) The Employer shall be deemed to have made available to the Contractor before the submission of the Tender all information on the nature of the ground and sub-soil including hydrological conditions obtained by or on behalf of the Employer from investigations undertaken relevant to the Works.

The Contractor shall be responsible for the interpretation of all such information for the purposes of constructing the Works and for any design which is the Contractor's responsibility under the Contract.

Inspection of Site

(2) The Contractor shall be deemed to have inspected and examined the Site and its surroundings and information available in connection therewith and to have satisfied

himself so far as is practicable and reasonable before submitting his Tender as to

    (a) the form and nature thereof including the ground and sub-soil
    (b) the extent and nature of work and materials necessary for constructing and completing the Works and
    (c) the means of communication with and access to the Site and the accommodation he may require

and in general to have obtained for himself all necessary information as to risks contingencies and all other circumstances which may influence or affect his Tender.

Basis and sufficiency of Tender

(3)   The Contractor shall be deemed to have

    (a) based his Tender on the information made available by the Employer and on his own inspection and examination all as aforementioned and
    (b) satisfied himself before submitting his Tender as to the correctness and sufficiency of the rates and prices stated by him in the Bill of Quantities which shall (unless otherwise provided in the Contract) cover all his obligations under the Contract.

Clause 11: Provision and Interpretation of Information

This clause is an important part of the placing of risks, and must be read with the provisions of clause 12, which entitles the Contractor to seek extra payment for unforeseen events. In previous editions of the I.C.E. Conditions, clause 11 has dealt primarily with examination of the site and any information provided. The clause now contains, in sub-clause (1), an apparent obligation upon the Employer to provide information. The drafting is based on clause 11.1 of the F.I.D.I.C. Civil Engineering Contract, 4th edition, 1987.

Clause 11(1).   *"The Employer shall be deemed to have made available ..."*

The words appear to constitute a promise by the Employer that he has provided all the information which has been obtained by him or on his behalf relevant to the Works. If this is correct, interesting questions of damages may arise in the event of breach. In principle, the Contractor is entitled to be put into the position he would have been in had the promise been performed, *i.e.* had the undisclosed information been provided. Prima facie, the measure of damage will, therefore, be the difference between the tender that would have been submitted had the information been available, and the tender that was submitted. What is the position if the Contractor would not have tendered at all, had all the information been available on the basis that the risk was unacceptable? In such a case, it is arguable that the breach should be regarded as fundamental, giving a right, upon discovery, to terminate the Contract.[44]

Clause 11(1).   *"... obtained by or on behalf of the Employer from investigations undertaken relevant to the Works."*

These words are potentially very wide and not necessarily limited to infor-

---

[44] See p. 207 for the consequences of such termination.

mation in the Employer's possession. Data concerning other sites, not necessarily adjoining the contract site, might be regarded as relevant. The obligation might include data obtained by Consultants engaged by the Employer on previous projects and not supplied in full to the Employer. All such information appears to be within the obligation. Employers who undertake successive capital projects in the same area will, therefore, be under an onerous duty carefully to record data obtained by or on their behalf, in order to comply with this obligation. It may be anticipated that Contractors will be keen to pursue the possible existence of undisclosed data through the discovery process.

Clause 11(1). *"The Contractor shall be responsible for the interpretation ..."*
Information relating to the ground and sub-soil typically consists of test data obtained from a series of identified locations. By clause 11(3)(a) the Contractor is deemed to base his tender on this information. To use such information at all, necessarily involves interpolation and sometimes extrapolation. There may be a fine line between "use" and "interpretation."

Clause 11(2). *"The Contractor shall be deemed to have inspected and examined the Site ... and to have satisfied himself ..."*
These are traditional words, found in public authority contracts going back into the 19th Century. Similar words have been held to protect an Employer where a limited amount of information was supplied which, although not incorrect, was misleading. There was held to be no implication that the information was complete or exhaustive.[45] The site cannot be limited to the surface, having regard to the definition[46] and to the following sub-paragraphs which refer expressly to "the ground and sub-soil." Subject to the effect of sub-clause (1) and clause 12 (see below), these provisions reaffirm the general principle, under English law at least, that the Contractor takes the risk in the ground and sub-soil.[47]

Clause 11(3). *"The Contractor shall be deemed to have ... based his Tender on the information made available ..."*
These words confirm the effect of the information as suggested above under sub-clause (1). The Contractor must use the information in order to base his tender on it. The Employer will therefore be responsible for such use, provided it is reasonable.[48] It is reasonably clear that in this sub-clause "made available" refers to the actual and not deemed provision of information (see the opening words of sub-clause (1)).

---

[45] *Dillingham Construction Pty* v. *Downs* (1972) 2 N.S.W.L.R. 49; see also p. 177.

[46] See clause 1(1)(v).

[47] *Thorn* v. *London Corporation* (1876) 1 App. Cas. 120; *Bottoms* v. *York Corporation* (1892) H.B.C. (4th ed.), Vol. 2, p. 208 and *cf. Morrison-Knudsen Co.* v. *State of Alaska* (1974) 519 P2d 834, discussed by I.N.D. Wallace, Proceedings of a Conference on Construction Contract Policy (Kings College, London, 1989).

[48] See also *Bacal* v. *Northampton Development Corporation* (1975) 8 B.L.R. 88 (C.A.), where the simple provision of borehole data with an invitation to tender gave rise to an implied warranty.

Clause 11(3). "*The Contractor shall be deemed to have . . . satisfied himself . . . as to the correctness and sufficiency of the rates and prices stated . . .*"

This provision will not affect the overall pricing of the Contract but may be important in relation to the application or refixing of rates under clause 52. It is submitted that the effect of this provision is that the rates are deemed to cover the work described notwithstanding evidence to the contrary, *e.g.* that the rates have been artificially weighted or adjusted.

ADVERSE PHYSICAL CONDITIONS AND ARTIFICIAL OBSTRUCTIONS

Adverse physical conditions and artificial obstructions

12 (1) If during the execution of the Works the Contractor shall encounter physical conditions (other than weather conditions or conditions due to weather conditions) or artificial obstructions which conditions or obstructions could not in his opinion reasonably have been foreseen by an experienced contractor the Contractor shall as early as practicable give written notice thereof to the Engineer.

Intention to claim

(2) If in addition the Contractor intends to make any claim for additional payment or extension of time arising from such condition or obstruction he shall at the same time or as soon thereafter as may be reasonable inform the Engineer in writing pursuant to clause 52(4) and/or clause 44(1) as may be appropriate specifying the condition or obstruction to which the claim relates.

Measures being taken

(3) When giving notification in accordance with sub-clauses (1) and (2) of this clause or as soon as practicable thereafter the Contractor shall give details of any anticipated effects of the condition or obstruction the measures he has taken is taking or is proposing to take their estimated cost and the extent of the anticipated delay in or interference with the execution of the Works.

Action by Engineer

(4) Following receipt of any notification under sub-clauses (1) (2) or (3) of this clause the Engineer may if he thinks fit inter alia

(a) require the Contractor to investigate and report upon the practicality cost and timing of alternative measures which may be available
(b) give written consent to measures notified under sub-clause (3) of this clause with or without modification
(c) give written instructions as to how the physical conditions or artificial obstructions are to be dealt with
(d) order a suspension under clause 40 or a variation under clause 51.

Conditions reasonably foreseeable

(5) If the Engineer shall decide that the physical conditions or artificial obstructions

could in whole or in part have been reasonably foreseen by an experienced contractor he shall so inform the Contractor in writing as soon as he shall have reached that decision but the value of any variation previously ordered by him pursuant to sub-clause (4)(d) of this clause shall be ascertained in accordance with clause 52 and included in the Contract Price.

Delay and extra cost

(6)   Where an extension of time or additional payment is claimed pursuant to sub-clause (2) of this clause the Engineer shall if in his opinion such conditions or obstructions could not reasonably have been foreseen by an experienced contractor determine the amount of any costs which may reasonably have been incurred by the Contractor by reason of such conditions or obstructions together with a reasonable percentage addition thereto in respect of profit and any extension of time to which the Contractor may be entitled and shall notify the Contractor accordingly with a copy to the Employer.

Clause 12: Adverse physical conditions and artificial obstructions

The essence of this clause is to place the particular defined risk of adverse conditions on the Employer and not the Contractor. There could be a substantial overlap between loss recoverable under this clause and a claim made pursuant to clause 11(1), and other claims such as misrepresentation.[49] There are two grounds on which the policy of this clause is open to serious questions, *viz.* firstly, whether the Contractor should be required to undertake any part of the risk in ground conditions, and secondly, whether the particular apportionment of risk is efficient and workable. As to the first point, contrary to what appears to be implicit in clause 11(2), modern tendering procedures do not permit Contractors to do more than examine the surface of the site and to consider the information concerning the sub-soil provided by the Employer. It is the Employer who decides how much money and effort to invest in the site investigation process, and this determines the reliability of the data provided. While the Contractor may be left with some responsibility for adverse ground conditions, the Employer often has no clear incentive to provide the best information possible.[50] As to the second point, the division between the Employer's risk and the Contractor's risk is such as to lead frequently to major and costly disputes. Further, there is no clear incentive on the Contractor, when adverse conditions are encountered, to minimise their effect. The ability to recover comparatively generous compensation under this clause could be seen as tending to inefficiency.

A solution which has been suggested is to utilise "reference conditions" against which the Contractor's prices are deemed to apply, with provision for pricing more adverse conditions in the Bill of Quantities. In this way, the

---

[49] And consider also the possibility, not yet recognised under English law, of a claim based on breach of duty of disclosure: see *Morrison-Knudsen* v. *State of Alaska* (1974) 519 P2d 834.

[50] See generally Methods of Procurement for Ground Investigation: CIRIA SP45, 1988.

Contractor is paid for what is actually encountered and the Employer has a positive incentive to make the reference conditions as accurate as possible.[51]

Drafting of clause 12. There are a number of amendments in the new edition of this clause, but none of substance. The 4th edition of the I.C.E. Conditions contained a provision that additional cost could be claimed only if incurred after the giving of notice. This provision was reversed in the 5th edition of the Conditions, and the present clause maintains that position. Much of the present clause is purely procedural and enabling, without substantive effect. The essential matters dealt with in the clause are (a) definition of the conditions which fall within the clause and (b) provisions governing compensation.

Clause 12(1). *"... physical conditions ..."*
These words are very wide. They suggest a state of affairs having a pre-existence before being "encountered." However, there is no justification for limiting the clause to conditions occurring after the Contract nor to pre-existing conditions.[52]

Clause 12(1). *"... other than weather conditions or conditions due to weather conditions ..."*
This provision is apt to exclude both heavy rainfall and succeeding floods. More difficult questions may arise where the adverse condition arises from the action of weather upon some other physical condition, *e.g.* a rising water table giving rise to instability in soil. The words "due to" appear to indicate an intention to exclude matters only where weather conditions are the effective or proximate cause.[53]

Clause 12(1). *"... artificial obstructions ..."*
These words are much more specific than "physical conditions", and must be limited to non-naturally occurring events which obstruct, *i.e.* hinder or stop, some part of the Contractor's operations. In their context, it is thought that the words must contemplate a physical occurrence and not matters such as statutory controls or even (as sometimes suggested) obstructive members of the professional team. A typical example of an artificial obstruction is buried services. The obstruction may, however, be transient.

Clause 12(1). *"... could not .... reasonably have been foreseen by an experienced contractor ..."*
Although expressed objectively, the intention is plainly to allow or disallow claims by reference to the particular circumstances of the Contract, but

---

[51] See further *New Civil Engineer*, July 6, 1989 and CIRIA Report R479, "Tunnelling—Improved contract practices", 1978.
[52] See *Holland Dredging* v. *Dredging & Construction* (1987) 37 B.L.R. 1 at 35 (C.A.).
[53] See *Wayne Tank & Pump* v. *Employer's Liability Assurance Corporation* [1974] Q.B. 57 (C.A.).

attributing to the real Contractor an objective degree of foresight. Thus the assessment of what could or could not reasonably have been foreseen must take into account all the available sources of information.[54] This must include the actual knowledge of the real Contractor, even if this goes beyond what an experienced Contractor would know, otherwise there would be recovery for conditions which the real Contractor should have foreseen or even did foresee.

Determining whether a condition could "reasonably" have been foreseen habitually gives rise to the greatest difficulty of interpretation in civil engineering arbitration. The words of the sub-clause seem to defy precise analysis and it is thought that little is to be gained from analysing the words in terms of probability. It is always worthwhile to bear in mind that a ruling that a condition could reasonably have been foreseen leaves the Contractor in a position of loss, while the opposite ruling may leave him in a position of unexpected profit. It is indeed unfortunate that there is virtually no authority on the application of this difficult test. It is thought that most Arbitrators in practice apply the clause by asking whether it is reasonable to expect this Contractor, assuming him to be experienced, to have foreseen the particular condition or obstruction.

Requirement for Notice.   The clause contains a number of notice provisions. Sub-clause (1) requires the Contractor to give written notice "as early as practicable" of the condition or obstruction encountered. Sub-clause (2) requires additional notice "pursuant to clause 52(4) and/or clause 44(1)" if the Contractor wishes to claim payment or an extension of time. Sub-clause (3) also requires notice "as soon as practicable thereafter" of the anticipated effects of the condition or obstruction, the measures proposed and their estimated cost. None of these notices, it is thought, can operate as a condition precedent to the right to press a claim. Clause 52(4) (see below) expressly permits claims out of time, provided that the Engineer has not been prejudiced.[55]

Clause 12(4): Action by the Engineer.   The Engineer is given a battery of express powers under this clause, notwithstanding the breadth of his powers under clauses 13(1) and 51 which are also exercisable, if necessary, under this clause. In practice, Engineers are usually extremely cautious in responding to claims under clause 12 because of the serious financial consequences. In many cases, the Contractor is left to pursue remedies of his own choosing and to seek to recover the costs subsequently by negotiation or arbitration.[56]

Clause 12(6): Sums payable.   This sub-clause has been greatly simplified. It permits the recovery of any costs[57] "which may reasonably have been

---

[54] See *C.J. Pearce* v. *Hereford Corporation* (1968) 66 L.G.R. 647, a case on the 4th edition of the I.C.E. Conditions.
[55] Clause 52(4)(e).
[56] For an alternative provision see *New Civil Engineer*, July 6, 1989.
[57] See clause 1(5) for definition.

835

incurred by the Contractor by reason of such conditions or obstructions." This formula avoids strict questions of causation. It may also place an onus on the Engineer to act under sub-clause (4) or otherwise to control the incurring of additional cost. The Contractor is entitled to an additional percentage for profit on the whole of his cost, a change from the previous edition where profit was allowed only on additional work or plant.

WORK TO BE TO SATISFACTION OF ENGINEER

Work to be to satisfaction of Engineer

13   (1)   Save insofar as it is legally or physically impossible the Contractor shall construct and complete the Works in strict accordance with the Contract to the satisfaction of the Engineer and shall comply with and adhere strictly to the Engineer's instructions on any matter connected therewith (whether mentioned in the Contract or not). The Contractor shall take instructions only from the Engineer or (subject to the limitations referred to in clause 2) from the Engineer's Representative.

Mode and manner of construction

(2)   The whole of the materials plant and labour to be provided by the Contractor under clause 8 and the mode manner and speed of construction of the Works are to be of a kind and conducted in a manner acceptable to the Engineer.

Delay and extra cost

(3)   If in pursuance of clause 5 or sub-clause (1) of this clause the Engineer shall issue instructions which involve the Contractor in delay or disrupt his arrangements or methods of construction so as to cause him to incur cost beyond that reasonably to have been foreseen by an experienced contractor at the time of tender then the Engineer shall take such delay into account in determining any extension of time to which the Contractor is entitled under clause 44 and the Contractor shall subject to clause 52(4) be paid in accordance with clause 60 the amount of such cost as may be reasonable except to the extent that such delay and extra cost result from the Contractor's default. Profit shall be added thereto in respect of any additional permanent or temporary work. If such instructions require any variation to any part of the Works the same shall be deemed to have been given pursuant to clause 51.

Clause 13

This clause contains a number of important general obligations and powers, and should be read with clauses 5, 8 and 14. Sub-clause (1) contains an important restriction on the Contractor's obligation to carry out the Works, where they become legally or physically impossible. Sub-clause (3) makes provision for additional payments in circumstances which may have wide application.

Clause 13(1).   *"... legally ... impossible ..."*

This applies to the construction process, as well as to the permanent and

---

[58] See clause 1(1)(p).

temporary works.[58] Thus the Contractor would be absolved from carrying out the work if the only means of doing it would contravene the Health and Safety at Work, etc., Act 1974. Similarly, if the permanent works or the temporary works would infringe a statutory provision such as the Public Health Acts, or a private right capable of protection by injunction, the Contractor would similarly be absolved to the extent of such impossibility.

Clause 13(1). *"... physically impossible ..."*

The effect of this provision was considered in the case of *Yorkshire Water Authority* v. *McAlpine*,[59] where it was held that if a method of construction which was contractually binding became impossible, clause 13(1) had the effect of entitling the Contractor to a variation and to payment under clauses 51 and 52. The same principle was applied in a dredging case, where an incorporated Method Statement was held to limit the area from which fill was to be obtained.[60] Where there are no constraints upon the Contractor's methods of working, the Contractor will rarely be in a position to allege physical impossibility. However, in *Turriff Ltd.* v. *Welsh National Water Development Authority*,[61] work consisting of constructing rectangular pre-cast concrete segments of a sewer to specific tolerances was held to be physically impossible within clause 13(1) where, although not absolutely impossible, the work was impossible in the ordinary commercial sense. The Contractor was, therefore, not bound to complete the relevant parts of the work.

Clause 13(1). *"... in strict accordance with the Contract to the satisfaction of the Engineer ..."*

These words are traditional, and are probably otiose. The Engineer cannot withhold his satisfaction where the work is fully defined in the Contract, nor can he give his satisfaction where the work does not comply with the requirements of the Contract.[62] The obligation to comply with the Contract is repeated in clause 8(1) and in the Tender and Form of Agreement.

Clause 13(1). *"... adhere strictly to the Engineer's instructions on any matter connected therewith (whether mentioned in the Contract or not)."*

These words are important because they appear to give the Engineer considerable powers to give instructions. The words empower the Engineer to give an instruction (a) on any matter connected with the Works, (b) which need not be mentioned in the Contract. However, the words do not mean, it is submitted, that any instruction connected with the Works is to be regarded as given under clause 13(1).[63] Under sub-clause (3), provision is made for payment for an instruction given "in pursuance of ... sub-clause (1) of this clause."

---

[59] (1985) 32 B.L.R. 114.
[60] *Holland Dredging* v. *Dredging and Construction* (1987) 37 B.L.R. 1 (C.A.).
[61] Unreported, save for Note at 32 B.L.R. 117, and see *New Civil Engineer*, February 7, 1980.
[62] See clause 2(1)(c).
[63] See commentary to clause 13(3).

Clause 13(2): Mode and manner of construction.   It is not clear what distinction, if any, is to be drawn between "mode and manner" and "method." The latter is dealt with in clause 8(2), where the Contractor is made responsible, and in clause 14, where the Engineer is empowered to require further detail and to impose restrictions. Clause 13(2) entitles the Engineer, without invoking clause 14, to withhold his acceptance.

Clause 13(3).   *"If in pursuance of clause 5 or sub-clause (1) of this clause the Engineer shall issue instructions ..."*

The ambit of instructions which are to be regarded as issued "in pursuance of" sub-clause (1) is not defined. Sub-clause (1) itself gives no assistance, since practically any instruction may come within its words. It is significant that the right to payment under sub-clause (3) is materially restricted compared with other clauses in the Contract, and this would indicate that instructions which could be regarded as issued under some other clause should be so regarded. The last sentence of the sub-clause is not wholly consistent with this view, but it may refer to a composite instruction which includes a variation to part of the Works. Note that under clause 2(6)(c) the Engineer or his representative must specify in writing the authority for any instruction given.

The instruction under sub-clause (3) requires no particular form, and need not even be in writing. The sub-clause has great potential for disputes, but, since its introduction in 1973, the clause does not appear to have been greatly used by Contractors. This may be a reflection of the limitation on recovery of cost, or alternatively a reflection on the availability of other grounds of claim.

Clause 13(3).   *"... beyond that reasonably to have been foreseen by an experienced contractor ..."*

These words appear, curiously, to qualify "cost", despite the fact that the Contractor is then entitled to payment of "such cost as may be reasonable", *i.e.* the cost recoverable is subject to two qualifications. The intention appears to be to allow claims only where the instruction, or the resulting disruption were unforeseeable, but the effect is far from clear. As indicated above, the clause has been little used.

PROGRAMME TO BE FURNISHED

Programme to be furnished

14   (1)   (a)   Within 21 days after the award of the Contract the Contractor shall submit to the Engineer for his acceptance a programme showing the order in which he proposes to carry out the Works having regard to the provisions of clause 42(1).
(b)   At the same time the Contractor shall also provide in writing for the information of the Engineer a general description of the arrangements and methods of construction which the Contractor proposes to adopt for the carrying out of the Works.
(c)   Should the Engineer reject any programme under sub-clause (2)(b) of this clause the Contractor shall within 21 days of such rejection submit a revised programme.

Action by Engineer

(2)   The Engineer shall within 21 days after receipt of the Contractor's programme

(a)   accept the programme in writing or
(b)   reject the programme in writing with reasons or
(c)   request the Contractor to supply further information to clarify or substantiate the programme or to satisfy the Engineer as to its reasonableness having regard to the Contractor's obligations under the Contract.

Provided that if none of the above actions is taken within the said period of 21 days the Engineer shall be deemed to have accepted the programme as submitted.

Provision of further information

(3)   The Contractor shall within 21 days after receiving from the Engineer any request under sub-clause (2)(c) of this clause or within such further period as the Engineer may allow provide the further information requested failing which the relevant programme shall be deemed to be rejected.

Upon receipt of such further information the Engineer shall within a further 21 days accept or reject the programme in accordance with sub-clauses (2)(a) or (2)(b) of this clause.

Revision of programme

(4)   Should it appear to the Engineer at any time that the actual progress of the work does not conform with the accepted programme referred to in sub-clause (1) of this clause the Engineer shall be entitled to require the Contractor to produce a revised programme showing such modifications to the original programme as may be necessary to ensure completion of the Works or any Section within the time for completion as defined in clause 43 or extended time granted pursuant to clause 44. In such event the Contractor shall submit his revised programme within 21 days or within such further period as the Engineer shall allow. Thereafter the provisions of sub-clauses (2) and (3) of this clause shall apply.

Design criteria

(5)   The Engineer shall provide to the Contractor such design criteria relevant to the Permanent Works or any Temporary Works design supplied by the Engineer as may be necessary to enable the Contractor to comply with sub-clauses (6) and (7) of this clause.

Methods of construction

(6)   If requested by the Engineer the Contractor shall submit at such times and in such further detail as the Engineer may reasonably require information pertaining to the methods of construction (including Temporary Works and the use of Contractor's Equipment) which the Contractor proposes to adopt or use and calculations of stresses strains and deflections that will arise in the Permanent Works or any parts thereof during construction so as to enable the Engineer to decide whether if these methods are adhered to the Works can be constructed and completed in accordance with the Contract and without detriment to the Permanent Works when completed.

839

Engineer's consent

(7)   The Engineer shall inform the Contractor in writing within 21 days after receipt of the information submitted in accordance with sub-clauses (1)(b) and (6) of this clause either

    (a)   that the Contractor's proposed methods have the consent of the Engineer or
    (b)   in what respects in the opinion of the Engineer they fail to meet the requirements of the Contract or will be detrimental to the Permanent Works.

In the latter event the Contractor shall take such steps or make such changes in the said methods as may be necessary to meet the Engineer's requirements and to obtain his consent. The Contractor shall not change the methods which have received the Engineer's consent without the further consent in writing of the Engineer which shall not be unreasonably withheld.

Delay and cost

(8)   If the Contractor unavoidably incurs delay or cost because

    (a)   the Engineer's consent to the proposed methods of construction is unreasonably delayed or
    (b)   the Engineer's requirements pursuant to sub-clause (7) of this clause or any limitations imposed by any of the design criteria supplied by the Engineer pursuant to sub-clause (5) of this clause could not reasonably have been foreseen by an experienced Contractor at the time of Tender

the Engineer shall take such delay into account in determining any extension of time to which the Contractor is entitled under clause 44 and the Contractor shall subject to clause 52(4) be paid in accordance with clause 60 such sum in respect of the cost incurred as the Engineer considers fair in all the circumstances. Profit shall be added thereto in respect of any additional permanent or temporary work.

Responsibility unaffected by acceptance or consent

(9)   Acceptance by the Engineer of the Contractor's programme in accordance with sub-clauses (2)(3) or (4) of this clause and the consent of the Engineer to the Contractor's proposed methods of construction in accordance with sub-clause (7) of this clause shall not relieve the Contractor of any of his duties or responsibilities under the Contract.

Clause 14

This clause covers two important matters, *viz.* programme and the method of working. The Employer, through the Engineer, needs to exercise some degree of control over each of these, but without relieving the Contractor from his overall responsibility to carry out and complete the Works within the stated time for completion.

Clause 14(1)–(3): Contractor's initial programme.   These sub-clauses contain elaborate provisions for the submission, consideration and revision of

840

an initial programme for the work. The drafting assumes that an acceptable programme will be produced by these means. There is no provision which applies otherwise, beyond requiring the Contractor to submit a revision. In practice, programming problems tend to occur during, rather than at the commencement of the Works. Note that sub-clause (1)(b) also requires the Contractor to provide "a general description of the arrangements and methods of construction." These are not subject to the review procedure which applies to the programme, but see commentary to sub-clause (7) below.

Clause 14(4): Requirement for revised programme. It should be noted that none of these programmes are contractually binding. The Contractor remains under an obligation to complete within the time stated, subject to any extension,[64] and to proceed with "due expedition and without delay."[65] The sanction or remedy provided against delay is set out in clause 46.

Clause 14(6). "*... information pertaining to the methods of construction ...*"
It is important to note that this sub-clause, and the procedure which follows, has to be invoked by the Engineer. He is perfectly entitled, as an alternative, to signify his non-acceptance of the mode or manner of construction under clause 13(2), without putting into effect the procedure which may lead to a claim for additional cost under this clause. If the Engineer decides to request information under this clause, it must include what may be elaborate stress and strain calculations. Note that under sub-clause (5), the Engineer is to provide relevant design criteria to enable the Contractor to comply with these obligations.

Clause 14(7): Engineer's response to information submitted. This sub-clause has an interesting history. When originally introduced with the 5th edition of the I.C.E. Conditions, it was part of the procedure which applied if (but only if) the Engineer decided to invoke sub-clause (6). It will be noted that these provisions now apply also to the information which the Contractor is bound to submit under sub-clause (1)(b). Accordingly, whether or not sub-clause (6) is invoked, the Engineer must now deal with information submitted about the methods of construction proposed by the Contractor, and either (a) give his consent or (b) indicate in what respects they fail to meet "the requirements of the Contract or will be detrimental to the Permanent Works."
It will be noted that this phrase turns into "the Engineer's requirements" in the latter part of the sub-clause. There does not appear to be any need for the Engineer to make requirements. He need only point out where the Contractor's method fails to meet the requirements of the Contract or will be detrimental to the Permanent Works.

Clause 14(7): Contractor not to change methods without consent. Approval of the Contractor's method under this clause does not render the

---

[64] Clause 43.
[65] Clause 41(2).

Employer responsible (see sub-clause (9)) nor is the Contractor entitled to a variation order if it becomes impossible to continue with the method.[66] The Engineer need only consent to a change of method.

Clause 14(8): Claim for delay and additional cost.   The grounds of claim include "Engineer's requirements" or design criteria being not reasonably foreseeable. As noted above, it is not clear why the Engineer should need to make requirements. Note that the sum recoverable is not the cost incurred, but what the Engineer considers "fair in all the circumstances." It is not clear how this is to be assessed, but presumably it is not to exceed the actual cost incurred.

Clause 14(9): Contractor's responsibility unaffected.   This clause confirms that the Contractor's responsibility under clauses 8(3) and 13(2) remain unaffected by the submission of information and the giving of the Engineer's consent. The Engineer should, however, be mindful of the dangers of going beyond the machinery of this clause as regards the method, having regard to the terms of clause 51(1).

CONTRACTOR'S SUPERINTENDENCE

Contractor's superintendence

15   (1)   The Contractor shall give or provide all necessary superintendence during the construction and completion of the Works and as long thereafter as the Engineer may consider necessary. Such superintendence shall be given by sufficient persons having adequate knowledge of the operations to be carried out (including the methods and techniques required the hazards likely to be encountered and methods of preventing accidents) as may be requisite for the satisfactory and safe construction of the Works.

Contractor's agent

(2)   The Contractor or a competent and authorized agent or representative approved of in writing by the Engineer (which approval may at any time be withdrawn) is to be constantly on the Works and shall give his whole time to the superintendence of the same. Such authorized agent or representative shall be in full charge of the Works and shall receive on behalf of the Contractor directions and instructions from the Engineer or (subject to the limitations of clause 2) the Engineer's Representative. The Contractor or such authorized agent or representative shall be responsible for the safety of all operations.

Removal of Contractor's employees

16   The Contractor shall employ or cause to be employed in and about the construction and completion of the Works and in the superintendence thereof only such persons as are careful skilled and experienced in their several trades and callings.

The Engineer shall be at liberty to object to and require the Contractor to remove or cause to be removed from the Works any person employed thereon who in the opinion

---

[66] *cf. Yorkshire Water Authority* v. *McAlpine* (1985) 32 B.L.R. 114.

of the Engineer misconducts himself or is incompetent or negligent in the performance of his duties or fails to conform with any particular provisions with regard to safety which may be set out in the Contract or persists in any conduct which is prejudicial to safety to health and such persons shall not be again employed upon the Works without the permission of the Engineer.

Clauses 15 and 16

The Contractor's obligations under these clauses are not such as may readily give rise to damages for breach. The Employer's only effective remedy lies in the threat of determination under clause 63, but this would be available only if the Contractor were "persistently or fundamentally" in breach of his obligations.[67]

Clause 15(2).   *"The Contractor or such authorised agent or representative shall be responsible . . ."*

This amounts to a statement of the authority which the agent is required to be given. It cannot relieve the Contractor of his primary responsibility under clause 8(3) "for the adequacy, stability and safety of all site operations and methods of construction."

SETTING-OUT

Setting-out

17   (1)   The Contractor shall be responsible for the true and proper setting-out of the Works and for the correctness of the position levels dimensions and alignment of all parts of the Works and for the provision of all necessary instruments appliances and labour in connection therewith.

(2)   If at any time during the progress of the Works any error shall appear or arise in the position levels dimensions or alignment of any part of the Works the Contractor on being required so to do by the Engineer shall at his own cost rectify such error to the satisfaction of the Engineer unless such error is based on incorrect data supplied in writing by the Engineer or the Engineer's Representative in which case the cost of rectifying the same shall be borne by the Employer.

(3)   The checking of any setting-out or of any line or level by the Engineer or the Engineer's Representative shall not in any way relieve the Contractor of his responsibility for the correctness thereof and the Contractor shall carefully protect and preserve all bench-marks sight rails pegs and other things used in setting out the Works.

Clause 17(2).   *". . . the Contractor on being required so to do by the Engineer shall at his own cost rectify such error . . ."*

This is a useful provision, apart from which the Engineer's only sanction is to refuse to certify payment for the erroneous work. Equivalent provisions for defective work or materials are contained in clause 39, which also includes power to employ others to do the work if the Contractor does not comply. Clause 17 does not contain such a provision.

---

[67] Clause 63(1)(b)(iv).

BOREHOLES

Boreholes and exploratory excavation

18   If at any time during the construction of the Works the Engineer shall require the Contractor to make boreholes or to carry out exploratory excavation such requirement shall be ordered in writing and shall be deemed to be a variation under clause 51 unless a Provisional Sum or Prime Cost Item in respect of such anticipated work shall have been included in the Bill of Quantities.

SAFETY AND SECURITY

Safety and security

19   (1)   The Contractor shall throughout the progress of the Works have full regard for the safety of all persons entitled to be upon the Site and shall keep the Site (so far as the same is under his control) and the Works (so far as the same are not completed or occupied by the Employer) in an orderly state appropriate to the avoidance of danger to such persons and shall inter alia in connection with the Works provide and maintain at his own cost all lights guards fencing warning signs and watching when and where necessary or required by the Engineer or the Engineer's Representative or by any competent statutory or other authority for the protection of the Works or for the safety and convenience of the public or others.

Employer's responsibilities

(2)   If under clause 31 the Employer shall carry out work on the Site with his own workmen he shall in respect of such work

   (a)   have full regard to the safety of all persons entitled to be upon the Site and
   (b)   keep the Site in an orderly state appropriate to the avoidance of danger to such persons.

   If under clause 31 the Employer shall employ other contractors on the Site he shall require them to have the same regard for safety and avoidance of danger.

Clause 19

Clause 19: Generally: This clause should be read with clauses 8(3), 15 and 22, and in the light of the general law relating to occupiers of premises.[68] If a failure to observe the requirements for safety results in a claim being brought against the Employer, there will be a claim over against the Contractor for breach of this clause. Alternatively, clause 22(1) requires the Contractor to indemnify the Employer against claims, etc., "which may arise out of or in consequence of the execution of the Works."

---

[68] See p. 260.

844

Clause 19(1).   "*. . . all persons entitled to be upon the Site . . .*"

The obligations under the clause should not be regarded as so limited. Both the Contractor and the Employer could attract liability in tort to trespassers.[69]

Clause 19(1).   "*. . . the Site (so far as the same is under his control) . . .*"

The Contractor will remain in control notwithstanding occupation by a Sub-Contractor. Note that clause 42(2) contemplates handover of the site in sections "as may be required." It is plainly in the interests of both parties to avoid any doubt or misunderstanding as to control and responsibility. Safety on construction sites has been the subject of much comment and some action within the United Kingdom, and a European Community directive on the subject is awaited.[70]

CARE AND INSURANCE OF THE WORKS

Care of the Works

20 (1)   (a)   The Contractor shall save as in paragraph (b) hereof and subject to sub-clause (2) of this clause take full responsibility for the care of the Works and materials plant and equipment for incorporation therein from the Works Commencement Date until the date of issue of a Certificate of Substantial Completion for the whole of the Works when the responsibility for the said care shall pass to the Employer.

(b)   If the Engineer issues a Certificate of Substantial Completion for any Section or part of the Permanent Works the Contractor shall cease to be responsible for the care of that Section or part from the date of issue of such Certificate of Substantial Completion when the responsibility for the care of that Section or part shall pass to the Employer.

(c)   The Contractor shall take full responsibility for the care of any outstanding work and materials plant and equipment for incorporation therein which he undertakes to finish during the Defects Correction Period until such outstanding work has been completed.

Excepted Risks

(2)   The Excepted Risks for which the Contractor is not liable are loss or damage to the extent that it is due to

(a)   the use or occupation by the Employer his agents servants or other contractors (not being employed by the Contractor) of any part of the Permanent Works

(b)   any fault defect error or omission in the design of the Works (other than a design provided by the Contractor pursuant to his obligations under the Contract)

(c)   riot war invasion act of foreign enemies or hostilities (whether war be declared or not)

(d)   civil war rebellion revolution insurrection or military or usurped power

(e)   ionizing radiations or contamination by radioactivity from any nuclear fuel or from any nuclear waste from the combustion of nuclear fuel radioactive toxic

---

[69] See Occupiers' Liability Act 1984.

[70] Construction sites are not presently covered by the framework directive on Health and Safety at Work adopted by the Commission on June 12, 1989. A subsidiary directive of the framework directive is expected to cover safety on construction sites.

explosive or other hazardous properties of any explosive nuclear assembly or nuclear component thereof and

(f) pressure waves caused by aircraft or other aerial devices travelling at sonic or supersonic speeds.

Rectification of loss or damage

(3) (a) In the event of any loss or damage to

    (i) the Works or any Section or part thereof or

    (ii) materials plant or equipment for incorporation therein

while the Contractor is responsible for the care thereof (except as provided in sub-clause (2) of this clause) the Contractor shall at his own cost rectify such loss or damage so that the Permanent Works conform in every respect with the provisions of the Contract and the Engineer's instructions. The Contractor shall also be liable for any loss or damage to the Works occasioned by him in the course of any operations carried out by him for the purpose of complying with his obligations under clauses 49 and 50.

(b) Should any such loss or damage arise from any of the Excepted Risks defined in sub-clause (2) of this clause the Contractor shall if and to the extent required by the Engineer rectify the loss or damage at the expense of the Employer.

(c) In the event of loss or damage arising from an Excepted Risk and a risk for which the Contractor is responsible under sub-clause (1)(a) of this clause then the Engineer shall when determining the expense to be borne by the Employer under the Contract apportion the cost of rectification into that part caused by the Excepted Risk and that part which is the responsibility of the Contractor.

Insurance of Works etc.

21 (1) The Contractor shall without limiting his or the Employers obligations and responsibilities under clause 20 insure in the joint names of the Contractor and the Employer the Works together with materials plant and equipment for incorporation therein to the full replacement cost plus an additional 10 per cent. to cover any additional costs that may arise incidental to the rectification of any loss or damage including professional fees cost of demolition and removal of debris.

Extent of cover

(2) (a) The insurance required under sub-clause (1) of this clause shall cover the Employer and the Contractor against all loss or damage from whatsoever cause arising other than the Excepted Risks defined in clause 20(2) from the Works Commencement Date until the date of issue of the relevant Certificate of Substantial Completion.

(b) The insurance shall extend to cover any loss or damage arising during the Defects Correction Period from a cause occurring prior to the issue of any Certificate of Substantial Completion and any loss or damage occasioned by the Contractor in the course of any operation carried out by him for the purpose of complying with his obligations under clauses 49 and 50.

(c) Nothing in this clause shall render the Contractor liable to insure against the necessity for the repair or reconstruction of any work constructed with materials or workmanship not in accordance with the requirements of the Contract unless the Bill of Quantities shall provide a special item for this insurance.

(d) Any amounts not insured or not recovered from insurers whether as excesses carried under the policy or otherwise shall be borne by the Contractor or the Employer in accordance with their respective responsibilities under clause 20.

Clauses 20 and 21

These clauses lay down responsibilities for damage to the Works, materials, plant and equipment, by making the Contractor generally liable, subject to specific exceptions. Insurance is required in the joint names of the Contractor and the Employer. Apart from this clause, the Contractor is *prima facie* liable for damage to the Works, through the overriding obligation to complete the Works.[71] The principal effect of clause 20 is to define those areas in which the Contractor is relieved of liability. These clauses have been rearranged and the drafting clarified for the 6th edition, which also contains some amendments.

Clause 20(1)(a). "... *full responsibility for the care of the Works* ..."
These words do not accurately reflect the Contractor's responsibility, which is not simply to exercise (reasonable) care. The Contractor is responsible irrespective of fault within the terms of the clause. The effect of sub-clause (1) is to define the period during which the Contractor is responsible before such responsibility passes to the Employer.

Clause 20(1): Period of Contractor's responsibility. This is stated in paragraph (a) as extending from the Works Commencement Date to the date of the issue of a Certificate of Substantial Completion for the whole of the Works. But by paragraph (b), a Certificate of Substantial Completion for any Section or part immediately transfers responsibility for that Section or part to the Employer. In each case, by paragraph (c), this is subject to any outstanding work, etc., remaining the Contractor's responsibility until it is complete. Note that a "Section" means a part of the Works separately identified in the Appendix,[72] but a part has no definition.[73]

Clause 20(2)(a). "... *use or occupation by the Employer his agents servants or other Contractors* ..."
This is a potentially wide exception, because use or occupation may occur informally. The words apply *ex hypothesi* to use or occupation not recognised by a Certificate of Substantial Completion.[74] But the exception operates only where the loss or damage in question is "due to" such use or occupation.

Clause 20(2)(b). "... *any fault defect error or omission in the design of the Works* ..."
These words are not limited to a failure by the designer to comply with

---

[71] Clause 8(1)(a), Tender and Form of Agreement.
[72] Clause 1(1)(u).
[73] See clause 48(3) and (4).
[74] See clause 20(1)(b) and 48(3).

accepted standards of skill, nor to a failure to take account of existing engineering knowledge. A "fault" in the design of the Works may exist where the only error consists in the inability of available knowledge or theory to predict the actual stresses to which a structure will be subjected.[75] Note that the exception applies to any part of the design other than one provided by the Contractor pursuant to his obligations under the Contract. Design which is not excluded, and which therefore remains the Contractor's responsibility, is the design of the temporary works (unless designed by the Engineer[76]), and design of the permanent works where the Contract contains an express obligation to carry out such design.[77] (See further, note to clause 21(2) below).

Clause 20(3)(a). *"In the event of any loss or damage ..."*

The clause now omits the words "from any cause whatsoever" which have appeared in previous editions of the form of Contract, and which have been held to render the Contractor liable for loss due to the Employer's negligence.[78] This omission does not cut down the Contractor's obligation to put right the loss or damage, but the present wording would not prevent the Contractor mounting a cross-claim for indemnity, either in contract or in tort[79] where the Employer is at fault.[80]

Clause 20(3). *"... the Contractor shall at his own cost rectify such loss or damage ..."*

Provided that the loss occurs while the Contractor is responsible, as defined by sub-clause (1), the Contractor is automatically required to reinstate the Works or any materials, plant or equipment. Where the damage is due to an Excepted Risk, the Contractor is required to rectify, at the Employer's expense, only if and to the extent instructed.

Clause 20(3)(c): Concurrent causes of loss. The power to apportion the cost of rectification may have the effect of preventing the Contractor (and the Insurer under clause 21) from avoiding liability where a cause of the loss (not being the sole cause) is one of the Excepted Risks.[81]

Clause 21(1): Insurance in joint names. The Employer, named as principal in the policy, can bring a claim in his own name. The Employer may also

---

[75] *Manufacturers' Mutual Insurance* v. *Queensland Government Railway* [1969] 1 Lloyd's Rep. 214 and see also *Pentagon Construction* v. *Fidelity & Guarantee Co.* [1978] 1 Lloyd's Rep. 93.
[76] Clause 8(2).
[77] See clause 8(2) and 58(3).
[78] *Farr* v. *The Admiralty* [1953] 1 W.L.R. 965; see, however, "Loss caused by negligence" at p. 60 and in particular n. 40, where it is suggested that *Farr* v. *The Admiralty* might not be followed today.
[79] See p. 62.
[80] But see *Candlewood Navigation* v. *Mitsui O.S.K. Lines* [1986] A.C. 1 (P.C.); *Leigh & Sillivan* v. *Aliakmon Shipping Co.* [1986] A.C. 785 (H.L.).
[81] See *Wayne Tank Co.* v. *Employers' Liability Ltd.* [1974] Q.B. 57 (C.A.); see also p. 194.

bring a claim against the Contractor under clause 20, but the Contractor (depending on its terms) will also be entitled to rely on the policy, so that the Insurer's right of subrogation will effectively disappear.[82] Insurance in the Employer's name is strictly unnecessary, because where the Contractor only is insured, the Employer has a statutory right to proceed against the Insurer in the event of the Contractor's insolvency.[83]

Clause 21(2). *". . . insurance . . . shall cover the Employer and Contractor against all loss or damage from whatsoever cause arising other than the Excepted Risks . . ."*
Note that the words "from whatsoever cause arising" have been reinserted in this clause, to ensure that the insurance cover is at least as wide as the liability provided under clause 20 (see commentary to clause 20(3)(a) above). Design provided by the Contractor pursuant to his obligations under the Contract is not within the excepted risks (see clause 20(2)(b)). The Contractor is therefore fully liable for any resulting loss or damage under clause 20, and should be covered by insurance under clause 21, without the need to prove negligence.[84] There is, however, a serious lacuna arising from the excepted risks. The potential liability of the Engineer for design fault will not normally extend beyond negligence[85] so that the Employer will have no cover against loss due to design fault which does not amount to negligence.

DAMAGE AND INSURANCE

Damage to persons and property

22 (1) The Contractor shall except if and so far as the Contract provides otherwise and subject to the exceptions set out in sub-clause (2) of this clause indemnify and keep indemnified the Employer against all losses and claims in respect of

(a) death of or injury to any person or
(b) loss of or damage to any property (other than the Works)

which may arise out of or in consequence of the execution of the Works and the remedying of any defects therein and against all claims demands proceedings damages costs charges and expenses whatsoever in respect thereof or in relation thereto.

Exceptions

(2) The exceptions referred to in sub-clause (1) of this clause which are the responsibility of the Employer are

(a) damage to crops being on the Site (save in so far as possession has not been given to the Contractor)

---

[82] See *Petrofina* v. *Magnaload* [1984] Q.B. 127.
[83] Third Parties (Rights against Insurers) Act 1930 and see *M/S Aswan Engineering* v. *Iron Trades Mutual Insurance* [1989] 1 Lloyds Rep. 289.
[84] See commentary to clause 8(2).
[85] See *Greaves Contractors* v. *Baynham Meikle* [1975] 1 W.L.R. 1095 (C.A.); *Manufacturers' Mutual Insurance* v. *Queensland Government Railway* [1969] 1 Lloyd's Rep. 214; see also *Wimpey* v. *Poole* [1984] 2 Lloyds Rep. 499.

(b) the use or occupation of land (provided by the Employer) by the Works or any part thereof or for the purpose of executing and maintaining the Works (including consequent losses of crops) or interference whether temporary or permanent with any right of way light air or water or other easement or quasi-easement which are the unavoidable result of the construction of the Works in accordance with the Contract
(c) the right of the Employer to construct the Works or any part thereof on over under in or through any land
(d) damage which is the unavoidable result of the construction of the Works in accordance with the Contract and
(e) death of or injury to persons or loss of or damage to property resulting from any act neglect or breach of statutory duty done or committed by the Employer his agents servants or other Contractors (not being employed by the Contractor) or for or in respect of any claims demands proceedings damages costs charges and expenses in respect thereof or in relation thereto.

Indemnity by Employer

(3) The Employer shall subject to sub-clause (4) of this clause indemnify the Contractor against all claims demands proceedings damages costs charges and expenses in respect of the matters referred to in the exceptions defined in sub-clause (2) of this clause.

Shared responsibility

(4) (a) The Contractor's liability to indemnify the Employer under sub-clause (1) of this clause shall be reduced in proportion to the extent that the act or neglect of the Employer his agents servants or other contractors (not being employed by the Contractor) may have contributed to the said death injury loss or damage.
(b) The Employer's liability to indemnify the Contractor under sub-clause (3) of this clause in respect of matters referred to in sub-clause (2)(e) of this clause shall be reduced in proportion to the extent that the act or neglect of the Contractor or his sub-contractors servants or agents may have contributed to the said death injury loss or damage.

Third party insurance

23 (1) The Contractor shall without limiting his or the Employer's obligations and responsibilities under clause 22 insure in the joint names of the Contractor and the Employer against liabilities for death of or injury to any person (other than any operative or other person in the employment of the Contractor or any of his sub-contractors) or loss of or damage to any property (other than the Works) arising out of the execution of the Contract other than the exceptions defined in clause 22(2)(a)(b)(c) and (d).

Cross liability clause

(2) The insurance policy shall include a cross liability clause such that the insurance shall apply to the Contractor and to the Employer as separate insured.

Amount of insurance

(3) Such insurance shall be for at least the amount stated in the Appendix to the Form of Tender.

Clauses 22 and 23

These clauses divide and apportion responsibility between the Contractor and the Employer for damage other than to the Works, etc. and provide for corresponding insurance. Clause 22 is the main indemnity clause of the Contract. Other indemnities which may overlap with this clause are contained in clauses 24 (Accident or Injury to Work People), 26(3) (Contractor to conform with statutes), 27(7) (Compliance with Public Utilities, etc., Act), 28(1) (Interference with Traffic, etc.), 28(2) (noise, disturbance and pollution) and 30(2) and (3) (claims arising from transport).

Clause 22(1)(b).   "... *loss of or damage to any property (other than the Works)* ..."
The Contractor's materials, plant and equipment are within the indemnity, which therefore duplicates the wider responsibility (and insurance) provided for in clauses 20 and 21.

Clause 22(1).   "... *which may arise out of or in consequence of the execution of the Works* ..."
Note that the indemnity is much narrower than the obligations in regard to the Works, etc., which cover "any loss or damage."[86] Equivalent words in the fourth edition were held not to permit the Employer to recover costs incurred in defending a third party claim for injury allegedly caused by the Works, but held not to be.[87]

Clause 22(2)(e): Liability for injury to persons or property resulting from neglect or breach of the statutory duty.   This exception to the Contractor's indemnity applies to neglect or breach "by the Employer, his agents, servants or other Contractors (not being employed by the Contractor)." Sub-clause (3) requires the Employer to indemnify the Contractor in regard to such matters, but sub-clause (4)(b) provides a limit to the Employer's liability, where the act or neglect of the Contractor, his Sub-Contractors, servants or agents may have contributed to the loss or damage. It is difficult to see any application for this latter restriction, since the original exception applies only to the act, neglect or breach of the Employer.

Clause 22(4)(a).   "*The Contractor's liability ... shall be reduced in proportion* ..."
Such words are necessary to preserve the right to indemnity, where the party claiming indemnity has been negligent.[88] The corresponding provision covering the Employer's liability is limited to the matter in sub-clause 2(e) (see above).

Clause 23(1): Insurance required.   Note that insurance is now required in joint names and with a cross liability clause (clause 23(2)). The cover excludes

---

[86] See commentary to clauses 20(3) and 21(2).
[87] *Richardson* v. *Buckinghamshire C.C.* (1971) 6 B.L.R. 58 (C.A.).
[88] *A.M.F. International* v. *Magnet Bowling* [1968] 1 W.L.R. 1028.

the matters set out in clause 22(2)(a), (b), (c) and (d), but includes (e). The risk to be insured is defined as that "arising out of the execution of the Contract", in contrast to the wider words (including "in consequence of") appearing in clause 22(1). It is not clear why there is a change in the wording. The Contractor may, of course, take out any insurance he wishes to, and the parties would be well advised to ensure that the relevant wording of the liability and insurance cover coincide. The period during which the policy is to be in force is not stated. The reference to "the execution of the contract" suggests that the policy should extend at least during the Defects Correction Period. Clause 22(1), however, includes "the remedying of any defects" in the Works, which might extend further. It is plainly in the interests of the parties to ensure that adequate insurance is available whenever there are third party risks.

Accident or injury to workpeople

24   The Employer shall not be liable for or in respect of any damages or compensation payable at law in respect or in consequence of any accident or injury to any operative or other person in the employment of the Contractor or any of his sub-contractors save and except to the extent that such accident or injury results from or is contributed to by any act or default of the Employer his agents or servants and the Contractor shall indemnify and keep indemnified the Employer against all such damages and compensation (save and except as aforesaid) and against all claims demands proceedings costs charges and expenses whatsoever in respect thereof or in relation thereto.

Clause 24

This provision should be read with clause 22. It does not affect the right of any workmen or other person employed by the Contractor or a sub-contractor to bring proceedings against the Employer, for example, under the Occupiers Liability Act 1957.[89] In the event of the Employer being found liable, he is entitled to indemnity from the Contractor except to the extent of the Employer's default. Such apportionment of liability is necessary to preserve the right to indemnity where the Employer has been negligent.[90] The clause makes no requirement for insurance, but the Contractor is obliged by statute[91] to insure against injury to employees arising out of the course of their employment.

Evidence and terms of insurance

25   (1)   The Contractor shall provide satisfactory evidence to the Employer prior to the Works Commencement Date that the insurances required under the Contract have been effected and shall if so required produce the insurance policies for inspection. The

---

[89] See also Occupiers' Liability Act 1984.
[90] *A.M.F. International* v. *Magnet Bowling* [1968] 1 W.L.R. 1028.
[91] Employers' Liability (Compulsory Insurance) Act 1969.

terms of all such insurances shall be subject to the approval of the Employer (which approval shall not unreasonably be withheld). The Contractor shall upon request produce to the Employer receipts for the payment of current insurance premiums.

Excesses

(2)   Any excesses on the policies of insurance effected under clauses 21 and 23 shall be as stated by the Contractor in the Appendix to the Form of Tender.

Remedy on Contractor's failure to insure

(3)   If the Contractor shall fail upon request to produce to the Employer satisfactory evidence that there is in force any of the insurances required under the Contract then and in any such case the Employer may effect and keep in force any such insurance and pay such premium or premiums as may be necessary for that purpose and from time to time deduct the amount so paid from any monies due or which may become due to the Contractor or recover the same as a debt due from the Contractor.

Compliance with policy conditions

(4)   Both the Employer and the Contractor shall comply with all conditions laid down in the insurance policies. In the event that the Contractor or the Employer fails to comply with any condition imposed by the insurance policies effected pursuant to the Contract each shall indemnify the other against all losses and claims arising from such failure.

Clause 25

Clause 25(3).   *". . . the Employer may effect . . . any such insurance . . ."*
    The Employer has no authority to insure in the Contractor's name, or in joint names, and must effect the necessary insurance in his own name. In any such case, the Insurer would be entitled to exercise his right of subrogation, where the Contractor is prima facie liable for the loss under the Contract. It is plainly in the Contractor's interest to ensure that all joint name policies are effected.

GIVING OF NOTICES AND PAYMENT OF FEES

Giving of notices and payment of fees

26 (1)   The Contractor shall save as provided in clause 27 give all notices and pay all fees required to be given or paid by any Act of Parliament or any Regulation or Bye-law of any local or other statutory authority in relation to the construction and completion of the Works and by the rules and regulations of all public bodies and companies whose property or rights are or may be affected in any way by the Works.

Repayment by Employer

(2)   The Employer shall repay or allow to the Contractor all such sums as the

Engineer shall certify to have been properly payable and paid by the Contractor in respect of such fees and also all rates and taxes paid by the Contractor in respect of the Site or any part thereof or anything constructed or erected thereon or on any part thereof or any temporary structures situated elsewhere but used exclusively for the purposes of the Works or any structures used temporarily and exclusively for the purposes of the Works.

Contractor to conform with Statutes etc.

(3)   The Contractor shall ascertain and conform in all respects with the provisions of any general or local Act of Parliament and the Regulations and Bye-laws of any local or other statutory authority which may be applicable to the Works and with such rules and regulations of public bodies and companies as aforesaid and shall keep the Employer indemnified against all penalties and liability of every kind for breach of any such Act Regulation or Bye-law. Provided always that

> (a)   the Contractor shall not be required to indemnify the Employer against the consequences of any such breach which is the unavoidable result of complying with the Contract or instructions of the Engineer
> (b)   if the Contract or instructions of the Engineer shall at any time be found not to be in conformity with any such Act Regulation or Bye-law the Engineer shall issue such instructions including the ordering of a variation under clause 51 as may be necessary to ensure conformity with such Act Regulation or Bye-law and
> (c)   the Contractor shall not be responsible for obtaining any planning permission which may be necessary in respect of the Permanent Works or any Temporary Works design supplied by the Engineer and the Employer hereby warrants that all the said permissions have been or will in due time be obtained.

Clause 26

Construction works are subject to many important statutory controls, and the consequences of non-compliance can be serious. This clause deals with the important question of liability for non-compliance. By sub-clause (3), the Contractor is made generally responsible for compliance subject to some important limitations. The question of liability in tort for non-compliance with statutes in relation to construction works has been the subject of considerable judicial activity over the past two decades. For the present position see page 374.

Clause 26(1).   "... *give all notices ... required to be given* ..."
The Contractor's obligation under this clause will not be limited to notices required under the relevant statute to be given by a Contractor or other person carrying out the physical work. The principal notices to which this clause will apply are those required by the Building Regulations 1985.[92] While the initial application under the Regulations for approval is termed a Notice, it is thought the clear intention of this sub-clause is to require the Contractor to

---

[92] Note that the Regulations now apply with very limited exceptions throughout the whole of England and Wales, including Inner London. See generally Chap. 15, Section 4.

give only those Notices in the nature of "notification" rather than "application." Under the London Building Acts, notices are also required to be served on adjoining owners at prescribed times before commencement of work.[93] Such notices are in practice normally served by the Employer or his Engineer or Surveyor. But the Contractor's obligation under this sub-clause must include such notices.

Clause 26(2). *". . . any structures used temporarily and exclusively for the purposes of the Works."*

The Employer is to repay rates and taxes for these structures, which need not be on the site. The ordinary meaning of "structure" is very wide, and is apt to include any building.[94] It is thought that use "for the purposes of the Works" would limit such structures or buildings to those used for physical operations rather than, for example, the Contractor's offices. But this is by no means clear.

Clause 26(3)(a). *"Provided . . . the Contractor shall not be required to indemnify the Employer against . . . the unavoidable result of complying with the Contract or instructions of the Engineer"*

This is the principal limitation on the Contractor's blanket obligation to comply with statutes and to indemnify the Employer. Note that the Contractor is absolved only from indemnifying the Employer. He remains liable to comply with the statute, subject to the effect of paragraph (b) (see below). The proviso will apply only where the Contractor has no choice regarding the nature of the work, so that the result becomes "unavoidable." When a breach arises from the method of working, the Contractor will not normally be confined to a particular method, unless through instructions of the Engineer.[95]

Clause 26(3)(b). *"Provided . . . if the Contract or instructions of the Engineer shall at any time be found not to be in conformity . . ."*

The Contractor is under an obligation, under sub-clause (3), to "ascertain" as well as to conform with the provisions of any applicable statutes. Consequently, it is thought that this proviso does not limit the Contractor's obligation, but rather the obligation of the Engineer to issue instructions.[96] The effect, it is submitted, is that the Contractor is entitled to payment only for work carried out, and varied as necessary, to achieve conformity with applicable statutes, and not to payment for work carried out in breach of statute, nor to the costs of demolition.[97]

---

[93] See London Building Acts (Amendment) Act 1939, Pt. VI.

[94] *Almond* v. *Birmingham Royal Institution for the Blind* [1968] A.C. 37 at 51 (H.L.).

[95] But see commentary to clauses 8(3) and 14(6), (7).

[96] Otherwise, the obligation to supply necessary instructions under clause 7(1) would prevail.

[97] Consider *Townsends (Builders) Ltd.* v. *Cinema News* [1959] 1 W.L.R. 119 (C.A.), and now fully reported at 20 B.L.R. 118; see also p. 87.

Clause 26(3)(c). *". . . the Employer hereby warrants . . ."*

Breach of such warranty will entitle the Contractor to damages including any loss or expense incurred by delay waiting for necessary planning permission. If planning permission is not obtained at all, the Contractor will generally be entitled to be paid the price of the work carried out.[98] Note that work done without planning consent is not *per se* unlawful, even though it may be the subject of enforcement proceedings.

PUBLIC UTILITIES STREET WORKS ACT 1950

Public Utilities Street Works Act 1950—definitions

27 (1) For the purposes of this clause

(a) the expression "the Act" shall mean and include the Public Utilities Street Works Act 1950 and any statutory modification or re-enactment thereof for the time being in force and

(b) all other expressions common to the Act and to this clause shall have the same meaning as those assigned to them by the Act.

Notifications by Employer to Contractor

(2) (a) The Employer shall before the commencement of the Works notify the Contractor in writing

(i) whether the Works or any parts thereof (and if so which parts) are Emergency Works and

(ii) which (if any) parts of the Works are to be carried out in Controlled Land or in a Prospectively Maintainable Highway.

(b) If any duly authorized variation of the Works shall involve the execution thereof in a Street or in Controlled Land or in a Prospectively Maintainable Highway or are Emergency Works the Employer shall notify the Contractor in writing accordingly at the time such variation is ordered.

Service of notices by Employer

(3) The Employer shall (subject to the obligations of the Contractor under sub-clause (4) of this clause) serve all such notices as may from time to time whether before or during the course of or after completion of the Works be required to be served under the Act.

Notices by Contractor to Employer

(4) The Contractor shall in relation to any part of the Works (other than Emergency Works) and subject to the compliance by the Employer with sub-clause (2) of this clause give not less that 21 days notice in writing to the Employer before

(a) commencing any part of the Works in a Street (as defined in Sections 1(3) and 38(1) of the Act) or

---

[98] See *Strongman (1945)* v. *Sincock* [1955] 2 Q.B. 525 (C.A.).

(b) commencing any part of the Works in Controlled Land or in a Prospectively Maintainable Highway or

(c) commencing in a Street or in Controlled Land or in a Prospectively Maintainable Highway any part of the Works which is likely to affect the apparatus of any Owning Undertaker (within the meaning of Section 26 of the Act).

Such notice shall state the date on which and the place at which the Contractor intends to commence the execution of the work referred to therein.

Failure to commence Street Works

(5) If the Contractor having given any such notice as is required by sub-clause (4) of this clause shall not commence the part of the Works to which such notice relates within 2 months after the date when such notice is given such notice shall be treated as invalid and compliance with the said sub-clause (4) shall be requisite as if such notice had not been given.

Delays attributable to variations

(6) In the event of such a variation of the Works as is referred to in sub-clause (2)(b) of this clause being ordered by or on behalf of the Employer and resulting in delay in the construction and completion of the Works by reason of the necessity of compliance by the Contractor with sub-clause (4) of this clause the Engineer shall in addition to valuing the variation under clause 52 take such delay into account in determining any extension of time to which the Contractor is entitled under clause 44 and the Contractor shall subject to clause 52(4) be paid in accordance with clause 60 such additional cost as the Engineer shall consider to have been reasonably attributable to such delay.

Contractor to comply with other obligations of Act

(7) Except as otherwise provided by this clause where in relation to the carrying out of the Works the Act imposes any requirements or obligations upon the Employer the Contractor shall comply with such requirements and obligations and shall indemnify the Employer against any liability which the Employer may incur in consequence of any failure to comply with the said requirements and obligations.

Clause 27: Public Utilities Street Works Act 1950

Part I of the Act creates a statutory code (Street Works Code) to regulate works carried out by statutory undertakers affecting highways. The purpose of the Act is to protect authorities affected by such works, and to enable certain works to be carried out on land abutting a highway (Controlled Land) instead of in the highway. Part II of the Act creates a code for the protection of statutory undertakers where works are carried out by an interested authority; and Part III provides for statutory undertakers' work which affects the apparatus of another undertaker (the owning undertaker).

The operation of the Act has given rise to much criticism in recent years, particularly from road users. A comprehensive review of the working of the Act was carried out for the Department of Transport by Professor M. R. Horne and published in 1985. It is reported (1990) that the Government intends to provide Parliamentary time for a new Bill, which is likely to require complete replacement of the present clause.

Clause 27(3). *"The Employer shall . . . serve all such notices . . ."*

The principal notices required to be served (subject to certain exceptions) by statutory undertakers are (i) 7 days' notice to the relevant authority prior to the start of works to which the Street Works Code relates; (ii) 3 days' notice to any other undertaker whose apparatus is likely to be affected by the proposed work; (iii) for emergency works, notices as soon as reasonably practicable, which may be given after start of the work.

Notice given under (i) above lapses if the work has not been substantially begun within 2 months, but by sub-clause (5), the Contractor's notice to the Employer will also have lapsed, so that the Employer is protected against a statutory breach by the Contractor.

Clause 27(7): Contractor to indemnify the Employer. See clauses 22 and 26(3) for other related indemnity provisions. The requirements or obligations placed upon the Employer by the Act and which, by sub-clause (7), devolve upon the Contractor may be very wide in their application. They include the obligation to make payments to undertakers who are required to move their apparatus or to authorities who elect to execute certain works to their own undertakings.[99]

PATENT RIGHTS

Patent Rights

28 (1) The Contractor shall save harmless and indemnify the Employer from and against all claims and proceedings for or on account of infringement of any patent right design trademark or name or other protected right in respect of any

    (a) Contractor's Equipment used for or in connection with the Works
    (b) materials plant and equipment for incorporation in the Works

and from and against all claims demands proceedings damages costs charges and expenses whatsoever in respect thereof or in relation thereto except where such infringement results from compliance with the design or Specification provided other than by the Contractor. In the latter event the Employer shall indemnify the Contractor from and against all claims and proceedings for or on account of infringement of any patent right design trademark or name or other protected right aforesaid.

Royalties

(2) Except where otherwise stated the Contractor shall pay all tonnage and other royalties rent and other payments or compensation (if any) for getting stone sand clay or other materials required for the Works.

---

[99] Public Utilities Street Works Act 1950, ss.10, 12, 22.

Clause 28

This clause deals with the increasingly important area of law compendiously known as "intellectual property" rights. Sub-clause (1) contains no provision for apportionment of liability[1] because the relevant design of equipment or plant will be provided by the Employer or the Contractor alone.

INTERFERENCE WITH TRAFFIC AND ADJOINING PROPERTIES

Interference with traffic and adjoining properties

29   (1)   All operations necessary for the construction and completion of the Works shall so far as compliance with the requirements of the Contract permits be carried on so as not to interfere unnecessarily or improperly with

(a)   the convenience of the public, or

(b)   the access to public or private roads footpaths or properties whether in the possession of the Employer or of any other person and with the use or occupation thereof.

The Contractor shall save harmless and indemnify the Employer in respect of all claims demands proceedings damages costs charges and expenses whatsoever arising out of or in relation to any such matters.

Noise disturbance and pollution

(2)   All work shall be carried out without unreasonable noise or disturbance or other pollution.

Indemnity by Contractor

(3)   To the extent that noise disturbance or other pollution is not the unavoidable consequence of constructing and completing the Works or performing the Contract the Contractor shall indemnify the Employer from and against any liability for damages on that account and against all claims demands proceedings damages costs charges and expenses whatsoever in regard or in relation to such liability.

Indemnity by Employer

(4)   The Employer shall indemnify the Contractor from and against any liability for damages on account of noise disturbance or other pollution which is the unavoidable consequence of carrying out the Works and from and against all claims demands proceedings damages costs charges and expenses whatsoever in regard or in relation to such liability.

Clause 29

Clause 29(1): Duty not to interfere with traffic.   The obligation to avoid inconvenience or interference with access is qualified by the words "unneces-

---

[1] See commentary to clause 22 above.

sarily" and "so far as compliance with the requirements of the Contract permits." No such qualifications are expressed in the indemnity which follows. It is thought that the words "whatsoever arising out of or in relation to" mean that the matters which are the subject of the indemnity cannot be limited by the qualifications referred to. However, the sub-clause must be read with and subject to clause 22, particularly the exceptions in sub-clause (2) and the Employer's Indemnity in sub-clause (3) of clause 22.

Clause 29(2) to (4): Noise and pollution. The scheme of cross-indemnity, depending upon whether the matter is an unavoidable consequence of performing the Contract, follows the scheme set out in clause 22.[2] Noise on construction sites may be the subject of action in nuisance by an aggrieved individual.[3] Noise is also subject to statutory control by a local authority under the Control of Pollution Act 1974.[4] This Act also contains provision for obtaining prior consent to particular methods of work, which may be subject to conditions.[5]

AVOIDANCE OF DAMAGE TO HIGHWAYS ETC.

Avoidance of damage to highways etc.

30 (1) The Contractor shall use every reasonable means to prevent any of the highways or bridges communicating with or on the routes to the Site from being subjected to extraordinary traffic within the meaning of the Highways Act 1980 or in Scotland the Roads (Scotland) Act 1984 or any statutory modification or re-enactment thereof by any traffic of the Contractor or any of his sub-contractors and in particular shall select routes and use vehicles and restrict and distribute loads so that any such extraordinary traffic as will inevitably arise from the moving of Contractor's Equipment and materials or manufactured or fabricated articles from and to the Site shall be limited as far as reasonably possible and so that no unnecessary damage or injury may be occasioned to such highways and bridges.

Transport of Contractor's Equipment

(2) Save insofar as the Contract otherwise provides the Contractor shall be responsible for and shall pay the cost of strengthening any bridges or altering or improving any highway communicating with the Site to facilitate the movement of Contractor's Equipment or Temporary Works required in the execution of the Works and the Contractor shall indemnify and keep indemnified the Employer against all claims for damage to any highway or bridge communicating with the Site caused by such movement including such claims as may be made by any competent authority directly against the Employer pursuant to any Act of Parliament or other Statutory Instrument and shall negotiate and pay all claims arising solely out of such damage.

---

[2] See clause 22(2)(d) and (3).
[3] See p. 365.
[4] ss.60 and 61: see also *City of London* v. *Bovis Construction Ltd.* (1988) 49 B.L.R. 1 (C.A.). See generally Chap. 15, Section 2.
[5] s.61.

Transport of materials

(3)   If notwithstanding sub-clause (1) of this clause any damage shall occur to any bridge or highway communicating with the Site arising from the transport of materials or manufactured or fabricated articles in the execution of the Works the Contractor shall notify the Engineer as soon as he becomes aware of such damage or as soon as he receives any claim from the authority entitled to make such claim.

Where under any Act of Parliament or other Statutory Instrument the haulier of such materials or manufactured or fabricated articles is required to indemnify the highway authority against damage the Employer shall not be liable for any costs charges or expenses in respect thereof or in relation thereto.

In other cases the Employer shall negotiate the settlement of and pay all sums due in respect of such claim and shall indemnify the Contractor in respect thereof and in respect of all claims demands proceedings damages costs charges and expenses in relation thereto. Provided always that if and so far as any such claim or part thereof shall in the opinion of the Engineer be due to any failure on the part of the Contractor to observe and perform his obligations under sub-clause (1) of this clause then the amount certified by the Engineer to be due to such failure shall be paid by the Contractor to the Employer or deducted from any sum due or which may become due to the Contractor.

Clause 30

Clause 30(1).   *"... extraordinary traffic ..."*
The Highways Act 1980 provides, by section 59, for recovery by the Highway Authority from any person "by or in consequence of whose order the traffic has been conducted" of the excess maintenance expenses arising from "excessive weight passing along the highway or other extraordinary traffic thereon." These latter terms are not defined in the Act, but are subject to much case law.[6] It is not apparent why sub-section (1) limits the Contractor's obligation of using "every reasonable means" to the avoidance of "extraordinary traffic" only, but the obligation is probably sufficiently wide to impose a general duty to prevent avoidable damage.

Clause 30(2) and (3).   The scheme of these sub-clauses is to require the Contractor, subject to sub-clause (1), to accept responsibility only for damage caused by transport of "Contractor's Equipment or Temporary Works"; and to place the corresponding liability for transport of "materials or manufactured or fabricated articles" upon the Employer, subject to possible liability of the haulier. Where claims arise, the Act makes provision for determination of liability by arbitration, or the appropriate County Court.[7]

FACILITIES FOR OTHER CONTRACTORS

Facilities for other contractors

31   (1)   The Contractor shall in accordance with the requirements of the Engineer or

---

[6] See *Hill* v. *Thomas* [1893] 2 Q.B. 333 (C.A.) and 20 *Halsbury* (4th ed.), p. 207.
[7] Highways Act 1980, s.59(3) and (4).

Engineer's Representative afford all reasonable facilities for any other Contractors employed by the Employer and their workmen and for the workmen of the Employer and of any other properly authorised authorities or statutory bodies who may be employed in the execution on or near the Site of any work not in the Contract or of any contract which the Employer may enter into in connection with or ancillary to the Works.

Delay and extra cost

(2)   If compliance with sub-clause (1) of this clause shall involve the Contractor in delay or cost beyond that reasonably to be foreseen by an experienced contractor at the time of tender then the Engineer shall take such delay into account in determining any extension of time to which the Contractor is entitled under clause 44 and the Contractor shall subject to clause 52(4) be paid in accordance with clause 60 the amount of such cost as may be reasonable. Profit shall be added thereto in respect of any additional permanent or temporary work.

Clause 31

Clause 31(1).   "*. . . afford all reasonable facilities . . .*"
  This obligation upon the Contractor does not, it is thought, displace the Employer's obligation under clause 42(2)(a), to give the Contractor possession of so much of the site "as may be required to enable the Contractor to commence and proceed with the construction of the Works."[8] Accordingly, if the other Contractors, etc., interfere with the Contractor's ability to proceed, a claim for compensation will be available under clause 42(3), as an alternative to the claim provided under sub-clause (2). A claim under clause 31(2) is limited to cost which was not reasonably foreseeable,[9] while a claim under 42 is not so limited.

FOSSILS ETC. AND CLEARANCE OF SITE

Fossils etc.

32   All fossils coins articles of value or antiquity and structures or other remains or things of geological or archaeological interest discovered on the Site shall as between the Employer and the Contractor be deemed to be the absolute property of the Employer and the Contractor shall take reasonable precautions to prevent his workmen or any other persons from removing or damaging any such article or thing and shall immediately upon discovery thereof and before removal acquaint the Engineer of such discovery and carry out at the expense of the Employer the Engineer's orders as to the disposal of the same.

Clearance of Site on completion

33   On the completion of the Works the Contractor shall clear away and remove from the

---

[8] See also clause 41(2), where the Contractor is to proceed "with due expedition and without delay."
[9] See also clause 13(3).

Site all Contractor's Equipment surplus material rubbish and Temporary Works of every kind and leave the whole of the Site and Permanent Works clean and in a workmanlike condition to the satisfaction of the Engineer.

Clause 34 (not used)

This clause formerly contained an obligation to comply with the fair wages resolution, which has now been repealed.

RETURNS OF LABOUR AND CONTRACTOR'S EQUIPMENT

Returns of labour and Contractor's Equipment

35 The Contractor shall if required by the Engineer deliver to the Engineer or the Engineer's Representative a return in such form and at such intervals as the Engineer may prescribe showing in detail the numbers of the several classes of labour from time to time employed by the Contractor on the Site and such information respecting Contractor's Equipment as the Engineer may require. The Contractor shall require his sub-contractors to observe the provisions of this clause.

WORKMANSHIP AND MATERIALS

Quality of materials and workmanship and tests

36 (1) All materials and workmanship shall be of the respective kinds described in the Contract and in accordance with the Engineer's instructions and shall be subjected from time to time to such tests as the Engineer may direct at the place of manufacture or fabrication or on the Site or such other place or places as may be specified in the Contract. The Contractor shall provide such assistance instruments machines labour and materials as are normally required for examining measuring and testing any work and the quality weight or quantity of any materials used and shall supply samples of materials before incorporation in the Works for testing as may be selected and required by the Engineer.

Cost of samples

(2) All samples shall be supplied by the Contractor at his own cost if the supply thereof is clearly intended by or provided for in the Contract but if not then at the cost of the Employer.

Cost of tests

(3) The cost of making any test shall be borne by the Contractor if such test is clearly intended by or provided for in the Contract and (in the cases only of a test under load or of a test to ascertain whether the design of any finished or partially finished work is appropriate for the purposes which it was intended to fulfil) is particularized in the Specification or Bill of Quantities in sufficient detail to enable the Contractor to have priced or allowed for the same in his Tender. If any test is ordered by the Engineer which is either

    (a) not so intended by or provided for or
    (b) (in the cases above mentioned) is not so particularized

863

then the cost of such test shall be borne by the Contractor if the test shows the workmanship or materials not to be in accordance with the provisions of the Contract or the Engineer's instructions but otherwise by the Employer.

Clause 36

Clause 36(1). *"... shall be of the respective kinds described in the Contract and in accordance with the Engineer's instructions ..."*

The Engineer has no general authority to give instructions regarding the quality of materials or workmanship. The Contractor's obligation is to comply with the descriptions contained in the Contract, and with the Engineer's instruction or direction thereon only where specific provision is made to this effect in the Contract. An instruction which makes requirements outside these limits would take effect, it is thought, under clause 13(1), giving rise to a claim for additional payment under clause 13(3).

Clause 36(3): Cost of tests. The apparently simple scheme set out does not always operate easily in practice. Consider the position where the Engineer entertains a reasonable suspicion about the quality of certain materials or work and orders tests which show defects in some cases but not in others. Should the Employer pay the cost of those tests which do not reveal defects? The same problem arises under clause 38(2) in relation to uncovering work, and clause 50 in relation to tests or trials to determine the cause of any defect. Under the present clause, it is submitted that where the Engineer orders a series of investigations, if they are sufficiently closely related, they may be regarded as one test for the purpose of determining whether or not they show "the workmanship or materials not to be in accordance with the provisions of the Contract or the Engineer's instruction." Where such a procedure is repeated, to widen the area of tests, it would be a matter of fact and degree to determine which tests should be paid for by whom, assuming that some tests revealed defects and others did not.

ACCESS TO SITE AND EXAMINATION OF WORK

Access to Site

37　The Engineer and any person authorized by him shall at all times have access to the Works and to the Site and to all workshops and places where work is being prepared or whence materials manufactured articles and machinery are being obtained for the Works and the Contractor shall afford every facility for and every assistance in obtaining such access or the right to such access.

Examination of work before covering up

38　(1)　No work shall be covered up or put out of view without the consent of the Engineer and the Contractor shall afford full opportunity for the Engineer to examine and measure any work which is about to be covered up or put out of view and to examine foundations before permanent work is placed thereon. The Contractor shall give due notice to the Engineer whenever any such work or foundations is or are ready or about to be ready for examination and the Engineer shall without unreasonable delay unless he considers it unnecessary and advises the Contractor accordingly attend for the purpose of examining and measuring such work or of examining such foundations.

Uncovering and making openings

(2)   The Contractor shall uncover any part or parts of the Works or make openings in or through the same as the Engineer may from time to time direct and shall reinstate and make good such part or parts to the satisfaction of the Engineer. If any such part or parts have been covered up or put out of view after compliance with the requirements of sub-clause (1) of this clause and are found to be executed in accordance with the Contract the cost of uncovering making openings in or through reinstating and making good the same shall be borne by the Employer but in any other case all such cost shall be borne by the Contractor.

Clause 38

Clause 38(1): Examination.   A necessary distinction is drawn between examination and measurement. In regard to the former, the Contractor must give "due notice" to the Engineer when work or foundations are ready, and afford full opportunity for examination. The work must not be covered up without consent. It is thought that consent would be implied from the Engineer's failure to examine within a reasonable time after notice. The sanction against the Contractor's failure to comply with the sub-clause is uncovering under sub-clause (2) at the Contractor's cost.

Clause 38(1): Measurement.   These provisions must be read with clause 56. The Engineer must give reasonable notice to the Contractor under clause 56(3) when he requires to measure any part of the work. Under clause 38(1), upon the Contractor giving notice that "any such work" (*i.e.* work which is about to be covered up) is ready for examination, the Engineer is bound (unless he considers it unnecessary) to attend for measurement. It is not thought that the Engineer could exercise his right to measure under clause 56(3) after the Works have been properly covered up.

Clause 38(2): Cost of making openings.   See commentary to clause 36(3). The same problem may arise in relation to making openings. It is thought that the wording of this sub-clause lends itself more readily to the conclusion suggested, namely that a series of openings could be regarded as a single operation for the purpose of determining who should bear the cost.

REMOVAL OF UNSATISFACTORY WORK AND MATERIALS

Removal of unsatisfactory work and materials

39   (1)   The Engineer shall during the progress of the Works have power to instruct in writing the

(a) removal from the Site within such time or times specified in the instruction of any materials which in the opinion of the Engineer are not in accordance with the Contract
(b) substitution with materials in accordance with the Contract and
(c) removal and proper re-execution notwithstanding any previous test thereof or interim payment therefor of any work which in respect of
    (i) material or workmanship or
    (ii) design by the Contractor or for which he is responsible
is not in the opinion of the Engineer in accordance with the Contract.

Default of Contractor in compliance

(2) In case of default on the part of the Contractor in carrying out such instruction the Employer shall be entitled to employ and pay other persons to carry out the same and all costs consequent thereon or incidental thereto as determined by the Engineer shall be recoverable from the Contractor by the Employer and may be deducted by the Employer from any monies due or to become due to him and the Engineer shall notify the Contractor accordingly with a copy to the Employer.

Failure to disapprove

(3) Failure of the Engineer or any person acting under him pursuant to clause 2 to disapprove any work or materials shall not prejudice the power of the Engineer or any such person subsequently to take action under this clause.

Clause 39

Clause 39(1). "... *during the progress of the Works* ..."
The expression is not defined, but it plainly refers to the period from commencement to the Completion Certificate.[10] Clause 49 contains parallel provisions to be operated during the Defects Correction Period.

Clause 39(1): Removal, substitution and re-execution. An express power is needed for the removal of non-conforming work. Withholding payment may not be effective and, on the assumption that defective work gives rise to an immediate legal right,[11] the Employer could otherwise enforce it only by stopping the work. The power to order substitution or re-execution is strictly unnecessary, in view of the Contractor's overriding obligation to complete the Contract.[12] The power to order substitution or re-execution should be exercised sparingly, since an incautiously drafted instruction might be alleged to constitute a variation.[13] If sub-clause (1)(c) is to be read as requiring the

---

[10] See also clauses 7(1), 40(1) and 46(1). Note also that clause 62 uses the expression "during the execution of the Works", which appears to have the same meaning.
[11] See *Kaye* v. *Hosier & Dickinson* [1972] 1 W.L.R. 146 at 157 (H.L.); *cf. Lintest Builders* v. *Roberts* (1980) 13 B.L.R. 38 (C.A.).
[12] The power has traditionally been omitted from the JCT Standard Form of Building Contract for the reason given.
[13] See *Simplex Concrete Piles* v. *St. Pancras B.C.* (1958) 14 B.L.R. 80; but see clause 51(3).

instruction to specify re-execution, the Engineer is entitled to order "re-execution in accordance with the Contract."

Clause 39(1)(c)(ii). *"... design by the Contractor or for which he is responsible is not ... in accordance with the Contract."*

This raises the question of the level of the Contractor's design responsibility. The Contract is neither clear nor consistent whether such responsibility is limited to taking reasonable care or achieving fitness for purpose (see notes to clause 8(2) and 20(3) above and 58(3) below). If the Engineer came to the conclusion that part of the work where the design was the Contractor's responsibility was unfit for purpose, it would be necessary to give a carefully worded instruction which would protect the Employer if the Contractor were found to be liable (and protect the Contractor if he were not).

Clause 39(2): Remedy for default. In addition to the power under sub-clause (2) to employ and pay other persons, clause 63(1)(b)(iii) gives a potential right of determination for matters falling within clause 39(1) where the Contractor fails to comply within 14 days of receiving notice. Note that where remedial or other work of repair is urgently necessary, the Engineer may act under clause 62 to have it done immediately.

Clause 39(3). *"Failure of the Engineer ... to disapprove any work or materials shall not prejudice ..."*

There is no implication that approval will prejudice the Engineer's right subsequently to disapprove the work. Neither failure to disapprove nor approval will prejudice the right of the Employer to bring a claim for defects after completion.[14]

SUSPENSION OF WORK

Suspension of work

40 (1) The Contractor shall on the written order of the Engineer suspend the progress of the Works or any part thereof for such time or times and in such manner as the Engineer may consider necessary and shall during such suspension properly protect and secure the work so far as is necessary in the opinion of the Engineer. Subject to clause 52(4) the Contractor shall be paid in accordance with clause 60 the extra cost (if any) incurred in giving effect to the Engineer's instructions under this clause except to the extent that such suspension is

　(a) otherwise provided for in the Contract or
　(b) necessary by reason of weather conditions or by some default on the part of the Contractor or
　(c) necessary for the proper execution or for the safety of the Works or any part thereof in as much as such necessity does not arise from any act or default of the Engineer or the Employer or from any of the Excepted Risks defined in clause 20(2).

---

[14] See also clause 60(8).

Profit shall be added thereto in respect of any additional permanent or temporary work.

The Engineer shall take any delay occasioned by a suspension ordered under this clause (including that arising from any act or default of the Engineer or the Employer) into account in determining any extension of time to which the Contractor is entitled under clause 44 except when such suspension is otherwise provided for in the Contract or is necessary by reason of some default on the part of the Contractor.

Suspension lasting more than three months

(2)   If the progress of the Works or any part thereof is suspended on the written order of the Engineer and if permission to resume work is not given by the Engineer within a period of 3 months from the date of suspension then the Contractor may unless such suspension is otherwise provided for in the Contract or continues to be necessary by reason of some default on the part of the Contractor serve a written notice on the Engineer requiring permission within 28 days from the receipt of such notice to proceed with the Works or that part thereof in regard to which progress is suspended. If within the said 28 days the Engineer does not grant such permission the Contractor by a further written notice so served may (but is not bound to) elect to treat the suspension where it affects part only of the Works as an omission of such part under clause 51 or where it affects the whole Works as an abandonment of the Contract by the Employer.

Clause 40

Suspension of work is an extreme remedy, only to be entertained where no other course is available, in view of the serious consequences which may ensue under sub-clause (2). The Engineer is never obliged under the Contract to order suspension. Such an order would normally be given after consultation with the Employer. It has been held in a case under the JCT Standard Form of Building Contract that an instruction nominating a Sub-Contractor on terms which involved stopping other work necessarily operated as a postponement (or suspension) order.[15]

Clause 40(2).   "... *elect to treat the suspension where it affects part only of the Works as an omission* ..."

The omission of the suspended part of the Works entitles the Contractor to compensation under clause 52, which permits a claim for new rates to be fixed for other work where the prices are rendered "unreasonable or inapplicable" by the variation (*i.e.* the omission).

Clause 40(2).   "... *or where it affects the whole Works* ..."

The apparent intention of these words is to permit the Contractor to be released from further performance where what has been suspended is the whole of the uncompleted Works.[16] A suspension is most unlikely to affect the

---

[15] *Harrison* v. *Leeds City Council* (1980) 14 BLR 118 (C.A.)—a decision described by Megaw L.J. as "unlikely to be repeated."

[16] See JCT Standard Form of Building Contract 1980, clause 28.1.3.

whole of the Works as defined in clause 1(1). However, it is thought that the palpable intention would be achieved by applying to the definition the opening words of clause 1(1)(p): "Except where the context otherwise requires."

Clause 40(2). "*. . . abandonment of the Contract by the Employer.*"

This term is not defined, nor is there any provision for its consequences.[17] The Contractor clearly ceases to be bound to complete the Works, but it is not clear whether the Contractor has any right to compensation, and if so, on what basis.[18]

COMMENCEMENT TIME AND DELAYS

Works Commencement Date

41　(1)　The Works Commencement Date shall be

(a)　the date specified in the Appendix to the Form of Tender or if no date is specified
(b)　a date within 28 days of the award of the Contract to be notified by the Engineer in writing or
(c)　such other date as may be agreed between the parties.

Start of Works

(2)　The Contractor shall start the Works on or as soon as is reasonably practicable after the Works Commencement Date. Thereafter the Contractor shall proceed with the Works with due expedition and without delay in accordance with the Contract.

Clause 41

Clause 41(2).　"*The Contractor shall start the Works on . . .*"

The actual start date does not affect the required Completion Date, which is calculated from the "Works Commencement Date." Failure to start the work at all may lead to notice of determination under clause 63(1)(b)(ii).

Clause 41(2).　"*. . . proceed with the Works with due expedition . . .*"

Clause 63(1)(b)(iv) gives a right of determination for failure to proceed with the Works "with due diligence." The two terms, whilst similar, are not the same. There is no sanction which attaches separately to the obligation to proceed with "due expedition." Clause 46 provides a limited remedy where the rate of progress of the Works is too slow. But the remedy is limited to requiring the Contractor to take unspecified steps to expedite progress. An appropriate measure of "due expedition" will be the Contractor's Programme submitted under clause 14.

---

[17] Compare clause 63(1)(b)(i), where express provision is made.
[18] See p. 207 for the position if the employer is to be treated as in breach.

POSSESSION OF SITE AND ACCESS

Possession of Site and access

42 (1) The Contract may prescribe

(a) the extent of portions of the Site of which the Contractor is to be given possession from time to time
(b) the order in which such portions of the Site shall be made available to the Contractor
(c) the availability and the nature of the access which is to be provided by the Employer
(d) the order in which the Works shall be constructed.

(2) (a) Subject to sub-clause (1) of this clause the Employer shall give to the Contractor on the Works Commencement Date possession of so much of the Site and access thereto as may be required to enable the Contractor to commence and proceed with the construction of the Works.

(b) Thereafter the Employer shall during the course of the Works give to the Contractor possession of such further portions of the Site as may be required in accordance with the programme which the Engineer has accepted under clause 14 and such further access as is necessary to enable the Contractor to proceed with the construction of the Works with due despatch.

Failure to give possession

(3) If the Contractor suffers delay and/or incurs additional cost from failure on the part of the Employer to give possession in accordance with the terms of this clause the Engineer shall determine

(a) any extension of time to which the Contractor is entitled under clause 44 and
(b) subject to clause 52(4) the amount of any additional cost to which the Contractor may be entitled. Profit shall be added thereto in respect of any additional permanent or temporary work.

The Engineer shall notify the Contractor accordingly with a copy to the Employer.

Access and facilities provided by the Contractor

(4) The Contractor shall bear all costs and charges for any access required by him additional to those provided by the Employer. The Contractor shall also provide at his own cost any additional facilities outside the Site required by him for the purposes of the Works.

Clause 42

Clause 42(2)(a). *"... so much of the site and access thereto as may be required to enable the Contractor to commence and proceed ..."*

This obligation is stated to be "subject to sub-clause (1)", which states that the Contract may prescribe the handing over of the site. Accordingly, the Contractor is entitled either to have the site delivered in accordance with a programme or otherwise to have possession of sufficient to allow the work to proceed. The latter option may give rise to dispute about the adequacy of the land available, for example, for purposes of storage and items of fixed plant. It is clearly preferable for the land which is to be made available to be clearly defined.

Clause 42(3). *"... failure ... to give possession in accordance with the terms of this clause ..."*

The obligation to give possession may be that arising under sub-clause (1) or (2). It is thought that the obligation to provide facilities for other Contractors under clause 31 does not override the Contractor's entitlement to possession of the site. Failure to give possession could give rise to an alternative claim for damages for breach of contract (see commentary to clause 31).

TIME FOR COMPLETION

Time for completion

43 The whole of the Works and any Section required to be completed within a particular time as stated in the Appendix to the Form of Tender shall be substantially completed within the time so stated (or such extended time as may be allowed under clause 44) calculated from the Works Commencement Date.

Clause 43

The Employer's remedy for non-compliance is liquidated damages as provided by clause 47. The Contractor is entitled to carry out the work faster and to complete earlier than is required by the Contract. The Employer under such circumstances is obliged to pay for the work as and when done, but is under no further obligation to facilitate earlier performance or pay compensation if the Contractor is unable to achieve an accelerated programme.[19]

Extension of time for completion

44 (1) Should the Contractor consider that

(a) any variation ordered under clause 51(1) or
(b) increased quantities referred to in clause 51(4) or
(c) any cause of delay referred to in these Conditions or
(d) exceptional adverse weather conditions or
(e) other special circumstances of any kind whatsoever which may occur

be such as to entitle him to an extension of time for the substantial completion of the Works or any Section thereof he shall within 28 days after the cause of any delay has arisen or as soon thereafter as is reasonable deliver to the Engineer full and detailed particulars in justification of the period of extension claimed in order that the claim may be investigated at the time.

---

[19] *Glenlion Construction* v. *The Guinness Trust* (1987) 39 B.L.R. 89.

Assessment of delay

(2)   (a)   The Engineer shall upon receipt of such particulars consider all the circumstances known to him at that time and make an assessment of the delay (if any) that has been suffered by the Contractor as a result of the alleged cause and shall so notify the Contractor in writing.
(b)   The Engineer may in the absence of any claim make an assessment of the delay that he considers has been suffered by the Contractor as a result of any of the circumstances listed in sub-clause (1) of this clause and shall so notify the Contractor in writing.

Interim grant of extension of time

(3)   Should the Engineer consider that the delay suffered fairly entitles the Contractor to an extension of the time for the substantial completion of the Works or any Section thereof such interim extension shall be granted forthwith and be notified to the Contractor in writing. In the event that the Contractor has made a claim for an extension of time but the Engineer does not consider the Contractor entitled to an extension of time he shall so inform the Contractor without delay.

Assessment at due date for completion

(4)   The Engineer shall not later than 14 days after the due date or extended date for completion of the Works or any Section thereof (and whether or not the Contractor shall have made any claim for an extension of time) consider all the circumstances known to him at that time and take action similar to that provided for in sub-clause (3) of this clause. Should the Engineer consider that the Contractor is not entitled to an extension of time he shall so notify the Employer and the Contractor.

Final determination of extension

(5)   The Engineer shall within 14 days of the issue of the Certificate of Substantial Completion for the Works or for any Section thereof review all the circumstances of the kind referred to in sub-clause (1) of this clause and shall finally determine and certify to the Contractor with a copy to the Employer the overall extension of time (if any) to which he considers the Contractor entitled in respect of the Works or the relevant Section. No such final review of the circumstances shall result in a decrease in any extension of time already granted by the Engineer pursuant to sub-clauses (3) or (4) of this clause.

Clause 44

Clause 44(1): Grounds for extension.   Apart from the four specific grounds referred to at (a), (b), (d) and (e), the following causes of delay are referred to in the Conditions:

Clause 7(4):   failure by the Engineer to issue necessary drawings or instructions at reasonable times;

Clause 12(2):   adverse physical conditions or artificial obstructions;

Clause 13(3):   instructions under clause 13(1) or clause 5;
Clause 14(8):   delay in giving consent or notifying requirements regarding
                 the method of work;
Clause 27(6):   variations involving street works;
Clause 31(2):   facilities for other Contractors;
Clause 40(1):   suspension of work;
Clause 42(1):   failure to give possession.

Clause 44(1)(e).   "*... other special circumstances ...*"

The words "of any kind whatsoever" mean that the circumstances need not be related to other enumerated grounds. Whether particulars facts amount to "special circumstances" will depend upon construction of the contract as a whole, including any special terms. Matters reasonably with the contemplation of the parties, such as delay by Sub-Contractors (whether nominated or not) will not rank as special.[20] Such general words will not be construed as entitling the Engineer to grant an extension for delay arising from the Employer's default.[21] Any such delay must be brought within one of the express grounds of extension. Failure to do so may invalidate the liquidated damages clause.

Clause 44(1).   "*... he shall within 28 days after the cause of any delay has arisen ...*"

This is not a condition precedent. The Contractor may deliver his claim "as soon thereafter as is reasonable." Further, under sub-clause (2)(b), the Engineer is empowered to make an extension in the absence of a claim, which presumably includes the absence of a valid or timely claim.

Clause 44(2) and (3).   These two sub-clauses govern the assessment and granting of extensions. The wording is not wholly clear, but the process appears to involve the following steps: (1) the Engineer must make an assessment of the delay suffered; (2) he must consider whether this delay fairly entitles the Contractor to an extension of the time for substantial completion. The Contractor is required to be notified of both matters. No further criteria are laid down. Presumably, the second step involves considering how far the individual delayed items are critical to progress of the Works or any relevant Section. Note that in assessing the delay suffered, the Engineer is required to consider "all the circumstances known to him at the time," which may include factors outside the grounds put forward by the Contractor.

Clause 44(3).   "*... or any Section thereof ...*"

The application and grant of extensions may be applied to Sections, *i.e.* a part of the Works separately identified in the Appendix to the tender.[22]

---

[20] See also clauses 4(4) and 59(3).
[21] *Peak Construction* v. *McKinney Foundations* (1970) 69 L.G.R. 1 and 1 B.L.R. 1 (C.A.).
[22] Clause 1(1)(u).

Liquidated damages may be provided separately for Sections pursuant to clause 47(2).

Clause 44(4): Reassessment of extension at Due Date.   This is required whether or not the Works are complete. The Engineer is required to assess an extension of time whether or not the Contractor has applied for one, and whether or not an interim extension has previously been granted. The purpose of this interim assessment is to fix the Employer's entitlement to deduct liquidated damages under clause 47 from the contractual completion date or extension thereof.

Clause 44(5): Final Determination.   This will be a final review of the extension which must be assessed under sub-clause (4). Note that the final review may not decrease extensions previously granted, whereas the assessment under sub-clause (4) may do so.

Effect of Revised Extensions.   While the provisions for interim and final assessments of extension of time recognise what must frequently occur in practice, some difficulties remain. The root of the problem is the nature of the "temporary" default where the Contractor is in delay and has not yet been granted an extension of time.[23] During the course of the work, this difficulty may give rise to requirements under clause 14(4) for a revised programme, or under clause 46 for steps to expedite progress. At completion, the question arises whether the Contractor is to be regarded as in breach of contract, pending the final determination of extension of time. The right to recover liquidated damages under these circumstances is expressly dealt with in clause 47. In regard to a claim for general damages, the point is free from authority.[24]

NIGHT AND SUNDAY WORK/RATE OF PROGRESS

Night and Sunday work

45   Subject to any provision to the contrary contained in the Contract none of the Works shall be executed during the night or on Sundays without the permission in writing of the Engineer save when the work is unavoidable or absolutely necessary for the saving of life or property or for the safety of the Works in which case the Contractor shall immediately advise the Engineer or the Engineer's Representative. Provided always that this clause shall not be applicable in the case of any work which it is customary to carry out outside normal working hours or by rotary or double shifts.

Clause 45

Clause 45.   "... *without the permission in writing of the Engineer* ..."
    Subject to the exceptions set out in the clause, the Contractor has no right to

---

[23] See reference by Lord Diplock to "temporary disconformity" in *Kaye* v. *Hosier & Dickinson* [1972] 1 W.L.R. 146 at 157 (H.L.).

[24] The point was argued but not decided by the Court of Appeal in *Rosehaugh Stanhope* v. *Redpath Dorman Long* and *Beaufort House* v. *Zimmcor* (1990) 50 B.L.R. 69 and 91 (C.A.).

carry out night or Sunday work. There is no implication that withholding of consent must be reasonable. See clause 46(2), however, where such permission is not to be unreasonably refused.

Rate of progress

46 (1)   If for any reason which does not entitle the Contractor to an extension of time the rate of progress of the Works or any Section is at any time in the opinion of the Engineer too slow to ensure substantial completion by the time or extended time for completion prescribed by clause 43 and 44 as appropriate the Engineer shall notify the Contractor in writing and the Contractor shall thereupon take such steps as are necessary and to which the Engineer may consent to expedite the progress so as substantially to complete the Works or such Section by that prescribed time or extended time. The Contractor shall not be entitled to any additional payment for taking such steps.

Permission to work at night or on Sundays

(2)   If as a result of any notice given by the Engineer under sub-clause (1) of this clause the Contractor shall seek the Engineer's permission to do any work on Site at night or on Sundays such permission shall not be unreasonably refused.

Provision for accelerated completion

(3)   If the Contractor is requested by the Employer or the Engineer to complete the Works or any Section within a revised time being less than the time or extended time for completion prescribed by clauses 43 and 44 as appropriate and the Contractor agrees so to do then any special terms and conditions of payment shall be agreed between the Contractor and the Employer before any such action is taken.

Clause 46

Clause 46(1).   Notice given under this clause is likely to result in the Contractor incurring expense to expedite progress. The question arises whether the Contractor is entitled to bring a claim where the basis of the notice given is removed by a later review of extensions of time, based on grounds existing at the date the notice was given. Although the matter is not free from doubt (see last note to clause 44 above) it is thought that an instruction under clause 46(1), which is retrospectively invalidated by an extension of time, could take effect under clause 13(1) and give rise to a claim for compensation under clause 13(3). It would be necessary, however, for the Contractor to have applied for the extension in order to demonstrate that there was an entitlement at the date of the clause 46(1) notice.

Clause 46(3): Acceleration Measures.   This provision, which is new to the 6th edition of the I.C.E. Conditions, merely records the possibility of agreement being reached.[25] Note that clause 51(1) empowers the Engineer to order

---

[25] For alternative clauses to similar effect see JCT Management Contract, 1987 edition, clause 3.6 and GC/Works/1—edition 3, 1989, clause 38.

a variation including "changes in any specified ... timing of construction required by the Contract."

LIQUIDATED DAMAGES FOR DELAY

Liquidated damages for delay in substantial completion of the whole of the Works

47   (1)   (a)   Where the whole of the Works is not divided into Sections the Appendix to the Form of Tender shall include a sum which represents the Employer's genuine pre-estimate (expressed per week or per day as the case may be) of the damages likely to be suffered by him if the whole of the Works is not substantially completed within the time prescribed by clause 43 or by any extension thereof granted under clause 44 or by any revision thereof agreed under clause 46(3) as the case may be.
 (b)   If the Contractor fails to complete the whole of the Works within the time so prescribed he shall pay to the Employer the said sum for every week or day (as the case may be) which shall elapse between the date on which the prescribed time expired and the date the whole of the Works is substantially completed.

Provided that if any part of the Works is certified as complete pursuant to clause 48 before the completion of the whole of the Works the said sum shall be reduced by the proportion which the value of the part so completed bears to the value of the whole of the Works.

Liquidated damages for delay in substantial completion where the whole of the Works is divided into Sections

 (2)   (a)   Where the Works is divided into Sections (together comprising the whole of the Works) which are required to be completed within particular times as stated in the Appendix to the Form of Tender sub-clause (1) of this clause shall not apply and the said Appendix shall include a sum in respect of each Section which represents the Employer's genuine pre-estimate (expressed per week or per day as the case may be) of the damages likely to be suffered by him if that Section is not substantially completed within the time prescribed by clause 43 or by any extension thereof granted under clause 44 or by any revision thereof agreed under clause 46(3) as the case may be.
 (b)   If the Contractor fails to complete any Section within the time so prescribed he shall pay to the Employer the appropriate stated sum for every week or day (as the case may be) which shall elapse between the date on which the prescribed time expired and the date of substantial completion of that Section.

Provided that if any part of that Section is certified as complete pursuant to clause 48 before the completion of the whole thereof the appropriate stated sum shall be reduced by the proportion which the value of the part so completed bears to the value of the whole of that Section.
 (c)   Liquidated damages in respect of two or more Sections may where circumstances so dictate run concurrently.

Damages not a penalty

 (3)   All sums payable by the Contractor to the Employer pursuant to this clause shall be paid as liquidated damages for delay and not as a penalty.

Limitation of liquidated damages

(4) (a) The total amount of liquidated damages in respect of the whole of the Works or any Section thereof shall be limited to the appropriate sum stated in the Appendix to the Form of Tender. If no such limit is stated therein then liquidated damages without limit shall apply.

(b) Should there be omitted from the Appendix to the Form of Tender any sum required to be inserted therein either by sub-clause (1)(a) or by sub-clause (2)(a) of this clause as the case may be or if any such sum is stated to be "nil" then to that extent damages shall not be payable.

Recovery and reimbursement of liquidated damages

(5) The Employer may

(a) deduct and retain the amount of any liquidated damages becoming due under the provision of this clause from any sums due or which become due to the Contractor or

(b) require the Contractor to pay such amount to the Employer forthwith.

If upon a subsequent or final review of the circumstances causing delay the Engineer grants a relevant extension or further extension of time the Employer shall no longer be entitled to liquidated damages in respect of the period of such extension.

Any sum in respect of such period which may already have been recovered under this clause shall be reimbursed forthwith to the Contractor together with interest at the rate provided for in clause 60(7) from the date on which such sums were recovered from the Contractor.

Intervention of variations etc.

(6) If after liquidated damages have become payable in respect of any part of the Works the Engineer issues a variation order under clause 51 or adverse physical conditions or artificial obstructions within the meaning of clause 12 are encountered or any other situation outside the contractor's control arises any of which in the Engineer's opinion results in further delay to that part of the Works

(a) the Engineer shall so inform the Contractor and the Employer in writing and

(b) the Employer's entitlement to liquidated damages in respect of that part of the Works shall be suspended until the Engineer notifies the Contractor and the Employer in writing that the further delay has come to an end.

Such suspension shall not invalidate any entitlement to liquidated damages which accrued before the period of delay started to run and any monies deducted or paid in accordance with sub-clause (5) of this clause may be retained by the Employer without incurring liability for interest thereon under clause 60(7).

Clause 47: Liquidated Damages for delay

This clause has been redrafted for the 6th edition of the I.C.E. Conditions. It provides for the deduction of liquidated damages upon the Contractor's failure to complete on time, with the following refinements:

(i) by sub-clause (1), liquidated damages for the whole of the Works, subject to proportional deduction for completed parts;

(ii) by sub-clause (2), liquidated damages for Sections as specified in the Appendix, each Section subject to proportional reduction for completed parts;

(iii) by sub-clause (4), limitation of the damages recoverable to a stated sum;

(iv) reimbursement of damages deducted, together with interest, arising from a subsequent review of extensions of time;

(v) by sub-clause (6), provision for variations etc., causing delay after liquidated damages have begun to accrue.

Clause 47(1)(a) and (2)(a). *". . . the Employer's genuine pre-estimate . . . of the damages likely to be suffered . . ."*

These are technical words which denote the type of damages which the Court will regard as liquidated damages as opposed to a penalty.[26] Note that sub-clause (3) states expressly that all sums payable under this clause "shall be paid as liquidated damages for delay and not as a penalty." No such words can prevent the Court inquiring whether the payment stipulated is in fact a penalty. The Employer should therefore be advised to ensure that the stipulated sums comply with the words of the Contract. It is unnecessary for a precise calculation to be made, and the damages will not become invalid because the Employer's loss is difficult or even impossible to calculate in money. Indeed, the difficulty of calculation may be a compelling reason for adopting liquidated damages. In practice, such clauses frequently operate as a limitation on the Contractor's liability.[27]

Clause 47(2): Liquidated damages for Sections. This provision operates by abrogating sub-clause (1) and treating the whole Contract as a series of independent parts, each subject to its own separate damages provision, each such provision subject to proportional reduction if part of the section is completed earlier. This approach avoids the considerable difficulties of attempting to combine an overall damages provision with separate provision for some sections, as was contained in the 5th edition of the Conditions.[28] The successful operation of these provisions depends also on sectional treatment of extensions of time, as provided for in clause 44, so that there is always a contractual completion date for each section.[29]

Clause 47(4)(a): Limitation of damages. The limitation applies once the liquidated damages have built up to a capping figure, beyond which there is to be no further increase. There can be no objection in principle to such a clause,

---

[26] Lord Dunedin in *Dunlop Ltd.* v. *New Garage Co. Ltd.* [1915] A.C. 79 at 86 (H.L.). For liquidated damages generally, see Chap. 9, Part B.

[27] See Lord Wilberforce in *Suisse & Atlantique* v. *NV Rotterdamsche Kolen* [1967] 1 A.C. 361 at 435 (H.L.).

[28] See commentary on clause 47 in the 4th edition of this book at pp. 497–499.

[29] See *Peak Construction* v. *McKinney Foundations* (1970) 69 L.G.R. 1 and 1 B.L.R. 111 (C.A.).

since liquidated damages frequently operate as a limit in any event. This method is greatly to be preferred to the practice, frequently adopted, of specifying the limit as a percentage of a figure which is itself variable.[30]

Clause 47(4)(b): Damages not specified. This provision covers the possibility of accidental omission and also the not infrequent practice of inserting "nil" in the relevant part of the Appendix. In the latter case, such a provision has been held to amount to an agreement that there should be no damages for delayed completion.[31] The position would be different in the case of omission where, subject to any other relevant provisions of the Contract, the Employer would normally retain the right to general damages. Sub-clause (4)(b) seeks to reverse this, by providing that in such a case, damages are not to be payable. While the objective of this provision is reasonably clear, the wording leaves some room for doubt.

Clause 47(5): Recovery of liquidated damages. This sub-clause refers to deduction of "any liquidated damages becoming due." Such damages become due by virtue of sub-clause (1)(b) or (2)(b), each of which contain the words "if the Contractor fails ... he shall pay the Employer...." The liquidated damages thus become due automatically without the need for any Certificate or other action by the Engineer or the Employer.[32]

Clause 47(5): Subsequent extension of time and return of damages. This provision deals with the difficulty referred to in the last note to clause 44. Note also that interest payable under clause 60(7) is to be payable at a commercial rate (2 per cent. above base lending rate). Accordingly, where there is thought to be a possibility that some part of the damages may become repayable with interest, the Employer might be best advised to defer deduction, or to place the money deducted on deposit.

Clause 47(6): Subsequent grounds of delay. This sub-clause deals with the difficult question of delay arising after the contractual completion date has passed. It is sometimes argued that, in such circumstances, the Contractor must be granted a full extension up to the end of the period of subsequent delay. This sub-clause does not deal as such with this argument, but rather assumes it to be invalid, as is the better view.[33] While the intention of the clause

---

[30] See Model Form A, for Mechanical and Electrical Erection, clause 26, which applies a capping percentage of the "Contract Value", which means the Contract Price adjusted for variations etc. In one case, the percentage limit was applied to a figure expressed in dual currencies subject to relative fluctuations, the liquidated damages being expressed in one currency only.

[31] *Temloc* v. *Errill Properties* (1987) 39 B.L.R. 30 (C.A.).

[32] Compare clause 47(4) of the 5th edition of the I.C.E. Conditions and equivalent provisions in the Standard Form of Building Contract.

[33] The argument depends upon construction of the extension of time clause, and it is not thought that it is maintainable under clause 44. But the position cannot be regarded as beyond argument.

879

is clear, its operation may result in difficulty, *e.g.* as to the precise date from which the "further delay" is operative, and therefore from which the further accrual of liquidated damages is suspended. Once the full period of the further delay has been ascertained, this difficulty should disappear.

Clause 47(6): "*... any other situation outside the Contractor's control ...*"

This is the general ground which suspends the accrual of liquidated damages. It is distinctly wider than the grounds for extension of time under clause 44(1) and may operate as a serious limitation on the Employer's right to recover liquidated damages.

Clause 47(6): Retention of liquidated damages without liability for interest. It is not clear what damages this provision applies to. Sub-clause (6) is intended to result in liquidated damages being frozen at the point when further delay occurs, and then continuing to accrue when the delay has come to an end, so that there should not be any question of damages being repaid. It may be that the provision is intended to deal with the case where the intervening delay is recognised and accepted only retrospectively, in which case the Employer will have deducted his liquidated damages too early. If this is the intention, the last paragraph of the sub-clause ought to read:

"But if the Employer has continued to deduct liquidated damages after the date on which they should have become suspended the Employer may retain such damages without incurring liability for interest thereon under clause 60(7), provided that the total liquidated damages deducted does not exceed the amount properly recoverable having regard to the further delay."

CERTIFICATE OF SUBSTANTIAL COMPLETION

Notification of substantial completion

48 (1) When the Contractor considers that

(a) the whole of the Works or
(b) any Section in respect of which a separate time for completion is provided in the Appendix to the Form of Tender

has been substantially completed and has satisfactorily passed any final test that may be prescribed by the Contract he may give notice in writing to that effect to the Engineer or to the Engineer's Representative. Such notice shall be accompanied by an undertaking to finish any outstanding work in accordance with the provisions of clause 49(1).

Certification of substantial completion

(2) The Engineer shall within 21 days of the date of delivery of such notice either

(a) issue to the Contractor (with a copy to the Employer) a Certificate of Substantial Completion stating the date on which in his opinion the Works were or the Section was substantially completed in accordance with the Contract or

(b)   give instructions in writing to the Contractor specifying all the work which ìn the Engineer's opinion requires to be done by the Contractor before the issue of such certificate.

If the Engineer gives such instructions the Contractor shall be entitled to receive a Certificate of Substantial Completion within 21 days of completion to the satisfaction of the Engineer of the work specified in the said instructions.

Premature use by Employer

(3)   If any substantial part of the Works has been occupied or used by the Employer other than as provided in the Contract the Contractor may request in writing and the Engineer shall issue a Certificate of Substantial Completion in respect thereof. Such certificate shall take effect from the date of delivery of the Contractor's request and upon the issue of such certificate the Contractor shall be deemed to have undertaken to complete any outstanding work in that part of the Works during the Defects Correction Period.

Substantial completion of other parts of the Works

(4)   If the Engineer considers that any part of the Works has been substantially completed and has passed any final test that may be prescribed by the Contract he may issue a Certificate of Substantial Completion in respect of that part of the Works before completion of the whole of the Works and upon the issue of such certificate the Contractor shall be deemed to have undertaken to complete any outstanding work in that part of the Works during the Defects Correction Period.

Reinstatement of ground

(5)   A Certificate of Substantial Completion given in respect of any Section or part of the Works before completion of the whole shall not be deemed to certify completion of any ground or surfaces requiring reinstatement unless such certificate shall expressly so state.

Clause 48: Certificate of Substantial Completion

Clause 48(1).   "... *substantially completed* ..."

This term (or equivalent words) now appears consistently throughout the Conditions, *inter alia*, in clauses 43 and 47. The term is not defined, but the expressed reference to "outstanding work" to be completed within the Defects Correction Period[34] indicates a state plainly falling short of literal completion.[35] Neither is there any definition of "outstanding work." There is no reason to limit it to work that has not been carried out. It may include work which is defective, but is to be re-executed or remedied in accordance with the Contract.

Clause 48(2): Entitlement to Certificate of Substantial Completion.

The lack of definition of the term may give rise to disputes as to when the

---

[34] See clause 49(1).

[35] Consider *Westminster Corporation* v. *Jarvis* [1970] 1 W.L.R. 637 (H.L.), a decision on the Standard Form of Building Contract.

Contractor is entitled to have the Certificate of Substantial Completion issued. What is the extent of "outstanding work" that may be permitted? The question will be of considerable importance when large liquidated damages are potentially claimable. Clearly the clause gives the Engineer a discretion as to the degree of outstanding work which should be accepted. But his decision may be reviewed by an Arbitrator who will have "full power to open up, review and revise any decision, opinion, instruction, direction, certificate or valuation of the Engineer."[36] It is suggested that the relevant criterion for accepting substantial completion is whether the Works have reached a state when they are fit to be taken into use by the Employer.[37]

Clause 48(3). *"If any substantial part of the Works has been occupied or used by the Employer ..."*

See sub-clause (4), where provision is made for parts of the Works to be accepted as substantially complete. Sub-clause (3) accordingly applies where a part of the Works would not otherwise qualify for a Certificate of Substantial Completion. The degree of occupation or use is not specified, but it is thought that it must be substantial.

Clause 48(4): Completion of parts. A part of the Works is a portion which is undefined.[38] The decision to issue the Certificate is discretionary. The Engineer and the Employer must, it is submitted, consider accepting completed parts in order to mitigate any claim for liquidated damages.[39]

OUTSTANDING WORK AND DEFECTS

Work outstanding

49 (1) The undertaking to be given under clause 48(1) may after agreement between the Engineer and the Contractor specify a time or times within which the outstanding work shall be completed. If no such times are specified any outstanding work shall be completed as soon as practicable during the Defects Correction Period.

Execution of work of repair etc.

(2) The Contractor shall deliver up to the Employer the Works and each Section and part thereof at or as soon as practicable after the expiry of the relevant Defects Correction Period in the condition required by the Contract (fair wear and tear excepted) to the satisfaction of the Engineer. To this end the Contractor shall as soon as practicable execute all work of repair amendment reconstruction rectification and

---

[36] Clause 66(8)(a).
[37] See I.C.E. Conditions of Contract for Minor Works, clause 4.5(1), which contains a useful definition to this effect.
[38] Compare definition of "section" in clause 1(1)(u).
[39] *British Westinghouse* v. *Underground Electric Railways* [1912] A.C. 673 at 689 (H.L.).

making good of defects of whatever nature as may be required of him in writing by the Engineer during the relevant Defects Correction Period or within 14 days after its expiry as a result of an inspection made by or on behalf of the Engineer prior to its expiry.

Cost of execution of work of repair etc.

(3) All work required under sub-clause (2) of this clause shall be carried out by the Contractor at his own expense if in the Engineer's opinion it is necessary due to the use of materials or workmanship not in accordance with the Contract or to neglect or failure by the Contractor to comply with any of his obligations under the Contract. In any other event the value of such work shall be ascertained and paid for as if it were additional work.

Remedy on Contractor's failure to carry out work required

(4) If the Contractor fails to do any such work as aforesaid the Employer shall be entitled to carry out such work by his own workpeople or by other contractors and if such work is work which the Contractor should have carried out at his own expense the Employer shall be entitled to recover the cost thereof from the Contractor and may deduct the same from any monies that are or may become due to the Contractor.

Clause 49: Outstanding work and defects

This clause in previous editions of the I.C.E. Conditions referred extensively to "maintenance," which has now been replaced by the term "defects correction." The clause refers to both work of repair and completion of outstanding work. As regards latent defects which come to light during the Defects Correction Period (or later) the Contractor will be in breach of contract and liable to the Employer in damages, *e.g.* if the defects are such as to prevent beneficial use of the Works.[40] The clause therefore gives the Contractor the right to mitigate any damages that might be claimable. As regards outstanding work, including patent defects existing at the date of Substantial Completion, clauses 48 and 49 give the Contractor a right effectively to defer such work to the Defects Correction Period, so that no question of breach of contract would arise. These clauses have no effect on the continuing liability of the Contractor for latent defects. Any damages recoverable will be general damages, not limited by any provision as to liquidated damages.

Clause 49(2). "*. . . defects of whatever nature as may be required of him in writing by the Engineer . . .*"

The Contractor is obliged to put right any defects including, *e.g.* defects attributable to the Engineer's design, if so instructed. Sub-clause (3) provides that the Contractor is to bear the cost only where the work is due to breach of the Contractor's obligations under the Contract. In other cases the work is to

---

[40] See Lord Diplock in *Kaye* v. *Hosier & Dickinson* [1972] 1 W.L.R. 146 at 157 (H.L.).

be paid for as additional work. Note that the effect of sub-clause (4) is that the Employer's remedy of calling in other contractors and charging the cost to the Contractor is available only for "work which the Contractor should have carried out at his own expense." It is thought that the Contractor would nevertheless be in breach of contract and liable in damages if he declined to carry out the rectification of other defects when properly instructed.

Contractor to search

50   The Contractor shall if required by the Engineer in writing carry out such searches tests or trials as may be necessary to determine the cause of any defect imperfection or fault under the directions of the Engineer. Unless such defect imperfection or fault shall be one for which the Contractor is liable under the Contract the cost of the work carried out by the Contractor as aforesaid shall be borne by the Employer. But if such defect imperfection or fault shall be one for which the Contractor is liable the cost of the work carried out as aforesaid shall be borne by the Contractor and he shall in such case repair rectify and make good such defect imperfection or fault at his own expense in accordance with clause 49.

Clause 50

Refer to the commentary to clauses 36(3) and 38(2). The same problem arises under this clause, *viz.* what is the position if a number of tests or trials are carried out, only some of which reveal fault on the part of the Contractor? Under the present clause, the position is clearer, because there must be a perceived "defect imperfection or fault," and provided that it is a matter for which the Contractor is liable, it is necessary only to establish that the searches, tests or trials were "necessary to determine the cause." However, difficult factual questions will arise in the same way as under clauses 36 and 38, where a defect or fault is known or suspected, but the cause and responsibility depend on the result of the searches, tests or trials. For example, if one of a group of foundation piles has failed a load test, the cause of failure, and therefore the nature of the fault or defect, can only be ascertained by carrying out tests, which may be elaborate and expensive, and may also cause costly delay to the project. These tests may reveal that some of the piles are defective and others not. In such cases, it is suggested that the same principles must apply as under clauses 36 and 38. If some defect, imperfection or fault is found for which the Contractor is liable, it is a question of fact and degree whether the tests or trials carried out should be regarded as reasonably arising from the Contractor's fault.

ALTERATIONS, ADDITIONS AND OMISSIONS

Ordered variations

51   (1)   The Engineer

(a)   shall order any variation to any part of the Works that is in his opinion necessary for the completion of the Works and

(b) may order any variation that for any other reason shall in his opinion be desirable for the completion and/or improved functioning of the Works.

Such variations may include additions omissions substitutions alterations changes in quality form character kind position dimension level or line and changes in any specified sequence method or timing of construction required by the Contract and may be ordered during the Defects Correction Period.

Ordered variations to be in writing

(2) All variations shall be ordered in writing but the provisions of clause 2(6) in respect of oral instructions shall apply.

Variation not to affect Contract

(3) No variation ordered in accordance with sub-clauses (1) and (2) of this clause shall in any way vitiate or invalidate the Contract but the value (if any) of all such variations shall be taken into account in ascertaining the amount of the Contract Price except to the extent that such variation is necessitated by the Contractor's default.

Changes in quantities

(4) No order in writing shall be required for increase or decrease in the quantity of any work where such increase or decrease is not the result of an order given under this clause but is the result of the quantities exceeding or being less than those stated in the Bill of Quantities.

Clause 51: Alterations Additions and Omissions

A clause permitting variation of the work (as opposed to the Contract) is an essential feature of any construction contract. Without it the Contractor is not bound to execute additional work or to make omissions or changes. Further, if extra work is carried out, the Contractor must seek payment outside the Contract. Changes may occur to the work without invoking this clause, *e.g.* under clause 13 or through a concession accepting work carried out otherwise than in accordance with the Contract. Clause 51, however, is the principal mode of changing the designated work.

Clause 51(1). *"The Engineer (a) shall order ..."*

These words are clearly imperative, in contrast to the words of paragraph (b) "may order." The obligation to give a variation order is, however, severely limited by the words which follow: "necessary for the completion of the Works." The Contractor is ordinarily obliged to achieve completion by whatever means may be necessary or appropriate. If the method of work chosen becomes impossible within the meaning of clause 13(1), the Contractor must find another method. The circumstances in which the Engineer will order a variation necessary for completion include:

885

(i) where, in the course of supplying further necessary details or instructions, the details or instructions amount to a variation to the existing Works[41];

(ii) where the Contract binds the Contractor to adopt a specified method of working, which method becomes impossible within the meaning of clause 13(1)[42];

(iii) where the work becomes physically impossible by any available method, or where the work becomes legally impossible[43];

(iv) where the Contract imposes some physical limit on the work, and it is necessary to go beyond such limit to achieve completion.[44]

Clause 51(1)(b). *". . . desirable for the completion and/or improved functioning of the Works"*

These words may limit the Engineer's power to order variations. The words do not easily cover, *e.g.* the omission of work in order to achieve a saving, unless perhaps the Employer cannot otherwise afford to complete the Works. It is not clear why such restrictive wording is employed. It may be that the Engineer could instruct a variation outside these words by using his powers under clause 13(1). Clause 13(3) provides that if an instruction under sub-clause (1) requires a variation, it is deemed to have been given under clause 51. Alternatively, if the Contractor acts on any variation which may be outside the ambit of clause 51(1)(b), he may waive the right to object.

Clause 51(1). *"Such variations may include . . . changes in any specified sequence method or timing of construction required by the Contract . . ."*

This is a new concept in variations, which has no parallel in other forms of contract. Similar words were included in the 5th edition of the I.C.E. Conditions, but the present edition adds the words "required by the Contract." These words will ensure that a variation can occur only in relation to a sequence, method or timing of construction which is binding on the Contractor and not, *e.g.* to a programme or method submitted under clause 14.[45] An interesting question which arises under this provision is whether the reference to "timing of construction required by the Contract" allows the Engineer to order a change to the time for completion, whether by advancing or retarding the work. Although the wording is less than clear, it is difficult to see what else these particular words could refer to. Clause 46(3) provides for accelerated completion by agreement, but there is no reason why it should not be ordered as a variation, with the accelerated work being valued by new rates under clause 52(2).

---

[41] See clause 7(1).

[42] See *Yorkshire Water Authority* v. *McAlpine* (1985) 32 B.L.R. 114, and see also commentary to clause 8(3).

[43] Clause 13(1).

[44] *Holland Dredging* v. *Dredging & Construction Co.* (1987) 37 B.L.R. 1 (C.A.).

[45] See clause 14(7), under which the Contractor requires the consent of the Engineer (not to be unreasonably withheld) to change methods which have previously received consent.

Clause 51(2): Variations to be in writing. Clause 2(6) requires oral instructions to be confirmed in writing by the Engineer or the Engineer's representative as soon as possible, and also permits the Contractor to confirm in writing, which confirmation is deemed to be an instruction in writing if not contradicted forthwith.

Clause 51(3). *"... except to the extent that such variation is necessitated by the Contractor's default."*

This provision is new to the 6th edition of the I.C.E. Conditions. It has been argued for and included in other forms of contract.[46] These words will prevent the Contractor relying on an unintended instruction to avoid the consequences of work not complying with the Contract.[47]

VALUATION OF ORDERED VARIATIONS

Valuation of ordered variations

52 (1)   The value of all variations ordered by the Engineer in accordance with clause 51 shall be ascertained by the Engineer after consultation with the Contractor in accordance with the following principles.

(a)   Where work is of similar character and executed under similar conditions to work priced in the Bill of Quantities it shall be valued at such rates and prices contained therein as may be applicable.

(b)   Where work is not of a similar character or is not executed under similar conditions or is ordered during the Defects Correction Period the rates and prices in the Bill of Quantities shall be used as the basis for valuation so far as may be reasonable failing which a fair valuation shall be made.

Failing agreement between the Engineer and the Contractor as to any rate or price to be applied in the valuation of any variation the Engineer shall determine the rate of price in accordance with the foregoing principles and he shall notify the Contractor accordingly.

Engineer to fix rates

(2)   If the nature or amount of any variation relative to the nature or amount of the whole of the contract work or to any part thereof shall be such that in the opinion of the Engineer or the Contractor any rate or price contained in the Contract for any item of work is by reason of such variation rendered unreasonable or inapplicable either the Engineer shall give to the Contractor or the Contractor shall give to the Engineer notice before the varied work is commenced or as soon thereafter as is reasonable in all the circumstances that such rate or price should be varied and the Engineer shall fix such rate or price as in the circumstances he shall think reasonable and proper.

Daywork

(3)   The Engineer may if in his opinion it is necessary or desirable order in writing that

---

[46] Particularly by Mr. I.N. Duncan Wallace Q.C., who has incorporated an equivalent provision in the Singapore Institute of Architects (SIA) Form of Building Contract.

[47] See *Simplex Concrete Piles* v. *Borough of St Pancras* (1958) 14 B.L.R. 80.

any additional or substituted work shall be executed on a daywork basis in accordance with the provisions of clause 56(4).

Notice of claims

(4)   (a)   If the Contractor intends to claim a higher rate or price than one notified to him by the Engineer pursuant to sub-clauses (1) and (2) of this clause or clause 56(2) the Contractor shall within 28 days after such notification give notice in writing of his intention to the Engineer.

(b)   If the Contractor intends to claim any additional payment pursuant to any clause of these Conditions other than sub-clauses (1) and (2) of this clause or clause 56(2) he shall give notice in writing of his intention to the Engineer as soon as may be reasonable and in any event within 28 days after the happening of the events giving rise to the claim. Upon the happening of such events the Contractor shall keep such contemporary records as may reasonably be necessary to support any claim he may subsequently wish to make.

(c)   Without necessarily admitting the Employer's liability the Engineer may upon receipt of a notice under this clause instruct the Contractor to keep such contemporary records or further contemporary records as the case may be as are reasonable and may be material to the claim of which notice has been given and the Contractor shall keep such records. The Contractor shall permit the Engineer to inspect all records kept pursuant to this clause and shall supply him with copies thereof as and when the Engineer shall so instruct.

(d)   After the giving of a notice to the Engineer under this clause the Contractor shall as soon as is reasonable in all the circumstances send to the Engineer a first interim account giving full and detailed particulars of the amount claimed to that date and of the grounds upon which the claim is based. Thereafter at such intervals as the Engineer may reasonably require the Contractor shall send to the Engineer further up to date accounts giving the accumulated total of the claim and any further grounds upon which it is based.

(e)   If the Contractor fails to comply with any of the provisions of this clause in respect of any claim which he shall seek to make then the Contractor shall be entitled to payment in respect thereof only to the extent that the Engineer has not been prevented from or substantially prejudiced by such failure in investigating the said claim.

(f)   The Contractor shall be entitled to have included in any interim payment certified by the Engineer pursuant to clause 60 such amount in respect of any claim as the Engineer may consider due to the Contractor provided that the Contractor shall have supplied sufficient particulars to enable the Engineer to determine the amount due. If such particulars are insufficent to substantiate the whole of the claim the Contractor shall be entitled to payment in respect of such part of the claim as the particulars may substantiate to the satisfaction of the Engineer.

Clause 52

This clause makes provision for two vital matters: valuation of variations and the procedure for claims generally, including claims arising under sub-clauses (1) and (2) of this clause. In regard to the valuation of variations, it is important to note that there is no provision under the Contract for recovery of additional costs arising from variations other than under this clause.[48] If the

---

[48] Compare clause 26 of the JCT 1980 Standard Form of Building Contract.

888

Contractor considers that variations have disrupted other non-varied work, then a claim must be made under sub-clause (2) in terms of adjustment of rates. There is no provision for claims based on cost.

Clause 52(1): Valuation of the varied work. This sub-clause deals with fixing appropriate rates and prices for the work within the variation. There are three possible approaches:

(i) if the varied work is both of similar character and executed under similar conditions to work in the Bill of Quantities, applicable rates in the Bill are to be used;

(ii) where either of these requirements is not met, or if the work is ordered during the Defects Correction Period, then rates and prices in the Bills are to be used "as the basis for valuation so far as may be reasonable." This formula contemplates adjustment to the specified rates to take account of any changed circumstances;

(iii) if it is not reasonable to use the rates and prices as a basis, the Contractor is entitled to a "fair valuation."

The sub-clause places emphasis on consultation between the Engineer and the Contractor. It may be necessary to ask for a breakdown of the Contractor's rates in order to determine to what extent it is reasonable to apply them. In the absence of agreement, however, the Engineer is to determine the appropriate rates, which may then be challenged by the Contractor.[49]

Clause 52(2): Engineer's power to fix rates. The power is exercisable for "any rate or price contained in the Contract for any item of work." The rate to be fixed is such price "as in the circumstances [the Engineer] shall think reasonable and proper." This is equivalent to the "fair valuation" under sub-clause (1), but applied to any other items of work.

The condition for operating rate fixing is that the nature or amount of the variation relative to the unvaried work is such as to render the rate or price "unreasonable or inapplicable." Note that either the Engineer or the Contractor can bring the clause into operation, claiming a decrease or increase in the rates as appropriate. Note also that notice is required from the party invoking the clause either "before the varied work is commenced or as soon thereafter as is reasonable in all the circumstances" (see below).

The Contract gives no further guidance for the method of rate fixing. It will normally be necessary to break down the quoted rates into the elements of plant, materials, labour and overheads, in order to make the appropriate adjustments.[50] Note that by clause 11(3)(b) the Contractor is deemed to have satisfied himself as to the correctness and sufficiency of the rates and prices in the Bill.

---

[49] See clause 52(4)(a).
[50] See C.K. Haswell, "Rate Fixing in Civil Engineering Contracts" Proc. I.C.E. February 1963 and Haswell & de Silva *Civil Engineering Contracts, Practice and Procedure* (1982).

Clause 52(2): Notice. The party invoking clause 52(2) is required to give notice either "before the varied work is commenced or as soon thereafter as is reasonable in all the circumstances." Such notice is a condition precedent to the ability to bring such a claim. The notice need only identify the rate or price required to be varied. There is no requirement to specify the rate claimed. As to the timing of notice, some assistance may be gained from the case of *Tersons* v. *Stevenage Development Corporation*,[51] where a wide interpretation was given to the words "as soon thereafter as is practicable" appearing in the equivalent clause of an earlier edition of the Conditions. In *Hersent Offshore* v. *Burmah Oil*,[52] where the contract was similar to the I.C.E. 4th edition, notice four months after completion of extra work was held not to be "as soon thereafter as is practicable."

Clause 52(4): Notice of claims. This sub-clause applies to claims throughout the Conditions of Contract, and is expressly invoked in many instances where provision is made for payment of additional cost, *e.g.* clauses 7(4), 12(5), 13(3), 14(8), 27(6), 31(2), 40(1) and 42(3). The key to the operation of this sub-clause is in paragraphs (f) and (e), which govern respectively the right to interim and final payment where the preceding requirements have not been fully complied with. The requirements of paragraphs (a)–(d) are procedural and apparently subject to paragraphs (f) and (e).

Clause 52(4)(a): Claims under clause 52(1) and (2) or 56(2). These claims relate to establishing appropriate rates arising from variations or changes in quantity. Both sub-clauses (a) and (b) appear to refer to rights to bring claims under the Contract. In regard to (b), there is a substantial number of express claims subject to clause 52(4) (see above). As regards (a), however, there is no express right under the Contract to claim a higher rate than that notified by the Engineer under the clauses mentioned. It may be that this clause indicates that the Engineer may review his first decision, or alternatively it may refer to the submission of a claim as a dispute under clause 66. In either case, the requirement for notice 28 days after the Engineer's notification is plainly subject to sub-clause (e). The provision is, therefore, of little effect.

Clause 52(4)(f): Interim payments. This requires the supply of particulars, which will presumably comply concurrently with sub-clause (d), and may further constitute written notice under (b). The only practical issue will therefore be what amount the Engineer "may consider due," having regard to the particulars supplied. Subject to this, it is submitted that the Contractor is entitled to interim payments.

---

[51] [1963] 2 Lloyd's Rep. 333 (C.A.), a case on the 2nd edition of the Conditions, but applicable to the 4th edition.
[52] [1978] 2 Lloyds Rep. 565 and 10 B.L.R. 1.

Clause 52(4)(e): Final payments.   If there has been a failure to comply with paragraphs (a)–(d), the Contractor is entitled to payment "only to the extent that the Engineer has not been prevented from or substantially prejudiced by such failure in investigating the said claim." If the Engineer excludes any part of the claim on the grounds of prevention or prejudice, it is necessary to consider the rights of the Contractor to submit further proof of the claim, and the effect of a reference under clause 66 to the Engineer and to an Arbitrator.

First, it should be noted that paragraph (e) sets no time limit on the Engineer's investigation. If the Contractor is able to furnish further proof, he may resubmit the claim under the relevant clause of the Contract at any time before the final certificate.[53] Secondly, where a claim has been rejected on the ground of prevention or prejudice, the dispute to be decided by an Arbitrator under clause 66 is whether the *Engineer* has been prevented or prejudiced.[54] It is irrelevant whether or not the Arbitrator is similarly prevented or prejudiced. However, the Arbitrator would be bound, it is submitted, to consider all information made available to the Engineer before the final certificate, whether or not there has been a formal resubmission of the claim under the Contract.

PROPERTY IN MATERIALS AND CONTRACTOR'S EQUIPMENT

Vesting of Contractor's Equipment

53   (1)   All Contractor's Equipment Temporary Works materials for Temporary Works or other goods or materials owned by the Contractor shall when on Site be deemed to be the property of the Employer and shall not be removed therefrom without the written consent of the Engineer which consent shall not unreasonably be withheld where the items in question are no longer immediately required for the purposes of the completion of the Works.

Liability for loss or damage to Contractor's Equipment

(2)   The Employer shall not at any time be liable save as mentioned in clauses 22 and 65 for the loss of or damage to any Contractor's Equipment Temporary Works goods or materials.

Disposal of Contractor's Equipment

(3)   If the Contractor fails to remove any of the said Contractor's Equipment Temporary Works goods or materials as required by clause 33 within such reasonable time after

---

[53] *I.e.* the Certificate issued under clause 60(4).

[54] It may be that this curious feature, which first appeared in the 5th edition, was accidental. It has been corrected in the 4th edition of the F.I.D.I.C. Conditions (clause 53.4) but not in the current edition of the I.C.E. Conditions.

completion of the Works as the Engineer may allow then the Employer may sell or otherwise dispose of such items. From the proceeds of the sale of any such items the Employer shall be entitled to retain any costs or expenses incurred in connection with their sale and disposal before paying the balance (if any) to the Contractor.

Clause 53: Property in Materials and Contractor's Equipment

Clause 53(1): Effect of sub-clause. For definitions of "Contractor's Equipment" and "Temporary Works" see clause 1(1)(w) and (o). The expression "other goods or materials owned by the Contractor" covers goods and materials intended for the Works themselves. The purpose of the sub-clause is to ensure that plant and materials are available to the Employer if the Contractor fails to perform the Contract. A clause providing for vesting upon the Contractor's insolvency is likely to be unenforceable.[55] The present sub-clause raises issues as to its enforceability against the Contractor and against third parties.

Enforceability of sub-clause (1). The effectiveness of words such as "deemed to be the property of . . ." has been doubted[56] but it is thought that the provision for vesting when on site would be enforced against the Contractor.[57] The sub-clause cannot and does not purport to bind third parties. Accordingly, plant and materials, etc., owned by Sub-Contractors and suppliers will be unaffected unless property in them has passed to the Contractor under a similar provision.

Clause 53(2)—Employer not liable for damage to Contractor's Equipment. The excepted clauses refer to the Employer's indemnities (clause 22) and the War clause (clause 65). The exclusion of liability applies, it is submitted, to accidental damage, but does not preclude a claim under the Contract which includes the cost of damage to Contractor's Equipment or Temporary Works, *e.g.* where this is part of a claim for unforeseen conditions under clause 12. All such plant and works will, however, be insured in joint names under clause 21.

VESTING OF GOODS AND MATERIALS

Vesting of goods and materials not on Site

54 (1) With a view to securing payment under clause 60(1)(c) the Contractor may (and shall if the Engineer so directs) transfer to the Employer the property in goods and materials listed in the Appendix to the Form of Tender before the same are delivered to the Site provided that the goods and materials

---

[55] *Re Harrison ex p. Jay* [1880] 14 Ch.D. 19 (C.A.); *Re Walker ex p. Barter* [1884] 26 Ch.D. 510 (C.A.); see also p. 379.

[56] *Bennett* v. *Sugar City* [1951] A.C. 786 at 814 (P.C.); *Re Keen ex p. Collins* [1902] 1 K.B. 555; *cf. Re Winter, ex p. Bolland* [1878] 8 Ch.D. 225; see also p. 244.

[57] For further discussion see H.B.C. (10th ed.), pp. 669-673.

(a) have been manufactured or prepared and are substantially ready for incorporation in the Works and

(b) are the property of the Contractor or the contract for the supply of the same expressly provides that the property therein shall pass unconditionally to the Contractor upon the Contractor taking the action referred to in sub-clause (2) to this clause.

Action by Contractor

(2) The intention of the Contractor to transfer the property in any goods or materials to the Employer in accordance with this clause shall be evidenced by the Contractor taking or causing the supplier of those goods or materials to take the following actions.

(a) Provide to the Engineer documentary evidence that the property in the said goods or materials has vested in the Contractor.

(b) Suitably mark or otherwise plainly identify the goods and materials so as to show that their destination is the Site that they are the property of the Employer and (where they are not stored at the premises of the Contractor) to whose order they are held.

(c) Set aside and store the said goods and materials so marked or identified to the satisfaction of the Engineer.

(d) Send to the Engineer a schedule listing and giving the value of every item of the goods and materials so set aside and stored and inviting him to inspect them.

Vesting in Employer

(3) Upon the Engineer approving in writing the transfer in ownership of any goods and materials for the purposes of this clause they shall vest in and become the absolute property of the Employer and thereafter shall be in possession of the Contractor for the sole purpose of delivering them to the Employer and incorporating them in the Works and shall not be within the ownership control or disposition of the Contractor.

Provided always that

(a) approval by the Engineer for the purposes of this clause or any payment certified by him in respect of goods and materials pursuant to clause 60 shall be without prejudice to the exercise of any power of the Engineer contained in this Contract to reject any goods or materials which are not in accordance with the provisions of the Contract and upon any such rejection the property in the rejected goods or materials shall immediately revest in the Contractor and

(b) the Contractor shall be responsible for any loss or damage to such goods and materials and for the cost of storing handling and transporting the same and shall effect such additional insurance as may be necessary to cover the risk of such loss or damage from any cause.

Lien on goods or materials

(4) Neither the Contractor nor a sub-contractor nor any other person shall have a lien on any goods or materials which have vested in the Employer under sub-clause (3) of this clause for any sum due to the Contractor Sub-Contractor or other person and the Contractor shall take all such steps as may reasonably be necessary to ensure that the title of the Employer and the exclusion of any such lien are brought to the notice of Sub-Contractors·and other persons dealing with any such goods or materials.

893

Delivery to the Employer of vested goods or materials

(5) Upon cessation of the employment of the Contractor under this Contract before the completion of the Works whether as a result of the operation of clause 63 or otherwise the Contractor shall deliver to the Employer any goods or materials the property in which has vested in the Employer by virtue of sub-clause (3) of this clause and if he shall fail to do so the Employer may enter any premises of the Contractor or of any Sub-Contractor and remove such goods and materials and recover the cost of so doing from the Contractor.

Incorporation in Sub-Contracts

(6) The Contractor shall incorporate provisions equivalent to those provided in this clause in every Sub-Contract in which provision is to be made for payment in respect of goods or materials before the same have been delivered to the Site.

Clause 54

This clause should be read with clause 60(1)(c) and 60(2)(b), which govern the Contractor's entitlement to payment. There is no limitation on when the Contractor may seek payment. But the clause applies only to goods, etc., expressly listed in the Appendix to the Tender. The amount to be paid is subject to the Engineer's discretion under clause 60(2) and to the percentage of the value stated in the Appendix to the Tender.[58] Provided the Engineer is satisfied that the goods comply with every requirement of this clause, the Engineer is bound to give his approval in writing under sub-clause (3). Such approval is, however, subject to the power subsequently to reject the goods and withhold payment by a later Certificate and under clause 60(8).

The vesting of property is no longer subject to the doctrine of reputed ownership.[59] However, the effective transfer of property remains subject to possible difficulties arising from retention of title clauses in supply contracts.[60]

MEASUREMENT

Quantities

55 (1) The quantities set out in the Bill of Quantities are the estimated quantities of the work but they are not to be taken as the actual and correct quantities of the Works to be executed by the Contractor in fulfilment of his obligations under the Contract.

Correction of errors

(2) Any error in description in the Bill of Quantities or omission therefrom shall not

---

[58] The payment is not subject to retention: see clause 60(2).

[59] Abolished by the Insolvency Act 1986.

[60] See *Aluminium Industrie Vaassen* v. *Romalpa Aluminium* [1976] 1 W.L.R. 676; *Pfeiffer* v. *Arbuthnot Factors* [1988] 1 W.L.R. 150; *Armour* v. *Thyssen Edelstahlwerke A.G.* [1990] 3 W.L.R. 810 (H.L (Sc.)); see also p. 242.

vitiate the Contract nor release the Contractor from the execution of the whole or any part of the Works according to the Drawings and Specification or from any of his obligations or liabilities under the Contract. Any such error or omission shall be corrected by the Engineer and the value of the work actually carried out shall be ascertained in accordance with clause 52. Provided that there shall be no rectification of any errors omissions or wrong estimates in the descriptions rates and prices inserted by the Contractor in the Bill of Quantities.

Measurement and valuation

56 (1) The Engineer shall except as otherwise stated ascertain and determine by admeasurement the value in accordance with the Contract of the work done in accordance with the Contract.

Increase or decrease of rate

(2) Should the actual quantities executed in respect of any item be greater or less than those stated in the Bill of Quantities and if in the opinion of the Engineer such increase or decrease of itself shall so warrant the Engineer shall after consultation with the Contractor determine an appropriate increase or decrease of any rates or prices rendered unreasonable or inapplicable in consequence thereof and shall notify the Contractor accordingly.

Attending for measurement

(3) The Engineer shall when he requires any part or parts of the work to be measured give reasonable notice to the Contractor who shall attend or send a qualified agent to assist the Engineer or the Engineer's Representative in making such measurement and shall furnish all particulars required by either of them. Should the Contractor not attend or neglect or omit to send such agent then the measurement made by the Engineer or approved by him shall be taken to be the correct measurement of the work.

Daywork

(4) Where any work is carried out on a daywork basis the Contractor shall be paid for such work under the conditions and at the rates and prices set out in the daywork schedule included in the Contract or failing the inclusion of a daywork schedule he shall be paid at the rates and prices and under the conditions contained in the "Schedule of Dayworks carried out incidental to Contract work" issued by The Federation of Civil Engineering Contractors current at the date of the execution of the daywork.

The Contractor shall furnish to the Engineer such records receipts and other documentation as may be necessary to prove amounts paid and/or costs incurred. Such returns shall be in the form and delivered at the times the Engineer shall direct and shall be agreed within a reasonable time.

Before ordering materials the Contractor shall if so required submit to the Engineer quotations for the same for his approval.

Method of measurement

57 Unless otherwise provided in the Contract or unless general or detailed description of

the work in the Bill of Quantities or any other statement clearly shows to the contrary the Bill of Quantities shall be deemed to have been prepared and measurements shall be made according to the procedure set out in the "Civil Engineering Standard Method of Measurement Second Edition 1985" approved by the Institution of Civil Engineers and the Federation of Civil Engineering Contractors in association with the Association of Consulting Engineers or such later or amended edition thereof as may be stated in the Appendix to the Form of Tender to have been adopted in its preparation.

Clauses 55, 56 and 57: Measurement

These clauses should be read together. Clauses 55(1) with clause 56(1) and (2) make it clear that the Contractor is to be paid for the actual quantities of work executed at the billed rates or at such other rates as may be determined under clause 56(2). Any inference to the contrary is removed by the absence of any sum being stated in the Tender. The Contract Agreement contains an obligation to pay to the Contractor the "Contract Price," which is defined as the sum to be ascertained and paid in accordance with the provisions of the Contract.[61] The Contract is accordingly a "remeasure" and not a "lump sum" Contract.

Clause 55(2).   "... *error in description in the Bill of Quantities or omission therefrom* ..."

The error or omission referred to will be in relation to the Standard Method of Measurement referred to in clause 57 (see below). By this provision, the drawings and specification are made to prevail over the Bill of Quantities contrary to the general rule (see clause 5). Errors in quantity are automatically accounted for in remeasurement.

Clause 56(2).   "... *increase or decrease of any rates or prices rendered unreasonable or inapplicable* ..."

The mechanism created by this clause is similar in effect to that created by clause 52(2), save that the change of rates or prices is more usually applicable to the item which has itself undergone the change of quantity. The clause nevertheless applies to "any rates or prices rendered unreasonable, etc." It is important to note that the clause applies only where the increase or decrease in quantities "of itself" warrants the adjustment of rate. Thus there can be no change simply on the ground that the Contractor is making an excessive profit or loss. The Contractor's rates are to be taken as correct and sufficient.[62] There must, it is thought, be some change in the nature of the work, *e.g.* requiring different plant or organisation. See clause 52(4)(a) for the notice required where the Contractor wishes to challenge the Engineer's decision.

Clause 56(3): Measurement.   See also clause 38(1) for examination and measurement before covering up. It is submitted that measurement which is to

---

[61] Clause 1(1)(j).
[62] Clause 11(3)(b).

be taken as correct under sub-clause (3) will bind both the Contractor and an arbitrator subsequently appointed.[63] However, what is to be taken as correct is limited to the physical measurements. Calculations made from measurements, *e.g.* volumes of excavation and fill, may not be binding. In practice, Bills of Quantities under Civil Engineering Contracts tend to be shorter than under Building Contracts, and less susceptible to disputes about measurement of quantities.

Clause 57: The Standard Method of Measurement. The effect of this clause, when read with clause 55(2), is to limit the Contractor's prices to the work described in the Bill of Quantities, assuming those descriptions to be in accordance with the Standard Method. Work which is required to be measured separately, but is not so measured, must be paid for as an extra.[64] There are two important exceptions. First, there may be some contrary provision in the contract to indicate that the billing is not in accordance with the Standard Method. Secondly, the general or detailed description of the work in the Bill itself may indicate to the contrary. In either case, the Contractor will be bound to do the work at the prices stated, including any work not specifically mentioned but reasonably to be inferred from the Contract.[65]

PROVISIONAL AND PRIME COST SUMS AND NOMINATED SUB-CONTRACTS

Use of Provisional Sums

58 (1)   In respect of every Provisional Sum the Engineer may order either or both of the following.

(a)   Work to be executed or goods materials or services to be supplied by the Contractor the value thereof being determined in accordance with clause 52 and included in the Contract Price.
(b)   Work to be executed or goods materials or services to be supplied by a Nominated Sub-Contractor in accordance with clause 59.

Use of Prime Cost Items

(2)   In respect of every Prime Cost Item the Engineer may order either or both of the following.

(a)   Subject to clause 59 that the Contractor employ a Sub-Contractor nominated by the Engineer for the execution of any work or the supply of any goods materials or services included therein.
(b)   With the consent of the Contractor that the Contractor himself execute any such work or supply any such goods materials or services in which event the

---

[63] See *Kaye* v. *Hosier & Dickinson* [1972] 1 W.L.R. 146 (H.L.).
[64] See *A.E. Farr* v. *Ministry of Transport* (1965) 5 B.L.R. 94 (H.L.).
[65] See clause 8(1)(b) and *Williams* v. *Fitzmaurice* (1858) 3 H. & N. 844.

Contractor shall be paid in accordance with the terms of a quotation submitted by him and accepted by the Engineer or in the absence thereof the value shall be determined in accordance with clause 52 and included in the Contract Price.

Design requirements to be expressly stated

(3)   If in connection with any Provisional Sum or Prime Cost Item the services to be provided include any matter of design or specification of any part of the Permanent Works or of any equipment or plant to be incorporated therein such requirement shall be expressly stated in the Contract and shall be included in any Nominated Sub-Contract. The obligation of the Contractor in respect thereof shall be only that which has been expressly stated in accordance with this sub-clause.

Nominated Sub-contractors—objection to nomination

59   (1)   The Contractor shall not be under any obligation to enter into a Sub-Contract with any Nominated Sub-Contractor against whom the Contractor may raise reasonable objection or who declines to enter into a Sub-Contract with the Contractor containing provisions

(a)   that in respect of the work goods materials or services the subject of the Sub-Contract the Nominated Sub-Contractor will undertake towards the Contractor such obligations and liabilities as will enable the Contractor to discharge his own obligations and liabilities towards the Employer under the terms of the Contract
(b)   that the Nominated Sub-Contractor will save harmless and indemnify the Contractor against all claims demands and proceedings damages costs charges and expenses whatsoever arising out of or in connection with any failure by the Nominated Sub-Contractor to perform such obligations or fulfil such liabilities
(c)   that the Nominated Sub-Contractor will save harmless and indemnify the Contractor from and against any negligence by the Nominated Sub-Contractor his agents workmen and servants and against any misuse by him or them of any Contractor's Equipment or Temporary Works provided by the Contractor for the purposes of the Contract and for all claims as aforesaid
(d)   that the Nominated Sub-Contractor will provide the Contractor with security for the proper performance of the Sub-Contract and
(e)   equivalent to those contaned in clause 63.

Engineer's action upon objection to nomination or upon determination of Nominated Sub-contract

(2)   If pursuant to sub-clause (1) of this clause the Contractor declines to enter into a Sub-Contract with a Sub-Contractor nominated by the Engineer or if during the course of the Nominated Sub-Contract the Contractor shall validly terminate the employment of the Nominated Sub-Contractor as a result of his default the Engineer shall

(a)   nominate an alternative Sub-Contractor in which case sub-clause (1) of this clause shall apply or
(b)   by order under clause 51 vary the Works or the work goods materials or services in question or
(c)   by order under clause 51 omit any or any part of such works goods materials or services so that they may be provided by workmen contractors or suppliers employed by the Employer either

      (i) concurrently with the Works (in which case clause 31 shall apply) or

      (ii) at some other date

and in either case there shall nevertheless be included in the Contract Price such sum (if any) in respect of the Contractor's charges and profit being a percentage of the estimated value of such omission as would have been payable had there been no such omission and the value thereof had been that estimated in the Bill of Quantities or inserted in the Appendix to the Form of Tender as the case may be or

(d) instruct the Contractor to secure a Sub-Contractor of his own choice and to submit a quotation for the work goods materials or services in question to be so performed or provided for the Engineer's consideration and action or

(e) invite the Contractor himself to execute or supply the work goods materials or services in question under clause 58(1)(a) or clause 58(2)(b) or on a daywork basis as the case may be.

Contractor responsible for Nominated Sub-Contractors

(3)   Except as otherwise provided in clause 58(3) the Contractor shall be as responsible for the work executed or goods materials or services supplied by a Nominated Sub-Contractor employed by him as if he had himself executed such work or supplied such goods materials or services.

Nominated Sub-Contractor's default

(4)   (a) If any event arises which in the opinion of the Contractor justifies the exercise of his right under the Forfeiture Clause to terminate the Sub-Contract or to treat the Sub-Contract as repudiated by the Nominated Sub-Contractor he shall at once notify the Engineer in writing.

Termination of Sub-Contract

    (b) With the consent in writing of the Engineer the Contractor may give notice to the Nominated Sub-Contractor expelling him from the Sub-Contract works pursuant to the Forfeiture Clause or rescinding the Sub-Contract as the case may be. If however the Engineer's consent is withheld the Contractor shall be entitled to appropriate instructions under clause 13.

Engineer's action upon termination

    (c) In the event that the Nominated Sub-Contractor is expelled from the Sub-Contract works the Engineer shall at once take such action as is required under sub-clause (2) of this clause.

Delay and extra expense

    (d) Having with the Engineer's consent terminated the Nominated Sub-contract the Contractor shall take all necessary steps and proceedings as are available to him to recover all additional expenses that are incurred from the Sub-Contractor or under the security provided pursuant to sub-clause (1)(d) of this clause. Such expenses shall include any additional expenses incurred by the Employer as a result of the termination.

Reimbursement of Contractor's loss

(e) If and to the extent that the Contractor fails to recover all his reasonable expenses of completing the Sub-Contract works and all his proper additional expenses arising from the termination the Employer will reimburse the Contractor his unrecovered expenses.

Provisions for payment

(5) For all work executed or goods materials or services supplied by Nominated Sub-contractors there shall be included in the Contract Price

(a) the actual price paid or due to be paid by the Contractor in accordance with the terms of the sub-contract (unless and to the extent that any such payment is the result of a default of the Contractor) net of all trade and other discounts rebates and allowances other than any discount obtainable by the Contractor for prompt payment
(b) the sum (if any) provided in the Bill of Quantities for labours in connection therewith and
(c) in respect of all other charges and profit a sum being a percentage of the actual price paid or due to be paid calculated (where provision has been made in the Bill of Quantities for a rate to be set against the relevant item of prime cost) at the rate inserted by the Contractor against that item or (where no such provision has been made) at the rate inserted by the Contractor in the Appendix to the Form of Tender as the percentage for adjustment of sums set against Prime Cost Items.

Production of vouchers etc.

(6) The Contractor shall when required by the Engineer produce all quotations invoices vouchers sub-Contract documents accounts and receipts in connection with expenditure in respect of work carried out by all Nominated Sub-Contractors.

Payment to Nominated Sub-Contractors

(7) Before issuing any certificate under clause 60 the Engineer shall be entitled to demand from the Contractor reasonable proof that all sums (less retentions provided for in the Sub-Contract) included in previous certificates in respect of the work executed or goods or materials or services supplied by Nominated Sub-Contractors have been paid to the Nominated Sub-Contractors or discharged by the Contractor in default whereof unless the Contractor shall

(a) give details to the Engineer in writing of any reasonable cause he may have for withholding or refusing to make such payment and
(b) produce to the Engineer reasonable proof that he has so informed such Nominated Sub-Contractor in writing

the Employer shall be entitled to pay such Nominated Sub-Contractor direct upon the certification of the Engineer all payments (less retentions provided for in the Sub-

Contract) which the Contractor has failed to make to such Nominated Sub-Contractor and to deduct by way of set-off the amount so paid by the Employer from any sums due or which become due from the Employer to the Contractor. Provided always that where the Engineer has certified and the Employer has made direct payment to the Nominated Sub-Contractor the Engineer shall in issuing any further certificate in favour of the Contractor deduct from the amount thereof the amount so paid but shall not withhold or delay the issue of the certificate itself when due to be issued under the terms of the Contract.

Clauses 58 and 59: Provisional and Prime Cost Sums and Nominated Sub-Contracts

These clauses need to be read together. Clause 58 follows closely the same clause of the 5th edition, but has been shortened by moving the definitions of "Provisional Sum," "Prime Cost (PC) Item" and "Nominated Sub-Contractor" to clause 1(1). Clause 59 covers substantially the same ground as the former clauses 59A, B and C, but has been shortened by the omission of the following:

(i) there is no longer provision enabling the Engineer to nominate on terms not complying with clause 59(1);

(ii) in place of the lengthy provisions of the former clause 59B(2) to (5), clause 59(4) now contains a much simplified procedure requiring instructions under clause 13, where the Engineer does not consent to termination;

(iii) the former clause 59A(6) is omitted and 59B(6) simplified.

The effect of these clauses is substantially unaltered with one major exception, *viz.* the Main Contractor is now fully responsible for a Nominated Sub-Contractor, unless his performance gives grounds for termination, whereupon the Employer effectively takes the risk. The Contractor's widened responsibility is mitigated by a new provision (clause 59(1)(d)) entitling the Main Contractor to ask for security from the Sub-Contractor.

Clause 58(1) and (2): Provisional Sums, Prime Cost Items. See clause 1(1)(l) and (k) for definitions. A Provisional Sum is a "contingency . . . which may be used in whole or in part or not at all at the direction and discretion of the Engineer." A Prime Cost Item includes "a sum . . . which will be used for the execution of work or the supply of goods, materials or services for the Works." What is the difference between these two definitions? It seems that the Contractor can only be ordered to execute Prime Cost work himself with consent (clause 58(2)(d)), no such consent being required for use of a Provisional Sum. A further distinction is that a Prime Cost Item may allow a nomination for any volume of work, provided it remains within the words defining the Prime Cost Item. But it is thought that a Provisional Sum may be utilised only up to its stated value.

Clause 58(3): Design Requirements. These are to be "expressly stated in the Contract" and to be included in any Nominated Sub-Contract. The last sentence of the sub-clause ensures that the Contractor's liability arises only if both these conditions are satisfied. This provision has not been amended in line with clause 8(2) to refer to "reasonable skill, care and diligence." Although the position is not clear, it is thought that clause 8(2) is not sufficient to prevent an obligation being created through a Nominated Sub-Contract to carry out design to the higher standard of "fitness for purpose."[66]

Clause 59(1): Reasonable objection to Nominated Sub-Contractor. There is no indication what matters may be taken into account in deciding whether the Contractor's objection is reasonable. It is thought that competence and reputation are relevant matters, and also financial standing (see, however, sub-clause (1)(d)).

Clause 59(1)(d): Sub-Contractor to provide security. This is a new ground of objection. There is no indication of the level of security contemplated or its terms. It is not thought that the provision contemplates an "on demand" bond, but there may be a wide disparity in what is regarded as "security", ranging, perhaps, from 10 per cent. upwards. It is relevant to consider the extent of the Contractor's risk, which is effectively limited to breach short of repudiation. But the Contractor is prima facie responsible for delay by the Nominated Sub-Contractor. This may lead to disputes unless some limit is placed on the security to be provided.

Clause 59(2): Engineer's action. This clause expressly requires the Engineer to take action, which may be to "re-nominate," where a Nominated Sub-Contract is validly terminated. It provides an express remedy for the situation which arose in the *Bickerton* case.[67] It is of interest to note that an express right of renomination was included in the 5th edition of the I.C.E. Conditions in 1973, while the JCT Form did not provide an express remedy until the publication of the 1980 edition. Note that the Engineer has a wide range of alternative options to renomination.

Clause 59(3). "*... the Contractor shall be as responsible ... as if he had himself executed such work ...*"

There is an important change to the Contractor's responsibility. In the 5th edition of the I.C.E. Conditions, clause 59A(6) prevented the Employer enforcing the Main Contract where a breach was due to a Nominated Sub-Contractor, unless the Main Contractor could recover under the Sub-Contract. This provision has gone, leaving the Main Contractor fully responsible for Nominated Sub-Contractors save for the restriction effectively imposed by sub-clause (4)(e) (see below). The further restriction provided by clause 58(3) relates to design requirements, which are unenforceable through the Main Contract, unless expressly included therein (see above).

---

[66] For the distinction see *Greaves Contractors* v. *Baynham Meikle* [1975] 1 W.L.R. 1095 (C.A.); see also p. 291.
[67] [1970] 1 W.L.R. 607 (H.L.).

Clause 59(4): Options on repudiation by Nominated Sub-Contractor.
The clause now provides two options only, *i.e.* termination with the Engineer's consent, or alternatively instructions being given under clause 13. The previous edition contained lengthy provisions covering termination by the Contractor without consent.[68] This is no longer an option, and a Contractor who terminates a Nominated Sub-Contract otherwise than in accordance with this sub-clause will remain responsible for completion subject, however, to contending that the Engineer should have given instructions under clause 13. It is submitted that a decision of the Engineer to withhold his consent to terminating the Sub-Contract is not open to arbitration.

Clause 59(4)(b). "*... appropriate instructions under clause 13.*"
This remedy is intended to cover the situation in which the Main Contractor is entitled to terminate the Sub-Contract, but the Engineer withholds his consent. Clause 13 contains a perfectly general power to give instructions "on any matter connected therewith (whether mentioned in the Contract or not)." In circumstances where the Sub-Contractor is in repudiatory breach, what instruction are "appropriate"? It is relevant to note that upon termination with consent, sub-clause (4)(e) protects the Contractor against loss, while the Contractor is himself responsible for breaches which do not lead to termination. It is thought that, at the least, the Engineer's instructions should be such as to facilitate continued performance and completion of the Sub-Contract Work, if necessary by instructing the Contractor himself to undertake parts, directly or through other Sub-Contractors. Note also that under clause 13(3), the Contractor is not entitled automatically to payment of additional cost incurred, but must show that it was "not reasonably to have been foreseen at the time of tender."

Clause 59(4)(d): Recovery of extra expense. This applies where the termination is with the Engineer's consent. The obligation to seek recovery from the Sub-Contractor should be read with the right under sub-clause (4)(e) to be reimbursed by the Employer in the event of non-recovery. The Contractor is also required to seek recovery of "any additional expenses incurred by the Employer as a result of the termination." The Main Contractor will not himself be liable for these additional expenses (unless they result from his breach of contract). The additional cost of renomination is not claimable against the Main Contractor, since the Main Contract provides expressly for these additional costs to be paid under clause 59(5). It is difficult to see what the Employer can effectively recover by virtue of this provision. The Employer should therefore be advised to protect himself against the possibility of repudiation by obtaining a direct warranty, which should expressly cover loss arising from termination of the Sub-Contract.[69]

---

[68] 5th edition 1973, clause 59B(2)–(5).
[69] For further discussion on warranties, see pp. 130 and 295.

Clause 59(4)(e): Reimbursement of Contractor's loss.   Contrary to the Employer's position, the Contractor is entitled to seek recovery first from the Sub-Contractor, and if unsuccessful, he is entitled virtually to a full indemnity from the Employer (subject only to the expenses being reasonable or proper). This clause is, in its effect, similar to clauses found in Management Contracts to the effect that the Main Contractor is liable only to the extent he can recover from the Sub-Contractor.[70] It is thought that objection to the enforceability of such clauses[71] would not apply under this clause, because the Contractor is prima facie liable, *e.g.* for the consequences of delay. The Employer's indemnity is similar to an insurance provision.

Clause 59(7): Payment to Nominated Sub-Contractors.   The right of direct payment arises only upon the Certificate of the Engineer, which must take into account "any reasonable cause for withholding payment." If the Contractor claims a right of set-off for breach by the Sub-Contractor the Engineer must, it is submitted, make an assessment of, and deduct the reasonable amount of the set-off before certifying to the Employer. The right of direct payment arises only where the sums in question have already been certified to the Contractor. The provision will not, therefore, entitle the Employer to make direct payments to Nominated Sub-Contractors upon the Contractor's insolvency without running the risk of double payment. It seems that the right of direct payment and the right of deduction may be exercised against the Contractor despite insolvency, where performance of the contract is continued.[72]

CERTIFICATES AND PAYMENT

Monthly statements

60   (1)   The Contractor shall submit to the Engineer at monthly intervals a statement (in such form if any as may be prescribed in the Specification) showing

(a)   the estimated contract value of the Permanent Works executed up to the end of that month
(b)   a list of any goods or materials delivered to the Site for but not yet incorporated in the Permanent Works and their value
(c)   a list of any of those goods or materials identified in the Appendix to the Form of Tender which have not yet been delivered to the Site but of which the property has vested in the Employer pursuant to clause 54 and their value and
(d)   the estimated amounts to which the Contractor considers himself entitled in connection with all other matters for which provision is made under the Contract including any Temporary Works or Contractor's Equipment for which separate amounts are included in the Bill of Quantities

---

[70] See JCT Management Contract 1987 edition, clause 3.21.
[71] See Liability for Default of Sub-Contractors see Peter Barber, "Proceedings of a Conference on Legal Obligations in Construction" (Kings College, London 1990).
[72] *Re Tout* v. *Finch* [1954] 1 W.L.R. 178; *Re Wilkinson ex p. Fowler* [1905] 2 K.B. 713.

unless in the opinion of the Contractor such values and amounts together will not justify the issue of an interim certificate.

Amounts payable in respect of Nominated Sub-Contracts are to be listed separately.

Monthly payments

(2)   Within 28 days of the date of delivery to the Engineer or Engineer's Representative in accordance with sub-clause (1) of this clause of the Contractor's monthly statement the Engineer shall certify and the Employer shall pay to the Contractor (after deducting any previous payments on account)

(a)   the amount which in the opinion of the Engineer on the basis of the monthly statement is due to the Contractor on account of sub-clauses (1)(a) and (1)(d) of this clause less a retention as provided in sub-clause (5) of this clause and
(b)   such amounts (if any) as the Engineer may consider proper (but in no case exceeding the percentage of the value stated in the Appendix to the Form of Tender) in respect of sub-clauses (1)(b) and (1)(c) of this clause.

The amounts certified in respect of Nominated Sub-Contracts shall be shown separately in the certificate.

Minimum amount of certificate

(3)   Until the whole of the Works has been certified as substantially complete in accordance with clause 48 the Engineer shall not be bound to issue an interim certificate for a sum less than that stated in the Appendix to the Form of Tender but thereafter he shall be bound to do so and the certification and payment of amounts due to the Contractor shall be in accordance with the time limits contained in this clause.

Final account

(4)   Not later than 3 months after the date of the Defects Correction Certificate the Contractor shall submit to the Engineer a statement of final account and supporting documentation showing in detail the value in accordance with the Contract of the Works executed together with all further sums which the Contractor considers to be due to him under the Contract up to the date of the Defects Correction Certificate.

Within 3 months after receipt of this final account and of all information reasonably required for its verification the Engineer shall issue a certificate stating the amount which in his opinion is finally due under the Contract from the Employer to the Contractor or from the Contractor to the Employer as the case may be up to the date of the Defects Correction Certificate and after giving credit to the Employer for all amounts previously paid by the Employer and for all sums to which the Employer is entitled under the Contract.

Such amount shall subject to clause 47 be paid to or by the Contractor as the case may require within 28 days of the date of the certificate.

Retention

(5)   The retention to be made pursuant to sub-clause (2)(a) of this clause shall be the difference beween

(a)   an amount calculated at the rate indicated in and up to the limit set out in the

Appendix to the Form of Tender upon the amount due to the Contractor on account of sub-clauses (1)(a) and (1)(d) of this clause and

(b) any payment which shall have become due under sub-clause (6) of this clause.

Payment of retention

(6) (a) Upon the issue of a Certificate of Substantial Completion in respect of any Section or part of the Works there shall become due to the Contractor one half of such proportion of the retention money deductible to date under sub-clause (5)(a) of this clause as the value of the Section or part bears to the value of the whole of the Works completed to date as certified under sub-clause (2)(a) of this clause and such amount shall be added to the amount next certified as due to the Contractor under sub-clause (2) of this clause.

The total of the amounts released shall in no event exceed one half of the limit of retention set out in the Appendix to the Form of Tender.

(b) Upon issue of the Certificate of Substantial Completion in respect of the whole of the Works there shall become due to the Contractor one half of the retention money calculated in accordance with sub-clause (5)(a) of this clause. The amount so due (or the balance thereof over and above such payments already made pursuant to sub-clause (6)(a) of this clause) shall be paid within 14 days of the issue of the said Certificate.

(c) Upon the expiry of the Defects Correction Period or if more than one the last of such periods the remainder of the retention money shall be paid to the Contractor within 14 days notwithstanding that at that time there may be outstanding claims by the Contractor against the Employer.

Provided that if at that time there remains to be executed by the Contractor any outstanding work referred to under clause 48 or any work ordered pursuant to clauses 49 or 50 the Employer may withhold payment until the completion of such work of so much of the said remainder as shall in the opinion of the Engineer represent the cost of the work remaining to be executed.

Interest on overdue payments

(7) In the event of

(a) failure by the Engineer to certify or the Employer to make payment in accordance with sub-clauses (2) (4) or (6) of this clause or

(b) any finding of an arbitrator to such effect

the Employer shall pay to the Contractor interest compounded monthly for each day on which any payment is overdue or which should have been certified and paid at a rate equivalent to 2 per cent. per annum above the base lending rate of the bank specified in the Appendix to the Form of Tender. If in an arbitration pursuant to clause 66 the arbitrator holds that any sum or additional sum should have been certified by a particular date in accordance with the aforementioned sub-clauses but was not so certified this shall be regarded for the purposes of this sub-clause as a failure to certify such sum or additional sum. Such sum or additional sum shall be regarded as overdue for payment 28 days after the date by which the arbitrator holds that the Engineer should have certified the sum or if no such date is identified by the arbitrator shall be regarded as overdue for payment from the date of the Certificate of Substantial Completion for the whole of the Works.

Correction and withholding of certificates

(8) The Engineer shall have power to omit from any certificate the value of any work

done goods or materials supplied or services rendered with which he may for the time being be dissatisfied and for that purpose or for any other reason which to him may seem proper may by any certificate delete correct or modify any sum previously certified by him. Provided that

(a) the Engineer shall not in any interim certificate delete or reduce any sum previously certified in respect of work done goods or materials supplied or services rendered by a Nominated Sub-contractor if the Contractor shall have already paid or be bound to pay that sum to the Nominated Sub-Contractor and

(b) if the Engineer in the final certificate shall delete or reduce any sum previously certified in respect of work done goods or materials supplied or services rendered by a Nominated Sub-Contractor which sum shall have been already paid by the Contractor to the Nominated Sub-Contractor the Employer shall reimburse to the Contractor the amount of any sum overpaid by the Contractor to the Sub-Contractor in accordance with the certificates issued under sub-clause (2) of this clause which the Contractor shall be unable to recover from the Nominated Sub-Contractor together with interest thereon at the rate stated in sub-clause (7) of this clause from 28 days after the date of the final certificate issued under sub-clause (4) of this clause until the date of such reimbursement.

Copy of certificate for Contractor

(9) Every certificate issued by the Engineer pursuant to this clause shall be sent to the Employer and at the same time copied to the Contractor with such detailed explanation as may be necessary.

Payment advice

(10) Where a payment made in accordance with sub-clause (2) of this clause differs in any respect from the amount certified by the Engineer the Employer shall notify the Contractor forthwith with full details showing how the amount being paid has been calculated.

Clause 60: Certificates and Payment

This clause requires the Contractor to submit at monthly intervals a valuation of the Works (sub-clause (1)) and requires the Engineer to issue an interim certificate within 28 days (sub-clause (2)). After issue of the Maintenance certificate the Engineer must give a certificate (no longer called the Final certificate) stating the amount finally due (sub-clause (4)). Interim payments are subject to retention (sub-clause (2)(a) and (4)), save that for goods and materials, the amount to be certified is not subject to retention but is to be the amount which the Engineer "may consider proper," not exceeding the percentage stated in the Appendix to the Tender (sub-clause (2)(b)). The retention is to be paid half on Substantial Completion (with provision for sectional arrangements) and the remainder 14 days after expiry of the Defects Correction Period, but subject to deductions (sub-clause (6)). There are provisions for payment of interest on over-due payments (sub-clause (7)) and for the correction and withholding of certificates (sub-clause (8)).

907

Clause 60(1). "... *goods or materials* ..."

The interim valuation may include goods or materials on site (paragraph (b)) and those not on site in which the property has vested in the Employer pursuant to clause 54 (paragraph (c)). In the latter case the vesting is to be signified by the Engineer's approval in writing under clause 54(3). Note that in each case the goods and materials are not subject to retention, but to a capping percentage, which is to be stated in the Appendix to the Tender (sub-clause (2)(b)).

Clause 60(1)(d). "... *all other matters for which provision is made under the Contract* ..."

This includes claims under various clauses of the Conditions: see commentary to clause 52(4) for claims expressed to be subject to that clause. Other claims or rights to additional payment may arise under clause 17 (setting out), 20(3) (reinstatement works), 22(3) (damage to persons or property), 26(2) (fees, rates), 30(3) (damage to highways), 32 (fossils), 36(3) (tests), 38(2) (uncovering), 49(3) (repair work), 50 (searches), 64 (frustration), 65 (war) and 69 (tax fluctuations). The Contractor is expressly required by clause 69(2) to inform the Engineer of changes in taxes, etc. VAT is dealt with under clause 70. The Engineer's certificate is required to be net of VAT, the Employer being required separately to identify and pay any VAT properly chargeable. The Contractor is not required himself to assess the VAT.

Clause 60(2). "... *the Engineer shall certify and the Employer shall pay* ..."

The question whether an interim certificate is a condition precedent to the right to payment has not been definitively decided.[73] However, in the light of the decision in the *Crouch* case,[74] the court could not entertain a claim for payment without a certificate, unless interference or other misconduct were also alleged.[75] Where a certificate has been given, the Court may, despite the *Crouch* case, entertain an application for Summary Judgment[76] on the basis that there is no dispute to be referred to arbitration.[77] A similar application may now be made under the I.C.E. Arbitration Procedure (1983), Rule 14, for a "Summary Award."[78] The advantage of an application to an arbitrator is that he is empowered to open up and revise any certificate or valuation of the Engineer,[79] which will include the power to supply any certificate that ought to have been given.

---

[73] See *Dunlop & Ranken Ltd.* v. *Hendall* [1957] 1 W.L.R. 1102 at 1106 (Q.B.D.); *Lubenham Fidelities* v. *South Pembrokeshire D.C.* (1986) 33 B.L.R. 39 (C.A.); see also *Gilbert-Ash* v. *Modern Engineering* [1974] A.C. 689 (H.L.).
[74] *Northern Regional Health Authority* v. *Derek Crouch* [1984] Q.B. 644 (C.A.)—see p. 389.
[75] See pp. 104 and 114 *et seq.*
[76] See *Ellis Mechanical* v. *Wates* [1978] 1 Lloyds Rep. 33 (C.A.); the *Kostas Melas* [1981] 1 Lloyds Rep. 18 at 27.
[77] But see *Hayter* v. *Nelson* [1990] 2 Lloyd's Rep. 265; *Mayer Newman* v. *Al Ferro*, *The Times*, April 9, 1990, noted at (1990) C.I.L.L. 577.
[78] See commentary to clause 66.
[79] Clause 66(8)(a).

The Employer retains the right of set-off.[80] The Engineer should certify the full amount due in accordance with sub-clause (2), leaving the Employer to make any deduction, *e.g.* for liquidated damages.

Clause 60(2)(b). *"... such amounts (if any) as the Engineer may consider proper ..."*
These words qualify the Contractor's right to payment for goods or materials. There is no indication of the matters which the Engineer may, or is bound to take into account. It is thought that the Engineer should take into account their conditions of storage and security of goods or materials delivered to the site. For materials both on site and off-site, the Engineer may take into account the date by which they are likely to be required and, where the goods are provided substantially in advance, the reasons for this.

Clause 60(4): Final Account. References to the "Final certificate" appearing in the 5th edition of the I.C.E. Conditions have been removed. The Engineer is required to issue a certificate (which will in fact be the final one issued) stating the amount finally due to or from the Contractor after making allowance for "all sums to which the Employer is entitled under the Contract." This appears to mean that the Engineer is to set-off cross-claims, which may include liquidated damages. However, the closing words of the sub-clause refer to payment "subject to clause 47," which would entitle the Employer to deduct liquidated damages from the certified sum. The sums to be deducted before giving the certificate do not include cross-claims for damages, which are not due "under the Contract," nor is the Engineer empowered to consider such claims save on a reference under clause 66. Whatever it is called, the last certificate is of no evidential effect as regards performance of the Contract, in contrast with the Final certificate under the Standard Form of Building Contract.[81]

Clause 60(5) and (6): Retention. The maximum recommended percentages stated in the Appendix are 5 per cent. with a limit of 3 per cent. of the "Tender Total,"[82] which will give a fixed monetary limit. Retention will be deducted pursuant to sub-clause (2)(a) on the value of work and other amounts due. There is an effective retention on goods and materials by virtue of sub-clause (2)(b), which is likely to be greater than the retention percentage, and this will be converted into a normal retention as the goods and materials become incorporated into the Works.
On any section or part reaching substantial completion, a proportional part of the retention deducted up to that date becomes payable. This may turn out to be more than would have been released had the capping figure been

---

[80] *Gilbert-Ash* v. *Modern Engineering* [1974] A.C. 689 (H.L.).
[81] See p. 610.
[82] See clause 1(1)(i).

reached, but it will be adjusted automatically for later sections or parts so that the Employer ends up holding half the limit of retention at substantial completion of the whole of the Works. Retention which is released is either to be added to the next interim certificate or, at substantial completion of the whole of the Works, any outstanding retention money up to the limit of one half becomes payable automatically 14 days after the Certificate of Substantial Completion. Note that the second half of retention is payable in one sum on expiry of the last of the Defects Correction Periods, subject to deduction for any outstanding work.

Clause 60(7): Interest on overdue payments. This redrafted clause has finally clarified the Contractor's entitlement to interest, which will run from the date on which the payment became due (if certified) or the date on which it should have been certified and paid (if not certified). The entitlement covers any sums capable of certification under clause 60(1), which includes all payments becoming due "under the Contract." It does not include claims for damages (see above). There is no provision for certifying interest under this sub-clause. It is payable automatically upon a failure to certify or make payment being admitted or established by arbitration. Interest will be payable under the sub-clause whether or not formally included in the Arbitrator's award. It will normally be convenient to include it in the Award, however, to facilitate payment or enforcement.

The new provisions avoid problems which have occurred under the equivalent clause in the 5th edition.[83] The contractual right to interest on overdue payments does not affect the question of interest being recovered as part of the cost incurred and payable under other provisions of the Contract.[84] Nor does the provision abrogate the power of an Arbitrator to award discretionary interest.[85] The Arbitrator's statutory power is, however, limited to the award of simple interest. Given a choice of statutory or contractual interest, there would seem to be no circumstances in which the Contractor would wish to opt for the former.

Clause 60(8): Correction and withholding of certificates. The Engineer has a wide discretion to modify previous certificates and to deduct sums accordingly from subsequent certificates. There is no inference that an interim certificate constitutes any approval or has any binding effect on either party.

The proviso to sub-clause (8) prevents reduction of sums for Nominated Sub-Contract work where the Contractor has paid or is bound to pay the Sub-Contractor. Where the Main Contractor has himself withheld payment by reason of a set-off, he is not "bound to pay" the sum in question and the

---

[83] See *Morgan Grenfell (Local Authority Finance)* v. *Seven Seas Dredging* (1990) C.I.L.L. 618.
[84] See commentary to clause 1(5).
[85] Arbitration Act 1950, s.19A.

Engineer may reduce the valuation accordingly. There is no restriction on the right of adjustment on the Final Account. The Employer may have to repay the sum with interest, but the obligation to repay will arise only when the Contractor can demonstrate that he is "unable to recover" from the Nominated Sub-Contractor. Where the Sub-Contractor remains solvent, it is thought this would require the Contractor to bring arbitration proceedings and to bear the cost of such proceedings himself.[86]

Defects Correction Certificate

61 (1) Upon the expiry of the Defects Correction Period or where there is more than one such period upon the expiration of the last of such periods and when all outstanding work referred to under clause 48 and all work of repair amendment reconstruction rectification and making good of defects imperfections shrinkages and other faults referred to under clauses 49 and 50 shall have been completed the Engineer shall issue to the Employer (with a copy to the Contractor) a Defects Correction Certificate stating the date on which the Contractor shall have completed his obligations to construct and complete the Works to the Engineer's satisfaction.

Unfulfilled obligations

(2) The issue of the Defects Correction Certificate shall not be taken as relieving either the Contractor or the Employer from any liability the one towards the other arising out of or in any way connected with the performance of their respective obligations under the Contract.

Clause 61

The Defects Correction Certificate (formerly known as the Maintenance Certificate) signifies completion to the Engineer's satisfaction. It further sets in train the procedure under clause 60(4) leading to the final account and final certificate (not actually called the final certificate). Sub-clause (2) makes clear that the Defects Correction Certificate has no substantive effect on the rights or obligations of either party. It is an administrative step only, but it affects the operation of other clauses under the contract. Thus the Contractor has no duty or right himself to carry out further remedial work under clause 49 once the Certificate has been given. In theory, this will leave the Employer having to sue for damages if further defects or outstanding work are discovered. In practice, there is nothing to prevent the parties coming to an agreement for the Contractor to carry out further work, and the Employer may fail to mitigate his loss if he does not so permit the Contractor to do so.

REMEDIES AND POWERS

Urgent repairs

62 If by reason of any accident or failure or other event occurring to in or in connection

---

[86] See also clause 59(4)(e), which applies only where a Nominated Sub-Contract has been terminated with the Engineer's consent.

with the Works or any part thereof either during the execution of the Works or during the Defects Correction Period any remedial or other work or repair shall in the opinion of the Engineer or the Engineer's Representative be urgently necessary and the Contractor is unable or unwilling at once to do such work or repair the Employer may by his own or other workpeople do such work or repair. If the work or repair so done by the Employer is work which in the opinion of the Engineer the Contractor was liable to do at his own expense under the Contract all costs and charges properly incurred by the Employer in so doing shall on demand be paid by the Contractor to the Employer or may be deducted by the Employer from any monies due or which may become due to the Contractor. Provided that the Engineer shall as soon after the occurrence of any such emergency as may be reasonably practicable notify the Contractor thereof in writing.

Clause 62

This useful power may be exercised by the Engineer or his Representative at any time up to the date of the Defects Correction Certificate. The right to bring in other people to do the work and to charge the Contractor therefor is dependant upon notice being given "as soon after the occurrence . . . as may be reasonably practicable." In the absence of notice, the Employer may not be entitled to set-off his costs unless it can be shown that the Contractor was in default.[87] Where the urgency is not immediate, the Engineer should consider acting under the alternative provisions of clauses 39(1) before the Certificate of Substantial Completion, or under clause 49 afterwards.

DETERMINATION OF THE CONTRACTOR'S EMPLOYMENT

Determination of the Contractor's employment

63 (1) If

    (a) the Contractor shall be in default in that he
        (i) becomes bankrupt or has a receiving order or administration order made against him or presents his petition in bankruptcy or makes an arrangement with or assignment in favour of his creditors or agrees to carry out the Contract under a committee of inspection of his creditors or (being a corporation) goes into liquidation (other than a voluntary liquidation for the purposes of amalgamation or reconstruction) or
        (ii) assigns the Contract without the consent in writing of the Employer first obtained or
        (iii) has an execution levied on his goods which is not stayed or discharged within 28 days

or

    (b) the Engineer certifies in writing to the Employer with a copy to the Contractor that in his opinion the Contractor
        (i) has abandoned the Contract or
        (ii) without reasonable excuse has failed to commence the Works in accordance with clause 41 or has suspended the progress of the Works for 14 days after receiving from the Engineer written notice to proceed or

---

[87] See commentary to clause 39(1).

(iii) has failed to remove goods or materials from the Site or to pull down and replace work for 14 days after receiving from the Engineer written notice that the said goods materials or work have been condemned and rejected by the Engineer or

(iv) despite previous warnings by the Engineer in writing is failing to proceed with the Works with due diligence or is otherwise persistently or fundamentally in breach of his obligations under Contract

then the Employer may after giving 7 days' notice in writing to the Contractor specifying the default enter upon the Site and the Works and expel the Contractor therefrom without thereby avoiding the Contract or releasing the Contractor from any of his obligations or liabilities under the Contract. Provided that the Employer may extend the period of notice to give the Contractor opportunity to remedy the default.

Where a notice of determination is given pursuant to this sub-clause it shall be given as soon as is reasonably possible after receipt of the Engineer's certificate.

Completing the Works

(2)   Where the Employer has entered upon the Site and the Works as hereinbefore provided he may himself complete the Works or may employ any other contractor to complete the Works and the Employer or such other contractor may use for such completion so much of the Contractor's Equipment Temporary Works goods and materials which have been deemed to become the property of the Employer under clauses 53 and 54 as he or they may think proper and the Employer may at any time sell any of the said Contractor's Equipment Temporary Works and unused goods and materials and apply the proceeds of sale in or towards the satisfaction of any sums due or which may become due to him from the Contractor under the Contract.

Assignment to Employer

(3)   By the said notice or by further notice in writing within 7 days of the date of expiry thereof the Engineer may require the Contractor to assign to the Employer and if so required the Contractor shall forthwith assign to the Employer the benefit of any agreement for the supply of any goods or materials and/or for the execution of any work for the purposes of this Contract which the Contractor may have entered into.

Payment after determination

(4)   If the Employer enters and expels the Contractor under this clause he shall not be liable to pay to the Contractor any money on account of the Contract until the expiration of the Defects Correction Period and thereafter until the costs of completion damages for delay in completion (if any) and all other expenses incurred by the Employer have been ascertained and the amount thereof certified by the Engineer.

The Contractor shall then be entitled to receive only such sum or sums (if any) as the Engineer may certify would have been due to him upon due completion by him after deducting the said amount. But if such amount shall exceed the sum which would have been payable to the Contractor on due completion by him then the Contractor shall upon demand pay to the Employer the amount of such excess and it shall be deemed a debt due by the Contractor to the Employer and shall be recoverable accordingly.

Valuation at date of determination

(5)   As soon as may be practicable after any such entry and expulsion by the Employer the Engineer shall fix and determine as at the time of such entry and expulsion

913

(a) the amount (if any) which had been reasonably earned by or would reasonably accrue to the Contractor in respect of work actually done by him under the Contract and

(b) the value of any unused or partially used goods and materials and any Contractor's Equipment and Temporary Works which had been deemed to become the property of the Employer under clauses 53 and 54

and shall certify accordingly.

The said determination may be carried out ex parte or by or after reference to the parties or after such investigation or enquiry as the Engineer may think fit to make or institute.

Clause 63

This clause has been rearranged and rewritten in part. It still suffers from a number of difficulties, largely through the possibility of there being a technical defect in the operation of the clause. This will usually mean that the Employer cannot rely on the clause, and unless it can be shown that the Contractor was in repudiatory breach of the Contract,[88] the Employer is likely to be held himself to be in repudiation by expelling the Contractor. Determination of the Contractor's employment does not terminate the Contract. Both parties remain bound to perform the secondary obligations under this clause which come into play upon a correct determination.

Clause 63(1)(a): Automatic right of determination. The grounds are matters of record which, if they occur, give an immediate right to serve the seven-day notice. The clause does not deal with the question of delay before giving notice. This is expressly dealt with where the Engineer gives a certificate. Nor does the clause deal with any delay in the Employer becoming aware of the relevant events. This may well be significant in the case of assignment without consent. Each case would depend on the particular facts, and the Employer should be advised to proceed with considerable caution where there is a possibility of waiver or estoppel being raised.[89]

Clause 63(1)(b): Grounds dependant upon the Engineer's certificate:

(i) ".. *has abandoned the contract* ..."

Abandonment is referred to in clause 40(2) in connection with a suspension of the progress of the Works. It is thought that abandonment denotes at least a suspension coupled with an apparent intention not to continue.

(ii) "... *failed to commence* ..."

Clause 41 requires the Contractor to start the Works "as soon as is reasonably practicable after the Works Commencement Date." The Engineer must therefore be satisfied that it is reasonably practicable to start and that there is

---

[88] See pp. 153 *et seq.*
[89] See pp. 262 *et seq.*

no reasonable excuse. It is not clear to what circumstances the 14-day suspension refers, and whether the Engineer's notice to proceed is simply the notice under clause 41(1)(b), or some specific notice.[90]

(iii) "*...failed to remove ... or to pull down and replace ...*"

This provision clearly links with clause 39. The 14-day period would seem to apply whether or not the Engineer's notice itself specified a period for compliance.[91] Clause 39 contains an alternative remedy of employing others to do the work, but there is no restriction on operation of the alternative remedy of determination.

(iv) "*... is failing to proceed with the Works with due diligence ...*"

Refer to commentary to clause 42(2), which uses the term "due expedition." This refers to the rate of progress, whereas it is thought that, to establish a lack of "due diligence," it would have to be shown that the Contractor was not putting enough effort or resources into the work. The distinction is therefore important in terms of the material and evidence which the Employer would need to rely upon in order to justify a disputed determination. Note that there must be "previous warnings" from the Engineer, which indicates at least two such warnings.

(v) "*... or is otherwise persistently or fundamentally in breach of his obligations under the contract ...*"

This appears also to require previous warnings. "Persistently" and "fundamentally" are alternatives. A breach need not be serious in order to be persistent, but it must involve either repeated or continuing occurrences, *e.g.* repeated execution of bad work or continuing failure to rectify. "Fundamentally" indicates a breach of a very serious nature going to the root of the Contract.[92]

Clause 63(1): Action by the Employer.   Provided that the relevant event under sub-clause 1(1)(a) has occurred or the Engineer's certificate under (b) has been given, the Employer must then himself give seven-days notice in writing "specifying the default." This is apparently the "notice of determination" which is to be given as soon as reasonably possible after receipt of the Engineer's certificate, *i.e.* the Employer must make up his mind at once whether to determine. Plainly, such a fundamental step is not to be taken without careful thought and planning. The Employer must be careful not to influence the Engineer in giving or withholding his certificate under clause 63(1)(b).[93] However, it is perfectly proper for the Employer, if he wishes to consider termination, to request the Engineer to consider whether he is

---

[90] Comparison with the equivalent provisions in the 5th and 4th editions of the I.C.E. Conditions suggests a connection which is, however, not readily apparent under the present edition.

[91] Compare clause 39(1)(a), where time may be specified, and (c), where apparently it may not.

[92] See p. 149.

[93] See pp. 114 *et seq.*

prepared to give a certificate under sub-clause 1(1)(b). The Employer should be advised to be quite open about his intentions, since correspondence with the Engineer will be discoverable in any subsequent arbitration proceedings.

It is unclear whether the Employer's right of determination crystallises when a correct notice is served, so that the Contractor may be expelled from the site irrespective of any steps taken to remedy the matters complained of during the seven-day notice period. The proviso allowing the Employer to extend "the period of notice to give the Contractor opportunity to remedy the default" suggests that the right of determination may be lost if the Contractor puts right his default. This question is of such importance that the clause ought to be clarified.

The contract gives no further guidance about what is meant by "enter upon the site and the Works" or "expel the Contractor therefrom." Since the Employer may be an occupier of the site, entry must contemplate an act going beyond mere occupation. The Employer must, it is thought, take such action as will leave no doubt that the right of entry and expulsion has been exercised. This will usually consist of locking up the site and taking other measures to secure materials and equipment which the Employer intends to claim as security.[94]

Clause 63(2): Completing the Works. The right to use or dispose of the Contractor's plant and materials, etc., is dependant upon the Employer being able to defeat any adverse claims thereto from other persons claiming property in them, including the Contractor's Receiver or Trustee in Bankruptcy. Note that materials under clause 54 should be the Employer's property beyond dispute, if the clause has been properly operated. However, the Employer will not have paid for such materials in full.[95]

Clause 63(3): Requirement to assign. It is not at all clear what is meant by "the said notice." The Engineer's notice under sub-clause 1(1)(b) is to be given to the Employer, and the notice of determination is given by the Employer. Nor is it at all clear when the said notice expires. These points are of little importance, save that they might be said to restrict the Engineer's right to require the Contractor to assign. There is nothing to prevent the Employer entering into direct arrangements with Sub-Contractors and suppliers. In practice, the arrangement will usually amount to a novation, and it will be necessary to consider carefully the payment obligations which the Employer is to take on.

Clause 63(4): Payment after determination: Determination is likely to lead to a large net deficit which the Employer must seek to recover from the Contractor. The accounting process does not appear to permit the Employer

---

[94] See clause 53.
[95] See clause 60(1)(c) and 60(2)(b).

to recover his loss until completion of the Works. An arbitration may be commenced at any time, and it may be that the parties can circumvent this procedural difficulty (if the reference proceeds before completion) by a preliminary hearing on the validity of the termination, assuming this to be in dispute. If the Employer alternatively relies on common law repudiation, there could be a damages claim brought immediately after termination.

FRUSTRATION

Payment in event of frustration

64 In the event of the Contract being frustrated whether by war or by any other supervening event which may occur independently of the will of the parties the sum payable by the Employer to the Contractor in respect of the work executed shall be the same as that which would have been payable under clause 65(5) if the Contract had been determined by the Employer under clause 65.

Clause 64

The term "frustrated" is used, it is thought, in the legal sense, meaning a supervening event which renders performance or further performance of the contract radically different from that contemplated.[96] The words "by any other supervening event which may occur independently of the will of the parties" confirm what would otherwise be the position at common law. It is thought that the provision entitling the Contractor to payment of a sum calculated by reference to clause 65(5) excludes the operation of section 1 of the Law Reform (Frustrated Contracts) Act 1943.[97] This section would otherwise require the Contractor to prove that the Employer had obtained a valuable benefit from the Contract in order to be able to recover even the value of work done.[98]

WAR CLAUSE

Works to continue for 28 days on outbreak of war

65 (1) If during the currency of the Contract there shall be an outbreak of war (whether war is declared or not) in which Great Britain shall be engaged on a scale involving general mobilization of the armed forces of the Crown the Contractor shall for a period of 28 days reckoned from midnight on the date that the order for general mobilization is given continue so far as is physically possible to execute the Works in accordance with the Contract.

---

[96] See p. 134.
[97] By s.2(3).
[98] s.1(2) and (3). See further "Law Reform (Frustrated Contracts) Act 1943" at p. 140.

Effect of completion within 28 days

(2) If at any time before the expiration of the said period of 28 days the Works shall have been completed or completed so far as to be usable all provisions of the Contract shall continue to have full force and effect save that

(a) the Contractor shall in lieu of fulfilling his obligations under clauses 49 and 50 be entitled at his option to allow against the sum due to him under the provisions hereof the cost (calculated at the prices ruling at the beginning of the said period of 28 days) as certified by the Engineer at the expiration of the Defects Correction Period of repair rectification and making good any work for the repair rectification or making good of which the Contractor would have been liable under the said clauses had they continued to be applicable

(b) the Employer shall not be entitled at the expiry of the Defects Correction Period to withhold payment under clause 60(5)(c) of the second half of the retention money or any part thereof except such sum as may be allowable by the Contractor under the provisions of the last preceding paragraph which sum may (without prejudice to any other mode of recovery thereof) be deducted by the Employer from such second half.

Right of Employer to determine Contract

(3) If the Works shall not have been completed as aforesaid the Employer shall be entitled to determine the Contract (with the exception of this clause and clauses 66 and 68) by giving notice in writing to the Contractor at any time after the aforesaid period of 28 days has expired and upon such notice being given the Contract shall (except as above mentioned) forthwith determine but without prejudice to the claims of either party in respect of any antecedent breach thereof.

Removal of Contractor's Equipment on determination

(4) If the Contract shall be determined under the provisions of the last preceding sub-clause the Contractor shall with all reasonable despatch remove from the Site all his Contractor's Equipment and shall give facilities to his sub-contractors to remove similarly all Contractor's Equipment belonging to them and in the event of any failure so to do the Employer shall have the like powers as are contained in clause 53(3) in regard to failure to remove Contractor's Equipment on completion of the Works but subject to the same condition as is contained in clause 53(3).

Payment on determination

(5) If the Contract shall be determined as aforesaid the Contractor shall be paid by the Employer (insofar as such amounts or items shall not have been already covered by payment on account made to the Contractor) for all work executed prior to the date of determination at the rates and prices provided in the Contract and in addition

(a) the amounts payable in respect of any preliminary items so far as the work or service comprised therein has been carried out or performed and a proper proportion as certified by the Engineer of any such items the work or service comprised in which has been partially carried out or performed

(b) the cost of materials or goods reasonably ordered for the Works which have been delivered to the Contractor or of which the Contractor is legally liable to accept delivery (such materials or goods becoming the property of the Employer upon such payment being made by him)

(c) a sum to be certified by the Engineer being the amount of any expenditure reasonably incurred by the Contractor in the expectation of completing the whole of the Works in so far as such expenditure shall not have been covered by the payments in this sub-clause before mentioned

(d) any additional sum payable under sub-clause (6)(b)(c) and (d) of this clause and

(e) the reasonable cost of removal under sub-clause (4) of this clause.

Provisions to apply as from outbreak of war

(6) Whether the Contract shall be determined under the provisions of sub-clause (3) of this clause or not the following provisions shall apply or be deemed to have applied as from the date of the said outbreak of war notwithstanding anything expressed in or implied by the other terms of the Contract viz

(a) The Contractor shall be under no liability whatsoever by way of indemnity or otherwise for or in respect of damage to the Works or to property (other than property of the Contractor or property hired by him for the purposes of executing the Works) whether of the Employer or of third parties or for or in respect of injury or loss of life to persons which is the consequence whether direct or indirect of war hostilities (whether war has been declared or not) invasion act of the Queen's enemies civil war rebellion revolution insurrection military or usurped power and the Employer shall indemnify the Contractor against all such liabilities and against all claims demands proceedings damages costs charges and expenses whatsoever arising thereout or in connection therewith.

(b) If the Works shall sustain destruction or any damage by reason of any of the causes mentioned in the last preceding paragraph the Contractor shall nevertheless be entitled to payment for any part of the Works so destroyed or damaged and the Contractor shall be entitled to be paid by the Employer the cost of making good any such destruction or damage so far as may be required by the Engineer or as may be necessary for the completion of the Works on a cost basis plus such profit as the Engineer may certify to be reasonable.

(c) In the event that the Contract includes the Contract Price Fluctuations Clause the terms of that clause shall continue to apply but if subsequent to the outbreak of war the index figures therein referred to shall cease to be published or in the event that the Contract shall not include a Contract Price Fluctuations Clause in that form the following paragraph shall have effect:

If under decision of the Civil Engineering Construction Conciliation Board or of any other body recognized as an appropriate body for regulating the rates of wages in any trade or industry other than the Civil Engineering Construction Industry to which Contractors undertaking works of civil engineering construction give effect by agreement or in practice or by reason of any Statute or Statutory Instrument there shall during the currency of the Contract be any increase or decrease in the wages or the rates of wages or in the allowances or rates of allowances (including allowances in respect of holidays) payable to or in respect of labour of any kind prevailing at the date of outbreak of war as then fixed by the said Board or such other body as aforesaid or by Statute or Statutory Instrument or any increase in the amount payable by the Contractor by virtue or in respect of any Scheme of State Insurance or if there shall be any increase or decrease in the cost prevailing at the date of the said outbreak of war of any materials consumable stores fuel or power (and whether for permanent or temporary works) which increase or increases decrease or decreases shall result in an

919

increase or decrease of cost to the Contractor in carrying out the Works the net increase or decrease of cost shall form an addition or deduction as the case may be to or from the Contract Price and be paid to or allowed by the Contractor accordingly.

(d)   If the cost of the Works to the Contractor shall be increased or decreased by reason of the provisions of any Statute or Statutory Instrument or other Government or Local Government Order or Regulation becoming applicable to the Works after the date of the said outbreak of war or by reason of any trade or industrial agreement entered in to after such date to which the Civil Engineering Construction Conciliation Board or any other body as aforesaid is party or gives effect or by reason of any amendment of whatsoever nature of the Working Rule Agreement of the said Board or of any other body as aforesaid or by reason of any other circumstance or thing attributable to or consequent on such outbreak of war such increase or decrease of cost as certified by the Engineer shall be reimbursed by the Employer to the Contractor or allowed by the Contractor as the case may be.

(e)   Damage or injury caused by the explosion whenever occurring of any mine bomb shell grenade or other projectile missile or munition of war and whether occurring before or after the cessation of hostilities shall be deemed to be the consequence of any of the events mentioned in sub-clause (6)(a) of this clause.

Clause 65

This clause applies to war involving general mobilisation. Its only practical importance is that, upon the Contract being frustrated under clause 64, the payment provisions of sub-clause (5) are to apply.

SETTLEMENT OF DISPUTES

Settlement of disputes

66   (1)   Except as otherwise provided in these Conditions if a dispute of any kind whatsoever arises between the Employer and the Contractor in connection with or arising out of the Contract or the carrying out of the Works including any dispute as to any decision opinion instruction direction certificate or valuation of the Engineer (whether during the progress of the Works or after their completion and whether before or after the determination abandonment or breach of the Contract) it shall be settled in accordance with the following provisions.

Notice of Dispute

(2)   For the purpose of sub-clauses (2) to (6) inclusive of this clause a dispute shall be deemed to arise when one party serves on the Engineer a notice in writing (hereinafter called the Notice of Dispute) stating the nature of the dispute. Provided that no Notice of Dispute may be served unless the party wishing to do so has first taken any steps or invoked any procedure available elsewhere in the Contract in connection with the subject matter of such dispute and the other party or the Engineer as the case may be has

(a)   taken such step as may be required or

(b)   been allowed a reasonable time to take any such action.

Engineer's decision

(3)   Every dispute notified under sub-clause (2) of this clause shall be settled by the Engineer who shall state his decision in writing and give notice of the same to the Employer and the Contractor within the time limits set out in sub-clause (6) of this clause.

Effect on Contractor and Employer

(4)   Unless the Contract has already been determined or abandoned the Contractor shall in every case continue to proceed with the Works with all due diligence and the Contractor and the Employer shall both give effect forthwith to every such decision of the Engineer. Such decisions shall be final and binding upon the Contractor and the Employer unless and until as hereinafter provided either

(a)   the recommendation of a conciliator has been accepted by both parties or
(b)   the decision of the Engineer is revised by an arbitrator and an award made and published.

Conciliation

(5)   In relation to any dispute notified under sub-clause (2) of this clause and in respect of which

(a)   the Engineer has given his decision or
(b)   the time for giving an Engineer's decision as set out in sub-clause (3) of this clause has expired

and no Notice to Refer under sub-clause (6) of this clause has been served either party may give notice in writing requiring the dispute to be considered under the Institution of Civil Engineers' Conciliation Procedure (1988) or any amendment or modification thereof being in force at the date of such notice and the dispute shall thereafter be referred and considered in accordance with the said Procedure. The recommendation of the conciliator shall be deemed to have been accepted in settlement of the dispute unless a written Notice to Refer under sub-clause (6) of this clause is served within one calendar month of its receipt.

Arbitration

(6)   (a)   Where a Certificate of Substantial Completion of the whole of the Works has not been issued and either
        (i)   the Employer or the Contractor is dissatisfied with any decision of the Engineer given under sub-clause (3) of this clause or
        (ii)   the Engineer fails to give such decision for a period of one calendar month after the service of the Notice of Dispute or
        (iii)   the Employer or the Contractor is dissatisfied with any recommendation of a conciliator appointed under sub-clause (5) of this clause
      then either the Employer or the Contractor may within 3 calendar months after receiving notice of such decision or within 3 calendar months after the expiry of the said period of one month or within one calendar month of receipt of the

conciliator's recommendation (as the case may be) refer the dispute to the arbitration of a person to be agreed upon by the parties by serving on the other party a written Notice to Refer.

(b) Where a Certificate of Substantial Completion of the whole of the Works has been issued the foregoing provisions shall apply save that the said periods of one calendar month referred to in (a) above shall be read as 3 calendar months.

President or Vice-President to act

(7) (a) If the parties fail to appoint an arbitrator within one calendar month of either party serving on the other party written Notice to Concur in the appointment of an arbitrator the dispute or difference shall be referred to a person to be appointed on the application of either party by the President for the time being of the Institution of Civil Engineers.

(b) If an arbitrator declines the appointment or after appointment is removed by order of a competent court or is incapable of acting or dies and the parties do not within one calendar month of the vacancy arising fill the vacancy then either party may apply to the President for the time being of the Institution of Civil Engineers to appoint another arbitrator to fill the vacancy.

(c) In any case where the President for the time being of the Institution of Civil Engineers is not able to exercise the functions conferred on him by this clause the said functions shall be exercised on his behalf by a Vice-President for the time being of the said Institution.

Arbitration—procedure and powers

(8) (a) Any reference to arbitration under this clause shall be deemed to be a submission to arbitration within the meaning of the Arbitration Acts 1950 to 1979 or any statutory re-enactment or amendment thereof for the time being in force. The reference shall be conducted in accordance with the Institution of Civil Engineers Arbitration Procedure (1983) or any amendment or modification thereof being in force at the time of the appointment of the arbitrator. Such arbitrator shall have full power to open up review and revise any decision opinion instruction direction certificate or valuation of the Engineer.

(b) Neither party shall be limited in the proceedings before such arbitrator to the evidence or arguments put before the Engineer for the purpose of obtaining his decision under sub-clause (3) of this clause.

(c) The award of the arbitrator shall be binding on all parties.

(d) Unless the parties otherwise agree in writing any reference to arbitration may proceed notwithstanding that the Works are not then complete or alleged to be complete.

Engineer as witness

(9) No decision given by the Engineer in accordance with the foregoing provisions shall disqualify him from being called as witness and giving evidence before the arbitrator on any matter whatsoever relevant to the dispute or difference so referred to the arbitrator.

Clause 66: Settlement of Disputes

Nature of clause. The Contract embodies a three or four stage dispute process. An issue will normally arise first under the Contract by one party making a claim or assertion. The Engineer will usually give a decision on such issue in the form of a certificate or other action as provided under the Contract. The second stage is the reference to the Engineer under sub-clauses (2) and (3) of this clause. His decision (or failure to give a decision) may then be followed by a reference to arbitration. There is an additional, fourth stage, of conciliation which may take place at the option of either party between reference to the Engineer and arbitration. In some circumstances, conciliation may result in a binding resolution of the issue.

Multi-stage dispute procedure was unique to I.C.E. Contracts. Its use has, however, become widespread internationally as a result of adoption in the International F.I.D.I.C. Conditions of Contract.[99] The current edition of these Conditions also provides a form of conciliation through a requirement that arbitration is not to commence until a period has elapsed during which the parties may attempt amicable settlement.[1] The complexity of these multi-stage disputes clauses is such that procedural and jurisdictional disputes are now common.[2]

Clause 66, after remaining virtually unchanged through five editions of the I.C.E. Conditions, has now undergone a number of substantial revisions. The version printed with the 5th edition provided a single timetable for the Engineer's decision and reference to arbitration, with a general embargo on proceeding with an arbitration until completion, save with the consent of the other party. Both these provisions were substantially amended in a revision published in March 1985.[3] That revision, for the first time, required the Engineer's decision to be given in one calendar month where a dispute was referred before completion and (most importantly) removed any bar to arbitration during the course of the work. The present clause adopts these changes and introduces the further option of conciliation. This provision, together with sub-clause (2) (Notice of Dispute), owes its origin to the I.C.E. Conditions of Contract for Minor Works, produced in 1988.

This clause, as other arbitration clauses under Construction Contracts, is of immense importance in the light of the *Crouch* case.[4] The clause must be read as defining the circumstances in which an arbitral dispute may be raised. Failure or inability to comply with the procedural requirements of this clause means, in general, that the parties are bound by existing decisions of the Engineer.[5]

---

[99] Federation Internationale des Ingenieurs-Conseils Conditions of Contract for Works of Civil Engineering Construction, 4th edition 1987.

[1] Clause 67.2.

[2] It is understood that significant numbers of disputes under the F.I.D.I.C. Form of Contract referred to the ICC concern or include jurisdictional questions. For ICC arbitration generally, see Chap. 16, Section 9.

[3] See Hawker, Uff and Timms, *Institution of Civil Engineer's Arbitration Practice* (1986), p. 207.

[4] *Northern Regional Health Authority* v. *Derek Crouch* [1984] Q.B. 644 (C.A.); see also *Finnegan* v. *Sheffield City Council* (1988) 43 B.L.R. 124.

[5] For exceptions see generally pp. 106 *et seq.* See also commentary to clause 66(6).

Clause 66(1). *"Except as otherwise provided in these conditions ..."*

These words are strictly unnecessary. Where the Contract does not permit a decision to be challenged there cannot, technically, be a "dispute."[6]

Clause 66(1). *"... dispute of any kind whatsoever ..."*

These are very wide words, and are widened further by the following words "in connection with or arising out of the contract or the carrying out of the Works...." Disputes arising out of the Contract may include the question whether the Contract has been frustrated (see clause 64) or repudiated[7] but not a dispute as to whether the Contract is void for illegality.[8] There may be a claim for rectification of the Contract,[9] or alternatively a dispute as to adjustment of the terms of the Contract as provided in clause 5 (see above). A dispute arising out of the carrying out of the Works may include a claim in tort.[10]

Clause 66(2): Notice of Dispute. The express requirement for Notice only after taking steps under the Contract should avoid uncertainty whether a matter has been referred to the Engineer.[11] There might still be a dispute whether the Notice of Dispute was premature. This could arise, *e.g.* where the Engineer or the Employer contends that a claim has not been properly formulated so as to require response. Alternatively, where a party is potentially barred through failure to give a Notice to Refer under sub-clause (6), there might be a challenge to the validity of the process through attacking the Notice of Dispute. Where doubt might exist, an arbitrator or conciliator would be well advised to ascertain and record the parties' acceptance that a dispute had arisen and also that it had been referred to the Engineer.

Clause 66(2) and (3): Notice and the Engineer's decision. The Notice of Dispute constitutes reference of the dispute to the Engineer, and therefore sets in motion the timetable in sub-clause (6), which may lead to the decision of the Engineer or the recommendation of a Conciliator becoming binding. This is different from the procedure under clause 11 of the I.C.E. Conditions of Contract for Minor Works (the origin of sub-clause (2)), where a further notice is required to continue the settlement process. Under this Contract, the timetable continues automatically. Consequently, parties to the Contract should consider carefully at what stage they wish to initiate the disputes procedure by serving the Notice of Dispute. Clause 66 permits a dispute to be processed to a final decision at any stage. But the party initiating the dispute

---

[6] See, *e.g.* clause 4(1) where sub-letting the whole of the Works is not permitted without consent of the Employer. But see also *Hayter* v. *Nelson* [1990] 2 Lloyd's Rep. 265; *Mayer Newman* v. *Al Ferro, The Times*, April 9, 1990 noted at (1990) C.I.L.L. 577.

[7] *Heyman* v. *Darwins* [1942] A.C. 356 (H.L.).

[8] *Ibid.*

[9] For rectification, see p. 266.

[10] *Ashville Investments* v. *Elmer Contractors* (1987) 37 B.L.R. 55 (C.A.); but see also *Blue Circle Industries* v. *Holland Dredging* (1987) 37 B.L.R. 40 (C.A.).

[11] See *Monmouth County Council* v. *Costelloe & Kemple* (1965) 63 L.G.R. 429 and 5 B.L.R. 83 (C.A.) and see also the decision at first instance of Mocatta J. at (1964) 63 L.G.R. 131.

may, of course, choose when to do so. See below for further comment on Interim Arbitration.

Nature of Engineer's decision.   The requirement for the dispute to be "settled" means no more than that he should give a decision on the basis of the matters referred to him. There is no obligation to afford the parties a hearing, nor to invite comment. The Engineer does not act as an Arbitrator.[12] There is, however, nothing to prevent the Engineer considering the views of the other party, nor of soliciting further information from the party initiating the reference. Plainly, the Engineer will take into account matters within his own knowledge arising from his position as Engineer under the Contract and it must be implicit that the parties expect him to do so. The Engineer's decision, if rendered binding by the Contract, should in principle be open to challenge in the same way as the decision of a valuer.[13] Thus the Engineer's decision might be questioned, *e.g.* if he had decided the wrong issues, or if the decision embodied a patent error of law.[14]

The Engineer's decision binds both parties unless and until changed by conciliation or arbitration. It follows that the monetary element of any such decision will create a debt immediately payable irrespective of any reference to arbitration or conciliation. There are no requirements for the form of the Engineer's decision. It has been said that clarity is required because of the possible forfeiting effect.[15] However, the clause may also produce a barring effect if there is no decision at all (see below). Note that the Engineer's decision is required to be given within one calendar month of the Notice of Dispute where the Certificate of Completion for the whole of the Works has not been issued.[16] The period of three calendar months, which formerly applied in all cases, now applies only after the Completion Certificate has been given.[17]

Failure to give a decision.   Sub-clauses (5) and (6) provide for the conciliation or arbitration timetable to proceed on the expiry of the period for the Engineer's decision if no decision is given. Sub-clause (4) does not deal with the position if (as is bound to occur from time to time) the Engineer fails to give a decision at all, or gives a decision outside the time limit. In the latter case, it is submitted that, in the absence of agreement by the parties to extend time, such decision is of no effect and is equivalent to a failure to give a decision. What is the position if, in the absence of a valid Engineer's decision, neither party refers the matter to conciliation or arbitration within the prescribed time limit?

---

[12] *Sutcliffe* v. *Thackrah* [1974] A.C. 727 at 737, 751 (H.L.).
[13] See *Collier* v. *Mason* (1858) 25 Beav. 200; *Dean* v. *Prince* [1954] Ch. 409 (C.A.); *Campbell* v. *Edwards* [1976] 1 W.L.R. 403 (C.A.); *Toepfer v. Continental Grain Co.* [1974] 1 Lloyd's Rep. 11 (C.A.): *Jones v. Sherwood Computer Services, The Times,* December 14, 1989 (C.A.).
[14] See generally Chap. 5 and in particular "Mistake by architect" at p. 113.
[15] See *Monmouth County Council* v. *Costelloe & Kemple* (1965) 63 L.G.R. 429 and 5 B.L.R. 83, especially the judgment of Harman L.J.
[16] Sub-clause (6)(a)(ii).
[17] Sub-clause (6)(b).

It remains arguable that the party aggrieved may serve a fresh Notice of Dispute under sub-clause (2). However, in the light of the *Crouch* decision[18] it is thought that a subsequent reference of the same dispute is not possible, and the parties, not having invoked arbitration, will remain bound by the Engineer's previous decision. The reason for this conclusion is that the arbitration machinery has to be regarded as the exclusive means of challenging decisions under the Contract which, in the absence of such machinery, are not open to challenge.[19] The position is less clear where there is no previous ruling by the Engineer to bind the parties in the absence of a decision under sub-clause (3). In such a case, the effect of the *Crouch* case must be taken as barring the right to bring the claim.

Clause 66(5): Conciliation.   This process is available so long as no Notice to Refer to Arbitration has been given by either party under sub-clause (6). Once either party has given notice under sub-clause (5), the matter is required to proceed to conciliation, and the time limit for subsequent arbitration will run from receipt of the conciliator's recommendation. The I.C.E. Conciliation Procedure (1988) was first published with the I.C.E. Conditions of Contract for Minor Works. It provides a set of rules, including time limits which are designed to result in a recommendation from the conciliator being produced within an overall period of 2 months from appointment.[20] The conciliator is not an arbitrator, nor is he a mediator.[21] The conciliator is required by the Rules to investigate the dispute including the parties' submissions and to produce a "recommendation." While this need not, it is thought, comprise a ruling on the disputes, it is intended to be a resolution in accordance with the merits, and not merely a recommendation for commercial settlement.[22]

The importance of the I.C.E. Conciliation Procedure and the conduct of the conciliation itself lies in the binding effect of the recommendation if no written Notice to Refer is given within one calendar month of receipt. Should there be such an unintended failure, an aggrieved party may seek to argue that the conciliation process was procedurally flawed. It is thought that the decision of the conciliator should, in principle, be susceptible to challenge on similar grounds to the Engineer's decision.[23]

Clause 66(6): Notice to Refer to Arbitration.   There is no indication what the Notice must contain. It must in principle identify the dispute, and contain sufficient wording to indicate the intention of the party giving notice to

---

[18] *Northern Regional Health Authority* v. *Derek Crouch* [1984] Q.B. 644 (C.A.).

[19] See *Oram Builders* v. *Pemberton* (1985) 29 B.L.R. 23; *Finnegan* v. *Sheffield City Council* (1988) 43 B.L.R. 124.

[20] For a brief account of the procedure, see Vincent Powell-Smith, *I.C.E. Conditions of Contract for Minor Works 1988* (ed.) (Legal Studies and Services (Publishing) Limited (1989), p. 66.

[21] See generally Philip Naughton Q.C., "Alternative Forms of Dispute Resolution—Their Strengths and Weaknesses," *Arbitration*, Vol. 56, No. 2, p. 76.

[22] This is usually taken to be the meaning of "mediation", although there is no uniform terminology.

[23] See n. 14 above.

exercise the right of arbitration. The Notice will also operate as the commencement of proceedings.[24] The High Court has jurisdiction to extend the time for commencing arbitration[25] but this will be exercised sparingly and only in cases of undue hardship.[26]

The I.C.E. Arbitration Procedure (1983). This is now mandatory. It vests the Arbitrator with powers which go considerably beyond those created by the Arbitration Acts. Under the Rules, the Arbitrator may order security for costs or security for the sum in dispute (Rule 6); he may debar a party in default (Rule 11); the Arbitrator may himself conduct the examination of experts (Rule 13). A *Summary Award* may be made on grounds similar to those where the High Court may order summary judgment or an interim payment[27] (Rule 14). The Arbitrator may order disclosure and exchange of proofs, and that proofs may stand as evidence in chief (Rule 16). There are new forms of procedure including a Short Procedure conducted largely on documents (Part F) and a Special Procedure for issues depending largely on technical expertise (Part G). Generally, the procedure has proved popular and beneficial in helping to speed up engineering arbitration.

Clause 66(8)(a): Power to open up, review and revise. These words are of great importance as a result of the *Crouch* case.[28] They define and limit the power of the parties to raise disputes through arbitration. The court will not normally exercise these powers subject, however, to the possibility of agreement.[29]

Clause 66(8)(b). *"Neither party shall be limited ..."*
These words empower, or confirm the power of the arbitrator to go beyond the grounds put to the Engineer.[30] The words may also allow the whole of an account or certificate to be reviewed even though part only has been formally challenged.[31]

APPLICATION TO SCOTLAND

Application to Scotland

67 (1) If the Works are situated in Scotland the Contract shall in all respects be

---

[24] Limitation Act 1980, s. 34(3).
[25] Arbitration Act 1950, s. 27.
[26] *Liberian Shipping* v. *King* [1967] 2 Q.B. 86 (C.A.); *Libra Shipping* v. *Northern Sales* [1981] 1 Lloyd's Rep. 273 (C.A.); *Comdel* v. *Siporex (No. 2)* [1990] 3 W.L.R. 1 (H.L.).
[27] See R.S.C., Ord. 14 and Ord. 29, Pt. II and see generally Chap. 17, Section 6.
[28] *Northern Regional Health Authority* v. *Derek Crouch* [1984] Q.B. 644 (C.A.).
[29] See s.43A of the Supreme Court Act 1981, inserted by s.100 of the Courts and Legal Services Act 1990 (not yet in force).
[30] See *Morgan Grenfell* v. *Seven Seas Dredging* (1989) 49 B.L.R. 31; but see *Wigan M.B.C.* v. *Sharkey Bros.* (1987) 43 B.L.R. 115.
[31] *Mid-Glamorgan County Council* v. *Land Authority for Wales* (1990) 49 B.L.R. 61.

construed and operate as a Scottish contract and shall be interpreted in accordance with Scots Law and the provisions of this clause shall apply.

(2)   In the application of these Conditions and in particular clause 66 thereof

(a)   the word "arbiter" shall be substituted for the word "arbitrator"

(b)   for any reference to the "Arbitration Acts" there shall be substituted reference to the "Arbitration (Scotland) Act 1894"

(c)   for any reference to the Institution of Civil Engineers Arbitration Procedure (1983) there shall be substituted a reference to the Institution of Civil Engineers Arbitration Procedure (Scotland) (1983) and

(d)   notwithstanding any of the other provisions of these Conditions nothing therein shall be construed as excluding or otherwise affecting the right of a party to arbitration to call in terms of Section 3 of the Administration of Justice (Scotland) Act 1972 for the arbiter to state a case.

Clause 67

The Contract is intended for use under Scots law without amendment. It should however be emphasised that this commentary is based on English law, and the Contract may not have the same effect under Scots law.

Clause 67(2): Arbitration.   The incorporation of Scottish Arbitration law and procedure applies, by virtue of sub-clause (1), "if the works are situated in Scotland." This would appear to take effect as an express choice of Scots law as the applicable procedural law,[32] even though the arbitration might be conducted elsewhere, such as in England. This will be the case whatever the nationality or domicile of the parties. There are important differences between English and Scottish law[33] including the availability of appeal by case stated under Section 3 of the Administration of Justice (Scotland) Act 1972.[34]

NOTICES

Service of notices on Contractor

68   (1)   Any notice to be given to the Contractor under the terms of the Contract shall be served in writing at the Contractor's principal place of business (or in the event of the Contractor being a Company to or at its registered office).

Service of notices on Employer

(2)   Any notice to be given to the Employer under the terms of the Contract shall be served in writing at the Employer's last known address (or in the event of the Employer being a Company to or at its registered office).

---

[32] *James Miller & Partners* v. *Whitworth Street Estate* [1970] A.C. 583 (H.L.).

[33] Although incorporation of the UNCITRAL model law has not been recommended in England, the position is still under consideration in Scotland.

[34] For the right of appeal under English law, see p. 412.

Clause 68

The service of notices under the Contract may be a matter of considerable importance. By virtue of this clause, all notices required under the Contract must be in writing, whether or not the relevant clause refers to a written notice. The equivalent clause in the 5th edition referred to notices being "served by sending the same by post to or leaving the same at. . . ." This passage has been truncated to "served in writing at" the Contractor's principal place of business. The words in the brackets have not, however, been amended, and this accounts for the curious inclusion of "to or at" at the end of each sub-clause. The important question that arises under the clause is whether the term "served" which now replaces the alternatives of sending by post or leaving, is to be construed as referring to some technical process analogous to service of legal proceedings[35] or simply to bringing the document effectively to the attention of the other party. It is thought the latter is intended, and this is consistent with the provisions for "communications" in clause 1(6). If this is so, notices may be "served" by post or other effective means. This question would, however, benefit from clarification. Note that the clause does not cover notices to be given to the Engineer. Clause 52(4) lays down general requirements for notice of claims. Other clauses in the Contract contain their own particular requirements for the form, content and timing of notices, *e.g.* clause 7(3) refers to "adequate notice in writing" of further information, and clause 38(1) requires the Contractor to give "due notice to the Engineer" when work is ready for examination.

TAX MATTERS

Labour-tax fluctuations

69 (1)   The rates and prices contained in the Bill of Quantities shall be deemed to take account of the levels and incidence at the date for return of tenders of the taxes levies contributions premiums or refunds (including national insurance contributions but excluding income tax and any levy payable under the Industrial Training Act 1964) which are by law payable by or to the Contractor and his sub-contractors in respect of their workpeople engaged on the Contract.

The rates and prices contained in the Bill of Quantities do not take account of any level or incidence of the aforesaid matters where at the date for return of tenders such level or incidence does not then have effect but although then known is to take effect at some later date.

(2)   If after the date for return of tenders there shall occur any change in the level and/or incidence of any such taxes levies contributions premiums or refunds the Contractor shall so inform the Engineer and the net increase or decrease shall be taken into account in arriving at the Contract Price. The Contractor shall supply the information necessary to support any consequent adjustment to the Contract Price. All certificates for payment issued after submission of such information shall take due account of the additions or deductions to which such information relates.

---

[35] See particularly R.S.C., Ord. 65.

Clause 69

This clause has been simplified and reduced from six to two sub-clauses compared with the version in the 5th edition. There is no longer any definition of "workpeople" for whom labour-tax fluctuations are payable. The definition in the previous version of the clause required the persons in question to be engaged in manual labour and normally on the site. This restriction has gone, and the clause now appears to cover anyone "engaged on the contract" which need not require them to work on the site. Nor is it limited to manual labour. Note that the clause operates both ways and the Contractor is required to give notice to the Engineer whether the net change is up or down. In the absence of notice where there is a net decrease, the Engineer would have to make an estimate. Alternatively, the Engineer might be justified in omitting work from the certificate under clause 60(8) until particulars are given.

Value Added Tax

70   (1)   The Contractor shall be deemed not to have allowed in his tender for the tax payable by him as a taxable person to the Commissioners of Customs and Excise being tax chargeable on any taxable supplies to the Employer which are to be made under the Contract.

Engineer's certificates net of Value Added Tax

(2)   All certificates issued by the Engineer under Clause 60 shall be net of Value Added Tax.

In addition to the payments due under such certificates the Employer shall separately identify and pay to the Contractor any Value Added Tax properly chargeable by the Commissioners of Customs and Excise on the supply to the Employer of any goods and/or services by the Contractor under the Contract.

Disputes

(3)   If any dispute difference or question arises between either the Employer or the Contractor and the Commissioners of Customs and Excise in relation to any tax chargeable or alleged to be chargeable in connection with the Contract or the Works each shall render to the other such support and assistance as may be necessary to resolve the dispute difference or question.

Clause 66 not applicable

(4)   Clause 66 shall not apply to any dispute difference or question arising under this Clause.

Clause 70

The effect of this clause is that the Engineer is not concerned with VAT and all Certificates are issued for the value of work net of VAT. Subsequently, the Employer is to pay any chargeable VAT on the goods or services supplied. The additional paperwork required to facilitate payment of VAT will depend on the current Regulations.[36] Any dispute between the Contractor and the Employer concerning VAT is not subject to arbitration under clause 66, and would have to be resolved initially by the Commissioners and subsequently in court if necessary.

SPECIAL CONDITIONS

Special conditions

71 The following special conditions form part of the Conditions of Contract.

(Note. Any special conditions including contract price fluctuation which it is desired to incorporate in the conditions of contract should be numbered consecutively with the foregoing conditions of contract).

Clause 71

There is a widespread practice of adding "special conditions" numbered as part of the Conditions of Contract. Clause 5 makes this unnecessary. Provisions incorporated into the Contract are to be given equal weight whether contained in the Conditions of Contract or elsewhere, *e.g.* in the Specification or Bills or in incorporated correspondence. Clauses do not acquire any added weight by being referred to as "special."

---

[36] See p. 687.

The Institution of	The Association of	The Federation of Civil
Civil Engineers	Consulting Engineers	Engineering Contractors

This clause has been prepared by the Institution of Civil Engineers, the Association of Consulting Engineers and the Federation of Civil Engineering Contractors, in consultation with the Government in its revised form, for use in appropriate cases as a Special Condition of the Conditions of Contract for use in connection with Works of Civil Engineering Construction SIXTH EDITION dated January 1991.

CONTRACT PRICE FLUCTUATIONS

(1)   The amount payable by the Employer to the Contractor upon the issue by the Engineer of an interim certificate pursuant to clause 60(2) or of the final certificate pursuant to clause 60(4) (other than amounts due under this clause) shall be increased or decreased in accordance with the provisions of this clause if there shall be any changes in the following Index Figures compiled by the Department of the Environment and published by Her Majesty's Stationery Office (HMSO) in the Monthly Bulletin of Construction Indices (Civil Engineering Works)

   (a)   the Index of the Cost of labour in civil engineering construction
   (b)   the Index of the Cost of providing and maintaining constructional plant and equipment
   (c)   the Indices of constructional material prices applicable to those materials in sub-clause (4) of this clause.

The net total of such increases and decreases shall be given effect to in determining the Contract Price.

(2)   For the purpose of this clause

   (a)   'Final Index Figure' shall mean any Index Figure appropriate to sub-clause (1) of this clause not qualified in the said bulletin as provisional
   (b)   'Base Index Figure' shall mean the appropriate Final Index Figure applicable to the date 42 days prior to the date for the return of Tenders
   (c)   'Current Index Figure' shall mean the appropriate Final Index Figure to be applied in respect of any certificate issued or due to be issued by the Engineer pursuant to clause 60 and shall be the appropriate Final Index Figure applicable to the date 42 days prior to
      (i)   the due date (or extended date) for completion or
      (ii) the date certified pursuant to clause 48 of completion of the whole of the Works or
      (iii) the last day of the period to which the certificate relates
   whichever is the earliest.

   Provided that in respect of any work the value of which is included in any such certificate and which work forms part of a Section for which the due date (or extended date) for completion or the date certified pursuant to clause 48 of completion of such Section precedes the last day of the period to which the certificate relates the Current Index Figure shall be the Final Index Figure applicable to the date 42 days prior to whichever of these dates is the earliest.

932

(d) The 'Effective Value' in respect of the whole or any Section of the Works shall be the difference between

  (i) the amount which in the opinion of the Engineer is due to the Contractor under clause 60(2) (before deducting retention) or the amount due to the Contractor under clause 60(4) (but in each case before deducting sums previously paid on account) less any amounts for Dayworks Nominated Sub-contractors or any other items based on actual cost or current prices and any sums for increases or decreases in the Contract Price under this clause and

  (ii) the amount calculated in accordance with (i) above and included in the last preceding interim certificate issued by the Engineer in accordance with clause 60.

  Provided that in the case of the first certificate the Effective Value shall be the amount calculated in accordance with sub-paragraph (i) above.

(3) The increase or decrease in the amounts otherwise payable under clause 60 pursuant to sub-clause (1) of this clause shall be calculated by multiplying the Effective Value by a Price Fluctuation Factor which shall be the net sum of the products obtained by multiplying each of the proportions given in (a) (b) and (c) of sub-clause (4) of this clause by a fraction the numerator of which is the relevant Current Index Figure minus the relevant Base Index Figure and the denominator of which is the relevant Base Index Figure.

(4) For the purpose of calculating the Price Fluctuation Factor the proportions referred to in sub-clause (3) of this clause shall (irrespective of the actual constituents of the work) be as follows and the total of such proportions shall amount to unity

  (a) 0.___ * in respect of labour and supervision costs subject to adjustment by reference to the Index referred to in sub-clause (1)(a) of this clause

  (b) 0.___ * in respect of costs of provision and use of all civil engineering plant road vehicles etc. which shall be subject to adjustment by reference to the Index referred to in sub-clause (1)(b) of this clause

  (c) the following proportions in respect of the materials named which shall be subject to adjustment by reference to the relevant indices referred to in sub-clause (1)(c) of this clause

      0.___ * in respect of Aggregates
      0.___ * in respect of Bricks and Clay Products generally
      0.___ * in respect of Cements
      0.___ * in respect of Cast Iron products
      0.___ * in respect of Coated Roadstone for road pavements and bituminous products generally
      0.___ * in respect of Fuel for plant to which the DERV Fuel Index will be applied
      0.___ * in respect of Fuel for plant to which the Gas Oil Index will be applied
      0.___ * in respect of Timber generally
      0.___ * in respect of Reinforcement (cut, bent and delivered)
      0.___ * in respect of other Metal Sections
      0.___ * in respect of Fabricated Structural Steel
      0.___ * in respect of Labour and Supervision in fabricating and erecting steelwork

  (d) 0.10 in respect of all other costs which shall not be subject to any adjustment

  Total 1.00 .

---

* To be filled in by the Employer prior to inviting tenders.

(5)   Provisional Index Figures in the Bulletin referred to in sub-clause (1) of this clause may be used for the provisional adjustment of interim valuations but such adjustments shall be subsequently recalculated on the basis of the corresponding Final Index Figures.

(6)   Clause 69—Tax Fluctuations—shall not apply except to the extent that any matter dealt with therein is not covered by the Index of the Cost of Labour in Civil Engineering Construction.

Revised March 1976   FSS Clause

The Institution of   The Association of   The Federation of Civil
Civil Engineers   Consulting Engineers   Engineering Contractors

This clause has been prepared by the Institution of Civil Engineers, the Associa-tion of Consulting Engineers and the Federation of Civil Engineering Contrac-tors, in consultation with the Government, for use in those cases where it is required to make special provision for adjustment of Price Fluctuation in respect of Fabricated Structural Steelwork only or predominantly Fabricated Structural Steelwork together with a negligible amount of Civil Engineering work, as a Special Condition of the Conditions of Contract for use in connection with Works of Civil Engineering Construction SIXTH EDITION dated January 1991.

CONTRACT PRICE FLUCTUATIONS FABRICATED STRUCTURAL STEELWORK

(1)   The amount payable by the Employer to the Contractor upon the issue by the Engineer of an interim certificate pursuant to clause 60(2) or of the final certificate pursuant to clause 60(4) (other than amounts due under this clause) shall be increased or decreased in accordance with the provisions of this clause if there shall be any changes in the following Index Figures compiled by the Department of the Environment and published by Her Majesty's Stationery Office (H.M.S.O.) in the Monthly Bulletin of Construction Indices (Civil Engineering Works)

      (a) the Index of the cost of labour in fabrication of steelwork and erection of steelwork
      (b) the Index for structural steel

The net total of such increases and decreases shall be given effect to in determining the Contract Price.

(2)   For the purpose of this clause

      (a) 'Fabricated Structural Steelwork' shall mean those items of work listed in sub-clause (6) of this clause and shall include any variations as may be ordered under clause 51 involving work of a description which in the opinion of the Engineer is similar to the description of the items so listed
      (b) 'Final Index Figure' shall mean any Index Figure appropriate to sub-clause (1) of this clause not qualified in the said bulletin as provisional
      (c) 'Base Index Figure' shall mean the appropriate Final Index Figure applic-able to the date 42 days prior to the date for the return of tenders
      (d) 'Current Index Figure' shall mean the appropriate Final Index Figure to be applied in respect of any certificate issued or due to be issued by the Engineer pursuant to clause 60 being such figure applicable

           (i)   in respect of labour employed in fabrication—to a date 56 days prior to the last day of the period to which the certificate relates or
           (ii) in respect of labour employed in erection—to a date 14 days prior to the last day of the period to which the certificate relates or
           (iii) in respect of materials specifically purchased for inclusion in the Works—to the date of delivery to the fabricator's premises (of which

935

date the Contractor shall produce such evidence relating to gross tonnages delivered as the Engineer may reasonably require) or

  (iv) in respect of materials (if any) not specifically purchased for inclusion in the Works—to the date of the last of the deliveries referred to in sub-paragraph (iii) of this paragraph

as the case may be

Provided always that should the due date (or extended date) for completion or the date certified pursuant to clause 48 of completion of the whole of the Works precede any of the aforesaid then such due date or extended date or certified date whichever is earliest shall be substituted for those aforesaid.

Provided further that if in respect of any work which forms part of a Section and whose value is included in any certificate the due date (or extended date) for completion of that Section or the date certified pursuant to clause 48 of completion of that Section precede any of the dates aforesaid in sub-paragraphs (i) to (iv) above then such due date or extended date or certified date whichever is the earliest in respect of that Section shall be substituted for those aforesaid

(e) The 'Effective Value' in respect of the whole or any Section of the Works shall be the difference between

  (i) the amount which in the opinion of the Engineer is due to the Contractor under clause 60(2) (before deducting retention) or the amount due to the Contractor under clause 60(4) (but in each case before deducting sums previously paid on account) less any amounts for Dayworks Nominated Sub-contractors or any other items based on actual cost or current prices and any sums for increases or decreases in the Contract Price under this clause and

  (ii) the amount calculated in accordance with (i) above and included in the last preceding interim certificate issued by the Engineer in accordance with clause 60.

Provided that in the case of the first certificate the Effective Value shall be the amount calculated in accordance with sub-paragraph (i) above.

(3) The Effective Value shall be apportioned between labour and materials in the following manner that is to say

  (a) labour
  (i) employed in erection—by multiplying the total tonnage erected during the period to which the certificate relates by the average cost per tonne entered at (b) of sub-clause (5) of this clause
  (ii) employed in fabrication and delivery—by deducting the summation of the values calculated in respect of materials and in respect of labour employed in erection from the Effective Value
  (b) materials
by multiplying the total tonnage of steel delivered to the Site for inclusion in the Works during the period to which the certificate relates by the average price per tonne entered at (a) of sub-clause (5) of this clause.

(4) (a) The increase or decrease in the amounts otherwise payable under clause 60 pursuant to sub-clause (1) of this clause shall be calculated by multiplying each portion of the Effective Value by a fraction the numerator of which is the product of 0.90 and the difference between the relevant Current Index Figure and the relevant Base Index Figure and the denominator of which is the relevant Base Index Figure.

(b) The relevant indices to be used in connection with this sub-clause are
  (i) for labour and supervision in fabrication and erection—the Index referred to in sub-clause (1)(a) of this clause

      (ii) for materials—the Index referred to in sub-clause (1)(b) of this clause.

(5)   For the purpose of the apportionment in sub-clause (3) of this clause the full average costs per tonne (inclusive of all associated labour plant power maintenance overheads and profit) to be used are

      (a) Materials delivered to fabricators premises   ...... £ per tonne*

      (b) Erection   ...... £ per tonne*

      (c) Subject to sub-paragraphs (i)(ii) and (iii) of this paragraph the relevant figures to be used in connection with this sub-clause shall be in accordance with sub-clause (2) of this clause.

Provided that in respect of materials

      (i)   the Current Index Figure subsequent to the first established Current Index Figure pursuant to sub-clause (2)(d)(iii) of this clause shall not be used until a tonnage of steel greater than the tonnage to which the Current Index Figure first established applies has been delivered to the Site for inclusion in the Works and

      (ii) for the purpose of establishing the appropriate subsequent Current Index Figures to apply to all later deliveries of steel to the Site for inclusion in the Works the provisions of sub-paragraph (i) of this paragraph shall apply mutatis mutandis and

      (iii) the Current Index Figure referred to in sub-clause (2)(d)(iv) of this clause shall not be used until the total tonnage of steel delivered to the Site for inclusion in the Works exceeds the total tonnage of steel specifically purchased for inclusion in the Works and delivered to the fabricator's premises.

(6)   For the purposes of this clause the expression 'Fabricated Structural Steelwork' shall comprise those items listed hereunder†

Bill No.†	Page No.†	Item No.†

(7)   Provisional Index Figures in the Bulletin referred to in sub-clause (1) of this clause may be used for the provisional adjustment of interim valuations but such adjustments shall be subsequently recalculated on the basis of the corresponding Final Index Figures.

(8)   Clause 69—Tax Fluctuations—shall not apply except to the extent that any matter dealt with therein is not covered by the Index of the Cost of labour in fabrication of steelwork and erection of steelwork.

---

* To be filled in by the Contractor at time of tendering.

† To be filled in by the Employer prior to inviting tenders.

The Institution of	The Association of	The Federation of Civil
Civil Engineers	Consulting Engineers	Engineering Contractors

This clause has been prepared by the Institution of Civil Engineers, the Association of Consulting Engineers and the Federation of Civil Engineering Contractors, in consultation with the Government, for use in those cases where it is required to make special provision for adjustment of Price Fluctuation in respect of both Civil Engineering work and Fabricated Structural Steelwork, as a Special Condition of the Conditions of Contract for use in connection with Works of Civil Engineering Construction SIXTH EDITION dated January 1991.

CONTRACT PRICE FLUCTUATIONS
CIVIL ENGINEERING WORK AND FABRICATED STRUCTURAL STEELWORK

(1)   This clause shall apply only to those contracts which incorporate the Contract Price Fluctuation Clause Revised March 1976 for Civil Engineering work and the Fabricated Structural Steelwork Clause Revised March 1976 (referred to in this clause as the CE Clause and the FSS Clause respectively).

(2)   For the purposes of this clause

       (a)   'Civil Engineering work' shall mean all Works with the exception of Fabricated Structural Steelwork and

       (b)   'Fabricated Structural Steelwork' shall mean the work defined in sub-clause (2)(a) of the FSS Clause.

(3)   The Effective Value (as defined both in the CE Clause and in the FSS Clause) shall be sub-divided to show the amounts included in respect of the Civil Engineering work and the Fabricated Structural Steelwork. The amount in respect of the former shall then be treated as if it were the Effective Value as defined in the CE Clause and adjusted in accordance with the provisions of that clause. The amount in respect of the latter shall then be treated as if it were the Effective Value as defined in the FSS Clause and adjusted in accordance with that clause.

Contract price fluctuations clauses

The printed version of the 6th edition of the I.C.E. Conditions does not include a fluctuations clause. Separate clauses are provided as inserts, which are identical (save for minor changes to clause numbers) with those published with the 5th edition.

The fluctuations provisions comprise three separate clauses. The first is for use alone where the work consists of civil engineering work which is not predominantly fabricated structural steelwork (the CE clause). The second clause is used alone where the work consists solely or predominantly of fabricated structural steelwork (the FSS clause). Where the work involves both civil engineering and fabricated structural steelwork, both of these clauses are to be used together with the third clause (the CE/FSS clause).

Outline of clauses. The price fluctuation clauses operate as simple algebraic formulae, whose resolution depends upon current cost and price index figures published by H.M.S.O. and upon the net value of work carried out by the Contractor. Irrespective of the actual constituents of that work in labour, plant costs and materials, the increase or decrease payable depends upon a predetermined apportionment. In the CE clause that apportionment is itself subject to adjustment by reference to the relevant published indices.

In the CE clause fluctuations are calculated on index changes from a base date 42 days prior to the date for return of tenders to a date 42 days prior to the end of the period to which the certificate relates (sub-clause (2)). In the FSS clause the relevant date for the current index figures depends upon whether the labour is engaged in fabrication or erection and upon whether materials are purchased specifically for the works or not (sub-clause (2)). In each case fluctuations are to be allowed only up to the due date, or extended date for completion, so that, if the contractor overruns, no further increases in price will be allowable.

CE and FSS clauses, sub-clause (1). *"The amount payable shall be increased or decreased in accordance with the provisions of this clause …"*

These words appear in both the CE and FSS clauses. They give the Contractor a right to payment of fluctuations in addition to the sums to be certified under clause 60(2) (interim) or 60(4) (final account). It follows that fluctuation payments need not be subject to retention. However the draughtsmen have indicated a different view,[37] and if fluctuations are included in the certificate under clause 60(2)(a) they will be subject to retention.

CE and FSS clauses, sub-clause (2): Effective Value. *"The amount which in the opinion of the Engineer is due to the Contractor under clause 60(2) …"*

The Engineer has a discretion over the monthly measurement and generally as to sums to be certified. Delayed certification does not necessarily prejudice the Contractor since later payment will attract higher fluctuation payments if the index is rising.

CE and FSS clauses, sub-clause (2): Effective Value *"… less any amounts for Dayworks, Nominated Sub-Contractors or any other items based on actual cost or current prices …"*

These words appear in both the CE and FSS clauses. They define the "effective value" on which fluctuations are to be calculated. It is submitted

---

[37] See Guidance Note (GN) 1: Contract Price Fluctuations, issued by the I.C.E. Conditions of Contract Standing Joint Committee.

that these words exclude from the effective value, goods and materials delivered to the site or in which the property has vested in the Employer pursuant to clause 60(1)(b) or (c), since the sums due are based on the value of the goods or materials.[38] Such goods or materials will be included in the effective value and therefore qualify for fluctuation payments when they are incorporated into the works.

---

[38] See Guidance Note (GN) 1, *ibid.*

SHORT DESCRIPTION OF WORKS

All Permanent and Temporary Works in connection with* . . . .

. . . .

. . . .

Form of Tender

(NOTE: The Appendix forms part of the Tender)

To . . . .

. . . .

. . . .

GENTLEMEN,

Having examined the Drawings, Conditions of Contract, Specification and Bill of Quantities for the construction of the above-mentioned Works (and the matters set out in the Appendix hereto) we offer to construct and complete the whole of the said Works in conformity with the said Drawings, Conditions of Contract, Specification and Bill of Quantities for such sum as may be ascertained in accordance with the said Conditions of Contract.

We undertake to complete and deliver the whole of the Permanent Works comprised in the Contract within the time stated in the Appendix hereto.

If our tender is accepted we will, if required, provide security for the due performance of the Contract as stipulated in the Conditions of Contract and the Appendix hereto.

Unless and until a formal Agreement is prepared and executed this tender together with your written acceptance thereof, shall constitute a binding Contract between us.

We understand that you are not bound to accept the lowest or any tender you may receive.

We are, Gentlemen,
Yours faithfully,

Signature . . . .

Address . . . .

. . . .

Date . . . .

* Complete as appropriate

FORM OF TENDER (APPENDIX)

(NOTE: Relevant clause numbers are shown in brackets)

Appendix—Part 1 (to be completed prior to the invitation of Tenders)

1   Name of the Employer (clause 1(1)(a)) ....

    Address ....

2   Name of the Engineer (clause 1(1)(c)) ....

    Address ....

3   Defects Correction Period (clause 1(1)(s))   ... weeks

4   Number and type of copies of Drawings to be provided (clause 6(1)(b)) ....

    ....

5   Contract Agreement (clause 9)   Required/Not required

6   Performance Bond (clause 10(1))   Required/Not required

    Amount of Bond (if required) to be   .... per cent. of Tender Total

7   Minimum amount of third party insurance   £ ....
    (persons and property) (clause 23(3))   each and every occurrence

8   Works Commencement Date (if known) (clause 41(1)(a)) ....

9   Time for Completion (clause 43)[a]

    EITHER for the whole of the Works   .... weeks
    OR for Sections of the Works (clause 1(1)(u))[b]

      Section A .... weeks

      Section B .... weeks

      Section C .... weeks

      Section D .... weeks

      the Remainder of the Works   .... weeks

10 Liquidated damages for delay (clause 47)

                           per day/week   limit of liability[c]
    EITHER for the whole of
    the Works   £ ....   £ ....

---

[a] If not stated is to be completed by Contractor in Part 2 of the Appendix

[b] to be completed if required, with brief description. Where Sectional completion applies the item for "the Remainder of the Works" must be used to cover the balance of the Works if the Sections described do not in total comprise the whole of the Works.

[c] Delete where not required.

942

OR for Section A (as
above)   £ . . . .   £ . . . .

Section B (as above)   £ . . . .   £ . . . .

Section C (as above)   £ . . . .   £ . . . .

Section D (as above)   £ . . . .   £ . . . .

the Remainder of the
Works (as above)   £ . . . .   £ . . . .

11   Vesting of materials not on Site (clauses 54(1) and 60(1)(c)) (if required by the Employer)[d]

1 . . . .   4 . . . .

2 . . . .   5 . . . .

3 . . . .   6 . . . .

12   Method of measurement adopted in preparation of Bills of Quantities (clause 57)[e] . .

. . . .

13   Percentage of the value of goods and materials to be included

in Interim Certificates (clause 60(2)(b))   . . . . per cent.

14   Minimum amount of Interim Certificates (clause
60(3))   £ . . . .

15   Rate of retention (recommended not to exceed 5 per
cent.) (clause 60(5))   . . . . per cent.

16   Limit of retention (per cent. of Tender Total) (clause 60(5)) (Recommended not to
exceed 3 per cent.) . . . . per cent.

17   Bank whose Base Lending Rate is to be used (clause 60(7)) . . . .

18   Requirement for prior approval by the Employer before the Engineer can act.
DETAILS TO BE GIVEN AND CLAUSE NUMBER STATED (clause 2(1)(b))[f]

. . . .

. . . .

. . . .

. . . .

. . . .

. . . .

---

[d] (If used) Materials to which the clauses apply must be listed in Part 1 (Employer's option) or Part 2 (Contractor's option)

[e] Insert here any amendment or modification adopted if different from that stated in clause 57.

[f] If there is any requirement that the Engineer has to obtain prior approval from the Employer before he can act full particulars of such requirements must be set out above.

Appendix—Part 2

(To be completed by Contractor)

1   Insurance Policy Excesses (clause 25(2))

     Insurance of the Works (clause 21(1))   £ ....

     Third party (property damage) (clause 23(1))   £ ....

2   Time for Completion (clause 43) (if not completed in Part 1 of the Appendix)

     EITHER for the whole of the Works   .... weeks

     OR for Sections of the Works (clause 1(1)(u)) (as detailed in Part 1 of the Appendix)

     Section A .... weeks

     Section B .... weeks

     Section C .... weeks

     Section D .... weeks

     the Remainder of the Works   .... weeks

3   Vesting of materials not on site (clauses 54(1) and 60(1)(c)) (at the option of the Contractor—see [d] in Part 1)

     1 ....   4 ....

     2 ....   5 ....

     3 ....   6 ....

4   Percentage(s) for adjustment of PC sums (clauses 59(2)(c) and 59(5)(c)) (with details if required)

     ....

     ....

Form of Tender and Appendix

Note that by clause 1(1)(e) the Tender and written acceptance thereof are full Contract Documents. The fourth paragraph of the Tender contemplates a simple contract being formed by written acceptance of the Tender. No sum is stated in the Tender, even though the definitions in clause 1 refer to the "Tender Total."[39]

---

[39] Clause 1(1)(i).

Form of Agreement

THIS AGREEMENT made the .... day of .... 19 ....
BETWEEN ....
of ....
in the County of .... (hereinafter called "the Employer")
and ....
of ....
in the County of .... (hereinafter called "the Contractor").
WHEREAS the Employer is desirous that certain Works should be constructed,
namely the Permanent and Temporary Works in connection with ....
....
and has accepted a Tender by the Contractor for the construction and completion of
such Works.

NOW THIS AGREEMENT WITNESSETH as follows

1. In this Agreement words and expressions shall have the same meanings as are respectively assigned to them in the Conditions of Contract hereinafter referred to.

2. The following documents shall be deemed to form and be read and construed as part of this Agreement, namely

(a) the said Tender and the written acceptance thereof
(b) the Drawings
(c) the Conditions of Contract
(d) the Specification
(e) the priced Bill of Quantities.

3. In consideration of the payments to be made by the Employer to the Contractor as hereinafter mentioned the Contractor hereby covenants with the Employer to construct and complete the Works in conformity in all respects with the provisions of the Contract.

4. The Employer hereby covenants to pay to the Contractor in consideration of the construction and completion of the Works the Contract Price at the times and in the manner prescribed by the Contract.

IN WITNESS whereof the parties hereto have caused this Agreement to be executed the day and year first above written.

SIGNED on behalf of the said .... Ltd/plc

Signature ....   Signature ....
Position ....   Position ....
In the presence of ....   In the presence of ....
or SIGNED SEALED AND DELIVERED AS A DEED
by the said .... Ltd/plc
in the presence of ....

Form of Agreement

The Agreement provides for execution as a deed, for which the only formality now required is a witnessing signature.[40] Otherwise, the Form of Agree-

---

[40] See p. 27.

ment is consistent with the Conditions of Contract. Many public authority employers use their own form of agreement. It is also a common practice to list in a formal agreement other documents to be incorporated, such as correspondence.

Form of Bond

BY THIS BOND [1]We ....
of ....
in the County of ....
We[2] .... Ltd/plc
whose registered office is at ....
in the County of ....
[3]We ....
and ....
carrying on business in partnership under the name or style of ....
....
at ....
in the County of .... (hereinafter called "the Contractor")
[4]and .... Ltd/plc
whose registered office is at ....
in the County of .... (hereinafter called "the Surety")
are held and firmly bound unto ....
(hereinafter called "the Employer") in the sum of
.... pounds
(£ ....) for the payment of which sum the Contractor and the Surety
bind themselves their successors and assigns jointly and severally by these presents.
　　Sealed with our respective seals and dated this
　　.......... day of .... 19 ....

WHEREAS the Contractor and the Employer have entered into a Contact (here-inafter called "the said Contract") for the construction and completion of the Works as therein mentioned in conformity with the provisions of the said Contract.

NOW THE CONDITIONS of the above-written Bond are such that if

(a) the Contractor shall subject to Condition (c) hereof duly perform and observe all the terms provisions conditions and stipulations of the said Contract on the Contractor's part to be performed and observed according to the true purport intent and meaning thereof or if

(b) on default by the Contractor the Surety shall satisfy and discharge the damages sustained by the Employer thereby up to the amount of the above-written Bond or if

(c) the Engineer defined in clause 1(1)(c) of the said Contract shall pursuant to the provisions of clause 61 thereof issue a Defects Correction Certificate then upon the date stated therein (hereinafter called "the Relevant Date")

this obligation shall be null and void but otherwise shall remain in full force and effect but no alteration in the terms of the said Contract made by agreement between the Employer and the Contractor or in the extent or nature of the Works to be constructed and completed thereunder and no allowance of time by the Employer or the Engineer under the said Contract nor any forbearance or forgiveness in or in respect of any matter or thing concerning the said Contract on the part of the Employer or the said Engineer shall in any way release the Surety from any liability under the above-written Bond.

---

[1] Is appropriate to an individual.
[2] to a Limited company and
[3] to a Firm. Strike out whichever two are inappropriate.
[4] Is appropriate where the Surety is a Bank or Insurance Company.

PROVIDED ALWAYS that if any dispute or difference shall arise between the Employer and the Contractor concerning the Relevant Date or otherwise as to the withholding of the Defects Correction Certificate then for the purpose of this Bond only and without prejudice to the resolution or determination pursuant to the provisions of the said Contract of any dispute or difference whatsoever between the Employer and Contractor the Relevant Date shall be such as may be.

(a) agreed in writing between the Employer and the Contractor or
(b) if either the Employer or the Contractor shall be aggrieved at the date stated in the said Defects Correction Certificate or otherwise as to the issue or with-holding of the said Defects Correction Certificate the party so aggrieved shall forthwith by notice in writing to the other refer any such dispute or difference to the arbitration of a person to be agreed upon between the parties or (if the parties fail to appoint an arbitrator within one calendar month of the service of the notice as aforesaid) a person to be appointed on the application of either party by the President for the time being of the Institution of Civil Engineers and such arbitrator shall forthwith and with all due expedition enter upon the reference and make an award thereon which award shall be final and conclusive to determine the Relevant Date for the purposes of this Bond. If the arbitrator declines the appointment or after appointment is removed by order of a competent court or is incapable of acting or dies and the parties do not within one calendar month of the vacancy arising fill the vacancy then the President for the time being of the Institution of Civil Engineers may on the application of either party appoint an arbitrator to fill the vacancy. In any case where the President for the time being of the Institution of Civil Engineers is not able to exercise the aforesaid functions conferred upon him the said functions may be exercized on his behalf by a Vice-President for the time being of the said Institution.

Signed Sealed and Delivered as a Deed by the
said .... Ltd/plc
in the presence of ....

(Similar form of Attestation Clause for the Surety)

Form of Bond[41]

The Form of Bond was amended and reissued in 1979. It deals with the difficult question of when the surety is to be released. Although of interest to the surety, this may be of even more interest to the Contractor, since there is likely to be a counter-guarantee. These provisions, in effect, entitle the Contractor to call for release of the Bond when the Defects Correction Period has expired and the work is apparently satisfactory (see clause 61(1)). The Employer is thus not intended to have the protection of the Bond against latent defects in the event of the Contractor's insolvency. The Bond provides for arbitration on the question of withholding the Defects Correction Certificate. The parties to such arbitration are to be the Contractor and the Employer. Clause 10 of the Conditions of Contract stipulates that the Employer is

---

[41] For Bonds generally, see Chap. 10, Section 5.

deemed to be a party to the Bond for the purpose of the arbitration provisions. Both the Bond and clause 10 provide that the resolution of such a dispute is not to affect any dispute under the Main Contract. But this is of no practical importance (see clause 61(2)).

ARCHITECT'S APPOINTMENT

(published for the Royal Institute of British Architects)

Foreword

The successful completion of a building project requires a clear understanding of the client's requirements, the nature of the service to be provided, and the responsibilities of all involved. This document has been designed to help achieve that understanding.

The education and training of architects prepares them to assist clients at all stages of a building project and to co-ordinate all the elements of the design and construction process.

The architect's primary professional responsibility is to act as the client's adviser and additionally to administer the building contract fairly between client and contractor.

The clients also have an important role. They must provide adequate information on the project, site and budget and fully understand and approve the architect's proposals at various stages of the work as it proceeds.

The most successful jobs are those which proceed in an atmosphere of mutual trust and goodwill. A statement of the client's and the architect's obligations is fundamental to the creation of such an atmosphere, and is essential for the protection of their respective interests. The RIBA recommends the use of the Schedule of Services and Fees and the Memorandum of Agreement (samples of which are included in the Architect's Appointment). Alternatively, letters of agreement may be used provided that the services, responsibilities and fee basis are fully defined. If the agreement is not comprehensive it may create uncertainties for either or both parties as the project progresses.

The work an architect normally undertakes during the course of a building project is described as the Basic Services. These services are common to large and small projects and none should be omitted if the project is to be completed successfully. Where for any reason partial services only are to be provided there should be a clear understanding as to their extent.

Many projects will require other services which the architect may or may not be able to provide. The extent to which additional consultant advice will be required depends on the nature and experience of the architect's practice and on the complexity of the project. The provision of such other services should be discussed at the outset of any project.

The recommended fee scales included in this document are based on a percentage of the total construction cost. The RIBA considers these fee scales to be fair and reasonable. The cost of providing architectural services is affected by many factors besides the cost of the building works concerned, so that the recommended fee scales may not apply to all types of work. However, where the architect provides the Basic Services the percentage framework is often the most appropriate fee basis.

For the purpose of fee calculation, buildings are classified into five categories according to their complexity and the demands on the architect's time, skill and professional knowledge. A list of buildings which typically fall into each category is published with the recommended fee scales.

Introduction

The RIBA requires of its members that when making an engagement for professional services they shall define and record the terms of the engagement including the scope of the service, the allocation of responsibilities and any limitation of liability, the method of calculation of remuneration and the provision for termination.

Architect's Appointment consists of four related parts:

Part 1 Architect's Services

Preliminary and Basic Services normally provided by the architect. These services progress through work stages based on the RIBA Plan of Work (RIBA Publications Limited). The sequence of work stages may be varied or two or more work stages may be combined to suit the particular circumstances.

Preliminary Services

Work stage A: Inception
Work stage B: Feasibility

Basic Services

Work stage C: Outline proposals

Work stage D: Scheme design

Work stage E: Detail design

Work stage F: Production information
Work stage G: Bills of quantities

Work stage H: Tender action
Work stage J: Project planning
Work stage K: Operations on site
Work stage L: Completion

Preliminary Services are normally charged on a time basis and Basic Services on a percentage basis, as described in Part 4.

Part 2 Other Services

Services which may augment the Preliminary and Basic Services or which may be the subject of a separate appointment. Fees for these services are normally charged on a time or lump sum basis as described in Part 4.

Part 3 Conditions of Appointment

Conditions which apply to an architect's appointment.

Part 4 Recommended Fees and Expenses

Recommended and not mandatory methods of calculating the architect's fees and expenses and of apportioning fees between work stages.

A sample **Memorandum of Agreement** and **Schedule of Services and Fees** are included with the document for information. They are published separately.

The client and the architect should discuss the architect's appointment and agree in writing the services, conditions and fee basis. These should be stated in the Schedule of Services and Fees and referred to in the Memorandum of Agreement between client and architect; alternatively, they should be stated in a letter of appointment.

Any question on or arising out of the information contained within this document may be referred for advice to:

The Director-General, RIBA, 66 Portland Place, London W1N 4AD; or

The Secretary, Royal Incorporation of Architects in Scotland, 15 Rutland Square, Edinburgh EH1 2BE; or

The Secretary, Royal Society of Ulster Architects, 2 Mount Charles, Belfast BT7 1NZ.

Part 1 Architect's Services

This part describes Preliminary and Basic Services which an architect will normally provide.

PRELIMINARY SERVICES

Work stage A: Inception

Brief

1.1   Discuss the client's requirements including timescale and any financial limits; assess these and given general advice on how to proceed; agree the architect's services.

Information to be provided by the client

1.2   Obtain from the client information on ownership and any lessors and lessees of the site, any existing buildings on the site, boundary fences and other enclosures, and any known easements, encroachments, underground services, rights of way, rights of support and other relevant matters.

Site appraisal

1.3   Visit the site and carry out an initial appraisal.

Advice on other consultants' services

1.4   Advise on the need for other consultants' services and on the scope of these services.

Design work by specialist firms

1.5   Advise on the need for specialist contractors, sub-contractors and suppliers to design and execute part of the works to comply with the architect's requirements.

Site staff

1.6   Advise on the need for site staff.

Timetable and fee basis

1.7 Prepare where required an outline timetable and fee basis for further services for the client's approval.

Work stage B: Feasibility

Feasibility studies

1.8 Carry out such studies as may be necessary to determine the feasibility of the client's requirements; review with the client alternative design and construction approaches and cost implications; advise on the need to obtain planning permissions, approvals under building acts or regulations, and other similar statutory requirements.

BASIC SERVICES

Work stage C: Outline proposals

Outline proposals

1.9 With other consultants where appointed, analyse the client's requirements; prepare outline proposals and an approximation of the construction cost for the client's preliminary approval.

Work Stage D: Scheme design

Scheme design

1.10 With other consultants where appointed, develop a scheme design from the outline proposals taking into account amendments requested by the client; prepare a cost estimate; where applicable given an indication of possible start and completion date for the building Contract. The scheme will illustrate the size and character of the project in sufficient detail to enable the client to agree the spatial arrangements, materials and appearance.

Changes in scheme design

1.11 With other consultants where appointed, advise the client of the implications of any subsequent changes on the cost of the project and on the overall programme.

Planning application

1.12 Make where required application for planning permission. The permission itself is beyond the architect's control and no guarantee that it will be granted can be given.

Work stage E: Detail design

Detail design

1.13 With other consultants where appointed, develop the scheme design; obtain the client's approval of the type of construction, quality of materials and standard of workmanship; co-ordinate any design work done by consultants, specialist contracts, sub-contractors and suppliers; obtain quotations and other information in connection with specialist work.

Cost checks and changes in detail design

1.14 With other consultants where appointed, carry out cost checks as necessary; advise the client of the consequences of any subsequent changes on the cost and programme.

Statutory approvals

1.15 Make and negotiate where required applications for approvals under building acts, regulations or other statutory requirements.

Work stages F and G: Production information and bills of quantities

Production information

1.16 With other consultants where appointed, prepare production information including drawings, schedules and specification of materials and workmanship; provide information for bills of quantities, if any, to be prepared: all information complete in sufficient detail to enable a contractor to prepare a tender.

Work stage H: Tender action

Other contracts

1.17 Arrange, where relevant, for other contracts to be let prior to the contractor commencing work.

Tender lists

1.18 Advise on and obtain the client's approval to a list of tenderers.

Tender action and appraisal

1.19 Invite tenders from approved contractors; appraise and advise on tenders submitted. Alternatively, arrange for a price to be negotiated with a contractor.

Work stage J: Project planning

Project planning

1.20 Advise the client on the appointment of the contractor and on the responsibilities of the client, contractor and architect under the terms of the building contract; where required prepare the building contract and arrange for it to be signed by the client and the contractor; provide production information as required by the building contract.

Work stage K: Operations on site

Contract administration

1.21 Administer the terms of the building contract during operations on site.

Inspections

1.22 Visit the site as appropriate to inspect generally the progress and quality of the work.

Financial appraisal

1.23 With other consultants where appointed, make where required periodic financial reports to the client including the effect of any variations on the construction cost.

Work stage L: Completion

Completion

1.24   Administer the terms of the building contract relating to the completion of the works.

Guidance on maintenance

1.25   Give general guidance on maintenance.

Record drawings

1.26   Provide the client with a set of drawings showing the building and the main lines of drainage; arrange for drawings of the services installations to be provided.

Part 2 Other Services

   This part describes services which may be provided by the architect to augment the Preliminary and Basic Services described in Part 1 or which may be the subject of a separate appointment. The list of services so described is not exhaustive.

Surveys and investigations

Building sites

2.1   Advise on the selection and suitability of sites; conduct negotiations concerned with sites and buildings.

Measured surveys

2.2   Make measured surveys, take levels and prepare plans of sites and buildings.

Soil investigations

2.3   Provide services in connection with soil and other similar investigations.

Condition of premises

2.4   Make inspections, prepare reports or give general advice on the condition of premises.

Schedules of dilapidations

2.5   Prepare schedules of dilapidations; negotiate them on behalf of landlords or tenants.

Structural surveys

2.6   Make structural surveys to ascertain whether there are defects in the walls, roof, floors, drains or other parts of a building which may materially affect its safety, life and value.

Building failures

2.7   Investigate building failures; arrange and supervise exploratory work by contractors or specialists.

Repairs and restoration work

2.8   Take particulars on site; prepare specifications and/or schedules for repairs and restoration work, and inspect their execution.

Problems in existing buildings

2.9   Investigate and advise on problems in existing buildings such as fire protection, floor loadings, sound insulation, or change of use.

Energy surveys

2.10   Advise on the efficient use of energy in new and existing buildings.

Cost in use

2.11   Carry out life cycle analyses of buildings to determine their cost in use.

Valuations

2.12   Make an inspection and valuation for mortgage or other purposes.

Development services

Special drawings and models

2.13   Prepare special drawings, models or technical information for the use of the client or for applications under planning, building act, building regulation or other statutory requirements, or for negotiations with ground landlords, adjoining owners, public authorities, licensing authorities, mortgagors and others; prepare plans for conveyancing, land registry and other legal purposes.

Development plans

2.14   Prepare development plans for a large building or complex of buildings; prepare a layout only, or prepare a layout for a greater area than that which is to be developed immediately.

Estate plans

2.15   Prepare layouts for housing, industrial or other estates showing the siting of buildings and other works such as roads and sewers.

Roads and sewers

2.16   Prepare drawings and specification of materials and workmanship for the construction of housing, industrial or other estate roads and sewers.

Demolitions

2.17   Provide services in connection with demolition works.

Environmental studies

2.18   Provide services in connection with environmental studies.

Design services

Furniture and fittings

2.19 Design or advise on the selection of furniture and fittings; inspect the making up of such furnishings.

Shopfitting and other works of special quality

2.20 Advise on and prepare detailed designs for works of special quality such as shopfitting or exhibition design, either independently or within the shell of an existing building.

Works of art

2.21 Advise on the commissioning or selection of works of art; supervise their installation.

Acoustical investigations

2.22 Carry out specialist acoustical investigations.

Special constructional research

2.23 Carry out special constructional research in connection with a scheme design, including the design, construction or testing of prototype buildings or models.

Building systems and components

2.24 Develop a building system or mass-produced building components; examine and advise on existing building systems; monitor the testing of prototype buildings and models.

Cost estimating and financial advisory services

Cost plans and cash flow requirements

2.25 Carry out cost planning for a building project, including the cost of associated design services, site development, landscaping, furniture and equipment; advise on cash flow requirements for design cost, construction cost, and cost in use.

Schedules of rates and quantities

2.26 Prepare schedules of rates or schedules of quantities for tendering purposes; value work executed where no quantity surveyor is appointed. Fees for this work are recommended to be in accordance with the Professional Charges of the Royal Institution of Chartered Surveyors.

Cost of replacement

2.27 Carry out inspections and surveys; prepare estimates for the replacement and reinstatement of buildings and plant; submit and negotiate claims following damage by fire or other causes.

Grant applications

2.28 Provide information; make applications for and conduct negotiations in connections with local authority, government or other grants.

Negotiations

Planning applications: exceptional negotiations

2.29   Conduct exceptional negotiations with a planning authority.

Planning appeals

2.30   Prepare and submit an appeal under planning acts; advise on other work in connection with planning appeals.

Building regulations: exceptional negotiations

2.31   Conduct exceptional negotiations for approvals under building acts or regulations; negotiation waivers or relaxations.

Royal Fine Art Commission

2.32   Make submissions to the Royal Fine Art Commission and other non-statutory bodies.

Landlords' approvals

2.33   Submit plans of proposed building works for approval of landlords, mortgagors, freeholders or others.

Rights of owners and lessees

2.34   Advise on the rights and responsibilities of owners or lessees including rights of light, rights of support, and rights of way; provide information; undertake any negotiations.

Party walls

2.35   Provide services in connection with party wall negotiations.

Litigation and arbitration

2.36   Prepare and give evidence; settle proofs; confer with solicitors and counsel; attend court and arbitrations; appear before other tribunals; act as arbitrator.

Administration and management of building projects

Site staff

2.37   Provide site staff for frequent or constant inspection of the works.

Project management

2.38   Provide management from inception to completion: prepare briefs; appoint and co-ordinate consultants, construction managers, agents and contractors; monitor time, cost and agreed targets; monitor progress of the works; hand over the building on completion; equip, commission and set up any operational organisations.

Design and build contracts

2.39   Provide services to the client, whether employer or contractor, in carrying out duties under a design and build contract.

Separate trades contracts

2.40   Provide services in connection with separate trades contracts; agree a programme of work; act as co-ordinator for the duration of the contracts.

Direct labour

2.41   Provide services in connection with labour employed directly by the client; agree a programme of work; co-ordinate the supply of labour and materials; provide general supervision; agree the final account.

"As built" drawings

2.42   Provide specially prepared drawings of a building "as built."

Maintenance manuals

2.43   Compile maintenance and operational manuals; incorporate information prepared by other consultants, specialist contractors, sub-contractors and suppliers.

Maintenance programme

2.44   Prepare a programme for the maintenance of a building; arrange maintenance contracts.

Services normally provided by consultants

Consultants' services

2.45   Provide such services as:

a   Quantity surveying
b   Structural engineering
c   Mechanical engineering
d   Electrical engineering
e   Landscape and garden design
f   Civil engineering
g   Town planning
h   Furniture design
j   Graphic design
k   Industrial design
l   Interior design

Where consultants' services are provided from within the architect's own office or by consultants in association with the architect it is recommended that fees be in accordance with the scales of charges of the relevant professional body.

Consultancy services

Consultant architect

2.46   Provide services as a consultant architect on a regular or intermittent basis.

Part 3 Conditions of appointment

This part describes the conditions which normally apply to an architect's

appointment. If different or additional conditions are to apply, they should be set out in the Schedule of Services and Fees or letter of appointment.

Duty of care

3.1 The architect will exercise reasonable skill and care in conformity with the normal standards of the architect's profession.

Architect's authority

Authority

3.2 The architect will act on behalf of the client in the matters set out or implied in the architect's appointment; the architect will obtain the authority of the client before initiating any service or work stage.

Variation of service

3.3 The architect shall not make any material alteration, addition to or omission from the approved design without the knowledge and consent of the client, except if found necessary during construction for constructional reasons in which case the architect shall inform the client without delay.

Variation of cost or time

3.4 The architect will inform the client if the total authorised expenditure or the building contract period is likely to be materially varied.

Consultants

Nomination of consultants

3.5 Consultants may be nominated by either the client or the architect, subject to acceptance by each party.

Consultants employed by client

3.6 Where the client employs the consultants, either directly or through the agency of the architect, the client will hold each consultant, and not the architect, responsible for the competence, general inspection and performance of the work entrusted to that consultant; provided that in relation to the execution of such work under the contract between the client and the contractor nothing in this clause shall affect any responsibility of the architect for issuing instructions or for other functions ascribed to the architect under that contract.

Co-ordination of consultants' services

3.7 The architect will have the authority to co-ordinate and integrate into the overall design the services provided by any consultant, however employed.

Contractors, sub-contractors and suppliers

Design work by specialist contractors, sub-contractors and suppliers

3.8 A specialist contractor, sub-contractor or supplier who is to be employed by the client to design any part of the works may be nominated by either the architect or the client, subject to acceptance by each party. The client will hold such contractor, sub-contractor or supplier, and not the architect, responsible for the competence, proper execution and performance of the work thereby entrusted to that contractor, sub-contractor or supplier. The architect will have the authority to co-ordinate and integrate such work into the overall design.

Responsibility of the contractor

3.9   The client will employ a contractor under a separate agreement to undertake construction or other works. The client will hold the contractor, and not the architect, responsible for the contractor's operational methods and for the proper execution of the works.

Site inspection

Inspection

3.10   The architect will visit the site at intervals appropriate to the stage of construction to inspect the progress and quality of the works and to determine that they are being executed generally in accordance with the contract documents. The architect will not be required to make frequent or constant inspections.

Site staff: Clerk of works

3.11   Where frequent or constant inspection is required a clerk or clerks of works will be employed. They may be employed either by the client or by the architect and will in either event be under the architect's direction and control.

Site staff: Resident architect

3.12   Where frequent or constant inspection by the architect is agreed to be necessary, a resident architect may be appointed by the architect on a part or full time basis.

Client's instructions

Information from the client

3.13   The client will provide the architect with such information and make such decisions as are necessary for the proper performance of the agreed service.

Client's representative

3.14   The client, if a firm or other body of persons, will, when requested by the architect, nominate a responsible representative through whom all instructions will be given.

Copyright

Copyright

3.15   Copyright in all documents and drawings prepared by the architect and in any works executed from those documents and drawings shall, unless otherwise agreed, remain the property of the architect.

Copyright entitlement

3.16   The client, unless otherwise agreed, will be entitled to reproduce the architect's design by proceeding to execute the project provide that:

—the entitlement applies only to the site or part of the site to which the design relates; and

—the architect has completed work stage D or has provided detail design and production information in work stages E, F and G; and

—any fees due to the architect have been paid or tendered.

This entitlement will also apply to the maintenance, repair and renewal of the works.

Entitlement restrictions

3.17 Where an architect has not completed work stage D, or where the client and the architect have agreed that clause 3.16 shall not apply, the client may not reproduce the design by proceeding to execute the project without the consent of the architect and payment of any additional fee that may be agreed in exchange for the architects consent.

Limited services

3.18 The architect shall not unreasonably withhold his consent under clause 3.17 but where his services are limited to making and negotiating planning applications he may withhold his consent unless otherwise determined by an arbitration appointed in accordance with clause 3.26.

Assignment

Asssignment

3.19 Neither the architect nor the client may assign the whole or any part of his duties without the other's written consent.

Suspension and termination

Suspension of services: Force majeure

3.20 The architect will give immediate notice in writing to the client of any situation arising from force majeure which makes it impracticable to carry out any of the agreed services, and agree with the client a suitable course of action.

Suspension of services: Client

3.21 The client may suspend the performance of any or all of the agreed services by giving reasonable notice in writing to the architect.

Resumption of services

3.22 If the architect has not been given instructions to resume any suspended service within six months from the date of suspension the architect will make written request for such instructions which must be given in writing. If these have not been received within 30 days of the date of such request the architect will have the right to treat the appointment as terminated upon the expiry of the 30 days.

Termination

3.23 The architect's appointment may be terminated by either party on the expiry of reasonable notice given in writing.

3.24   Should the architect through death or incapacity be unable to provide the agreed services, the appointment will thereby be terminated. In such an event the client may, on payment or tender of all outstanding fees and expenses, make full use of reports, drawings or other documents prepared by the architect in accordance with and for use under the agreement, but only for the purpose for which they were prepared.

Settlement of disputes

Opinion on a joint statement

3.25   A difference or dispute arising on the application of the Architect's Appointment to fees charged by a member may, by agreement between the parties, be referred to the RIBA, RIAS or RSUA for an opinion provided that:

—the member's appointment is based on this document and has been agreed and confirmed in writing; and

—the opinion is sought on a joint statement of undisputed facts; and

—the parties undertake to accept the opinion as final and binding upon them.

Arbitration

3.26   Any other difference or dispute arising out of the appointment and any difference or dispute arising on the fees charged which cannot be resolved in accordance with clause 3.25 shall be referred to arbitration by a person to be agreed between the parties or, failing agreement within 14 days after either party has given to the other a written request to concur in the appointment of an arbitrator, a person to be nominated at the request of either party by the President of the Chartered Institute of Arbitrators, provided that in a difference or dispute arising out of provisions relating to copyright, clauses 3.15 to 3.18 above, the arbitrator shall, unless otherwise agreed, be an architect.

or

Alternative for Scotland

.26S   *In Scotland, any other difference or dispute arising out of the appointment and any difference or dispute arising on the fees charged which cannot be resolved in accordance with clause 3.25 shall be referred to arbitration by a person to be agreed between the parties or, failing agreement within 14 days after either party has given to the other a written request to concur in the appointment of an arbiter, a person to be nominated at the request of either party by the Dean of the Faculty of Advocates, provided that in a difference or dispute arising out of provisions relating to copyright, clauses 3.15 to 3.18 above, the arbiter shall, unless otherwise agreed, be an architect.*

By agreement

3.27   Nothing herein shall prevent the parties agreeing to settle any difference or dispute arising out of the appointment without recourse to arbitration.

Governing laws

England and Wales

3.28   The application of these conditions shall be governed by the laws of England and Wales.

or

Alternative for Scotland

3.28S   *The application of these conditions shall be governed by the laws of Scotland.*

or

Alternative for Northern Ireland

3.28NI   *The application of these conditions shall be governed by the laws of Northern Ireland.*

Part 4 Recommended fees and expenses

This part describes the recommended and not mandatory methods of calculating fees for the architect's services and expenses. Fees may be based on a percentage of the total construction cost or on time expended, or may be a lump sum. This part should be read in conjunction with Parts 1, 2 and 3.

Percentage fees

New works

4.1   The percentage fee scales shown in Figure 1 (graph) are for use where the architect's appointment is for the Basic Services described in Part 1 for new works having a total construction cost between £20,000 and £5,000,000. Where the total construction cost is less than £20,000 or more than £5,000,000 client and architect should agree an appropriate fee basis at the time of appointment.

Percentage fees

4.2   Percentage fees are based on the total construction cost of the works; on the issue of the final certificate fees should be recalculated on the actual total construction cost.

Total construction cost

4.3   Total construction cost is defined as the cost, as certified by the architect, of all works including site works executed under the architect's direction, subject to the following:

a   The total construction cost includes the cost of all work designed by consultants and co-ordinated by the architect, irrespective of whether such work is carried out under separate building contracts for which the architect may not be responsible. The architect will be informed of the cost of any such separate contracts.

b   The total construction cost does not include specialist sub-contractors' design fees for work on which consultants would otherwise have been employed. Where such fees are not known, the architect will estimate a reduction from the total construction cost.

c   For the purpose of calculating the appropriate fee, the total construction cost:

—includes the actual or estimated cost of any work executed which is excluded from the contract but otherwise designed by the architect;

964

—is not subject to any deductions made in respect of work not in accordance with the building contract.

d The total construction cost includes the cost of built-in furniture and equipment. Where the cost of any special equipment is excluded from the total construction cost, the architect may charge additionally for work in connection with such items.

e Where any material, labour or carriage is supplied by a client who is not the contractor, the cost will be estimated by the architect as if it were supplied by the contractor, and included in the total cost.

f Where the client is the contractor, a statement of the ascertained gross cost of the works may be used in calculating the total construction cost of the works. In the absence of such a statement, the architect's own estimate will be used. In both a statement of the ascertained gross cost and an architect's estimate there will be included an allowance for the contractor's profits and overheads.

Classification of buildings

4.4 Buildings are divided into five classes for fee calculation purposes. For guidance only the building types most likely to fall into each class are shown in Figure 3.

Repetition

Repetition

4.5 The classification of buildings in Figure 3 takes account of reduced design work arising from the nature of the building.

Repeated buildings

4.6 Where a building is repeated for the same client the recommended fee for the super-structure may be reduced on all except the first three of any houses of the same design and on all accept the first of all other building types of the same design.

Identical compartments

4.7 Where a single building incorporates a number of identical compartments such as floors or complete structural bays the recommended fee may be reduced on all identical compartments in excess of ten.

Fee reduction

4.8 Reductions should be made by waiving the fee for work stages E, F and G where a complete design can be re-used without modification other than the handing of a plan.

Time charge fees

Time charges: Principals and technical staff

4.9 Time charges are based on hourly rates for principals and other technical staff. In assessing the hourly rate all relevant factors should be considered, including the complexity of the work, the qualifications, experience and responsibility of the architect, and the character of any negotiations. Hourly rates for principals shall be agreed.

The hourly rate for technical staff should be not less than 18 pence per £100 of gross annual income.

Technical staff

4.10   Technical staff are defined as architectural and other professional and technical staff, where the architect is responsible for deducting PAYE and National Insurance contributions from those persons' salaries on behalf of the Inland Revenue.

Gross annual income

4.11   Gross annual income includes bonus payments plus the employer's share of contributions towards National Insurance, pension and private medical schemes and other emoluments such as car and accommodation allowances.

Agency staff

4.12   Where staff are provided by an agency hourly rates shall be agreed.

Site staff

4.13   Where site staff are employed by the architect hourly rates shall be agreed.

Secretarial and administrative staff

4.14   Unless otherwise agreed no separate time charges will be made for secretarial staff or staff engaged on general accountancy or administrative duties.

Architect's records

4.15   The architect will maintain records of time spent on services performed on a time basis. The architect will make such records available to the client on reasonable request.

Lump sum fees

Lump sum fee

4.16   The architect may agree with the client to charge a lump sum fee for any of the services described in Parts 1 and 2 in appropriate circumstances, for example where:

—the client's requirements are provided in a form such that the architect is not obliged to undertake any additional preparatory work;

—the full extent of the service can be determined when the architect is appointed; and

—the architect's service can be completed within an agreed period.

Works to existing buildings

Alterations or extensions

4.17   The percentage fee scales shown in Figure 2 (graph) are for use where the architect's appointment is for the Basic Services described in Part 1 for alterations or extensions to an existing building having a total construction cost of between £20,000 and

£5,000,000. Where the total construction cost is less than £20,000 or more than £5,000,000 client and architect should agree an appropriate fee basis at the time of the appointment.

Extensions substantially independent

4.18 Where extensions to existing buildings are substantially independent, percentage fees should be as Figure 1 for new works, but the fee for those sections of the works which marry existing buildings to the new should be charged separately as Figure 2 applicable to an independent commission of similar value.

Repair and restoration work

4.19 Where the architect's appointment is for repair and restoration work fees should be on a time basis; alternatively a percentage fee may be agreed.

Historic or listed buildings

4.20 Where the architect's appointment is in connection with works to a building of architectural or historic interest, or to a building in a conservation area, higher fees may be charged.

Compounding of fees

Compounding of fees

4.21 By agreement the percentage or lump sum fee may be compounded to cover all or any part of the architect's services and expenses.

Interim payments

Fee instalments

4.22 Fees and expenses should be paid in instalments either at regular intervals or on completion of work stages of the Basic Services (Part 1).

Fee apportionment

4.23A Where interim payment of percentage or lump sum fees is related to completion of work stages of the Basic Services the recommended apportionment is as follows:

Work stage	Proportion of fee	Cumulative total
C	15%	15%
D	20%	35%
E	20%	55%
F G	20%	75%
H J K L	25%	100%

Fees in respect of work stages E to L should be paid in instalments proportionate to the work completed or the value of the works certified from time to time. Interim payments should be based on the current estimated cost of the works.

The apportionment of fees is a means of assessing interim payments and does not necessarily reflect the amount of work completed in any work stage. By agreement an adjustment in the apportionment may be made.

Interest

4.23B   Any sum remaining unpaid at the expiry of 30 days from the date of submission of the fee account shall bear interest thereafter, such interest to accrue from day to day at the rate of 2 per cent. per annum above the current base rate of the architect's principal bank.

Partial services

Partial services

4.24   The architect may be required to provide part only of the Basic Services (Part 1). In such cases the architect will be entitled to a commensurate fee.

Work done by client

4.25   Where work is to be done by or on behalf of the client, resulting in the omission of part of work stages C to L, or a sponsored constructional method is to be used, a commensurate reduction in the recommended percentage fee may be agreed. In assessing the reduction, due account should be taken of the need for the architect to become thoroughly familiar with the work done by others, and a familiarisation fee will be charged for this work.

Partial service fee basis

4.26   All percentage fees for partial services should be based on the architect's current estimate of the total construction cost of the works. Such estimates may be based on an accepted tender or, subject to the following, on the lowest of unaccepted tenders. Where partial services are provided in respect of works for which the executed cost is not known and no tender has been accepted, percentage fees should be based either on the architect's estimated total construction cost or on the most recent cost limit agreed with the client, whichever, is the lower.

Alternative fee arrangements

4.27   Fees for partial services may alternatively be on a time or lump sum basis.

Suspension, resumption and termination

Fees on suspension or termination

4.28   On suspension or termination of the architect's appointment the architect will be entitled to fees for all work completed at that time. Fees will be charged on a partial service basis.

Reimbursing during suspension

4.29   During such period of suspension the architect will be reimbursed by the client for all expenses and disbursements necessarily incurred under the appointment.

Fees on resumption

4.30   On the resumption of a suspended service within six months, previous payments will be regarded solely as payments on account towards the total fee.

Reimbursement on termination

4.31 Where the architect's appointment is terminated by the client the architect will be reimbursed by the client for all expenses and disbursements necessarily incurred in connection with work then in progress and arising as a result of the termination.

Expenses and disbursements

Expenses and disbursements

4.32 In addition to the fees charged the architect will be reimbursed for all expenses and disbursements properly incurred in connection with the appointment, including the following:

a Printing, reproduction or purchase costs of all documents, drawings, maps, models, photographs, and other records, including all those used in communication between architect, client, consultants and contractors, and for enquiries to contractors, sub-contractors and suppliers, notwithstanding any obligation on the part of the architect to supply such documents to those concerned, except that contractors will pay for any prints additional to those to which they are entitled under the contract.

b Hotel and travelling expenses, including mileage allowance for cars at rates stated in the Schedule of Service and Fees and other similar disbursements.

c All payments made on behalf of the client, such as expenses incurred in advertising for tenders and resident site staff including the time and expenses of interviewers and reasonable expenses for interviewees.

d Fees and other charges for specialist professional advice, including legal advice, which have been incurred by the architect with the specific authority of the client.

e The cost of postage, telephone charges, telex messages, telegrams, cables, facsimiles, air-freight and courier services.

f Rental and hire charges for specialised equipment, including computers, where required and agreed by the client.

g Where work charged on a percentage fee is at such a distance that an exceptional amount of time is spent travelling, additional charges may be made.

Records

4.33 The architect will maintain records of all such expenses and disbursements and will make these records available to the client on reasonable request.

Compounding of expenses

4.34 Expenses and disbursements may by agreement be estimated or standardised in whole or in part, or compounded for an increase in the percentage or lump sum fee.

Payment of statutory fees

4.35 The client will pay all fees in respect of applications under planning and buildings acts and other statutory requirements.

Variations

Variation of fees

4.36   Where the scope of the architect's services is varied fees may be adjusted accordingly.

Extra work and expense

4.37   Where the architect is involved in extra work and expense for reasons beyond the architect's control and for which the architect would not otherwise be remunerated additional fees are due. Any of the following is likely to involve the architect in extra work and expense:

a   The need to revise reports, drawings, specifications or other documents due to changes in interpretation or enactment or revisions of laws, statutory or other regulations.

b   Changes in the client's instructions, or delay by the client in providing information.

c   Consideration of notices, applications or claims by the contractor under a building contract; delays in the building contract operations; delays resulting from defects or deficiencies in the work of the contractor, sub-contractors or suppliers; default, bankruptcy or liquidation of the contractor, sub-contractors or suppliers.

d   Any other cause beyond the architect's control.

Value Added Tax

Value Added Tax

4.38   The amount of any Value Added Tax on the services and expenses of the architect arising under the Finance Act 1972 will be chargeable to the client in addition to the architect's fees and expenses.

[Figures 1, 2 and 3, showing Recommended percentage fee scales and Classification of buildings are not reproduced.]

INDEX

973

974